LAW AND MORALITY:

READINGS IN LEGAL PHILOSOPHY

Second Edition

This is the second edition of an anthology that fills a longstanding need for a contemporary Canadian textbook in the philosophy of law. It includes articles, readings, and cases in legal philosophy that give students the conceptual tools necessary to consider the general problems of jurisprudence.

The collection begins with general questions about morality and law, drawing on both traditional literature on legal positivism and contemporary debates about the role of law in the pursuit of equality. It explores the tensions between law as a protector of individual liberty and as a tool of democratic self-rule. The second part deals with these philosophical questions as they apply to contemporary issues. Included is an extensive sampling of the feminist writings that have been influential in legal theory and Canadian law. Transcripts of judicial decisions are presented throughout to give students an appropriate sense of the complexity of legal reasoning.

This book strikes a balance between practical problems and the more analytic, philosophical frameworks. Its treatment of the philosophy of law as a branch of political philosophy enables students to understand law in its function as a social institution. A valuable text in both departments of philosophy and faculties of law, the second, much-expanded edition brings the debates up to date, fills gaps in the first edition, and adds to the array of contemporary issues.

DAVID DYZENHAUS and ARTHUR RIPSTEIN are professors of law and philosophy at the University of Toronto.

EDITED BY DAVID DYZENHAUS
AND ARTHUR RIPSTEIN

Law and Morality:
Readings in Legal Philosophy

Second Edition

UNIVERSITY OF TORONTO PRESS
Toronto Buffalo London

First edition published 1996; reprinted 1998

ISBN 0-8020-3576-0 (cloth)
ISBN 0-8020-8447-8 (paper)

Printed on acid-free paper

Toronto Studies in Philosophy
Editors: James R. Brown and Calvin Normore

National Library of Canada Cataloguing in Publication Data

Main entry under title:

Law and morality: readings in legal philosophy

2nd ed.
(Toronto studies in philosophy)
Includes bibliographical references.
ISBN 0-8020-3576-0 (bound)
ISBN 0-8020-8447-8 (pbk.)

1. Law – Philosophy. 2. Law and ethics. I. Dyzenhaus, David.
II. Ripstein, Arthur. III. Series

K235L39 2001   340'112   C2001-901262-4

University of Toronto Press acknowledges the financial assistance to its
publishing program of the Canada Council and the Ontario Arts Council.

University of Toronto Press acknowledges the financial support for its
publishing activities of the Government of Canada through the Book
Publishing Industry Development Program (BPIDP).

Contents

Preface to the Second Edition

The five years since the first edition of *Law and Morality* have been momentous for Canadian law and legal culture. The Supreme Court has broken new ground on many of the issues explored in the first edition. The most prominent decision was the *Quebec Secession Reference*, in which the Court both decided that Quebec has no constitutional right to unilateral secession, and considered between the legal and political obligations of the Canadian state in the event that Quebec declares independence unilaterally. We have included the *Secession Reference*, and to complement it a series of further readings on challenges to the legitimacy of the legal order. These include two essays concerning the particular challenges posed by Canada's Aboriginal Peoples.

In addition, a case about foetal rights, which was discussed in one of the reading questions in the first edition, has now been decided by the Court. A new case on sexual orientation discrimination has also been decided. Excerpts from both cases have been included.

Other debates have risen to new prominence. Although the *Butler* pornography decision purported to incorporate Catharine MacKinnon's feminist analysis of pornography, another group of feminists has objected to it, in part in response to issues of enforcement to which it gave rise. We include an article on that topic.

We have also modified our selection of more theoretical material, including a discussion of legal authority, and a further piece from the critical legal studies movement. And we have made numerous other small additions and as many deletions, all prompted by our and others' experience in teaching from this book.

We are grateful to our editor, Ron Schoeffel, for his help and support at every stage of this project.

THE EDITORS

David Dyzenhaus is Professor of Law and Philosophy at the University of Toronto. He was a Humboldt Fellow at the University of Heidelberg in 1992–3, and a Connaught Fellow in 1998. He is the author of *Hard Cases in Wicked Legal Systems: South African Law in the Perspective of Legal Philosophy; Legality and Legitimacy: Carl Schmitt, Hans Kelsen,* and *Hermann Heller in Weimar; Judging the Judges, Judging Ourselves: Truth, Reconciliation and the Apartheid Legal Order,* and two edited collections of essays, *Law as Politics: Carl Schmitt's Critique of Liberalism* and *Recrafting the Rule of Law: The Limits of Legal Order*. He is a Fellow of the Royal Society of Canada.

Arthur Ripstein is Professor of Law and Philosophy at the University of Toronto. He was Laurance Rockefeller Visiting Fellow at Princeton in 1995–6, and held a Connaught fellowship for the 2000 spring term. His research areas include political philosophy, philosophy of law, and moral philosophy. He is the author of *Equality, Responsibility and the Law* (Cambridge 1999) and co-editor of *Preference and Practical Reason*. He has also published numerous articles in legal theory and political philosophy. He is an associate editor of *Ethics*.

Preface to the First Edition

For most students, a course in legal philosophy marks their first encounter with a rigorous examination of the conceptual apparatus of the law. Yet it is hardly their first encounter with many of the law's central questions. Law has long shaped ordinary life. From regulations concerning auto emissions to common-law rules governing warranties and product liability, the law affects our everyday existence. Indeed, these rules and regulations are so pervasive that most people seldom notice them, let alone reflect on them. By providing conceptual tools with which to consider the general problems of jurisprudence, this book aims to be an aid to students both in their intellectual pursuits and in their role as informed citizens.

Courses in the philosophy of law often break up into two sharply divided sections, one exploring conceptual questions about the nature of law, the other looking at a series of questions concerning the proper limits of the criminal law. These two sections sometimes sit together uneasily. In our view, the philosophy of law is far too important a subject to be treated in such a disjointed way. Part of the difficulty is that most discussion of the nature of law focuses on administrative rules or grand questions of constitutional theory. As a result, questions about the reach of the criminal law too often seem unrelated to those about its nature. A deeper reason for avoiding the usual approach is that it probably rests on a particular resolution to one of the problems considered in the first part of such courses in the philosophy of law. Standard versions of legal positivism suppose that the law can take on any content whatsoever. One consequence of such a view is that questions about the appropriate reach of the criminal law are in principle open to any sort of argumentation, because the concept of law by itself provides no constraints on its content. Yet legal reasoning often employs reasoning from other areas of the law, and these often seem to constrain the law's content. An adequate understanding of these challenges to positivism, or a version of positivism adequate to meet them, allows for a more sophisticated approach to contemporary issues. While we do not offer this anthology for use only by anti-positivists, we regard it as a virtue of our approach that it is neutral on those questions. Our central organizing assumption in compiling this anthology is that questions about morality and the law are at root questions of political theory.

The traditional questions of jurisprudence concern the distinguishing features of a legal order. What makes a legal order different from other types of social order? Answers to those questions, in turn, make a difference to the ways in which law can be used. For example, different views of legal order have profound implications for any account of the relation between democracy and the rule of law, and so for questions about the limits to criminalization. Again, views about the nature of law have implications for the ways in which the law might appropriately address those who object to it on moral grounds. Of course, there is no direct relationship – one might be a positivist or anti-positivist and still suppose the criminal law should be limited. But views about the general relation between law, morality, and democracy give shape to the types of arguments that are available, and assumptions about the nature of law will sometimes dictate which of those arguments seem most compelling. At the same time, views about the appropriate limits of state action may well lend credence to views about what is or is not an acceptable account of the nature of law. Again, questions about the nature of adjudication seem to straddle both sets of issues. In the end, all of the issues revolve around whether, or under what conditions, law is an appropriate place to pin our hopes for justice.

Since the introduction of the *Charter of Rights and Freedoms* in 1982, Canada's legal and political culture has changed dramatically. The political vocabulary of Canadians has become increasingly legalized. Perhaps the most noticeable feature is the way in which claims about fundamental justice and individual rights are traded in debates about most issues of public concern. But there have been subtler and deeper changes also. Although this collection contains brief excerpts from and discussions of American cases, its main focus will be Canadian. While some critics have described the introduction of the *Charter* as the "Americanization" of Canadian law, such a characterization is at best misleading. Judicial review has assumed an increased importance since the *Charter* was introduced, but the content of Canadian and American legal thought is very different. The differences are perhaps most obvious on issues of freedom of expression, where Canadian and American courts have come to such different conclusions. Those conclusions reveal yet deeper differences in their views of equality and the rule of law more generally. The central debates of legal theory and public policy that face Canadians in the 1990s are not the same as those that divided the United States in the 1960s. While those American struggles, especially the struggle for racial equality, are worthy of serious study, America's specific political and constitutional history has given these issues a shape that does not transfer readily to the rest of the world. Canada's legal culture is distinctive and important, and must be taken seriously in its own right. For similar reasons, we include a sample of the feminist writings which have been so influential in both legal theory and Canadian law.

The collection is divided into two sections. The first deals with general questions about morality and law, drawing both on the traditional literature discussing legal positivism and on contemporary debates about the role of law as a tool in pursuit of equality. Then it looks at a series of questions revolving around the tensions between the role of law as a protector of individual liberty and as a tool of democratic self-rule. Law has been defended as each of these, yet they are in apparent tension. The second section considers a series of contemporary issues in which the questions considered in the first section present themselves especially forcefully. The collection contains somewhat more material than would ordinarily be included in a one-semester course, so as to allow instructors some flexibility in designing a course using it, and in varying the course from year to year. For example, different contemporary problems might be covered, and the conceptual and practical materials integrated in a number of ways. At the same time, it does not contain so much material as to make prohibitive the cost of using additional material, either because this is better suited to the particular instructor's aims or because the instructor wishes to use the collection as the basis for a full-year course.

We have included reading questions for each of the selections. We have not suggested additional readings, leaving that instead to the discretion of instructors using the book.

PART ONE

MORALITY AND THE RULE OF LAW

1

Positivism, Legal Ordering, and Morality

Careful reflection about the law's relationship to morality requires inquiry into a variety of questions about its other features. Lawyers regularly make claims about what the law requires in a particular case. What other facts fix the truth of such claims? Does moral argument enter into them? If so, what sorts of moral argument? What determines whether a moral argument is admissible? Must every legal system incorporate moral arguments?

Philosophical thought about the nature of law has fallen into two broad camps. Legal positivism is the view that law is best understood as a sociological phenomenon, a particular way of structuring social life. For the positivist, it is essential to the nature of law that it can be identified without appeal to controversial moral arguments. Law is thus identified with positive law, that is law that has been promulgated or enacted in appropriate ways. Different positivists have different views of the necessary and sufficient conditions for appropriate enactment. Some make the command of a sovereign essential; others the existence of structures for changing laws, and others the availability of non-controversial ways of applying the law to particular cases. Whatever their other differences, positivists share the view that it is essential to a legal system that what the law *is* can be established without considering what the law morally *ought to be.*

Opposed to positivists are defenders of natural law, according to whom a system of official power only qualifies as a legal system if it meets certain moral demands. Natural lawyers differ on what those demands might be, but share an insistence that the difference between the rule of law and other ways of organizing power can only be drawn in terms of the fundamental moral conceptions at the heart of a legal system.

So described, the traditional questions of jurisprudence sometimes seem narrowly conceptual and lacking in political implications. At one level, this is plainly true: answers to them do not, by themselves, dictate answers to pressing political disputes. Yet jurisprudence was born of political ferment, and many people continue to see it as profoundly related to questions of justice and legitimacy. The connection can be found in the issue of adjudication. Any account of the nature of law is thereby also an account of the distinction between a judge or other official *applying* established law and *making* new law. One of the core ideals of the rule of law is that the task of judges is to apply the law rather than to make it. Depending on how this distinction is drawn, the role of courts can be seen as anything from a usurpation of majority rule (or a bulwark against tyranny), to a direct instrument of state control. Positivists will regard most intrusions of morality into official decisions as making law rather than applying it; natural lawyers will suppose that correctly applying the law requires moral argument. The distinction between making and applying law also has important implications for understanding the demands placed on judges as legal actors. Does the law allow a judge to reach morally desirable results contrary to the wishes of the state? Does it ever require such results?

Both positivists and their opponents sometimes accuse each other of authoritarianism. Positivists claim that seeing law as essentially moral is likely to lead to either of two pathologies. It may lead to authoritarianism, because people will suppose that whatever law is on the books is therefore just, and thus blindly obey it. Alternatively, it may lead to anarchy, as people suppose themselves to be the appropriate judges of whether or not to obey. For their part, anti-positivists sometimes charge that positivism leads to a sort of rule-worship, and an implicit moral admiration for order, regardless of its injustices.

In the seventeenth century, Thomas Hobbes first articulated legal positivism in support of the consolidation of state power. Virtually all human societies have resolved disputes by granting authority to people not involved in the disputes. Such courts are not necessarily directly connected with either state power or the more general directions of public policy. Our own legal system is a descendent of a system in which nobles held courts of their own in addition to the royal courts. In the English-speaking world, religious courts remained a separate center of legal power well into the nineteenth century. Similar systems of adjudication can be found today in the form of disciplinary procedures in workplaces and universities. The idea that the state should be the only lawmaking institution is thus comparatively new.

On Hobbes's view, law cannot be understood as anything but the command of a sovereign. If courts lie outside the direct control of the state, judges are making law rather than applying it. The result is divided sovereignty and conflict. A century and a half later, Jeremy Bentham offered a different version of positivism in support of a forward-looking version of public policy. The role of law is to provide incentives to behavior, and laws must have coercive sanctions attached to them in order to qualify as laws. For both Hobbes and Bentham, courts can only properly apply the law if judges follow clear instructions from the state.

Recent versions of positivism have had less of a tone of political urgency about them. H.L.A. Hart's influential development of positivism emphasizes the role of rules in a legal system. According to Hart, a legal system must contain both "primary" rules regulating behavior and "secondary" rules regulating the changing of the primary rules. In order to govern behavior effectively, these rules must be largely accepted by both the population they govern and the officials applying them. For Hart, any such system of rules will face cases to which they do not straightforwardly apply. In such circumstances, the judge will have no choice but to exercise discretion, making law rather than simply applying it. Hart maintains that these distinctions are descriptive and conceptual, but politically important, because keeping them in mind enables us to evaluate existing law with an open mind, rather than seeing it as either a nightmare of power politics or a noble dream of perfect justice.

The readings explore the political charges made by both positivists and their critics. Those issues come to a head in the issue of wicked legal systems. Whether the example is Nazi law, South African law under Apartheid, or slavery in the United States, positivists insist that wicked legal systems must nonetheless be seen as involving law. Opponents of positivism have two options: some insist that such systems are not legal systems at all; others insist that precisely because they are legal systems, they cannot consistently enforce their unjust dictates. According to the anti-positivist, positivist judges serve unjust regimes when they suppose that their choices are to either enforce the wishes of their political masters or give up on being judges.

The debate about whether the law is an instrument of justice carries over into recent feminist scholarship about the law. The readings approach the same set of issues in light of recent feminist scholarship. Historically, the law has treated women badly. At common law, women were not allowed to own property, husbands were allowed to beat their wives, and victims of sexual assault were presumed to have consented. Feminist scholarship has criticized these implicit (sometimes explicit) biases. Some feminist scholarship has supposed that the law can nonetheless be reclaimed for feminist purposes; other feminists take a less optimistic view.

The selections in this opening chapter look at the traditional jurisprudential question, "What is law?" Both positivists and anti-positivists agree that law is a distinctive type of social ordering, but disagree about what makes it distinctive. Positivists suppose that law can be identified solely by its sources, while their critics suppose it must be identified by its particular moral content.

Thomas Hobbes
Leviathan (1651)

Hobbes is widely regarded as the greatest of the English political philosophers. He is also plausibly credited with being the founder of modern legal philosophy. Various forms of dispute resolution, legislation, and punishment have been found in all human societies. In early modern England, the church had its own laws and courts, as did various nobles, just as universities and workplaces have analogous disciplinary practices to this day. Hobbes, writing at the dawn of the modern age, was the first philosopher to identify law as a type of order exercised above all by the state. Thus, Hobbes understands legal order in terms of its sources, rather than its particular content. The selections included here set the context for Hobbes's view of law with his description of what he calls "the natural condition of mankind." Hobbes views the state as the solution to a practical problem of order. Laws provide predictability, and are backed with threats. As a result, they change the structure of social life from one of opposition and distrust to one of coordination. For Hobbes, such coordination is only possible if there is a single sovereign charged with making, applying, and enforcing law. Anything else, including any kind of moral limitation on the sovereign, risks controversy and eventual war. As a result, law must be identified with whatever the sovereign commands.

CHAPTER 5

And as in Arithmetique, unpractised men must, and Professors them-selves may often erre, and cast up false; so also in any other subject of Reasoning, the ablest, most attentive, and most practised men, may deceive themselves, and inferre false Conclusions; Not but that Reason it selfe is always Right Reason, as well as Arithmetique is a certain and infallible Art: But no one mans Reason, nor the Reason of any one number of men, makes the certaintie; no more than an account is there-fore well cast up, because a great many men have unanimously ap-proved it. And therefore, as when there is a controversy in [19] an account, the parties must by their own accord, set up for right Reason, the Reason of some Arbitrator, or Judge, to whose sentence they will both stand, or their controversie must either come to blowes, or be un-decided, for want of a right Reason constituted by Nature; so is it also in all debates of what kind soever: And when men that think them-selves wiser than all others, clamour and demand right Reason for judge; yet seek no more, but that things should be determined, by no other mens reason but their own, it is as intolerable in the society of men, as it is in play after trump is turned, to use for trump on every occasion, that suite whereof they have most in their hand. For they do nothing els, that will have every of their passions, as it comes to bear sway in them, to be taken for right Reason, and that in their own con-troversies: bewraying their want of right Reason, by the claym they lay to it.

CHAPTER 6

But whatsoever is the object of any mans Appetite or Desire; that is it, which he for his part calleth *Good:* And the object of his Hate, and Aversion, *Evill;* And of his Contempt, *Vile, and Inconsiderable.* For these words of Good, Evill, and Contemptible, are ever used with relation to the person that useth them: There being nothing simply and absolutely so; nor any common Rule of Good and Evill, to be taken from the nature of the objects themselves; but from the Person of the man (where there is no Common-wealth;) or, (in a Common-wealth,) from the Person that representeth it; or from an Arbitrator or Judge, whom men disagreeing shall by consent set up, and make his sentence the Rule thereof.

CHAPTER 13: OF THE NATURALL CONDITION OF *MANKIND, AS CONCERNING THEIR FELICITY, AND MISERY*

Nature hath made men so equall, in the faculties of body, and mind; as that though there bee found one man sometimes manifestly stronger in body, or of quicker mind than another; yet when all is reckoned together, the difference between man, and man, is not so considerable, as that one man can thereupon claim to himselfe any benefit, to which another may not pretend, as well as he. For as to the strength of body, the weakest has strength enough to kill the strongest, either by secret machination, or by confederacy with others, that are in the same danger with himselfe.

And as to the faculties of the mind, (setting aside the arts grounded upon words, and especially that skill of proceeding upon generall, and infallible rules, called Science; which very few have, and but in few things; as being not a native faculty, born with us; nor attained, (as Prudence,) while we look after somewhat els,) I find yet a greater equality amongst men, than that of strength. For Prudence, is but Experience; which equall time, equally bestows on all men, in [61] those things they equally apply themselves unto. That which may perhaps make such equality incredible, is but a vain conceit of ones own wisdom, which almost all men think they have in a greater degree, than the Vulgar; that is, than all men but themselves, and a few others, whom by Fame, or for concurring with themselves, they approve. For such is the nature of men, that howsoever they may acknowledge many others to be more witty, or more eloquent, or more learned; Yet they will hardly believe there be many so wise as themselves: For they see their own wit at hand, and other mens at a distance. But this proveth rather that men are in that point equall, than unequall. For there is not ordinarily a greater signe of the equall distribution of any thing, than that every man is contented with his share.

From this equality of ability, ariseth equality of hope in the attaining of our Ends. And therefore if any two men desire the same thing, which neverthelesse they cannot both enjoy, they become enemies; and in the way to their End, (which is principally their owne conservation, and sometimes their delectation only,) endeavour to destroy, or subdue one an other. And from hence it comes to passe, that where an Invader hath no more to feare, than an other mans single power; if one plant, sow, build, or possesse a convenient Seat, others may probably be expected to come prepared with forces united, to dispossesse, and deprive him, not only of the fruit of his labour, but also of his life, or liberty. And the Invader again is in the like danger of another.

And from this diffidence of one another, there is no way for any man to secure himselfe, so reasonable, as Anticipation; that is, by force, or wiles, to master the persons of all men he can, so long, till he see no other power great enough to endanger him: And this is no more than his own conservation requireth, and is generally allowed. Also because there be some, that taking pleasure in contemplating their own power in the acts of conquest, which they pursue farther than their security requires; if others, that otherwise would be glad to be at ease within modest bounds, should not by invasion increase their power, they would not be able, long time, by standing only on their defence, to subsist. And by consequence, such augmentation of dominion over men, being necessary to a mans conservation, it ought to be allowed him.

Againe, men have no pleasure, (but on the contrary a great deale of griefe) in keeping company, where there is no power able to over-awe them all. For every man looketh that his companion should value him, at the same rate he sets upon himselfe: And upon all signes of contempt, or undervaluing, naturally endeavours, as far as he dares (which amongst them that have no common power, to keep them in quiet, is far enough to make them destroy each other,) to extort a greater value from his contemners, by dommage; and from others, by the example.

So that in the nature of man, we find three principall causes of quarrell. First, Competition; Secondly, Diffidence; Thirdly, Glory.

[62] The first, maketh men invade for Gain; the second, for Safety; and the third, for Reputation. The first use Violence, to make themselves Masters of other mens persons, wives, children, and cattell; the second, to defend them; the third, for trifles, as a word, a smile, a different opinion, and any other signe of undervalue, either direct in their Persons, or by reflexion in their Kindred, their Friends, their Nation, their Profession, or their Name.

Hereby it is manifest, that during the time men live without a common Power to keep them all in awe, they are in that condition which is called Warre; and such a warre, as is of every man, against every man. For Warre, consisteth not in Battell onely, or the act of fighting; but in a tract of time, wherein the Will to contend by Battell is sufficiently known: and therefore the notion of *Time*, is to be considered in the nature of Warre; as it is in the nature of Weather. For as the nature of Foule weather, lyeth not in a showre or two of rain; but in an inclination thereto of many days together: So the nature of War, consisteth not in actuall fighting; but in the known disposition thereto, during all the time there is no assurance to the contrary. All other time is Peace.

Whatsoever therefore is consequent to a time of Warre, where every man is Enemy to every man; the same is consequent to the time, wherein men live without other security, than what their own strength, and their own invention shall furnish them withall. In such condition, there is no place for Industry; because the fruit thereof is uncertain: and consequently no Culture of the Earth; no Navigation, nor use of the commodities that may be imported by Sea; no commodious Building; no Instruments of moving, and removing such things as require much force; no Knowledge of the face of the Earth; no account of Time; no Arts; no Letters; no Society; and which is worst of all, continuall feare, and danger of violent death; And the life of man, solitary, poore, nasty, brutish, and short.

It may seem strange to some man, that has not well weighed these things; that Nature should thus dissociate, and render men apt to invade, and destroy one another: and he may therefore, not trusting to this Inference, made from the Passions, desire perhaps to have the same confirmed by Experience. Let him therefore consider with himselfe, when taking a journey, he armes himselfe, and seeks to go well accompanied; when going to sleep, he locks his dores; when even in his house he locks his chests; and this when he knows there bee Lawes, and publike Officers, armed, to revenge all injuries shall bee done him; what opinion he has of his fellow subjects, when he rides armed; of his fellow Citizens, when he locks his dores; and of his children, and servants, when he locks his chests. Does he not there as much accuse mankind by his actions, as I do by my words? But neither of us accuse mans nature in it. The Desires, and other Passions of man, are in themselves no Sin. No more are the Actions, that proceed from those Passions, till they know a Law that forbids them: which till Lawes be made they cannot know: nor can any Law be made, till they have agreed upon the Person that shall make it.

[63] It may peradventure be thought, there was never such a time, nor condition of warre as this; and I believe it was never generally so, over all the world: but there are many places, where they live so now. For the savage people in many places of *America*, except the government of small Families, the concord whereof dependeth on naturall lust, have no government at all; and live at this day in that brutish manner, as I said before. Howsoever, it may be perceived what manner of life there

would be, where there were no common Power to feare; by the manner of life, which men that have formerly lived under a peacefull government, use to degenerate into, in a civill Warre.

But though there had never been any time, wherein particular men were in a condition of warre one against another; yet in all times, Kings, and Persons of Soveraigne authority, because of their Independency, are in continuall jealousies, and in the state and posture of Gladiators; having their weapons pointing, and their eyes fixed on one another; that is, their Forts, Garrisons, and Guns upon the Frontiers of their Kingdomes; and continuall Spyes upon their neighbours; which is a posture of War. But because they uphold thereby, the Industry of their Subjects; there does not follow from it, that misery, which accompanies the Liberty of particular men.

To this warre of every man against every man, this also is consequent; that nothing can be Unjust. The notions of Right and Wrong, Justice and Injustice have there no place. Where there is no common Power, there is no Law: where no Law, no Injustice. Force, and Fraud, are in warre the two Cardinall vertues. Justice, and Injustice are none of the Faculties neither of the Body, nor Mind. If they were, they might be in a man that were alone in the world, as well as his Senses, and Passions. They are Qualities, that relate to men in Society, not in Solitude. It is consequent also to the same condition, that there be no Propriety, no Dominion, no *Mine* and *Thine* distinct; but onely that to be every mans that he can get; and for so long, as he can keep it. And thus much for the ill condition, which man by meer Nature is actually placed in; though with a possibility to come out of it, consisting partly in the Passions, partly in his Reason.

The Passions that encline men to Peace, are Feare of Death; Desire of such things as are necessary to commodious living; and a Hope by their Industry to obtain them. And Reason suggesteth convenient Articles of Peace, upon which men may be drawn to agreement. These Articles, are they, which otherwise are called the Lawes of Nature: whereof I shall speak more particularly, in the two following Chapters. [64]

CHAPTER 14: *OF THE FIRST AND SECOND* NATURALL LAWES, *AND OF* CONTRACTS

The Right of Nature, which Writers commonly call *Jus Naturale*, is the Liberty each man hath, to use his own power, as he will himselfe, for the preservation of his own Nature; that is to say, of his own Life; and consequently, of doing any thing, which in his own Judgement, and Reason, hee shall conceive to be the aptest means thereunto.

By Liberty, is understood, according to the proper signification of the word, the absence of externall Impediments: which Impediments, may oft take away part of a mans power to do what hee would; but cannot hinder him from using the power left him, according as his judgement, and reason shall dictate to him.

A Law of Nature, *(Lex Naturalis,)* is a precept, or generall Rule, found out by Reason, by which a man is forbidden to do, that, which is destructive of his life, or taketh away the means of preserving the same; and to omit, that, by which he thinketh it may be best preserved. For though they that speak of this subject, use to confound *Jus*, and *Lex*, *Right* and *Law;* yet they ought to be distinguished; because RIGHT, consisteth in liberty to do, or to forbeare; Whereas LAW, determineth, and bindeth to one of them: so that Law, and Right, differ as much, as Obligation, and Liberty; which in one and the same matter are inconsistent.

And because the condition of Man, (as hath been declared in the precedent Chapter) is a condition of Warre of every one against every one; in which case every one is governed by his own Reason; and there is nothing he can make use of, that may not be a help unto him, in preserving his life against his enemyes; It followeth, that in such a condition, every man has a Right to every thing; even to one anothers body. And therefore, as long as this naturall Right of every man to every thing endureth, there can be no security to any man, (how strong or wise soever he be,) of living out the time, which Nature ordinarily alloweth men to live. And consequently it is a precept, or generall rule of Reason, *That every man, ought to endeavour Peace, as farre as he has hope of obtaining it; and when he cannot obtain it, that he may seek, and use, all helps, and advantages of Warre.* The first branch of which Rule, containeth the first, and Fundamentall Law of Nature; which is, *to seek Peace, and follow it.* The Second, the summe of the Right of Nature; which is, By *all means we can, to defend our selves.*

From this Fundamentall Law of Nature, by which men are commanded to endeavour Peace, is derived this second Law; *That a man be willing, when others are so too, as farre-forth, as for Peace, and* [65] *defence of himselfe he shall think it necessary, to lay down this right to all things; and be contented with so much liberty against other men, as he would allow other men against himselfe.* For as long as every man holdeth this Right, of doing any thing he liketh; so long are all men in the condition of Warre. But if other men will not lay down their Right, as well as he; then there is no Reason for any one, to devest himselfe of his: For that were to expose himselfe to Prey, (which no man is bound to) rather than to dispose himselfe to Peace. This is that Law of the Gospell; *Whatsoever you require that others should do to you, that do ye to them.* And that Law of all men, *Quod tibi fieri non vis, alteri ne feceris ...*

A Covenant not to defend my selfe from force, by force, is alwayes voyd. For (as I have shewed before) no man can transferre or lay down his Right to save himselfe from Death, Wounds, and Imprisonment, (the avoyding whereof is the onely End of laying [70] down any Right, and therefore the promise of not resisting force, in no Covenant transferreth any right; nor is obliging. For though a man may Covenant thus, *Unlesse I do so, or so, kill* me; he cannot Covenant thus, *Unlesse I do so, or so, I will not resist you, when you come to kill me.* For man by nature chooseth the lesser evill, which is danger of death in resisting; rather than the greater, which is certain and present death in not resisting. And this is granted to be true by all men, in that they lead Criminals to Execution, and Prison, with armed men, notwithstanding that such Criminals have consented to the Law, by which they are condemned.

CHAPTER 15: OF OTHER LAWES OF NATURE

From that law of Nature, by which we are obliged to transferre to another, such Rights, as being retained, hinder the peace of Mankind, there followeth a Third; which is this, *That men performe their Covenants made*: without which, Covenants are in vain, and but Empty words; and the Right of all men to all things remaining, wee are still in the condition of Warre.

And in this law of Nature, consisteth the Fountain and Originall of JUSTICE. For where no Convenant hath preceded, there hath no Right been transferred, and every man has right to every thing; and consequently, no action can be Unjust. But when a Covenant is made, then to break it is *Unjust*: And the definition of INJUSTICE, is no other than *the not Performance of Covenant*. And whatsoever is not Unjust, is *Just*.

But because Covenants of mutuall trust, where there is a feare of not performance on either part, (as hath been said in the former Chapter,) are invalid; though the Originall of Justice be the making of Covenants; yet Injustice actually there can be none, till the cause of such feare be taken away; which while men are in the naturall condition of Warre, cannot be done. Therefore before the names of Just, and Unjust can have place, there must be some coercive Power, to compell men equally to the performance of their Covenants, by the terrour of some punishment, greater than the benefit they expect [72] by the breach of their Covenant; and to make good that Propriety, which by mutuall Contract men acquire, in recompence of the universall Right they abandon: and such power there is none before the erection of a Commonwealth. And this is also to be gathered out of the ordinary definition of Justice in the Schooles; For they say, that *Justice is the constant Will of giving to every man his own*. And therefore where there is no *Own*, that is, no Propriety, there is no Injustice; and where there is no coërceive Power erected, that is, where there is no Common-wealth, there is no Propriety; all men having Right to all things: Therefore where there is no Common-wealth, there nothing is Unjust. So that the nature of Justice, consisteth in keeping of valid Covenants; but the Validity of Covenants begins not but with the Constitution of a Civill Power, sufficient to compell men to keep them: And then it is also that Propriety begins.

The Foole hath sayd in his heart, there is no such thing as Justice; and sometimes also with his tongue; seriously alleaging, that every mans conservation, and contentment, being committed to his own care, there could be no reason, why every man might not do what he thought conduced thereunto: and therefore also to make, or not make; keep, or not keep Covenants, was not against Reason, when it conduced to ones benefit. He does not therein deny, that there be Covenants; and that they are sometimes broken, sometimes kept; and that such breach of them may be called Injustice, and the observance of them Justice: but he questioneth, whether Injustice, taking away the feare of God, (for the same Foole hath said in his heart there is no God,) may not sometimes stand with that Reason, which dictateth to every man his own good; and particularly then, when it conduceth to such a benefit, as shall put a man in a condition, to neglect not onely the dispraise, and revilings, but also the power of other men. The Kingdome of God is gotten by violence: but what if it could be gotten by unjust violence? were it against Reason so to get it, when it is impossible to receive hurt by it? And if it be not against Reason, it is not against Justice: or else Justice is not to be approved for good. From such reasoning as this, Successful wickednesse hath obtained the name of Vertue: and some that in all other things have disallowed the violation of Faith; yet have allowed it, when it is for the getting of a Kingdome. And the Heathen that believed, that *Saturn* was deposed by his son *Jupiter*, believed neverthelesse the same *Jupiter* to be the avenger of Injustice: Somewhat like to a piece of Law in *Cokes* Commentaries on *Litleton*; where he sayes, If the right Heire of the Crown be attainted of Treason; yet the Crown shall descend to him, and *eo instante* the Atteynder be voyd: From which instances a man will be very prone to inferre; that when the Heire apparent of a Kingdome, shall kill him that is in possession, though his father; you may call it Injustice, or by what other name you will; yet it can never be against reason, seeing all the voluntary actions of men tend to the benefit of themselves; and those actions are most reasonable, that conduce most to their [73] ends. This specious reasoning is neverthelesse false.

For the question is not of promises mutuall, where there is no security of performance on either side; as when there is no Civill Power erected over the parties promising; for such promises are no Covenants: But either where one of the parties has performed already; or where there is a Power to make him performe; there is the question whether it be against reason, that is, against the benefit of the other to performe, or not. And I say it is not against reason. For the manifestation whereof, we are to consider; First, that when a man doth a thing, which notwithstanding any thing can be foreseen, and reckoned on, tendeth to his own destruction, howsoever some accident which he could not expect, arriving may turne it to his benefit; yet such events do not make it reasonably or wisely done. Secondly, that in a condition of Warre, wherein every man to every man, for want of a common Power to keep them all in awe, is an Enemy, there is no man can hope by his own strength, or wit, to defend himselfe from destruction, without the help of Confederates; where every one expects the same defence by the Confederation, that any one else does: and therefore he which declares he thinks it reason to deceive those that help him, can in reason expect no other means of safety, than what can be had from his own single Power. He therefore that breaketh his Covenant, and consequently declareth that he thinks he may with reason do so, cannot be received into any Society, that unite themselves for Peace and Defence, but by the errour of them that receive him; nor when he is received, be retayned in it, without seeing the danger of their errour; which errours a man cannot reasonably reckon upon as the means of his security: and therefore if he be left, or cast out of Society, he perisheth; and if he live in Society, it is by the errours of other men, which he could not foresee, nor reckon upon; and consequently against the reason of his preservation; and so, as all men that contribute not to his destruction, forbear him only out of ignorance of what is good for themselves.

As for the Instance of gaining the secure and perpetuall felicity of Heaven, by any way; it is frivolous: there being but one way imaginable; and that is not breaking, but keeping of Covenant.

And for the other Instance of attaining Soveraignty by Rebellion; it is manifest, that though the event follow, yet because it cannot reasonably be expected, but rather the contrary; and because by gaining it so, others are taught to gain the same in like manner, the attempt thereof is against reason. Justice therefore, that is to say, Keeping of Covenant, is a Rule of Reason, by which we are forbidden to do any thing destructive to our life; and consequently a law of Nature.

There be some that proceed further; and will not have the Law of Nature, to be those Rules which conduce to the preservation of mans life on earth; but to the attaining of an eternall felicity after death; to which they think the breach of Covenant may conduce; and consequently be just and reasonable; (such are they that think it a work of [74] merit to kill, or depose, or rebell against, the Soveraigne Power constituted over them by their own consent.) But because there is no naturall knowledge of mans estate after death; much lesse of the reward that is then to be given to breach of Faith; but onely a beliefe grounded upon other mens saying, that they know it supernaturally, or that they know those, that knew them, that knew others, that knew it supernaturally; Breach of Faith cannot be called a Precept of Reason, or Nature.

Others, that allow for a Law of Nature, the keeping of Faith, do neverthelesse make exception of certain persons; as Heretiques, and such as use not to performe their Covenant to others; And this also is against reason. For if any fault of a man, be sufficient to discharge our Covenant made; the same ought in reason to have been sufficient not to have hindred the making of it.

The names of Just, and Injust, when they are attributed to Men, signifie one thing; and when they are attributed to actions, another. When they are attributed to Men, they signifie Conformity, or Inconformity of Manners, to Reason. But when they are attributed to Actions, they signifie the Conformity, or Inconformity to Reason, not of Manners, or manner of life, but of particular Actions. A Just man therefore, is he that taketh all the care he can, that his Actions may be all Just: and an Unjust man, is he that neglecteth it. And such men are more often in our Language stiled by the names of Righteous, and Unrighteous; then Just, and Unjust; though the meaning be the same. Therefore a Righteous man, does not lose that Title, by one, or a few unjust Actions, that proceed from sudden Passion, or mistake of Things, or Persons: nor does an Unrighteous man, lose his character, for such Actions, as he does, or forbeares to do, for feare: because his Will is not framed by the Justice, but by the apparant benefit of what he is to do. That which gives to humane Actions the relish of Justice, is a certain Noblenesse or Gallantnesse of courage, (rarely found,) by which a man scorns to be beholding for the contentment of his life, to fraud, or breach of promise. This Justice of the Manners, is that which is meant, where Justice is called a Vertue; and Injustice a Vice.

But the Justice of Actions denominates man, not Just, but *Guiltlesse*: and the Injustice of the same, (which is also called Injury,) gives them but the name of *Guilty*.

Again, the Injustice of Manners, is the disposition, or aptitude to do Injurie; and is Injustice before it proceed to Act; and without supposing any individuall person injured. But the Injustice of an Action, (that is to say Injury,) supposeth an individuall person Injured; namely him, to whom the Covenant was made: And therefore many times the injury is received by one man, when the dammage redoundeth to another. As when the Master commandeth his servant to give mony to a stranger; if it be not done, the Injury is done to the Master, whom he had before Covenanted to obey; but the dammage redoundeth to the stranger, to whom he had no Obligation; and therefore could not Injure him. And so also in Common-[75]wealths, private men may remit to one another their debts; but not robberies or other violences, whereby they are endammaged; because the detaining of Debt, is an Injury to themselves; but Robbery and Violence, are Injuries to the Person of the Commonwealth.

Whatsoever is done to a man, conformable to his own Will signified to the doer, is no Injury to him. For if he that doeth it, hath not passed away his originall right to do what he please, by some Antecedent Covenant, there is no breach of Covenant; and therefore no Injury done him. And if he have; then his Will to have it done being signified, is a release of that Covenant; and so again there is no Injury done him.

Justice of Actions, is by Writers divided into *Commutative*, and *Distributive*: and the former they say consisteth in proportion Arithmeticall; the later in proportion Geometricall. Commutative therefore, they place in the equality of value of the things contracted for; and Distributive, in the distribution of equall benefit, to men of equall merit. As if it were Injustice to sell dearer than we buy; or to give more to a man than he merits. The value of all things contracted for, is measured by the Appetite of the Contractors: and therefore the just value, is that which they be contented to give. And Merit (besides that which is by Covenant, where the performance on one part, meriteth the performance of the other part, and falls under Justice Commutative, not Distributive,) is not due by Justice; but is rewarded of Grace onely. And therefore this distinction, in the sense wherein it useth to be expounded, is not right. To speak properly, Commutative Justice, is the Justice of a Contractor; that is, a Performance of Covenant, in Buying, and Selling; Hiring, and Letting to Hire; Lending, and Borrowing; Exchanging, Bartering and other acts of Contract.

And Distributive Justice, the Justice of an Arbitrator; that is to say, the act of defining what is Just. Wherein, (being trusted by them that make him Arbitrator), if he performe his Trust, he is said to distribute to every man his own: and this is indeed Just Distribution, and may be called (though improperly) Distributive Justice; but more properly Equity; which also is a Law of Nature, as shall be shewn in due place.

As Justice dependeth on Antecedent Covenant; so does GRATITUDE depend on Antecedent Grace; that is to say, Antecedent Free-gift: and is the fourth Law of Nature; which may be conceived in this Forme, *That a man which receiveth Benefit from another of meer Grace, Endeavour that he which giveth it, have no reasonable cause to repent him of his good will.* For no man giveth, but with intention of Good to himself; because Gift is Voluntary; and of all Voluntary Acts, the Object is to every man his own Good; of which if men see they shall be frustrated, there will be no beginning of benevolence, or trust; nor consequently of mutuall help; nor of reconciliation of one man to another; and therefore they are to remain still in the condition of *War*; which is contrary to the first and Fundamentall Law of Nature, which commandeth men to *Seek Peace*. The breach of this Law, [76] is called *Ingratitude*; and hath the same relation to Grace, that Injustice hath to Obligation by Covenant.

A fifth Law of Nature, is COMPLEASANCE; that is to say, *That every man strive to accommodate himselfe to the rest.* For the understanding whereof, we may consider, that there is in mens aptnesse to Society; a diversity of Nature, rising from their diversity of Affections; not unlike to that we see in stones brought together for building of an Ædifice. For as that stone which by the asperity, and irregularity of Figure, takes more room from others, than it selfe fills; and for the hardnesse, cannot be easily made plain, and thereby hindereth the building, is by the builders cast away as unprofitable, and troublesome: so also, a man that by asperity of Nature, will strive to retain those things which to himselfe are superfluous, and to others necessary; and for the stubbornness of his Passions, cannot be corrected, is to be left, or cast out of Society, as combersome thereunto. For seeing every man, not onely by Right, but also by necessity of Nature, is supposed to endeavour all he can, to obtain that which is necessary for his conservation; He that shall oppose himselfe against it, for things superfluous, is guilty of the warre that thereupon is to follow; and therefore doth that, which is contrary to the fundamentall Law of Nature, which commandeth *to seek Peace*. The observers of this Law, may be called SOCIABLE, (the Latines call them *Commodi;*) The contrary, *Stubborn, Insociable, Froward, Intractable*.

A sixth law of Nature is this, *That upon caution of the Future time, a man ought to pardon the offences past of them that repenting, desire it*. For PARDON, is nothing but granting of Peace; which though granted to them that persevere in their hostility, be not Peace, but Feare; yet not granted to them that give caution of the Future time, is signe of an aversion to Peace; and therefore contrary to the Law of Nature.

A seventh is, *That in Revenges*, (that is, retribution of Evil for Evil,) *Men look not at the greatnesse of the evill past, but the greatnesse of the good to follow*. Whereby we are forbidden to inflict punishment with any other designe, than for correction of the offender, or direction of others. For this Law is consequent to the next before it, that commandeth Pardon, upon security of the Future time. Besides, Revenge without respect to the Example, and profit to come, is a triumph, or glorying in the hurt of another, tending to no end; (for the End is always somewhat to Come;) and glorying to an end, is vain-glory, and contrary to reason; and to hurt without reason, tendeth to the introduction of Warre; which is against the Law of Nature; and is commonly stiled by the name of *Cruelty*.

And because all signes of hatred, or contempt, provoke to fight; insomuch as most men choose rather to hazard their life, than not to be revenged; we may in the eighth place, for a Law of Nature, set down this Precept, *That no man by deed, word, countenance, or gesture, declare Hatred, or Contempt of another*. The breach of which Law, is commonly called *Contumely*.

The question who is the better man, has no place in the condition of meer Nature; where, (as has been shewn before,) all men are equall. [77] The inequallity that now is, has bin introduced by the Lawes civill. I know that *Aristotle* in the first books of his politiques, for a foundation of his doctrine, maketh men by Nature, some more worthy to Command, meaning the wiser sort (such as he thought himselfe to be for his Philosophy;) others to Serve, (meaning those that had strong bodies, but were not Philosophers as he;) as if Master and Servant were not introduced by consent of men, but by difference of Wit: which is not only against reason; but also against experience. For there are very few so foolish, that had not rather governe themselves, than be governed by others: Nor when the wise in their own conceit, contend by force, with them who distrust their owne wisdome, to they alwaies, or often, or almost at any time, get the Victory. If Nature therefore have made men equall, that equalitie is to be acknowledged: or if Nature have made men unequall; yet because men that think themselves equall, will not enter into conditions of Peace, but upon Equall termes, such equalitie must be admitted. And therefore for the ninth law of Nature, I put this, *That every man acknowledge other for his Equall by Nature.* The breach of this Precept is *Pride.*

On this law, dependeth another, *That at the entrance into conditions of Peace, no man require to reserve to himselfe any Right, which he is not content should be reserved to every one of the rest.* As it is necessary for all men that seek peace, to lay down certaine Rights of Nature; that is to say, not to have libertie to do all they list: so is it necessarie for mans life, to retaine some; as right to governe their owne bodies; enjoy aire, water, motion, waies to go from place to place; and all things else without which a man cannot live, or not live well. If in this case, at the making of Peace, men require for themselves, that which they would not have to be granted to others, they do contrary to the precedent law, that commandeth the acknowledgment of naturall equalitie, and therefore also against the law of Nature. The observers of this law, are those we call *Modest,* and the breakers *Arrogant* men. The Greeks call the violation of this law πλεονεξία; that is, a desire of more than their share.

Also if *a man be trusted to judge between man and man,* it is a precept of the Law of Nature, *that he deale Equally between them.* For without that, the Controversies of men cannot be determined but by Warre. He therefore that is partiall in judgment, doth what in him lies, to deterre men from the use of Judges, and Arbitrators; and consequently, (against the fundamentall Lawe of Nature) is the cause of Warre.

The observance of this law, from the equall distribution to each man, of that which in reason belongeth to him, is called EQUITY, and (as I have sayd before) distributive Justice: the violation, *Acception of persons,* προσωποληψία.

And from this followeth another law, *That such things as cannot be divided, be enjoyed in Common, if it can be; and if the quantity of the thing per-*

mit, without Stint; otherwise Proportionably to the number of them that have Right. For otherwise the distribution is Unequall, and contrary to Equitie.

But some things there be, that can neither be divided, nor enjoyed in common. Then, The Law of Nature, which prescribeth Equity, requireth, *That the Entire Right; or else, (making the use alternate,) the First Possession, be determined by Lot.* For equall distribution, is of the Law of Nature; and other means of equall distribution cannot be imagined.

Of *Lots* there be two sorts, *Arbitrary,* and *Naturall.* Arbitrary, is that which is agreed on by the Competitors; Naturall is either *Primogeniture,* (which the Greek calls Κληρονομία, which signifies, *Given by Lot;*) or *First Seisure.*

And therefore those things which cannot be enjoyed in common, nor divided, ought to be adjudged to the First Possessor; and in some cases to the First-Borne, as acquired by Lot.

It is also a Law of Nature, *That all men that mediate Peace, be allowed safe Conduct.* For the Law that commandeth Peace, as the *End,* commandeth Intercession, as the *Means;* and to Intercession the Means is safe Conduct.

And because, though men be never so willing to observe these Lawes, there may neverthelesse arise questions concerning a mans action; First, whether it were done, or not done; Secondly (if done) whether against the Law, or not against the Law; the former whereof, is called a question *Of Fact;* the later a question *Of Right;* therefore unlesse the parties to the question, Covenant mutually to stand to the sentence of another, they are as farre from Peace as ever. This other, to whose Sentence they submit, is called an ARBITRATOR. And therefore it is of the Law of Nature, *That they that are at controversie, submit their Right to the judgement of an Arbitrator.*

And seeing every man is presumed to do all things in order to his own benefit, no man is a fit Arbitrator in his own cause: and if he were never so fit; yet Equity allowing to each party equall benefit, if one be admitted to be Judge, the other is to be admitted also; & so the controversie, that is, the cause of War, remains, against the Law of Nature.

For the same reason no man in any Cause ought to be received for Arbitrator, to whom greater profit, or honour, or pleasure apparently ariseth out of the victory of one part, than of the other: for hee hath taken (though an unavoydable bribe, yet) a bribe; and no man can be obliged to trust him. And thus also the controversie, and the condition of War remaineth, contrary to the Law of Nature.

And in a controversie of *Fact*, the Judge being to give no more credit to one, than to the other, (if there be no other Arguments) must give credit to a third; or to a third and fourth; or more: For else the question is undecided, and left to force, contrary to the Law of Nature.

There are the Lawes of Nature, dictating Peace, for a means of the conservation of men in multitudes; and which onely concern the doctrine of Civill Society. There be other things tending to the destruction of particular men; as Drunkenness, and all other parts of Intemperance; which may therefore also be reckoned amongst those things which the Law of Nature hath forbidden; but are not neces[79]sary to be mentioned, nor are pertinent enough to this place.

And though this may seem too subtile a deduction of the Lawes of Nature, to be taken notice of by all men; whereof the most part are too busie in getting food, and the rest too negligent to understand; yet to leave all men unexcusable, they have been contracted into one easie sum, intelligible, even to the meanest capacity; and that is, *Do not that to another, which thou wouldest not have done to they selfe*; which sheweth him, that he has no more to do in learning the Lawes of Nature, but when weighing the actions of other men with his own, they seem too heavy, to put them into the other part of the ballance, and his own into their place, that his own passions, and selfe-love, may adde nothing to the weight; and then there is none of these Lawes of Nature that will not appear unto him very reasonable.

The Lawes of Nature oblige *in foro interno*; that is to say, they bind to a desire they should take place: but *in foro externo*; that is, to the putting them in act, not alwayes. For he that should be modest, and tractable, and performe all he promises, in such time, and place, where no man els should do so, should but make himselfe a prey to others, and procure his own certain ruine, contrary to the ground of all Lawes of Nature, which tend to Natures preservation. And again, he that having sufficient Security, that others shall observe the same Lawes towards him, observes them not himselfe, seeketh not Peace, but War; & consequently the destruction of his Nature by Violence.

And whatsoever Lawes bind *in foro interno*, may be broken, not onely by a fact contrary to the Law but also by a fact according to it, in case a man think it contrary. For though his Action in this case, be according to the Law; yet his Purpose was against the Law; which where the Obligation is *in foro interno*, is a breach.

The Lawes of Nature are Immutable and Eternall; For Injustice, Ingratitude, Arrogance, Pride, Iniquity, Acception of persons, and the rest, can never be made lawfull. For it can never be that Warre shall preserve life, and Peace destroy it.

The same Lawes, because they oblige onely to a desire, and endeavour, I mean an unfeigned and constant endeavour, are easie to be observed. For in that they require nothing but endeavour; he that endeavoureth their performance, fulfilleth them; and he that fulfilleth the Law, is Just.

And the Science of them, is the true and onely Moral Philosophy. For Morall Philosophy is nothing else but the Science of what is *Good*, and *Evill*, in the conversation, and society of mankind. *Good*, and *Evill*, are names that signifie our Appetites, and Aversions; which in different tempers, customes, and doctrines of men, are different: And divers men, differ not onely in their Judgement, on the senses of what is pleasant, and unpleasant to the tast, smell, hearing, touch, and sight; but also of what is conformable, or disagreeable to Reason, in the actions of common life. Nay, the same man, in divers times, differs from himselfe; and one time praiseth, that is, calleth Good, what another time he dispraiseth, and calleth Evil: [80] From whence arise Disputes, Controversies, and at last War. And therefore so long a man is in the condition of meer Nature, (which is a condition of War,) as private Appetite is the measure of Good, and Evill: and consequently all men agree on this, that Peace is Good, and therefore also the way, or means of Peace, which (as I have shewed before) are *Justice, Gratitude, Modesty, Equity, Mercy*, & the rest of the Laws of Nature, are good; that is to say, *Morall Vertues*; and their contrarie *Vices*, Evill. Now the science of Vertue and Vice, is Morall Philosophie; and therefore the true Doctrine of the Lawes of Nature, is the true Morall Philosophie. But the Writers of Morall Philosophie, though they acknowledge the same Vertues and Vices; Yet not seeing wherein consisted their Goodnesse; nor that they come to be praised, as the meanes of peaceable, sociable, and comfortable living; place them in a mediocrity of passions: as if not the Cause, but the Degree of daring, made Fortitude; or not the Cause, but the Quantity of a gift, made Liberality.

These dictates of Reason, men use to call by the name of Lawes; but improperly: for they are but Conclusions, or Theoremes concerning what conduceth to the conservation and defence of themselves; wheras Law, properly is the word of him, that by right hath command over others. But yet if we consider the same Theoremes, as delivered in the word of God, that by right commandeth all things; then are they properly called Lawes.

CHAPTER 21

... Again, the Consent of a Subject to Soveraign Power, is contained in these words, *I Authorise, or take upon me, all his actions*; in which there is no restriction at all, of his own former naturall Liberty: For by allowing him to *kill me*, I am not bound to kill my selfe when he commands me. 'Tis one thing to say, *Kill me, or my fellow, if you please*; another thing to say, *I will kill my selfe, or my fellow*. It followeth therefore, that

No man is bound by the words themselves, either to kill himselfe, or any other man; And consequently, that the Obligation a man may sometimes have, upon the Command of the Soveraign to execute any dangerous, or dishonourable Office, dependeth not on the Words of our submission; but on the Intention; which is to be understood by the End thereof. When therefore our refusall to obey, frustrates the End for which the Soveraignty was ordained; then there is no Liberty to refuse: otherwise there is.

CHAPTER 25

Command is, where a man saith, *Doe this, or Doe not this*, without expecting other reason than the Will of him that sayes it. From this it followeth manifestly, that he that Commandeth, pretendeth thereby his own Benefit: For the reason of his Command is his own [132] Will onely, and the proper object of every mans Will, is some Good to himselfe.

Counsell, is where a man saith, *Doe, or Doe not this*, and deduceth his reasons from the benefit that arriveth by it to him to whom he saith it. And from this it is evident, that he that giveth Counsell, pretendeth onely (whatsoever he intendeth) the good of him, to whom he giveth it ...

CHAPTER 26: *OF* CIVILL LAWES

By Civill Lawes, I understand the Lawes, that men are therefore bound to observe, because they are Members, not of this, or that Common-wealth in particular, but of a Common-wealth. For the knowledge of particular Lawes [137] belongeth to them, that professe the study of the Lawes of their severall Countries; but the knowledge of Civill Law in generall, to any man. The antient Law of *Rome* was called their *Civil Law*, from the word *Civitas*, which signifies a Common-wealth: And those Countries, which having been under the Roman Empire, and governed by that Law, retaine still such part thereof as they think fit, call that part the Civill Law, to distinguish it from the rest of their own Civill Lawes. But that is not it I intend to speak of here; my designe being not to shew what is Law here, and there; but what is Law; as *Plato, Aristotle, Cicero*, and divers others have done, without taking upon them the profession of the study of the Law.

And first it is manifest, that Law in generall, is not Counsell, but Command; nor a Command of any man to any man; but only of him, whose Command is addressed to one formerly obliged to obey him. And as for Civill Law, it addeth only the name of the person Commanding, which is *Persona Civitatis*, the Person of the Common-wealth.

Which considered, I define Civill Law in this manner. Civill Law, *Is to every Subject, those Rules, which the Common-wealth hath Commanded him, by Word, Writing, or other sufficient Sign of the Will, to make use of, for the Distinction of Right, and Wrong; that is to say, of what is contrary, and what is not contrary to the Rule.*

In which definition, there is nothing that is not at first sight evident. For every man seeth, that some Lawes are addressed to all the Subjects in generall; some to particular Provinces; some to particular Vocations; and some to particular Men; and are therefore Lawes, to every of those to whom the Command is directed; and to none else. As also, that Lawes are the Rules of Just, and Unjust; nothing being reputed Unjust, that is not contrary to some Law. Likewise, that none can make Lawes but the Common-wealth; because our Subjection is to the Common-wealth only: and that Commands, are to be signified by sufficient Signs; because a man knows not otherwise how to obey them. And therefore, whatsoever can from this definition by necessary consequence be deduced, ought to be acknowledged for truth. Now I deduce from it this that followeth.

1. The Legislator in all Common-wealths, is only the Soveraign, be he one Man, as in a Monarchy, or one Assembly of men, as in a Democracy, or Aristocracy. For the Legislator, is he that maketh the Law. And the Common-wealth only, præscribes, and commandeth the observation of those rules, which we call Law: Therefore the Common-wealth is the Legislator. But the Common-wealth is no Person, nor has capacity to doe any thing, but by the Representative, (that is, the Soveraign;) and therefore the Soveraign is the sole Legislator. For the same reason, none can abrogate a Law made, but the Soveraign; because a Law is not abrogated, but by another Law, that forbiddeth it to be put in execution.

2. The Soveraign of a Common-wealth, be it an Assembly, or one Man, is not Subject to the Civill Lawes. For having power to [138] make, and repeale Lawes, he may when he pleaseth, free himselfe from that subjection, by repealing those Lawes that trouble him, and making of new; and consequently he was free before. For he is free, that can be free when he will: Nor is it possible for any person to be bound to himselfe; because he that can bind, can release; and therefore he that is bound to himselfe onely, is not bound.

3. When long Use obtaineth the authority of a Law, it is not the Length of Time that maketh the Authority, but the Will of the Soveraign signified by his silence, (for Silence is sometimes an argument of Consent;) and it is no longer Law, then the Soveraign shall be silent therein. And therefore if the Soveraign shall have a question of Right grounded, not upon his present Will, but upon the Lawes formerly made; the Length of Time shal bring no prejudice to his Right; but the question shal be judged by Equity. For many unjust Actions, and unjust Sentences, go uncontrolled a longer time, than any man can remember. And our Lawyers account no Customes Law, but such as are reasonable, and that eville Customes are to be abolished: But the Judgement of what is reasonable, and of what is to be abolished, belongeth to him that maketh the Law, which is the Soveraign Assembly, or Monarch.

4. The Law of Nature, and the Civill Law, contain each other, and are of equall extent. For the Lawes of Nature, which consist in Equity, Justice, Gratitude, and other morall Vertues on these depending, in the condition of meer Nature (as I have said before in the end of the 15th Chapter,) are not properly Lawes, but qualities that dispose men to peace, and to obedience. When a Common-wealth is once settled, then are they actually Lawes, and not before; as being then the commands of the Common-wealth; and therefore also Civill Lawes: For it is the Soveraign Power that obliges men to obey them. For in the differences of private men, to declare, what is Equity, what is Justice, and what is morall Vertue, and to make them binding, there is need of the Ordinances of Soveraign Power, and Punishments to be ordained for such as shall break them; which Ordinances are therefore part of the Civill Law. The Law of Nature therefore is a part of the Civill Law in all Common-wealths of the world. Reciprocally also, the Civill Law is a part of the Dictates of Nature. For Justice, that is to say, Performance of Covenant, and giving to every man his own, is a Dictate of the Law of Nature. But every subject in a Common-wealth, hath covenanted to obey the Civill Law, (either one with another, as when they assemble to

make a common Representative, or with the Representative it selfe one by one, when subdued by the Sword they promise obedience, that they may receive life;) And therefore Obedience to the Civill Law is part also of the Law of Nature. Civill, and Naturall Law are not different kinds, but different parts of Law; whereof one part being written, is called Civill, the other unwritten, Naturall. But the Right of Nature, that is, the naturall Liberty of man, may by the Civill Law be abridged, and re-strained: nay, the end of making Lawes, is no other, but such Restraint; without the which there cannot possibly be any Peace. And Law was brought into the world for nothing else, [139] but to limit the naturall liberty of particular men, in such manner, as they might not hurt, but assist one another, and joyn together against a common Enemy.

5. If the Soveraign of one Common-wealth, subdue a People that have lived under other written Lawes, and afterwards govern them by the same Lawes, by which they were governed before; yet those Lawes are the Civill Lawes of the Victor, and not of the Vanquished Common-wealth. For the Legislator is he, not by whose authority the Lawes were first made, but by whose authority they now continue to be Lawes. And therefore where there be divers Provinces, within the Dominion of a Common-wealth, and in those Provinces diversity of Lawes, which commonly are called the Customes of each severall Province, we are not to understand that such Customes have their force, onely from Length of Time; but that they were antiently Lawes written, or otherwise made known, for the Constitutions, and Statutes of their Soveraigns; and are now Lawes, not by vertue of the Præscription of time, but by the Con-stitutions of their present Soveraigns. But if an unwritten Law, in all the Provinces of a Dominion, shall be generally observed, and no iniquity appear in the use thereof; that Law can be no other but a Law of Nature, equally obliging all man-kind.

6. Seeing then all Lawes, written, and unwritten, have their Author-ity, and force, from the Will of the Common-wealth; that is to say, from the Will of the Representative; which in a Monarchy is the Monarch, and in other Common-wealths the Soveraign Assembly; a man may wonder from whence proceed such opinions, as are found in the Books of Lawyers of eminence in several Commonwealths, directly, or by consequence making the Legislative Power depend on private men, or subordinate Judges. As for example, *That the Common Law, hath no Controuler but the Parlament;* which is true onely where a Parlament has the Soveraign Power, and cannot be assembled, not dissolved, but by their own discretion. For if there be a right in any else to dissolve them,

there is a right also to controule them, and consequently to controule their controulings. And if there be no such right, then the Controuler of Lawes is not *Parlamentum*, but *Rex in Parlamento*. And where a Parlament is Soveraign, if it should assemble never so many, or so wise men, from the Countries subject to them, for whatsoever cause; yet there is no man will believe, that such an Assembly hath thereby acquired to themselves a Legislative Power. *Item*, that the two arms of a Common-wealth, are *Force, and Justice; the first whereof is in the King; the other deposited in the hands of the Parlament.* As if a Common-wealth could consist, where the Force were in any hand, which justice had not the Authority to command and govern.

7. That Law can never be against Reason, our Lawyers are agreed; and that not the Letter, (that is every construction of it,) but that which is according to the Intention of the Legislator, is the Law. And it is true: but the doubt is, of whose Reason it is, that shall be received for Law. It is not meant of any private Reason; for [140] then there would be as much contradiction in the Lawes, as there is in the Schooles; nor yet, (as Sr. *Ed. Coke* makes it,) an *Artificiall perfection of Reason, gotten by long study, observation, and experience,* (as his was.) For it is possible long study may encrease, and confirm erroneous Sentences: and where men build on false grounds, the more they build, the greater is the ruine: and of those that study, and observe with equall time, and diligence, the reasons and resolutions are, and must remain discordant: and therefore it is not that *Juris prudentia,* or wisedome of subordinate Judges; but the Reason of this our Artificiall Man the Common-wealth, and his Command, that maketh Law: And the Common-wealth being in their Representative but one Person, there cannot easily arise any contradiction in the Lawes; and when there doth, the same Reason is able, by interpretation, or alteration, to take it away. In all Courts of Justice, the Soveraign (which is the Person of the Common-wealth,) is he that Judgeth: The subordinate Judge, ought to have regard to the reason, which moved his Soveraign to make such Law, that his Sentence may be according thereunto; which then is his Soveraigns Sentence; otherwise it is his own, and an unjust one.

8. From this, that the Law is a Command, and a Command consisteth in declaration, or manifestation of the will of him that commandeth, by voyce, writing, or some other sufficient argument of the same, we may understand, that the Command of the Common-wealth, is Law onely to those, that have means to take notice of it. Over naturall fooles, children, or mad-men there is no Law, no more than over brute beasts; nor

are they capable of the title of just, or unjust; because they had never power to make any covenant, or to understand the consequences thereof; and consequently never took upon them to authorise the actions of any Soveraign, as they must do that make to themselves a Common-wealth. And as those from whom Nature, or Accident hath taken away the notice of all Lawes in generall; so also every man, from whom any accident, not proceeding from his own default, hath taken away the means to take notice of any particular Law, is excused, if he observe it not; And to speak properly, that Law is no Law to him. It is therefore necessary, to consider in this place, what arguments, and signes be sufficient for the knowledge of what is the Law; that is to say, what is the will of the Soveraign, as well in Monarchies, as in other formes of government.

And first, if it be a Law that obliges all the Subjects without exception, and is not written, nor otherwise published in such places as they may take notice thereof, it is a Law of Nature. For whatsoever men are to take knowledge of for Law, not upon other mens words, but every one from his own reason, must be such as is agreeable to the reason of all men; which no Law can be, but the Law of Nature. The Lawes of Nature therefore need not any publishing, nor Proclamation; as being contained in this one Sentence, approved by all the world, *Do not that to another, which thou thinkest unreasonable to be done by another to thy selfe.*

[141] Secondly, if it be a Law that obliges only some condition of men, or one particular man, and be not written, nor published by word, then also it is a Law of Nature; and known by the same arguments, and signs, that distinguish those in such a condition, from other Subjects. For whatsoever Law is not written, or some way published by him that makes it Law, can be known no way, but by the reason of him that is to obey it; and is therefore also a Law not only Civill, but Naturall. For Example, if the Soveraign employ a Publique Minister, without written Instructions what to doe; he is obliged to take for Instructions the Dictates of Reason; As if he make a Judge, The Judge is to take notice, that his Sentence ought to be according to the reason of his Soveraign, which being alwaies understood to be Equity, he is bound to it by the Law of Nature: Or if an Ambassador, he is (in all things not conteined in his written Instructions) to take for Instruction that which Reason dictates to be most conducing to his Soveraigns interest; and so of all other Ministers of the Soveraignty, publique and private. All which Instructions of naturall Reason may be comprehended under one name of *Fidelity*; which is a branch of naturall Justice ...

Nor is it enough the Law be written, and published; but also that there be manifest signs, that it proceedeth from the will of the Soveraign. For private men, when they have, or think they have force enough to secure their unjust designes, and convoy them safely to their ambitious ends, may publish for Lawes what they please, without, or against the Legislative Authority. There is therefore requisite, not only a Declaration of the Law, but also sufficient signes of the Author, and Authority. The Author, or Legislator is supposed in every Commonwealth to be evident, because he is the Soveraign, who having been Constituted by the consent of every one, is supposed by every one to be sufficiently known. And though the ignorance, and security of men be such, for the most part, as that when [142] the memory of the first Constitution of their Common-wealth is worn out, they doe not consider, by whose power they use to be defended against their enemies, and to have their industry protected, and to be righted when injury is done them; yet because no man that considers, can make question of it, no excuse can be derived from the ignorance of where the Soveraignty is placed. And it is a Dictate of Naturall Reason, and consequently an evident Law of Nature, that no man ought to weaken that power, the protection whereof he hath himself demanded, or wittingly received against others. Therefore of who is Soveraign, no man, but by his own fault, (whatsoever evill men suggest,) can make any doubt. The difficulty consisteth in the evidence of the Authority derived from him; The removing whereof, dependeth on the knowledge of the publique Registers, publique Counsels, publique Ministers, and publique Seales; by which all Lawes are sufficiently verified; Verifyed, I say, not Authorised: for the Verification, is but the Testimony and Record; not the Authority of the Law; which consisteth in the Command of the Soveraign only.

If therefore a man have a question of Injury, depending on the Law of Nature; that is to say, on common Equity; the Sentence of the Judge, that by Commission hath Authority to take cognisance of such causes, is a sufficient Verification of the Law of Nature in that individuall case. For though the advice of one that professeth the study of the Law, be usefull for the avoyding of contention; yet it is but advice: tis the Judge must tell men what is Law, upon the hearing of the Controversy.

But when the question is of injury, or crime, upon a written Law; every man by recourse to the Registers, by himself, or others, may (if he will) be sufficiently enformed, before he doe such injury, or commit the crime, whither it be an injury, or not: Nay he ought to doe so: For when a man doubts whether the act he goeth about, be just, or injust; and may informe himself, if he will; the doing is unlawfull. In like manner, he that supposeth himself injured, in a case determined by the written Law, which he may by himself, or others see and consider; if he complaines before he consults with the Law, he does unjustly, and bewrayeth a disposition rather to vex other men, than to demand his own right.

If the question be of Obedience to a publique Officer; To have seen his Commission, with the Publique Seale, and heard it read; or to have had the means to be informed of it, if a man would, is a sufficient Verification of his Authority. For every man is obliged to doe his best endeavour, to informe himself of all written Lawes, that may conceme his own future actions.

The Legislator known; and the Lawes, either by writing, or by the light of Nature, sufficiently published; there wanteth yet another very materiall circumstance to make them obligatory. For it is not the Letter, but the Intendment, or Meaning; that is to say, the authentique Interpretation of the Law (which is the sense of the Legislator,) in which the nature of the Law consisteth; And therefore [143] the Interpretation of all Lawes dependeth on the Authority Soveraign; and the Interpreters can be none but those, which the Soveraign, (to whom only the Subject oweth obedience) shall appoint. For else, by the craft of an Interpreter, the Law may be made to beare a sense, contrary to that of the Soveraign; by which means the Interpreter becomes the Legislator.

All Laws, written, and unwritten, have need of Interpretation. The unwritten Law of Nature, though it be easy to such, as without partiality, and passion, make use of there naturall reason, and therefore leaves the violaters thereof without excuse; yet considering there be very few, perhaps none, that in some cases are not blinded by self love, or some other passion, it is now become of all Laws the most obscure; and has consequently the greatest need of able Interpreters. The written Laws, if they be short, are easily mis-interpreted, from the divers significations of a word, or two: if long, they be more obscure by the diverse significations of many words: in so much as no written Law, delivered in few, or many words, can be well understood, without a perfect understanding of the finall causes, for which the Law was made; the knowledge of which finall causes is in the Legislator. To him therefore there can not be any knot in the Law, insoluble; either by finding out the ends, to undoe it by; or else by making what ends he will, (as *Alexander* did with his sword in the Gordian Knot,) by the Legislative power; which no other Interpreter can doe.

The Interpretation of the Lawes of Nature, in a Common-wealth, dependeth not on the books of Morall Philosophy. The Authority of writers, without the Authority of the Common-wealth, maketh not their opinions Law, by they never so true. That which I have written in this Treatise, concerning the Morall Vertues, and of their necessity, for the procuring, and maintaining peace, though it bee evident Truth, is not therefore presently Law; but because in all Common-wealths in the world, it is part of the Civill Law: For though it be naturally reasonable; yet it is by the Soveraigne Power that it is Law: Otherwise, it were a great errour, to call the Lawes of Nature unwritten Law; whereof wee see so many volumes published, and in them so many contradictions of one another, and of themselves.

The Interpretation of the Law of Nature, is the Sentence of the Judge constituted by the Soveraign Authority, to heare and determine such controversies, as depend thereon; and consisteth in the application of the Law to the present case. For in the act of Judicature, the Judge doth no more but consider, whither the demand of the party, be consonant to naturall reason, and Equity; and the Sentence he giveth, is therefore the Interpretation of the Law of Nature; which Interpretation is Authentique; not because it is his private Sentence; but because he giveth it by Authority of the Soveraign, whereby it becomes the Soveraigns Sentence; which is Law for that time, to the parties pleading.

[144] But because there is no Judge Subordinate, nor Soveraign, but may erre in a Judgement of Equity; if afterward in another like case he find it more consonant to Equity to give a contrary Sentence, he is obliged to doe it. No mans error becomes his own Law; nor obliges him to persist in it. Neither (for the same reason) becomes it a Law to other Judges, though sworn to follow it. For though a wrong Sentence given by authority of the Soveraign, if he know and allow it, in such Lawes as are mutable, be a constitution of a new Law, in cases, in which every little circumstance is the same; yet in Lawes immutable, such as are the Lawes of Nature, they are no Lawes to the same, or other Judges, in the like cases for ever after. Princes succeed one another; and one Judge passeth, another commeth; nay, Heaven and Earth shall passe; but not one title of the Law of Nature shall passe; for it is the Eternall Law of God. Therefore all the Sentences of precedent Judges that have ever been, cannot all altogether make a Law contrary to naturall Equity: Nor any Examples of former Judges, can warrant an unreasonable Sentence, or discharge the present Judge of the trouble of studying what is Equity (in the case he is to Judge,) from the principles of his own naturall

reason. For example sake, 'Tis against the Law of Nature, *To punish the Innocent;* and Innocent is he that acquitteth himselfe Judicially, and is acknowledged for Innocent by the Judge. Put the case now, that a man is accused of a capitall crime, and seeing the power and malice of some enemy, and the frequent corruption and partiality of Judges, runneth away for feare of the event, and afterwards is taken, and brought to a legall triall, and maketh it sufficiently appear, he was not guilty of the crime, and being thereof acquitted, is neverthelesse condemned to lose his goods; this is a manifest condemnation of the Innocent. I say therefore, that there is no place in the world, where this can be an interpretation of a Law of Nature, or be made a Law by the Sentences of precedent Judges, that had done the same. For he that judged it first, judged unjustly; and no Injustice can be a pattern of Judgement to succeeding Judges. A written Law may forbid innocent men to fly, and they may be punished for flying: But that flying for feare of injury, should be taken for presumption of guilt, after a man is already absolved of the crime Judicially, is contrary to the nature of a Presumption, which hath no place after Judgement given. Yet this is set down by a great Lawyer for the common Law of *England. If a man* (saith he) *that is Innocent, be accused of Felony, and for feare flyeth for the same; albeit he judicially acquitteth himselfe of the Felony; yet if it be found that he fled for the Felony, he shall notwithstanding his Innocency, Forfeit all his goods, chattells, debts, and duties. For as to the Forfeiture of them, the Law will admit no proofe against the Presumption in Law, grounded upon his flight.* Here you see, *An Innocent man, Judicially acquitted, notwithstanding his Innocency,* (when no written Law forbad him to fly) after his acquittall, *upon a Presumption in Law,* condemned to lose all the goods he hath. If the Law ground upon his flight a Presumption of the fact, (what was Capitall,) the Sen[145] tence ought to have been Capitall: if the Presumption were not of the Fact, for what then ought he to lose his goods? This therefore is no Law of *England;* nor is the condemnation grounded upon a Presumption of Law, but upon the Presumption of the Judges. It is also against Law, to say that no Proofe shall be admitted against a Presumption of Law. For all Judges, Soveraign and subordinate, if they refuse to heare Proofe, refuse to do Justice: for though the Sentence be Just, yet the Judges that condemn without hearing the Proofes offered, are Unjust Judges; and their Presumption is but Prejudice; which no man ought to bring with him to the Seat of Justice, whatsoever precedent judgements, or examples he shall pretend to follow. There be other things of this nature, wherein mens Judgements have been perverted, by trusting to

Precedents: but this is enough to shew, that though the Sentence of the Judge, be a Law to the party pleading, yet it is no Law to any Judge, that shall succeed him in that Office.

In like manner, when question is of the Meaning of written Lawes, he is not the Interpreter of them, that writeth a Commentary upon them. For Commentaries are commonly more subject to cavill, than the Text; and therefore need other Commentaries; and so there will be no end of such Interpretation. And therefore unlesse there be an Interpreter authorised by the Soveraign, from which the subordinate Judges are not to recede, the Interpreter can be no other than the ordinary Judges, in the same manner, as they are in cases of the unwritten Law; and their Sentences are to be taken by them that plead, for Lawes in that particular case; but not to bind other Judges, in like cases to give like judgements. For a Judge may erre in the Interpretation even of written Lawes; but no errour of a subordinate Judge, can change the Law, which is the generall Sentence of the Soveraigne.

In written Lawes, men use to make a difference between the Letter, and the Sentence of the Law: And when by the Letter, is meant whatsoever can be gathered from the bare words, 'tis well distinguished. For the significations of almost all words, are either in themselves, or in the metaphoricall use of them, ambiguous; and may be drawn in argument, to make many senses; but there is onely one sense of the Law. But if by the Letter, be meant the literall sense, then the Letter, and the Sentence or intention of the Law, is all one. For the literall sense is that, which the Legislator intended, should by the letter of the Law be signified. Now the Intention of the Legislator is always supposed to be Equity: For it were a great contumely for a Judge to think otherwise of the Soveraigne. He ought therefore, if the Word of the Law doe not fully authorise a reasonable Sentence, to supply it with the Law of Nature; or if the case be difficult, to respit Judgement till he have received more ample authority. For Example, a written Law ordaineth, that he which is thrust out of his house by force, shall be restored by force: It happens that a man by negligence leaves his house empty, and returning is kept out by force, in which case there is no speciall Law ordained. It is evi[146]dent, that this case is contained in the same Law: for else there is no remedy for him at all; which is to be supposed against the Intention of the Legislator. Again, the word of the Law, commandeth to Judge according to the Evidence: A man is accused falsly of a fact, which the Judge saw himself done by another; and not by him that is accused. In this case neither shall the Letter of the Law be followed to the condemnation of the Innocent, nor shall the Judge give Sentence against the evidence of the Witnesses; because the Letter of the Law is to the contrary: but procure of the Soveraign that another be made Judge, and himselfe Witnesse. So that the incommodity that follows the bare words of a written Law, may lead him to the Intention of the Law, whereby to interpret the same the better; though no Incommodity can warrant a Sentence against the Law. For every Judge of Right, and Wrong, is not Judge of what is Commodious, or Incommodious to the Common-wealth.

The abilities required in a good Interpreter of the Law, that is to say, in a good Judge, are not the same with those of an Advocate; namely the study of the Lawes. For a Judge, as he ought to take notice of the Fact, from none but the Witnesses; so also he ought to take notice of the Law, from nothing but the Statutes, and Constitutions of the Soveraign, alledged in the pleading, or declared to him by some that have authority from the Soveraign Power to declare them; and need not take care before-hand, what hee shall Judge; for it shall bee given him what hee shall say concerning the Fact, by Witnesses; and what hee shall say in point of Law, from those that shall in their pleadings shew it, and by authority interpret it upon the place. The Lords of Parlament in *England* were Judges, and most difficult causes have been heard and determined by them; yet few of them were much versed in the study of the Lawes, and fewer had made profession of them: and though they consulted with Lawyers, that were appointed to be present there for that purpose; yet they alone had the authority of giving Sentence. In like manner, in the ordinary trialls of Right, Twelve men of the common People, are the Judges, and give Sentence, not onely of the Fact, but of the Right; and pronounce simply for the Complaynant, or for the Defendant; that is to say, are Judges not onely of the Fact, but also of the Right: and in a question of crime, not onely determine whether done, or not done; but also whether it be *Murder, Homicide, Felony, Assault*, and the like, which are determinations of Law: but because they are not supposed to know the Law of themselves, there is one that hath Authority to enforme them of it, in the particular case they are to Judge of. But yet if they judge not according to that he tells them, they are not subject thereby to any penalty; unlesse it be made appear, they did it against their consciences, or had been corrupted by reward.

The things that make a good Judge, or good Interpreter of the Lawes, are, first, *A right understanding* of that principall Law of Nature called *Equity*; which depending not on the reading of other mens Writings, but on the goodnesse of a mans own naturall [147] Reason, and Meditation, is presumed to be in those most, that have had most leisure, and had the most inclination to meditate thereon. Secondly, *Contempt of unnecessary Riches,* and Preferments. Thirdly, *To be able in judgement to devest himselfe of all feare, anger, hatred, love,* and *compassion.* Fourthly, and lastly, *Patience to heare; diligent attention in hearing, and memory to retain, digest and apply what he hath heard ...*

CHAPTER 30: *OF THE* OFFICE *OF THE SOVERAIGN REPRESENTATIVE*

The Office of the Soveraign, (be it a Monarch, or an Assembly), consisteth in the end, for which he was trusted with the Soveraign Power, namely the procuration of *the safety of the people;* to which he is obliged by the Law of Nature, and to render an account thereof to God, the Author of that Law, and to none but him. But by Safety here, is not meant a bare Preservation, but also all other Contentments of life, which every man by lawfull Industry, without danger, or hurt to the Common-wealth, shall acquire to himselfe.

And this is intended should be done, not by care applyed to Individualls, further than their protection from injuries, when they shall complain; but by a generall Providence, contained in publique Instruction, both of Doctrine, and Example; and in the making, and executing of good Lawes, to which individuall persons may apply their own cases.

And because, if the essentiall Rights of Soveraignty (specified before in the eighteenth Chapter) be taken away, the Common-wealth is thereby dissolved, and every man returneth into the condition, and calamity of a warre with every other man, (which is the greatest evill that can happen in this life;) it is the Office of the Soveraign, to maintain those Rights entire; and consequently against his duty, First, to transferre to another, or to lay from himselfe any of them. For he that deserteth the Means, deserteth the Ends; and he deserteth the Means, that being the Soveraign, acknowledgeth himselfe subject to the Civill Lawes; and renounceth the Power of Supreme Judicature; or of making Warre, or Peace by his own Authority; or of Judging of the Necessities of the Common-wealth; or of levying Mony, and Souldiers, when, and as much as in his own conscience he shall judge necessary; or of making Officers, and Ministers both of Warre, and Peace; or of appointing Teachers, and examining what Doctrines are conformable, or contrary to the Defence, Peace, and Good of the people. Secondly, it is against his

Duty, to let the people be ignorant, or mis-informed of the grounds, and reasons of those his essentiall Rights; because thereby men are easie to be seduced, and drawn to resist him, when the Common-wealth shall require their use and exercise.

And the grounds of these Rights, have the rather need to be diligently, and truly taught; because they cannot be maintained by any Civill Law, or terrour of legal punishment. For a Civill Law, that shall forbid Rebellion, (and such is all resistance to the essentiall Rights of Soveraignty,) is not (as a Civill Law) any obligation, [176] but by vertue onely of the Law of Nature, that forbiddeth the violation of Faith; which naturall obligation if men know not, they cannot know the Right of any Law the Soveraign maketh. And for the Punishment, they take it but for an act of Hostility; which when they think they have strength enough, they will endeavour by acts of Hostility, to avoyd.

As I have heard some say, that Justice is but a word, without substance; and that whatsoever a man can by force, or art, acquire to himself, (not onely in the condition of warre, but also in a Common-wealth,) is his own, which I have already shewed to be false: So there be also that maintain, that there are no grounds, nor Principles of Reason, to sustain those essentiall Rights, which make Soveraignty absolute. For if there were, they would have been found out in some place, or other; whereas we see, there has not hitherto been any Common-wealth, where those Rights have been acknowledged, or challenged. Wherein they argue as ill, as if the Savage people of America, should deny there were any grounds, or Principles of Reason, so to build a house, as to last as long as the materials, because they never yet saw any so well built. Time, and Industry, produce every day new knowledge. And as the art of well building, is derived from Principles of Reason, observed by industrious men, that had long studied the nature of materials, and the divers effects of figure, and proportion, long after mankind began (though poorly) to build: So, long time after men have begun to constitute Common-wealths, imperfect, and apt to relapse into disorder, there may, Principles of Reason be found out, by industrious meditation, to make their constitution (excepting by externall violence) everlasting. And such are those which I have in this discourse set forth: Which whether they come not into the sight of those that have Power to make use of them, or be neglected by them, or not, concerneth my particular interest, at this day, very little. But supposing that these of mine are not such Principles of Reason; yet I am sure they are Principles from Authority of Scripture;

as I shall make it appear, when I shall come to speak of the Kingdome of God, (administered by *Moses*,) over the Jewes, his peculiar people by Covenant.

But they say again, that though the Principles be right, yet Common people are not of capacity enough to be made to understand them. I should be glad, that the Rich, and Potent Subjects of a Kingdome, or those that are accounted the most Learned, were no lesse incapable than they. But all men know, that the obstructions to this kind of doctrine, proceed not so much from the difficulty of the matter, as from the interest of them that are to learn. Potent men, digest hardly any thing that setteth up a Power to bridle their affections; and Learned men, any thing that discovereth their errours, and thereby lesseneth their Authority: whereas the Common-peoples minds, unlesse they be tainted with dependance on the Potent, or scribbled over with the opinions of their Doctors, are like clean paper, fit to receive whatsoever by Publique Authority shall be imprinted in them. Shall whole Nations be brought to *acquiesce* [177] in the great Mysteries of Christian Religion, which are above Reason; and millions of men be made believe, that the same Body may be in innumerable places, at one and the same time, which is against Reason; and shall not men be able, by their teaching, and preaching, protected by the Law, to make that received, which is so consonant to Reason, that any unprejudicated man, needs no more to learn it, than to hear it? I conclude therefore, that in the instruction of the people in the Essentiall Rights (which are the Naturall, and Fundamentall Lawes) of Soveraignty, there is no difficulty, (whilest a Soveraign has his Power entire,) but what proceeds from his own fault, or the fault of those whom he trusteth in the administration of the Common-wealth; and consequently, it is his Duty, to cause them so to be instructed; and not onely his Duty, but his Benefit also, and Security, against the danger that may arrive to himselfe in his naturall Person, from Rebellion.

And (to descend to particulars) the People are to be taught, First, that they ought not to be in love with any forme of Government they see in their neighbour Nations, more than with their own, nor (whatsoever present prosperity they behold in Nations that are otherwise governed than they,) to desire change. For the prosperity of a People ruled by an Aristocraticall, or Democraticall assembly, commeth not from Aristocracy, nor from Democracy, but from the Obedience, and Concord of the Subjects: nor do the people flourish in a Monarchy, because one man has the right to rule them, but because they obey him. Take away in any kind of State, the Obedience, (and consequently the Concord of the People,) and they shall not onely not flourish, but in short time be dissolved. And they that go about by disobedience, to doe no more than reforme the Common-wealth, shall find they do thereby destroy it; like the foolish daughters of *Peleus* (in the fable;) which desiring to renew the youth of their decrepit Father, did by the Counsell of *Medea*, cut him in pieces, and boyle him, together with strange herbs, but made not of him a new man. This desire of change, is like the breach of the first of Gods Commandements: For there God sayes, *Non habebis Deos alienos*; Thou shalt not have the Gods of other Nations; and in another place concerning *Kings*, that they are *Gods*.

Secondly, they are to be taught, that they ought not to be led with admiration of the vertue of any of their fellow Subjects, how high soever he stand, nor how conspicuously soever he shine in the Common-wealth; nor of any Assembly, (except the Soveraign Assembly,) so as to deferre to them any obedience, or honour, appropriate to the Soveraign onely, whom (in their particular stations) they represent; nor to receive any influence from them, but such as is conveighed by them from the Soveraign Authority. For that Soveraign, cannot be imagined to love his People as he ought, that is not Jealous of them, but suffers them by the flattery of Popular men, to be seduced from their loyalty, as they have often been, not onely secretly, but openly, so as to proclaime Marriage with them *in facie Ecclesiæ* by Preachers; and by publishing the same in the open streets: which [178] may fitly be compared to the violation of the second of the ten Commandements.

Thirdly, in consequence to this, they ought to be informed, how great a fault it is, to speak evill of the Soveraign Representative, (whether One man, or an Assembly of men;) or to argue and dispute his Power, or any way to use his Name irreverently, whereby he may be brought into Contempt with his People, and their Obedience (in which the safety of the Common-wealth consisteth) slackened. Which doctrine the third Commandement by resemblance pointeth to.

Fourthly, seeing people cannot be taught this, nor when 'tis taught, remember it, nor after one generation past, so much as know in whom the Soveraign Power is placed, without setting a part from their ordinary labour, some certain times, in which they may attend those that are appointed to instruct them; It is necessary that some such times be determined, wherein they may assemble together, and (after prayers and praises given to God, the Soveraign of Soveraigns) hear those their Duties told them, and the Positive Lawes, such as generally concern them all, read and expounded, and be put in mind of the authority that maketh them Lawes. To this end had the *Jewes* every seventh day, a *Sabbath*, in which the Law was read and expounded; and in the solemnity whereof they were put in mind, that their King was God; that having created the world in six dayes, he rested the seventh day; and by their resting on it from their labour, that that God was their King, which redeemed them from their servile, and painfull labour in *Egypt*, and gave them a time, after they had rejoyced in God, to take joy also in themselves, by lawfull recreation. So that the first Table of the Commandements, is spent all, in setting down the summe of Gods absolute Power; not onely as God, but as King by pact, (in peculiar) of the Jewes; and may therefore give light, to those that have Soveraign Power conferred on them by the consent of men, to see what doctrine they Ought to teach their Subjects.

And because the first instruction of Children, dependeth on the care of their Parents; it is necessary that they should be obedient to them, whilest they are under their tuition; and not onely so, but that also afterwards (as gratitude requireth,) they acknowledge the benefit of their education, by externall signes of honour. To which end they are to be taught, that originally the Father of every man was also his soveraign Lord, with power over him of life and death; and that the Fathers of families, when by instituting a Common-wealth, they resigned that absolute Power, yet it was never intended, they should lose the honour due unto them for their education. For to relinquish such right, was not necessary to the Institution of Soveraign Power; nor would there be any reason, why any man should desire to have children, or take the care to nourish, and instruct them, if they were afterwards to have no other benefit from them, than from other men. And this accordeth with the fifth Commandement.

[179] Again, every Soveraign Ought to cause Justice to be taught, which (consisting in taking from no man what is his) is as much as to say, to cause men to be taught not to deprive their Neighbours, by violence, or fraud, of any thing which by the Soveraign Authority is theirs. Of things held in propriety, those that are dearest to a man are his own life, & limbs; and in the next degree, (in most men,) those that concern conjugall affection; and after them riches and means of living. Therefore the People are to be taught, to abstain from violence to one anothers person, by private revenges; from violation of conjugall honour; and from forcible rapine, and fraudulent surreption of one anothers goods. For which purpose also it is necessary they be shewed

the evill consequences of false Judgement, by corruption either of Judges or Witnesses, whereby the distinction of propriety is taken away, and Justice becomes of no effect; all which things are intimated in the sixth, seventh, eighth, and ninth Commandements.

Lastly, they are to be taught, that not onely the unjust facts, but the designes and intentions to do them, (though by accident hindred,) are Injustice; which consisteth in the pravity of the will, as well as in the irregularity of the act. And this is the intention of the tenth Commandement, and the summe of the Second Table; which is reduced all to this one Commandement of mutuall Charity, *Thou shalt love thy neighbour as thy selfe*: as the summe of the first Table is reduced to *the love of God*; whom they had then newly received as their King.

As for the Means, and Conduits, by which the people may receive this Instruction, wee are to search, by what means so many Opinions, contrary to the peace of Man-kind, upon weak and false Principles, have neverthelesse been so deeply rooted in them. I mean those, which I have in the precedent Chapter specified; as That men shall Judge of what is lawfull and unlawfull, not by the Law it selfe, but by their own Consciences; that is to say, by their own private Judgements: that Subjects sinne in obeying the Commands of the Common-wealth, unlesse they themselves have first judged them to be lawfull: That their Propriety in their riches is such, as to exclude the Dominion, which the Common-wealth hath over the same: That it is lawfull for Subjects to kill such, as they call Tyrants: That the Soveraign Power may be divided, and the like; which come to be instilled into the People by this means. They whom necessity, or covetousnesse keepeth attent on their trades, and labour; and they, on the other side, whom superfluity, or sloth carrieth after their sensuall pleasures, (which two sorts of men take up the greatest part of Man-kind,) being diverted from the deep meditation, which the learning of truth, not onely in the matter of Naturall Justice, but also of all other Sciences necessarily requireth, receive the Notions of their duty, chiefly from Divines in the Pulpit, and partly from such of their Neighbours, or familiar acquaintance, as having the Faculty of discoursing readily, and plausibly, seem wiser and better learned in cases of Law, and Conscience, than themselves. And the Divines, and such others as make shew of Learning, derive their [18] knowledge from the Universities, and from the Schooles of Law, or from the Books, which by men eminent in those Schooles, and Universities have been published. It is therefore manifest, that the Instruction of the people, dependeth wholly, on the right teaching of

Youth in the Universities. But are not (may some man say) the Universities of *England* learned enough already to do that? or is it you will undertake to teach the Universities? Hard questions. Yet to the first, I doubt not to answer; that till towards the later end of *Henry the eighth*, the Power of the Pope, was alwayes upheld against the Power of the Common-wealth, principally by the Universities; and that the doctrines maintained by so many Preachers, against the Soveraign Power of the King, and by so many Lawyers, and others, that had their education there, is a sufficient argument, that though the Universities were not authors of those false doctrines, yet they knew not how to plant the true. For in such a contradiction of Opinions, it is most certain, that they have not been sufficiently instructed; and 'tis no wonder, if they yet retain a relish of that subtile liquor, wherewith they were first seasoned, against the Civill Authority. But to the later question, it is not fit, nor needfull for me to say either I, or No: for any man that sees what I am doing, may easily perceive what I think.

The safety of the People, requireth further, from him, or them that have the Soveraign Power, that Justice be equally administred to all degrees of People; that is, that as well the rich, and mighty, as poor and obscure persons, may be righted of the injuries done them; so as the great, may have no greater hope of impunity, when they doe violence, dishonour, any Injury to the meaner sort, than when one of these, does the like to one of them: For in this consisteth Equity; to which, as being a Precept of the Law of Nature, a Soveraign is as much subject, as any of the meanest of his People. All breaches of the Law, are offences against the Common-wealth; but there be some, that are also against private Persons. Those that concern the Common-wealth onely, may without breach of Equity be pardoned; for every man may pardon what is done against himselfe, according to his own discretion. But an offence against a private man, cannot in Equity be pardoned, without the consent of him that is injured; or reasonable satisfaction.

CHAPTER 37

A private man has alwaies the liberty, (because thought is free,) to beleeve, or not beleeve in his heart, those acts that have been given out for Miracles according as he shall see, what benefit can accrew by mens belief, to those that pretend, or countenance them, and thereby conjecture, whether they be Miracles, or Lies. But when it comes to confession of that faith, the Private Reason must submit to the Publique; that is to say, to Gods Lieutenant.

CONCLUSION

And thus I have brought to an end my Discourse of Civill and Ecclesiasticall Government, occasioned by the disorders of the present time, without partiality, without application, and without other designe, than to set before mens eyes the mutuall Relation be[396]tween Protection and Obedience.

READING QUESTIONS ON HOBBES

1   How realistic is Hobbes's view of the "Natural Condition of Mankind"? (Don't ask yourself if Hobbes accurately describes your motives; ask instead if he describes other people you know.)
2   Can the Hobbesian sovereign appeal to moral considerations?
3   What is the role of judges in Hobbes's theory? Could someone actually carry out the task of judging as Hobbes describes it?
4   Hobbes reserves individual freedoms of conscience and rights to self-defence even against the sovereign. Is this consistent with his view of the importance of legal order and stability?
5   Hobbes appeals to ideas of equity in deciding cases. How is this related to his more general positivism? Is there a tension in his view? Can you think of any way it might be resolved?

H.L.A. Hart
"Positivism and the Separation of Law and Morals" (1958)

Jurisprudence had lain moribund for close to half a century before Hart's classic essay. Hart's aim is to offer a rigorous statement of legal positivism, the view that law and morality are distinct modes of social ordering. Hart's essay is important both for its historical place and because of its emphasis on the importance, both moral and conceptual, of keeping law and morality apart. In *The Concept of Law*, Hart elaborates his idea of a fundamental rule which has to be accepted by legal officials.

Positivism and the Separation of Law and Morals

... I shall present the subject as part of the history of an idea ...

Bentham's general recipe for life under the government of laws was simple: it was *"to obey punctually; to censure freely."* But Bentham was especially aware, as an anxious spectator of the French revolution, that this was not enough: the time might come in any society when the law's commands were so evil that the question of resistance had to be faced, and it was then essential that the issues at stake at this point should neither be oversimplified nor obscured. Yet this was precisely what the confusion between law and morals had done, and Bentham found that the confusion had spread symmetrically in two different directions. On the one hand Bentham had in mind the anarchist who argues thus: "This ought not to be the law, therefore it is not and I am free not merely to censure but to disregard it." On the other hand he thought of the reactionary who argues: "This is the law, therefore it is what it ought to be," and thus stifles criticism at its birth. Both errors, Bentham thought, were to be found in Blackstone: there was his incautious statement that human laws were invalid if contrary to the law of God, and "that spirit of obsequious *quietism* that seems constitutional in our Author" which "will scarce ever let him recognise a difference" between what is and what ought to be. This indeed was for Bentham the occupational disease of lawyers: "[I]n the eyes of lawyers – not to speak their dupes – that is to say, as yet, the generality of non-lawyers – the *is* and the *ought to be* ... were one and indivisible." There are therefore two dangers between which insistence on this distinction will help us to steer: the danger that law and its authority may be dissolved in man's conceptions of what law ought to be and the danger that the existing law may supplant morality as a final test of conduct and so escape criticism.

In view of later criticisms it is also important to distinguish several things that the Utilitarians did not mean by insisting on their separation of law and morals. They certainly accepted many of the things that might be called "the intersection of law and morals." First, they never denied that, as a matter of historical fact, the development of legal systems had been powerfully influenced by moral opinion, and, conversely, that moral standards had been profoundly influenced by law, so that the content of many legal rules mirrored moral rules or principles. It is not in fact always easy to trace this historical causal connection, but Bentham was certainly ready to admit its existence; so too

Austin spoke of the "frequent coincidence" of positive law and morality and attributed the confusion of what law is with what law ought to be to this very fact.

Second, neither Bentham nor his followers denied that by explicit legal provisions moral principles might at different points be brought into a legal system and form part of its rules, or that courts might be legally bound to decide in accordance with what they thought just or best. Bentham indeed recognized, as Austin did not, that even the supreme legislative power might be subjected to legal restraints by a constitution and would not have denied that moral principles, like those of the Fifth Amendment, might form the content of such legal constitutional restraints. Austin differed in thinking that restraints on the supreme legislative power could not have the force of law, but would remain merely political or moral checks; but of course he would have recognized that a statute, for example, might confer a delegated legislative power and restrict the area of its exercise by reference to moral principles.

What both Bentham and Austin were anxious to assert were the following two simple things: first, in the absence of an expressed constitutional or legal provision, it could not follow from the mere fact that a rule violated standards of morality that it was not a rule of law; and, conversely, it could not follow from the mere fact that a rule was morally desirable that it was a rule of law ...

So much for the doctrine in the heyday of its success. Let us turn now to some of the criticisms. Undoubtedly, when Bentham and Austin insisted on the distinction between law as it is and as it ought to be, they had in mind *particular* laws, the meanings of which were clear and so not in dispute, and they were concerned to argue that such laws, even if morally outrageous, were still laws. It is, however, necessary, in considering the criticisms which later developed, to consider more than those criticisms which were directed to this particular point if we are to get at the root of the dissatisfaction felt; we must also take account of the objection that, even if what the Utilitarians said on this particular point were true, their insistence on it, in a terminology suggesting a general cleavage between what is and ought to be law, obscured the fact that at other points there is an essential point of contact between the two. So in what follows I consider not only criticisms of the particular point which the Utilitarians had in mind, but also the claim that an essential connection between law and morals emerges if we examine how laws, the meanings of which are in dispute, are interpreted and applied in concrete cases; and that this connection emerges again if we widen our point of view and ask, not whether every particular rule of law must satisfy a moral minimum in order to be a law, but whether a system of rules which altogether failed to do this could be a legal system.

There is, however, one major initial complexity by which criticism has been much confused. We must remember that the Utilitarians combined with their insistence on the separation of law and morals two other equally famous but distinct doctrines. One was the important truth that a purely analytical study of legal concepts, a study of the meaning of the distinctive vocabulary of the law, was as vital to our understanding of the nature of law as historical or sociological studies, though of course it could not supplant them. The other doctrine was the famous imperative theory of law – that law is essentially a command.

These three doctrines constitute the utilitarian tradition in jurisprudence; yet they are distinct doctrines. It is possible to endorse the separation between law and morals and to value analytical inquiries into the meaning of legal concepts and yet think it wrong to conceive of law as essentially a command. One source of great confusion in the criticism of the separation of law and morals was the belief that the falsity of any one of these three doctrines in the utilitarian tradition showed the other two to be false; what was worse was the failure to see that there were three quite separate doctrines in this tradition. The indiscriminate use of the label "positivism" to designate ambiguously each one of these three separate doctrines (together with some others which the Utilitarians never professed) has perhaps confused the issue more than any other single factor ...[1]

The famous theory that law is a command was a part of a wider and more ambitious claim. Austin said that the notion of a command was "the *key* to the sciences of jurisprudence and moral," and contemporary attempts to elucidate moral judgments in terms of "imperative" or "prescriptive" utterances echo this ambitious claim. But the command theory, viewed as an effort to identify even the quintessence of law, let alone the quintessence of morals, seems breathtaking in its simplicity and quite inadequate. There is much, even in the simplest legal system, that is distorted if presented as a command. Yet the Utilitarians thought that the essence of a legal system could be conveyed if the notion of a command were supplemented by that of a habit of obedience. The simple scheme was this: What is a command? It is simply an expression by one person of the desire that another person should do or abstain from some action, accompanied by a threat of punishment which is likely to follow disobedience. Commands are laws if two conditions are satisfied: first, they must be general; second they must be commanded by what (as both Bentham and Austin claimed) exists in every political society whatever its constitutional form, namely, a person or a group of persons who are in receipt of habitual obedience from most of the society but pay no such obedience to others. These persons are its sovereign. Thus law is the command of the uncommanded commanders of society – the creation of the legally untrammelled will of the sovereign who is by definition outside the law.

It is easy to see that this account of a legal system is threadbare. One can also see why it might seem that its inadequacy is due to the omission of some essential connection with morality. The situation which the simple trilogy of command, sanction, and sovereign avails to describe, if you take these notions at all precisely, is like that of a gunman saying to his victim, "Give me your money or your life." The only difference is that in the case of a legal system the gunman says it to a large number of people who are accustomed to the racket and habitually surrender to it. Law surely is not the gunman situation writ large, and legal order is surely not to be thus simply identified with compulsion.

This scheme, despite the points of obvious analogy between a statute and a command, omits some of the most characteristic elements of law. Let me cite a few. It is wrong to think of a legislature (and *a fortiori* an electorate) with a changing membership as a group of persons habitually obeyed: this simple idea is suited only to a monarch sufficiently long-lived for a "habit" to grow up. Even if we waive this point, nothing which legislators do makes law unless they comply with fundamental accepted rules specifying the essential law-making procedures. This is true even in a system having a simple unitary constitution like the British. These fundamental accepted rules specifying what the legislature must do to legislate are not commands habitually obeyed, nor can they be expressed as habits of obedience to persons. They lie at the root of a legal system, and what is most missing in the utilitarian scheme is an analysis of what it is for a social group and its officials to accept such rules. This notion, not that of a command as Austin claimed, is the "key to the science of jurisprudence," or at least one of the keys.

Again, Austin, in the case of a democracy, looked past the legislators to the electorate as "the sovereign" (or in England as part of it). He thought that in the United States the mass of the electors to the state and federal legislatures were the sovereign whose commands, given by their "agents" in the legislatures, were law. But on this footing the whole notion of the sovereign outside the law being "habitually obeyed" by the "bulk" of the population must go: for in this case the "bulk" obeys the bulk, that is, it obeys itself. Plainly the general acceptance of the authority of a law-making procedure, irrespective of the changing individuals who operate it from time to time, can be only distorted by an analysis in terms of mass habitual obedience to certain persons who are by definition outside the law, just as the cognate but much simpler phenomenon of the general social acceptance of a rule, say of taking off the hat when entering a church, would be distorted if represented as habitual obedience by the mass to specific persons.

Other critics dimly sensed a further and more important defect in the command theory, yet blurred the edge of an important criticism by assuming that the defect was due to the failure to insist upon some important connection between law and morals. This more radical defect is as follows. The picture that the command theory draws of life under law is essentially a simple relationship of the commander to the commanded, of superior to inferior, of top to bottom; the relationship is vertical between the commanders or authors of the law conceived of as essentially outside the law and those who are commanded and subject to the law. In this picture no place, or only an accidental or subordinate place, is afforded for a distinction between types of legal rules which are in fact radically different. Some laws require men to act in certain ways or to abstain from acting whether they wish to or not. The criminal law consists largely of rules of this sort: like commands they are simply "obeyed" or "disobeyed." But other legal rules are presented to society in quite different ways and have quite different functions. They provide facilities more or less elaborate for individuals to create structures of rights and duties for the conduct of life within the coercive framework of the law. Such are the rules enabling individuals to make contracts, wills, and trusts, and generally to mould their legal relations with others. Such rules, unlike the criminal law, are not factors designed to obstruct wishes and choices of an antisocial sort. On the contrary, these rules provide facilities for the realization of wishes and choices. They do not say (like commands) "do this whether you wish it or no not," but rather "if you wish to do this, here is the way to do it." Under these rules we exercise powers, make claims, and assert rights. These phrases mark off characteristic features of laws that confer rights and powers; they are laws which are, so to speak, put at the disposition of individuals in a way in which the criminal law is not. Much ingenuity has gone into the task of "reducing" laws of this second sort to some complex variant of laws of the first sort. The effort to show that laws conferring rights are "really" only conditional stipulations of sanctions to be exacted from the person ultimately under a legal duty characterizes much of Kelsen's work. Yet to urge this is really just to exhibit dogmatic determination to suppress one aspect of the legal system in order to maintain the theory that the stipulation of a sanction, like Austin's command, represents the quintessence of law. One might as well urge that the rules of baseball were "really" only complex conditional directions to the scorer and that this showed their real or "essential" nature.

One of the first jurists in England to break with the Austinian tradition, Salmond, complained that the analysis in terms of commands left the notion of a right unprovided with a place. But he confused the point. He argued first, and correctly, that if laws are merely commands it is inexplicable that we should have come to speak of legal rights and powers as conferred or arising under them, but then wrongly concluded that the rules of a legal system must necessarily be connected with moral rules or principles of justice and that only on this footing could the phenomenon of legal rights be explained. Otherwise, Salmond thought, we would have to say that a mere "verbal coincidence" connects the concepts of legal and moral right. Similarly, continental critics of the Utilitarians, always alive to the complexity of the notion of a subjective right, insisted that the command theory gave it no place. Hägerström insisted that if laws were merely commands the notion of an individual's right was really inexplicable, for commands are, as he said, something which we either obey or we do not obey; they do not confer rights. But he, too, concluded that moral, or, as he put it, common-sense, notions of justice must therefore be necessarily involved in the analysis of any legal structure elaborate enough to confer rights.

Yet, surely these arguments are confused. Rules that confer rights, though distinct from commands, need not be moral rules or coincide with them. Rights, after all, exist under the rules of ceremonies, games, and in many other spheres regulated by rules which are irrelevant to the question of justice or what the law ought to be. Nor need rules which confer rights be just or morally good rules. The rights of a master over his slaves show us that. "Their merit or demerit," as Austin termed it, depends on how rights are distributed in society and over whom or what they are exercised. These critics indeed revealed the inadequacy of the simple notions of command and habit for the analysis of law; at many points it is apparent that the social acceptance of a rule or standard of authority (even if it is motivated only by fear or superstition or rests on inertia) must be brought into the analysis and cannot itself be reduced to the two simple terms. Yet nothing in this showed the utilitarian insistence on the distinction between the existence of law and its "merits" to be wrong.

III

I now turn to a distinctively American criticism of the separation of the law that is from the law that ought to be. It emerged from the critical study of the judicial process with which American jurisprudence has been on the whole so beneficially occupied. The most sceptical of these critics – the loosely named "Realists" of the 1930s – perhaps too naively accepted the conceptual framework of the natural sciences as adequate for the characterization of law and for the analysis of rule-guided action of which a living system of law at least partly consists. But they opened men's eyes to what actually goes on when courts decide cases, and the contrast they drew between the actual facts of judicial decision and the traditional terminology for describing it as if it were a wholly logical operation was usually illuminating; for in spite of some exaggeration the Realists made us acutely conscious of one cardinal feature of human language and human thought, emphasis on which is vital not only for the understanding of law but in areas of philosophy far beyond the confines of jurisprudence. The insight of this school may be presented in the following example. A legal rule forbids you to take a vehicle into the public park. Plainly this forbids an automobile, but what about bicycles, roller skates, toy automobiles? What about aeroplanes? Are these, as we say, to be called "vehicles" for the purpose of the rule or not? If we are to communicate with each other at all, and if, as in the most elementary form of law, we are to express our intentions that a certain type of behaviour be regulated by rules, then the general words we use – like "vehicle" in the case I consider – must have some standard instance in which no doubts are felt about its application. There must be a core of settled meaning, but there will be, as well, a penumbra of debatable cases in which words are neither obviously applicable nor obviously ruled out. These cases will each have some features in common with the standard case; they will lack others or be accompanied by features not present in the standard case. Human invention and natural processes continually throw up such variants on the familiar, and if we are to say that these ranges of facts do or do not fall under existing rules, then the classifier must make a decision which is not dictated to him, for the facts and phenomena to which we fit our words and apply our rules are as it were *dumb*. The toy automobile cannot speak up and say, "I am a vehicle for the purpose of this legal rule," nor can the roller skates chorus, "We are not a vehicle." Fact situations do not await us neatly labelled, creased, and folded; nor is their legal classification written on them to be simply read off by the judge. Instead, in applying legal rules, someone must take the responsibility of deciding that words do or do not cover some case in hand, with all the practical consequences involved in this decision.

We may call the problems which arise outside the hard core of standard instances or settled meaning "problems of the penumbra"; they are always with us whether in relation to such trivial things as the regulation of the use of the public park or in relation to the multidimensional generalities of a constitution. If a penumbra of uncertainty must surround all legal rules, then their application to specific cases in the penumbral area cannot be a matter of logical deduction, and so deductive reasoning, which for generations has been cherished as the very perfection of human reasoning, cannot serve as a model for what judges, or indeed anyone, should do in bringing particular cases under general rules. In this area men cannot live by deduction alone. And it follows that if legal arguments and legal decisions of penumbral questions are to be rational, their rationality must lie in something other than a logical relation to premises. So if it is rational or "sound" to argue and to decide that for the purposes of this rule an aeroplane is not a vehicle, this argument must be sound or rational without being logically conclusive. What is it then that makes such decisions correct or at least better than alternative decisions? Again, it seems true to say that the criterion which makes a decision sound in such cases is some concept of what the law ought to be; it is easy to slide from that into saying that it must be a moral judgment about what law ought to be. So here we touch upon a point of necessary "intersection between law and morals" which demonstrates the falsity or, at any rate, the misleading character of the Utilitarians' emphatic insistence on the separation of law as it is and ought to be. Surely, Bentham and Austin could only have written as they did because they misunderstood or neglected this aspect of the judicial process, because they ignored the problems of the penumbra.

The misconception of the judicial process which ignores the problems of the penumbra and which views the process as consisting preeminently in deductive reasoning is often stigmatized as the error of "formalism" or "literalism." My question now is, how and to what extent does the demonstration of this error show the utilitarian distinction to be wrong or misleading? Here there are many issues which have been confused, but I can only disentangle some. The charge of formalism has been levelled both at the "positivist" legal theorist and at the courts, but of course it must be a very different charge in each case. Levelled at the legal theorist, the charge means that he has made a theoretical mistake about the character of legal decision; he has thought of the reasoning involved as consisting in deduction from premises in which the judges' practical choices or decisions play no part. It would be easy to show that Austin was guiltless of this error; only an entire misconception of what analytical jurisprudence is and why he thought it important has led to the view that he, or any other analyst, believed that the law was a closed logical system in which judges deduced their decisions from premises. On the contrary, he was very much alive to the character of language, to its vagueness or open character; he thought that in the penumbral situation judges must necessarily legislate, and, in accents that sometimes recall those of the late Judge Jerome Frank, he berated the common-law judges for legislating feebly and timidly and for blindly relying on real or fancied analogies with past cases instead of adapting their decisions to the growing needs of society as revealed by the moral standard of utility. The villains of this piece, responsible for the conception of the judge as an automaton, are not the utilitarian thinkers. The responsibility, it if is to be laid at the door of any theorist, is with thinkers like Blackstone and, at an earlier stage, Montesquieu. The root of this evil is preoccupation with the separation of powers and Blackstone's "childish fiction" (as Austin termed it) that judges only "find," never "make," law.

But we are concerned with "formalism" as a vice not of jurists but of judges. What precisely is it for a judge to commit this error, to be a "formalist," "automatic," a "slot machine"? Curiously enough the literature, which is full of the denunciation of these vices, never makes this clear in concrete terms; instead we have only descriptions which cannot mean what they appear to say; it is said that in the formalist error courts make an excessive use of logic, take a thing to "a dryly logical extreme," or make an excessive use of analytical methods. But just how in being a formalist does a judge make an excessive use of logic? It is clear that the essence of his error is to give some general term an interpretation which is blind to social values and consequences (or which is in some other way stupid or perhaps merely disliked by critics). But logic does not prescribe interpretation of terms; it dictates neither the stupid nor intelligent interpretation of any expression. Logic only tells you hypothetically that *if* you give a certain term a certain interpretation then a certain conclusion follows. Logic is silent on how to classify particulars – and this is the heart of a judicial decision. So this reference to logic and to logical extremes is a misnomer for something else, which must be this. A judge has to apply a rule to a concrete case – perhaps the rule that one may not take a stolen "vehicle" across State lines, and in this case an aeroplane has been taken. He either does not see or pretends not to see that the general terms of this rule are susceptible of different interpretations and that he has a choice left open uncontrolled by linguistic conventions. He ignores, or is blind to, the fact that he is in the area of the penumbra and is not dealing with a standard case. Instead of choosing in the light of social aims the judge fixes the meaning in a different way. He either takes the meaning that the word most obviously suggests in its ordinary non-legal context to ordinary men, or one which the word has been given in some other legal context, or, still worse, he thinks of a standard case and then arbitrarily identifies certain features in it – for example, in the case of a vehicle, (1) normally used on land, (2) capable of carrying a human person, (3) capable of being self-propelled – and treats these three as always necessary and always sufficient conditions for the use in all contexts of the word "vehicle," irrespective of the social consequences of giving it this interpretation. This choice, not "logic," would force the judge to include a toy motor car (if electrically propelled) and to exclude bicycles and the aeroplane. In all this there is possibly great stupidity, but no more "logic," and no less, than in cases in which the interpretation given to a general term and the consequent application of some general rule to a particular case is consciously controlled by some identified social aim.

Decisions made in a fashion as blind as this would scarcely deserve the name of decisions; we might as well toss a penny in applying a rule of law. But it is at least doubtful whether any judicial decisions (even in England) have been quite as automatic as this. Rather, either the interpretations stigmatized as automatic have resulted from the conviction that it is fairer in a criminal statute to take a meaning which would jump to the mind of the ordinary man at the cost even of defeating other values, and this itself is a social policy (though possibly a bad one); or much more frequently, what is stigmatized as "mechanical" and "automatic" is a determined choice made indeed in the light of a social aim but of a conservative social aim. Certainly many of the Supreme Court decisions at the turn of the century which have been so stigmatized represent clear choices in the penumbral area to give effect to a policy of a conservative type. This is peculiarly true of Mr Justice Peckham's opinions defining the spheres of police power and due process.

But how does the wrongness of deciding cases in an automatic and mechanical way and the rightness of deciding cases by reference to social purposes show that the utilitarian insistence on the distinction between what the law is and what it ought to be is wrong? I take it that no one who wished to use these vices of formalism as proof that the distinction between what is and what ought to be is mistaken would deny that the decisions stigmatized as automatic are law; nor would he deny that the system in which such automatic decisions are made is a legal system. Surely he would say that they are law, but they are bad law; they ought not to be law. But this would be to use the distinction, not to refute it; and of course both Bentham and Austin used it to attack judges for failing to decide penumbral cases in accordance with the growing needs of society.

Clearly, if the demonstration of the errors of formalism is to show the utilitarian distinction to be wrong, the point must be drastically re-stated. The point must be not merely that a judicial decision to be rational must be made in the light of some conception of what ought to be, but that the aims, the social policies and purposes to which judges should appeal if their decisions are to be rational, are themselves to be considered as part of the law in some suitably wide sense of "law" which is held to be more illuminating than that used by the Utilitarians. This restatement of the point would have the following consequence: instead of saying that the recurrence of penumbral questions shows us that legal rules are essentially incomplete, and that, when they fail to determine decisions, judges must legislate and so exercise a creative choice between alternatives, we shall say that the social policies which guide the judges' choice are in a sense there for them to discover; the judges are only "drawing out" of the rule what, if it is properly under-stood, is "latent" within it. To call this judicial legislation is to obscure some essential continuity between the clear cases of the rule's applica-tion and the penumbral decisions. I shall question later whether this way of talking is salutary, but I wish at this time to point out something obvious, but likely, if not stated, to tangle the issues. It does not follow that, because the opposite of a decision reached blindly in the formalist or literalist manner is a decision intelligently reached by reference to some conception of what ought to be, we have a junction of law and morals. We must, I think, beware of thinking in a too simple-minded fashion about the word "ought." This is not because there is no distinction to be made between law as it is and ought to be. Far from it. It is because the distinction should be between what is and what from many different points of view ought to be. The word "ought" merely reflects the presence of some standard of criticism; one of these standards is a moral standard, but not all standards are moral. We say to our neighbour, "You ought not to lie," and that may certainly be a moral judgment, but we should remember that the baffled poisoner may say, "I ought to have given her a second dose." The point here is that intelligent decisions which we oppose to mechanical or formal decisions are not necessarily identical with decisions defensible on moral grounds. We may say of many a decision: "Yes, that is right; that is as it ought to be," and we may mean only that some accepted purpose or policy has been thereby advanced; we may not mean to endorse the moral propriety of the policy or the decision. So the contrast between the mechanical decision and the intelligent one can be reproduced inside a system dedicated to the pursuit of the most evil aims. It does not exist as a contrast to be found only in legal systems which, like our own, widely recognize principles of justice and moral claims of individuals.

An example may make this point plainer. With us the task of sentencing in criminal cases is the one that seems most obviously to demand from the judge the exercise of moral judgment. Here the factors to be weighed seem clearly to be moral factors: society must not be exposed to wanton attack; too much misery must not be inflicted on either the victim or his dependents; efforts must be made to enable him to lead a better life and regain a position in the society whose laws he has violated. To a judge striking the balance among these claims, with all the discretion and perplexities involved, his task seems as plain an example of the exercise of moral judgment as could be; and it seems to be the polar opposite of some mechanical application of a tariff of penalties fixing a sentence careless of the moral claims which in our system have to be weighed. So here intelligent and rational decision is guided however uncertainly by moral aims. But we have only to vary the example to see that this need not necessarily be so and surely, if it need not necessarily be so, the utilitarian point remains unshaken. Under the Nazi regime men were sentenced by courts for criticism of the regime. Here the choice of sentence might be guided exclusively by consideration of what was needed to maintain the state's tyranny effectively. What sentence would both terrorize the public at large and keep the friends and family of the prisoner in suspense so that both hope and fear would cooperate as factors making for subservience? The prisoner of such a system would be regarded simply as an object to be used in pursuit of these aims. Yet, in contrast with a mechanical decision, decision on these grounds would be intelligent and purposive, and from one point of view the decision would be as it ought to be. Of course, I am not unaware that a whole philosophical tradition has sought to demonstrate the fact that we cannot correctly call decisions or behaviour truly rational unless they are in conformity with moral aims and principles. But the example I have used seems to me to serve at least as a warning that we cannot use the errors of formalism as something which *per se* demonstrates the falsity of the utilitarian insistence on the distinction between law as it is and law as *morally* it ought to be.

We can now return to the main point. If it is true that the intelligent decision of penumbral questions is one made not mechanically but in the light of aims, purposes, and policies, though not necessarily in the light of anything we would call moral principles, is it wise to express this important fact by saying that the firm utilitarian distinction between what the law is and what it ought to be should be dropped? Perhaps the claim that it is wise cannot be theoretically refuted, for it is, in effect, an *invitation* to revise *our conception* of what a legal rule is. We are invited to include in the "rule" the various aims and policies in the light of which its penumbral cases are decided on the ground that these aims have, because of their importance, as much right to be called law as the core of legal rules whose meaning is settled. But though an invitation cannot be refuted, it may be refused, and I would proffer two reasons for refusing this invitation. First, everything we have learned about the judicial process can be expressed in other less mysterious ways. We can say laws are incurably incomplete and we must decide the penumbral cases rationally by reference to social aims. I think Holmes, who had such a vivid appreciation of the fact that "general propositions do not decide concrete cases," would have put it that way. Secondly, to insist on the utilitarian distinction is to emphasize that the hard core of settled meaning is law in some centrally important sense and that even if there are borderlines, there must first be lines. If this were not so the notion of rules controlling courts' decisions would be senseless, as some of the "Realists" – in their most extreme moods, and, I think, on bad grounds – claimed.

By contrast, to soften the distinction, to assert mysteriously that there is some fused identity between law as it is and as it ought to be, is to suggest that all legal questions are fundamentally like those of the penumbra. It is to assert that there is no central element of actual law to be seen in the core of central meaning which rules have, that there is nothing in the nature of a legal rule inconsistent with *all* questions being open to reconsideration in the light of social policy. Of course, it is good to be occupied with the penumbra. Its problems are rightly the daily diet of the law schools. But to be occupied with the penumbra is one thing, to be preoccupied with it another. And preoccupation with the penumbra is, if I may say so, as rich a source of confusion in the American legal tradition as formalism in the English. Of course we might abandon the notion that rules have authority; we might cease to attach force or even meaning to an argument that a case falls clearly within a rule and the scope of a precedent. We might call all such reasoning "automatic" or "mechanical," which is already the routine invective of the courts. But until we decide that this *is* what we want, we should not encourage it by obliterating the utilitarian distinction ...

IV

The third criticism of the separation of law and morals is of a very different character; it certainly is less an intellectual argument against the utilitarian distinction than a passionate appeal supported not by detailed reasoning but by reminders of a terrible experience. For it consists of the testimony of those who have descended into Hell, and, like Ulysses or Dante, brought back a message for human beings. Only in this case the Hell was not beneath or beyond earth, but on it; it was a Hell created on earth by men for other men.

This appeal comes from those German thinkers who lived through the Nazi regime and reflected upon its evil manifestations in the legal system. One of these thinkers, Gustav Radbruch, had himself shared the "positivist" doctrine until the Nazi tyranny, but he was converted by this experience and so his appeal to other men to discard the doctrine of the separation of law and morals has the special poignancy of a recantation. What is important about this criticism is that it really does confront the particular point which Bentham and Austin had in mind in urging the separation of law as it is and as it ought to be. These German thinkers put their insistence on the need to join together what the Utilitarians separated just where this separation was of most importance in the eyes of the Utilitarians; for they were concerned with the problem posed by the existence of morally evil laws.

Before his conversion Radbruch held that resistance to law was a matter for the personal conscience, to be thought out by the individual as a moral problem, and the validity of a law could not be disproved by showing that its requirements were morally evil or even by showing that the effect of compliance with the law would be more evil than the effect of disobedience. Austin, it may be recalled, was emphatic in condemning those who said that if human laws conflicted with the fundamental principles of morality then they cease to be laws, as talking "stark nonsense."

The most pernicious laws, and therefore those which are most opposed to the will of God, have been and are continually enforced as laws by judicial tribunals. Suppose an act innocuous, or positively beneficial, be prohibited by the sovereign under the penalty of death; if I commit this act, I shall be tried and condemned, and if I object to the sentence, that it is contrary to the law of God ... the court of justice will demonstrate the inconclusiveness of my reasoning by hanging me up, in pursuance of the law of which I have impugned the validity. An exception, demurrer, or plea, founded on the law of God was never heard in a Court of Justice, from the creation of the world down to the present moment.

These are strong, indeed brutal words, but we must remember that they went along – in the case of Austin and, of course, Bentham – with the conviction that if laws reached a certain degree of iniquity then there would be a plain moral obligation to resist them and to withhold obedience. We shall see, when we consider the alternatives, that this simple presentation of the human dilemma which may arise has much to be said for it.

Radbruch, however, had concluded from the ease with which the Nazi regime had exploited subservience to mere law – expressed, as he thought, in the "positivist" slogan "law as law" (*Gesetz als Gesetz*) – and from the failure of the German legal profession to protest against the enormities which they were required to perpetrate in the name of law, that "positivism" (meaning here the insistence on the separation of law as it is from law as it ought to be) had powerfully contributed to the horrors. His considered reflections led him to the doctrine that the fundamental principles of humanitarian morality were part of the very concept of *Recht* or Legality and that no positive enactment or statute, however clearly it was expressed and however clearly it conformed with the formal criteria of validity of a given legal system, could be valid if it contravened basic principles of morality. This doctrine can be appreciated fully only if the nuances imported by the German word *Recht* are grasped. But it is clear that the doctrine meant that every lawyer and judge should denounce statutes that transgressed the fundamental principles not as merely immoral or wrong but as having no legal character, and enactments which on this ground lack the quality of law should not be taken into account in working out the legal position of any given individual in particular circumstances. The striking recantation of his previous doctrine is unfortunately omitted from the translation of his works, but it should be read by all who wish to think afresh on the question of the interconnection of law and morals.

It is impossible to read without sympathy Radbruch's passionate demand that the German legal conscience should be open to the demands of morality and his complaint that this has been too little the case in the German tradition. On the other hand there is an extraordinary naïvety in the view that insensitiveness to the demands of morality and subservience to state power in a people like the Germans should have arisen from the belief that law might be law though it failed to conform with the minimum requirements of morality. Rather this terrible history prompts inquiry into why emphasis on the slogan "law is law," and the distinction between law and morals, acquired a sinister character in Germany, but elsewhere, as with the Utilitarians themselves, went along with the most enlightened liberal attitudes. But something more disturbing than naïvety is latent in Radbruch's whole presentation of the issues to which the existence of morally iniquitous laws give rise. It is not, I think, uncharitable to say that we can see in his argument that he has only half digested the spiritual message of liberalism which he is seeking to convey to the legal profession. For everything that he says is really dependent upon an enormous overvaluation of the importance of the bare fact that a rule may be said to be a valid rule of law, as if this, once declared, was conclusive of the final moral question: "Ought this rule of law to be obeyed?" Surely the truly liberal answer to any sinister use of the slogan "law is law" or of the distinction between law and morals is, "Very well, but that does not conclude the question. Law is not morality; do not let it supplant morality."

However, we are not left to a mere academic discussion in order to evaluate the plea which Radbruch made for the revision of the distinction between law and morals. After the war Radbruch's conception of law as containing in itself the essential moral principle of humanitarianism was applied in practice by German courts in certain cases in which local war criminals, spies, and informers under the Nazi regime were punished. The special importance of these cases is that the persons accused of these crimes claimed that what they had done was not illegal under the laws of the regime in force at the time these actions were performed. This plea was met with the reply that the laws upon which they relied were invalid as contravening the fundamental principles of morality. Let me cite briefly one of these cases.

In 1944 a woman, wishing to be rid of her husband, denounced him to the authorities for insulting remarks he had made about Hitler while home on leave from the German army. The wife was under no legal duty to report his acts, though what he had said was apparently in violation of statutes making it illegal to make statements detrimental to the government of the Third Reich or to impair by any means the military defence of the German people. The husband was arrested and sentenced to death, apparently pursuant to these statutes, though he was not executed but was sent to the front. In 1949 the wife was prosecuted in a West German court for an offence which we would describe as illegally depriving a person of his freedom (*rechtswidrige Freiheitsberaubung*). This was punishable as a crime under the German Criminal Code of 1871 which had remained in force continuously since its enactment. The wife pleaded that her husband's imprisonment was pursuant to the Nazi statutes and hence that she had committed no crime. The court of appeal to which the case ultimately came held that the wife was guilty of procuring the deprivation of her husband's liberty by denouncing him to the German courts, even though he had been sentenced by a court for having violated a statute, since, to quote the words of the court, the statute "was contrary to the sound conscience and sense of justice of all decent human beings." This reasoning was followed in many cases which have been hailed as a triumph of the doctrines of natural law and as signalling the overthrow of positivism. The unqualified satisfaction with this result seems to me to be hysteria. Many of us might applaud the objective – that of punishing a woman for an outrageously immoral act – but this was secured only by declaring a statute established since 1934 not to have the force of law, and at least the wisdom of this course must be doubted. There were, of course, two other choices. One was to let the woman go unpunished; one can sympathize with and endorse the view that this might have been a bad thing to do. The other was to face the fact that if the woman were to be punished it must be pursuant to the introduction of a frankly retrospective law and with a full consciousness of what was sacrificed in securing her punishment in this way. Odious as retrospective criminal legislation and punishment may be, to have pursued it openly in this case would at least have had the merits of candour. It would have made plain that in punishing the woman a choice had to be made between two evils, that of leaving her unpunished and that of sacrificing a very precious principle of morality endorsed by most legal systems. Surely if we have learned anything from the history of morals it is that the thing to do with a moral quandary is not to hide it. Like nettles, the occasions when life forces us to choose the lesser of two evils must be grasped with the consciousness that they are what they are. The vice of this use of the principle that, at certain limiting points, what is utterly immoral cannot be law or lawful is that it will serve to cloak the true nature of the problems with which we are faced and will encourage the romantic optimism that all the values we cherish ultimately will fit into a single system, that no one of them has to be sacrificed or compromised to accommodate another.

> All Discord Harmony not understood
> All Partial Evil Universal Good

This is surely untrue, and there is an insincerity in any formulation of our problem which allows us to describe the treatment of the dilemma as if it were the disposition of the ordinary case.

It may seem perhaps to make too much of forms, even perhaps of words, to emphasize one way of disposing of this difficult case as compared with another which might have led, so far as the woman was concerned, to exactly the same result. Why should we dramatize the difference between them? We might punish the woman under a new retrospective law and declare overtly that we were doing something inconsistent with our principles as the lesser of two evils; or we might allow the case to pass as one in which we do not point out precisely where we sacrifice such a principle. But candour is not just one among many minor virtues of the administration of law, just as it is not merely a minor virtue of morality. For if we adopt Radbruch's view, and with him and the German courts make our protest against evil law in the form of an assertion that certain rules cannot be law because of their moral iniquity, we confuse one of the most powerful, because it is the simplest, forms of moral criticism. If with the Utilitarians we speak plainly, we say that laws may be law but too evil to be obeyed. This is a moral condemnation which everyone can understand and it makes an immediate and obvious claim to moral attention. If, on the other hand, we formulate our objection as an assertion that these evil things are not law, here is an assertion which many people do not believe, and if they are disposed to consider it at all, it would seem to raise a whole host of philosophical issues before it can be accepted. So perhaps the most important single lesson to be learned from this form of the denial of the utilitarian distinction is the one that the Utilitarians were most concerned to teach; when we have the ample resources of plain speech we must not present the moral criticism of institutions as propositions of a disputable philosophy.

V

I have endeavoured to show that, in spite of all that has been learned and experienced since the Utilitarians wrote, and in spite of the defects of other parts of their doctrine, their protest against the confusion of what is and what ought to be law has a moral as well as an intellectual value. Yet it may well be said that, though this distinction is valid and important if applied to any particular law of a system, it is at least misleading if we attempt to apply it to "law," that is, to the notion of a legal system, and that if we insist, as I have, on the narrower truth (or truism), we obscure a wider (or deeper) truth. After all, it may be urged, we have learned that there are many things which are untrue of laws taken separately, but which are true and important in a legal system considered as a whole. For example, the connection between law and sanctions and between the existence of law and its "efficacy" must be understood in this more general way. It is surely not arguable (without some desperate extension of the word "sanction" or artificial narrowing of the word "law") that every law in a municipal legal system must have a sanction, yet it is at least plausible to argue that a legal system must, to be a legal system, provide sanctions for certain of its rules. So too, a rule of law may be said to exist though enforced or obeyed in only a minority of cases, but this could not be said of a legal system as a whole. Perhaps the differences with respect to laws taken separately and a legal system as a whole are also true of the connection between moral (or some other) conceptions of what law ought to be and law in this wider sense.

This line of argument, found (at least in embryo form) in Austin, where he draws attention to the fact that every developed legal system contains certain fundamental notions which are "necessary" and "bottomed in the common nature of man," is worth pursuing – up to a point – and I shall say briefly why and how far this is so.

We must avoid, if we can, the arid wastes of inappropriate definition, for, in relation to a concept as many-sided and vague as that of a legal system, disputes about the "essential" character, or necessity to the whole, of any single element soon begin to look like disputes about whether chess could be "chess" if played without pawns. There is a wish, which may be understandable, to cut straight through the question whether a legal system, to be a legal system, must measure up to some moral or other standard with simple statements of fact: for example, that no system which utterly failed in this respect has ever existed or could endure; that the normally fulfilled assumption that a legal system aims at some form of justice colours the whole way in which we interpret specific rules in particular cases, and if this normally fulfilled assumption were not fulfilled no one would have any reason to obey except fear (and probably not that), and still less, of course, any moral obligation to obey. The connection between law and moral standards and principles of justice is therefore as little arbitrary and as "necessary" as the connection between law and sanctions, and the pursuit of the question whether this necessity is logical (part of the "meaning" of law) or merely factual or causal can safely be left as an innocent pastime for philosophers.

Yet in two respects I should wish to go further (even though this involves the use of a philosophical fantasy) and show what could intelligibly be meant by the claim that certain provisions in a legal system are "necessary". The world in which we live, and we who live in it, may one day change in many different ways; and if this change were radical enough not only would certain statements of fact now true be false and vice versa, but whole ways of thinking and talking which constitute our present conceptual apparatus, through which we see the world and each other, would lapse. We have only to consider how the whole of our social, moral, and legal life, as we understand it now, depends on the contingent fact that though our bodies do change in shape, size, and other physical properties they do not do this so drastically nor with such quicksilver rapidity and irregularity that we cannot identify each other as the same persistent individual over considerable spans of time. Though this is but a contingent fact which may one day be different, on it at present rest huge structures of our thought and principles of action and social life. Similarly, consider the following possibility (not because it is more than a possibility but because it reveals why we think certain things necessary in a legal system and what we mean by this): suppose that men were to become invulnerable to attack by each other, were clad perhaps like giant land crabs with an impenetrable carapace, and could extract the food they needed from the air by some internal chemical process. In such circumstances (the details of which can be left to science fiction) rules forbidding the free use of violence and rules constituting the minimum form of property – with its rights and duties sufficient to enable food to grow and be retained until eaten – would not have the necessary non-arbitrary status which they have for us, constituted as we are in a world like ours. At present, and until such radical changes supervene, such rules are so fundamental that if a legal system did not have them there would be no point in having any other rules at all. Such rules overlap with basic moral principles vetoing murder, violence, and theft; and so we can add to the factual statement that all legal systems in fact coincide with morality at such vital points, the statement that this is, in this sense, necessarily so. And why not call it a "natural" necessity?

Of course even this much depends on the fact that in asking what content a legal system must have we take this question to be worth asking only if we who consider it cherish the humble aim of survival in close proximity to our fellows. Natural-law theory, however, in all its protean guises, attempts to push the argument much further and to assert that human beings are equally devoted to and united in their conception of aims (the pursuit of knowledge, justice to their fellow men) other than that of survival and these dictate a further necessary content to a legal system (over and above my humble minimum) without which it would be pointless. Of course we must be careful not to exaggerate the differences among human beings, but it seems to me that above this minimum the purposes men have for living in society are too conflicting and varying to make possible much extension of the argument that some fuller overlap of legal rules and moral standards is "necessary" in this sense.

Another aspect of the matter deserves attention. If we attach to a legal system the minimum meaning that it must consist of general rules – general both in the sense that they refer to courses of action, not single actions and to multiplicities of men, not single individuals – this meaning connotes the principle of treating like cases alike, though the criteria of when cases are alike will be, so far, only the general elements specified in the rules. It is, however, true that *one* essential element of the concept of justice is the principle of treating like cases alike. This is justice in the administration of the law, not justice of the law. So there is, in the very notion of law consisting of general rules, something which prevents us from treating it as if morally it is utterly neutral, without any necessary contact with moral principles. Natural procedural justice consists therefore of those principles of objectivity and impartiality in the administration of the law which implement just this aspect of law and which are designed to ensure that rules are applied only to what are genuinely cases of the rule or at least to minimize the risks of inequalities in this sense.

These two reasons (or excuses) for talking of a certain overlap between legal and moral standards as necessary and natural, of course, should not satisfy anyone who is really disturbed by the utilitarian or "positivist" insistence that law and morality are distinct. This is so because a legal system that satisfied these minimum requirements might apply, with the most pedantic impartiality as between the persons affected, laws which were hideously oppressive, and might deny to a vast rightless slave population the minimum benefits of protection from violence and theft. The stink of such society is, after all, still in our nostrils, and to argue that they have (or had) no legal system would only involve the repetition of the argument. Only if the rules failed to provide these essential benefits and protection for anyone – even for a slave-owning group – would the minimum be unsatisfied and the system sink to the status of a set of meaningless taboos. Of course no one denied those benefits would have any reason to obey except fear and would have every moral reason to revolt.

VI

... When rules are recognized as applying to instances beyond any that legislators did or could have considered, their extension to such new cases often presents itself not as a deliberate choice or fiat on the part of those who so interpret the rule. It appears neither as a decision to give the rule a new or extended meaning nor as a guess as to what legislators, dead perhaps in the eighteenth century, would have said had they been alive in the twentieth century. Rather, the inclusion of the new case under the rule takes its place as a natural elaboration of the rule, as something implementing a "purpose" which it seems natural to attribute (in some sense) to the rule itself rather than to any particular person dead or alive. The utilitarian description of such interpretative extension of old rules to new cases as judicial legislation fails to do justice to this phenomenon; it gives no hint of the differences between a deliberate fiat or decision to treat the new case in the same way as past cases and a recognition (in which there is little that is deliberate or even voluntary) that inclusion of the new case under the rule will implement or articulate a continuing and identical purpose, hitherto less specifically apprehended.

Perhaps many lawyers and judges will see in this language something that precisely fits their experience; others may think it a romantic gloss on facts better stated in the utilitarian language of judicial "legislation" or in the modern American terminology of "creative choice."

To make the point clear Professor Fuller uses a non-legal example from the philosopher Wittgenstein which is, I think, illuminating.

Someone says to me: "Show the children a game." I teach them gaming with dice and the other says "I did not mean that sort of game." Must the exclusion of the game with dice have come before his mind when he gave me the order?

Something important does seem to me to be touched on in this example. Perhaps there are the following (distinguishable) points. First, we normally do interpret not only what people are trying to do but what they say in the light of assumed common human objectives, so that unless the contrary were expressly indicated we would not interpret an instruction to show a young child a game as a mandate to introduce him to gambling even though in other contexts the word "game" would be naturally so interpreted. Secondly, very often, the speaker whose words are thus interpreted might say: "Yes, that's what I mean [or "that's what I meant all along"] though I never thought of it until you put this particular case to me." Third, when we thus recognize, perhaps after argument or consultation with others, a particular case not specifically envisaged beforehand as falling within the ambit of some vaguely expressed instruction, we may find this experience falsified by description of it as a mere decision on our part so to treat the particular case, and that we can only describe this faithfully as coming to realize and to articulate what we "really" want or our "true purpose" – phrases which Professor Fuller uses later in the same article.

I am sure that many philosophical discussions of the character of moral argument would benefit from attention to cases of the sort instanced by Professor Fuller. Such attention would help to provide a corrective to the view that there is a sharp separation between "ends" and "means" and that in debating "ends" we can only work on each other non-rationally, and that rational argument is reserved for discussion of "means." But I think the relevance of his point to the issue whether it is correct or wise to insist on the distinction between law as it is and law as it ought to be is very small indeed. Its net effect is that in interpreting legal rules there are some cases which we find after reflection to be so natural an elaboration or articulation of the rule that to think of and refer to this as "legislation," "making law," or a "fiat" on our part would be misleading. So, the argument must be, it would be misleading to distinguish in such cases between what the rule is and what it ought to be – at least in some sense of ought. We think it ought to include the new case and come to see after reflection that it really does. But even if this way of presenting a recognizable experience as an example of a fusion between is and ought to be is admitted, two caveats must be borne in mind. The first is that "ought" in this case need have nothing to do with morals for the reasons explained already in section III: there may be just the same sense that a new case will implement and articulate the purpose of a rule in interpreting the rules of a game or some hideously immoral code of oppression whose immorality is appreciated by those called in to interpret it. They too can see what the "spirit" of the game they are playing requires in previously unenvisaged cases. More important is this: after all is said and done we must remember how rare in the law is the phenomenon held to justify this way of talking, how exceptional is this feeling that one way of deciding a case is imposed upon us as the only natural or rational elaboration of some rule. Surely it cannot be doubted that, for most cases of interpretation, the language of choice between alternatives, "judicial legislation" or even "fiat" (though not arbitrary fiat), better conveys the realities of the situation.

Within the framework of relatively well-settled law there jostle too many alternatives too nearly equal in attraction between which judge and lawyer must uncertainly pick their way to make appropriate here language which may well describe those experiences which we have in interpreting our own or others' principles of conduct, intention, or wishes, when we are not conscious of exercising a deliberate choice, but rather of recognizing something awaiting recognition. To use in the description of the interpretation of laws the suggested terminology of a fusion or inability to separate what is law and ought to be will serve (like earlier stories that judges only find, never make, law) only to conceal the facts, that here if anywhere we live among uncertainties between which we have to choose, and that the existing law imposes only limits on our choice and not the choice itself.

NOTE

1   It may help to identify five (there may be more) meanings of "positivism" bandied about in contemporary jurisprudence:

(1) the contention that laws are commands of human beings; see 46–50 *infra;*

(2) the contention that there is no necessary connection between law and morals or law as it is and ought to be; see 44–5 *supra;*

(3) the contention that the analysis (or study of the meaning) of legal concepts is (a) worth pursuing and (b) to be distinguished from historical inquiries into the causes or origins of laws, from sociological inquiries into the relation of law and other social phenomena, and from the criticism or appraisal of law whether in terms of morals, social aims, "functions," or otherwise; see 50–5 *infra;*

(4) the contention that a legal system is a "closed logical system" in which correct legal decisions can be deduced by logical means from predetermined legal rules without reference to social aims, policies, moral standards; see 50–5 *infra,* and

(5) the contention that moral judgments cannot be established or defended, as statements of facts can, by rational argument, evidence, or proof ('noncognitivism" in ethics).

Bentham and Austin held the views described in (1), (2), and (3), but not those in (4) and (5). Opinion (4) is often ascribed to analytical jurists; see 50–5 *infra,* but I know of no "analyst" who held this view.

H.L.A. Hart
The Concept of Law (1961)

PRIMARY AND SECONDARY RULES

The Elements of Law

It is, of course, possible to imagine a society without a legislature, courts or officials of any kind. Indeed, there are many studies of primitive communities which not only claim that this possibility is realized but depict in detail the life of a society where the only means of social control is that general attitude of the group towards its own standard modes of behaviour in terms of which we have characterized rules of obligation. A social structure of this kind is often referred to as one of "custom"; but we shall not use this term, because it often implies that the customary rules are very old and supported with less social pressure than other rules. To avoid these implications we shall refer to such a social structure as one of primary rules of obligation. If a society is to live by such primary rules alone, there are certain conditions which, granted a few of the most obvious truisms about human nature and the world we live in, must clearly be satisfied. The first of these conditions is that the rules must contain in some form restrictions on the free use of violence, theft, and deception to which human beings are tempted but which they must, in general, repress, if they are to coexist in close proximity to each other. Such rules are in fact always found in the primitive societies of which we have knowledge, together with a variety of others imposing on individuals various positive duties to perform services or make contributions to the common life. Secondly, though such a society may exhibit the tension, already described, between those who accept the rules and those who reject the rules except where fear of social pressure induces them to conform, it is plain that the latter cannot be more than a minority, if so loosely organized a society of persons, approximately equal in physical strength, is to endure: for otherwise those who reject the rules would have too little social pressure to fear. This too is confirmed by what we know of primitive communities where, though there are dissidents and malefactors, the majority live by the rules seen from the internal point of view.

More important for our present purpose is the following consideration. It is plain that only a small community closely knit by ties of kinship, common sentiment, and belief, and placed in a stable environment, could live successfully by such a régime of unofficial rules. In any other conditions such a simple form of social control must prove defective and will require supplementation in different ways. In the first place, the rules by which the group lives will not form a system, but will simply be a set of separate standards, without any identifying or common mark, except of course that they are the rules which a particular group of human beings accepts. They will in this respect resemble our own rules of etiquette. Hence if doubts arise as to what the rules are or as to the precise scope of some given rule, there will be no procedure for settling this doubt, either by reference to an authoritative text or to an official whose declarations on this point are authoritative. For, plainly, such a procedure and the acknowledgement of either authoritative text or persons involve the existence of rules of a type different from the rules of obligation or duty which *ex hypothesi* are all that the group has. This defect in the simple social structure of primary rules we may call its *uncertainty*.

A second defect is the *static* character of the rules. The only mode of change in the rules known to such a society will be the slow process of growth, whereby courses of conduct once thought optional become first habitual or usual, and then obligatory, and the converse process of decay, when deviations, once severely dealt with, are first tolerated and then pass unnoticed. There will be no means, in such a society, of deliberately adapting the rules to changing circumstances, either by eliminating old rules or introducing new ones: for, again, the possibility of doing this presupposes the existence of rules of a different type from the primary rules of obligation by which alone the society lives. In an extreme case the rules may be static in a more drastic sense. This, though never perhaps fully realized in any actual community, is worth considering because the remedy for it is something very characteristic of law. In this extreme case, not only would there be no way of deliberately changing the general rules, but the obligations which arise under the rules in particular cases could not be varied or modified by the deliberate choice of any individual. Each individual would simply have fixed obligations or duties to do or abstain from doing certain things. It might indeed very often be the case that others would benefit from the performance of these obligations; yet if there are only primary rules of obligation they would have no power to release those bound from performance or to transfer to others the benefits which would accrue from performance. For such operations of release or transfer create changes in the initial positions of individuals under the primary rules of obligation, and for these operations to be possible there must be rules of a sort different from the primary rules.

The third defect of this simple form of social life is the *inefficiency of* the diffuse social pressure by which the rules are maintained. Disputes as to whether an admitted rule has or has not been violated will always occur and will, in any but the smallest societies, continue interminably, if there is no agency specially empowered to ascertain finally, and authoritatively, the fact of violation. Lack of such final and authoritative determinations is to be distinguished from another weakness associated with it. This is the fact that punishments for violations of the rules, and other forms of social pressure involving physical effort or the use of force, are not administered by a special agency but are left to the individuals affected or to the group at large. It is obvious that the waste of time involved in the group's unorganized efforts to catch and punish offenders, and the smouldering vendettas which may result from self help in the absence of an official monopoly of "sanctions," may be serious. This history of law does, however, strongly suggest that the lack of official agencies to determine authoritatively the fact of violation of the rules is a much more serious defect; for many societies have remedies for this defect long before the other.

The remedy for each of these three main defects in this simplest form of social structure consists in supplementing the *primary* rules of obligation with *secondary* rules which are rules of a different kind. The introduction of the remedy for each defect might, in itself, be considered a step from the pre-legal into the legal world; since each remedy brings with it many elements that permeate law: certainly all three remedies together are enough to convert the régime of primary rules into what is indisputably a legal system. We shall consider in turn each of these remedies and show why law may most illuminatingly be characterized as a union of primary rules of obligation with such secondary rules. Before we do this, however, the following general points should be noted. Though the remedies consist in the introduction of rules which are certainly different from each other, as well as from the primary rules of obligation which they supplement, they have important features in common and are connected in various ways. Thus they may all be said to be on a different level from the primary rules, for they are all *about* such rules; in the sense that while primary rules are concerned with the actions that individuals must or must not do, these secondary rules are all concerned with the primary rules themselves. They specify the ways in which the primary rules may be conclusively ascertained, introduced, eliminated, varied, and the fact of their violation conclusively determined.

The simplest form of remedy for the *uncertainty* of the régime of primary rules is the introduction of what we shall call a "rule of recognition." This will specify some feature or features possession of which by a suggested rule is taken as a conclusive affirmative indication that it is a rule of the group to be supported by the social pressure it exerts. The existence of such a rule of recognition may take any of a huge variety of forms, simple or complex. It may, as in the early law of many societies, be no more than that an authoritative list or text of the rules is to be found in a written document or carved on some public monument. No doubt as a matter of history this step from the pre-legal to the legal may be accomplished in distinguishable stages, of which the first is the mere reduction to writing of hitherto unwritten rules. This is not itself the crucial step, though it is a very important one: what is crucial is the acknowledgement of reference to the writing or inscription as *authoritative,* i.e., as the *proper* way of disposing of doubts as to the existence of the rule. Where there is such an acknowledgement there is a very simple form of secondary rule: a rule for conclusive identification of the primary rules of obligation.

In a developed legal system the rules of recognition are of course more complex; instead of identifying rules exclusively by reference to a text or list they do so by reference to some general characteristic possessed by the primary rules. This may be the fact of their having been enacted by a specific body, or their long customary practice, or their relation to judicial decisions. Moreover, where more than one of such general characteristics are treated as identifying criteria, provision may be made for their possible conflict by their arrangement in an order of superiority, as by the common subordination of custom or precedent to statute, the latter being a "superior source" of law. Such complexity may make the rules of recognition in a modern legal system seem very different from the simple acceptance of an authoritative test: yet even in this simplest form, such a rule brings with it many elements distinctive of law. By providing an authoritative mark it introduces, although in embryonic form, the idea of a legal system: for the rules are now not just a discrete unconnected set but are, in a simple way, unified. Further, in the simple operation of identifying a given rule as possessing the required feature of being an item on an authoritative list of rules we have the germ of the idea of legal validity.

The remedy for the *static* quality of the régime of primary rules consists in the introduction of what we shall call "rules of change." The simplest form of such a rule is that which empowers an individual or body of persons to introduce new primary rules for the conduct of the life of the group, or of some class within it, and to eliminate old rules. As we have already argued in Chapter IV it is in terms of such a rule, and not in terms of orders backed by threats, that the ideas of legislative enactment and repeal are to be understood. Such rules of change may be very simple or very complex: the powers conferred may be unrestricted or limited in various ways: and the rules may, besides specifying the persons who are to legislate, define in more or less rigid terms the procedure to be followed in legislation. Plainly, there will be a very close connexion between the rules of change and the rules of recognition: for where the former exists the latter will necessarily incorporate a reference to legislation as an identifying feature of the rules, though it need not refer to all the details of procedure involved in legislation. Usually some official certificate or official copy will, under the rules of recognition, be taken as a sufficient proof of due enactment. Of course if there is a social structure so simple that the only "source of law" is legislation, the rule of recognition will simply specify enactment as the unique identifying mark or criterion of validity of the rules. This will be the case for example in the imaginary kingdom of Rex I depicted in Chapter IV: there the rule of recognition would simply be that whatever Rex I enacts is law.

We have already described in some detail the rules which confer on individuals power to vary their initial positions under the primary rules. Without such private power-conferring rules society would lack some of the chief amenities which law confers upon it. For the operations which these rules make possible are the making of wills, contracts, transfers of property, and many other voluntarily created structures of rights and duties which typify life under law, though of course an elementary form of power-conferring rule also underlies the moral institution of a promise. The kinship of these rules with the rules of change involved in the notion of legislation is clear, and as recent theory such as Kelsen's has shown, many of the features which puzzle us in the institutions of contract or property are clarified by thinking of the operations of making a contract or transferring property as the exercise of limited legislative powers by individuals.

The third supplement to the simple régime of primary rules, intended to remedy the *inefficiency* of its diffused social pressure, consists of secondary rules empowering individuals to make authoritative determinations of the question whether, on a particular occasion, a primary rule has been broken. The minimal form of adjudication consists in such determinations, and we shall call the secondary rules which confer the power to make them "rules of adjudication." Besides identifying the individuals who are to adjudicate, such rules will also define the procedure to be followed. Like the other secondary rules these are on a different level from the primary rules: though they may be reinforced by further rules imposing duties on judges to adjudicate, they do not impose duties but confer judicial powers and a special status on judicial declarations about the breach of obligations. Again these rules, like the other secondary rules, define a group of important legal concepts: in this case the concepts of judge or court, jurisdiction and judgment. Besides these resemblances to the other secondary rules, rules of adjudication have intimate connexions with them. Indeed, a system which has rules of adjudication is necessarily also committed to a rule of recognition of an elementary and imperfect sort. This is so because, if courts are empowered to make authoritative determinations of the fact that a rule has been broken, these cannot avoid being taken as authoritative determinations of what the rules are. So the rule which confers jurisdiction will also be a rule of recognition, identifying the primary rules through the judgments of the courts and these judgments will become a "source" of law. It is true that this form of rule of recognition, inseparable from the minimum form of jurisdiction, will be very imperfect. Unlike an authoritative text or a statute book, judgments may not be couched in general terms and their use as authoritative guides to the rules depends on a somewhat shaky inference from particular decisions, and the reliability of this must fluctuate both with the skill of the interpreter and the consistency of the judges.

It need hardly be said that in few legal systems are judicial powers confined to authoritative determinations of the fact of violation of the primary rules. Most systems have, after some delay, seen the advantages of further centralization of social pressure; and have partially prohibited the use of physical punishments or violent self help by private individuals. Instead they have supplemented the primary rules of obligation by further secondary rules, specifying or at least limiting the penalties for violation, and have conferred upon judges, where they have ascertained the fact of violation, the exclusive power to direct the application of penalties by other officials. These secondary rules provide the centralized official "sanctions" of the system ...

New Questions

Once we abandon the view that the foundations of a legal system consist in a habit of obedience to a legally unlimited sovereign and substitute for this the conception of an ultimate rule of recognition which provides a system of rules with its criteria of validity, a range of fascinating and important questions confronts us. They are relatively new questions; for they were veiled so long as jurisprudence and political theory were committed to the older ways of thought. They are also difficult questions, requiring for a full answer, on the one hand a grasp of some fundamental issues of constitutional law and on the other an appreciation of the characteristic manner in which legal forms may silently shift and change. We shall therefore investigate these questions only so far as they bear upon the wisdom or unwisdom of insisting, as we have done, that a central place should be assigned to the union of primary and secondary rules in the elucidation of the concept of law.

The first difficulty is that of classification; for the rule which, in the last resort, is used to identify the law escapes the conventional categories used for describing a legal system, though these are often taken to be exhaustive. Thus, English constitutional writers since Dicey have usually repeated the statement that the constitutional arrangements of the United Kingdom consist partly of laws strictly so called (statutes, orders in council, and rules embodied in precedents) and partly of conventions which are mere usages, understandings or customs. The latter include important rules such as that the Queen may not refuse her consent to a bill duly passed by Peers and Commons; there is, however, no legal duty on the Queen to give her consent and such rules are called conventions because the courts do not recognize them as imposing a legal duty. Plainly the rule that what the Queen in Parliament enacts is law does not fall into either of these categories. It is not a convention, since the courts are most intimately concerned with it and they use it in identifying the law; and it is not a rule on the same level as the "laws strictly so called" which it is used to identify. Even if it were enacted by statute, this would not reduce it to the level of a statute; for the legal status of such an enactment necessarily would depend on the fact that the rule existed antecedently to and independently of the enactment. Moreover, as we have shown in the last section, its existence, unlike that of a statute, must consist in an actual practice.

This aspect of things extracts from some a cry of despair: how can we show that the fundamental provisions of a constitution which are surely law are really law? Others reply with the insistence that at the base of legal systems there is something which is "not law," which is "pre-legal," "meta-legal," or is just "political fact." This uneasiness is a sure sign that the categories used for the description of this most important feature in any system of law are too crude. The case for calling the rule of recognition "law" is that the rule providing criteria for the identification of other rules of the system may well be thought a defining feature of a legal system, and so itself worth calling "law"; the case for calling it "fact" is that to assert that such a rule exists is indeed to make an external statement of an actual fact concerning the manner in which the rules of an "efficacious" system are identified. Both these aspects claim attention but we cannot do justice to them both by choosing one of the labels "law" or "fact." Instead, we need to remember that the ultimate rule of recognition may be regarded from two points of view: one is expressed in the external statement of fact that the rule exists in the actual practice of the system; the other is expressed in the internal statements of validity made by those who use it in identifying the law.

A second set of questions arises out of the hidden complexity and vagueness of the assertion that a legal system *exists* in a given country or among a given social group. When we make this assertion we in fact refer in compressed, portmanteau form to a number of heterogeneous social facts, usually concomitant. The standard terminology of legal and political thought, developed in the shadow of a misleading theory, is apt to over-simplify and obscure the facts. Yet when we take off the spectacles constituted by this terminology and look at the facts, it becomes apparent that a legal system, like a human being, may at one stage be unborn, at a second not yet wholly independent of its mother, then enjoy a healthy independent existence, later decay and finally die. These half-way stages between birth and normal, independent existence and, again, between that and death, put out of joint our familiar ways of describing legal phenomena. They are worth our study because, baffling as they are, they throw into relief the full complexity of what we take for granted when, in the normal case, we make the confident and true assertion that in a given country a legal system exists.

One way of realizing this complexity is to see just where the simple, Austinian formula of a general habit of obedience to orders fails to reproduce or distorts the complex facts which constitute the minimum conditions which a society must satisfy if it is to have a legal system. We may allow that this formula does designate one necessary condition: namely, that where the laws impose obligations or duties these should be generally obeyed or at any rate not generally disobeyed. But, though essential, this only caters for what we may term the "end product" of the legal system, where it makes its impact on the private citizen; whereas its day-to-day existence consists also in the official creation, the official identification, and the official use and application of law. The relationship with law involved here can be called "obedience" only if that word is extended so far beyond its normal use as to cease to characterize informatively these operations. In no ordinary sense of "obey" are legislators obeying rules when, in enacting laws, they conform to the rules conferring their legislative powers, except of course when the rules conferring such powers are reinforced by rules imposing a duty to follow them. Nor, in failing to conform with these rules do they "disobey" a law, though they may fail to make one. Nor does the word "obey" describe well what judges do when they apply the system's rule of recognition and recognize a statute as valid law and use it in the determination of disputes. We can of course, if we wish, preserve the simple terminology of "obedience" in face of the facts by many devices. One is to express, e.g. the use made by judges of general criteria of validity in recognizing a statute, as a case of obedience to orders given by the "Founders of the Constitution," or (where there are no "Founders") as obedience to a "depsychologized command," i.e., a command without a commander. But this last should perhaps have no more serious claims on our attention than the notion of a nephew without an uncle. Alternatively we can push out of sight the whole official side to law and forgo the description of the use of rules made in legislation and adjudication, and instead, think of the whole official world as one person (the "sovereign") issuing orders, through various agents or mouthpieces, which are habitually obeyed by the citizen. But this is either no more than a convenient shorthand for complex facts which still await description, or a disastrously confusing piece of mythology.

It is natural to react from the failure of attempts to give an account of what it is for a legal system to exist, in the agreeably simple terms of the habitual obedience which is indeed characteristic of (though it does not always exhaustively describe) the relationship of the ordinary citizen to law, by making the opposite error. This consists in taking what is characteristic (though again not exhaustive) of the official activities, especially the judicial attitude or relationship to law, and treating this as an adequate account of what must exist in a social group which has a legal system. This amounts to replacing the simple conception that the bulk of society habitually obey the law with the conception that they must generally share, accept, or regard as binding the ultimate rule of recognition specifying the criteria in terms of which the validity of laws are ultimately assessed. Of course we can imagine, as we have done in Chapter III, a simple society where knowledge and understanding of the sources of law are widely diffused. There the "constitution" was so simple that no fiction would be involved in attributing knowledge and acceptance of it to the ordinary citizen as well as to the officials and lawyers. In the simple world of Rex I we might well say that there was more than mere habitual obedience by the bulk of the population to his word. There it might well be the case that both they and the officials of the system "accepted," in the same explicit, conscious way, a rule of recognition specifying Rex's word as the criterion of valid law for the whole society, though subjects and officials would have different roles to play and different relationships to the rules of law identified by this criterion. To insist that this state of affairs, imaginable in a simple society, always or usually exists in a complex modern state would be to insist on a fiction. Here surely the reality of the situation is that a great proportion of ordinary citizens – perhaps a majority – have no general conception of the legal structure or of its criteria of validity. The law which he obeys is something which he knows of only as "the law." He may obey it for a variety of different reasons and among them may often, though not always, be the knowledge that it will be best for him to do so. He will be aware of the general likely consequences of disobedience: that there are officials who may arrest him and others who will try him and send him to prison for breaking the law. So long as the laws which are valid by the system's tests of validity are obeyed by the bulk of the population this surely is all the evidence we need in order to establish that a given legal system exists.

But just because a legal system is a complex union of primary and secondary rules, this evidence is not all that is needed to describe the relationships to law involved in the existence of a legal system. It must be supplemented by a description of the relevant relationship of the officials of the system to the secondary rules which concern them as officials. Here what is crucial is that there should be a unified or shared official acceptance of the rule of recognition containing the system's criteria of validity. But it is just here that the simple notion of general obedience, which was adequate to characterize the indispensable minimum in the case of ordinary citizens, is inadequate. The point is not, or not merely, the "linguistic" one that "obedience" is not naturally used to refer to the way in which these secondary rules are respected as rules by courts and other officials. We could find, if necessary, some wider expression like "follow," "comply," or "conform to" which would characterize both what ordinary citizens do in relation to law when they report for military service and what judges do when they identify a particular statute as law in their courts, on the footing that what the Queen in Parliament enacts is law. But these blanket terms would merely mask vital differences which must be grasped if the minimum conditions involved in the existence of the complex social phenomenon which we call a legal system is to be understood.

What makes "obedience" misleading as a description of what legislators do in conforming to the rules conferring their powers, and of what courts do in applying an accepted ultimate rule of recognition, is that obeying a rule (or an order) *need* involve no thought on the part of the person obeying that what he does is the right thing both for himself and for others to do: he need have no view of what he does as a fulfilment of a standard of behaviour for others of the social group. He need not think of his conforming behaviour as "right," "correct," or "obligatory." His attitude, in other words, need not have any of that critical character which is involved whenever social rules are accepted and types of conduct are treated as general standards. He need not, though he may, share the internal point of view accepting the rules as standards for all to whom they apply. Instead, he may think of the rule only as something demanding action from *him* under threat of penalty; he may obey it out of fear of the consequences, or from inertia, without thinking of himself or others as having an obligation to do so and without being disposed to criticize either himself or others for deviations. But this merely personal concern with the rules, which is all the ordinary citizen *may* have in obeying them, cannot characterize the attitude of the courts to the rules with which they operate as courts. This is most patently the case with the ultimate rule of recognition in terms of which the validity of other rules is assessed. This, if it is to exist at all, must be regarded from the internal point of view as a public, common standard of correct judicial decision, and not as something which each judge merely obeys for his part only. Individual courts of the system though they may, on occasion, deviate from these rules must, in general, be critically concerned with such deviations as lapses from standards, which are essentially common or public. This is not merely a matter of the efficiency or health of the legal system, but is logically a necessary condition of our ability to speak of the existence of a single legal system. If only some judges acted "for their part only" on the footing that what the Queen in Parliament enacts is law, and made no criticisms of those who did not respect this rule of recognition, the characteristic unity and continuity of a legal system would have disappeared. For this depends on the acceptance, at this crucial point, of common standards of legal validity. In the interval between these vagaries of judicial behaviour and the chaos which would ultimately ensue when the ordinary man was faced with contrary judicial orders, we would be at a loss to describe the situation. We would be in the presence of a *lusus naturae* worth thinking about only because it sharpens our awareness of what is often too obvious to be noticed.

There are therefore two minimum conditions necessary and sufficient for the existence of a legal system. On the one hand those rules of behaviour which are valid according to the system's ultimate criteria of validity must be generally obeyed, and, on the other hand, its rules of recognition specifying the criteria of legal validity and its rules of change and adjudication must be effectively accepted as common public standards of official behaviour by its officials. The first condition is the only one which private citizens *need* satisfy: they may obey each "for his part only" and from any motive whatever; though in a healthy society they will in fact often accept these rules as common standards of behaviour and acknowledge an obligation to obey them, or even trace this obligation to a more general obligation to respect the constitution. The second condition must also be satisfied by the officials of the system. They must regard these as common standards of official behaviour and appraise critically their own and each other's deviations as lapses. Of course it is also true that besides these there will be many primary rules which apply to officials in their merely personal capacity which they need only obey.

The assertion that a legal system exists is therefore a Janus-faced statement looking both towards obedience by ordinary citizens and to the acceptance by officials of secondary rules as critical common standards of official behaviour. We need not be surprised at this duality. It is merely the reflection of the composite character of a legal system as compared with a simpler decentralized pre-legal form of social structure which consists only of primary rules. In the simpler structure, since there are no officials, the rules must be widely accepted as setting critical standards for the behaviour of the group. If, there, the internal point of view is not widely disseminated there could not logically be any rules. But where there is a union of primary and secondary rules, which is, as we have argued, the most fruitful way of regarding a legal system, the acceptance of the rules as common standards for the group may be split off from the relatively passive matter of the ordinary individual acquiescing in the rules by obeying them for his part alone. In an extreme case the internal point of view with its characteristic normative use of legal language ("This is a valid rule") might be confined to the official world. In this more complex system, only officials might accept and use the system's criteria of legal validity. The society in which this was so might be deplorably sheeplike; the sheep might end in the slaughter-house. But there is little reason for thinking that it could not exist or for denying it the title of a legal system ...

READING QUESTIONS ON HART

1 What are Hart's criticisms of the command theory?
2 What is the "internal point of view"? Is there a difference between it and a moral point of view?
3 Why are secondary rules important to a legal system?

Whitely v Chapel
(1868) LR 4 QB 147

In this nineteenth-century English case, the accused had used the names of people recently deceased whose names appeared on the voting list; the issue was whether that constituted personating another for purposes of the statute. (Footnotes omitted.)

By 14 & 15 Vict. c. 105, s. 3, if any person, pending or after the election of any guardian [of the poor], shall wilfully, fraudulently, and with intent to affect the result of such election ... "personate any person entitled to vote at such election," he is made liable on conviction to imprisonment for not exceeding three months.

The appellant was charged with having personated one J. Marston, a person entitled to vote at an election of guardians for the township of Bradford; and it was proved that Marston was duly qualified as a rate-payer on the rate book to have voted at the election, but that he had died before the election. The appellant delivered to the person appointed to collect the voting papers a voting paper apparently duly signed by Marston.

The magistrate convicted the appellant.

The question for the Court was, whether the appellant was rightly convicted.

Mellish, QC (with him *McIntyre*), for the appellant. A dead person cannot be said to be "a person entitled to vote;" and the appellant therefore could not be guilty of personation under 14 & 15 Vict. c. 105, s. 3. Very possibly he was within the spirit, but he was not within the letter, of the enactment, and in order to bring a person within a penal enactment, both must concur. In Russell on Crimes (vol. ii. p. 1013, 4th ed., p. 541,

3rd ed.), under a former statute, in which the words were similar to those of 2 Wm. 4, c. 53, s. 49, which makes it a misdemeanor to personate "a person entitled or supposed to be entitled to any prize money," &c., *Brown's Case* is cited, in which it was held that the personation must be of some person prima facie entitled to prize money. In the Parliamentary Registration Act (6 Vict. c. 18), s. 83, the words are "any person who shall knowingly personate ... any person whose name appears on the register of voters, whether such person be alive or dead;" but under the present enactment the person must be entitled, that is, could have voted himself.

Crompton, for the respondent. *Brown's Case* is, in effect, overruled by the later cases of *Rex v Martin, and Rex v Cramp*, in which the judges decided that the offence of personating a person "supposed to be entitled" could be committed, although the person, to the knowledge or belief of the authorities, was dead. Those cases are directly in point. The gist of the offence is the fraudulently voting under another's name; the mischief is the same, whether the supposed voter be alive or dead; and the Court will put a liberal construction on such an enactment: *Reg. v Hague.*

Mellish, QC, in reply. "Supposed to be entitled" must have been held by the judges in the cases cited to mean supposed by the person personating.

Lush, J: – I do not think we can, without straining them, bring the case within the words of the enactment. The legislature has not used words wide enough to make the personation of a dead person an offence. The words "a person entitled to vote" can only mean, without a forced construction, a person who is entitled to vote at the time at which the personation takes place; in the present case, therefore, I feel bound to say the offence has not been committed. In the cases of *Rex v Martin,* and *Rex v Cramp,* the judges gave no reasons for their decision; they probably held that "supposed to be entitled" meant supposed by the person personating.

Hannen, J: – I regret that we are obliged to come to the conclusion that the offence charged was not proved; but it would be wrong to strain words to meet the justice of the present case, because it might make a precedent, and lead to dangerous consequences in other cases.

Hayes, J, concurred.

Lon L. Fuller
The Morality of Law (1969)

Fuller disputes Hart's claim that a legal order can take on any content whatsoever. The excerpt included here offers the example of a hypothetical tyrant, who decides to use law as a tool to enforce his wishes. Fuller argues that such a tyrant would quickly run into difficulties because the institutional structure of a legal system cannot help but include a minimal morality of fairness. He also accuses positivism of adopting an authoritarian concept of the authority of law.

THE MORALITY THAT MAKES LAW POSSIBLE

[A] law which a man cannot obey, nor act according to it, is void and no law: and it is impossible to obey contradictions, or act according to them. – Vaughan, CJ
In *Thomas v. Sorrell*, 1677

It is desired that our learned lawyers would answer these ensuing queries ... whether ever the Commonwealth, when they chose the Parliament, gave them a lawless unlimited power, and at their pleasure to walk contrary to their own laws and ordinances before they have repeated them? – Lilburne, *England's Birth-Right Justified*, 1645

This chapter will begin with a fairly lengthy allegory. It concerns the unhappy reign of a monarch who bore the convenient, but not very imaginative and not even very regal sounding name of Rex.

Eight Ways to Fail to Make Law

Rex came to the throne filled with the zeal of a reformer. He considered that the greatest failure of his predecessors had been in the field of law. For generations the legal system had known nothing like a basic reform. Procedures of trial were cumbersome, the rules of law spoke in the archaic tongue of another age, justice was expensive, the judges were slovenly and sometimes corrupt. Rex was resolved to remedy all this and to make his name in history as a great lawgiver. It was his unhappy fate to fail in this ambition. Indeed, he failed spectacularly, since not only did he not succeed in introducing the needed reforms, but he never even succeeded in creating any law at all, good or bad.

His first official act was, however, dramatic and propitious. Since he needed a clean slate on which to write, he announced to his subjects the immediate repeal of all existing law, of whatever kind. He then set about drafting a new code. Unfortunately, trained as a lonely prince, his education had been very defective. In particular he found himself incapable of making even the simplest generalizations. Though not lacking in confidence when it came to deciding specific controversies, the effort to give articulate reasons for any conclusion strained his capacities to the breaking point.

Becoming aware of his limitations, Rex gave up the project of a code and announced to his subjects that henceforth he would act as a judge in any disputes that might arise among them. In this way under the stimulus of a variety of cases he hoped that his latent powers of generalization might develop and, proceeding case by case, he would gradually work out a system of rules that could be incorporated in a code. Unfortunately the defects in his education were more deep-seated than he had supposed. The venture failed completely. After he had handed down literally hundreds of decisions neither he nor his subjects could detect in those decisions any pattern whatsoever. Such tentatives toward generalization as were to be found in his opinions only compounded the confusion, for they gave false leads to his subjects and threw his own meager powers of judgment off balance in the decision of later cases.

After this fiasco Rex realized it was necessary to take a fresh start. His first move was to subscribe to a course of lessons in generalization. With his intellectual powers thus fortified, he resumed the project of a code and, after many hours of solitary labor, succeeded in preparing a fairly lengthy document. He was still not confident, however, that he had fully overcome his previous defects. Accordingly, he announced to his subjects that he had written out a code and would henceforth be governed by it in deciding cases, but that for an indefinite future the contents of the code would remain an official state secret, known only to him and his scrivener. To Rex's surprise this sensible plan was deeply resented by his subjects. They declared it was very unpleasant to have one's case decided by rules when there was no way of knowing what those rules were.

Stunned by this rejection Rex undertook an earnest inventory of his personal strengths and weaknesses. He decided that life had taught him one clear lesson, namely, that it is easier to decide things with the aid of hindsight than it is to attempt to foresee and control the future. Not only did hindsight make it easier to decide cases, but – and this was of supreme importance to Rex – it made it easier to give reasons. Deciding to capitalize on this insight, Rex hit on the following plan. At the beginning of each calendar year he would decide all the controversies that had arisen among his subjects during the preceding year. He would accompany his decisions with a full statement of reasons. Naturally, the reasons thus given would be understood as not controlling decisions in future years, for that would be to defeat the whole purpose of the new arrangement, which was to gain the advantages of hindsight. Rex confidently announced the new plan to his subjects, observing that he was going to publish the full text of his judgments with the rules applied by him, thus meeting the chief objection to the old plan. Rex's subjects received this announcement in silence, then quietly explained through their leaders that when they said they needed to know the rules, they meant they needed to know them *in advance* so they could act on them. Rex muttered something to the effect that they might have made that point a little clearer, but said he would see what could be done.

Rex now realized that there was no escape from a published code declaring the rules to be applied in future disputes. Continuing his lessons in generalization, Rex worked diligently on a revised code, and finally announced that it would shortly be published. This announcement was received with universal gratification. The dismay of Rex's subjects was all the more intense, therefore, when his code became available and it was discovered that it was truly a masterpiece of obscurity. Legal experts who studied it declared that there was not a single sentence in it that could be understood either by an ordinary citizen or by a trained lawyer. Indignation became general and soon a picket appeared before the royal palace carrying a sign that read, "How can anybody follow a rule that nobody can understand?"

The code was quickly withdrawn. Recognizing for the first time that he needed assistance, Rex put a staff of experts to work on a revision. He instructed them to leave the substance untouched, but to clarify the expression throughout. The resulting code was a model of clarity, but as it was studied it became apparent that its new clarity had merely brought to light that it was honeycombed with contradictions. It was reliably reported that there was not a single provision in the code that was not nullified by another provision inconsistent with it. A picket again appeared before the royal residence carrying a sign that read, "This time the king made himself clear – in both directions."

Once again the code was withdrawn for revision. By now, however, Rex had lost his patience with his subjects and the negative attitude they seemed to adopt toward everything he tried to do for them. He decided to teach them a lesson and put an end to their carping. He instructed his experts to purge the code of contradictions, but at the same time to stiffen drastically every requirement contained in it and to add a long list of new crimes. Thus, where before the citizen summoned to the throne was given ten days in which to report, in the revision the time was cut to ten seconds. It was made a crime, punishable by ten years' imprisonment, to cough, sneeze, hiccough, faint or fall down in the presence of the king. It was made treason not to understand, believe in, and correctly profess the doctrine of evolutionary, democratic redemption.

When the new code was published a near revolution resulted. Leading citizens declared their intention to flout its provisions. Someone discovered in an ancient author a passage that seemed apt: "To command what cannot be done is not to make law; it is to unmake law, for a command that cannot be obeyed serves no end but confusion, fear and chaos." Soon this passage was being quoted in a hundred petitions to the king.

The code was again withdrawn and a staff of experts charged with the task of revision. Rex's instructions to the experts were that whenever they encountered a rule requiring an impossibility, it should be revised to make compliance possible. It turned out that to accomplish this result every provision in the code had to be substantially rewritten. The final result was, however, a triumph of draftsmanship. It was clear, consistent with itself, and demanded nothing of the subject that did not lie easily within his powers. It was printed and distributed free of charge on every street comer.

However, before the effective date for the new code had arrived, it was discovered that so much time had been spent in successive revisions of Rex's original draft, that the substance of the code had been seriously overtaken by events. Ever since Rex assumed the throne there had been a suspension of ordinary legal processes and this had brought about important economic and institutional changes within the country. Accommodation to these altered conditions required many changes of substance in the law. Accordingly as soon as the new code became legally effective, it was subjected to a daily stream of amendments. Again popular discontent mounted; an anonymous pamphlet appeared on the streets carrying scurrilous cartoons of the king and a leading article with the title: "A law that changes every day is worse than no law at all."

Within a short time this source of discontent began to cure itself as the pace of amendment gradually slackened. Before this had occurred to any noticeable degree, however, Rex announced an important decision. Reflecting on the misadventures of his reign, he concluded that much of the trouble lay in bad advice he had received from experts. He accordingly declared he was reassuming the judicial power in his own person. In this way he could directly control the application of the new code and insure his country against another crisis. He began to spend practically all of his time hearing and deciding cases arising under the new code.

As the king proceeded with this task, it seemed to bring to a belated blossoming his long dormant powers of generalization. His opinions began, indeed, to reveal a confident and almost exuberant virtuosity as he deftly distinguished his own previous decisions, exposed the principles on which he acted, and laid down guide lines for the disposition of future controversies. For Rex's subjects a new day seemed about to dawn when they could finally conform their conduct to a coherent body of rules.

This hope was, however, soon shattered. As the bound volumes of Rex's judgments became available and were subjected to closer study, his subjects were appalled to discover that there existed no discernible relation between those judgments and the code they purported to apply. Insofar as it found expression in the actual disposition of controversies, the new code might just as well not have existed at all. Yet in virtually every one of his decisions Rex declared and redeclared the code to be the basic law of his kingdom.

Leading citizens began to hold private meetings to discuss what measures, short of open revolt, could be taken to get the king away from the bench and back on the throne. While these discussions were going on Rex suddenly died, old before his time and deeply disillusioned with his subjects.

The first act of his successor, Rex II, was to announce that he was taking the powers of government away from the lawyers and placing them in the hands of psychiatrists and experts in public relations. This way, he explained, people could be made happy without rules.

The Consequences of Failure

Rex's bungling career as legislator and judge illustrates that the attempt to create and maintain a system of legal rules may miscarry in at least eight ways; there are in this enterprise, if you will, eight distinct routes to disaster. The first and most obvious lies in a failure to achieve rules at all, so that every issue must be decided on an ad hoc basis. The other routes are: (2) a failure to publicize, or at least to make available to the affected party, the rules he is expected to observe; (3) the abuse of retroactive legislation, which not only cannot itself guide action, but undercuts the integrity of rules prospective in effect, since it puts them under the threat of retrospective change; (4) a failure to make rules understandable; (5) the enactment of contradictory rules or (6) rules that require conduct beyond the powers of the affected party; (7) introducing such frequent changes in the rules that the subject cannot orient his action by them; and, finally, (8) a failure of congruence between the rules as announced and their actual administration.

A total failure in any one of these eight directions does not simply result in a bad system of law; it results in something that is not properly called a legal system at all, except perhaps in the Pickwickian sense in which a void contract can still be said to be one kind of contract. Certainly there can be no rational ground for asserting that a man can have a moral obligation to obey a legal rule that does not exist, or is kept secret from him, or that came into existence only after he had acted, or was unintelligible, or was contradicted by another rule of the same system, or commanded the impossible, or changed every minute. It may not be impossible for a man to obey a rule that is disregarded by those charged with its administration, but at some point obedience becomes futile – as futile, in fact, as casting a vote that will never be counted. As the sociologist Simmel has observed, there is a kind of reciprocity between government and the citizen with respect to the observance of rules. Government says to the citizen in effect, "These are the rules we expect you to follow. If you follow them, you have our assurance that they are the rules that will be applied to your conduct." When this bond of reciprocity is finally and completely ruptured by government, nothing is left on which to ground the citizen's duty to observe the rules.

The citizen's predicament becomes more difficult when, though there is no total failure in any direction, there is a general and drastic deterioration in legality, such as occurred in Germany under Hitler. A situation begins to develop, for example, in which though some laws are published, others, including the most important, are not. Though most laws are prospective in effect, so free a use is made of retrospective legislation that no law is immune to change ex post facto if it suits the convenience of those in power. For the trial of criminal cases concerned with loyalty to the regime, special military tribunals are established and these tribunals disregard, whenever it suits their convenience, the rules that are supposed to control their decisions. Increasingly the principal object of government seems to be, not that of giving the citizen rules by which to shape his conduct, but to frighten him into impotence. As such a situation develops, the problem faced by the citizen is not so simple as that of a voter who knows with certainty that his ballot will not be counted. It is more like that of the voter who knows that the odds are against his ballot being counted at all, and that if it is counted, there is a good chance that it will be counted for the side against which he actually voted. A citizen in this predicament has to decide for himself whether to stay with the system and cast his ballot as a kind of symbolic act expressing the hope of a better day. So it was with the German citizen under Hitler faced with deciding whether he had an obligation to obey such portions of the laws as the Nazi terror had left intact.

In situations like these there can be no simple principle by which to test the citizen's obligation of fidelity to law, any more than there can be such a principle for testing his right to engage in a general revolution. One thing is, however, clear. A mere respect for constituted authority must not be confused with fidelity to law. Rex's subjects, for example, remained faithful to him as king throughout his long and inept reign. They were not faithful to his law, for he never made any.

The Aspiration toward Perfection in Legality

So far we have been concerned to trace out eight routes to failure in the enterprise of creating law. Corresponding to these are eight kinds of legal excellence toward which a system of rules may strive. What appear at the lowest level as indispensable conditions for the existence of law at all, become, as we ascend the scale of achievement, increasingly demanding challenges to human capacity. At the height of the ascent we are tempted to imagine a utopia of legality in which all rules are perfectly clear, consistent with one another, known to every citizen, and never retroactive. In this utopia the rules remain constant through time, demand only what is possible, and are scrupulously observed by courts, police, and everyone else charged with their administration. For reasons that I shall advance shortly, this utopia, in which all eight of the principles of legality are realized to perfection, is not actually a useful target for guiding the impulse toward legality; the goal of perfection is much more complex. Nevertheless it does suggest eight distinct standards by which excellence in legality may be tested.

In expounding in my first chapter the distinction between the morality of duty and that of aspiration, I spoke of an imaginary scale that starts at the bottom with the most obvious and essential moral duties and ascends upward to the highest achievements open to man. I also spoke of an invisible pointer as marking the dividing line where the pressure of duty leaves off and the challenge of excellence begins. The inner morality of law, it should now be clear, presents all of these aspects. It too embraces a morality of duty and a morality of aspiration. It too confronts us with the problem of knowing where to draw the boundary below which men will be condemned for failure, but can expect no praise for success, and above which they will be admired for success and at worst pitied for the lack of it.

In applying the analysis of the first chapter to our present subject, it becomes essential to consider certain distinctive qualities of the inner morality of law. In what may be called the basic morality of social life, duties that run toward other persons generally (as contrasted with those running toward specific individuals) normally require only forbearances, or as we say, are negative in nature: Do not kill, do not injure, do not deceive, do not defame, and the like. Such duties lend themselves with a minimum of difficulty to formalized definition. That is to say, whether we are concerned with legal or moral duties, we are able to develop standards which designate with some precision – though it is never complete – the kind of conduct that is to be avoided.

The demands of the inner morality of the law, however, though they concern a relationship with persons generally, demand more than forbearances; they are, as we loosely say, affirmative in nature: make the law known, make it coherent and clear, see that your decisions as an official are guided by it, etc. To meet these demands human energies must be directed toward specific kinds of achievement and not merely warned away from harmful acts.

Because of the affirmative and creative quality of its demands, the inner morality of law lends itself badly to realization through duties, whether they be moral or legal. No matter how desirable a direction of human effort may appear to be, if we assert there is a duty to pursue it, we shall confront the responsibility of defining at what point that duty has been violated. It is easy to assert that the legislator has a moral duty to make his laws clear and understandable. But this remains at best an exhortation unless we are prepared to define the degree of clarity he must attain in order to discharge his duty. The notion of subjecting clarity to quantitative measure presents obvious difficulties. We may content ourselves, of course, by saying that the legislator has at least a moral duty to try to be clear. But this only postpones the difficulty, for in some situations nothing can be more baffling than to attempt to measure how vigorously a man intended to do that which he has failed to do. In the morality of law, in any event, good intentions are of little avail, as King Rex amply demonstrated. All of this adds up to the conclusion that the inner morality of law is condemned to remain largely a morality of aspiration and not of duty. Its primary appeal must be to a sense of trusteeship and to the pride of the craftsman.

To these observations there is one important exception. This relates to the desideratum of making the laws known, or at least making them available to those affected by them. Here we have a demand that lends itself with unusual readiness to formalization. A written constitution may prescribe that no statute shall become law until it has been given a specified form of publication. If the courts have power to effectuate this provision, we may speak of a legal requirement for the making of law. But a moral duty with respect to publication is also readily imaginable. A custom, for example, might define what kind of promulgation of laws is expected, at the same time leaving unclear what consequences attend a departure from the accepted mode of publication. A formalization of the desideratum of publicity has obvious advantages over uncanalized efforts, even when they are intelligently and conscientiously pursued. A formalized standard of promulgation not only tells the lawmaker where to publish his laws; it also lets the subject – or a lawyer representing his interests – know where to go to learn what the law is.

One might suppose that the principle condemning retroactive laws could also be very readily formalized in a simple rule that no such law should ever be passed, or should be valid if enacted. Such a rule would, however, disserve the cause of legality. Curiously, one of the most obvious seeming demands of legality – that a rule passed today should govern what happens tomorrow, not what happened yesterday – turns out to present some of the most difficult problems of the whole internal morality of law.

With respect to the demands of legality other than promulgation, then, the most we can expect of constitutions and courts is that they save us from the abyss; they cannot be expected to lay out very many compulsory steps toward truly significant accomplishment ...

Do the Principles of Legality Constitute an "Internal Morality of Law"?

The title of my second chapter, *The Morality that Makes Law Possible*, represents a thesis my four reviewers find thoroughly unacceptable. In attempting a response to their criticisms I shall strive to avoid any escalation of polemics, for the level I confront on this issue is already uncomfortably high. "Axe-grinding," "absurd," "bizarre," "grotesque" – these are some of the terms my critics find necessary in characterizing my thesis that there is such a thing as an internal morality of law.

According to my four critics the notion of an internal morality of law betrays a basic confusion between efficacy and morality. Some respect for the eight principles of legality is essential if law is to be effective, but that does not mean that these principles are moral in nature, any more than holding a nail straight in order to hit it right is a matter of morality. You won't drive the nail properly if you don't hold it straight and so also you won't achieve an effective system of law unless you give some heed to what I have called principles of legality. Neither of these exercises of common prudence has anything to do with morality.

So runs the argument of my critics. They are not content, however, with any such prosaic comparison as that offered by the driving of nails. Instead, they assert that if there is such a thing as an internal morality of law-making and law-administering, then there must also be an internal morality of even the most disreputable and censurable of human activities. Cohen asks whether there is a lapse in morality when a would-be assassin forgets to load his gun.[1] Dworkin raises a similar question about an inept attempt at blackmail.[2] As usual, Hart is at once the most eloquent and most explicit of my critics:

the author's insistence on classifying these principles of legality as a "moral-ity" is a source of confusion both for him and his readers ... the crucial ob-jection to the designation of these principles of good legal craftsmanship as morality, in spite of the qualification "inner," is that it perpetrates a confu-sion between two notions that it is vital to hold apart: the notions of purpos-ive activity and morality. Poisoning is no doubt a purposive activity, and re-flections on its purpose may show that it has its internal principles. ("Avoid poisons however lethal if they cause the victim to vomit," or "Avoid poisons however lethal if their shape, color, or size is likely to attract notice.") But to call these principles of the poisoner's art "the morality of poisoning" would simply blur the distinction between the notion of efficiency for a purpose and those final judgments about activities and purposes with which morality in its various forms is concerned.[3]

I must confess that this line of argument struck me at first as being so bizarre, and even perverse, as not to deserve an answer. Reflection has, however, convinced me that I was mistaken in this. As I now view the matter no issue in the exchange between me and my critics reveals more clearly the tacit presuppositions that each side brings to the debate; taking seriously this argument that the alleged internal morality of law is merely a matter of efficacy has helped me to clarify not only the unarticulated "Starting points" of my critics, but my own as well.

That something is here involved more basic than any mere quibble about the word "morality" becomes apparent when we note the fundamental obscurity of my critics' position. Just what do they have in mind when they speak of efficacy? It is not hard to see what is meant by efficacy when you are trying to kill a man with poison; if he ends up dead, you have succeeded; if he is still alive and able to strike back, you have failed. But how do we apply the notion of efficacy to the creation and administration of a thing as complex as a whole legal system? Let me offer an example drawn from the recent history of the Soviet Union that will suggest some of the difficulties involved in answering that question.

At the beginning of the 1960s the problem of economic crimes (including illegal transactions in foreign currencies) had apparently reached such proportions in Russia that the Soviet authorities decided drastic countermeasures were in order. Accordingly in May and July of 1961 statutes were passed subjecting such crimes to the death penalty. These statutes were then applied retrospectively and convicted men were put to death for acts which, while not lawful when committed, were not then subject to the death penalty.

The purpose of the Soviet authorities was obviously to make people quit stealing from the state. Was a retrospective application of the death penalty "inefficacious" for this purpose? One of the problems of criminal law is to convey to the prospective criminal that you are not engaged in a game of idle threats, that you mean what you say. Is there any more effective way of conveying that message than the retrospective application of a criminal penalty? The very fact that it marks a drastic departure from ordinary practice is, in effect, a pledge of the earnestness of the lawgiver. Yet there were Russians who were disturbed by this action of the authorities, as my colleague Harold Berman reports in the following passage:

I asked a leading Soviet jurist if he could explain the decision of the Supreme Court of the Russian Republic applying the July law retroactively – in clear violation, it seemed to me, of the 1958 Fundamental Principles of Criminal Procedure. He replied, "We lawyers didn't like that" – a statement as interesting for the "we lawyers" as for the "didn't like that."[4]

Now it is reasonable to suppose, I think, that the Soviet lawyer was not asserting that the action of the authorities was an ineffective measure for combating economic crime. He was saying that it involved a compromise of principle, an impairment of the integrity of the law. As Berman remarks with reference to this conversation: "it is the lawyers who understand best of all, perhaps, the integrity of law, the universality of legal standards – in other words, the threat to legality *in general* which is posed by any *particular* infringement of legality."[5]

At this point I can imagine my critics pulling at my sleeve: "Ah, but you have misunderstood what we meant by efficacy. We did not have in mind short-run efficacy in meeting some passing emergency. The Soviet action impaired the efficacy of law because it tended to undermine public confidence in legal rules generally and reduced the incentive to obey them. It achieved an immediate gain at a cost in the damage done to the institution of law generally." But plainly if my critics begin to expand the notion of efficacy in this direction, they will soon find themselves drifting across the boundary they have so painstakingly set up to distinguish morality from efficacy. They are likely to get themselves into the predicament of those who try to convert all morality into enlightened selfishness and who end up with so much enlightenment, and so little selfishness, that they might have saved themselves a good deal of trouble by simply talking about morality in the first place.

I do not think, therefore, that in discussing problems of legality any useful joinder of issue is achieved by opposing efficacy to morality; certainly nothing is attained that justifies treating the use of the word "morality" in this connection as an exercise in obfuscation. In truth, the appeal of "efficacy" does not lie in any definiteness of its meaning, but in the tough-sounding, positivistic flavor of the word; it suggests an observer clear-eyed and result-oriented, not easily misled by fuzzy concepts of purpose. In other words, my critics' preference for "efficacy" over "morality" reflects the influence of deep-seated and largely unarticulated resolutions of the mind, rather than any reasoned-out conclusion about a specific issue.

I confront therefore the most unwelcome task of demonstrating that my critics' rejection of an internal morality of law rests on premises they have not themselves brought to expression in their writings. Let me make it clear, however, that I do not purport to explore unavowed emotional biases; my efforts lie in the realm of the intellect, in the exploration of an implicit structure that shapes my critics' thought processes. If their conclusions do not imply the premises I ascribe to them, they are at liberty to set me straight.

Proceeding then to the task at hand, I perceive *two* assumptions underlying my critics' rejection of "the internal morality of law." The *first* of these is a belief that the existence or non-existence of law is, from a moral point of view, a matter of indifference. The *second* is an assumption I have already described as characteristic of legal positivism generally. This is the assumption that law should be viewed not as the product of an interplay of purposive orientations between the citizen and his government but as a one-way projection of authority, originating with government and imposing itself upon the citizen.

In the literature of legal positivism it is of course standard practice to examine at length the relations of law and morals. With respect to the influence of morals on law it is common to point out that moral conceptions may guide legislation, furnish standards for the criticism of existing law, and may properly be taken into account in the interpretation of law. The treatment of the converse influence – that of law on morality – is generally more meager, being confined chiefly to the observation that legal rules long established tend, through a kind of cultural conditioning, to be regarded as morally right.

What is generally missing in these accounts is any recognition of the role legal rules play in making possible an effective realization of morality in the actual behavior of human beings. Moral principles cannot function in a social vacuum or in a war of all against all. To live the good life requires something more than good intentions, even if they are generally shared; it requires the support of firm base lines for human interaction, something that – in modern society at least – only a sound legal system can supply ...

So when we speak of "the moral neutrality of law" we cannot mean that the existence and conscientious administration of a legal system are unrelated to a realization of moral objectives in the affairs of life. If respect for the principles of legality is essential to produce such a system, then certainly it does not seem absurd to suggest that those principles constitute a special morality of role attaching to the office of lawmaker and law-administrator. In any event the responsibilities of that office deserve some more flattering comparison than that offered by the practices of the thoughtful and conscientious poisoner who never forgets to tear the chemist's label off before he hands the bottle to his victim.

To regard as morally indifferent the existence or non-existence of law is to assume that moral precepts retain the same meaning regardless of the social context into which they are projected. It thus illustrates what I have previously described as an abstraction from the social dimension; it brings to expression a distaste for phenomena of interaction characteristic of positivistic thought. This bent of mind comes openly to the fore in the second assumption underlying my critics' rejection of the notion of an internal morality of law. This is the assumption that the essential reality of law is perceived when we picture it as a one-way projection of authority originating with government and imposing itself upon the citizen. Since this assumption is shared by unreflective common sense, and finds tacit recognition in the ordinary usages of language, it will be well to examine in some detail what is wrong with it.

Let me begin by putting in opposition to one another two forms of social ordering that are often confounded. One of these is *managerial direction*, the other is *law*. Both involve the direction and control of human activity; both imply subordination to authority. An extensive vocabulary is shared by the two forms: "authority," "orders," control," "jurisdiction," "obedience," "compliance," "legitimacy" – these are but a few of the terms whose double residence is a source of confusion.

A general and summary statement of the distinction between the two forms of social ordering might run somewhat as follows: The directives issued in a managerial context are *applied* by the subordinate in order to serve a purpose set by his superior. The law-abiding citizen, on the other hand, does not *apply* legal rules to serve specific ends set by the lawgiver, but rather *follows* them in the conduct of his own affairs, the interests he is presumed to serve in following legal rules being those of society generally. The directives of a managerial system regulate primarily the relations between the subordinate and his superior and only collaterally the relations of the subordinate with third persons. The rules of a legal system, on the other hand, normally serve the primary purpose of setting the citizen's relations with other citizens and only in a collateral manner his relations with the seat of authority from which the rules proceed. (Though we sometimes think of the criminal law as defining the citizen's duties toward his government, its primary function is to provide a sound and stable framework for the interactions of citizens with one another.)

The account just given could stand much expansion and qualification; the two forms of social ordering present themselves in actual life in many mixed, ambiguous, and distorted forms. For our present purposes, however, we shall attempt to clarify the essential difference between them by presupposing what may be called "ideal types." We shall proceed by inquiring what implications the eight principles of legality (or analogues thereof) have for a system of managerial direction as compared with their implications for a legal order.

Now five of the eight principles are quite at home in a managerial context. If the superior is to secure what he wants through the instrumentality of the subordinate he must, first of all, communicate his wishes, or "promulgate" them by giving the subordinate a chance to know what they are, for example, by posting them on a bulletin board. His directives must also be reasonably clear, free from contradiction, possible of execution and not changed so often as to frustrate the efforts of the subordinate to act on them. Carelessness in these matters may seriously impair the "efficacy" of the managerial enterprise.

What of the other three principles? With respect to the requirement of generality, this becomes, in a managerial context, simply a matter of expediency. In actual practice managerial control is normally achieved by standing orders that will relieve the superior from having to give a step-by-step direction to his subordinate's performance. But the subordinate has no justification for complaint if, in a particular case, the superior directs him to depart from the procedures prescribed by some general order. This means, in turn, that in a managerial relation there is no room for a formal principle demanding that the actions of the superior conform to the rules he has himself announced; in this context the principle of "congruence between official action and declared rule" loses its relevance. As for the principle against retrospectivity, the problem simply does not arise; no manager retaining a semblance of sanity would direct his subordinate today to do something on his behalf yesterday.

From the brief analysis just presented it is apparent that the managerial relation fits quite comfortably the picture of a one-way projection of authority. Insofar as the principles of legality (or, perhaps I should say, their managerial analogues) are here applicable they are indeed "principles of efficacy"; they are instruments for the achievement of the superior's ends. This does not mean that elements of interaction or reciprocity are ever wholly absent in a managerial relation. If the superior habitually overburdens those under his direction, confuses them by switching signals too frequently, or falsely accuses them of departing from instructions they have in fact faithfully followed, the morale of his subordinates will suffer and they may not do a good job for him; indeed, if his inconsiderateness goes too far, they may end by deserting his employ or turning against him in open revolt. But this tacit reciprocity of reasonableness and restraint is something collateral to the basic relation of order-giver and order-executor.

With a legal system the matter stands quite otherwise, for here the existence of a relatively stable reciprocity of expectations between lawgiver and subject is part of the very idea of a functioning legal order. To see why and in what sense this is true it is essential to continue our examination of the implications of the eight principles, turning now to their implications for a system of law. Though the principles of legality are in large measure interdependent, in distinguishing law from managerial direction the key principle is that I have described as "congruence between official action and declared rule."

Surely the very essence of the Rule of Law is that in acting upon the citizen (by putting him in jail, for example, or declaring invalid a deed under which he claims title to property) a government will faithfully apply rules previously declared as those to be followed by the citizen and as being determinative of his rights and duties. If the Rule of Law does not mean this, it means nothing. Applying rules faithfully implies, in turn, that rules will take the form of general declarations; it would make little sense, for example, if the government were today to enact a special law whereby Jones should be put in jail and then tomorrow were "faithfully" to follow this "rule" by actually putting him in jail. Furthermore, if the law is intended to permit a man to conduct his own affairs subject to an obligation to observe certain restraints imposed by superior authority, this implies that he will not be told at each turn what to do; law furnishes a baseline for self-directed action, not a detailed set of instructions for accomplishing specific objectives.

The twin principles of generality and of faithful adherence by government to its own declared rules cannot be viewed as offering mere counsels of expediency. This follows from the basic difference between law and managerial direction; law is not, like management, a matter of directing other persons how to accomplish tasks set by a superior, but is basically a matter of providing the citizenry with a sound and stable framework for their interactions with one another, the role of government being that of standing as a guardian of the integrity of this system.

I have previously said that the principle against retrospective rule-making is without significance in a context of managerial direction simply because no manager in his right mind would be tempted to direct his subordinate today to do something yesterday. Why do things stand differently with a legal system? The answer is, I believe, both somewhat complex and at the same time useful for the light it sheds on the differences between managerial direction and law.

The first ingredient of the explanation lies in the concept of legitimation. If *A* purports to give orders to *B*, or to lay down rules for his conduct, *B* may demand to know by what title *A* claims the power to exercise a direction over the conduct of other persons. This is the kind of problem Hart had in mind in formulating his Rule of Recognition. It is a problem shared by law-making and managerial direction alike, and may be said to involve a principle of *external* legitimation. But the Rule of Law demands of a government that it also legitimate its actions toward citizens by a second and *internal* standard. This standard requires that within the general area covered by law acts of government toward the citizen be in accordance with (that is, be authorized or validated by) general rules previously declared by government itself. Thus, a lawful government may be said to accomplish an internal validation of its acts by an exercise of its own legislative power. If a prior exercise of that power can effect this validation, it is easy to slip into the belief that the same validation can be accomplished retrospectively.

What has just been said may explain why retrospective legislation is not rejected out of hand as utterly nonsensical. It does not, however, explain why retrospective law-making can in some instances actually serve the cause of legality. To see why this is so we need to recall that under the Rule of Law control over the citizen's actions is accomplished, not by specific directions, but by *general* rules expressing the principle that like cases should be given like treatment. Now abuses and mishaps in the operations of a legal system may impair this principle and require as a cure retrospective legislation. The retrospective statute cannot serve as a baseline for the interactions of citizens with one another, but it can serve to heal infringements of the principle that like cases should receive like treatment. I have given illustrations of this in my second chapter. As a further example one may imagine a situation in which a new statute, changing the law, is enacted and notice of this statute is conveyed to all the courts in the country except those in *Province X*, where through some failure of communication the courts remain uninformed of the change. The courts of this province continue to apply the old law; those in the remaining portions of the country decide cases by the new law. The principle that like cases should be given like treatment is seriously infringed, and the only cure (at best involving a choice of evils) may lie in retrospective legislation. Plainly problems of this sort cannot arise in a managerial context, since managerial direction is not in principle required to act by general rule and has no occasion to legitimate specific orders by showing that they conform to previously announced general rules.

We have already observed that in a managerial context it is difficult to perceive anything beyond counsels of expediency in the remaining principles of legality – those requiring that rules or orders be promulgated, clear in meaning, noncontradictory, possible of observance, and not subject to too frequent change. One who thinks of law in terms of the managerial model will assume as a matter of course that these five principles retain the same significance for law. This is particularly apt to be true of the desideratum of clarity. What possible motive, one may ask, other than sheer slovenliness, would prompt a legislator to leave his enactments vague and indefinite in their coverage?

The answer is that there are quite understandable motives moving him in that direction. A government wants its laws to be clear enough to be obeyed, but it also wants to preserve its freedom to deal with situations not readily foreseeable when the laws are enacted. By publishing a criminal statute government does not merely issue a directive to the citizen; it also imposes on itself a charter delimiting its powers to deal with a particular area of human conduct. The loosely phrased criminal statute may reduce the citizens' chance to know what is expected of him, but it expands the powers of government to deal with forms of misbehavior which could not be anticipated in advance. If one looks at the matter purely in terms of "efficacy" in the achievement of governmental aims, one might speak of a kind of optimum position between a definiteness of coverage that is unduly restrictive of governmental discretion and a vagueness so pronounced that it will not only fail to frighten the citizen away from a general area of conduct deemed undesirable, but may also rob the statute of its power to lend a meaningful legitimation to action taken pursuant to it.

Opposing motivations of this sort become most visible in a bureaucratic context where men deal, in some measure, face to face. Often managerial direction is accompanied by, and intertwined with miniature legal systems affecting such matters as discipline and special privileges. In such a context it is a commonplace of sociological observation that those occupying posts of authority will often resist not only the clarification of rules, but even their effective publication. Knowledge of the rules, and freedom to interpret them to fit the case at hand, are important sources of power. One student in this field has even concluded that the "toleration of illicit practices actually enhances the controlling power of superiors, paradoxical as it may seem."[6] It enhances the superior's power, of course, by affording him the opportunity to obtain gratitude and loyalty through the grant of absolutions, at the same time leaving him free to visit the full rigor of the law on those he considers in need of being brought into line. This welcome freedom of action would not be his if he could not point to rules as giving significance to his actions; one cannot, for example, forgive the violation of a rule unless there is a rule to violate. This does not mean, however, that the rule has to be free from obscurity, or widely publicized, or consistently enforced. Indeed, any of these conditions may curtail the discretion of the man in control – a discretion from which he may derive not only a sense of personal power but also a sense, perhaps not wholly perverse, of serving well the enterprise of which he is a part.

It may seem that in the broader, more impersonal processes of a national or state legal system there would be lacking any impulse toward deformations or accommodations of the sort just suggested. This is far from being the case. It should be remembered, for example, that in drafting almost any statute, particularly in the fields of criminal law and economic regulation, there is likely to occur a struggle between those who want to preserve for government a broad freedom of action and those whose primary concern is to let the citizen know in advance where he stands. In confronting this kind of problem there is room in close cases for honest differences of opinion, but there can also arise acute problems of conscience touching the basic integrity of legal processes. Over wide areas of governmental action a still more fundamental question can be raised: whether there is not a damaging and corrosive hypocrisy in pretending to act in accordance with preestablished rules when in reality the functions exercised are essentially managerial and for that reason demand – and on close inspection are seen to exhibit – a rule-free response to changing conditions.

What has just been said can offer only a fleeting glimpse of the responsibilities, dilemmas, and temptations that confront those concerned with the making and administering of laws. These problems are shared by legislators, judges, prosecutors, commissioners, probation officers, building inspectors, and a host of other officials, including – above all the patrolman on his beat. To attempt to reduce these problems to issues of "efficacy" is to trivialize them beyond recognition.

Why, then, are my critics so intent on maintaining the view that the principles of legality represent nothing more than maxims of efficiency for the attainment of governmental aims? The answer is simple. The main ingredients of their analysis are not taken from law at all, but from what has here been called managerial direction. One searches in vain in their writings for any recognition of the basic principle of the Rule of Law – that the acts of a legal authority toward the citizen must be legitimated by being brought within the terms of a previous declaration of general rules.

This omission is conspicuous throughout Hart's *Concept of Law*. His only extended treatment of the principle of generality, for example, seems plainly inspired by the managerial model:

Even in a complex large society, like that of a modern state, there are occasions when an official, face to face with an individual, orders him to do something. A policeman orders a particular motorist to stop or a particular beggar to move on. But these simple situations are not, and could not be, the standard way in which law functions, if only because no society could support the number of officials necessary to secure that every member of society was officially and separately informed of every act which he was required to do. Instead such particularized forms of control are either exceptional or reinforcements of general forms of directions which do not name, and are not addressed to, particular individuals, and do not indicate a particular act to be done. (pp. 20–1)

Other comments by Hart on the principle of generality, while less explicit, in no way qualify the statement just quoted. (See pp. 38, 121, 202, 236.) All run in terms of providing "instruments of social control" and of enabling "social control to function."

With respect to what I have called the principle requiring "congruence between official action and declared rule," Hart's comments again relate to the problem of achieving "effective control" over the citizen's actions; failure of this control is said to be illustrated when the criminal law is so laxly enforced that the public ends by ignoring it. (See pp. 23, 82, 141.) The only departure from what may be called the managerial frame of reference is found in some remarks (pp. 156, 202) about an abstract affinity between the ideal of justice and an efficiently run legal system; both are said to respect the principle that like cases should be given like treatment. Thus "we have, in the bare notion of applying a general rule of law, the germ at least of justice." There is no intimation that a government has toward the citizen any obligation to realize this "germ of justice" in the way it makes and administers laws; the point seems to be simply that if we happen to observe a well-run legal system in operation we shall discover in it a certain formal resemblance to justice.

Thus, it will be seen that Hart's concept of law, being based essentially on the managerial model,[7] contains no element inconsistent with the view that law is a one-way projection of authority. This does not mean, of course, that the lawgiver can bring a legal system into existence by himself; like the manager he requires the acquiescence and cooperation of those subject to his direction. This is recognized quite explicitly and with his usual aptness of phrasing by Hart himself:

if a system of rules is to be imposed by force on any, there must be a sufficient number who accept it voluntarily. Without their voluntary cooperation, thus creating *authority*, the coercive power of law and government cannot be established. (p. 196)

There is no suggestion here that the citizen's voluntary cooperation must be matched by a corresponding cooperative effort on the part of government. There is no recognition in Hart's analysis that maintaining a legal system in existence depends upon the discharge of interlocking responsibilities – of government toward the citizen and of the citizen toward government.

If we assume, as I do here, that an element of commitment by the lawgiver is implicit in the concept of law, then it will be well to attempt to spell out briefly in what form this commitment manifests itself. In a passage headed by his translator "Interaction in the Idea of Law," Simmel suggests that underlying a legal system is a contract between lawgiver and subject. By enacting laws government says to the citizen, "These are the rules we ask you to follow. If you will obey them, you have our promise that they are the rules we will apply to your conduct." Certainly such a construction contains at least this much truth:

if the citizen knew in advance that in dealing with him government would pay no attention to its own declared rules, he would have little incentive himself to abide by them. The publication of rules plainly carries with it the "social meaning" that the rulemaker will himself abide by his own rules. On the other hand, any attempt to conceive of a legal system as resting on a contract between lawgiver and subject not only stirs inconvenient historical associations, but has a certain incongruity about it, especially when we recall that in a democratic society the same citizen may be both lawgiver and legal subject.

There is an old-fashioned legal term that may offer an escape from our predicament. This is the word "intendment." Our institutions and our forenamed interactions with one another are accompanied by certain interlocking expectations that may be called intendments, even though there is seldom occasion to bring these underlying expectations across the threshold of consciousness. In a very real sense when I cast my vote in an election my conduct is directed and conditioned by an anticipation that my ballot will be counted in favor of the candidate I actually vote for. This is true even though the possibility that my ballot will be thrown in the wastebasket, or counted for the wrong man, may never enter my mind as an object of conscious attention. In this sense the institution of elections may be said to contain an intendment that the votes cast will be faithfully tallied, though I might hesitate to say, except in a mood of rhetoric, that the election authorities had entered a contract with me to count my vote as I had cast it.

NOTES

1   "The Morality of Law – A Symposium," 10 *Villanova Law Review* 631-78 (1965) at p. 651. Individual contributions were Murray, "Introduction to the Morality of Law," 624-30; Dworkin, 'The Elusive Morality of Law,'" 631–9; Cohen, "Law, Morality and Purpose," 640–54; Fuller, "A Reply to Professors Cohen and Dworkin," 655–66; with comments by John E. Murray, Jr., 667–70; E. Russell Naughton 671–2; Francis H. Parker, 673–5; and Donald A. Giannella, 676–8.
2   Supra n.1 at p. 634.
3   78 *Harvard Law Review* 1281–96 (1965) at pp. 1285–6.
4   Berman, "The Struggle of Soviet Jurists Against a Return to Stalinist Terror," 22 *Slavic Review* 314–20, at p. 315 (1963).
5   Ibid., p. 320.

6 Blau, *The Dynamics of Bureaucracy* (2d ed. 1963), p. 215.
7 It may be well at this point to mention briefly one possible source of
misunderstanding. A reader generally familiar with Hart's *Concept of Law*
may recall that he explicitly rejects Austin's "command theory of law."
To one who does not have in mind just what this rejection implies, it may
seem that in disapproving of the command theory Hart is also rejecting
what I have here described as a managerial theory of law. This would,
however, be to misunderstand Hart's argument. Hart rejects the command theory chiefly on two grounds: (1) it sees the force of law as residing in the threat of sanctions, rather than in an acceptance of authority;
(2) Austin's theory presupposes direct communication between lawgiver
and legal subject. But, plainly, effective managerial direction rests, much
more obviously than does law, on a willingness to accept authoritative
direction. Furthermore, managerial directions need not be conveyed in a
face-to-face manner; they are in fact commonly embodied in something
like a manual of operations or may be set forth on a bulletin board. The
crucial point in distinguishing law from managerial direction lies in a
commitment by the legal authority to abide by its own announced rules
in judging the actions of the legal subject. I can find no recognition of this
basic notion in *The Concept of Law*.

READING QUESTIONS ON FULLER

1 Fuller argues that at a minimum, any legal system will include
certain procedural safeguards. How much of a morality is this?
Could there nonetheless be an utterly wicked legal system?
2 Do you think that Fuller correctly describes the positivist concept
of authority as "managerial"?
3 Does Hart's "internal point of view" address Fuller's concerns
about reciprocity?

Ronald Dworkin
"Law's Ambitions for Itself" (1985)

Dworkin seeks to expand Fuller's point, arguing that fundamental values of
fairness are implicated in every legal decision. Law's ambition is to work

itself pure and rid itself of all morally arbitrary distinctions. Dworkin argues that positivist judges make bad decisions when they try to steer clear of making substantive judgments of fairness.

The 1984 McCorkle Lecture
Law's Ambitions for Itself

I

My title is meant to remind you of a set of metaphors that were once cherished by lawyers but now seem both old-fashioned and silly. "Law works itself pure." "There is a higher law, within and yet beyond positive law, toward which positive law grows." "Law has its own ambitions."

Three mysteries live in these metaphors; they all recognize the obvious fact that in some sense law changes through adjudication as well as explicit legislation. Judges often describe the law, that is, as different from what people had taken it to be before, and use their novel description to decide the very case in which it is announced. The first mystery argues that these changes are (or at least can be) guided by the law itself, personified, playing out an internal program or design. The second adds that changes guided in this way by the law itself are also improvements, that law purer is law better. The third is more mysterious yet: that such changes are not really changes at all, but on the contrary discoveries of an underlying identity, so that a judge who announces a novel rule may actually be describing existing law more accurately.

There are political claims in each of these mysteries; but the practical claim of the third is most evident because it figures in the political justification of what judges do in hard cases. It seems unfair for judges to change the law in the course of litigation. If change is really self-realization, however, if apparent change is only the discovery of deeper identity, then this complaint is misplaced. On the contrary judges would be acting unfairly in the way the complaint assumes – acting against the idea of legality – if they did not recognize and enforce the apparent change.

This entire set of ideas will strike many of you as not only mysterious but idiotic. It has played no important role in formal legal theory for the better part of a century. It was ridiculed and, so most academic lawyers think, destroyed by the movement that began with the legal positivists, led by Jeremy Bentham and his energetic disciple John Austin in Britain, and by the legal realists of American jurisprudence. Their attack was direct. They argued that the mysterious claims I described employ an illegitimate personification: there is no such thing as the law that can have its own ambitions, that can guide the course of its own change. There are only judges who change the law, from time to time, in order to make it better, in their own entirely human view, or simply to repair its gaps enough to decide cases at hand. We do much better, these critics said, to junk the obscurantism, and to insist that the law already in the books, with all its faults and gaps, is the only law we have. Judges do legislate when they change that law, they do apply new law retrospectively, and we must criticize and explain what they do with our eyes open to those simple facts.

This jurisprudential battle, which almost everyone thinks the positivists and the realists won, had a political dimension. Positivists and realists saw themselves as reformers. They said that the older theorists, who celebrated the metaphors and the mysteries, were formalists blind to the practical consequences of judicial decisions for the community at large, or worse, that they were conscious or unconscious agents of oppressive capitalism who protected the status quo by pretending that their political decisions were the unfolding of the law's own necessity. I mention this political dimension because the old battle has been rejoined in our time and the political alignments are now strikingly different, indeed reversed.

The battle has been rejoined mainly in a new theater: constitutional adjudication. The famous decisions of the "Warren Court" built a jurisprudence of individual constitutional rights against the state; the justices who wrote the famous opinions said these rights were created not by the bare text of the Constitution, nor by the specific, concrete intentions of its "framers," nor by their own fiat, but instead by the constitutional structure itself working itself pure. They relied, that is, on the mysteries latent in the antique metaphors. They have been attacked with the same arguments, and all the fervor and ridicule, the earlier positivists and realists used against what they called natural law; but now the attack comes from the right, not the left, of the political spectrum. Today's skeptics are conservative, not progressive or even liberal.

The nation's attention is drawn to this argument, at least languidly, every four years, because presidential elections concentrate the public's mind on the Supreme Court. Attention was greater during the recent election, because five members of the Court are now at least seventy-five years old, and also because the lawyers President Reagan is tipped to appoint to fill the coming vacancies include several who have declared their judicial philosophies with unusual candor and academic thoroughness. Some of these are former professors of law Reagan has already appointed to the federal circuit courts of appeal, like Richard Posner and Robert Bork, and it is these I have particularly in mind when I say that the banners of positivism now march with the right.

I shall later illustrate the new political alignment by describing, in some detail, a recent decision by Judge Bork in the circuit court for the District of Columbia. But I should first mention two competing explanations of the political reversal. Some of you will think it shows that jurisprudence is epiphenomenal in the following way. If people like the recent drift of law, if they want judges to continue in the spirit of the last few decades, they will be drawn to the old metaphors about law's internal ambitions. If they do not, if they think law has been moving very much in the wrong direction, they will strike realist postures and condemn the metaphors as empty and mischievous personifications. I am not myself attracted to that cynical view of the connection between jurisprudence and legal practice. (You may think I dislike it because it makes my job pointless.) I prefer an alternative explanation: that the realignment is a natural consequence of the growing attraction, to liberals, of the idea that minorities of different types have political rights against the majority. This development, I believe, itself makes the older attitude to law more attractive to liberals and the positivist attitude correspondingly more attractive to conservatives. (I return to this alternate explanation toward the end of this discussion.)

II

I shall now try to rehabilitate the old idea expressed in the metaphors and developed in the mysteries I described. The nerve of my suggestion is this: we can understand the metaphors and mysteries, and also account for their appeal, if we take them to express an *interpretive* model of adjudication. I cannot describe that model in any detail here, though I have tried to do so elsewhere[1] can only summarize it here with the caution that needed detail, as well as response to obvious objections, has been left out. The omissions will not, I hope, defeat my present ambition, which is to show how the mysteries I describe become less mysterious, and less vulnerable to the ridicule of the realist attack, if taken to express a model of adjudication of the general character I describe.

The model distinguishes between the positive law – the law in the books, the law declared in the clear statements of statutes and past court decisions – and the full law, which it takes to be the set of principles of political morality that taken together provide the best interpretation of the positive law. It insists on a certain understanding of the idea of interpretation: a set of principles provides the best interpretation of the positive law if it provides the best justification available for the political decisions the positive law announces. It provides the best interpretation, in other words, if it shows the positive law in the best possible light.

That will seem an odd account of interpretation to those of you who believe that interpretation, in its very nature, is the process of recovering the "intention" of the historical author of the material being interpreted. For the positive law is the product of a great many different officials at different times who were moved by very different ambitions and purposes, and retrieving these often conflicting ambitions and purposes would be a very different enterprise from the one I have just described. But the assumption that interpretation, in its very nature, is a process of recovering intentions confuses two different levels at which the character of interpretation can be studied.

Even in the case of literary interpretation, when the "author's intention" account seems most plausible, it is only one of the several competing accounts of interpretation we find in the literature. Some scholars argue, for example, that interpretation is better understood as an attempt to capture the effect a literary work has on contemporary readers. So we must try to find some description of interpretation more abstract than any of these contending theories, a description we can use to explain the argument among them; to explain, that is, both what they are disagreeing about, and how they can all be seen as theories of the same activity. The account I gave – that interpretation seeks to show the material being interpreted as the best it can be – is meant as a candidate for that more abstract description embracing, in that way, the rival theories rather than contending with them. It explains why the author's intention theory seems appealing to some critics but not others. The former believe or assume that the point of literature is essentially communicative, so that discovering an author's communicative intentions, and showing how these are realized in his or her work, is the best way of showing the value that work can properly be claimed to have. The latter hold different views about the sources of value in literature, and these different views spawn rival ideas about which techniques of interpretation show a work in its best light. This view of the matter – this account of the level at which the author's intention thesis provides a theory of interpretation – is, I believe, suggested by the work of Professor Hirsch of the University of Virginia, who is the most powerful and illuminating exponent of that thesis.

If we keep the more abstract account of interpretation in mind, that an interpretation seeks to make of the material being interpreted the best it can be, then we insist that any interpretation of any material must be tested on two dimensions. First, it must fit that material. No interpretation of the positive law can be successful unless it can justify, broadly, the judicial decisions that have actually been reached; otherwise it cannot claim to show *these* decisions in their best light. We can state that requirement by imagining what we know not to be true, that the various decisions that form the positive law were all taken by a single official. Then the first requirement tests a proposed interpretation by asking whether that single official, guided by the principles set out in the proposed interpretation, could have made those decisions. We cannot insist on an exact fit: that every actual decision be explainable in that way. But we do insist that the fit be at least general, that no fundamental or important part of the positive law run contrary to a proposed interpretation, at least if another interpretation, much more successful in this respect, is available.

The second requirement lies on the dimension of justification. An interpretation of positive law is unsuccessful unless it offers a justification of that law, and if, as will ordinarily be the case, two competing interpretations both satisfy the first requirement of fit to an adequate degree, this second requirement of justification will discriminate between them because it will prefer the interpretation that provides the better justification. In the case of law, of course, the justification in question is one of political morality. Showing positive law in its best light means showing it as the best course of statesmanship possible.

That fact will confirm, for many of you, a suspicion that must have been growing throughout this brief account of interpretation. You will think that it makes interpretation irredeemably subjective, that since two interpreters of the law may very well have different convictions about whether a particular interpretation fits well enough to succeed on the first dimension, and are very likely to have different political convictions about which provides a better justification in political morality on the second, interpretation is just a matter of opinion and no one's interpretation could claim to be "objectively" any better than any one else's. I believe that this is the wrong conclusion to draw, that this use of the troublesome distinction between "subjective" and "objective" is confused and adds nothing useful to any discussion of either interpretation or political morality. I have tried to defend that view elsewhere[2] but I will not expand on it now, because I can continue my argument without it.

Construe, if you like, my description of the interpretive model of adjudication "subjectively." It then becomes an account of the questions a judge should put to himself and answer from his own "subjective" convictions about fit and political morality. Since these are in any case different from the questions the positivist model requires him to put to himself, and draws on a different set of "subjective" convictions, the difference between the two models will be preserved, and so will the question I shall shortly consider, which is whether we have any basis for choosing between the two models.

III

My discussion of interpretation, and of the interpretive model of adjudication, has been exceedingly abstract. I shall try to make it somewhat more concrete by showing how a judge who accepted the interpretive model would attack the problem posed by the recent case I referred to earlier, which is *Dronenburg*.[3] The facts of that case can be stated quickly enough. Dronenburg served with distinction in the Navy for many years, but was discharged when he admitted homosexual acts in a barracks. He sued the Navy claiming that his discharge for that reason violated his constitutional rights.

The interpretive model recommends the following method of studying his claim. We begin by identifying the positive law in the neighborhood of the problem. This consists, first, in the text of the constitutional clauses Dronenburg cited, and then in the past decisions of the Supreme Court under those clauses. For our illustration we may limit the positive law to the text of the Due Process Clause and the set of decisions usually called the "privacy" decisions. *Griswold*[4] decided that states, may not prohibit the use of contraceptives by married couples. *Eisenstad*[5] confirmed that the right to contraception extends to unmarried couples as well, and *Carey*[6] condemned a New York statute requiring contraceptives to be bought only from licensed pharmacists and prohibiting their sale to children under sixteen. The Court has upheld the right to "privacy" in other contexts: for example, in *Loving*,[7] which held a Virginia statute prohibiting interracial marriage unconstitutional. The most dramatic of the "privacy" decisions so far, however, is the abortion issue, *Roe v Wade*.[8] Court cited the contraception decisions and *Loving* to justify its ruling that the states could not constitutionally prohibit abortion in the first trimester of pregnancy.

This limited description of the positive law provides our preinterpretive base, and we must now ask which set of principles would provide the best interpretation, that is to say the best justification, of it. Which political principles would satisfy the requirement of the first dimension, the requirement of fit? I can think of two principles that might well be thought to fit, and I shall consider only these, though you might well be able to think of more. First, the decisions just described could have been made by a single statesman acting to enforce a version of Mill's famous principle, which holds that the state must not prohibit acts that harm no one just because these acts are widely considered immoral or sinful. Second, they could have been made by a statesman who accepted the narrower principle that the state may not legislate to restrict liberty touching decisions about procreation.

Suppose, each of these two principles does fit the decisions of the positive law.[9] It matters very much which we accept as the better interpretation of that law. If Mill's principle is a better interpretation, then the full or genuine law protects Dronenburg through the constitutional right he claims. If the second principle, limited to procreation, is superior, then it does not (unless some other principle favoring him can be found elsewhere in constitutional law) because the choice of homosexual sex cannot plausibly be treated as a choice about procreation even though it has consequences for it. So our attention shifts to the second dimension of interpretation; we must ask which of our two putative interpretations provides a better justification of the decisions from the point of view of political morality. Can there be much doubt that the first is superior? It states a recognizable ideal of moral independence that will have considerable appeal even to those who cannot accept it in full. The second principle, which declares only that the state may not intervene in personal decisions about procreation, is not really, on a second look, a principle at all. It sets out an arbitrary line unconnected to any recognizable distinction of moral importance. It offers no reason why intimate personal decisions about procreation should be protected from state regulation though other intimate decisions need not be so protected, and we have no reason at hand in either the literature or common culture of morality that could justify that distinction.

Though, as I emphasized earlier, the interpretive model will often produce different results for different people, because the convictions they bring to bear on the questions the model provides are different, *Dronenburg* strikes me as an easy case within that model.[10] Under that model the full, genuine law holds for Dronenburg. Now please reconsider, in the light of this example, the three "mysteries" I described at the beginning of this lecture.

On the surface a decision for Dronenburg, under the claim that the constitutional right of privacy extends to homosexuals, is a change in the law, because that right is not explicit in the text of the Constitution and had not before been recognized by the Supreme Court. But we can now, I hope, see the sense in the claim that if the interpretive argument justifying this change is a good argument the change was directed by the positive law itself, realizing what can sensibly be called its own ambitions. That is only a way – I agree that it is not the most pellucid way – of saying that the positive law constrains what can count as its best interpretation, and this is patently so. The second claim we found mysterious argues that a change produced through adjudication is not neutral but an improvement, that law purer is law better. This, too, can be restated as a feature of the interpretive model we have developed, for it claims only the converse of the second requirement of interpretation we distinguished. Since an interpretation is better if it provides a better justification in political morality, then a change guided by a better interpretation will for that reason alone be an improvement. Our third "mystery" insisted that change guided by the law itself is not genuine change but only clarification of law as it stands already. That is simply the contrast between positive and full law made to sound more mysterious than it is, and the practical upshot we noticed survives the demystification. For the interpretive model insists that if the best interpretation of the positive law, and therefore the most accurate statement of the full law, yields a constitutional right for Dronenburg, then denying him that right is not merely refusing to make a change in the law that would improve it, but is itself a denial of legality, an insult to the rule of law.

IV

So the interpretive model does give point to the old metaphors and does show the illuminating power of the attitudes towards adjudication and the law they expressed. The positivist assault on those attitudes rejected not a patently absurd metaphysics but a perfectly practical style of judging. I said that the positivist critique had become the weapon of conservative lawyers in their opposition to the use of our Constitution to protect individual rights against the state. The judge who actually decided *Dronenburg* is, as it happens, a self-conscious member of the school of conservative positivists, and we may therefore turn to his opinion hoping to sharpen our sense of the contrast between the two styles of adjudication we have now distinguished.

Indeed, the contrast could hardly be more complete. Judge Bork set out the positive law I have described, but only to show that it did not contain, as positive law, any explicit recognition of a constitutional right protecting homosexuals. That, for him, was decisive of whether Dronenburg already had the constitutional right he claimed. He did not. So the only question left for adjudication was whether lower-court federal judges should create a new right in his favor, and this question, for Bork, answered itself. He allowed himself to say that, in his opinion, even the justices of the Supreme Court should not create new constitutional rights because in so doing they exceed their legitimate powers as judges. But he thought it obvious that, whatever the Supreme Court should or should not do, lower-court justices should not usurp powers not rightfully theirs. He decided, on that ground alone, against Dronenburg's claim. This opinion is remarkable for its crude positivist character. The positive law is all the law there is, and any change would be a piece of legislation merely, in this case, a constitutional amendment in defiance of the amending procedures that document itself provides.

V

So we have two models for adjudication: the interpretive model that, in this instance at least, argues for improved protection of individual rights and the positivist model that argues, at least here, against that development. What grounds could we have for choosing between these two models? It is easier to describe the grounds we do *not* have for that choice.

Positivists often appeal to skepticism as a reason for rejecting the ideas that come together in the interpretive model. This is sometimes metaphysical skepticism, expressed in comments like Holmes' scornful remark that law is not a brooding omnipresence in the sky. But this form of skepticism is available only so long as positivism can treat its opponent as committed to some ghostly form of natural law. It is not appropriate when the older tradition is restated as the interpretive model. That model seems to encourage a different form of skepticism, however, which is moral skepticism in the shape of the following argument. If two lawyers disagree about which set of principles shows positive law in the best light, there can be no right answer to that question, and therefore no single answer dictated by the interpretive model. That argument seems to me a poor one, as I said; but even if it were sound it would provide no argument for positivism against interpretation as general styles of adjudication. For positivism requires judges to make controversial judgments of political morality just as often as the interpretive model does. It is true – and important – that the questions of political morality the interpretive model puts to judges are different, and invoke different convictions, from the questions of morality positivism puts, but if there can be no right answer to the former there can be none to the latter either. So moral skepticism provides as strong – or as weak – an objection to each of the two styles of adjudication, and offers no ground for choosing between them (or, indeed, between either of them and any other theory about how judges should decide hard cases).

Legal philosophers once thought that the choice between theories of adjudication could be made on semantic grounds or (what comes to much the same thing) on grounds of conceptual clarity or convenience. Positivism was supposed to capture how lawyers use the word "law," or at least to provide a superior way to use that word. But these claims foundered for two reasons. First, they are false as claims about how lawyers talk: it is not true that almost all lawyers use "law" to refer only to positive law. (Indeed, positivists have had to invent implausible epicycles of linguistic theory to explain why they do not.) Second, since our two models are substantively different – the difference is illustrated dramatically by the different consequences of the two models in *Dronenburg* – the choice we must make is between the models themselves, not how we should speak about or within them.

We can dismiss a third suggestion, about how to choose between the two models of adjudication, equally quickly. I mean the argument Bork relied on so heavily in *Dronenburg*, that the interpretive model he refused to follow is *illegitimate* in the constitutional context because judges who follow that model usurp powers of constitutional amendment. That argument simply and directly begs the question at issue, for what the constitution actually is, at any moment, depends on which model of adjudication is the proper one to use in constitutional adjudication. If the interpretive model is the right one, for us, then our Constitution already consists of what that model identifies as the full constitutional law, and then it is *Bork's* decision declining to enforce the full law that is illegitimate, that amends the Constitution by fiat.

I anticipated this point in remarking, early in this lecture, this practical consequence of the set of ideas we have now restated in the interpretive model: it makes the scope of the rule of law, and therefore the legitimate power of judges, turn on what it identifies as the full law rather than the positive law it takes as the object of interpretation. Of course it would beg the question in the opposite direction if I were to argue, on behalf of the interpretive model, that Bork's positivistic decision was a piece of illegitimate usurpation because it amended the constitution. Claims of legitimacy or illegitimacy are part of the conclusion of an argument for a model of adjudication, and so cannot themselves figure in that argument.

It is time I turned from arguments we should reject for choosing one of our two models over the other, however, to consider whether there are any we should accept. We might well be tempted to ask which model itself provides a better interpretation of our constitutional practice. It seems plain that the interpretive model fits that practice much better. It is, indeed, a large complaint of the conservative positivists that the Supreme Court has too often decided cases in the interpretive spirit. We should not rely too heavily on that observation, however, because these conservatives might reply that the positivist model fits enough of constitutional practice – or, if not, that it fits enough of legal practice in the United States more generally – to remain eligible on the dimension of fit. So we should compare the two models on the other dimension of interpretation by asking which provides a better justification, in political morality, for the practices it claims to fit. We have an even stronger reason for turning at once to that directly political question. Positivists may claim that it begs the question, in much the way I just said Bork's argument does, to argue for the interpretive model on interpretive grounds. But if we reject the interpretive test, for that reason, then the test of political morality, where the interpretive test was already leading us, would be the only remaining method of comparing the two models.

We might begin the political test by noticing that the interpretive model supposes and serves a distinct political virtue: political integrity. The model assumes that the state, as policeman, must speak with one voice in the following sense. If it relies on one set of political principles to justify its use of coercive power in one area, it must allow those principles their natural extension. If it must rely on some version of Mill's principle, for example, to justify denying the majority the decision whether people should be permitted to use contraceptives, or to marry interracially, or to have abortions in the first trimester of pregnancy, it must extend the protection of that principle to homosexuals as well.

Can we find a comparable underlying political virtue for the positivist model of constitutional adjudication expressed in Bork's opinion? I believe so: it is the virtue of economic efficiency, conceived as the goal of satisfying the preferences of the community overall, including its political and moral as well as its more narrowly economic preferences. It is no accident that the foremost academic supporters of conservative constitutional policy are also the most obdurate advocates of what is called economic analysis in other areas of the law. Their conviction that the majority's political power should be limited as little as possible – that it should be limited only by the explicit text of the Constitution or the unambiguous intentions of its framers – reflects the same unexpressed political theory as their ambition that the rules of contract, tort, and property be constructed so as to maximize social wealth. Both reflect an unrestricted utilitarianism that allows the preferences of many people to override those of a few, in some overall calculation of a social preference, and denies any constraint on the kind of preferences that must be counted in that calculation. My preferences about how you lead your life, in other words, count as much as yours.

The conflict between the underlying virtues we have now identified for our two models – integrity for the interpretive model and efficiency for the positivist model – is clear enough. Integrity is, from the point of view of efficiency, both arbitrary and irrational: arbitrary because it cannot be drawn from unrestricted utilitarianism, and irrational because it will prove, except in the rarest cases, incompatible with it. A social engineer anxious to achieve the fullest possible satisfaction of everyone's preferences in the long run could not accept integrity as a constraint, because the preferences he seeks to satisfy are unlikely themselves to be disciplined by the principled coherence integrity would impose on them. Our leading example shows this dramatically. Many people prefer that others not have contraceptives, abortions, or homosexual sex. But the phenomenological profiles of these different "external" preferences are very different: they differ in their popularity, emotional charge, and connection to other "moral" views. Perhaps the overall satisfaction of preferences would be improved, in the long run, by some constitutional constraint prohibiting temporary majorities from banning contraception. But it hardly follows that a constraint prohibiting punishing homosexuals would have the same consequence, because the mix and character of preferences, not to mention side effects, is so different in that case.

The conflict between the two virtues seems sharper still when we reflect on the ideals of community associated with each. In a community regulated by efficiency each person sees other people as resources and competitors: resources because his preferences include and are supported by preferences about how they should act, competitors because the satisfaction of their preferences is likely to impinge on the satisfaction of his. There is no sorority or fraternity in this picture of society; it is the picture of politics as commerce by other means. A society dedicated to integrity, on the contrary, aims at the most intense version of community compatible with moral diversity.

We are not a community tied together by a concrete moral settlement, by shared opinions about the details of what justice and fairness and a decent and valuable life require. (We would, I believe, be a worse community if we did achieve consensus about these matters.) We debate about justice and fairness through the institutions we have, seeking, as part of that debate, to reform these institutions as we use them, acknowledging that any institutional structure we achieve is provisional, that no decision of majority or executive or court is right just because it has been taken, or right just because it must be respected so long as it stands. We march in this way toward what we hope is a better community, fairer and more just; we march we hope forward though we can believe some steps are backward. But we nevertheless recognize community in our present diversity, and so accept, in the name of community, a special and further constraint. We march together so that the settlements of principle we reach from time to time, as plateaus for further campaigns, extend to everyone. We leave no wounded behind, no abandoned minorities of race or gender or sexual disposition, even when bringing them along delays the gains of others.

If you find that vision of community more attractive than the community of efficiency, as I do, then you will find in it the only kind of argument we can have for one conception of law over another. It points us toward the interpretive model, toward the set of ideas locked in the old metaphors about law's ambitions for itself. You may find one feature of my argument odd. You may find it odd that the lawyers' contest about styles of adjudication finally turns in the way I claim of ideals of community, that volumes of philosophy speak in the fall of every judge's gavel. It may be odd, but I'm sure it's true, and even a little thrilling ...

NOTES

1 See, e.g., R. Dworkin, "Law as Interpretation," in *A Matter of Principle*, Pt. 2 (Harvard Univ. Press, 1985).
2 Ibid., p. 167.
3 *Dronenburg v Zech*, 741 F.2d 1388 (DC Cir. 1984).
4 *Griswold v Connecticut*, 381 US 479 (1965).
5 *Eisenstadt v Baird*, 405 US 438 (1971).
6 *Carey v Population Servs. Int'l*, 431 US 678 (1977).
7 *Loving v Virginia*, 388 US 1 (1967).
8 410 US 113 (1973).
9 The assumption that the first interpretation, which appeals to Mill's principle, fits the abortion decision requires the controversial further assumption that a fetus is not a person within the first trimester, and this assumption might therefore be a necessary part of any competent interpretation of the full set of privacy decisions. Or, perhaps, Mill's principle might be used to justify the other decisions in the "privacy" group and some further principle found, if any could be, to justify the abortion decision independently. In either case Mill's principle would then be *part* of an interpretation of the decisions as a whole, though not exhaustive of it.
10 I should repeat, however, that this claim is not necessary to my main purpose, which is to show the model at work and how it differs from the positivist model I shall shortly use Bork's actual decision in *Dronenburg* to illustrate.

Ronald Dworkin
Law's Empire (1986)

THE CHAIN OF LAW

The Chain Novel

I argued in Chapter 2 that creative interpretation takes its formal structure from the idea of intention, not (at least not necessarily) because it aims to discover the purposes of any particular historical person or group but because it aims to impose purpose over the text or data or tradition being interpreted. Since all creative interpretation shares this feature, and therefore has a normative aspect or component, we profit from comparing law with other forms or occasions of interpretation. We can usefully compare the judge deciding what the law is on some issue not only with the citizens of courtesy deciding what the tradition requires, but with the literary critic teasing out the various dimensions of value in a complex play or poem.

Judges, however, are authors as well as critics. A judge deciding *McLoughlin* or *Brown* adds to the tradition he interprets; future judges confront a new tradition that includes what he has done. Of course literary criticism contributes to the traditions of art in which authors work; the character and importance of that contribution are themselves issues in critical theory. But the contribution of judges is more direct, and the distinction between author and interpreter more a matter of different aspects of the same process. We can find an even more fruitful comparison between literature and law, therefore, by constructing an artificial genre of literature that we might call the chain novel.

In this enterprise a group of novelists writes a novel *seriatim*; each novelist in the chain interprets the chapters he has been given in order to write a new chapter, which is then added to what the next novelist receives, and so on. Each has the job of writing his chapter so as to make the novel being constructed the best it can be, and the complexity of this task models the complexity of deciding a hard case under law as integrity. The imaginary literary enterprise is fantastic but not unrecognizable. Some novels have actually been written in this way, though mainly for a debunking purpose, and certain parlor games for rainy weekends in English country houses have something of the same structure. Television soap operas span decades with the same characters and some minimal continuity of personality and plot, though they are written by different teams of authors even in different weeks. In our example, however, the novelists are expected to take their responsibilities of continuity more seriously; they aim jointly to create, so far as they can, a single unified novel that is the best it can be.

Each novelist aims to make a single novel of the material he has been given, what he adds to it, and (so far as he can control this) what his successors will want or be able to add. He must try to make this the best novel it can be construed as the work of a single author rather than, as is the fact, the product of many different hands. That calls for an overall judgment on his part, or a series of overall judgments as he writes and rewrites. He must take up some view about the novel in progress, some working theory about its characters, plot, genre, theme, and point, in order to decide what counts as continuing it and not as beginning anew. If he is a good critic, his view of these matters will be complicated and multifaceted, because the value of a decent novel cannot be captured from a single perspective. He will aim to find layers and currents of meaning rather than a single, exhaustive theme. We can, however, in our now familiar way give some structure to any interpretation he adopts, by distinguishing two dimensions on which it must be tested. The first is what we have been calling the dimension of fit. He cannot adopt any interpretation, however complex, if he believes that no single author who set out to write a novel with the various readings of character, plot, theme, and point that interpretation describes could have written substantially the text he has been given. That does not mean his interpretation must fit every bit of the text. It is not disqualified simply because he claims that some lines or tropes are accidental, or even that some events of plot are mistakes because they work against the literary ambitions the interpretation states. But the interpretation he takes up must nevertheless flow throughout the text; it must have general explanatory power, and it is flawed if it leaves unexplained some major structural aspect of the text, a subplot treated as having great dramatic importance or a dominant and repeated metaphor. If no interpretation can be found that is not flawed in that way, then the chain novelist will not be able fully to meet his assignment; he will have to settle for an interpretation that captures most of the text, conceding that it is not wholly successful. Perhaps even that partial success is unavailable; perhaps every interpretation he considers is inconsistent with the bulk of the material supplied to him. In that case he must abandon the enterprise, for the consequence of taking the interpretive attitude toward the text in question is then a piece of internal skepticism; that nothing can count as continuing the novel rather than beginning anew.

He may find, not that no single interpretation fits the bulk of the text, but that more than one does. The second dimension of interpretation then requires him to judge which of these eligible readings makes the work in progress best, all things considered. At this point his more substantive aesthetic judgments, about the importance or insight or realism or beauty of different ideas the novel might be taken to express, come into play. But the formal and structural considerations that dominate on the first dimension figure on the second as well, for even when neither of two interpretations is disqualified out of hand as explaining too little, one may show the text in a better light because it fits more of the text or provides a more interesting integration of style and content. So the distinction between the two dimensions is less crucial or profound than it might seem. It is a useful analytical device that helps us give structure to any interpreter's working theory or style. He will form a sense of when an interpretation fits so poorly that it is unnecessary to consider its substantive appeal, because he knows that this cannot outweigh its embarrassments of fit in deciding whether it makes the novel better, everything taken into account, than its rivals. This sense will define the first dimension for him. But he need not reduce his intuitive sense to any precise formula; he would rarely need to decide whether some interpretation barely survives or barely fails, because a bare survivor, no matter how ambitious or interesting it claimed the text to be, would almost certainly fail in the overall comparison with other interpretations whose fit was evident.

We can now appreciate the range of different kinds of judgments that are blended in this overall comparison. Judgments about textual coherence and integrity, reflecting different formal literary values, are interwoven with more substantive aesthetic judgments that themselves assume different literary aims. Yet these various kinds of judgments, of each general kind, remain distinct enough to check on another in an overall assessment, and it is that possibility of contest, particularly between textual and substantive judgments, that distinguishes a chain novelist's assignment from more independent creative writing. Nor can we draw any flat distinction between the stage at which a chain novelist interprets the text he has been given and the stage at which he adds his own chapter, guided by the interpretation he has settled on. When he begins to write he might discover in what he has written a different, perhaps radically different, interpretation. Or he might find it impossible to write in the tone or theme he first took up, and that will lead him to reconsider other interpretations he first rejected. In either case he returns to the text to reconsider the lines it makes eligible.

Scrooge

We can expand this abstract description of the chain novelist's judgment through an example. Suppose you are a novelist well down the chain. Suppose Dickens never wrote *A Christmas Carol*, and the text you are furnished, though written by several people, happens to be the first part of that short novel. You consider these two interpretations of the central character: Scrooge is inherently and irredeemably evil, an embodiment of the untarnished wickedness of human nature freed from the disguises of convention he rejects; or Scrooge is inherently good but progressively corrupted by the false values and perverse demands of high capitalist society. Obviously it will make an enormous difference to the way you continue the story which of these interpretations you adopt. If you have been given almost all of *A Christmas Carol* with only the very end to be written – Scrooge has already had his dreams, repented, and sent his turkey – it is too late for you to make him irredeemably wicked, assuming you think, as most interpreters would, that the text will not bear that interpretation without too much strain. I do not mean that no interpreter could possibly think Scrooge inherently evil after his supposed redemption. Someone might take that putative redemption to be a final act of hypocrisy, though only at the cost of taking much else in the text not at face value. This would be a poor interpretation, not because no one could think it a good one, but because it is in fact, on all the criteria so far described, a poor one ...

READING QUESTIONS ON DWORKIN

1 What is Dworkin's middle ground between history and moral recommendation?
2 Can Dworkin really rely on law to work itself pure? There's an old saying "garbage in, garbage out." Dworkin seems confident that any legal system starts with enough good to generate freedom and equality in the end. What features of a legal system make him so confident? Is his belief realistic?
3 Positivists have conceded that legal systems often include moral values, but insist those values simply reflect the views of those with the power to make law. How might Dworkin reply to such a challenge?

Mark Tushnet
"Following the Rules Laid Down:
A Critique of Interpretivism and Neutral Principles" (1983)

Tushnet argues that the idea of law as a system of rules, and the related idea that the task of judges is to apply the law, do not stand up to serious scrutiny, because rules provide no significant constraint on behaviour. He argues that such regularity as can be found in judicial decision making is the result of the shared social background and sensibilities of judges, rather than in the application of either rules or principles to particular cases.

The rule of law, according to the liberal conception, is meant to protect us against the exercise of arbitrary power. The theory of neutral principles asserts that a requirement of consistency, the core of the ideal of the rule of law, places sufficient bounds on judges to reduce the risk of arbitrariness to an acceptable level. The question is whether the concepts of neutrality and consistency can be developed in ways that are adequate for the task. My discussion examines various candidates for a definition of neutrality, beginning with a crude definition and moving toward more sophisticated ones. Yet each candidate suffers from similar defects: each fails to provide the kinds of constraints on judges that liberalism requires. Some candidates seek to limit the results judges might reach, others the methods they may use. The supposed substantive bounds that consistency imposes on judges, however, are either empty or parasitic on other substantive theories of constitutional law, and the methodological bounds are either empty or dependent on a sociology of law that undermines liberalism's assumptions about society.

If neutrality is to serve as a meaningful guide, it must be understood not as a standard for the content of principles, but rather as a constraint on the process by which principles are selected, justified, and applied. Thus, the remaining candidate explications of neutrality all focus on the judicial process and the need for "neutral application." This focus transfers our attention from the principles themselves to the judges who purport to use them.

1. Prospective Application – What then are methodologically neutral principles? To Wechsler, such principles are identified primarily by a forward-looking aspect: a judge who invokes a principle in a specific instance commits himself or herself to invoking it in future cases that are relevantly identical. For example, a judge who justifies the holding in *Brown v Board of Education* that segregated schools are unconstitutional by invoking the principle that the state may not take race into account in any significant policy decision is thereby also committed to holding state-developed affirmative action programs unconstitutional. The judge's interior monologue involves specifying the principle about to be invoked, imagining future cases and their proper resolution, de-

termining whether those cases are different from the present one in any ways that the proposed principle itself says are relevant, and asking whether the principle yields the proper results.

The ... conceptual difficulty with the theory of neutral principles was foreshadowed by the example of a case whose result could be justified by either of two principles. Neutral application requires that we be able to identify the principle that justified the result in case 1 in order to be sure that it is neutrally applied in case 2. This requirement, however, cannot be fulfilled, because there are always a number of justificatory principles available to make sense of case 1 and a number of techniques to select the "true" basis of case 1. Of course, the opinion in case 1 will articulate a principle that purports to support the result. But the thrust of introductory law courses is to show that the principles offered in opinions are never good enough. And this indefiniteness bedevils – and liberates – not only the commentators and the lawyers and judges subsequently dealing with the decision; it equally affects the author of the opinion.

... At the moment a decision is announced, we cannot identify the principle that it embodies. Even when we take account of the language of the opinion, each decision can be traced to many different possible principles, and we often learn the justifying principle of case 1 only when a court in case 2 states it. Behind the court's statement of what case 1 meant lies all the creativity to which the hermeneutic theory of historical understanding directed our attention. When *Roe* was decided, we might have thought that it rested on Perry's principle, but the funding cases show us that we were "wrong" and that *Roe* "in fact" rested on one of the alternatives spelled out above. The theory of neutral principles thus loses almost all of its constraining force when neutrality has a prospective meaning. What is left is something like a counsel to judges that they be sincere within the limits of their ability. But this formulation hardly provides a reassuring constraint on judicial willfulness.

2. Retrospective Application – Although Wechsler framed the neutral principles theory in prospective terms, it might be saved by recasting it in retrospective terms. The theory would then impose as a necessary condition for justification the requirement that a decision be consistent with the relevant precedents. This tack links the theory to general approaches to precedent-based judicial decisionmaking in nonconstitutional areas. It also captures the natural way in which we raise

questions about neutrality. The prospective theory requires that we pose hypothetical future cases, apply the principle, and ask whether the judges really meant to resolve the hypothetical cases as the principle seems to require. Because the hypothetical cases have not arisen, we cannot know the answer; we can do little more than raise our eyebrows, as Wechsler surely did, and emphasize the "really" as we ask the question in a skeptical tone.

In contrast, the retrospective theory encourages concrete criticism of the sort that Perry produced. We need only compare case 2, which is now decided, with case 1 to see if a principle from case 1 has been neutrally applied in case 2. But if the retrospective demand is merely that the opinion in case 2 deploy some reading of the earlier case from which the holding in case 2 follows, the openness of the precedents means that the demand can always be satisfied. And if the demand is rather that the holding be derived from the principles actually articulated in the relevant precedents, differences between case 2 and the precedents will inevitably demand a degree of reinterpretation of the old principles. New cases always present issues different from those settled by prior cases. Thus, to decide a new case, a judge must take some liberties with the old principles, if they are to be applied at all. There is, however, no principled way to determine how many liberties can be taken; hence this second reading of the retrospective approach likewise provides no meaningful constraints.

The central problem here is that, given the difficulty of isolating a single principle for which a given precedent stands, we lack any criteria for distinguishing between cases that depart from and those that conform to the principles of their precedents. In fact, any case can compellingly be placed in either category. Although such a universal claim cannot be validated by example, examples can at least make the claim plausible. Therefore, the following paragraphs present several instances of cases that simultaneously depart from and conform to their precedents.

The first is *Griswold v Connecticut*, in which the Supreme Court held that a state could not constitutionally prohibit the dissemination of contraceptive information or devices to married people. Griswold relied in part on *Pierce v Society of Sisters*, which held unconstitutional a requirement that children attend public rather than private schools, and *Meyer v Nebraska*, which held that a state could not prohibit the teaching of foreign languages to young children. In *Griswold*, the Court said that these cases relied on a constitutionally protected interest, conveniently labeled "privacy," that was identical to the interest implicated in the contraceptive case.

On one view, *Griswold* tortures these precedents. Both were old-fashioned due process cases, which emphasized interference "with the calling of modern language teachers ... and with the power of parents to control the education of their own." On this view, the most one can fairly find in *Meyer* and *Pierce* is a principle about freedom of inquiry that is rather narrower than a principle of privacy. Yet of course one can say with equal force that *Griswold* identifies for us the true privacy principle of *Meyer* and *Pierce*, in the same way that the abortion funding cases identify the true principle of *Roe v Wade* ... [T]he retrospective approach to neutral principles must recognize the extensive creativity exercised by a judge when he or she imputes to a precedent "the" principle that justifies both the precedent and the judge's present holding.

Once again the examples illustrate a general point. In a legal system with a relatively extensive body of precedent and with well-developed techniques of legal reasoning, it will always be possible to show how today's decision is consistent with the relevant past decisions. Conversely, however, it will also always be possible to show how today's decision is inconsistent with the precedents. This symmetry, of course, drains "consistency" of any normative content. Just as we were forced to abandon content neutrality and prospective neutrality of application, we are now also forced to abandon retrospective neutrality of application as a source of meaningful constraints in a mature legal system like ours.

The preceding discussion has reminded us that each decision reworks its precedents. A decision picks up some threads that received little emphasis before, and places great stress on them. It deprecates what seemed important before by emphasizing the factual setting of the precedents. The techniques are well known; indeed, learning them is at the core of a good legal education. But they are techniques. This recognition suggests that we attempt to define consistency as a matter of craft. When push comes to shove, in fact, adherents of neutral principles simply offer us lyrical descriptions of the sense of professionalism in lieu of sharper characterizations of the constraints on judges. Charles Black, for example, attempts to resolve the question whether law can rely on neutral principles by depicting "the art of law" living between the two poles of subjective preference and objective validation in much the same way that "the art of music has its life somewhere between traffic noise and a tuning fork – more disciplined by far than the one, with an unfathomably complex inner discipline of its own, far richer than the other, with inexhaustible variety of resource." The difficulty then is to specify the limits to permissible craftiness. One limit may be that a judge cannot lie about the precedents – for example, by grossly mischaracterizing the facts. And Black adds that "decision [must] be taken in knowledge of and with consideration of certainly known facts of public life," such as the fact that segregation necessarily degrades blacks. But these limits are clearly not terribly restrictive, and no one has suggested helpful others.

If the craft interpretation cannot specify limits to craftiness, another alternative is to identify some decisions that are within and some that are outside the limits in order to provide the basis for an inductive and intuitive generalization. As the following discussion indicates, however, it turns out that the limits of craft are so broad that in any interesting case any reasonably skilled lawyer can reach whatever result he or she wants. The craft interpretation thus fails to constrain the results that a reasonably skilled judge can reach, and leaves the judge free to enforce his or her personal values, as long as the opinions enforcing those values are well written. Such an outcome is inconsistent with the requirements of liberalism in that, once again, the demand for neutral principles fails in any appreciable way to limit the possibility of judicial tyranny.

The debate over the propriety of the result in *Roe v Wade* illustrates this problem. It seems to be generally agreed that, as a matter of simple craft, Justice Blackmun's opinion for the Court was dreadful. The central issue before the Court was whether a pregnant woman had a constitutionally protected interest in terminating her pregnancy. When his opinion reached that issue, Justice Blackmun simply listed a number of cases in which "a right of personal privacy, or a guarantee of certain areas or zones of privacy," had been recognized. Then he said, "This right of privacy, whether it be founded in the Fourteenth Amendment's concept of personal liberty ... or ... in the Ninth Amendment's reservation of rights to the people, is broad enough to encompass a woman's decision whether or not to terminate her pregnancy." And that was it. I will provisionally concede that this "argument" does not satisfy the requirements of the craft.

But the conclusion that we are to draw faces two challenges: it is either uninteresting or irrelevant to constitutional theory. Insofar as *Roe* gives us evidence, we can conclude that Justice Blackmun is a terrible judge. The point of constitutional theory, though, would seem to be to keep judges in line. If the result in *Roe* can be defended by judges more skilled than Justice Blackmun, the requirements of the craft would mean only that good judges can do things that bad judges cannot without subjecting themselves to professional criticism. For example, John Ely argues that, although *Roe* is beyond acceptable limits, *Griswold* is within them, though perhaps near the edge. Justice Douglas' opinion for the Court in *Griswold* identified a number of constitutional provisions that in his view explicitly protected one or another aspect of personal privacy. The opinion then noted that the Court had in the past protected other interests closely related to those expressly protected. By arguing that those "penumbral" interests overlapped in the area of marital use of contraceptives, Justice Douglas could hold the challenged statute unconstitutional.

If *Griswold* is acceptable, we need only repeat its method in *Roe*. Indeed, Justice Douglas followed just that course in a brilliant concurring opinion. And even if *Griswold's* logic is rejected, skilled lawyers could still rewrite *Roe* to defend Justice Blackmun's outcome. There is in fact a cottage industry of constitutional law scholars who concoct revised opinions for controversial decisions. Thus, the craft interpretation of neutrality in application is ultimately uninteresting for reasons that we have already seen. At most it provides a standard to measure the competence of judges, a standard that by itself is insufficient to constrain adequately the risk of tyranny.

The other difficulty with the craft interpretation runs deeper. Craft limitations make sense only if we can agree what the craft is. But consider the craft of "writing novels." Its practice includes Trollope writing *The Eustace Diamonds*, Joyce writing *Finnegan's Wake*, and Mailer writing *The Executioner's Song*. We might think of Justice Blackmun's opinion in *Roe* as an innovation akin to Joyce's or Mailer's. It is the totally unreasoned judicial opinion. To say that it does not look like Justice Powell's decision in some other case is like saying that a Cubist "portrait" does not look like its subject as a member of the Academy would paint it. The observation is true, but irrelevant both to the enterprise in which the artist or judge was engaged and to our ultimate assessment of his product.

C RULES AND INSTITUTIONS

We can now survey our progress in the attempt to define "neutral principles." Each proposed definition left us with judges who could enforce their personal values unconstrained by the suggested version of the neutrality requirement. Some of the more sophisticated candidates, such as the craft interpretation, seemed plausible because they appealed to an intuitive sense that the institution of judging involves people who are guided by and committed to general rules applied consistently. But the very notions of generality and consistency can be specified only by reference to an established institutional setting. We can know what we mean by "acting consistently" only if we understand the institution of judging in our society. Thus, neutral principles theory proves unable to satisfy its demand for rule-guided judicial decisionmaking in a way that can constrain or define the judicial institution; in the final analysis, it is the institution – or our conception of it – that constrains the concept of rule-guidedness.

Consider the following multiple choice question: "Which pair of numbers comes next in the series 1, 3, 5, 7? (a) 9, 11; (b) 11, 13; (c) 25, 18." It is easy to show that any of the answers is correct. The first is correct if the rule generating the series is "list the odd numbers"; the second is correct if the rule is "list the odd prime numbers"; and the third is correct if a more complex rule generates the series. Thus, if asked to follow the underlying rule – the "principle" of the series – we can justify a tremendous range of divergent answers by constructing the rule so that it generates the answer that we want. As the legal realists showed, this result obtains for legal as well as mathematical rules. The situation in law might be thought to differ, because judges try to articulate the rules they use. But even when an earlier case identifies the rule that it invokes, only a vision of the contours of the judicial role constrains judges' understanding of what counts as applying the rule. Without such a vision, there will always be a diversity of subsequent uses of the rule that could fairly be called consistent applications of it.

There is, however, something askew in this anarchic conclusion. After all, we know that no test maker would accept (c) as an answer to the mathematical problem; and indeed we can be fairly confident that test makers would not include both (a) and (b) as possible answers, because the underlying rules that generate them are so obvious that they make the question fatally ambiguous. Another example may sharpen the point. The examination for those seeking driver's licenses in the District of Columbia includes this question: "What is responsible for most automobile accidents? (a) The car; (b) the driver; (c) road conditions." Anyone who does not know immediately that the answer is (b) does not understand what the testing enterprise is all about.

In these examples, we know something about the rule to follow only because we are familiar with the social practices of intelligence testing and drivers' education. That is, the answer does not follow from a rule that can be uniquely identified without specifying something about the substantive practices. Similarly, although we can, as I have argued elsewhere, use standard techniques of legal argument to draw from the decided cases the conclusion that the Constitution requires socialism, we know that no judge will in the near future draw that conclusion. But the failure to reach that result is not ensured because the practice of "following rules" or neutral application of the principles inherent in the decided cases precludes a judge from doing so. Rather, it is ensured because judges in contemporary America are selected in a way that keeps them from thinking that such arguments make sense. This branch of the argument thus makes a sociological point about neutral principles. Neither the principles nor any reconstructed version of a theory that takes following rules as its focus can be neutral in the sense that liberalism requires, because taken by itself, an injunction to follow the rules tells us nothing of substance. If such a theory constrains judges, it does so only because judges, before they turn to the task of finding neutral principles for the case at hand, have implicitly accepted some image of what their role in shaping and applying rules in controverted cases ought to be.

There is something both odd and important here. The theory of neutral principles is initially attractive because it affirms the openness of the courts to all reasonable arguments drawn from decided cases. But if the courts are indeed open to such arguments, the theory allows judges to do whatever they want. If it is only in consequence of the pressures exerted by a highly developed, deeply entrenched, homeostatic social structure that judges seem to eschew conclusions grossly at odds with the values of liberal capitalism, sociological analysis ought to destroy the attraction of neutral principles theory. Principles are "neutral" only in the sense that they are, as a matter of contingent fact, unchallenged, and the contingencies have obvious historical limits.

At the same time, however, the theory shows us an institution at the heart of liberalism that contains the potential for destroying liberalism by revealing the institution's inconsistencies and its dialectical instability. The neutral rule of law was Locke's solution to the Hobbesian problem of order. But the rule of law requires that preexisting rules be followed. If we accept substantive limitations on the rules that courts can adopt, we abandon the notion of rule-following as a neutral enter-prise with no social content; yet if we truly allow all reasonable arguments to be made and possibly accepted, we abandon the notion of rule-following entirely, and with it we abandon the ideal of the rule of law. What is odd is that liberalism has generated an institution that reveals these irresolvable tensions.

The theory of neutral principles requires that judges be able to rely on a shared conception of the proper role of judicial reasoning. The critiques have established that there are no determinate continuities derivable from history or legal principle. Rather, judges must choose which conceptions to rely on. Their choice is constrained, but explaining the constraints demands a sociological explanation of the ways in which the system within which they operate is deeply entrenched and resistant to change. If this sociological explanation is to have not merely descriptive validity, but normative force as well, we find ourselves drawn into the domain of conservative social theory, in which variable individual conceptions are seen to be derivative from – and subsidiary to – an underlying societal perspective.

The problem faced by both judge and constitutional theorist is how to find or construct the requisite shared conceptions. This problem is analogous to the interpretive difficulties that confront us in many aspects of our social experience. Consider an ordinary conversation between two people. Alice hears Arthur use the word "arbogast." She thinks she knows what he means, but as the conversation continues Alice realizes that Arthur is using the word in a way that comes to seem a little strange. She interrupts, so that Arthur can explain what he means. But things get worse. His explanation shows that his entire vocabulary rests on the way that he has lived until that moment. Because Arthur's life is by definition different from Alice's, Alice finds herself left with only an illusory understanding of what Arthur says. Her task is then to identify the point at which she can, so to speak, think her way into Arthur's life, so that she can understand what he means through understanding how he has developed. In this story, "under-standing what Arthur means when he says 'arbogast'" plays the role of "following the rule in *Roe v Wade*" or "remaining faithful to the framers' meaning of 'due process.'"

The question in each case is how to overcome the gaps that reflection has revealed. Of course, we go along each day with some taken-for-granted understandings of the world. But anyone can disrupt what is taken for granted simply by placing it in question. Courts are institutions in which challenges to the taken-for-granted may be made as a matter of course, and the individualist premises of the liberal vision both make such challenges inevitable and demand that they be heard. But if society is to be stable, those challenges must be rebuffed in ways that preserve the shared societal understandings.

Here the parable of the conversation is central. As experience has taught us, Alice and Arthur need not give up in despair; if they keep talking, they can build bridges between their two idiosyncratic dialects. Just as the historian can understand the past through hermeneutic efforts, so can we understand each other by creating a community of understanding. But the parable also reminds us that we cannot assume that people who talk to each other are part of such a community merely because they seem to be speaking the same language. Similarly, communities of understanding are not defined by geographical boundaries or by allegiance to a single constitution. They are painstakingly created by people who enter into certain kinds of relations and share certain kinds of experiences.

Some have argued that such relations demand complete equality of power and of access to material resources; others identify the requisite experiences as confrontations with scarcity or similar natural kinds of human experience. For my purposes, I need not identify exactly what the prerequisites for a community of understanding are. It is enough simply to recognize that we must develop a shared system of meanings to make either interpretivism or neutral principles coherent. But in developing such a system, we will destroy the need for constitutional theory, predicated as that need is on liberal individualism; the problem identified by Hobbes, Locke, and liberal thought in general disappears in a society in which such a shared understanding exists. In the end we may decide to retrieve individualism in order to reaffirm its insistence on the otherness of other people, but we can do so only after we have thought through the implications of our dependence on each other.

READING QUESTIONS ON TUSHNET

1 Why does Tushnet suppose that the liberal conception of the rule of law requires consistency and neutrality? How much inconsistency could a liberal regime tolerate?
2 Is Tushnet right in his claim that it is always possible to find precedents to get to the result one desires? How would one go about testing such a claim? How might Dworkin reply?

3 What do you make of Tushnet's analogy with mathematics? Is mathematics really non-neutral in the ways he suggests? If not, why not? If so, do you think the argument strengthens or weakens his claims about law?
4 Tushnet concludes his essay by proposing shared understandings as the basis of a legal regime. Would this solve the problems of indeterminacy he identifies for other views? Or could there be controversy about how to extend those understandings to cases where the legitimacy of some policy was contested?

Riggs v Palmer 22 N.E. 188 (1889)

A nineteenth-century New York case involving the right of an heir to inherit from the grandfather he had murdered. This case raises the question of the relation between moral principles and statutory interpretation.

RIGGS ET AL. V PALMER ET AL.

(Court of Appeals of New York. Oct. 1889)

Rights of Legatees   Murder of Testator

The Laws of New York relating to the probate of wills and the distributions of estates will not be construed so as to secure the benefit of a will to a legatee who has killed the testator in order to prevent a revocation of the will. Gray and Danforth, JJ, dissenting.

Appeal from supreme court, general term, third department.
Leslie W. Russell, for appellants. *W. M. Hawkins*, for respondents.

Earl, J: On the 13th day of August, 1880, Francis B. Palmer made his last will and testament, in which he gave small legacies to his two daughters, Mrs Riggs and Mrs Preston, the plaintiffs in this action, and the remainder of his estate to his grandson, the defendant Elmer E. Palmer, subject to the support of Susan Palmer, his mother, with a gift over to the two daughters, subject to the support of Mrs Palmer in case Elmer should survive him and die under age, unmarried, and without any issue. The testator, at the date of his will, owned a farm, and considerable personal property. He was a widower, and thereafter, in March, 1882 he was married to Mrs Bresee, with whom, before his marriage, he entered into an ante-nuptial contract, in which it was agreed that in lieu of dower and all other claims upon his estate in case she survived him she should have her support upon his farm during her life, and such support was expressly charged upon the farm. At the date of the will, and subsequently to the death of the testator, Elmer lived with him as a member of his family, and at his death was 16 years old. He knew of the provisions made in his favor in the will, and, that he might prevent his grandfather from revoking such provisions, which he had manifested some intention to do, and to obtain the speedy enjoyment and immediate possession of his property, he willfully murdered him by poisoning him. He now claims the property, and the sole question for our determination is, can he have it?

The defendants say that the testator is dead; that his will was made in due form, and has been admitted to probate; and that therefore it must have effect according to the letter of the law. It is quite true that statutes regulating the making, proof, and effect of wills and the devolution of property, if literally construed, and if their force and effect can in no way and under no circumstances be controlled or modified, give this property to the murderer. The purpose of those statutes was to enable testators to dispose of their estates to the objects of their bounty at death, and to carry into effect their final wishes legally expressed; and in considering and giving effect to them this purpose must be kept in view ...

In 1 Bl. Comm. 91, the learned author, speaking of the construction of statutes, says: "If there arise out of them collaterally any absurd consequences manifestly contradictory to common reason, they are with regard to those collateral consequences void ... Where some collateral matter arises out of the general words, and happens to be unreasonable, there the judges are in decency to conclude that this consequence was not foreseen by the parliament, and therefore they are at liberty to expound the statute by equity, and only *quo ad hoc* disregard it"; and he gives as an illustration, if an act of parliament gives a man power to try all causes that arise within his manor of Dale, yet, if a cause should arise in which he himself is party, the act is construed not to extend to that, because it is unreasonable that any man should determine his own quarrel. There was a statute in Bologna that whoever drew blood in the streets should be severely punished, and yet it was held not to apply to the case of a barber who opened a vein in the street. It is commanded in the decalogue that no work shall be done upon the Sabbath, and yet giving the command a rational interpretation founded upon its design the Infallible Judge held that it did not prohibit works of necessity, charity, or benevolence on that day.

What could be more unreasonable than to suppose that it was the legislative intention in the general laws passed for the orderly, peaceable, and just devolution of property that they should have operation in favor of one who murdered his ancestor that he might speedily come into the possession of his estate? Such an intention is inconceivable. We need not, therefore, be much troubled by the general language contained in the laws. Besides, all laws, as well as all contracts, may be controlled in their operation and effect by general, fundamental maxims of the common law. No one shall be permitted to profit by his own fraud, or to take advantage of his own wrong, or to found any claim upon his own iniquity, or to acquire property by his own crime. These maxims are dictated by public policy, have their foundation in universal law administered in all civilized countries, and have nowhere been superseded by statutes. They were applied in the decision of the case of *Insurance Co. v Armstrong*. There it was held that the person who procured a policy upon the life of another, payable at his death, and then murdered the assured to make the policy payable, could not recover thereon ...

Here there was no certainty that this murderer would survive the testator, or that the testator would not change his will, and there was no certainty that he would get this property if nature was allowed to take its course. He therefore murdered the testator expressly to vest himself with an estate. Under such circumstances, what law, human or divine, will allow him to take the estate and enjoy the fruits of his crime? The will spoke and became operative at the death of the testator. He caused that death, and thus by his crime made it speak and have operation. Shall it speak and operate in his favor? If he had met the testator, and taken his property by force, he would have had no title to it. Shall he acquire title by murdering him? If he had gone to the testator's house, and by force compelled him, or by fraud or undue influence had induced him, to will him his property, the law would not allow him to hold it. But can he give effect and operation to a will by murder, and yet take the property? To answer these questions in the affirmative it seems to me would be a reproach to the jurisprudence of our state, and an offense against public policy ...

In the Civil Code of Lower Canada the provisions on the subject in the Code Napoleon have been substantially copied. But, so far as I can find, in no country where the common law prevails has it been deemed important to enact a law to provide for such a case. Our revisers and law-makers were familiar with the civil law, and they did not deem it important to incorporate into our statutes its provisions upon this subject. This is not a *casus omissus*. It was evidently supposed that the maxims of the common law were sufficient to regulate such a case, and that a specific enactment for that purpose was not needed. For the same reasons the defendant Palmer cannot take any of this property as heir. Just before the murder he was not an heir, and it was not certain that he ever would be. He might have died before his grandfather, or might have been disinherited by him. He made himself an heir by the murder, and he seeks to take property as the fruit of his crime. What has before been said as to him as legatee applies to him with equal force as an heir. He cannot vest himself with title by crime. My view of this case does not inflict upon Elmer any greater or other punishment for his crime than the law specifies. It takes from him no property, but simply holds that he shall not acquire property by his crime, and thus be rewarded for its commission.

Gray, J (*dissenting*): – This appeal presents an extraordinary state of facts, and the case, in respect of them, I believe, is without precedent in this state. The respondent, a lad of 16 years of age, being aware of the provisions in his grandfather's will, which constituted him the residuary legatee of the testator's estate, caused his death by poison, in 1882. For this crime he was tried, and was convicted of murder in the second degree, and at the time of the commencement of this action he was serving out his sentence in the state reformatory. This action was brought by two of the children of the testator for the purpose of having those provisions of the will in the respondent's favor canceled and annulled. The appellants' argument for a reversal of the judgment, which dismissed their complaint, is that the respondent unlawfully prevented a revocation of the existing will, or a new will from being made, by his crime; and that he terminated the enjoyment by the testator of his property, and effected his own succession to it, by the same crime. They say that to permit the respondent to take the property willed to him would be to permit him to take advantage of his own wrong. To sustain their position the appellants' counsel has submitted an able and elaborate brief, and, if I believed that the decision of the question could be effected by consideration of an equitable nature, I should not hesitate to assent to views which commend themselves to the conscience. But the matter does not lie within the domain of conscience. We are bound by the rigid rules of law, which have been established by the legislature, and within the limits of which the determination of this question is confined. The question we are dealing with is whether a testamentary disposition can be altered, or a will revoked, after the testator's death, through an appeal to the courts, when the legislature has by its enactments prescribed exactly when and how wills may be made, altered, and revoked, and apparently, as it seems to me, when they have been fully complied with, has left no room for the exercise of an equitable jurisdiction by courts over such matters. Modern jurisprudence, in recognizing the right of the individual, under more or less restrictions, to dispose of his property after his death, subjects it to legislative control, both as to extent and as to mode of exercise. Complete freedom of testamentary disposition of one's property has not been and is not the universal rule, as we see from the provisions of the Napoleonic Code, from the systems of jurisprudence in countries which are modeled upon the Roman law, and from the statutes of many of our states. To the statutory restraints which are imposed upon the disposition of one's property by will are added strict and systematic statutory rules for the execution, alteration, and revocation of the will, which must be, at least substantially, if not exactly, followed to insure validity and performance. The reason for the establishment of such rules, we may naturally assume, consists in the purpose to create those safeguards about these grave and important acts which experience has demonstrated to be the wisest and surest. That freedom which is permitted to be exercised in the testamentary disposition of one's estate by the laws of the state is subject to its being exercised in conformity with the regulations of the statutes. The capacity and the power of the individual to dispose of his property after death, and the mode by which that power can be exercised, are matters of which the legislature has assumed the entire control, and has undertaken to regulate with comprehensive particularity.

The appellants' argument is not helped by reference to those rules of the civil law, or to those laws of other governments, by which the heir, or legatee, is excluded from benefit under the testament if he has been convicted of killing, or attempting to kill, the testator.

In the absence of such legislation here, the courts are not empowered to institute such a system of remedial justice. The deprivation of the heir of his testamentary succession by the Roman law, when guilty of such a crime, plainly was intended to be in the nature of a punishment imposed upon him. The succession, in such a case of guilt, escheated to the exchequer. See Dom. Civil Law, pt. 2, bk. 1, tit. 1, s. 3. I concede that rules of law which annul testamentary provisions made for the benefit of those who have become unworthy of them may be based on principles of equity and of natural justice. It is quite reasonable to suppose that a testator would revoke or alter his will, where his mind has been so angered and changed as to make him unwilling to have his will executed as it stood. But these principles only suggest sufficient reasons for the enactment of laws to meet such cases.

The statutes of this state have prescribed various ways in which a will may be altered or revoked; but the very provision defining the modes of alteration and revocation implies a prohibition of alteration or revocation in any other way. The words of the section of the statute are: "No will in writing, except in the cases hereinafter mentioned, nor any part thereof, shall be revoked or altered otherwise," etc. Where, therefore, none of the cases mentioned are met by the facts, and the revocation is not in the way described in the section, the will of the testator is unalterable. I think that a valid will must continue as a will always, unless revoked in the manner provided by the statutes. Mere intention to revoke a will does not have the effect of revocation.

READING QUESTIONS ON *RIGGS V PALMER*

1 Earl, J says that the law will not allow a man to profit from his own wrongdoing. Where does he find this principle? Can you think of exceptions to it? If so, in what sense is it supposed to be binding?
2 Putting aside the question of Riggs's wrongdoing and the appropriate punishment for it, do you find Grey, J's view of the judicial role more appealing?

2

Adjudication

This chapter explores the relationship between law and morality in adjudication by looking at two cases in which judges found that they were compelled to come to conclusions of which they disapproved. The question here is whether a theory like Dworkin's, which presupposes a link between law and morality, is helpful to judges who find themselves in such a predicament.

Herman Melville
Billy Budd, Sailor **(1929)**

Melville's novella tells the story of a sailor who strikes a superior officer who has severely provoked him. The officer dies from a blow almost anyone would have survived. The central drama of the story comes when the Captain, who has witnessed the death, decides that Budd must be executed, despite the fact he is morally innocent. Vere feels compelled to enforce the law, though he regards it as profoundly unjust.

The court was held in the same cabin where the unfortunate affair had taken place. This cabin, the commander's, embraced the entire area under the poop deck. Aft, and on either side, was a small stateroom, the one now temporarily a jail and the other a dead-house, and a yet smaller compartment, leaving a space between expanding forward into a goodly oblong of length coinciding with the ship's beam. A skylight of moderate dimension was overhead, and at each end of the oblong space were two sashed porthole windows easily convertible back into embrasures for short carronades.

All being quickly in readiness, Billy Budd was arraigned, Captain Vere necessarily appearing as the sole witness in the case, and as such temporarily sinking his rank, though singularly maintaining it in a matter apparently trivial, namely, that he testified from the ship's weather side, with that object having caused the court to sit on the lee side. Concisely he narrated all that had led up to the catastrophe, omitting nothing in Claggart's accusation and deposing as to the manner in which the prisoner had received it. At this testimony the three officers glanced with no little surprise at Billy Budd, the last man they would have suspected either of the mutinous design alleged by Claggart or the undeniable deed he himself had done. The first lieutenant, taking judicial primacy and turning toward the prisoner, said, "Captain Vere has spoken. Is it or is it not as Captain Vere says?"

In response came syllables not so much impeded in the utterance as might have been anticipated. They were these: "Captain Vere tells the truth. It is just as Captain Vere says, but it is not as the master-at-arms said. I have eaten the King's bread and I am true to the King."

"I believe you, my man," said the witness, his voice indicating a suppressed emotion not otherwise betrayed.

"God will bless you for that, your honor!" not without stammering said Billy, and all but broke down. But immediately he was recalled to self-control by another question, to which with the same emotional difficulty of utterance he said, "No, there was no malice between us. I never bore malice against the master-at-arms. I am sorry that he is dead. I did not mean to kill him. Could I have used my tongue I would not have struck him. But he foully lied to my face and in presence of my captain, and I had to say something, and I could only say it with a blow, God help me!"

In the impulsive aboveboard manner of the frank one the court saw confirmed all that was implied in words that just previously had perplexed them, coming as they did from the testifier to the tragedy and promptly following Billy's impassioned disclaimer of mutinous intent Captain Vere's words, "I believe you, my man."

Next it was asked of him whether he knew of or suspected aught savoring of incipient trouble (meaning mutiny, though the explicit term was avoided) going on in any section of the ship's company.

The reply lingered. This was naturally imputed by the court to the same vocal embarrassment which had retarded or obstructed previous answers. But in main it was otherwise here, the question immediately recalling to Billy's mind the interview with the afterguardsman in the forechains. But an innate repugnance to playing a part at all approaching that of an informer against one's own shipmates – the same erring sense of uninstructed honor which had stood in the way of his reporting the matter at the time, though as a loyal man-of-war's man it was incumbent on him, and failure so to do, if charged against him and proven, would have subjected him to the heaviest of penalties; this, with the blind feeling now his that nothing really was being hatched, prevailed with him. When the answer came it was a negative.

"One question more," said the officer of marines, now first speaking and with a troubled earnestness. "You tell us that what the master-at-arms said against you was a lie. Now why should he have so lied, so maliciously lied, since you declare there was no malice between you?"

At that question, unintentionally touching on a spiritual sphere wholly obscure to Billy's thoughts, he was nonplussed, evincing a confusion indeed that some observers, such as can readily be imagined, would have construed into involuntary evidence of hidden guilt. Nevertheless, he strove some way to answer, but all at once relinquished the vain endeavor, at the same time turning an appealing glance towards Captain Vere as deeming him his best helper and friend. Captain Vere, who had been seated for a time, rose to his feet, addressing the interrogator. "The question you put to him comes naturally enough. But how can he rightly answer it? – or anybody else, unless indeed it be he who lies within there," designating the compartment where lay the corpse. "But the prone one there will not rise to our summons. In effect, though, as it seems to me, the point you make is hardly material. Quite aside from any conceivable motive actuating the master-at-arms, and irrespective of the provocation to the blow, a martial court must needs in the present case confine its attention to the blow's consequence, which consequence justly is to be deemed not otherwise than as the striker's deed."

This utterance, the full significance of which it was not at all likely that Billy took in, nevertheless caused him to turn a wistful interrogative look toward the speaker, a look in its dumb expressiveness not unlike that which a dog of generous breed might turn upon his master, seeking in his face some elucidation of a previous gesture ambiguous to the canine intelligence. Nor was the same utterance without marked effect upon the three officers, more especially the soldier. Couched in it seemed to them a meaning unanticipated, involving a prejudgment on the speaker's part. It served to augment a mental disturbance previously evident enough.

The soldier once more spoke, in a tone of suggestive dubiety addressing at once his associates and Captain Vere: "Nobody is present – none of the ship's company, I mean – who might shed lateral light, if any is to be had, upon what remains mysterious in this matter."

"That is thoughtfully put," said Captain Vere; "I see your drift. Ay, there is a mystery; but, to use a scriptural phrase, it is a 'mystery of iniquity,' a matter for psychologic theologians to discuss. But what has a military court to do with it? Not to add that for us any possible investigation of it is cut off by the lasting tongue-tie of – him – in yonder," again designating the mortuary stateroom. "The prisoner's deed – with that alone we have to do."

To this, and particularly the closing reiteration, the marine soldier, knowing not how aptly to reply, sadly abstained from saying aught. The first lieutenant, who at the outset had not unnaturally assumed primacy in the court, now overrulingly instructed by a glance from Captain Vere, a glance more effective than words, resumed that primacy. Turning to the prisoner, "Budd," he said, and scarce in equable tones, "Budd, if you have aught further to say for yourself, say it now."

Upon this the young sailor turned another quick glance toward Captain Vere; then, as taking a hint from that aspect, a hint confirming his own instinct that silence was now best, replied to the lieutenant, "I have said all, sir."

The marine – the same who had been the sentinel without the cabin door at the time that the foretopman, followed by the master-at-arms, entered it – he, standing by the sailor throughout these judicial proceedings, was now directed to take him back to the after compartment originally assigned to the prisoner and his custodian. As the twain disappeared from view, the three officers, as partially liberated from some inward constraint associated with Billy's mere presence, simultaneously stirred in their seats. They exchanged looks of troubled indecision, yet feeling that decide they must and without long delay. For Captain Vere, he for the time stood – unconsciously with his back toward them, apparently in one of his absent fits – gazing out from a sashed porthole to windward upon the monotonous blank of the twilight sea. But the court's silence continuing, broken only at moments by brief consultations, in low earnest tones, this served to arouse him and energize him. Turning, he to-and-fro paced the cabin athwart; in the returning ascent to windward climbing the slant deck in the ship's lee roll, without knowing it symbolizing thus in his action a mind resolute to surmount difficulties even if against primitive instincts strong as the wind and the sea. Presently he came to a stand before the three. After scanning their faces he stood less as mustering his thoughts for expression than as one inly deliberating how best to put them to well-meaning men not intellectually mature, men with whom it was necessary to demonstrate certain principles that were axioms to himself. Similar impatience as to talking is perhaps one reason that deters some minds from addressing any popular assemblies.

When speak he did, something, both in the substance of what he said and his manner of saying it, showed the influence of unshared studies modifying and tempering the practical training of an active career. This, along with his phraseology, now and then was suggestive of the grounds whereon rested that imputation of a certain pedantry socially alleged against him by certain naval men of wholly practical cast, captains who nevertheless would frankly concede that His Majesty's navy mustered no more efficient officer of their grade than Starry Vere.

What he said was to this effect: "Hitherto I have been but the witness, little more; and I should hardly think now to take another tone, that of your coadjutor for the time, did I not perceive in you – at the crisis too a troubled hesitancy, proceeding, I doubt not, from the clash of military duty with moral scruple – scruple vitalized by compassion. For the compassion, how can I otherwise than share it? But, mindful of paramount obligations, I strive against scruples that may tend to enervate decision. Not, gentlemen, that I hide from myself that the case is an exceptional one. Speculatively regarded, it well might be referred to a jury of casvists. But for us here, acting not as casvists or moralists, it is a case practical, and under martial law practically to be dealt with.

"But your scruples: do they move as in a dusk? Challenge them. Make them advance and declare themselves. Come now; do they import something like this: If, mindless of palliating circumstances, we are bound to regard the death of the master-at-arms as the prisoner's deed, then does that deed constitute a capital crime whereof the penalty is a mortal one. But in natural justice is nothing but the prisoner's overt act to be considered? How can we adjudge to summary and shameful death a fellow creature innocent before God, and whom we feel to be so? Does that state it aright? You sign sad assent. Well, I too feel that, the full force of that. It is Nature. But do these buttons that we wear attest that our allegiance is to Nature? No, to the King. Though the ocean, which is inviolate Nature primeval, though this be the element where we move and have our being as sailors, yet as the King's officers lies our duty in a sphere correspondingly natural? So little is that true, that in receiving our commissions we in the most important regards ceased to be natural free agents. When war is declared are we the commissioned fighters previously consulted? We fight at command. If our judgments approve the war, that is but coincidence. So in other particulars. "So now. For suppose condemnation to follow these present proceedings. Would it be so much we ourselves that would condemn as it would be martial law operating through us? For that law and the rigor of it, we are not responsible. Our vowed responsibility is in this: That however pitilessly that law may operate in any instances, we nevertheless adhere to it and administer it.

"But the exceptional in the matter moves the hearts within you. Even so too is mine moved. But let not warm hearts betray heads that should be cool. Ashore in a criminal case, will an upright judge allow himself off the bench to be waylaid by some tender kinswoman of the accused seeking to touch him with her tearful plea? Well, the heart here, sometimes the feminine in man, is as that piteous woman, and hard though it be, she must here be ruled out."

He paused, earnestly studying them for a moment; then resumed.

"But something in your aspect seems to urge that it is not solely the heart that moves in you, but also the conscience, the private conscience. But tell me whether or not, occupying the position we do, private conscience should not yield to that imperial one formulated in the code under which alone we officially proceed?"

Here the three men moved in their seats, less convinced than agitated by the course of an argument troubling but the more the spontaneous conflict within.

Perceiving which, the speaker paused for a moment; then abruptly changing his tone, went on.

"To steady us a bit, let us recur to the facts. – In wartime at sea a man-of-war's man strikes his superior in grade, and the blow kills. Apart from its effect the blow itself is, according to the Articles of War, a capital crime. Furthermore –"

"Ay, sir," emotionally broke in the officer of marines, "in one sense it was. But surely Budd proposed neither mutiny nor homicide."

"Surely not, my good man. And before a court less arbitrary and more merciful than a martial one, that plea would largely extenuate. At the Last Assizes it shall acquit. But how here? We proceed under the law of the Mutiny Act. In feature no child can resemble his father more than that Act resembles in spirit the thing from which it derives – War. In His Majesty's service – in this ship, indeed – there are Englishmen forced to fight for the King against their will. Against their conscience, for aught we know. Though as their fellow creatures some of us may appreciate their position, yet as navy officers what reck we of it? Still less recks the enemy. Our impressed men he would fain cut down in the same swath with our volunteers. As regards the enemy's naval conscripts, some of whom may even share our own abhorrence of the regicidal French Directory, it is the same on our side. War looks but to the frontage, the appearance. And the Mutiny Act, War's child, takes after the father. Budd's intent or non-intent is nothing to the purpose.

"But while, put to it by those anxieties in you which I cannot but respect, I only repeat myself – while thus strangely we prolong proceedings that should be summary – the enemy may be sighted and an engagement result. We must do; and one of two things must we do – condemn or let go."

"Can we not convict and yet mitigate the penalty?" asked the sailing master, here speaking, and falteringly, for the first.

"Gentlemen, were that clearly lawful for us under the circumstances, consider the consequences of such clemency. The people" (meaning the ship's company) "have native sense; most of them are familiar with our naval usage and tradition; and how would they take it? Even could you explain to them – which our official position forbids – they, long molded by arbitrary discipline, have not that kind of intelligent responsiveness that might qualify them to comprehend and discriminate. No, to the people the foretopman's deed, however it be worded in the announcement, will be plain homicide committed in a flagrant act of mutiny. What penalty for that should follow, they know. But it does not follow. *Why?* they will ruminate. You know what sailors are. Will they not revert to the recent outbreak at the Nore? Ay. They know the well-founded alarm – the panic it struck throughout England. Your clement sentence they would account pusillanimous. They would think that we flinch, that we are afraid of them – afraid of practicing a lawful rigor singularly demanded at this juncture, lest it should provoke new troubles. What shame to use such a conjecture on their part, and how deadly to discipline. You see then, whither, prompted by duty and the law, I steadfastly drive. But I beseech you, my friends, do not take me amiss. I feel as you do for this unfortunate boy. But did he know our hearts, I take him to be of that generous nature that he would feel even for us on whom in this military necessity so heavy a compulsion is laid."

With that, crossing the deck he resumed his place by the sashed porthole, tacitly leaving the three to come to a decision. On the cabin's opposite side the troubled court sat silent. Loyal lieges, plain and practical, though at bottom they dissented from some points Captain Vere had put to them, they were without the faculty, hardly had the inclination, to gainsay one whom they felt to be an earnest man, one too not less their superior in mind than in naval rank. But it is not improbable that even such of his words as were not without influence over them, less came home than his closing appeal to their instinct as sea officers: in the forethought he threw out as to the practical consequences to discipline, considering the unconfirmed tone of the fleet at the time, should a man-of-war's man's violent killing at sea of a superior in grade be allowed to pass for aught else than a capital crime demanding prompt infliction of the penalty.

Not unlikely they were brought to something more or less akin to that harassed frame of mind which in the year 1842 actuated the commander of the U.S. brig-of-war *Somers* to resolve, under the so-called Articles of War, Articles modelled upon the English Mutiny Act, to resolve upon the execution at sea of a midshipman and two sailors as mutineers designing the seizure of the brig. Which resolution was carried out though in a time of peace and within not many days' sail of home. An Act vindicated by a naval court of inquiry subsequently convened ashore. History, and here cited without comment. True, the circumstances on board the *Somers* were different from those on board the *Bellipotent*. But the urgency felt, well-warranted or otherwise, was much the same.

Says a writer whom few know, "Forty years after a battle it is easy for a noncombatant to reason about how it ought to have been fought. It is another thing personally and under fire to have to direct the fighting while involved in the obscuring smoke of it. Much so with respect to other emergencies involving considerations both practical and moral, and when it is imperative promptly to act. The greater the fog the more it imperils the steamer, and speed is put on though at the hazard of running somebody down. Little ween the snug card players in the cabin of the responsibilities of the sleepless man on the bridge."

In brief, Billy Budd was formally convicted and sentenced to be hung at the yardarm in the early morning watch, it being now night. Otherwise, as is customary in such cases, the sentence would forthwith have been carried out. In wartime on the field or in the fleet, a mortal punishment decreed by a drumhead court – on the field sometimes decreed by but a nod from the general – follows without delay on the heel of conviction, without appeal.

...

Of a series of incidents with a brief term rapidly following each other, the adequate narration may take up a term less brief, especially if explanation or comment here and there seem requisite to the better understanding of such incidents. Between the entrance into the cabin of him who never left it alive, and him who when he did leave it left it as one condemned to die; between this and the closeted interview just given, less than an hour and a half had elapsed. It was an interval long enough, however, to awaken speculations among no few of the ship's company.

READING QUESTIONS ON MELVILLE

1 Did Captain Vere really have no other option but to convict Billy? What argument might he have used to acquit him?
2 Captain Vere seems less concerned about whether or not the sailors will mutiny than about the duties of his office. He says that if he condemns Billy and the sailors mutiny, it will not be his responsibility. What view of law does this suggest?

Robert Cover
"Of Creon and Captain Vere" (1976)

Cover explores the similarities between Captain Vere's plight and that of Lemuel Shaw, an abolitionist judge in nineteenth-century Massachusetts, who felt compelled to enforce the *Fugitive Slave Acts*. Shaw's situation raised deep puzzles for theories of law. Like Captain Vere, he sees himself as torn between moral and legal duties. On the one hand, he believes slavery is immoral. On the other, he believes he is bound to uphold the rule of law. The two duties come into conflict because the United States Constitution explicitly allowed each state to decide whether or not to allow slavery.

Shaw's commitment to the rule of law did not stand in the way of him campaigning for the legislative abolition of slavery in states that still allowed it. Nor did it prevent him from preventing slaveowners forcibly returning slaves they had voluntarily brought into states that did not allow slavery. In cases involving the return of escaped slaves, Shaw had a more difficult time. The *Fugitive Slave Acts* required their return to their owners; in so doing it also seemed to require that free states participate in a system of slavery.

PRELUDE: OF CREON AND CAPTAIN VERE

I

Antigone's star has shown brightly through the millennia. The archetype for civil disobedience has claimed a constellation of first-magnitude emulators. The disobedient – whether Antigone, Luther, Gandhi, King, or Bonhoeffer – exerts a powerful force upon us. The singular act, the risk, the dramatic appeal to a juster justice, all contribute to the high drama of the moment and the power of the actor's role. No wonder then, that such men and women are celebrated in literature and history. No wonder that a great psychiatrist like Erikson, upon embarking on a venture in history and biography, chose Luther and Gandhi as his first subjects.

Yet, in a curious way, to focus upon the disobedient and the process of disobedience is to accept the perspective of the established order. It is a concession that it is the man who appeals beyond law that is in need of explanation. With the sole exception of Nazi atrocities, the phenomenon of complicity in oppressive legal systems (oppressive from the actor's own perspective) has seldom been studied. Thus, Creon is present only as a foil for Antigone, not himself the object of the artist's study of human character. In *Antigone* note the curious one-dimensional character of the King. How he comes to make his law and at what cost in psychic terms is not treated at all. Indeed, Creon's first conflict is not between right and law, but between his son and his pride. And even in the midst of that conflict he betrays his singular obtuseness to the complexity of the situation he created by crying filial impiety and anarchy in one breath. He is astounded by the possibility of Haemon's sympathy to an affront to authority. Much of the simplicity of Creon lies in the choice of a tyrant as model for legal system. The making of law and its applications are wholly confined to a single will unconstrained by any but the most personal of considerations such as the feelings and actions of a son.

Melville's Captain Vere in *Billy Budd* is one of the few examples of an attempt to portray the conflict patterns of Creon or Creon's minions in a context more nearly resembling the choice situations of judges in modern legal systems. Billy Budd, radical innocence personified, is overwhelmed by a charge of fomenting mutiny, falsely levied against him by the first mate Claggart. Claggart seems to personify dark and evil forces. Struck dumb by the slanderous charges, Billy strikes out and kills the mate with a single blow. Captain Vere must instruct a drum-head court on the law of the Mutiny Act as it is to be applied to Billy Budd – in some most fundamental sense "innocent," though perpetrator of the act of killing the first mate. In what must be, for the legal scholar, the high point of the novella, Vere articulates the "scruples" of the three officers (and his own) and rejects them.

How can we adjudge to summary and shameful death a fellow creature innocent before God, and whom we feel to be so? – Does that state it aright? You sign sad assent. Well, I too feel that, the full force of that. It is Nature. But do these buttons that we wear attest that our allegiance is to Nature? No, to the King.

And, but a few paragraphs farther on, Vere asks the three whether "occupying the position we do, private conscience should not yield to that imperial one formulated in the code under which alone we officially proceed."

In Vere's words we have a positivist's condensation of a legal system's formal character. Five aspects of that formalism may be discerned and specified: First, there is explicit recognition of the role character of the judges – a consciousness of the formal element. It is a uniform, not nature, that defines obligation. Second, law is distinguished from both the transcendent and the personal sources of obligation. The law is neither nature nor conscience. Third, the law is embodied in a readily identifiable source which governs transactions and occurrences of the sort under consideration: here an imperial code of which the Mutiny Act is a part. Fourth, the will behind the law is vague, uncertain, but *clearly not* that of the judges. It is here "imperial will" which, in (either eighteenth- or) nineteenth-century terms as applied to England, is not very easy to describe except through a constitutional law treatise. But, in any event, it is not the will of Vere and his three officers. Fifth, a corollary of the fourth point, the judge is not responsible for the content of the law but for its straightforward application.

For that law and the rigor of it, we are not responsible. Our vowed responsibility is in this: That however pitilessly that law may operate in any instances, we nevertheless adhere to it and administer it.

These five elements are part of Vere's arguments. But *Billy Budd* is a literary work and much that is most interesting about Vere is not in what he says but in what he is, in overtones of character. For example, we have intimations from the outset of a personality committed to fearful symmetries. His nickname, derived from Marvell's lines

Under the discipline severe
Of Fairfax and the starry Vere

suggests an impersonal and unrelaxed severity. And his intellectual bent, too, reinforces this suggestion of rigidity. He eschewed innovations "disinterestedly" and because they seemed "insusceptible of embodiment in lasting institutions." And he lacked "companionable quality." A man emerges who is disposed to approach life institutionally, to avoid the personal realm even where it perhaps ought to hold sway, to be inflexibly honest, righteous, and duty bound.

It is this man who, seeing and appreciating Budd's violent act, exclaimed, "Struck dead by an angel of God! Yet the angel must hang." And, characteristically, it is Vere who assumes the responsibility of conveying the dread verdict to the accused. Melville's speculations on that "interview" are revealing. He stresses the likelihood that Vere revealed his own full part in the "trial." He goes on to speculate that Vere might well have assumed a paternal stance in the manner of Abraham embracing Isaac "on the brink of resolutely offering him up in obedience to the exacting behest." Such a religious conviction of duty characterizes our man. Neither conventional morality, pity, nor personal agony could bend him from a stern duty. But in Vere's case the master is not God but the King. And the King is but a symbol for a social order.

Righteous men, indeed, suffer the agonies of their righteousness. Captain Vere betrayed just such agony in leaving his meeting with Billy Budd. But there is no indication that Vere suffered the agony of doubt about his course. When Billy died uttering "God Bless Captain Vere," there is no intimation that the Captain sensed any irony (whether intended or not) in the parting benediction. If Captain Vere is Abraham, he is the biblical version, not Kierkegaard's shadow poised achingly at the chasm.

Melville has been astonishingly successful in making his readers ask dreadful questions of Vere and his behavior. What deep urge leads a man to condemn unworldly beauty and innocence? To embrace, personally, the opportunity to do an impersonal, distasteful task? How reconcile the flash of recognition of "the angel must die" and the seizing of the opportunity to act Abraham, with declared protestations, unquestionably sincere, that only plain and clear duty overcomes his sense of the victim's cosmic innocence? We have so many doubts about a man who hears and obeys the voice of the Master so quickly, and our doubts are compounded when it is a harsh social system that becomes the Lord.

I venture to suggest that Melville had a model for Captain Vere that may bring us very close to our main story. Melville's father-in-law was Chief Justice Lemuel Shaw of the Massachusetts Supreme Judicial Court. A firm, unbending man of stem integrity, Shaw dominated the Massachusetts judicial system very much as Captain Vere ran his ship. The Chief Justice was a noted, strong opponent to slavery and expressed his opposition privately, in print, and in appropriate judicial opinions. Yet, in the great causes célèbres involving fugitive slaves, Shaw came down hard for an unflinching application of the harsh and summary law. The effort cost Shaw untold personal agony. He was vilified by abolitionists. I cannot claim that Vere is Lemuel Shaw (though he might be), for there is no direct evidence. I can only say that it would be remarkable that in portraying a man caught in the horrible conflict between duty and conscience, between role and morality, between nature and positive law, Melville would be untouched by the figure of his father-in-law in the *Sims Case*, the Latimer affair, or the Burns controversy. We know Melville's predilection to the ship as microcosm for the social order. He used the device quite plainly with respect to slavery in *Benito Cereno*.

The fugitive slave was very Budd-like, though he was as black as Billy was blonde. The Mutiny Act admitted of none of the usual defenses, extenuations, or mitigations. If the physical act was that of the defendant, he was guilty. The Fugitive Slave Act similarly excluded most customary sorts of defenses. The alleged fugitive could not even plead that he was not legally a slave so long as he was the person *alleged* to be a fugitive. The drumhead court was a special and summary proceeding; so was the fugitive rendition process. In both proceedings the fatal judgment was carried out immediately. There was no appeal.

More important, Billy's fatal flaw was his innocent dumbness. He struck because he could not speak. So, under the Fugitive Slave Acts, the alleged fugitive had no right to speak. And, as a rule, slaves had no capacity to testify against their masters or whites, generally. Billy Budd partakes of the slave, generalized. He was seized, impressed, from the ship *Rights of Man* and taken abroad the *Bellipotent*. Aboard the *Bellipotent* the Mutiny Act and Captain Vere held sway. The Mutiny Act was justified because of its necessity for the order demanded on a ship in time of war. So the laws of slavery, often equally harsh and unbending, were justified as necessary for the social order in antebellum America. Moreover, the institution itself was said to have its origin in war.

But most persuasive is Vere and his dilemma – the subject matter of this book. For, if there was a single sort of case in which judges during Melville's lifetime struggled with the moral-formal dilemma, it was slave cases. In these cases, time and again, the judiciary paraded its helplessness before the law; lamented harsh results; intimated that in a more perfect world, or at the end of days, a better law would emerge, but almost uniformly, marched to the music, steeled themselves, and hung Billy Budd.

Of course, *Billy Budd*, like any great work of literature, exists on many levels. I would not deny the theology in the work, nor the clash of elemental good and elemental evil in Budd and Claggart. But the novella is also about a judgment, within a social system, and about the man, who, dimly perceiving the great and abstract forces at work, bears responsibility for that judgment. It is about starry-eyed Vere and Lemuel Shaw.

II

The rest of this book is not about literature, but about Lemuel Shaw and many judges like him. It is the story of earnest, well-meaning pillars of legal respectability and of their collaboration in a system of oppression – Negro slavery. I have chosen to analyze at length only the dilemma of the antislavery judge – the man who would, in some sense, have agreed with my characterization of slavery as oppression. It was he who confronted Vere's dilemma, the choice between the demands of role and the voice of conscience. And it was he who contributed so much to the force of legitimacy that law may provide, for he plainly acted out of impersonal duty.

In a static and simplistic model of law, the judge caught between law and morality has only four choices. He may apply the law against his conscience. He may apply conscience and be faithless to the law. He may resign. Or he may cheat: He may state that the law is not what he believes it to be and, thus preserve an appearance (to others) of conformity of law and morality. Once we assume a more realistic model of law and of the judicial process, these four positions become only poles setting limits to a complex field of action and motive. For in a dynamic model, law is always becoming. And the judge has a legitimate role in determining what it is that the law will become. The flux in law means also that the law's content is frequently unclear. We must speak of direction and of weight as well as of position. Moreover, this frequent lack of clarity makes possible "ameliorist" solutions. The judge may introduce his own sense of what "ought to be" interstitially, where no "hard" law yet exists. And, he may do so without committing the law to broad doctrinal advances (or retreats).

In a given historical context the way in which judges are likely to respond to the moral-formal dilemma is going to be determined by a wide variety of intellectual and institutional variables. Judges, more than most men, are conscious of the baggage of the past. Thus, the traditions that they inherit will be important. For both slavery and the judicial role in antebellum America the judge had a library of works that influenced the idiom in which he thought. The nature of that intellectual tradition is my first inquiry. I shall examine the natural law tradition on slavery as it stood in the late eighteenth century. I shall then explore the actual uses of principled preferences for liberty in the first thirty or forty years of the nineteenth century. This exploration will delineate the areas of accepted usage of preference for liberty in judicial opinion and the areas where the judge could move the law in the direction of freedom. I shall then explore the sorts of demands that were made upon the judiciary to go beyond those accepted areas and the judicial refusal to do so. That refusal will be traced on the cognitive level to carefully formulated ideas about the judicial function that are themselves the products of a heritage of conflict over the values that ought to govern judging. The dialectical context for the judge's response was not constant, and it is necessary to examine responses to many demands varying, in part, with the ideology of the lawyers and the movements they represented.

Finally, I shall confront directly the question of personality. With Captain Vere we have the sense that it is not logic alone that leads him to his response. So, with Lemuel Shaw, John McLean, Joseph Story, and others, we must inquire into the internal forces that produced an almost uniform response of role fidelity. The theory of cognitive dissonance provides a suggestive framework for integrating the uniform response, the personalities of these men, and the professional and intellectual milieu in which they worked.

Make no mistake. The judges we shall examine really squirmed; were intensely uncomfortable in hanging Billy Budd. But they did the job. Like Vere, they were Creon's faithful minions. We must understand them – as much as Antigone – if we are to understand the processes of injustice.

Commonwealth v Aves 35 Mass. 193 (1836)

A case decided by Shaw, which holds that a slave brought into a free state by his owner is thereby set free. Shaw argues that the alternative would be to allow slave states to export their slavery to free ones.

... The precise question presented by the claim of the respondent is, whether a citizen of any one of the United States, where negro slavery is established by law, coming into this State, for any temporary purpose of business or pleasure, staying some time, but not acquiring a domicil here, who brings a slave with him as a personal attendant, may restrain such slave of his liberty during his continuance here, and convey him out of this State on his return, against his consent. It is not contended that a master can exercise here any other of the rights of a slave owner, than such as may be necessary to retain the custody of the slave during his residence, and to remove him on his return.

Until this discussion, I had supposed that there had been adjudged cases on this subject in this Commonwealth; and it is believed to have been a prevalent opinion among lawyers, that if a slave is brought voluntarily and unnecessarily within the limits of this State, he becomes free, if he chooses to avail himself of the provisions of our laws; not so much because his coming within our territorial limits, breathing our air, or treading on our soil, works any alteration in his *status*, or his condition, as settled by the law of his domicile as because by the operation of our laws, there is no authority on the part of the master, either to restrain the slave of his liberty, whilst here, or forcibly to take him into custody in order to his removal. There seems, however, to be no decided case on the subject reported ...

Without pursuing this inquiry farther, it is sufficient for the purposes of the case before us, that by the constitution adopted in 1780, slavery was abolished in Massachusetts, upon the ground that it is contrary to natural right and the plain principles of justice. The terms of the first article of the declaration of rights are plain and explicit. "All men are born free and equal, and have certain natural, essential, and unalienable rights, which are, the right of enjoying and defending their lives and liberties, that of acquiring, possessing, and protecting property." It would be difficult to select words more precisely adapted to the abolition of negro slavery. According to the laws prevailing in all the States, where slavery is upheld, the child of a slave is not deemed to be born free, a slave has no right to enjoy and defend his own liberty, or to acquire, possess, or protect property. That the description was broad enough in its terms to embrace negroes, and that it was intended by the framers of the constitution to embrace them, is proved by the earliest contemporaneous construction, by an unbroken series of judicial decisions, and by a uniform practice from the adoption of the constitution to the present time. The whole tenor of our policy, of our legislation and jurisprudence, from that time to the present, has been consistent with this construction, and with no other.

Such being the general rule of law, it becomes necessary to inquire how far it is modified or controlled in its operation; either,

1 By the law of other nations and states, as admitted by the comity of
   nations to have a limited operation within a particular state; or
2 By the constitution and laws of the United States ...

Upon a general review of the authorities, and upon an application of the well established principles upon this subject, we think they fully maintain the point stated, that though slavery is contrary to natural right, to the principles of justice, humanity and sound policy, as we adopt them and found our own laws upon them, yet not being contrary to the laws of nations, if any other state or community see fit to establish and continue slavery by law, so far as the legislative power of that country extends, we are bound to take notice of the existence of those laws, and we are not at liberty to declare and hold an act done within those limits, unlawful and void, upon our views of morality and policy, which the sovereign and legislative power of the place has pronounced to be lawful. If, therefore, an unwarranted interference and wrong is done by our citizens to a foreigner, acting under the sanction of such laws, and within their proper limits, that is, within the local limits of the power by whom they are thus established, or on the high seas, which each and every nation has a right in common with all others to occupy, our laws would no doubt afford a remedy against the wrong done. So, in pursuance of a well known maxim, that in the construction of contracts, the *lex loci contractus* shall govern, if a person, having in other respects a right to sue in our courts, shall bring an action against another, liable in other respects to be sued in our courts, upon a contract made upon the subject of slavery in a state where slavery is allowed by law, the law here would give it effect. As if a note of hand made in New Orleans were sued on here, and the defence should be, that it was on a bad consideration, or without consideration, because given for the price of a slave sold, it may well be admitted, that such a defence could not prevail, because the contract was a legal one by the law of the place where it was made.

This view of the law applicable to slavery, marks strongly the distinction between the relation of master and slave, as established by the local law of particular states, and in virtue of that sovereign power and independent authority which each independent state concedes to every other, and those natural and social relations, which are every-where and by all people recognized, and which, though they may be modified and regulated by municipal law, are not founded upon it such as the relation of parent and child, and husband and wife. Such also is the principle upon which the general right of property is founded, being in some form universally recognized as a natural right, independently of municipal law.

This affords an answer to the argument drawn from the maxim, that the right of personal property follows the person, and therefore, where by the law of a place a person there domiciled acquires personal property, by the comity of nations the same must be deemed his property everywhere. It is obvious, that if this were true, in the extent in which the argument employs it, if slavery exists anywhere, and if by the laws of any place a property can be acquired in slaves, the law of slavery must extend to every place where such slaves may be carried. The maxim, therefore, and the argument can apply only to those commodities which are everywhere, and by all nations, treated and deemed subjects of property. But it is not speaking with strict accuracy to say, that a property can be acquired in human beings, by local laws. Each state may, for its own convenience, declare that slaves shall be deemed property, and that the relations and laws of personal chattels shall be deemed to apply to them; as, for instance, that they may be bought and sold, delivered, attached, levied upon, that trespass will lie for an injury done to them, or trover for converting them. But it would be a perversion of terms to say, that such local laws do in fact make them personal property generally; they can only determine that the same rules of law shall apply to them as are applicable to property, and this effect will follow only so far as such laws *proprio vigore* can operate ...

Sims's Case 7 **Cush. 285 (1851)**

Another Shaw case, which holds that a fugitive slave must be returned to his master, just as a fugitive from justice must be. The issue is presented in terms of the powers of the commissioner who is charged with deciding whether an alleged fugitive is to be returned. The commissioner's decision is conclusive. Part of the argument in the case concerned whether the commissioner's appointment was an unconstitutional exercise of judicial power; part turned on the fact that fugitive slaves were not entitled to a jury trial. (By contrast, fugitives from justice could only be returned for trial by a jury.) Shaw makes short work of these arguments, arguing instead that the *Fugitive Slave Act is* prerequisite to the stability of the nation. The report includes an *obiter dictum* on the injustice of slavery.

... Shaw, CJ: – This is a petition for a writ of *habeas corpus* to bring the petitioner before this court, with a view to his discharge from imprisonment, upon the grounds stated in the petition. We were strongly urged to issue the writ, without inquiry into its cause, and to hear an argument upon the petitioner's right to a discharge, on the return of the writ. This we declined to do, on grounds of principle, and common and well settled practice. Before a writ of *habeas corpus* is granted, sufficient probable cause must be shown; but when it appears upon the party's own showing that there is no sufficient ground *prima facie* for his discharge, the court will not issue the writ ...

The evils existing immediately before the adoption of the constitution, and the greater and more appalling evils in prospect, indicated the absolute necessity of forming a more perfect union, in order to secure the peace and prosperity of all the states. This could only be done by the several states renouncing and relinquishing a portion of their powers of sovereignty; and these were the right of war and peace, the right of making treaties with foreign powers and with each other, and the right of exercising absolute power and dominion over all persons and things within their own territories respectively. In order to form this more perfect union, delegates from the several states met together. It was obvious that the renunciation of some of the powers of sovereignty, at least to the extent above mentioned, was the first step to be taken, and was absolutely essential to the success of any scheme of union. Still, it could not but be perceived that the great difference in the condition of the states in regard to the institution of slavery, and the prospect that many of the states would soon become free, from causes then in operation, constituted a difference in their relative condition, which must first be provided for. So long as the states remained sovereign, they could assert their rights in regard to fugitive slaves by war or treaty; and, therefore, before renouncing and surrendering such sovereignty, some substitute, in the nature of a treaty or compact, must necessarily be devised and agreed to. The clause above cited from the constitution seems to have been, in character, precisely such a treaty. It was a solemn compact, entered into by the delegates of states then sovereign and independent, and free to remain so, on great deliberation, and on the highest considerations of justice and policy, and reciprocal benefit, and in order to secure the peace and prosperity of all the states. It carries with it, therefore, all the sanction which can belong to it, either as an international or a social compact, made by parties invested with full powers to deliberate and act; or as a fundamental law, agreed on as the basis of a government, irrepealable, and to be changed only by the power that made it, in the form prescribed by it.

Such being the circumstances, under which this provision of the constitution was adopted; such the relations of the several states to each other; such the manifest object which the framers of the constitution had in view; we are to look at the clause in question, to ascertain its true meaning and effect. We think it was intended to guaranty to the owner of a slave, living within the territory of a state in which slavery is permitted, the rights conferred upon such owner, by the laws of such state; and that no state should make its own territory an asylum and sanctuary for fugitive slaves, by any law or regulation, by which a slave, who had escaped from a state where he owed labor or service into such state or territory, should avoid being reclaimed; it was designed also to provide a practicable and peaceable mode, by which such fugitive, upon the claim of the person to whom such labor or service should be due, might be delivered up ...

And the theory of the general government is, that these subjects, in their full extent and entire details, being placed under the jurisdiction of the general government, are necessarily withdrawn from the jurisdiction of the state, and the jurisdiction of the general government therefore becomes exclusive. And this is necessary to prevent constant collision and interference; and it is obvious that it must be so, because two distinct governments cannot exercise the same power, at the same time, on the same subject matter. This is not left to mere implication. It is expressly declared, in art. 1, s. 8, that congress shall have power to make all laws which shall be necessary and proper, for carrying into execution all the powers vested by the constitution in the government of the United States, or in any department or officer thereof. And by art. 6, "this constitution, and the laws of the United States which shall be made in pursuance thereof, and all treaties made, or which shall be made, under the authority of the United States, shall be the supreme law of the land; and the judges in every state shall be bound thereby, any thing in the constitution or laws of any state to the contrary notwithstanding." All such laws made by the general government, upon the rights, duties and subjects, specially enumerated and confided to their jurisdiction, are necessarily exclusive and supreme, as well by express provision, as by necessary implication. And the general government is provided with its executive, legislative and judicial departments, not only to make laws regulating the rights, duties and subjects thus confided to them, but to administer right and justice respecting them in a regular course of judicature, and cause them to be carried into full execution, by its own powers, without dependence upon state authority, and without any let or restraint imposed by it.

It was, as we believe, under this view of the right of regaining specifically the custody of one from whom service or labor is due by the laws of one state, and who has escaped into another, and under this view of the powers of the general government, and the duty of congress, that the law of February 12, 1793, was passed ...

The manifest intent of this act of congress was, to regulate and give effect to the right given by the constitution. It secured to the claimant the aid and assistance of certain magistrates and officers, to enable him to exercise his right in a more regular and orderly manner, and without being chargeable with a breach of the peace. It obviously contemplated a prompt and summary proceeding, adapted to the exigency of the occasion, in aid of a power, in terms conferred by the constitution on the claimant. It vested the power of inquiry, (whether regarded as judicial or otherwise,) the same power which is now drawn in question, in magistrates of counties, cities or towns corporate. As to the mode of trial contemplated by this act, it is described by Mr Justice McLean, in his opinion in *Prigg v Pennsylvania*, 16 Peters, 539, 667, in these terms: "Both the constitution and the act of 1793 require the fugitive from labor to be delivered up on claim being made by the party, or his agent, to whom the service is due. Not that a suit should be regularly instituted. The proceeding authorized by the law is summary and informal. The fugitive is seized and taken before a judge or magistrate within the state, and on proof, parol or written, that he owes labor to the claimant, it is made the duty of the judge or magistrate to give the certificate, which authorizes the removal of the fugitive to the state from whence he absconded"...

We have thought it important thus to inquire into the validity and constitutionality of the act of 1793, because it appears to be decisive of that in question. In the only particular in which the constitutionality of the act of congress of 1850 is now called in question, that of 1793 was obnoxious to the same objection, viz., that of authorizing a summary proceeding before officers and magistrates not qualified under the constitution to exercise the judicial powers of the general government. Congress may have thought it necessary to change the preexisting law, not in principle but in detail, because, as we have seen in the case of *Prigg v Pennsylvania*, some of the judges were of opinion that state magistrates could not act under the authority conferred on them by the act of 1793, when prohibited from doing so by the laws of their own state, and some states had in fact passed such prohibitory laws. The present fugitive slave law may vary in other respects, and provide other and more rigorous means for carrying its provisions into effect, but these are not made grounds of objection to its constitutionality.

We do not mean to say that this court will in no case issue a writ of *habeas corpus* to bring in a party, held under color of process from the courts of the United States, or whose services, and the custody of whose person, are claimed under authority derived from the laws of the United States. This is constantly done, in cases of soldiers and sailors, held by military and naval officers, under enlistments complained of as illegal and void. But it is manifest that this ought to be done only in a clear case, and in a case where it is necessary to the security of personal liberty from illegal restraint.

Since the argument in court, this morning, I am reminded by one of the counsel for the petitioner, that the law in question ought to be regarded as unconstitutional, because it makes no provision for a trial by jury. We think that this cannot vary the result. The law of 1850 stands, in this respect, precisely on the same ground with that of 1793, and the same grounds of argument which tend to show the unconstitutionality of one apply with equal force to the other; and the same answer must be made to them.

The principle of adhering to judicial precedent, especially that of the supreme court of the United States, in a case depending upon the constitution and laws of the United States, and thus placed within their special and final jurisdiction, is absolutely necessary to the peace, union and harmonious action of the state and general governments. The preservation of both, with their full and entire powers, each in its proper sphere, was regarded by the framers of the constitution, and has ever since been regarded, as essential to the peace, order and prosperity of all the United States.

If this were a new question, now for the first time presented, we should desire to pause and take time for consideration. But though this act, the construction of which is now drawn in question, is recent, and this point, in the form in which it is now stated, is new, yet the solution of the question depends upon reasons and judicial decisions, upon legal principles and a long course of practice, which are familiar, and which have often been the subject of discussion and deliberation.

Considering, therefore, the nature of the subject, the urgent necessity for a speedy and prompt decision, we have not thought it expedient to delay the judgment. I have, therefore, to state, in behalf of the court, under the weighty responsibility which rests upon us, and as the unanimous opinion of the court, that the writ of *habeas corpus* prayed for cannot be granted ...

Writ refused.

By the received laws of nations, it seems to be well established, that however odious we may consider slavery and the slave trade, however abhorrent to the dictates of humanity and the plainest principles of justice and natural right, yet each nation has a right, in this respect, to judge for itself, and to allow or prohibit slavery by its own laws, at its own will; and that whenever slavery is thus established by positive law within the limits of such state, all other nations and people are bound to respect it, and cannot rightfully interfere, either by forcibly seizing, or artfully enticing away slaves, within the limits of the territory of the nation establishing it, or on the high seas, which are the common highway of nations. In the case cited, the language of this court is this: "In considering the law of nations, we may assume that the law of this state is analogous to the law of England in this respect; that while slavery is considered as unlawful and inadmissible in both, because contrary to natural right, and the laws designed for the security of personal liberty, yet, in both, the existence of slavery in other countries is recognized, and the claims of foreigners, growing out of that condition, are, to a certain extent, respected." In *Sommersett's case*, before Lord Mansfield, in 1771, 20 Howells's State Trials, 1, 82, which is the leading case on this subject, and establishes the doctrine of the natural right to personal liberty in its fullest extent, we find a clear intimation of the principle above stated. Slavery, said Lord Mansfield, "is of such a nature that it is incapable of being introduced on any reasons, moral or political, but only by positive law." "It is so odious, that nothing can be suffered to support it, but positive law." But this is a clear admission, and indeed this is manifest throughout his opinion, that although odious and contrary to natural right, it may exist by force of positive law. And this may be mere customary law, as well as the enactment of a statute. The term "positive law," in this sense, may be understood to designate those rules, established by long and tacit acquiescence, or by the legislative act of any state, and which derive their force and effect as law from such acquiescence or legislative enactment, and are acted upon as such, whether conformable to the dictates of natural justice or otherwise.

The principle is, that although slavery and the slave trade are contrary to justice and natural right, yet each nation, in this respect, may establish its own law, within its own territory. And even the slave trade is not regarded as piracy, even by those states who regard it in the abstract as unjust, except when it has been declared so by statute, which can only operate within its own limits; or except when it has been so declared by treaty between two or more powers, in which case it may be so regarded as between such powers, their citizens and subjects. This is confirmed by the English and American authorities, although the governments of both the United States and England have made strong declarations and passed very severe laws against the slave trade ...

If then these states, prior to the adoption of the constitution, would have been sovereign and independent, these views of the established and recognized laws of nations indicate clearly what would have been their relative condition, and their respective rights. Slavery was likely to subsist in some states, and to be abolished in others. Each would have been clothed with certain rights, and bound to the performance of certain duties, which each would have a right to defend and enforce by war, to which there would be a constant temptation; and this could only have been avoided by treaty, regulating and providing for the enjoyment and security of such rights. It would have been in vain to say, that slavery being founded in wrong and injustice, any treaty tending to assent to, uphold and sanction it, would be itself immoral and wrong, and so could not conscientiously be made. Nations cannot elect the subjects on which they will treat; treaties are often made under great exigencies, as the best alternative which can be resorted to in order to avoid greater evils. In the infancy of our commerce and of our political power, we thought it not wrong to make treaties with the Algerines, and other piratical powers of the coast of Barbary, who had committed depredations on our commerce, and carried our citizens into captivity. We made treaties for ransoming our citizens held in slavery, and paid tribute to these acknowledged pirates, to induce them to forbear plundering our commerce, although such payments contributed directly to the upholding and encouragement of robbery and piracy. Having made such treaties, nobody would doubt that it was our duty to fulfil them to the letter, any more than they would doubt our perfect right to refuse renewing them, the moment we were able to defend our own rights by our own strength. No; in making a treaty, we must take our relations with others as we find them; and make the best provision for our rights which is practicable under the circumstances. The question is, in adopting or rejecting a proposed mutual stipulation, not whether it is the most desirable on general grounds of expediency, but whether it is preferable to that which is the inevitable alternative if this is rejected.

But if no binding treaty could be made on the subject of slavery, what would have been the necessary alternative? It would have been a state of things in which acknowledged rights were in constant danger of being drawn into conflict between neighboring states, leading to a war likely to be perpetual, or perhaps to a still more disastrous result – that of some states being subjugated by others of superior physical strength, in a contest in which right and wrong would be disregarded, and violence and brute force would supersede the government of law and the reign of peace. Can this be regarded as an inflamed or exaggerated view of the condition of these states, as independent, but without compact with each other, if the views of the laws of nations above stated are correct? The states were equal in right, but unequal in power. In view of the laws of nations, there was no difference between Rhode Island and Virginia, or Pennsylvania and Delaware. With equal rights, constantly in danger of being brought into conflict, with radical differences of opinion and views, both of justice and policy, on the subject of slavery, the danger of hostile collision was imminent. What alternative was there, but either a general treaty of alliance or a league, or a union under one government, to whom should be confided all these subjects of common and mutual interest. The latter expedient was adopted. The several states agreed to renounce their rights of sovereignty to a limited extent; among other subjects, the regulation of their intercourse with foreign powers, with the Indian tribes and with each other; the right of war and peace, and that of making treaties either with foreign powers or with each other. Certain other subjects of common interest were also surrendered, and placed under the exclusive control and jurisdiction of the common government. Instead of enforcing their rights, as they could have done before, only by war, it was agreed to establish a general government, furnished with full and complete legislative, judicial and executive powers, to take cognizance of these rights, to provide by law for the regulation of them, to declare and apply them in an orderly course of judicature, and to carry them into full effect. On coming to this arrangement, it could not be kept out of view, that some states had large numbers of slaves, and were disposed to uphold and sanction the existence of slavery by their laws; whilst others denounced it and held it in abhorrence, as unjust and criminal, alike opposed to natural right and to good policy. It could not, however, but be known to the framers of the constitution, that in the states where slavery was allowed by law, certain rights attached to its citizens, which were recognized by the laws of nations, and which could not be taken away without their consent. They therefore provided for the limited enjoyment of that right, as it existed before, so as to prevent persons owing service under the laws of one state, and escaping therefrom into another, from being discharged by the laws of the latter;

and authorized the general government to prescribe means for their restoration. This is the *casus fœderis*; to this extent the states are bound by their compact, but no further. Slavery was not created, established or perpetuated by the constitution. It existed before; it would have existed if the constitution had not been made. The framers of the constitution could not abrogate slavery, or the qualified rights claimed under it; they took it as they found it, and regulated it to a limited extent. The constitution, therefore, is not responsible for the origin or continuance of slavery. The provision it contains was the best adjustment which could be made of conflicting rights and claims, and was absolutely necessary to effect what may now be considered as the general pacification, by which harmony and peace should take the place of violence and war. These were the circumstances, and this the spirit, in which the constitution was made; the regulation of slavery so far as to prohibit states by law from harboring fugitive slaves, was an essential element in its formation; and the union intended to be established by it was essentially necessary to the peace, happiness and highest prosperity of all the states. In this spirit, and with these views steadily in prospect, it seems to be the duty of all judges and magistrates to expound and apply these provisions in the constitution and laws of the United States; and in this spirit it behooves all persons, bound to obey the laws of the United States, to consider and regard them.

The duties and relations of the states to each other, by the laws of nations, anterior to the making of the constitution, and the qualified but acknowledged right arising from the establishment of slavery in some states, and its exclusion in others, having been alluded to briefly in the opinion of the court, it was thought advisable, in this note, to expand the argument somewhat, arising from that consideration, but more especially to state the judicial authorities upon which it rests.

READING QUESTIONS ON SHAW

1 How can Shaw reach what seem to be opposite conclusions in the two cases?
2 Charles-Henri Sanson was appointed executioner of Paris by Louis XVI, and served him faithfully. After the French Revolution he served new political masters, and became the king's executioner in a new sense. In the counter-terror, he beheaded another former employer, Robespierre. Sanson insisted on professional

detachment at his task, and is said to have argued that were he to have refused to execute those he thought unworthy, he would have been no better than a murderer for those he did behead. Compare his situation with those of Judge Shaw and Captain Vere.

Anthony Sebok
'Judging the Fugitive Slave Acts" (1991)

Sebok argues that Judge Shaw could have decided Sims's case differently had he reasoned in the way that Dworkin recommends.

Robert Cover argues in *Justice Accused* that the *Fugitive Slave Acts* created a "moral/formal" dilemma for Northern judges. As judges, these men had sworn to uphold the Constitution and the laws of the United States. It seemed apparent to many judges that the federal government's intentions were clear, that the Acts had been passed by valid majorities in Congress, and that they were sanctioned by the Constitution. But, as Northern elites, many of them held strong abolitionist beliefs and considered slavery (and, by extension, the capture of Blacks for return to a life of slavery) evil. These judges lived in a world where, with increasing frequency, many politicians, state judges, and other legal elites were arguing for the rejection of the *Fugitive Slave Acts*. The dilemma, then, lay between the judges' moral beliefs and their formal legal obligations ...

Cover's conclusion is that the leading legal theory of the age – legal positivism – so dominated these judges that they could see but not act upon the appeals made from natural law in their courtrooms. Cover concludes that it was the very same technical skill that led these men to be judges that barred them from acting on their beliefs and rejecting the slave laws. The conscientious application of positivism led to "cognitive dissonance" amongst many judges of 1850. Cover suggests that these judges responded in two ways. First, they exaggerated the mechanical operation of the law, so as to deny to themselves any discretion and thereby excuse their failure to act. Second, they "raised the formal stakes" in the cases before them by claiming that if political or moral values were introduced into the process of adjudication, the authority of the state over all citizens would be eroded. Put most starkly, Cover depicts the Northern federal judges of 1850 as saying that in such morally charged cases as those concerning fugitive slaves, adjudication did not require moral judgment, and worse, moral judgment would imperil the state's authority.

Cover implicitly reaffirms the dichotomy ... natural law (normative communal vision) on the one side; positivism (bureaucracy and order) on the other. Cover thus finds the moral/formal dilemma a necessary element of American constitutional interpretation. To rebut Cover's view of adjudication, one would either have to dissolve the moral/formal dichotomy or show why the dichotomy is in fact not a dilemma ...

Dworkin believes that the moral/formal dilemma embraced by Cover is a trap set up by the positivist in order to make positivism attractive. The trap creates two artificial categories which bear little relation to legal practice: legal positivism ("which insists that law and morals are made wholly distinct by ... rules everyone accepts for using 'law'") and natural law ("which insists, on the contrary, that [law and morality] are united"). The false dichotomy poses a choice between positivism and natural law, or between setting out the judge's responsibility as searching for what the law "is" as opposed to what it "ought to be" ...

With the exception of some Constitutional Utopians, few argued that the Constitution, with its implicit references to slavery, did not actually permit slavery in some parts of the country. Further, it would have been hard for someone to argue in 1840 that the Constitution actively forbade slavery. Slavery was a matter of state law, and it is unlikely that Dworkin could generate not only a federal prohibition against slavery, but also some theory of federal common law or federal rights applicable to the states to enforce that prohibition. The Constitution did not approve of slavery, nor did it disapprove of it: its three mentions of the institution regulated a practice which the text could have outlawed but did not (until the Thirteenth Amendment) ...

A combination of these two prongs rebuts the objections to Dworkin's arguments by offering the following claim: the *Fugitive Slave Act* of 1850 was not constitutional because its application, given the conditions of 1850, violated the principle of comity that allowed the free states to tolerate slavery without compromising the demands of their own legal practices ...

Little information exists about the intentions and purposes of the Framers of the fugitive slave clause. As we saw above, however,

Dworkin argues that the goal of constitutional interpretation is not to describe the specific state of affairs the Framers intended, but rather to describe the general principle they hoped to build into the Constitution. Just as Dworkin was able to describe a general principle of the Fourteenth Amendment that was "correctly" instantiated by different theories of racial equality at different times, he can do the same with the principle expressed by the fugitive slave clause. The Clause required – most generally – that each state respect the laws of its neighbor; more specifically, it required the states that forbid slavery to deliver runaway slaves to the states that had slavery. But as with the "principle" of racial equality contained in the Fourteenth Amendment, this "principle" of fugitive comity could have had many different theoretical instantiations. One theory Dworkin could advance is as follows: The Constitution, in order to leave questions of the treatment of Blacks within their borders up to each state, could not replace the laws governing the internal regulation of Blacks with federal laws that, in effect, substituted the laws of another state.

If the Clause is read to refer to this theory, then Dworkin's attack on the 1850 Act can be made on two fronts. First, the Clause, which at root was concerned with the states' obligation to return runaways, cannot be read as having granted the federal courts the power to invalidate state processes simply because they were slow or – in the eyes of other states – obstructionist. Thus, the Clause should never have been read to forbid state governments from making fundamental choices about the process necessary for a slave to be "delivered up" to a slave state. Second, the due process clause of the Fifth Amendment limited the sort of processes the federal government could erect to ensure the return of runaway slaves. Unless the process due an accused Black was at least equal to that of the state in which the federal proceeding took place, the "home" state's "pro-Black" processes were being derogated in favor of a Southern state's "anti-Black" processes. These two issues, however, are merely logical extensions of the same central issue, which is: what limits did the fugitive slave clause place on the federal government's power to decide how alleged slaves were to be treated within the Northern states' territory?

The theory of interstate comity available to judges in the 1790s and the early nineteenth century may have been something like the following: In order to respect each state's views on slavery, federal law guarantees the slave states their citizens' property rights in slaves in the United States. This theory assumes that the protection of Southern property rights would not conflict with Northern states' domestic law. This assumption may have been credible when Northern states had no body of domestic law designed to address the treatment of accused slaves by domestic or foreign actors. If the laws of Northern states did not conflict with the extraterritorial claims of residents of Southern states, and federal law went no further than to enforce Southern claims, then the principle of comity described above would be consistent with the 1793 Act. A change in conditions – in both the nature of the Northern states' relation to slave-catching and the attitude of Northern governments toward slave-catching – made the Clause's principle of comity incompatible with either Act, however.

The principle of comity changed between 1793 and 1850 as the world changed. In the early years of the 1793 Act there were few Northern laws about slave-catching to conflict with Southern laws. There was simply much less reason for the Northern states to legislate on the issue of fugitives: the lack of an organized abolition movement meant fewer slaves coming across the border and less popular outrage at the slave-catchers who would enter Northern towns and forcibly remove Blacks to Southern states and inevitably to bondage. The gradual transformation in Northern political morality is illustrated by the rise of "personal liberty" laws, as well as an increase in both the frequency and severity of Northern reaction to the use of the 1793 Act by Southern slave-owners.

In the face of this changing political morality in the North, the Clause forced judges into an inescapable dilemma. On the one hand, the Clause specifically called upon states to cooperate in the return of slaves; one could see this federal instruction as a commitment on the part of the federal government to ensure that conflicts over slaves were regulated by more than the usual "interstate comity" rules that governed choice of law disputes. On the other hand, as Northern states passed more laws regulating how slaves were to be caught within their territory, the federal involvement in slave-catching necessarily had to express a preference in upholding either the North's or the South's conception of how slaves were to be caught. Since the activity always took place in the North, to uphold the Southern conception would increasingly void Northern laws regulating conduct within their own borders.

[F]or Northern states to curb their personal liberty laws (or to choose not to pass them out of regard for the Clause) would have violated the Clause's commitment to the principle of comity described above. It would be misleading to say that the free states were, in any significant way, adopting a view about the treatment of Blacks simply by omitting to act in a way that opposed a slave state's interests. However, once the free states developed and articulated a view – upon which they based positive state action – about how alleged slaves should be treated, then each time they curbed their sense of what process was due, and acted because of the slave state's interests, they were coerced into choosing the Southern regime over their own. That is why Dworkin can say that the change in the political morality and actions in the North made demands on the Clause that exposed its incompatibility with the Acts. Once that point was reached, to the extent that the Northern states were obliged to act because of the Constitution, the Constitution was not just protecting the slaveholder's interest in his slave, but forcing the North to respect that interest through procedures infected with the assumptions of slavery.

Northern states had begun to develop a coherent policy as to the treatment of fugitive slaves such that in regulating civil life within their territory, these states were taking positive steps toward preventing slavecatching. The Court's optimism that federal law could coexist with state inactivity became untenable as soon as state regulation with regard to the due process necessary to remove a fugitive slave began to look more and more like Pennsylvania's unconstitutional antikidnapping law.

[B] THE CLAUSE AND DUE PROCESS

... [B]y 1850, the Clause could not have been read to allow unconstrained federal regulation of slave-catching. A related and important point is that even if the Clause were viewed as giving the federal government the power to enforce the Northern states' obligations as set out in the Clause (to "deliver up" slaves), this still does not mean that the federal process used could violate contemporary state standards of due process. A conflict still remained concerning the extent to which the federal rules should reflect the Northern states' belief that any Black brought before a court in the North should enjoy the presumption that she was free until proven otherwise, and the Southern belief that proceedings in the North were little more than summary extradition hearings, where the presumption was reversed, and that any alleged slave could get a full and fair hearing once they were returned to the state of their alleged master.

We should recall what we determined to be the Clause's general principle: comity between the states with regard to how Blacks were to be treated within their borders. Until 1850, there was no special federal procedure for slave-catching, since there were no special federal officers like commissioners. Until 1850, federal judges (if they ever heard a runaway case) applied the procedure of the state in which they sat. This reflected the Clause's general commitment to comity. Under the pre-1850 scheme, as conceptions of due process changed in a Northern state, the federal procedure, which relied on state procedure, thus changed accordingly. Until 1850, a Dworkinian interpreter could claim that the Clause did not permit a person domiciled in Pennsylvania to receive federal procedural protections so thin that, in effect, that person's only real hearing was in South Carolina, with South Carolina "procedure." The denial of this interpretation would provide slave-catchers with guaranteed access to Southern slave law in every fugitive slave case: upon seizing a Black in the North, they then would need only to invoke a shred of federal procedure in order legitimately to introduce Southern law. On the other hand, obedience to the principle of comity would, according to our Dworkinian interpretation, require that federal due process treat Blacks with at least that process they would have received in the state in which they were seized ...

Dworkin's specific argument about the 1850 Act suggests that Cover's depiction of adjudication in hard cases is a misdescription with serious political consequences. If adjudication in hard cases requires estrangement from one's political commitments, then Cover simultaneously discourages people with political commitments from choosing to become, or remain, judges, while licensing those who remain judges to discount the role of political commitment in the interpretation of the Constitution. Cover's pessimistic view of adjudication is not necessarily correct. Judges in 1850 were not trapped between the formalism of following evil rules or the moral commands of their consciences.

READING QUESTIONS ON SEBOK

1 Summarize Sebok's argument in your own words. What steps in the argument might a positivist reject?
2 Suppose the *Fugitive Slave Act* had been designed to block the response Sebok suggests. What then?

Kindler v Canada (Minister of Justice) [1991] 2 SCR 779

The majority of the Supreme Court holds that Canadian judges are obliged to send convicted criminals back to the United States of America even though they will almost certainly be executed there.

The reasons of Lamer, CJ and Cory, J were delivered by

Cory, J (dissenting): – This appeal involves a challenge to the decision of the Minister of Justice, rendered pursuant to s. 25 of the Extradition Act, RSC 1985, c E-23, to surrender a fugitive charged with an offence punishable by death without first seeking assurances under Article 6 of the *Extradition Treaty between Canada and the United States of America*, Can. T.S. 1976 No. 3 (the *Treaty*), that the death penalty will not be imposed or, if imposed, not executed. The principal issue to be resolved is whether the Minister's decision to surrender the appellant to the United States without obtaining Article 6 assurances violates the appellant's rights under the *Canadian Charter of Rights and Freedoms*. In addressing this issue, two main questions arise. First, does the death penalty itself violate rights guaranteed under the *Charter*? Second, if so, what is the significance of this finding to the constitutional status of the Minister's decision?

Before dealing with the substantive issues raised on this appeal a few words must be said about extradition. Extradition treaties have long been recognized as both sound and necessary for the effective prosecution and enforcement of criminal law. It must be remembered that it is not the salutary scheme of extradition which is challenged on this appeal; rather, the question to be resolved is whether a fugitive subject to capital punishment in the requesting state should be surrendered without death penalty assurances.

I FACTUAL BACKGROUND

On November 15, 1983, in Philadelphia, Pennsylvania, Kindler was found guilty of first degree murder, conspiracy to commit murder and kidnapping. Following his conviction, the jury heard further evidence and recommended the imposition of the death penalty. Before the formal imposition of the sentence, Kindler escaped from prison and fled to Canada in September 1984.

He was arrested near Ste Adèle, Quebec, on April 26, 1985 and charged with offences under the Immigration Act, 1976, SC 1976-77, c 52, and the Criminal Code, RSC 1970, c C-34. On May 27, 1985, Kindler made an application to the Federal Court to prohibit the holding of an enquiry which had been commenced under s. 28 of the Immigration Act, 1976. Rouleau, J granted the application on July 23, 1985: [1985] 1 FC 676.

In the meantime, on July 3, 1985, the United States made a request for the extradition of Kindler pursuant to the *Treaty*. Kindler was arrested and an extradition hearing was set for August 26 in Montreal.

The hearing was held before Pinard, J of the Quebec Superior Court. It was agreed by counsel for Kindler that the evidence supplied by the United States complied with the conditions and requirements of the *Treaty* for the extradition of Kindler as a convicted fugitive. The sole issue raised was whether Article 6 of the *Treaty* required the extradition judge or the Minister of Justice to seek death penalty assurances from the United States before surrendering Kindler. Article 6 provides:

Article 6
When the offense for which extradition is requested is punishable by death under the laws of the requesting State and the laws of the requested State do not permit such punishment for that offense, extradition may be refused unless the requesting State provides such assurances as the requested State considers sufficient that the death penalty shall not be imposed, or, if imposed, shall not be executed.

On August 30, 1985, Pinard, J determined that he had no jurisdiction to request the Article 6 assurances and committed Kindler to custody to await the Minister's decision to surrender: [1985] CS 1117. That same day he sent a report of the case with a copy of his judgment to the Minister of Justice.

Kindler sought review of the decision of Pinard, J pertaining to Article 6 of the *Treaty* and brought an application for habeas corpus. This application was dismissed by Greenberg, J on September 20, 1985. He too was of the opinion that only the Minister of Justice could seek the assurances referred to in Article 6 of the *Treaty*. However, he added that in his view Kindler was entitled to be dealt with in accordance with the principles of fundamental justice pursuant to the provisions of s. 7 of the *Charter*. This clearly implied that the Minister's decision could be subject to judicial review. He determined that it was premature to decide whether extradition which could lead to the imposition of the death penalty constituted cruel and unusual punishment and was thus in conflict with s. 12 of the *Charter*.

The then Minister of Justice, the Honourable John Crosbie, in the exercise of his authority under s. 25 of the Extradition Act, agreed to entertain representations. Section 25 provides:

25. Subject to this Part, the Minister of Justice, on the requisition of the foreign state, may, under his hand and seal, order a fugitive who has been committed for surrender to be surrendered to the person or persons who are, in the Minister's opinion, duly authorized to receive the fugitive in the name and on behalf of the foreign state, and the fugitive shall be so surrendered accordingly.

Written material was supplied to the Minister, including letters from Kindler's parents, his wife, and from Dr Fugère and Dr Cormier of the McGill University Clinic in Forensic Psychiatry relating to their examination of Kindler. An affidavit was filed by Kindler's counsel, who had been scheduled to handle his post-trial motions in Pennsylvania. It was her opinion that Kindler would not succeed in the appeals of his convictions and sentence and that as a result he would be executed as soon as the appeal procedure had been completed.

Counsel for Kindler also sought to have Kindler give evidence at the hearing before the Minister and to submit studies on the death penalty. The Minister refused the application to present oral testimony or to hear Kindler in person, but considered the written material.

By letter to counsel for Kindler dated January 17, 1986, the Minister of Justice expressed the opinion that Canada should surrender Kindler without seeking any assurance from the United States authorities that the death penalty would not be imposed or, if imposed, would not be carried out. The Minister stated that in the interest of the Canadian public, those who commit murder in a foreign state should be discouraged from seeking haven in Canada as a means of reducing or limiting the severity of the penalty that might be exacted under the laws of the state in which their crime was committed.

V EARLY HISTORY OF THE DEATH PENALTY

At the very heart of this appeal is a conflict between two concepts. On one side is the concept of human dignity and the belief that this concept is of paramount importance in a democratic society. On the other side is the concept of retributive justice and the belief that capital punishment is necessary to deter murderers. An historical review reveals an increasing tendency to resolve this tension in favour of human dignity.

The Conduct of Juries

In England until the last century the death penalty was, at least in theory, the punishment imposed for all felonies. However, even a cursory review of the history of the death penalty indicates that from the earliest times there was a marked resistance by juries to the death sentence ...

This marked resistance to the death penalty speaks volumes for the basic decency and compassion of jurors. It is reflected in their decisions over the centuries and constitutes a long and lasting record of social values that is worthy of consideration. The compassionate views of the jurors are echoed in over three hundred years of writings by reformers.

Calls for Reform of the Death Penalty

There is a long history of opposition to the death penalty by reformers ... In summary it can be seen that from the 12th century forward there was a reluctance on the part of jurors to impose the death sentence. The jurors, the very people who might have been expected to be most interested in enforcing the criminal law particularly with regard to property offences, were loathe to condemn the accused to death. Their verdicts gave early recognition to the fundamental importance of human dignity and of the need to accord that dignity to all. As well, reformers for over 300 years advocated not only the reduction but the total abolition of the death penalty. This review demonstrates that opposition to the imposition of the death penalty has a long and honoured history.

VI TWENTIETH-CENTURY DEVELOPMENTS: THE INTERNATIONAL PROTECTION
OF HUMAN DIGNITY

The Commitment of the International Community

The end of hostilities following World War II signalled a massive movement towards the greater protection of human rights. Prior to the war,
international law paid scant attention to human rights. However, the
atrocities committed during the war led to international recognition of
the fundamental importance of human dignity and human rights ... On
the other hand, the position of the United States stands in marked
contrast to that of western countries. A majority of American states and
the United States Congress have opted to retain the death penalty for
some civil offences. Moreover, in *Gregg v Georgia*, 428 US 153 (1976), the
United States Supreme Court ruled that the death penalty was not, per
se, invalid. The Court noted that the text of the Constitution acknowledged the existence of capital punishment and, that, for 200 years the
Supreme Court had repeatedly found that capital punishment was not
invalid per se.

The commitment of the international community to human dignity
and the trend of western nations to abolish the death penalty parallels
Canada's own international stance.

Canada's International Commitment

Canada's commitment to human dignity has a lengthy and respected
history in international affairs. This commitment is exemplified by its
accession to the United Nations Charter on November 9, 1945, its vote
in favour of the Universal Declaration of Human Rights on December
10, 1948, its accession to the International Covenant on Civil and Political Rights and the Optional Protocol to the International Covenant on
Civil and Political Rights, 999 UNTS 302, on May 19, 1976, and its
accession to the Convention against Torture and Other Cruel, Inhuman,
or Degrading Treatment or Punishment on June 24, 1987.

In the United Nations Economic and Social Council on December 10,
1971, Canada voted in favour of the resolution affirming the goal of
abolition of capital punishment. Canada has also voted in favour of the
Second Optional Protocol to the International Covenant on Civil and
Political Rights, aiming at the Abolition of the Death Penalty (the

"Second Optional Protocol") on December 15, 1989. The Second Optional Protocol provides:

The States Parties to the Present Protocol,

Believing that abolition of the death penalty contributes to enhancement of human dignity and progressive development of human rights,

Recalling article 3 of the Universal Declaration of Human Rights, adopted on 10 December 1948, and article 6 of the International Covenant on Civil and Political Rights, adopted on 16 December 1966,

Noting that article 6 of the International Covenant on Civil and Political Rights refers to abolition of the death penalty in terms that strongly suggest that abolition is desirable,

Convinced that all measures of abolition of the death penalty should be considered as progress in the enjoyment of the right to life,

Desirous to undertake hereby an international commitment to abolish the death penalty,

Have Agreed as follows:

Article 1
1 No one within the jurisdiction of a State Party to the present Protocol shall be executed.
2 Each State party shall take all necessary measures to abolish the death penalty within its jurisdiction.

Article 2
1 No reservation is admissible to the present Protocol, except for a reservation made at the time of ratification or accession that provides for the application of the death penalty in time of war pursuant to a conviction for a most serious crime of a military nature committed during wartime.

In supporting the Second Optional Protocol, Canada stated that the United Nations would be honouring human dignity by enshrining the abolition of the death penalty in an international instrument. Canada's position was put this way in the United Nations Economic and Social Council, Commission on Human Rights, *Elaboration of a second optional protocol to the International Covenant on Civil and Political Rights, aiming at the abolition of the death penalty* on June 29, 1987, at p. 27:

Canada, having abolished the death penalty in 1977, believed that there was merit in the elaboration of a second optional protocol. The subject was a difficult one and raised passions in a number of countries, but it deserved the attention of the General Assembly even if all States would not be in a position to adopt such a second optional protocol immediately. There was no doubt that the United Nations would be honouring human dignity by enshrining the principle of the abolition of the death penalty in an international instrument.

Apart from Canada's international commitments, it is worthy of note that two other international organizations have taken steps similar to those of the United Nations to abolish capital punishment. The European Community enacted Protocol No. 6 to the European Convention for the Protection of Human Rights and Fundamental Freedoms Concerning the Abolition of the Death Penalty, Europ. TS No. 114, which came into force on March 3, 1985, and the Organization of American States approved the Protocol to the American Convention on Human Rights to Abolish the Death Penalty on June 8, 1990.

Summary

The international community has affirmed its commitment to the principle of human dignity through the various international instruments discussed above. Except for the United States, the western world has reinforced this commitment to human dignity, both internationally and nationally, through the express abolition of the death penalty. Canada's actions in the international forum affirms its own commitment to the preservation and enhancement of human dignity and to the abolition of the death penalty.

Let us now turn to the position within Canada.

VII THE CANADIAN POSITION

A consideration of the place of the death penalty in Canadian society must now take place in the context of the *Charter*. In particular, it must be determined whether the death penalty violates the *Charter* proscription against cruel and unusual punishment. Section 12 of the *Charter* provides:

12. Everyone has the right not to be subjected to any cruel and unusual treatment or punishment.

The constitutional status of capital punishment under s. 12 of the *Charter* is to be derived from the Canadian experience with respect to both the death penalty and the broader concept of cruel and unusual punishment.

The House of Commons Votes to Abolish the Death Penalty

In free votes in both 1976 and 1987, a majority of the members of the House of Commons supported the abolition of the death penalty. These votes, held after extensive and thorough debate, demonstrate that the elected representatives of the Canadian people found the death penalty for civil crimes to be an affront to human dignity which cannot be tolerated in Canadian society. These votes are a clear indication that capital punishment is considered to be contrary to basic Canadian values.

The rejection of the death penalty by the majority of the members of the House of Commons on two occasions can be taken as reflecting a basic abhorrence of the infliction of capital punishment either directly, within Canada, or through Canadian complicity in the actions of a foreign state.

The Position under the Charter

What then is the constitutional status of the death penalty under s. 12 of the *Charter*?

The American experience provides no guidance. Cases dealing with the constitutional validity of the death penalty were decided on very narrow bases unique to the wording of the American Constitution and rooted in early holdings of the United States Supreme Court. Canadian courts should articulate a distinct Canadian approach with respect to cruel and unusual punishment based on Canadian traditions and values.

The approach to be taken by this Court in determining whether capital punishment contravenes s. 12 of the *Charter* should, in my view, be guided by two central considerations. First is the principle of human dignity which lies at the heart of s. 12. It is the dignity and importance of the individual which is the essence and the cornerstone of democratic government. Second is the decision of this Court in *Smith*, supra.

1 Human Dignity under the *Charter*

The fundamental importance of human dignity in Canadian society has been recognized in numerous cases. In *R v Oakes*, [1986] 1 SCR 103

Dickson, CJ, at p. 136 referred to the basic principles and values which are enshrined in the *Charter*. He wrote:

The Court must be guided by the values and principles essential to a free and democratic society which I believe embody, to name but a few, respect for the inherent dignity of the human person, commitment to social justice and equality, accommodation of a wide variety of beliefs, respect for cultural and group identity, and faith in social and political institutions which enhance the participation of individuals and groups in society. The underlying values and principles of a free and democratic society are the genesis of the rights and freedoms guaranteed by the *Charter* and the ultimate standard against which a limit on a right or freedom must be shown, despite its effect, to be reasonable and demonstrably justified.

In her reasons in *R v Morgentaler*, [1986] 1 SCR 30, at p. 166, Wilson, J stressed the importance of human dignity in understanding the protections afforded by the *Charter*. She wrote:

The idea of human dignity finds expression in almost every right and freedom guaranteed in the *Charter*. Individuals are afforded the right to choose their own religion and their own philosophy of life, the right to choose with whom they will associate and how they will express themselves, the right to choose where they will live and what occupation they will pursue.

Let us now turn to consider the second guiding consideration, the decision of this Court in *R v Smith*, [1987] 1 SCR 1045.

2 Section 12 and the *Smith* Case

In *Smith*, supra, this Court considered a challenge to the minimum sentencing provision of the Narcotic Control Act, RSC 1970, c N-1. The penalty prescribed by the Narcotic Control Act for importing a narcotic into Canada was imprisonment for a minimum of seven years up to life. The minimum term was challenged on the ground that it constituted cruel and unusual punishment contrary to s. 12 of the *Charter*. It was argued that the punishment was unduly severe and disproportionate to the offence committed. The decision focused upon the element of proportionality.

Lamer, J, as he then was, carefully considered the nature of the protection afforded by s. 12 of the *Charter*. In giving a broad interpretation to the s. 12 right, Lamer, J, at p. 1072, held that punishments "must not be grossly disproportionate to what would have been appropriate." He later held, at pp. 1073–74, that certain punishments will by their very nature always be grossly disproportionate:

Finally, I should add that some punishments or treatments will always be grossly disproportionate and will always outrage our standards of decency: for example, the infliction of corporal punishment, such as the lash, irrespective of the number of lashes imposed, or, to give examples of treatment, the lobotomisation of certain dangerous offenders or the castration of sexual offenders.

From this decision two principles emerge. First, punishments must never be grossly disproportionate to that which would have been appropriate to punish, rehabilitate, or deter the particular offender or to protect the public from that offender. Second, and more importantly for the purposes of this case, punishments must not in themselves be unacceptable no matter what the crime, no matter what the offender. Although any form of punishment may be a blow to human dignity, some form of punishment is essential for the orderly functioning of society. However, when a punishment becomes so demeaning that all human dignity is lost, then the punishment must be considered cruel and unusual. At a minimum, the infliction of corporal punishment, lobotomisation of dangerous offenders and the castration of sexual offenders will not be tolerated.

3   Does the Death Penalty Violate Section 12 of the *Charter*?

In light of both the decisions stressing the importance of human dignity under the *Charter* and the principles espoused in the *Smith* case, it remains to be determined whether the death penalty violates s. 12 of the *Charter*. In my view, there can be no doubt that it does.

A consideration of the effect of the imposition of the death penalty on human dignity is enlightening. Descriptions of executions demonstrate that it is state-imposed death which is so repugnant to any belief in the importance of human dignity. The methods utilized to carry out the execution serve only to compound the indignities inflicted upon the individual.

In his book *Condemned to Die: Life Under Sentence of Death* (1981), at pp. 86–87, Johnson makes this reference to executions in the electric chair:

Electrocution has been described by one medical doctor as "a form of torture [that] rivals burning at the stake." Electrocutions have been known to drag on interminably, literally cooking the prisoners. In one instance, a man's brain "was found to be 'baked hard,' the blood in his head had turned to charcoal, and his entire back was burnt black." One man somehow survived electrocution and was returned months later, with the approval of the Supreme Court, for a second (and unsuccessful) encounter with the chair. More recently, John Spenkelink's electrocution lasted over six minutes and required three massive surges of electricity before he finally died. Although we have no accounts of the damage to Spenkelink's body caused by his execution, allegations that Florida prison officials stuffed his anus with cotton and taped his mouth shut suggest that they may have anticipated the forbidding spectacle typically provided by electrocution, and made every effort to make the sanction cosmetically acceptable.

This description of the imposition of the death penalty clearly indicates that persons executed by the state are deprived of all semblance of human dignity. The stuffing of the anus with cotton wool and the taping shut of the mouth suggest that even the authorities carrying out the execution were not only insensitive to human dignity but fully expected a horrible reaction to a dreadful punishment. Even so, these indignities are simply adjuncts to the ultimate attack on human dignity, the destruction of life by the state.

The following description by the Reverend Myer Tobey of the execution by lethal gas of Eddie Daniels is to similar effect:

In the chamber now, he was strapped to the chair. The cyanide had been prepared, and was placed beneath his chair, over a pan of acid that would later react with the cyanide to form the deadly gas. Electrocardiographic wires were attached to Daniels' forearms and legs, and connected to a monitor in the observation area. This lets the doctor know when the heart stops beating.

This done, the prison guards left the room, shutting the thick door, and sealing it to prevent the gas from leaking. I took my place at one of the windows, and looked at Eddie, and he looked at me. We said the prayer together, over and over.

At a motion of the warden, a prison guard then pulled a lever releasing the cyanide crystals beneath the chair. Eddie heard the chemical pellets drop, and he braced himself. We did not take our eyes off each other.

In an instant, puffs of light white smoke began to rise. Daniels saw the smoke, and moved his head to try to avoid breathing it in. As the gas continued to rise he moved his head this way and that way, thrashing as much as his straps would allow still in an attempt to avoid breathing. He was like an animal in a trap, with no escape, all the time being watched by his fellow humans in the windows that lined the chamber. He could steal only glimpses of me in his panic, but I continued to repeat "My Jesus I Love You," and he too would try to mouth it.

Then the convulsions began. His body strained as much as the straps would allow. He had inhaled the deadly gas, and it seemed as if every muscle in his body was straining in reaction. His eyes looked as if they were bulging, much as a choking man with a rope cutting off his windpipe. But he could get no air in the chamber.

Then his head dropped forward. The doctor in the observation room said that that was it for Daniels. This was within the first few minutes after the pellets had dropped. His head was down for several seconds. Then, as we had thought it was over, he again lifted his head in another convulsion. His eyes were open, he strained and he looked at me. I said one more time, automatically, "My Jesus I Love You." And he went with me, mouthing the prayer. He was still alive after those several minutes, and I was horrified. He was in great agony. Then he strained and began the words with me again. I knew he was conscious, this was not an automatic response of an unconscious man. But he did not finish. His head fell forward again.

There were several more convulsions after this, but his eyes were closed. I could not tell if he were conscious or not at that point. Then he stopped moving, approximately ten minutes after the gas began to rise, and was officially pronounced dead.

The death penalty not only deprives the prisoner of all vestiges of human dignity, it is the ultimate desecration of the individual as a human being. It is the annihilation of the very essence of human dignity.

Let us now consider the principles set out in *Smith* to determine whether the death penalty is of the same nature as corporal punishment, lobotomy or castration which were designated as cruel and unusual punishment.

What is acceptable as punishment to a society will vary with the nature of that society, its degree of stability and its level of maturity. The punishments of lashing with the cat-o-nine tails and keel-hauling were accepted forms of punishment in the 19th century in the British navy. Both of those punishments could, and not infrequently, did result in death to the recipient. By the end of the 19th century, however, it was unthinkable that such penalties would be inflicted. A more sensitive society had made such penalties abhorrent.

Similarly, corporal punishment is now considered cruel and unusual yet it was an accepted form of punishment in Canada until it was abolished in 1973. The explanation, it seems to me, is that a maturing society has recognized that the imposition of the lash would now be a cruel and intolerable punishment.

If corporal punishment, lobotomy and castration are no longer acceptable and contravene s. 12 then the death penalty cannot be considered to be anything other than cruel and unusual punishment. It is the supreme indignity to the individual, the ultimate corporal punishment, the final and complete lobotomy and the absolute and irrevocable castration.

As the ultimate desecration of human dignity, the imposition of the death penalty in Canada is a clear violation of the protection afforded by s. 12 of the *Charter*. Capital punishment is per se cruel and unusual.

If Kindler had committed the murder in Canada, then not simply the abolition of the death penalty in this country but, more importantly, the provisions of s. 12 of the *Charter* would prevent his execution. The next question is whether the fact that American, not Canadian, authorities would carry out the execution is fatal to Kindler's s. 12 claim. That is, does the Minister's decision to surrender Kindler to American authorities who may impose the death penalty "subject" him, within the meaning of s. 12, to cruel and unusual punishment?

VIII THE RELEVANCE OF THE FACT THAT THE DEATH PENALTY WOULD BE INFLICTED BY THE UNITED STATES AND NOT CANADA

The respondent contends that even if it is assumed that the death penalty constitutes cruel punishment, the *Charter* protections should not apply to a fugitive. In support of this position it was said that the surrender of Kindler did not mean that the Government of Canada would be subjecting the fugitive to cruel and unusual punishment, since the punishment would be inflicted by the requesting state. It was argued that so long as the trial procedure the fugitive had undergone or would undergo in the requesting state was fair, the punishment that followed a finding of guilt was not something which could be subject to the provisions of the *Charter*. Based on the *Charter* jurisprudence of this Court, this argument must be rejected.

The Approach that Should Be Taken in Applying the Charter

Although the *Charter* has no extraterritorial application, persons in Canada who are subject to extradition proceedings must be accorded all the rights which flow from the Charter. The approach to be taken is indicated by this Court in *Singh v Minister of Employment and Immigration*, [1985] 1 SCR 177. In that case the refugee claimants contended that Canada's decision not to extend convention refugee status to them placed them at risk that they would be prosecuted in their home country for their political beliefs. Wilson, J, for the plurality, found that this decision deprived the claimants of their s. 7 right to security of the person and that this was sufficient to trigger the protection of the *Charter*. Specifically, Wilson, J stressed that the *Charter* affords freedom not only from actual punishment but also from the threat of punishment.

The *Singh* principle was applied in the extradition context in *Schmidt*, supra, where La Forest, J held that the manner in which the foreign state will deal with the fugitive upon surrender may, in some situations, violate the *Charter*. When such a likelihood arises, Canada, as the extraditing state, must accept responsibility for the ultimate consequence of the extradition. This, I believe, is the conclusion to be drawn from the reasons of La Forest, J, at p. 522:

> I have no doubt either that in some circumstances the manner in which the foreign state will deal with the fugitive on surrender, whether that course of conduct is justifiable or not under the law of that country, may be such that it would violate the principles of fundamental justice to surrender an accused under those circumstances. To make the point, I need only refer to a case that arose before the European Commission on Human Rights, *Altun v Germany* (1983), 5 EHRR 611, where it was established that prosecution in the requesting country might involve the infliction of torture. Situations falling far short of this may well arise where the nature of the criminal procedures or penalties in a foreign country sufficiently shocks the conscience as to make a decision to surrender a fugitive for trial there one that breaches the principles of fundamental justice enshrined in s. 7
> ... The same conclusion has been reached in Europe, where arguments similar to those of the respondent have been firmly rejected.

The European Position

While the European cases are to a large extent determined by the provisions of the *European Convention for the Protection of Human Rights and Fundamental Freedoms*, 213 UNTS 222, they are useful in their indication of a judicial trend in the consideration of extradition cases where a fugitive may be subjected to cruel and unusual punishment or treatment.

Article 3 of the *European Convention* provides that "[n]o one shall be subjected to torture or to inhuman or degrading treatment or punishment."

In summary, the position taken under the *European Convention* is that a decision to surrender a fugitive to a country in which that fugitive may face torture, or inhuman, or degrading treatment or punishment is a violation of the fugitive's right not to be "subjected" to such treatment. If extradition will result in a risk that Article 3 will be contravened then a contracting party to the *European Convention* must, in the absence of an appropriate undertaking, refuse the request to extradite. Further, the exposure to the death penalty which results in "death row phenomenon" constitutes a breach of Article 3. Thus it is clear that a decision to surrender a fugitive to face a cruel and unusual punishment constitutes the *subjection* of the fugitive to that punishment. If the same reasoning were applied in the Canadian context, a decision to surrender a fugitive who, on conviction, might be subjected to the death penalty would contravene the provisions of s. 12 of the *Charter*.

The Responsibility of the Extraditing State

Given all of the above, the respondent's contention that the *Charter* would not apply to cruel and unusual punishments inflicted by the requesting state must be rejected. In my view, since the death penalty is a cruel punishment, that argument is an indefensible abdication of moral responsibility. Historically such a position has always been condemned. The ceremonial washing of his hands by Pontius Pilate did not relieve him of responsibility for the death sentence imposed by others and has found little favour over the succeeding centuries. Notwithstanding the fact that it is the United States and not Canada which would impose the death penalty, Canada has the obligation not to extradite a person to face a cruel and unusual treatment or punishment. To surrender a fugitive who may be subject to the death penalty violates s. 12 of the *Charter* just as surely as would the execution of the fugitive in Canada. Therefore, the Minister's decision to extradite Kindler without obtaining Article 6 assurances violates Kindler's s. 12 rights. The only remaining question is whether this violation can be justified under s. 1 of the *Charter*.

IX SECTION 1 OF THE *CHARTER*

The death penalty for civil crimes cannot be justified under s. 1 of the *Charter*. Indeed, it is difficult to imagine how it could ever be justified. However, let us assume that there could be a s. 1 justification for a punishment which would be, per se, a violation of s. 12. Even then, capital punishment could not meet the proportionality test except, perhaps, in very rare circumstances such as conviction for a very serious military offence committed during time of war or emergency.

The Safe Haven Argument

The primary s. 1 justification put forth by the respondent was the so-called "safe haven" argument. The respondent argued that if the death penalty was found to be cruel and unusual punishment per se, then to require the Minister to insist upon an Article 6 assurance in every case where the death penalty might be imposed would result in Canada becoming a safe haven for murderers. It was said that to retain such a ministerial discretion constitutes a reasonable limit on the *Charter* proscription against punishment which would be, per se, a breach of s. 12.

I cannot accept this contention. This submission is an *in terrorem* argument put forward without any evidentiary basis.

It is not an unreasonable supposition that people facing criminal charges may flee. But in Europe the decision not to extradite without death penalty assurances has not lead to any known exodus of violent criminals from one state to another. The respondent would exclude any comparison to Europe because of the stricter enforcement of national boundaries and its language differences which make it more difficult for a fugitive to flee. However, even if the relatively open border and the similarity in language invites flight from the United States to Canada, the reasons for flight are not necessarily dependent on a presumption that Canada will seek an Article 6 assurance before surrendering a fugitive. Flight may often be undertaken to avoid detection or trial. These are reasons enough to flee without an Article 6 assurance. It should be remembered that any fugitive must first escape from the authorities in the United States and then successfully enter Canada. With that accomplished the fugitive still has to avoid detection in this country.

The respondent alleges that Canada is seeking to prevent an influx of murderers in the future. An allegation that there will be a future danger can best be substantiated by past history. In this case the past history gives little indication of a flood of future problems. Article 6 has been in existence since 1976 yet only two instances are known of American murderers or alleged murderers fleeing to Canada: Kindler and Ng. In the case of Ng it was not surprising that he would attempt to flee to Calgary where his sister resided. There is simply no evidence that the existence of Article 6 has led to a flood of American murderers into Canada. Nor is there any reason to believe that this would occur if Ministers of Justice uniformly sought Article 6 assurances.

The respondent does not contend that Article 6 assurances should never be sought; rather it is said that the decision whether to make the request should be made on a case-by-case basis. However, once it is known that Canada will, on some occasions, seek assurances, there will be just as strong an incentive for American fugitives to flee to Canada as if assurances were uniformly sought. The difference between a requirement for a uniform request for assurances and an occasional request is a difference only in quantity.

The respondent's position cannot be said to rest on principle. The notion that certain individuals will arbitrarily be subjected to cruel and unusual punishment solely to serve as an apparent deterrent to American murderers contemplating flight to Canada cannot be accepted. Granting an arbitrary discretion to the Minister occasionally to seek Article 6 assurances cannot constitute a s. 1 justification. To say that it is justifiable to seek assurances only in some cases cannot meet the proportionality test required to establish a reasonable limit prescribed by law. This argument must be rejected.

Treaty Obligations

It was also argued that, in order to comply with its international commitments arising out of the *Treaty*, Canada should not uniformly seek Article 6 assurances. In essence the respondent argues that Kindler is an evil man. Regardless of the fact that he is subject to the death penalty, it is said, he should be extradited to the United States in order to fulfil Canada's obligations under the *Treaty*.

However, it must be remembered that, no matter how vile the killing, Kindler would not be executed in Canada had he committed the murder in this country. Further, Canada has committed itself in the international community to the recognition and support of human dignity and to the abolition of the death penalty. These commitments were not lightly made. They reflect Canadian values and principles. Canada cannot, on the one hand, give an international commitment to support the abolition of the death penalty and at the same time extradite a fugitive without seeking the very assurances contemplated by the *Treaty*. To do so would mean that Canada either was not honouring its international commitments or was applying one standard to the United States and another to other nations. Neither alternative is acceptable. Both would contravene Canadian values and commitments.

X SUMMARY

Capital punishment for murder is prohibited in Canada. Section 12 of the *Charter* provides that no one is to be subjected to cruel and unusual punishment. The death penalty is per se a cruel and unusual punishment. It is the ultimate denial of human dignity. No individual can be subjected to it in Canada. The decision of the Minister to surrender a fugitive who may be subject to execution without obtaining an assurance pursuant to Article 6 is one which can be reviewed under s. 12 of the *Charter*. It follows that the Minister must not surrender Kindler without obtaining the undertaking described in Article 6 of the *Treaty*. To do so would render s. 25 of the Extradition Act inconsistent with the *Charter* in its application to fugitives who would be subject to the death penalty.

This conclusion is based upon the historical reluctance displayed by jurors over the centuries to impose the death penalty; the provisions of s. 12 of the *Charter*; the decisions of this Court pertaining to that section; the pronouncements of this Court emphasizing the fundamental importance of human dignity; and the international statements and commitments made by Canada stressing the importance of the dignity of the individual and urging the abolition of the death penalty.

The *Charter*, the judicial pronouncements upon it and the international statements and commitments made by Canada reflect Canadian principles. The preservation of Canada's integrity and reputation in the international community require that extradition be refused unless an undertaking is obtained pursuant to Article 6. To take this position does not constitute an absolute refusal to extradite. It simply requires the requesting state to undertake that it will substitute a penalty of life imprisonment for the execution of the prisoner if that prisoner is found to be guilty of the crime.

La Forest, JL: – I have had the advantage of reading the reasons of my colleagues, Cory, J and McLachlin, J, and I am substantially in accord with McLachlin, J. I wish, however, to add reasons of my own ...

The judgment of L'Heureux-Dubé, Gonthier and McLachlin, JJ was delivered by

McLachlin, J: – This appeal and the companion case, *Reference Re Ng Extradition (Can.)*, raise the issue of whether the Minister of Justice can order the extradition of fugitives to the United States without obtaining an assurance from that country's authorities that the death penalty will not be imposed. Canadian law does not impose the death penalty, except for certain military offences. The question is whether our government is obliged, in all cases, to obtain assurances from the state requesting extradition that the death penalty will not be carried out by them. In my view the two cases raise the same issues. I have therefore chosen to deal with the cases together in the reasons for this appeal.

I THE PLACE OF EXTRADITION IN OUR SYSTEM OF JUSTICE

Extradition occupies a unique and important position in the structure of law enforcement ... Extradition is a practice which has deep historical roots in this country. The long border with the United States has meant that effective measures for the return of alleged criminals and other fugitives have been a necessary component of the administration of justice since before Confederation ...

While the extradition process is an important part of our system of criminal justice, it would be wrong to equate it to the criminal trial process. It differs from the criminal process in purpose and procedure and, most importantly, in the factors which render it fair. Extradition procedure, unlike the criminal procedure, is founded on the concepts of reciprocity, comity and respect for differences in other jurisdictions.

This unique foundation means that the law of extradition must accommodate many factors foreign to our internal criminal law. While our conceptions of what constitutes a fair criminal law are important to the process of extradition, they are necessarily tempered by other considerations.

Most importantly, our extradition process, while premised on our conceptions of what is fundamentally just, must accommodate differences between our system of criminal justice and the systems in place in reciprocating states. The simple fact is that if we were to insist on strict conformity with our own system, there would be virtually no state in the world with which we could reciprocate. Canada, unable to obtain extradition of persons who commit crimes here and flee elsewhere, would be the loser. For this reason, we require a limited but not absolute degree of similarity between our laws and those of the reciprocating state. We will not extradite for acts which are not offences in this country. We sign treaties only with states which can assure us that their systems of criminal justice are fair and offer sufficient procedural protections to accused persons. We permit our Minister to demand assurances relating to penalties where the Minister considers such a demand appropriate. But beyond these basic conditions precedent of reciprocity, much diversity is, of necessity, tolerated.

Thus this Court, per La Forest, J, recognized in *Canada v Schmidt*, [1987] 1 SCR 500 at pp. 522–23, that our extradition process does not require conformity with Canadian norms and standards. The foreign judicial system will not necessarily be considered fundamentally unjust because it operates without, for example, the presumption of innocence and other legal safeguards we demand in our own system of criminal justice.

For the same reasons, this Court has emphasized that we must avoid extraterritorial application of the guarantees in our *Charter* under the guise of ruling extradition procedures unconstitutional. As La Forest, J put it in *Schmidt*, at p. 518, "the *Charter* cannot be given extraterritorial effect to govern how criminal proceedings in a foreign country are to be conducted."

These considerations affect the applicability of the *Charter* in these cases and the determination of whether our extradition law offends the fundamental principles of justice which the *Charter* enshrines. It is to these issues that I now turn.

II WHICH SECTIONS OF THE CHARTER APPLY?

The *Charter* clearly applies to extradition matters, including the executive decision of the Minister that effects the fugitive's surrender ... The narrower question is what provisions of the *Charter* apply to extradition proceedings – s. 12, s. 7, or both?

In my view, the guarantee against cruel and unusual punishment found in s. 12 of the *Charter* does not apply to s. 25 of the Extradition

Act or to ministerial acts done pursuant to s. 25. The *Charter*'s reach is confined to the legislative and executive acts of Canadian governments. The question then is whether the decision to surrender a fugitive under s. 25 can constitute the imposition of cruel and unusual punishment by a Canadian government. In my view, it cannot. Neither s. 25 nor orders made under it impose or authorize punishment. The purpose and effect of the provision is to permit the fugitive to be extradited to face the consequences of the judicial process elsewhere. Any punishment which is imposed will be the result of laws and actions in that jurisdiction.

The fact that the Minister may seek assurances that the death penalty will not be demanded or enforced in the foreign jurisdiction does not change this situation. The punishment, if any, to which the fugitive is ultimately subject will be punishment imposed, not by the Government of Canada, but by the foreign state. To put it another way, the effect of any Canadian law or government act is too remote from the possible imposition of the penalty complained of to attract the attention of s. 12. To apply s. 12 directly to the act of surrender to a foreign country where a particular penalty may be imposed, is to overshoot the purpose of the guarantee and to cast the net of the *Charter* broadly in extraterritorial waters. Effective relations between different states require that we respect the differences of our neighbors and that we refrain from imposing our constitutional guarantees on other states under the guise of refusing to assist them (and extradition is a form of assistance) unless they conform to our *Charter*.

This Court has in the past refused to apply *Charter* guarantees to defects in proceedings outside the country. In *Schmidt*, supra, the majority, per La Forest, J, rejected the argument that s. 11 rights could serve as an independent ground of *Charter* review, since the fugitive had not been charged with a crime in Canada. La Forest, J examined the opening words of s. 11, which grant the various rights contained within it to "[a]ny person charged with an offence." In his view, the rights under s. 11 apply only to criminal proceedings conducted by the governments referred to in s. 32 of the *Charter*, i.e., Parliament and the provincial legislatures. To go beyond this would be to give the section extraterritorial effect: *Schmidt*, supra, at pp. 518–19 ...

This is not to say that extradition will never attract scrutiny on account of an objectionable procedure or punishment in the requesting country. While s. 12 of the *Charter* may not apply since the acts to which it is directed occur outside Canada, our law of extradition and the Minister's acts pursuant to that law do fall under the *Charter* and the general guarantees found in s. 7. They must meet the requirements of s. 7 of the *Charter* that no one be deprived of his or her life, liberty or security of person except in accordance with the fundamental principles of justice. Section 12 may affect the interpretation of s. 7 ... But s. 12 is not the only factor to be considered in determining the constitutionality of an extradition procedure. Just as the extradition process involves considerations which go beyond our internal criminal law, so must an assessment of its fundamental fairness take account of those factors.

III DOES SECTION 25 OF THE EXTRADITION ACT VIOLATE THE CHARTER?

A The Test under Section 7

To ascertain the applicable principles of fundamental justice under s. 7 of the *Charter*, we must look to the basic tenets of our judicial system and the system under scrutiny – in this case our extradition system ...

Thus the Court in defining the principles of fundamental justice relevant to the extradition draws upon the principles and policies underlying extradition law and procedure. Is the impugned provision consistent with extradition practices, viewed historically and in the light of current conditions? Does the provision serve the purposes and concerns which lie at the heart of extradition policy? The question is whether, based on these considerations, the power conferred by s. 25 to extradite without imposing a condition which would preclude capital punishment, is consonant with the fundamental conceptions of what is fair and right in Canadian society.

In recognition of the various and complex considerations which necessarily enter into the extradition process, this Court has developed a more cautious approach in the review of executive decisions in the extradition area, holding that judicial scrutiny should not be over-exacting. As the majority in *Schmidt* pointed out, the reviewing court must recognize that extradition involves interests and complexities with which judges may not be well equipped to deal (p. 523). The superior placement of the executive to assess and consider the competing interests involved in particular extradition cases suggests that courts should be especially careful before striking down provisions conferring discretion on the executive. · Thus the court must be "extremely circumspect" to avoid undue interference with an area where the executive is well placed to make these sorts of decisions: *Schmidt*, at p. 523. It must, moreover, avoid extraterritorial application of the *Charter*: *Schmidt*, supra.

The test for whether an extradition law or action offends s. 7 of the *Charter* on account of the penalty which may be imposed in the requesting state, is whether the imposition of the penalty by the foreign state "sufficiently shocks" the Canadian conscience: *Schmidt*, per La Forest, J, at p. 522 ... Thus the reviewing court must consider the offence for which the penalty may be prescribed, as well as the nature of the justice system in the requesting jurisdiction and the safeguards and guarantees it affords the fugitive. Other considerations such as comity and security within Canada may also be relevant to the decision to extradite and if so, on what conditions. At the end of the day, the question is whether the provision or action in question offends the Canadian sense of what is fair, right and just, bearing in mind the nature of the offence and the penalty, the foreign justice system and considerations of comity and security, and according due latitude to the Minister to balance the conflicting considerations.

In determining whether, bearing all these factors in mind, the extradition in question is "simply unacceptable," the judge must avoid imposing his or her own subjective views on the matter, and seek rather to objectively assess the attitudes of Canadians on the issue of whether the fugitive is facing a situation which is shocking and fundamentally unacceptable to our society.

B Applying the Section 7 Test to Section 25 of the Extradition Act

Section 25 of the Extradition Act is attacked because it permits the Minister to order the extradition of a fugitive to a state where he or she may, if convicted, face capital punishment. To allow this, it is said, is to offend the principles of fundamental justice. I do not agree. The question, I reiterate, is not whether the death penalty is constitutional, or even desirable in this country, but whether returning a fugitive to face it in another jurisdiction offends the Canadian sense of what is fair and right. The answer to this question turns on attitudes in this country toward the death penalty, and toward extradition, considered along with other factors such as the need to preserve an effective extradition policy and to deter American criminals fleeing to Canada as a "safe haven."

The practice of extradition, as has been noted, has deep roots in this country, and the practice per se has never been controversial. This reflects a strong belief that crime must not go unpunished. Fairness requires that alleged criminals be brought to justice and extradition is the normal means by which this is achieved when the offence was committed in a foreign jurisdiction.

When an accused person is to be tried in Canada there will be no conflict between our desire to see an accused face justice, and our desire that the justice he or she faces conforms to the most exacting standards which have emerged from our judicial system. However, when a fugitive must face trial in a foreign jurisdiction if he or she is to face trial at all, the two desires may come into conflict. In some cases the social consensus may clearly favour one of these values above the other, and the resolution of the conflict will be straightforward. This would be the case if, for instance, the fugitive faced torture on return to his or her home country. In many cases, though, neither value will be able to claim absolute priority; rather, one will serve to temper the other. There may be less unfairness in requiring an accused to face a judicial process which may be less than perfect according to our standards, than in having him or her escape the judicial process entirely.

For this reason, in considering the attitude of Canadians toward the death penalty we must consider not only whether Canadians consider it unacceptable, but whether they consider it to be so absolutely unacceptable that it is better that a fugitive not face justice at all rather than face the death penalty.

With this in mind I turn to consider Canadian attitudes to the death penalty. Much has been said and written in this country on the death penalty. While it is difficult to generalize about a subject so controverted, this much can be ventured. There is no clear consensus in this country that capital punishment is morally abhorrent and absolutely unacceptable.

Capital punishment was a component of Canadian criminal law from this country's colonial beginnings until it was abolished by Parliament in 1976. For most of that period the penalty was accepted with little question, although executions became increasingly rare in the latter years of its existence in Canada. The last execution in Canada was in 1962. Yet, while the death penalty has been formally abolished in this country, its possible return continues to be debated. In 1987, in response to persistent calls to bring back the death penalty, Members of Parliament conducted a free vote on a resolution to reinstate capital punishment. The result was a defeat of the motion, but the vote – 148 to 127 – fell far short of reflecting a broad consensus even among Parliamentarians.

To this day, capital punishment continues to apply to certain military offences. At the same time, public opinion polls continue to show considerable support among Canadians for the return of the death penalty for certain offences. Can it be said, in light of such indications as these, that the possibility that a fugitive might face the death penalty in California or Pennsylvania "shocks" the Canadian conscience or leads Canadians to conclude that the situation the fugitive faces is "simply unacceptable"? The case is far from plain.

When other considerations are brought into the picture, the matter becomes even less clear. In some cases, the unconditional surrender of a fugitive to face the death penalty may "sufficiently shock" the national conscience as to render it mandatory that the Minister seek an assurance that the penalty will not be imposed. But in other cases, this may not be so. These instances provide an example. Both fugitives are sought for crimes involving brutal, and in the case of Ng, multiple, murders. In both Pennsylvania and California the legal system is the product of democratic government, and includes the substantial protections of a constitutional rights document which dates back over two centuries. The variance between cases supports legislation which accords to the Minister a measure of discretion on the question of whether an assurance that the death penalty will not be imposed should be demanded.

The importance of maintaining effective extradition arrangements with other countries in a world where law enforcement is increasingly international in scope, likewise supports the ministerial discretion found in s. 25. As discussed above, an effective extradition process is founded on respect for sovereignty and differences in the judicial systems among various nations. Canada displays confidence in the fairness of the justice systems of other nations by entering into treaties with them. If Canada is to be assured of cooperation when it seeks extradition from states whose laws may not conform exactly to ours, it must be prepared to reciprocate.

Another relevant consideration in determining whether surrender without assurances regarding the death penalty would be a breach of fundamental justice is the danger that if such assurances were mandatory, Canada might become a safe haven for criminals in the United States seeking to avoid the death penalty. This is not a new concern. The facility with which American offenders can flee to Canada has been recognized since the nineteenth century ...

It was argued that there was little statistical evidence that criminals routinely cross the border into Canada. On the other hand, there must be few cases indeed where a person facing the death penalty in the United States is able to escape and make his or her way to the border.

What is certain is that this is precisely what happened in the two cases before the Court, and that the result endangered Canadians; Ng, arrested in the course of committing a crime here, shot and wounded a security guard. Given our long undefended common border with the United States, it is not unreasonable for the Minister, in deciding whether to seek the assurance that the death penalty will not be imposed, to consider the danger of encouraging other fugitives to do what Ng and Kindler did.

The fugitives, in suggesting that s. 25 should be struck down, in effect urge that the only constitutional law is one which absolutely forbids extradition in the absence of assurances that the death penalty will not be imposed. The foregoing discussion suggests that such a law might well prove too inflexible to permit the Government of Canada to deal with particular situations in a way which maintains the required comity with other nations, while at the same time going beyond what is required to conform to our fundamental sense of fairness. What is required is a law which permits the Minister, in the particular case before her, to act in a way which preserves the effectiveness of the extradition process, while conforming to the Canadian sense of what is fundamentally just. Section 25 does this; the less flexible alternative proposed by the fugitives would not.

I conclude that the fugitives have not established that the law which permits their extradition without assurances that the death penalty will not be applied in the requesting states offends the fundamental principles of justice enshrined in s. 7 of the *Charter*.

IV DID THE MINISTER'S ORDER OF UNCONDITIONAL EXTRADITION VIOLATE THE CHARTER?

I have concluded that s. 25 of the Extradition Act does not violate the *Charter*. The question remains whether the Minister, in the exercise of his discretion under s. 25, violated s. 7 of the Charter.

In making this determination, a court must remain sensitive to the dangers of over-zealous interference with the extradition system alluded to in *Canada v Schmidt*, per La Forest, J. These include the need not to compromise the integrity of the judicial process, the proper role of the Minister in assessing the competing considerations bearing on a particular extradition, and the need to ensure that the Court is not, in reality, giving the *Charter* extraterritorial effect. As La Forest, J put it in *Schmidt*, at p. 522:

I see nothing unjust in surrendering to a foreign country a person accused of having committed a crime there for trial in the ordinary way in accordance with the system for the administration of justice prevailing in that country simply because that system is substantially different from ours with different checks and balances. The judicial process in a foreign country must not be subjected to finicky evaluations against the rules governing the legal process in this country.

Given these concerns, judicial interference with decisions of the executive on matters of extradition must be limited. To quote La Forest, J in *Schmidt* (at p. 523) once again:

What has to be determined is whether or not, in the particular circumstances of the case, surrender of a fugitive for a trial offends against the basic demands of justice. In determining that issue, the courts must begin with the notion that the executive must first have determined that the general system for the administration of justice in the foreign country sufficiently corresponds to our concepts of justice to warrant entering into the treaty in the first place, and must have recognized that it too has a duty to ensure that its actions comply with constitutional standards. Blind judicial deference to executive judgment cannot, of course, be expected. The courts have the duty to uphold the Constitution. Nonetheless, this is an area where the executive is likely to be far better informed than the courts, and where the courts must be extremely circumspect so as to avoid interfering unduly in decisions that involve the good faith and honour of this country in its relations with other states. *In a word, judicial intervention must be limited to cases of real substance.* [Emphasis added]

In my view, the Minister's decisions in these cases do not violate s. 7. The crimes alleged to have been perpetrated by Ng in the State of California are among the worst imaginable. If the state's contention is correct, these were deliberate, cold-blooded murders of a series of random and innocent victims for no motive other than personal gratification. The crimes of which Kindler stands convicted are also brutal and shocking. The justice systems in California and Pennsylvania are founded on constitutional provisions not dissimilar to ours giving reasonable assurance of a fair trial. This leaves only the fact that at the end of the process, the fugitive may face the death penalty. But, as we have seen, that possibility alone in the context of the extradition system of this country is insufficient to render the decision unconstitutional. On the facts of these cases, where the reasons for extradition are compelling and the procedural guarantees in the reciprocating state high, I am satisfied that the Minister's decision did not infringe the *Charter*.

The Minister's decision to extradite without assurances that the death penalty would not be imposed or carried out is not out of step with the international community. The United Kingdom, for example, has twice extradited fugitives charged with murder to the United States without demanding such assurances ...

As for the other arguments, it has not been demonstrated that the Minister erred in law or exercised his discretion upon an inadmissible basis in either case ...

I conclude that it has not been established that the Minister's orders infringe the *Charter* or are otherwise invalid.

READING QUESTIONS ON *KINDLER*

1 How do you think Cover would evaluate the judgments?
2 Does the distinction between the majority and the minority here in part rest on how repugnant they found the death penalty?
3 Should it make a difference to you or to the judges that the fugitive slaves were morally justified in seeking their freedom while Kindler had been convicted of awful crimes?

John Finnis
"Natural Law and Legal Reasoning" (1994)

Finnis, the leading contemporary exponent of natural law theory, argues that natural law theory provides a sound basis for legal reasoning.

Moral reasoning, legal reasoning, and their interrelationships can scarcely be understood reflectively without attention to two different sources of ambiguity. The source is, in each case, well known: the distinction between reasons and feelings; and the distinction between doing (the shaping of one's own "existence" by one's choices) and making (the exercise of technique by activity on some form of "cultural" object or method). But the distinctions are commonly not well understood, and the traps they lay for the analysis of morality and adjudication are usually neglected.

I

We are animals, but intelligent. Our actions all have an emotional motivation, involve our feelings and imagination and other aspects of our bodiliness, and can all be observed (if only, in some cases, by introspection) as pieces of behaviour. But rationally motivated actions also have an intelligent motivation – seek to realize (protect, promote) an intelligible good.

So our purposes, the states of affairs we seek to bring about, typically have a double aspect: the goal which we imagine and which engages our feelings, and the intelligible benefit which appeals to our rationality by promising to instantiate, either immediately or instrumentally, some basic human good. While some of the purposes we employ intelligence to pursue may be motivated ultimately by nothing more than feeling, others are motivated ultimately by (an understanding of) a basic human good. The idiom in which "reason" refers to purposes – "the reason he did that," equivalent to "his purpose in doing that" – fails to mark this distinction. But none of common speech's related terms – "purpose," "goal," "intention" – is free from the same ambiguity. So I stipulate that when I speak of "reasons" in this chapter, I refer (except when discussing technical reasons) to reason(s) as giving ground for intelligent action motivated ultimately by a basic human good (more precisely, by the intelligible benefit promised by the instantiation of a basic good).

An account of basic reasons for action should not be rationalistic. Human flourishing is not to be portrayed in terms only of exercising capacities to reason. As animals, we are organic substances part of whose well-being is *bodily life*, maintained in health, vigour, and safety, and transmitted to new human beings. To regard human life as a basic reason for action is to understand it as a good in which indefinitely many beings can participate in indefinitely many ways, going far beyond any goal or purpose which anyone could envisage and pursue, but making sense of indefinitely many purposes, and giving rational support to indefinitely many goals.

This sense of "(basic) reason for action" holds for all the other basic human goods: *knowledge* of reality (including aesthetic appreciation of it); *excellence in work and play* whereby one transforms natural realities to express meanings and serve purposes; harmony *between individuals and groups* of persons (peace, neighbourliness, and friendship); *harmony between one's feelings and one's judgements and choices* (inner peace); *harmony between one's choices and judgements and one's behaviour* (peace of conscience and authenticity in the sense of consistency between one's self and its expression); and *harmony between oneself and the wider reaches of reality* including the reality constituted by the world's dependence on *a more-than-human source of meaning and value.*

Such a statement of the basic human goods entails an account of human nature. But it does not presuppose such an account. It is not an attempt to deduce reasons for action from some preexisting theoretical conception of human nature. Such an attempt would vainly defy the logical truth (well respected by the ancients) that "ought" cannot be deduced from "is" – a syllogism's conclusion cannot contain what is not in its premises. Rather, a full account of human nature can only be given by one who understands the human goods practically, i.e., as reasons for choice and action, reasons which make full sense of supporting feelings and spontaneities.

An account of practical reasonableness can be called a theory of "natural law" because practical reasoning's very first principles are those basic reasons which identify the basic human goods as ultimate reasons for choice and action – reasons for actions which will instantiate and express human nature precisely because participating in those goods, i.e., instantiating (actualizing, realizing) those ultimate aspects of human flourishing.

II

To the extent that legal reasoning derives from and participates in practical reasonableness, a sound theory of legal reasoning must differ from some theories now current ...

But, in reality, it is the diversity of *rationally* appealing human goods which makes free choice both possible and frequently necessary. Like every other term concerning human activity, "choice" is afflicted, in common idiom, by ambiguities originating particularly in the distinction between reason and feeling. In its strong, central sense, free choice is the adoption of one amongst two or more rationally appealing and incompatible, alternative options, such that nothing but the choosing itself settles which option is chosen and pursued. Many aspects of individual and social life, and many individual and social obligations, are structured by choice between rationally appealing options whose rational appeal can be explained only in terms, ultimately, of basic human opportunities understood to be objectively good (though variously realizable). No sound sense can be made of "objectivity" and "truth," here or elsewhere, otherwise than in terms of rational judgement, open to all relevant questions.

But if the basic human goods, for all their objectivity and truth, open up so much to free choice, what can be the basis for identifying choices which, though rational, ought to be rejected because unreasonable, wrong, immoral?

Moral thought is simply rational thought at full stretch, integrating emotions and feelings but *undeflected* by them. Practical rationality's fundamental principle is: take as a premise at least one of the basic reasons for action, and follow through to the point at which you some-how bring about the instantiation of that good in action. Do not act pointlessly. The fundamental principle of moral thought is simply the demand to be fully rational: in so far as it is in your power, allow nothing but the basic reasons for action to shape your practical thinking as you find, develop, and use your opportunities to pursue human flourishing through your chosen actions. Be entirely reasonable. Aristotle's phrase *orthos logos*, and his later followers' *recta ratio*, right reason, should simply be understood as "unfettered reason," reason undetected by emotions and feelings. And so undeflected reason, and the morally good will, are guided by the first moral principle: that one ought to choose (and otherwise will) those and only those possibilities whose willing is compatible with a will towards the fulfilment of all human persons in all the basic goods, towards the ideal of integral human fulfilment.

Take a simple, paradigmatic form of immorality. Emotion may make one wish to destroy or damage the good life in someone one hates, or the good of knowledge; so one kills or injures, or deceives, that person just out of feelings of aversion. It is immoral, because hereabouts there is a general, so to speak methodological, moral principle intermediate between the most basic principles of practical reason (the basic goods or reasons for action, and the first moral principle) and particular moral norms against killing or lying. This intermediate moral principle, which some call a mode of responsibility, will exclude meeting injury with injury, or responding to one's own weakness or setbacks with self-destructiveness.

Perhaps more immediately relevant to political and legal theory is the intermediate moral principle requiring that one act fairly: that one not limit one's concern for basic human goods simply by one's feelings of self-preference or preference for those who are near and dear. Fair-ness (and its paradigmatic formulation in the Golden Rule) does not exclude treating different persons differently; it requires only that the differential treatment be justified either by inevitable limits on one's action or by intelligible requirements of the basic goods themselves. I shall say more (VII below) about the legitimate role of feelings in making fair choices in which one prioritizes goods (or instantiations of basic goods) by one's feelings without prioritizing persons simply by feelings.

There are other intermediate moral principles. Very important to the structuring of legal thought is the principle which excludes acting against a basic reason by choosing to destroy or damage any basic good in any of its instantiations in any human person (VI below). A basic human good always is a reason for action and always gives a reason *not* to choose to destroy, damage, or impede some instantiation of that good; but since the instantiations of human good at stake in any morally significant choice are not commensurable by *reason* prior to choice, there can never be a sufficient reason not to take that reason-not-to as decisive for choice. Only emotional factors such as desire or aversion could motivate a choice rejecting it.

Of course, the basic reasons for action, as the phrase suggests, present one with many reasons for choice and action, many reasons to ... And since one is finite, one's choice of any purpose, however far-reaching, will inevitably have as a side-effect some negative impact on (minimally, the non-realization of) other possible instantiations of this and other basic goods. In that sense, every choice is "against some basic reason." But only as a side-effect. In the choices which are excluded by the intermediate moral principle now in question, the damaging or destruction or impeding of an instantiation of a basic good – the harming of some basic aspect of someone's existence and well-being – is chosen, as a means, i.e., *as part* of the description of the option adopted by choice. Whereas the first intermediate principle excludes making such damage or destruction one's end, the present principle excludes making it one's means. The concepts of (the) end and means (defining an option) come together in the conception so fundamental to our law: intention.

III

Even so rapid a sketch begins to make clear that a theory of natural law, while primarily a theory of human goods as principles of practical reasoning, must accommodate within its account – as practical reasoning itself must take into account – certain features of our world.

Among these features are the reality of free choice, and the significance of choices as lasting in the character of the chooser beyond the time of the behaviour which executes them; and the distinction between what is chosen as end or means (i.e., as intended) and what is foreseen and accepted as a side-effect (i.e., an unintended effect). Again, there are such basic facts as that which Robert Nozick overlooked in declaring that (virtually) everything comes into the world already attached to someone having an entitlement over it – the reality, being, on the contrary, that the natural resources from which everything made has been made pre-exist all entitlements and "came into the world" attached to nobody in particular; the world's resources are fundamentally common and no theory of entitlements can rightly appropriate any resource to one person so absolutely as to negate that original commonality of the world's stock.[1]

A further feature of the world to be accommodated by a sound natural law theory is the distinction between the orders of reality with which human reason is concerned. In attending to this set of distinctions, we shall be noticing the second of the two sources of ambiguity I mentioned at the outset.

Almost any interesting human state of affairs instantiates the four orders of reality with which human reason is concerned. Consider, for example, a lecture. (1) One hears the *sounds* produced by the speaker's vocal chords: there is an order of nature which we in no way establish by our understanding but which we can investigate by our understanding, as in the natural sciences or (as right now) in metaphysics. (2) One hears the speaker's *expositions, arguments, and explanations* and brings one's understanding into line with them (if only to the extent necessary to reject them as mistaken): there is an order which one can bring into one's own enquiries, understanding, and reasoning, the order studied by logic, methodology, and epistemology. (3) One hears *the lecturer*, who (like the audience) is freely engaging in an activity and thereby participating in a human relationship: there is an order which one can bring into one's own dispositions, choices, and actions – one's *praxis*, one's doing, one's *Existenz* – the "existential" order studied by some parts of psychology, by biography and the history of human affairs, and by moral and political philosophy. (4) One hears the *English language* and statements ordered by an expository or rhetorical technique, making and decoding the formalized symbols of a language and the less formalized but still conventional symbols and expressive routines of a cultural form and technique: the order one can intelligently bring into matter which is subject to our power, so as to make objects such as phonemes, words, poems, boats, software, ballistic missiles and their inbuilt trajectories – the order of *poiesis*, of making, of culture – studied in the arts and technologies, and in linguistics and rhetoric. (Corresponding to these four orders are four irreducibly distinct senses of "hearing.")

Almost every form of reductionist deformation in social (say, political) theory, and many destructive misunderstandings in almost every aspect of, say, legal theory, can be traced to oversight of the complexities and ambiguities created by the irreducible distinctions between these four orders – whose irreducibility to one another is disguised by the fact that each in a sense includes all the others.

The distinction particularly relevant to legal theory is that between the third (existential, moral) order and the fourth (cultural, technical) order. Few morally significant choices can be carried out without employing some culturally formed technique; and no technique can be put to human use without some morally significant choice. But every technique has an integral, fourth-order intelligibility which can be fully explicated without referring to the morally significant choices by which it might be put to use and the moral principles of practical reasonableness pertinent to such choices.

Amongst the ambiguities created by the distinctions between the third and fourth orders is the ambiguity of the term "rational choice." It has (at least) three important, distinct senses:

1 choice which is fully reasonable, complies with all the requirements of practical reasonableness, and is thus morally upright;
2 choice which is rationally motivated in the sense that its object has been shaped by practical intelligence and has rational appeal, even if it is in some respect(s) motivated ultimately by feeling rather than reason, feelings which have to some extent fettered and instrumentalized reason, and is therefore unreasonable and immoral, though rational;
3 decision and action which is technically (technologically) right, i.e., is identifiable according to some art or technique as the most effective for attaining the relevant technical objective – typically, the decision for which there is, within this technique (e.g., this game), a dominant reason which can be commensurated with the reasons for alternative options and which includes all that these offer and some more.

Sense 3 is the only sense in which economists and exponents of "game" or "decision" theory commonly use the phrase "rational choice." I have used the terms "rational" (and its cognates) and "choice," in Section II above, in sense 2 (or senses 1 and 2) but never in sense 3. Here is rich opportunity for misunderstanding. In senses 1 and 2, what makes rational choice necessary is the incommensurability of the intelligible goods and bads involved in alternative options; if options were fully commensurable, alternatives could be identified as unqualifiedly superior and inferior, and the unqualifiedly inferior would lose its rational appeal, fall out of rational deliberation; rational choice would be unnecessary and, in a significant sense, impossible (VI below). But in sense 3, rational choice is possible only when one option can be identified as unqualifiedly superior.

IV

Legal reasoning and rationality has, I suggest, its distinctiveness and its peculiar elusiveness because, in the service of a third-order, existential, moral, and chosen purpose – of living together in a just order of fair and right relationships – there has been and is being constructed a fourth-order object, "the law" (as in "the law of England"). This is a vastly complex cultural object, comprising a vocabulary with many artfully assigned meanings, rules identifying permitted and excluded arguments and decision, and correspondingly very many technical routines or processes (such as pleading, trial, conveyancing, etc.) constituted and regulated according to those formulae, their assigned meanings, and the rules of argument and decision.

This cultural object, constructed or (as we say) posited by creative human choices, is an instrument, a technique adopted for a moral purpose, and adopted because there is no other available way of agreeing over significant spans of time about precisely how to pursue the moral project well. Political authority in all its manifestations, including legal institutions, is a technique for doing without unanimity in making social choices – where unanimity would almost always be unattainable or temporary – in order to secure practical (near-)unanimity about how to coordinate the actions (including forbearances) of members of the society.

Legal reasoning, then, is (at least in large part) technical reasoning – not moral reasoning. Like all technical reasoning, it is concerned to achieve a particular purpose, a definite state of affairs attainable by efficient dispositions of means to end. The particular end here is the resolution of disputes (and other allegations of misconduct) by the provision of a directive sufficiently definite and specific to identify one party as right (in-the-right) and the other as wrong (not-in-the-right).

Hence the law's distinctive devices: defining terms, and specifying rules, with sufficient and necessarily artificial clarity and definiteness to establish the "bright lines" which make so many real-life legal questions *easy questions*. Legal definitions and rules are to provide the citizen, the legal adviser, and the judge with an algorithm for deciding as many questions as possible – in principle every question – yes (or no), this course of action would (or would not) be lawful; this arrangement is valid; this contract is at an end; these losses are compensable in damages and those are not; and so forth. As far as it can, the law is to provide sources of reasoning – statutes and statute-based rules, common law rules, and customs – capable of ranking (commensurating) alternative dispute-resolutions as right or wrong, and thus better and worse.

Lawyers' tools of trade – their ability to find and use the authoritative sources – are means in the service of a purpose sufficiently definite to constitute a technique, a mode of technical reasoning. The purpose, again, is the unequivocal resolution of every dispute (and other question for just decision) which can be in some way foreseen and provided for. Still, this quest for certainty, for a complete set of uniquely correct answers, is itself in the service of a wider good which, like all basic human goods, is not reducible to a definite goal but is rather an open-ended good which persons and their communities can participate in without ever capturing or exhausting the good of just harmony. This good is a moral good just in so far as it is itself promoted and respected as one aspect of the ideal of integral human fulfilment. As a moral good its implications are specified by all the moral principles which could bear upon it.

Thus there emerges the tension around which Ronald Dworkin's work on legal reasoning revolves.

V

Dworkin seeks to resolve the tension between law's and legal reasoning's character as a culturally specified technique of attaining predictable answers to problems of social co-ordination and its character as, in each of its decisive legislative, executive and judicial moments, a moral act participating in justice (or injustice). His attempted resolution fails, I think, to grasp the real nature and implications of that tension.

In judicial reasoning as portrayed by Dworkin, two criteria of judgement are in use; as we shall see, there is between these two criteria a kind of incommensurability analogous to the incommensurability between the human goods involved in morally significant, rationally motivated choices. One of these criteria or dimensions belongs to what I have called the third (moral) order or rationality, and the other to the fourth (technical) order. The first dimension Dworkin calls "fit": coherence with the existing legal "materials" created by past political decisions, i.e., with legislation and authoritative judicial decision (precedent). The second dimension he now calls "justification."[2] And he tries to show that a *uniquely* correct ("the right") answer is available in "most" hard cases.

One can deny this last thesis without committing oneself to any scepticism about the objectivity of human good(s) or of correct judgements about right and wrong. Nor need one's denial be predicated on the popular argument which Dworkin is rightly concerned to scorn and demolish – the argument that disagreement is endemic and ineradicable. (For disagreement is a mere fact about people, and is logically irrelevant to the merits of any practical or other interpretative claim.) Nor need a denial of Dworkin's one-right-answer thesis rest on the fact that no one has the "superhuman" powers of Dworkin's imaginary judge.

Even an ideal human judge, with superhuman powers, could not sensibly search for a uniquely correct answer to a hard case (as lawyers in sophisticated legal systems use the term "hard case"). For in such a case, the search for the one right answer is practically incoherent and senseless, in much the same way as a search for the English novel which is "most romantic and shortest" (or "funniest and best," or "most English and most profound").

Assuming with Dworkin that there are two "dimensions" or criteria of judicial assessment, we can say that a case for judicial decision is hard (not merely novel) when not only is there more than one answer which is not in evident violation of an applicable rule, but also the answers which are in that sense available can be ranked in different orders along each of the relevant criteria of evaluation: for novels, their brevity and their Englishness (or humour, or profundity, or ...); for judicial judgements their fit with previous legislation and precedent, and – let us grant (not concede) to Dworkin – their *inherent* moral soundness. In such a case there is found what theorists of "rational choice" (in sense 3) call "intransitivity," a phenomenon which such

theories confessedly cannot really handle: solution A is better than solution B on the scale of legal fit, and B than C, but C is better than A on
the scale of "moral soundness"; so there is no sufficient reason to declare A, or B, or C the overall "best judicial decision." If the rank order
was the same on both dimensions, of course, the case was not a hard
one at all, and the legal system already had what one always desires of
it: a uniquely correct answer.

In his works before *Law's Empire*, Dworkin tried to overcome this
incommensurability of the dimensions or criteria of assessment by proposing a kind of lexicographical (in Rawls's terminology "lexical") ordering. Candidates for the "best account" of the law of England in 1980
must fit the then existing English legal materials adequately, and of
those which satisfy this threshold criterion, that which ranks highest on
the other criterion (moral soundness) is overall, absolutely, "the best,"
even though it fits less well than (an)other(s). But this solution was
empty, since he identified no criteria, however sketchy or "in principle,"
for specifying when fit is "adequate," i.e., for locating the threshold (of
fit) beyond which the criterion of soundness would prevail. (It was like
being told to search for the funniest novel among those that are "short
enough.") Presumably, candidates for the one right answer to the question "When is fit adequate?" would themselves be ranked in terms both
of fit and of soundness. An infinite regress, of the vicious sort which
nullifies purported rational explanations, was well under way.

In *Law's Empire*, Dworkin abandons the simple picture of a lexical
ordering between these two criteria. We are left with little more than a
metaphor: "balance" – as in "the general balance of political virtues"
embodied in competing interpretations or accounts of the law (of
England (in 1990)). But in the absence of any metric which could
commensurate the different criteria, the instruction to balance (or, earlier to weigh) can legitimately mean no more than "Bear in mind,
conscientiously, all the relevant factors, and *choose*." Or, in the legal
sphere, "Hear the arguments, sitting in the highest court, and then
vote."

In understanding practical rationality in all its forms, one should
notice a feature of the experience of choice. *After* one has chosen, the
factors favouring the chosen option will usually seem to outweigh,
overbalance, those favouring the rejected alternative options. The option chosen – to do *x*, to adopt rule or interpretation *y* – will commonly
seem (to the person who chose, if not to onlookers) to have a supremacy, a unique rightness. But this sense of the supremacy, the rightness

of one (the chosen) option will not alter the truth that the choice was not rationally determined, i.e., was not guided by an identification of one option or answer as "the right one." (And this does not mean that it was irrational; it was between rationally appealing options.) Rather, the choice established the "right" answer – i.e., established it in, and by reference ultimately to, the dispositions and sentiments of the chooser. When the choice in a hard case is made by (the majority in the) highest appeal court (a mere brute fact), the unique rightness of the answer is established not only by and for the attitude of those who have chosen it, but also for the legal system or community for which it has thus been authoritatively decided upon, and laid down as or in a *rule*.

VI

The incommensurability of Dworkin's two dimensions or criteria for judicial judgement has significant similarities to the incommensurability of the goods (and reasons) at stake in alternative options available for morally significant choice in any context. The moral and political rationality which underpins (though does not exhaust) legal rationality cannot be understood without an understanding of incommensurability.

Incommensurability, the absence of any *rationally* identified metric for measuring, or scale for "weighing," the goods and bads in issue, is much more pervasive and intense than one would imagine from the simple Dworkinian picture of legal reasoning along the two dimensions of legal fit and moral soundness. One meets incommensurability in humble contexts, such as having to choose between going to a lecture, reading a good book, going to the cinema, and talking to friends. One meets it in relation to grand social choices, such as whether to reject or renounce a nuclear deterrent: exploring such a choice will amply illustrate the impotence of all forms of aggregative reasoning towards morally significant choice – choice outside the purely technical or technological task of identifying the most cost-efficient means to a single limited goal.

The reasoning most characteristic of technical rationality is "cost-benefit analysis," comparing the costs of alternative options with the probable benefits. This can be carried through with full rationality only when (*a*) goals are well defined, (*b*) costs can be compared with some definite unit (e.g., money), (*c*) benefits can also be quantified in a way that renders them commensurable with one another, and (*d*) differences among means, other than their efficiency, measurable costs, and measurable benefits, are not counted as significant. None of these conditions is fulfilled in moral reasoning.

Indeed, morally significant choice would be unnecessary and, with one qualification, impossible if one option could be shown to be *the best* on a single scale which, as all aggregative reasoning does, ranks options in a single, transitive order. If there were a reason (for doing *x*) which some rational method of comparison (e.g., aggregation of goods and bads in a complete cost-benefit analysis) identified as rationally preferable, the alternative reason (against doing *x*), being thus identified as rationally inferior, would cease to be rationally appealing in that situation of choice. The reason thus identified as dominant, as unqualifiedly preferable, and the option favoured by that reason, would be rationally unopposed. There would remain *no choice* of the sort that moral theories seek to guide. For, the morally significant choices which moral theories seek to guide are between alternative options which have rational appeal.

To identify options as morally wrong does not entail identifying one option as (morally) uniquely right. Indeed, even when one option can be judged the only (morally) right option for a given person (a moral judgement which only that person's prior commitments and dispositions will make possible), this entails only that the alternative, immoral options are not fully reasonable. It in no way entails that these alternative options are irrational, i.e., lack rational appeal in terms of genuine, intelligible human goods which would be secured by the immoral options and sacrificed by the morally upright option. Thus rationally motivated, morally significant choice remains possible – indeed characterstic of the human situation – even in the perhaps relatively uncommon case of the moral "one right answer (option)."

But when technical reasonings identify one option as uniquely correct, i.e., as dominant, they do so by demonstrating that it offers *all that the other options offer and some more*; it is unqualifiedly better. The other options then lack *rational* appeal. Such deliberation ends not in choice – in the rich, central sense of that ambiguous term – but rather in insight, "decision" (not choice, but rationally compelled judgement), and action.

One of morality's principles, I have said (II above), excludes acting against a basic reason by choosing to destroy or damage any basic human good in any of its instantiations in any human person. For these instantiations are nothing other than aspects of human persons, present and future, and human persons cannot rationally be reduced to the commensurable factors captured by technical reasoning. These instantiations of human good constitute *reasons against* any option which involves choosing (intending) to destroy or damage any of them. The significance of the incommensurability of goods involved in such morally significant options is that no reason *for* such an option can be rationally preferable to such a reason against. And the same is true of the *reason against* an option which is constituted by that option's unfairness.

What, it may be asked, are the grounds for regulating one's choice according to the reason-*against* rather than by any reason *for*? Once again, they cannot be stated without reference to some features of our world, the fundamental context of all human choosing. Options which there are reasons *for* my choosing are infinite in number. Being finite, I simply cannot do everything, cannot choose every option for which there are reasons. But I can refrain from doing anything; I can respect every serious reason-against. So, an unconditional or absolute affirmative duty (duty *to* ...) would impose an impossible burden and be irrational; but negative moral absolutes (duties *not* to ...), if correctly stated with attention to the distinction between intention and side-effect, can all be adhered to in any and every circumstance.

Moreover, many human goods (e.g., the lives of others) are gifts, givens, which we can destroy or damage, but cannot create. Here, too, is a ground of the intelligible asymmetry between reasons-for and reasons-against. Nor does the priority, within their ambit, of reasons-against give morality as a whole a negative case, or elevate "moral purity" to the rank of a supreme goal. The first limb of practical reason's first principle remains that human good is to be done and pursued. Its second limb is that evil is to be avoided. But a full respect for and adherence to the absolute duties to forbear from evil leaves open a wide field of (more numerous) individual and social positive responsibilities.

VII

The moral absolutes give legal reasoning its backbone: the exclusion of intentional killing, of intentional injury to the person and even the economic interests of the person, of deliberate deception for the sake of securing desired results, of enslavement which treats a human person as an object of a lower rank of being than the autonomous human subject. These moral absolutes, which *are* rationally determined and essentially determinate, constitute the most basic human rights, and the foundations of the criminal law and the law of intentional torts or delicts, not to mention all the rules, principles, and doctrines which penalize intentional deception, withdraw from it all direct legal support, and exclude it from the legal process.

The rationality of all these moral and legal norms depends upon the incommensurability of the human goods and bads at stake in morally significant options for choice. This incommensurability has further implications of importance to legal reasoning.

The core of the moral norm of fairness is the Golden Rule: "Do to others as you would have them do to you; do not impose on others what you would not want to be obliged by them to accept." This has two aspects. First: practical rationality, outside the limited technical context of competitive games, includes a rational norm of impartiality. This norm excludes not all forms and corresponding feelings of preference for oneself and those who are near and dear, but rather all those forms of preference which are motivated only by desires, aversions, or hostilities which do not correspond to intelligible aspects of the real *reasons* for action, the basic human goods realizable in the lives of other human beings as in the lives of oneself or those close to one's heart.

The Golden Rule's second aspect is this. Although fairness is thus a rational norm requiring one to transcend all rationally unintegrated feelings, its concrete application in personal life presupposes a commensuration of benefits and burdens which reason is impotent to commensurate. For, to apply the Golden Rule one must know what burdens one considers too great to accept. And this knowledge, constituting a pre-moral commensuration, cannot be by rational commensuration. Therefore, it can only be one's intuitive awareness, one's discernment, of one's own differentiated *feelings* towards various goods and bads as concretely remembered, experienced, or imagined. This, I repeat, is not a rational and objective commensuration of goods and bads; but once established in one's feelings and identified in one's self-awareness, it enables one to measure one's options by a rational and objective standard of inter-personal impartiality.

Analogously, in the life of a community, the preliminary commensuration of rationally incommensurable factors is accomplished not by rationally determined judgements, but by *decisions* (choices). Is it fair to impose on others the risks inherent in driving at more than 10 m.p.h.? Yes, in our community, since our community has by custom and law *decided* to treat those risks and harms as *not too great*. Have we a rational critique of a community which decided to limit road traffic to 10 m.p.h. and to accept all the economic and other costs of that decision? Or not to have the institution of trusts, or constructive trusts? No, we have no rational critique of such a community. But we do have a rational critique of someone who drives at 60 m.p.h. but who, when struck by another, complains and alleges that the mere fact that the other's speed exceeded 10 m.p.h. established that other's negligence. Or of someone willing to receive the benefits (e.g., the tax benefits) of trusts but not willing to accept the law's distinction between trust and contract in his bankruptcy.

And, in general, we have a rational critique of one who accepts the benefits of this and other communal decisions but rejects the burdens as they bear on him and those in whom he feels interested. In short, the decision to permit road traffic to proceed faster than 10 m.p.h., or to define trusts just as English law does, was rationally underdetermined. (That is not to say that it was or is wholly unguided by reason; the good of human bodily life and integrity is a genuine reason always practically relevant, and the rational demand for consistency with our individual and communal tolerance or intolerance of other – non-traffic - threats to that good provides some rational criteria for decision. And similarly with the trust, whose rationality defied many legislative attempts, for centuries, to suppress this peculiar double ownership.) Still, though rationally underdetermined, the decision to permit fast-moving traffic, once made, provides an often fully determinate rational standard for treating those accused of wrongful conduct or wrongfully inflicting injury. Likewise with trusts, in bankruptcy.

In the working of the legal process, much turns on the principle – a principle of fairness – that litigants (and others involved in the process) should be treated by judges (and others with power to decide) *impartially*, in the sense that they are as nearly as possible to be treated by each judge as they would be treated by every other judge. It is this above all, I believe, that drives the law towards the artificial, the *techne* rationality of laying down and following a set of positive norms identifiable as far as possible simply by their "sources" (i.e., by the fact of their enactment or other constitutive event) and applied so far as possible according to their publicly stipulated meaning, itself elucidated with as little as possible appeal to considerations which, because not controlled by facts about sources (constitutive events), are inherently likely to be appealed to differently by different judges. This drive to insulate legal from moral reasoning can never, however, be complete.

Incommensurability has further, related implications for legal reasoning. It rules out the proposed technique of legal reasoning known as Economic Analysis of Law. For it is central to that technique that every serious question of social order can be resolved by aggregating the overall net good promised by alternative options, in terms of a simple commensurating factor (or maximand), namely wealth measured in terms of the money which relevant social actors would be willing and able to pay to secure their preferred option. Equally central to Economic Analysis is the assumption, or thesis, that there is no difference of principle between buying the right to inflict injury intentionally and buying the right not to take precautions which would eliminate an equivalent number of injuries caused accidentally. A root and branch critique of Economic Analysis of Law will focus on these two features of it.

Less fundamental critiques, such as Dworkin's (helpful and worth while though it is), leave those features untouched. Indeed, Dworkin's own distinction between rights and collective goals (the latter being proposed by Dworkin as the legitimate province of legislatures) is a distinction which uncritically assumes that collective goals can rationally be identified and preferred to alternatives by aggregation of value, without regard to principles of distributive fairness and other aspects of justice – principles which themselves constitute rights, and which cannot be traded off, according to some rational methodology, against measurable quantities of value.

VIII

In sum: much academic theory about legal reasoning greatly exaggerates the extent to which reason can settle what is greater good and lesser evil. At the same time, such theory minimizes the need for authoritative sources. Such sources, so far as they are clear, and respect the few absolute moral rights and duties, are to be respected as the only reasonable basis for judicial reasoning and decision, in relation to those countless issues which do not directly involve those absolute rights and duties. A natural law theory in the classical tradition makes no pretence that natural reason can identify the one right answer to those countless questions which arise for the judge who finds the sources unclear.

In the classical view, expressed by Aquinas with a clear debt to Aristotle, there are many ways of going wrong and doing wrong; but in very many, perhaps most situations of personal and social life there are a number of incompatible *right* (i.e., not-wrong) options. Prior personal choice(s) or authoritative social decision-making can greatly reduce this variety of options for the person who has made that commitment or the community which accepts that authority. Still, those choices and decisions, while rational and reasonable, were in most cases not required by reason. They were not preceded by any rational judgement that *this* option is *the* right answer, or the best solution.

NOTES

1 Robert Nozick, *Anarchy, State and Utopia* (Oxford: Blackwell, 1974), 160.
2 See Ronald Dworkin, *Law's Empire* (Cambridge, Mass.: Harvard University Press, 1986), 255. This term seems confusing, since both dimensions are, on his account, necessary to justify a judicial decision. His previous name for the second dimension (inherent substantive moral), "soundness," better: see Dworkin, *Taking Rights Seriously* (Cambridge, Mass.: Harvard University Press, 1978), 340–1. Still, the labels adopted by Dworkin have the merit of making it clear that fit, although relevant precisely because a necessary condition for securing certain moral and political goods and requirements such as community and integrity, is itself a matter of historical fact, namely, the facts about what judgements and decisions have been made by the relevant institutions in a given span of time, and the extent to which some actual or hypothetical judgement or decision corresponds in content to earlier judgements and decisions.

READING QUESTIONS ON FINNIS

1 Do you find Finnis's account of the incommensurability of values a convincing basis for his critique of Dworkin?
2 How does Finnis's critique of Dworkin relate to Hart's account of discretion? If there is a relationship, does this bring Finnis's natural law project closer to positivism than to Dworkin's understanding of the moral basis of law?

3

Feminist Approaches to the Rule of Law

Feminist scholars and lawyers have made important contributions to legal thought and legal change in the past two decades. There are many different strands in contemporary feminist thought about law. Some feminists are critical of the detachment to which law claims to aspire, others of its implicit bias against women, still others of its emphasis on rights and the separateness of persons rather than their connectedness. These selections are not meant to be representative of all of these trends. Instead, they touch on some of the issues already considered about the general relation between morality and the rule of law. Later sections include feminist engagements with particular issues.

Catharine A. MacKinnon
"The Liberal State" (1989)

MacKinnon sees the law as a potentially powerful medium of progressive change, one that has historically not been in women's hands and has largely sided against women.

The difference between the judges and Sir Isaac [Newton] is that a mistake by Sir Isaac in calculating the orbit of the earth would not send it spinning around the sun with an increased velocity... while if the judges... come to a wrong result, it is none the less law.
– John Chipman Gray (1909)

Political revolutions aim to change political institutions in ways that those institutions themselves prohibit.
– Thomas Kuhn (1962)

Feminism has no theory of the state. Just as feminism has a theory of power but lacks a specific theory of its state form, marxism has a theory of value which (through the organization of work in production) becomes class analysis, but also a problematic theory of the state. Marx himself did not address the state much more explicitly than he addressed women. Women were substratum, the state epiphenomenon. He termed the state "a concentrated expression of economics," a reflection of the real action, which occurred elsewhere; it was "the official résumé of society," a unity of ruptures; it, or its "executive," was "but a committee for managing the common affairs of the whole bourgeoisie." Engels frontally analyzed women and the state, and together. But just as he presumed the subordination of women in every attempt to reveal its roots, he presupposed something like the state, or statelike society, in every attempt to find its origins.

Marx tended to use the term *political* narrowly to refer to the state or its laws, criticizing as exclusively political interpretations of the state's organization or behavior which took them as sui generis, as if they were to be analyzed apart from economic conditions. He termed "political power" as embodied in the modern state "the official expression of antagonism in civil society." Changes on this level could, therefore, emancipate the individual only within the framework of the existing social order, termed "civil society." Revolution on this level was "partial, merely political revolution." Accordingly, until recently, most marxist theory has tended to consider as political that which occurs between classes and the state as the instrument of the economically dominant class. That is, it has interpreted the political in terms of the marxist view of social inequality and the state in terms of the class that controls it. The marxist theory of social inequality has been its theory of politics. The state as such was not seen as furthering particular interests through its form. This theory does not so much collapse the state into society (although it goes far in that direction) as conceive the state as determined by the totality of social relations of which the state is one determined and determining part – without specifying which, or how much, is which.

After 1848, having seen the bourgeoisie win revolutions but then not exercise state power directly, Marx tried to understand how states could plainly serve the bourgeoisie's interest yet not represent it as a class. His attempts form the basis for much contemporary marxist work that has tried to grasp the specificity of the institutional state: how it wields class power or operates within class strictures or supplements or moderates class rule or transforms class society or responds to approach by a left aspiring to rulership or other changes. While much liberal theory has seen the state as emanating power, and traditional marxism has seen the state as expressing power constituted elsewhere, recent marxism, much of it structuralist, has tried to analyze state power as specific to the state as a form, yet integral to a determinate social whole understood in class terms.

Politics becomes "an autonomous phenomenon that is constrained by economics but not reducible to it." This state is found "relatively autonomous," that is, the state, expressed through its functionaries, has a definite class character, is definitely capitalist or socialist, but also has its own interests, which are to some degree independent of those of the ruling class and even of the class structure. The state as such, in this view, has a specific power and interest, termed "the political," such that class power, class interest expressed by and in the state, and state behavior, though inconceivable in isolation from one another, are nevertheless not linearly linked or strictly coextensive. Thus Jon Elster argues that Marx saw that the bourgeoisie perceived their interests best furthered "if they remain outside politics." Much of this work locates "the specificity of the political" in a mediate "region" between the state and its own ground of power (which alone, as in the liberal conception, would set the state above or apart from class) and the state as possessing no special supremacy or priority in terms of power, as in the more orthodox marxist view. For Nicos Poulantzas, for example, the "specific autonomy which is characteristic of the function of the state ... is the basis of the specificity of the political" – whatever that means.

The idea that the state is relatively autonomous, a kind of first among equals of social institutions, has the genius of appearing to take a stand on the issue of reciprocal constitution of state and society while straddling it. Is the state essentially autonomous of class but partly determined by it, or is it essentially determined by class but not exclusively so? Is it relatively constrained within a context of freedom or relatively free within a context of constraint? As to who or what fundamentally moves and shapes the realities and instrumentalities of domination, and where to go to do something about it, what qualifies what is as ambiguous as it is crucial. When this work has investigated law as a particular form of state expression, it has served to relieve the compulsion to find all law – directly or convolutedly, nakedly or clothed in unconscious or devious rationalia – to be simply "bourgeois," without undercutting the notion that it, with all state emanations, is determinately driven by interest.

Feminism has not confronted, on its own terms, the relation between the state and society within a theory of social determination specific to sex. As a result, it lacks a jurisprudence, that is, a theory of the substance of law, its relation to society, and the relationship between the two. Such a theory would comprehend how law works as a form of state power in a social context in which power is gendered. It would answer the questions: What is state power? Where, socially, does it come from? How do women encounter it? What is the law for women? How does law work to legitimate the state, male power, itself? Can law do anything for women? Can it do anything about women's status? Does how the law is used matter?

In the absence of answers, feminist practice has oscillated between a liberal theory of the state on the one hand and a left theory of the state on the other. Both theories treat law as the mind of society: disembodied reason in liberal theory, reflection of material interest in left theory. In liberal moments, the state is accepted on its own terms as a neutral arbiter among conflicting interests. The law is actually or potentially principled, meaning predisposed to no substantive outcome, or manipulable to any ends, thus available as a tool that is not fatally twisted. Women implicitly become an interest group within pluralism, with specific problems of mobilization and representation, exit and voice, sustaining incremental gains and losses. In left moments, the state becomes a tool of dominance and repression, the law legitimating ideology, use of the legal system a form of utopian idealism or gradualist reform, each apparent gain deceptive or cooptive, and each loss inevitable.

Liberalism applied to women has supported state intervention on behalf of women as abstract persons with abstract rights, without scrutinizing the content and limitations of these notions in terms of gender. Marxism applied to women is always on the edge of counseling abdication of the state as an arena altogether – and with it those women whom the state does not ignore or who are in no position to ignore it. As a result, feminism has been left with these tacit alternatives: either the state is a primary tool of women's betterment and status transformation, without analysis (hence strategy) of it as male; or women are left to civil society, which for women has more closely resembled a state of nature. The state, and with it the law, have been either omnipotent or impotent: everything or nothing. The feminist posture toward the state has therefore been schizoid on issues central to women's status. Rape, abortion, pornography, and sex discrimination are examples. To grasp the inadequacies for women of liberalism on the one hand and marxism on the other is to begin to comprehend the role of the liberal state and liberal legalism within a post-marxist feminism of social transformation.

Gender is a social system that divides power. It is therefore a political system. That is, over time, women have been economically exploited, relegated to domestic slavery, forced into motherhood, sexually objectified, physically abused, used in denigrating entertainment, deprived of a voice and authentic culture, and disenfranchised and excluded from public life. Women, by contrast with comparable men, have systematically been subjected to physical insecurity; targeted for sexual denigration and violation; depersonalized and denigrated; deprived of respect, credibility, and resources; and silenced – and denied public presence, voice, and representation of their interests. Men as men have generally not had these things done to them; that is, men have had to be Black or gay (for instance) to have these things done to them as men. Men have done these things to women. Even conventional theories of power – the more individuated, atomistic, and decisional approaches of the pluralists, as well as the more radical theories, which stress structural, tacit, contextual, and relational aspects of power – recognize such conditions as defining positions of power and powerlessness. If one defines politics with Harold Lasswell, who defines a political act as "one performed in power perspectives," and with Robert Dahl, who defines a political system as "any persistent pattern of human relationships that involves, to a significant extent, power, rule, or authority," and with Kate Millett, who defines political relationships as "power structured relationships," the relation between women and men is political.

Unlike the ways in which men systematically enslave, violate, dehumanize, and exterminate other men, expressing political inequalities among men, men's forms of dominance over women have been accomplished socially as well as economically, prior to the operation of law, without express state acts, often in intimate contexts, as everyday life. So what is the role of the state in sexual politics? Neither liberalism nor marxism grants women, as such, a specific relation to the state. Feminism has described some of the state's treatment of the gender difference but has not analyzed the state's role in gender hierarchy. What, in gender terms, are the state's norms of accountability, sources of power, real constituency? Is the state to some degree autonomous of the interests of men or an integral expression of them? Does the state embody and serve male interests in its form, dynamics, relation to society, and specific policies? Is the state constructed upon the subordination of women? If so, how does male power become state power? Can such a state be made to serve the interests of those upon whose powerlessness its power is erected? Would a different relation between state and society, such as may exist under socialism, make a difference? If not, is masculinity inherent in the state form as such, or is some other form of state, or some other way of governing, distinguishable or imaginable? In the absence of answers to these questions, feminism has been caught between giving more power to that state in each attempt to claim it for women and leaving unchecked power in the society to men. Undisturbed, meanwhile, like the assumption that women generally consent to sex, is the assumption that women consent to this government. The question for feminism is: what is this state, from women's point of view?

The state is male in the feminist sense: the law sees and treats women the way men see and treat women. The liberal state coercively and authoritatively constitutes the social order in the interest of men as a gender – through its legitimating norms, forms, relation to society, and substantive policies. The state's formal norms recapitulate the male point of view on the level of design. In Anglo-American jurisprudence, morals (value judgments) are deemed separable and separated from politics (power contests), and both from adjudication (interpretation). Neutrality, including judicial decision making that is dispassionate, impersonal, disinterested, and precedential, is considered desirable and descriptive. Courts, forums without predisposition among parties and with no interest of their own, reflect society back to itself resolved. Government of laws, not of men, limits partiality with written constraints and tempers force with reasonable rule-following.

At least since Langdell's first casebook in 1871, this law has aspired to be a science of rules and a science with rules, a science of the immanent generalization subsuming the emergent particularity, of prediction and control of social regularities and regulations, preferably codified. The formulaic "tests" of "doctrine" aspire to mechanism, classification to taxonomy, legislators to Linnaeus. Courts intervene only in properly "factualized" disputes, cognizing social conflicts as if collecting empirical data; right conduct becomes rule-following. But these demarcations between morals and politics, science and politics, the personality of the judge and the judicial role, bare coercion and the rule of law, tend to merge in women's experience. Relatively seamlessly they promote the dominance of men as a social group through privileging the form of power – the perspective on social life – which feminist consciousness reveals as socially male. The separation of form from substance, process from policy, adjudication from legislation, judicial role from theory or practice, echoes and reechoes at each level of the regime its basic norm: objectivity.

Formally, the state is male in that objectivity is its norm. Objectivity is liberal legalism's conception of itself. It legitimates itself by reflecting its view of society, a society it helps make by so seeing it, and calling that view, and that relation, rationality. Since rationality is measured by point-of-viewlessness, what counts as reason is that which corresponds to the way things are. Practical rationality, in this approach, means that which can be done without changing anything. In this framework, the task of legal interpretation becomes "to perfect the state as mirror of the society." Objectivist epistemology is the law of law. It ensures that the law will most reinforce existing distributions of power when it most closely adheres to its own ideal of fairness. Like the science it emulates, this epistemological stance cannot see the social specificity of reflexion as method or its choice to embrace that which it reflects. Such law not only reflects a society in which men rule women; it rules in a male way insofar as "the phallus means everything that sets itself up as a mirror." Law, as words in power, writes society in state form and writes the state onto society. The rule form, which unites scientific knowledge with state control in its conception of what law is, institutionalizes the objective stance as jurisprudence.

The state is male jurisprudentially, meaning that it adopts the standpoint of male power on the relation between law and society. This stance is especially vivid in constitutional adjudication, thought legitimate to the degree it is neutral on the policy content of legislation. The foundation for its neutrality is the pervasive assumption that conditions that pertain among men on the basis of gender apply to women as well – that is, the assumption that sex inequality does not really exist in society. The Constitution – the constituting document of this state society – with its interpretations assumes that society, absent government intervention, is free and equal; that its laws, in general, reflect that; and that government need and should right only what government has previously wronged. This posture is structural to a constitution of absti- nence: for example, "Congress shall make no law abridging the freedom of ... speech." Those who have freedoms like equality, liberty, privacy, and speech socially keep them legally, free of governmental intrusion. No one who does not already have them socially is granted them legally.

In this light, once gender is grasped as a means of social stratifica- tion, the status categories basic to medieval law, thought to have been superseded by liberal regimes in aspirational nonhierarchical constructs of abstract personhood, are revealed deeply unchanged. Gender as a status category was simply assumed out of legal existence, suppressed into a presumptively pre-constitutional social order through a constitu- tional structure designed not to reach it. Speaking descriptively rather than functionally or motivationally, the strategy is first to constitute society unequally prior to law; then to design the constitution, including the law of equality, so that all its guarantees apply only to those values that are taken away by law; then to construct legitimating norms so that the state legitimates itself through noninterference with the status quo. Then, so long as male dominance is so effective in society that it is unnecessary to impose sex inequality through law, such that only the most superficial sex inequalities become *de jure*, not even a legal guar- antee of sex equality will produce social equality.

The posture and presumptions of the negative state, the view that government best promotes freedom when it stays out of existing social arrangements, reverberates throughout constitutional law. Doctrinally, it is embodied in rubrics like the "state action" requirement of equal protection law, in the law of freedom of speech, and in the law of privacy. The "state action" requirement restricts the Constitution to securing citizens' equality rights only from violations by governments, not by other citizens. The law of the First Amendment secures freedom of speech only from governmental deprivation. In the law of privacy, governmental intervention itself is unconstitutional.

In terms of judicial role, these notions are defended as the "passive virtues": courts should not (and say they do not) impose their own substantive views on constitutional questions. Judges best vindicate the Constitution when they proceed as if they have no views, when they reflect society back to itself from the angle of vision at which society is refracted to them. In this hall of mirrors, only in extremis shall any man alter what any other man has wrought. The offspring of proper passiv- ity is substancelessness. Law produces its progeny immaculately, with- out messy political intercourse.

Philosophically, this posture is expressed in the repeated constitutional invocation of the superiority of "negative freedom" – staying out, letting be – over positive legal affirmations. Negative liberty gives one the right to be "left to do or be what [he] is able to do or be, without interference from other persons." The state that pursues this value promotes freedom when it does not intervene in the social status quo. Positive freedom, freedom to do rather than to keep from being done to, by distinction, gives one the right to "control or ... determine someone to do, or be, this rather than that." If one group is socially granted the positive freedom to do whatever it wants to another group, to determine that the second group will be and do this rather than that, no amount of negative freedom legally guaranteed to the second group will make it the equal of the first. For women, this has meant that civil society, the domain in which women are distinctively subordinated and deprived of power, has been placed beyond reach of legal guarantees. Women are oppressed socially, prior to law, without express state acts, often in intimate contexts. The negative state cannot address their situation in any but an equal society – the one in which it is needed least.

This posture is enforced through judicial methodology, the formative legal experience for which is *Lochner v New York,* a case that arose out of the struggle of the working class to extract livable working conditions from a capitalist state through legislated reform. Invalidating legislation that would have restricted the number of hours bakers could work on grounds of freedom of contract, the Supreme Court sided with capitalism over workers. The dissenters' view, ultimately vindicated, was that the majority had superimposed its own views on the Constitution; they, by contrast, would passively reflect the Constitution by upholding the legislation. Soon after, in *Muller v Oregon,* the Supreme Court upheld restrictive hours legislation for women only. The opinion distinguished *Lochner* on the basis that women's unique frailty, dependency, and breeding capacity placed her "at a disadvantage in the struggle for subsistence." A later ruling, *West Coast Hotel v Parrish,* generally regarded as ending the *Lochner* era, also used women as a lever against capitalism. Minimum-wage laws were upheld for women because "the exploitation of a class of workers who are in an unequal position with respect to bargaining power and are thus relatively defenseless against the denial of a living wage ... casts a direct burden for their support upon the community."

Concretely, it is unclear whether these special protections, as they came to be called, helped or hurt women. These cases did do something for some workers (female) concretely; they also demeaned all women ideologically. They did assume that women were marginal and second-class members of the workforce; they probably contributed to keeping women marginal and second-class workers by keeping some women from competing with men at the male standard of exploitation. This benefited both male workers and capitalists. These rulings supported one sector of workers against all capitalists by benefiting male workers at the expense of female workers. They did help the working class by setting precedents that eventually supported minimum-wage and maximum-hours laws for all workers. They were a victory against capitalism and for sexism, for some women perhaps at the expense of all women (maybe including those they helped), for the working class perhaps at women's expense, at least so long as they were "women only."

The view of women in *Muller* and *West Coast Hotel* was that of the existing society: demeaning, paternalistic, and largely unrealistic; as with most pedestalization, its concrete benefits were equivocal at best. The view of workers in *Lochner* left capitalism unchecked and would have precluded most New Deal social reforms men wanted. (Protecting all workers was not considered demeaning by anyone.) For these reasons, these cases have come to stand for a critique of substantivity in adjudication as such. But their methodological solution – judicial neutrality – precludes from constitutional relief groups who are socially abject and systematically excluded from the usual political process. Despite universal rejections of "Lochnering," this substantive approach in neutral posture has continued to be incorporated in constitutional method, including in the law of equality. If over half the population has no voice in the Constitution, why is upholding legislation to give them a voice impermissibly substantive and activist, while striking down such legislation is properly substanceless and passive? Is permitting such an interpretation of, for example, the equality principle in a proper case activism, while not permitting it is properly nonsubstantive? Overruling *Lochner* was at least as judicially active as *Lochner* itself was. Further, why are legislation and adjudication regarded as exercises of state power, but passivity in the face of social inequality – even under a constitutional equality principle – is not? The result is, substantivity and activism are hunted down, flailed, and confined, while their twins, neutrality and passivity, roam at large.

To consider the "passive virtues" of judicial restraint as a tool for social change suggests that change for workers was constitutional only because workers were able to get power in legislatures. To achieve such changes by constitutional principle before achieving them socially and politically would be to engage in exactly the kind of substantive judicial activism that those who supported the changes said they opposed. The reasoning was: if courts make substantive decisions, they will express their prejudices, here, exploitive of workers, demeaning and unhelpful of women. The alternatives have been framed, then, as substantive adjudication that demeans and deprives on the one hand, or as substanceless adjudication that, passively virtuous, upholds whatever power can get out of the political process as it is.

The underlying assumption of judicial neutrality is that a status quo exists which is preferable to judicial intervention – a common law status quo, a legislative status quo, an economic status quo, or a gender status quo. For women, it also tends to assume that access to the conventional political realm might be available in the absence of legal rights. At the same time it obscures the possibility that a substantive approach to women's situation could be adequate to women's distinctive social exploitation – ground a claim to civil equality, for example – and do no more to license judicial arbitrariness than current standards do. From women's point of view, adjudications are already substantive; the view from nowhere already has content. *Lochner* saw workers legally the way capitalists see workers socially: as free agents, bargaining at arm's length. *Muller* saw women legally the way men see women socially: as breeders, marginal workers, excludable. If one wants to claim no more for a powerless group than what can be extracted under an established system of power, one can try to abstract them into entitlement by blurring the lines between them and everyone else. Neutrality as pure means makes some sense. If, however, the claim is against the definition and distribution of power itself, one needs a critique not so much of the substantivity of cases like *Lochner* and *Muller*, but of their substance. Such a critique must also include that aspect of the liberal tradition in which one strategy for dominance has been substancelessness.

If the content of positive law is surveyed more broadly from women's point of view, a pattern emerges. The way the male point of view frames an experience is the way it is framed by state policy. Over and over again, the state protects male power through embodying and ensuring existing male control over women at every level – cushioning, qualifying, or *de jure* appearing to prohibit its excesses when necessary to its normalization. *De jure* relations stabilize de facto relations. Laws that touch on sexuality provide illustrations of this argument. As in society, to the extent possession is the point of sex, rape in law is sex with a woman who is not yours, unless the act is so as to make her yours. Social and legal realities are consistent and mutually determinate: since law has never effectively interfered with men's ability to rape women on these terms, it has been unnecessary to make this an express rule of law. Because part of the kick of pornography involves eroticizing the putatively prohibited, obscenity law putatively prohibits pornography enough to maintain its desirability without ever making it unavailable or truly illegitimate. Because the stigma of prostitution is the stigma of sexuality is the stigma of the female gender, prostitution may be legal or illegal, but so long as women are unequal to men and that inequality is sexualized, women will be bought and sold as prostitutes, and law will do nothing about it.

Women as a whole are kept poor, hence socially dependent on men, available for sexual or reproductive use. To the extent that abortion exists to control the reproductive consequences of intercourse, hence to facilitate male sexual access to women, access to abortion will be controlled by "a man or The Man." So long as this is effectively done socially, it is unnecessary to do it by law. Law need merely stand passively by, reflecting the passing scene. The law of sex equality stays as far away as possible from issues of sexuality. Rape, pornography, prostitution, incest, battery, abortion, gay and lesbian rights: none have been sex equality issues under law. In the issues the law of sex discrimination does treat, male is the implicit reference for human, maleness the measure of entitlement to equality. In its mainstream interpretation, this law is neutral: it gives little to women that it cannot also give to men, maintaining sex inequality while appearing to address it. Gender, thus elaborated and sustained by law, is maintained as a division of power. The negative state views gender and sexual relations as neutrally as *Lochner* viewed class relations.

The law on women's situation produced in this way views women's situation from the standpoint of male dominance. It assumes that the conditions that pertain among men on the basis of sex – consent to sex, comparative privacy, voice in moral discourse, and political equality on the basis of gender – apply to women. It assumes on the epistemic level that sex inequality in society is not real. Rape law takes women's usual response to coercion – acquiescence, the despairing response to hopelessness to unequal odds – and calls that consent. Men coerce women; women "consent." The law of privacy treats the private sphere as a sphere of personal freedom. For men, it is. For women, the private is the distinctive sphere of intimate violation and abuse, neither free nor particularly personal. Men's realm of private freedom is women's realm of collective subordination. The law of obscenity treats pornography as "ideas." Whether or not ideas are sex for men, pornography certainly is sex for men. From the standpoint of women, who live the sexual abuse in pornography as everyday life, pornography is reality. The law of obscenity treats regulation of pornography from the standpoint of what is necessary to protect it: as regulation of morals, as some men telling other men what they may not see and do and think and say about sex. From the standpoint of women, whose torture pornography makes entertainment, pornography is the essence of a powerless condition, its effective protection by the state the essence of sexual politics. Obscenity law's "moral ideas" are a political reality of women's subordination. Just as, in male law, public oppression masquerades as private freedom and coercion is guised as consent, in obscenity law real political domination is presented as a discourse in ideas about virtue and vice.

Rape law assumes that consent to sex is as real for women as it is for men. Privacy law assumes that women in private have the same privacy men do. Obscenity law assumes that women have the access to speech men have. Equality law assumes that women are already socially equal to men. Only to the extent women have already achieved social equality does the mainstream law of equality support their inequality claims. The laws of rape, abortion, obscenity, and sex discrimination show how the relation between objectification, understood as the primary process of the subordination of women, and the power of the state is the relation between the personal and the political at the level of government. These laws are not political because the state is presumptively the sphere of politics. They are integral to sexual politics because the state, through law, institutionalizes male power over women through institutionalizing the male point of view in law. Its first state act is to see women from the standpoint of male dominance; its next act is to treat them that way. This power, this state, is not a discrete location, but a web of sanctions throughout society which "control[s] the principal means of coercion" that structures women's everyday lives. The Weberian monopoly on the means of legitimate coercion, thought to distinguish the state as an entity, actually describes the power of men over women in the home, in the bedroom, on the job, in the street, throughout social life. It is difficult, actually, to find a place it does not circumscribe and describe. Men are sovereign in society in the way Austin describes law as sovereign: a person or group whose commands are habitually obeyed and who is not in the habit of obeying anyone else. Men are the group that has had the authority to make law, embodying H.L.A. Hart's "rule of recognition" that, in his conception, makes law authoritative. Distinctively male values (and men) constitute the authoritative interpretive community that makes law distinctively lawlike to the likes of Ronald Dworkin. If one combines "a realistic conception of the state with a revolutionary theory of society," the place of gender in state power is not limited to government, nor is the rule of law limited to police and courts. The rule of law and the rule of men are one thing, indivisible, at once official and unofficial – officially circumscribed, unofficially not. State power, embodied in law, exists throughout society as male power at the same time as the power of men over women throughout society is organized as the power of the state.

Perhaps the failure to consider gender as a determinant of state behavior has made the state's behavior appear indeterminate. Perhaps the objectivity of the liberal state has made it appear autonomous of class. Including, but beyond, the bourgeois in liberal legalism, lies what is male about it. However autonomous of class the liberal state may appear, it is not autonomous of sex. Male power is systemic. Coercive, legitimated, and epistemic, it *is* the regime.

READING QUESTIONS ON MACKINNON

1 What exactly is the tension MacKinnon identifies in the law?
2 Can the tension she identifies form the basis of a progressive legal strategy?

Martha Minow
"Foreword [to The Supreme Court 1986 Term]: Justice Engendered" (1987)

Minow examines legal assumptions about what is and is not normal, and explores opportunities to better realize law's ambitions.

I INTRODUCTION

A What's the Difference?

The use of anesthesia in surgery spread quickly once discovered. Yet the nineteenth-century doctors who adopted anesthesia selected which patients needed it and which deserved it. Both the medical literature and actual medical practices distinguished people's need for painkillers based on race, gender, ethnicity, age, temperament, personal habits, and economic class. Some people's pain was thought more serious than others; some people were thought to be hardy enough to withstand pain. Doctors believed that women, for example, needed painkillers more than men and that the rich and educated needed painkillers more than the poor and uneducated. How might we, today, evaluate these examples of discrimination? What differences between people should matter, and for what purposes? ...

The dilemma of difference appears unresolvable. The risk of non-neutrality – the risk of discrimination – accompanies efforts both to ignore and to recognize difference in equal treatment and special treatment; in color- or gender-blindness and in affirmative action; in governmental neutrality and in governmental preferences; and in decision-makers' discretion and in formal constraints on discretion. Yet the dilemma is not as intractable as it seems. What makes it seem so difficult are unstated assumptions about the nature of difference. Once articulated and examined, these assumptions can take their proper place among other choices about how to treat difference. I will explore here the assumptions underlying the dilemma of difference, assumptions that usually go without saying.

First, we often assume that "differences" are intrinsic, rather than viewing them as expressions of comparisons between people. We are all different from one another in innumerable ways. Each of these differences is an implicit comparison we draw. And the comparisons themselves depend upon and reconfirm socially constructed meanings about what traits should matter for purposes of comparison.

Second, typically we adopt an unstated point of reference when assessing others. From the point of reference of this norm, we determine who is different and who is normal. Women are different in relation to the unstated male norm. Blacks, Mormons, Jews, and Arabs are different in relation to the unstated white, Christian norm. Handicapped persons are different in relation to the unstated norm of able-bodiedness, or, as some have described it, the vantage point of the "Temporarily Able Persons." The unstated point of comparison is not neutral, but particular, and not inevitable, but only seemingly so when left unstated. A notion of equality that demands disregarding a "difference" calls for assimilation to an unstated norm. To strip away difference, then, often is to remove or ignore a feature distinguishing an individual from a presumed norm – like a white, able-bodied Christian man – but leaving that norm in place as the measure for equal treatment.

Third, we treat the perspective of the person doing the seeing or judging as objective, rather than as subjective. Although a person's perspective does not collapse into his or her demographic characteristics, no one is free from perspective, and no one can see fully from another's point of view.

Fourth, we assume that the perspectives of those being judged are either irrelevant or are already taken into account through the perspective of the judge. That is, we regard a person's self-conception or world view as unimportant to our treatment of that person.

Finally, there is an assumption that the existing social and economic arrangements are natural and neutral. We presume that individuals are free to form their own preferences and act upon them. In this view, any departure from the status quo risks non-neutrality and interference with free choice.

These related assumptions, once made explicit, must contend with some contrary ones. Consider these alternative starting points. Difference is relational, not intrinsic. Who or what should be taken as the point of reference for defining differences is debatable. There is no single, superior perspective for judging questions of difference. No perspective asserted to produce "the truth" is objective, but rather will obscure the power of the person attributing a difference while excluding important competing perspectives. Social arrangements can be changed: maintaining the status quo is not neutral and cannot be justified by the claim that everyone has freely chosen it.

A THE FIVE UNSTATED ASSUMPTIONS

1 Assumption 1: Difference Is Intrinsic, Not Relational

[M]any of us have never conceived of ourselves only as somebody's other.
– Barbara Christian

Can and should the questions about who is different be resolved by a process of discovering intrinsic differences? Is difference an objective, verifiable matter rather than something constructed by social attitudes? By posing legal claims through the difference dilemma, litigants and judges treat the problem of difference as what society or a given decisionmaker should do about the "different person" – a formulation that implicitly assigns the label of difference to that person.

The difference inquiry functions by pigeonholing people into sharply distinguished categories based on selected facts and features. Categorization helps people cope with complexity and understand each other. The legal analyst tends to treat the difference question as one of discovery rather than of choice. The judge asks: "Into what category does a given person or feature belong?" The categories then determine the significance of the persons or features situated within them. The distinguishing features behind critical perceptions and behind the categories themselves appear natural rather than chosen. It is hard, if not impossible, to find commonalities across differences, and to argue for the same treatment across difference. Responsibility for the consequences of identifying difference, then, is dispersed through the process of perception and categorization, even as the process of categorization itself can create new perceptions and realities.

Legal analysis of difference, and its focus on categorization, bears much similarity to legal analysis in general. Legal analysis, cast in a judicial mode, typically addresses whether a given situation "fits" in a category defined by a legal rule or instead belongs outside of it. Many questions presented to the Supreme Court, for example, take the form, "Is this a that?" A leading expositor of the nature of legal reasoning explains the three steps involved: "similarity is seen between cases; next the rule of law inherent in the first case is announced; then the rule of law is made applicable to the second case ... The finding of similarity or difference is the key step in the legal process." Again, as critics have noted for nearly a century, these patterns of legal analysis imply that legal reasoning yields results of its own accord, beyond human control.

For both legal difference and difference in general, a difference "discovered" is more aptly a statement of a relationship, expressing one person's deviation from an unstated norm assumed by the other. But where do these criteria for comparison come from, and why do they seem so natural that they escape debate? Especially when legal analysis overlaps with social analysis of difference, the criteria for comparison may express perceptions and prejudices of those with the power to define and name others.

In some cases, members of the Court have acknowledged that differences are not intrinsic but socially constructed, which implies in turn that the criteria for comparison are not "real" but humanly chosen. Thus, in *School Board v Arline*, the Court concluded that co-workers' perceptions of an individual's contagious disease actually help constitute the handicap, impairment, or difference, triggering legal protection. The Court thereby acknowledged that much of what is called disability is created by social attitudes that are themselves mutable. Similarly, many of the stereotypes we often associate with differences of race or sex are also changeable social constructs, rather than intrinsic traits.

Yet the Court has not entirely abandoned the assumption that at least some differences are intrinsic and verifiable. In *Arline,* the Court emphasized that the Rehabilitation Act protects only persons who are both "handicapped *and* otherwise qualified" and called for individualized review of persons who claim that their contagious disease constitutes a handicap. The Court thus sharpened the judicial tools for challenging mistaken attributions of difference, without abandoning the idea that people have real, objective differences.

The Court also acknowledged the socially and historically contingent construction of difference in *Shaare Tefila* and *Saint Francis.* The Court reasoned that objective, scientific sources could not resolve whether Arabs and Jews represent distinct races for the purposes of civil rights statutes. In essence, the Court acknowledged that racial identity is socially constrained and yet, oddly, the Justices turned to middle and late nineteenth-century notions of racial identity, prevalent when the remedial statutes were adopted, rather than examining contemporary assumptions and current prejudices.

In both *Shaare Tefila* and *Saint Francis,* members of minority groups sought to obtain protection by reinvoking the categories that had been used to denigrate them. As the cases thus illustrate, groups that seek to challenge socially assigned stigmas and stereotypes run into this dilemma: "How do you protest a socially imposed categorization, except by organizing around the category?" Although some people have resisted and challenged the meanings assigned to them, recipients of labels are often unable to control the many layers of negative association those labels carry. The web of negative associations assigned to the outsider complicates any effort to resist the denigration implied by difference.

What *Shaare Tefila* and *Saint Francis College* neglect to state is that attributions of difference reflect choices by those in power about what characteristics should matter. Ann Scales has noted: "To characterize similarities and differences among situations is a key step in legal judgments. That step, however, is not a mechanistic manipulation of essences. Rather, that step always has a moral crux." Some have argued that the assignment of differences in Western thought entails not just relationships and comparisons but also imposition of hierarchies. To explore this idea, we need the next unstated assumption: the implicit norm or reference point for the comparisons through which difference is assigned.

2 Assumption 2: The Unstated Norm ...

To treat someone as different means to accord them treatment that is different from treatment of someone else; to describe someone as "the same" implies "the same as" someone else. When differences are discussed without explicit reference to the person or trait on the other side of the comparison, an unstated norm remains. Usually, this default reference point is so powerful and well-established that it need not be specified.

Some remedial statutes explicitly state the norm: in 42 USC section 1981, the norm is "white citizens" – with an emphasis on both terms, implicitly establishing the terms of sameness and difference in this very statement of the norm. Claimants invoking the statute must show themselves to be relatively similar to "white citizens." Hence, these cases focus on whether the claimant is a member of a race.

When women argue for rights, the implicit reference point used in discussions of sameness and difference is the privilege accorded some males. This reference point can present powerful arguments for overcoming the exclusion of women from activities and opportunities available to men. For example, reform efforts on behalf of women during both the nineteenth and the twentieth centuries asserted women's fundamental similarities to privileged, white men as a tactic for securing equal treatment. Unfortunately for the reformers, embracing the theory of "sameness" meant that any sign of difference between women and men could be used to justify treating women differently from men. Men remained the unstated norm.

A prominent "difference" assigned to women, by implicit comparison with men, is pregnancy, especially as experienced by women working for pay outside their homes. The Supreme Court's treatment of issues concerning pregnancy and the workplace highlights the power of the unstated male norm in analyses of problems of difference. In 1975, the Court accepted the similarity of women to the male norm in striking down a Utah statute that disqualified a woman from receiving unemployment compensation for a specified period surrounding child-

birth, even if her reasons for leaving work were unrelated to the pregnancy.[1] Although the capacity to become pregnant is a difference between women and men, this fact alone did not justify treating women
and men differently on matters unrelated to pregnancy. Using men as
the norm, the Court reasoned that any woman who can perform like a
man can be treated like a man. A woman could not be denied unemployment compensation for different reasons than a man would.

What, however, is equal treatment for the woman who is correctly
identified within the group of pregnant persons, not simply stereotyped
as such, and who is different from nonpregnant persons in ways that
are relevant to the workplace? The Court first grappled with these
issues in two cases that posed the question of whether discrimination
on the basis of pregnancy amounted to discrimination on the basis of
sex. In both instances, the Court answered negatively, arguing that
pregnancy marks a division between the groups of pregnant and
nonpregnant persons and that women fall into both categories.[2]
Congress responded by enacting the Pregnancy Discrimination Act
(PDA), which amended title VII to include discrimination on the basis
of pregnancy within the range of impermissible sex discrimination. Yet
even under these new statutory terms, the power of the unstated male
norm persists in debates over the definition of discrimination ...

The dissenters, on the other hand, countered by emphasizing that the
PDA's commitment to equal treatment bans preferential treatment on
the basis of pregnancy. The dissenters persisted in using the male norm
as the measure for equal treatment in the workplace.

By contrast, the Court in *Wimberly*[3] used just such an implicit male
standard in concluding that the federal law against discriminating on
the basis of pregnancy in unemployment compensation provides no
check against states that refuse to provide compensation for a broad
range of situations, including pregnancy. In a work world designed
without pregnancy in mind, requiring women to be treated like men
means that there is no discrimination when women, as well as men,
receive no benefits for unemployment due to pregnancy.[4] At a doctrinal
level, the Court's holding that a state need not provide unemployment
compensation to a woman who left her job because of pregnancy rested
on the conclusion that the state treated pregnant women the same as all
other persons who left for reasons unconnected with work. There was
no discrimination when pregnancy was not singled out for detrimental
treatment. The federal antidiscrimination statute did not demand "pref-

erential treatment," and thus did not require that benefits be provided for pregnant persons when they would not be provided for others.

Wimberly is not an illogical ruling; a plausible theory of equality would call for a comparison between pregnant persons and other similarly situated persons. But what, exactly, is a situation similar to pregnancy? Unlike in *CalFed*, where the Court used a statute prohibiting pregnancy discrimination to establish the pregnant person as the point of comparison, the Court in *Wimberly* laid a neutral nondiscrimination demand on top of a workplace world and a state statute modeled without pregnancy in mind. Missing altogether was the equality norm that combined the work and family worlds and called for no difference in the abilities of men and women to work and have a family ...

Similar, unstated reference points appear in many other contexts. These implicit norms often work subtly, through the categories manifested in language. Reasoning processes tend to treat categories as clear, bounded, and sharp-edged; a given item either fits within the category or it does not. Instead of considering the entire individual, we often select one characteristic as representative of the whole. George Lakoff illustrates this phenomenon with the term "mother." Although "mother" appears to be a general category, with subcategories like working mother and unwed mother, the very need for modifying adjectives demonstrates an implicit prototype of the married housewife. The unstated prototype structures expectations about and valuations of members of the general category, yet treats these expectations and valuations as mere reflections of reality ...

Legal language seeks universal applicability, regardless of the particular traits of an individual. Yet abstract universalism often "takes the part for the whole, the particular for the universal and essential, the present for the eternal."[5] Making explicit the unstated points of reference is the first step in addressing this problem; the next is challenging the presumed neutrality of the observer who in fact sees from an unacknowledged perspective.

3 Assumption 3: The Observer Can See without a Perspective ...

If differences are intrinsic, then anyone can see them; if there is an objective reality, then any impartial observer can make judgments unaffected and untainted by his or her own perspective or experience. Once rules are selected, regardless of disputes over the rules themselves, a distinct aspiration is that they will be applied evenhandedly. This aspiration to impartiality, however, is just that – an aspiration rather than a description – because it may suppress the inevitability of the existence of a perspective and thus make it harder for the observer, or anyone else, to challenge the absence of objectivity.

What interests us, given who we are and where we stand, affects our ability to perceive. Philosophers such as A.J. Ayer and W.V. Quine note that although we can alter the theory we use to frame our perceptions of the world, we cannot see the world unclouded by preconceptions. The impact of the observer's perspective may be crudely oppressive. Yet, we continue to believe in neutrality.

For example, in *Johnson v Transportation Agency*, in which the Court upheld an affirmative action plan for women, the press reported that the employer promoted a woman less qualified than a man, even though their scores differed by merely two points after a first interview. Johnson, the male applicant, earned the second highest score (with another applicant), whereas Joyce, the female applicant, had the next highest score. A second interview was conducted by three agency supervisors, two of whom had either harassed or made sexist comments to Joyce. Based on all the evidence and the recommendation of the affirmative action office, the employer promoted Joyce. To treat this as a case of a less qualified woman getting the job over a more qualified man perpetuates the mythology of neutral observers. The Court itself criticized this myth, noting that for unexceptional middle-level craft positions, final selection decisions are inevitably subjective, once a pool of fully qualified candidates is assembled ...

4 Assumption 4: The Irrelevance of Other Perspectives ...

Glimpsing contrasting perspectives helps resolve problems of difference. Several of the Justices have tried, on different occasions, to glimpse the point of view of a minority group or a person quite different from themselves; some have articulated eloquently the difficulty or even impossibility of knowing another's perspective, and have developed legal positions that take into account this difficulty. Others have rejected as irrelevant or relatively unimportant the experience of "difference" people and have denied their own partiality, often by using stereotypes as though they were real.

Justice Powell's majority opinion in *McCleskey v Kemp*[6] for example, ignored its own partial perspective in upholding the death penalty against a black defendant, despite strong statistical evidence of racial discrimination in capital sentencing generally. The petitioner, explained Justice Powell, failed to show that the decisionmakers in *his* case acted with a discriminatory purpose. This formulation takes seriously the vantage point of decisionmakers like the reviewing court and the jury, but not the perspective of the criminal defendant. From the black defendant's point of view, however, proof of the intent of the individual jury is much less important than the disproportionate risk of the death penalty.

The rarity of glimpses of such minority perspectives is underscored by their power when taken seriously. For example, consider Justice Brennan's dissent in *McCleskey*. Perhaps knowing that neither he nor many of his readers could fully grasp the defendant's perspective, Justice Brennan in his dissent tried to look through the eyes of the defense attorney who is asked by the black defendant about the chances of a death sentence. Adopting that viewpoint, Justice Brennan concluded that "counsel would feel bound to tell McCleskey that defendants charged with killing white victims in Georgia are 4.3 times as likely to be sentenced to death as defendants charged with killing blacks" and that "there was a significant chance that race would play a prominent role in determining if he lived or died." From the defendant's angle, Justice Powell's concluding fears about the unmanageability of more challenges to the criminal sentencing process should McCleskey prevail look strikingly confined by his perspective, prompting the question, unmanageable for whom? ...

Thus, some Justices, on some occasions, have tried to see beyond the dominant perspective and reach an alternative construction of reality. In many other instances, however, the Justices presume that the perspective they adopt is either universal or superior to others. A perspective may go unstated because it is so powerful and pervasive that it may be presumed without defense; it may also go unstated because it is so unknown to those in charge that they do not recognize it as a perspective. Presumptions about whose perspective matters ultimately may be embedded in the final, typically unstated assumption: when in doubt, the status quo is preferred, and is indeed presumed natural and free from coercion.

5 Assumption 5: The Status Quo Is Natural, Uncoerced, and Good ...

Connected with many of the other assumptions is the idea that critical features of the status quo – general social and economic arrangements

are natural and desirable. From this assumption follow three propositions: first, the goal of governmental neutrality demands the status quo
because existing societal arrangements are assumed to be neutral. Second, governmental actions that change the status quo have a different
status than omissions, or failures to act, that maintain the status quo.
Third, prevailing social and political arrangements are not forced on
anyone. Individuals are free to make choices and to assume responsibility for those choices. These propositions are rarely stated, both because
they are deeply entrenched and because they view the status quo as
good, natural, and freely chosen ...

Judges operating under the assumption that the world is neutral do
not find discrimination unless it is specifically proven. In *McCleskey v
Kemp*, for example, the Court refused to find discrimination in the case
before it, despite strong statistical evidence that the race of the victim
and of the defendant often determines who receives the death penalty.
...

For the most part, unstated assumptions work in subtle and complex
ways. Assumptions fill the basic human need to simplify and to make
our world familiar and unsurprising. Yet, by their very simplification,
assumptions exclude contrasting views. Moreover, they contribute to
the dilemma of difference by frustrating legislative and constitutional
commitments to change the treatment of differences in race, gender,
ethnicity, religion, and handicap. Before justice can be done, judges
need to hear and understand contrasting points of view about the
treatment of difference.

IV PERSPECTIVES ON PERSPECTIVES ...

The difference dilemma seems paralyzing if framed by the unstated
assumptions described in Part III. Those assumptions so entrench one
point of view as natural and orderly that any conscious decision to
notice or to ignore difference breaks the illusion of a legal world free of
perspective. The assumptions make it seem that departures from
unstated norms violate commitments to neutrality. Yet adhering to the
unstated norms undermines commitments to neutrality – and to
equality. Is it possible to proceed differently, putting these assumptions
into question?

I will suggest that it is possible, even if difficult, to move beyond the
constricting assumptions.

NOTES

1 The case was decided on due process grounds. See *Turner v Department of Employment Sec.*, 423 US 44 (1975) (per curiam); see also *Cleveland Bd. of Educ. v LaFleur*, 414 US 632 (1974) (invalidating a local school board rule requiring pregnant teachers to take unpaid maternity leaves as a violation of due process).
2 See *General Electric Co v Gilbert*, 429 US 125 (1976) (title VII); *Geduldig v Aiello*, 417 US 484 (1974) (equal protection).
3 *Wimberly v Labor & Indus. Relations Comm'n*, 107 SCt 821 (1987).
4 See *General Elec. Co v Gilbert*, 429 US 125 (1976); *Geduldig v Aiello*, 417 US 484 (1974). One could seriously debate whether a man's prostate surgery or fatherhood is comparable to pregnancy and maternity.
5 Gould, "The Woman Question: Philosophy of Liberation and the Liberation of Philosophy," in *Women and Philosophy: Toward a Theory of Liberation* 21 (C. Gould & M. Wartofsky, eds. 1976).
6 107 SCt 1756 (1987).

READING QUESTIONS ON MINOW

1 What are the five assumptions Minow questions? What do they share?
2 Is there a relation between Minow's project and Dworkin's idea of the law "working itself pure"?

Patricia Williams
The Alchemy of Race and Rights (1991)

Williams's narrative tells of the importance for the oppressed of a certain formality to law.

Some time ago, Peter Gabel and I taught a contracts class together. (He was one of the first to bring critical theory to legal analysis and so is considered a "founder" of Critical Legal Studies.) Both recent transplants from California to New York, each of us hunted for apartments in between preparing for class. Inevitably, I suppose, we got into a discussion of trust and distrust as factors in bargain relations. It turned out that Peter had handed over a $900 deposit in cash, with no lease, no exchange of keys, and no receipt, to strangers with whom he had no ties other than a few moments of pleasant conversation. He said he didn't need to sign a lease because it imposed too much formality. The handshake and the good vibes were for him indicators of trust more binding than a form contract. At the time I told Peter he was mad, but his faith paid off. His sublessors showed up at the appointed time, keys in hand, to welcome him in. There was absolutely nothing in my experience to prepare me for such a happy ending. (In fact I remain convinced that, even if I were of a mind to trust a lessor with this degree of informality, things would not have worked out so successfully for me: many Manhattan lessors would not have trusted a black person enough to let me in the door in the first place, paperwork, references, and credit check notwithstanding.)

I, meanwhile, had friends who found me an apartment in a building they owned. In my rush to show good faith and trustworthiness, I signed a detailed, lengthily negotiated, finely printed lease firmly establishing me as the ideal arm's-length transactor.

As Peter and I discussed our experiences, I was struck by the similarity of what each of us was seeking, yet with such polar approaches. We both wanted to establish enduring relationships with the people in whose houses we would be living; we both wanted to enhance trust of ourselves and to allow whatever closeness was possible. This similarity of desire, however, could not reconcile our very different relations to the tonalities of law. Peter, for example, appeared to be extremely self-conscious of his power potential (either real or imagistic) as white or male or lawyer authority figure. He therefore seemed to go to some length to overcome the wall that image might impose. The logical ways of establishing some measure of trust between strangers were an avoidance of power and a preference for informal processes generally.

On the other hand, I was raised to be acutely conscious of the likelihood that no matter what degree of professional I am, people will greet and dismiss my black femaleness as unreliable, untrustworthy, hostile, angry, powerless, irrational, and probably destitute. Futility and despair are very real parts of my response. So it helps me to clarify boundary; to show that I can speak the language of lease is my way of enhancing trust of me in my business affairs. As black, I have been given by this society a strong sense of myself as already too familiar, personal, subordinate to white people. I am still evolving from being treated as three-fifths of a human, a subpart of the white estate. I grew up in a neighborhood where landlords would not sign leases with their poor black tenants, and demanded that rent be paid in cash; although superficially resembling Peter's transaction, such informality in most white-on-black situations signals distrust, not trust. Unlike Peter, I am still engaged in a struggle to set up transactions at arm's length, as legitimately commercial, and to portray myself as a bargainer of separate worth, distinct power, sufficient *rights* to manipulate commerce.

Peter, I speculate, would say that a lease or any other formal mechanism would introduce distrust into his relationships and he would suffer alienation, leading the commodification of his being and the degradation of his person to property. For me, in contrast, the lack of formal relation to the other would leave me estranged. It would risk a figurative isolation from that creative commerce by which I may be recognized as whole, by which I may feed and clothe and shelter myself, by which I may be seen as equal – even if I am stranger. For me, stranger-stranger relations are better than stranger-chattel.

READING QUESTIONS ON WILLIAMS

1 Does Williams's argument support or undermine what either MacKinnon or Minow have to say about the nature of law?

Lavallée v The Queen [1990] 555 CCC (3d) 97

Lynn Lavallée killed her abusive spouse and successfully argued that she was defending herself. The case, decided by the Supreme Court of Canada, reveals ways in which the law has attempted to integrate the sort of concerns raised by MacKinnon and Minow.

Wilson, J: – The narrow issue raised on this appeal is the adequacy of a trial judge's instructions to the jury regarding expert evidence. The broader issue concerns the utility of expert evidence in assisting a jury confronted by a plea of self-defence to a murder charge by a common law wife who had been battered by the deceased.

1 THE FACTS

The appellant, who was 22 years old at the time, had been living with Kevin Rust for some three to four years. Their residence was the scene of a boisterous party on August 30, 1986. In the early hours of August 31, after most of the guests had departed, the appellant and Rust had an argument in the upstairs bedroom which was used by the appellant. Rust was killed by a single shot in the back of the head from a .303 calibre rifle fired by the appellant as he was leaving the room.

The appellant did not testify but her statement made to police on the night of the shooting was put in evidence. Portions of it read as follows:

Me and Wendy argued as usual and I ran in the house after Kevin pushed me. I was scared, I was really scared. I locked the door. Herb was downstairs with Joanne and I called for Herb but I was crying when I called him. I said, "Herb come up here please." Herb came up to the top of the stairs and I told him that Kevin was going to hit me actually beat on me again. Herb said he knew and that if I was his old lady things would be different, he gave me a hug. OK, we're friends, there's nothing between us. He said, "Yeah, I know" and he went outside to talk to Kevin leaving the door unlocked. I went upstairs and hid in my closet from Kevin. I was so scared ... My window was open and I could hear Kevin asking questions about what I was doing and what I was saying. Next thing I know he was coming up the stairs for me. He came into my bedroom and said, "Wench, where are you?" And he turned on my light and he said, "Your purse is on the floor," and he kicked it. OK then he turned and he saw me in the closet. He wanted me to come out but I didn't want to come out because I was scared. I was so scared. [The officer who took the statement then testified that the appellant started to cry at this point and stopped after a minute or two.] He grabbed me by the arm right there. There's a bruise on my face also where he slapped me. He didn't slap me right then. First he yelled at me then he pushed me and I pushed him back and he hit me twice on the right-hand side of my head. I was scared. All I thought about was all the other times he used to beat me, I was scared, I was shaking as usual. The rest is a blank, all I remember is he gave me the gun and a shot was fired through my screen. This is all so fast. And then the guns were in another room, and he loaded it the second shot and gave it to me. And I was going to shoot myself. I pointed it to myself, I was so upset. OK and then he went and I was sitting on the bed and he started going like this with his finger [the appellant made a shaking motion with an index finger] and said something like "You're my old lady and you do as you're told" or something like that. He said, "Wait till everybody leaves, you'll get it then," and he said something to the effect of "either you kill me or I'll get you" that was what it was. He kind of smiled and then he turned around. I shot him but I aimed out. I thought I aimed above him and a piece of his head went that way.

... The relationship between the appellant and Rust was volatile and punctuated by frequent arguments and violence. They would apparently fight for two or three days at a time or several times a week. Considerable evidence was led at trial indicating that the appellant was frequently a victim of physical abuse at the hands of Rust. Between 1983 and 1986, the appellant made several trips to hospital for injuries including severe bruises, a fractured nose, multiple contusions and a black eye. One of the attending physicians, Dr Dirks testified that he disbelieved the appellant's explanation on one such occasion that she had sustained her injuries by falling from a horse.

A friend of the deceased, Robert Ezako, testified that he had witnessed several fights between the appellant and the deceased and that he had seen the appellant point a gun at the deceased twice and threaten to kill him if he ever touched her again. Under cross-examination Ezako admitted to seeing or hearing the deceased beat up the appellant on several occasions and, during the preliminary inquiry, described her screaming during one such incident like "a pig being butchered"...

At one point on the night of his death Rust chased the appellant outside the house and a mutual friend, Norman Kolish, testified that the appellant pleaded with Rust to "leave me alone" and sought Kolish's protection by trying to hide behind him. A neighbour overheard Rust and the appellant arguing and described the tone of the former as "argumentative" and the latter as "scared." Later, between the first and second gunshot, he testified that he could hear that "somebody was beating up somebody" and the screams were female. Another neighbour testified to hearing noises like gunshots and then a woman's voice sounding upset saying, "Fuck. He punched me in the face. He punched me in the face." He looked out the window and saw a woman matching the description of the appellant.

... [T]he appellant was seen visibly shaken and upset and was heard to say, "Rooster [the deceased] was beating me so I shot him," and, "You know how he treated me, you've got to help me." The arresting officer testified that en route to the police station the appellant made various comments in the police car, including, "He said if I didn't kill him first he would kill me. I hope he lives. I really love him," and, "He told me he was gonna kill me when everyone left."

The police officer who took the appellant's statement testified to seeing a red mark on her arm where she said the deceased had grabbed her. When the coroner who performed an autopsy on the deceased was shown pictures of the appellant (who had various bruises), he testified that it was "entirely possible" that bruises on the deceased's left hand were occasioned by an assault on the appellant. Another doctor noted an injury to the appellant's pinkie finger consistent with those sustained by the adoption of a defensive stance.

... The expert evidence which forms the subject-matter of the appeal came from Dr Fred Shane, a psychiatrist with extensive professional experience in the treatment of battered wives. At the request of defence counsel Dr Shane prepared a psychiatric assessment of the appellant. The substance of Dr Shane's opinion was that the appellant had been terrorized by Rust to the point of feeling trapped, vulnerable, worthless, and unable to escape the relationship despite the violence. At the same time, the continuing pattern of abuse put her life in danger. In Dr Shane's opinion the appellant's shooting of the deceased was a final desperate act by a woman who sincerely believed that she would be killed that night:

I think she felt, she felt in the final tragic moment that her life was on the line, that unless she defended herself, unless she reacted in a violent way that she would die. I mean he made it very explicit to her, from what she told me and from the information I have from the material that you forwarded to me, that she had, I think, to defend herself against his violence.

Dr Shane stated that his opinion was based on four hours of formal interviews with the appellant, a police report of the incident (including the appellant's statement), hospital reports documenting eight of her visits to emergency departments between 1983 and 1985, and an interview with the appellant's mother. In the course of his testimony Dr Shane related many things told to him by the appellant for which there was no admissible evidence. They were not in the appellant's statement to the police, and she did not testify at trial. For example, Dr Shane mentioned several episodes of abuse described by the appellant for which there were no hospital reports. He also related the appellant's disclosure to him that she had lied to doctors about the cause of her injuries. Dr Shane testified that such fabrication was typical of battered women. The appellant also recounted to Dr Shane occasions on which Rust would allegedly beat her, then beg her forgiveness, and ply her with flowers and temporary displays of kindness. Dr Shane was aware of the incidents described by Ezako about the appellant's pointing a gun at Rust on two occasions and explained it as "an issue for trying to defend herself. She was afraid that she would be assaulted." The appellant denied to Dr Shane that she had homicidal fantasies about Rust and mentioned that she had smoked some marijuana on the night in question. These facts were related by Dr Shane in the course of his testimony.

... The appellant was acquitted by a jury but the verdict was overturned by a majority of the Manitoba Court of Appeal and the case sent back for retrial ...

3 RELEVANT LEGISLATION

Criminal Code, RSC 1985, c. C-46:

34(2) Every one who is unlawfully assaulted and who causes death or grievous bodily harm in repelling the assault is justified if
(a) he causes it under reasonable apprehension of death or grievous bodily harm from the violence with which the assault was originally made or with which the assailant pursues his purposes, and
(b) he believes on reasonable and probable grounds, that he cannot otherwise preserve himself from death or grievous bodily harm.

4 ISSUES ON APPEAL

It should be noted that two bases for ordering a new trial are implicit in the reasons of the majority of the Court of Appeal. In finding that "absent the evidence of Dr Shane, it is unlikely that the jury, properly instructed, would have accepted the accused's plea of self-defence" the Court of Appeal suggests that the evidence of Dr Shane ought to have been excluded entirely. The alternative ground for allowing the Crown's appeal was that Dr Shane's testimony was properly admitted but the trial judge's instructions with respect to it were deficient. Thus, the issues before this court are as follows:

1 Did the majority of the Manitoba Court of Appeal err in concluding that the jury should have considered the plea of self-defence
   absent the expert evidence of Dr Shane?
2 Did the majority of the Manitoba Court of Appeal err in holding
   that the trial judge's charge to the jury with respect to Dr Shane's
   expert evidence did not meet the requirements set out by this
   court in *Abbey*, thus warranting a new trial?

5 ANALYSIS

(i) Admissibility of Expert Evidence

In *Kelliher v Smith*, this court adopted the principle that in order for
expert evidence to be admissible "the subject-matter of the inquiry must
be such that ordinary people are unlikely to form a correct judgment
about it, if unassisted by persons with special knowledge." More recently, this court addressed the admissibility of expert psychiatric evidence in criminal cases in *R v Abbey*, *supra*. At p. 409 of the unanimous
judgment Dickson J (as he then was) stated the rule as follows:

With respect to matters calling for special knowledge, an expert in the field
may draw inferences and state his opinion. An expert's function is precisely
this: to provide the judge and jury with a ready-made inference which the
judge and jury, due to the technical nature of the facts, are unable to formulate ...

Where expert evidence is tendered in such fields as engineering or
pathology, the paucity of the layperson's knowledge is uncontentious.
The long-standing recognition that psychiatric or psychological testimony also falls within the realm of expert evidence is predicated on the
realization that in some circumstances the average person may not have
sufficient knowledge of or experience with human behaviour to draw
an appropriate inference from the facts before him or her.

The need for expert evidence in these areas can, however, be obfus-
cated by the belief that judges and juries are thoroughly knowledgeable
about "human nature" and that no more is needed. They are, so to
speak, their own experts on human behaviour. This, in effect, was the
primary submission of the Crown to this court.

The bare facts of this case, which I think are amply supported by the
evidence, are that the appellant was repeatedly abused by the deceased

but did not leave him (although she twice pointed a gun at him), and ultimately shot him in the back of the head as he was leaving her room. The Crown submits that these facts disclose all the information a jury needs in order to decide whether or not the appellant acted in self-defence. I have no hesitation in rejecting the Crown's submission.

Expert evidence on the psychological effect of battering on wives and common law partners must, it seems to me, be both relevant and necessary in the context of the present case. How can the mental state of the appellant be appreciated without it? The average member of the public (or of the jury) can be forgiven for asking: Why would a woman put up with this kind of treatment? Why should she continue to live with such a man? How could she love a partner who beat her to the point of requiring hospitalization? We would expect the woman to pack her bags and go. Where is her self-respect? Why does she not cut loose and make a new life for herself? Such is the reaction of the average person confronted with the so-called battered wife syndrome. We need help to understand it and help is available from trained professionals.

The gravity, indeed, the tragedy of domestic violence can hardly be overstated. Greater media attention to this phenomenon in recent years has revealed both its prevalence and its horrific impact on women from all walks of life.

... Laws do not spring out of a social vacuum. The notion that a man has a right to "discipline" his wife is deeply rooted in the history of our society. The woman's duty was to serve her husband and to stay in the marriage at all costs "till death do us part" and to accept as her due any "punishment" that was meted out for failing to please her husband. One consequence of this attitude was that "wife battering" was rarely spoken of, rarely reported, rarely prosecuted, and even more rarely punished. Long after society abandoned its formal approval of spousal abuse, tolerance of it continued and continues in some circles to this day.

Fortunately, there has been a growing awareness in recent years that no man has a right to abuse any woman under any circumstances. Legislative initiatives designed to educate police, judicial officers, and the public, as well as more aggressive investigation and charging policies all signal a concerted effort by the criminal justice system to take spousal abuse seriously. However, a woman who comes before a judge or jury with the claim that she has been battered and suggests that this may be a relevant factor in evaluating her subsequent actions still faces the prospect of being condemned by popular mythology about domestic violence. Either she was not as badly beaten as she claims or she would have left the man long ago. Or, if she was battered that severely, she must have stayed out of some masochistic enjoyment of it.

(ii) The Relevance of Expert Testimony to the Elements of Self-Defence

In my view, there are two elements of the defence under s. 34(2) of the *Code* which merit scrutiny for present purposes. The first is the temporal connection in s. 34(2)(a) between the apprehension of death or grievous bodily harm and the act allegedly taken in self-defence. Was the appellant "under reasonable apprehension of death or grievous bodily harm" from Rust as he was walking out of the room? The second is the assessment in s. 34(2)(b) of the magnitude of the force used by the accused. Was the accused's belief that she could not "otherwise preserve herself from death or grievous bodily harm" except by shooting the deceased based "on reasonable grounds"?

The feature common to both para. (a) and para. (b) of s. 34(2) is the imposition of an objective standard of reasonableness on the apprehension of death and the need to repel the assault with deadly force ...

If it strains credulity to imagine what the "ordinary man" would do in the position of a battered spouse, it is probably because men do not typically find themselves in that situation. Some women do, however. The definition of what is reasonable must be adapted to circumstances which are, by and large, foreign to the world inhabited by the hypothetical "reasonable man."

... I turn now to a consideration of the specific components of self--defence under s. 34(2) of the *Criminal Code*.

A Reasonable Apprehension of Death

Section 34(2)(a) requires that an accused who intentionally causes death or grievous bodily harm in repelling an assault is justified if he or she does so "under reasonable apprehension of death or grievous bodily harm." In the present case, the assault precipitating the appellant's alleged defensive act was Rust's threat to kill her when everyone else had gone.

It will be observed that s. 34(2)(a) does not actually stipulate that the accused apprehend imminent danger when he or she acts. Case-law has, however, read that requirement into the defence. The sense in which "imminent" is used conjures up the image of "an uplifted knife" or a pointed gun. The rationale for the imminence rule seems obvious. The law of self-defence is designed to ensure that the use of defensive force is really necessary. It justifies the act because the defender reasonably believed that he or she had no alternative but to take the attacker's life. If there is a significant time interval between the original unlawful assault and the accused's response, one tends to suspect that the accused was motivated by revenge rather than self-defence. In the paradigmatic case of a one-time bar-room brawl between two men of equal size and strength, this inference makes sense. How can one feel endangered to the point of firing a gun at an unarmed man who utters a death threat, then turns his back and walks out of the room? One cannot be certain of the gravity of the threat or his capacity to carry it out. Besides, one can always take the opportunity to flee or to call the police. If he comes back and raises his fist, one can respond in kind if need be. These are the tacit assumptions that underlie the imminence rule.

... According to the testimony of Dr Shane these assaults [by the deceased] were not entirely random in their occurrence ... Dr Shane acknowledged his debt to Dr [Lenore] Walker in the course of establishing his credentials as an expert at trial. Dr Walker first describes the cycle in the book *The Battered Woman* (1979). In her 1984 book, *The Battered Woman Syndrome*, Dr Walker reports the results of a study involving 400 battered women. Her research was designed to test empirically the theories expounded in her earlier book. At pp. 95-6 of *The Battered Woman Syndrome*, she summarizes the Cycle Theory as follows:

A second major theory that was tested in this project is the Walker Cycle Theory of Violence (Walker, 1979). This tension reduction theory states that there are three distinct phases associated in a recurring battering cycle: (1) tension building, (2) the acute battering incident, and (3) loving contrition. During the first phase, there is a gradual escalation of tension displayed by discrete acts causing increased friction such as name-calling, other mean intentional behaviors, and/or physical abuse. The batterer expresses dissatisfaction and hostility but not in an extreme or maximally explosive form. The woman attempts to placate the batterer, doing what she thinks might please him, calm him down, or at least, what will not further aggravate him. She tries not to respond to his hostile actions and uses general anger reduction techniques. Often she succeeds for a little while which reinforces her unrealistic belief that she can control this man ...

The tension continues to escalate and eventually she is unable to continue controlling his angry response pattern. "Exhausted from the constant stress, she usually withdraws from the batterer, fearing she will inadvertently set off an explosion. He begins to move more oppressively toward her as he observes her withdrawal ... Tension between the two becomes unbearable" (Walker, 1979, p. 59). The second phase, the acute battering incident, becomes inevitable without intervention. Sometimes, she precipitates the inevitable explosion so as to control where and when it occurs, allowing her to take better precautions to minimize her injuries and pain.

"Phase two is characterized by the uncontrollable discharge of the tensions that have built up during phase one" (p. 59). The batterer typically unleashes a barrage of verbal and physical aggression that can leave the woman severely shaken and injured. In fact, when injuries do occur it usually happens during this second phase. It is also the time police become involved, if they are called at all. The acute battering phase is concluded when the batterer stops, usually bringing with its cessation a sharp physiological reduction in tension. This in itself is naturally reinforcing. Violence often succeeds because it does work.

In phase three which follows, the batterer may apologize profusely, try to assist his victim, show kindness and remorse, and shower her with gifts and/or promises. The batterer himself may believe at this point that he will never allow himself to be violent again. The woman wants to believe the batterer and, early in the relationship at least, may renew her hope in his ability to change. This third phase provides the positive reinforcement for remaining in the relationship, for the woman. In fact, our results showed that phase three could also be characterized by an absence of tension or violence, and no observable loving-contrition behaviour, and still be reinforcing for the woman.

Given the relational context in which the violence occurs, the mental state of an accused at the critical moment she pulls the trigger cannot be understood except in terms of the cumulative effect of months or years of brutality. As Dr Shane explained in his testimony, the deterioration of the relationship between the appellant and Rust in the period immediately preceding the killing led to feelings of escalating terror on the part of the appellant:

But their relationship some weeks to months before was definitely escalating in terms of tension and in terms of the discordant quality about it. They were sleeping in separate bedrooms. Their intimate relationship was lacking and things were building and building and to a point, I think, where it built to that particular point where she couldn't – she felt so threatened and so overwhelmed that she had to – that she reacted in a violent way because of her fear of survival and also because, I think because of her, I guess, final sense that she was – that she had to defend herself and her own sense of violence towards this man who had really desecrated her and damaged her for so long.

... Another aspect of the cyclical nature of the abuse is that it begets a degree of predictability to the violence that is absent in an isolated violent encounter between two strangers. This also means that it may in fact be possible for a battered spouse to accurately predict the onset of violence before the first blow is struck, even if an outsider to the relationship cannot. Indeed, it has been suggested that a battered woman's knowledge of her partner's violence is so heightened that she is able to anticipate the nature and extent (though not the onset) of the violence by his conduct beforehand.

Where evidence exists that an accused is in a battering relationship, expert testimony can assist the jury in determining whether the accused had a "reasonable" apprehension of death when she acted by explaining the heightened sensitivity of a battered woman to her partner's acts. Without such testimony I am skeptical that the average fact-finder would be capable of appreciating why her subjective fear may have been reasonable in the context of the relationship. After all, the hypothetical "reasonable man" observing only the final incident may have been unlikely to recognize the batterer's threat as potentially lethal. Using the case at bar as an example the "reasonable man" might have thought, as the majority of the Court of Appeal seemed to, that it was unlikely that Rust would make good on his threat to kill the appellant that night because they had guests staying overnight.

The issue is not, however, what an outsider would have reasonably perceived but what the accused reasonably perceived, given her situation and her experience.

... Even accepting that a battered woman may be uniquely sensitized to danger from her batterer, it may yet be contended that the law ought to require her to wait until the knife is uplifted, the gun pointed, or the fist clenched before her apprehension is deemed reasonable. This would allegedly reduce the risk that the woman is mistaken in her fear, although the law does not require her fear to be correct, only reasonable. In response to this contention, I need only point to the observation made by Huband JA that the evidence showed that when the appellant and Rust physically fought, the appellant "invariably got the worst of it." I do not think it is an unwarranted generalization to say that due to their size, strength, socialization, and lack of training, women are typically no match for men in hand-to-hand combat. The requirement imposed in *Whynot* that a battered woman wait until the physical assault is "under way" before her apprehensions can be validated in law would, in the words of an American court, be tantamount to sentencing her to "murder by installment":

B Lack of Alternatives to Self-Help

Section 34(2) requires an accused who pleads self-defence to believe "on reasonable grounds" that it is not possible to otherwise preserve him or herself from death or grievous bodily harm. The obvious question is if the violence was so intolerable, why did the appellant not leave her abuser long ago? This question does not really go to whether she had an alternative to killing the deceased at the critical moment. Rather, it plays on the popular myth already referred to that a woman who says she was battered yet stayed with her batterer was either not as badly beaten as she claimed or else she liked it. Nevertheless, to the extent that her failure to leave the abusive relationship earlier may be used in support of the proposition that she was free to leave at the final moment, expert testimony can provide useful insights. Dr Shane attempted to explain in his testimony how and why, in the case at bar, the appellant remained with Rust:

She had stayed in this relationship, I think, because of the strange, almost unbelievable, but yet it happens, relationship that sometimes develops between people who develop this very disturbed, I think, very disturbed quality of a relationship. Trying to understand it, I think, isn't always easy and there's been a lot written about it recently, in the recent years, in psychiatric literature. But basically it involves two people who are involved in what appears to be an attachment which may have sexual or romantic or affectionate overtones.

And the one individual, and it's usually the women in our society, but there have been occasions where it's been reversed, but what happens is the spouse who becomes battered, if you will, stays in the relationship probably because of a number of reasons.

One is that the spouse gets beaten so badly – so badly – that he or she loses the motivation to react and becomes helpless and becomes powerless. And it's also been shown sometimes, you know, in – not that you can compare animals to human beings, but in laboratories, what you do if you shock an animal, after a while it can't respond to a threat of its life. It becomes just helpless and lies there in an amotivational state, if you will, where it feels there's no power and there's no energy to do anything.

So in a sense it happens in human beings as well. It's almost like a concentration camp, if you will. You get paralyzed with fear.

The other thing that happens often in these types of relationships with human beings is that the person who beats or assaults, who batters, often tries – he makes up and begs for forgiveness. And this individual, who basically has a very disturbed or damaged self-esteem, all of a sudden feels that he or she – we'll use women in this case because it's so much more common – the spouse feels that she again can do the spouse a favour and it can make her feel needed and boost her self-esteem for a while and make her feel worthwhile and the spouse says he'll forgive her and whatnot.

The account given by Dr Shane comports with that documented in the literature. Reference is often made to it as a condition of "learned helplessness," a phrase coined by Dr Charles Seligman, the psychologist who first developed the theory by experimenting on animals in the manner described by Dr Shane in his testimony. A related theory used to explain the failure of women to leave battering relationships is described by psychologist and lawyer Charles Patrick Ewing, in his book *Battered Women Who Kill* (1987). Ewing describes a phenomenon labelled "traumatic bonding" that has been observed between hostages and captors, battered children and their parents, concentration camp prisoners and guards, and batterers and their spouses.

The situation of the battered woman as described by Dr Shane strikes me as somewhat analogous to that of a hostage. If the captor tells her that he will kill her in three days' time, is it potentially reasonable for her to seize an opportunity presented on the first day to kill the captor or must she wait until he makes the attempt on the third day? I think the question the jury must ask itself is whether, given the history, circumstances and perceptions of the appellant, her belief that she could not preserve herself from being killed by Rust that night except by killing him first was reasonable. To the extent that expert evidence can assist the jury in making that determination, I would find such testimony to be both relevant and necessary.

In light of the foregoing discussion I would summarize as follows the principles upon which expert testimony is properly admitted in cases such as this:

1 Expert testimony is admissible to assist the fact-finder in drawing
   inferences in areas where the expert has relevant knowledge or
   experience beyond that of the layperson.
2 It is difficult for the layperson to comprehend the battered-wife
   syndrome. It is commonly thought that battered women are not
   really beaten as badly as they claim; otherwise they would have
   left the relationship. Alternatively, some believe that women enjoy
   being beaten, that they have a masochistic strain in them. Each of
   these stereotypes may adversely affect consideration of a battered
   woman's claim to have acted in self-defence in killing her mate.
3 Expert evidence can assist the jury in dispelling these myths.
4 Expert testimony relating to the ability of an accused to perceive
   danger from her mate may go to the issue of whether she "reasonably apprehended" death or grievous bodily harm on a particular
   occasion.
5 Expert testimony pertaining to why an accused remained in the
   battering relationship may be relevant in assessing the nature and
   extent of the alleged abuse.
6 By providing an explanation as to why an accused did not flee
   when she perceived her life to be in danger, expert testimony may
   also assist the jury in assessing the reasonableness of her belief
   that killing her batterer was the only way to save her own life.

... In my view, the trial judge did not err in admitting Dr Shane's
expert testimony in order to assist the jury in determining whether the
appellant had a reasonable apprehension of death or grievous bodily
harm and believed on reasonable grounds that she had no alternative
but to shoot Kevin Rust on the night in question.

Obviously the fact that the appellant was a battered woman does not
entitle her to an acquittal. Battered women may well kill their partners
other than in self-defence. The focus is not on who the woman is, but on
what she did.

(iii) Adequacy of Trial Judge's Charge to the Jury

The second issue raised in this case is the adequacy of the trial judge's
charge to the jury with respect to the expert evidence furnished by Dr
Shane. It appears that Dr Shane relied on various sources in formulating
his opinion – his series of interviews with the appellant, an interview

with her mother, a police report of the incident (including information regarding her statement to the police), and hospital records documenting eight of her visits to emergency departments between 1983 and 1986. Neither the appellant nor her mother testified at trial. The contents of their statements to Dr Shane were hearsay ...

Where the factual basis of an expert's opinion is a melange of admissible and inadmissible evidence the duty of the trial judge is to caution the jury that the weight attributable to the expert testimony is directly related to the amount and quality of admissible evidence on which it relies. The trial judge openly acknowledged to counsel the inherent difficulty in discharging such a duty in the case at bar. In my view, the trial judge performed his task adequately in this regard. A new trial is not warranted on the basis of the trial judge's charge to the jury.

I would accordingly allow the appeal, set aside the order of the Court of Appeal, and restore the acquittal.

Appeal allowed; acquittal restored.

READING QUESTIONS ON LAVALLÉE

1 Madame Justice Wilson compares Lavallée's situation to that of a hostage. In what ways are the situations parallel? Do you see any disanalogies?
2 Are there dangers connected to the idea of a "battered woman syndrome"? Does the defensibility of Lavallée's acts turn on her suffering from a condition, or can it be justified purely in light of the situation in which she finds herself?
3 Johnny Frank Buggs was attacked and threatened by members of the Crips gang, who were notorious for carrying grudges and using guns. When he saw them again shortly after the attack, he shot them. Can he claim self-defence? (State v Buggs 806 P. 2d 1381)
4 Nellie Eyapaise, who had been in a variety of abusive relationships, stabbed a man she barely knew when he made advances at her. Can she claim self-defence? (R v Eyapaise 20 CR (4th) 246 (Alta. QB) (1993))
5 In the movie Cape Fear, a lawyer is harassed by a recently released former client. The client threatens to kill the lawyer's family. The audience knows the convict will eventually do something terrible. Although the police tell the lawyer that he can only kill the convict during a confrontation, they cannot guarantee that they will be able to protect him. Compare this lawyer's situation to those of Lavallée, Eyapaise, and Buggs. Should the lawyer be allowed to act pre-emptively?

4

Law and Values: Liberty, Democracy, and the Rule of Law

This chapter looks at a series of questions revolving around the tensions between the role of law as a protector of individual liberty and as a tool of democratic self-rule. Law has been defended as each of these, yet they are in constant tension. Individual rights are sometimes endangered by policies chosen by majorities. As a result, almost everyone supposes that some limits should be placed on majority rule. Still, profound disagreements arise about how to think about the appropriate limits. Some defenders of the rule of law insist on severe limits. They argue that the law can only protect liberty if it has clear and readily identifiable rules that enable people to plan their own affairs. This understanding of liberty has been criticized on a number of fronts. From one direction, critics have suggested that such a view of liberty sets appropriate limits to the reach of the law, but that more than the protection of liberty is needed if a society is to survive. Defenders of such views may disagree about what more is needed. Some of them suppose that what is important is that the members of the society share some conception of the good life, while others may insist that the material conditions for the meaningful exercise of liberty be guaranteed. Others argue that the very idea of negative liberty is flawed, resting on an unrealistic view of the importance of choice. From still another direction, difficulties with the idea of negative liberty have led some critics to question the very idea of the rule of law. Sometimes this criticism takes the form of a rejection of the distinction between making law and applying it, and concludes that the idea of law as a rule-governed activity makes no sense. In the eyes of these critics, law is always an exercise of power, and at best bears a contingent relation to justice and democracy.

John Stuart Mill
On Liberty (1859)

In the classic work of nineteenth-century liberalism, Mill argues that the only legitimate restrictions on individual liberty are those that will prevent harms to others.

CHAPTER I: INTRODUCTORY

The Subject of this Essay is not the so-called Liberty of the Will, so unfortunately opposed to the misnamed doctrine of Philosophical Necessity; but Civil, or Social Liberty: the nature and limits of the power which can be legitimately exercised by society over the individual. A question seldom stated, and hardly ever discussed, in general terms, but which profoundly influences the practical controversies of the age by its latent presence, and is likely soon to make itself recognised as the vital question of the future. It is so far from being new, that, in a certain sense, it has divided mankind, almost from the remotest ages; but in the stage of progress into which the more civilized portions of the species have now entered, it presents itself under new conditions, and requires a different and more fundamental treatment.

The struggle between Liberty and Authority is the most conspicuous feature in the portions of history with which we are earliest familiar, particularly in that of Greece, Rome, and England. But in old times this contest was between subjects, or some classes of subjects, and the Government. By liberty, was meant protection against the tyranny of the political rulers. The rulers were conceived (except in some of the popular governments of Greece) as in a necessarily antagonistic position to the people whom they ruled. They consisted of a governing One, or a governing tribe or caste, who derived their authority from inheritance or conquest, who, at all events, did not hold it at the pleasure of the governed, and whose supremacy men did not venture, perhaps did not desire, to contest, whatever precautions might be taken against its oppressive exercise. Their power was regarded as necessary, but also as highly dangerous; as a weapon which they would attempt to use against their subjects, no less than against external enemies. To prevent the weaker members of the community from being preyed upon by innumerable vultures, it was needful that there should be an animal of prey stronger than the rest, commissioned to keep them down. But as the king of the vultures would be no less bent upon preying on the flock than any of the minor harpies, it was indispensable to be in a perpetual attitude of defence against his beak and claws. The aim, therefore, of patriots was to set limits to the power which the ruler should be suffered to exercise over the community; and this limitation was what they meant by liberty. It was attempted in two ways. First, by obtaining a recognition of certain immunities, called political liberties or rights, which it was to be regarded as a breach of duty in the ruler to infringe, and which, if he did infringe, specific resistance, or general rebellion, was held to be justifiable. A second, and generally a later expedient, was the establishment of constitutional checks, by which the consent of the community, or of a body of some sort, supposed to represent its interests, was made a necessary condition to some of the more important acts of the governing power. To the first of these modes of limitation, the ruling power, in most European countries, was compelled, more or less, to submit. It was not so with the second; and, to attain this, or when already in some degree possessed, to attain it more completely, became everywhere the principal object of the lovers of liberty. And so long as mankind were content to combat one enemy by another, and to be ruled by a master, on condition of being guaranteed more or less efficaciously against his tyranny, they did not carry their aspirations beyond this point.

A time, however, came, in the progress of human affairs, when men ceased to think it a necessity of nature that their governors should be an independent power, opposed in interest to themselves. It appeared to them much better that the various magistrates of the State should be their tenants or delegates, revocable at their pleasure. In that way alone, it seemed, could they have complete security that the powers of government would never be abused to their disadvantage. By degrees this new demand for elective and temporary rulers became the prominent object of the exertions of the popular party, wherever any such party existed; and superseded, to a considerable extent, the previous efforts to limit the power of rulers. As the struggle proceeded for making the ruling power emanate from the periodical choice of the ruled, some persons began to think that too much importance had been attached to the limitation of the power itself. *That* (it might seem) was a resource against rulers whose interests were habitually opposed to those of the people. What was now wanted was, that the rulers should be identified with the people; that their interest and will should be the interest and will of the nation. The nation did not need to be protected against its own will. There was no fear of its tyrannizing over itself. Let the rulers be effectually responsible to it, promptly removable by it, and it could afford to trust them with power of which it could itself dictate the use to be made. Their power was but the nation's own power, concentrated, and in a form convenient for exercise. This mode of thought, or rather perhaps of feeling, was common among the last generation of European liberalism, in the Continental section of which it still apparently predominates. Those who admit any limit to what a government may do, except in the case of such governments as they think ought not to exist, stand out as brilliant exceptions among the political thinkers of the Continent. A similar tone of sentiment might by this time have been prevalent in our own country, if the circumstances which for a time encouraged it, had continued unaltered.

But, in political and philosophical theories, as well as in persons, success discloses faults and infirmities which failure might have concealed from observation. The notion, that the people have no need to limit their power over themselves, might seem axiomatic, when popular government was a thing only dreamed about, or read of as having existed at some distant period of the past. Neither was that notion necessarily disturbed by such temporary aberrations as those of the French Revolution, the worst of which were the work of an usurping few, and which, in any case, belonged, not to the permanent working of popular institutions, but to a sudden and convulsive outbreak against monarchical and aristocratic despotism. In time, however, a democratic republic came to occupy a large portion of the earth's surface, and made itself felt as one of the most powerful members of the community of nations; and elective and responsible government became subject to the observations and criticisms which wait upon a great existing fact. It was now perceived that such phrases as "self-government," and "the power of the people over themselves," do not express the true state of the case. The "people" who exercise the power are not always the same people with those over whom it is exercised; and the "self-government" spoken of is not the government of each by himself, but of each by all the rest. The will of the people, moreover, practically means the will of the most numerous or the most active *part* of the people; the majority, or those who succeed in making themselves accepted as the majority; the people, consequently, *may* desire to oppress a part of their number; and precautions are as much needed against this as against any other abuse of power. The limitation, therefore, of the power of government over individuals loses none of its importance when the holders of power are regularly accountable to the community, that is, to the strongest party therein. This view of things, recommending itself equally to the intelligence of thinkers and to the inclination of those important classes in European society to whose real or supposed interests democracy is adverse, has had no difficulty in establishing itself; and in political speculations "the tyranny of the majority" is now generally included among the evils against which society requires to be on its guard.

Like other tyrannies, the tyranny of the majority was at first, and is still vulgarly, held in dread, chiefly as operating through the acts of the public authorities. But reflecting persons perceived that when society is itself the tyrant – society collectively, over the separate individuals who compose it – its means of tyrannizing are not restricted to the acts which it may do by the hands of its political functionaries. Society can and does execute its own mandates: and if it issues wrong mandates instead of right, or any mandates at all in things with which it ought not to meddle, it practises a social tyranny more formidable than many kinds of political oppression, since, though not usually upheld by such extreme penalties, it leaves fewer means of escape, penetrating much more deeply into the details of life, and enslaving the soul itself. Protection, therefore, against the tyranny of the magistrate is not enough: there needs protection also against the tyranny of the prevailing opinion and feeling; against the tendency of society to impose, by other means than civil penalties, its own ideas and practices as rules of conduct on those who dissent from them; to fetter the development, and, if possible, prevent the formation, of any individuality not in harmony with its ways, and compel all characters to fashion themselves upon the model of its own. There is a limit to the legitimate interference of collective opinion with individual independence: and to find that limit, and maintain it against encroachment, is as indispensable to a good condition of human affairs, as protection against political despotism.

But though this proposition is not likely to be contested in general terms, the practical question, where to place the limit – how to make the fitting adjustment between individual independence and social control – is a subject on which nearly everything remains to be done. All that makes existence valuable to any one, depends on the enforcement of restraints upon the actions of other people. Some rules of conduct, therefore, must be imposed, by law in the first place, and by opinion on many things which are not fit subjects for the operation of law. What these rules should be, is the principal question in human affairs; but if we except a few of the most obvious cases, it is one of those which least progress has been made in resolving. No two ages, and scarcely any two countries, have decided it alike; and the decision of one age or country is a wonder to another. Yet the people of any given age and country no more suspect any difficulty in it, than if it were a subject on which mankind had always been agreed. The rules which obtain among themselves appear to them self-evident and self-justifying. This all but universal illusion is one of the examples of the magical influence of custom, which is not only, as the proverb says, a second nature, but is continually mistaken for the first. The effect of custom, in preventing any misgiving respecting the rules of conduct which mankind impose on one another, is all the more complete because the subject is one on which it is not generally considered necessary that reasons should be given, either by one person to others, or by each to himself. People are accustomed to believe, and have been encouraged in the belief by some who aspire to the character of philosophers, that their feelings, on subjects of this nature, are better than reasons, and render reasons unnecessary. The practical principle which guides them to their opinions on the regulation of human conduct, is the feeling in each person's mind that everybody should be required to act as he, and those with whom he sympathizes, would like them to act. No one, indeed, acknowledges to himself that his standard of judgment is his own liking; but an opinion on a point of conduct, not supported by reasons, can only count as one person's preference; and if the reasons, when given, are a mere appeal to a similar preference felt by other people, it is still only many people's liking instead of one. To an ordinary man, however, his own preference, thus supported, is not only a perfectly satisfactory reason, but the only one he generally has for any of his notions of morality, taste, or propriety, which are not expressly written in his religious creed; and his chief guide in the interpretation even of that. Men's opinions, accordingly, on what is laudable or blameable, are affected by all the multifarious causes which influence their wishes in regard to the conduct of others, and which are as numerous as those which determine their wishes on any other subject. Sometimes their reason – at other times their prejudices or superstitions: often their social affections, not seldom their antisocial ones, their envy or jealousy, their arrogance or contemptuousness: but most commonly, their desires or fears for themselves – their legitimate or illegitimate self-interest. Wherever there is

an ascendant class, a large portion of the morality of the country ema-
nates from its class interests, and its feelings of class superiority. The
morality between Spartans and Helots, between planters and negroes,
between princes and subjects, between nobles and roturiers, between
men and women, has been for the most part the creation of these class
interests and feelings: and the sentiments thus generated, react in turn
upon the moral feelings of the members of the ascendant class, in their
relations among themselves. Where, on the other hand, a class, formerly
ascendant, has lost its ascendancy, or where its ascendancy is unpopular, the prevailing moral sentiments frequently bear the impress of an
impatient dislike of superiority. Another grand determining principle
of the rules of conduct, both in act and forbearance, which have been
enforced by law or opinion, has been the servility of mankind towards
the supposed preferences or aversions of their temporal masters, or of
their gods. This servility, though essentially selfish, is not hypocrisy; it
gives rise to perfectly genuine sentiments of abhorrence; it made men
burn magicians and heretics. Among so many baser influences, the
general and obvious interests of society have of course had a share, and
a large one, in the direction of the moral sentiments: less, however, as
a matter of reason, and on their own account, than as a consequence of
the sympathies and antipathies which grew out of them: and sympathies and antipathies which had little or nothing to do with the interests
of society, have made themselves felt in the establishment of moralities
with quite as great force.

The likings and dislikings of society, or of some powerful portion of
it, are thus the main thing which has practically determined the rules
laid down for general observance, under the penalties of law or opinion. And in general, those who have been in advance of society in
thought and feeling, have left this condition of things unassailed in
principle, however they may have come into conflict with it in some of
its details. They have occupied themselves rather in inquiring what
things society ought to like or dislike, than in questioning whether its
likings or dislikings should be a law to individuals. They preferred
endeavouring to alter the feelings of mankind on the particular points
on which they were themselves heretical, rather than make common
cause in defence of freedom, with heretics generally. The only case in
which the higher ground has been taken on principle and maintained
with consistency, by any but an individual here and there, is that of
religious belief: a case instructive in many ways, and not least so as
forming a most striking instance of the fallibility of what is called the

moral sense: for the *odium theologicum*, in a sincere bigot, is one of the most unequivocal cases of moral feeling. Those who first broke the yoke of what called itself the Universal Church, were in general as little willing to permit difference of religious opinion as that church itself. But when the heat of the conflict was over, without giving a complete victory to any party, and each church or sect was reduced to limit its hopes to retaining possession of the ground it already occupied; minorities, seeing that they had no chance of becoming majorities, were under the necessity of pleading to those whom they could not convert, for permission to differ. It is accordingly on this battle field, almost solely, that the rights of the individual against society have been asserted on broad grounds of principle, and the claim of society to exercise authority over dissentients, openly controverted. The great writers to whom the world owes what religious liberty it possesses, have mostly asserted freedom of conscience as an indefeasible right, and denied absolutely that a human being is accountable to others for his religious belief. Yet so natural to mankind is intolerance in whatever they really care about, that religious freedom has hardly anywhere been practically realized, except where religious indifference, which dislikes to have its peace disturbed by theological quarrels, has added its weight to the scale. In the minds of almost all religious persons, even in the most tolerant countries, the duty of toleration is admitted with tacit reserves. One person will bear with dissent in matters of church government, but not of dogma; another can tolerate everybody, short of a Papist or an Unitarian; another, every one who believes in revealed religion, a few extend their charity a little further, but stop at the belief in a God and in a future state. Wherever the sentiment of the majority is still genuine and intense, it is found to have abated little of its claim to be obeyed.

In England, from the peculiar circumstances of our political history, though the yoke of opinion is perhaps heavier, that of law is lighter, than in most other countries of Europe; and there is considerable jealousy of direct interference, by the legislative or the executive power, with private conduct; not so much from any just regard for the independence of the individual, as from the still subsisting habit of looking on the government as representing an opposite interest to the public. The majority have not yet learnt to feel the power of the government their power, or its opinions their opinions. When they do so, individual liberty will probably be as much exposed to invasion from the government, as it already is from public opinion. But, as yet, there is a considerable amount of feeling ready to be called forth against any attempt of the law to control individuals in things in which they have not hitherto been accustomed to be controlled by it; and this with very little discrimination as to whether the matter is, or is not, within the legitimate sphere of legal control; insomuch that the feeling, highly salutary on the whole, is perhaps quite as often misplaced as well grounded in the particular instances of its application. There is, in fact, no recognised principle by which the propriety or impropriety of government interference is customarily tested. People decide according to their personal preferences. Some, whenever they see any good to be done, or evil to be remedied, would willingly instigate the government to undertake the business; while others prefer to bear almost any amount of social evil, rather than add one to the departments of human interests amenable to governmental control. And men range themselves on one or the other side in any particular case, according to this general direction of their sentiments; or according to the degree of interest which they feel in the particular thing which it is proposed that the government should do, or according to the belief they entertain that the government would, or would not, do it in the manner they prefer; but very rarely on account of any opinion to which they consistently adhere, as to what things are fit to be done by a government. And it seems to me that in consequence of this absence of rule or principle, one side is at present as often wrong as the other; the interference of government is, with about equal frequency, improperly invoked and improperly condemned.

The object of this Essay is to assert one very simple principle, as entitled to govern absolutely the dealings of society with the individual in the way of compulsion and control, whether the means used be physical force in the form of legal penalties, or the moral coercion of public opinion. That principle is, that the sole end for which mankind are warranted, individually or collectively, in interfering with the liberty of action of any of their number, is self-protection. That the only purpose for which power can be rightfully exercised over any member of a civilized community, against his will, is to prevent harm to others. His own good, either physical or moral, is not a sufficient warrant. He cannot rightfully be compelled to do or forbear because it will be better for him to do so, because it will make him happier, because, in the opinions of others, to do so would be wise, or even right. These are good reasons for remonstrating with him, or reasoning with him, or persuading him, or entreating him, but not for compelling him, or visiting him with any evil in case he do otherwise. To justify that, the conduct from which it is desired to deter him, must be calculated to produce evil to some one else. The only part of the conduct of any one, for which he is amenable to society, is that which concerns others. In the part which merely concerns himself, his independence is, of right, absolute. Over himself, over his own body and mind, the individual is sovereign.

It is, perhaps, hardly necessary to say that this doctrine is meant to apply only to human beings in the maturity of their faculties. We are not speaking of children, or of young persons below the age which the law may fix as that of manhood or womanhood. Those who are still in a state to require being taken care of by others, must be protected against their own actions as well as against external injury. For the same reason, we may leave out of consideration those backward states of society in which the race itself may be considered as in its nonage. The early difficulties in the way of spontaneous progress are so great, that there is seldom any choice of means for overcoming them; and a ruler full of the spirit of improvement is warranted in the use of any expedients that will attain an end, perhaps otherwise unattainable. Despotism is a legitimate mode of government in dealing with barbarians, provided the end be their improvement, and the means justified by actually effecting that end. Liberty, as a principle, has no application to any state of things anterior to the time when mankind have become capable of being improved by free and equal discussion. Until then, there is nothing for them but implicit obedience to an Akbar or a Charlemagne, if they are so fortunate as to find one. But as soon as mankind have attained the capacity of being guided to their own improvement by conviction or persuasion (a period long since reached in all nations with whom we need here concern ourselves), compulsion, either in the direct form or in that of pains and penalties for non-compliance, is no longer admissible as a means to their own good, and justifiable only for the security of others.

It is proper to state that I forego any advantage which could be derived to my argument from the idea of abstract right, as a thing independent of utility. I regard utility as the ultimate appeal on all ethical questions; but it must be utility in the largest sense, grounded on the permanent interests of man as a progressive being. Those interests, I contend, authorize the subjection of individual spontaneity to external control, only in respect to those actions of each, which concern the interest of other people. If any one does an act hurtful to others, there is a *primâ facie* case for punishing him, by law, or, where legal penalties are not safely applicable, by general disapprobation. There are also many positive acts for the benefit of others, which he may rightfully be compelled to perform; such as, to give evidence in a court of justice; to bear his fair share in the common defence, or in any other joint work necessary to the interest of the society of which he enjoys the protection; and to perform certain acts of individual beneficence, such as saving a fellow-creature's life, or interposing to protect the defenceless against ill-usage, things which whenever it is obviously a man's duty to do, he may rightfully be made responsible to society for not doing. A person may cause evil to others not only by his actions, but by his inaction, and in either case he is justly accountable to them for the injury. The latter case, it is true, requires a much more cautious exercise of compulsion than the former. To make any one answerable for doing evil to others, is the rule; to make him answerable for not preventing evil, is, comparatively speaking, the exception. Yet there are many cases clear enough and grave enough to justify that exception. In all things which regard the external relations of the individual, he is *de jure* amenable to those whose interests are concerned, and if need be, to society as their protector. There are often good reasons for not holding him to the responsibility; but these reasons must arise from the special expediencies of the case: either because it is a kind of case in which he is on the whole likely to act better, when left to his own discretion, than when controlled in any way in which society have it in their power to control him; or because the attempt to exercise control would produce other evils, greater than those which it would prevent. When such reasons as these preclude the enforcement of responsibility, the conscience of the agent himself should step into the vacant judgment seat, and protect those interests of others which have no external protection; judging himself all the more rigidly, because the case does not admit of his being made accountable to the judgment of his fellow-creatures.

But there is a sphere of action in which society, as distinguished from the individual, has, if any, only an indirect interest; comprehending all that portion of a person's life and conduct which affects only himself, or if it also affects others, only with their free, voluntary, and undeceived consent and participation. When I say only himself, I mean directly, and in the first instance: for whatever affects himself, may affect others through himself; and the objection which may be grounded on this contingency, will receive consideration in the sequel. This, then, is the appropriate region of human liberty. It comprises, first, the inward domain of consciousness; demanding liberty of conscience, in the most comprehensive sense; liberty of thought and feeling; absolute freedom of opinion and sentiment on all subjects, practical or speculative, scientific, moral, or theological. The liberty of expressing and publishing opinions may seem to fall under a different principle, since it belongs to that part of the conduct of an individual which concerns other people; but, being almost of as much importance as the liberty of thought itself, and resting in great part on the same reasons, is practically inseparable from it. Secondly, the principle requires liberty of tastes and pursuits; of framing the plan of our life to suit our own character; of doing as we like, subject to such consequences as may follow: without impediment from our fellow-creatures, so long as what we do does not harm them, even though they should think our conduct foolish, perverse, or wrong. Thirdly, from this liberty of each individual, follows the liberty, within the same limits, of combination among individuals; freedom to unite, for any purpose not involving harm to others: the persons combining being supposed to be of full age, and not forced or deceived.

No society in which these liberties are not, on the whole, respected, is free, whatever may be its form of government; and none is completely free in which they do not exist absolute and unqualified. The only freedom which deserves the name, is that of pursuing our own good in our own way, so long as we do not attempt to deprive others of theirs, or impede their efforts to obtain it. Each is the proper guardian of his own health, whether bodily, or mental and spiritual. Mankind are greater gainers by suffering each other to live as seems good to themselves, than by compelling each to live as seems good to the rest.

Though this doctrine is anything but new, and, to some persons, may have the air of a truism, there is no doctrine which stands more directly opposed to the general tendency of existing opinion and practice. Society has expended fully as much effort in the attempt (according to its lights) to compel people to conform to its notions of personal, as of social excellence. The ancient commonwealths thought themselves entitled to practise, and the ancient philosophers countenanced, the regulation of every part of private conduct by public authority, on the ground that the State had a deep interest in the whole bodily and mental discipline of every one of its citizens; a mode of thinking which may have been admissible in small republics surrounded by powerful enemies, in constant peril of being subverted by foreign attack or internal commotion, and to which even a short interval of relaxed energy and selfcommand might so easily be fatal, that they could not afford to wait for the salutary permanent effects of freedom. In the modern world, the greater size of political communities, and above all, the separation between spiritual and temporal authority (which placed the direction of men's consciences in other hands than those which controlled their worldly affairs), prevented so great an interference by law in the details of private life; but the engines of moral repression have been wielded more strenuously against divergence from the reigning opinion in self-regarding, than even in social matters; religion, the most powerful of the elements which have entered into the formation of moral feeling, having almost always been governed either by the ambition of a hierarchy, seeking control over every department of human conduct, or by the spirit of Puritanism. And some of those modern reformers who have placed themselves in strongest opposition to the religions of the past, have been noway behind either churches or sects in their assertion of the right of spiritual domination: M. Comte, in particular, whose social system, as unfolded in his *Système de Politique Positive*, aims at establishing (though by moral more than by legal appliances) a despotism of society over the individual, surpassing anything contemplated in the political ideal of the most rigid disciplinarian among the ancient philosophers.

Apart from the peculiar tenets of individual thinkers, there is also in the world at large an increasing inclination to stretch unduly the powers of society over the individual, both by the force of opinion and even by that of legislation: and as the tendency of all the changes taking place in the world is to strengthen society, and diminish the power of the individual, this encroachment is not one of the evils which tend spontaneously to disappear, but, on the contrary, to grow more and more formidable. The disposition of mankind, whether as rulers or as fellow-citizens, to impose their own opinions and inclinations as a rule of conduct on others, is so energetically supported by some of the best and by some of the worst feelings incident to human nature, that it is hardly ever kept under restraint by anything but want of power; and as the power is not declining, but growing, unless a strong barrier of moral conviction can be raised against the mischief, we must expect, in the present circumstances of the world, to see it increase.

It will be convenient for the argument, if, instead of at once entering upon the general thesis, we confine ourselves in the first instance to a single branch of it, on which the principle here stated is, if not fully, yet to a certain point, recognised by the current opinions. This one branch is the Liberty of Thought: from which it is impossible to separate the cognate liberty of speaking and of writing. Although these liberties, to some considerable amount, form part of the political morality of all countries which profess religious toleration and free institutions, the grounds, both philosophical and practical, on which they rest, are perhaps not so familiar to the general mind, nor so thoroughly appreciated by many even of the leaders of opinion, as might have been expected. Those grounds, when rightly understood, are of much wider application than to only one division of the subject, and a thorough consideration of this part of the question will be found the best introduction to the remainder. Those to whom nothing which I am about to say will be new, may therefore, I hope, excuse me, if on a subject which for now three centuries has been so often discussed, I venture on one discussion more.

CHAPTER II: OF THE LIBERTY OF THOUGHT AND DISCUSSION

The time, it is to be hoped, is gone by, when any defence would be necessary of the "liberty of the press" as one of the securities against corrupt or tyrannical government. No argument, we may suppose, can now be needed, against permitting a legislature or an executive, not identified in interest with the people, to prescribe opinions to them, and determine what doctrines or what arguments they shall be allowed to hear. This aspect of the question, besides, has been so often and so triumphantly enforced by preceding writers, that it needs not be specially insisted on in this place. Though the law of England, on the subject of the press, is as servile to this day as it was in the time of the Tudors, there is little danger of its being actually put in force against political discussion, except during some temporary panic, when fear of insurrection drives ministers and judges from their propriety; and, speaking generally, it is not, in constitutional countries, to be apprehended, that the government, whether completely responsible to the people or not, will often attempt to control the expression of opinion, except when in doing so it makes itself the organ of the general intolerance of the public. Let us suppose, therefore, that the government is entirely at one with the people, and never thinks of exerting any power of coercion unless in agreement with what it conceives to be their voice. But I deny the right of the people to exercise such coercion, either by themselves or by their government. The power itself is illegitimate. The best government has no more title to it than the worst. It is as noxious, or more noxious, when exerted in accordance with public opinion, than when in opposition to it. If all mankind minus one, were of one opinion, and only one person were of the contrary opinion, mankind would be no more justified in silencing that one person, than he, if he had the power, would be justified in silencing mankind. Were an opinion a personal possession of no value except to the owner; if to be obstructed in the enjoyment of it were simply a private injury, it would make some difference whether the injury was inflicted only on a few persons or on many. But the peculiar evil of silencing the expression of an opinion is, that it is robbing the human race; posterity as well as the existing generation; those who dissent from the opinion, still more than those who hold it. If the opinion is right, they are deprived of the opportunity of exchanging error for truth: if wrong, they lose, what is almost as great a benefit, the clearer perception and livelier impression of truth, produced by its collision with error.

It is necessary to consider separately these two hypotheses, each of which has a distinct branch of the argument corresponding to it. We can never be sure that the opinion we are endeavouring to stifle is a false opinion; and if we were sure, stifling it would be an evil still.

First: the opinion which it is attempted to suppress by authority may possibly be true. Those who desire to suppress it, of course deny its truth; but they are not infallible. They have no authority to decide the question for all mankind, and exclude every other person from the means of judging. To refuse a hearing to an opinion, because they are sure that it is false, is to assume that *their* certainty is the same thing as *absolute* certainty. All silencing of discussion is an assumption of infallibility. Its condemnation may be allowed to rest on this common argument, not the worse for being common.

Unfortunately for the good sense of mankind, the fact of their fallibility is far from carrying the weight in their practical judgment, which is always allowed to it in theory; for while every one well knows himself to be fallible, few think it necessary to take any precautions against their own fallibility, or admit the supposition that any opinion, of which they feel very certain, may be one of the examples of the error to which they acknowledge themselves to be liable. Absolute princes, or others who are accustomed to unlimited deference, usually feel this complete confidence in their own opinions on nearly all subjects. People more happily situated, who sometimes hear their opinions disputed, and are not wholly unused to be set right when they are wrong, place the same unbounded reliance only on such of their opinions as are shared by all who surround them, or to whom they habitually defer: for in proportion to a man's want of confidence in his own solitary judgment, does he usually repose, with implicit trust, on the infallibility of "the world" in general. And the world, to each individual, means the part of it with which he comes in contact; his party, his sect, his church, his class of society: the man may be called, by comparison, almost liberal and large-minded to whom it means anything so comprehensive as his own country or his own age. Nor is his faith in this collective authority at all shaken by his being aware that other ages, countries, sects, churches, classes, and parties have thought, and even now think, the exact reverse. He devolves upon his own world the responsibility of being in the right against the dissentient worlds of other people; and it never troubles him that mere accident has decided which of these numerous worlds is the object of his reliance, and that the same causes which make him a Churchman in London, would have made him a Buddhist or a Confucian in Pekin. Yet it is as evident in itself, as any amount of argument can make it, that ages are no more infallible than individuals; every age having held many opinions which subsequent ages have deemed not only false but absurd; and it is as certain that many opinions, now general, will be rejected by future ages, as it is that many, once general, are rejected by the present.

The objection likely to be made to this argument, would probably take some such form as the following. There is no greater assumption of infallibility in forbidding the propagation of error, than in any other thing which is done by public authority on its own judgment and responsibility. Judgment is given to men that they may use it. Because it may be used erroneously, are men to be told that they ought not to use it at all? To prohibit what they think pernicious, is not claiming exemption from error, but fulfilling the duty incumbent on them, although fallible, of acting on their conscientious conviction. If we were never to act on our opinions, because those opinions may be wrong, we should leave all our interests uncared for, and all our duties unperformed. An objection which applies to all conduct, can be no valid objection to any conduct in particular. It is the duty of governments, and of individuals, to form the truest opinions they can; to form them carefully, and never impose them upon others unless they are quite sure of being right. But when they are sure (such reasoners may say), it is not conscientiousness but cowardice to shrink from acting on their opinions, and allow doctrines which they honestly think dangerous to the welfare of mankind, either in this life or in another, to be scattered abroad without restraint, because other people, in less enlightened times, have persecuted opinions now believed to be true. Let us take care, it may be said, not to make the same mistake: but governments and nations have made mistakes in other things, which are not denied to be fit subjects for the exercise of authority: they have laid on bad taxes, made unjust wars. Ought we therefore to lay on no taxes, and, under whatever provocation, make no wars? Men, and governments, must act to the best of their ability. There is no such thing as absolute certainty, but there is assurance sufficient for the purposes of human life. We may, and must, assume our opinion to be true for the guidance of our own conduct: and it is assuming no more when we forbid bad men to pervert society by the propagation of opinions which we regard as false and pernicious.

I answer, that it is assuming very much more. There is the greatest difference between presuming an opinion to be true, because, with every opportunity for contesting it, it has not been refuted, and assuming its truth for the purpose of not permitting its refutation. Complete liberty of contradicting and disproving our opinion, is the very condition which justifies us in assuming its truth for purposes of action; and on no other terms can a being with human faculties have any rational assurance of being right ...

Let us now pass to the second division of the argument, and dismissing the supposition that any of the received opinions may be false, let us assume them to be true, and examine into the worth of the manner in which they are likely to be held, when their truth is not freely and openly canvassed. However unwillingly a person who has a strong opinion may admit the possibility that his opinion may be false, he ought to be moved by the consideration that however true it may be, if it is not fully, frequently, and fearlessly discussed, it will be held as a dead dogma, not a living truth.

There is a class of persons (happily not quite so numerous as formerly) who think it enough if a person assents undoubtingly to what they think true, though he has no knowledge whatever of the grounds of the opinion, and could not make a tenable defence of it against the most superficial objections. Such persons, if they can once get their creed taught from authority, naturally think that no good, and some harm, comes of its being allowed to be questioned. Where their influence prevails, they make it nearly impossible for the received opinion to be rejected wisely and considerately, though it may still be rejected rashly and ignorantly; for to shut out discussion entirely is seldom possible, and when it once gets in, beliefs not grounded on conviction are apt to give way before the slightest semblance of an argument. Waving, however, this possibility – assuming that the true opinion abides in the mind, but abides as a prejudice, a belief independent of and proof against, argument – this is not the way in which truth ought to be held by a rational being. This is not knowing the truth. Truth, thus held, is but one superstition the more, accidentally clinging to the words which enunciate a truth.

If the intellect and judgment of mankind ought to be cultivated, a thing which Protestants at least do not deny, on what can these faculties be more appropriately exercised by any one, than on the things which concern him so much that it is considered necessary for him to hold opinions on them? If the cultivation of the understanding consists in one thing more than in another, it is surely in learning the grounds of one's own opinions. Whatever people believe, on subjects on which it is of the first importance to believe rightly, they ought to be able to defend against at least the common objections. But, some one may say, "Let them be *taught* the grounds of their opinions. It does not follow that opinions must be merely parroted because they are never heard controverted. Persons who learn geometry do not simply commit the theorems to memory, but understand and learn likewise the demonstrations; and it would be absurd to say that they remain ignorant of the grounds of geometrical truths, because they never hear any one deny, and attempt to disprove them." Undoubtedly: and such teaching suffices on a subject like mathematics, where there is nothing at all to be said on the wrong side of the question. The peculiarity of the evidence of mathematical truths is, that all the argument is on one side. There are not objections, and no answers to objections. But on every subject on which difference of opinion is possible, the truth depends on a balance to be struck between two sets of conflicting reasons. Even in natural philosophy, there is always some other explanation possible of the same facts; some geocentric theory instead of heliocentric, some phlogiston instead of oxygen; and it has to be shown why that other theory cannot be the true one: and until this is shown, and until we know how it is shown, we do not understand the grounds of our opinion. But when we turn to subjects infinitely more complicated, to morals, religion, politics, social relations, and the business of life, three-fourths of the arguments for every disputed opinion consist in dispelling the appearances which favour some opinion different from it. The greatest orator, save one, of antiquity, has left it on record that he always studied his adversary's case with as great, if not with still greater, intensity than even his own.

What Cicero practised as the means of forensic success, requires to be imitated by all who study any subject in order to arrive at the truth. He who knows only his own side of the case, knows little of that. His reasons may be good, and no one may have been able to refute them. But if he is equally unable to refute the reasons on the opposite side; if he does not so much as know what they are, he has no ground for preferring either opinion. The rational position for him would be suspension of judgment, and unless he contents himself with that, he is either led by authority, or adopts, like the generality of the world, the side to which he feels most inclination. Nor is it enough that he should hear the arguments of adversaries from his own teachers, presented as they state them, and accompanied by what they offer as refutations. That is not the way to do justice to the arguments, or bring them into real contact with his own mind. He must be able to hear them from persons who actually believe them; who defend them in earnest, and do their very utmost for them. He must know them in their most plausible and persuasive form; he must feel the whole force of the difficulty which the true view of the subject has to encounter and dispose of; else he will never really possess himself of the portion of truth which meets and removes that difficulty. Ninety-nine in a hundred of what are called educated men are in this condition; even of those who can argue fluently for their opinions. Their conclusion may be true, but it might be false for anything they know: they have never thrown themselves into the mental position of whose who think differently from them, and considered what such persons may have to say; and consequently they do not, in any proper sense of the word, know the doctrine which they themselves profess. They do not know those parts of it which explain and justify the remainder; the considerations which show that a fact which seemingly conflicts with another is reconcilable with it, or that, of two apparently strong reasons, one and not the other ought to be preferred. All that part of the truth which turns the scale, and decides the judgment of a completely informed mind, they are strangers to; nor is it ever really known, but to those who have attended equally and impartially to both sides, and endeavoured to see the reasons of both in the strongest light. So essential is this discipline to a real understanding of moral and human subjects, that if opponents of all important truths do not exist, it is indispensable to imagine them, and supply them with the strongest arguments which the most skilful devil's advocate can conjure up.

CHAPTER III: OF INDIVIDUALITY, AS ONE OF THE ELEMENTS OF WELL-BEING

Such being the reasons which make it imperative that human beings should be free to form opinions, and to express their opinions without reserve; and such the baneful consequences to the intellectual, and through that to the moral nature of man, unless this liberty is either conceded, or asserted in spite of prohibition; let us next examine whether the same reasons do not require that men should be free to act upon their opinions – to carry these out in their lives, without hindrance, either physical or moral, from their fellow-men, so long as it is at their own risk and peril. This last proviso is of course indispensable. No one pretends that actions should be as free as opinions. On the contrary, even opinions lose their immunity, when the circumstances in which they are expressed are such as to constitute their expression a positive instigation to some mischievous act. An opinion that corn-dealers are starvers of the poor, or that private property is robbery, ought to be unmolested when simply circulated through the press, but may justly incur punishment when delivered orally to an excited mob assembled before the house of a corn-dealer, or when handed about among the same mob in the form of a placard. Acts, of whatever kind, which, without justifiable cause, do harm to others, may be, and in the more important cases absolutely require to be, controlled by the unfavourable sentiments, and, when needful, by the active interference of mankind. The liberty of the individual must be thus far limited; he must not make himself a nuisance to other people. But if he refrains from molesting others in what concerns them, and merely acts according to his own inclination and judgment in things which concern himself, the same reasons which show that opinion should be free, prove also that he should be allowed, without molestation, to carry his opinions into practice at his own cost. That mankind are not infallible; that their truths, for the most part, are only half-truths; that unity of opinion, unless resulting from the fullest and freest comparison of opposite opinions, is not desirable, and diversity not an evil, but a good, until mankind are much more capable than at present of recognising all sides of the truth, are principles applicable to men's modes of action, not less than to their opinions. As it is useful that while mankind are imperfect there should be different opinions, so is it that there should be different experiments of living; that free scope should be given to varieties of character, short of injury to others; and that the worth of different modes of life should be proved practically, when any one thinks fit to try them. It is desirable, in short, that in things which do not primarily concern others, individuality should assert itself. Where, not the person's own character, but the traditions or customs of other people are the rule of conduct, there is wanting one of the principal ingredients of human happiness, and quite the chief ingredient of individual and social progress ...

CHAPTER IV: OF THE LIMITS TO THE AUTHORITY OF SOCIETY OVER THE INDIVIDUAL

What, then, is the rightful limit to the sovereignty of the individual over himself? Where does the authority of society begin? How much of human life should be assigned to individuality, and how much to society?

Each will receive its proper share, if each has that which more particularly concerns it. To individuality should belong the part of life in which it is chiefly the individual that is interested; to society, the part which chiefly interests society.

Though society is not founded on a contract, and though no good purpose is answered by inventing a contract in order to deduce social obligations from it, every one who receives the protection of society owes a return for the benefit, and the fact of living in society renders it indispensable that each should be bound to observe a certain line of conduct towards the rest. This conduct consists first, in not injuring the interests of one another; or rather certain interests, which, either by express legal provision or by tacit understanding, ought to be considered as rights; and secondly, in each person's bearing his share (to be fixed on some equitable principle) of the labours and sacrifices incurred for defending the society or its members from injury and molestation. These conditions society is justified in enforcing at all costs to those who endeavour to withhold fulfilment. Nor is this all that society may do. The acts of an individual may be hurtful to others, or wanting in due consideration for their welfare, without going the length of violating any of their constituted rights. The offender may then be justly punished by opinion, though not by law. As soon as any part of a person's conduct affects prejudicially the interests of others, society has jurisdiction over it, and the question whether the general welfare will or will not be promoted by interfering with it, becomes open to discussion. But there is no room for entertaining any such question when a person's conduct affects the interests of no persons besides himself, or needs not affect them unless they like (all the persons concerned being of full age, and the ordinary amount of understanding). In all such cases there should be perfect freedom, legal and social, to do the action and stand the consequences ...

READING QUESTIONS ON MILL

1 How broadly or narrowly must harm be construed for Mill's view to provide a defence of liberty?
2 What implications does Mill's focus on social injustice, rather than the injustice of the state, have for the liberal claim that the state should be neutral?
3 How are Mill's views about freedom of expression related to his understanding of individual autonomy?

Charles Taylor
"What's Wrong with Negative Liberty" (1985)

Taylor criticizes the coherence of the idea of negative liberty. In particular, he questions its usefulness to liberalism's aim of enabling individuals to flourish.

... Doctrines of positive freedom are concerned with a view of freedom which involves essentially the exercising of control over one's life. On this view, one is free only to the extent that one has effectively determined oneself and the shape of one's life. The concept of freedom here is an exercise-concept.

By contrast, negative theories can rely simply on an opportunity concept, where being free is a matter of what we can do, of what it is open to us to do, whether or not we do anything to exercise these options. This certainly is the case of the crude, original Hobbesian concept. Freedom consists just in there being no obstacle. It is a sufficient condition of one's being free that nothing stand in the way.

But we have to say that negative theories *can* rely on an opportunity-concept, rather than that they necessarily do so rely, for we have to allow for that part of the gamut of negative theories mentioned above which incorporates some notion of self-realization. Plainly this kind of view cannot rely simply on an opportunity-concept. We cannot say that someone is free, on a self-realization view, if he is totally unrealized, if for instance he is totally unaware of his potential, if fulfilling it has never even arisen as a question for him, or if he is paralysed by the fear of breaking with some norm which he has internalized but which does not authentically reflect him. Within this conceptual scheme, some degree of exercise is necessary for a man to be thought free. Or if we want to think of the internal bars to freedom as obstacles on all fours with the external ones, then being in a position to exercise freedom, having the opportunity, involves removing the internal barriers; and this is not possible without having to some extent realized myself. So that with the freedom of self-realization, having the opportunity to be free requires that I already be exercising freedom. A pure opportunity-concept is impossible here.

But if negative theories can be grounded on either an opportunity- or an exercise-concept, the same is not true of positive theories. The view that freedom involves at least partially collective self-rule is essentially grounded on an exercise-concept. For this view (at least partly) identifies freedom with self-direction, that is, the actual exercise of directing control over one's life.

But this already gives us a hint towards illuminating the above paradox, that while the extreme variant of positive freedom is usually pinned on its protagonists by their opponents, negative theorists seem prone to embrace the crudest versions of their theory themselves. For if an opportunity-concept is not combinable with a positive theory, but either it or its alternative can suit a negative theory, then one way of ruling out positive theories in principle is by firmly espousing an opportunity concept. One cuts off the positive theories by the root, as it were, even though one may also pay a price in the atrophy of a wide range of negative theories as well. At least by taking one's stand firmly on the crude side of the negative range, where only opportunity-concepts are recognized, one leaves no place for a positive theory to grow.

Taking one's stand here has the advantage that one is holding the line around a very simple and basic issue of principle, and one where the negative view seems to have some backing in common sense. The basic institution here is that freedom is a matter of being able to do something or other, of not having obstacles in one's way, rather than being a capacity that we have to realize. It naturally seems more prudent to fight the Totalitarian Menace at this last-ditch position, digging in behind the natural frontier of this simple issue, rather than engaging the enemy on the open terrain of exercise-concepts, where one will have to fight to discriminate the good from the bad among such concepts; fight, for instance, for a view of individual self-realization, against various notions of collective self-realization, of a nation, or a class. It seems easier and safer to cut all the nonsense off at the start by declaring all self-realization views to be metaphysical hog-wash. Freedom should just be tough-mindedly defined as the absence of external obstacles.

Of course, there are independent reasons for wanting to define freedom tough-mindedly. In particular there is the immense influence of the anti-metaphysical, materialist, natural-science-oriented temper of thought in our civilization. Something of this spirit at its inception induced Hobbes to take the line that he did, and the same spirit goes marching on today. Indeed, it is because of the prevalence of this spirit that the line is so easy to defend, forensically speaking, in our society.

Nevertheless, I think that one of the strongest motives for defending the crude Hobbes-Bentham concept, that freedom is the absence of external obstacles, physical or legal, is the strategic one above. For most of those who take this line thereby abandon many of their own intuitions, sharing as they do with the rest of us in a post-Romantic civilization which puts great value on self-realization, and values freedom largely because of this. It is fear of the Totalitarian Menace, I would argue, which has led them to abandon this terrain to the enemy.

I want to argue that this not only robs their eventual forensic victory of much of its value, since they become incapable of defending liberalism in the form we in fact value it, but I want to make the stronger claim that this Maginot Line mentality actually ensures defeat, as is often the case with Maginot Line mentalities. The Hobbes-Bentham view, I want to argue, is indefensible as a view of freedom.

To see this, let us examine the line more closely, and the temptation to stand on it. The advantage of the view that freedom is the absence of external obstacles is its simplicity. It allows us to say that freedom is being able to do what you want, where what you want is unproblematically understood as what the agent can identify as his desires. By contrast an exercise-concept of freedom requires that we discriminate among motivations. If we are free in the exercise of certain capacities, then we are not free, or less free, when these capacities are in some way unfulfilled or blocked. But the obstacles can be internal as well as external. And this must be so, for the capacities relevant to freedom must involve some self-awareness, self-understanding, moral discrimination and self-control, otherwise their exercise could not amount to freedom in the sense of self-direction; and this being so, we can fail to be free because these internal conditions are not realized. But where this happens, where, for example, we are quite self-deceived, or utterly fail to discriminate properly the ends we seek, or have lost self-control, we can quite easily be doing what we want in the sense of what we can identify as our wants, without being free; indeed, we can be further entrenching our unfreedom.

Once one adopts a self-realization view, or indeed any exercise-concept of freedom, then being able to do what one wants can no longer be accepted as a sufficient condition of being free. For this view puts certain conditions on one's motivation. You are not free if you are motivated, through fear, inauthentically internalized standards, or false consciousness, to thwart your self-realization.

...

There are some considerations one can put forward straight off to show that the pure Hobbesian concept will not work, that there are some discriminations among motivations which are essential to the concept of freedom as we use it. Even where we think of freedom as the absence of external obstacles, it is not the absence of such obstacles *simpliciter*. For we make discriminations between obstacles as representing more or less serious infringements of freedom. And we do this, because we deploy the concept against a background understanding that certain goals and activities are more significant than others.

Thus we could say that my freedom is restricted if the local authority puts up a new traffic light at an intersection close to my home; so that where previously I could cross as I liked, consistently with avoiding collision with other cars, now I have to wait until the light is green. In a philosophical argument, we might call this a restriction of freedom, but not in a serious political debate. The reason is that it is too trivial, the activity and purposes inhibited here are not really significant. It is not just a matter of our having made a trade-off, and considered that a small loss of liberty was worth fewer traffic accidents, or less danger for the children; we are reluctant to speak here of a loss of liberty at all; what we feel we are trading off is convenience against safety.

By contrast a law which forbids me from worshipping according to the form I believe in is a serious blow to liberty; even a law which tried to restrict this to certain times (as the traffic light restricts my crossing of the intersection to certain times) would be seen as a serious restriction. Why this difference between the two cases? Because we have a background understanding, too obvious to spell out, of some activities and goals as highly significant for human beings and others as less so. One's religious belief is recognized, even by atheists, as supremely important, because it is that by which the believer defines himself as a moral being. By contrast my rhythm of movement through the city traffic is trivial. We do not want to speak of these two in the same breath. We do not even readily admit that liberty is at stake in the traffic light case. For *de minimis non curat libertas.*

But this recourse to significance takes us beyond a Hobbesian scheme. Freedom is no longer just the absence of external obstacle *tout court*, but the absence of external obstacle to significant action, to what is important to man. There are discriminations to be made; some restrictions are more serious than others, some are utterly trivial. About many, there is of course controversy. But what the judgement turns on is some sense of what is significant for human life. Restricting the expression of people's religious and ethical convictions is more significant than restricting their movement around uninhabited parts of the country; and both are more significant than the trivia of traffic control.

But the Hobbesian scheme has no place for the notion of significance. It will allow only for purely quantitative judgements. On the toughest-minded version of his conception, where Hobbes seems to be about to define liberty in terms of the absence of physical obstacles, one is presented with the vertiginous prospect of human freedom being measurable in the same way as the degrees of freedom of some physical object, say a lever. Later we see that this will not do, because we have to take account of legal obstacles to my action. But in any case, such a quantitative conception of freedom is a non-starter.

Consider the following diabolical defence of Albania as a free country. We recognize that religion has been abolished in Albania, whereas it hasn't been in Britain. But on the other hand there are probably far fewer traffic lights per head in Tirana than in London. (I haven't checked for myself, but this is a very plausible assumption.) Suppose an apologist for Albanian socialism were nevertheless to claim that this country was freer than Britain, because the number of acts restricted was far smaller. After all, only a minority of Londoners practise some religion in public places, but all have to negotiate their way through traffic. Those who do practise a religion generally do so on one day of the week, while they are held up at traffic lights every day. In sheer quantitative terms, the number of acts restricted by traffic lights must be greater than that restricted by a ban on public religious practice. So if Britain is considered a free society, why not Albania?

Thus the application even of our negative notion of freedom requires a background conception of what is significant, according to which some restrictions are seen to be without relevance for freedom altogether, and others are judged as being of greater and lesser importance. So some discrimination among motivations seems essential to our concept of freedom. A minute's reflection shows why this must be so. Freedom is important to us because we are purposive beings. But then there must be distinctions in the significance of different kinds of freedom based on the distinction in the significance of different purposes.

But of course, this still does not involve the kind of discrimination mentioned above, the kind which would allow us to say that someone who was doing what he wanted (in the unproblematic sense) was not really free, the kind of discrimination which allows us to put conditions on people's motivations necessary to their being free, and hence to second-guess them. All we have shown is that we make discriminations between more or less significant freedoms, based on discriminations among the purposes people have.

This creates some embarrassment for the crude negative theory, but it can cope with it by simply adding a recognition that we make judgements of significance. Its central claim that freedom just is the absence of external obstacles seems untouched, as also its view of freedom as an opportunity-concept. It is just that we now have to admit that not all opportunities are equal.

But there is more trouble in store for the crude view when we examine further what these qualitative discriminations are based on. What lies behind our judging certain purposes/feelings as more significant than others? One might think that there was room here again for another quantitative theory; that the more significant purposes are those we want more. But this account is either vacuous or false.

It is true but vacuous if we take wanting more just to mean being more significant. It is false as soon as we try to give wanting more an independent criterion, such as, for instance, the urgency or force of a desire, or the prevalence of one desire over another, because it is a matter of the most banal experience that the purposes we know to be more significant are not always those which we desire with the greatest urgency to encompass, nor the ones that actually always win out in cases of conflict of desires.

When we reflect on this kind of significance, we come up against what I have called elsewhere the fact of strong evaluation, the fact that we human subjects are not only subjects of first-order desires, but of second-order desires, desires about desires. We experience our desires and purposes as qualitatively discriminated, as higher or lower, noble or base, integrated or fragmented, significant or trivial, good and bad. This means that we experience some of our desires and goals as intrinsically more significant than others: some passing comfort is less important than the fulfilment of our life-time vocation, our *amour propre* less important than a love relationship; while we experience some others as bad, not just comparatively but absolutely: we desire not to be moved by spite, or some childish desire to impress at all costs. And these judgements of significance are quite independent of the strength of the respective desires: the craving for comfort may be overwhelming at this moment, we may be obsessed with our *amour propre*, but the judgement of significance stands.

But then the question arises whether this fact of strong evaluation doesn't have other consequences for our notion of freedom, than just that it permits us to rank freedoms in importance. Is freedom not at stake when we find ourselves carried away by a less significant goal to over-ride a highly significant one? Or when we are led to act out of a motive we consider bad or despicable?

The answer is that we sometimes do speak in this way. Suppose I have some irrational fear, which is preventing me from doing something I very much want to do. Say the fear of public speaking is preventing me from taking up a career that I should find very fulfilling, and that I should be quite good at, if I could just get over this "hangup." It is clear that we experience this fear as an obstacle, and that we feel we are less than we would be if we could overcome it.

Or again, consider the case where I am very attached to comfort. To go on short rations, and to miss my creature comforts for a time, makes me very depressed. I find myself making a big thing of this. Because of this reaction I cannot do certain things that I should like very much to do, such as going on an expedition over the Andes, or a canoe trip in the Yukon. Once again, it is quite understandable if I experience this attachment as an obstacle, and feel that I should be freer without it.

Or I could find that my spiteful feelings and reactions which I almost cannot inhibit are undermining a relationship which is terribly important to me. At times, I feel as though I am almost assisting as a helpless witness at my own destructive behaviour, as I lash out again with my unbridled tongue at her. I long to be able not to feel this spite. As long as I feel it, even control is not an option, because it just builds up inside until it either bursts out, or else the feeling somehow communicates itself, and queers things between us. I long to be free of this feeling.

These are quite understandable cases, where we can speak of freedom or its absence without strain. What I have called strong evaluation is essentially involved here. For these are not just cases of conflict, even cases of painful conflict. If the conflict is between two desires with which I have no trouble identifying, there can be no talk of lesser freedom, no matter how painful or fateful. Thus if what is breaking up my relationship is my finding fulfilment in a job which, say, takes me away from home a lot, I have indeed a terrible conflict, but I would have no temptation to speak of myself as less free.

Even seeing a great difference in the significance of the two terms doesn't seem to be a sufficient condition of my wanting to speak of freedom and its absence. Thus my marriage may be breaking up because I like going to the pub and playing cards on Saturday nights with the boys. I may feel quite unequivocally that my marriage is much more important than the release and comradeship of the Saturday night bash. But nevertheless I would not want to talk of my being freer if I could slough off this desire.

The difference seems to be that in this case, unlike the ones above, I still identify with the less important desire, I still see it as expressive of myself, so that I could not lose it without altering who I am, losing something of my personality. Whereas my irrational fear, my being quite distressed by discomfort, my spite – these are all things which I can easily see myself losing without any loss whatsoever to what I am. This is why I can see them as obstacles to my purposes, and hence to my freedom, even though they are in a sense unquestionably desires and feelings of mine.

Before exploring further what is involved in this, let us go back and keep score. It would seem that these cases make a bigger breach in the crude negative theory. For they seem to be cases in which the obstacles to freedom are internal; and if this is so, then freedom cannot simply be interpreted as the absence of *external* obstacles; and the fact that I am doing what I want, in the sense of following my strongest desire, is not sufficient to establish that I am free. On the contrary, we have to make discriminations among motivations, and accept that acting out of some motivations, for example irrational fear or spite, or this too great need for comfort, is not freedom, is even a negation of freedom ...

Thus we can experience some desires as fetters, because we can experience them as not ours. And we can experience them as not ours because we see them as incorporating a quite erroneous appreciation of our situation and of what matters to us. We can see this again if we contrast the case of spite with that of another emotion which partly overlaps, and which is highly considered in some societies, the desire for revenge. In certain traditional societies this is far from being considered a despicable emotion. On the contrary, it is a duty of honour on a male relative to avenge a man's death. We might imagine that this too might give rise to conflict. It might conflict with the attempts of a new regime to bring some order to the land. The government would have to stop people taking vengeance, in the name of peace.

But short of a conversion to a new ethical outlook, this would be seen as a trade-off, the sacrifice of one legitimate goal for the sake of another. And it would seem monstrous were one to propose reconditioning people so that they no longer felt the desire to avenge their kin. This would be to unman them.[1]

Why do we feel so different about spite (and for that matter also revenge)? Because the desire for revenge for an ancient Icelander was his sense of a real obligation incumbent on him, something it would be dishonourable to repudiate; while for us, spite is the child of a distorted perspective on things.

We cannot therefore understand our desires and emotions as all brute, and in particular we cannot make sense of our discrimination of some desires as more important and fundamental, or of our repudiation of others, unless we understand our feelings to be import-attributing. This is essential to there being what we have called strong evaluation. Consequently the half-way position which admits strong evaluation, admits that our desires may frustrate our deeper purposes, admits therefore that there may be inner obstacles to freedom, and yet will not admit that the subject may be wrong or mistaken about these purposes – this position does not seem tenable. For the only way to make the subject's assessment incorrigible in principle would be to claim that there was nothing to be right or wrong about here; and that could only be so if experiencing a given feeling were a matter of the qualities of brute feeling. But this it cannot be if we are to make sense of the whole background of strong evaluation, more significant goals, and aims that we repudiate. This whole scheme requires that we understand the emotions concerned as import-attributing, as, indeed, it is clear that we must do on other grounds as well.

But once we admit that our feelings are import-attributing, then we admit the possibility of error, or false appreciation. And indeed, we have to admit a kind of false appreciation which the agent himself detects in order to make sense of the cases where we experience our own desires as fetters. How can we exclude in principle that there may be other false appreciations which the agent does not detect? That he may be profoundly in error, that is, have a very distorted sense of his fundamental purposes? Who can say that such people cannot exist? All cases are, of course, controversial; but I should nominate Charles Manson and Andreas Baader for this category, among others. I pick them out as people with a strong sense of some purposes and goals as incomparably more fundamental as others, or at least with a propensity to act the having such a sense so as to take in even themselves a good part of the time, but whose sense of fundamental purpose was shot through with confusion and error. And once we recognize such extreme cases, how avoid admitting that many of the rest of mankind can suffer to a lesser degree from the same disabilities?

What has this got to do with freedom? Well, to resume what we have seen: our attributions of freedom make sense against a background sense of more and less significant purposes, for the question of freedom/unfreedom is bound up with the frustration/fulfilment of our purposes. Further, our significant purposes can be frustrated by our own desires, and where these are sufficiently based on misappreciation, we consider them as not really ours, and experience them as fetters. A man's freedom can therefore be hemmed in by internal, motivational obstacles, as well as external ones. A man who is driven by spite to jeopardize his most important relationships, in spite of himself, as it were, or who is prevented by unreasoning fear from taking up the career he truly wants, is not really made more free if one lifts the external obstacles to his venting his spite or acting on his fear. Or at best he is liberated into a very impoverished freedom ...

NOTE

1 Compare the unease we feel at the reconditioning of the hero of Anthony Burgess's *A Clockwork Orange*.

READING QUESTION ON TAYLOR

1 Does Taylor's argument give us any basis for choosing between legal positivism and Dworkin's or Fuller's alternatives to it?

Joseph Raz
The Rule of Law and Its Virtue* (1979)

Raz, the leading legal positivist since H.L.A. Hart, claims that the rule of law is a precondition of individual liberty. Nevertheless, he argues that there is no inherent moral worth to the rule of law and that it is often good to sacrifice it.

F.A. Hayek has provided one of the clearest and most powerful formulations of the ideal of the rule of law: "stripped of all technicalities this means that government in all its actions is bound by rules fixed and announced beforehand – rules which make it possible to foresee with fair certainty how the authority will use its coercive powers in given circumstances, and to plan one's individual affairs on the basis of this knowledge.[1] At the same time the way he draws certain conclusions from this ideal illustrates one of the two main fallacies in the contemporary treatment of the doctrine of the rule of law: the assumption of its overriding importance. My purpose is to analyse the ideal of the rule of law in the spirit of Hayek's quoted statement of it and to show why some of the conclusions which he drew from it cannot be thus supported. But first we must be put on our guard against the other common fallacy concerning the rule of law.

Not uncommonly when a political ideal captures the imagination of large numbers of people its name becomes a slogan used by supporters of ideals which bear little or no relation to the one it originally designated. The fate of "democracy" not long ago and of "privacy" today are just two examples of this familiar process. In 1959 the International Congress of Jurists meeting in New Delhi gave official blessing to a similar perversion of the doctrine of the rule of law.

The function of the legislature in a free society under the Rule of Law is to create and maintain the conditions which will uphold the dignity of man as an individual. This dignity requires not only the recognition of his civil and political rights but also the establishment of the social, economic, educational, and cultural conditions which are essential to the full development of his personality.[2]

The report goes on to mention or refer to just about every political ideal which has found support in any part of the globe during the post-war years.

If the rule of law is the rule of the good law then to explain its nature is to propound a complete social philosophy. But if so the term lacks any useful function. We have no need to be concerned to the rule of law just in order to discover that to believe in it is to believe that good should triumph. The rule of law is a political ideal which a legal system may lack or may possess to a greater or lesser degree. That much is common ground. It is also to be insisted that the rule of law is just one of the virtues which a legal system may possess and by which it is to be judged. It is not to be confused with democracy, justice, equality (before the law or otherwise), human rights of any kind or respect for persons or for the dignity of man. A non-democratic legal system, based on the denial of human rights, on extensive poverty, on racial segregation, sexual inequalities, and religious persecution may, in principle, conform to the requirements of the rule of law better than any of the legal systems of the more enlightened Western democracies. This does not mean that it will be better than those Western democracies. It will be an immeasurably worse legal system, but it will excel in one respect: in its conformity to the rule of law.

Given the promiscuous use made in recent years of the expression "the rule of law" it is hardly surprising that my claim will alarm many. We have reached the stage in which no purist can claim that truth is on his side and blame the others for distorting the notion of the rule of law. All that I can claim for my account is, first, that it presents a coherent view of one important virtue which legal systems should possess and, secondly, that it is not original, that I am following in the footsteps of Hayek and of many others who understood "the rule of law" in similar ways.

I THE BASIC IDEA

"The rule of law" means literally what is says: the rule of the law. Taken in its broadest sense this means that people should obey the law and be ruled by it.[3] But in political and legal theory it has come to be read in a narrower sense, that the government shall be ruled by the law and subject to it. The ideal of the rule of law in this sense is often expressed by the phrase "government by law and not by men." No sooner does one use these formulas than their obscurity becomes evident. Surely government must be both by law and by men. It is said that the rule of law means that all government action must have foundation in law, must be authorized by law. But is not that a tautology? Actions not authorized by law cannot be the actions of the government as a government. They would be without legal effect and often unlawful.

It is true that we can elaborate a political notion of government which is different from the legal one: government as the location of real power in the society. It is in this sense that one can say that Britain is governed by The City or by the trade unions. In this sense of "government" it is not a tautology to say that government should be based on law. If the trade union ruling a country breaks an industrial relations law in order to impose its will on the Parliament or if the President or the F.B.I. authorize burglaries and conspire to pervert justice they can be said to violate the rule of law. But here "the rule of law" is used in its original sense of obedience to law. Powerful people and people in government, just like anybody else, should obey the law. This is no doubt correct, and yet does it exhaust the meaning of the rule of law? There is more to the rule of law than the law and order interpretation allows. It means more even than law and order applied to the government. I shall proceed on the assumption that we are concerned with government in the legal sense and with the conception of the rule of law which applies to government and to law and is no mere application of the law and order conception.

The problem is that now we are back with our initial puzzle. If government is, by definition, government authorized by law the rule of law seems to amount to an empty tautology, not a political ideal.

The solution to this riddle is in the difference between the professional and the lay sense of "law." For the lawyer anything is the law if it meets the conditions of validity laid down in the system's rules of recognition or in other rules of the system.[4] This includes the constitution, parliamentary legislation, ministerial regulations, policemen's orders, the regulations of limited companies, conditions imposed in trading licences, etc. To the layman the law consists only of a subclass of these. To him the law is essentially a set of open, general, and relatively stable laws. Government by law and not by men is not a tautology if "law" means general, open, and relatively stable law. In fact, the danger of this interpretation is that the rule of law might set too strict a requirement, one which no legal system can meet and which embodies very little virtue. It is humanly inconceivable that law can consist only of general rules and it is very undesirable that it should. Just as we need government both by laws and by men, so we need both general and particular laws to carry out the jobs for which we need the law.

The doctrine of the rule of law does not deny that every legal system should consist of both general, open, and stable rules (the popular conception of law) and particular laws (legal orders), an essential tool in the hands of the executive and the judiciary alike. As we shall see, what the doctrine requires is the subjection of particular laws to general, open, and stable ones. It is one of the important principles of the doctrine that *the making of particular laws should be guided by open and relatively stable general rules.*

This principle shows how the slogan of the rule of law and not of men can be read as a meaningful political ideal. The principle does not, however, exhaust the meaning of "the rule of law" and does not by itself illuminate the reasons for its alleged importance. Let us, therefore, return to the literal sense of "the rule of law." It has two aspects: (1) that people should be ruled by the law and obey it, and (2) that the law should be such that people will be able to be guided by it. As was noted above, it is with the second aspect that we are concerned: the law must be capable of being obeyed. A person conforms with the law to the extent that he does not break the law. But he obeys the law only if part of his reason for conforming is his knowledge of the law. Therefore, if the law is to be obeyed *it must be capable of guiding the behaviour of its subjects.* It must be such that they can find out what it is and act on it.

This is the basic intuition from which the doctrine of the rule of law derives: the law must be capable of guiding the behaviour of its subjects. It is evident that this conception of the rule of law is a formal one. It says nothing about how the law is to be made: by tyrants, democratic majorities, or any other way. It says nothing about fundamental rights, about equality, or justice. It may even be thought that this version of the doctrine is formal to the extent that it is almost devoid of content. This is far from the truth. Most of the requirements which were associated with the rule of law before it came to signify all the virtues of the state can be derived from this one basic idea.

II SOME PRINCIPLES

Many of the principles which can be derived from the basic idea of the rule of law depend for their validity or importance on the particular circumstances of different societies. There is little point in trying to enumerate them all, but some of the more important ones might be mentioned:

(1) *All laws should be prospective, open, and clear.* One cannot be guided by a retroactive law. It does not exist at the time of action. Sometimes it is then known for certain that a retroactive law will be enacted. When this happens retroactivity does not conflict with the rule of law (though it may be objected to on other grounds). The law must be open and adequately publicized. If it is to guide people they must be able to find out what it is. For the same reason its meaning must be clear. An ambiguous, vague, obscure, or imprecise law is likely to mislead or confuse at least some of those who desire to be guided by it.

(2) *Laws should be relatively stable.* They should not be changed too often. If they are frequently changed people will find it difficult to find out what the law is at any given moment and will be constantly in fear that the law has been changed since they last learnt what it was. But more important still is the fact that people need to know the law not only for short-term decisions (where to park one's car, how much alcohol is allowed duty free, etc.) but also for long-term planning. Knowledge of at least the general outlines and sometimes even of details of tax law and company law are often important for business plans which will bear fruit only years later. Stability is essential if people are to be guided by law in their long-term decisions.[5]

Three important points are illustrated by this principle. First, conformity to the rule of law is often a matter of degree, not only when the conformity of the legal system as a whole is at stake, but also with respect to single laws. A law is either retroactive or not, but it can be more or less clear, more or less stable, etc. It should be remembered, however, that by asserting that conformity to the principles is a matter of degree, it is not meant that the degree of conformity can be quantitatively measured by counting the number of infringements, or some such method. Some infringements are worse than others. Some violate the principles in a formal way only, which does not offend against the spirit of the doctrine. Secondly, the principles of the rule of law affect primarily the content and form of the law (it should be prospective, clear, etc.) but not only them. They also affect the manner of government beyond what is or can usefully be prescribed by law. The requirement of stability cannot be usefully subject to complete legal regulation. It is largely a matter for wise governmental policy. Thirdly, though the rule of law concerns primarily private citizens as subject to duties and governmental agencies in the exercise of their powers (on which more below), it is also concerned with the exercise of private powers. Power-conferring rules are designed to guide behaviour and should conform to the doctrine of rule of law if they are to be capable of doing so effectively.

(3) *The making of particular laws (particular legal orders) should be guided by open, stable, clear, and general rules.* It is sometimes assumed that the requirement of generality is of the essence of the rule of law. This notion derives (as noted above) from the literal interpretation of "the rule of law" when "law" is read in its lay connotations as being restricted to general, stable, and open law. It is also reinforced by a belief that the rule of law is particularly relevant to the protection of equality and that equality is related to the generality of law. The last belief is, as has often been noted before, mistaken. Racial, religious, and all manner of discrimination are not only compatible but often institutionalized by general rules.

The formal conception of the rule of law which I am defending does not object to particular legal orders as long as they are stable, clear, etc. But of course particular legal orders are mostly used by government agencies to introduce flexibility into the law. A police constable regulating traffic, a licensing authority granting a licence under certain conditions, all these and their like are among the more ephemeral parts of the law. As such they run counter to the basic idea of the rule of law. They make it difficult for people to plan ahead on the basis of their knowledge of the law. This difficulty is overcome to a large extent if particular laws of an ephemeral status are enacted only within a framework set by general laws which are more durable and which impose limits on the unpredictability introduced by the particular orders.

Two kinds of general rules create the framework for the enactment of particular laws: those which confer the necessary powers for making valid orders and those which impose duties instructing the power-holders how to exercise their powers. Both have equal importance in creating a stable framework for the creation of particular legal orders.

Clearly, similar considerations apply to general legal regulations which do not meet the requirement of stability. They too should be circumscribed to conform to a stable framework. Hence the requirement that much of the subordinate administrative law-making should be made to conform to detailed ground rules laid down in framework laws. It is essential, however, not to confuse this argument with democratic arguments for the close supervision of popularly elected bodies over law-making by non-elected ones. These further arguments may be valid but have nothing to do with the rule of law, and though sometimes they reinforce rule of law type arguments, on other occasions they support different and even conflicting conclusions.

(4) *The independence of the judiciary must be guaranteed.* It is of the essence of municipal legal systems that they institute judicial bodies charged, among other things, with the duty of applying the law to cases brought before them and whose judgments and conclusions as to the legal merits of those cases are final. Since just about any matter arising under any law can be subject to a conclusive court judgment, it is obvious that it is futile to guide one's action on the basis of the law if when the matter comes to adjudication the courts will not apply the law and will act for some other reasons. The point can be put even more strongly. Since the court's judgment establishes conclusively what is the law in the case before it, the litigants can be guided by law only if the judges apply the law correctly.[6] Otherwise people will only be able to be guided by their guesses as to what the courts are likely to do – but these guesses will not be based on the law but on other considerations.

The rules concerning the independence of the judiciary – the method of appointing judges, their security of tenure, the way of fixing their salaries, and other conditions of service – are designed to guarantee that they will be free from extraneous pressures and independent of all authority save that of the law. They are, therefore, essential for the preservation of the rule of law.

(5) *The principles of natural justice must be observed.* Open and fair hearing, absence of bias, and the like are obviously essential for the correct application of the law and thus, through the very same considerations mentioned above, to its ability to guide action.

(6) *The courts should have review powers over the implementation of the other principles.* This includes review of both subordinate and parliamentary legislation and of administrative action, but in itself it is a very limited review – merely to ensure conformity to the rule of law.

(7) *The courts should be easily accessible.* Given the central position of the courts in ensuring the rule of law (see principles 4 and 6) it is obvious that their accessibility is of paramount importance. Long delays, excessive costs, etc., may effectively turn the most enlightened law to a dead letter and frustrate one's ability effectively to guide oneself by the law.

(8) *The discretion of the crime-preventing agencies should not be allowed to pervert the law.* Not only the courts but also the actions of the police and

the prosecuting authorities can subvert the law. The prosecution should not be allowed, for example, to decide not to prosecute for commission of certain crimes, or for crimes committed by certain classes of offenders. The police should not be allowed to allocate its resources so as to avoid all effort to prevent and detect certain crimes or prosecute certain classes of criminals.

This list is very incomplete. Other principles could be mentioned and those which have been mentioned need further elaboration and further justification (why – as required by the sixth principle – should the courts and not some other body be in charge of reviewing conformity to the rule of law? etc.)[7] My purpose in listing them was merely to illustrate the power and fruitfulness of the formal conception of the rule of law. It should, however, be remembered that in the final analysis the doctrine rests on its basic idea that the law should be capable of providing effective guidance. The principles do not stand on their own. They must be constantly interpreted in the light of the basic idea.

The eight principles listed fall into two groups. Principles 1 to 3 require that the law should conform to standards designed to enable it effectively to guide action. Principles 4 to 8 are designed to ensure that the legal machinery of enforcing the law should not deprive it of its ability to guide through distorted enforcement and that it shall be capable of supervising conformity to the rule of law and provide effective remedies in cases of deviation from it. All the principles directly concern the system and method of government in matters directly relevant to the rule of law. Needless to say, many other aspects in the life of a community may, in more indirect ways, either strengthen or weaken the rule of law. A free press run by people anxious to defend the rule of law is of great assistance in preserving it, just as a gagged press or one run by people wishing to undermine the rule of law is a threat to it. But we need not be concerned here with these more indirect influences.

III THE VALUE OF THE RULE OF LAW

One of the merits of the doctrine of the rule of law I am defending is that there are so many values it does not serve. Conformity to the rule of law is a virtue, but only one of the many virtues a legal system should possess. This makes it all the more important to be clear on the values which the rule of law does serve.

The rule of law is often rightly contrasted with arbitrary power. Arbitrary power is broader than the rule of law. Many forms of arbitrary rule are compatible with the rule of law. A ruler can promote general rules based on whim or self-interest, etc., without offending against the rule of law. But certainly many of the more common manifestations of arbitrary power run foul of the rule of law. A government subjected to the rule of law is prevented from changing the law retroactively or abruptly or secretly whenever this suits its purposes. The one area where the rule of law excludes all forms of arbitrary power is in the law-applying function of the judiciary where the courts are required to be subject only to the law and to conform to fairly strict procedures.[8] No less important is the restraint imposed by the rule of law on the making of particular laws and thus on the powers of the executive. The arbitrary use of power for personal gain, out of vengeance or favouritism, is most commonly manifested in the making of particular legal orders. These possibilities are drastically restricted by close adherence to the rule of law.

"Arbitrary power" is a difficult notion. We have no cause to analyse it here. It seems, however, that an act which is the exercise of power is arbitrary only if it was done either with indifference as to whether it will serve the purposes which alone can justify use of that power or with belief that it will not serve them. The nature of the purposes alluded to varies with the nature of the power. This condition represents "arbitrary power" as a subjective concept. It all depends on the state of mind of the men in power. As such the rule of law does not bear directly on the extent of arbitrary power. But around its subjective core the notion of arbitrary power has grown a hard objective edge. Since it is universally believed that it is wrong to use public powers for private ends any such use is in itself an instance of arbitrary use of power. As we have seen the rule of law does help to curb such forms of arbitrary power.

But there are more reasons for valuing the rule of law. We value the ability to choose styles and forms of life, to fix long-term goals and effectively direct one's life towards them. One's ability to do so depends on the existence of stable, secure frameworks for one's life and actions. The law can help to secure such fixed points of reference in two ways: (1) by stabilizing social relationships which but for the law may disintegrate or develop in erratic and unpredictable ways; (2) by a policy of self-restraint designed to make the law itself a stable and safe basis for individual planning. This last aspect is the concern of the rule of law.

This second virtue of the rule of law is often, notably by Hayek, identified as the protection of individual freedom. This is right in the sense of freedom in which it is identified with an effective ability to choose between as many options as possible. Predictability in one's environment does increase one's power of action.[9] If this is freedom well and good. The important thing is to remember that this sense of freedom differs from what is commonly meant by political freedom. Political freedom consists of: (1) the prohibition of certain forms of behaviour which interfere with personal freedom and (2) the limits imposed on the powers of public authorities in order to minimize interference with personal freedom. The criminal offences against the person are an example of the first mode of protecting personal freedom, the disability of the government to restrict freedom of movement – an example of the second. It is in connection with political freedom in this sense that constitutionally guaranteed rights are of great importance. The rule of law may be yet another mode of protecting personal freedom. But it has no bearing on the existence of spheres of activity free from governmental interference and is compatible with gross violations of human rights.

More important than both these considerations is the fact that observance of the rule of law is necessary if the law is to respect human dignity. Respecting human dignity entails treating humans as persons incapable of planning and plotting their future. Thus, respecting people's dignity includes respecting their autonomy, their right to control their future. A person's control over his life is never complete. It can be incomplete in any one of several respects. The person may be ignorant of his options, unable to decide what to do, incapable of realizing his choices or frustrated in his attempts to do so, or he may have no choice at all (or at least none which is worth having). All these failures can occur through natural causes or through the limitations of the person's own character and abilities.

Naturally, there are many ways in which one person's action may affect the life of another. Only some such interferences will amount to an offence to the dignity or a violation of the autonomy of the person thus affected. Such offences can be divided into three classes: insults, enslavement, and manipulation. (I am using the last two terms in a somewhat special sense.) An insult offends a person's dignity if it consists of or implies a denial that he is an autonomous person or that he deserves to be treated as one. An action enslaves another if it practically denies him all options through the manipulation of the environment. (Though it may be for a length of time – as in real slavery – I mean to include here also coercing another to act in a certain way on a single occasion.) One manipulates a person by intentionally changing his tastes, his beliefs or his ability to act or decide. Manipulation – in other words – is manipulation of the person, of those factors relevant to his autonomy which are internal to him. Enslavement is the elimination of control by changing factors external to the person.

The law can violate people's dignity in many ways. Observing the rule of law by no means guarantees that such violations do not occur. But it is clear that deliberate disregard for the rule of law violates human dignity. It is the business of law to guide human action by affecting people's options. The law may, for example, institute slavery without violating the rule of law. But deliberate violation of the rule of law violates human dignity. The violation of the rule of law can take two forms. It may lead to uncertainty or it may lead to frustrated and disappointed expectations. It leads to the first when the law does not enable people to foresee future deployments or to form definite expectations (as in cases of vagueness and most cases of wide discretion). It leads to frustrated expectations when the appearance of stability and certainty which encourages people to rely and plan on the basis of the existing law is shattered by retroactive law-making or by preventing proper law-enforcement, etc. The evils of uncertainty are in providing opportunities for arbitrary power and restricting people's ability to plan for their future. The evils of frustrated expectations are greater. Quite apart from the concrete harm they cause they also offend dignity in expressing disrespect for people's autonomy. The law in such cases encourages autonomous action only in order to frustrate its purpose. When such frustration is the result of human action or the result of the activities of social institutions then it expresses disrespect. Often it is analogous to entrapment: one is encouraged innocently to rely on the law and then that assurance is withdrawn and one's very reliance is turned into a cause of harm to one. A legal system which does in general observe the rule of law treats people as persons at least in the sense that it attempts to guide their behaviour through affecting the circumstances of their action. It thus presupposes that they are rational autonomous creatures and attempts to affect their actions and habits by affecting their deliberations.

Conformity to the rule of law is a matter of degree. Complete conformity is impossible (some vagueness is inescapable) and maximal possible conformity is on the whole undesirable (some controlled administrative discretion is better than none). It is generally agreed that general conformity to the rule of law is to be highly cherished. But one should not take the value of the rule of law on trust nor assert it blindly. Disentangling the various values served by the rule of law helps to assess intelligently what is at stake in various possible or actual violations. Some cases insult human dignity, give free rein to arbitrary power, frustrate one's expectations, and undermine one's ability to plan. Others involve only some of these evils. The evil of different violations of the rule of law is not always the same despite the fact that the doctrine rests on the solid core of its basic idea.

IV THE RULE OF LAW AND ITS ESSENCE

Lon Fuller[10] has claimed that the principles of the rule of law which he enumerated are essential for the existence of law. This claim if true is crucial to our understanding not only of the rule of law but also of the relation of law and morality. I have been treating the rule of law as an ideal, as a standard to which the law ought to conform but which it can and sometimes does violate most radically and systematically. Fuller, while allowing that deviations from the ideal of the rule of law can occur, denies that they can be radical or total. A legal system must of necessity conform to the rule of law to a certain degree, he claims. From this claim he concludes that there is an essential link between law and morality. Law is necessarily moral, at least in some respects.

It is, of course, true that most of the principles enumerated in section 2 above cannot be violated altogether by any legal system.[11] Legal systems are based on judicial institutions. There cannot be institutions of any kind unless there are general rules setting them up. A particular norm can authorize adjudication in a particular dispute, but no number of particular norms can set up an institution. Similarly retroactive laws can exist only because there are institutions enforcing them. This entails that there must be prospective laws instructing those institutions to apply the retroactive laws if the retroactive laws are to be valid. In the terminology of H.L.A. Hart's theory one can say that at least some of the rules of recognition and of adjudication of every system must be general and prospective. Naturally they must also be relatively clear if they are to make any sense at all, etc.

Clearly, the extent to which generality, clarity, prospectivity, etc., are essential to the law is minimal and is consistent with gross violations of the rule of law. But are not considerations of the kind mentioned sufficient to establish that there is necessarily at least some moral value in every legal system? I think not. The rule of law is essentially a negative value. The law inevitably creates a great danger of arbitrary power – the rule of law is designed to minimize the danger created by the law itself. Similarly, the law may be unstable, obscure, retrospective, etc., and thus infringe people's freedom and dignity. The rule of law is designed to prevent this danger as well. Thus the rule of law is a negative virtue in two senses: conformity to it does not cause good except through avoiding evil and the evil which is avoided is evil which could only have been caused by the law itself. It is thus somewhat analogous to honesty when this virtue is narrowly interpreted as the avoidance of deceit. (I do not deny that honesty is normally conceived more broadly to incorporate other virtuous acts and inclinations.) The good of honesty does not include the good of communication between people, for honesty is consistent with a refusal to communicate. Its good is exclusively in the avoidance of the harm of deceit – and not deceit by others but by the honest person himself. Therefore, only a person who can deceive can be honest. A person who cannot communicate cannot claim any moral merit for being honest. A person who through ignorance or inability cannot kill another by poison deserves no credit for it. Similarly, that the law cannot sanction arbitrary force or violations of freedom and dignity through total absence of generality, prospectivity, or clarity is no moral credit to the law. It only means that there are some kinds of evil which cannot be brought about by the law. But this is no virtue in the law just as it is no virtue in the law that it cannot rape or murder (all it can do is sanction such actions).

Fuller's attempt to establish a necessary connection between law and morality fails. In so far as conformity to the rule of law is a moral virtue it is an ideal which should but may fail to become a reality. There is another argument, however, which establishes an essential connection between the law and the rule of law, though it does not guarantee any virtue to the law. Conformity to the rule of law is essential for securing whatever purposes the law is designed to achieve. This statement should be qualified. We could divide the purposes a law is intended to serve into two kinds: those which are secured by conformity with the law in itself and those further consequences of conformity with the law of knowledge of its existence which the law is intended to secure.[12] Thus a law prohibiting racial discrimination in government employment has as its direct purpose the establishment of racial equality in the hiring, promotion, and conditions of service of government employees (since discriminatory action is a breach of law.) Its indirect purposes may well be to improve race relations in the country in general, prevent a threat of a strike by some trade unions, or halt the decline in popularity of the government.

Conformity to the rule of law does not always facilitate realization of the indirect purposes of the law, but it is essential to the realization of its direct purposes. These are achieved by conformity with the law which is secured (unless accidentally) by people taking note of the law and guiding themselves accordingly. Therefore, if the direct purposes of the law are not to be frustrated it must be capable of guiding human behaviour, and the more it conforms to the principles of the rule of law the better it can do so.

In section 2 we saw that conformity to the rule of law is one among many moral virtues which the law should possess. The present consideration shows that the rule of law is not merely a moral virtue – it is a necessary condition for the law to be serving directly any good purpose at all. Of course, conformity to the rule of law also enables the law to serve bad purposes. That does not show that it is not a virtue, just as the fact that a sharp knife can be used to harm does not show that being sharp is not a good-making characteristic for knives. At most it shows that from the point of view of the present consideration it is not a moral good. Being sharp is an inherent good-making characteristic of knives. A good knife is, among other things, a sharp knife. Similarly, conformity to the rule of law is an inherent value of laws, indeed it is their most important inherent value. It is of the essence of law to guide behaviour through rules and courts in charge of their application. Therefore, the rule of law is the specific excellence of the law. Since conformity to the rule of law is the virtue of law in itself, law as law regardless of the purposes it serves, it is understandable and right that the rule of law is though of as among the few virtues of law which are the special responsibility of the courts and the legal profession.

Regarding the rule of law as the inherent or specific virtue of law is a result of an instrumental conception of law. The law is not just a fact of life. It is a form of social organization which should be used properly and for the proper ends. It is a tool in the hands of men differing from many others in being versatile and capable of being used for a large variety of proper purposes. As with some other tools, machines, and instruments a thing is not of the kind unless it has at least some ability to perform its function. A knife is not a knife unless it has some ability to cut. The law to be law must be capable of guiding behaviour, however inefficiently. Like other instruments, the law has a specific virtue which is morally neutral in being neutral as to the end to which the instrument is put. It is the virtue of efficiency; the virtue of the instrument as an instrument. For the law this virtue is the rule of law. Thus the rule of law is an inherent virtue of the law, but not a moral virtue as such.

The special status of the rule of law does not mean that conformity with it is of no moral importance. Quite apart from the fact that conformity to the rule of law is also a moral virtue, it is a moral requirement when necessary to enable the law to perform useful social function; just as it may be of moral importance to produce a sharp knife when it is required for a moral purpose. In the case of the rule of law this means that it is virtually always of great moral value.

V SOME PITFALLS

The undoubted value of conformity to the rule of law should not lead one to exaggerate its importance. We saw how Hayek noted correctly its relevance for the protection of freedom. We also saw that the rule of law itself does not provide sufficient protection of freedom. Consider, however, Hayek's position. He begins with a grand statement which inevitably leads to exaggerated expectations:

> The conception of freedom under the law that is the chief concern of this book rests on the contention that when we obey laws, in the sense of general abstract rules laid down irrespective of their application to us we are not subject to another man's will and are therefore free. It is because the law-giver does not know the particular cases to which his rules will apply, and it is because the judge who applies them has no choice in drawing the conclusions that follow from the existing body of rules and the particular facts of the case, that it can be said that laws and not men rule ... As a true law should not name any particulars, so it should especially not single out any specific persons or group of persons.[13]

Then, aware of the absurdity to which this passage leads, he modifies his line, still trying to present the rule of law as the supreme guarantor of freedom:

> The requirement that the rules of true law be general does not mean that sometimes special rules may not apply to different classes of people if they

refer to properties that only some people possess. There may be rules that can apply only to women or to the blind or to persons above a certain age. (In most instances it would not even be necessary to name the class of people to whom the rule applies: only a woman, for example, can be raped or got with child.) Such distinctions will not be arbitrary, will not subject one group to the will of others, if they are equally recognized as justified by those inside and those outside the group. This does not mean that there must be unanimity as to the desirability of the distinction, but merely that individual views will not depend on whether the individual is in the group or not.[14]

But here the rule of law is transformed to encompass a form of government by consent and it is this which is alleged to guarantee freedom. This is the slippery slope leading to the identification of the rule of law with the rule of the good law.

Hayek's main objection is to governmental interference with the economy:

We must now turn to the kinds of governmental measures which the rule of law excludes in principle because they cannot be achieved by merely enforcing general rules but, of necessity, involve arbitrary discrimination between persons. The most important among them are decisions as to who is to be allowed to provide different services or commodities, at what prices or in what quantities – in other words, measures designed to control the access to different trades and occupations, the terms of sale, and the amounts to be produced or sold.

There are several reasons why all direct control of prices by government is irreconcilable with a functioning free system, whether the government actually fixes prices or merely lays down rules by which the permissible prices are to be determined. In the first place, it is impossible to fix prices according to long-term rules which will effectively guide production. Appropriate prices depend on circumstances which are constantly changing and must be continually adjusted to them. On the other hand, prices which are not fixed outright but determined by some rule (such as that they must be in a certain relation to cost) will not be the same for all sellers and, for this reason, will prevent the market from functioning. A still more important consideration is that, with prices different from those that would form on a free market, demand and supply will not be equal, and if the price control is to be effective, some method must be found for deciding who is to be allowed to buy or sell. This would necessarily be discretionary and must consist of *ad hoc* decisions that discriminate between persons on essentially arbitrary grounds.[15]

Here again it is clear that arguments which at best show that certain policies are wrong for economic reasons are claimed to show that they infringe the rule of law and the making of supposedly misguided but perfectly principled particular orders is condemned as an arbitrary exercise of power.

Since the rule of law is just one of the virtues the law should possess, it is to be expected that it possesses no more than prima facie force. It has always to be balanced against competing claims of other values. Hence Hayek's arguments, to the extent that they show no more than that some other goals inevitably conflict with the rule of law, are not the sort of arguments which could, in principle, show that pursuit of such goals by means of law is inappropriate. Conflict between the rule of law and other values is just what is to be expected. Conformity to the rule of law is a matter of degree, and though, other things being equal, the greater the conformity the better – other things are rarely equal. A lesser degree of conformity is often to be preferred precisely because it helps realization of other goals.

In considering the relation between the rule of law and other values the law should serve, it is of particular importance to remember that the rule of law is essentially a negative value. It is merely designed to minimize the harm to freedom and dignity which the law may cause in its pursuit of its goals however laudable these may be. Finally, regarding the rule of law as the inherent excellence of the law means that it fulfils essentially a subservient role. Conformity to it makes the law a good instrument for achieving certain goals, but conformity to the rule of law is not itself an ultimate goal. This subservient role of the doctrine shows both its power and its limitations. On the one hand, if the pursuit of certain goals is entirely incompatible with the rule of law, then these goals should not be pursued by legal means. But on the other hand one should be wary of disqualifying the legal pursuit of major social goals in the name of the rule of law. After all, the rule of law is meant to enable the last to promote social good, and should not be lightly used to show that it should not do so. Sacrificing too many social goals on the altar of the rule of law may make the law barren and empty.

NOTES

* First published in *The Law Quarterly Review* (1977). A draft of this paper was presented to a conference sponsored by the Liberty Fund and the University of San Francisco. I am grateful to Rolf Sartorious, Douglas

Hutchinson, and David Libling for useful suggestions on ways to improve an early draft of the paper.

1 *The Road to Serfdom* (London, 1944), p. 54.
2 Clause 1 of the report of Committee I of the International Congress of Jurists at New Delhi, 1959.
3 Cf., on this sense of the phrase, Jennings, *The Law and the Constitution* (London, 1933), pp. 42–5.
4 I am here following Hart, *The Concept of Law* (Oxford, 1961), pp. 97–107.
5 Of course, uncertainty generated by instability of law also affects people's planning and action. If it did not, stability would not have any impact either. The point is that only if the law is stable are people guided by *their knowledge of the content of the law.*
6 I am not denying that courts also make law. This principle of the rule of law applies to them primarily in their duty to apply the law. As lawmakers they are subject to the same principles as all law-makers.
7 Similar lists of principles have been discussed by various authors. English writers have been mesmerized by Dicey's unfortunate doctrine for too long. For a list similar to mine see Lon Fuller's *The Morality of Law*, 2nd ed., ch. 2. His discussion of many of the principles is full of good sense. My main reason for abandoning some of his principles is a difference of views on conflicts between the laws of one system.
8 The rule of law itself does not exclude all the possibilities of arbitrary law-making by the courts.
9 But then welfare law and governmental manipulation of the economy also increase freedom by increasing – if successful – people's welfare. If the rule of law is defended as the bulwark of freedom in this sense, it can hardly be used to oppose in principle governmental management of the economy.
10 In *The Morality of Law*, 2nd ed. (Yale, 1969), Fuller's argument is complex and his claims are numerous and hard to disentangle. Many of his claims are weak and unsupportable. Others are suggestive and useful. It is not my purpose to analyse or evaluate them. For a sympathetic discussion see R.E. Sartorius, *Individual Conduct and Social Norms* (Encino, California, 1975), ch. 9.
11 I am not adopting here Fuller's conception of the law, but rather I am following my own adaptation of Hart's conception. Cf. Hart's *The Concept of Law* and my *Practical Reason and Norms* (1975), pp. 132–54. Therefore, the discussion which follows is not a direct assessment of Fuller's own claims.
12 See further on this distinction Essay 9 above.

13 F.A. Hayek, *The Constitution of Liberty* (Chicago, 1960), pp. 153–4.
14 Ibid., p. 154.
15 F.A. Hayek, *The Constitution of Liberty*, pp. 227–8.

READING QUESTIONS ON RAZ

1 Does Raz's conception of the rule of law fit well with Taylor's critique of negative liberty?
2 Do you find Raz's response to Fuller convincing?

Patrick Devlin
"Morals and the Criminal Law" (1965)

Devlin advocates a vision of democracy in which justice is determined by the will of the majority. He argues that a society is no less entitled to protect itself against moral decay than against treason.

I MORALS AND THE CRIMINAL LAW

The Report of the Committee on Homosexual Offences and Prostitution, generally known as the Wolfenden Report, is recognized to be an excellent study of two very difficult legal and social problems. But it has also a particular claim to the respect of those interested in jurisprudence; it does what law reformers so rarely do; it sets out clearly and carefully what in relation to its subjects it considers the function of the law to be. Statutory additions to the criminal law are too often made on the simple principle that "there ought to be a law against it." The greater part of the law relating to sexual offences is the creation of statute and it is difficult to ascertain any logical relationship between it and the moral ideas which most of us uphold. Adultery, fornication, and prostitution are not, as the Report points out, criminal offences: homosexuality between males is a criminal offence, but between females it is not. Incest was not an offence until it was declared so by statute only fifty years ago. Does the legislature select those offences haphazardly or are there some principles which can be used to determine what part of the moral law should be embodied in the criminal? There is, for example, being now considered a proposal to make A.I.D., that is, the practice of artificial insemination of a woman with the seed of a man who is not her husband, a criminal offence; if, as is usually the case, the woman is married, this is in substance, if not in form, adultery. Ought it to be made punishable when adultery is not? This sort of question is of practical importance, for a law that appears to be arbitrary and illogical, in the end and after the wave of moral indignation that has put it on the statute book subsides, forfeits respect. As a practical question it arises more frequently in the field of sexual morals than in any other, but there is no special answer to be found in that field. The inquiry must be general and fundamental. What is the connexion between crime and sin and to what extent, if at all, should the criminal law of England concern itself with the enforcement of morals and punish sin or immorality as such?

The statements of principle in the Wolfenden Report provide an admirable and modern starting-point for such an inquiry. In the course of my examination of them I shall find matter for criticism. If my criticisms are sound, it must not be imagined that they point to any shortcomings in the Report. Its authors were not, as I am trying to do, composing a paper on the jurisprudence of morality; they were evolving a working formula to use for reaching a number of practical conclusions. I do not intend to express any opinion one way or the other about these; that would be outside the scope of a lecture on jurisprudence. I am concerned only with general principles; the statement of these in the Report illuminates the entry into the subject and I hope that its authors will forgive me if I carry the lamp with me into places where it was not intended to go.

Early in the Report the Committee put forward:

Our own formulation of the function of the criminal law so far as it concerns the subjects of this enquiry. In this field, its function, as we see it, is to preserve public order and decency, to protect the citizen from what is offensive or injurious, and to provide sufficient safeguards against exploitation and corruption of others, particularly whose who are specially vulnerable because they are young, weak in body or mind, inexperienced, or in a state of special physical, official or economic dependence.

It is not, in our view, the function of the law to intervene in the private lives of citizens, or to seek to enforce any particular pattern of behaviour, further than is necessary to carry out the purposes we have outlined.

The Committee preface their most important recommendation

that homosexual behaviour between consenting adults in private should no longer be a criminal offence, [by stating the argument] which we believe to be decisive, namely, the importance which society and the law ought to give to individual freedom of choice and action in matters of private morality. Unless a deliberate attempt is to be made by society, acting through the agency of the law, to equate the sphere of crime with that of sin, there must remain a realm of private morality and immorality which is, in brief and crude terms, not the law's business. To say this is not to condone or encourage private immorality.

Similar statements of principle are set out in the chapters of the Report which deal with prostitution. No case can be sustained, the Report says, for attempting to make prostitution itself illegal. The Committee refer to the general reasons already given and add: "We are agreed that private immorality should not be the concern of the criminal law except in the special circumstances therein mentioned." They quote with approval the report of the Street Offences Committee, which says: "As a general proposition it will be universally accepted that the law is not concerned with private morals or with ethical sanctions." It will be observed that the emphasis is on *private* immorality. By this is meant immorality which is not offensive or injurious to the public in the ways defined or described in the first passage which I quoted. In other words, no act of immorality should be made a criminal offence unless it is accompanied by some other feature such as indecency, corruption, or exploitation. This is clearly brought out in relation to prostitution: "It is not the duty of the law to concern itself with immorality as such ... it should confine itself to those activities which offend against public order and decency or expose the ordinary citizen to what is offensive or injurious."

These statements of principle are naturally restricted to the subject matter of the Report. But they are made in general terms and there seems to be no reason why, if they are valid, they should not be applied to the criminal law in general. They separate very decisively crime from sin, the divine law from the secular, and the moral from the criminal. They do not signify any lack of support for the law, moral or criminal, and they do not represent an attitude that can be called either religious or irreligious. There are many schools of thought among those who may think that morals are not the law's business. There is first of all the agnostic or free-thinker. He does not of course disbelieve in morals, nor in sin if it be given the wider of the two meanings assigned to it in the *Oxford English Dictionary* where it is defined as "transgression against divine law or the principles of morality." He cannot accept the divine law; that does not mean that he might not view with suspicion any departure from moral principles that have for generations been accepted by the society in which he lives; but in the end he judges for himself. Then there is the deeply religious person who feels that the criminal law is sometimes more of a hindrance than a help in the sphere of morality, and that the reform of the sinner – at any rate when he injures only himself – should be a spiritual rather than a temporal work. Then there is the man who without any strong feeling cannot see why, where there is freedom in religious belief, there should not logically be freedom in morality as well. All these are powerfully allied against the equating of crime with sin.

I must disclose at the outset that I have as a judge an interest in the result of the inquiry which I am seeking to make as a jurisprudent. As a judge who administers the criminal law and who has often to pass sentence in a criminal court, I should feel handicapped in my task if I thought that I was addressing an audience which had no sense of sin or which thought of crime as something quite different. Ought one, for example, in passing sentence upon a female abortionist to treat her simply as if she were an unlicensed midwife? If not, why not? But if so, is all the panoply of the law erected over a set of social regulations? I must admit that I begin with a feeling that a complete separation of crime from sin (I use the term throughout this lecture in the wider meaning) would not be good for the moral law and might be disastrous for the criminal. But can this sort of feeling be justified as a matter of jurisprudence? And if it be a right feeling, how should the relationship between the criminal and the moral law be stated? Is there a good theoretical basis for it, or is it just a practical working alliance, or is it a bit of both? That is the problem which I want to examine, and I shall begin by considering the standpoint of the strict logician. It can be supported by cogent arguments, some of which I believe to be unanswerable and which I put as follows.

Morals and religion are inextricably joined – the moral standards generally accepted in Western civilization being those belonging to Christianity. Outside Christendom other standards derive from other religions. None of these moral codes can claim any validity except by virtue of the religion on which it is based. Old Testament morals differ in some respects from New Testament morals. Even within Christianity there are differences. Some hold that contraception is an immoral practice and that a man who has carnal knowledge of another woman while his wife is alive is in all circumstances a fornicator; others, including most of the English-speaking world, deny both these propositions. Between the great religions of the world, of which Christianity is only one, there are much wider differences. It may or may not be right for the State to adopt one of these religions as the truth, to found itself upon its doctrines, and to deny to any of its citizens the liberty to practise any other. If it does, it is logical that it should use the secular law wherever it thinks it necessary to enforce the divine. If it does not, it is illogical that it should concern itself with morals as such. But if it leaves matters of religion to private judgement, it should logically leave matters of morals also. A State which refuses to enforce Christian beliefs has lost the right to enforce Christian morals.

If this view is sound, it means that the criminal law cannot justify any of its provisions by reference to the moral law. It cannot say, for example, that murder and theft are prohibited because they are immoral or sinful. The State must justify in some other way the punishments which it imposes on wrongdoers and a function for the criminal law independent of morals must be found. This is not difficult to do. The smooth functioning of society and the preservation of order require that a number of activities should be regulated. The rules that are made for that purpose and are enforced by the criminal law are often designed simply to achieve uniformity and convenience and rarely involve any choice between good and evil. Rules that impose a speed limit or prevent obstruction on the highway have nothing to do with morals. Since so much of the criminal law is composed of rules of this sort, why bring morals into it at all? Why not define the function of the criminal law in simple terms as the preservation of order and decency and the protection of the lives and property of citizens, and elaborate those terms in relation to any particular subject in the way in which it is done in the Wolfenden Report? The criminal law in carrying out these objects will undoubtedly overlap the moral law. Crimes of violence are morally wrong and they are also offences against good order; therefore they offend against both laws. But this is simply because the two laws in pursuit of different objectives happen to cover the same area. Such is the argument.

Is the argument consistent or inconsistent with the fundamental principles of English criminal law as it exists today? That is the first way of testing it, though by no means a conclusive one. In the field of jurisprudence one is at liberty to overturn even fundamental conceptions if they are theoretically unsound. But to see how the argument fares under the existing law is a good starting-point.

It is true that for many centuries the criminal law was much concerned with keeping the peace and little, if at all, with sexual morals. But it would be wrong to infer from that that it had no moral content or that it would ever have tolerated the idea of a man being left to judge for himself in matters of morals. The criminal law of England has from the very first concerned itself with moral principles. A simple way of testing this point is to consider the attitude which the criminal law adopts towards consent.

Subject to certain exceptions inherent in the nature of particular crimes, the criminal law has never permitted consent of the victim to be used as a defence. In rape, for example, consent negatives an essential element. But consent of the victim is no defence to a charge of murder. It is not a defence to any form of assault that the victim thought his punishment well deserved and submitted to it; to make a good defence the accused must prove that the law gave him the right to chastise and that he exercised it reasonably. Likewise, the victim may not forgive the aggressor and require the prosecution to desist; the right to enter a *nolle prosequi* belongs to the Attorney-General alone.

Now, if the law existed for the protection of the individual, there would be no reason why he should avail himself of it if he did not want it. The reason why a man may not consent to the commission of an offence against himself beforehand or forgive it afterwards is because it is an offence against society. It is not that society is physically injured; that would be impossible. Nor need any individual be shocked, corrupted, or exploited; everything may be done in private. Nor can it be explained on the practical ground that a violent man is a potential danger to others in the community who have therefore a direct interest in his apprehension and punishment as being necessary to their own protection. That would be true of a man whom the victim is prepared to forgive but not of one who gets his consent first; a murderer who acts only upon the consent, and maybe the request, of his victim is no menace to others, but he does threaten one of the great moral principles upon which society is based, that is, the sanctity of human life. There is only one explanation of what has hitherto been accepted as the basis of the criminal law and that is that there are certain standards of behaviour or moral principles which society requires to be observed; and the breach of them is an offence not merely against the person who is injured but against society as a whole.

Thus, if the criminal law were to be reformed so as to eliminate from it everything that was not designed to preserve order and decency or to protect citizens (including the protection of youth from corruption), it would overturn a fundamental principle. It would also end a number of specific crimes. Euthanasia or the killing of another at his own request, suicide, attempted suicide and suicide pacts, duelling, abortion, incest between brother and sister, are all acts which can be done in private and without offence to others and need not involve the corruption or exploitation of others. Many people think that the law on some of these subjects is in need of reform, but no one hitherto has gone so far as to suggest that they should all be left outside the criminal law as matters of private morality. They can be brought within it only as a matter of moral principle. It must be remembered also that although there is much immorality that is not punished by the law, there is none that is condoned by the law. The law will not allow its processes to be used by those engaged in immorality of any sort. For example, a house may not be let for immoral purposes; the lease is invalid and would not be enforced. But if what goes on inside there is a matter of private morality and not the law's business, why does the law inquire into it at all?

I think it is clear that the criminal law as we know it is based upon moral principle. In a number of crimes its function is simply to enforce a moral principle and nothing else. The law, both criminal and civil, claims to be able to speak about morality and immorality generally. Where does it get its authority to do this and how does it settle the moral principles which it enforces? Undoubtedly, as a matter of history, it derived both from Christian teaching. But I think that the strict logician is right when he says that the law can no longer rely on doctrines in which citizens are entitled to disbelieve. It is necessary therefore to look for some other source.

In jurisprudence, as I have said, everything is thrown open to discussion and, in the belief that they cover the whole field, I have framed three interrogatories addressed to myself to answer:

1 Has society the right to pass judgement at all on matters of morals? Ought there, in other words, to be a public morality, or are morals always a matter for private judgement?

2 If society has the right to pass judgement, has it also the right to use the weapon of the law to enforce it?
3 If so, ought it to use that weapon in all cases or only in some; and if only in some, on what principles should it distinguish?

I shall begin with the first interrogatory and consider what is meant by the right of society to pass a moral judgement, that is, a judgement about what is good and what is evil. The fact that a majority of people may disapprove of a practice does not of itself make it a matter for society as a whole. Nine men out of ten may disapprove of what the tenth man is doing and still say that it is not their business. There is a case for a collective judgement (as distinct from a large number of individual opinions which sensible people may even refrain from pronouncing at all if it is upon somebody else's private affairs) only if society is affected. Without a collective judgement there can be no case at all for intervention. Let me take as an illustration the Englishman's attitude to religion as it is now and as it has been in the past. His attitude now is that a man's religion is his private affair; he may think of another man's religion that it is right or wrong, true or untrue, but not that it is good or bad. In earlier times that was not so; a man was denied the right to practise what was thought of as heresy, and heresy was thought of as destructive of society.

The language used in the passages I have quoted from the Wolfenden Report suggests the view that there ought not to be a collective judgement about immorality *per se*. Is this what is meant by "private morality" and "individual freedom of choice and action"? Some people sincerely believe that homosexuality is neither immoral nor unnatural. Is the "freedom of choice and action" that is offered to the individual, freedom to decide for himself what is moral or immoral, society remaining neutral; or is it freedom to be immoral if he wants to be? The language of the Report may be open to question, but the conclusions at which the Committee arrive answer this question unambiguously. If society is not prepared to say that homosexuality is morally wrong, there would be no basis for a law protecting youth from "corruption" or punishing a man for living on the "immoral" earnings of a homosexual prostitute, as the Report recommends. This attitude the Committee make even clearer when they come to deal with prostitution. In truth, the Report takes it for granted that there is in existence a public morality which condemns homosexuality and prostitution. What the

Report seems to mean by private morality might perhaps be better described as private behaviour in matters of morals.

This view – that there is such a thing as public morality – can also be justified by *a priori* argument. What makes a society of any sort is community of ideas, not only political ideas but also ideas about the way its members should behave and govern their lives; these latter ideas are its morals. Every society has a moral structure as well as a political one: or rather, since that might suggest two independent systems, I should say that the structure of every society is made up both of politics and morals. Take, for example, the institution of marriage. Whether a man should be allowed to take more than one wife is something about which every society has to make up its mind one way or the other. In England we believe in the Christian idea of marriage and therefore adopt monogamy as a moral principle. Consequently the Christian institution of marriage has become the basis of family life and so part of the structure of our society. It is there not because it is Christian. It has got there because it is Christian, but it remains there because it is built into the house in which we live and could not be removed without bringing it down. The great majority of those who live in this country accept it because it is the Christian idea of marriage and for them the only true one. But a non-Christian is bound by it, not because it is part of Christianity but because, rightly or wrongly, it has been adopted by the society in which he lives. It would be useless for him to stage a debate designed to prove that polygamy was theologically more correct and socially preferable; if he wants to live in the house, he must accept it as built in the way in which it is.

We see this more clearly if we think of ideas or institutions that are purely political. Society cannot tolerate rebellion; it will not allow argument about the rightness of the cause. Historians a century later may say that the rebels were right and the Government was wrong and a percipient and conscientious subject of the State may think so at the time. But it is not a matter which can be left to individual judgement.

The institution of marriage is a good example for my purpose because it bridges the division, if there is one, between politics and morals. Marriage is part of the structure of our society and it is also the basis of a moral code which condemns fornication and adultery. The institution of marriage would be gravely threatened if individual judgements were permitted about the morality of adultery; on these points there must be a public morality. But public morality is not to be confined to those moral principles which support institutions such as marriage. People do not think of monogamy as something which has to be supported because our society has chosen to organize itself upon it; they think of it as something that is good in itself and offering a good way of life and that it is for that reason that our society has adopted it. I return to the statement that I have already made, that society means a community of ideas; without shared ideas on politics, morals, and ethics no society can exist. Each one of us has ideas about what is good and what is evil; they cannot be kept private from the society in which we live. If men and women try to create a society in which there is no fundamental agreement about good and evil they will fail; if, having based it on common agreement, the agreement goes, the society will disintegrate. For society is not something that is kept together physically; it is held by the invisible bonds of common thought. If the bonds were too far relaxed the members would drift apart. A common morality is part of the bondage. The bondage is part of the price of society; and mankind, which needs society, must pay its price ...

You may think that I have taken far too long in contending that there is such a thing as public morality, a proposition which most people would readily accept, and may have left myself too little time to discuss the next question which to many minds may cause greater difficulty: to what extent should society use the law to enforce its moral judgements? But I believe that the answer to the first question determines the way in which the second should be approached and may indeed very nearly dictate the answer to the second question. If society has no right to make judgements on morals, the law must find some special justification for entering the field of morality: if homosexuality and prostitution are not in themselves wrong, then the onus is very clearly on the law-giver who wants to frame a law against certain aspects of them to justify the exceptional treatment. But if society has the right to make a judgement and has it on the basis that a recognized morality is as necessary to society as, say, a recognized government, then society may use the law to preserve morality in the same way as it uses it to safeguard anything else that is essential to its existence. If therefore the first proposition is securely established with all its implications, society has a prima facie right to legislate against immorality as such.

The Wolfenden Report, notwithstanding that it seems to admit the right of society to condemn homosexuality and prostitution as immoral, requires special circumstances to be shown to justify the intervention of the law. I think that this is wrong in principle and that any attempt to approach my second interrogatory on these lines is bound to break down. I think that the attempt by the Committee does break down and that this is shown by the fact that it has to define or describe its special circumstances so widely that they can be supported only if it is accepted that the law *is* concerned with immorality as such.

The widest of the special circumstances are described as the provision of "sufficient safeguards against exploitation and corruption of others, particularly those who are specially vulnerable because they are young, weak in body or mind, inexperienced, or in a state of special physical, official or economic dependence." The corruption of youth is a well-recognized ground for intervention by the State and for the purpose of any legislation the young can easily be defined. But if similar protection were to be extended to every other citizen, there would be no limit to the reach of the law. The "corruption and exploitation of others" is so wide that it could be used to cover any sort of immorality which involves, as most do, the co-operation of another person. Even if the phrase is taken as limited to the categories that are particularized as "specially vulnerable," it is so elastic as to be practically no restriction. This is not merely a matter of words. For if the words used are stretched almost beyond breaking-point, they still are not wide enough to cover the recommendations which the committee make about prostitution.

Prostitution is not in itself illegal and the Committee do not think that it ought to be made so. If prostitution is private immorality and not the law's business, what concern has the law with the ponce or the brothel-keeper or the householder who permits habitual prostitution? The Report recommends that the laws which make these activities criminal offences should be maintained or strengthened and brings them (so far as it goes into principle; with regard to brothels it says simply that the law rightly frowns on them) under the head of exploitation. There may be cases of exploitation in this trade, as there are or used to be in many others, but in general a ponce exploits a prostitute no more than an impressario exploits an actress. The Report finds that "the great majority of prostitutes are women whose psychological makeup is such that they choose this life because they find in it a style of living which is to them easier, freer and more profitable than would be provided by any other occupation ... In the main the association between prostitute and ponce is voluntary and operates to mutual advantage." The Committee would agree that this could not be called exploitation in the ordinary sense. They say: "It is in our view an oversimplification to think that those who live on the earnings of prostitution are exploiting the prostitute as such. What they are really exploiting is the whole complex of the relationship between prostitute and customer; they are, in effect, exploiting the human weaknesses which cause the customer to seek the prostitute and the prostitute to meet the demand."

All sexual immorality involves the exploitation of human weaknesses. The prostitute exploits the lust of her customers and the customer the moral weakness of the prostitute. If the exploitation of human weaknesses is considered to create a special circumstance, there is virtually no field of morality which can be defined in such a way as to exclude the law.

I think, therefore, that it is not possible to set theoretical limits to the power of the State to legislate against immorality. It is not possible to settle in advance exceptions to the general rule or to define inflexibly areas of morality into which the law is in no circumstances to be allowed to enter. Society is entitled by means of its laws to protect itself from dangers, whether from within or without. Here again I think that the political parallel is legitimate. The law of treason is directed against aiding the king's enemies and against sedition from within. The justification for this is that established government is necessary for the existence of society and therefore its safety against violent overthrow must be secured. But an established morality is as necessary as good government to the welfare of society. Societies disintegrate from within more frequently than they are broken up by external pressures. There is disintegration when no common morality is observed and history shows that the loosening of moral bonds is often the first stage of disintegration, so that society is justified in taking the same steps to preserve its moral code as it does to preserve its government and other essential institutions.[1] The suppression of vice is as much the law's business as the suppression of subversive activities; it is no more possible to define a sphere of private morality than it is to define one of private subversive activity. It is wrong to talk of private morality or of the law not being concerned with immorality as such or to try to set rigid bounds to the part which the law may play in the suppression of vice. There are no theoretical limits to the power of the State to legislate against treason and sedition, and likewise I think there can be no theoretical limits to legislation against immorality. You may argue that if a man's sins affect only himself it cannot be the concern of society. If he chooses to get drunk every night in the privacy of his own home, is any one except himself the worse for it? But suppose a quarter or a half of the population got drunk every night, what sort of society would it be? You cannot set a theoretical limit to the number of people who can get drunk before society is entitled to legislate against drunkenness. The same may be said of gambling. The Royal Commission on Betting, Lotteries, and Gaming took as their test the character of the citizen as a member of society. They said: "Our concern with the ethical significance of gambling is confined to the effect which it may have on the character of the gambler as a member of society. If we were convinced that whatever the degree of gambling this effect must be harmful we should be inclined to think that it was the duty of the state to restrict gambling to the greatest extent practicable."

In what circumstances the State should exercise its power is the third of the interrogatories I have framed. But before I get to it I must raise a point which might have been brought up in any one of the three. How are the moral judgements of society to be ascertained? By leaving it until now, I can ask it in the more limited form that is now sufficient for my purpose. How is the law-maker to ascertain the moral judgements of society? It is surely not enough that they should be reached by the opinion of the majority; it would be too much to require the individual assent of every citizen. English law has evolved and regularly uses a standard which does not depend on the counting of heads. It is that of the reasonable man. He is not to be confused with the rational man. He is not expected to reason about anything and his judgement may be largely a matter of feeling. It is the viewpoint of the man in the street or to use an archaism familiar to all lawyers – the man in the Clapham omnibus. He might also be called the right-minded man. For my purpose I should like to call him the man in the jury box, for the moral judgement of society must be something about which any twelve men or women drawn at random might after discussion be expected to be unanimous. This was the standard the judges applied in the days before Parliament was as active as it is now and when they laid down rules of public policy. They did not think of themselves as making law but simply as stating principles which every right-minded person would accept as valid. It is what Pollock called "practical morality," which is based not on theological or philosophical foundations but "in the mass of continuous experience half-consciously or unconsciously accumulated and embodied in the morality of common sense." He called it also "a certain way of thinking on questions of morality which we expect to find in a reasonable civilized man or a reasonable Englishman, taken at random."[2]

Immorality then, for the purpose of the law, is what every right-minded person is presumed to consider to be immoral. Any immorality is capable of affecting society injuriously and in effect to a greater or lesser extent it usually does; this is what gives the law its *locus standi*. It cannot be shut out. But – and this brings me to the third question – the individual has a *locus standi* too; he cannot be expected to surrender to the judgement of society the whole conduct of his life. It is the old and familiar question of striking a balance between the rights and interests of society and those of the individual. This is something which the law is constantly doing in matters large and small. To take a very down-to-earth example, let me consider the right of the individual whose house adjoins the highway to have access to it; that means in these days the right to have vehicles stationary in the highway, sometimes for a considerable time if there is a lot of loading or unloading. There are many cases in which the courts have had to balance the private right of access against the public right to use the highway without obstruction. It cannot be done by carving up the highway into public and private areas. It is done by recognizing that each have rights over the whole; that if each were to exercise their rights to the full, they would come into conflict; and therefore that the rights of each must be curtailed so as to ensure as far as possible that the essential needs of each are safeguarded.

I do not think that one can talk sensibly of a public and private morality any more than one can of a public or private highway. Morality is a sphere in which there is a public interest and a private interest, often in conflict, and the problem is to reconcile the two. This does not mean that it is impossible to put forward any general statements about how in our society the balance ought to be struck. Such statements cannot of their nature be rigid or precise; they would not be designed to circumscribe the operation of the law-making power but to guide those who have to apply it. While every decision which a court of law makes when it balances the public against the private interest is an *ad hoc* decision, the cases contain statements of principle to which the court should have regard when it reaches its decision. In the same way it is possible to make general statements of principle which it may be thought the legislature should bear in mind when it is considering the enactment of laws enforcing morals.

I believe that most people would agree upon the chief of these elastic principles. There must be toleration of the maximum individual freedom that is consistent with the integrity of society. It cannot be said that this is a principle that runs all through the criminal law. Much of the criminal law that is regulatory in character – the part of it that deals with *malum prohibitum* rather than *malum in se* – is based upon the opposite principle, that is, that the choice of the individual must give way to the convenience of the many. But in all matters of conscience the principle I have stated is generally held to prevail. It is not confined to thought and speech; it extends to action, as is shown by the recognition of the right to conscientious objection in war-time; this example shows also that conscience will be respected even in times of national danger. The principle appears to me to be peculiarly appropriate to all questions of morals. Nothing should be punished by the law that does not lie beyond the limits of tolerance. It is not nearly enough to say that a majority dislike a practice; there must be a real feeling of reprobation. Those who are dissatisfied with the present law on homosexuality often say that the opponents of reform are swayed simply by disgust. If that were so it would be wrong, but I do not think one can ignore disgust if it is deeply felt and not manufactured. Its presence is a good indication that the bounds of toleration are being reached. Not everything is to be tolerated. No society can do without intolerance, indignation, and disgust; they are the forces behind the moral law, and indeed it can be argued that if they or something like them are not present, the feelings of society cannot be weighty enough to deprive the individual of freedom of choice. I suppose that there is hardly anyone nowadays who would not be disgusted by the thought of deliberate cruelty to animals. No one proposes to relegate that or any other form of sadism to the realm of private morality or to allow it to be practised in public or in private. It would be possible no doubt to point out that until a comparatively short while ago nobody thought very much of cruelty to animals and also that pity and kindliness and the unwillingness to inflict pain are virtues more generally esteemed now than they have even been in the past. But matters of this sort are not determined by rational argument. Every moral judgement, unless it claims a divine source, is simply a feeling that no right-minded man could behave in any other way without admitting that he was doing wrong. It is the power of a common sense and not the power of reason that is behind the judgements of society. But before a society can put a practice beyond the limits of tolerance there must be a deliberate judgement that the practice is injurious to society. There is, for example, a general abhorrence of homosexuality. We should ask ourselves in the first instance whether, looking at it calmly and dispassionately, we regard it as a vice so abominable that its mere presence is an offence. If that is the genuine feeling of the society in which we live, I do not see how society can be denied the right to eradicate it. Our feeling may not be so intense as that. We may feel about it that, if confined, it is tolerable, but that if it spread it might be gravely injurious; it is in this way that most societies look upon fornication, seeing it as a natural weakness which must be kept within bounds but which cannot be rooted out. It becomes then a question of balance, the danger to society in one scale and the extent of the restriction in the other. On this sort of point the value of an investigation by such a body as the Wolfenden Committee and of its conclusions is manifest.

The limits of tolerance shift. This is supplementary to what I have been saying but of sufficient importance in itself to deserve statement as a separate principle which law-makers have to bear in mind. I suppose that moral standards do not shift; so far as they come from divine revelation they do not, and I am willing to assume that the moral judgements made by a society always remain good for that society. But the extent to which society will tolerate – I mean tolerate, not approve – departures from moral standards varies from generation to generation. It may be that over-all tolerance is always increasing. The pressure of the human mind, always seeking greater freedom of thought, is outwards against the bonds of society forcing their gradual relaxation. It may be that history is a tale of contraction and expansion and that all developed societies are on their way to dissolution. I must not speak of things I do not know; and anyway as a practical matter no society is willing to make provision for its own decay. I return therefore to the simple and observable fact that in matters of morals the limits of tolerance shift. Laws, especially those which are based on morals, are less easily moved. It follows as another good working principle that in any new matter of morals the law should be slow to act. By the next generation the swell of indignation may have abated and the law be left without the strong backing which it needs. But it is then difficult to alter the law without giving the impression that moral judgement is being weakened. This is now one of the factors that is strongly militating against any alteration to the law on homosexuality.

A third elastic principle must be advanced more tentatively. It is that as far as possible privacy should be respected. This is not an idea that has ever been made explicit in the criminal law. Acts or words done or said in public or in private are all brought within its scope without distinction in principle. But there goes with this a strong reluctance on the part of judges and legislators to sanction invasions of privacy in the detection of crime. The police have no more right to trespass than the ordinary citizen has; there is no general right of search; to this extent an Englishman's home is still his castle. The Government is extremely careful in the exercise even of those powers which it claims to be undisputed. Telephone tapping and interference with the mails afford a good illustration of this. A Committee of three Privy Councillors who recently inquired into these activities found that the Home Secretary and his predecessors had already formulated strict rules governing the exercise of these powers and the Committee were able to recommend that they should be continued to be exercised substantially on the same terms. But they reported that the power was "regarded with general disfavour."

This indicates a general sentiment that the right to privacy is something to be put in the balance against the enforcement of the law. Ought the same sort of consideration to play any part in the formation of the law? Clearly only in a very limited number of cases. When the help of the law is invoked by an injured citizen, privacy must be irrelevant; the individual cannot ask that his right to privacy should be measured against injury criminally done to another. But when all who are involved in the deed are consenting parties and the injury is done to morals, the public interest in the moral order can be balanced against the claims of privacy. The restriction on police powers of investigation goes further than the affording of a parallel; it means that the detection of crime committed in private and when there is no complaint is bound to be rather haphazard and this is an additional reason for moderation. These considerations do not justify the exclusion of all private immorality from the scope of the law. I think that, as I have already suggested, the test of "private behaviour" should be substituted for "private morality" and the influence of the factor should be reduced from that of a definite limitation to that of a matter to be taken into account. Since the gravity of the crime is also a proper consideration, a distinction might well be made in the case of homosexuality between the lesser acts of indecency and the full offence, which on the principles of the Wolfenden Report it would be illogical to do.

The last and the biggest thing to be remembered is that the law is concerned with the minimum and not with the maximum; there is much in the Sermon on the Mount that would be out of place in the Ten Commandments. We all recognize the gap between the moral law and the law of the land. No man is worth much who regulates his conduct with the sole object of escaping punishment, and every worthy society sets for its members standards which are above those of the law. We recognize the existence of such higher standards when we use expressions such as "moral obligation" and "morally bound." The distinction was well put in the judgement of African elders in a family dispute: "We have power to make you divide the crops, for this is our law, and we will see this is done. But we have not power to make you behave like an upright man.[3]

It can only be because this point is so obvious that it is so frequently ignored. Discussion among law-makers, both professional and amateur, is too often limited to what is right or wrong and good or bad for society. There is a failure to keep separate the two questions I have earlier posed – the question of society's right to pass a moral judgement and the question of whether the arm of the law should be used to enforce the judgement. The criminal law is not a statement of how people ought to behave; it is a statement of what will happen to them if they do not behave; good citizens are not expected to come within reach of it or to set their sights by it, and every enactment should be framed accordingly.

The arm of the law is an instrument to be used by society, and the decision about what particular cases it should be used in is essentially a practical one. Since it is an instrument, it is wise before deciding to use it to have regard to the tools with which it can be fitted and to the machinery which operates it. Its tools are fines, imprisonment, or lesser forms of supervision (such as Borstal and probation) and – not to be ignored – the degradation that often follows upon the publication of the crime. Are any of these suited to the job of dealing with sexual immorality? The fact that there is so much immorality which has never been brought within the law shows that there can be no general rule. It is a matter for decision in each case; but in the case of homosexuality the Wolfenden Report rightly has regard to the views of those who are experienced in dealing with this sort of crime and to those of the clergy who are the natural guardians of public morals.

The machinery which sets the criminal law in motion ends with the verdict and the sentence; and a verdict is given either by magistrates or by a jury. As a general rule, whenever a crime is sufficiently serious to justify a maximum punishment of more than three months, the accused has the right to the verdict of a jury. The result is that magistrates administer mostly what I have called the regulatory part of the law.

They deal extensively with drunkenness, gambling, and prostitution, which are matters of morals or close to them, but not with any of the graver moral offences. They are more responsive than juries to the ideas of the legislature; it may not be accidental that the Wolfenden Report, in recommending increased penalties for solicitation, did not go above the limit of three months. Juries tend to dilute the decrees of Parliament with their own ideas of what should be punishable. Their province of course is fact and not law, and I do not mean that they often deliberately disregard the law. But if they think it is too stringent, they sometimes take a very merciful view of the facts. Let me take one example out of many that could be given. It is an offence to have carnal knowledge of a girl under the age of sixteen years. Consent on her part is no defence; if she did not consent, it would of course amount to rape. The law makes special provision for the situation when a boy and girl are near in age. If a man under twenty-four can prove that he had reasonable cause to believe that the girl was over the age of sixteen years, he has a good defence. The law regards the offence as sufficiently serious to make it one that is triable only by a judge at assizes. "Reasonable cause" means not merely that the boy honestly believed that the girl was over sixteen but also that he must have had reasonable grounds for his belief. In theory it ought not to be an easy defence to make out but in fact it is extremely rare for anyone who advances it to be convicted. The fact is that the girl is often as much to blame as the boy. The object of the law, as judges repeatedly tell juries, is to protect young girls against themselves; but juries are not impressed.

The part that the jury plays in the enforcement of the criminal law, the fact that no grave offence against morals is punishable without their verdict, these are of great importance in relation to the statements of principle that I have been making. They turn what might otherwise be pure exhortation to the legislature into something like rules that the law-makers cannot safely ignore. The man in the jury box is not just an expression; he is an active reality. It will not in the long run work to make laws about morality that are not acceptable to him.

This then is how I believe my third interrogatory should be answered – not by the formulation of hard and fast rules, but by a judgement in each case taking into account the sort of factors I have been mentioning. The line that divides the criminal law from the moral is not determinable by the application of any clear-cut principle. It is like a line that divides land and sea, a coastline of irregularities and indentations. There are gaps and promontories, such as adultery and fornication, which the law has for centuries left substantially untouched. Adultery of the sort that breaks up marriage seems to be just as harmful to the social fabric as homosexuality or bigamy. The only ground for putting it outside the criminal law is that a law which made it a crime would be too difficult to enforce; it is too generally regarded as a human weakness not suitably punished by imprisonment. All that the law can do with fornication is to act against its worst manifestations; there is a general abhorrence of the commercialization of vice, and that sentiment gives strength to the law against brothels and immoral earnings. There is no logic to be found in this. The boundary between the criminal law and the moral law is fixed by balancing in the case of each particular crime the pros and cons of legal enforcement in accordance with the sort of considerations I have been outlining. The fact that adultery, fornication, and lesbianism are untouched by the criminal law does not prove that homosexuality ought not to be touched. The error of jurisprudence in the Wolfenden Report is caused by the search for some single principle to explain the division between crime and sin. The Report finds it in the principle that the criminal law exists for the protection of individuals; on this principle fornication in private between consenting adults is outside the law and thus it becomes logically indefensible to bring homosexuality between consenting adults in private within it. But the true principle is that the law exists for the protection of society. It does not discharge its function by protecting the individual from injury, annoyance, corruption, and exploitation; the law must protect also the institutions and the community of ideas, political and moral, without which people cannot live together. Society cannot ignore the morality of the individual any more than it can his loyalty; it flourishes on both and without either it dies.

I have said that the morals which underly the law must be derived from the sense of right and wrong which resides in the community as a whole; it does not matter whence the community of thought comes, whether from one body of doctrine or another or from the knowledge of good and evil which no man is without. If the reasonable man believes that a practice is immoral and believes also – no matter whether the belief is right or wrong, so be it that it is honest and dispassionate – that no right-minded member of his society could think otherwise, then for the purpose of the law it is immoral. This, you may say, makes immorality a question of fact – what the law would consider as self-evident fact no doubt, but still with no higher authority than any other doctrine of public policy. I think that this is so, and indeed the law does not distinguish between an act that is immoral and one that is contrary to public policy. But the law has never yet had occasion to inquire into the differences between Christian morals and those which every right-minded member of society is expected to hold. The inquiry would, I believe, be academic. Moralists would find differences; indeed they would find them between different branches of the Christian faith on subjects such as divorce and birth-control. But for the purpose of the limited entry which the law makes into the field of morals, there is no practical difference. It seems to me therefore that the free-thinker and the non-Christian can accept, without offence to his convictions, the fact that Christian morals are the basis of the criminal law and that he can recognize, also without taking offence, that without the support of the churches the moral order, which has its origin in and takes its strength from Christian beliefs, would collapse.

This brings me back in the end to a question I posed at the beginning. What is the relationship between crime and sin, between the Church and the Law? I do not think that you can equate crime with sin. The divine law and the secular have been disunited, but they are brought together again by the need which each has, for the other. It is not my function to emphasize the Church's need of the secular law; it can be put tersely by saying that you cannot have a ceiling without a floor. I am very clear about the law's need for the Church. I have spoken of the criminal law as dealing with the minimum standards of human conduct and the moral law with the maximum. The instrument of the criminal law is punishment; those of the moral law are teaching, training, and exhortation. If the whole dead weight of sin were ever to be allowed to fall upon the law, it could not take the strain. If at any point there is a lack of clear and convincing moral teaching, the administration of the law suffers. Let me take as an illustration of this the law on abortion. I believe that a great many people nowadays do not understand why abortion is wrong. If it is right to prevent conception, at what point does it become sinful to prevent birth and why? I doubt if anyone who has not had a theological training would give a satisfactory answer to that question. Many people regard abortion as the next step when by accident birth-control has failed; and many more people are deterred from abortion not because they think it sinful or illegal but because of the difficulty which illegality puts in the way of obtaining it. The law is powerless to deal with abortion *per se*; unless a tragedy occurs or a "professional" abortionist is involved – the parallel between the "professional" in abortions and the "professional" in fornication is quite close – it has to leave it alone. Without one or other of these features the crime is rarely detected; and when detected, the plea *ad misericordiam* is often too strong. The "professional" abortionist is usually the unskilled person who for a small reward helps girls in trouble; the man and the girl involved are essential witnesses for the prosecution and therefore go free; the paid abortionist generally receives a very severe sentence, much more severe than that usually given to the paid assistant in immorality, such as the ponce or the brothel-keeper. The reason is because unskilled abortion endangers life. In a case in 1949[4] Lord Chief Justice Goddard said: "It is because the unskilful attentions of ignorant people in cases of this kind often result in death that attempts to produce abortion are regarded by the law as very serious offences." This gives the law a twist which disassociates it from morality and, I think, to some extent from sound sense. The act is being punished because it is dangerous, and it is dangerous largely because it is illegal and therefore performed only by the unskilled.

The object of what I have said is not to criticise theology or law in relation to abortion. That is a large subject and beyond my present scope. It is to show what happens to the law in matters of morality about which the community as a whole is not deeply imbued with a sense of sin, the law sags under a weight which it is not constructed to bear and may become permanently warped.

I return now to the main thread of my argument and summarize it. Society cannot live without morals. Its morals are those standards of conduct which the reasonable man approves. A rational man, who is also a good man, may have other standards. If he has no standards at all he is not a good man and need not be further considered. If he has standards, they may be very different; he may, for example, not disapprove of homosexuality or abortion. In that case he will not share in the common morality; but that should not make him deny that it is a social necessity. A rebel may be rational in thinking that he is right but he is irrational if he thinks that society can leave him free to rebel.

A man who concedes that morality is necessary to society must support the use of those instruments without which morality cannot be maintained. The two instruments are those of teaching, which is doctrine, and of enforcement, which is the law. If morals could be taught simply on the basis that they are necessary to society, there would be no social need for religion; it could be left as a purely personal affair. But morality cannot be taught in that way. Loyalty is not taught in that way either. No society has yet solved the problem of how to teach morality without religion. So the law must base itself on Christian morals and to the limit of its ability enforce them, not simply because they are the morals of most of us, nor simply because they are the morals which are taught by the established Church – on these points the law recognizes the right to dissent – but for the compelling reason that without the help of Christian teaching the law will fail.

NOTES

1 It is somewhere about this point in the argument that Professor Hart in *Law, Liberty and Morality* discerns a proposition which he describes as central to my thought. He states the proposition and his objection to it as follows (p. 51). "He appears to move from the acceptable proposition that *some* shared morality is essential to the existence of any society [this I take to be the proposition on p. 12] to the unacceptable proposition that a society is identical with its morality as that is at any given moment of its history, so that a change in its morality is tantamount to the destruction of a society. The former proposition might be even accepted as a necessary rather than an empirical truth depending on a quite plausible definition of society as a body of men who hold certain moral views in common. But the latter proposition is absurd. Taken strictly, it would prevent us saying that the morality of a given society had changed, and would compel us instead to say that one society had disappeared and another one taken its place. But it is only on this absurd criterion of what it is for the same society to continue to exist that it could be asserted without evidence that any deviation from a society's shared morality threatens its existence." In conclusion (p. 82) Professor Hart condemns the whole thesis in the lecture as based on "a confused definition of what a society is."

I do not assert that *any* deviation from a society's shared morality threatens its existence any more than I assert that *any* subversive activity threatens its existence. I assert that they are both activities which are capable in their nature of threatening the existence of society so that neither can be put beyond the law.

For the rest, the objection appears to me to be all a matter of words. I would venture to assert, for example, that you cannot have a game without rules and that if there were no rules there would be no game. If I am asked whether that means that the game is "identical" with the rules, I would be willing for the question to be answered either way in the belief that the answer would lead to nowhere. If I am asked whether a change in the rules means that one game has disappeared and another has taken its place, I would reply probably not, but that it would depend on the extent of the change.

Likewise I should venture to assert that there cannot be a contract without terms. Does this mean that an "amended" contract is a "new" contract in the eyes of the law? I once listened to an argument by an ingenious counsel that a contract, because of the substitution of one clause for another, had "ceased to have effect" within the meaning of a statutory provision. The judge did not accept the argument; but if most of the fundamental terms had been changed, I daresay he would have done.

The proposition that I make in the text is that if (as I understand Professor Hart to agree, at any rate for the purposes of the argument) you cannot have a society without morality, the law can be used to enforce morality as something that is essential to a society. I cannot see why this proposition (whether it is right or wrong) should mean that morality can never be changed without the destruction of society. If morality is changed, the law can be changed. Professor Hart refers (p. 72) to the proposition as "the use of legal punishment to freeze into immobility the morality dominant at a particular time in a society's existence." One might as well say that the inclusion of a penal section into a statute prohibiting certain acts freezes the whole statute into immobility and prevents the prohibitions from ever being modified.

2 *Essays in Jurisprudence and Ethics* (1882), Macmillan, pp. 278 and 353.
3 A case in the Saa-Katengo Kuta at Lialiu, August 1942, quoted in *The Judicial Process among the Barotse of Northern Rhodesia* by Max Gluckman, Manchester University Press, 1955, p. 172.
4 *R v Tate, The Times*, 22 June 1949.

READING QUESTIONS ON DEVLIN

1 Why does Devlin suppose that "intolerance, indignation, and disgust" are important?
2 Does the toleration of things that disgust many people carry the risks that Devlin suggests?
3 In Phoenix, Arizona, it is against the law to kill a pony within the city limits. There is a Tongan tradition of roasting a pony to celebrate weddings. Should the law be enforced against Tongans living in Phoenix? What would Devlin say?
4 Does Devlin provide a way of replacing the gap left by negative liberty if Taylor is right about its incoherence?

Ronald Dworkin
"Liberty and Moralism" (1977)

Dworkin examines the relation between law and democracy, arguing that democracy requires certain limits on the types of argument that can be put forward. He challenges Devlin's understanding of a moral position.

My purpose is not to settle issues of political morality by the fiat of a dictionary, but to exhibit what I believe to be mistakes in Lord Devlin's moral sociology. I shall try to show that our conventional moral practices are more complex and more structured than he takes them to be, and that he consequently misunderstands what it means to say that the criminal law should be drawn from public morality. This is a popular and appealing thesis, and it lies near the core not only of Lord Devlin's, but of many other, theories about law and morals. It is crucial that its implications be understood.

THE CONCEPT OF A MORAL POSITION

We might start with the fact that terms like "moral position" and "moral conviction" function in our conventional morality as terms of justification and criticism, as well as of description. It is true that we sometimes speak of a group's "morals," or "morality," or "moral beliefs," or "moral positions" or "moral convictions," in what might be called an anthropological sense, meaning to refer to whatever attitudes the group displays about the propriety about human conduct, qualities or goals. We say, in this sense, that the morality of Nazi Germany was based on prejudice, or was irrational. But we also use some of these terms, particularly "moral position" and "moral conviction," a discriminatory sense, to contrast the positions they describe with prejudices, rationalizations, matters of personal aversion or taste, arbitrary stands, and the like. One use – perhaps the most characteristic use – of this discriminatory sense is to offer a limited but important sort of justification for an act, when the moral issues surrounding that act are unclear or in dispute.

Suppose I tell you that I propose to vote against a man running for

a public office of trust because I know him to be a homosexual and because I believe that homosexuality is profoundly immoral. If you disagree that homosexuality is immoral, you may accuse me of being about
to cast my vote unfairly, acting on prejudice or out of a personal repugnance which is irrelevant to the moral issue. I might then try to convert
you to my position on homosexuality, but if I fail in this I shall still want
to convince you of what you and I will both take to be a separate point
– that my vote was based on a moral position, in the discriminatory
sense, even though one which differs from yours. I shall want to
persuade you of this, because if I do I am entitled to expect that you will
alter your opinion of me and of what I am about to do. Your judgment
of my character will be different – you might still think me eccentric (or
puritanical or unsophisticated) but these are types of character and not
faults of character. Your judgment of my act will also be different, in
this respect. You will admit that so long as I hold my moral position, I
have a moral right to vote against the homosexual, because I have a
right (indeed a duty) to vote my own convictions. You would not admit
such a right (or duty) if you were still persuaded that I was acting out
of a prejudice or a personal taste.

I am entitled to expect that your opinion will change in these ways,
because these distinctions are a part of the conventional morality you
and I share, and which forms the background for our discussion. They
enforce the difference between positions we must respect, although we
think them wrong, and positions we need not respect because they
offend some ground rule of moral reasoning. A great deal of debate
about moral issues (in real life, although not in philosophy texts) consists of arguments that some position falls on one or the other side of
this crucial line.

It is this feature of conventional morality that animates Lord Devlin's
argument that society has the right to follow its own lights. We must
therefore examine that discriminatory concept of a moral position
more closely, and we can do so by pursuing our imaginary conversation. What must I do to convince you that my position is a moral
position?

(a) I must produce some reasons for it. This is not to say that I have to
articulate a moral principle I am following or a general moral theory
to which I subscribe. Very few people can do either, and the ability to
hold a moral position is not limited to those who can. My reason need
not be a principle or theory at all. It must only point out some aspect or

feature of homosexuality which moves me to regard it as immoral: the fact that the Bible forbids it, for example, or that one who practices homosexuality becomes unfit for marriage and parenthood. Of course, any such reason would presuppose my acceptance of some general principle or theory, but I need not be able to state what it is, or realize that I am relying upon it.

Not every reason I might give will do, however. Some will be excluded by general criteria stipulating sorts of reasons which do not count. We might take note of four of the most important such criteria:

1 If I tell you that homosexuals are morally inferior because they do not have heterosexual desires, and so are not "real men," you would reject that reason as showing one type of prejudice. Prejudices, in general, are postures of judgment that take into account considerations our conventions exclude. In a structured context, like a trial or a contest, the ground rules exclude all but certain considerations, and a prejudice is a basis of judgment which violates these rules. Our conventions stipulate some ground rules of moral judgment which obtain even apart from such special contexts, the most important of which is that a man must not be held morally inferior on the basis of some physical, racial or other characteristic he cannot help having. Thus a man whose moral judgements about Jews, or Negroes, or Southerners, or women, or effeminate men are based on his belief that any member of these classes automatically deserves less respect, without regard to anything he himself has done, is said to be prejudiced against that group.

2 If I base my view about homosexuals on a personal emotional reaction ("they make me sick") you would reject that reason as well. We distinguish moral positions from emotional reactions, not because moral positions are supposed to be unemotional or dispassionate – quite the reverse is true – but because the moral position is supposed to justify the emotional reaction, not vice versa. If a man is unable to produce such reasons, we do not deny the fact of his emotional involvement, which may have important social or political consequences, but we do not take this involvement as demonstrating his moral conviction. Indeed, it is just this sort of position – a severe emotional reaction to a practice or a situation for which one cannot account – that we tend to describe, in lay terms, as a phobia or an obsession.

3 If I base my position on a proposition of fact ("homosexual acts are physically debilitating") which is not only false, but is so implausible that it challenges the minimal standards of evidence and argument I generally accept and impose upon others, then you would regard my belief, even though sincere, as a form of rationalization, and disqualify my reason on that ground. (Rationalization is a complex concept, and also includes, as we shall see, the production of reasons which suggest general theories I do not accept.)

4 If I can argue for my own position only by citing the beliefs of others ("everyone knows homosexuality is a sin") you will conclude that I am parroting and not relying on a moral conviction of my own. With the possible (though complex) exception of a deity, there is no moral authority to which I can appeal and so automatically make my position a moral one. I must have my own reasons, though of course I may have been taught these reasons by others.

No doubt many readers will disagree with these thumbnail sketches of prejudice, mere emotional reaction, rationalization and parroting. Some may have their own theories of what these are. I want to emphasize now only that these are distinct concepts, whatever the details of the differences might be, and that they have a role in deciding whether to treat another's position as a moral conviction. They are not merely epithets to be pasted on positions we strongly dislike.

(b) Suppose I do produce a reason which is not disqualified on one of these (or on similar) grounds. That reason will presuppose some general moral principle or theory, even though I may not be able to state that principle or theory, and do not have it in mind when I speak. If I offer, as my reason, the fact that the Bible forbids homosexual acts, or that homosexual acts make it less likely that the actor will marry and raise children, I suggest that I accept the theory my reason presupposes, and you will not be satisfied that my position is a moral one if you believe that I do not. It may be a question of my sincerity – do I in fact believe that the injunctions of the Bible are morally binding as such, or that all men have a duty to procreate? Sincerity is not, however, the only issue, for consistency is also in point. I may believe that I accept one of these general positions, and be wrong, because my other beliefs, and my own conduct on other occasions, may be inconsistent with it. I may reject certain Biblical injunctions, or I may hold that men have a right to remain bachelors if they please or use contraceptives all their lives.

Of course, my general moral positions may have qualifications and exceptions. The difference between an exception and an inconsistency is that the former can be supported by reasons which presuppose other moral positions I can properly claim to hold. Suppose I condemn all homosexuals on Biblical authority, but not all fornicators. What reason can I offer for the distinction? If I can produce none which supports it, I cannot claim to accept the general position about Biblical authority. If I do produce a reason which seems to support the distinction, the same sorts of question may be asked about that reason as were asked about my original reply. What general position does the reason for my exception presuppose? Can I sincerely claim to accept that further general position? Suppose my reason, for example, is that fornication is now very common, and has been sanctioned by custom. Do I really believe that what is immoral becomes moral when it becomes popular? If not, and if I can produce no other reason for the distinction, I cannot claim to accept the general position that what the Bible condemns is immoral. Of course, I may be persuaded, when this is pointed out, to change my views on fornication. But you would be alert to the question of whether this is a genuine change of heart, or only a performance for the sake of the argument.

In principle there is no limit to these ramifications of my original claim, though of course no actual argument is likely to pursue very many of them.

(c) But do I really have to have a reason to make my position a matter of moral conviction? Most men think that acts which cause unnecessary suffering, or break a serious promise with no excuse, are immoral, and yet they could give no reason for these beliefs. They feel that no reason is necessary, because they take it as axiomatic or self-evident that these are immoral acts. It seems contrary to common sense to deny that a position held in this way can be a moral position.

Yet there is an important difference between believing that one's position is self-evident and just not having a reason for one's position. The former presupposes a positive belief that no further reason is necessary, that the immorality of the act in question does not depend upon its social effects, or its effects on the character of the actor, or its proscription by a deity, or anything else, but follows from the nature of the act itself. The claim that a particular position is axiomatic, in other words, does supply a reason of a special sort, namely that the act is immoral in and of itself, and this special reason, like the others we considered, may be inconsistent with more general theories I hold.

The moral arguments we make presuppose not only moral principles, but also more abstract positions about moral reasoning. In particular, they presuppose positions about what kinds of acts can be immoral in and of themselves. When I criticize your moral opinions, or attempt to justify my own disregard of traditional moral rules I think are silly, I will likely proceed by denying that the act in question has any of the several features that can make an act immoral – that it involves no breach of an undertaking or duty, for example, harms no one including the actor, is not proscribed by any organized religion, and is not illegal. I proceed in this way because I assume that the ultimate grounds of immorality are limited to some such small set of very general standards. I may assert this assumption directly or it may emerge from the pattern of my argument. In either event, I will enforce it by calling positions which can claim no support from any of these ultimate standards *arbitrary*, as I should certainly do if you said that photography was immoral, for instance, or swimming. Even if I cannot articulate this underlying assumption, I shall still apply it, and since the ultimate criteria I recognize are among the most abstract of my moral standards, they will not vary much from those my neighbors recognize and apply. Although many who despise homosexuals are unable to say why, few would claim affirmatively that one needs no reason, for this would make their position, on their own standards, an arbitrary one.

(d) This anatomy of our argument could be continued, but it is already long enough to justify some conclusions. If the issue between us is whether my views on homosexuality amount to a moral position, and hence whether I am entitled to vote against a homosexual on that ground, I cannot settle the issue simply by reporting my feelings. You will want to consider the reasons I can produce to support my belief, and whether my other views and behavior are consistent with the theories these reasons presuppose. You will have, of course, to apply your own understanding, which may differ in detail from mine, of what a prejudice or a rationalization is, for example, and of when one view is inconsistent with another. You and I may end in disagreement over whether my position is a moral one, partly because of such differences in understanding, and partly because one is less likely to recognize these illegitimate grounds in himself than in others.

We must avoid the skeptical fallacy of passing from these facts to the conclusion that there is no such thing as a prejudice or a rationalization or an inconsistency, or that these terms mean merely that the one who uses them strongly dislikes the positions he describes this way. That would be like arguing that because different people have different understandings of what jealousy is, and can in good faith disagree about whether one of them is jealous, there is no such thing as jealousy, and one who says another is jealous merely means he dislikes him very much.

LORD DEVLIN'S MORALITY

We may now return to Lord Devlin's second argument. He argues that when legislators must decide a moral issue (as by his hypothesis they must when a practice threatens a valued social arrangement), they must follow any consensus of moral position which the community at large has reached, because this is required by the democratic principle, and because a community is entitled to follow its own lights. The argument would have some plausibility if Lord Devlin meant, in speaking of the moral consensus of the community, those positions which are moral positions in the discriminatory sense we have been exploring.

But he means nothing of the sort. His definition of a moral position shows he is using it in what I called the anthropological sense. The ordinary man whose opinion we must enforce, he says, "is not expected to reason about anything and his judgment may be largely a matter of feeling." "If the reasonable man believes," he adds, "that a practice is immoral and believes so – no matter whether the belief is right or wrong, so be it that it is honest and dispassionate – that no right-minded member of his society could think otherwise, then for the purpose of the law it is immoral." Elsewhere he quotes with approval Dean Rostow's attribution to him of the view that "the common morality of a society at any time is a blend of custom and conviction, of reason and feeling, of experience and prejudice." His sense of what a moral conviction is emerges most clearly of all from the famous remark about homosexuals. If the ordinary man regards homosexuality "as a vice so abominable that its mere presence is an offence," this demonstrates for him that the ordinary man's feelings about homosexuals are a matter of moral conviction.

His conclusions fail because they depend upon using "moral position" in this anthropological sense. Even if it is true that most men think homosexuality an abominable vice and cannot tolerate its presence, it remains possible that this common opinion is a compound of prejudice (resting on the assumption that homosexuals are morally inferior creatures because they are effeminate), rationalization (based on assumptions of fact so unsupported that they challenge the community's own standards of rationality), and personal aversion (representing no conviction but merely blind hate rising from unacknowledged self-suspicion). It remains possible that the ordinary man could produce no reason for his view, but would simply parrot his neighbor who in turn parrots him, or that he would produce a reason which presupposes a general moral position he could not sincerely or consistently claim to hold. If so, the principles of democracy we follow do not call for the enforcement of the consensus, for the belief that prejudices, personal aversions and rationalizations do not justify restricting another's freedom itself occupies a critical and fundamental position in our popular morality. Nor would the bulk of the community then be entitled to follow its own lights, for the community does not extend that privilege to one who acts on the basis of prejudice, rationalization, or personal aversion. Indeed, the distinction between these and moral convictions, in the discriminatory sense, exists largely to mark off the former as the sort of positions one is not entitled to pursue.

A conscientious legislator who is told a moral consensus exists must test the credentials of that consensus. He cannot, of course, examine the beliefs of behavior of individual citizens; he cannot hold hearings on the Clapham omnibus. That is not the point.

The claim that a moral consensus exists is not itself based on a poll. It is based on an appeal to the legislator's sense of how his community reacts to some disfavored practice. But this same sense included an awareness of the grounds on which that reaction is generally supported. If there has been a public debate involving the editorial columns, speeches of his colleagues, the testimony of interested groups, and his own correspondence, these will sharpen his awareness of what arguments and positions are in the field. He must sift these arguments and positions, trying to determine which are prejudices or rationalizations, which presuppose general principles or theories vast parts of the population could not be supposed to accept, and so on. It may be that when he has finished this process of reflection he will find that the claim of a moral consensus has not been made out. In the case of homosexuality, I expect, it would not be, and that is what makes Lord Devlin's undiscriminating hypothetical so serious a misstatement. What is shocking and wrong is not his idea that the community's morality counts, but his idea of what counts as the community's morality.

Of course the legislator must apply these tests for himself. If he shares the popular views he is less likely to find them wanting, though if he is self-critical the exercise may convert him. His answer, in any event, will depend upon his own understanding of what our shared morality requires. That is inevitable, for whatever criteria we urge him to apply, he can apply them only as he understands them.

A legislator who proceeds in this way, who refuses to take popular indignation, intolerance and disgust as the moral conviction of his community, is not guilty of moral elitism. He is not simply setting his own educated views against those of a vast public which rejects them. He is doing his best to enforce a distinct, and fundamentally important, part of his community's morality, a consensus more essential to society's existence in the form we know it than the opinion Lord Devlin bids him follow.

No legislator can afford to ignore the public's outrage. It is a fact he must reckon with. It will set the boundaries of what is politically feasible, and it will determine his strategies of persuasion and enforcement within these boundaries. But we must not confuse strategy with justice, nor facts of political life with principles of political morality. Lord Devlin understands these distinctions, but his arguments will appeal most, I am afraid, to those who do not.

READING QUESTION ON DWORKIN

1 Does Dworkin's view give judges too much power? Alternatively, does he give democratic assemblies too much power?

Allan C. Hutchinson and Patrick Monahan
"Democracy and the Rule of Law" (1987)

Hutchinson and Monahan argue that the rule of law stands in the way of democracy. They offer two reasons for distrusting courts. They suggest that surrendering power to courts leads to apathy, and they also argue that when courts have appeared to be in the forefront of social change, the results have been more apparent than real. In place of courts and the rule of law, Hutchinson and Monahan advocate citizen juries and democracy.

The practice and theory of liberal democracy is in disarray. Condemned as utopian, ideals of full public participation and control have been preempted by an ethic of expertise. This contemporary orthodoxy holds that public policy should be formulated only by those properly qualified for the task; the role of the people is limited to choosing the elites who make the choices for them. The link between government policy and popular sentiment is, at best, obscure, with electoral apathy and disaffection the norm. For instance nearly a third of the Canadian electorate believe that politics either makes things worse or else has no effect in solving social problems.[1] In America, almost half the electorate does not vote in presidential elections. Public trust and confidence in government has fallen to the point where less than one-quarter of Americans believe that government is run for the "benefit of all."[2]

This is nothing new. There has never been a "golden age" of popular democracy except in the wishful thoughts of the nostalgic few. Thus the current apathy and elitism which dominates liberal democratic thinking lends scant support to critics who claim that present conditions constitute an exceptional crisis for democracy. Indeed, liberal democratic institutions have continually managed to confound critics, who have underestimated their resiliency and stamina. Representative democracy has flourished in the face of widespread citizen ennui precisely because public participation and interest are dispensable to its survival and performance. Limited public participation and apathy are even regarded in a positive light, since they minimize conflict and promote stability. Democratic politics is seen as the legitimate preserve of specialists, whose only expertise happens to be that they have made a habit of engaging in political activity.

Whether by design or default, the courts have been proclaimed by many theorists as a proxy for a genuine democratic dialogue. The American Supreme Court has long been cast in the role of the nation's moral conscience. With the advent of an entrenched *Charter of Rights and Freedoms* in 1982, the Supreme Court of Canada is assuming a similar mantle. No longer seen merely as a means of constraining democratic debate and argument, courts act as elite forums for the enactment and resolution of this dialogue. Judicial review celebrates the triumph of detached philosophical deliberation over heated political haggling. Although a travesty of the democratic ideal, the judiciary's elevation to the status of moral prophet is defended and extolled by many in the name of democracy itself.[3]

Thomas Paine's assertion that "in America law is king" has never been more pertinent, not only in America but in Canada as well. Long a central feature of American's self-image, respect for the Rule of Law is becoming a vaunted article of Canadian constitutional faith. Indeed, the preamble to the *Canadian Charter of Rights and Freedoms* states that "Canada is founded upon principles that recognize the supremacy of God and the [R]ule of [L]aw." Law has been the gavel wielded to bring to order (or silence) competing voices in the cause of justice. In recent decades, the American Supreme Court has moved to front and centre on the political stage, intervening in heated political controversies. Paradoxically, the American Court's landmark decisions in *Brown* (desegregation) and *Roe v Wade* (abortion) have worn pretty thin its claims to be acting within the bounds of constitutional propriety. Rising to the challenge, legal and political theorists have championed the relocation of political debate from the legislative crucible of communal controversy to the judicial "forum of principle." The judicialization of politics has been justified under the banner of the Rule of Law. Within this projected scenario, there is no conflict between an activist judiciary and democratic governance. Indeed, the Rule of Law is welcomed as a necessary component of a properly functioning democratic polity. Checking popular excesses, litigation is thought to provide a privileged occasion for the renewal of society's commitment to continuing moral discourse.

Notwithstanding recent valiant attempts to reconcile the Rule of Law with democratic theory, this gambit fails. The Rule of Law functions as a clear check on the flourishing of a rigorous democracy. Attempts to characterize the Rule of Law as the butler of democracy are false and misleading. Liberal legalism is premised on the same logic of expertise which has made popular control over public policy dispensable. It is simply more evidence of the demise of contestability as the touchstone of politics. The first part of the essay will trace the historical and theoretical connections between the Rule of Law and liberal democracy. The second part will offer a more searching criticism of the elite and marginal practice of constitutional adjudication. The final section reasserts the primacy of democratic over legalistic values and seeks to sketch a tical vision of democratic practice.

1 THE BRIDLE OF POWER: LAW AND POLITICS

(a) Liberalism, Law, and Democracy

The sonorous and majestic ring of the appeal to the Rule of Law has resonated through the centuries. It has operated as a potent call to moral arms, a clarion-call for constitutional justice by a whole host of political actors and combatants. At times, the Rule of Law has been used to legitimize and galvanize a challenge to entrenched power; at others, the ruling elite has relied upon it to sanction its power and resistance to would-be usurpers. Like any ideal, it only exists in the political consciousness and conscience. But, like every other ideal, it exercises a tenacious grip on the imagination and actions of its adherents. Indeed, its ideological attraction and political durability are largely attributable to its historical plasticity, the facility to accommodate itself to changing governmental situations and political forces. In short, it is the will-o'-the-wisp of constitutional history.

Notwithstanding its protean nature, the rich historical tapestry of the Rule of Law has been loosely connected by a strong liberal thread: it has been used as a seductive slogan in the struggle to establish or preserve individual liberty and action. On many occasions, this appeal to liberty has amounted to nothing more than moralistic window-dressing for otherwise naked attempts to seize political power, a rhetorical gambit in a continuing power-play. But to reduce the appeal to the Rule of Law to simply and always an exercise in mystification is to distort the historical record; it impugns the honourable motives of many and overestimates the credulity of even more.[4] Over the last millennium, the Rule of Law has occasionally proved to be an effective principle to check the indulgent abuse of power by the few over the many. However, over the long haul, the Rule of Law has been activated as a "principled" counter in the shuffling of power among elite groups; it has served to inhibit the flourishing of any governmental system of direct democracy.

The Rule of Law is more concerned with and committed to individual liberty than democratic governance. The historical development of any kind of democracy has been the by-product of a preoccupation with private autonomy. The Rule of Law is premised on the ideal of limited government; it has stood as a constitutional barrier between the governors and the governed, between power and people. The existence and extent of democratic governance is only justified insofar as it better serves the enhanced liberty of individuals; it is a recent recruit on the proclaimed march to the truly liberal state. Indeed, universal suffrage is a decidedly twentieth century phenomenon. Even today, representative democracy only extends to about 20 per cent of the world's nations (not population) and, in many of these states, the arrangements are extremely fragile and incomplete.

The compulsion to reason within a closed system of premises is said to guarantee the enduring integrity and efficacy of the constitutional compact and insulate the judges from ideological controversy. Within this constitutional scenario, adherence to the Rule of Law has come to be synonymous with compliance with a liberal scheme of constitutional governance. Although some form of representative democracy has become a modern component of this model, the history of the Rule of Law's theory and practice reveals that it is more an optional extra than an essential condition. Indeed, the opposite often seems to be true: the Rule of Law has functioned as a clear check on the actual impact and expansion of a rigorous democracy.

(b) The Thick and the Thin

If not non-democratic in aspiration and orientation, the Rule of Law is democratically indifferent in character and scope. The enduring concerns of the Rule of Law are the limitation of state power, the maintenance of a broad sphere of private liberty and the preservation of a market-exchange economy. In its many academic manifestations, it has been connected, to greater and lesser extents, to an individualistic theory of political justice and jurisprudence. Ostensibly, there have been two versions of the Rule of Law, but they both represent a commitment to liberalism; it is simply that one tends to be more explicit and marked than the other.

The "thin" version of the Rule of Law amounts to a constitutional principle of legality. It demands that government be conducted in accordance with established and performable norms; its voice remains silent or, at best, whispered on the issue of substantive policies. Rule must be by law and not discretion. Also, and especially, the lawmaker itself must be under the law, at least until it changes the law. In this "thin" form, the Rule of Law is targeted against arbitrary government and palm-tree justice. Its critical logo is "a government of laws, not men"; its operative axioms are the generality of official rules and the faithful adherence by government to those declared standards of conduct. The modern defence of such a "thin" version is that the preferred system of governance is that in which "the law furnishes a base-line for self-directed action, not a detailed set of instructions for accomplishing specific objectives."[5]

Although far from explicit or necessarily so, its substantive tendency is clearly toward a liberal society in which the best government is the one which governs least. However, unless such a constitutional requirement of official legality is supplemented by a "thicker" theory of political justice, the Rule of Law will be a weak restraint on an ambitiously unjust regime. It might even tend to legitimate its substantive excesses under a patina of formal justice. Unrepresentative government and the Rule of Law are not mutually exclusive; democracy is an entirely dispensable feature of this form of the Rule of Law. As Herbert Hart has observed, "however great the aura of majesty or authority which the official system may have, its demands in the end must be submitted to moral scrutiny."[6] Accordingly, a full and proper defence and understanding of the Rule of Law must be based on its foundational and substantive political connections.

The "thick" version of the Rule of Law incorporates the thinner one as merely one dimension of a liberal theory of justice. This conception of the Rule of Law goes back to the Greeks and Romans, but finds its modern roots in the Enlightenment.[7] Indeed, there is an almost direct line of descent from the theory and practice of 17th century England to that of late 20th century Anglo-America. The intellectual lineage runs almost unbroken from John Locke and Thomas Hobbes to John Rawls and Ronald Dworkin, through Thomas Paine, John Stuart Mill, A.V. Dicey and Friedrich Hayek. The modern defence of this "thick" version posits the necessary connection between procedural and substantive justice. The Rule of Law demands that positive law embody a particular vision of social justice, structured around the moral rights and duties which citizens have against each other and the state as a whole.

(c) 1215 and All That

Modern scholarship and constitutional practice can be traced back to the Glorious Revolution and, even beyond that, to the Magna Carta. Before the 17th century, increased individual liberty was more an incidental cost of the political struggle than the result of any deliberate strategy. Beginning with the Magna Carta in 1215, the barons sought to restrain the monarchical monopoly by demanding that the sovereign act only *per legem terrae*. And, as early as the 13th century, jurists like Henry de Bracton argued that even the king was *sub Deo et lege;* "law is the bridle of power."[8] However, by the 15th century at latest, the Magna Carta had become an obscure and hollow proclamation, only later to be romanticised by some modern legal historians. It was not until after the Tudor Reformation, when the Stuarts sought to re-invoke the divine right of kings, that the Rule of Law came into its own as an influential and effective piece of constitutional rhetoric for curbing royal power.

Within this encounter, the idea and establishment of some democratic dimension to political governance was of little consequence or concern.[9]

1610 was a banner year for the Rule of Law. Sir Edward Coke, later to be dismissed as Chief Justice and become a parliamentarian committed to reviving the memory of the Magna Carta as the great charter of English freedom, held in *Dr. Bonham's Case* that "the Common Law will controll Acts of Parliament, and sometimes adjudge them to be utterly void."[10] Also, in that year, the House of Commons presented James I with the Petition of Grievances, insisting that he continue the tradition of being "guided and governed by certain rule of law." Matters did not come to a head until 1625 when Charles I assumed the throne. As so often, the major bone of contention was the right to levy taxes. The price for Parliament's compliance with Charles' fiscal demands was royal assent to the Petition of Right. This enacted that the king would govern according to the laws and statutes of the realm; that no one could be arrested by the king's order, but only for the breach of a specific offence; that only Parliament could impose taxes; and that civilians could not be made subject to martial law.

It must not be forgotten that, although these events have been regarded by generations of constitutional lawyers as laying the foundations for the modern Rule of Law, they were motivated more by a revolutionary than a legal spirit. Nevertheless, they did establish that henceforth law was the "instrument and prize; he who would control the constitution would have first to control the law."[11] But, importantly, it has to be added that Parliament did not embark on this course of action as part of a campaign to transfer power to the general populace; the progressive tenor of the times was resoundingly libertarian and not democratic.

For the next two centuries, the English constitution remained a pragmatic melange of monarchical, aristocratic and democratic ingredients, bound together by a strong libertarian commitment ... Yet, the half century after 1628 demonstrated an important historical lesson that many societies, including our own, continue to overlook: a law is worth little more than the paper it is written on unless it is accompanied by sufficient willingness *and power* to translate its promises into practice. Indeed, after the Petition of Right, Charles almost immediately dissolved Parliament and ruled alone for 11 years. Although Parliament was briefly recalled, England was soon riven by Civil War. The country was not returned to some semblance of normality until the Glorious Revolution of 1688. Significantly, the monarch was restored, but only on terms laid down by Parliament.

A major instrument of government and statement of political intent was the Bill of Rights. While this is the closest England has ever come to adopting a written constitution, it was never more than another piece of legislation, repealable by any later Parliament. The central thrust of the legislation was to force the Crown to rule through Parliament. Its constitutional ambition was not to popularize government, but to restore and conserve "the true auntient and indubitable rights and liberties of the people." It dispensed with the Stuart's extravagant claims to rule by prerogative writ, ensuring that every parliamentarian had freedom of speech and that "cruel and unusual punishments" were prohibited. These provisions were supplemented by the Act of Settlement in 1701; a major clause was that judges no longer held office at the king's whim, but *quamdiu se bene gesserint* (during good behaviour).

The undisputed apologist for these constitutional developments was John Locke, the father of modern liberalism. In his *Second Treatise on Government*, he provided the enduring account of how people created civil society to protect better their individual rights enjoyed in a state of nature. Within such a constitutional scheme, the limited role of government was to enact law "as guards and fences to the properties of all the members of society." The Rule of Law was a pivotal principle. Laws were to be general in scope and operation; "freedom of men under government is ... not to be subject to the inconstant, unknown, arbitrary will of another man." While Locke justified the initial success, it was 18th century writers, like David Hume, Edmund Burke and William Paley, who consolidated the constitutional position of the Rule of Law. Yet, it was the Americans who were to embrace and implement most directly the Lockean teachings.

(d) The American Experiment

Although England had proceeded on the path to parliamentary supremacy, the American colonists were more inclined to resuscitate the Magna Carta and its libertarian underpinnings against a recalcitrant English Parliament. After the Revolution, America set about establishing its own constitutional order. Despite significant divisions, the preferred basis for republican government was not democracy. While, by existing standards, America was enviably more representative in governance than most nations, the Founders' rabid libertarianism was only matched by its faint-hearted commitment to popular rule. As one prominent Philadelphia Conventioneer, Elbridge Gerry, put it, "the evils we experience flow from the excess of democracy."[12] People's

supposed natural rights were to be put beyond the imagined vicissi-
tudes of majoritarian politics. In particular, private property was not to
be open to governmental interference. After all, the War of Independence had been fought over this very principle. The relation between
personal liberty and popular democracy has been neatly described by
Martin Diamond:

> ... for the founding generation it was liberty that was the comprehensive good,
> the end against which political things had to be measured; and democracy
> was only a form of government which, like any other form of government,
> had to prove itself adequately instrumental to the security of liberty.[13]

This liberal theory of democracy has continued to dominate American constitutional life. In effect, the American Revolution only managed
to replace the dominion of a foreign power with that of a domestic
document.[14] Entrenched individual rights always trump any collective
concerns of the democratic process. Enforcing this social compact, the
courts were to function as the guardians of the Rule of Law. But, in the
process, they were not to turn themselves into an independent centre of
constitutional power. As John Marshall announced, "judicial power, as
contradistinguished from the power of laws, has no existence. Courts
are the mere instruments of the law, and can will nothing."[15] Rule of
Law demanded a scrupulously objective and formalistic judiciary.

While the upholding of the Rule of Law in the United States was
being increasingly entrusted to the judicial interpreters of the written
constitution, the English constitution remained proudly and defiantly
unwritten. Indeed, A.V. Dicey maintained that the Constitution is not
"the source, but the consequence of the rights of individuals."[16] Writing
at the dusk of the Victorian laissez-faire era and at pains to check the
runaway development of a collectivistically-inclined bureaucracy, he
symbolized the modern attempt to reinvigorate the Rule of Law as a set
of constitutional postulates devoted to safeguarding individual interests
and liberty. Dicey's Rule of Law comprised "three distinct though
kindred conceptions:[17] no one can be punished except for a breach of the
ordinary law, established in the ordinary legal manner before the
ordinary courts; no one is above the law and everyone, especially
officials, is amenable to the ordinary law; and the general principles of
the constitution, protecting private rights, are the result of the ordinary
laws. The combined force and design of Dicey's principles was to make
the Rule of Law into a bridle for a supposedly rampant administrative
arm of government.

The Diceyian tradition of Lockean conservatism has been continued by Friedrich Hayek in the contemporary debate over the Rule of Law. For him, the Rule of Law stands in unequivocal opposition to state redistribution and planning; it is the essential and most important condition of individual freedom.[18]It is not simply a constitutional principle of "legality," but comprises a substantive vision of the correct and just relations between individuals and society:

Nothing distinguishes more clearly conditions in a free country from those in a country under arbitrary government than the observance in the former of the great principles known as the [R]ule of [L]aw. Stripped of all technicalities this means that government in all its actions is bound by rules fixed and announced beforehand – rules which make it possible to see with fair certainty how the authority will use its coercive powers in given circumstances, and to plan one's individual affairs on the basis of this knowledge.[19]

Not surprisingly, Hayek identifies the inter-war years, culminating in the New Deal, as the period when America began to renege on its original constitutional compact and to subvert the Rule of Law. For him, an activist government, let alone an activist judiciary, is anathema to the Rule of Law and its libertarian foundations.

This tradition has been continued by contemporary writers. Although the emphasis has become more liberal than libertarian, democracy remains very much a secondary feature of the constitutional order. Most writers agree that the Rule of Law is a vital protective and facilitative constitutional device for a fundamental scheme of individual rights; disagreement is over the scope and character of those rights. In this sense, the protean quality of the Rule of Law has allowed it to be extended beyond civil and political rights to social and economic entitlements without sacrificing its essential nature. The product of a multinational conference, the Declaration of Delhi in 1958 stated that the Rule of Law is, apart from its traditional concerns, intended "to establish social, economic, educational and cultural conditions under which [individuals'] legitimate aspirations and dignity may be realized."[20]

(d) The Contemporary Debate: Democratizing the Rule of Law

The work of Ronald Dworkin, temporarily at least, dominates the animated contemporary debate over the judicial role under the Rule of Law. Adjudication is claimed to satisfy the Rule of Law by meeting the democratic demand for judicial objectivity and the popular need for political equity. While some rail that an activist judiciary is antithetical to democratic governance,[21]Dworkin argues that, if judges are to fulfil their democratic responsibilities under the Rule of Law, they must make political decisions, albeit not personal or partisan ones. His claim is bold and brilliant. The traditional formalistic, rule-book conception of the Rule of Law requires judges in hard cases to be unconstrainedly creative or to dissemble. Dworkin's rights conception of the Rule of Law incorporates a dimension of substantive fairness and thereby appropriately constrains and guides the judge in the resolution of hard cases. In defending such a version of the Rule of Law, Dworkin keeps himself firmly within the tradition of Locke and the constitutional priority of liberty; "the idea of individual rights ... is the zodiac sign under which America was born."[22]

For Dworkin, judges are political actors whose power is limited by a legal system's history and its liberal character. The state does not give them a blank check on which to write in the political currency of their choice; they must interpret the regnant legal materials in their best light as a theory of political morality. The judge breathes political vitality into the lifeless words of legal texts by applying the twin tests of "formal fit" and "substantive justice." Any interpretation must be able to demonstrate some plausible connection with society's legal history. However, the better theory is not necessarily the one that accounts for the most decisions or statutes; "formal fit" is only a heuristic device or rule-of-thumb. This requirement acts as a threshold and combines with the test of "substantive justice." This obliges the judge to develop a scheme of rights which a just state would establish and enforce. While this task can only be provisionally and partially performed, the conscious striving for such a perfected theory is the hallmark of adjudication under the Dworkinian conception of the Rule of Law. Accordingly, judicial power is legitimated by this commitment to uphold the existing political order of rights and only to extend it in a consistent and principled manner. In this way, law is and remains rational, just and objective.

It is to Dworkin's credit that he does not disguise his individualistic revitalization of the Rule of Law. He openly concedes that his conception might well exact a price in the development of a communitarian spirit. Yet, anxious to deflect charges of being insufficiently democratic, he reminds us that his conception of the Rule of Law "enriches democracy by adding an independent forum of principle ... [where] justice is in the end a matter of individual right, and not independently a matter of the public good."[23] He casts the Supreme Court as the central constitutional institution through which the citizenry can debate, articulate and implement its collective standards for social justice. Dworkin is not alone in elevating legal conversation to a privileged form of democratic discourse. Joined by other writers, like Owen Fiss and Laurence Tribe, Bruce Ackerman has gone so far as to suggest that:

Not that a vigorous and constructive legal dialogue can ever hope to compensate for an apathetic and muddled political debate. Yet the reverse is also true: political commitment is no substitute for legal deliberation. While the future of America depends on the American people, the future of American law depends, in a special way, on the way American lawyers interpret their calling.[24]

2 DEMOCRATIC INDIVIDUALISM AND THE RULE OF LAW

(a) Democracy and Community

Liberalism has always been ambivalent about the significance and the desirability of the value of community. For liberal theory, all roads begin with atomic, prepolitical individuals maximizing their self-interest. Thus, social contract theorists like Hobbes and Locke justified the creation of the state by analogy to a self-interested bargain between autonomous individuals in a state of nature. There was little emphasis on the possibility of the state helping to forge communal values or common ends. The state was necessary merely as a means of establishing order in a universe in which the interests of rational maximizers inevitably collided with each other.[25] The order that resulted was always in possible jeopardy, since it depended on a delicate and evenhanded resort to carrots and sticks.

This emphasis on the self-interested and autonomous individual receives its highest and most explicit expression in contemporary theories of democratic institutions and behaviour. Current analyses of "polyarchal" forms of democracy lack any genuine conception of public, communal values. Democracy is simply a mechanism for choosing governments in which sets of elites compete for the right to rule. According to some observers, there is no necessary connection between the choices made by the elites and the desires of the electorate. Instead, the elites themselves formulate and resolve the issues. The demands of the voters are not the ultimate data of the system since these demands are themselves shaped or manufactured; the public's demand for political goods "does not flow from its initiative but is being shaped, and the shaping of it is an essential part of the democratic process."[26]

Other analyses of democracy do not adopt such an impoverished conception of the community and its values. Yet even when the volitions of the electorate are seen as independent rather than manufactured, the analysis continues to be framed in market terms. Individual consumers "spend" their votes so as to maximize their individual self-interest, rather than to further the ends of the community as a whole. In fact, the invocation of the "public interest" is simply an ideological masquerade for the aggregation of private interests. Citizenship involves striking bargains in one's own interest rather than forging and debating the fundamental values of the community.[27]

Polyarchal forms of democracy reinforce the very consumer mentality they purport to serve. Because effective decision-making occurs at the elite rather than the mass level, the average citizen assumes no responsibility for shaping the values, beliefs and actions of the community. Even the act of voting, the one form of citizen participation which is sanctioned and encouraged, is a jealously guarded private activity; there is no necessity for individuals to discuss or justify their choices to others.[28] In polyarchical politics, spectacle has eclipsed substance. Given an electorate unaccustomed to participating in meaningful debate over public values, election campaigns have become prized occasions for the marketing of "leadership" rather than informed discussion and choice by citizens. To the extent that issues are discussed at all, they are framed in such abstract terms (for example, "inflation" or "the deficit") as to be virtually unintelligible and have only ephemeral impact on voter choice.[29] The stunted character of this public discourse on values calls to mind Rousseau's dictum that without informed and active citizens, you have nothing but "debased slaves, from the rulers of the state downwards."[30]

The great challenge for modern democratic theory has been to justify this elitist version of democratic practice. Most justifications centre on the "realism" of representative forms of democracy. Since citizens are largely apathetic about public affairs; it is thought to be appropriate that decision-making be left to the discretion of representative elites. It is considered utopian to require all issues of public policy to be submitted for electoral debate and decision.

Notions of law and legality have played a subsidiary but significant role in the justification of polyarchal forms of democracy. Adherents to the "thick" Rule of Law have suggested that there is no necessary tension between their proposals and democratic decision-making; the Rule of Law has an important role to play in tempering and modifying the elitism in modern liberal democracies.

This might be accomplished in a variety of ways. On one view, the Rule of Law serves as a guarantee to individuals that their rights will not be ignored by the bureaucracies of the state, the corporation or the trade union. The Rule of Law requires that fundamental issues of political morality be debated as issues of principle and not simply issues of political power. The positive effects of judicial review are thought to extend far beyond the particular case or dispute before a court. The claim is that "rights talk" is a means of uplifting and revitalizing political and moral discourse in our society generally. By forcing the political process to confront the question of individual rights, public morality will become more reflective and self-critical.[31] Cast as the high priests of moral discourse, the judiciary encourages and orchestrates meaningful public debate on moral issues.

These claims that the Rule of Law can serve as an indispensable means of popular control are profoundly mistaken. The Rule of Law sustains elitist politics, with its impoverished sense of community. It does so in at least two related, but distinct ways. First, the Rule of Law's language of rights reinforces the assumption that communities are nothing more than aggregations of private interests. Rightholders are defined in contradistinction to the community rather than as integral components of it. Second, and more significantly, a politics dominated by the Rule of Law is a politics with limited scope for popular participation and control. It cramps and compresses the ability of individuals to debate and define the conditions of their communal life. In attempting to avoid the tyranny of the majority, it mistakenly embraces a doctrine of expertise and dependency which carries with it a subtle, yet despotic dominion of its own.

(b) Citizens as Rightholders

Democratic politics is not guaranteed to produce "right answers." No matter how much debate and discussion is encouraged or exists, there is still the possibility that the community will make a choice that is mean-spirited or unenlightened. This is implicit in democratic politics. A choice for democracy means that the community has a right to be wrong. Even if a citizen vehemently disagrees with a particular democratic outcome, that outcome is still entitled to a measure of respect simply by virtue of the fact that it embodies the democratic will of the community.

The notion that decisions that are "wrong" should nevertheless be entitled to respect may seem paradoxical or unsettling.[32] Consider a case where a citizen believed not only that the community's decision was wrong-headed, but that the error could be demonstrated through appeal to an uncontroversial or "neutral" form of reasoning. In such a case, that person might find it particularly galling if the collective decision were permitted to stand. He or she might struggle to discover some way of maintaining a general commitment to democracy, while disavowing the legitimacy of the community's choice on this particular occasion.

In essence, this is the attitude of those theorists who accord a central, primary role to considerations of legality and constitutionalism. Defenders of the Rule of Law do not deny that the democratic community has the right to be wrong. They simply contend that this prerogative exists within a closely circumscribed sphere. If the democratic community strays outside its appointed area and trespasses onto prohibited turf, the appropriate response is self-evident: like antibodies attacking a foreign substance, the judiciary should move swiftly to excise the offending contagion before it spreads uncontrollably throughout the body politic.

Of course, the perennial difficulty is to define the alleged boundaries of democratic politics. Contemporary political philosophy claims to have noticed these boundaries lurking in the interstices of Kantian moral theory. The argument runs a typical course.[33] Individuals are entitled to be treated as ends in themselves, rather than as a means to someone else's ends. In order to give effect to this background political ideal, it is necessary to specify the conditions under which each individual's qualities of moral agency and personality are recognized. These political conditions form a coherent whole. They can be expressed in the form of a series of entitlements or rights which must be respected by the community if it is to be true to the notion of individual autonomy. A community cannot be said to be just or rightly ordered until and unless it recognizes and guarantees these individual rights. Such a schema represents the fixed fulcrum around which democratic politics must swing.

Although this rights theory purports to leave basic democratic principles intact, it frustrates and paralyzes them. This results as much from what is excluded as included in the theory. Significantly, a rights-based conception of the Rule of Law has an impoverished or non-existent conception of communal politics. There is very little respect and a good deal of anxiety surrounding attempts on the part of the community to define its collective identity. For the rights theorist, wherever collectivities gather together to express their moral beliefs in law, there lurks the stale, but unmistakable whiff of totalitarianism on the political breeze. Questions of morality and values are considered to be inescapably relative. Such matters of taste must be left in the hands of individuals, freed from the tyranny of the opinions of others regarding their lifestyles.

The constitutional analysis of Ronald Dworkin exemplifies this impoverished conception of community with its corresponding emphasis on the privatization of morality.[34] Dworkin's analysis is premised on the notion that everyone has the right to be treated with equal concern and respect. This concern for equality is violated when the community allows a "corrupting" element to contaminate its calculation of general welfare. The corrupting element can be identified on the basis of a distinction between personal and external preferences. Individuals' personal preferences relate to the assignment of goods or advantages to themselves, while external preferences relate to the assignment of goods or advantages to others. According to Dworkin, a utilitarianism that counts both personal and external preferences is vulgar and corrupt. External preferences do not respect the right of everyone to be treated with equal concern and respect; they suppose that a particular form of life or community is more valuable than any other. For instance, to take one of Dworkin's examples, if there is a proposal to build a swimming pool, only the votes of those who want to use the pool may properly be counted in its favour. Non-swimmers who might support the construction of the pool because they wish to promote the activity of swimming should be ignored. This is because the non-swimmers are suggesting that a certain lifestyle or activity is inherently more valuable than another.

Far from purifying utilitarian discourse, Dworkin's proposal debases it. In the guise of offering a political discourse that is neutral and egalitarian, Dworkin has simply ordained that only certain values or ideals may be tolerated in political debate and argument. The accepted ideolect is that employed by individuals bargaining in their own self interest. They are entitled to be heard only if they frame their claims in terms of what they hope to gain personally from a decision. Any appeal to the values or interests of the community as a whole is corrupting. Apparently, to invoke public as opposed to private considerations is to violate the norm of equal concern and respect.

Dworkin exhibits a profound antipathy for common consciousness amongst citizens. Politics becomes nothing more than a lackey for private interest. Pluralism and relativism are constitutionally mandated because there can be no genuine public interests. The result is an aggregate of individuals secure in their abstract rights and liberties but divorced from each other. This, of course, is entirely predictable given the background theory of personality which underlies contemporary liberal accounts of politics. The common starting point of these accounts is a fictitious choosing self, stripped of all particularity. This abstract self belongs to no particular family or community, has no set of allegiances or commitments and possesses no life plan. Although liberalism fetes the individual and celebrates personal freedom, it recommends a set of social organizing principles that rests on a pessimistic notion of human personality. By depicting individuals as indifferent to others, it establishes an ephemeral lifestyle that stifles the ameliorating potential in them; "the limits of liberal democracy are the limits of self-preoccupied imagination."[35] In a liberal regime, individuals become exiles in their own society, only united in their separateness and self-interestedness. The dominant motif of liberal society is its tendency to anomie; individuals drift with no communal connections. Bereft of any sense of community, "our society may have become so anomic that explicit occasions for mutual recognition among strangers on public streets are more feared than sought."[36]

The difficulty with this individualistic ideology is that it ignores and suppresses actual human experience.[37] Individuals are located in history, within a context of allegiances. They are not abstract or bloodless, but are in part constituted by their social context. To divorce individuals from this structure of allegiances is to rob them of the "railings to which [individuals] can cling as they walk into the mist of their social lives."[38] It stunts the possibility of developing a set of shared ends and values, a precondition to the emergence of a genuine populist democratic practice. By developing a moral sense and practical experience of community, individuals will be better able to contribute to the growth of a shared set of values and institutions in accordance with which social life could be organized. Persons might come to be respected as themselves and not as simply rightholders. In this way, society could develop a modus vivendi that encourages caring and sharing and actualizes the possibility for meaningful connection with others.

(c) Adjudication and Social Change

Notwithstanding the corrosive implications of rights-based theories for communal aspirations, the Rule of Law might still be characterized as the ally of democracy. Democratic politics is usually thought to involve a utilitarian calculus of the general welfare. There is no guarantee that this calculus will be conducted in a principled manner. Individual claims to autonomy and personhood might be ignored or bypassed simply in order to further the ephemeral interests of the community as a whole. On this view, the Rule of Law is required in order to ensure that considerations of principle and individual right enter into the societal calculus. The institution of judicial review is an attempt to transform a jungle of deals into a world of rights. As Ronald Dworkin urges, judicial review promises that "the deepest, most fundamental conflicts between individual and society will once, someplace, finally, become questions of justice."[39]

A sensitivity for individual rights might be seen as particularly apposite and necessary in contemporary society. Individual life is dominated and permeated by large and complex bureaucracies, principally the state and the business corporation. The challenge to individual rights is no longer the lynch mob crying for blood, but the coolly rational bureaucrat, armed with spread sheets and cost-benefit studies. Regard for the Rule of Law is thought to ensure that "social managers" will not trample individuals in the march toward so-called organizational progress. Yet, while bureaucracy represents one of the greatest threats to genuine democratic values, there is little reason to suppose that the Rule of Law offers any refuge from the dangers of unbridled bureaucracy.

The Rule of Law is premised on a set of beliefs about the relation between adjudication and social behaviour. It assumes that judicial decisions are a significant and positive instrument for shaping popular attitudes and social action. As an explanation of social change, the account is simplistic and lacks any empirical foundation. Indeed, the gathering of social data to ground their instrumental assumptions forms no part of the agenda of traditional jurisprudence. The limited available evidence suggests that the public is only vaguely aware of judicial activity and that there is little correlation between judicial pronouncements and societal life. For instance, numerous opinion surveys confirm that the public has only marginal awareness of legal institutions and decisions. Only half of Americans can recall any Supreme Court decision. Those who can have an unfavourable opinion of it, by a margin of at least two to one. Further, Americans have less public confidence in the Supreme Court than the Presidency or Congress.[40]

It is instructive to track the direction of public opinion over time towards visible court decisions that are thought to be liberally enlightened. In the 1960s, both the school desegregation and reapportionment decisions of the American Supreme Court were favoured by about 60 per cent of respondents, while the school prayer decisions were opposed by a margin of about three to one.[41] By the 1970s, large majorities remained opposed to the school prayer decisions. In contrast, the reapportionment decisions were no longer visible to the public, while public support for the Court's desegregation decisions had eroded drastically. Although a majority of respondents remained committed to desegregation in schools, the judicial remedy of busing was opposed by 82 per cent of whites and 33 per cent of blacks.

Not surprisingly, in view of this ignorance or hostility towards adjudication, judicial decisions have not tended to bring about large-scale social change. For instance, although only about school desegregation, *Brown* is heralded by received jurisprudential wisdom as a turning point in relations between American blacks and whites and as a victory over Southern institutional racism. Yet, for almost a decade after *Brown*, the local situation of blacks remained appalling: "the Southern caste system remained intact ... [and] the federal government's efforts on behalf of oppressed blacks were sporadic and ineffective."[42] It was not until the blacks mobilized themselves en masse in the early 1960s that their situation improved. The contribution that the *Brown* decision made to this state of affairs is moot and certainly not explained by the causally reductive accounts of Rule of Law theorists.

While racist attitudes and overt institutional practices may have improved, systemic racism persists. Some hard facts make for distressing reading. The poverty rate for black Americans is three times that of whites; non-white American men earn about 80 per cent of the wages of their white counterparts; the income gap between white and black families has widened since 1977; not only is the unemployment rate among blacks more than double that for whites, this unemployment inequality has itself doubled in the last thirty years; and while 26 per cent of young black high school graduates are unemployed, the exact same proportion of young white high school dropouts are unemployed.[43] Even in the limited area of school desegregation itself, the immediate and long-term effects of *Brown* are moot. Like Dickens's Jarndyce v. Jarndyce, the *Brown* saga "drones on" and "still drags its dreary length before the Court."[44] The gap between legal doctrine and social change is striking. The rosy picture of social life painted by the legal materials is far removed from its sombre actuality.

(d) Of Vitamins and Virtues

The reasons for discussing the impact of court decisions is not to suggest that the American Supreme Court's civil rights or school prayer decisions were somehow "wrong." Such a conclusion would be beside the point. The meaningful issue is why an elite judiciary should have responsibility for making such decisions in the first place. Reliance on the Supreme Court undermines popular control and participation in the policy-making process. Although the Supreme Court receives extensive attention in the media and the law reviews, publicity is no substitute for participation and does not overcome the exclusion of citizens from such debate. The media is dominated by much the same elite voices and institutional actors as litigation. For citizens, Supreme Court judges seem to resemble inscrutable Platonic figures who make decisions in which they have no part and of which they are largely ignorant. When a decision does come to their attention, they are likely to disagree with it. This further decreases the extent to which individuals have control over their own lives.

The citizens' role as distant spectators is exacerbated by the arcane and stylized language of constitutional litigation. As disputes move into the magnetic field of law, they are translated into the received argot. To partake of the law's special privileges and prizes, citizens must become proficient in its idioms and nuances. In this way, legal discourse enforces its own canons of relevance, rationality and reasonableness. The lawyerly sentinels of power ensure that citizens comport to the rules of constitutional grammar; those who do not are deprived of a voice and are rendered powerless. The courts' historical function has not been to express popular justice, but rather "to ensnare it, control it and to strangle it, by re-inscribing it within institutions which are typical of a state apparatus."[45]

Defenders of this "elitist" approach to the Rule of Law must inevitably rely on some version of the claim that the ends justify the means. Although the elimination of popular control might be lamentable in the abstract, in cases like *Brown* it was the only realistic means available to counter deep-rooted and widespread public prejudice. Popular control, it is argued, would have been a recipe for the continued denial of justice and equality towards blacks. As such, it was simply unacceptable.

There is a good deal of force in these arguments. Given the harsh and brutal history of discrimination in the American South, it is difficult not to welcome the intervention of the Supreme Court as an antidote to racial intolerance. The difficulty with framing the debate in these terms is that it portrays the courts as an enlightened oracle proclaiming the gospel to the stupefied masses. Such an assumption is unwarranted and ahistorical; advances in social justice have been achieved through legislative rather than judicial action. Both Canadian and American courts have been as much a source of reaction and chauvinism as of edification and enlightenment. Much of the social welfare legislation enacted by the federal government in the 1930s was ruled unconstitutional by the courts as an intrusion on provincial jurisdiction. The practical effect of these decisions, such as the *Unemployment Insurance Reference* of 1937, was to make the enactment of such legislation impossible since the provinces lacked the fiscal resources to undertake such costly programs. The judicial decision in this particular instance was overcome only after the political branches of government secured a constitutional amendment which specifically empowered the federal government to put in place an unemployment insurance scheme.

The evolution of American First Amendment doctrine provides further illustration of this. Prior to World War I, the Court ruled in favour of a free speech claimant on only one occasion.[46] In subsequent decades the Court became more sensitive to free speech issues, but it cut back or ignored these doctrines during the so-called Red Scare in the 1950s. The 1960s was a period of renewed first amendment activism by the Court, coincident with the civil rights movement. However, in recent years the first amendment has been enlisted as a potent weapon in the defence of the entrenched status of power and privilege. The ability of corporations and the wealthy to dominate the political process has been constitutionally guaranteed;[47] privately-owned public areas have been excluded from first amendment scrutiny,[48] while commercial advertising has been protected.[49] In short, while popular decision-making does not guarantee enlightened answers to political questions, neither does deference to an elite judiciary.

Even in the so-called "progressive" constitutional decisions, the difficult question is whether the elimination of popular control in favour of an elite institution like the Supreme Court will actually promote the long-term cause of justice and equality. At the institutional level, there may be a marked negative effect. Because judicial decisions tend to persuade people that things are being done, reformative energy may be frustrated and other governmental institutions may feel relieved of the pressure and responsibility to initiate and facilitate social change. More-over, the assumption seems to be that values such as justice and free-dom can be defined in some external forum, like the Supreme Court, and then simply foisted on a recalcitrant public. But the reality is pre-cisely the opposite. Public values cannot be abstractly manufactured in some antiseptic political laboratory and administered, like vitamin tab-lets, to a malnourished and lethargic mass.

Values such as justice and equality are the products of politics, not its antecedents. They take root in a public that engages in debate and argument and that is given the opportunity to nurture notions of reasonableness and commonality. Deprived of such empowerment, public values corrode and civic energy dissipates. Deferring to "spe-cialists," citizens lose the capacity to define their own values and traditions. Public morality will atrophy rather than be energized. The appointment of the judicial philosopher king exacerbates the problem it was intended to remedy.

Democracy means the greatest possible engagement by people in the greatest possible range of communal tasks and public action. As people reclaim control over their own lives, they will develop an appetite and a talent for more. This rejects the prevailing pessimism about the com-petence of ordinary citizens; their present apathy and disaffection is a product of their current powerlessness rather than any natural infir-mity. This insight is easily forgotten in a setting in which the opportuni-ties for meaningful popular participation are few. The central impor-tance of participation and debate in the shaping of public morality can only be grasped by focusing on an institution which rejects values of expertise and elitism in favour of participatory self-government.

Such an institution is the jury system. To suggest that the jury system represents a paradigm of democratic practice may seem anachronistic or naive. Critics on both the right and the left have condemned the jury as a device to legitimate bigotry, ignorance or racism. These criticisms of the jury parallel those issued against democracy in general; the basic complaints are that these institutions produce decisions that are oppressive and that individual citizens are incapable of making such decisions.

Yet, whatever the failings of individual juries, the jury system as a whole embodies to a remarkable degree values of self-government.[50] The jury system rejects rule by experts; people assume the responsibility for making important civic decisions on a rotating basis. Discussion and argument are central to the success of the institution. The jurors do not simply observe the trial and then cast their votes individually in the privacy of a polling booth. They are expected to arrive at a common verdict, through persuasion and argument. Without such debate, "the jury system as a whole would be devalued, and ... individual jurors would value their own roles less."[51] The jury system represents a commitment to the principle that the ordinary citizen is competent to debate and decide important issues in the community. As E.P. Thompson states,[52]

I can imagine better laws and I can imagine better jurors, but I cannot imagine a better system. I would like to think of the jury system as a lingering paradigm of an alternative mode of participatory self-government, a nucleus around which analogous modes might grow in our town halls, factories and streets.

With its emphasis on persuasion, argument and consensus, it is democratic rule writ small. True, the jury often acts as a rubber stamp for state values, but it can also act as a lamp of liberty which might illuminate the potential and power of ordinary people.

There is no quick fix for bigotry or prejudice. Certainly, it would be naive to suppose that such deplorable attitudes would simply disappear with the dawn of a genuine democratic community. Democracy does not guarantee civil enlightenment. But if communal morality is to become more informed and developed, this will be achieved through more rather than less democracy. It is only through public talk that small minded or superficial attitudes might be exposed and attacked. The ambition is not to attain some romantic or utopian harmony, but a political order which facilitates individual participation in the continuing social deliberation over political ends.

Judicial musing, enforced by fiat, is no substitute for civil deliberation. Rule by judiciary supposes that the only way to deter oppression is to impose external restraints on the political process. But because such restraints deny the moral competence of citizens, they undermine the very process of reflection and self-criticism which might lead to a more mature collective morality. Elitist politics breed only a mob; the nurturing of citizens demands democratic culture.

3 CONSTRUCTION AND CONSTRAINT

The Rule of Law democrat lives in a society bereft of community. Given its historical obsession with abstract individual rights and liberties, liberal legalism stymies the establishment of a truly communal modus vivendi in which people can satisfy their collective and personal aspirations. Within a legalistic ethic, communal ambitions are destined to remain etiolated. We have tried to free democracy from its bondage to the Rule of Law. Emancipated, it might serve rather than stifle the flourishing of communal life and fulfilled citizens.

A concrete and constructive example illustrates our claims. The way modern society defines "health" and "need" and establishes standards for health care both exposes the elitism of present arrangements and suggests the possibilities for democratic involvement. Currently, the medical and legal professions have come together in an unholy alliance to monopolize the process of health decision-making. People have become "limp and mystified voyeur[s]"[53] on the treatment of their own bodies, the passive objects of clinical therapy rather than active participants in its prescription and administration. In contrast to present practice, democracy demands that people must be fully integrated into the formulation of any preventative and rehabilitative program. All individuals must become "welfare workers"; "a society which ignores [that health care involves mutual learning, mutual help and mutual responsibility] may stave off, for a time, the effects of illness and injury, only to pave a better road to ill-health."[54]

Even the fully democratic society will have to make "tragic choices" about the allocation of scarce resources. While medical technology advances apace, its direction and nature are not open to public control. Much medical research has been devoted to the reduction of mortality, but this has meant a corresponding increase in morbidity, especially among the elderly. Choices about the treatment of defective babies, geriatrics, paraplegics and other afflicted individuals have been made in the elite forums of the medical and legal establishment; they deserve to be the subject of a more thoroughgoing democratic debate. The target must be the introduction of communal health care services which work toward a local and supportive environment for recovery or readjustment to changed health circumstances.

There must develop a greater appreciation that health and welfare are as much socially caused as individually experienced. This means the fostering of a more holistic approach to well-being. This would not merely treat individual symptoms, but would concern itself with the total environment in which people live, work, play and die. The control of risk would be of, at least, the same importance as the treatment of injury and misfortune. Whereas the democratic society takes an integrated and coherent stance on risk and well-being, the liberal society adopts a divided and contradictory position.[55]

A commitment to democracy does not mean that constraints on popular decision making must always and everywhere be condemned. It is important that the basic institutions and practices of democracy – free elections, debate and assembly – be guaranteed and extended. Further, democracy implies the necessity for general laws which do not single out particular groups or individuals for special treatment and which are applied in nondiscriminatory fashion across the whole community. But there is a distinction between constitutional safeguards which constrain democratic activity in the name of democracy and those which constrain democratic activity in the name of "right answers." The latter type of constraints seek to substitute the judgments of philosophy for those of the people simply because the popular judgments are regarded as tainted. As Michael Walzer observes,[56]

... any extensive incorporation of philosophical principles into the law ... is ... to take them out of the political arena where they properly belong. The interventions of philosophers should be limited to the gifts they bring. Else they are like Greeks bringing gifts, of whom the people should beware, for what they have in mind is the capture of the city.

Democrats should always be wary of constraints that seek to substitute the cold hand of philosophy for popular judgment, no matter how presently plausible or attractive they might appear. Of course, instances will arise in which public sentiments appear so wrong-headed that they demand instant repudiation. Even a committed democrat would likely be tempted by the siren song of the Rule of Law. But to tie oneself to the post of "principle" is to court seduction rather than salvation. Far from purifying public morality, it would merely ensure its continued debasement.

NOTES

1 See J. Cohen and J. Rogers, On *Democracy: Toward a Transformation of American Society* (1983), pp. 32–5.
2 See H. Clarke et al., *Absent Mandate: The Politics of Discontent in Canada* (1984), pp. 32–3.
3 See, for example, M. Perry, *The Constitution, the Courts and Human Rights: An Inquiry into the Legitimacy of Constitutional Policymaking by the Judiciary* (1982), pp. 91–145.

4 See, for example, E.P. Thompson, *Whigs and Hunters* (1975).
5 L. Fuller, *The Morality of Law* (rev. ed., 1969), p. 210.
6 H.L.A. Hart, *The Concept of Law* (1961), p. 206.
7 For a historical introduction to these events, see H. Berman, *Law and Revolution: The Formation of the Western Legal Tradition* (1983).
8 *On The Laws and Customs of England*, vol. 2 (S. Thorne trans., 1968), p. 305.
9 For an accessible and informed account of this history, see J. Ridley, *The History of England* (1981), and E. Schnapper, "The Parliament of Wonders" (1984), 83 Colum. L. Rev. 1665.
10 (1610), 77 ER 638, 652.
11 H. Nenner, *By Colour of Law* (1977), p. xi.
12 *The Records of the Federal Convention of 1787*, vol. 1, ed. M. Farrand (1937), p. 48. Roger Sherman's response was to the democratic point. Bills of Rights were "mere paper protection"; "the only real security that you can have for all your important rights must be in the nature of your government ... If you are about to trust your liberties with people whom it is necessary to bind by stipulation ... your stipulation is not even worth the trouble of writing." "Letters of a Countryman, November 22, 1787," reprinted in *Essays on the Constitution of the United States*, ed. P. Ford (1910), p. 220.
13 "The Declaration and The Constitution: Liberty, Democracy and The Founders" in *The American Commonwealth*, ed. N. Glazer (1976), p. 47.
14 See E. Corwin, *The "Higher Law" Background of American Constitutional Law* (1965).
15 *Osborn v Bank of the United States*, 22 US 738, 866 (1824).
16 *The Law of the Constitution* (1885), p. 46. Reference will be made to the 10th ed., E. Wade (1965).
17 Ibid., at 188–203.
18 See *The Constitution of Liberty* (1960) and *The Political Ideal of the Rule of Law* (1955).
19 *The Road to Serfdom* (1946), p. 54.
20 International Commission of Jurists, *The Rule of Law in a Free Society* (1959), p. 3.
21 See John Hart Ely, *Democracy and Distrust* (1980), p. 67 ("we may rant until we're blue in the face that legislatures aren't wholly democratic, but that isn't going to make courts more democratic than legislatures").
22 R. Dworkin, "Political Judges and the Rule of Law" in *A Matter of Principle* (1985), p. 31.
23 Ibid., at p. 32. In his most recent book, Dworkin develops and elaborates on these themes and emphasizes that the Rule of Law is "the parent and guardian of democracy." See *Law's Empire* (1986), p. 399.
24 *Reconstructing American Law* (1984), p. 110.

25 See generally, C.B. Macpherson, *The Life and Times of Liberal Democracy* (1977) and *Democratic Theory: Essays in Retrieval* (1973).
26 Schumpeter, *Capitalism, Socialism and Democracy* (1943), p. 282. For a useful discussion of the extent to which volitions of citizens are constrained in liberal democracies, see Lindblom, *Politics and Markets* (1977), pp. 208–13.
27 For examples of this economic and interest group theory of democracy, see Anthony Downs, *An Economic Theory of Democracy* (1957); Mancur Olson Jr, *The Logic of Collective Action* (1965); Robert Dahl, *Dilemmas of Pluralist Democracy: Autonomy versus Control* (1982).
28 "... our primary electoral act, voting, is rather like using a public toilet: we wait in line with a crowd in order to close ourselves up in a small compartment where we can relieve ourselves in solitude and in privacy of our burden, pull a lever, and then, yielding to the next in line, go silently home." B. Barber, *Direct Democracy* (1984), p. 188.
29 For instance, a recent analysis of voter attitudes in Canada found that issues which were seen as central in the 1974 election were barely mentioned in the 1979 campaign. When a third election was held some nine months later in 1980, a whole new set of concerns was seen as central. These shifts in public perceptions were closely related to the agenda of discussion set by the media and the political leaders. See Clarke, *supra*, note 2 at pp. 77–99.
30 J.J. Rousseau, "A Discourse on Political Economy" in *Social Contract and Discourses*, p. 251.
31 For arguments to this effect see Ackerman, *supra*, note 24.
32 See, for example, R. Wollheim, "A Paradox in the Theory of Democracy," in P. Laslett and W.G. Runciman, eds., *Philosophy, Politics and Society* (2nd Series, 1962), pp. 71–87.
33 For instances of the line of argument described in this paragraph, see J. Rawls, *A Theory of Justice* (1971); and R. Nozick, *Anarchy, State, and Utopia* (1974).
34 See R. Dworkin, *Taking Rights Seriously (1977)*.
35 Barber, *supra*, note 28 at p. 18.
36 R. Burt, *Taking Care of Strangers* (1979), p. 41.
37 For a development of this argument, see A. Hutchinson and P. Monahan, "The 'Rights' Stuff: Roberto Unger and Beyond" (1984), 62 Texas L. Rev. 1477 at 1534–37.
38 R . Dahrendorf, *Life Chances: Approaches to Social and Political Theory* (1979), p. 32.
39 Dworkin, *supra*, note 22 at p. 71.

40 See Adamany and Grossman, "Support for the Supreme Court as a National Policymaker" (1983), 5 Law and Policy Quarterly 405.

41 The survey data is collected and analysed in Adamany and Grossman, ibid. at 422–24.

42 S. Bachmann, "Lawyers, Law, and Social Change" (1985), 13 NY Rev. of Law & Soc. Change 1.

43 See Cohen and Rogers, *supra*, note 1 at 30–2.

44 See *Bleak House* (1853), ch. 1. See *Brown v Bd. of Ed.*, 84 FRD 383 (D. Kan. 1979) (seeking intervention in original Topeka desegregation case on behalf of class represented by Linda Brown's daughter); *Clark v Bd. of Ed.*, 705 F. 2d 265 (8th Cir. 1983) (continuation of Little Rock desegregation case).

45 M. Foucault, *Power/Knowledge: Selected Interviews and Other Writings*, ed. C. Gordon (1980), p. 1.

46 *American School of Magnetic Healing v McAnnulty*, 187 US 94 (1902). For a discussion, see Rabban, "The First Amendment in Its Forgotten Years" (1981), 90 Yale Law Journal 514.

47 *Buckley v Valeo*, 424 US 1 (1976).

48 *Hudgens v NLRB*, 424 US 507 (1976).

49 *Virginia Pharmacy Board v Virginia Consumer Council*, 425 US 748 (1976).

50 For discussion, see E.P. Thompson, *Writing by Candlelight* (1980), pp. 167–70; M. Walzer, *Spheres of Justice: A Defense of Pluralism and Equality* (1983), pp. 308–9.

51 Walzer, ibid., at 309.

52 Thompson, *supra*, note 50 at 170.

53 I. Illich, *Limits to Medicine*, ch. 3 (1976).

54 A.V. Campbell, *Medicine, Health and Justice: The Problem of Priorities* (1978), p. 88.

55 These ideas are developed further in A. Hutchinson, "Beyond No-Fault" (1985), 60 Cal. L. Rev. 755. See also, R. Abel, "A Socialist Approach to Risk" (1982), 41 Maryland L. Rev. 695.

56 M. Walzer, "Philosophy and Democracy" (1981), 9 Political Theory 379 at 392–3.

READING QUESTIONS ON HUTCHINSON AND MONAHAN

1 Do you think juries are more or less trustworthy than judges?
2 How does Hutchinson and Monahan's position differ from Devlin's?
3 Is their position consistent with legal positivism?

Hofer v Hofer (1970) 13 DLR 3d 1

Members of a Hutterite colony were expelled when they converted to another religion. They sued, claiming that they were entitled to their proportionate share of the colony's land. The colony insisted that their freedom of religion entitled them to hold all land in common. The decision, by the Supreme Court of Canada, provides a clear illustration of the debate between the two models of freedom that the earlier readings in this section explore. If religious freedom is construed as a negative liberty, the community has no say over the activities of its members. As a result, a certain way of life may prove to be impossible to sustain. By contrast, if freedom of religion is seen as a positive liberty, the community will have power over its members, but the negative liberty of individuals will suffer.

Ritchie, J: – ... It will be seen from the above that, in my view, adherence to the Hutterite faith was a prerequisite to membership in the Colony which by its very nature was required to be composed exclusively of Hutterian Brethren and their families. I am also of opinion that the decision as to whether or not any individual was a Hutterian Brethren so as to be entitled to continue as a member of the community was a decision which could only be made by the Hutterite Church. In the present case, as I have indicated, the decision to expel the appellants from the Colony was made by the church, but it had the effect of making the appellants ineligible for continued membership in the Colony. It follows from this that the appellants' contention to the effect that the articles of association were not properly complied with in regard to expulsion is without merit, and in my view the alternative plea with respect to the unlimited power and control of the ministers of the church over the personal life and property, being contrary to public policy, is equally invalid.

I am also of opinion, as I have indicated, that the Interlake Colony was not a partnership in the accepted legal sense of that term.

There is no doubt that the Hutterian way of life is not that of the vast majority of Canadians, but it makes manifest a form of religious philosophy to which any Canadian can subscribe and it appears to me that if any individual either through birth within the community or by choice wishes to subscribe to such a rigid form of life and to subject himself to the harsh disciplines of the Hutterian Church, he is free to do so. I can see nothing contrary to public policy in the continued existence of these communities living as they do in accordance with their own rules and beliefs, and as I have indicated, I think it is for the church to determine who is and who is not an acceptable member of any of its communities.

For all these reasons, as well as for those so fully expressed by the learned trial Judge and the Court of Appeal, I would dismiss this appeal with costs ...

Pigeon, J (dissenting): – The appellants and the respondents were all Hutterian Brethren. They lived at and were members of the Rock Lake Colony. In 1960, the Rock Lake Colony had grown to such size that it was decided, in accordance with established practice, to split the Colony and form a "daughter" colony at Interlake, Manitoba. The members of Rock Lake Colony divided into two groups, neither of which knew whether it would go to the new colony or stay at Rock Lake Colony. This was decided by lot. The assets of Rock Lake Colony were then divided roughly in proportion to membership and 2,080 acres of land were purchased for the new Colony at $76 per acre.

The seven parties to this action formed the group moving to the new Colony. In May, 1961, they signed a document entitled "Articles of Association of the Interlake Colony of Hutterian Brethren of the Post Office of Teulon in the Province of Manitoba, Dominion of Canada." Those articles of association include the following provisions:

2. The purposes for which the said Colony is formed are: To promote, engage in and carry on the Christian religion, Christian worship, and religious education and teachings, and to worship God according to the religious belief of the members thereof; and to engage in and carry on farming, stock-raising, milling, and all branches of these industries, and to manufacture and deal in such products and by-products as may be considered by the Directors to be in the best interests of the Colony and for the purposes aforesaid, to hold, own, and possess such real and personal property as may be necessary.

3. The Colony shall be comprised of all persons who sign these Articles. No person shall become a member of the Colony and be permitted to sign these Articles, until he or she shall have:

    (a) Attained the full age of seventeen years.

    (b) Become a member and communicant of the Hutterian Brethren Church.

(c) Been chosen and elected to Membership upon a majority vote of all
the male members of the Colony present at any annual, general, or
special meeting of the Colony.

30. All the property, real and personal, of said Colony from whomsoever,
whensoever and howsoever it may have been obtained, shall forever be
owned, used, occupied, controlled and possessed by the said Colony for the
common use, interest, and benefit of each and all members thereof, for the
purposes of said Colony.

31. All the property both real and personal, that each and every member of
the said Colony has or may have, own, possess or may be entitled to at the
time that he or she joins such Colony, or becomes a member thereof, and all
the property both real and personal, that each and every member of the said
Colony may have, obtain, inherit, possess or be entitled to, after he or she
becomes a member of the said Colony, shall be and become the property of
the said Colony for the common use, interest, and benefit of each and all of
the members thereof as aforesaid.

32. None of the property, either real or personal, of the said Colony shall
ever be taken, held, owned, removed or withdrawn from the said Colony, or
be granted, sold, transferred or conveyed otherwise than by the Board of
Directors, and if any member of the said Colony shall be expelled therefrom,
or cease to be a member thereof, he or she shall not have, take, withdraw,
grant, sell, transfer or convey, or be entitled to any of the property of the
said Colony, or any interest therein; and if any member of the said Colony
shall die, be expelled therefrom, or cease to be a member thereof, he or she,
or his or her representatives, heirs-at-law, legatees or devisees or creditors or
any other person shall not be entitled to, or have any of the property of the
said Colony, or interest therein, whether or not he or she owned, possessed
or had any interest in or to any of the property of the said Colony at the time
he or she became member thereof, or at any time thereafter, or had given,
granted, conveyed or transferred any property or property interest to the
said Colony at any time.

33. Each and every member of the said Colony shall give and devote all his
or her time, labor, services, earnings and energies to the said Colony, and
the purposes for which it is formed, freely, voluntarily, and without compensation or reward of any kind whatsoever, other than as herein expressed.

34. The members of the said Colony shall be entitled to have their husbands,
wives and children, who are not members thereof, reside with them, and be
supported, maintained, instructed and educated by the said Colony, according to the rules, regulations and requirements of the said Colony, and the
Christian religion, Christian worship, religious education, teachings and

belief promoted, engaged in and carried on by the said Colony, during the time and so long as they obey, abide by and conform to the rules, regulations, instructions, and requirements of the said Colony.

35. Whenever any member of the said Colony shall die then his or her husband, wife and children who are not members thereof, shall have the right to remain with, and be supported, instructed and educated by the said Colony, during the time and so long as they give and devote all of their time, labor, services, earnings, and energies to the said Colony, and the purposes thereof, and obey and conform to the rules, regulations and requirements of the said Colony, the same as if the said member had lived.

37. The Community, or Association, or Colony hereby created shall not be dissolved without the consent of all of the members thereof.

The parties with their families moved to the Interlake Colony on December 20, 1961. Benjamin Hofer, one of the appellants, had by that time begun to be attracted by the teachings of the Radio Church of God and by March, 1964, he and David Hofer, another appellant, had both become converted to the beliefs of that church. These differed from those of the Hutterite Church in many respects. For instance, the Radio Church of God did not regard community of property as a part of its faith. It did not believe in the Christian festivals as observed by the Hutterian Brethren and it condemned the eating of pork. The two dissidents became subscribers to a monthly magazine published by the Radio Church of God and entitled *The Plain Truth*.

On March 3, 1964, no less than 20 ministers of the Hutterite Church came from other colonies to Interlake and talked to the two dissidents in an attempt to re-establish their faith. A second and unavailing effort was made on March 13th, when 24 ministers came from other colonies and the two dissidents were asked if they did accept a church penalty of "unfrieden." Both dissidents refused and challenged the authority of the ministers to impose it. The penalty was, however, imposed and meant that the two dissidents were shunned by the rest of the Colony and their families were subjected to various indignities.

On June 13, 1964, the two dissidents, Benjamin and David Hofer, were expelled.

A year later, it became apparent that the other two appellants, John Hofer and Joseph Hofer, had also abandoned the Hutterite faith in favour of the Radio Church of God. Attempts to bring them back to the Hutterian faith were unsuccessful and in the end they were also expelled.

By their action, the appellants sought a declaration that they were still members of the Interlake Colony together with an order for the winding-up of its affairs, the appointment of a receiver, an accounting of its assets and liabilities, and a direction that its assets should be distributed equally among each of the appellants and respondents. The respondents counterclaimed for a declaration that the appellants are no longer members of the Colony, and are not entitled to any portion of its property and directing them to vacate the real property owned by the Colony and deliver up possession of all personal property owned by it which may have come into their possession.

Appellants' action was dismissed and respondents' counterclaim was allowed by Dickson, J [59 DLR (2d) 723], and this judgment was affirmed by the Court of Appeal of Manitoba [65 DLR (2d) 607].

In my view, the first question to be considered is the legal nature of the Colony. Having heard a great deal of evidence respecting the beliefs of the Hutterian Brethren Church, the trial Judge found as a fact that the Interlake Colony is a congregation of that church. I have no doubt that if the question is approached as the trial Judge did, namely, by looking how the matter is considered according to the teachings of the Hutterians, this is the correct conclusion. However, it appears to me that this is not the manner in which the question must be approached for legal purposes. What is religion, what is a church in the eyes of the law does not depend on the religious beliefs of any confession, at least under a regime of freedom of religion.

In Walter et al. v A.-G. Alta., 3 DLR (3d) 1, [1969] SCR 383, 66 WWR 513, this Court decided that the fact that Hutterites consider as part of their religion the holding of land as communal property does not mean that legislation controlling such holding is in relation to religion. Martland, J, said for the Court (at p. 9):

The fact that a religious group upholds tenets which lead to economic views in relation to land holding does not mean that a provincial Legislature, enacting land legislation which may run counter to such views, can be said, in consequence, to be legislating in respect of religion and not in respect of property.

Religion, as the subject-matter of legislation, wherever the jurisdiction may lie, must mean religion in the sense that it is generally understood in Canada. It involves matters of faith and worship, and freedom of religion involves freedom in connection with the profession and dissemination of religious faith and the exercise of religious worship.

In *Robertson and Rosetanni v The Queen*, 41 DLR (2d) 485, [1964] 1 CCC 1, [1963] SCR 651, Ritchie, J, said for the majority (at p. 494):

It is said on behalf of the appellants that freedom of religion means "freedom to enjoy the freedom which my own religion allows without being confined by restrictions imposed by Parliament for the purpose of enforcing the tenets of a faith to which I do not subscribe." It is further pointed out that Orthodox Jews observe Saturday as the Sabbath and as a day of rest from their labours, whereas Friday is the day so observed by the members of the Mohammedan faith, and it is said that the *Lord's Day Act* imposes an aspect of the Christian faith, namely, the observance of Sunday on some citizens who do not subscribe to that faith.

My own view is that the *effect* of the *Lord's Day Act* rather than its *purpose* must be looked to in order to determine whether its application involves the abrogation, abridgment or infringement of religious freedom, and I can see nothing in that statute which in any way affects the liberty of religious thought and practice of any citizen of this country. Nor is the "untrammelled affirmations of religious belief and its propagation" in any curtailed.

The practical result of this law on those whose religion requires them to observe a day of rest other than Sunday, is a purely secular and financial one in that they are required to refrain from carrying on or conducting their business on Sunday as well as on their own day of rest. In some cases this is no doubt a business inconvenience, but it is neither an abrogation nor an abridgment nor an infringement of religious freedom, and the fact that it has been brought about by reason of the existence of a statute enacted for the purpose of preserving the sanctity of Sunday, cannot, in my view, be construed as attaching some religious significance to an effect which is purely secular in so far as non-Christians are concerned.

If the evidence respecting the operations of the Colony is considered on the basis that the legal nature of that association is to be determined by reference to generally accepted principles and not by reference to the tenets of the Hutterians, it becomes evident that it is a commercial undertaking, not a church. The land is used essentially for growing crops and raising livestock and while some part of the production is consumed by the members of the Colony and their families, the major part is sold in the same manner as the product of any similar undertaking whether owned by an individual, a joint stock company or a co-operative association. Of course, some small part of the land is used for a place of worship but it is clear that looking at the matter according to ordinary principles, this is only an extremely minor part. For legal purposes, it can no more be controlling than the use of two small rooms, one for the chaplain's office, the other for board meetings, in a large building otherwise occupied for commercial purposes could be considered as putting a property in the class of "properties occupied by a youth association" in *L'Association Catholique de la Jeunesse Canadienne - Française v Chicoutimi*, [1940] 4 DLR 348, [1940] SCR 510.

It must also be noted that if the articles of association rather than the teachings and theories of the Hutterian Church are examined, it becomes apparent that two distinct purposes are enumerated in art. 2: religion and industry, the industrial purpose being described in the following way:

... to engage in and carry on farming, stock-raising, milling, and all branches of these industries, and to manufacture and deal in such products and by-products as may be considered by the Directors to be in the best interest of the Colony.

It is therefore contrary to the articles of association to say that the Colony was set up as a church. The articles of association as well as the facts properly considered show that the Colony was set up both for a religious purpose and the object of operating a communal farm. In respect of the agricultural operations, the Colony cannot be considered otherwise than as a secular undertaking; it is not a charitable undertaking. Because it has among its purposes an object that cannot be classified as charitable, it follows that it must in law be treated as a commercial undertaking.

With great deference to the trial Judge and the Judges of the Court of Appeal, it was wrong to decide the case by the application of rules of law governing churches. In my view, the situation from the point of view of religion must be said to be that the members of the Colony and their families formed a congregation of the Hutterian Brethren Church. This distinction between the church and the Colony is fully recognized in the articles of association. One of the qualifications for becoming a member of the Colony is to have "(b) Become a member and communicant of the Hutterian Brethren Church." It is clear that the church in this provision of the articles means the unincorporated religious community. This is not to be identified with the Hutterian Brethren Church, a corporation incorporated by the Parliament of Canada (1950-51 (Can.), c. 77).

From a religious point of view, the dissenting tendencies of Benjamin and David Hofer were obviously of concern to the whole church and not merely to the Interlake congregation and that may explain why a large number of ministers of other congregations together with the local minister concerned themselves with the situation, and in fact made the decision first to impose a church penalty and ultimately, when the appellants did not repent from their dissent, to expel them from the church.

Before considering the effect of that decision with respect to the subsequent expulsion from the Colony, it seems convenient to examine the status of churches in Canada. It is clear that the basic principle is freedom of religion. I see no reason for not applying in Manitoba the following statement of the legal situation in Quebec that was made by the Privy Council in *Despatie v Tremblay*, 58 DLR 27 at pp. 37-8 [1921] 1 AC 702, 47 Que. KB 305:

The religious position in the Province of Quebec in 1774, was therefore that every individual had the right to profess and practise the Catholic religion without let or hindrance. But it must be borne in mind that this is a privilege granted to the individual. There is no legislative compulsion of any kind whatever. He may change his religion at will. If he remains in the Roman Catholic community he may, so far as the law is concerned, choose to be orthodox or not, subject to the inherent power of any voluntary community, such as the Roman Catholic Church, to decide the conditions on which he may remain a member of that community unless that power has been limited in some way by the past acts of the community itself. In other words, each member of the Roman Catholic community in Quebec possessed the same privileges as any other citizen so far as religious freedom is concerned, save that he was not subject to any of the disabilities which then and, for a long time after, attached to Protestant dissenters. The Legislature did not put over him as a citizen any ecclesiastical jurisdiction. The decisions of the ecclesiastical Courts that existed in the Roman Church bound him solely as a matter of conscience. The Legislature gave to their decrees no civil effect nor bound any of its subjects to obey them. Indeed, the Act in art. 17 expressly reserves to His Majesty the power to set up Courts of ecclesiastical jurisdiction in the Province and to appoint Judges thereof, although that power seems never to have been acted upon. But what has just been said must not be misunderstood. The law did not interfere in any way with the jurisdiction of any ecclesiastical Courts of the Roman Catholic religion over the members of that communion so far as questions of conscience were concerned. But it gave to them no civil operation. Whether the persons affected chose to recognize those decrees or not was a matter of individual choice which might, or might not, affect their continuance as members of that religious communion. But that was a matter which concerned themselves alone.

It will be noted that freedom of religion includes the right for each individual to change his religion at will. While churches are otherwise free like other voluntary associations to establish whatever rules they may see fit, freedom of religion means that they cannot make rules having the effect of depriving their members of this fundamental freedom. In my view, this is precisely what these Hutterians have been attempting to do. With respect to the indignities suffered by appellants and their families, the learned trial Judge said [59 DLR (2d) 723 at p. 731]:

The application of pressures upon a deviant, through shunning, deprivation of privileges, and the like, follows Hutterian custom and was intended to make the non-conforming deviant once more conform. Some of the indignities and mistreatment suffered by plaintiffs and members of their families appear strange and repellant, and on occasion excessive, although there can be no doubt that within a religious community stern discipline must be observed if the community is to survive.

With deference, it appears to me that the learned Judge's comments are based on a misconception of the extent of the power that may properly be exercised by church authorities on communicants. He is clearly assuming that this may be whatever the rules of a church provide for. In other words, the decision in the Courts below proceeds on the assumption that religion extends to whatever a particular congregation may choose to include in it and that the religious authority is coextensive with such definition. This is contrary to the proper legal conception of religion whereby its scope is limited to what is commonly so considered and the extent of religious authority is limited to what is consistent with freedom of religion as properly understood, that is freedom for the individual not only to adopt a religion but also to abandon it at will.

The evidence shows that the rules and practices of this religious group make it as nearly impossible as can be for those who are born in it to do otherwise than embrace its teachings and remain forever within it. As the trial Judge has noted, it is unusual for Hutterian children to be allowed to go beyond Grade 8 education. They have no right at any time in their life to leave the Colony where they are living unless they abandon literally everything. Even the clothes they are wearing belong to the Colony and, according to the judgments below, they are to be returned to it as its property by anyone who ceases to be a member of the church.

Such a construction of the contractual relationship between the members of the Colony means that they really cannot exercise their right of freedom of religion. If the rights of the church and of the Colony are fully enforceable as the Courts below have held them to be, it is really legally impossible for them to leave because to do so they must do what the respondents did not hesitate to characterize as "stealing from the Church," in other words committing a crime *(Criminal Code*, ss. 2, 37, 269, 280). It does not seem to me that it is a proper answer to say that these rights will not be enforced to the limit. This is precisely what the British Court of Appeal refused to admit with respect to a contract with a money-lender that was not nearly as harsh as the contract embodied in the articles of association: *Horwood v Millar's Timber & Trading Co. Ltd.*, [1917] 1 KB 305. In that case, the Master of the Rolls [Lord Cozens-Hardy] said (at p. 311):

Is it open for a man in consideration of a sum of cash to bind himself not to leave the house where he is, not to sell any of his furniture and effects in the house or in any future house he may move into, which furniture is not the subject of any charge in favour of the mortgagee; is it open to him to say "Whatever property I may have I will not give any kind of security upon it for any sum of money or for any debt which legally or morally I may desire to pay"? Such a covenant would prevent the man from employing a doctor or a surgeon in the case of illness in his family, and would prevent him from raising money for the maintenance of his wife and children, or for the education of the latter. I think this is a deed which the law must recognize as bad on grounds of public policy of the most well-established kind.

He had previously stated the applicable principle in the following words (at p. 311):

It seems to me that if as a matter of construction I come to the conclusion that the contract is one which puts the covenanter in the position – I cannot think of a better word at the moment to express my view – of *adscriptus glebae*, as the villein used to be called in mediaeval times, on the ground of public policy the law will not recognize such a thing. No one has a right so to deal with a man's liberty of action as well as his property, and the law says it is contrary to public policy.

In the present case, through the articles of association if construed and applied as embodying therein the rules of the Hutterian Church, each of the appellants was literally made *adscriptus glebae* and, in my view, such a result is contrary to public policy ...

I cannot agree that on their proper construction the articles of association provide for automatic expulsion of any member who is expelled from the church. Such expulsion would be in the nature of a forfeiture of the whole of appellants' worldly possessions and would divest them without compensation of an important share in very valuable assets. Under ordinary rules of construction this could not be inferred, explicit words would be required which I cannot find. In any event, I am of the opinion that such a provision would be unenforceable as contrary to freedom of religion and also contrary to public policy in the context of such an association or partnership as these colonies existing for commercial purposes as opposed to church bodies or other religious or charitable organizations that may be subject to the rules applicable to churches and as to which no opinion is expressed.

In the Court of Appeal, Freedman, JA, said [65 DLR (2d) at p. 613]:

Here, however, the vital point is that Benjamin and his brothers had by their own free and voluntary act precluded themselves, so long as they continued to be members of the Colony, from the luxury of adopting or espousing doctrines alien to Hutterianism. Outside the Hutterian Brethren Church, and not as members of the Colony, they possessed (and still possess) the ordinary rights of free citizens to follow any religious beliefs they might desire, or indeed no religious beliefs, if that should be their inclination. But within the Colony they were Hutterites, pledged by solemn obligation and specific covenants to adhere to the religion of the Hutterian Brethren Church. Their rejection of that religion and their acceptance in its place of the doctrines of the Church of God could only be a disruptive influence in a close-knit and united Colony.

With respect, I fail to see on what basis freedom of religion can be so circumscribed. Of course, inside a church no one can be allowed to disrupt services by challenging the tenets of the religion according to which they are conducted. But, as this Court in effect held in the *Barick-*

man Colony case, the Colony is a farm, not a Church. No one can contract out of freedom of religion, no one can by acquiring a large tract of land establish one religion over that area and exclude freedom of religion therefrom. The authorities already cited make it abundantly clear that such freedom is a matter of public policy.

It is of some significance that in Manitoba the *Religious Societies' Lands Act*, RSM 1940, c. 180 [RSM 1954, c. 225], limits the land that a religious society may hold to a maximum area that is small by comparison with that which is held by the Interlake Colony. The following provisions of that Act are to be noted:

2   (1) In this Act,
(c) "religious society" means a religious society, church, or congregation, of Christians or Jews in Manitoba.
3   (1) A religious society may, in the name of trustees subject to this Act hold
(a) land not exceeding three hundred acres to be used for the site of a church, chapel, meeting house, residence of a minister, or for the support of public worship and the propagation of Christian knowledge or for other like religious or congregational purposes;
(b) lands not exceeding twenty acres to be used [subject to subsection (2)] for a cemetery.

Those provisions show that if the Colony was considered as a church it would be holding land largely in excess of the maximum area fixed by law. I do not find it necessary to consider what the legal consequences would be in that view because I agree with Freedman, JA, that the proper rule to apply in the instant case is that which was enunciated by Wynn-Parry, J, in the case of *Re Hartley Baird Ltd.*, [1955] Ch. 143 at p. 146, as follows:

In the interpretation of such a commercial document as articles of association, the maxim ut res magis valeat quam pereat [it is better for a thing to have effect than to be made void] should certainly be applied, and I propose to interpret these articles in the light of that maxim.

It appears to me that the application of that rule supports the view already expressed that the Colony is a farmers' association, not a church, and that members are not subject to expulsion for the reason that they cease to be members of the Hutterian Church. It follows that the resolutions whereby the appellants were expelled should be declared void and they should be declared to be members.

Because, in the opinion of the majority, this appeal fails, it becomes unnecessary to consider what further remedies should be allowed.

As to costs, this is a case where all parties throughout appear to have acted in accordance with their sincere view of what their respective religious beliefs required. I would therefore order the costs of all parties in all Courts to be paid out of the assets of the Colony.

Appeal dismissed.

READING QUESTIONS ON *HOFER V HOFER*

1 Do you think that the court reaches the right balance between individual and group freedoms?
2 Suppose that the Hutterites, like many agrarian religious communities, held land individually. Would the tension between the two understandings of freedom of religion still arise? To what extent is the tension between competing views of property, rather than about religious freedom?

Jean Hampton
"Democracy and the Rule of Law" (1994)

Hampton argues that a combination of Hobbes and Hart yields a democratic account of the rule of law.

Prominent Soviet supporters of Boris Yeltsin who defeated the coup of August 1991, when questioned by Western reporters, argued that its defeat vindicated the Soviet people's commitment to two important ideals: first, the ideal of democracy, and second, the ideal of the "rule of law." The thesis of this paper is that these two ideals are connected, and that we should understand contemporary democracy as a style of government quite unlike the ancient Greek democracies heavily criticized by early modern political theorists, insofar as it is based on the idea of the rule of law and not, as ancient Greek democracies were, on the rule of human will. Indeed, as I shall explain in what follows, it is because James Madison identified democracy as a species of will-directed human government that he was so concerned to deny that a United States under the Constitution would be an instance of it.

I shall explicate and defend my thesis in part by arguing against Thomas Hobbes's contention that all political societies must be founded on human will in order properly to be considered political societies. Hobbes maintained that it was logically impossible to have something called a government that was founded on a rule, or set of precepts, put forward in some kind of constitution or contract between the people and the ruler. Ironically, I will argue that implicit in Hobbes's own contract method is the idea not only that law can be the ultimate governor in a political society but also that the ruling law can and should have what I will call a certain "democratic" content. In a strange way, one might even consider Hobbes the father of modern democracy, although he would have been horrified to have received such a title.

I THE TRADITIONAL DEFINITION OF DEMOCRACY

Consider Hobbes's definition of democracy, the main lines of which would be approved by political theorists of ancient Greece and Rome and the Middle Ages:

The difference of Common-wealths, consisteth in the difference of the Sov-eraign or the Person representative of all and every one of the Multitude. And because the Soveraignty is either in one Man, or in an Assembly either every man hath right to enter, or not every one, but Certain men distin-guished from the rest; it is manifest, there can be but Three kinds of Common-wealth. For the Representative must needs be One man, or More: and if more, then it is the Assembly of All, or but of a Part. When the Repre-sentative is One man, then is the Common-wealth a MONARCHY: when an Assembly of All that will come together, then it is a DEMOCRACY, or Popular Common-wealth: when an Assembly of a Part onely, then it is called an ARISTOCRACY. Other kind of Common-wealth there can be none: for either One, or More, or All must have the Soveraign Power (which I have shewn to be indivisible) entire.[1]

Note that Hobbes's categorization assumes that political authority is ultimately a human-directed phenomenon: the three kinds of political authority are merely three ways in which human beings can rule over others. Either all of them can rule, or only some of them, or only one of them. And when all of them rule, the resulting government is defined as a democracy. Thus for Hobbes, *democracy is a species of government based on human will – and in this case, the human will is constituted by all the people.*

Hobbes's definition of governments in terms of *how many humans are doing the ruling* is consciously based upon an argument to the effect that there cannot be a nonhuman, rule-based political authority. The best statement of this argument is to be found in *De Cive*, in the following passage:

It is therefore manifest, that in every city there is some one man, or council, or court, who by right hath as great a power over each single citizen, as each man hath over himself considered out of that civil state; that is, supreme and absolute, to be limited only by the strength and forces of the city itself, and by nothing else in the world. For if his power were limited, that limitation must necessarily proceed from some greater power. For he that prescribes limits, must have a greater power than he who is confined by them. Now that confining power is either without limit, or is again restrained by some other greater than itself; and so we shall at length arrive to a power, which hath no other limit but that which is the *terminus ultimus* of the forces of all the citizens together. That same is called the supreme command; and if it be committed to a council, a supreme council, but if to one man, the supreme lord of the city.[2]

This "regress argument" is briefly summarized in a passage in *Leviathan*:

[W]hosoever thinking Soveraign Power too great, will seek to make it lesse, must subject himselfe, to the Power, that can limit it; that is to say, to a greater.[3]

The conclusion of this argument is that in a political society there is a single source of power, beyond which no subject can appeal, and which is authorized to decide any question, resolve any dispute, no matter the content, the history, or the parties involved. This single source of power, called the "Sovereign," must be a kind of human will: either it is a single human will or a collective of human wills acting as one.

But hasn't Hobbes made an obvious mistake here? Even if we grant that a political society must be a "closed" system, with an ultimate authority, must that ultimate authority be human? Why can't it also be a constitution or set of laws, as Kelsen or H.L.A. Hart have argued, which acts as the "final decider" in the regime?[4]

In his expansion of the regress argument in *Leviathan*, Hobbes attempts to show that a final non-human decider is impossible. The problems of conflict and disorder that the political society is supposed to cure cannot be cured unless that political society rests on an ultimate and undivided *human* will. After all, argues Hobbes, in any controversy between human beings, only another human being is in a position to decide it, and to enforce that decision. A rule is inherently powerless; it only takes on life if it is interpreted, applied, and enforced by individuals. That set of human beings that has final say over what the rules are, how they should be applied, and how they should be enforced has ultimate control over what these rules actually *are. So human beings control the rules*, and not vice versa. Hence, if we agree with Hobbes that the central reason for having a political society is to resolve conflict, and if we agree with his observation that laws alone are unable to resolve anything because their meaning and their power over us are entirely a function of how they are defined, applied, and enforced, then we must accept the conclusion of the regress argument that only a regime with a final human decider who (either directly or through delegates) defines, applies, and enforces these laws is in a position to effect peace, and thus actually *be* a political society. And so, to those who propose that a constitution (limiting the power of a ruler) could be the final decider in a regime, Hobbes insists that this is not a viable form of polity because

> to be subject to Laws, is to be subject to the Common-wealth, that is to the Soveraign Representative, that is, to himselfe; which is not subjection, but freedom from the Lawes. Which errour, because it setteth the Lawes above the Soveraign, setteth also a *Judge* above him, and *a power to punish him*; which is to make a new Soveraign; and again for the same reason a third, to punish the second; and so continually without end, to the Confusion, and Dissolution of the Common-wealth.[5]

Note that Hobbes assumes that a political regime is only in place when one has an authority established that has the potential power to resolve all controversies that could potentially threaten the union. And he argues that laws cannot do this because their nature is such that they are just as able to generate conflict as to resolve it.

In part 2 of *Leviathan*, Hobbes elaborates on why he regards all laws, no matter their content, as worthless as an ultimate foundation of a political unit. Hobbes's position on the inefficacy of laws as governors is based on the following three beliefs:

1 Laws can never be rendered so completely clear that it is obvious to every human being what they mean. Hence they can themselves be the source of conflict unless there is a human being authorized to give the definitive interpretation of them. And if such a human being exists, then *he* is the ultimate authority, and not the laws he interprets, because he has control over them, rather than vice versa.

2 Laws can never be written so that their application to every situation is obvious to every human being. Thus, the question of how they are to be applied can generate controversy, which can only be resolved if a human being is authorized to decide their application in a definitive fashion.

3 Even if it were possible to define laws in a completely clear way, such that their application to any situation would be obvious, Hobbes would still maintain that human nature is such that those who stood to be disadvantaged by their application would be motivated by self-love to insist on defining them in some other, more advantageous way. So laws are often the source of conflict because of the way human nature responds to normative rules that get in the way of self-interest.

Relying on these three assumptions, Hobbes responds to opponents who argue, as Locke was to do later in the century, on behalf of rule-based (and sometimes morally motivated) limits on government power over the people it rules. First, to those who insist that there can and should be a contract between ruler and people, or else some sort of overarching constitution that defines and potentially limits the ruler's power, Hobbes replies in chapter 18 of *Leviathan* that this is merely an attempt to establish a set of rules as ultimate deciders in a regime, and is therefore doomed to fail because it does not incorporate into a political regime the kind of solution to the problem that such regimes are supposed to solve, namely, a final decider. Indeed, it not only neglects to incorporate that solution but also contributes to the social problem of disorder by interjecting into the social fabric yet another source of controversy.

Second, to those who want to divide sovereignty – for example, between a king and a parliament, or between a king, a parliament, and a court – Hobbes points out that sovereignty can only be divided via laws or rules setting out the division and the relative jurisdiction of each branch of government. So, argues Hobbes, if someone were to propose that, for example, sovereignty be divided into judicial, executive, and legislative units, he would be advocating, in effect,

not government ... not one independent Common-wealth, but three independent Factions; not one Representative Person, but three. In the Kingdome of God, there may be three Persons independent, without breach of unity in God that Reigneth, but where men Reigne, *that be subject to a diversity of opinion*, it cannot be so.[6]

So if the point of creating a political regime is to create an institution that will resolve all union-threatening controversy in a society, then one simply fails to create such an institution if one sets about to divide sovereignty, because such division must be accomplished by laws that are inevitably conflict generating.

Third and finally, if constitutional laws cannot be the final deciders of a political regime, this is even more true of moral laws. While Hobbes is willing to admit the existence of "laws of nature" that he regards as hypothetical imperatives dictating various forms of peaceful behavior that, when performed in concert with others, will promote peaceful and commodious living, once again he argues that, insofar as those laws are the subject of great controversy, they cannot be the final solution of conflict.

All Laws, written, and unwritten, have need of Interpretation. The unwritten Law of Nature, though it be easy to such, as without partiality, and passion, make use of their naturall reason, and therefore leave the violators thereof without excuse; yet considering there be few, perhaps none, that in some cases are not blinded by self love, or some other passion, it is now become of all Laws the most obscure; and has consequently the greatest need of able Interpreters.[7]

So Hobbes would think it fruitless to try to amend or clarify moral rules intended as fundamental legal rules in a society so as to minimize conflict over how they are to be understood and applied because human nature makes the obvious response to them impossible when self-interest is at stake.

Let me restate Hobbes's regress argument so that we understand exactly what assumptions about laws and about human nature that argument rests upon:

1 A political institution exists if and only if it has the ability to resolve or forestall all conflict among human beings who interact in a certain territory.
2 An institution, purporting to be political, whose ultimate authority is some set of rules, whether moral rules, rules dividing power among branches of government, or rules limiting the power of political officials, cannot resolve conflict among human beings because these rules will themselves be the source of conflict, and this is because
   a) it is virtually impossible to define such rules clearly enough to eliminate all controversies about what they mean;
   b) it is virtually impossible to define rules clearly enough to eliminate all controversies about how and when they should be applied;
   c) human nature is such that, even if a rule is clear and easy to apply, if its application to one's own case is disadvantageous, one will strive to argue for a different application, thereby coming into conflict with those who are intent on understanding and applying it properly.
3 A political institution will be able to resolve all conflict only if total power (or sovereignty) is invested in a human will – the will of either one person or a group of persons or all the people.
4 Therefore, only those institutions in which total power is invested in a human will (in any of these three ways) can count as political institutions.

II WHO SHALL JUDGE?

Hobbes's argument is best understood as one salvo in a theoretical war waged in many sectors of European life during the seventeenth century concerning what kinds of government are possible. This was a frequent topic of discussion in the pamphlets written by politically interested people, from clergyman to lords, in seventeenth-century England. One pamphlet, written by Philip Hunton, which argued in favor of divided sovereignty, is particularly interesting because of the way it struggles with the issues raised by Hobbes's regress argument. Hunton maintained that England should divide powers between the king and the Parliament, with the king's power limited by the latter. However, he was aware that this position was attacked by royalists convinced that it was a recipe for anarchy. If the king is in effect a servant of the people insofar as he is subject to the power of Parliament, how can he hope to rule over them? Won't they ignore those of his rulings that they dislike, or remove him from power altogether if their self-interest so dictates? Hunton replies to this objection as follows:

[I]f I convey an estate of Land to another, it doth not hold that after such conveyance I have a better estate remayning in me then that other, but rather the contrary; because what was in one is passed to the other: The servant who at the year of *Jubile* would ... give his master a full Lordship over him: can we argue, that he had afterward more power over himselfe then his Master, because he gave his Master that power over him, by that act of Oeconomical Contract[?][8]

Hunton's idea seems to be that although the people are responsible for the king's power, nonetheless, when they create that power the people *give up* their right to govern themselves, and pass it entirely on to him. Nonetheless Hunton also wants to argue that the king's power is limited and subject, in part, to the control of Parliament. So what will happen if the king's behavior is perceived as extending beyond the legal prerogatives of his power? *Who decides* whether or not he has over-stepped his bounds? Note that this last question asks for the person or persons entitled to apply what is in effect a rule defining the king's jurisdiction of power.

Hunton struggles mightily to answer the question. The decider, he notes, cannot be any foreign power, because if it were, the autonomy of the state would be destroyed. And one cannot grant the right to decide to the king himself, because that would, in effect, make the monarch absolute in power. Finally, he considers whether or not the people should judge the rule, *and he rejects this option also*, because this would turn the people into the ruler and make the king their servant, who could only govern them subject to their whims and pleasures (which are sufficiently dangerous to justify the creation of a ruling power over them in the first place). So in the end, Hunton says that in the kind of regime he would install in England, *no one* has the right to judge whether the monarch is abusing his powers! This is a remarkable example of intellectual honesty but seems so foolish as to indirectly make Hobbes's own case for him. The royalist Robert Filmer ridicules Hunton's position as follows: "Thus our Author hath caught himself in a plaine *dilemma*: if the King be judge, then he is no limited Monarch. If the people be judge, then he is no Monarch at all. So farewell *limited Monarchy*, nay farewell *all government* if there be no Judge."[9]

Hunton realized the unsatisfactory nature of this position, and thus tacked on the following codicil to it, maintaining that while the people cannot judge the ruler in any legal sense, they do have the *moral* right to judge him:

And this power of judging argues not a superiority of those who Judge, over him who is Judged; for it is not Authoritative and Civill, but morall, residing in reasonable Creatures and lawfull for them to execute, because never devested and put off by any act in the constitution of a legall Government, but rather the reservation of it intended: For when they define the Superiour to a Law, and constitute no Power to Judge of his Excesses from that Law, it is evident they reserve to themselves, not a Formall Authoritative Power but a morall Power, such as they had originally before the Constitution of the Government; which must needs remaine, being not conveyed away in the Constitution.[10]

But the reader is puzzled: at first Hunton describes the king as the *master* of the people, who are his slaves, and now he is granting these slaves the moral right not only to judge the king's performance but also to depose him if they think it necessary! Filmer attacks Hunton's position: "Thus at the last, every man is brought by this Doctrine of our Authors, to be his owne judge. And I also appeal to the consciences of mankinde, whether the end of this be not utter confusion, and Anarchy."[11]

Hobbes would argue that all of Hunton's problems stem from the fact that he would make government rest on a law defining and limiting a king's power. With any such government, one must ask the question, "Who shall judge the law?", and as the regress argument shows, either the answer to this question will establish who the *real* (human) authority in the regime is, insofar as it is the law's deciders who establish what will prevail in the regime, or it will show that there are no deciders of these laws, in which case the regime is doomed to collapse and thus cannot count as a genuine government. Note that if the decider is the king, then it is his will that is the foundation of the regime. But if the decider is the people, Hobbes would insist that the king can't be the ultimate ruler, since it is not he, but the people, who effectively constitute the human will calling the shots in the society. Hobbes has a dim view of the viability of democratic rule so understood, given that the people's tendency to misbehave or fail to coordinate effectively is the very reason for creating a political society in the first place. I suspect he would agree with James Madison, who maintained, in the context of explaining why the United States

Constitution did not establish a democracy in the style of the Greeks, that "[d]emocracies have ever been spectacles of turbulence and contention: have ever been found incompatible with personal security or in the rights of property; and have in general been as short in their lives, as they have been violent in their deaths."[12]

After the seventeenth century many theorists took Hobbes to be right. For example, it was commonplace in the nineteenth century to analyze modern regimes in the Hobbesian manner, by identifying the sovereign. Many believed this was easy to do in the case of Britain, insofar as Parliament by that time had become, to all intents and purposes, the sole legislative body in the country. But it was not easy to do for countries such as the United States, where the Supreme Court, the Congress, and the president are supposed to "share" power by performing separate (but equal) governmental functions. Indeed, the United States seems to be an example of a regime that Hobbes thought was impossible: namely, a regime in which the sovereignty is divided according to an ultimate rule, which acts as a "final decider." If Hobbes is right that such a regime is impossible and that laws cannot rule, there must be an ultimate human decider somewhere in this country. Indeed, perhaps in this regime it would make sense to say that the decider is the will of the entire people. (And this may be the correct analysis of countries such as Britain, in which most of the members of Parliament are, after all, popularly elected.)

But if the people are continually called "sovereign" in these regimes, how does it make sense to consider the people "ruled"? Hunton's dilemma returns. If babysitters are hired to supervise a bunch of unruly children, and in reality the babysitters turn out to *be* unruly children, the supervision is useless. And similarly, if the reason for creating a political institution is that people cannot govern themselves satisfactorily, and the political regime that is created is one in which the people rule, the exercise appears useless. James Buchanan, whose own contractarian analysis of the state gives the people the last word in government, calls this "the paradox of sovereignty":

Man's universal thirst for freedom is a fact of history, and his ubiquitous reluctance to "be governed" insures that his putative masters, who are also men, face never-ending threats of rebellion against and disobedience to any rules that attempt to direct and order individual behavior.[13]

But the idea that each of us lives in a political regime under a master whom the people believe they are both able and right to master themselves when he gets out of line is not a benign paradox for theorists such as Hobbes; it is a straightforward inconsistency. We who live in regimes in which this seems to be true dismiss the charges of inconsistency without, however, understanding why we are justified in doing so, or indeed, why these regimes work, despite their paradoxical character. The fact that we have so little to say to defend our regimes against Hobbesian attack suggests that we don't yet understand how they work, why they cohere so well, and why they are capable of being highly stable, despite the force of Hobbes's attacks. In a curious way, we are in the same position as Philip Hunton: we know what polity we like, but we don't know how to defend it coherently against Hobbesian attacks.

III A HOBBESIAN RULE OF RECOGNITION

So we must understand the polity of the contemporary modern democracy better. To do so, let us begin with H.L.A. Hart's famous argument that a political society must have at least one rule, namely, the rule of recognition, which identifies what counts as law in that society. Hart's charge against Austin's positivist theory of law, namely, that it neglected to recognize the existence of the rule of recognition, is also an argument against Hobbes's entirely will-based analysis of government. Hobbes had hoped to avoid laws at the foundation of a regime, but in Hart's view, such an attempt is futile, because in each of the types of political regime Hobbes recognizes, there must be at least one law prevailing in order to identify who the sovereign is, and thus who has the power to decide all conflicts in a regime. That rule authorizes either one person or a group of persons or every person to make the law. Upon that rule rests the very fact that there is a political regime, and not simply a group of hoodlums with superior might ordering around a population.

To accommodate Hart's conclusion, therefore, we might amend the Hobbesian argument as follows:

In order for a group of people to be considered to constitute a political society, there must be a rule of recognition identifying as law whatever arises from some kind of human will, whether that be a single person's will, or the will of some group less than the entire population, or the population. No other rule of recognition will result in the creation of a legal system, and therefore of genuinely effective law.

This revision attributes to Hobbes the position that the rule of recognition, in order to be understood to define a political regime, must have a certain content. His regress argument is therefore reinterpreted as a thesis about how the socially recognized and followed rule of recognition must identify law if government is to be created: namely, that it must specify the law as the product of some kind of human will.

But can we reconcile Hobbes's attack on governments founded in law with this revised position's reliance on the rule of recognition? Perhaps. Although Hobbes takes a dim view of the possibility of human beings cooperating in the interpretation of a rule, if the rule of recognition is as simple and straightforward as the revised position above would make it, then even Hobbes might think it possible for human beings to agree on what it means. This is particularly true in the case of monarchical government, where the rule might simply specify one individual as ruler.[14]

But must a rule of recognition have this form in order to define government effectively? And even if our post-Hartian Hobbes isn't right that a legal society *must* be so defined, is he right that it *ought* to be so defined if the ends of political society are to be effectively achieved?

IV THE STRATIFICATION SOLUTION

In order to begin the process of finding answers to these questions, I want to return to Buchanan's "paradox of being governed." I shall offer a solution to that paradox here,[15] and then go on to use it to evaluate the effectiveness of Hobbes's arguments against rules of recognition that rely either entirely or in part on something other than human will to define law. That evaluation will then allow us to analyze and defend an interpretation of the structure of modern democratic regimes.

This paradox should be solved in the same way that linguistic paradoxes are standardly solved: namely, by differentiating levels of inquiry and analysis. Consider the famous "liar's paradox," which one can illustrate with the sentence "This sentence is false." The sentence cannot be true when it tells us it is false; but if it is false, then given the assertion it is making, it would seem to be true. Tarski resolved this paradox by distinguishing two kinds of language, which he called the "object" language and the "meta" language. The meta language is used to talk about the object language but is not itself part of that language. By understanding the predicates "is true" and "is false" to belong only to the meta language, one avoids the paradox. An assertion in the object language may not involve these words, which are properly employed only as part of evaluations at the meta level.

We can employ the same "stratification" solution to the paradox of being governed. Let us start by distinguishing two levels of government, the object level and the meta level. The object level is the level of laws made by those with legislative power in a regime: call this the level of the "legal system." That which defines this system is the rule of recognition – a rule that is part of the meta level, not the object level. Hart himself calls the rule of recognition a "secondary" rule, one that is about the "primary rules." So, as Hart noted, there are two kinds of laws in the legal system, the kind that defines what the system is, that is, the rule of recognition, and the kind that is created in the system, as specified by the system-defining rule. As I've discussed, if we revise Hobbes's regress argument along Hartian lines, that argument concludes that the system-defining rule must operate by identifying who the makers, interpreters, and enforcers of the primary (or "object") law are. Those who are not authorized by the rule of recognition to perform some aspect of governing would be appropriately considered "the ruled," pure and simple.

But how does such a rule of recognition, even if it has the kind of content Hobbes would recommend, get to be authoritative? And who is the person or group that shall judge whether those who are ruling have respected their role as defined by the rules of recognition? These are twentieth-century versions of the questions that troubled Hobbes and Hunton.

In a recent article, Jules Coleman argues that the rule of recognition is "authoritative only if there is a social practice in regard to it among relevant officials."[16] That is, it isn't authoritative insofar as it derives its validity from some higher law: "It is not valid or in some other sense correct; it just is."[17] Instead, to use Coleman's phrase, its authoritativeness is a "social fact," and he refers to the rule as a kind of social "convention."

Now surely Coleman is right that a rule of recognition is a social fact, one that sociologists or anthropologists or historians would be concerned to discover were they trying to understand the political society that it defined. But how is it that this social fact comes into existence, and how does that generation explain the authority of this social convention? Coleman's language above (which he takes to be suggested by Hart) seems to support the thesis that this fact is generated and maintained by the officials who are operating according to the rule of recognition. But surely this is to get the cart before the horse. The person who is identified as having a certain role in government by the rule of recognition doesn't make that law authoritative over her by obeying it; quite the contrary – it is *because* she understands it as authoritative over her that she obeys it as she performs that role. Of course, were she to fail to do so, she might be contributing to a weakening of that rule's authority. But whether or not this is true, if she does not obey it, she is flouting a law whose authority derives from something other than her prior obedience to it. This is only to say that, as Hart himself noted, the rule of recognition is a genuine *rule*, not a mere custom or social regularity but a normative requirement, and one that those who are empowered by it are obligated to respect.[18] So where does its normativity come from?

Hart himself suggests that its normativity comes from those who make up the regime when he discusses the source of the "acceptance" of the rule of recognition in a legal society: "Plainly, general acceptance [of the rule of recognition] is here a complex phenomenon, in a sense divided between official and ordinary citizens, who contribute to it in different ways."[19] Hart goes on to say that whereas the officials contribute by explicitly acknowledging what this law is, and what it means, as they play their roles in the system, in contrast, "The ordinary citizen manifests his acceptance largely by acquiescence in the results of these official operations."[20]

Now this last passage grants the people a role in maintaining the rule of recognition that appears to be quite passive – that is, acquiescence as opposed to active interpretation of its meaning. But elsewhere Hart suggests that "acquiescence" must be understood in a more active way, when he relates what is, in essence, a contractarian story to explain the origination and legitimacy of a legal system.[21] If a group of people were in a prelegal state, argues Hart, they would agree that, as a way of promoting order, instituting a government was desirable, and they would therefore create it by specifying a secondary rule – the rule of recognition – defining what would count as the primary rules in the legal society. This story essentially makes people the ultimate source of the legal system itself, and therefore the party that not only maintains it but also ultimately decides whether or not it will continue (and if so, under what form). The people's "acquiescence" is therefore analogous to the "acquiescence" of someone who has hired a lawyer to look after her affairs. The lawyer decides what to do, and acts under this person's authority, and as long as he does so satisfactorily, his client will be prepared to "acquiesce" in his decisions. But just as he holds his office only as long as she retains him in her service, so too does the ruler maintain his power only as long as the people retain him in their service (and indeed retain the very definition of the office he holds). So Hart's answer is that of a contractarian: the secondary rule has its source in and derives its authority from the people – including not only the officials who are rulers but also the people who are being ruled.

If the people are the source of the rules, mustn't they also be the ones who should judge it? Here we must be aware: to say that "[t]he people who are ruled are also the ones who rule" is just as misleading as to say, "This sentence is false." To answer this question, we must specify *which* rules we're talking about. The people in most societies don't have the job of interpreting any of the primary or object rules. That job is performed by someone who occupies a certain legal office. But the people *do* decide the rule of recognition, and as they do so they are performing a meta-level action – that is, they are engaged in an action that is about the operation of the object level.

But have I solved the paradox of being governed by a mere verbal trick? I would insist that I have not, because the analysis I have just given doesn't merely generate labels, but does so in a way that allows us to *describe and understand the relationship between fundamentally different kinds of political activity*. Imagine a group of children who are playing a game of baseball in a vacant lot and who periodically stop the game to argue about the rules (they might want to make up new rules, argue about the interpretation of existing rules, or object to the application of the existing rules by the person they've appointed umpire). We know the difference between "playing baseball" and "arguing about the rules of baseball." And similarly, this analysis helps us to see the difference between "being subject to primary rules" and "participating in activities that seek to change how such rules are generated" in political societies. We are engaged in "being ruled" when we follow the law and experience sanctions set by legal authorities. And we are engaged in "interpreting the rule of recognition" either when we participate in activities that "create and maintain" our governments, or when we do what we can to overthrow them. I have discussed at length elsewhere the particular activities that constitute "creation and maintenance" of political structures: they can include everything from voting to doing jury duty to assisting in the punishment of those who have violated the primary laws to attempting to make constitutional changes (a process in which we behave most like the children arguing over the baseball rules in the vacant lot) to, perhaps most important, refraining from performing, advocating, or assisting in violent activities designed to overthrow the government.[22]

In a curious way, I think that this analysis might be what Philip Hunton was trying to get at in his remarks. He was right that no one in a political regime has the *legal* right to judge the fundamental rule of recognition defining the powers of government – that is, no one has that right in the "object legal system" itself, because at this level the rules are the foundation of government. But he was also right that the people have the "moral" right – or better, the "extralegal right" – to decide these rules in the sense that they have a right *outside* the legal system itself as they scrutinize the government at the meta level.

Why does the stratification analysis assume that the people are the ones who decide how well the object game is going at the meta level? Why doesn't it allow the possibility that it could be a right held only by a few individuals, or a small group? The answer to this question is, I would argue, implicit in the contractarian's methodology. One of the covert messages being sent by those, such as Hobbes, who justify the existence of the state on the basis of what we "could agree to," is that – in fact – a state exists *only* because enough of the people who constitute it either have created it and/or continue to maintain it, which means they behave such that the rule of recognition does not change, or changes only minimally. Creating a political system is like creating a game: the creators set out the rules that provide for the roles each person will play in the game (and most of us play the role of "ruled" in the political system), and everyone plays his or her part for as long as a sufficient number are satisfied with how it's going. So, contractarians are saying that, in fact, a political system is the "people's game" because (whether or not rulers wish to acknowledge this fact) the people will decide how well the game is going, and in particular, how well any ruler is adhering to the rules defining the extent of his jurisdiction and power. And this is not a normative thesis, but *a descriptive thesis*. A political system isn't something built into nature, created by God, or designed and maintained by only a few individuals, who naturally rule other human beings in the way that a farmer rules over the animals in his herds. It is a thoroughly human institution, whose existence depends, in a variety of ways, on the behavior of those who constitute it.

This thesis was highly radical in the seventeenth century because it essentially insists that, as a matter of *fact*, the authority of the state is not something that can be derived from some sort of natural or innate authority possessed by some set of supposedly superior persons, nor is it something that is derived solely from the word of God. Instead, it maintains that the authority of the state is the creation of the people who constitute it (albeit perhaps also a creation that God endorses). The creation of the state is the creation of rules, or authoritative norms, that define the legal system and establish the obligations of those who would serve in it. Only officials who are empowered by this set of norms are correctly known as "legal authorities." Although no contractarian believes that *all* authorities are human creations (Locke maintained that parental authority was natural; and even Hobbes accepted that God's authority is natural and not a human creation), the thrust of their argument is that the authority of a *legal* system is a human invention – and yet one to which we nonetheless believe we owe great allegiance.

The issue of how far Hobbes should be understood to endorse the conception of the state I have just described is complicated. I've been representing the contractarian methodology in a very Lockean way – a way that Hobbes himself tried self-consciously not to endorse. Hobbes wanted to say that when the people create the government they *give up* their right to rule themselves, so that they can never get it back, which means that they can never be justified in staging a revolution to replace the ruler. Or, in other words, he perceived the people as *alienating* their right to govern themselves.[23] In contrast, Locke saw people not as giving up their right to rule to the persons they named rulers, but rather as *entrusting* that right to the rulers, fully prepared to take it back if they were not satisfied with their rulers' use of it. On Locke's view, the people make the rulers their *agents*.[24] Clearly Hart's contract argument is in the Lockean tradition. But remarkably, at a number of points in *Leviathan* Hobbes himself cannot resist an agency conception of political rule, at one point claiming,

The obligation of Subjects to the Sovereign is understood to last as long, and no longer, [sic] than the power lasteth, by which he is able to protect them. For the right men have by Nature to protect themselves, when none else can protect them, can by no Covenant be relinquished.[25]

Such passages caused conservative royalists such as Bishop Bramhall to label Hobbes's *Leviathan* a "rebel's catechism."[26] But how can a philosopher who has maintained that the people *give up* their right to govern themselves slip into language that is supportive of rebellion? In my book I argue at length that an alienation interpretation of the contract argument cannot be consistently maintained by Hobbes, given his psychological assumptions – particularly the assumption that we will and ought to do whatever we need to do to insure our preservation (which, as Hobbes recognizes in the quotation above, might conceivably require deposing the sovereign in certain circumstances).[27]

So both the premises of his argument and the contractarian assumption that the state is the people's creation push Hobbes in the direction of the main outlines of an agency approach. The royalist Robert Filmer was surely right that if Hobbes wanted to defend an absolutist government, his contractarian method was exactly the wrong one to use to do it.[28] That method suggests not only a new descriptive account of the nature of a state but also a new understanding of the source of government's legitimacy. Indeed, it may even be the case, as I shall now explain, that these two implications of the contract method played a role in the development of the new concept of democratic polity in the eighteenth century.

V THE STRUCTURE OF A MODERN DEMOCRACY

Let us now turn to the analysis of the structure of a modern democracy. What does the rule of recognition in a political society with this kind of polity look like? I will argue that it is substantially different from the kind of rule a post-Hartian Hobbes would endorse. In this section I will set out the central components of this rule, relying on the stratification analysis just developed. And in the next section, I will defend the analysis against Hobbesian attack.

In the old days, those theorists, such as Hobbes, Hunton, or John Locke, who maintained, contra the divine rights theorists, that it was the people, and not God, who established and legitimized political power, also assumed that, as a matter of fact (albeit perhaps not of right), what the people did when they didn't like a regime was to stage a revolution, preferably bloodless, in which rulers were overthrown and, if necessary (as in 1688), the political rules changed. But what if one could design a political system in which "revolution" was an organized and regular part of the political process? This is the idea that inspired the founders of modern democratic societies (and particularly the founders of the American polity); it is at the heart of the structure of contemporary democratic states.

Defenders of modern democracy self-consciously recognize that *political societies are created and maintained by the people who are ruled in them*. And as I've discussed, this creation-and-maintenance process involves the creation and maintenance of a set of authoritative norms that define the legal system and the obligations of the officials who work within it. However, *democracies operate so that the people have continual control over the process of creating and maintaining the regime*. In modern democracies, the people have created not only the "legal game" but also another game that defines how to play the "creation and maintenance" game. Let me explain.

Consider the standard coup: Ruler X has power because there is a rule, accepted by the people, that he is authorized to have it. But when some or all of the people no longer accept that rule, they engage in various power-retracting activities, and if enough people (or enough of the people who have most control over the present rulership convention) engage in these activities, Ruler X is gone. (So, for example, in the case of the Soviet coup, when too many people in powerful positions refused to obey orders – for example, Russian and Baltic soldiers in the army, political officers in various Soviet states, and various people involved in the economic life of the nation – the coup collapsed.) How such activities can come to be possible, and even coordinated despite the opposition of rulers, is a fascinating story; communication among opponents of a ruler is critical (and thus some pundits argued that one of the reasons the Soviet coup failed was the existence of the FAX machine). In another place I have described this kind of revolutionary activity at length and labeled it "convention-dissolving," in virtue of the fact that it unravels the convention defining who is to hold power – which is just to say that it destroys the society's rule of recognition.[29]

The experience of England in the seventeenth century was that political convention-dissolving could be difficult, lengthy, and even dangerous for those involved in it. This lesson was not lost on the American revolutionaries. But what the framers essentially asked themselves was this: what if the people could get control of convention-dissolving activity – establishing rules that would actually allow it to occur on a periodic basis if the people so decided, and that would regulate it so that the dissolution would be as peaceful and orderly as possible? If there could be a "system of revolution" that was attached to the legal system, both rules and rulers could be changed quickly with minimal cost and disruption to the people. And the possibility of replacing them peacefully and painlessly would increase the people's control over the shape of their political game and thus allow them to better supervise their leaders (who would know that their being fired was not a particularly costly action for the people, and who would thus be under pressure, if they wanted to retain their jobs, to perform them as the people required). By and large, this "controlled convention-dissolving activity" involves what is commonly referred to as "voting," as I shall now explain.

Consider how the American Constitution works. This document not only sets up a certain kind of government, with offices that involve distinctive kinds of power and jurisdiction, but it also sets up rules for creating and dissolving conventions about *who* holds these offices. Through these rules our various government officials are empowered; but through these rules they can also be peacefully and effectively deprived of power. *Voting is therefore a form of controlled revolutionary activity.* Socialist radicals of the early twentieth century were right when they referred to votes as "paper stones."[30] Our elected "representatives" don't represent us in any literal sense – as if we were doing the ruling "through them." This is nonsense. They rule and we don't. But it is because we can easily deprive them of power – depose them, if you will – at certain regular intervals that they have (at least theoretically) the incentive to rule in a way responsive to our interests. Just like any other employee, if they want to keep their jobs they must work to the satisfaction of their employer. They therefore "represent" us in the way that any agent represents those who authorize her. In modern democratic regimes, representation is actually a form of agency.[31] Thus, those who would rule us are, in a democracy, in a continual competition with one another, attempting to gather votes that will, each hopes, be sufficient, according to the rules, to hire him or her as ruler. In democracies, more than in any other kind of regime, rulers don't have tenure.[32]

So our government is by the people, for the people, and of the people – except that this last preposition is misleading. Unlike in ancient Athens, most of us aren't actually in the government – only a few of us are. What makes this a government of the people is the fact that built into the rule of recognition are not only the rules that define the object political game but also rules that grant the people the power to create and dissolve portions of that object political game if they choose to do so with relatively little cost. Creating these rules is a novel way of extending the activity involved in creating and maintaining government. Such rules allow the people to play their "meta" role as definers of their political society in a more effective and controlled way. Those who fashioned modern democracies came to see that not only such activities as criminal punishment and tort litigation but also the very process of adding to or changing the political game itself could be made part of a large conception of the "political game." Or, to put it another way, they discovered that revolutionary activity could be an everyday part of the operation of a political society. (Other democracies besides the United States might be better exemplars of this point; one thinks for example of Italy.)

To appreciate the precise structure of these regimes, we need to examine more closely the content of the rules of recognition that define them. As Hart appreciated, any rule of recognition is a *type* of rule – that is, it is a rule about rules, or what Hart calls a "secondary" rule. Now Hart notes that there are other secondary rules (about rules) that operate *within* a legal system, for example, contract rules (which are rules about how to create "private" transactional rules between two or more parties), or rules about how to make wills (which define rules about the distribution of property). The rule of recognition is not only a rule about rules, but more generally a rule about how to recognize and/or produce *any* rule in the legal system defined by it.

However, I will now argue that in a democracy, this rule is actually a *set* of rules that can be divided into types, as follows:

First, as Hart noted, this set of rules includes those rules that identify what is to count as the law in the object political regime. In democratic societies, these rules operate by defining offices that perform legislative, executive, and judicial functions, offices that, taken together, generate the primary laws in this society. Let me call such rules "structural" in virtue of the way they set out the institutions that perform these functions. They are, as Hart notes, a type of secondary (or meta) rule.

However, there is a second type of rule that Hart failed to explicitly recognize, and whose addition transforms any regime into a modern democracy. This type of rule defines how it is that the people control and/or change the operation of the political regime as defined by the first type of rule, and it does so in two ways. First, these rules dictate how the people install or replace those who hold the offices defined by the structural type of rule just discussed, through either direct or indirect voting procedures. Second, these rules set out the procedures for changing the rules that define these offices and the procedures for filling them. (For example, the U.S. Constitution sets out an elaborate process for constitutional amendment.) By including these rules in the rule of recognition, the people not only define the object political game but also determine the system by which the people can revise that game, and under what circumstances they will be warranted to do so. So with the addition of these latter rules, the overall rule of recognition now contains components that are *tertiary* as well as secondary: that is, it contains rules about rules about rules (i.e., "meta meta rules") insofar as it defines not merely the object political game and the primary rules generated in that game, but also the game of changing the object political game. Politics becomes a three-tier, not merely a two-tier, activity.

Now all political societies have a three-tiered structure. What makes democratic societies different is that *the way one engages in third-tier activities is now governed by rules*. That is, in a nondemocratic regime, the citizen's role as member of the population that creates, maintains, or destroys the rule of recognition defining this object game is ill defined, often little understood, often thwarted by the ruler to any extent possible, and something she and her fellow citizens "make up as they go along." In a modern democracy, the citizen not only plays a role in the object game and not only plays a role as a member of the population that creates, maintains, and changes the rule of recognition defining the first game but also performs the latter role according to well-defined procedures laid out in other parts of the rule of recognition, procedures that can involve elections, plebiscites, constitutional conventions, and so forth. And indeed, in some democracies, she plays the fourth-tier role of creating, maintaining, or changing those rules that define these election procedures, and that also define how to create, maintain, or destroy any other part of the rule of recognition. And when she plays either of these last two roles, she is part of a population that has taken it upon itself to structure and abide by rules that it uses to "revolution-ize" the government.

Disgruntled members of a democratic regime are supposed to follow the procedures laid down by the rule of recognition for changing their rulers, or the offices they hold, or these procedures themselves. But they might not do so; and if they attempt to change the rule of recognition – including those rules that tell the population how to change rulers or offices in the regime – by taking certain actions (including violent actions) or by following procedures not laid down in that rule, they are engaging in what might be called "extralegal revolution." Such "old-fashioned" revolution is still possible in modern democratic states and occurs whenever the citizenry strives to revise or destroy the rule of recognition *without* respecting the rules it contains for carrying out a revision process. But insofar as the rule of recognition's procedures for revision are perceived as reasonable and are endorsed by most of the population, such revolutionaries will appear as opponents not only of the present rulers of the regime but also of the vast majority who support and maintain the way the rule of recognition defines the process of overseeing the regime's operation. Such a position makes their revolutionary activity seem unlikely to succeed, and contributes to what many see as the remarkable stability of modern democratic states.

There is one other type of rule that can be a constituent of a rule of recognition in modern democracies – but this type of rule need not be present in order for the regime to be appropriately called a democracy. It requires those who are to govern to do so in conformity to certain moral requirements. This type of rule is morally loaded to the extent that it partially articulates or partially points to a moral theory as the proper source of the content of object law created by the legislature. Coleman has rightly pointed out that there is no reason such rules cannot be part of (or even all of) the rule of recognition, and Randy Barnett argues that the presence of the Bill of Rights, and particularly the ninth amendment, indicates that the framers of the U.S. Constitution were convinced that moral reality was sufficiently clear to enable the American people to recognize and operate from that part of it circumscribed by these amendments.[33] Modern democracies do not have to incorporate such moral rules in order to be democracies, since their democratic structure is basically created by the tertiary rules discussed above. Nor do they need these rules to be explicitly written down in order for them to play an operational role in defining the nature of the object political society established by the rule of recognition. But they are a common part of many such societies, especially in written form, because they help to provide a moral yardstick that the people can use to judge the performance of those whom they are able to peacefully depose at the voting booth.

In my judgement the contribution of social contract arguments to the development of this modern conception of democracy is enormous. Historical documentation must await another paper, but consider that even though the image of an explicit social contract as the basis of government is make-believe, nonetheless that image must surely have generated in the minds of those who constructed modern democracies the idea that a well-run polity is one that recognizes and allows for the control of the people over that which is their creation – the political regime.

VI THE STABILITY OF MODERN DEMOCRACIES

Hobbes would certainly question how a rule of recognition with the democratic structure I have outlined could be either long lived or stable. After all, his regress argument establishes that the law alone, uninterpreted and unenforced, cannot rule. In a sense he would be right – the types of rules that together constitute the rule of recognition in modern democracies can govern only because the people of the political society understand them in more or less the same fashion and are prepared to do what is required to ensure that they are followed. So human will is behind the democratic rule of recognition, and the kinds of law making it up.

But one of the most important lessons we learn from the stratification analysis is that the particular kinds of behavior that human beings must perform to insure that a modern democratic political system survives are ones that all human beings – even the "bad" ones – are capable of performing. As I've described, these behaviors all come under the rubric "maintaining the rule of recognition," and as people engage in these behaviors, they are engaged in a meta game of controlling the political game, which, in modern democracies, now includes procedures for revolution itself.[34] The people's control over this political game need not be tight; if the political system (and those who rule within it) is/are perceived as performing satisfactorily, public apathy is likely. This is Hart's "acquiescence." After all, why participate actively in meta activities if the political game is going well and the officials are performing (in the people's view) ably in interpreting the rule of recognition? However, such apathy can encourage power-hungry or incompetent government officials to make changes in the operation of that game and/or in the interpretation of that rule in ways that benefit them or the interest groups that they represent, and thus damage the people's ability to supervise them. (This can involve everything from trying to pack the Supreme Court to manipulating rules about campaign contributions in order to make incumbents' reelection highly likely.) As anyone who has been hurt by a bad lawyer will recognize, if the people fail to supervise their agents properly, they may wind up at their agents' mercy. Nonetheless, the object political game is the people's to lose.

But Hobbes would wonder why that loss wouldn't be inevitable, given that effective control of these agents is only possible when the population of the democratic regime by and large share a common understanding of what these normative conventions mean, so that they are able to reach a consensus on whether they are being followed and when they are being flouted. Despite the stratification analysis, this may seem problematic. Even assuming that the people are playing a meta role when they judge the officials of the regimes in which they live, nonetheless, as they play this role they will have to cooperate and agree with one another to a large degree about what components of the rule of recognition mean and how well the officials are playing the roles that this rule sets out. But this means the rule will have to be interpreted and enforced by the very people whose inability to cooperate and agree with one another is the fundamental reason for installing a government in the first place. So how can such a regime last for any length of time?

We can reply to these Hobbesian worries by pointing out that a modern democracy is explicitly designed to deal with and resolve the sort of disagreements about the performance of the rulers that Hobbes thought were inevitable. A democracy controls these disagreements, channels them into peaceful political paths, and makes the deposing of leaders rather easy if dissatisfaction is great. Rather than rely on a sovereign to banish such disagreement (a solution that post-Hobbesians thought unlikely to work, and in any case, unacceptable), the framers of modern democracies set up rules that would resolve disagreements about the performance of rulers through the use of various voting procedures. And although there is no voting procedure that can by itself persuade everyone that the outcome of the vote is the correct one, voting can provide a means of evaluating the operation of various parts of the object game that can strike people as "fair" in the sense that it grants everyone a say, and thus allows the opposition to state its case – even while leading in the end to a decision. And the opposition knows that this decision is reversible (in their favor) if they can garner enough votes for their side in the future, a fact that encourages them to remain supportive of the system that nonetheless produced, in their eyes, a bad outcome. Moreover, a society has a *democratic culture* when every citizen, including those with large differences in political outlook, can nonetheless follow and agree on the interpretation of those tertiary (or quaternary) constituents of the rule of recognition that set out procedures for resolving that controversy in favor of only one party.

Granted, in order for this style of government to work, the people must be in rough agreement about the correct interpretation of the meta rules defining these voting procedures. And even if the interpretation of these rules is, by and large, relegated to "expert" officials, the people must generally support their interpretive practices if the regime is to be stable and peaceful. Of course, one must remember that creating an object political game involves (as I've argued at length elsewhere[35]) the creation of a coercive policing power that, once installed, may be difficult to remove. (After all, those who govern are supposed to have more force than you, so that they will be able to prevail upon you were you to break the law. But such an advantage can also be used to undermine revolutionary activity against them.) So even considerable unhappiness in the population about how the tertiary rules are being interpreted may still be consistent with the stable and peaceful operation of the regime. Nonetheless, because even the policing power of a state relies on people either being actively involved in policing activities or else refraining from interfering with the operation of this policing power, the continued health of even this institution relies on the people's support of it and their ability to create and sustain at least some rough conventions about what rules mean and how rulers are doing. However, the success and stability of this style of government in the modern world is proof that at least this minimal cooperation is something human beings are quite capable of, contra Hobbes's cynical assertions to the contrary.

So, to summarize, modern democracies are highly successful in today's world because the remedy that will inevitably accompany publicity about the private citizenry's evaluations of their government's performance is not the use of political coercion to try to banish all but one point of view, as Hobbes proposed, but the creation of (meta) rules that allow the people to reconcile their differing points of view, and to build those rules into the political process. And perhaps the increasing capacity of human beings to communicate and thus coordinate with one another has made this type of regime not only possible but also inevitable, given that governments based upon unconstrained human will cannot survive in a society where it is commonly known that dissatisfaction among the people is rampant. There is, of course, no guarantee that all such governments will remain stable and unified indefinitely, in part because there is no guarantee that the people will be able to maintain a commitment to following and commonly interpreting the meta rules defining how to reconcile their disagreements over its operation. But the fact that such highly stratified states are both possible and surprisingly robust permits us to be optimistic about both the future of fledgling democracies and the continued health of older ones, in the face of Hobbes's "proof" that such regimes fall quickly and inevitably into ruins.

NOTES

1 *Leviathan,* ch. 19, par. 1, p. 94 of 1651 ed. (Henceforth, all page references in *Leviathan* will be to the 1651 ed., but I will also give the number of the paragraph of the chapter in which the passage occurs, to assist those whose editions do not preserve the pagination of the 1651 ed.)
2 See *The English Works of Thomas Hobbes,* vol. 2, *De Cive,* ed. W. Molesworth (London: Bohn, 1840), ch. 6, par. 18, p. 88.
3 *Leviathan,* 20, 18, 107.
4 H.L.A. Hart, *The Concept of Law* (Oxford: Clarendon, 1961), 97–107; and Hans Kelsen, *The General Theory of Law and the State,* trans. Anders Wedberg (Cambridge, MA: Harvard University Press, 1945), 110–16.
5 *Leviathan,* 29, 9, 169.
6 Ibid., 29, 16, 172.
7 Ibid., 26, 21, 143.
8 Philip Hunton, *A Treatise of Monarchy* (London, 1643), 15–16.
9 Robert Filmer, *The Anarchy of a Limited or Mixed Monarchy* (London, 1648), 20; reprinted in *Patriarcha and other Political Works by Robert Filmer,* ed. Peter Laslett (Oxford: Blackwell, 1949).
10 Hunton, *Treatise,* 18.
11 Filmer, *Anarchy,* 22.
12 From *The Federal Papers,* Paper No. 10, written by Madison. (Quotation from Mentor ed. [New York: New American Library, 1961], 81.)
13 James Buchanan, *The Limits of Liberty* (Chicago: University of Chicago Press, 1975), 92.
14 However, if this were all the rule did, then the political regime would last only as long as this ruler lived. There would be no rule requiring a certain procedure for transferring power. Moreover, if the rule established a democracy or aristocracy, the problem of succession would be removed, but we would now face the problem of defining how the aristocratic group or the entire population of citizenry must cooperate internally to create law. Rules would certainly be necessary to clarify how this would be done; and such rules would be open to interpretive controversy. Hobbes fails to realize that democracies and aristocracies require rules of recognition with substantial content.
15 This solution is based on the one that I offered in ch. 9 of my *Hobbes and the Social Contract Tradition* (Cambridge: Cambridge University Press, 1986).

16 Jules Coleman, "Rules and Social Facts," *Harvard Journal of Law and Public Policy* 14, no. 3 (Summer 1991), 721.

17 Randy Barnett, "Unenumerated Constitutional Rights and the Rule of Law," *Harvard Journal of Law and Public Policy* 14, no. 3 (Summer 1991), 719.

18 Coleman himself sometimes characterizes the rule as a social "convention," but conventions are often normative in character (and indeed called "rules"), e.g., traffic conventions, conventions about constructing a legal document such as a will or a contract.

19 Hart, *Concept of Law*, 59.

20 Hart, *Concept of Law*, 60.

21 See ibid., *Concept of Law*, 89ff.

22 See my "The Contractarian Explanation of the State," in *Midwest Studies in Philosophy: The Philosophy of the Social Sciences*, ed. T. Ueling (Minneapolis: University of Minnesota Press, 1990).

23 I discuss the many passages in which Hobbes uses language suggesting alienation in chapter 5 of my *Hobbes and the Social Contract Tradition*.

24 Locke actually uses the metaphor of trust rather than of agency, but from the legal point of view, the latter relationship better captures Locke's own understanding of the ruler/subject relationship than the former. For more on this, see note 31 below.

25 *Leviathan*, 21, 21, 272.

26 Bishop John Bramhall, *The Catching of Leviathan ... Appendix to Castigations of Mister Hobbes ... Concerning Liberty and Universal Necessity* (London, 1658), 515.

27 See my *Hobbes and the Social Contract Tradition*, esp. chs. 6–8.

28 As Filmer himself puts it, "I consent with him about the Rights of exercising government, but I cannot agree to his meanes of acquring it ... [I] praise his building, and yet mislike his Foundation." From preface to *Observations concerning the Original of Government* (London, 1652); reprinted in Laslett, *Patriarcha* (see note 9 above).

30 See the book *Paper Stones* by Adam Przeworski and John Sprague for a discussion of this term.

31 This is not unlike Hannah Pitkin's view of the nature of representation in modern democratic societies, as put forth in her book *The Concept of Representation* (Berkeley: University of California Press, 1967). However, Pitkin tends to use the metaphor of trust, and that metaphor is problematic. A trustor does not own that which is used on his behalf by the trustee. Moreover, unlike in an agent/client relationship, the trustee/ trustor relationship is one in which the trustor does not have sufficient standing to fire the trustee, and is generally regarded as inferior to or less

competent than the trustee, such that he must be subject to the trustee's care. (So children are assigned trustees; and in nineteenth-century England women could only hold property in trust, in virtue of what was taken to be their inferior reasoning abilities.) The assumptions of the rights of citizens in modern democratic societies are at odds with the presumption of the trustor's incompetence.

32 I am grateful to Pasquale Pasquino for the tenure metaphor here.

33 See Coleman and R. Barnett, notes 16 and 17 above.

34 So members of Western democracies can never be considered subjects; the word is misused because at best one could say that they are subjects not to any political office holder but to rules that they have made, some of which give them control over the office holder.

35 See my "Contractarian Explanation of the State."

READING QUESTIONS ON HAMPTON

1 How do you think Hobbes and Hart would react to Hampton's use of their theories?

2 Are Dworkin's and Devlin's accounts of the rule of law in tension with Hampton's?

PART TWO

SOME CONTEMPORARY ISSUES

5

Defining Family

Family structure is sometimes said to be a purely private matter. Yet the state has always played some role in enabling some intimate arrangements and discouraging others. For example, certain benefits are conferred on only married couples, such as the ability to gain landed immigrant status for a spouse, or the right to adopt the biological children of one's spouse, or to receive survivor benefits of the spouse's pension plan. In addition, various employment benefits, such as dental plans and bereavement leaves, typically apply only to family members. While these are not government benefits per se, human rights codes require that they not be enforced in a discriminatory fashion. As a result, questions arise about whether a government can draw a distinction, or allow employers to draw one, between traditional and non-traditional families. Even if the state does not act to directly outlaw non-traditional families, issues of fairness may arise concerning their treatment under the law.

In Canada, these questions have been the subject of recent litigation concerning the rights of same-sex couples. Some of the issues are related to Devlin's claim that a majority is entitled to enforce its moral understandings simply because it is a majority. Thus, Devlin would presumably have no complaint about the result in *Bowers v Hardwick*, below, in which an American court upheld a law prohibiting homosexual sodomy. Other issues are tied to Dworkin's idea of the law "working itself pure" by getting rid of arbitrary distinctions. The difficult question is which distinctions count as arbitrary. Are distinctions based on sexual orientation arbitrary?

Canada (Attorney General) v Mossop [1993] 1 SCR 554

A gay federal government employee applied for bereavement leave when his lover's father died. The employee and his lover had known each other for more than ten years and owned their home together. The collective agreement between the government and Mossop's union limited bereavement leave to the death of a member of an employee's "immediate family." That included a common-law spouse but the agreement restricted the definition of "common-law spouse" to persons of the opposite sex. As a result, Mossop's request was denied. When his subsequent grievance failed, he filed a complaint with the Canadian Human Rights Commission. The Commission concluded that he had been the victim of a discriminatory practice committed contrary to the *Canadian Human Rights Act* (*CHRA*) which prohibited discrimination on the basis of "family status." It ordered that the day of the funeral be designated as a day of bereavement leave, and that the collective agreement be amended so as to include persons of the same sex in the definition of common-law spouse if they satisfy the definitional in all other respects. The government appealed this decision, and the issue eventually reached the Supreme Court, which held that "family status" had to be understood in terms of the implicit legislative decision to exclude homosexuals from the protection of the Human Rights Act. (Note that the complainant did not argue that the agreement was contrary to the *Charter*. Rather, he claimed that if the phrase "family status" in the *Human Rights Act* agreement was interpreted in the spirit of the *Charter*, it clearly would not permit excluding gay couples.)

Lamer, CJ: – ... The appellant chose not to take this approach [of a constitutional challenge to the section], however, and insisted that this Court dispose of its action solely on the basis of the meaning of "family status." In these circumstances ... I can do no more than to dispose of this appeal on the basis of the law as it stood at the time of the events in question. Accordingly, the issue to be determined, on the facts of this case, is whether there was discrimination on the basis of Mr Mossop's "family status" under the *CHRA* as it stood at the time the events occurred.

When Mr Mossop was denied bereavement leave in June 1985, the *CHRA* did not prohibit discrimination on the basis of sexual orientation.

In my opinion, this fact is a highly relevant part of the context in which the phrase "family status" in the Act must be interpreted. It is interesting to note in this regard that there was a recommendation by the Canadian Human Rights Commission that sexual orientation be made a prohibited ground of discrimination. Nevertheless, at the time of the 1983 amendments to the *CHRA*, no action was taken to implement this recommendation.

It is thus clear that when Parliament added the phrase "family status" to the English version of the *CHRA* in 1983, it refused at the same time to prohibit discrimination on the basis of sexual orientation in that Act. In my opinion, this fact is determinative. I find it hard to see how Parliament can be deemed to have intended to cover the situation now before the Court in the *CHRA* when we know that it specifically excluded sexual orientation from the list of prohibited grounds of discrimination contained in the Act. In the case at bar, Mr Mossop's sexual orientation is so closely connected with the grounds which led to the refusal of the benefit that this denial could not be condemned as discrimination on the basis of "family status" without indirectly introducing into the *CHRA* the prohibition which Parliament specifically decided not to include in the Act, namely, the prohibition of discrimination on the basis of sexual orientation.

While, with respect, I am not in agreement with all of Marceau, JA's judgment [in the Court of Appeal], I believe that he correctly identified the relationship which exists between sexual orientation and the discrimination at issue in this case (at p. 37):

... should it be admitted that a homosexual couple constitutes a family in the same manner as a husband and wife, it then becomes apparent that the disadvantage that may result to it by a refusal to treat it as a heterosexual couple is inextricably related to the sexual orientation of its members. It is sexual orientation which has led the complainant to enter with Popert into a "familial relationship" (to use the expression of the expert sociologist) and sexual orientation, therefore, which has precluded the recognition of his family status with regard to his lover and that man's father. So in final analysis, sexual orientation is really the ground of discrimination involved.

While it may be argued that the discrimination here applies to homosexual couples through their familial relationship or in their "family status" and does not apply to the sexual orientation of Mr Mossop as an individual as such, I am not persuaded by this distinction. I cannot conclude that by omitting sexual orientation from the list of prohibited grounds of discrimination contained in the *CHRA*, Parliament intended to exclude from the scope of that Act only discrimination on the basis of the sexual orientation of individuals. If such an interpretation were to be given to the *CHRA*, the result would be somewhat surprising: while homosexuals who are not couples would receive no protection under the Act, those who are would be protected.

Whatever may be my personal views in that regard, I find that Parliament's clear intent throughout the *CHRA*, before and at the time of the amendment of 1983, was to not extend to anyone protection from discrimination based on sexual orientation.

Absent a *Charter* challenge of its constitutionality, when Parliamentary intent is clear, courts and administrative tribunals are not empowered to do anything else but to apply the law. If there is some ambiguity as to its meaning or scope, then the courts should, using the usual rules of interpretation, seek out the purpose of the legislation and if more than one reasonable interpretation consistent with that purpose is available, that which is more in conformity with the *Charter* should prevail.

But, I repeat, absent a *Charter* challenge, the *Charter* cannot be used as an interpretative tool to defeat the purpose of the legislation or to give the legislation an effect Parliament clearly intended it not to have.

Of course, if the effect of the legislation is in violation of the *Charter*, and a challenge of the constitutionality of the law is made before the courts, then the courts are commanded under s. 52 of the *Constitution Act*, 1982 to declare the section inoperative or to amend it when permissible ...

Before concluding, I should add that this does not mean that the hypothesis of overlapping grounds of discrimination should be ruled out in other contexts. Indeed, in this case, if Parliament had decided to include sexual orientation in the list of prohibited grounds of discrimination, my interpretation of the phrase "family status" might have been entirely different and I might perhaps then have concluded that Mr Mossop's situation included both his sexual orientation and his "family status." For the reasons I have given, however, and in particular as there is no challenge under the *Charter*, I am unable to come to such a conclusion in the case at bar.

Nor should this decision be interpreted as meaning that homosexual couples cannot constitute a "family" for the purposes of legislation other than the *CHRA*. In this regard, each statute must be interpreted in its own context.

IV CONCLUSION

For these reasons, I would dismiss the appeal.

L'Heureux-Dubé, J (dissenting): – It is well established in the jurisprudence of this Court that human rights legislation has a unique quasi-constitutional nature, and that it is to be given a large, purposive, and liberal interpretation ... This long line of cases mandates that courts interpret human rights legislation in a manner consistent with its overarching goals ... In interpreting a statute, *Charter* values must not be ignored ...

The respondent Attorney General of Canada argued that, although the Act should be interpreted as remedial legislation, the ordinary rules of interpretation should apply ... I would agree that the rules of interpretation which have guided the courts to this day have not been set aside, and that they continue to play a role in the interpretation of legislation, including constitutional and quasi-constitutional documents ...

The Court has repeatedly warned of the dangers of strict or legalistic approaches which would restrict or defeat the purpose of quasi-constitutional documents ... In short, though traditional interpretational tools ought not be ignored, they must be applied in the context of a broad and purposive approach.

2 PURPOSE OF THE ACT

The purpose of the Act, set out in s. 2 recited earlier, is to ensure that people have an equal opportunity to make for themselves the life that they are able and wish to have without being hindered by discriminatory practices. The social cost of discrimination is insupportably high, and these insidious practices are damaging not only to the individuals who suffer the discrimination, but also to the very fabric of our society. This Court decried the multiple harms caused by discrimination in the context of hate promotion in *R v Keegstra*, [1990] 3 SCR 697. Dickson, CJ remarked, at pp. 746–47, that the consequences of such discriminatory practices "bear heavily in a nation that prides itself on tolerance and the fostering of human dignity through, among other things, respect for the many racial, religious and cultural groups in our society" ... The Act, in prohibiting certain forms of discrimination, has the express purpose of promoting the value of equality which lies at the centre of a free and democratic society. Our society is one of rich diversity, and the Act fosters the principle that all members of the community deserve to be treated with dignity, concern, respect, and consideration, and are entitled to a community free from discrimination.

The Tribunal did not fail to appreciate these factors, and understood the importance of interpreting the Act in light of its purpose ...

Against this framework, I would like to briefly address the arguments advanced before us that, in its interpretation, the Tribunal failed to adequately consider both textual context and legislative intent, and that this failure constituted an error of law.

3 TEXTUAL INTERPRETATION

It was argued that a correct interpretive approach would warrant that a textual interpretation be determinative, and that the coupling of the terms "family" and "status" in the English text of s. 3 of the Act required the Tribunal to construe "family status" as including only those families who have recognizable status at law. This is the way that the Court of Appeal approached the matter. Leaving aside for the moment the broad and purposive approach which, in my view, should guide the interpretation of human rights legislation, even if one were to take a textual approach to the interpretation of s. 3 of the Act, the result of such an interpretive exercise would not lead to the conclusions of the Court of Appeal, but rather would, in my view, support the Tribunal's findings.

First, the word "status" is capable of bearing several meanings. The *Concise Oxford Dictionary*, 7th ed., provides the following definition:

1 social position, rank, relation to others, relative importance; ...
2 (Law). person's relation to others as fixed by law. 3. position of affairs;

While the term "status" may be used to indicate status at law, it may indicate more factual matters of rank, social position, or relation to others. The use of the term "status" is not sufficient by itself to restrict the notion of "family status" to only those families that are recognized at law. Reference to the French version of the term, "situation de famille" is warranted here. *Le Petit Robert* provides the following definitions of the term "situation":

1 Le fait d'être en un lieu; manière dont une chose est disposée, située ou orientée.

2 Ensemble des circonstances dans lesquelles une personne se trouve.
3 Emploi, post rémunérateur régulier et stable ...

'Situation" is not a legal term, is broader than the English term "status," and encompasses a host of meanings. When the meaning of the French term is considered, it is apparent that the scope of "family status" has potential to be very broad. In French, the term "situation de famille" would not be used to express a legal notion. "État matrimonial" would.

As noted in the Court of Appeal reasons, until 1983, the French text of the Act prohibited discrimination on the basis of "situation de famille" while the English text of the Act prohibited discrimination on the basis of "marital status." In 1983 the Act was amended, the French text to include both "situation de famille" and "état matrimonial," the English text to include both "marital status" and "family status." The amendment did not simply modify the existing terms, but in fact expanded the Act. Had the intention been to narrow the scope of protection, it would have been simple to use one term or the other. In my view the purpose of the amendment could only have been to envelop the two notions. Furthermore, if both terms "situation de famille" and "état matrimonial," "marital status" and "family status," in the French or in the English texts, were similar, there would have been no need to juxtapose them. One such expression would have been sufficient as the legislator is not presumed to use meaningless words (P.A. Côté, *The Interpretation of Legislation in Canada* (2nd ed. 1992), at p. 232).

In any event, I have difficulty with the Court of Appeal's proposition that the meaning of "family status" and its French equivalent can be determined through reference to what it found to be the more restrictive English term. First, as I have noted above, the English term is not necessarily more restrictive. Second, even if it could be said that "family status" encompassed only families with legal status, it would be highly inappropriate to interpret the term by relying on the more narrow meaning of the French and English texts. It is an established principle of interpretation in Canada that French and English texts of legislation are deemed to be equally authoritative (*R v Turpin*, [1989] 1 SCR 1296), and where there is a discrepancy between the two, it is the meaning which furthers the purpose of the legislation which must prevail ... In this case, given that the purpose of the Act is to prevent discrimination and provide an equal opportunity to make the type of life one wishes, the broader of the two meanings should prevail.

A textual interpretation seems to me to support the conclusion of the Tribunal that "family status" should not be restricted to a narrow legal meaning. Nothing in the textual context indicates that the protection of the Act is to be extended only to certain types of legally validated families. On the contrary, the term "family status" suggests a broader protection that would prohibit discrimination against individuals on the basis on the internal structuring of their families. But, as I said above, a strict textual interpretation is not warranted here. That leaves then the argument concerning legislative intent.

4 PURPOSE AND INTENT

[H]ad Parliament intended that the protection for families be restricted to legally recognized families, the amendment to the Act could have made this clear. However, this was not done. Instead, the amendment increased the scope of protection by adding a new ground of discrimination to each text: both "marital status" and "family status" became prohibited grounds. As the terms are juxtaposed, it is reasonable to conclude that "family status" must be something other than "marital status," just as "situation de famille" must be something other than "état matrimonial." Since "état matrimonial" is closer to a legal notion, "situation de famille" or "family status" can only be broader. It was, of course, open to Parliament to define the concept of "family status" within the Act. It did not choose to do so, even in the face of debate about the meaning of the term. Instead, Parliament determined that the task of dealing with any ambiguity in any concepts in the Act should be left to the administrative board charged with the task of implementing the Act ... Though the members of Parliament may perhaps not at that precise moment have envisaged that "family status" would be interpreted by the Tribunal so as to extend to same-sex couples, the decision to leave the term undefined is evidence of clear legislative intent that the meaning of "family status," like the meaning of other undefined concepts in the Act, be left for the Commission and its Tribunals to define. In my view, if the legislative record helps here in the search for legislative intent, it rather supports the Tribunal's wide and broad discretion in the interpretation of the provisions of its own Act.

An interpretation of a human rights document, or for that matter any legislation, that may not conform with Parliament's intention can be easily cured by Parliament itself. Because legislation can be amended more readily than a Constitution, legislatures who find the interpretations given by administrative tribunals inconsistent with legislative intent can always amend the legislation, or pass new legislation in order to modify that interpretation ...

Even if Parliament had in mind a specific idea of the scope of "family status," in the absence of a definition in the Act which embodies this scope, concepts of equality and liberty which appear in human rights documents are not bounded by the precise understanding of those who drafted them. Human rights codes are documents that embody fundamental principles, but which permit the understanding and application of these principles to change over time. These codes leave ample scope for interpretation by those charged with that task. The "living-tree" doctrine, well understood and accepted as a principle of constitutional interpretation, is particularly well suited to human rights legislation. The enumerated grounds of discrimination must be examined in the context of contemporary values, and not in a vacuum. As with other such types of legislation, the meaning of the enumerated grounds in s. 3 of the Act is not "frozen in time," and the scope of each ground may evolve.

Textual context should not detract from the purposive approach mandated by human rights documents, and legislative intent is best inferred from the legislation itself. Any ambiguities as to the exact boundaries of the enumerated grounds of discrimination were specifically left to the Tribunal's interpretation. Consequently, the Tribunal cannot be reproached for having applied recognized principles of interpretation of human rights legislation, in light of the particular purpose of its Act ...

That being said, I turn now to the Tribunal's actual interpretation of "family status" in s. 3. of the Act, to determine whether, according to the proper standard of review, it was patently unreasonable.

5 THE MEANING OF "FAMILY STATUS"

Across the political spectrum, there is broad appreciation of the vital importance of strong, stable families ...

This "unexamined consensus" leads many to feel that the term "family" in fact has a plain meaning. This belief is reflected in the decision of the Court of Appeal where Marceau, JA asks the question, "Is it not to be acknowledged that the basic concept signified by the word has always been a group of individuals with common genes, common blood, common ancestors?" However, the unexamined consensus begins to fall apart when one is required to define the concepts which are embedded in the term "family" in the context of "family status." How are the boundaries of that status to be drawn? Is there a plain meaning for "family status"? Could it not be said that "family status" is an attribute of those who live as if they were a family, in a family relationship, caring for each other?

Those who support a formalistic or more restrictive meaning for the term "family" point out that there is a dominant conception of family that has been traditionally enforced by laws and social custom. The form taken by this dominant conception is commonly referred to as the traditional family. It is widely understood that the traditional family is one composed of a married man and woman and their children ...

The multiplicity of definitions and approaches to the family illustrates clearly that there is no consensus as to the boundaries of family, and that "family status" may not have a sole meaning, but rather may have varied meanings depending on the context or purpose for which the definition is desired. This same diversity in definition can be seen in a review of Canadian legislation affecting the "family." The law has evolved and continues to evolve to recognize an increasingly broad range of relationships. Different pieces of legislation contain more or less restrictive definitions depending on the benefit or burden of the law to be imposed. These definitions of family vary with legislative purpose, and depend on the context of the legislation. By way of ex-ample, one may be part of a family for the purpose of receiving income assistance under welfare legislation, but not for the purpose of income tax legislation.

Despite the demonstrable range of definitions for family, the respon-dent Attorney General of Canada took a more narrow approach, argu-ing that the legal status of same-sex partners, either as family or as spouses, has not received extensive judicial consideration. Furthermore, he submits that where it has been considered, courts have almost con-sistently rejected the proposition that the concept of spouse can include same-sex partners.

The Tribunal, of course, was not concerned here with the definition of "spouse" but rather with "family status" in the particular context of an employee benefit. Be that as it may, both legislatures and courts have long been involved in the process of defining the relationships which will or will not be recognized for various purposes. The resulting legislation and decisions have often had an impact on the ways that families structure themselves. However, the family is not merely a creation of law, and while law may affect the ways in which families behave or structure themselves, the changing nature of family relationships also has an impact on the law. A review of our own legislation reveals the extent to which laws have changed to reflect the realities of families. The treatment of common law spouses is but one example. Law and Family have long been engaged in an Escherian dialectic, each shaping the other while at the same time being shaped. Therefore, in attempting to define "family status," the Tribunal found that it would be inadequate to consider the law without examining the family itself. In this case, the Tribunal considered that the interpretation of "family status" in the Act must account not only for current legal and societal conceptions, but also for the lived experience of family.

While it is arguable that the "traditional family" has an ideological stronghold, it is clear that a large number of Canadians do not live within traditional families. One cannot ignore the fact, that, between 1970 and 1987, the divorce rate in Canada rose from 18.6% to 43.1% ... *The Statistics Canada 1990 Family and Friends* survey indicated that half of divorcees aged 30–39 and more than one-third of those aged 40–49 were living common-law (Marriage and Conjugal Life in Canada, *supra*, at p. 50). Many children do not live in nuclear families. For example, in the United States in 1982, it was reported that 25% of children under the age of 18 did not live with both biological parents ... Single-parent families, especially mother-led, are prevalent; an increasing number of parents never marry; divorce is common; as is remarriage; significant numbers of families are comprised of a husband and wife with no children at home; lesbians and homosexuals establish long-term and committed relationships, and many are involved in raising and nurturing children ...

The evidence before the Tribunal was that the traditional family form is not the only family form, but co-exists with numerous others. Though there are Canadians whose experience of family does in fact accord with the traditional model, the way many people in Canada currently experience family does not necessarily fit with this model ...

While the structure of the family may be a question of choice for some, for others the structure of family may be in part a natural response to social and political pressures. The definition of "family" is thus capable of adapting to changes in the family structure which are caused by such pressures.

In defining the scope of the protection for "family status," the Tribunal considered it essential not only look at families in the traditional sense, but also to consider the values that lie at the base of our support for families. To look beyond the specific forms a family might take is to ask what value one sees in the family and what lies at the base of society's desire to recognize the support families. In order to define "family status," it is no error to examine the underlying values of families so that, as Lisa R. Zimmer says in "Family, Marriage, and the Same Sex Couple" (1990), 12 *Cardozo L Rev* 681, at p. 699, "actual families, rather than theoretical stereotypes, may enjoy their protected status."

There are a variety of values that may lie at the base of society's support of the family. The state focuses on the family as an organizing structure of society. It is argued that the state has an interest in family as a vehicle to promote social stability. The comments made in *Moge v Moge*, SCC, No. 21979, December 17,1992, at p. 32, are germane here:

Many believe that marriage and the family provide for the emotional, economic, and social well-being of its members. It may be the location of safety and comfort, and it may be the place where its members have their most intimate human contact. Marriage and the family act as an emotional and economic support system as well as a forum for intimacy. In this regard, it serves vital personal interests, and may be linked to building a "comprehensive sense of personhood." Marriage and the family are a superb environment for raising and nurturing the young of our society by providing the initial environment for the development of social skills. These institutions also provide a means to pass on the values that we deem to be central to our sense of community.

The Tribunal found that these values are not exclusive to the traditional family and can be advanced in other types of families. For example, while many see marriage as an indicator of stability, it appears from the current rate of marriage breakdown that heterosexual union is not an absolute guarantee of stability ...

Stability is a desirable value, but it may be achieved in a variety of family forms ... It could certainly not have been lost on the Tribunal that long-lasting and stable relationships have been maintained outside the bounds of legal marriage, as well as within same-sex relationships.

These comments also apply to intimate and emotional relationships. These relationships are often conceptualized as heterosexual, and it is often thought that people will form their most intimate and emotionally rewarding relationships with a heterosexual partner. However, the Tribunal was of the view that many individuals have found their most fulfilling relationships outside of marriage, and even outside of sexual relationships completely. In its view, it is to be bound by myth to assume that only heterosexual couples are capable of forming loving caring stable relationships ... If there is value in encouraging individuals to form stable and emotionally intimate relationships, such relationships can be forged and maintained in a wide variety of family forms. The emotional and economic safety nets forged by same-sex couples and their families were found not to be without value to society at large.

It was argued by the intervener Focus on the Family that one of the values of the family is its importance to society in fostering procreation, and that procreation requires families to be heterosexual. The argument is that procreation is somehow necessary to the concept of family, and that same-sex couples cannot be families as they are incapable of procreation. Though there is undeniable value in procreation, the Tribunal could not have accepted that the capacity to procreate limits the boundaries of family. If this were so, childless couples and single parents would not constitute families. Further, this logic suggests that adoptive families are not as desirable as natural families. The flaws in this position must have been self-evident. Though procreation is an element in many families, placing the ability to procreate as the inalterable basis of family could result in an impoverished rather than enriched vision.

It was also argued by the interveners Focus on the Family that the traditional family provides the most favourable environment for raising children. Many people in society are still influenced by myth and stereotype concerning the ability of same-sex couples to raise and nurture the children of one or the other ... What is important is that children be nurtured. The critical factor is not the family form, nor the presence of mixed-sex role models, but the provision of a loving and nurturing environment. From this perspective, the ideal family is one which meets the needs of its members, and best attempts to realize the values that lie at the base of family ...

Families, both traditional and otherwise, have not always succeeded in the promotion of these values. As Adrienne Rich notes in "Husband-Right and Father-Right" in *On Lies, Secrets and Silence* (1979), at p. 219:

The "preservation of the family" is quoted as an abstract principle without considering the quality of life within the family, or the fact that families may be held together by force, legally sanctioned terrorism, and the threat of violence.

Not all families are or have been sites of happiness, fulfilment, and joy for their members. This Court has had many occasions to consider incidents of emotional, physical, and sexual violence within families. It goes without saying that the values that lie at the base of society's desire to protect families are not always or even necessarily met within the family.

The reality is, as Didi Herman writes, in "Are We Family?: Lesbian Rights and Women's Liberation" (1990), 28 *Osgoode Hall LJ* 789, at p. 802, that families are "sites of contradiction." Some people find family life oppressive, others seek supportive family relations but cannot find them. While the family may provide emotionally satisfying experiences, it may also be the site of brutal, violent, and terrifying experiences. However, despite the very real potential for oppression within the family, most people continue to believe that the family also has the potential to be the site of our most important human connections, and that it is these intimate connections that offer the greatest possibilities for individual fulfilment. It is the connections themselves, not simply the form they take, that are important ...

Given the range of human preferences and possibilities, it is not unreasonable to conclude that families may take many forms. It is important to recognize that there are differences which separate as well as commonalities which bind. The differences should not be ignored, but neither should they be used to de-legitimize those families that are thought to be different, and as Audre Lorde puts it in "Age, Race, Class and Sex: Women Redefining Difference" in *Sister Outsider* (1984) 114 at p. 122:

We must recognize differences among [people] who are our equals, neither inferior nor superior, and devise ways to use each others' differences to enrich our visions and our joint struggles.

Though not all people structure their family relations in the same manner, it is clear that there are common problems. Today, families of all descriptions are subject to pressures that are often shattering. Changes in the economy mean that most families feel that they need the wages of two adult workers. At the same time, families must often care for the young, elderly, and ill, with little help from the larger community. Although these problems are shared by all forms of families, they are further exacerbated in families whose legitimacy is called into question. Given these pressures and responsibilities, it would seem that it is in society's interest to improve conditions to enable families to function as they can, free from discrimination.

In light of all this, it is interesting to note that, in some ways, the debate about family presents society with a false choice. It is possible to be pro-family without rejecting less traditional family forms. It is not anti-family to support protection for non-traditional families. The traditional family is not the only family form, and non-traditional family forms may equally advance true family values.

The above discussion is not intended to provide an authoritative definition of what constitutes the family, but is rather to illustrate that a purposive approach to the term "family status" can result in an interpretation that can vary depending on the specific context. In the context of the claim made by Mr Mossop, the Tribunal found that a unilateral and inflexible definition of "family status" could not accord with the purpose of the Act. As the Tribunal explained, "[t]he possibilities inherent in the term family are many and complex" (p. D/6092). Cognizant that the purpose of the Act could be subverted by an inappropriate definition, the Tribunal fully appreciated the values at the base of "family," and had a clear understanding of the need to interpret the term in a manner that would accord with the purpose of the Act ...

The Tribunal did not conclude that there is one definition which will serve for all purposes, but rather determined that the task was to find a reasonable meaning which advanced the rights contained in the Act ... On the evidence before it and in the context of the Act, the Tribunal concluded that the potential scope of the term "family status" is broad enough that it does not prima facie exclude same-sex couples. In making this finding, the Tribunal used the proper interpretational approach, considered the purpose of the Act, and the values at the base of the protection of families ... Whatever definition I myself would have adopted, I would not substitute my opinion for the Tribunal's conclusion based on its specialized field of expertise and the evidence before it. Its conclusion is in accord with the broad and purposive interpretation warranted in human rights legislation and is one that, given its purpose, the Act can bear.

READING QUESTIONS ON *MOSSOP*

1 In light of *Egan*, below, is the majority judgment in *Mossop* convincing when it implies that its decision might well have been different had the case been brought as a *Charter* challenge?
2 What views of the judicial role (positivist, anti-positivist, or feminist) do the majority judgment and the dissent presume? Can these views be mapped onto the different views in *Riggs v Palmer*, above?
3 To what extent do you think the different views of statutory interpretation offered by the judges are rooted in different political commitments?

Egan v Canada [1995] 2 SCR 513

A case in which the Supreme Court of Canada upheld the constitutionality of a law that defined "spouse" in a way which excluded homosexual couples. A narrow majority of the court held that the law did not unfairly discriminate against homosexuals since it also excluded benefits to other cohabiting pairs not joined in heterosexual unions, such as siblings.

La Forest, J: – This appeal concerns the constitutionality of ss. 2 and 19(l) of the *Old Age Security Act*, RSC, 1985, c. 0-9, which accord to spouses of pensioners under the Act whose income falls below a stipulated amount, an allowance when they reach the age of 60, payable until they themselves become pensioners at age 65. The appellants maintain these provisions violate s. 15 of the *Canadian Charter of Rights and Freedoms* as discriminating against persons living in a homosexual relationship because the effect of the definition of "spouse" in s. 2 is to restrict the allowances to spouses in a heterosexual union, i.e., those who are legally married or who live in a common-law relationship ...

The provision providing for the payment of the allowance is s. 19(l), which reads as follows:

19. (1) Subject to this Act and the regulations, for each month in any fiscal year, a spouse's allowance may be paid to the spouse of a pensioner if the spouse
(a) is not separated from the pensioner;
(b) has attained sixty years of age but has not attained sixty-five years of age; and
(c) has resided in Canada after attaining eighteen years of age and prior to the day on which the spouse's application is approved for an aggregate period of at least ten years and, where that aggregate period is less than twenty years, was resident in Canada on the day preceding the day on which the spouse's application is approved.

That provision, without more, would be confined – as the term "spouse" had been interpreted in the Act before the original enactment of s. 19(l) in 1975 – to spouses in a legal marriage. At the time of the enactment of s. 19(l), however, s. 2 of the Act was amended to define the term "spouse" for the purposes of the Act to include common-law spouses described in the definition. The definition reads:

2. In this Act ...
"spouse", in relation to any person, includes a person of the opposite sex who is living with that person,

> having lived with that person for at least one year, if the two persons have publicly represented themselves as husband and wife;

The effect of this new definition was to extend the allowances to spouses living in a common-law relationship as well as those in a legal marriage.

The appellants, James Egan and John Norris Nesbit, are homosexuals who have since 1948 lived together in a relationship marked by commitment and interdependence similar to that which one expects to find in a marriage. When Egan became 65 in 1986, he began to receive old age security and guaranteed income supplements under the Act. On reaching age 60, Nesbit applied for a spousal allowance under s. 19(1), which as I mentioned is available to spouses as defined in the Act between the ages of 60 and 65 whose combined income falls below a fixed level. His application was rejected because the relationship between Nesbit and Egan did not fall within the Act.

The appellants' claim before this Court is that the Act contravenes s. 15 of the *Charter* in that it discriminates on the basis of sexual orientation. To establish that claim, it must first be determined that s. 15's protection of equality without discrimination extends to sexual orientation as a ground analogous to those specifically mentioned in the section. This poses no great hurdle for the appellants; the respondent Attorney General of Canada conceded this point. While I ordinarily have reservations about concessions of constitutional issues, I have no difficulty accepting the appellants' contention that whether or not sexual orientation is based on biological or physiological factors, which may be a matter of some controversy, it is a deeply personal characteristic that is either unchangeable or changeable only at unacceptable personal costs, and so falls within the ambit of s. 15 protection as being analogous to the enumerated grounds ...

The nature of discrimination within the meaning of s. 15(1) of the *Charter* was first discussed by this Court in the seminal case of *Andrews v Law Society of British Columbia*, [1989] 1 SCR 143. In the principal reasons in that case, McIntyre, J, at p. 175, underlined the importance in a constitutional document, which is not easily modified, of achieving a workable balance that permits government to perform effectively its function of making ongoing choices in the interests of society and the work of the courts in ensuring protection for the equality rights described in s. 15. As he stated, what we must do is "to provide a 'continuing framework for the legitimate exercise of governmental power' and, at the same time, for 'the unremitting protection' of equality rights." And he warned (see p. 168), as I did in my separate reasons, that not all distinctions resulting in disadvantage to a particular group will constitute discrimination. It would bring the legitimate work of our legislative bodies to a standstill if the courts were to question every distinction that had a disadvantageous effect on an enumerated or analogous group. This would open up a s. 1 inquiry in every case involving a protected group. As I put it in *Andrews*, at p. 194, "It was never intended in enacting s. 15 that it become a tool for the wholesale subjection to judicial scrutiny of variegated legislative choices in no way infringing on values fundamental to a free and democratic society."

When then is discrimination? There are several comments in the course of McIntyre, J's remarks in *Andrews* that go a long way towards clarifying the concept. Thus, at p. 174, he stated:

I would say then that discrimination may be described as a distinction, whether intentional or not but based on grounds relating to personal characteristics of the individual or group, which has the effect of imposing burdens, obligations, or disadvantages on such individual or group not imposed upon others, or which withholds or limits access to opportunities, benefits, and advantages available to other members of society.

This statement cannot, however, be looked at in isolation. It must be read in conjunction with McIntyre, J's earlier comment, at p. 165, as follows:

In other words, the admittedly unattainable ideal [of equality] should be that a law expressed to bind all should not because of irrelevant personal differences have a more burdensome or less beneficial impact on one than another.

Similarly in my separate reasons, at p. 193, I observed that "the relevant question ... is ... whether the impugned provision amounts to discrimination in the sense in which my colleague has defined it, i.e., on the basis of 'irrelevant personal differences' such as those listed in s. 15." As Gonthier, J has noted in *Miron v Trudel* [[1995] 2 SCR 418], this involves a three-step analysis, which he puts this way (at p. 435):

The first step looks to whether the law has drawn a distinction between the claimant and others. The second step then questions whether the distinction results in disadvantage, and examines whether the impugned law imposes a burden, obligation or disadvantage on a group of persons to which the claimant belongs which is not imposed on others, or does not provide them with a benefit which it grants others *(Andrews, supra)*.

The third step assesses whether the distinction is based on an irrelevant personal characteristic which is either enumerated in s. 15(l) or one analogous thereto.

There is no question that the first step is satisfied in this case. Parliament has clearly made a distinction between the claimant and others. This, of course, does not carry one very far. Parliament is in the business of making such distinctions in developing programs and policies which is the task assigned to it in our democratic system. Further ingredients must be added to warrant a distinction being discriminatory.

The second step will also, in general at least, not be of great assistance. Ordinarily decisions do result in advantages or disadvantages to individuals and groups, sometimes intentionally, sometimes unintentionally. Parliament, as I mentioned, is in the business of making choices, and this inevitably involves the distribution of benefits and burdens in our society.

In this case, however, the respondent contends that the appellants have suffered no prejudice because by being treated as individuals they have received considerably more in combined federal and provincial benefits than they would have received had they been treated as "spouses." I would simply dispose of this argument on the ground that, while this may be true in this specific instance, there is nothing to show that this is generally the case with homosexual couples, which is the point the respondent must establish ...

I turn then to the third step of the analysis described by Gonthier, J. Since it has already been accepted that "sexual orientation" is an analogous ground under s. 15(l), all that remains to be considered under this step is whether the distinction made by Parliament is relevant, what Gonthier, J describes in *Miron v Trudel*, at p. 436, as the second aspect of this third step. He there notes that in assessing relevancy for this purpose one must look at "the nature of the personal characteristic and its relevancy to the functional values underlying the law." At this stage, he adds, one must necessarily undertake a form of comparative analysis to determine whether particular facts give rise to inequality... This proposition, too, derives from McIntyre, J's reasons in *Andrews, supra,* who, at p. 164, states:

It [equality] is a comparative concept, the condition of which may only be attained or discerned by comparison with the condition of others in the social and political setting in which the question arises. It must be recognized at once, however, that every difference in treatment between individuals under the law will not necessarily result in inequality and, as well, that identical treatment may frequently produce serious inequality.

Gonthier, J adds ... that this comparative analysis must be linked to an examination of the larger context ...

In embarking upon this comparative analysis, I shall begin with an examination of the statute with a view to determining "the functional values underlying the law." I shall then examine the personal characteristic here in issue to determine its relevancy to these functional values.

In undertaking an examination of the statute, it is now settled that one must not focus narrowly on a provision that has the effect of depriving a group of a benefit that others who initially appear to be in a similar position are accorded. This is the "similarly situated test" which has been categorically rejected by this Court ... McIntyre, J in *Andrews* immediately stated that such a fixed rule or formula cannot be accepted, and then concluded by setting forth how the relevant statute must be approached in the following remarks, at p. 168:

Consideration must be given to the content of the law, to its purpose, and its impact upon those to whom it applies, and also upon those whom it excludes from its application. The issues which will arise from case to case are such that it would be wrong to attempt to confine these considerations within such a fixed and limited formula.

It is in that spirit that I propose to examine the *Old Age Security Act.*

... As is evident ... Parliament, in addition to providing greater benefits to the elderly in need, long ago took special account of married couples in need; as I mentioned earlier, before 1975 the term "spouse" only applied to persons who were legally married. This special interest is clearly expressed by the Minister of National Health and Welfare, the Honourable Marc Lalonde, when testifying before the *Standing Committee on Health, Welfare, and Social Affairs* in relation to the amendment adding the spousal allowance in 1975. He stated:

Its objective is clear and singular in purpose. It is to ensure that when a couple is in a situation where one of the spouses has been forced to retire, and that couple has to live on the pension of a single person, that there should be a special provision, when the breadwinner has been forced to retire at or after 65, to make sure that particular couple will be able to rely upon an income which would be equivalent to both members of the couple being retired or 60 [sic] years of age and over. That is the purpose of this Bill, no more than that, no less than that.

See Minutes of Proceedings and Evidence, June 12, 1975, at p. 25:7.

I add that other evidence of Parliament's continuing concern for the needs of married couples is the benefits for widows and widowers. To complete the picture, I repeat that in 1975 Parliament, by defining spouse as above described, extended the benefits under the Act beyond those who were legally married to common-law couples, and it is that definition that has formed the principal focus of the appellants' attack. As I earlier noted, however, it is dangerous to focus narrowly on a particular provision. A more comprehensive contextual approach must be taken to determine the relevancy of the personal characteristic in question to the functional values underlying the law. That is how I propose to proceed.

The singling out of legally married and common-law couples as the recipients of benefits necessarily excludes all sorts of other couples living together such as brothers and sisters or other relatives, regardless of sex, and others who are not related, whatever reasons these other couples may have for doing so and whatever their sexual orientation ...

What reason or purpose, then, can be assigned to the distinction made by Parliament? It seems to me that it is both obvious and deeply rooted in our fundamental values and traditions, values and traditions that could not have been lost on the framers of the *Charter*. Simply stated, what Parliament clearly had in mind was to accord support to married couples who were aged and elderly, and this for the advancement of public policy central to society. Moreover, in recognition of changing social realities, s. 2 was amended so that whenever the term "spouse" was used in the Act it was to be construed to extend beyond legal married couples to couples in a common-law marriage.

My colleague Gonthier, J in *Miron v Trudel* has been at pains to discuss the fundamental importance of marriage as a social institution, and I need not repeat his analysis at length or refer to the authorities he cites. Suffice it to say that marriage has from time immemorial been firmly grounded in our legal tradition, one that is itself a reflection of long-standing philosophical and religious traditions. But its ultimate *raison d'être* transcends all of these and is firmly anchored in the biological and social realities that heterosexual couples have the unique ability to procreate, that most children are the product of these relationships, and that they are generally cared for and nurtured by those who live in that relationship. In this sense, marriage is by nature heterosexual. It would be possible to legally define marriage to include homosexual couples, but this would not change the biological and social realities that underlie the traditional marriage.

The marital relationship has special needs with which Parliament and the legislatures and indeed custom and judge-made law have long been concerned. The legal institution of marriage exists both for the protection of the relationship and for defining the obligations that flow from entering into a legal marriage. Because of its importance, legal marriage may properly be viewed as fundamental to the stability and well-being of the family and, as such, as Gonthier, J argued in *Miron v Trudel*, Parliament may quite properly give special support to the institution of marriage. It is spouses in legal marriage who constitute the bulk of the beneficiaries of spousal allowances.

But many of the underlying concerns that justify Parliament's support and protection of legal marriage extend to heterosexual couples who are not legally married. Many of these couples live together indefinitely, bring forth children, and care for them in response to familial instincts rooted in the human psyche. These couples have need for support just as legally married couples do in performing this critical task, which is of benefit to all society. Language has long captured the essence of this relationship by the expression "common-law marriage."

Faced with the social reality that increasing numbers choose not to enter a legal marriage but live together in a common-law relationship, Parliament has elected to support these relationships. The legal institution of marriage has long been viewed as the fundamental instrument to promote the underlying values I have referred to. But Parliament cannot force people to get married, and I see no reason why it should not take the necessary means to promote the basic social interests and policies that inform the institution of legal marriage through other instrumentalities. Support of common-law relationships with a view to promoting their stability seems well devised to advance many of the underlying values for which the institution of marriage exists. For example, children brought up by single parents more often end up in poverty and impose greater burdens on society. Parliament, it seems to me, is wholly justified in extending support to heterosexual couples like this, which is not to say, however, that it is obligated to do so and may not treat married and unmarried couples differently ...

Viewed in the larger context, then, there is nothing arbitrary about the distinction supportive of heterosexual family units. And for the reasons set forth by Gonthier, J in *Miron*, I am not troubled by the fact that not all these heterosexual couples in fact have children. It is the social unit that uniquely has the capacity to procreate children and generally cares for their upbringing, and as such warrants support by Parliament to meet its needs. This is the only unit in society that expends resources to care for children on a routine and sustained basis. As counsel for the intervener the Inter-Faith Coalition on Marriage and the Family put it, whether the mother or the father leaves the paid work force or whether both parents are paying after-tax dollars for day care, this is the unit in society that fundamentally anchors other social relationships and other aspects of society. I add that I do not think the courts should attempt to require meticulous line drawing that would ensure that only couples that had children were included. This could impose on Parliament the burden of devising administrative procedures to ensure conformity that could be both unnecessarily intrusive and difficult to administer, thereby depriving Parliament of that "reasonable room to manoeuvre" which this Court has frequently recognized as necessary ... This I think is wholly consistent with the workable balance between Parliament and the courts sought to be achieved in *Andrews, supra*, to which I have earlier referred.

Neither in its purpose or effect does the legislation constitute an infringement of the fundamental values sought to be protected by the *Charter*. None of the couples excluded from benefits under the Act are capable of meeting the fundamental social objectives thereby sought to be promoted by Parliament. These couples undoubtedly provide mutual support for one another, and that, no doubt, is of some benefit to society. They may, it is true, occasionally adopt or bring up children, but this is exceptional and in no way affects the general picture. I fail to see how homosexuals differ from other excluded couples in terms of the fundamental social reasons for which Parliament has sought to favour heterosexuals who live as married couples. Homosexual couples, it is true, differ from other excluded couples in that their relationships include a sexual aspect. But this sexual aspect has nothing to do with the social objectives for which Parliament affords a measure of support to married couples and those who live in a common-law relationship.

In a word, the distinction made by Parliament is grounded in a social relationship, a social unit that is fundamental to society. That unit, as I have attempted to explain, is unique. It differs from all other couples, including homosexual couples. Other excluded couples, it is true, do not have to be described by reference to sex or sexual preferences, but this is of no moment. The distinction adopted by Parliament is relevant, indeed essential, to describe the relationship in the way the statute does so as to differentiate the couples described in the statute from all couples that do not serve the social purposes for which the legislature has made the distinction. Homosexual couples are not, therefore, discriminated against; they are simply included with these other couples.

I add that this distinction exists in a plethora of statutes, both federal and provincial, and, indeed, it directly or indirectly forms the substratum of an abundance of legal principles and rules at common law and under the civil law system. I realize, of course, that the distinction could in certain circumstances be used in a discriminatory manner, but that is not this case. It is relevant here to describe a fundamental social unit, indeed the fundamental unit in society, to which some measure of support is given. I add, interstitially, that this support does not exacerbate an historic advantage; rather it ameliorates an historic economic disadvantage, both for couples who are legally married and those who live in a common-law relationship. If the distinction is thought to be irrelevant here, this would, in my view, mean that the courts would have to embark upon a s. 1 justification every time a distinction was made on the basis of marriage, legal or common law. Moreover, it would interfere with the appropriate balance between legislative and judicial power described in *Andrews*, which I have discussed earlier in these reasons.

Had I concluded that the impugned legislation infringed s. 15 of the *Charter*, I would still uphold it under s. 1 of the *Charter* ...

I would dismiss the appeal and would answer the constitutional questions as follows:

Question 1: Does the definition of "spouse" in s. 2 of the *Old Age Security Act*, RSC, 1985, c. 0-9, infringe or deny s. 15(l) of the *Canadian Charter of Rights and Freedoms?*

Answer: No.

Question 2: If the answer to question 1 is yes, is the infringement or denial demonstrably justified in a free and democratic society pursuant to s. 1 of the *Canadian Charter of Rights and Freedoms?*

Answer: Assuming it is an infringement, it is justifiable under s. 1 of the *Charter*.

READING QUESTIONS ON *EGAN*

1 How plausible do you find the court's arguments about the discrimination not being unfair?
2 Would it be more appropriate to allow any pair of people, regardless of their sexual relations (or lack thereof) to form domestic partnerships?
3 The *Globe and Mail* (August 17, 1995) carried a report of a decision on a *Charter* challenge to the constitutional validity of the crime of incest. The Nova Scotia Supreme Court rejected a family's claim that its adult members were constitutionally entitled to have sex with each other. The argument was that, while incest may be morally wrong, it is a matter of individual choice for the parties when they are adults and use contraception to prevent the danger of genetic defects in children. The Crown Attorney argued that incest strikes at the heart of the family and the rights of society far outweigh the rights of the individual. Judge Carver agreed. He said that while *Charter* rights provide an individual with the freedom to move and act freely within an imaginary fence: "When an individual lives in a society outside that fence, the legislature is free to pass legislation for the good of society." What do you think of this holding? Is there any analogy between it and the argument of the majority in *Egan?* Would Dworkin classify Judge Carver's argument as a moral position?

Bowers v Hardwick (1986) 478 U.S. 186 [1986]

A case in which the U.S. Supreme Court upheld the Georgia law outlawing consensual sodomy. The majority argues that, because homosexuality has traditionally been judged to be immoral, the state is entitled to prohibit it.

Justice White delivered the opinion of the Court: – In August 1982, respondent Hardwick (hereafter respondent) was charged with violating the Georgia statute criminalizing sodomy[1] by committing that act with another adult male in the bedroom of respondent's home. After a preliminary hearing, the District Attorney decided not to present the matter to the grand jury unless further evidence developed. Respondent then brought suit in the Federal District Court, challenging the constitutionality of the statute insofar as it criminalized consensual sodomy.[2]

This case does not require a judgment on whether laws against sodomy between consenting adults in general, or between homosexuals in particular, are wise or desirable. It raises no question about the right or propriety of state legislative decisions to repeal their laws that criminalize homosexual sodomy, or of state-court decisions invalidating those laws on state constitutional grounds. The issue presented is whether the Federal Constitution confers a fundamental right upon homosexuals to engage in sodomy and hence invalidates the laws of the many States that still make such conduct illegal and have done so for a very long time. The case also calls for some judgment about the limits of the Court's role in carrying out its constitutional mandate.

We first register our disagreement with the Court of Appeals and with respondent that the Court's prior cases have construed the Constitution to confer a right of privacy that extends to homosexual sodomy and for all intents and purposes have decided this case ...

Precedent aside, however, respondent would have us announce, as the Court of Appeals did, a fundamental right to engage in homosexual sodomy. This we are quite unwilling to do.

Striving to assure itself and the public that announcing rights not readily identifiable in the Constitution's text involves much more than the imposition of the Justices' own choice of values on the States and the

Federal Government, the Court has sought to identify the nature of the rights qualifying for heightened judicial protection. In *Palko v Connecticut*, it was said that this category includes those fundamental liberties that are "implicit in the concept of ordered liberty," such that "neither liberty nor justice would exist if [they] were sacrificed." A different description of fundamental liberties appeared in *Moore v East Cleveland*, where they are characterized as those liberties that are "deeply rooted in this Nation's history and tradition."

It is obvious that neither of these formulations would extend a fundamental right to homosexuals to engage in acts of consensual sodomy. Proscriptions against that conduct have ancient roots ... Sodomy was a criminal offense at common law and was forbidden by the laws of the original 13 States when they ratified the Bill of Rights. In 1868, when the Fourteenth Amendment was ratified, all but 5 of the 37 States in the Union had criminal sodomy laws.

In fact, until 1961, all 50 States outlawed sodomy, and today, 24 States and the District of Columbia continue to provide criminal penalties for sodomy performed in private and between consenting adults ... Against this background, to claim that a right to engage in such conduct is "deeply rooted in this Nation's history and tradition" or "implicit in the concept of ordered liberty" is, at best, facetious.

Victimless crimes, such as the possession and use of illegal drugs, do not escape the law where they are committed at home ... Offered no protection for the possession in the home of drugs, firearms, or stolen goods. And if respondent's submission is limited to the voluntary sexual conduct between consenting adults, it would be difficult, except by fiat, to limit the claimed right to homosexual conduct while leaving exposed to prosecution adultery, incest, and other sexual crimes even though they are committed in the home. We are unwilling to start down that road.

... This is essentially not a question of personal "preferences" but rather of the legislative authority of the State. I find nothing in the Constitution depriving a State of the power to enact the statute challenged here.

Dissent: Justice Blackmun – This case is no more about "a fundamental right to engage in homosexual sodomy," as the Court purports to declare, than *Stanley v Georgia* was about a fundamental right to watch obscene movies, or *Katz v United States* was about a fundamental right to place interstate bets from a telephone booth. Rather, this case is about "the most comprehensive of rights and the right most valued by civilized men," namely, "the right to be let alone."

... I believe that "[it] is revolting to have no better reason for a rule of law than that so it was laid down in the time of Henry IV. It is still more revolting if the grounds upon which it was laid down have vanished long since, and the rule simply persists from blind imitation of the past."[3] I believe we must analyze respondent Hardwick's claim in the light of the values that underlie the constitutional right to privacy. If that right means anything, it means that, before Georgia can prosecute its citizens for making choices about the most intimate aspects of their lives, it must do more than assert that the choice they have made is an "abominable crime not fit to be named among Christians."

I cannot agree that either the length of time a majority has held its convictions or the passions with which it defends them can withdraw legislation from this Court's scrutiny. That certain, but by no means all, religious groups condemn the behavior at issue gives the State no license to impose their judgments on the entire citizenry. The legitimacy of secular legislation depends instead on whether the State can advance some justification for its law beyond its conformity to religious doctrine. ... Thus, far from buttressing his case, petitioner's invocation of Leviticus, Romans, St Thomas Aquinas, and sodomy's heretical status during the Middle Ages undermines his suggestion that s. 16-6-2 represents a legitimate use of secular coercive power.

NOTES

1 Georgia Code Ann. at 16-6-2 (1984) provides, in pertinent part, as follows: "(a) A person commits the offense of sodomy when he performs or submits to any sexual act involving the sex organs of one person and the mouth or anus of another ... (b) A person convicted of the offense of sodomy shall be punished by imprisonment for not less than one nor more than 20 years ..."

2 John and Mary Doe were also plaintiffs in the action. They alleged that they wished to engage in sexual activity proscribed by 16-6-2 in the privacy of their home, App. 3, and that they had been "chilled and deterred" from engaging in such activity by both the existence of the statute and Hardwick's arrest. Ibid., at 5. The District Court held, however, that because they had neither sustained, nor were in immediate danger of sustaining, any direct injury from the enforcement of the statute, they did not have proper standing to maintain the action. Ibid., at

18. The Court of Appeals affirmed the District Court's judgment dismissing the Does' claim for lack of standing, 760 F.2d 1202, 1206–1207 (CA11 1985), and the Does do not challenge that holding in this Court.

3 Holmes, *The Path of the Law*, 10 Harv L Rev 457, 469 (1897).

Michael H. v Gerald D. 491 U.S. 110 (1989)

The U.S. Supreme Court upheld a California law establishing a conclusive presumption that the husband of the mother of a child was the child's father for legal purposes. The excerpt concerns the question of how broadly or narrowly traditions are to be interpreted in addressing issues of due process.

Justice Scalia announced the judgment of the Court:

Under California law, a child born to a married woman living with her husband is presumed to be a child of the marriage ... The presumption of legitimacy may be rebutted only by the husband or wife, and then only in limited circumstances. The instant appeal presents the claim that this presumption infringes upon the due process rights of a man who wishes to establish his paternity of a child born to the wife of another man, and the claim that it infringes upon the constitutional right of the child to maintain a relationship with her natural father.

I

The facts of this case are, we must hope, extraordinary. On May 9, 1976, in Las Vegas, Nevada, Carole D., an international model, and Gerald D., a top executive in a French oil company, were married. The couple established a home in Playa del Rey, California, in which they resided as husband and wife when one or the other was not out of the country on business. In the summer of 1978, Carole became involved in an adulterous affair with a neighbor, Michael H. In September 1980, she conceived a child, Victoria D., who was born on May 11, 1981. Gerald was listed as father on the birth certificate and has always held Victoria out to the world as his daughter. Soon after delivery of the child, however, Carole informed Michael that she believed he might be the father.

In the first three years of her life, Victoria remained always with Carole, but found herself within a variety of quasi-family units. In October 1981, Gerald moved to New York City to pursue his business interests, but Carole chose to remain in California. At the end of that month, Carole and Michael had blood tests of themselves and Victoria, which showed a 98.07% probability that Michael was Victoria's father ... In November 1982, rebuffed in his attempts to visit Victoria, Michael filed a filiation action in California Superior Court to establish his paternity and right to visitation ...

We address first the claims of Michael. At the outset, it is necessary to clarify what he sought and what he was denied. California law, like nature itself, makes no provision for dual fatherhood. Michael was seeking to be declared the father of Victoria. The immediate benefit he evidently sought to obtain from that status was visitation rights ... But if Michael were successful in being declared the father, other rights would follow – most importantly, the right to be considered as the parent who should have custody ...

The presumption of legitimacy was a fundamental principle of the common law. Traditionally, that presumption could be rebutted only by proof that a husband was incapable of procreation or had had no access to his wife during the relevant period. As explained by Blackstone, nonaccess could only be proved "if the husband be out of the kingdom of England (or, as the law somewhat loosely phrases it, extra quatuor maria [beyond the four seas]) for above nine months ..." And, under the common law both in England and here, "neither husband nor wife [could] be a witness to prove access or nonaccess." The primary policy rationale underlying the common law's severe restrictions on rebuttal of the presumption appears to have been an aversion to declaring children illegitimate, and likely making them wards of the state. A secondary policy concern was the interest in promoting the "peace and tranquillity of States and families," a goal that is obviously impaired by facilitating suits against husband and wife asserting that their children are illegitimate ... We have found nothing in the older sources, nor in the older cases, addressing specifically the power of the natural father to assert parental rights over a child born into a woman's existing marriage with another man. Since it is Michael's burden to establish that such a power (at least where the natural father has established a relationship with the child) is so deeply embedded within our traditions as to be a fundamental right, the lack of evidence alone might defeat his case. But the evidence shows that even in modern times – when, as we have noted, the rigid protection of the marital family has in other respects been relaxed – the ability of a person in Michael's position to claim paternity has not been generally acknowledged.

Moreover, even if it were clear that one in Michael's position generally possesses, and has generally always possessed, standing to challenge the marital child's legitimacy, that would still not establish Michael's case. As noted earlier, what is at issue here is not entitlement to a state pronouncement that Victoria was begotten by Michael. It is no conceivable denial of constitutional right for a State to decline to declare facts unless some legal consequence hinges upon the requested declaration. What Michael asserts here is a right to have himself declared the natural father and thereby to obtain parental prerogatives. What he must establish, therefore, is not that our society has traditionally allowed a natural father in his circumstances to establish paternity, but that it has traditionally accorded such a father parental rights, or at least has not traditionally denied them. Even if the law in all States had always been that the entire world could challenge the marital presumption and obtain a declaration as to who was the natural father, that would not advance Michael's claim. Thus, it is ultimately irrelevant, even for purposes of determining current social attitudes towards the alleged substantive right Michael asserts, that the present law in a number of States appears to allow the natural father – including the natural father who has not established a relationship with the child – the theoretical power to rebut the marital presumption ... What counts is whether the States in fact award substantive parental rights to the natural father of a child conceived within, and born into, an extant marital union that wishes to embrace the child. We are not aware of a single case, old or new, that has done so. This is not the stuff of which fundamental rights qualifying as liberty interests are made.[1]

Justice Brennan (dissenting): – Once we recognized that the "liberty" protected by the Due Process Clause of the Fourteenth Amendment encompasses more than freedom from bodily restraint, today's plurality opinion emphasizes, the concept was cut loose from one natural limitation on its meaning. This innovation paved the way, so the plurality hints, for judges to substitute their own preferences for those of elected officials. Dissatisfied with this supposedly unbridled and uncertain state of affairs, the plurality casts about for another limitation on the concept of liberty.

It finds this limitation in "tradition." Apparently oblivious to the fact that this concept can be as malleable and as elusive as "liberty" itself, the plurality pretends that tradition places a discernible border around the Constitution. The pretense is seductive; it would be comforting to believe that a search for "tradition" involves nothing more idiosyncratic or complicated than poring through dusty volumes on American history. Yet, as Justice White observed in his dissent in *Moore v East Cleveland*, "What the deeply rooted traditions of the country are is arguable." Indeed, wherever I would begin to look for an interest "deeply rooted in the country's traditions," one thing is certain: I would not stop (as does the plurality) at Bracton, or Blackstone, or Kent, or even the American Law Reports in conducting my search. Because reasonable people can disagree about the content of particular traditions, and because they can disagree even about which traditions are relevant to the definition of "liberty," the plurality has not found the objective boundary that it seeks.

Even if we could agree, moreover, on the content and significance of particular traditions, we still would be forced to identify the point at which a tradition becomes firm enough to be relevant to our definition of liberty and the moment at which it becomes too obsolete to be relevant any longer. The plurality supplies no objective means by which we might make these determinations. Indeed, as soon as the plurality sees signs that the tradition upon which it bases its decision (the laws denying putative fathers like Michael standing to assert paternity) is crumbling, it shifts ground and says that the case has nothing to do with that tradition, after all. "[W]hat is at issue here," the plurality asserts after canvassing the law on paternity suits, "is not entitlement to a state pronouncement that Victoria was begotten by Michael." But that is precisely what is at issue here, and the plurality's last-minute denial of this fact dramatically illustrates the subjectivity of its own analysis.

It is ironic that an approach so utterly dependent on tradition is so indifferent to our precedents. Citing barely a handful of this Court's numerous decisions defining the scope of the liberty protected by the Due Process Clause to support its reliance on tradition, the plurality acts as though English legal treatises and the American Law Reports always have provided the sole source for our constitutional principles. They have not. Just as common-law notions no longer define the "property" that the Constitution protects, neither do they circumscribe the "liberty" that it guarantees ...

It is not that tradition has been irrelevant to our prior decisions. Throughout our decision making in this important area runs the theme that certain interests and practices – freedom from physical restraint, marriage, childbearing, childrearing, and others – form the core of our definition of "liberty." Our solicitude for these interests is partly the result of the fact that the Due Process Clause would seem an empty promise if it did not protect them, and partly the result of the historical and traditional importance of these interests in our society. In deciding cases arising under the Due Process Clause, therefore, we have considered whether the concrete limitation under consideration impermissibly impinges upon one of these more generalized interests.

Today's plurality, however, does not ask whether parenthood is an interest that historically has received our attention and protection; the answer to that question is too clear for dispute. Instead, the plurality asks whether the specific variety of parenthood under consideration – a natural father's relationship with a child whose mother is married to another man – has enjoyed such protection.

If we had looked to tradition with such specificity in past cases, many a decision would have reached a different result ...

The plurality's interpretive method is more than novel; it is misguided. It ignores the good reasons for limiting the role of "tradition" in interpreting the Constitution's deliberately capacious language. In the plurality's constitutional universe, we may not take notice of the fact that the original reasons for the conclusive presumption of paternity are out of place in a world in which blood tests can prove virtually beyond a shadow of a doubt who sired a particular child and in which the fact of illegitimacy no longer plays the burdensome and stigmatizing role it once did. Nor, in the plurality's world, may we deny "tradition" its full scope by pointing out that the rationale for the conventional rule has changed over the years ... Instead, our task is simply to identify a rule denying the asserted interest and not to ask whether the basis for that rule – which is the true reflection of the values undergirding it – has changed too often or too recently to call the rule embodying that rationale a "tradition." Moreover, by describing the decisive question as whether Michael's and Victoria's interest is one that has been "traditionally protected by our society," rather than one that society traditionally has thought important (with or without protecting it), and by suggesting that our sole function is to "discern the society's views," the plurality acts as if the only purpose of the Due Process Clause is to confirm the importance of interests already protected by a majority of the States. Transforming the protection afforded by the Due Process Clause into a redundancy mocks those who, with care and purpose, wrote the Fourteenth Amendment.

In construing the Fourteenth Amendment to offer shelter only to those interests specifically protected by historical practice, moreover, the plurality ignores the kind of society in which our Constitution exists. We are not an assimilative, homogeneous society, but a facilitative, pluralistic one, in which we must be willing to abide someone else's unfamiliar or even repellent practice because the same tolerant impulse protects our own idiosyncracies. Even if we can agree, therefore, that "family" and "parenthood" are part of the good life, it is absurd to assume that we can agree on the content of those terms and destructive to pretend that we do. In a community such as ours, "liberty" must include the freedom not to conform. The plurality today squashes this freedom by requiring specific approval from history before protecting anything in the name of liberty.

The document that the plurality construes today is unfamiliar to me. It is not the living charter that I have taken to be our Constitution; it is instead a stagnant, archaic, hidebound document steeped in the prejudices and superstitions of a time long past. This Constitution does not recognize that times change, does not see that sometimes a practice or rule outlives its foundations. I cannot accept an interpretive method that does such violence to the charter that I am bound by oath to uphold.

The plurality's reworking of our interpretive approach is all the more troubling because it is unnecessary. This is not a case in which we face a "new" kind of interest, one that requires us to consider for the first time whether the Constitution protects it. On the contrary, we confront an interest – that of a parent and child in their relationship with each other – that was among the first that this Court acknowledged in its cases defining the "liberty" protected by the Constitution, and I think I am safe in saying that no one doubts the wisdom or validity of those decisions. Where the interest under consideration is a parent-child relationship, we need not ask, over and over again, whether that interest is one that society traditionally protects.

Thus, to describe the issue in this case as whether the relationship existing between Michael and Victoria "has been treated as a protected family unit under the historic practices of our society, or whether on any other basis it has been accorded special protection," is to reinvent the wheel. The better approach – indeed, the one commanded by our prior cases and by common sense – is to ask whether the specific parent-child relationship under consideration is close enough to the interests that we already have protected to be deemed an aspect of "liberty" as well. On the facts before us, therefore, the question is not what "level of generality" should be used to describe the relationship between Michael and Victoria, see ante, n. 6, but whether the relationship under consideration is sufficiently substantial to qualify as a liberty interest under our prior cases.

    ... The plurality's exclusive rather than inclusive definition of the "unitary family" is out of step with other decisions as well. This pinched conception of "the family," crucial as it is in rejecting Michael's and Victoria's claims of a liberty interest, is jarring in light of our many cases preventing the States from denying important interests or statuses to those whose situations do not fit the government's narrow view of the family. [W]e have declined to respect a State's notion, as manifested in its allocation of privileges and burdens, of what the family should be. Today's rhapsody on the "unitary family" is out of tune with such decisions.

    ... The plurality has wedged itself between a rock and a hard place. If it limits its holding to those situations in which a wife and husband wish to raise the child together, then it necessarily takes the State's interest into account in defining "liberty"; yet if it extends that approach to circumstances in which the marital union already has been dissolved, then it may no longer rely on the State's asserted interest in protecting the "unitary family" in denying that Michael and Victoria have been deprived of liberty.

NOTES

1 Justice Brennan criticizes our methodology in using historical traditions specifically relating to the rights of an adulterous natural father, rather than inquiring more generally "whether parenthood is an interest that historically has received our attention and protection." ... We do not understand why, having rejected our focus upon the societal tradition regarding the natural father's rights vis-à-vis a child whose mother is married to another man, Justice Brennan would choose to focus instead upon "parenthood." Why should the relevant category not be even more general – perhaps "family relationships"; or "personal relationships"; or

even "emotional attachments in general"? Though the dissent has no basis for the level of generality it would select, we do: We refer to the most specific level at which a relevant tradition protecting, or denying protection to, the asserted right can be identified. If, for example, there were no societal tradition, either way, regarding the rights of the natural father of a child adulterously conceived, we would have to consult, and (if possible) reason from, the traditions regarding natural fathers in general. But there is such a more specific tradition, and it unqualifiedly denies protection to such a parent. One would think that Justice Brennan would appreciate the value of consulting the most specific tradition available, since he acknowledges that "[e]ven if we can agree ... that 'family' and 'parenthood' are part of the good life, it is absurd to assume that we can agree on the content of those terms and destructive to pretend that we do." Because such general traditions provide such imprecise guidance, they permit judges to dictate rather than discern the society's views. We need, if arbitrary decisionmaking is to be avoided, to adopt the most specific tradition as the point of reference – or at least to announce, as Justice Brennan declines to do, some other criterion for selecting among the innumerable relevant traditions that could be consulted.

READING QUESTION ON *BOWERS* AND MICHAEL H.

1   Why does the court suppose tradition is important? How broadly or narrowly should it be interpreted? Is there a principled answer to this question?

Jody Freeman
"Defining Family in *Mossop v DSS*: The Challenge of Anti-Essentialism and Interactive Discrimination for Human Rights Litigation" (1994)

Freeman argues that the law should reflect different contemporary understandings of the family. Her article provides insight into *Charter* litigation in a progressive cause, as well as outlining a "post-modern" basis for such litigation.

INTRODUCTION

This article is a narrative about the construction of a legal argument: a close analysis of the intervenors' factum in *Mossop v DSS*, a case recently decided by the Supreme Court of Canada, in which a gay man argued that his exclusion from an employment benefit constituted discrimination on the basis of family status in contravention of the *Canadian Human Rights Act (CHRA)*. The intervention brought together a broad and diverse coalition of interests, including Equality for Gays and Lesbians Everywhere, the National Action Committee on the Status of Women, the Canadian Disability Rights Council, the National Association of Women and the Law, and the Canadian Rights and Liberties Federation. The coalition's intervention in *Mossop* can be understood from a variety of perspectives. For some, it is a gay rights test case; for others, it is an attempt to demythologize the traditional family; and for still others, it represents an attempt to infuse human rights interpretation with notions of anti-essentialism and interactive discrimination. The factum is interesting both methodologically and substantively; one of its lessons is that a self-conscious and critical process is essential to the development of a self-conscious and critical legal argument.

Collaborating on this project blurred for me the already suspect distinction between legal practice and legal scholarship. Virtually every paragraph of the factum is the product of heated debate about the appropriateness of a particular theoretical framework, the symbolic importance of a word choice, the long-term implications of one argument over another, the likelihood of persuading the audience, and the chance of "winning." Each of these debates usually led to another, deeper discussion about why theory is important in the first place, to what extent word choice or long-term considerations ought to matter, whether we really agreed about who the audience was, and what "winning" might be in the context. The experience of contributing to this factum was extraordinarily rich for me for a number of reasons: the inclusive and collaborative process established by Gwen Brodsky, the intervenors' counsel, at the outset; the combination of powerful intellects working on the factum from a variety of perspectives; and the challenges presented by the legal and social issues. *Mossop* was treated by Ms Brodsky in keeping with the tradition of her *Charter* and human rights litigation to date. She calls her procedural method "participatory litigation," by which she means that the litigation process is substantially democratized and inclusive, compared with the traditional model of solicitor/ client relations: "I believe that this transformation of the litigation process is essential to the realization of the egalitarian goals that drive the equality rights movement." The factum was constructed with ongoing consultation among the five groups comprising the coalition, Ms Brodsky, and her staff. The intervenors participated in a serious and substantive way, reviewing drafts of the factum, voicing their concerns, and approving the direction of the litigation. The process facilitated a thoughtful and energetic treatment of some very complicated issues, both technical and deeply philosophical. It enabled participants, regardless of status and formal rank, to advance novel conceptual paradigms or legal arguments without fear that they would be prematurely dismissed as too risky or unreasonable. This experience, and others, have convinced me that test case litigation benefits immeasurably from a process that mirrors its substantive social vision. Not only do the participants feel that their contribution, and the litigation in general, is meaningful, but the final product is inevitably superior to one conceived and borne of a closed, non-consultative process. As I explain, elaborate upon, and then critique the factum, the link between methodology and substance should be clear.

THE PROBLEM

Although most people have an image of what constitutes a "traditional" family, neither legislation nor the common law reflects a consistent definition. In fact, the legal definition of family continues to evolve over time along with the reality of social life. And yet, the field of "family" law is implicitly based on a heterosexual norm. Although no statute explicitly defines "family" for all purposes, and despite the fact that one can find inconsistency in the definition if one searches for it, an impressive variety of legislation, legal holdings, rules, and omission, taken together, nonetheless reinforce the notion that a "normal" family comprises two heterosexual parents and their children.[1] These legal interpretations are only part of the vast array of cultural messages that are responsible for the dominance of the image of "normality" that most people draw upon when asked to define family. As part of culture, both legislation and judge-made law contribute to the social pressure to conform to a mythologized traditional family, but law is not the only, nor is it necessarily the most powerful, social force. Popular culture overwhelmingly reinforces the dominance of the "traditional" family form, as reflected in the media, advertising, television, music, and theatre. Single-parent families are represented as anomalous and unfortunate; they are held in contempt, vilified, and blamed for a number of social ills including maladjusted children and welfare dependency. Positive cultural representations of counterexamples to the traditional, heterosexual, two-parent family are relatively rare. Social institutions, to the extent that they are "family-friendly" at all, are designed to meet the needs of traditional, and not alternative, families. This broader cultural message is often most strictly enforced in the context of our own families. Who of us can claim to have been raised in an environment where remaining single, getting a divorce, or being gay would not be viewed as a failure, or where choosing not to have children would be greeted with the same enthusiasm as the announcement that one is pregnant?

In its factum, the coalition exposes this paradox – that despite inconsistent and evolving definitions of family in legislation, and a great variety of families in contemporary society, a dominant conception of the family persists. The intervenors' argument is that no single, all-purpose definition of family is accurate or defensible. Families that do not conform to the traditional model might include single-parent families, extended families, unmarried people who consider themselves family but do not meet common law criteria, and gay men and lesbians. In order to include such relationships, the intervenors advance an anti-essentialist definition of family, one that is non-discriminatory and justifiable in the light of the legislative provision or specific regulation to which the definition is linked.

The coalition makes a conscious attempt in its factum to discredit the pervasive notion that only heterosexual couples with children are families, while resisting the temptation to supply the Court with a new universal definition. In marked contrast to the appellant, the Canadian Human Rights Commission (CHRC), and in direct opposition to the respondent, the Department of the Secretary of State (DSS) and its supporting intervenors,[2] the factum challenges essentialist understandings of family in general, and socially constructed stereotypes of gay men and lesbians in particular. In addition, by asserting that sexual orientation and family status discrimination are inseparable in this case, it invites the Court to acknowledge the interactive and multiple nature of discrimination. Finally, the intervenors' factum might be viewed as an example of postmodern legal argument.[3] Although postmodernism means different things to different people, and is met with hostility by those who view its critique of modernity as potentially nihilist, a post-modern "stance" in difficult cases like *Mossop* makes it possible to see contradictions and impasses as opportunities for contesting settled meanings and suggesting creative remedies. This stance is borne out in a number of the factum's features: its insistence on the falsity of universals; its refusal to choose between dichotomized alternatives; its emphasis on the indeterminacy of interpretation; and its reliance on context-ualized argument. Confronted with the confines and limitations of legal argument in general, and rights discourse in particular, lawyers and academics are sometimes tempted to abandon it entirely as a means of progressive social change, or to condemn its radical transformative po-tential in a fit of antirationalism. The intervenors' factum in *Mossop* resists that temptation without ignoring the critical lessons which lead to it. In my view, this factum's innovative strategies sit, albeit uncom-fortably, somewhere between the scepticism of those with no faith in the liberatory potential of the legal system, and the hope of those who wish to see it transformed from within. My own justification for engag-ing in test case litigation is that law is a critical site of struggle over meaning, although by no means the only one. And although the factum is vulnerable to critiques that it is either too radical, too liberal, too moderate, or inadequately feminist, it represents a laudable attempt to place anti-essentialism and intersection theory at the heart of the inter-pretation of human rights legislation ...

THE PERSPECTIVE IN THE SUPREME COURT OF CANADA OF THE
INTERVENORS

Two goals seemed to me to inform the construction of the factum dur-ing its early stages: that it perform an educative function by exposing both the variety of families currently existing in Canadian society and the ideological role that the dominant conception of family plays in our socialization; and that it demonstrate convincingly how the denial of bereavement leave was experienced by Mossop as a denial of his family, such that he suffered *both* family status discrimination and discrimi-nation on the basis of sexual orientation. The coalition's position was supportive of Mossop's desire for legal recognition of his family, but over time, the intervenors' factum differed substantially from that of the CHRC by challenging the coherence of the conception of family itself. The coalition rejected not only the CHRC's philosophical approach, but also its analysis of the legal and ideological issues before the Court and the CHRC's choice of remedy. The CHRC adopted what could be described as a "sameness" approach to equality, arguing that Mossop's relationship with Popert was "just like" a heterosexual relationship, and that this equivalence entitled the two men to inclusion within the ground family status. If the Court were to accept this argument, an appropriate remedy would be to amend the definition of family in the collective agreement to include same-sex couples. Although such an amendment would have satisfied the order of the human rights tribunal, it would have imposed criteria on same-sex relationships that many could not meet, and the result would still amount to discrimination on the basis of family status. The remedies sought by the intervenors, to eliminate the family relationship qualification for granting bereavement leave, or to define family in an open-ended way, were also consistent with the tribunal's order. They had the advantage, as well, of eliminating entirely family status discrimination. The CHRC's remedial approach, in the end, left the ideological force of the dominant conception of family unexplored and did not fully ameliorate the discriminatory impact of the sameness strategy.

THE SOCIAL REALITY OF FAMILIES

Demographic research demonstrates that intimate relationships do not overwhelmingly fit the dominant norm for family. In fact, there is a variety of "family" forms in Canadian society: many children do not live in traditional nuclear families with two heterosexual parents; single parents with children and step-parent or step-sibling relationships are prevalent and on the rise; divorce statistics are high; and many couples are childless. There are no statistics available for how many families are non-traditional, because official census definitions reflect only the traditional model. Organizations of people into what they call their families occurs for a number of highly contingent reasons that vary with age, circumstance, religion, economics, race, and gender, among other considerations. Variety exists not only in terms of the form of relationships (some of which people can consciously alter through decisions to marry, divorce, remarry, adopt, cohabit, etc., and others of which are "inherited") but also in terms of how they function. Some families are more affectionate than others, for example, or more abusive than others. They are bound together with different degrees of emotional, intellectual, and economic dependence. Some relationships are more easily recognized as family by outsiders and by the legal regime. Although one could provide a list of features that are common to many self-regarding families, it is difficult to define the "essence" of family. Some couples have children, while others do not; some related individuals share a residence, while others do not; some married people share their finances, while others do not; and so on. In the face of this diversity, the notion of a "core" definition of family becomes increasingly unworkable.

As noted earlier, however, neither federal nor provincial legislation reflects a consistent definition of family, even if the definition of spouse is consistently heterosexual. The meaning of family varies with legislative purpose. For example, individuals may be deemed a family for the purpose of receiving income assistance under welfare legislation, but not for the purpose of income tax legislation. Further, over time, legal definitions of family have evolved, along with social attitudes. Legislative reforms, both federal and provincial, have extended the status of family to common law spouses. "Illegitimate" children are no longer denied status as equal to "legitimate" ones. Social resistance to interracial marriage has declined over time as well. In the face of this legislative and social history, in the light of the broad purpose of the *CHRA*, and given that legislative intent is neither clear nor determinative, it is remarkable that the Federal Court of Appeal and the federal government could insist that family has a single, all-purpose meaning. Family is less a fact than it is a product of legal and social regulation and ideology. Only by blinding itself both to the lack of consistency in the legal regulation of the family and to the existing diversity of people's affiliations could the Court interpret family status in the *CHRA* to be limited to heterosexuals.

A restrictive interpretation of family status would effectively freeze human rights legislation and significantly widen the gap between law and social life. The coalition's factum argues that it would exclude from the reach of the *CHRA* those who most need protection from discrimination, precisely because they have historically lacked "status." The coalition argued that this interpretation would be inconsistent with the purposes of human rights legislation, which include the amelioration of group disadvantage, the breakdown of negative stereotypes, and the recognition of the inherent dignity and value of all persons. The Supreme Court has approached the interpretation of human rights legislation purposively, with a view to furthering its goals, and it has focused on the effects of the discrimination complained of, regardless of whether it was intentional or not. Moreover, the Court has taken pains to assess the effects of discrimination in its specific context, and from the perspective of those victimized by it. The intervenors argued that it was fully consistent with the Court's recent jurisprudence to consider the meaning of family status from the perspective of those most affected by exclusion from the category, including gay men and lesbians.

Implicit in the coalition's position is the notion that a legal decision about what constitutes a family is necessarily normative, and has an important symbolic or legitimating force. Judicial decisions proclaim "truths" in the course of resolving particular disputes. Even if only indirectly or diffusely, judicial pronouncements can reinforce and alter social views. Of course, it is virtually impossible to measure the isolated impact of a single decision; but as part of the barrage of authoritative messages from the State, the Supreme Court's refusal to acknowledge the diversity of affiliative relationships and accord them human rights protection would send a powerful message to society about what an "appropriate" and "normal" family relationship looks like. Individuals are likely to internalize authoritative proclamations emanating from courts and other institutions that are seen as neutral and rational, and that have achieved a special cultural status. As a result, their impact can be hurtful personally, as well as inhibiting to movement building. An adverse decision in a case like *Mossop* could provide the legal backdrop against which oppressive actions emanating from the State, private organizations, and individuals might seem justifiable.[4]

The coalition's factum describes the increasing variety of family life and juxtaposes it with the idealized, traditional model of the two-heterosexual-parent family with children. The factum demythologizes the family, and provides the Court with a more realistic image of the diversity of affiliative relationships. Demythologizing the family meant exposing the function of family ideology and explaining how its pervasiveness insulates conventional families from criticism, helps maintain the invisibility of child and spousal abuse, reinforces heterosexuality as the only legitimate sexual identity (thereby fuelling and legitimizing homophobia), and denies non-conforming families the material and psychological benefits of recognition and legitimation.

This section of the factum relies heavily on "fact," including data collected to contradict prevailing beliefs about family, beliefs that appear to be obvious and to make "common sense" until interrogated. Here the factum contrasts the model of family that pervades our legal and political rhetoric with empirical facts about the prevalence of single-parent families, families comprising gay people both with and without children, and childless families, all of which deviate from the imagined norm. The Court's interpretation of family status in the *CHRA*, the intervenors argued, should be informed by social reality, not fiction and ideology.

The factum also provides the Court with positive images of gay men and lesbians ...

This strategy directly confronts, and seeks to correct, assumptions that often lurk in the minds of even well-intentioned people: that gay men and lesbians do not reproduce; that they are bad parents; that they do not love; or that if they do, it is a lesser love than that shared between heterosexuals. It seemed possible that the judges' subconscious views might influence their ability even to imagine family status in an inclusive way. Ideally, the factum provided judges the impetus for careful scrutiny of their own, perhaps unintentional, biases.[5]

ANTI-ESSENTIALISM

The demographic evidence made it increasingly difficult to imagine that any single definition of family could capture the diversity of relationships that regard each other as such, even if providing one might have comforted the Court. To me, the factum's educative function gave birth to its anti-essentialism. Being anti-essentialist in this context meant refusing to use an abstract and universal definition intended to capture the "essence" of family because it would be indefensibly reductive and exclude a wide variety of affiliations.

And yet, even armed with social science evidence, reaching the rather destabilizing conclusion that family has no core meaning was a struggle for some of us working on the factum in its early stages. It seemed, intuitively, that family had to be "fundamentally" about something. Some of us agonized over this problem, trying on, and then discarding, a series of possible definitions. At one point, it seemed that the only common denominator of all families was love, and a moving paragraph to this effect was written into the factum. Although it survived several overhauls and rewrites, the love paragraph was eventually criticized as idealistic, factually wrong, and, as with many other definitions of family, essentialist. At one meeting it was even referred to as "romantic drivel." In an ideal world, love might lie at the heart of all families, but in reality, many relationships endure for a variety of reasons that have nothing to do with love. Rather, they are sustained by the desire for companionship, the needs of children, a sense of obligation, or convenience, among other things. Still, relationships held together for these reasons, rather than love, are not less worthy of respect and recognition than those that fit the romantic model. The love paragraph was, in the end, deleted.

The process of letting the love paragraph go forced me to confront my own discomfort with the idea that family eluded an essence, and perhaps any attempt at definition, a discomfort that I suspected judges might feel more intensely. It seemed to follow logically from the anti-essentialist argument that the definition of family was arbitrary, even meaningless, and that any group of people could plausibly argue that they were one. The heart of the debate was whether there should be any minimal requirements that people must meet to "qualify" for the label family. To some extent, however, getting lost in the question of what "counts" as family in general was unnecessary to resolve the problem of providing employees bereavement leave in a manner that did not discriminate on the basis of family status.

Why, many of us wondered during the construction of the factum, use the category of "family" at all? Should I not receive paid leave to attend, say, Elvis Presley's funeral, I asked at one point, if his death means more to me than the death of someone whom others would regard as a member of my "family"? Would my unrequited regard for Elvis make him a member of my family? It may be true that people take leave more often to mourn the death of those others regard as closest to them, but was the determination of who "counted most," in this way, not very subjective? The example was not meant to be funny; it raised a serious issue and forced me, and others, to think through the factum's position. The idea that there are no limits on the definition of family would likely bother any judge, and might be raised by the bench in oral argument.

The factum's response to the "Elvis Presley problem" as the concern about limits came to be known, is that the definition of family need not be meaningless or arbitrary, but should be linked to the purpose of the legislation, or the benefit at issue. For example, the purpose of bereavement leave is to acknowledge that individual's need to mourn the loss of those close to them, or support others who must mourn. Limiting the class of relationships one is entitled to mourn without losing a day's pay to an employer-imposed definition of family might undermine this purpose. The crux of the argument is that a definition of family in the context of employment benefits ought not to be limited to those whom the state, or an employer recognizes as a family member but expanded to include people the employee cares about, respects, depends upon, or with whom he or she shares a special relationship. That relationship, in my view (although this was not stated in the factum), need not even be reciprocal to be considered close enough to merit this special status. Even in many traditional family relationships, the degree of closeness is not mutual. Two remedies would solve this problem: the employer could limit the number of days of bereavement leave for all employees, to be used at their discretion, avoiding entirely the need to define family. Or, if the employer were wed to the idea of bereavement leave only for a category of people known as "family members," the employer could permit employees to supply a list of those they regarded as family, honouring the subjectivity of the definition.

Although both of these solutions would work, in the sense of fulfilling the purpose of the benefit without imposing a limited definition of family on employees, it seemed that the Elvis Presley problem would not go away. This was because it raised two questions that often became intertwined: for what deaths should employees be permitted to take bereavement leave, and, if that leave is restricted to "immediate family" members, as in the case at bar, could any relationship qualify as "immediate family" just because someone makes that claim? The first question seemed easier to answer, but the second was more important because the intervenors were accepting Mossop's contention that he and the Poperts were a family, and arguing that he had suffered discrimination on the basis of family status. If Mossop and Popert's relationship were defensible as a "family," would the Court not expect the intervenors to say why, and to set limits on what relationships would qualify? Would this not lead to a comparison between their relationship and that of conventional heterosexual couples, in effect, the approach taken by the tribunal? In the end, the factum did not supply a single definition of family but it did insist that Mossop, Popert, and Popert, Sr, were a family because Mossop regarded them as such, and it did suggest that in the context of bereavement leave, the definition of immediate family should be subjectively determined.

Thus, the Elvis Presley problem had troublesome ripple effects. Having gone down a path from anti-essentialism to meaninglessness, and back again, it seemed potentially contradictory to argue that Mossop and Popert were a family, a claim which arguably presumes the coherence and stability of the category. It was as if we had destroyed the club to which we now demanded entry. But closer analysis revealed that these two aspects of the coalition's position were not inconsistent. The point of arguing against abstract universal definitions and in favour of context-based, purposive definitions is to recognize and include families that are excluded from legal and social recognition simply because they are seen to deviate from the established norm. The argument is not that "family" is meaningless, but that its meaning is subjective and shifting. The challenge was to achieve recognition of Mossop's family, but not at the cost of reinforcing an exclusionary definition.

Despite the absence of a "core" meaning, particular definitions of family might be defensible in terms of the purpose of legislation. The prohibition on family status discrimination might have a broader reach than benefits or burdens assigned on the basis of membership in a family. For example, as counsel for the intervenors argued, government entitlements intended for children might be available only to relationships involving children. Such legislation could justifiably prevent all self-regarding families, or singles without children, from claiming the entitlement, but it need not distinguish between families on the basis of the parents' sexual orientation. This approach would at least require the government to justify their definitions of family with reference to the purpose of any given benefit. An explicitly homophobic purpose would arguably violate section 15 of the *Charter*.

There are three common reactions to this position: first, that if the meaning of family is so unstable, laws will be inconsistent, and inconsistency leads to unpredictability, which is a bad thing; second, that extending the category of family to those not traditionally thought of as family might suggest that family includes even single people, which seems ludicrous at first glance; and third, that adopting a flexible definition of family may permit "selective opting-in," where people would pick and choose when they want to be considered family, in order to claim the benefits and avoid the burdens of such a status. In response to the first point, a historical analysis reveals that instability and inconsistency already plague legislation. More importantly, however, inconsistency is far preferable to an imposed definition of family that discriminates against some families in favour of others, providing it is justifiable in the light of the purpose of the legislation.

On the second point, it seems very plausible that family status protection could extend to singles in some case, if, for example, they were excluded from employment benefits, or access to housing arbitrarily, simply because of their non-married status. Again, a particular context might require a broader or narrower definition of what constitutes a family. The factum uses the *Charter* guarantee of freedom of religion as a useful analogy here. It seems clear that atheists should be protected by the *Charter* guarantee of freedom of religion, even though one might think of them as not having a religion, and as therefore outside the scope of the right. Discrimination against atheists because they do not partake of dominant religion can still interfere with their freedom from religion. Singles might be thought of, then, as the atheists of familial ideology.

Finally, concerns about abuse should be confronted directly by employers, and should apply to heterosexuals as well as to gay men and lesbians. There is no evidence to support the assertion that lesbians and gay men would take more advantage of flexible bereavement leave provisions than would heterosexuals, but safeguards could be put in place if they were deemed necessary (a position the coalition did not support). An employer concerned about abuse might have to police *everyone* who claims to be a family, a practice which, although raising privacy concerns, is at least non-discriminatory. Judges might also be reluctant to accord to non-traditional families what they see as benefits, without assigning them the perceived burdens associated with marriage. Although this differs from an employee who takes advantage of flexible definitions, it might be viewed by judges as another potential form of abuse. Precisely this reasoning, even though it is deeply flawed, has been employed to prevent the recognition of same-sex marriage.

There is, in fact, no reason to believe that people who form non-traditional families want all of the advantages and none of the disadvantages of legal recognition, nor is it entirely clear what counts, or ought to count, as an advantage. Fear that the disadvantages of being deemed a family by the state will outweigh the advantages, particularly for those with lower incomes, may be one reason why some gay men and lesbians do not want recognition as family. But for those who seek legal recognition, burdens may be as welcome as benefits. Still, the question of concomitant burdens is irrelevant to whether the denial of employment benefits in this case contravened human rights legislation. The issue is not discussed in the factum because, as Ms Brodsky put it, even having to raise it would impose on the appellants an unfair burden. Those who suffer discrimination should not be required to agree to "package deals" as a condition of obtaining their rights.

Although they were not explicit in the factum, counsel in oral argument addressed the problems associated with a functional definition of family, and rejected it as both discriminatory and administratively unworkable. This approach isolated common features of the traditional family (for example, a joint bank account, a shared residence, the public holding out of the relationship) and uses them as a checklist against which people claiming to be a family are measured. The coalition rejected, on the basis of this argument, the CHRC's proposed remedy of including same-sex couples within the definition of common law spouse because it would not solve the problem of imposing discriminatory criteria on only some relationships.

Some people, gay rights advocates among them, would argue that a functional approach makes sense because some indicators of "family" are, in fact, fairly common. A checklist of features might even appear to pose less of an administrative burden than a vague, shifting notion of family. Most importantly, a functional approach may be palatable as a compromise of sorts: it introduces some flexibility into the definition of family, without conceding the idea that family cannot be objectively determined. On a narrow interpretation of the functional approach, if a gay couple functions like a heterosexual couple, that is, if they do the things families are meant to do, and look the way families are meant to look (apart from being of the same gender, of course), they ought to be recognized as a family.

Although the hurdles established by a functional test could be cleared by some gay men and lesbians, it is problematic. Embracing such an approach strikes some as requiring that gays argue they are essentially "the same" as heterosexuals; it forces them to mimic heterosexual relationships and confines them to a narrow, unimaginative conception of family life. And even if this were not a serious concern, it remains true that the most common features of the traditional family, such as a shared residence or pooled finances, are by no means universal. The checklist test is often criticized for being both internally flawed and assimilationist: internally flawed, because even married heterosexuals do not consistently meet its standards and are nonetheless assumed to be families; assimilationist, because it forces families to look the same in order for them to receive benefits heterosexuals get just because they are heterosexual.

Although in theory a broader functionalist approach might be defensible (a more creative and flexible list might include love, intimacy, respect, and the provision of care, for example, along with shared assets, mutual dependency, cohabitation, a sexual relationship, children, and so forth), its application in practice is what worries most people. Even a broad test represents an administrative morass, since it would call for inquiries into the most intimate aspects of people's lives. How would the state or an employer test for the "intention to continue to be spouses," which is required even of common law couples under the definition of "immediate family" in the collective agreement? What amounts to a public "holding out" as spouses? Would gay couples have to prove, somehow, their sexual fidelity, or their love of each other? Would they need to pool their finances, and jointly own all property? If they had no assets, what would count as a commitment to partnership? Although some gay people would certainly benefit from the application of such a test, its effect would be to create a dichotomy between "good" gay people and "bad" gay people, the former being those who behave in ways that make their relationships recognizable to heterosexuals.

Many gay men and lesbians do not share a residence, use joint bank accounts, or hold themselves out to the public as a "couple" precisely because they risk being victimized on the basis of their sexual orientation and family status. And even though many heterosexual married couples do not conform to these criteria, they are nonetheless automatically recognized as family. The question is, why should a test be applied to homosexual couples, and not to heterosexual ones? The only explanation for such differential treatment is that heterosexual couples are viewed as the norm, and as more natural than gay and lesbian couples. Thus, families that have not been legally or socially recognized must "qualify" as families by achieving the heterosexual standard. Common law couples are still routinely subject to these kinds of discriminatory tests, such as the requirement that they hold themselves out as spouses and intend to remain together. People who regard themselves as a family are no less so simply because they arrange their relationship differently from the traditional norm. A checklist of features used to determine who is "in" and who is "out" of family normalizes the dominant conception of family, and reinforces the notion that difference is deviance. Resort to such a test leaves intact the hierarchy of heterosexual over same-sex relationships. It thus preserves the exclusionary function of family, albeit with slightly adjusted boundaries.

In other words, if the recognition of gay couples as families only reinforces the already idealized conception of family without challenging it, and if inclusion in the prohibited ground family status means looking, acting, and functioning like traditional families, many lesbians and gay men would undoubtedly forgo legal and social recognition. Not that such a view is universal. Some people would be perfectly content to submit to a functional test. They would claim to be just like heterosexuals in all relevant ways and argue for similar treatment. Counsel for the CHRC effectively adopted this position in his submissions to the Supreme Court of Canada, arguing that Mossop was entitled to bereavement leave because his relationship was *analogous* to that of a traditional family. Critics would call it an assimilationist argument.

This issue provokes vigorous disagreement within gay, lesbian, and heterosexual communities, which extends to the question of what acceptance as "family" would mean. While some argue that asking for legal and social recognition as "family" reinforces the norm of the traditional family, others say that the inclusion of gay men and lesbians within the concept would necessarily change that norm. In a related debate, many gay men and lesbians staunchly oppose the idea of same-sex marriage as a tribute to a sexist and homophobic institution. It should be resisted, even dismantled, but certainly not embraced, they say. Others argue that recognizing marriage between gay men or lesbians would revolutionize its meaning. Some gay men and lesbians reject any attempt at "inclusion" on the basis that their relationships *are* different from the norm, just as they are different from each other. Proponents of this view prefer not to be compared to heterosexuals, and do not want their relationships legalized and regulated.

The intervenors' factum rejects both sides of the "inclusion/exclusion" dichotomy, and argues that recognition as family need not amount to the acceptance of its traditional meaning. Exposing the harmful, exclusionary effect of popular mythology about the family, the coalition seems to be saying, is consistent with the notion that being recognized as family for the purpose of human rights protection is important to some gay men and lesbians. In fact, legal recognition can represent significant material, psychological, and symbolic benefits. And (although the factum does not make the point, for reasons stated earlier) even if legal recognition would eventually be accompanied by the imposition of some burdens on gay couples, such as support obligations, these would be welcomed by some individuals if the result yielded a reduction in social stigma and discrimination. Some activists think concerns about assimilation are inflated and misplaced. The important thing, they say, is to win the legal argument and get the benefit desired, not to insist on an anti-assimilationist position for its own sake. The factum, however, does not support this view. Instead, it claims inclusion and attempts to alter the category of family at the same time.

INTERACTIVE DISCRIMINATION

Another critical feature of the factum is its insistence on the multiplicity and inseparability of discrimination. The intervenors claimed two things that might seem contradictory in the light of the conventional way lawyers argue about discrimination: that Mossop was denied bereavement leave because he is gay, *and* that because his family was not recognized, he experienced the denial as discrimination on the basis of his family status. The Federal Court of Appeal held that the denial of bereavement leave constituted sexual orientation discrimination, and not family status discrimination. This technique of either/or characterization allowed the Federal Court to avoid dealing with the reality of how discrimination operates and is experienced, a reality which is infinitely more complex than its reflection in the tidy categories used to delineate different grounds of discrimination in human rights legislation. More specifically, it allowed the court to avoid considering family status entirely, as if, because Mossop is gay, non-recognition of his family ceases to be an issue.

Conveying to a court how different "kinds" of discrimination overlap and intersect is an enormous challenge. Jurisprudence and legal scholarship about discrimination have not, as a rule, been geared to determining how discrimination on the basis of race and sex, for example, work together. Equality analysis has paid scant attention to the ways in which discrimination may occur on multiple grounds. And yet, people often experience discrimination in precisely this way. They are denied a benefit or an opportunity because of their gender *and* their race, or their disability *and* their sexuality, or their race *and* their class. The effects of multiple discrimination are so entangled that they seem intransigent in the face of analytical attempts to separate them. Even if judges understand additive discrimination, that is, two different kinds of discrimination added together, they may not grasp the notion of interactive or overlapping discrimination, which is qualitatively different. For example, when women of colour are systematically excluded from certain job classifications, it may not be purely because they are women, or purely because they are not white, but due to the interaction of both. Similarly, when an openly gay man living with AIDS is denied housing, one might argue that it is because he is gay, or, alternatively, because of his disability, but in fact, it might be very difficult to separate the two.

This is not to say that discrimination can always be expressed in terms of two grounds. Some forms of discrimination on the basis of sexual orientation are unrelated to family status, or less related than others. For example, if an employee is refused a job because the employer assumes he is gay, and the employer dislikes gay men because he thinks them inadequately "male," the employee would have a difficult time establishing a claim that he suffered discrimination on the basis of his family status. Here, the discrimination arguably had nothing to do with the prospective employee's relationships, but stemmed from his perceived membership in the class "homosexual." Similarly, if an HIV-positive man is refused service in a restaurant because the owner knows or suspects he has the AIDS virus, it would be difficult to characterize the denial of service as family status discrimination, as opposed to discrimination on the basis of sexual orientation and/or disability.

But even if these examples are unconvincing, and one could imagine how every example of discrimination against gay men and lesbians could *potentially* involve both family status and sexual orientation discrimination, it would be at least a stretch to describe, say, physical assault, or a denial of health care of the basis of HIV-positivity, as discrimination on the basis of "family status." The strongest case for a "family status" argument arises where the benefit or opportunity sought hinges on membership in a family. Denying gay men and lesbians a benefit that flows to people *because* of their family relationships, a benefit triggered by a definition of family, such as bereavement leave, is the clearest instance of discrimination on both grounds.

Again, as with the Elvis Presley problem, the concern that recognizing interactive discrimination will cause uncertainty, or complicate legal decisions, is a concern about abuse. Acknowledging that interactive discrimination exists does not, realistically, raise the spectre of lawyers hopping arbitrarily from one combination of prohibited grounds to another, until they hit one that works. ("Well, my Lord, if it wasn't race and sex discrimination, then how about, um, religious and family status discrimination?") Courts are capable of distinguishing between fatuous and legitimate claims. Acknowledgment likely does mean, however, that judges will begin to understand the qualitative differences between people's experience of discrimination, enabling courts to recognize harms to which until now, they have been blind. And even if the concept of a continuum of grounds of discrimination (or better yet, a three-dimensional model) did create new possibilities for successful arguments based on interactive or coexisting kinds of discrimination, that is not necessarily a bad development. It could represent an important evolution in the judicial understanding of discrimination, one that should not be stunted by a "floodgates" paranoia.

The argument about interactive discrimination answers the Federal Court of Appeal's concern that Mossop and the intervenors were attempting to amend the *CHRA* "through the back door." The court was of the view that an inclusive interpretation of family status would effectively add sexual orientation to the statute. But this is simply not true. Family status protection would not provide a remedy for gay men and lesbians who face a wide variety of discriminatory practices, many of which are unrelated to their relationships. An interpretation of "family status" that acknowledges interactive discrimination would not necessarily provide a remedy to people who are physically assaulted, fired, and denied housing, among other things, simply because they are homosexual. Those interested in protecting gay men and lesbians from the entire spectrum of public and private abuses would still press the federal and provincial governments to amend human rights legislation to include sexual orientation as a prohibited ground. They would also continue to challenge the constitutionality of legislation and other state action that discriminates on the basis of sexual orientation, in violation of the *Charter's* equality guarantees.

The intervenors' factum admonishes judges not simply to characterize discrimination away, in an effort to avoid dealing with its felt effects. For example, if a jurisdiction were to prohibit discrimination on the ground of disability, but not sexual orientation, a court could find that the exclusion of a gay man with AIDS from housing constitutes discrimination on the basis of sexual orientation alone, which would not contravene the legislation. In *Mossop*, the easiest way out of the perplexing dilemma of defining family was to understand the discrimination as stemming solely from sexual orientation, as the Federal Court of Appeal did, since the *CHRA* does not prohibit discrimination on this ground. The simple fact is that it will always be open to courts to prefer the least problematic categorization available, without regard for how discrimination is experienced by those subjected to it.

Obviously, the categorization game, like all interpretive techniques, is highly manipulable. If sexual orientation were a prohibited ground in the *CHRA*, instead of family status, the attorney general arguing *Mossop* would undoubtedly have claimed that the definition of "immediate family" in the collective agreement discriminates on the basis of family status, not sexual orientation. One can be homosexual as much as one wants, he would argue, pointing to the fact that the employer makes no inquiry whatsoever into an employee's sexual practices under the terms of the collective agreement. He would assert that what matters is whether an employee's formal family arrangements conform to the definition in the collective agreement, not, technically, one's sexual preferences. Confronted with this argument, the intervenors would be forced to demonstrate how disingenuous this was, and how integral sexual orientation is to one's family arrangements, again highlighting the inseparability of sexual orientation and family status discrimination in this case. And so it goes. In this reverse situation, the characterization game still enables the Court to avoid addressing the injury done to Mossop.

POSTMODERN LEGAL ARGUMENT

This case points to the possibility of postmodernism as a strategic para- digm, even if it cannot be a specific agenda or a consistent methodol- ogy. Perhaps it is best understood in this context as a sensitivity to perspective and contingency, combined with a dislike for closure, topped off with a deep scepticism about the process of naturalization. I view the factum's anti-essentialism, its critical approach to the dominant conception of family, and its acknowledgment of interactive discrimination as postmodern because it challenges the notion that what is tradition is natural and therefore good, and advances the proposition that seemingly obvious meanings suppress others. The methodology of the factum is to argue from the margins (the experience of families who have no social or legal status), in a specific context (bereavement leave), without making overreaching, universal claims (anti-essentialism). Substantively, this translated into the argument that "family" means different things in different legislative contexts, and that legal defini- tions, which tend to presume static subjects and conditions, do not correspond to the realities in which people lead their lives. The best we can do in the light of the shifting models of family is to adopt a flexible approach to its definition.

Although characterization is an inevitable part of identifying the source and nature of discrimination, the intervenors' factum argued that, at a minimum, the characterization should be informed by the view of those affected by the exclusion or denial. By focusing on the effects of discrimination instead of the discriminatory intent of the perpetrator, both Canadian constitutional and human rights jurisprudence has already laid the basis for appreciating the interplay of different prohibited grounds. Rooting human rights analysis in the *impact* of the impugned behaviour may enable courts to acknowledge that discrimination can be both additive and interactive. Thus, rather than cancelling each other out, multiple grounds of discrimination reinforce each other.

I do not know whether anyone collaborating on the factum consciously tried to implement postmodern theory; certainly no one invoked it in discussion. It did lurk in the background for me, however, more as a set of related beliefs and a methodological stance than a coherent ideology. Postmodern art and architecture and poststructuralist philosophy and literary criticism expose the contingent status of dominant ideologies and suggest, implicitly, that resistance to them is possible. One critical insight is that dominant representations of reality emerge from a closed, self-referential system in which meaning is relative. For example, "deviance" has meaning only in the context of its opposite, "normality." Words and concepts have meaning, then only *in relation* to each other. In my view, this factum explores the implications of poststructuralist thought by explaining how the relationship between normality and deviance (family and not family) is hierarchical, and socially constructed.

It also challenges the rationality and integrity of legal categories and the objectivity of legal reasoning. I understand its central points as challenges to traditional legal arguments and as an attempt to stretch the limits of the form of argument itself: family cannot be defined as if it had a stable meaning, the way courts are inclined to define concepts; discrimination is not unidimensional, the way courts have historically understood it; and merely amending the definition of common law spouse is insufficient as a remedy because it leaves intact a standard to which all "deviant" families must be measured. These arguments were a critique of the Court's *approach* to problems of interpretation, as much as they were about obtaining a particular outcome. In the course of explaining how the Court of Appeal erred, the factum contests its representation of social reality and challenges the integrity of the distinctions upon which its decision relied, such as "family/not family" or "real/imitation." For example, who is family and who is not is a product of legal among other, discourses; it is not a product of nature. And what makes a family real, as opposed to an imitation, depends on what we have historically privileged as natural. This line of argument ultimately contests the very notion of the "real."

It may be possible, however, to practise litigation in a postmodern manner. After all, the coalition's submissions were packaged in familiar legal discourse, filed in a factum written according to the rules of civil procedure, and then put to the Court in oral argument which, no matter how creative and persuasive, was confined by the customs and conventions of practice, both formal and informal. One might think that regardless of the technical quality of the product and the deftness of counsel's advocacy, this deference to authority, both in substance (the pursuit of a legal remedy) and form (using the terms of legal discourse), is hardly postmodern, or that, at best, it is what one legal scholar has dubbed "postmodernism-lite." The notion of persuading a higher authority by using legal argument itself depends upon a belief in the possibility of rationality, and reinforces a hierarchical process of decision-making that ultimately establishes truths. At a minimum, however, postmodernism's central tenets, to the extent that they can be discerned at all, can provide a theoretical framework from which progressive lawyers can challenge conventional meanings, interrogate the production of "normality," and give voice to suppressed accounts of experience. Perhaps because I do not fully embrace the "version" of postmodernism that would make rationality and agency impossible, I believe in the possibility of a partial and self-conscious, if instrumental, "use" of its insights. Rather than absolute moral relativism, which is one potential product of postmodernism's hypercritical approach to settled meanings, I prefer continuous self-reflective criticism applied to goals that are always subject to revision.

CRITIQUES FROM THE RIGHT

The Perceived Assault on the Family

In both the United States and Canada, it is a time of antifeminist backlash, rising hate crimes against sexual minorities, outrageous scapegoating against the least powerful in society, and surging support for reactionary politicians. In this climate, unconventional families, and gay men and lesbians in particular, are seen as threats to an already unstable way of life. It is, to say the least, an especially bad time to be mounting what is perceived as an "attack" on the family. The intervenors' factum could undoubtedly be seen as part of an antifamily campaign.

In the last American presidential campaign "family values" became a critical battleground. Preserving traditional families was the rallying cry for the conservative right, which depicted the "liberal" left as sympathetic to deviant and immoral "life style" choices. America was in cultural crisis, and the conservative right's agenda could save the country. All of this rhetoric translated into furious "gay bashing" and self-righteous criticism of single mothers by the Republican Party, both at its National Convention in August 1992 and throughout the campaign for George Bush's reelection. The Republican's unmistakable message was that single mothers (implicitly – although erroneously – understood to be overwhelmingly African-American), and gay men and lesbians, were the enemies of the American family. Even though this performance was generally considered a failure by observers and apparently alienated many voters, that it dominated the convention at all was shocking.

As a Canadian in the United States, I was exceedingly contemptuous watching the discourse erupt into a national debate about who "really" was a family and whether only traditional ones were worthy of respect. When I returned to Canada and began working on the intervenors' factum, this kind of rhetoric had not taken centre stage on the Canadian political scene and I could not imagine that it would. In the last two years, however, the family caucus of the Conservative Party has sounded increasingly like the Republican right, going as far as proposing to entrench the "importance of family" in a preamble to the Constitution, and attempting to amend federal laws to include an "official definition of the family, specifying that the couple must be male and female."[6] Ironically, a chilling story about the caucus's accomplishments and ambitions appeared on the front page of the Toronto *Globe and Mail* the very day the *Mossop* appeal was heard by the Supreme Court.

Whether the intervenors' argument in *Mossop* is "pro-family" or "antifamily" depends entirely upon how family is defined. The factum is clearly pro-family on its own terms. And attaching labels like this only avoids the central questions: what *is* a family anyway? The argument that Mossop and Popert are a family in the context of an employment benefits scheme can be characterized, as argued earlier, as a claim for inclusion, which is meant to expand, and not destroy, the concept of family. If the factum is anti-family, it is only anti this narrow, exclusive, rigidly heterosexual, and purely procreative family. The notion that groups like the coalition are trying to "destroy" conventional families is at best the product of paranoia and at worst intentional hate-mongering. It is simply not credible to claim that legal recognition of unconventional families will lead to the breakup of traditional ones, even though this reasoning is usually implicit in arguments against homosexual marriage or progressive notions of family. The right's attempt to blame all the problems of our troubled times (a failing economy, drugs, sexual abuse, racial conflict) on, for example, the breakdown of the traditional family, the feminist agenda, and sexual "deviance," instead of on ill-conceived policies, a culture of greed and violence, or a lack of political will, is just shameless scapegoating. What is really threatened here, and the reason the right is so defensive, is an ideology of superiority.

CRITIQUES FROM THE LEFT

The Radical Critique

The factum might be criticized from the left for not being radical enough. According to this view, the coalition should have approached this project as an opportunity to oppose more strenuously the idea that family status is relevant to employment or other benefits. The heart of the radical critique is a scepticism about any appeal to family, given its oppressive ideological function. Neither the state nor employers should have the power to define family, and legislation should not distinguish between "family" and "not family" for the purpose of allocating benefits and burdens. The construct itself, in other words, is the problem. Proponents of this view would, I imagine, support the allotment of a fixed number of days of bereavement leave for each employee to use at their discretion.

As noted above, the coalition did suggest this remedy to the court. Still, the factum does not argue that the concept of family should be abandoned; in fact, in oral argument, counsel took pains to make clear that its meaning should be assessed in the light of its context, the legislative purpose. The coalition may simply have not been prepared to argue that the conception of family is inherently destructive and should be abandoned for all purposes. For my part, I believed that some of the things "family" *might* connote are good things, such as intimacy, emotional support, mutual dependence, and shared responsibility. Perhaps the state has a place encouraging these aspects of relationship under the term family, as long as it does so in a non-discriminatory way. This is essentially an argument that the category can be rehabilitated. Another concern might be that abandoning family as an organizational category and adopting a radically individualistic approach to benefits is unrealistic, because it ignores the fact that people do live constantly in relationships, and that they have responsibilities as a result.

One could also argue that the prospect of entirely eliminating the concept of family from legal and social discourse seems very remote, and that an attempt to do so in the factum might be perceived as extreme. Perhaps more significantly, even if it could be achieved, the elimination of state regulation of the family might lead to its reprivatization, a daunting prospect to the women and children who are often abused within it. Finally, as long as legal and social significance attach to "family status," and benefits or protections flow to those entitled to the label, it will be necessary, even if only from a defensive stance, to engage in the debate about what the term means. Disengaging from the struggle to define family will lead not to the abandonment of the category; instead the concept will be used by those with the power of definition to impose their categorizations on others, and further marginalize disadvantaged individuals and groups.

Finally, some critics might think that the intervenors should have focused more sharply on the connection between homophobia and the domination of women by men. The factum could have explained how a restrictive definition of family is central to the efficient policing of gender boundaries, which define women as different from and "less than" men. To some extent, the factum did this by pointing out how the idealization of the "traditional" family masks its problems. The intervenors argued, for example, that for many women and children the family is a site of gender role stereotyping, inequality, domination, physical and emotional violence, and incest. But in the end, the link between homophobia and misogyny did take a back seat to the more primary argument that the denial of bereavement leave was indeed family status discrimination. This prioritization made sense given the facts of the case; Mossop is, after all, a gay man.

THE LIBERAL CRITIQUE

Perhaps predictably, the factum is vulnerable to a number of very potent critiques from the left, including the anti-assimilation argument described earlier. Significantly, however, the factum explicitly rejects a "similarly-situated" approach to family status precisely to avoid a comparative paradigm that would reinforce the superiority of the traditional family. It is very different to argue that people who conform to an imposed norm should be entitled to the same rights as the dominant group, than it is to throw the notion of "sameness" into question, which is what we did in this case. The factum's anti-essentialism does not fit easily with liberal legalism, and had the Court adopted the intervenors' argument, it would have marked an important step away from it.

Among those who would refer to the intervenors' position as consistent with liberal pluralism – and mean it disparagingly – another concern would be that the factum appears agnostic about the relative value of different family arrangements. If all families are equal, these critics say, on what basis could one condemn abusive families and applaud loving ones? Indeed, the factum does support diversity in and among families and declines to prefer, say, a family of heterosexual people to a family of gay people, or a family without children to one with children. But this in no way advocates tolerance of family members that abuse and neglect others. Child abuse and spousal assault are unacceptable regardless of a family's composition or the sexuality of its members, and should be penalized on that basis.

Other critics, who may or may not overlap with those concerned about assimilation, might reject the notion that human rights litigation has anything substantive to offer members of marginalized groups. They are sceptical about the possibility of deconstructing or subverting traditional meanings within the conceptual framework and discourse of rights. Material gains, they would argue, rarely flow from legal decisions. Most attempts to secure rights for marginalized individuals and groups fail, and participating in conventional litigation only reinforces the legitimacy of judges and the authority of the liberal-legal state.

I must confess my deep sympathy with many of these views. And yet, although I realize that even progressive interpretations of the *Charter* and human rights codes are not the answer to all of our social ills, I am not persuaded that test case litigation is necessarily self-defeating.[7] The symbolic power of law is potentially too enormous, and its influence on culture too profound, to abandon it as a site of dialogue, confrontation, and resistance. It makes for both good law and policy that legal decisions be informed by the reality of the social life they regulate. I simply disagree with conventional leftist wisdom about the impossibility of achieving significant social change through, among other things, rights arguments because I see them, from a historical perspective, as an indispensable part of the political strategies of social movements. I also believe that it is important to challenge established meanings within legal discourse, because representations of reality are created and fixed in the form of judicial decisions and are then absorbed into the fabric of society, with broad and unpredictable effects. Finally, I am one of those who places value on the secondary or "ripple" effects of litigation: it can create opportunities for coalition work both within and around lawsuits, and provide marginalized individuals and groups with a sense of entitlement and legitimacy that fuels their political engagement. Even adverse decisions may ultimately contribute to social change by mobilizing previously quiescent constituencies.

In addition, at least *some* material gains can result from legal decisions; gay men and lesbians stood to gain employment benefits from which they were excluded, had Mossop won his case. Granted, this may not be their most significant problem, and some people fear that the price to be paid in terms of assimilation is too onerous, but formal recognition of an entitlement can still be an important victory and change people's lives. The fact that the issue was litigated could provide the impetus for hesitant private and public employers to independently extend benefits to lesbians and gay men. The case also arguably added to the pressure on the federal government to amend the *CHRA,* and it forced an important discussion onto the public agenda by attracting media coverage. Ultimately, of course, the willingness to engage in test case litigation, and to make rights claims in particular, depends on one's personal beliefs about the scope and value of their impact, but it is a false argument to suggest that they must be embraced *in place of* some other strategy. In reality, test case litigation coexists with a number of equally problematic and potentially helpful alternatives.

To be sure, there are different arenas in which to pursue one's vision of social change, including the legal, the political, and the personal. The categories are not, however, very neatly divisible, and the power of legal discourse is ignored at our peril. In other words, were it up to me, I would rather advance the argument articulated in the intervenors' factum, discuss its risks, and admit its shortcomings, than wait for the Court to interpret the meaning of "family status" based on arguments from the CHRC and the Salvation Army. I have not decided yet whether my attitude towards legal strategies is best described as defensive cynicism, quasi-liberal optimism, or postmodern pragmatism, but it is driven by a deep scepticism about the possibility that other forums are somehow more compatible to these arguments than is law.

CONCLUSION

All of these critiques are sound to some extent and should be taken seriously. I honestly believe that most people involved in the litigation on the coalition's behalf struggled daily with just such issues. Among other things, the critiques bring into focus the premium placed by some activists and lawyers on ideology when writing a factum and pursuing legal remedies. For my part, the self-imposed need to be ideologically consistent created an enormous pressure that was not always productive. I am learning that ideological purity for its own sake may be debilitating, even if it is partly what leads people to test case litigation or political activism in the first place. It can blind advocates to strategic compromises or different forms of expression, to the possibility of achieving less than complete victories, and to making improvements on the margins and in the interstices of the existing legal regime. Whether or not it is important to insist on an ideological point, or simply to do whatever it takes to win the case, will depend on what the clients and lawyers see as their goals. Views on this may vary with the characteristics of the litigants, the lawyers, and the perceived audience. Some people are interested in short-term tangible results, and others value ideological or symbolic victories which, although not always mutually exclusive, can conflict at times. For example, if the goal is to secure employment benefits at any cost, then an "assimilationist" argument will be acceptable. It might be important to speak the familiar language of the court, to use contentional legal strategies, even if they are not ideologically consistent with the clients' or the lawyers' perspectives. By contrast, if the point is to give voice to an excluded perspective, and to give the clients a sense of having asserted their "rights," then risking a novel argument might make sense. Intervenors arguably have more latitude for both creativity and ideology.

A willingness to question the role of ideology in the context of the progressive use of litigation makes one vulnerable to aggressive (and sometimes dismissive) critiques of one's commitment to the issues at stake. One might be accused of being a minimalist, a sellout, lacking in backbone, ad hoc in approach, and empty of vision. But at least considering the possible conflicts between ideology and tactics forces public interest lawyers and their clients to ask important questions about strategy. What are the interests at stake? What are the responsibilities of advocates to the class of people ostensibly represented by the clients, but which is larger and more diverse than they are? Is the purpose of the factum to confront the court with a different picture of reality, or secure the remedy sought? These are not new questions. *Charter* litigation often involves controversial social issues and the factums usually reflect a balancing of strategic and ideological choices. But the nature of the balance is a product of the people who do the work and it cannot possibly speak to the concerns of every interested party. The only certainty that emerges from such work is the impossibility of pleasing all of the people any of the time.

I doubt that anyone involved in producing the intervenors' factum believed that a single legal decision, even from the Supreme Court, would change social attitudes and lead to the acceptance of non-conforming families. Perhaps an inclusive interpretation of family would ultimately backfire by reinforcing the dominance of the traditional model, resulting in increased "tolerance" for "alternative" families that are in some ways like "real" families. It might in time, applied more generally and beyond the employment context in which counsel sought to confine this case, deprive gay men and lesbians of an important form of dissent from the category of family, as even those who would rather not be regarded as family find family status imposed upon them, like common law spouses. This could happen, notwithstanding the intervenors' argument that what weighs most in the determination of family, at least in the context of employment benefits, are the subjective views of the parties. Perhaps, for example, same-sex couples would be the first to lose entitlements under welfare legislation on the reasoning that they are family, and obligated to support each other. The long-term, although unintended, result could be increased state intervention into the lives of gay men and lesbians, with no concomitant amelioration of their inferior social status. The intervenors' factum alone would neither cause nor prevent this, but the negative possibilities of the litigation's ultimate impact gave me, personally, pause.

The discussion about what constitutes a family and whether marginalized groups should claim inclusion has only just begun. Even if there were consensus in the gay and lesbian communities, or the larger progressive community, on whether gay men and lesbians should or should not argue that they "are" families (which is highly unlikely in the near future), doubts about the strategic utility of test case litigation would still exist. The attempt to argue for inclusion in an institution like the family, while simultaneously deconstructing it, is an unquestionably high-risk position. People may misunderstand the coalition's position as a purely liberal claim for equality and tolerance on the basis of sameness, while ignoring the deconstructive aspect, or may purposely simplify it, for political reasons, as dangerously threatening to "real" families. Resorting to litigation will always be criticized by some as a doomed attempt to change the system from within.

Resisting the temptation to take an inflexible position on what can be subversive or challenging to existing notions of naturalness, rationality, objectivity, and hierarchy is a very postmodern and, to my mind, very advisable view. Thus, although I would be the first to stress the importance of carefully gauging the effects of any strategy, they will always be, at best, contingent. It is very possible that legal recognition for unconventional families under the category "family status" in human rights legislation will be simultaneously (or alternately or occasionally) liberating and assimilationist, depending on the context, the audience, and the issues at stake. There is no reliable way to test the "ultimate" meaning of the inclusion/deconstruction strategy employed by the coalition, and the notion of it having any single meaning seems hopelessly naive. Before the Supreme Court's decision was rendered, I had no idea whether the arguments about interactive discrimination and anti-essentialism would be misinterpreted, partly adopted, or completely ignored by the Court. I always understood that the result in *Mossop* might lead us towards more acceptance of unconventional families, or might prompt a backlash against them, and specifically against gay men and lesbians. But to me such uncertainty is a reason to engage in legal argument and not abandon it ...

NOTES

1 Same-sex couples are excluded from the definition of spouse in all provincial and federal legislation and are therefore deprived of the benefits and entitlements that flow to people on the basis of spousal status. Challenges to this exclusion have systematically failed.
2 These were the Salvation Army, Focus on the Family Association of Canada, REAL Women, and the Pentecostal Assemblies of Canada.
3 Postmodernism is difficult to define, but it refers generally to a movement/critique/methodology/ideology that spans art, architecture, dance, history, literary criticism, philosophy, and a variety of other fields. Although it has different inflections in every discipline, postmodernism

represents a critique of modernist rationalism, rejects the notion of objectivity and neutrality, insists that meaning is a product of perspective, stipulates that universalism and "meta-narratives" suppress different accounts of reality and truth, and understands subjectivity to be socially and discursively produced and reproduced. Needless to say, such tenets (shamelessly reduced here to mere slogans) pose a direct challenge to traditional understandings of rationality, truth, subjectivity, and universality. See Jacques Derrida "Structure, Sign and Play in the Discourse of Human Sciences" in *Writing and Difference* (1967; trans. 1978). Derrida is religiously cited as the pre-eminent poststructuralist philosopher and the father of deconstruction, a methodology that reveals how meaning is deferred and relative, and that inverts the dichotomies on which any intelligible reading of a text depends. Derrida's own style upsets the presumption of a stable interpretive context to which a reader can appeal for a determination of reason. The reader's desire for rationality, or for "closure," according to Derrida, represses other notions of rationality and privileges some meanings over others.

4   A good example is the aftermath of the United States Supreme Court's decision in *Bowers v Hardwick* 478 US 186 (1986) upholding a Georgia sodomy statute on the basis that sexual behaviour between two gay men in the privacy of their home is not constitutionally protected by the due process clause of the Fourteenth Amendment. This case provided a justificatory backdrop for other laws or policies that penalize gay men and lesbians. It has arguably exacerbated the difficulty of convincing the American military to repeal its ban on gay men and lesbians, and dimmed the prospects of persuading courts that homosexuality ought to be a suspect class for the purpose of equal protection analysis. The argument against including sexual orientation in anti-discrimination legislation is strengthened when gay sexual behaviour is criminal (22 states retain sodomy statutes). If the Court finds in *Mossop* that gay men and lesbians are not included in the term "family status" it could be interpreted very broadly, by traditionalists and reactionaries, to mean that gay men and lesbians are less worthy as human beings.

5   The factum also uses the term "sexual identity" along with "sexual orientation," which undermines the idea that sexuality is biologically fixed (and that whether it is fixed or not should be irrelevant to human rights protection).

6   *Globe and Mail* June 3 1992. With respect to the definition in federal laws, Don Blenkarn, MP for Mississauga South, said, "It should define a family as a male and a female, living together to raise children. And that's the

only kind of family that ought to be defined." Ibid. This caucus, dating
back, according to the article, to 1989, is credited with eliminating tax
benefits from common law couples, scrapping a long-term Conservative
commitment to a national day-care program, and introducing a targeted
system of child benefits, measures which the caucus sees as encouraging
women to stay home with children. The family caucus also ran a campaign against amending the *CHRA* to prohibit discrimination against gay
men and lesbians. Blenkarn stated in an interview, "You don't give
privileges to homosexuals if they derogate from the family." Ibid.

7   I have been called both naive and hopelessly liberal when I espouse this
point of view, but I think people who respond dismissively are not listen-
ing carefully to my understanding of useful or worthwhile litigation.
They often, for their part, display an amazingly single-minded confidence in electoral politics, or in education, which I do not share. The difference is that I see *all* of these discourses as sources of domination and
possible sources of liberation. I think they are related, and I believe it is a
mistake to concede the territory of any one of them without a struggle.

READING QUESTION ON FREEMAN

1   Reflect back on the readings by MacKinnon, Minow, and Williams. How does Freeman's post-modernism fit with their views
about law?

Vriend v Alberta [1998] 1 SCR 493

Vriend was dismissed from his job in a private religious school on the basis
of his sexual orientation. The *Charter of Rights and Freedoms* only limits state
action, so he could not bring a case against his employers under the *Charter*.
He sought to bring a complaint under Alberta's *Individual Rights Protections
Act*, but the Alberta Human Rights Commission (a government body)
refused to hear his complaint because sexual orientation was not among the
enumerated grounds of discrimination it was charged with prohibiting.
Vriend argued that failure to include sexual orientation among the prohibited grounds of discrimination was a violation of his equality rights under
the *Charter*.

Cory, J: – The *Individual's Rights Protection Act*, RSA 1980, c I-2 ("*IRPA*" or the "Act"), prohibits discrimination in a number of areas of public life, and establishes the Human Rights Commission to deal with complaints of discrimination. In 1990, the Act included the following list of prohibited grounds of discrimination: race, religious beliefs, colour, gender, physical disability, mental disability, age, ancestry and place of origin. At the present time it also includes marital status, source of income and family status.

Despite repeated calls for its inclusion sexual orientation has never been included in the list of those groups protected from discrimination ... The reasons given for declining to take this action include the assertions that sexual orientation is a "marginal" ground; that human rights legislation is powerless to change public attitudes; and that there have only been a few cases of sexual orientation discrimination in employment brought to the attention of the Minister. In 1992, the Human Rights Commission decided to investigate complaints of discrimination on the basis of sexual orientation. This decision was immediately vetoed by the Government and the Minister directed the Commission not to investigate the complaints.

B Vriend's Dismissal From King's College and Complaint to the Alberta Human Rights Commission

In December 1987 the appellant Delwin Vriend was employed as a laboratory coordinator by King's College in Edmonton, Alberta. He was given a permanent, full-time position in 1988. Throughout his term of employment he received positive evaluations, salary increases and promotions for his work performance. On February 20, 1990, in response to an inquiry by the President of the College, Vriend disclosed that he was homosexual. In early January 1991, the Board of Governors of the College adopted a position statement on homosexuality, and shortly thereafter, the President of the College requested Vriend's resignation. He declined to resign, and on January 28, 1991, Vriend's employment was terminated by the College. The sole reason given for his termination was his non-compliance with the policy of the College on homosexual practice. Vriend appealed the termination and applied for reinstatement, but was refused.

On June 11, 1991, Vriend attempted to file a complaint with the Alberta Human Rights Commission on the grounds that his employer discriminated against him because of his sexual orientation. On July 10, 1991, the Commission advised Vriend that he could not make a complaint under the *IRPA*, because the Act did not include sexual orientation as a protected ground.

II RELEVANT STATUTORY PROVISIONS

Since the time the appellant made his claim in 1992, the relevant statute was amended (*Individual's Rights Protection Amendment Act, 1996*, S.A. 1996, c. 25). The Act is now known as the *Human Rights, Citizenship and Multiculturalism Act*. In these reasons, however, we refer to the statute, as amended, as the *Individual's Rights Protection Act* or *IRPA*, since that is how the legislation was most often referred to by the parties on this appeal. For the sake of convenience, the provisions are set out below first as they existed at the time the action commenced, and then as they currently stand.

Individual's Rights Protection Act, RSA 1980, c I-2, am. SA 1985, c 33, SA 1990, c 23

Preamble

Whereas recognition of the inherent dignity and the equal and inalienable rights of all persons is the foundation of freedom, justice and peace in the world; and
Whereas it is recognized in Alberta as a fundamental principle and as a matter of public policy that all persons are equal in dignity and rights without regard to race, religious beliefs, colour, gender, physical disability, mental disability, age, ancestry or place of origin; and
Whereas it is fitting that this principle be affirmed by the Legislature of Alberta in an enactment whereby those rights of the individual may be protected ...

7(1) No employer or person acting on behalf of an employer shall
(a) refuse to employ or refuse to continue to employ any person, or
(b) discriminate against any person with regard to employment or any term or condition of employment, because of the race, religious beliefs, colour, gender, physical disability, mental disability, marital status, age, ancestry or place of origin of that person or of any other person.
(2) Subsection (1) as it relates to age and marital status does not affect the operation of any bona fide retirement or pension plan or the terms or conditions of any bona fide group or employee insurance plan.
(3) Subsection (1) does not apply with respect to a refusal, limitation, specification or preference based on a bona fide occupational requirement.

8(1) No person shall use or circulate any form of application for employment or publish any advertisement in connection with employment or prospective employment or make any written or oral inquiry of an applicant
(a) that expresses either directly or indirectly any limitation, specification or preference indicating discrimination on the basis of the race, religious beliefs, colour, gender, physical disability, mental disability, marital status, age, ancestry or place of origin of any person, or
(b) that requires an applicant to furnish any information concerning race, religious beliefs, colour, gender, physical disability, mental disability, marital status, age, ancestry or place of origin.
(2) Subsection (1) does not apply with respect to a refusal, limitation, specification or preference based on a bona fide occupational requirement ...

Canadian Charter of Rights and Freedoms

1. The *Canadian Charter of Rights and Freedoms* guarantees the rights and freedoms set out in it subject only to such reasonable limits prescribed by law as can be demonstrably justified in a free and democratic society.

15. (1) Every individual is equal before and under the law and has the right to the equal protection and equal benefit of the law without discrimination and, in particular, without discrimination based on race, national or ethnic origin, colour, religion, sex, age or mental or physical disability.

24. (1) Anyone whose rights or freedoms, as guaranteed by this Charter, have been infringed or denied may apply to a court of competent jurisdiction to obtain such remedy as the court considers appropriate and just in the circumstances.

32. (1) This Charter applies
(a) to the Parliament and government of Canada in respect of all matters within the authority of Parliament including all matters relating to the Yukon Territory and Northwest Territories; and
(b) to the legislature and government of each province in respect of all matters within the authority of the legislature of each province.

Constitution Act, 1982

52.(1) The Constitution of Canada is the supreme law of Canada, and any law that is inconsistent with the provisions of the Constitution is, to the extent of the inconsistency, of no force or effect.

III DECISIONS BELOW

A Alberta Court of Queen's Bench (1994), 152 A.R. 1

The appellants applied to Russell, J, as she then was, for an order (1) declaring that ss. 2(1), 3, 4 and 7(1) of the *IRPA* are inconsistent with s. 15(1) of the *Charter* and infringe the appellants' rights, as a result of the absence of sexual orientation from the list of proscribed grounds of discrimination; (2) that Vriend has the right to file a complaint under the *IRPA* alleging discrimination on the grounds of sexual orientation; and (3) that lesbians and gays have the right to the protections of the *IRPA*.

Russell, J noted also that discrimination does not depend on a finding of invidious intent ...

B Alberta Court of Appeal (1996), 181 A.R. 16

McClung, JA held that the first question to be resolved was whether the *IRPA* is "answerable, as it stands" to the *Charter* (at p. 22). He was of the opinion that the omission of "sexual orientation" from the discrimination provisions of the *IRPA* does not amount to governmental action for the purpose of s. 32(1) of the *Charter*.

IV ISSUES

The constitutional questions which have been stated by this Court are:

1 Do (a) decisions not to include sexual orientation or (b) the non-inclusion of sexual orientation, as a prohibited ground of discrimination in the preamble and ss. 2(1), 3, 4, 7(1), 8(1), 10 and 16(1) of the *Individual's Rights Protection Act*, R.S.A. 1980, c. I-2, as am., now called the *Human Rights, Citizenship and Multiculturalism Act*, R.S.A. 1980, c. H-11.7, infringe or deny the rights guaranteed by s. 15(1) of the *Canadian Charter of Rights and Freedoms*?
2 If the answer to Question 1 is "yes," is the infringement or denial demonstrably justified as a reasonable limit pursuant to s. 1 of the *Canadian Charter of Rights and Freedoms*?

The parties have also raised issues with respect to standing, the application of the *Charter* and the appropriate remedy.

V ANALYSIS

1 Application of the Charter to a Legislative Omission

Does s. 32 of the *Charter* prohibit consideration of a s. 15 violation when that issue arises from a legislative omission? ...

Confusion results when arguments concerning the respective roles of the legislature and the judiciary are introduced into the s. 32 analysis. These arguments put forward the position that courts must defer to a decision of the legislature not to enact a particular provision, and that the scope of *Charter* review should be restricted so that such decisions will be unchallenged. I cannot accept this position. Apart from the very problematic distinction it draws between legislative action and inaction, this argument seeks to substantially alter the nature of considerations of legislative deference in *Charter* analysis. The deference very properly due to the choices made by the legislature will be taken into account in deciding whether a limit is justified under s. 1 and again in determining the appropriate remedy for a *Charter* breach. My colleague Iacobucci, J deals with these considerations at greater length more fully in his reasons.

The notion of judicial deference to legislative choices should not, however, be used to completely immunize certain kinds of legislative decisions from *Charter* scrutiny. McClung, JA in the Alberta Court of Appeal criticized the application of the *Charter* to a legislative omission as an encroachment by the courts on legislative autonomy. He objected to what he saw as judges dictating provincial legislation under the pretext of constitutional scrutiny. In his view, a choice by the legislature not to legislate with respect to a particular matter within its jurisdiction, especially a controversial one, should not be open to review by the judiciary: "When they choose silence provincial legislatures need not march to the *Charter* drum. In a constitutional sense they need not march at all ... The *Canadian Charter of Rights and Freedoms* was not adopted by the provinces to promote the federal extraction of subsidiary legislation from them but only to police it once it is proclaimed – if it is proclaimed" (pp. 25 and 28).

There are several answers to this position. The first is that in this case, the constitutional challenge concerns the *IRPA*, legislation that has been proclaimed.

It is suggested that this appeal represents a contest between the power of the democratically elected legislatures to pass the laws they see fit, and the power of the courts to disallow those laws, or to dictate that certain matters be included in those laws. To put the issue in this way is misleading and erroneous. Quite simply, it is not the courts which limit the legislatures. Rather, it is the Constitution, which must be interpreted by the courts, that limits the legislatures. This is necessarily true of all constitutional democracies. Citizens must have the right to challenge laws which they consider to be beyond the powers of the legislatures. When such a challenge is properly made, the courts must, pursuant to their constitutional duty, rule on the challenge ...

The respondents contend that a deliberate choice not to legislate should not be considered government action and thus does not attract *Charter* scrutiny. This submission should not be accepted ...

The relevant subsection, s. 32(1)(b), states that the *Charter* applies to "the legislature and government of each province in respect of all matters within the authority of the legislature of each province." There is nothing in that wording to suggest that a *positive act* encroaching on rights is required; rather the subsection speaks only of *matters within the authority of the legislature* ... The *IRPA* is being challenged as unconstitutional because of its failure to protect *Charter* rights, that is to say its underinclusiveness. The mere fact that the challenged aspect of the Act is its underinclusiveness should not necessarily render the *Charter* inapplicable. If an omission were not subject to the *Charter*, underinclusive legislation which was worded in such a way as to simply omit one class rather than to explicitly exclude it would be immune from *Charter* challenge. If this position was accepted, the form, rather than the substance, of the legislation would determine whether it was open to challenge. This result would be illogical and more importantly unfair ...

It might also be possible to say in this case that the deliberate decision to omit sexual orientation from the provisions of the *IRPA* is an "act" of the Legislature to which the *Charter* should apply.

2 *Application of the Charter to Private Activity*

The respondents further argue that the effect of applying the *Charter* to the *IRPA* would be to regulate private activity ... The respondents' submission has failed to distinguish between "private activity" and "laws that regulate private activity." The former is not subject to the *Charter*, while the latter obviously is. It is the latter which is at issue in this appeal.

C Section 15(1)

1. Approach to Section 15(1). The rights enshrined in s. 15(1) of the *Charter* are fundamental to Canada. They reflect the fondest dreams, the highest hopes and finest aspirations of Canadian society. When universal suffrage was granted it recognized to some extent the importance of the individual. Canada by the broad scope and fundamental fairness of the provisions of s. 15(1) has taken a further step in the recognition of the fundamental importance and the innate dignity of the individual. That it has done so is not only praiseworthy but essential to achieving the magnificent goal of equal dignity for all. It is the means of giving Canadians a sense of pride. In order to achieve equality the intrinsic worthiness and importance of every individual must be recognized regardless of the age, sex, colour, origins, or other characteristics of the person. This in turn should lead to a sense of dignity and worthiness for every Canadian and the greatest possible pride and appreciation in being a part of a great nation ...Yet, if any enumerated or analogous group is denied the equality provided by s. 15 then the equality of every other minority group is threatened. That equality is guaranteed by our constitution. If equality rights for minorities had been recognized, the all too frequent tragedies of history might have been avoided. It can never be forgotten that discrimination is the antithesis of equality and that it is the recognition of equality which will foster the dignity of every individual.

How then should the analysis of s. 15 proceed? ... The essential requirements of all these cases will be satisfied by enquiring first, whether there is a distinction which results in the denial of equality before or under the law, or of equal protection or benefit of the law; and second, whether this denial constitutes discrimination on the basis of an enumerated or analogous ground.

2. The IRPA Creates a Distinction Between the Claimant and Others Based on a Personal Characteristic, and Because of That Distinction, It Denies the Claimant Equal Protection or Equal Benefit of the Law.

(a) Does the IRPA Create a Distinction? The respondents have argued that because the *IRPA* merely omits any reference to sexual orientation, this "neutral silence" cannot be understood as creating a distinction. They contend that the *IRPA* extends full protection on the grounds contained within it to heterosexuals and homosexuals alike, and therefore there is no distinction and hence no discrimination. It is the respondents' position that if any distinction is made on the basis of sexual orientation that distinction exists because it is present in society and not because of the *IRPA*.

These arguments cannot be accepted ... It has been repeatedly held that identical treatment will not always constitute equal treatment (see for example *Andrews, supra,* at p. 164). It is also clear that the way in which an exclusion is worded should not disguise the nature of the exclusion so as to allow differently drafted exclusions to be treated differently ...

The respondents concede that if homosexuals were excluded altogether from the protection of the *IRPA* in the sense that they were not protected from discrimination on any grounds, this would be discriminatory. Clearly that would be discrimination of the most egregious kind. It is true that gay and lesbian individuals are not entirely excluded from the protection of the *IRPA*. They can claim protection on some grounds. Yet that certainly does not mean that there is no discrimination present. For example, the fact that a lesbian and a heterosexual woman are both entitled to bring a complaint of discrimination on the basis of gender does not mean that they have *equal* protection under the Act ...

If the mere silence of the legislation was enough to remove it from s. 15(1) scrutiny then any legislature could easily avoid the objects of s. 15(1) simply by drafting laws which omitted reference to excluded groups ... It is clear that the *IRPA*, by reason of its underinclusiveness, does create a distinction. The distinction is simultaneously drawn along two different lines. The first is the distinction between homosexuals, on one hand, and other disadvantaged groups which are protected under the Act, on the other. Gays and lesbians do not even have formal equality with reference to other protected groups, since those other groups are explicitly included and they are not.

The second distinction, and, I think, the more fundamental one, is between homosexuals and heterosexuals. This distinction may be more difficult to see because there is, on the surface, a measure of formal equality: gay or lesbian individuals have the same access as heterosexual individuals to the protection of the *IRPA* in the sense that they could complain to the Commission about an incident of discrimination on the basis of any of the grounds currently included. However, the exclusion of the ground of sexual orientation, considered in the context of the social reality of discrimination against gays and lesbians, clearly has a disproportionate impact on them as opposed to heterosexuals. Therefore the *IRPA* in its underinclusive state denies substantive equality to the former group.

Finally, the respondents' contention that the distinction is not created by law, but rather exists independently of the *IRPA* in society, cannot be accepted. It is, of course, true that discrimination against gays and lesbians exists in society. The reality of this cruel and unfortunate discrimination was recognized in *Egan*. Indeed it provides the context in which the legislative distinction challenged in this case must be analysed. The reality of society's discrimination against lesbians and gay men demonstrates that there is a distinction drawn in the *IRPA* which denies these groups equal protection of the law by excluding lesbians and gay men from its protection, the very protection they so urgently need because of the existence of discrimination against them in society. It is not necessary to find that the legislation *creates* the discrimination existing in society in order to determine that it creates a potentially discriminatory distinction.

 Although the respondents try to distinguish this case from *Bliss v. Attorney General of Canada*, [1979] 1 SCR 183, the reasoning they put forward is very much reminiscent of the approach taken in that case ... There it was held that a longer qualifying period for unemployment benefits relating to pregnancy was not discriminatory because it applied to all pregnant individuals, and that if this category happened only to include women, that was a distinction created by nature, not by law. This reasoning has since been emphatically rejected (see, e.g., *Brooks*).

The omission of sexual orientation as a protected ground in the *IRPA* creates a distinction on the basis of sexual orientation. The "silence" of the *IRPA* with respect to discrimination on the ground of sexual orientation is not "neutral." Gay men and lesbians are treated differently from other disadvantaged groups and from heterosexuals. They, unlike gays and lesbians, receive protection from discrimination on the grounds that are likely to be relevant to them.

(b) Denial of Equal Benefit and Protection of the Law. It is apparent that the omission from the *IRPA* creates a distinction. That distinction results in a denial of the equal benefit and equal protection of the law. It is the exclusion of sexual orientation from the list of grounds in the *IRPA* which denies lesbians and gay men the protection and benefit of the Act in two important ways. They are excluded from the government's statement of policy against discrimination, and they are also denied access to the remedial procedures established by the Act. Therefore, the *IRPA*, by its omission or underinclusiveness, denies gays and lesbians the equal benefit and protection of the law on the basis of a personal characteristic, namely sexual orientation.

3. The Denial of Equal Benefit and Equal Protection Constitutes Discrimination Contrary to Section 15(1). In *Egan*, it was said that there are two aspects which are relevant in determining whether the distinction created by the law constitutes discrimination. First, "whether the equality right was denied on the basis of a personal characteristic which is either enumerated in s. 15(1) or which is analogous to those enumerated." Second "whether that distinction has the effect on the claimant of imposing a burden, obligation or disadvantage not imposed upon others or of withholding or limiting access to benefits or advantages which are available to others" (para. 131) ...

(a) The Equality Right is Denied on the Basis of a Personal Characteristic Which Is Analogous to Those Enumerated in Section 15(1). In *Egan*, it was held, on the basis of "historical social, political and economic disadvantage suffered by homosexuals" and the emerging consensus among legislatures (at para. 176), as well as previous judicial decisions (at para. 177), that sexual orientation is a ground analogous to those listed in s. 15(1). Sexual orientation is "a deeply personal characteristic that is either unchangeable or changeable only at unacceptable personal costs" (para. 5). It is analogous to the other personal characteristics enumerated in s. 15(1); and therefore this step of the test is satisfied ... It may at first be difficult to recognize the significance of being excluded from the protection of human rights legislation. However it imposes a heavy and disabling burden on those excluded ...

Apart from the immediate effect of the denial of recourse in cases of discrimination, there are other effects which, while perhaps less obvious, are at least as harmful. In *Haig*, the Ontario Court of Appeal based its finding of discrimination on both the "failure to provide an avenue for redress for prejudicial treatment of homosexual members of society" and "the possible inference from the omission that such treatment is acceptable" (p. 503). It can be reasonably inferred that the absence of any legal recourse for discrimination on the ground of sexual orientation perpetuates and even encourages that kind of discrimination. The respondents contend that it cannot be assumed that the "silence" of the *IRPA* reinforces or perpetuates discrimination, since governments "cannot legislate attitudes." However, this argument seems disingenuous in light of the stated purpose of the *IRPA*, to prevent discrimination. It cannot be claimed that human rights legislation will help to protect individuals from discrimination, and at the same time contend that an exclusion from the legislation will have no effect.

However, let us assume, contrary to all reasonable inferences, that exclusion from the *IRPA*'s protection does not actually contribute to a greater incidence of discrimination on the excluded ground. Nonetheless that exclusion, deliberately chosen in the face of clear findings that discrimination on the ground of sexual orientation does exist in society, sends a strong and sinister message ... to all Albertans that it is permissible, and perhaps even acceptable, to discriminate against individuals on the basis of their sexual orientation. The effect of that message on gays and lesbians is one whose significance cannot be underestimated ... Fear of discrimination will logically lead to concealment of true identity and this must be harmful to personal confidence and self-esteem. Compounding that effect is the implicit message conveyed by the exclusion, that gays and lesbians, unlike other individuals, are not worthy of protection. This is clearly an example of a distinction which demeans the individual and strengthens and perpetrates the view that gays and lesbians are less worthy of protection as individuals in Canada's society. The potential harm to the dignity and perceived worth of gay and lesbian individuals constitutes a particularly cruel form of discrimination.

4. *"Mirror" Argument.* The respondents take the position that if the appellants are successful, the result will be that human rights legislation will always have to "mirror" the *Charter* by including all of the enumerated and analogous grounds of the *Charter*. This would have the undesirable result of unduly constraining legislative choice and allowing the *Charter* to indirectly regulate private conduct, which should be left to the legislatures.

... However, the notion of "mirroring" is too simplistic. Whether an omission is unconstitutional must be assessed in each case, taking into account the nature of the exclusion, the type of legislation, and the context in which it was enacted. The determination of whether a particular exclusion complies with s. 15 of the *Charter* would not be made through the mechanical application of any "mirroring" principle, but rather, as in all other cases, by determining whether the exclusion was proven to be discriminatory in its specific context and whether the discrimination could be justified under s. 1. If a provincial legislature chooses to take legislative measures which do not include all of the enumerated and analogous grounds of the *Charter*, deference may be shown to this choice, so long as the tests for justification under s. 1, including rational connection, are satisfied.

5. Conclusion Regarding Section 15. In summary, this Court has no choice but to conclude that the *IRPA*, by reason of the omission of sexual orientation as a protected ground, clearly violates s. 15 of the *Charter*. The *IRPA* in its underinclusive state creates a distinction which results in the denial of the equal benefit and protection of the law on the basis of sexual orientation, a personal characteristic which has been found to be analogous to the grounds enumerated in s. 15. It is therefore necessary to determine whether this violation can be justified under s. 1. This analysis will be undertaken by my colleague.

Iacobucci, J: – Section 1 of the *Charter* guarantees the rights and freedoms set out therein, but allows for *Charter* infringements provided that the state can establish that they are reasonably justifiable in a free and democratic society. The analytical framework for determining whether a statutory provision is a reasonable limit on a *Charter* right or freedom has been set out many times since it was first established in *R. v Oakes*, [1986] 1 SCR 103. It was recently restated in *Egan, supra*, at para. 182, which was quoted with approval in *Eldridge, supra*, at para. 84: A limitation to a constitutional guarantee will be sustained once two conditions are met. First, the objective of the legislation must be pressing and substantial. Second, the means chosen to attain this legislative end must be reasonable and demonstrably justifiable in a free and democratic society. In order to satisfy the second requirement, three criteria must be satisfied: (1) the rights violation must be rationally connected to the aim of the legislation; (2) the impugned provision must minimally impair the *Charter* guarantee; and (3) there must be a proportionality between the effect of the measure and its objective so that the attainment of the legislative goal is not outweighed by the abridgement of the right. In all s. 1 cases the burden of proof is with the government to show on a balance of probabilities that the violation is justifiable.

1. Pressing and Substantial Objective. In my view, where, as here, a law has been found to violate the *Charter* owing to underinclusion, the legislation as a whole, the impugned provisions, and the omission itself are all properly considered.

Section 1 of the *Charter* states that it is the *limits* on *Charter* rights and freedoms that must be demonstrably justified in a free and democratic society. It follows that under the first part of the *Oakes* test, the analysis must focus upon the objective of the impugned limitation, or in this case, the omission ... However, in my opinion, the objective of the omission cannot be fully understood in isolation. It seems to me that some consideration must also be given to both the purposes of the Act as a whole and the specific impugned provisions so as to give the objective of the omission the context that is necessary for a more complete understanding of its operation in the broader scheme of the legislation.

Applying these principles to the case at bar, the preamble of the *IRPA* suggests that the object of the Act in its entirety is the recognition and protection of the inherent dignity and inalienable rights of Albertans through the elimination of discriminatory practices. Clearly, the protection of human rights in our society is a laudable goal and is aptly described as pressing and substantial. As to the impugned provisions, their objective can generally be described as the protection against discrimination for Albertans belonging to specific groups in various settings, for example, employment and accommodation. This too is properly regarded as a pressing and substantial objective.

Against this backdrop, what can be said of the objective of the omission? The respondents submit that only the overall goal of the Act need be examined and offer no direct submissions in answer to this question. In the Court of Appeal, absent any evidence on this point, Hunt, JA relied on the factum of the respondents from which she gleaned several possible reasons why, when the matter was debated by the Alberta Legislature in 1985 and considered at various other times, a decision was made not to add sexual orientation to the *IRPA*. Some of these same reasons appear in the factum that the respondents have submitted to this Court and include the following:

- The *IRPA* is inadequate to address some of the concerns expressed by the homosexual community (e.g., parental acceptance) (paragraph 57);

- Attitudes cannot be changed by order of the Human Rights Commission (paragraph 57);
- Despite the Minister asking for examples which would be ameliorated by the inclusion of sexual orientation in the *IRPA* (e.g., employment), only a few illustrations were provided (paragraph 57);
- Codification of marginal grounds which affect few persons raises objections from larger numbers of others, adding to the number of exemptions that would have been needed to satisfy both groups (paragraph 66).

In my view, although these statements go some distance toward explaining the Legislature's choice to exclude sexual orientation from the *IRPA*, this is not the type of evidence required under the first step of the *Oakes* test. At the first stage of that test, the government is asked to demonstrate that the "objective" of the omission is pressing and substantial. An "objective," being a goal or a purpose to be achieved, is a very different concept from an "explanation" which makes plain that which is not immediately obvious. In my opinion, the above statements fall into the latter category and hence are of little help.

In his reasons for judgment, McClung, JA alludes to "moral" considerations that likely informed the Legislature's choice. However, even if such considerations could be said to amount to a pressing and substantial objective (a position which I find difficult to accept in this case), I note that it is well established that the onus of justifying a *Charter* infringement rests on the government (see, e.g., *Andrews v Law Society of British Columbia, supra*). In the absence of any submissions regarding the pressing and substantial nature of the objective of the omission, the respondents have failed to discharge their evidentiary burden, and thus, I conclude that their case must fail at this first stage of the s. 1 analysis.

... Even if I were to put the evidentiary burden aside in an attempt to discover an objective for the omission from the provisions of the *IRPA*, in my view, the result would be the same. As I noted above, the overall goal of the *IRPA* is the protection of the dignity and rights of all persons living in Alberta. The exclusion of sexual orientation from the Act effectively denies gay men and lesbians such protection.

2. Proportionality Analysis

(a) Rational Connection. On the basis of my conclusion above, it is not necessary to analyse the second part of the *Oakes* test to dispose of this appeal. However, to deal with this matter more fully, I will go on to consider the remainder of the test. I will assume, solely for the sake of the analysis, that the respondents correctly argued that where the objective of the whole of the legislation is pressing and substantial, this is sufficient to satisfy the first stage of the inquiry under s. 1 of the *Charter*.

At the second stage of the *Oakes* test, the preliminary inquiry is a consideration of the rationality of the impugned provisions (*Oakes*, *supra*, at p. 141). The party invoking s. 1 must demonstrate that a rational connection exists between the objective of the provisions under attack and the measures that have been adopted. Thus, in the case at bar, it falls to the Legislature to show that there is a rational connection between the goal of protection against discrimination for Albertans belonging to specific groups in various settings, and the exclusion of gay men and lesbians from the impugned provisions of the *IRPA*.

Far from being rationally connected to the objective of the impugned provisions, the exclusion of sexual orientation from the Act is antithetical to that goal ...

(b) Minimal Impairment. The respondents contend that an *IRPA* which is silent as to sexual orientation minimally impairs the appellants' s. 15 rights. The *IRPA* is alleged to be the type of social policy legislation that requires the Alberta Legislature to mediate between competing groups. It is suggested that the competing interests in the present case are religious freedom and homosexuality. Relying upon Sopinka, J's reasons in *Egan*, the respondents advocate judicial deference in these circumstances. I reject these submissions for several reasons.

To begin, I cannot accede to the suggestion that the Alberta Legislature has been cast in the role of mediator between competing groups. To the extent that there may be a conflict between religious freedom and the protection of gay men and lesbians, the *IRPA* contains internal mechanisms for balancing these rival concerns. Section 11.1 of the *IRPA* provides a defence where the discrimination was "reasonable and justifiable in the circumstances." In addition, ss. 7(3) and 8(2) excuse discrimination which can be linked to a *bona fide* occupational requirement. The balancing provisions ensure that no conferral of rights is absolute. Rather, rights are recognized in tandem, with no one right being automatically paramount to another ... Thus, in the present case it is no answer to say that rights cannot be conferred upon one group because of a conflict with the rights of others. A complete solution to any such conflict already exists within the legislation.

In any event, although this Court has recognized that the Legislatures ought to be accorded some leeway when making choices between competing social concerns ... judicial deference is not without limits.

(c) Proportionality Between the Effect of the Measure and the Objective of the Legislation. The respondents did not address this third element of the proportionality requirement. However, in my view, the deleterious effects of the exclusion of sexual orientation from the *IRPA*, as noted by Cory, J, are numerous and clear. As the Alberta Government has failed to demonstrate any salutary effect of the exclusion in promoting and protecting human rights, I cannot accept that there is any proportionality between the attainment of the legislative goal and the infringement of the appellants' equality rights. I conclude that the exclusion of sexual orientation from the *IRPA* does not meet the requirements of the *Oakes* test and accordingly, it cannot be saved under s. 1 of the *Charter*.

II REMEDY

A Introduction: The Relationship Between the Legislatures and the Courts Under the Charter

Having found the exclusion of sexual orientation from the *IRPA* to be an unjustifiable violation of the appellants' equality rights, I now turn to the question of remedy under s. 52 of the *Constitution Act, 1982*. Before discussing the jurisprudence on remedies, I believe it might be helpful to pause to reflect more broadly on the general issue of the relationship between legislatures and the courts in the age of the *Charter*.

Much was made in argument before us about the inadvisability of the Court interfering with or otherwise meddling in what is regarded as the proper role of the legislature, which in this case was to decide whether or not sexual orientation would be added to Alberta's human rights legislation. Indeed, it seems that hardly a day goes by without some comment or criticism to the effect that under the *Charter* courts are wrongfully usurping the role of the legislatures. I believe this allegation misunderstands what took place and what was intended when our country adopted the *Charter* in 1981–82. When the *Charter* was introduced, Canada went, in the words of former Chief Justice Brian

Dickson, from a system of Parliamentary supremacy to constitutional supremacy ("Keynote Address," in *The Cambridge Lectures 1985* (1985), at pp. 3–4). Simply put, each Canadian was given individual rights and freedoms which no government or legislature could take away. However, as rights and freedoms are not absolute, governments and legislatures could justify the qualification or infringement of these constitutional rights under s. 1 as I previously discussed. Inevitably disputes over the meaning of the rights and their justification would have to be settled and here the role of the judiciary enters to resolve these disputes. Many countries have assigned the important role of judicial review to their supreme or constitutional courts ... We should recall that it was the deliberate choice of our provincial and federal legislatures in adopting the *Charter* to assign an interpretive role to the courts and to command them under s. 52 to declare unconstitutional legislation invalid ...

The leading case on constitutional remedies is *Schachter, supra*. Writing on behalf of the majority in *Schachter*, Lamer, CJ stated that the first step in selecting a remedial course under s. 52 is to define the extent of the *Charter* inconsistency which must be struck down.

Because the *Charter* violation in the instant case stems from an omission, the remedy of reading down is simply not available. Further, I note that given the considerable number of sections at issue in this case and the important roles they play in the scheme of the *IRPA* as a whole, severance of these sections from the remainder of the Act would be akin to striking down the entire Act.

As I discussed above, the purpose of the *IRPA* is the recognition and protection of the inherent dignity and inalienable rights of Albertans through the elimination of discriminatory practices. It seems to me that the remedy of reading in would minimize interference with this clearly legitimate legislative purpose and thereby avoid excessive intrusion into the legislative sphere whereas striking down the *IRPA* would deprive all Albertans of human rights protection and thereby unduly interfere with the scheme enacted by the Legislature.

... I agree with K. Roach who noted that the legislature "can always subsequently intervene on matters of detail that are not dictated by the Constitution" (*Constitutional Remedies in Canada* (1994 (loose-leaf), at p. 14–64.1). I therefore conclude on this point that, in the present case, there is sufficient remedial precision to justify the remedy of reading in.

Turning to budgetary repercussions, in the circumstances of the present appeal, such considerations are not sufficiently significant to warrant avoiding the reading in approach ...

Where a statute has been found to be unconstitutional, whether the court chooses to read provisions into the legislation or to strike it down, legislative intent is necessarily interfered with to some extent. Therefore, the closest a court can come to respecting the legislative intention is to determine what the legislature would likely have done if it had known that its chosen measures would be found unconstitutional. As I see the matter, a deliberate choice of means will not act as a bar to reading in save for those circumstances in which the means chosen can be shown to be of such centrality to the aims of the legislature and so integral to the scheme of the legislation, that the legislature would not have enacted the statute without them.

... When a court remedies an unconstitutional statute by reading in provisions, no doubt this constrains the legislative process and therefore should not be done needlessly, but only after considered examination. However, in my view, the "parliamentary safeguards" remain. Governments are free to modify the amended legislation by passing exceptions and defences which they feel can be justified under s. 1 of the *Charter*.

III CONCLUSIONS AND DISPOSITION

I would answer the constitutional questions as follows:

1 Do (a) decisions not to include sexual orientation or (b) the non-inclusion of sexual orientation, as a prohibited ground of discrimination in the preamble and ss. 2(1), 3, 4, 7(1), 8(1), 10 and 16(1) of the *Individual's Rights Protection Act*, R.S.A. 1980, c. I-2, as am., now called the *Human Rights, Citizenship and Multiculturalism Act*, R.S.A. 1980, c. H-11.7, infringe or deny the rights guaranteed by s. 15(1) of the *Canadian Charter of Rights and Freedoms*?
   Answer: Yes.
2 If the answer to Question 1 is "yes," is the infringement or denial demonstrably justified as a reasonable limit pursuant to s. 1 of the *Canadian Charter of Rights and Freedoms*?
   Answer: No.

L'Heureux-Dubé, J:–I am in general agreement with the results reached by my colleagues, Cory and Iacobucci, JJ.

I do not agree with the centrality of enumerated and analogous grounds in Cory, J's approach to s. 15(1). Although the presence of enumerated or analogous grounds may be indicia of discrimination, or may even raise a presumption of discrimination, it is in the appreciation of the nature of the individual or group who is being negatively affected that they should be examined. Of greatest significance to a finding of discrimination is the effect of the legislative distinction on that individual or group.

This being said, I agree with Cory and Iacobucci, JJ to allow the appeal and dismiss the cross-appeal with costs.

Major, J (dissenting in part): – ... Reading in may be appropriate where it can be safely assumed that the legislature itself would have remedied the underinclusiveness by extending the benefit or protection to the previously excluded group. That assumption cannot be made in this appeal. The issue may be that the Legislature would prefer no human rights Act over one that includes sexual orientation as a prohibited ground of discrimination, or the issue may be *how* the legislation ought to be amended to bring it into conformity with the *Charter* ... There are numerous ways in which the legislation could be amended to address the underinclusiveness. Sexual orientation may be added as a prohibited ground of discrimination to each of the impugned provisions. In so doing, the Legislature may choose to define the term "sexual orientation," or it may devise constitutional limitations on the scope of protection provided by the *IRPA*. As an alternative, the Legislature may choose to override the *Charter* breach by invoking s. 33 of the *Charter*, which enables Parliament or a legislature to enact a law that will operate notwithstanding the rights guaranteed in s. 2 and ss. 7 to 15 of the *Charter*. Given the persistent refusal of the Legislature to protect against discrimination on the basis of sexual orientation, it may be that it would choose to invoke s. 33 in these circumstances. In any event it should lie with the elected Legislature to determine this issue. They are answerable to the electorate of that province and it is for them to choose the remedy whether it is changing the legislation or using the notwithstanding clause. That decision in turn will be judged by the voters.

READING QUESTIONS ON *VRIEND*

1 Cory, J cites *Egan*, above, in support of his judgment. Are *Vriend* and *Egan* consistent?
2 What is the "mirror" argument that Cory, J rejects? Is there more to be said for the worry than he allows?

3 Iacobucci, J rejects the contention that the Alberta legislature made its decision on moral grounds, saying that the onus is on the legislature to explain its grounds. How do you think he would have decided the s. 1 issue if Alberta had made an explicit Devlin-style argument?

4 L'Heureux-Dubé, J says that a *Charter* finding of discrimination does not require showing that the situation of the individual or group discriminated against is analgous to that of others receiving legal protection. How else might one identify discrimination?

5 The Court decides to "read in" the missing provisions of the *Individual Rights Protection Act*. What does this mean? Why does Major, J object? What would the Court do if the legislature decided to repeal the Act? Would Vriend have any recourse against his employer or the government?

John M. Finnis
Law, Morality, and "Sexual Orientation" (1994)

I

During the past thirty years there has emerged in Europe a standard of legal regulation of sexual conduct. This standard form or scheme, which I shall call the "standard modern [European] position," is accepted by the European Court of Human Rights and the European Commission of Human Rights (the two supra-national judicial and quasi-judicial institutions of the European Convention for the Protection of Human rights and Fundamental Freedoms (1950), to which almost all European states are party, whether or not they are also party to the European [Economic] Community now known as the European Union). The standard modern European position has two limbs. On the one hand, the state is not authorized to, and does not, make it a punishable offence for adult consenting persons to engage, in private, in immoral sexual acts (for example, homosexual acts). On the other hand, states do have the authority to discourage, say, homosexual conduct and "orientation" (i.e., overtly manifested active willingness to engage in homosexual conduct). And typically, though not universally, they do so. That is to say, they maintain various criminal and administrative laws and policies which have as part of their purpose the discouraging of such conduct. Many of these laws, regulations, and policies discriminate (i.e. distinguish) between heterosexual and homosexual conduct adversely to the latter.

In England, for example, well after Parliament's decriminalization of private adult homosexual conduct by the Sexual Offences Act 1967, the highest court (the House of Lords) reaffirmed that a jury may lawfully convict on a charge of conspiring to corrupt public morals by publishing advertisements by private individuals of their availability for (noncommercial) private homosexual acts.[1] The Court of Appeal has constantly reaffirmed, notably in 1977, 1981 and 1990,[2] that public soliciting of adult males by adult males falls within the statutory prohibition of "importuning in a public place for an immoral purpose."[3] Parliament has peacefully accepted both these judicial interpretations of the constitutional, statutory and common law position. It has also voted more than once to maintain the legal position whereby the age of consent for lawful intercourse is 21 for homosexual but 16 for heterosexual intercourse;[4] in February 1994 the House of Commons voted to make the homosexual age of consent 18, which would reduce but retain the differentiation between homosexual and heterosexual conduct.[5] In 1988, Parliament specifically prohibited local governments in England from doing anything to "intentionally promote homosexuality" or "promote the teaching in any maintained school of the acceptability of homosexuality as a pretended family relationship."[6] The provisions of English law relating to marriage and to adoption similarly manifest a purpose or at least a willingness to discourage homosexual conduct and impede its promotion by any form of invitatory activity other than between consenting adults and in a truly private milieu.

The English position as outlined above is in full conformity with the position upheld by the European human rights institutions. When the European Court of Human Rights in 1981 adopted (and in 1988 reaffirmed) the position which Parliament in England had taken in 1967, it ruled that penal prohibition of private adult homosexual activity is not necessary for the securing of the state's legitimate aim of protecting morals.[7] In doing so, the court expressly left unscathed, and in principle confirmed, the decision of March 13, 1980 of the European Commission of Human Rights (and of the Commission on October 12, 1978 and the Council of Ministers by Resolution DH (79) 5 of June 12, 1979) that states can properly prohibit private consensual homosexual acts involving a male under 21 notwithstanding the Convention right of non-discrimination in the legal protection of rights and notwithstanding that the state law in question made 16 the "age of consent" for heterosexual intercourse (and 18 the age of majority for other purposes).

The Commission has subsequently reaffirmed that decision and has declared unarguable ("inadmissible" for further judicial process) complaints made, under the Convention's anti-discrimination provisions, against the long-standing Swiss law which criminalizes homosexual prostitution (male or female) but not heterosexual prostitution.[8]

II

The standard modern [European] position is consistent with the view that (apart perhaps from special cases and contexts) it is unjust for A to impose any kind of disadvantage on B simply because A believes (perhaps correctly) that B has sexual inclinations (which he may or may not act on) towards persons of the same sex. (Special cases are more likely to arise, for example, where B's inclination is towards "man-boy love," i.e., pederasty.) The position does not give B the widest conceivably legal protection against such unjust discrimination (just as it generally does not give wide protection against needless acts of adverse private discrimination in housing or employment to people with unpopular or eccentric political views). But the position does not itself encourage, sponsor or impose any such unjust burden. (And it is accompanied by many legal protections for homosexual persons with respect to assaults, threats, unreasonable discrimination by public bodies and officials, etc.)

The concern of the standard modern position itself is not with inclinations but entirely with certain decisions to express or manifest deliberate promotion of, or readiness to engage in, homosexual activity or conduct, including promotion of forms of life (e.g., purportedly marital cohabitation) which both encourage such activity and present it as a valid or acceptable alternative to the committed heterosexual union which the state recognizes as marriage. Subject only to the written or unwritten constitutional requirement of freedom of discussion of ideas, the state laws and state policies which I have outlined are intended to discourage decisions which are thus deliberately oriented towards homosexual conduct and are manifested in public ways.

The standard modern position differs from the position which it replaced, which made adult consensual sodomy and like acts crimes per se. States which adhere to the standard modern position make it clear by laws and policies such as I have referred to that the state has by no means renounced its legitimate concern with public morality and the education of children and young people towards truly worthwhile and against alluring but bad forms of conduct and life. Nor have such states renounced the judgment that a life involving homosexual conduct is bad even for anyone unfortunate enough to have innate or quasi-innate homosexual inclinations.

The difference between the standard modern position and the position it has replaced can be expressed as follows. The standard modern position considers that the state's proper responsibility for upholding true worth (morality) is a responsibility subsidiary (auxiliary) to the primary responsibility of parents and non-political voluntary associations. The subsidiary character of government is widely emphasized and increasingly accepted, at least in principle, in contemporary European politics. (It was, for example, a cornerstone of the Treaty of Maastricht of 1992.) This conception of the proper role of government has been taken to exclude the state from assuming a directly parental disciplinary role in relation to consenting adults. That role was one which political theory and practice formerly ascribed to the state on the assumption that the role followed by logical necessity from the truth that the state should encourage true worth and discourage immorality. That assumption is now judged to be mistaken (a judgment for which I shall argue in the final part of this lecture).

So the modern theory and practice draws from a distinction not drawn in the former legal arrangements, a distinction between (a) supervising the truly private conduct of adults and (b) supervising the public realm or environment. The importance of the latter includes the following considerations: (1) this is the environment or public realm in which young people (of whatever sexual inclinations) are educated; (2) it is the context in which and by which everyone with responsibility for the well being of young people is helped or hindered in assisting them to avoid bad forms of life; (3) it is the milieu in which and by which all citizens are encouraged and helped, or discouraged and undermined, in their own resistance to being lured by temptation into falling away from their own aspirations to be people of integrated good character, and to be autonomous, self-controlled persons rather than slaves to impulse and sensual gratification.

While the type (a) supervision of truly private adult consensual conduct is now considered to be outside the state's normal proper role (with exceptions such as sado-masochistic bodily damage, and assistance in suicide), type (b) supervision of the moral-cultural-educational environment is maintained as a very important part of the state's justification for claiming legitimately the loyalty of its decent citizens.

III

The standard modern position is part of a politico-legal order which systematically outlaws many forms of discrimination. Thus, the European Convention on Human Rights (model for several dozen constitutions enacted over the past thirty-five years by the British authorities, for nations gaining independence) provides that the protection of the rights it sets out is to be enjoyed without discrimination on any ground such as "sex, race, colour, language, religion, political or other opinion, national or social origin, association with a national minority, property, birth or other status."

But the standard modern position deliberately rejects proposals to include in such lists the item "sexual orientation." The explanation commonly given (correctly, in my opinion) is this. The phrase "sexual orientation" is radically equivocal. Particularly used by promoters of "gay rights," the phrase ambiguously assimilates two things which the standard modern position carefully distinguishes: (I) a psychological or psychosomatic disposition inwardly orienting one towards homosexual activity; (II) the deliberate decision so to orient one's public behavior as to express or manifest one's active interest in and endorsement of homosexual conduct and/or forms of life which presumptively involve such conduct.

It is also widely observed that laws or proposed laws outlawing "discrimination based on sexual orientation" are always interpreted by "gay rights" movements as going far beyond discrimination based merely on A's belief that B is sexually attracted to persons of the same sex. Instead (it is observed), "gay rights" movements interpret the phrase as extending full legal protection to public activities intended specifically to promote, procure and facilitate homosexual conduct.

It has been noticed in public circles in Europe that such laws have indeed been interpreted by American courts as having just such an implication. An example which has been widely reported is the Georgetown University case,[9] requiring a religiously affiliated educational institution to give equal access to its facilities to organizations "partici-pating in and promoting homosexual lifestyles [which necessarily include homosexual conduct]" in manifest opposition to the moral beliefs and teachings of the religion with which that institution professed an association.

So, while the standard position accepts that acts of type (I) discrimi-nation are unjust, it judges that there are compelling reasons to both deny that such injustice would be appropriately remedied by laws against "discrimination based on sexual orientation," and to hold that such a "remedy" would work significant discrimination and injustice against (and would indeed damage) families, associations and institu-tions which have organized themselves to live out and transmit ideals of family life that include a high conception of the worth of truly conjugal sexual intercourse.

It is in fact accepted by almost everyone, on both sides of the political debate, that the adoption of a law framed to prohibit "discrimination on grounds of sexual orientation" would require the prompt abandonment of all attempts by the political community to discourage homosexual conduct by means of educational policies, restrictions on prostitution, non-recognition of homosexual "marriages" and adoptions, and so forth. It is judged (and in my view soundly) that the law itself would perforce have changed from teaching, in many ways, that homosexual conduct is bad to teaching, massively, that it is a type of sexual activity as good as any other (and per se much less involved with onerous responsibilities than is the sexual union of husband and wife or, in perhaps other ways, the life of those who live in unmarried chastity).

IV

The standard modern position involves a number of explicit or implicit judgments about the proper role of law and the compelling interests of political communities, and about the evil of homosexual conduct. Can these be defended by reflective, critical, publicly intelligible and rational arguments? I believe they can. Since even the advocates of "gay rights" do not seriously assert that the state can never have any compelling interests in public morality or the moral formation of its young people or the moral environment in which parents, other educators, and young people themselves must undertake this formation, I shall in this lecture focus rather on the underlying issue which receives far too little public discussion: What is wrong with homosexual conduct? Is the judgment that it is morally wrong inevitably a manifestation either of merely hostility to a hated minority, or of purely religious, theological, and sectarian belief which can ground no constitutionally valid determination disadvantaging those who do not conform to it?

I have been using and shall continue to use the terms "homosexual activity," "homosexual acts" and "homosexual conduct" synonymously, to refer to bodily acts, on the body of a person of the same sex, which are engaged in with a view to securing orgasmic sexual satisfaction for one or more of the parties.

Let me begin by noticing a too little noticed fact. All three of the greatest Greek philosophers, Socrates, Plato and Aristotle, regarded homosexual conduct as intrinsically shameful, immoral, and indeed depraved or depraving. That is to say, all three rejected the linchpin of modern "gay" ideology and lifestyle ...

At the heart of the Platonic-Aristotelian and later ancient philosophical rejections of all homosexual conduct, and thus of the modern "gay" ideology, are three fundamental theses: (1) The commitment of a man and woman to each other in the sexual union of marriage is intrinsically good and reasonable, and is incompatible with sexual relations outside marriage. (2) Homosexual acts are radically and peculiarly non-marital, and for that reason intrinsically unreasonable and unnatural. (3) Furthermore, according to Plato, if not Aristotle, homosexual acts have a special similarity to solitary masturbation, and both types of radically non-marital acts are manifestly unworthy of the human being and immoral.

V

I want now to offer an interpretation of these three theses which articulates them more clearly than was ever attempted by Plato or, so far as we can tell, by Aristotle. It is, I think, an interpretation faithful to what they do say, but takes up suggestions in Plutarch and in the eighteenth century Enlightenment philosophy of Immanuel Kant (who likewise rejected all homosexual conduct), though even these writers' indications, too, remain relatively terse. My account also articulates thoughts which have historically been implicit in the judgments of many non-philosophical people, and which have been held to justify the laws adopted in many nations and states both before and after the period when Christian beliefs as such were politically and socially dominant. And it is an application of the theory of morality and natural law developed over the past thirty years by Germain Grisez and others. A fuller exposition can be found in the chapter on marriage, sexual acts, and family life, in the new second volume of Grisez's great work on moral theology.[10]

Plato's mature concern, in the Laws, for familiarity, affection and love between spouses in a chastely exclusive marriage, Aristotle's representation of marriage as an intrinsically desirable friendship between quasi-equals, and as a state of life even more natural to human beings than political life,[11] and Musonuis Rufus's conception of the inseparable double goods of marriage, all find expression in Plutarch's celebration of marriage as a union not of mere instinct but of reasonable love, and not merely for procreation but for mutual help, goodwill and cooperation for their own sake.[12] Plutarch's severe critiques of homosexual conduct (and of the disparagement of women implicit in homosexual ideology),[13] develop Plato's critique of homosexual and all other extra-marital sexual conduct. Like Musonius Rufus, Plutarch does so by bringing much closer to explicit articulation the following thought. Genital intercourse between spouses enables them to actualize and experience (and in that sense express)[14] their marriage itself, as a single reality with two blessings (children and mutual affection). Non-marital intercourse, especially but not only homosexual, has no such point and therefore is unacceptable.

The core of this argument can be clarified by comparing it with Saint Augustine's treatment of marriage in his De Bono Coniugali. The good of marital communion is here an instrumental good, in the service of the procreation and education of children so that the intrinsic, non-instrumental good of friendship will be promoted and realized by the propagation of the human race, and the intrinsic good of inner integration be promoted and realized by the "remedying" of the disordered desires of concupiscence.[15] Now, when considering sterile marriages, Augustine had identified a further good of marriage, the natural societas (companionship) of the two sexes.[16] Had he truly integrated this into his synthesis, he would have recognized that in sterile and fertile marriages alike, the communion, companionship, societas and amicitia of the spouses – their being married – is the very good of marriage, and is an intrinsic, basic human good, not merely instrumental to any other good. And this communion of married life, this integral amalgamation of the lives of the two persons (as Plutarch[17] put it before John Paul II),[18] has as its intrinsic elements, as essential parts of one and the same good, the goods and ends to which the theological tradition, following Augustine, for a long time subordinated that communion. It took a long and gradual process of development of doctrine, through the Catechism of the Council of Trent, the teachings of Pius XI and Pius XII, and eventually those of Vatican II – a process brilliantly illuminated by Germain Grisez[19] – to bring the tradition to the position that procreation and children are neither the end (whether primary or secondary) to which marriage is instrumental (as Augustine taught), nor instrumental to the good of the spouses (as much secular and "liberal Christian" thought supposes), but rather: Parenthood and children and family are the intrinsic fulfillment of a communion which, because it is not merely instrumental, can exist and fulfill the spouses even if procreation happens to be impossible for them.

Now if, as the recent encyclical on the foundations of morality, Veritatis Splendor, teaches, "the communion of persons in marriages" which is violated by every act of adultery is itself a "fundamental human good,"[20] there fall into place not only the elements of the classic philosophical judgments on non-marital sexual conduct but also the similar judgments reached about such conduct by decent people who cannot articulate explanatory premises for those judgments, which they reach rather by an insight into what is and is not consistent with realities whose goodness they experience and understand at least sufficiently to will and choose. In particular, there fall into place the elements of an answer to the question: Why cannot non-marital friendship be promoted and expressed by sexual acts? Why is the attempt to express affection by orgasmic non-marital sex the pursuit of an illusion? Why did Plato and Socrates, Xenophon, Aristotle, Musonius Rufus, and Plutarch, right at the heart of their reflections on the homoerotic culture around them, make the very deliberate and careful judgment that homosexual conduct (and indeed all extra-marital sexual gratification) is radically incapable of participating in, actualizing, the common good of friendship?

Implicit in the philosophical and common-sense rejection of extra-marital sex is the answer: The union of the reproductive organs of husband and wife really unites them biologically (and their biological reality is part of, not merely an instrument of, their personal reality); reproduction is one function and so, in respect of that function, the spouses are indeed one reality, and their sexual union therefore can actualize and allow them to experience their real common good – their marriage with the two goods, parenthood and friendship, which (leaving aside the order of grace) are the parts of its wholeness as an intelligible common good even if, independently of what the spouses will, their capacity for biological parenthood will not be fulfilled by that act of genital union. But the common good of friends who are not and cannot be married (for example, man and man, man and boy, woman and woman) has nothing to do with their having children by each other, and their reproductive organs cannot make them a biological (and therefore personal) unit.[21] So their sexual acts together cannot do what they may hope and imagine. Because their activation of one or even each of their reproductive organs cannot be an actualizing and experiencing of the marital good – as marital intercourse (intercourse between spouses in a marital way) can, even between spouses who happen to be sterile – it can do no more than provide each partner with an individual gratification. For want of a common good that could be actualized and experienced by and in this bodily union, that conduct involves the partners in treating their bodies as instruments to be used in the service of their consciously experiencing selves; their choice to engage in such conduct thus disintegrates each of them precisely as acting persons.[22]

Reality is known in judgment, not in emotion, and in reality, whatever the generous hopes and dreams and thoughts of giving with which some same-sex partners may surround their sexual acts, those acts cannot express or do more than is expressed or done if two strangers engage in such activity to give each other pleasure, or a prostitute pleasures a client to give him pleasure in return for money, or (say) a man masturbates to give himself pleasure and a fantasy of more human relationships after a gruelling day on the assembly line. This is, I believe, the substance of Plato's judgment – at that moment in the *Gorgias* which is also decisive for the moral and political philosophical critique of hedonism[23] – that there is no important distinction in essential moral worthlessness between solitary masturbation, being sodomized as a prostitute, and being sodomized for the pleasure of it. Sexual acts cannot in reality be self-giving unless they are acts by which a man and a woman actualize and experience sexually the real giving of themselves to each other – in biological, affective and volitional union in mutual commitment, both open-ended and exclusive – which like Plato and Aristotle and most people we call marriage.

In short, sexual acts are not unitive in their significance unless they are marital (actualizing the all-level unity of marriage) and (since the common good of marriage has two aspects) they are not marital unless they have not only the generosity of acts of friendship but also the procreative significance, not necessarily of being intended to generate or capable in the circumstances of generating but at least of being, as human conduct, acts of the reproductive kind – actualizations, so far as the spouses then and there can, of the reproductive function in which they are biologically and thus personally one.

The ancient philosophers do not much discuss the case of sterile marriages, or the fact (well known to them) that for long periods of time (e.g. throughout pregnancy) the sexual acts of a married couple are naturally incapable of resulting in reproduction. They appear to take for granted what the subsequent Christian tradition certainly did, that such sterility does not render the conjugal sexual acts of the spouses non-marital. (Plutarch indicates that intercourse with a sterile spouse is a desirable mark of marital esteem and affection.)[24] For: A husband and wife who unite their reproductive organs in an act of sexual intercourse which, so far as they then can make it, is of a kind suitable for generation, do function as a biological (and thus personal) unit and thus can be actualizing and experiencing the two-in-one-flesh common good and reality of marriage, even when some biological condition happens to prevent that unity resulting in the generation of a child. Their conduct thus differs radically from the acts of a husband and wife whose intercourse is masturbatory, for example sodomitic or by fellatio or coitus interruptus.[25] In law such acts do not consummate a marriage, because in reality (whatever the couple's illusions of intimacy and self-giving in such acts) they do not actualize the one-flesh, two-part marital good.

Does this account seek to "make moral judgments based on natural facts?"[26] Yes and no. No, in the sense that it does not seek to infer normative conclusions or theses from non-normative (natural-fact) premises. Nor does it appeal to any norm of the form "Respect natural facts or natural function." But yes, it does apply the relevant practical reasons (especially that marriage and inner integrity are basic human goods) and moral principles (especially that one may never intend to destroy, damage, impede, or violate any basic human good, or prefer and illusory instantiation of a basic human good to a real instantiation of that or some other human good) to facts about the human personal organism.

VI

Societies such as classical Athens and contemporary England (and virtually every other) draw a distinction between behavior found merely (perhaps extremely) offensive (such as eating excrement), and behavior to be repudiated as destructive of human character and relationships. Copulation of humans with animals is repudiated because it treats human sexual activity and satisfaction as something appropriately sought in a manner as divorced from the actualizing of an intelligible common good as is the instinctive coupling of beasts – and so treats human bodily life, in one of its most intense activities, as appropriately lived as merely animal. The deliberate genital coupling of persons of the same sex is repudiated for a very similar reason. It is not simply that it is sterile and disposes the participants to an abdication of responsibility for the future of humankind. Nor is it simply that it cannot really actualize the mutual devotion which some homosexual persons hope to manifest and experience by it, and that it harms the personalities of its participants by its disintegrative manipulation of different parts of their one personal reality. It is also that it treats human sexual capacities in a way which is deeply hostile to the self-understanding of those members of the community who are willing to commit themselves to real marriage in the understanding that its sexual joys are not mere instruments or accompaniments to, or mere compensations for, the accomplishment of marriage's responsibilities, but rather enable the spouses to actualize and experience their intelligent commitment to share in those responsibilities, in that genuine self-giving.

Now, as I have said before, "homosexual orientation," in one of the two main senses of that highly equivocal term, is precisely the deliberate willingness to promote and engage in homosexual acts – the state of mind, will, and character whose self-interpretation came to be expressed in the deplorable but helpfully revealing name "gay." So this willingness, and the whole "gay" ideology, treats human sexual capacities in a way which is deeply hostile to the self-understanding of those members of the community who are willing to commit themselves to real marriage.

Homosexual orientation in this sense is, in fact, a standing denial of the intrinsic aptness of sexual intercourse to actualize and in that sense give expression to the exclusiveness and open-ended commitment of marriage as something good in itself. All who accept that homosexual acts can be a humanly appropriate use of sexual capacities must, if consistent, regard sexual capacities, organs and acts as instruments for gratifying the individual "selves" who have them. Such an acceptance is commonly (and in my opinion rightly) judged to be an active threat to the stability of existing and future marriages; it makes nonsense, for example, of the view that adultery is per se (and not merely because it may involve deception), and in an important way, inconsistent with conjugal love. A political community which judges that the stability and protective and educative generosity of family life is of fundamental importance to that community's present and future can rightly judge that it has a compelling interest in denying that homosexual conduct – a "gay lifestyle" – is a valid, humanly acceptable choice and form of life, and in doing whatever it properly can, as a community with uniquely wide but still subsidiary functions, to discourage such conduct.

VII

I promised to defend the judgment that the government of political communities is subsidiary, and rationally limited not only by constitutional law and by the moral norms which limit every decent person's deliberation and choice, but also by the inherent limits of its general justifying aim, purpose or rationale. That rationale is, of course, the common good of the political community. And that common good, I shall argue, is not basic, intrinsic or constitutive, but rather is instrumental.

Every community is constituted by the communication and cooperation between its members. To say that a community has a common good is simply to say that communication and cooperation have a point which the members more or less concur in understanding, valuing and pursuing. There are three types of common good which each provide the constitutive point of a distinctive type of open-ended community and directly instantiate a basic human good: (1) the affectionate mutual help and shared enjoyment of the friendship and communio of "real friends"; (2) the sharing of husband and wife in married life, united as complementary, bodily persons whose activities make them apt for parenthood – the communio of spouses and, if their marriage is fruitful, their children; (3) the communio of religious believers cooperating in the devotion and service called for by what they believe to be the accessible truths about the ultimate source of meaning, value and other realities, and about the ways in which human beings can be in harmony with that ultimate source. Other human communities either are dedicated to accomplishing a specific goal or set of goals (like a university or hospital) and so are not in the open-ended service of their members, or have a common good which is instrumental rather than basic. One should notice here that association and cooperation, even when oriented towards goals which are both specific and instrumentally rather than basically and intrinsically good (as, e.g., in a business enterprise), have a more than merely instrumental character inasmuch as they instantiate the basic good of friendship in one or other of its central or non-central forms.

The political community – properly understood as one of the forms of collaboration needed for the sake of the basic goods identified in the first principles of natural law – is a community cooperating in the service of a common good which is instrumental, not itself basic. True, it is a good which is "great and god-like"[27] in its ambitious range: "to secure the whole ensemble of material and other conditions, including forms of collaboration, that tend to favor, facilitate, and foster the realization by each individual in that community of his or her personal development"[28] (which will in each case include, constitutively, the flourishing of the family, friendship and other communities to which that person belongs). True too, its proper range includes the regulation of friendships, marriage, families, and religious associations, as well as of all the many organizations and associations which are dedicated to specific goals or which, like the state itself, have only an instrumental (e.g., an economic) common good. But such regulation of these associations should never (in the case of the associations with a non-instrumental common good) or only exceptionally (in the case of instrumental associations) be intended to take over the formation, direction, or management of these personal initiatives and interpersonal associations. Rather, its purpose must be to carry out the subsidiary (i.e. helping from the Latin subsidium, help) function[29] of assisting individuals and groups to coordinate their activities for the objectives and commitments they have chosen, and to do so in ways consistent with the other aspects of the common good of this community, uniquely complex, far-reaching and demanding in its rationale, its requirements of cooperation, and its monopolization of force: the political community.[30]

The fundamentally instrumental character of the political common good is indicated by both parts of the Second Vatican Council's teaching about religious liberty, a teaching considered by the Council to be a matter of natural law (i.e., of "reason itself").[31] The first part of the teaching is that everyone has the right not to be coerced in matters of religious belief and practice. For, to know the truth about the ultimate matters compendiously called by the Council "religious," and to adhere to and put into practice the truth one has come to know, is so significant a good and so basic a responsibility, and the attainment of that "good of the human spirit"[32] is so inherently and non-substitutably a matter of personal assent and conscientious decision, that if a government intervenes coercively in people's search for true religious beliefs, or in people's expression of the beliefs they suppose true, it will harm those people and violate their dignity even when its intervention is based on the correct premise that their search has been negligently conducted and/or has led them into false beliefs. Religious acts, according to the Council, "transcend" the sphere which is proper to government; government is to care for the temporal common good, and this includes the subsidiary function of acknowledging and fostering the religious life of its citizens; but governments have no responsibility or right to direct religious acts, and "exceed their proper limits" if they presume to do so.[33]

The second part of the Council's teaching concerns the proper restrictions on religious freedom, namely those restrictions which are required for [i] the effective protection of the rights of all citizens and of their peaceful coexistence, [ii] a sufficient care for the authentic public peace of an ordered common life in true justice, and [iii] a proper upholding of public morality. All these factors constitute the fundamental part of the common good, and come under the notion of ordre public.[34]

Here, too, the political common good is presented as instrumental, serving the protection of human and legal rights, public peace and public morality – in other words, the preservation of a social environment conducive to virtue. Government is precisely not presented here as dedicated to the commanding of virtue and the repressing of vice, as such, even though virtue (and vice) are of supreme and constitutive importance for well-being (or otherwise) of individual persons and the worth (or otherwise) of their associations.

Is the Council's natural law teaching right? Or should we rather adhere to the uncomplicated theory of Aquinas's treatise On Princely Government, that government should command whatever leads people towards their ultimate (heavenly) end, forbid whatever deflects them from it, and coercively deter people from evil-doing and induce them to morally decent conduct?[35] Perhaps the most suasive short statement of that teaching is still Aristotle's famous attack on theories which, like the sophist Lycophron's, treat the state as a mere mutual insurance arrangement?[36] But in two crucial respects, at least, Aristotle (and with him the tradition) has taken things too easily.

First: If the object, point or common good of the political community were indeed a self-sufficient life, and if self-sufficiency (autarcheia) were indeed what Aristotle defines it to be – a life lacking in nothing, of complete fulfillment[37] – then we would have to say that the political community has a point it cannot hope to achieve, a common good utterly beyond its reach. For subsequent philosophical reflection has confirmed what one might suspect from Aristotle's own manifest oscillation between different conceptions of eudaimonia (and thus of autarcheia): Integral human fulfillment is nothing less than the fulfillment of (in principle) all human persons in all communities and cannot be achieved in any community short of the heavenly kingdom, a community envisaged not by unaided reason (natural law theory) but only by virtue of divine revelation and attainable only by a divine gift which transcends the capacities of nature. To be sure, integral human fulfillment can and should be a conception central to a natural law theory of morality and thus of politics, and should be envisaged as a kind of ideal community (to which will answer the reality of the Kingdom which Christian faith's first moral norm directs us to seek).[38] But that ideal community is not, as early natural law theories such as Aristotle's prematurely proposed, the political community.

Second: When Aristotle speaks of "making" people good, he constantly[39] uses the word *poiesis* which he has so often contrasted with praxis and reserved for techniques ("arts") of manipulating matter.[40] But helping citizens to choose and act in line with integral human fulfillment must involve something which goes beyond any art or technique. For only individual acting persons can by their own choices make themselves good or evil. Not that their life should or can be individualistic; their deliberating and choosing will be shaped, and helped or hindered, by the language of their culture, by their family, their friends, their associates and enemies, the customs of their communities, the laws of their polity, and by the impress of human influences of many kinds from beyond their homeland. Their choices will involve them in relationships just or unjust, generous or illiberal, vengeful or charitable, with other persons in all these communities. And as members of all these communities they have some responsibility to encourage their fellow-members in morally good and discourage them from morally bad conduct.

To be sure, the political community is a cooperation which undertakes the unique tasks of giving coercive protection to all individuals and lawful associations within its domain, and of securing an economic and cultural environment in which all these persons and groups can pursue their own proper good. To be sure, this common good of the political community makes it far more than a mere arrangement for "preventing mutual injury and exchanging goods." But it is one thing to maintain, as reason requires, that the political community's rationale requires that its public managing structure, the state, should deliberately and publicly identify, encourage, facilitate and support the truly worthwhile (including moral virtue), should deliberately and publicly identify, discourage and hinder the harmful and evil, and should, by its criminal prohibitions and sanctions (as well as its other laws and policies), assist people with parental responsibilities to educate children and young people in virtue and to discourage their vices. It is another things to maintain that that rationale requires or authorizes the state to direct people to virtue and deter them from vice by making even secret and truly consensual adult acts of vice a punishable offence against the state's laws.[41]

So there was a sound and important distinction of principle which the Supreme Court of the United States overlooked in moving from *Griswold v Connecticut*[42] (private use of contraceptives by spouses) to *Eisenstadt v Baird* (public distribution of contraceptives to unmarried people).[43] The truth and relevance of that distinction, and its high importance for the common good, would be overlooked again if laws criminalizing private acts of sodomy between adults were to be struck down by the Court on any ground which would also constitutionally require the law to tolerate the advertising or marketing of homosexual services, the maintenance of places of resort for homosexual activity, or the promotion of homosexual-ist "lifestyles" via education and public media of communication, or to recognize homosexual "marriages" or permit the adoption of children by homosexually active people, and so forth.

NOTES

1 *Knuller (Publishing, Printing and Promotions) Ltd. v. Director of Pub. Prosecutions*, [1973] A.C. 435 (1972).
2 *Regina v. Goddard*, 92 Crim. App. R. 185 (1990); Regina v. Gray 74 Crim. App. R. 324 (1981); Regina v. Ford, 66 Crim. App. R. 46 (1977).
3 Sexual Offences Act 1956, 4 & 5 Eliz. 2, ch. 69, § 32 (Eng.).
4 Id. § 6(1) (heterosexual acts: age of consent 16); Sexual Offences Act, 1967, ch. 60, § 1(1) (Eng.) (homosexual acts: age of consent 21).
5 The bill has yet to be passed by the House of Lords.
6 The statute states:
    2A(1) A local authority shall not:

(a) intentionally promote homosexuality or publish material with the intention of promoting homosexuality;

(b) promote the teaching in any maintained school of the acceptability of homosexuality as a pretended family relationship.

Local Government Act 1986, ch. 10, § 2A (Eng.), inserted by Local Government Act 1988, ch. 9, § 28(Eng.).

A "maintained school" is any school funded by a local governmental authority and includes most of the schools in England.

7 *Dudgeon v. United Kingdom*, 45 Eur. Ct. H.R. 21 (ser.A) (1981); Norris v. Ireland, 142 Eur. Ct. H.R. 20 (ser.A) (1988).

8 Application 11680/85, decision of March 10, 1988, unpublished; see Mireille Delmas-Marty, *The European Convention for the Protection of Human Rights; International Protection versus National Restrictions* 253–54 (1992).

9 *Gay Rights Coalition of Georgetown Univ. Law Ctr. v. Georgetown Univ.*, 536 A.2d 1 (D.C. 1987).

10 Germain Grisez, *The Way of the Lord Jesus, Living a Christian Life* 555–574, 633–680 (1993).

11 Aristotle, *Nicomachean Ethics*, VIII, 12: 1162a16–30; see also the probably pseudo-Aristotle, *Oeconomica* I, 3–4; 1343b12–1344a22; III.

12 Plutarch reads this conception back to the dawn of Athenian civilization and, doubtless anachronistically, ascribes it to the great original Athenian law-giver, Solon: Marriage should be "a union of life between man and woman for the delights of love and the getting of children." Plutarch, *Life of Solon* 20, 4. See also Plutarch, *Erotikos* 769:

In the case of lawful wives, physical union is the beginning of friendship, a sharing, as it were, in great mysteries. [The] pleasure is short [or unimportant: mikron], but the respect and kindness and mutual affection and loyalty that daily spring from it [conjugal sex] convicts neither the Delphians of raving when they call Aphrodite "Harmony" nor Homer when he designates such a union "friendship." It also proves that Solon was a very experienced legislator of marriage laws. He prescribed that a man should consort with his wife not less than three times a month – not for the pleasure surely, but as cities renew their mutual agreements from time to time, just so he must have wished this to be a renewal of marriage and with such an act of tenderness to wipe out the complaints that accumulate from everyday living.

13 See Plutarch, *Erotikos* 768D–770A; IX *Moralia* 427 (Loeb ed., 1961); see also the fine translation in D.A. Russell, *Plutarch* 92 (1973).

14 Plutarch speaks of the union of husband and wife as an "integral amalgamation" [di' holon krasis]. Plutarch, *Erotikos* 769F; *Coniugalia Praecepta* 142F.

15 St. Augustine, *De Bono Coniugali*, 9.9.

16 Id. at 3.3.

17 Plutarch, *Erotikos* 769f; *Coniugalia Praecepta* 142f.

18 John Paul II, Address to Young Married Couples at Taranto (October 1989), quoted in Grisez, *supra* note 10, at 571 n.46 ("a great project: fusing your persons to the point of becoming 'one flesh'").

19 Grisez, *supra* note 10, at 556–69.

20 John Paul II, *Veritas Splendor* § §13, 48 (1984); see also id. at § § 50, 67, 78, 79.

21 Steven Macedo, The New Natural Lawyers, *The Harv. Crimson*, Oct. 28, 1993, writes:

> In effect, gays can have sex in a way that is open to procreation, and to new life. They can be, and many are, prepared to engage in the kind of loving relations that would result in procreation – were conditions different. Like sterile married couples, many would like nothing better. Here, fantasy has taken leave of reality. Anal or oral intercourse, whether between spouses or between males, is no more a biological union "open to procreation" than is intercourse with a goat by a shepherd who fantasizes about breeding a faun; each "would" yield the desired mutant "were conditions different." Biological union between humans is the inseminatory union of male genital organ with female genital organ; in most circumstances it does not result in generation, but it is the behavior that unites biologically because it is the behavior which, as behavior, is suitable for generation.

22 For the whole argument, see Grisez, *supra* note 10, at 634–9, 662–4.

23 Plato, *Gorgias* 494–5, especially 494el–5, 495b3.

24 Plutarch, *Life of Solon*, 20, 3. The post-Christian moral philosophy of Kant identified the wrongfulness of masturbation and homosexual (and bestial) conduct as consisting in the instrumentalisation of one's body, and thus ("since a person is an absolute unity") the "wrong to humanity in our own person." But Kant, though he emphasizes the equality of husband and wife (impossible in concubinage or more casual prostitution), did not integrate this insight with an understanding of marriage as a single two-part good involving, inseparably, friendship as well as procreation. Hence he was puzzled by the question why marital intercourse is right when the woman is pregnant or beyond the menopause.

See Immanuel Kant, *The Metaphysics of Morals* 277–9, 424–6 (Mary Gregor trans., Cambridge Univ. Press 1991, 96–7, 220–2) (1797). The deep source of his puzzlement is his refusal to allow intelligible goods any structural role in his ethics, a refusal which sets him against a classical moral philosophy such as Aristotle's, and indeed against any adequate theory of natural law, and in turn is connected with his dualistic separation of body from mind and body, a separation which conflicts with his own insight, just quoted, that the person is a real unity.

25 Or deliberately contracepted, which I omit from the list in the text only because it would no doubt not now be accepted by secular civil law as preventing consummation – a failure of understanding. See discussion, *supra* note 21.

26 Macedo, *supra* note 21, at 2:

> All we can say is that conditions would have to be more radically different in the case of gay and lesbian couples than sterile married couples for new life to result from sex ... but what is the moral force of that? The new natural law theory does not make moral judgments based on natural facts.

Macedo's phrase "based on" equivocates between the first premises of normative arguments (which must be normative) and other premise(s) (which can and normally should be factual and, where appropriate, can refer to natural facts such as that the human mouth is not a reproductive organ).

27 Aristotle, *Nicomachean Ethics*, I, 1: 1094b9.

28 John Finnis, *Natural Law and Natural Rights* 147 (1980). As I indicate, this account of the common good of the political community is close to that worked out by French commentators on Aquinas in the early mid-twentieth century. Id. at 160. A similar account was adopted by the Second Vatican Council: "the sum of those conditions of social life which allow social groups and their individual members relatively thorough and ready access to their own fulfillment." *Gaudium et Spes* § 26 (1965); see also *Dignitatis Humanae* § 6 (1965).

29 See *Finnis, supra,* note 28, at 146–7, 159.

30 Of course, the common good of the political community has important elements which are scarcely shared with any other community within the polity: for example, the restoration of justice by punishment of those who have offended against just laws; the coercive repelling and restraint of those whose conduct (including negligent omissions) unfairly threatens the interests of others, particularly those interests identified as moral

("human") or legal rights, and corresponding compulsory measures to secure restitution, compensation or reparation for violations of rights; and the specifying and upholding of a system of holding or property rights which respects the various interests, immediate and vested or remote and contingent, which everyone has in each holding. But the fact that these and various other elements of the political common good are peculiar to the political community and the proper responsibility of its leaders, the government, in no way entails that these elements are basic human goods or that the political common good is other than in itself instrumental.

31 *Dignitatis Humanae* § 2. In the succeeding part, the Declaration treats the matter as one of divine revelation. Id. at § § 9–14.

32 It is one of the animi humani bona mentioned in id., § 1.

33 "Potestas igitur civilis, cuilus finis proprius est bonum commune tempo-rale curare, religiosam quidem civium vitam agnoscere eique favere debet, sed limites suos excedere dicenda est, si actus religiosos dirigere vel impedire praesumat." Id. at § 3.

34 Id. at § 7.

35 *De Regimine Principum* c.14 (... ab iniquitate coerceat et ad opera virtuosa inducat). This thesis is qualified, thought not abandoned, in other works of Aquinas. Thus Summa Theologiae II-II q. 104 a.5c teaches that human government has no authority over people's minds and the interior motives of their wills. Id. I-II q.96 a.2 teaches that governmental pursuit of virtue should be gradual and should not ask too much of the average citizen (who is not virtuous).

36 It states:

[T]he polis was formed not for the sake of life only but rather for the good life ... and ... its purpose is not [merely] military alliance for defence ... and it does not exist [merely] for the sake of trade and business rela-tions ... any polis which is truly so called, and is not one merely in name, must have virtue/excellence as an object of its care [peri aretes epimeles einai: be solicitous about virtue]. Otherwise a polis sinks into a mere alli-ance, differing only in space from other forms of alliance where the mem-bers live at a distance from one another. Otherwise, too, the law becomes a mere social contract [syntheke: covenant] – or (in the phrase of the sophist Lycophron) "a guarantor of justice as between one man and another" – instead of being, as it should be, such as will make [poiein] the citizens good and just ... The polis is not merely a sharing of a common locality for the purpose of preventing mutual injury and exchanging goods. These are necessary preconditions of the existence of a polis ... but a polis is a communio [kiononia] of clans [and neighborhoods] in living well, with the object of a full and self-sufficient [autarkous] life ... it must therefore be for the sake of truly good [kalon] actions, not of merely living together.

Aristotle, *Politics*, III.5: 1280a32, a35, 1280b7–13, b30–31, b34, 1281a1–4.

37 Aristotle, *Nicomachean Ethics*, I, 7:1097b8. This, incidentally, differs widely from what Stephen Macedo, *Liberal Virtues* 215–17 (1990), means by "an autarchic person."

38 For nothing less than integral human fulfillment, the fulfillment of all persons in all the basic human goods, answers to reason's full knowledge of, and the will's full interest in, the human good in which one can participate by action. And so the first principle of a sound morality must be: In voluntarily acting for human goods and avoiding what is opposed to them, one ought to choose and will those and only those possibilities whose willing is compatible with integral human fulfillment. To say that immorality is constituted by cutting back on, fettering, reason by passions is equivalent to saying that the sway of feelings over reason constitutes immorality by deflecting one to objectives not in line with integral human fulfillment. This ideal community is thus the good will's most fundamental orienting ideal.

39 Apart from the passage just cited, see Aristotle, *Nicomachean Ethics*, I, 10; 1099b32; II, 1: 110364; X, 9: 1180b24.

40 Aristotle, *Nicomachean Ethics*, VI, 5: 1140a2; Aristotle, *Politics*, 1, 2: 1254a5.

41 So a third way in which Aristotle takes things too easily in his slide from upholding government's responsibility to assist or substitute for the direct parental discipline of youth, to claiming that this responsibility continues, and in the same direct coercive form, "to cover the whole of a lifetime, since most people obey necessity rather than argument, and punishments rather than the sense of what is truly worthwhile." Aristotle, *Nicomachean Ethics*, X.9:1180a1–3.

42 381 U.S. 479 (1965).

43 405 U.S. 438 (1972). The law struck down in *Griswold* was the law forbidding use of contraceptives even by married persons; Griswold's conviction as an accessory to such use fell with the fall of the substantive law against the principals in such use. Very different, in principle, would have been a law directly forbidding Griswold's activities as a public promoter of contraceptive information and supplies. If American constitutional law fails to recognize such distinctions, it shows, I suggest, its want of sound principle.

Professor Finnis would like it noted that a more general and more detailed account of his understanding of the morality of sexual relations, and references to matters omitted in the excerpt, can be found in his "The Good of Marriage and the Morality of Sexual Relations: Some Philosophical and Historical Observations" 42 *American Journal of Jurisprudence* (1998) 97–134.

READING QUESTIONS ON FINNIS

1　Compare Finnis's argument to Lord Devlin's position and also to Dworkin, both "Law's Ambitions for Itself" and Dworkin's response to Devlin. Finnis is the leading contemporary exponent on natural law and his vision of community is clearly not the positivistic one Dworkin attributes to Bork. Does Finnis present a "moral position" and if so on what grounds would Dworkin object to that position? Or is Finnis's position – especially the distinction he draws at the end of his article – consistent with Dworkin's and Mill's principle of privacy? If the position is so consistent, is the Supreme Court of Canada now illiberal?

2　Do we want the state involved in a debate about the connection between intimacy and legal protection for relationships? Has the Supreme Court of Canada entered that debate?

6

Civil Disobedience

Civil disobedience has a long and distinguished history. Henry David Thoreau wrote a classic defence of breaking the law while in prison for refusal to pay taxes that supported slavery. Thoreau argued that there were some circumstances in which the only place an honest person could feel comfortable is in jail. Mahatma Gandhi directed a massive campaign of non-violent non-cooperation in the attempt to end British rule in India. In the 1960s, Martin Luther King, Jr, organized a campaign of civil disobedience to end discrimination against African Americans.

In each of these examples, the nobility of the cause and the eloquence of its leaders makes the choice of tactics strike us as obviously appropriate (at least in retrospect). Not surprisingly, more recent opponents of what are perceived to be illegitimate government policies have engaged in activities that they too describe as civil disobedience. Opponents of everything from nuclear weapons development to Sunday closing laws have claimed the mantle of civil disobedience. At one level, the description plainly fits: in the service of what is believed to be a "higher" law, laws are broken, but violence is generally not employed. Yet if the concept of civil disobedience is to have any moral purchase, there must be some limits to its application. Not every illegal act done in the service of what is thought to be moral principle deserves either our support or the lenience of courts in sentencing. The readings in this section explore a variety of ways of thinking about civil disobedience as a moral and legal category. They seek to determine which acts are worthy of special support. They also consider whether, and when, courts should treat morally motivated disobedience differently.

John Rawls
"Civil Disobedience" (1971)

Rawls suggests that any theory of democracy and the rule of law needs to include an account of the legitimate occasions of civil disobedience. He argues that civil disobedience is justified when it serves to remind citizens of injustices in a society that is largely just.

55 THE DEFINITION OF CIVIL DISOBEDIENCE

... The problem of civil disobedience, as I shall interpret it, arises only within a more or less just democratic state for those citizens who recognize and accept the legitimacy of the constitution. The difficulty is one of a conflict of duties. At what point does the duty to comply with laws enacted by a legislative majority (or with executive acts supported by such a majority) cease to be binding in view of the right to defend one's liberties and the duty to oppose injustice? This question involves the nature and limits of majority rule. For this reason the problem of civil disobedience is a crucial test case for any theory of the moral basis of democracy.

A constitutional theory of civil disobedience has three parts. First, it defines this kind of dissent and separates it from other forms of opposition to democratic authority. These range from legal demonstrations and infractions of law designed to raise test cases before the courts to instant action and organized resistance. A theory specifies the place of civil disobedience in this spectrum of possibilities. Next, it sets out the grounds of civil disobedience and the conditions under which such action is justified in a (more or less) just democratic regime. And finally, a theory should explain the role of civil disobedience within a constitutional system and account for the appropriateness of this mode of protest within a free society.

Before I take up these matters, a word of caution. We should not expect too much of a theory of civil disobedience, even one framed for special circumstances. Precise principles that straightway decide actual cases are clearly out of the question. Instead, a useful theory defines a perspective within which the problem of civil disobedience can be approached; it identifies the relevant considerations and helps us to assign them their correct weights in the more important instances. If a theory about these matters appears to us, on reflection, to have cleared our vision and to have made our considered judgments more coherent, then it has been worthwhile. The theory has done what, for the present, one may reasonably expect it to do: namely, to narrow the disparity between the conscientious convictions of those who accept the basic principles of a democratic society.

I shall begin by defining civil disobedience as a public, nonviolent, conscientious yet political act contrary to law usually done with the aim of bringing about a change in the law or policies of the government. By acting in this way one addresses the sense of justice of the majority of the community and declares that in one's considered opinion the principles of social cooperation among free and equal men are not being respected. A preliminary gloss on this definition is that it does not require that the civilly disobedient act breach the same law that is being protested. It allows for what some have called indirect as well as direct civil disobedience. And this a definition should do, as there are sometimes strong reasons for not infringing on the law or policy held to be unjust. Instead, one may disobey traffic ordinances or laws of trespass as a way of presenting one's case. Thus, if the government enacts a vague and harsh statute against treason, it would not be appropriate to commit treason as a way of objecting to it, and in any event, the penalty might be far more than one should reasonably be ready to accept. In other cases there is no way to violate the government's policy directly, as when it concerns foreign affairs, or affects another part of the country. A second gloss is that the civilly disobedient act is indeed thought to be contrary to law, at least in the sense that those engaged in it are not simply presenting a test case for a constitutional decision; they are prepared to oppose the statute even if it should be upheld. To be sure, in a constitutional regime, the courts may finally side with the dissenters and declare the law or policy objected to unconstitutional. It often happens, then, that there is some uncertainty as to whether the dissenters' action will be held illegal or not. But this is merely a complicating element. Those who use civil disobedience to protest unjust laws are not prepared to desist should the courts eventually disagree with them, however pleased they might have been with the opposite decision.

It should also be noted that civil disobedience is a political act not only in the sense that it is addressed to the majority that holds political power, but also because it is an act guided and justified by political principles, that is, by the principles of justice which regulate the constitution and social institutions generally. In justifying civil disobedience one does not appeal to principles of personal morality or to religious doctrines, though these may coincide with and support one's claims; and it goes without saying that civil disobedience cannot be grounded solely on group or self-interest. Instead one invokes the commonly shared conception of justice that underlies the political order. It is assumed that in a reasonably just democratic regime there is a public conception of justice by reference to which citizens regulate their political affairs and interpret the constitution. The persistent and deliberate violation of the basic principles of this conception over any extended period of time, especially the infringement of the fundamental equal liberties, invites either submission or resistance. By engaging in civil disobedience a minority forces the majority to consider whether it wishes to have its actions construed in this way, or whether, in view of the common sense of justice, it wishes to acknowledge the legitimate claims of the minority.

A further point is that civil disobedience is a public act. Not only is it addressed to public principles, it is done in public. It is engaged in openly with fair notice; it is not covert or secretive. One may compare it to public speech, and being a form of address, an expression of profound and conscientious political conviction, it takes place in the public forum. For this reason, among others, civil disobedience is nonviolent. It tries to avoid the use of violence, especially against persons, not from the abhorrence of the use of force in principle, but because it is a final expression of one's case. To engage in violent acts likely to injure and to hurt is incompatible with civil disobedience as a mode of address. Indeed, any interference with the civil liberties of others tends to obscure the civilly disobedient quality of one's act. Sometimes if the appeal fails in its purpose, forceful resistance may later be entertained. Yet civil disobedience is giving voice to conscientious and deeply held convictions; while it may warn and admonish, it is not itself a threat.

Civil disobedience is nonviolent for another reason. It expresses disobedience to law within the limits of fidelity to law, although it is at the outer edge thereof. The law is broken, but fidelity to law is expressed by the public and nonviolent nature of the act, by the willingness to accept the legal consequences of one's conduct. This fidelity to law helps to establish to the majority that the act is indeed politically conscientious and sincere, and that is intended to address the public's sense of justice. To be completely open and nonviolent is to give bond of one's sincerity, for it is not easy to convince another that one's acts are conscientious, or even to be sure of this before oneself. No doubt it is possible to imagine a legal system in which conscientious belief that the law is unjust is accepted as a defense for noncompliance. Men of great honesty with full confidence in one another might make such a system work. But as things are, such a scheme would presumably be unstable even in a state of near justice. We must pay a certain price to convince others that our actions have, in our carefully considered view, a sufficient moral basis in the political convictions of the community.

Civil disobedience has been defined so that it falls between legal protest and the raising of test cases on the one side, and conscientious refusal and the various forms of resistance on the other. In this range of possibilities it stands for that form of dissent at the boundary of fidelity to law. Civil disobedience, so understood, is clearly distinct from militant action and obstruction; it is far removed from organized forcible resistance. The militant, for example, is much more deeply opposed to the existing political system. He does not accept it as one which is nearly just or reasonably so; he believes either that it departs widely from its professed principles or that it pursues a mistaken conception of justice altogether. While his action is conscientious in its own terms, he does not appeal to the sense of justice of the majority (or those having effective political power), since he thinks that their sense of justice is erroneous, or else without effect. Instead, he seeks by well-framed militant acts of disruption and resistance, and the like, to attack the prevalent view of justice or to force a movement in the desired direction. Thus the militant may try to evade the penalty, since he is not prepared to accept the legal consequences of his violation of the law; this would not only be to play into the hands of forces that he believes cannot be trusted, but also to express a recognition of the legitimacy of the constitution to which he is opposed. In this sense militant action is not within the bounds of fidelity to law, but represents a more profound opposition to the legal order. The basic structure is thought to be so unjust or else to depart so widely from its own professed ideals that one must try to prepare the way for radical or even revolutionary change. And this is to be done by trying to arouse the public to an awareness of the fundamental reforms that need to be made. Now in certain circumstances militant action and other kinds of resistance are surely justified. I shall not, however, consider these cases. As I have said, my aim here is the limited one of defining a concept of civil disobedience and understanding its role in a nearly just constitutional regime.

56 THE DEFINITION OF CONSCIENTIOUS REFUSAL

Although I have distinguished civil disobedience from conscientious refusal, I have yet to explain the latter notion. This will now be done. It must be recognized, however, that to separate these two ideas is to give a narrower definition to civil disobedience than is traditional; for it is customary to think of civil disobedience in a broader sense as any noncompliance with law for conscientious reasons, at least when it is not covert and does not involve the use of force. Thoreau's essay is characteristic, if not definitive, of the traditional meaning. The usefulness of the narrower sense will, I believe, be clear once the definition of conscientious refusal is examined.

Conscientious refusal is noncompliance with a more or less direct legal injunction or administrative order. It is refusal since an order is addressed to us and, given the nature of the situation, whether we accede to it is known to the authorities. Typical examples are the refusal of the early Christians to perform certain acts of piety prescribed by the pagan state, and the refusal of the Jehovah's Witnesses to salute the flag. Other examples are the unwillingness of a pacifist to serve in the armed forces, or of a soldier to obey an order that he thinks is manifestly contrary to the moral law as it applies to war. Or again, in Thoreau's case, the refusal to pay a tax on the grounds that to do so would make him an agent of grave injustice to another. One's sanction is assumed to be known to the authorities, however much one might wish, in some cases, to conceal it. Where it can be covert, one might speak of conscientious evasion rather than conscientious refusal. Covert infractions of a fugitive slave law are instances of conscientious evasion.

There are several contrasts between conscientious refusal (or evasion) and civil disobedience. First of all, conscientious refusal is not a form of address appealing to the sense of justice of the majority. To be sure, such acts are not generally secretive or covert, as concealment is often impossible anyway. One simply refuses on conscientious grounds to obey a command or to comply with a legal injunction. One does not invoke the convictions of the community, and in this case conscientious refusal is not an act in the public forum. Those ready to withhold obedience recognize that there may be no basis for mutual understanding; they do not seek out occasions for disobedience as a way to state their cause. Rather, they bide their time hoping that the necessity to disobey will not arise. They are less optimistic than those undertaking civil disobedience and they may entertain no expectation of changing laws or policies. The situation may allow no time for them to make their case, or again there may not be any chance that the majority will be receptive to their claims.

Conscientious refusal is not necessarily based on political principles; it may be founded on religious or other principles at variance with the constitutional order. Civil disobedience is an appeal to a commonly shared conception of justice, whereas conscientious refusal may have other grounds. For example, assuming that the early Christians would not justify their refusal to comply with the religious customs of the Empire by reasons of justice but simply as being contrary to their religious convictions, their argument would not be political; nor, with similar qualifications, are the views of a pacifist, assuming that wars of self-defense at least are recognized by the conception of justice that underlies a constitutional regime. Conscientious refusal may, however, be grounded on political principles. One may decline to go along with a law thinking that it is so unjust that complying with it is simply out of the question. This would be the case if, say, the law were to enjoin our being the agent of enslaving another, or to require us to submit to a similar fate. These are patent violations of recognized political principles.

It is a difficult matter to find the right course when some men appeal to religious principles in refusing to do actions which, it seems, are required by principles of political justice. Does the pacifist possess an immunity from military service in a just war, assuming that there are such wars? Or is the state permitted to impose certain hardships for noncompliance? There is a temptation to say that the law must always respect the dictates of conscience, but this cannot be right. As we have seen in the case of the intolerant, the legal order must regulate men's pursuit of their religious interests so as to realize the principle of equal liberty; and it may certainly forbid religious practices such as human sacrifice, to take an extreme case. Neither religiosity nor conscientiousness suffices to protect this practice. A theory of justice must work out from its own point of view how to treat those who dissent from it. The aim of a well-ordered society, or one in a state of near justice, is to preserve and strengthen the institutions of justice. If a religion is denied its full expression, it is presumably because it is in violation of the equal liberties of others. In general, the degree of tolerance accorded opposing moral conceptions depends upon the extent to which they can be allowed an equal place within a just system of liberty.

If pacifism is to be treated with respect and not merely tolerated, the explanation must be that it accords reasonably well with the principles of justice, the main exception arising from its attitude toward engaging in a just war (assuming here that in some situations wars of self-defense are justified). The political principles recognized by the community have a certain affinity with the doctrine the pacifist professes. There is a common abhorrence of war and the use of force, and a belief in the equal status of men as moral persons. And given the tendency of nations, particularly great powers, to engage in war unjustifiably and to set in motion the apparatus of the state to suppress dissent, the respect accorded to pacifism serves the purpose of alerting citizens to the wrongs that governments are prone to commit in their name. Even though his views are not altogether sound, the warnings and protests that a pacifist is disposed to express may have the result that on balance the principles of justice are more rather than less secure. Pacifism as a natural departure from the correct doctrine conceivably compensates for the weakness of men living up to their professions.

It should be noted that there is, of course, in actual situations no sharp distinction between civil disobedience and conscientious refusal. Moreover the same action (or sequence of actions) may have strong elements of both. While there are clear cases of each, the contrast between them is intended as a way of elucidating the interpretation of civil disobedience and its role in a democratic society. Given the nature of this way of acting as a special kind of political appeal, it is not usually justified until other steps have been taken within the legal framework. By contrast this requirement often fails in the obvious cases of legitimate conscientious refusal. In a free society no one may be compelled, as the early Christians were, to perform religious acts in violation of equal liberty, nor must a soldier comply with inherently evil commands while awaiting an appeal to higher authority. These remarks lead up to the question of justification.

57 THE JUSTIFICATION OF CIVIL DISOBEDIENCE

With these various distinctions in mind, I shall consider the circumstances under which civil disobedience is justified. For simplicity I shall limit the discussion to domestic institutions and so to injustices internal to a given society. The somewhat narrow nature of this restriction will be mitigated a bit by taking up the contrasting problem of conscientious refusal in connection with the moral law as it applies to war. I shall begin by setting out what seem to be reasonable conditions for engaging in civil disobedience, and then later connect these conditions more systematically with the place of civil disobedience in a state of near justice. Of course, the conditions enumerated should be taken as presumptions; no doubt there will be situations when they do not hold, and other arguments could be given for civil disobedience.

The first point concerns the kinds of wrongs that are appropriate objects of civil disobedience. Now if one views such disobedience as a political act addressed to the sense of justice of the community, then it seems reasonable, other things equal, to limit it to instances of substantial and clear injustice, and preferably to those which obstruct the path to removing other injustices. For this reason there is a presumption in favor of restricting civil disobedience to serious infringements of the first principle of justice, the principle of equal liberty, and to blatant violations of the second part of the second principle, the principle of fair equality of opportunity. Of course, it is not always easy to tell whether these principles are satisfied. Still, if we think of them as guaranteeing the basic liberties, it is often clear that these freedoms are not being honored. After all, they impose certain strict requirements that must be visibly expressed in institutions. Thus when certain minorities are denied the right to vote or to hold office, or to own property and to move from place to place, or when certain religious groups are repressed and others denied various opportunities, these injustices may be obvious to all. They are publicly incorporated into the recognized practice, if not the letter, of social arrangements. The establishment of these wrongs does not presuppose an informed examination of institutional effects.

By contrast infractions of the difference principle are more difficult to ascertain. There is usually a wide range of conflicting yet rational opinion as to whether this principle is satisfied. The reason for this is that it applies primarily to economic and social institutions and policies. A choice among these depends upon theoretical and speculative beliefs as well as upon a wealth of statistical and other information, all of this seasoned with shrewd judgment and plain hunch. In view of the complexities of these questions, it is difficult to check the influence of self-interest and prejudice; and even if we can do this in our own case, it is another matter to convince others of our good faith. Thus unless tax laws, for example, are clearly designed to attack or to abridge a basic equal liberty, they should not normally be protested by civil disobedience. The appeal to the public's conception of justice is not sufficiently clear. The resolution of these issues is best left to the political process provided that the requisite equal liberties are secure. In this case a reasonable compromise can presumably be reached. The violation of the principle of equal liberty is, then, the more appropriate object of civil disobedience. This principle defines the common status of equal citizenship in a constitutional regime and lies at the basis of the political order. When it is fully honored the presumption is that other injustices, while possibly persistent and significant, will not get out of hand.

A further condition for civil disobedience is the following. We may suppose that the normal appeals to the political majority have already been made in good faith and that they have failed. The legal means of redress have proved of no avail. Thus, for example, the existing political parties have shown themselves indifferent to the claims of the minority or have proved unwilling to accommodate them. Attempts to have the laws repealed have been ignored and legal protests and demonstrations have had no success. Since civil disobedience is a last resort, we should be sure that it is necessary. Note that it has not been said, however, that legal means have been exhausted. At any rate, further normal appeals can be repeated; free speech is always possible. But if past actions have shown the majority immovable or apathetic, further attempts may reasonably be thought fruitless, and a second condition for justified civil disobedience is met. This condition is, however, a presumption. Some cases may be so extreme that there may be no duty to use first only legal means of political opposition. If, for example, the legislature were to enact some outrageous violation of equal liberty, say by forbidding the religion of a weak and defenseless minority, we surely could not expect that sect to oppose the law by normal political procedures. Indeed, even civil disobedience might be much too mild, the majority having already convicted itself of wantonly unjust and overtly hostile aims.

The third and last condition I shall discuss can be rather complicated. It arises from the fact that while the two preceding conditions are often sufficient to justify civil disobedience, this is not always the case. In certain circumstances the natural duty of justice may require a certain restraint. We can see this as follows. If a certain minority is justified in engaging in civil disobedience, then any other minority in relevantly similar circumstances is likewise justified. Using the two previous conditions as the criteria of relevantly similar circumstances, we can say that, other things equal, two minorities are similarly justified in resorting to civil disobedience if they have suffered for the same length of time from the same degree of injustice and if their equally sincere and normal political appeals have likewise been to no avail. It is conceivable, however, even if it is unlikely, that there should be many groups with an equally sound case (in the sense just defined) for being civilly disobedient, but that, if they were all to act in this way, serious disorder would follow which might well undermine the efficacy of the just constitution. I assume here that there is a limit on the extent to which civil disobedience can be engaged in without leading to a breakdown in the respect for law and the constitution, thereby setting in motion consequences unfortunate for all. There is also an upper bound on the ability of the public forum to handle such forms of dissent; the appeal that civilly disobedient groups wish to make can be distorted and their intention to appeal to the sense of justice of the majority lost sight of. For one or both of these reasons, the effectiveness of civil disobedience as a form of protest declines beyond a certain point; and those contemplating it must consider these constraints.

The ideal solution from a theoretical point of view calls for a cooperative political alliance of the minorities to regulate the overall level of dissent. For consider the nature of the situation: there are many groups each equally entitled to engage in civil disobedience. Moreover they all wish to exercise this right, equally strong in each case; but if they all do so, lasting injury may result to the just constitution to which they each recognize a natural duty of justice. Now when there are many equally strong claims which if taken together exceed what can be granted, some fair plan should be adopted so that all are equitably considered. In simple cases of claims to goods that are indivisible and fixed in number, some rotation or lottery scheme may be the fair solution when the number of equally valid claims is too great. But this sort of device is completely unrealistic here. What seems called for is a political understanding among the minorities suffering from injustice. They can meet their duty to democratic institutions by coordinating their actions so that while each has an opportunity to exercise its right, the limits on the degree of civil disobedience are not exceeded. To be sure, an alliance of this sort is difficult to arrange; but with perceptive leadership, it does not appear impossible.

Certainly the situation envisaged is a special one, and it is quite possible that these sorts of considerations will not be a bar to justified civil disobedience. There are not likely to be many groups similarly entitled to engage in this form of dissent while at the same time recognizing a duty to a just constitution. One should note, however, that an injured minority is tempted to believe its claims as strong as those of any other; and therefore even if the reasons that different groups have for engaging in civil disobedience are not equally compelling, it is often wise to presume that their claims are indistinguishable. Adopting this maxim, the circumstance imagined seems more likely to happen. This kind of case is also instructive in showing that the exercise of the right to dissent, like the exercise of rights generally, is sometimes limited by others having the very same right. Everyone's exercising this right would have deleterious consequences for all, and some equitable plan is called for.

Suppose that in the light of the three conditions, one has a right to appeal one's case by civil disobedience. The injustice one protests is a clear violation of the liberties of equal citizenship, or of equality of opportunity, this violation having been more or less deliberate over an extended period of time in the face of normal political opposition, and any complications raised by the question of fairness are met. These conditions are not exhaustive; some allowance still has to be made for the possibility of injury to third parties, to the innocent, so to speak. But I assume that they cover the main points. There is still, of course, the question whether it is wise or prudent to exercise this right. Having established the right, one is now free, as one is not before, to let these matters decide the issue. We may be acting within our rights but nevertheless unwisely if our conduct only serves to provoke the harsh retaliation of the majority. To be sure, in a state of near justice, vindictive repression of legitimate dissent is unlikely, but it is important that the action be properly designed to make an effective appeal to the wider community. Since civil disobedience is a mode of address taking place in the public forum, care must be taken to see that it is understood. Thus the exercise of the right to civil disobedience should, like any other right, be rationally framed to advance one's ends or the ends of those one wishes to assist. The theory of justice has nothing specific to say about these practical considerations. In any event questions of strategy and tactics depend upon the circumstances of each case. But the theory of justice should say at what point these matters are properly raised.

Now in this account of the justification of civil disobedience I have not mentioned the principle of fairness. The natural duty of justice is the primary basis of our political ties to a constitutional regime. As we noted before (s. 52), only the more favored members of society are likely to have a clear political obligation as opposed to a political duty. They are better situated to win public office and find it easier to take advantage of the political system. And having done so, they have acquired an obligation owed to citizens generally to uphold the just constitution. But members of subjected minorities, say, who have a strong case for civil disobedience will not generally have a political obligation of this sort. This does not mean, however, that the principle of fairness will not give rise to important obligations in their case. For not only do many of the requirements of private life derive from this principle, but it comes into force when persons or groups come together for common political purposes. Just as we acquire obligations to others with whom we have joined in various private associations, those who engage in political action assume obligatory ties to one another. Thus while the political obligation of dissenters to citizens generally is problematical, bonds of loyalty and fidelity still develop between them as they seek to advance their cause. In general, free association under a just constitution gives rise to obligations provided that the ends of the group are legitimate and its arrangements fair. This is as true of political as it is of other associations. These obligations are of immense significance and they constrain in many ways what individuals can do. But they are distinct from an obligation to comply with a just constitution. My discussion of civil disobedience is in terms of the duty of justice alone; a fuller view would note the place of these other requirements.

58 THE JUSTIFICATION OF CONSCIENTIOUS REFUSAL

In examining the justification of civil disobedience I assumed for simplicity that the laws and policies protested concerned domestic affairs. It is natural to ask how the theory of political duty applies to foreign policy. Now in order to do this it is necessary to extend the theory of justice to the law of nations. I shall try to indicate how this can be done. To fix ideas I shall consider briefly the justification of conscientious refusal to engage in certain acts of war, or to serve in the armed forces. I assume that this refusal is based upon political and not upon religious or other principles; that is, the principles cited by way of justification are those of the conception of justice underlying the constitution. Our problem, then, is to relate the just political principles regulating the conduct of states to the contract doctrine and to explain the moral basis of the law of nations from this point of view ...

I can give only an indication of the principles that would be acknowledged. But, in any case, there would be no surprises, since the principles chosen would, I think, be familiar ones. The basic principle of the law of nations is a principle of equality. Independent peoples organized as states have certain fundamental equal rights. This principle is analogous to the equal rights of citizens in a constitutional regime. One consequence of this equality of nations is the principle of self-determination, the right of a people to settle its own affairs without the intervention of foreign powers. Another consequence is the right to self-defense against attack, including the right to form defensive alliances to protect this right. A further principle is that treaties are to be kept, provided they are consistent with the other principles governing the relations of states. Thus treaties for self-defense, suitably interpreted, would be binding, but agreements to cooperate in an unjustified attack are void *ab initio*.

These principles define when a nation has a just cause in war or, in the traditional phrase, its *jus ad bellum*. But there are also principles regulating the means that a nation may use to wage war, its *jus in bello*. Even in a just war certain forms of violence are strictly inadmissible; and where a country's right to war is questionable and uncertain, the constraints on the means it can use are all the more severe. Acts permissible in a war of legitimate self-defense, when these are necessary, may be flatly excluded in a more doubtful situation. The aim of war is a just peace, and therefore the means employed must not destroy the possibility of peace or encourage a contempt for human life that puts the safety of ourselves and of mankind in jeopardy. The conduct of war is to be constrained and adjusted to this end. The representatives of state would recognize that their national interest, as seen from the original position, is best served by acknowledging these limits on the means of war. This is because the national interest of a just state is defined by the principles of justice that have already been acknowledged. Therefore such a nation will aim above all to maintain and to preserve its just institutions and the conditions that make them possible. It is not moved by the desire for world power or national glory; nor does it wage war for purposes of economic gain or the acquisition of territory. These ends are contrary to the conception of justice that defines a society's legitimate interest, however prevalent they have been in the actual conduct of states. Granting these presumptions, then, it seems reasonable to suppose that the traditional prohibitions incorporating the natural duties that protect human life would be chosen.

Now if conscientious refusal in time of war appeals to these principles, it is founded upon a political conception, and not necessarily upon religious or other notions. While this form of denial may not be a political act, since it does not take place in the public forum, it is based upon the same theory of justice that underlies the constitution and guides its interpretation. Moreover, the legal order itself presumably recognizes in the form of treaties the validity of at least some of these principles of the law of nations. Therefore if a soldier is ordered to engage in certain illicit acts of war, he may refuse if he reasonably and conscientiously believes that the principles applying to the conduct of war are plainly violated. He can maintain that, all things considered, his natural duty not to be made the agent of grave injustice and evil to another outweighs his duty to obey. I cannot discuss here what constitutes a manifest violation of these principles. It must suffice to note that certain clear cases are perfectly familiar ...

A somewhat different question is whether one should join the armed forces at all during some particular war. The answer is likely to depend upon the aim of the war as well as upon its conduct. In order to make the situation definite, let us suppose that conscription is in force and that the individual has to consider whether to comply with his legal duty to enter military service. Now I shall assume that since conscription is a drastic interference with the basic liberties of equal citizenship, it cannot be justified by any needs less compelling than those of national security. In a well-ordered society (or in one nearly just) these needs are determined by the end of preserving just institutions. Conscription is permissible only if it is demanded for the defense of liberty itself, including here not only the liberties of the citizens of the society in question, but also those of persons in other societies as well. Therefore if a conscript army is less likely to be an instrument of unjustified foreign adventures, it may be justified on this basis alone despite the fact that conscription infringes upon the equal liberties of citizens. But in any case, the priority of liberty (assuming serial order to obtain) requires that conscription be used only as the security of liberty necessitates. Viewed from the standpoint of the legislature (the appropriate stage for this question), the mechanism of the draft can be defended only on this ground. Citizens agree to this arrangement as a fair way of sharing the burdens of national defense. To be sure, the hazards that any particular individual must face are in part the result of accident and historical happenstance. But in a well-ordered society anyway, these evils arise externally, that is, from unjustified attacks from the outside. It is impossible for just institutions to eliminate these hardships entirely. The most that they can do is to try to make sure that the risks of suffering from these imposed misfortunes are more or less evenly shared by all members of society over the course of their life, and that there is no avoidable class bias in selecting those who are called for duty.

Imagine, then, a democratic society in which conscription exists. A person may conscientiously refuse to comply with his duty to enter the armed forces during a particular war on the ground that the aims of the conflict are unjust. It may be that the objective sought by war is economic advantage or national power. The basic liberty of citizens cannot be interfered with to achieve these ends. And, of course, it is unjust and contrary to the law of nations to attack the liberty of other societies for these reasons. Therefore a just cause for war does not exist, and this may be sufficiently evident that a citizen is justified in refusing to discharge his legal duty. Both the law of nations and the principles of justice for his own society uphold him in this claim. There is sometimes a further ground for refusal based not on the aim of the war but upon its conduct. A citizen may maintain that once it is clear that the moral law of war is being regularly violated, he has a right to decline military service on the ground that he is entitled to insure that he honors his natural duty. Once he is in the armed forces, and in a situation where he finds himself ordered to do acts contrary to the moral law of war, he may not be able to resist the demand to obey. Actually, if the aims of the conflict are sufficiently dubious and the likelihood of receiving fragrantly unjust commands is sufficiently great, one may have a duty and not only a right to refuse. Indeed, the conduct and aims of states in waging war, especially large and powerful ones, are in some circumstances so likely to be unjust that one is forced to conclude that in the foreseeable future one must abjure military service altogether. So understood a form of contingent pacifism may be a perfectly reasonable position: the possibility of a just war is conceded but not under present circumstances.

What is needed, then, is not a general pacifism but a discriminating conscientious refusal to engage in war in certain circumstances. States have not been loath to recognize pacifism and to grant it a special status. The refusal to take part in all war under any conditions is an unworldly view bound to remain a sectarian doctrine. It no more challenges the state's authority than the celibacy of priests challenges the sanctity of marriage. By exempting pacifists from its prescriptions the state may even seem to display a certain magnanimity. But conscientious refusal based upon the principles of justice between peoples as they apply to particular conflicts is another matter. For such refusal is an affront to the government's pretensions, and when it becomes widespread, the continuation of an unjust war may prove impossible. Given the often predatory aims of state power, and the tendency of men to defer to their government's decision to wage war, a general willingness to resist the state's claims is all the more necessary.

59 THE ROLE OF CIVIL DISOBEDIENCE

The third aim of a theory of civil disobedience is to explain its role within a constitutional system and to account for its connection with a democratic polity. As always, I assume that the society in question is one that is nearly just; and this implies that it has some form of democratic government, although serious injustices may nevertheless exist. In such a society I assume that the principles of justice are for the most part publicly recognized as the fundamental terms of willing cooperation among free and equal persons. By engaging in civil disobedience one intends, then, to address the sense of justice of the majority and to serve fair notice that in one's sincere and considered opinion the conditions of free cooperation are being violated. We are appealing to others to reconsider, to put themselves in our position, and to recognize that they cannot expect us to acquiesce indefinitely in the terms they impose upon us.

Now the force of this appeal depends upon the democratic conception of society as a system of cooperation among equal persons. If one thinks of society in another way, this form of protest may be out of place. For example, if the basic law is thought to reflect the order of nature and if the sovereign is held to govern by divine right as God's chosen lieutenant, then his subjects have only the right of suppliants. They can plead their cause but they cannot disobey should their appeal be denied. To do this would be to rebel against the final legitimate moral (and not simply legal) authority. This is not to say that the sovereign cannot be in error but only that the situation is not one for his subjects to correct. But once society is interpreted as a scheme of cooperation among equals, those injured by serious injustice need not submit. Indeed, civil disobedience (and conscientious refusal as well) is one of the stabilizing devices of a constitutional system, although by definition an illegal one. Along with such things as free and regular elections and an independent judiciary empowered to interpret the constitution (not necessarily written), civil disobedience used with due restraint and sound judgment helps to maintain and strengthen just institutions. By resisting injustice within the limits of fidelity to law, it serves to inhibit departures from justice and to correct them when they occur. A general disposition to engage in justified civil disobedience introduces stability into a well-ordered society, or one that is nearly just ...

One distinction between medieval and modern constitutionalism is that in the former the supremacy of law was not secured by established institutional controls. The check to the ruler who in his judgments and edicts opposed the sense of justice of the community was limited for the most part to the right of resistance by the whole society, or any part. Even this right seems not to have been interpreted as a corporate act; an unjust king was simply put aside. Thus the Middle Ages lacked the basic ideas of modern constitutional government, the idea of the sovereign people who have final authority and the institutionalizing of this authority by means of elections and parliaments, and other constitutional forms. Now in much the same way that the modern conception of constitutional government builds upon the medieval, the theory of civil disobedience supplements the purely legal conception of constitutional democracy. It attempts to formulate the grounds upon which legitimate democratic authority may be dissented from in ways that while admittedly contrary to law nevertheless express a fidelity to law and appeal to the fundamental political principles of a democratic regime. Thus to the legal forms of constitutionalism one may adjoin certain modes of illegal protest that do not violate the aims of a democratic constitution in view of the principles by which such dissent is guided. I have tried to show how these principles can be accounted for by the contract doctrine.

Some may object to this theory of civil disobedience that it is unrealistic. It presupposes that the majority has a sense of justice, and one might reply that moral sentiments are not a significant political force. What moves men are various interests, the desires for power, prestige, wealth, and the like. Although they are clever at producing moral arguments to support their claims, between one situation and another their opinions do not fit into a coherent conception of justice. Rather their views at any given time are occasional pieces calculated to advance certain interests. Unquestionably there is much truth in this contention, and in some societies it is more true than in others. But the essential question is the relative strength of the tendencies that oppose the sense of justice and whether the latter is ever strong enough so that it can be invoked to some significant effect.

A few comments may make the account presented more plausible. First of all, I have assumed throughout that we have to do with a nearly just society. This implies that there exists a constitutional regime and a publicly recognized conception of justice. Of course, in any particular situation certain individuals and groups may be tempted to violate its principles but the collective sentiment in their behalf has considerable strength when properly addressed. These principles are affirmed as the necessary terms of cooperation between free and equal persons. If those who perpetrate injustice can be clearly identified and isolated from the larger community, the convictions of the greater part of society may be of sufficient weight. Or if the contending parties are roughly equal, the sentiment of justice of those not engaged can be the deciding factor. In any case, should circumstances of this kind not obtain, the wisdom of civil disobedience is highly problematic. For unless one can appeal to the sense of justice of the larger society, the majority may simply be aroused to more repressive measures if the calculation of advantages points in this direction. Courts should take into account the civilly disobedient nature of the protester's act, and the fact that it is justifiable (or may seem so) by the political principles underlying the constitution, and on these grounds reduce and in some cases suspend the legal sanction. Yet quite the opposite may happen when the necessary background is lacking. We have to recognize then that justifiable civil disobedience is normally a reasonable and effective form of dissent only in a society regulated to some considerable degree by a sense of justice.

There may be some misapprehension about the manner in which the sense of justice is said to work. One may think that this sentiment expresses itself in sincere professions of principle and in actions requiring a considerable degree of self-sacrifice. But this supposition asks too much. A community's sense of justice is more likely to be revealed in the fact that the majority cannot bring itself to take the steps necessary to suppress the minority and to punish acts of civil disobedience as the law allows. Ruthless tactics that might be contemplated in other societies are not entertained as real alternatives. Thus the sense of justice affects, in ways we are often unaware of, our interpretation of political life, our perception of the possible courses of action, our will to resist the justified protests of others, and so on. In spite of its superior power, the majority may abandon its position and acquiesce in the proposals of the dissenters; its desire to give justice weakens its capacity to defend its unjust advantages. The sentiment of justice will be seen as a more vital political force once the subtle forms in which it exerts its influence are recognized, and in particular its role in rendering certain social positions indefensible.

In these remarks I have assumed that in a nearly just society there is a public acceptance of the same principles of justice. Fortunately this assumption is stronger than necessary. There can, in fact, be considerable differences in citizens' conceptions of justice provided that these conceptions lead to similar political judgments. And this is possible, since different premises can yield the same conclusion. In this case there exists what we may refer to as overlapping rather than strict consensus. In general, the overlapping of professed conceptions of justice suffices for civil disobedience to be a reasonable and prudent form of political dissent. Of course, this overlapping need not be perfect; it is enough that a condition of reciprocity is satisfied. Both sides must believe that however much their conceptions of justice differ, their views support the same judgment in the situation at hand, and would do so even should their respective positions be interchanged. Eventually, though, there comes a point beyond which the requisite agreement in judgment breaks down and society splits into more or less distinct parts that hold diverse opinions on fundamental political questions. In this case of strictly partitioned consensus, the basis for civil disobedience no long obtains. For example, suppose those who do not believe in toleration, and who would not tolerate others had they the power, wish to protest their lesser liberty by appealing to the sense of justice of the majority which holds the principle of equal liberty. While those who accept this principle should, as we have seen, tolerate the intolerant as far as the safety of free institutions permits, they are likely to resent being reminded of this duty by the intolerant who would, if positions were switched, establish their own dominion. The majority is bound to feel that their allegiance to equal liberty is being exploited by others for unjust ends. This situation illustrates once again the fact that a common sense of justice is a great collective asset which requires the cooperation of many to maintain. The intolerant can be viewed as free-riders, as persons who seek the advantages of just institutions while not doing their share to uphold them. Although those who acknowledge the principles of justice should always be guided by them, in a fragmented society as well as in one moved by group egoisms, the conditions for civil disobedience do not exist. Still, it is not necessary to have strict consensus, for often a degree of overlapping consensus allows the reciprocity condition to be fulfilled.

There are, to be sure, definite risks in the resort to civil disobedience. One reason for constitutional forms and their judicial interpretation is to establish a public reading of the political conception of justice and an explanation of the application of its principles to social questions. Up to a certain point it is better that the law and its interpretation be settled than that it be settled rightly. Therefore it may be protested that the preceding account does not determine who is to say when circumstances are such as to justify civil disobedience. It invites anarchy by encouraging everyone to decide for himself, and to abandon the public rendering of political principles. The reply to this is that each person must indeed make his own decision. Even though men normally seek advice and counsel, and accept the injunctions of those in authority when these seem reasonable to them, they are always accountable for their deeds. We cannot divest ourselves of our responsibility and transfer the burden of blame to others. This is true on any theory of political duty and obligation that is compatible with the principles of a democratic constitution. The citizen is autonomous yet he is held responsible for what he does (s. 78). If we ordinarily think that we should comply with the law, this is because our political principles normally lead to this conclusion. Certainly in a state of near justice there is a presumption in favor of compliance in the absence of strong reasons to the contrary. The many free and reasoned decisions of individuals fit together into an orderly political regime.

But while each person must decide for himself whether the circumstances justify civil disobedience, it does not follow that one is to decide as one pleases. It is not by looking to our personal interest, or to our political allegiances narrowly construed, that we should make up our minds. To act autonomously and responsibly a citizen must look to the political principles that underlie and guide the interpretation of the constitution. He must try to assess how these principles should be applied in the existing circumstances. If he comes to the conclusion after due consideration that civil disobedience is justified and conducts himself accordingly, he acts conscientiously. And though he may be mistaken, he has not done as he pleased. The theory of political duty and obligation enables us to draw these distinctions.

There are parallels with the common understandings and conclusions reached in the sciences. Here, too, everyone is autonomous yet responsible. We are to assess theories and hypotheses in the light of the evidence by publicly recognized principles. It is true that there are authoritative works, but these sum up the consensus of many persons each deciding for himself. The absence of a final authority to decide, and so of an official interpretation that all must accept, does not lead to confusion, but is rather a condition of theoretical advance. Equals accepting and applying reasonable principles need have no established superior. To the question, who is to decide? The answer is: all are to decide, everyone taking counsel with himself, and with reasonableness, comity, and good fortune, it often works out well enough.

In a democratic society, then, it is recognized that each citizen is responsible for his interpretation of the principles of justice and for his conduct in the light of them. There can be no legal or socially approved rendering of these principles that we are always morally bound to accept, not even when it is given by a supreme court or legislature. Indeed each constitutional agency, the legislature, the executive, and the court, puts forward its interpretation of the constitution and the political ideals that inform it. Although the court may have the last say in settling any particular case, it is not immune from powerful political influences that may force a revision of its reading of the constitution. The court presents its doctrine by reason and argument; its conception of the constitution must, if it is to endure, persuade the major part of the citizens of its soundness. The final court of appeal is not the court, or the executive, nor the legislature, but the electorate as a whole. The civilly disobedient appeal in a special way to this body. There is no danger of anarchy so long as there is a sufficient working agreement in citizens' conceptions of justice and the conditions for resorting to civil disobedience are respected. That men can achieve such an understanding and honor these limits when the basic political liberties are maintained is an assumption implicit in a democratic polity. There is no way to avoid entirely the danger of divisive strife, any more than one can rule out the possibility of profound scientific controversy. Yet if justified civil disobedience seems to threaten civic concord, the responsibility falls not upon those who protest but upon those whose abuse of authority and power justifies such opposition. For to employ the coercive apparatus of the state in order to maintain manifestly unjust institutions is itself a form of illegitimate force that men in due course have a right to resist.

With these remarks we have reached the end of our discussion of the content of the principles of justice. Throughout this part my aim has been to describe a scheme of institutions that satisfies these principles and to indicate how duties and obligations arise. These things must be done to see if the theory of justice put forward matches our considered judgments and extends them in an acceptable way. We need to check whether it defines a workable political conception and helps to focus our reflections on the most relevant and basic moral concerns. The account in this part is still highly abstract, but I hope to have provided some guidance as to how the principles of justice apply in practice. However, we should not forget the limited scope of the theory presented. For the most part I have tried to develop an ideal conception, only occasionally commenting on the various cases of nonideal theory. To be sure the priority rules suggest directives in many instances, and they may be useful if not pressed too far. Even so, the only question of nonideal theory examined in any detail is that of civil disobedience in the special case of near justice. If ideal theory is worthy of study, it must be because, as I have conjectured, it is the fundamental part of the theory of justice and essential for the nonideal part as well. I shall not pursue these matters further. We have still to complete the theory of justice by seeing how it is rooted in human thought and feeling, and tied in with our ends and aspirations.

READING QUESTIONS ON RAWLS

1 Why does Rawls suppose that non-violence is so important to civil disobedience?
2 Paul Magder stayed open in defiance of Ontario's Sunday closing laws, and claimed to be engaged in an act of civil disobedience. How would Rawls assess his claim? *(Paul Magder Furs Ltd v Ontario (Attorney-General)* (1993) 107 DLR 4th 634).

Ronald Dworkin
"Civil Disobedience" (1979)

Dworkin suggests that civil disobedience has an important place in a constitutional regime, because it serves to raise test cases about laws that some believe to be unjust. Because he believes that the law always has a moral content, Dworkin argues that when citizens believe a law is unjust, they may be justified in believing that it is not a law at all.

How should the government deal with those who disobey the draft laws out of conscience? Many people think the answer is obvious: The government must prosecute the dissenters, and if they are convicted it must punish them. Some people reach this conclusion easily, because they hold the mindless view that conscientious disobedience is the same as lawlessness. They think that the dissenters are anarchists who must be punished before their corruption spreads. Many lawyers and intellectuals come to the same conclusion, however, on what looks like a more sophisticated argument. They recognize that disobedience to law may be *morally* justified, but they insist that it cannot be *legally* justified, and they think that it follows from this truism that the law must be enforced. Erwin Griswold, once Solicitor General of the United States, and before that Dean of the Harvard Law School, appears to have adopted this view. "[It] is of the essence of law," he said, "that is equally applied to all, that it binds all alike, irrespective of personal motive. For this reason, one who contemplates civil disobedience out of moral conviction should not be surprised and must not be bitter if a criminal conviction ensues. And he must accept the fact that organized society cannot endure on any other basis."

The *New York Times* applauded that statement. A thousand faculty members of several universities had signed a *Times* advertisement calling on the Justice Department to quash the indictments of the Rev. William Sloane Coffin, Dr Benjamin Spock, Marcus Raskin, Mitchell Goodman, and Michael Ferber, for conspiring to counsel various draft offenses. The *Times* said that the request to quash the indictments "confused moral rights with legal responsibilities."

But the argument that, because the government believes a man has committed a crime, it must prosecute him is much weaker than it seems. Society "cannot endure" if it tolerates all disobedience; it does not follow, however, nor is there evidence, that it will collapse if it tolerates some. In the United States prosecutors have discretion whether to enforce criminal laws in particular cases. A prosecutor may properly decide not to press charges if the lawbreaker is young, or inexperienced, or the sole support of a family, or is repentant, or turns state's evidence, or if the law is unpopular or unworkable or generally disobeyed, or if the courts are clogged with more important cases, or for dozens of other reasons. This discretion is no license – we expect prosecutors to have good reasons for exercising it – but there are, at least *prima facie*, some good reasons for not prosecuting those who disobey the draft laws out of conscience. One is the obvious reason that they act out of better motives than those who break the law out of greed or a desire to subvert government. If motive can count in distinguishing between thieves, then why not in distinguishing between draft offenders? Another is the practical reason that our society suffers a loss if it punishes a group that includes – as the group of draft dissenters does – some of its most loyal and law-respecting citizens. Jailing such men solidifies their alienation from society, and alienates many like them who are deterred by the threat. If practical consequences like these argued for not enforcing prohibition, why do they not argue for tolerating offenses of conscience?

Those who think that conscientious draft offenders should always be punished must show that these are not good reasons for exercising discretion, or they must find contrary reasons that outweigh them. What arguments might they produce? There are practical reasons for enforcing draft laws, and I shall consider some of these later. But Dean Griswold and those who agree with him seem to rely on a fundamental moral argument that it would be unfair, not merely impractical, to let the dissenters go unpunished. They think it would be unfair, I gather, because society could not function if everyone disobeyed laws he disapproved of or found disadvantageous. If the government tolerates those few who will not "play the game," it allows them to secure the benefits of everyone else's deference to law, without shouldering the burdens, such as the burden of the draft.

This argument is a serious one. It cannot be answered simply by saying that the dissenters would allow everyone else the privilege of disobeying a law he believed immoral. In fact, few draft dissenters would accept a changed society in which sincere segregationists were free to break civil rights laws they hated. The majority want no such change, in any event, because they think that society would be worse off for it; until they are shown this is wrong, they will expect their officials to punish anyone who assumes a privilege which they, for the general benefit, do not assume.

There is, however, a flaw in the argument. The reasoning contains a hidden assumption that makes it almost entirely irrelevant to the draft cases, and indeed to any serious case of civil disobedience in the United States. The argument assumes that the dissenters know that they are breaking a valid law, and that the privilege they assert is the privilege to do that. Of course, almost everyone who discusses civil disobedience recognizes that in America a law may be invalid because it is unconstitutional. But the critics handle this complexity by arguing on separate hypotheses: If the law is invalid, then no crime is committed, and society may not punish. If the law is valid, then a crime has been committed, and society must punish. This reasoning hides the crucial fact that the validity of the law may be doubtful. The officials and judges may believe that the law is valid, the dissenters may disagree, and both sides may have plausible arguments for these positions. If so, then the issues are different from what they would be if the law were clearly valid or clearly invalid, and the argument of fairness, designed for these alternatives, is irrelevant.

Doubtful law is by no means special or exotic in cases of civil disobedience. On the contrary. In the United States, at least, almost any law which a significant number of people would be tempted to disobey on moral grounds would be doubtful – if not clearly invalid – on constitutional grounds as well. The constitution makes our conventional political morality relevant to the question of validity; any statute that appears to compromise that morality raises constitutional questions, and if the compromise is serious, the constitutional doubts are serious also.

The connection between moral and legal issues was especially clear in the draft cases of the last decade. Dissent was based at the time on the following moral objections: (a) The United States is using immoral weapons and tactics in Vietnam. (b) The war has never been endorsed by deliberate, considered, and open vote of the peoples' representatives. (c) The United States has no interest at stake in Vietnam remotely strong enough to justify forcing a segment of its citizens to risk death there. (d) If an army is to be raised to fight that war, it is immoral to raise it by a draft that defers or exempts college students, and thus discriminated against the economically underprivileged. (e) The draft exempts those who object to all wars on religious grounds, but not those who object to particular wars on moral grounds; there is no relevant difference between these positions, and so the draft, by making the distinction, implies that the second group is less worthy of the nation's respect than the first. (f) The law that makes it a crime to counsel draft resistance stifles those who oppose the war, because it is morally impossible to argue that the war is profoundly immoral, without encouraging and assisting those who refuse to fight it.

Lawyers will recognize that these moral positions, if we accept them, provide the basis for the following constitutional arguments: (a) The constitution makes treaties part of the law of the land, and the United States is a party to international conventions and covenants that make illegal the acts of war the dissenters charged the nation with committing. (b) The constitution provides that Congress must declare war; the legal issue of whether our action in Vietnam was a "war" and whether the Tonkin Bay Resolution was a "declaration" is the heart of the moral issue of whether the government had made a deliberate and open decision. (c) Both the due process clause of the Fifth and Fourteenth Amendments and equal protection clause of the Fourteenth Amendment condemn special burdens placed on a selected class of citizens when the burden or the classification is not reasonable; the burden is unreasonable when it patently does not serve the public interest, or when it is vastly disproportionate to the interest served. If our military action in Vietnam was frivolous or perverse, as the dissenters claimed, then the burden we placed on men of draft age was unreasonable and unconstitutional. (d) In any event, the discrimination in favor of college students denied to the poor the equal protection of the law that is guaranteed by the constitution. (e) If there is no pertinent difference between religious objection to all wars and moral objection to some wars, then the classification the draft made was arbitrary and unreasonable, and unconstitutional on that ground. The "establishment of religion" clause of the First Amendment forbids governmental pressure in favor of organized religion; if the draft's distinction coerced men in this direction, it was invalid on that count also. (f) The First Amendment also condemns invasions of freedom of speech. If the draft law's prohibition on counseling did inhibit expression of a range of views on the war, it abridged free speech.

The principal counterargument, supporting the view that the courts ought not to have held the draft unconstitutional, also involves moral issues. Under the so-called political question doctrine, the courts deny their own jurisdiction to pass on matters – such as foreign or military policy – whose resolution is best assigned to other branches of the government. The Boston court trying the Coffin, Spock case declared, on the basis of this doctrine, that it would not hear arguments about the legality of the war. But the Supreme Court has shown itself (in the reapportionment cases, for example) reluctant to refuse jurisdiction when it believed that the gravest issues of political morality were at stake and that no remedy was available through the political process. If the dissenters were right, and the war and the draft were state crimes of profound injustice to a group of citizens, then the argument that the courts should have refused jurisdiction is considerably weakened.

We cannot conclude from these arguments that the draft (or any part of it) was unconstitutional. When the Supreme Court was called upon to rule on the question, it rejected some of them, and refused to consider the others on grounds that they were political. The majority of lawyers agreed with this result. But the arguments of unconstitutionality were at least plausible, and a reasonable and competent lawyer might well think that they present a stronger case, on balance, than the counterarguments. If he does, he will consider that the draft was not constitutional, and there will be no way of proving that he is wrong.

Therefore we cannot assume, in judging what should have been done with the draft dissenters, that they were asserting a privilege to disobey valid laws. We cannot decide that fairness demanded their punishment until we try to answer further questions: What should a citizen do when the law is unclear, and when he thinks it allows what others think it does not? I do not mean to ask, of course, what it is *legally* proper for him to do, or what his *legal* rights are – that would be begging the question, because it depends upon whether he is right or they are right. I mean to ask what his proper course is as a citizen, what, in other words, we would consider to be "playing the game." That is a crucial question, because it cannot be unfair not to punish him if he is acting as, given his opinions, we think he should.[1]

There is no obvious answer on which most citizens would readily agree, and that is itself significant. If we examine our legal institutions and practices, however, we shall discover some relevant underlying principles and policies. I shall set out three possible answers to the question, and then try to show which of these best fits our practices and expectations. The three possibilities I want to consider are these:

1 If the law is doubtful, and it is therefore unclear whether it permits someone to do what he wants, he should assume the worst, and act on the assumption that it does not. He should obey the executive authorities who command him, even though he thinks they are wrong, while using the political process, if he can, to change the law.

2 If the law is doubtful, he may follow his own judgment, that is, he may do what he wants if he believes that the case that the law permits this is stronger than the case that it does not. But he may follow his own judgment only until an authoritative institution, like a court, decides the other way in a case involving him or someone else. Once an institutional decision has been reached, he must abide by that decision, even though he thinks that it was wrong. (There are, in theory, many subdivisions of this second possibility. We may say that the individual's choice is foreclosed by the contrary decision of any court, including the lowest court in the system if the case is not appealed. Or we may require a decision of some particular court or institution. I shall discuss this second possibility in its most liberal form, namely that the individual may properly follow his own judgment until a contrary decision of the highest court competent to pass on the issue, which, in the case of the draft, was the United States Supreme Court.)

3 If the law is doubtful, he may follow his own judgment, even after
   a contrary decision by the highest competent court. Of course, he
   must take the contrary decision of any court into account in making
   his judgment of what the law requires. Otherwise the judgment
   would not be an honest or reasonable one, because the doctrine of
   precedent, which is an established part of our legal system, has the
   effect of allowing the decision of the courts to *change* the law. Suppose, for example, that a taxpayer believes that he is not required to
   pay tax on certain forms of income. If the Supreme Court decides to
   the contrary, he should, taking into account the practice of according great weight to the decisions of the Supreme Court on tax matters, decide that the Court's decision has itself tipped the balance,
   and that the law now requires him to pay the tax.

Someone might think that this qualification erases the difference between the third and the second models, but it does not. The doctrine of
precedent gives different weights to the decisions of different courts,
and greatest weight to the decisions of the Supreme Court, but it does
not make the decisions of any court conclusive. Sometimes, even after
a contrary Supreme Court decision, an individual may still reasonably
believe that the law is on his side; such cases are rare, but they are most
likely to occur in disputes over constitutional law when civil disobedience is involved. The Court has shown itself more likely to overrule its
past decisions if these have limited important personal or political
rights, and it is just these decisions that a dissenter might want to
challenge.

We cannot assume, in other words, that the Constitution is always
what the Supreme Court says it is. Oliver Wendell Holmes, for example,
did not follow such a rule in his famous dissent in the *Gitlow* case. A
few years before, in *Abrams,* he had lost his battle to persuade the court
that the First Amendment protected an anarchist who had been urging
general strikes against the government. A similar issue was presented
in *Gitlow,* and Holmes once again dissented. "It is true," he said, "that
in my opinion this criterion was departed from [in *Abrams*] but the
convictions that I expressed in that case are too deep for it to be possible
for me as yet to believe that it ... settled the law." Holmes voted for
acquitting Gitlow, on the ground that what Gitlow had done was no
crime, even though the Supreme Court had recently held that it was.

Here then are three possible models for the behavior of dissenters
who disagree with the executive authorities when the law is doubtful.
Which of them best fits our legal and social practices?

I think it plain that we do not follow the first of these models, that is, that we do not expect citizens to assume the worst. If no court has decided the issue, and a man thinks, on balance, that the law is on his side, most of our lawyers and critics think it perfectly proper for him to follow his own judgment. Even when many disapprove of what he does – such as peddling pornography – they do not think he must desist just because the legality of his conduct is subject to doubt.

It is worth pausing a moment to consider what society would lose if it did follow the first model or, to put the matter the other way, what society gains when people follow their own judgment in cases like this. When the law is uncertain, in the sense that lawyers can reasonably disagree on what a court ought to decide, the reason usually is that different legal principles and policies have collided, and it is unclear how best to accommodate these conflicting principles and policies.

Our practice, in which different parties are encouraged to pursue their own understanding, provides a means of testing relevant hypotheses. If the question is whether a particular rule would have certain undesirable consequences, or whether these consequences would have limited or broad ramifications, then, before the issue is decided, it is useful to know what does in fact take place when some people proceed on that rule. (Much anti-trust and business regulation law has developed through this kind of testing.) If the question is whether and to what degree a particular solution would offend principles of justice or fair play deeply respected by the community, it is useful, again, to experiment by testing the community's response. The extent of community indifference to anti-contraception laws, for example, would never have become established had not some organizations deliberately flouted those laws.

If the first model were followed, we would lose the advantages of these tests. The law would suffer, particularly if this model were applied to constitutional issues. When the validity of a criminal statute is in doubt, the statute will almost always strike some people as being unfair or unjust, because it will infringe some principle of liberty or justice or fairness which they take to be built into the Constitution. If our practice were that whenever a law is doubtful on these grounds, one must act as if it were valid, then the chief vehicle we have for challenging the law on moral grounds would be lost, and over time the law we obeyed would certainly become less fair and just, and the liberty of our citizens would certainly be diminished.

We would lose almost as much if we used a variation of the first model, that a citizen must assume the worst unless he can anticipate that the courts will agree with his view of the law. If everyone deferred to his guess of what the courts would do, society and its law would be poorer. Our assumption in rejecting the first model was that the record a citizen makes in following his own judgment, together with the arguments he makes supporting that judgment when he has the opportunity, are helpful in creating the best judicial decision possible. This remains true even when, at the time the citizen acts, the odds are against his success in court. We must remember, too, that the value of the citizen's example is not exhausted once the decision has been made. Our practices require that the decision be criticized, by the legal profession and the law schools, and the record of dissent may be invaluable here.

Of course a man must consider what the courts will do when he decides whether it would be *prudent* to follow his own judgment. He may have to face jail, bankruptcy, or opprobrium if he does. But it is essential that we separate the calculation of prudence from the question of what, as a good citizen, he may properly do. We are investigating how society ought to treat him when its courts believe that he judged wrong; therefore we must ask what he is justified in doing when his judgment differs from others. We beg the question if we assume that what he may properly do depends on his guess as to how society will treat him.

We must also reject the second model, that if the law is unclear a citizen may properly follow his own judgment until the highest court has ruled that he is wrong. This fails to take into account the fact that any court, including the Supreme Court, may overrule itself. In 1940 the Court decided that a West Virginia law requiring students to salute the Flag was constitutional. In 1943 it reversed itself, and decided that such a statute was unconstitutional after all. What was the duty as citizens, of those people who in 1941 and 1942 objected to saluting the Flag on grounds of conscience, and thought that the Court's 1940 decision was wrong? We can hardly say that their duty was to follow the first decision. They believed that saluting the Flag was unconscionable, and they believed, reasonably, that no valid law required them to do so. The Supreme Court later decided that in this they were right. The Court did not simply hold that after the second decision failing to salute would not be a crime; it held (as in a case like this it almost always would) that it was no crime after the first decision either.

Some will say that the flag-salute dissenters should have obeyed the Court's first decision, while they worked in the legislatures to have the law repealed, and tried in the courts to find some way to challenge the law again without actually violating it. That would be, perhaps, a plausible recommendation if conscience were not involved, because it would then be arguable that the gain in orderly procedure was worth the personal sacrifice of patience. But conscience was involved, and if the dissenters had obeyed the law while biding their time, they would have suffered the irreparable injury of having done what their conscience forbade them to do. It is one thing to say that an individual must sometimes violate his conscience when he knows that the law commands him to do it. It is quite another to say that he must violate his conscience even when he reasonably believes that the law does not require it, because it would inconvenience his fellow citizens if he took the most direct, and perhaps the only, method of attempting to show that he is right and they are wrong.

Since a court may overrule itself, the same reasons we listed for rejecting the first model count against the second as well. If we did not have the pressure of dissent, we would not have a dramatic statement of the degree to which a court decision against the dissenter is felt to be wrong, a demonstration that is surely pertinent to the question of whether it was right. We would increase the chance of being governed by rules that offend the principles we claim to serve.

These considerations force us, I think, from the second model, but some will want to substitute a variation of it. They will argue that once the Supreme Court has decided that a criminal law is valid, then citizens have a duty to abide by that decision until they have a reasonable belief, not merely that the decision is a bad law, but that the Supreme Court is likely to overrule it. Under this view the West Virginia dissenters who refused to salute the Flag in 1942 were acting properly, because they might reasonably have anticipated that the Court would change its mind. But once the Court held laws like the draft laws constitutional, it would be improper to continue to challenge these laws, because there would be no great likelihood that the Court would soon change its mind. This suggestion must also be rejected, however. For once we say that a citizen may properly follow his own judgment of the law, in spite of his judgment that the courts will probably find against him, there is no plausible reason why he should act differently because a contrary decision is already on the books.

Thus the third model, or something close to it, seems to be the fairest statement of a man's social duty in our community. A citizen's allegiance is to the law, not to any particular person's view of what the law is, and he does not behave unfairly so long as he proceeds on his own considered and reasonable view of what the law requires. Let me repeat (because it is crucial) that this is not the same as saying that an individual may disregard what the courts have said. The doctrine of precedent lies near the core of our legal system, and no one can make a reasonable effort to follow the law unless he grants the courts the general power to alter it by their decisions. But if the issue is one touching fundamental personal or political rights, and it is arguable that the Supreme Court has made a mistake, a man is within his social rights in refusing to accept that decision as conclusive.

One large question remains before we can apply these observations to the problems of draft resistance. I have been talking about the case of a man who believes that the law is not what other people think, or what the courts have held. This description may fit some of those who disobey the draft laws out of conscience, but it does not fit most of them. Most of the dissenters are not lawyers or political philosophers; they believe that the laws on the books are immoral, and inconsistent with their country's legal ideals, but they have not considered the question of whether they may be invalid as well. Of what relevance to their situation, then, is the proposition that one may properly follow one's own view of the law?

To answer this, I shall have to return to the point I made earlier. The Constitution, through the due process clause, the equal protection clause, the First Amendment, and the other provisions I mentioned, injects an extraordinary amount of our political morality into the issue of whether a law is valid. The statement that most draft dissenters are unaware that the law is invalid therefore needs qualification. They hold beliefs that, if true, strongly support the view that the law is on their side; the fact that they have reached that further conclusion can be traced, in at least most cases, to their lack of legal sophistication. If we believe that when the law is doubtful people who follow their own judgment of the law may be acting properly, it would seem wrong not to extend that view to those dissenters whose judgments come to the same thing. No part of the case that I made for the third model would entitle us to distinguish them from their more knowledgeable colleagues.

We can draw several tentative conclusions from the argument so far: When the law is uncertain, in the sense that a plausible case can be made on both sides, then a citizen who follows his own judgment is not behaving unfairly. Our practices permit and encourage him to follow his own judgment in such cases. For that reason, our government has a special responsibility to try to protect him, and soften his predicament, whenever it can do so without great damage to other policies. It does not follow that the government can guarantee him immunity – it cannot adopt the rule that it will prosecute no one who acts out of conscience, or convict no one who reasonably disagrees with the courts. That would paralyze the government's ability to carry out its policies; it would, moreover, throw away the most important benefit of following the third model. If the state never prosecuted, then the courts could not act on the experience and the arguments the dissent has generated. But it does follow that when the practical reasons for prosecuting are relatively weak in a particular case, or can be met in other ways, the path of fairness lies in tolerance. The popular view that the law is the law and must always be enforced refuses to distinguish the man who acts on his own judgment of a doubtful law, and thus behaves as our practices provide, from the common criminal. I know of no reason, short of moral blindness, for not drawing a distinction in principle between the two cases.

I anticipate a philosophical objection to these conclusions: that I am treating law as a "brooding omnipresence in the sky." I have spoken of people making judgments about what the law requires, even in cases in which the law is unclear and undemonstrable. I have spoken of cases in which a man might think that the law requires one thing, even though the Supreme Court has said that it requires another, and even when it was not likely that the Supreme Court would soon change its mind. I will therefore be charged with the view that there is always a "right answer" to a legal problem to be found in natural law or locked up in some transcendental strongbox.

The strongbox theory of law is, of course, nonsense. When I say that people hold views on the law when the law is doubtful, and that these views are not merely predictions of what the courts will hold, I intend no such metaphysics. I mean only to summarize as accurately as I can many of the practices that are part of our legal process.

Lawyers and judges make statements of legal right and duty, even when they know these are not demonstrable, and support them with arguments even when they know that these arguments will not appeal to everyone. They make these arguments to one another, in the professional journals, in the classrooms, and in the courts. They respond to these arguments, when others make them, by judging them good or bad or mediocre. In so doing they assume that some arguments for a given doubtful position are better than others. They also assume that the case on one side of a doubtful proposition may be stronger than the case on the other, which is what I take a claim of law in a doubtful case to mean. They distinguish, without too much difficulty, these arguments from predictions of what the courts will decide.

These practices are poorly represented by the theory that the judgments of law on doubtful issues are nonsense, or are merely predictions of what the courts will do. Those who hold such theories cannot deny the fact of these practices; perhaps these theorists mean that the practices are not sensible, because they are based on suppositions that do not hold, or for some other reason. But this makes their objection mysterious, because they never specify what they take the purposes underlying these practices to be; and unless these goals are specified, one cannot decide whether the practices are sensible. I understand these underlying purposes to be those I described earlier: the development and testing of the law through experimentation by citizens and through the adversary process.

Our legal system pursues these goals by inviting citizens to decide the strengths and weaknesses of legal arguments for themselves, or through their own counsel, and to act on these judgments, although that permission is qualified by the limited threat that they may suffer if the courts do not agree. Success in this strategy depends on whether there is sufficient agreement within the community on what counts as good or bad argument, so that, although different people will reach different judgments, these differences will be neither so profound nor so frequent as to make the system unworkable, or dangerous for those who act by their own lights. I believe there is sufficient agreement on the criteria of the argument to avoid these traps, although one of the main tasks of legal philosophy is to exhibit and clarify these criteria. In any event, the practices I have described have not yet been shown to be misguided; they therefore must count in determining whether it is just and fair to be lenient to those who break what others think is the law.

I have said that the government has a special responsibility to those who act on a reasonable judgment that a law is invalid. It should make accommodation for them as far as possible, when this is consistent with other policies. It may be difficult to decide what the government ought to do, in the name of that responsibility, in particular cases. The decision will be a matter of balance, and flat rules will not help. Still, some principles can be set out.

I shall start with the prosecutor's decision whether to press charges. He must balance both his responsibility to be lenient and the risk that convictions will rend the society, against the damage to the law's policy that may follow if he leaves the dissenters alone. In making his calculation he must consider not only the extent to which others will be harmed, but also how the law evaluates that harm; and he must therefore make the following distinction. Every rule of law is supported, and presumably justified, by a set of policies it is supposed to advance and principles it is supposed to respect. Some rules (the laws prohibiting murder and theft, for example) are supported by the proposition that the individuals protected have a moral right to be free from the harm proscribed. Other rules (the more technical anti-trust rules, for example) are not supported by any supposition of any underlying right; their support comes chiefly from the alleged utility of the economic and social policies they promote. These may be supplemented with moral principles (like the view that it is a harsh business practice to undercut a weak competitor's prices) but these fall short of recognizing a moral right against the harm in question.

The point of the distinction here is this: if a particular rule of law represents an official decision that individuals have a moral right to be free from some harm, then that is a powerful argument against tolerating violations that inflict those injuries. Laws protecting people from personal injury or the destruction of their property, for example, do represent that sort of decision, and this is a very strong argument against tolerating civil disobedience that involves violence.

It may be controversial, of course, whether a law does rest on the assumption of a moral right. The question is whether it is reasonable to suppose, from the background and administration of the law, that its authors recognized such a right. There are cases, in addition to rules against violence, where it is plain that they did; the civil rights laws are examples. Many sincere and ardent segregationists believe that the civil rights laws and decisions are unconstitutional, because they compromise principles of local government and of freedom of association. This is an arguable, though not a persuasive, view. But these laws and decisions clearly embody the view that Negroes, as individuals, have a right not to be segregated. They do not rest simply on the judgment that other national policies are best pursued by preventing racial segregation. If we take no action against the man who blocks the school house door, therefore, we violate the moral rights, confirmed by law, of the schoolgirl he blocks. The responsibility of leniency cannot go this far.

The schoolgirl's position is different, however, from that of the draftee who may be called up sooner or given a more dangerous post if draft offenders are not punished. The draft laws, taken as a whole and with an eye to their administration, cannot be said to reflect the judgment that a man has a moral right to be drafted only after certain other men or groups have been called. The draft classifications, and the order-of-call within classifications, are arranged for social and administrative convenience. They also reflect considerations of fairness, like the proposition that a mother who has lost one of two sons in war ought not to be made to risk losing the other. But they presuppose no fixed rights. The draft boards are given considerable discretion in the classification process, and the army, of course, has almost complete discretion in assigning dangerous posts. If the prosecutor tolerates draft offenders, he makes small shifts in the law's calculations of fairness and utility. These may cause disadvantage to others in the pool of draftees but that is a different matter from contradicting their moral rights.

This difference between segregation and the draft is not an accident of how the laws happen to have been written. It would run counter to a century of practice to suppose that citizens have moral rights with respect to the order in which they are called to serve; the lottery system of selection, for example, would be abhorrent under that supposition. If our history had been different, and if the community had recognized such a moral right, it seems fair to suppose that some of the draft dissenters, at least, would have modified their acts so as to try to respect these rights. So it is wrong to analyze draft cases in the same way as cases of violence or civil rights cases, as many critics do when considering whether tolerance is justified. I do not mean that fairness to others is irrelevant in draft cases; it must be taken into account, and balanced against fairness to dissenters and the long-term benefit to society. But it does not play the commanding role here that it does when rights are at stake.

Where, then, does the balance of fairness and utility lie in the case of those who counseled draft resistance? If these men had encouraged violence or otherwise trespassed on the rights of others, then there would have been a strong case for prosecution. But in the absence of such actions, the balance of fairness and utility seems to me to lie the other way, and I therefore think that the decision to prosecute Coffin, Spock, Raskin, Goodman, and Ferber was wrong. It might have been argued that if those who counsel draft resistance are free from prosecution, the number who resist induction will increase; but not, I think, much beyond the number of those who would resist in any event.

If this is wrong, and there is much greater resistance, then a sense of this residual discontent is of importance to policy makers, and it ought not to have been hidden under a ban on speech. Conscience is deeply involved – it is hard to believe that many who counseled resistance did so on any other grounds. The case is strong that the laws making counseling a crime are unconstitutional; even those who do not find the case persuasive will admit that its arguments have substance. The harm to potential draftees, both those who may have been persuaded to resist and those who may have been called earlier because others have been persuaded, was remote and speculative.

The cases of men who refused induction when drafted are more complicated. The crucial question is whether a failure to prosecute will lead to wholesale refusals to serve. It may not – there were social pressures, including the threat of career disadvantages, that would have forced many young Americans to serve if drafted, even if they knew they would not go to jail if they refused. If the number would not much have increased, then the State should have left the dissenters alone, and I see no great harm in delaying any prosecution until the effect of that policy became clearer. If the number of those who refuse induction turned out to be large, this would argue for prosecution. But it would also make the problem academic, because if there had been sufficient dissent to bring us to that pass, it would have been most difficult to pursue the war in any event, except under a near-totalitarian regime.

There may seem to be a paradox in these conclusions. I argued earlier that when the law is unclear citizens have the right to follow their own judgment, partly on the grounds that this practice helps to shape issues for adjudication; now I propose a course that eliminates or postpones adjudication. But the contradiction is only apparent. It does not follow from the fact that our practice facilitates adjudication, and renders it more useful in developing the law, that a trial should follow whenever citizens do act by their own lights. The question arises in each case whether the issues are ripe for adjudication, and whether adjudication would settle these issues in a manner that would decrease the chance of, or remove the grounds for, further dissent.

In the draft cases, the answer to both these questions was negative: there was much ambivalence about the war, and ignorance about the scope of the moral issues involved in the draft. It was far from the best time for a court to pass on these issues, and tolerating dissent for a time was one way of allowing the debate to continue until it produced something clearer. Moreover, it was plain that an adjudication of the constitutional issues would not settle the law. Those who had doubts whether the draft was constitutional had the same doubts even after the Supreme

Court said that it was. This is one of those cases, touching fundamental rights, in which our practices of precedent encourage such doubts.

Even if the prosecutor does not act, however, the underlying problem will be only temporarily relieved. So long as the law appears to make acts of dissent criminal, a man of conscience will face danger. What can Congress, which shares the responsibility of leniency, do to lessen this danger?

Congress can review the laws in question to see how much accommodation can be given to dissenters. Every program a legislature adopts is a mixture of policies and restraining principles. We accept loss of efficiency in crime detection and urban renewal, for example, so that we can respect the rights of accused criminals and compensate property owners for their damages. Congress may properly defer to its responsibility toward the dissenters by adjusting or compromising other policies. The relevant questions are these: What means can be found for allowing the greatest possible tolerance of conscientious dissent while minimizing its impact on policy? How strong is the government's responsibility for leniency in this case – how deeply is conscience involved, and how strong is the case that the law is invalid after all? How important is the policy in question – is interference with that policy too great a price to pay? These questions are no doubt too simple, but they suggest the heart of the choices that must be made.

For the same reasons that those who counseled resistance should not have been prosecuted, I think that the law that makes this a crime should be repealed. The case is strong that this law abridges free speech. It certainly coerces conscience, and it probably serves no beneficial effect. If counseling would persuade only a few to resist who otherwise would not, the value of the restraint is small; if counseling would persuade many, that is an important political fact that should be known.

The issues are more complex, again, in the case of draft resistance itself. Those who believed that the war in Vietnam was itself a grotesque blunder would have favoured any change in the law that made peace more likely. But if we take the position of those who think the war was necessary, then we must admit that a policy that continued the draft but wholly exempted dissenters would have been unwise. Two less drastic alternatives should have been considered, however: a volunteer army, and an expanded conscientious objector category that included those who found the war immoral. There is much to be said against both proposals, but once the requirement of respect for dissent is recognized, the balance of principle may be tipped in their favor.

So the case for not prosecuting conscientious draft offenders, and for changing the laws in their favor, was a strong one. It would have been unrealistic to expect this policy to prevail, however, for political pressures opposed it.

We must consider, therefore, what the courts could and should have done. A court might, of course, have upheld the arguments that the draft laws were in some way unconstitutional, in general or as applied to the defendants in the case at hand. Or it might acquit the defendants because the facts necessary for conviction are not proved. I shall not argue the constitutional issues, or the facts of any particular case. I want instead to suggest that a court ought not to convict, at least in some circumstances, even if it sustains the statutes and finds the facts as charged. The Supreme Court had not ruled on the chief arguments that the draft was unconstitutional, nor had it held that these arguments raised political questions that are not within its jurisdiction, when several of the draft cases arose. There are strong reasons why a Court should acquit in these circumstances even if it does then sustain the draft. It ought to acquit on the ground that before its decision the validity of the draft was doubtful, and it is unfair to punish men for disobeying a doubtful law.

There would be precedent for a decision along these lines. The Court has several times reversed criminal convictions, on due process grounds, because the law in question was too vague. (It has overturned convictions, for example, under laws that made it a crime to charge "unreasonable prices" or to be a member of a "gang." Conviction under a vague criminal law offends the moral and political ideals of due process in two ways. First, it places a citizen in the unfair position of either acting at his peril or accepting a more stringent restriction on his life than the legislature may have authorized: As I argued earlier, it is not acceptable, as a model of social behavior, that in such cases he ought to assume the worst. Second, it gives power to the prosecutor and the courts to make criminal law, by opting for one or the other possible interpretations after the event. This would be a delegation of authority by the legislature that is inconsistent with our scheme of separation of powers.

Conviction under a criminal law whose terms are not vague, but whose constitutional validity is doubtful, offends due process in the first of these ways. It forces a citizen to assume the worst, or act at his peril. It offends due process in something like the second way as well. Most citizens would be deterred by a doubtful statute if they were to risk jail by violating it. Congress, and not the courts, would then be the effective voice in deciding the constitutionality of criminal enactments, and this also violates the separation of powers.

If acts of dissent continue to occur after the Supreme Court has ruled that the laws are valid, or that the political question doctrine applies, then acquittal on the grounds I have described is no longer appropriate. The Court's decision will not have finally settled the law, for the reasons given earlier, but the Court will have done all that can be done to settle it. The courts may still exercise their sentencing discretion, however, and impose minimal or suspended sentences as a mark of respect for the dissenters' position.

Some lawyers will be shocked by my general conclusion that we have a responsibility toward those who disobey the draft laws out of conscience, and that we may be required not to prosecute them, but rather to change our laws or adjust our sentencing procedures to accommodate them. The simple Draconian propositions, that crime must be punished, and that he who misjudges the law must take the consequences, have an extraordinary hold on the professional as well as the popular imagination. But the rule of law is more complex and more intelligent than that and it is important that it survive.

NOTE

1 I do not mean to imply that the government should always punish a man who deliberately breaks a law he knows is valid. There may be reasons of fairness or practicality, like those I listed in the third paragraph, for not prosecuting such men. But cases like the draft cases present special arguments for tolerance; I want to concentrate on these arguments and therefore have isolated these cases.

READING QUESTIONS ON DWORKIN

1 How are Dworkin's views about civil disobedience related to his view of law?
2 Could something qualify as civil disobedience on Dworkin's view despite being morally unjustified in the final analysis?
3 Protesters at Clayoquot sound sought to disrupt block clear-cut logging, and claimed to be engaged in civil disobedience. How would Dworkin assess their claim? (*MacMillan Bloedel Ltd v Simpson,* (1994) 89 CCC 3d 217)

7

The Limits of the Legal Order

The last chapter dealt with the issue of morally motivated disobedience to particular unjust laws. This chapter deals with challenges to the legitimacy of entire legal orders, either because they are shot through with injustice or because particular groups regard themselves as illegitimately subject to the law of the land.

Nelson Mandela
"Speech from the Dock" (1962)

Mandela was charged with inciting workers to act illegally and with leaving the country without a valid permit. In his statement to the court, Mandela challenges the legitimacy of the court to try people without political rights.

Your Worship, before I plead to the charge, there are one or two points I would like to raise.

CONDUCTS OWN DEFENCE

Firstly, Your Worship will recall that this matter was postponed last Monday at my request until today, to enable Counsel to make the arrangements to be available here today. Although Counsel is now available, after consultation with him and my attorneys, I have elected to conduct my own defence. Some time during the progress of these proceedings, I hope to be able to indicate that this case is a trial of the aspirations of the African people, and because of that I thought it proper to conduct my own defence. Nevertheless, I have decided to retain the services of Counsel, who will be here throughout these proceedings, and I also would like my attorney to be available in the course of these proceedings as well, but subject to that I will conduct my own defence.

RECUSAL

The second point I would like to raise is an application which is addressed to Your Worship. Now at the outset, I want to make it perfectly clear that the remarks I am going to make are not addressed to Your Worship in his personal capacity, nor are they intended to reflect upon the integrity of the Court. I hold Your Worship in high esteem and I do not for one single moment doubt your sense of fairness and justice. I must also mention that nothing I am going to raise in this application is intended to reflect against the Prosecutor in his personal capacity.

The point I wish to raise in my argument is based not on personal considerations, but on important questions that go beyond the scope of this present trial. I might also mention that in the course of this application I am frequently going to refer to the White man and the White people. I want at once to make it plain that I am no racialist, and I detest racialism, because I regard it as a barbaric thing, whether it comes from a Black man or from a White man. The terminology that I am going to employ will be compelled on me by the nature of the application I wish to make.

I want to apply for Your Worship's recusal from this case. I challenge the right of this Court to hear my case on two grounds.

I challenge it firstly because I fear that I will not be given a fair and proper trial. I challenge it in the second place because I consider myself neither legally nor morally bound to obey laws made by a Parliament in which I have no representation. In a political trial such as the present one which involves a clash of the aspirations of the African people and those of the Whites, the country's courts as presently constituted cannot be impartial and fair. In such cases Whites are interested parties. To have a White judicial officer presiding, however high his esteem, and however strong his sense of justice and fairness, is to make Whites judge their own case. It is improper and against the elementary principles of justice to entrust Whites with cases involving the denial by them of basic human rights to the African people. What sort of justice is this that enables the aggrieved to sit in judgement upon those whom they accused, a judiciary controlled entirely by Whites and enforcing laws enacted by a White Parliament in which we have no representation: laws, which in most cases are passed in the face of unanimous opposition from Africans.

By the Court: I am wondering whether I shouldn't interfere with you at this stage, Mr Mandela. Aren't we going beyond the scope of the proceedings? After all is said and done, there is only one Court today and that is the White Man's Court. There is no other Court. What purpose does it serve you to make an application when there is only one Court, as you know yourself. What Court do you wish to be tried by?

By the Accused: Well, Your Worship, firstly I would like Your Worship to bear in mind that in a series of cases our Courts have laid it down that the right of a litigant to ask for a recusal of a judicial officer is an extremely important right, which must be given full protection by the Court, as long as that right is exercised honestly. Now I honestly have apprehensions, as I am going to demonstrate just now, that this unfair discrimination throughout my life has been responsible for very grave injustices, and I am going to contend that that race discrimination which outside this Court has been responsible for all my troubles, I fear in this Court is going to do me the same injustice. Now Your Worship may disagree with that, but Your Worship is perfectly entitled, in fact, obliged to listen to me, and because of that I feel that Your Worship –

By the Court: I would like to listen, but I would like you to give me the grounds for your application for me to recuse myself.

By the Accused: Well, these are the grounds, I am developing them, sir. If Your Worship will give me time –

By the Court: I don't wish you to go out of the scope of the proceedings.

By the Accused: Of the scope of the application. I am within the scope of the application, because I am putting forward grounds which in my opinion are likely not to give me a fair and proper trial.

By the Court: Anyway, proceed.

By the Accused: As Your Worship pleases. I was developing the point that a judiciary controlled entirely by Whites and enforcing laws enacted by a White Parliament in which we have no representation, laws which in most cases are passed in the face of unanimous opposition from Africans, cannot be regarded as an impartial tribunal in a political trial where an African stands as an accused.

The Universal Declaration of Human Rights provides that all men are equal before the law, and are entitled without any discrimination to equal protection of the law. In May, 1951, Dr D.F. Malan, then Prime Minister, told the Union Parliament that this provision of the Declaration applies in this country. Similar statements have been made on numerous occasions in the past by prominent Whites in this country, including Judges and Magistrates. But the real truth is that there is in fact no equality before the law whatsoever as far as our people are concerned, and statements to the contrary are definitely incorrect and misleading.

EQUALITY BEFORE THE LAW

It is true that an African who is charged in a court of law enjoys on the surface the same rights and privileges as a White accused, insofar as the conduct of his trial is concerned. He is governed by the same rules of procedure and evidence as apply to a White accused. But it will be grossly inaccurate to conclude from this fact that an African consequently enjoys equality before the law. In its proper meaning equality before the law means the right to participate in the making of the laws by which one is governed. It means a constitution which guarantees democratic rights to all sections of the population, the right to approach the Court for protection or relief in the case of the violation of the rights guaranteed in the Constitution, and the right to take part in the administration of justice as Judges, Magistrates, Attorney-General, Prosecutors, law advisers and similar positions. In the absence of these safeguards the phrase "equal before the law" insofar as it is intended to apply to us, is meaningless and misleading.

All the rights and privileges to which I have referred are monopolised in this country exclusively by Whites, and we enjoy none of them. The White Man makes all the laws, he drags us before his courts and accuses us, and he sits in judgement over us. Now it is fit and proper to ask the question, Sir, what is this rigid colour bar in the administration of justice all about? Why is it that in this Courtroom I am facing a White Magistrate, confronted by a White Prosecutor, escorted by White Orderlies? Can anybody honestly and seriously suggest that in this type of atmosphere the scales of justice are evenly balanced? Why is it that no African in the history of this country has ever had the honour of being tried by his own kith and kin, by his own flesh and blood? I will tell Your Worship why: the real purpose of this rigid colour code is to ensure that the justice dispensed by the courts should conform to the policy of the country, however much that policy might be in conflict with the norms of justice accepted in judiciaries throughout the civilised world.

"THE ATMOSPHERE OF WHITE DOMINATION"

I feel oppressed by the atmosphere of White domination that is around me in this Courtroom. Somehow this atmosphere recalls to mind the inhuman injustice caused to my people outside this Courtroom by the same White domination. It reminds me that I am voteless because there is a Parliament in this country that is White-controlled. I am without land because the White minority has taken the lion's share of my country, and I am forced to occupy poverty stricken reserves which are over populated and over stocked. We are ravished by starvation and disease because our country's worth –

By the Court: What has that got to do with the case, Mr Mandela?

By the Accused: With the last point, Sir, it hangs together, if Your Worship will give me the chance to develop it.

By the Court: You have been developing for quite a while now, and I feel you are going beyond the scope of your application.

By the Accused: Your Worship, this to me is an extremely important ground which the Court must consider.

By the Court: I fully realise your position, Mr Mandela, but you must confine yourself to the application and not go beyond it. I don't want to know about starvation. That in my view has got nothing to do with the case at the present moment.

By the Accused: Well, Your Worship has already raised the point that here in this country there is only a White Court. What is the purpose of all this? Now if I demonstrate to Your Worship that outside this Courtroom race discrimination has been used in such a way as to deprive me of my rights, not to treat me fairly, certainly this is a relevant fact from which to infer that wherever race discrimination is practised, this will be the same result, and this is the only reason why I am using this point.

By the Court: I am afraid that I will have to interrupt you, and you will have to confine yourself to the reasons, the real reasons for asking me to recuse myself.

By the Accused: Your Worship, the next point which I want to make is this: I raise the question, how can I be expected to believe that this same racial discrimination which has been the cause of so much injustice and suffering right through the years should now operate here to give me a fair and open trial? Is there no danger that an African accused may regard the courts not as impartial tribunals, dispensing justice without fear or favour, but as instruments used by the White man to punish those amongst us who clamour for deliverance from the fiery furnace of White rule. I have grave fears that this system of justice may enable the guilty to drag the innocent before the courts. It enables the unjust to prosecute and demand vengeance against the just. It may tend to lower the standards of fairness and justice applied in the country's courts by White judicial officers to Black litigants. This is the first ground for this application: that I will not receive a fair and proper trial.

Now the second ground for this application is that I consider myself neither morally nor legally bound to obey laws made by a Parliament in which I have no representation. That the will of the people is the basis of the authority of government is a principle universally acknowledged as sacred throughout the civilised world, and constitutes the basic foundation of freedom and justice. It is understandable why citizens who have the vote as well as the right of direct representation in the country's governing bodies should be morally and legally bound by the laws governing the country. It should be equally understandable why we as Africans should adopt the attitude that we are neither morally nor legally bound to obey laws which were not made with our consent, nor can we be expected to have confidence in courts that interpret and enforce such laws.

I am aware, Your Worship, that in many cases of this nature in the past South African courts have upheld the right of the African people to work for democratic changes. Some of our judicial officers have even openly criticised the policy which refuses to acknowledge that all men are born free and equal, and fearlessly condemned the denial of opportunities to our people. But such exceptions, Your Worship, exist in spite, not because of the grotesque system of justice that has been built up in this country. These exceptions furnish yet another proof that even among the country's Whites there are honest men, whose sense of fairness and justice revolt against the cruelties perpetrated by their own White brothers to our people. The existence of genuine democratic values among some of the country's Whites in the judiciary, however slender they may be, is welcomed by me, but I have no illusions about the significance of this fact, healthy a sign as it may be. Such honest and upright men are few, and they have certainly not succeeded in convincing the vast majority of the rest of the White population that White supremacy leads to dangers and disasters.

"I HATE RACIAL DISCRIMINATION –"

Your Worship, I hate racial discrimination most intensely and in all its manifestations. I have fought it all along my life. I fight it now, and I will do so until the end of my days. I detest most intensely the set-up that surrounds me here. It makes me feel that I am a Black man in a White man's Court. This should not be. I should feel perfectly free and at ease with the assurance that I am being tried by a fellow South African who does not regard me as inferior, entitled to a special type of justice. This is not the type of atmosphere most conducive to feelings of security and confidence in the impartiality of the Court.

Now the Court might reply to this part of my argument by assuring me that it will try my case fairly and without fear or favour, that in deciding whether or not I am guilty of the offence charged by the State, the Court will not be influenced by the colour of my skin or by any improper motive. That might well be so. But such a reply will completely miss the whole point of my argument. As already indicated, my objection is not directed to Your Worship in his personal capacity, nor is it intended to reflect upon the integrity of the Court. My objection is based upon the fact that our courts as presently constituted create grave doubts in the mind of an African accused whether he will receive a fair and a proper trial. This doubt springs from objective facts relating to the practice of unfair discrimination against the Black man in the constitution of the country's courts. Such doubts cannot be allayed by mere verbal assurances from a presiding officer, however sincere such assurances may be. There is only one way, and one way only of allaying such

doubts: By removing discrimination, particularly in judicial appoint-
ments. This is my first difficulty.

WHITE AND BLACK ETHICS

I have yet another difficulty about similar assurances Your Worship
might give. Broadly speaking Africans and Whites in this country have
no common standard of fairness, morality and ethics, and it will be very
difficult for me to determine what standard of fairness and justice Your
Worship has in mind. In relationships with us, South African Whites
regard as fair and just to pursue policies which have outraged the
conscience of mankind, and of honest and upright men throughout the
civilised world. They suppress our aspirations, bar our way to freedom
and deny us opportunities in our moral and material progress, to secure
ourselves from fear and want. All the good things of life are reserved
for the White folk, and we Blacks are expected to be content to nourish
our bodies with such pieces of food as drop from the tables of men with
a White skin. This is the White man's standard of fairness and justice.
Herein lies his conception of ethics. Whatever he himself may say in his
defence, the White man's moral standards in this country must be
judged by the extent to which he has condemned the vast majority of its
citizens to serfdom and inferiority.

We, on the other hand, Your Worship, regard the struggle against
colour discrimination and for the pursuit of freedom as the highest
aspiration of all men. Through bitter experience we have learnt to regard the White man as a harsh and merciless type of human being,
whose contempt for our rights and whose utter indifference to the promotion of our welfare makes his assurances to us absolutely meaningless and hypocritical.

I have the hope and the confidence that Your Worship will not treat
this objection lightly, nor regard it as a frivolous one. I have decided to
speak frankly and honestly, because the injustices I have referred to
tend to undermine our confidence in the impartiality of our courts in
cases of this nature, and they contain the seeds of an extremely dangerous situation for our country and people. I make no threats, Your Worship, when I say that unless these wrongs to which I have pointed are
remedied without delay, we might well find that even plain talk before
the country's courts is too timid a method to draw attention to our
grievances.

Finally, I need only say that the courts have said that the possibility of bias and not actual bias is all that need be proved to ground an application of this nature. In this application I have merely referred to certain objective facts, from which I submit that the possibility be inferred that I will not receive a fair and proper trial.

By the Court: Mr Prosecutor, have you anything to say?

By the Prosecutor: Very briefly, Your Worship, I just wish to point out that there are certain legal grounds upon which an accused person is entitled to apply for the recusal of a judicial officer from the case in which he is to be tried. I submit that the Accused's application is not based on one of those principles, and I ask the Court to reject it.

By the Court: Your application is dismissed. Will you now plead to your charges?

By the Accused: I plead NOT GUILTY to both charges, to all the charges.

READING QUESTIONS ON MANDELA

1 How broad is the reach of Mandela's view? Does it only apply to politically motivated disobedience? Or does an illegitimate state lose its right to try people for any crimes?
2 What theory of the state is Mandela working with?
3 Reread *Lavallée*, above. Are Lavallée's duties to refrain from defending herself changed by the fact that the state has failed to protect her in the past?

Christine M. Korsgaard
"Taking the Law into Our Own Hands:
Kant on the Right to Revolution"

Korsgaard examines Kant's argument that there can be neither a moral or legal right to revolution. She concludes by arguing that in some cases revolutionary activity can be justified by its success.

If we place ourselves at the end of this tremendous process, where the tree at last brings forth fruit, where society and the morality of custom at last reveal *what* they have simply been the means to: then we discover that the ripest fruit is the *sovereign individual*, like only to himself, liberated again from the morality of custom, autonomous and supramoral.

Nietzsche[1]

I TAKING THE LAW INTO OUR OWN HANDS

Morality is unconditional and overriding. Its demands are uncompromising and its claims take priority over all others. Yet we can all think of situations in which, for reasons that seem to us honorable, unselfish, or conscientious, we would do things which morality seems to forbid. I want to ask how we can account for this fact.

There are two attempts to deal with the problem which, for obvious reasons, I will call skepticism and dogmatism. The skeptic denies that morality is unconditional and overriding. The dogmatist insists that it is, and argues that either the actions in question are not wrong, or, if they are, a good person just won't do them.[2]

Some skeptics and dogmatists are merely trying to domesticate the phenomena. The skeptic may have pretensions to being worldly and realistic, laughing at the ponderous claims of moralists. The dogmatist may simply be a moralistic prig. But there are serious and attractive versions of both views. The skeptic may think, as Bernard Williams does, that a life in which moral considerations can always override love and the cherished projects of a lifetime is not recognizably human.[3] The dogmatist may think that suitably refined and sensitive moral theory will show us that the actions in question are not wrong after all, but, in the complex or terrible situations in which we are tempted to choose them, simply the right things to do.

A Kantian's job is to find the path between skepticism and dogmatism. In this essay, I try to construct an account of one category of cases in which a good person will do a terrible thing: cases in which she judges that, for moral reasons, she must take the law into her own hands. There are many such cases, but the one I will examine is the standout in the category: the case of the conscientious revolutionary. From Kant I will derive an account of this case that, unlike skepticism and dogmatism, preserves at least something of both of the thoughts with which I began. Morality is unconditional and overriding, and revolution is always wrong. Yet sometimes the good person finds she must rebel.

I have another motive for examining this category of cases. It is that human beings seem to find them profoundly interesting and somehow attractive. Literature and the movies are full of them. We are shown a good person who, rather than violate his own standards, submits to the unjust treatment of himself and others. He holds out against solicitations to rebel long enough to convince us that his honor is real. And then a moment finally comes when, breaking the rules he has set for himself, he takes up his weapons and fights. Fletcher Christian finally mutinies against Captain Bligh. Ransom Stoddard, who came to the West to bring it law, picks up his gun and heads to the street for a shootout with Liberty Valance.[4] Instead of feeling disappointed at their defection, these are moments that we find *thrilling*.

Neither skepticism nor dogmatism can give an adequate account of this fact. The skeptic thinks that the hero has awakened to a more realistic view of the role of morality in human life. The dogmatist thinks that the hero has arrived at a more sensitive and refined conception of what morality demands. Both see these stories as what are sometimes called "coming of age" stories, in which the hero advances to maturity. This seems to me to be wrong in every way. Although the heroes of these stories have not previously taken the law into their own hands, they are not morally immature characters who have finally seen what they ought to do. And it is important to us that they do what they do with a sense not of rightness but of profound loss and pain. If Fletcher Christian rebelled any earlier, we wouldn't admire and sympathize with him nearly as much as we do. The moments when someone arrives at a more sensitive view of what morality demands, or of its role in human life, are no doubt important and deeply formative. But they are not thrilling, like the moment when the hero takes the law into his own hands.

II KANT ON REVOLUTION

Kant's attitude toward revolution, both in his work and in his life, are notoriously paradoxical. In many of his published works, revolution is roundly condemned. In the *Metaphysical Principles of Justice*, Kant argues that "there is no right of sedition, much less a right of revolution" and concludes that "it is the people's duty to endure even the most intolerable abuse of supreme authority" (*MPJ* 320).[5] In "On the Common Saying: 'This May Be True in Theory, but It Does not Apply in Practice,'" Kant says:

all resistance against the supreme legislative power, all incitement of the subjects to violent expressions of discontent, all defiance which breaks out into rebellion, is the greatest and most punishable crime in a commonwealth, for it destroys its very foundation. This prohibition is absolute. And even if the power of the state or its agent, the head of state, has violated the original contract by authorizing the government to act tyrannically, and has thereby, in the eyes of the subject, forfeited the right to legislate, the subject is still not entitled to offer counter-resistance. (*TP* 81)

And yet if a revolution succeeds, Kant thinks, the new government immediately becomes legitimate. In the *Metaphysical Principles of Justice* he writes:

if a revolution has succeeded and a new constitution has been established, the illegitimacy of its beginning and of its success cannot free the subjects from being bound to accept the new order of things as good citizens, and they cannot refuse to honor and obey the suzerain who now possesses the authority. (*MPJ* 323)

So even a regime newly established by an overthrow may not in turn be overthrown.

This may make it seem as if Kant were trying to defend quietism at any cost. And yet when Kant looked to history for a sign that would show whether the human race was making moral progress, he found encouragement in a phenomenon of his own day: the enthusiasm of the spectators of the French Revolution. In his essay "An Old Question Raised Again: Is the Human Race Constantly Progressing?" Kant writes:

The revolution of a gifted people which we have seen unfolding in our day may succeed or miscarry; it may be filled with misery and atrocities to the point that a sensible man, were he boldly to hope to execute it successfully the second time, would never resolve to make the experiment as such cost – this revolution, I say, nonetheless finds in the hearts of all spectators (who are not engaged in the game themselves) a wishful participation which borders on enthusiasm, the very expression of which is fraught with danger; this sympathy, therefore, can have no other cause than a moral disposition in the human race. (*OQ* 85)

Granted, it is the spectators, not the revolutionaries themselves, whose enthusiastic sympathy Kant thinks testifies to our moral nature. But if revolution is wrong, how can "wishful participation" in it be right? And we know that Kant himself was one of the most enthusiastic of these wishful participants. His personal obsession with both the French and the American Revolutions, his constant eagerness for the latest news from France, his persistent championship of the French Revolution even in the face of the Terror, won him the nickname "the Old Jacobin." Indeed according to one report "he said that all the horrors in France were unimportant compared with the chronic evil of despotism from which France had suffered, and the Jacobins were probably right in all they were doing."[6] Kant not only could sympathize with those aroused to violence by injustice; he could even cheer for them.

So here we have Kant's three views: revolution is unconditionally wrong; yet if it succeeds the government it establishes is a legitimate authority to which the citizens owe their obedience; and, finally, our enthusiasm for the French Revolution, even our wishful participation in it, is an outward sign of the presence of a moral disposition in our nature, from which we may derive hope for our own moral progress. In what follows, I try to show how this trio of views can make sense.

III JUSTICE AND THE POLITICAL STATE

Some background is necessary to my account. In the *Metaphysics of Morals*, Kant distinguishes two kinds of duties: duties of virtue and duties of justice (*MM* 218–21). Duties of justice are derived from the "Universal Principle of Justice" (*MPJ* 230), a restricted version of the categorical imperative. The Universal Principle of Justice tells us to act in a way that is compatible with the freedom of everyone according to a universal law (*MPJ* 231). Everyone is to have equal freedom of action, and the duties of justice are duties to avoid actions which violate that condition. According to Kant, the duties of justice are external duties. They are duties to perform or avoid certain outward acts. Insofar as a given action is regarded as a duty of justice, the duty is just to *do* it. The doctrine of right, in which the duties of justice are studied, is completely unconcerned about our motives. The sense in which the duties of justice are *duties* is cashed out entirely in terms of the right to use force or coercion to stop you (*MPJ* 231). In the sphere of law and justice, "this is your duty" means "we have the right to demand this of you." This stands in sharp contrast to the sphere of ethics, which concerns the duties of virtue. There "this is your duty" means "insofar as you are autonomous, you demand this of yourself" (*MPV* 379–80).

Why is it permissible for others to force or coerce you to conform to the duties of justice? The Universal Principle of Justice in effect says that the *only* restriction on freedom is consistency with the freedom of everyone else. Anything that is consistent with universal freedom is just, and you therefore have a right to do it. If someone tries to interfere with that right, he is interfering with your freedom and so violating the Universal Principle of Justice. Violations of the Universal Principle of Justice may be opposed by coercion for the simple reason that anything that hinders a hindrance to freedom is consistent with freedom, and anything that is consistent with universal freedom is just. It follows that rights are coercively enforceable. Indeed, coercive enforceability is not something attached to rights; it is constitutive of their very nature (*MPJ* 232). To have a right just is to have the executive authority to enforce a certain claim. This in turn is the foundation of the executive or coercive authority of the political state.

Kant's political philosophy is a social contract theory, in obvious ways in the tradition of Locke. But the differences are important. In Locke's view, individuals have rights in the state of nature, and may enforce those rights. But when each person determines and enforces his own rights the result is social disorder. Since this disorder is contrary to our interest, people join together into a political state, transferring our executive authority to a government.[7]

Kant also believes that there is a sense in which we have rights in the state of nature. We have a natural right to our freedom (*MPJ* 237), and, Kant thinks, the Universal Principle of Justice allows us to claim rights in land and, more generally, in external objects, in property. Kant argues that it would be inconsistent with freedom to *deny* the possibility of property rights, on the grounds that unless we can claim rights to objects, those objects cannot be used (*MPJ* 246).[8] This would be a restriction on freedom not based in freedom itself, which we should therefore reject, and this leads us to postulate that objects may be owned. But unlike Locke, Kant argues that in the state of nature these rights are only "provisional" (*MPJ* 256). In this, Kant is partly following Rousseau. In contrast to Locke, Rousseau argues that rights are created by the social contract, and, in a sense, relative to it. My possessions will become my property, so far as you and I are concerned, when you and I have given each other certain reciprocal guarantees: I will keep my hands off your possessions if you will keep your hands off mine.[9] Rights are not acquired by the metaphysical act of mixing one's labor with the land, but instead are constructed from the human relations among people who have made such agreements.[10] Kant adopts this idea, at least as far as the executive authority associated with a property right is concerned. I may indeed coercively enforce my rights. But if my doing so is to be consistent with the Universal Principle of Justice, it cannot be an act of *unilateral* coercion. To claim a right to a piece of property is to make a kind of law; for it is to lay it down that all others must refrain from using the object or land in question without my permission. But to view my claim as a *law* I must view it as the object of a contract between us, a contact in which we reciprocally commit ourselves to guaranteeing each other's rights. It is this fact that leads us to enter – or, more precisely, to view ourselves as already having entered – political society.

In making this argument, Kant evokes Rousseau's concept of the general will. He argues that a general will to the coercive enforcement of the rights of all concerned is *implicitly* involved in every property claim.

> Now, with respect to an external and contingent possession, a unilateral Will cannot serve as a coercive law for everyone, since that would be a violation of freedom in accordance with universal laws. Therefore, only a Will binding everyone else – that is, a collective, universal (common), and powerful Will – is the kind of Will that can provide the guarantee required. The condition of being subject to general external (that is, public) legislation that is backed by power is the civil society. Accordingly, a thing can be externally yours or mine [that is, can be property] only in a civil society. (*MPJ* 256)

It is because the idea of the general will to the reciprocal enforcement of rights is implicit in any claim of right that Kant argues that rights in the state of nature are only provisional. They are provisional because this general will has not yet been *instituted* by setting up a common authority to enforce everyone's right. The act that institutes the general will is the social contract.

Kant concludes from this argument that when the time comes to enforce your rights coercively, in the state of nature, the only legitimate way to do that is by joining in political society with those with whom you are in dispute. In fact, you enforce your right by first forcing them to join in political society with you so that the dispute can be settled by reciprocal rather than unilateral coercion:

> If it must be *de jure* possible to have an external object as one's own, then the subject must also be allowed to compel everyone else with whom he comes

into conflict over the question of whether such an object is his to enter, together with him, a society under a civil constitution. (*MPJ* 256)

Suppose we are in the state of nature and we get into a dispute about rights. My goat has kids, and I take them to be mine because I was caring for the mother goat when they were born. However, one of them escaped, and you found it wandering around apparently unowned in the state of nature, took possession of it, fed it, and cared for it for many years. Now we have discovered the matter, and each of us thinks she has a right to this particular goat. Since I think I have a right, I also think I may prosecute my right by coercive action. And you think the same. So what can we do? Perhaps I have a gun and you do not, so I can simply take the goat away from you. However, there are two ways to understand my action. One is: I am using unilateral force to take the goat away from you. Such an action would be illegitimate, a use of violence that interferes with your freedom. I cannot regard my action as an enforcement of my *right* without acknowledging that you have rights too, which also must be enforced. So if I am to claim that what I am doing is enforcing my right, I must understand my own action differently. The other way to understand the action is that I am forcing you to enter into political society with me. That gets us to the first step; the act of enforcing my right involves the establishment of a juridical condition (*rechtlicher Zustand*) between us and so establishes civil society. The second step, of course, is to settle the particular dispute in question in some lawful way.

This means that Kant's conception is different from Locke's in important ways. According to Kant a juridical condition – a condition in which human rights are upheld and enforced – can exist only in political society. And therefore existence in political society is not merely, as Locke had it, in our interest. It is a duty of justice to live in political society. That is to say, others have the right to require this of you, because that is the form that their authority to enforce their own rights takes. And you, reciprocally, have the right to require membership in political society of others with whom you might have such disputes. Since we will that our rights be enforced, reciprocal coercion, and therefore political society, can be seen as the object of a general will.

Kant does not take himself to be telling an historical story. He is answering a transcendental question: how is coercive political authority possible? His answer is that the idea of a general will to the reciprocal enforcement of rights is what makes coercive political authority possible. Governments are legitimate because human beings who live in proximity, who must therefore work out what their respective rights are, must form a general will. To put it another way, justice, which is the condition in which we have guaranteed one another our rights, exists only where there is government. Government, then, is founded on our presumptive general will to justice.

IV ALL GOVERNMENTS ARE LEGITIMATE

Kant's account of the state, as I have just said, is transcendental: it is an account of how political authority is possible. But of course we need to know something more than that: we need to know when political authority is actual. Which regimes are legitimate governments, and which are mere Mafias ruling the people by main force? Kant's view is that *all* governments should be taken to be legitimate. That is, any regime's decisions are the voice of the general will of its people; and its procedures for making those decisions must be taken to be ones the people have agreed to.

Kant of course does not mean that all governments and all of their decisions are perfectly just. In fact, Kant thinks that his theory of the political state implies an ideal of the state that is not generally realized. The state must embody the general will of the people to the reciprocal enforcement of those rights that constitute the freedom of everyone. In order to do this, Kant argues, the state must be a republic, characterized by a constitution and by the separation of powers, in which legislation is carried on by representatives of the citizens. Although Kant has some negative things to say about "democratic" government, these must be understood in terms of his rather complex account of political authority. Kant asserts that "legislative authority can be attributed only to the united Will of the people" (*MPJ* 313). This authority is then invested in a sovereign authority or ruler, which may be constituted by all, some, or one of the people (*MPJ* 338–9; *PP* 352), making the form of sovereignty democratic, aristocratic, or autocratic, respectively. Members of the sovereign are citizens and must therefore be fit to vote (*MPJ* 314); Kant criticizes the autocratic form of sovereignty, which concentrates it in a single person's hands, because "none of the subjects are citizens" (*MPJ* 339). The sovereign is responsible for administering the government. If the sovereign "himself" carries out all three functions of government directly, the government is despotic; if, however, the sovereign adopts a constitution establishing legal and institutional forms through which it performs the three functions of government separately, then the government is republican.[11] A republican constitution, Kant says, is the "one and only legitimate constitution" (*MPJ* 340) since it is "the only enduring constitution in which the law is autonomous and not annexed to any particular person" and in which therefore "each person receives his due peremptorily" (*MPJ* 341). In a republican constitution, that is, every person is bound by the law and so one's rights do not depend on everyone's (not even the majority's) will. And therefore:

Every true republic is and can be nothing else than a representative system of the people if it is to protect the rights of its citizens in the name of the people. Under a representative system, these rights are protected by the citizens themselves, united and acting through their representatives (deputies). As soon, however, as the chief of state in person (whether it be a king, the nobility, or the whole population – the democratic union) allows himself to be represented, then the united people do not merely *represent* the sovereign, but they themselves *are* the sovereign. (*MPJ* 341)

Once such constitutional forms are established, the united people no longer have to invest the sovereignty in any other "person," not even the collectivity of the whole people themselves. Instead the people govern themselves *directly* through their constitutional forms. Outwardly, of course, somebody must administer the functions of government, but those who do so are now regarded as magistrates who work for the people, not as sovereign authorities. The magistrate who runs the government may still be a "monarch," and Kant sometimes suggests that he thinks this is the best arrangement (*PP* 352–3). Yet it seems clear enough that this ideal requires that the magistrates be responsive to the demands of the people. For instance Kant argues that the establishment of republican forms of government will bring war to an end, because a declaration of war will require "the consent of the citizens," who are unlikely to give it (*PP* 351). This result seems to depend on the idea that the citizens will have some actual influence on the political process. Thus Kant's ideal state appears to be most closely realized by our own modern constitutional "democracies." Legislation is to be carried on by more or less direct delegates of the citizens, while the other functions of government are to be separated from the legislative function and the magistrates who perform all three functions are to understand themselves as representing the united will of the people.[12]

Why then does Kant think we must treat every regime, and all of its decisions, as the voice of the general will? To understand this, we need to consider Kant's responses to two possible challenges to the legitimacy of a government, one based on its history – on the illegitimacy of its origins – and the other on its present imperfections, as measured by the ideal.

Start with the historical challenge. I have already said that Kant is not proposing that there was an actual contractarian origin to the state. His social contract is a hypothetical or, perhaps better, a transcendental one, which explains how such things as governments are possible. Kant signals this by grounding the state in what he calls a "postulate." Earlier in the *Metaphysical Principles of Justice*, Kant had also grounded the possibility of property in a postulate. The notion of a postulate is introduced in the *Critique of Practical Reason*, in connection with Kant's account of practical religious faith. Suppose we have some rational concept, but we do not have theoretical grounds for assigning it "objective reality" – that is, for asserting that it could apply to any actual object. In some cases, we may nevertheless have practical grounds for doing so, based on the considerations that (i) moral practice is intelligible or possible only if we assume that this concept has objective reality, and (ii) moral practice is absolutely obligatory. In the second *Critique*, this is our basis for assigning objective reality to God, Freedom, and Immortality, concepts that cannot be applied theoretically because their objects could not be part of the sensible world (*KpV* 119–46).[13] In the *Metaphysical Principles of Justice*, Kant argues that both "property" (or right) and "government" are moral or normative, and so intelligible or rational rather than sensible or empirical, concepts. Empirically, all we can identify is *possession* in the one case and *ruling power* in the other: people have certain objects in their possession, or under their control, and some people rule over others. Yet it is essential for moral practice, as we have seen, that we treat some of these empirical relations as having normative force: that we treat some possessions as rightful property, and some cases of ruling power as cases of legitimate political authority. For we cannot have freedom without property rights, and we cannot have rights without government. The "Juridical Postulate of Practical Reason" (*MPJ* 246) and the "Postulate of Public Law" (*MPJ* 307) establish the objective reality of rights and government respectively.

In contrast to the religious postulates, however, these postulates license us to assign their concepts to objects we encounter in the natural world. And in both cases, a problem springs from the fact that the concept invokes a kind of hypothetical history. Kant's account of the possibility of property follows the usual strategy of appealing to the legitimacy of an individual's taking first possession of some land in the state of nature, rightfully laying claim to an object hitherto unowned. The individual then of course has the right to transfer this property to others. This kind of story can make it seem as if the correctness of a property-claim depends on an object's entire history and ancestry. Ownership of an object must be the result of a series of legitimate transactions stretching all the way back to the beginning of human history, when someone took first possession of the land.

Suppose someone challenges my right to a book. I say it's mine, but he says it's not; it's stolen property. He doesn't mean that *I* stole it; but that there's an illegitimate move *somewhere* in its history. Imagine that a congress of Native Americans demands that immigrant Americans return all of the books made from paper made from American trees to them. They say: you stole the forests, and the forests were ours; so the paper is ours; and the books are ours. And of course they've got a point. If we traced the ancestry of the property each of us owns, it would be full of illegitimate transactions. No one would be found to be the legitimate owner of anything. The history of the human race is a history of war and looting and theft and violence, not a history of legitimate transactions. So here's what we do. We simply take it for granted that, generally speaking, what people now have is their property. And we try to ensure that, from here on in, transactions will be legitimate and just.[14]

Kant thinks that this is what we should do with governments too. We should take it for granted that the existing governments are legitimate representatives of the general will of the people who are ruled by them, as if they originated in social contracts. "One ought to obey the legislative authority that now exists regardless of its origin" (*MPJ* 319). Kant says in several places that it is criminal even to *research* the origin of a government if you do it with an eye to challenging its legitimacy (*MPJ* 318–19; 372). Now of course there is also an important difference between the two cases. Kant thinks that if a revolution succeeds, we should take it that the new government is legitimate. The policy of treating any extant political power as legitimate is an absolutely blanket one. But of course if a theft or a swindle succeeds, we do not take it that the new distribution of property is legitimate. We do trace ownership back in time, within limits. But there is also an obvious explanation of this disanalogy. When someone is accused of stealing property, there is a duly constituted authority, namely the state itself, to decide the case. So this kind of conflict can be handled in a just manner. But of course after a revolution, there is no duly constituted authority to settle the question whether the old government or the new government is legitimate. The question which one is legitimate just is the question what the general will of the people is. And that, of course, can be settled only by consulting the true government – the voice of the general will – which is exactly what is at issue here.

Now we come to the second possible kind of challenge. Even if we don't deem the governments illegitimate because of their histories, we might challenge the legitimacy of those that fall short of the republican ideal to which the idea of government points us. Kant also argues against doing this. In an appendix attached to later editions of *The Metaphysical Principles of Justice*, Kant quotes a reviewer, Friedrich Bouterwek, who among other things called it "the most paradoxical of all paradoxes" that "the mere Idea of sovereignty should necessitate me to obey as my lord anyone who has imposed himself upon me as a lord, without my asking who has given him the right to command me" (*MPJ* 371).[15] And Kant replies:

Every matter of fact is an object that is an appearance (of sense); on the other hand, that which can be represented only through pure reason and which must be included among the Ideas – that is the thing in itself. *No object in experience can be given that adequately corresponds to an Idea.* A perfect juridical [just] constitution among men would be an example of such an Idea. (*MPJ* 370; my emphasis)

The claim is that no existing government adequately corresponds to the idea of a government. And yet:

When a people are united through laws under a suzerain, then the people are given as an object of experience conforming to the *Idea in general* of the unity of the people under a supreme powerful Will. Admittedly, this is only an appearance; that is, a juridical constitution in the most general sense of the term is present. Although the [actual] constitution may contain grave defects and gross errors and may need to be gradually improved in important respects, still, as such, it is absolutely unpermitted and culpable to oppose it. If the people were to hold that they were justified in using violence against a constitution, however defective it might be, and against the supreme authority, they would be supposing that they had a right to put violence as the supreme prescriptive act of legislation in the place of every right and Law. (*MPJ* 371–2)

There are two possible ways to understand this argument. One might read it, first, as a kind of slippery slope argument. Suppose that Kant is correct in saying that *no* extant government meets the ideal. If we then ask how close a government must come to the ideal before it counts as legitimate, there is no obvious place to draw the line. If we look for a minimum criterion of legitimacy, we find that the most natural one – universal adult suffrage – rules out nearly every "government" that has existed in the history of the world before the twentieth century.[16] So perhaps Kant thinks it is too dangerous to make such judgments.

This reading, however, does not sit well with the obviously Platonic character of the passage.[17] When Kant says that actual governments are only "appearances" he does not mean that they are not real. He means that they are imperfect participants, in the Platonic sense, in the form of justice, a form that is given by the ideal of the republic described earlier. When Kant contrasts autocracy, aristocracy, and democracy to the true form of government, he even calls them "those old ... empirical forms of the state" in contradistinction to the "original (rational) form" that is the republic (*MPJ* 340). Kant is clearly confident that, despite their imperfections, we recognize these objects as governments, as imperfect approximations to a perfect form.[18]

In order to understand why, it helps to reflect that there is a kind of tension inherent in our very concept of justice: a tension between what I will call the procedural and the substantive elements of the concept. On the one hand, the idea of justice essentially involves the idea of following certain procedures. In the state, these are the procedures by which the three functions of government are carried out. In order to be just, any sort of decision, outcome, or verdict – any political judgment – must be the result of *actually following* these procedures. That is a *law* which has been passed in form by a duly constituted legislature; this law is *constitutional* if (say) the supreme court says that it is; a person is *innocent* of a certain crime when he has been deemed so by a jury; someone is *the president* if he meets the qualifications and has been duly voted in, and so forth. These are all normative judgments – the terms I have italicized imply the existence of certain reasons for action – and the normativity of these judgments *derives from* the procedures that have established them.

On the other hand, however, there are many cases in which we have an independent idea of how these procedures ought to turn out. These independent criteria form our more substantive judgments – in some cases, of what is just, in other cases, simply of what is right or best. Perhaps the law is unconstitutional, though the legislature has passed it; perhaps the defendant is guilty, though the jury has set him free; perhaps the candidate elected is not the best person for the job, or even the best of those available, or perhaps due to the accidents of voter turnout he does not really represent the majority will. As this last example shows, the distinction between the procedurally just and the substantively just, right, or best, is a rough and ready one, and relative to the case under consideration. Who should be elected? The best person for the job, the best of those who actually run, the one preferred by the majority of the registered voters, the one elected by the majority of those who actually turn out on election day ... As we go down the list, the answer to the question becomes increasingly procedural; the answer above it is, relatively, more substantive. We may try to design our procedures to secure the substantively right, best, or just outcome. But – and here is the important point – the normativity on these procedures nevertheless does not spring from the efficiency, goodness, *or even the substantive justice* of the outcomes they produce. The reverse is true: it is the procedures themselves that confer normativity on those results. The person who gets elected holds the office, no matter how far he is from being the best person for the job. The jury's acquittal stands, though we later discover new evidence that the defendant was guilty after all. And the normativity of the procedures themselves springs not from the quality of their outcomes but rather from the fact that we must have such procedures if we are going to form a general will. In order to act together – to make laws and policies, apply them, enforce them, in a way that represents, not some of use imposing our private wills on others, but all of us acting together from a collective general will – we must have certain procedures that make collective decision and action possible, and, normatively speaking, we must stand by their actual results.

This point has some weight in any collective decision – even when we make a decision, say, with a group of friends. But it applies most forcefully to cases of right and justice, to decisions backed by coercive authority. For if we reserve ourselves the right to ignore the outcomes of such procedures when we believe them to be substantively wrong, then we are still in the state of nature. And this idea is reflected in our actual practice, leaving Kant aside, for it is a basic rule of citizenship, of living in accordance with the rule of law, that procedural judgments have a coercive normative force against which substantive ones have *no weight at all*. Your judgment that a law is stupid does not justify a lynching; your belief that your candidate is the better man is no grounds whatever for a takeover.

When the substantive ideal that opposes the procedural outcome is also an ideal of justice itself, and not merely one, say, of efficiency or qualification, this gives rise to a tension. It's bad enough when the jury lets the guilty go free, but suppose you are sure they have convicted the innocent. The law passed by congress is not just stupid or inefficient or incoherent, but – you think – plainly unconstitutional; only the Supreme Court, called upon to decide the case, does not agree with you here. Where then does justice lie? When we are judging the very institutions of government themselves, this kind of tension can rise to the level of paradox, illustrated by a simple example. Suppose we are convinced that the idea that government should represent the general will of the people requires that some group of people, hitherto helplessly subjected to a powerful tyrant, be allowed to choose their own political institutions in a democratic election. And suppose that having been liberated from their tyrant and allowed to vote for their political institutions, they unanimously vote the democracy out, and their tyrant right back in again. Where now does justice lie? Shall we force upon these people a form of government they do not choose to have, in the *name* of respecting their general will?[19] We may be convinced, and for good reasons, that constitutional democracy is the best way for a people to express its general will. But the absence of democratic institutions cannot be taken as proof or even as evidence that a government does not represent the general will of its people.

"When a people are united through laws under a suzerain, then the people are given as an object of experience conforming to the Idea in general of the unity of the people under a supreme powerful Will" (*MPJ* 371–2). What makes a people unified is that there are procedures under which they are unified, procedures that make collective decision and action possible, and give them a general will. Kant's view is that wherever we see such an arrangement, we see an imperfect empirical realization of the form of justice, of the idea of a general will. If someone has enough authority to make and execute laws, and the people are living and acting and relating to one another under those laws, then that is their general will. The failure of their institutions to meet our more substantive ideals of justice is simply irrelevant.

It's worth pointing out that, in the international sphere, we accept this conclusion. Although we may agree with Kant that the modern constitutional democracy is the substantively best form of government, we do not think that this licenses us to impose it on other nations, or even to refuse recognition to those who neither have nor aspire to this ideal. It would, for the reasons just given, be not just wrong, but paradoxical, since the very idea embodied in the ideal of constitutional democracy is that government should be by the consent of the governed, or an expression of the general will. That idea demands that we recognize that the peoples of other nations must decide for themselves what kind of political institutions they will have.[20] If we are to recognize them as sovereign states at all, we must simply take it that their governments are expressions of their general wills.

To arrive at Kant's position you need only see that the individual subject, when considered only as a private individual with his own private ideas about what constitutes good government, is in exactly the same position as an outsider toward his *own* government.[21] He must acknowledge its procedures, as they stand, to be the expression of the general will, if he is to see his country as having a general will and so a government at all. And according to Kant he must see himself as living under a government because, as we saw earlier, it is our duty to live in a political society.

V WHY THERE IS NO RIGHT TO REVOLUTION

Since Kant thinks that any government represents the general will of the people, his argument against the right to revolution is an immediate, simple, conceptual one. He says:

For in order for the people to be able to judge the supreme political authority with the force of law, they must already be viewed as united under a general legislative Will; hence they can and may not judge otherwise than the present chief of state wills. (*MPJ* 318)

The pont is plain. The government is the representative of the general will. But if *it* represents the general will, whatever it says is the voice of the general will. To revolt, where that means to oppose the decisions of the government, is therefore to oppose the general will. And to oppose the general will is to dissolve the judicial condition among human beings, and so to return to the state of nature. Revolution "is not an alteration of the civil constitution, but the dissolution of it" (*MPJ* 340). This is wrong, for, as we have seen, Kant thinks that living in political society is not, as Locke thought, a mere remedy for inconvenience, but instead is a duty of justice.

However paradoxical it seems, this argument has real force. If government exists by the general will, a revolution could be legitimate only if it in turn were in accordance with the general will. Otherwise, it is just a few lawless individuals making war against the nation. But we should ask how it could be established that a revolution *is* in accordance with the general will. Kant's argument shows how serious this problem is. The government contains agencies for both determining and interpreting what the general will is. Of course the people may decide that the government is not doing a good job of this. But this judgment can be made only by someone who has the right to speak for the people, and that right belongs to the government itself.[22] Therefore, the government can reform itself, but the people *as subjects* cannot reform the government.

The problem arises because the will of the people must be represented. A people cannot literally speak with one voice. They must speak through a representative who has their mandate. What makes the problem of revolution so acute is that what is in question here *is* who represents the people. And the people cannot literally speak with one voice about *this* any more than they can about anything else. Until we settle the question who represents the people the general will has no voice to speak with. So we cannot start with the will of the people; to know what the will of the people is, we must start with someone taken to be their representative, their voice. This can make it seem strangely arbitrary who we take to represent them. Kant's solution to this problem is to say that the representative of the people *just is* the extant government, whatever it is.

If we accept Kant's solution, a revolution is necessarily opposed to the general will and so it is illegitimate. To see this, imagine the best possible case for revolution. Suppose we have a small nation ruled by a single tyrant and his army. The revolutionary, hoping to establish legitimacy, assembles the entire population and takes a vote. Everyone except the dictator and his army votes for a new regime. If the dictator does not bow out, do the people have the right to revolt? The answer is no. In this country, the procedure for determining the general will is to consult the dictator, not to take a vote. Votes can determine what the general will is only where they are the duly constituted procedure for determining the general will. So for these people to revolt on the basis of this vote would be a raw act of the tyranny of the majority over the minority. The majority only represents the general will where it has been established that they do; and in this case, it has not.

Kant's argument, as I've suggested, depends on a deeply procedural conception of the general will. Our general will, according to this argument, just is whatever follows from the procedures that make collective action possible, and so, in Rousseau's extravagant language, it can do no wrong.[23] Suppose we allow, instead, that there is such a thing as the general will, independently of our procedures, and that our procedures should be viewed as fallible devices for ascertaining it. Then we can allow, contrary to Kant, that the extant regime may not represent the will of the people and so may fail to be legitimate. Even so, we get the problem. It is still true that the people cannot speak as a people until they have a voice. A revolutionary who claims to be the representative of the people merely because of the spirit he senses among them or even because he has taken a favorable vote is misdescribing the situation. The people can give their mandate only through some duly constituted voice, through someone who has the right to represent them. If we admit the possibility that the extant regime does not represent the general will then there is *no way* to tell what the general will is. The general will has lost its voice, and there are only two ways to make it speak again. One is if the people arrive at actual unanimity – in which case, of course, there could be no need for revolution, since the people of a nation include its governors. The other is by the essentially arbitrary choice of a representative. So even if we grant the possibility that a government might be illegitimate, we can never say that the revolution is in accordance with the general will. Now all we have is a raw clash of arbitrary powers at war with each other in a world without justice. We have still not established that revolution is something to which there could be a *right*.

VI WHAT FOLLOWS FROM THE FACT THAT THERE IS NO RIGHT TO REVOLUTION

Let's say Kant has made his case. There is no right to revolution. What follows?

It follows from the fact that there is no right to revolution that there is a duty not to revolt. This duty is a duty of justice. It is important now to recall what this means. A duty of justice is a duty in the sense that others may coercively require your performance. To say that something is a duty of justice is to say that its violation is punishable. So the first thing that follows is that if you participate in a revolution, it fails, and you are caught, you may be punished. As Kant says, revolution is the "most punishable crime in a commonwealth, for it destroys its very foundations" (*TP* 81). So far, this is unproblematic. It would be extraordinary to believe that people may not be punished for revolting. Of course if people get out their guns and shoot at others and make mayhem in society they may be punished. The fact that their motives were political rather than venal may make us judge them less harshly as human beings, but for all that they may be punished.[24] The whole point of a government is to enforce people's rights in a way that is orderly and grounded in reciprocal coercion, rather than in a disorderly and unilaterally coercive way. Executive authority is supposed to be concentrated in a government; and so the idea of a government which is not allowed to enforce its own decisions is incoherent. As Kant himself points out, a right to revolution would involve a kind of contradiction, rather like the Liar's Paradox: "the supreme legislation would have to contain a stipulation that it is not supreme" (*MPJ* 320).[25]

There is also a second consequence, which follows from Kant's views about responsibility for actions and their consequences. Kant argues that one must do what the moral law demands, let the consequences be what they may. If you do what is required of you, you are not responsible for the consequences. On the other hand, if you do something other than what the moral law demands, then you are responsible for the consequences. In the *Metaphysics of Morals*, Kant says:

The good or bad consequences of an action owed, as well as the consequences of omitting a meritorious action, cannot be imputed to the subject.

The good consequences of a meritorious action as well as the bad consequences of an unlawful action can be imputed to the subject. (*MM* 228)

In other words, if you do your perfect duties, you are not responsible for the results; if you do an imperfect duty, such as helping someone, you count as the author of the good result; and if you violate perfect duty and the results are bad, the consequences are on your head. In the *Lectures on Ethics*, Kant puts the point more simply:

If we do either more or less than is required of us we can be held accountable for the consequences, but not otherwise – not if we only do what is required, neither more nor less. (*LE* 59)[26]

Now the duties of justice are all perfect duties, and so when you violate them, you are responsible for the results. Revolutionaries who are caught may be held legally liable not only for the crime of sedition but for the death, injury, and mayhem that result. But Kant makes it clear that this is not merely a legal point. He says that the consequences of violating a perfect duty should also be imputed to the agent "by his own conscience" (*MPV* 431). So someone who undertakes to start or participate in a revolution must regard himself as responsible for the results. A revolutionary must see himself as the author of the loss of life and limb, the social disorder, and the suspension of the juridical condition that results from revolution.

Although this is a more controversial point, this too, seems to me to be correct. Even those who are inclined to argue for a "right to revolution" cannot think that revolution is something to be undertaken lightly. Justice exists only where there is government; the revolutionary undertakes to destroy the government, and so undertakes to destroy justice. Of course his aim is to improve the juridical condition. He thinks that justice will rise revivified from its own ashes, like the Phoenix; he hopes to bring about a new and better system of justice, which will come closer to doing its job, which is guaranteeing freedom. As Kant says, revolutionaries undertake "to be unjust once and for all, in order thereafter to establish legal justice on a foundation that is so much more secure" (*MPJ* 353). But for however short a time, there will be a condition in which there is no justice. During this period, as a result of conditions the revolutionary himself has instigated or supported, lives will be lost, injuries sustained, property rights violated, careers interrupted and destroyed. During this period, the victims of these disasters will have neither recourse nor compensation. He may fail, and if he fails, all of this will have been for nothing. Surely the victims of social upheaval may rightly regard the revolutionaries as the authors of their injuries. And surely the revolutionary cannot just say: the consequences were not my fault, since I was doing what I had a right to do.

So far, we have two consequences. First, the conclusion that there is no right to revolution, in Kant's sense of a right, is unproblematic. Of course revolutionaries, if they fail or are caught on time, may be punished. The idea of a government that is not entitled to defend itself in this way makes no sense. But this is not merely a matter of what the law has to say, of whether there can be a legal right to revolution. Even from a purely moral point of view, a just revolution would have to be in accordance with the general will of the people, and we have seen that this is impossible. Either the government is the voice of the general will of the people, or there is no voice; in neither case can the revolutionary claim the mandate of the general will. So the revolutionary is doing something he has no right to do. And that means that all the consequences of the revolution are imputable to him. If he wins, his party becomes the legitimate government, and as such they are not legally answerable for their actions; and morally, then, he at least has an excuse. But if he loses, he is nothing more than a murderer and a thief. And this last should be not only in the government's eyes, but in his own.

But there is one consequence that does not follow. So far, I have said nothing that implies that there are no circumstances in which a good person would revolt.

VII WHEN THE VIRTUOUS PERSON REVOLTS

More than any other philosopher in the tradition, Kant gives us an agent-centered moral philosophy. His primary question is not who shall we praise or blame, or which actions are right and which wrong. He has things to say about these questions, but they fall out of the discussion of what he takes to be the central question of moral philosophy: what must I do? So far, we have remained on the territory of duties of justice, and have discussed what we say *about* revolutionaries and revolution. But we have not yet addressed the main question: should *we* ever revolt? Nor could we address that question, so long as we kept the discussion to the duties of justice. To approach this question we must turn to the doctrine of virtue, to ethics.

Again we will need some background. Earlier I said that the duties of justice are external duties. The sense in which they are duties is that we may legitimately be forced to do them. The duties of virtue, by contrast, are internal duties. The sense in which they are duties is that morality requires them of us, which is to say that we require them of ourselves. Duties of virtue are concerned with our motives and attitudes. They arise from the command that we should not only do certain things, but do them for moral reasons: in Kantian language, they command us to make duty itself the incentive of our action. As the constitutive aim of the duties of justice is the achievement of external freedom, so the constitutive aim of the duties of virtue is internal freedom: for through the cultivation of virtue we achieve freedom of the will (*MPV* 379–84).[27]

Kant believes that all human action is purposive (*G* 427; *MPV* 381, 385; *R* 4, *R* 6–7n). This does not mean that we always act for the sake of some end in which we have taken a prior interest; but it does mean that we always act with some end in view. When we undertake an action, there is always some end to that action which we represent to ourselves as good. It does not have to be an end we are trying to bring about – it may be an end we wish not to act against, or wish to respect. In the moral case, for instance, we may simply see our action as expressing respect for humanity as an end in itself. Because morally good actions as well as others are purposive, Kant argues that the cultivation of virtue is achieved through the adoption of morally obligatory ends (*MPV* 380–1; 384–5).

Kant thinks that there are duties, and so ends, that belong specifically to the territory of virtue: the pursuit of the happiness of others, and the cultivation of our own talents, powers, and character (*MPV* 385–9). But ethics encompasses all of our duties. It is a duty of virtue to do the duties of justice from the motive of duty. In other words, justice itself is a virtue. And Kant says that the virtue of justice is possessed by one *who makes the rights of humanity his end* (*MPV* 390).

In ordinary circumstances, this is the end we have in view when we carry out the moral duty to obey the law. If you keep your hands off your neighbor's property, even thinking he has more than his fair share; if you refrain from stuffing ballot boxes, even when that means the better candidate will lose; if you pay your debts, even when you could get away with not doing so, this is because you care about the rights of others. The end you have in view is that their rights should be respected.

It is because justice is a virtue that there is an ethical duty, as well as a duty of justice, not to revolt. The just person respects the rights of humanity, and for this reason respects the government that enforces those rights, and the juridical condition that makes their enforcement possible. But it is by no means obvious that a person who makes the rights of humanity his end would never, under any circumstances, oppose the extant government. If this is correct, nothing in Kant's theory absolutely commits him to the view that a good person would *never* revolt. Nor, I believe, is this what he himself thought.[28]

Justice exists to preserve the rights and freedom of everyone: this is the idea, and the substantive ideal, of justice. But we all know that the procedures of justice may used *against these very ends*. Apartheid South Africa horrified us more, perhaps, than more egregious despotisms, because of its outward forms of legality, its caricature of a modern Western democracy. The same is true of America before the Civil War. A master recapturing a runaway slave is brutal; but a court's ordering the slave's return is a mockery of justice. Women and children have often been returned to the legal custody of the very husbands and fathers who have abused them; Captain Bligh does not just beat his men, but does it with the King's authority. There is a special kind of horror associated with such cases. For in such cases the very language of rights, and the robes and wigs and forms and ceremonies with which we celebrate our will to form a general will, are used to corner the helpless. The agencies of justice are used to reinforce injustice; and what should be the recourse of the oppressed is the very tool of the oppressor. In such cases, justice is turned against itself, perverted; human rights need protection from the law itself.

Kant does not say this, of course, but he was keenly sensitive to the special kind of horror I am talking about here. This shows up, interestingly, in a footnote to the very section of the *Metaphysical Principles of Justice* in which Kant argues that revolution is always wrong. He says:

Of all the abominations involved in the overthrow of a state through revolution, the *murder* of the monarch is still not the worst, because it is possible to imagine that the people are motivated by the fear that, were he to remain alive, he might regain his power and give them the punishment they deserve; in that case, this deed would not be an act of penal justice, but only one of self-preservation. It is the *formal execution* of a monarch that fills the soul, conscious of the Idea of human justice, with horror, and this horror returns whenever one thinks of scenes like those in which the fate of Charles I or Louis XVI was sealed. (*MPJ* 321n; my emphases)

Kant proceeds to examine the sources of this particular kind of horror. In the *Groundwork*, Kant had argued that since we cannot consistently will an evil maxim as a universal law, a person who acts wrongly cannot be doing *that*, but instead is making himself an exception to the law (*G* 424). Recalling these ideas, Kant argues here that to *get rid* of the ruler is to violate justice, and so to make yourself an exception to the law, but to *punish* the ruler (and to execute the supreme executive) is to subvert justice – not just to make yourself an exception to the law, but actually to repudiate it, and so to make a kind of law of unlawfulness itself. In *Religion within the Limits of Reason Alone*, Kant distinguishes human evil, which consists in making yourself an exception to the law for the sake of satisfying some contingent interest, from the possession of a malevolent will, one that wills evil for its own sake, that wills evil as a law. Contrary to Augustine, Kant does not think that human beings choose evil for its own sake (*R* 30). Yet here Kant argues that the execution of the monarch is like an exhibition of a malevolent will, because it presents an evil act in the outward forms of a lawful one. This is why we find it so horrifying.

Revolutionaries who formally execute a monarch perform an unjust act while dressed in the robes and wigs of justice; in so doing, they seem not just to ignore justice, but to mock it. But in cases of the sort I have mentioned, the state may seem to do this too. And then the just subject may find herself locked in exactly the sort of horror that Kant describes. When the very institutions whose purpose is to realize human rights is used to trample them, when justice is turned against itself, the virtue of justice will be turned against itself too. Concern for human rights leads the virtuous person to accept the authority of the law, but in such circumstances adherence to the law will lead her to support institutions that systematically violate human rights.[29] The person with the virtue of justice, the lover of human rights, unable to turn to the actual laws for their enforcement, has nowhere else to turn. She may come to feel that there is nothing for it but for her to take human rights under her own protection, and so to take the law into her own hands.

The decision to revolt would be a hard one to make because a person who loves the rights of humanity necessarily places a high value on the actual procedures of justice as well as on the substantive ideal of protecting human rights. And as I argued earlier, the procedures of justice are important not just because they approximate our substantive ideals, but because without such procedures there is no justice at all. Nor, of course, will the achievement of more substantive ideals be the result of the sacrifice. At the very best, revolution will bring only a closer approximation to the ideal. At the very worst, the result will be an extended period in which there is no justice at all, the rights of humanity are trampled underfoot, and a new excuse for tyranny will have been created. Short of that, there may be only marginal improvements, not obviously worth the ruined and ended lives we paid for it. The revolutionary risks this, and knows that she does, when she decides to revolt.

Two things make this decision different from most of the decisions we make, at least as those are envisioned in Kantian ethics. The first is that the universalization test cannot serve as a guide when we make it. The imperfections of the actual state of affairs are no excuse for revolution – if they were, revolution would always be in order. It is the perversion of justice, not merely its imperfections, that turns the virtue of justice against itself. But the difference between imperfect justice and perverted justice is a matter of pure judgment. There is no criterion for deciding when imperfection has become perversion, when things have gone too far. If we turn for help to the Universal Principle of Justice, all it says is: Do not revolt. The revolutionary cannot claim he has a justification, in the sense of an account of his action that other reasonable people must accept. That consolation is denied him. It is as if a kind of gap opens up in the moral world in which the moral agent must stand alone.

The revolutionary's stance, in fact, is one of paternalism toward a whole society, when paternalism, which after all is a kind of despotism, is what he hates the most. And this reminds us that revolution is only one case, the most vivid perhaps, in which good people take the law into their own hands. Another, much more common and familiar sort of case, is when we paternalize an adult human being who is engaged in some sort of self-destructive behavior. Most of us, for instance, would take action to prevent a suicide (at least unless the person was hopelessly ill and in great pain) even if we didn't think the person had simply gone crazy, but was really acting from his own choice. And many of us would be prepared to take action to prevent a close friend from going too far with self-destructive activities like abusing drugs. The structure of the problem we face in these cases is exactly the same as that of the problem faced by the revolutionary. When we see someone perverting or destroying the humanity or autonomy in his own person, our respect for his humanity or autonomy is turned against itself. Respect for his autonomy demands that we respect his right to choose. But if we respect his autonomy we cannot stand quietly by and watch while he destroys it. Like justice in an unjust state, his autonomy requires protection against itself. And so like the revolutionary, the paternalist violates his respect for autonomy in order to save its object. Paternalists too take the law into their own hands. Here too, there is no way of deciding exactly when the moment has come, when things have gone too far. Morality cannot tell you when to leave the moral law behind, in order to make sure that the world remains a place where morality can flourish. In making this kind of decision, you are entirely on your own.

And this brings us to the second thing that makes this decision different from others. Since these decisions necessarily involve stepping outside of the law, they involve what Bernard Williams has called "moral luck."[30] For as Kant says, if you do more or less than the law requires, the consequences are on your head. The form of moral luck Williams describes exists in a case with these features: the agent does something that is, on the face of it, wrong, but may be justified by success. If the project fails, the agent will simply be wrong, and the consequences will be, in his own eyes ad those of his victims, on his head. But if the project succeeds, he may at least be justified in his own eyes and in the eyes of outsiders, if not of those of his immediate victims. Williams thinks that the concept of moral luck is a notion inimical to Kantianism, but the case of the revolutionary has exactly this structure. Success makes the revolutionary, legally, the new voice of the general will, and, morally, one who has promoted the cause of justice on earth. In his own eyes and the eyes of the spectators this will justify him, though the victims of the revolution will still have a complaint. Failure, on the other hand, means that he has destroyed justice for nothing, that he is guilty of murder and treason, an assailant of the general will, and the enemy of everyone. Revolution may be justified, but only if you win.

Perhaps it will be doubted whether the view I have put forward could possibly be Kant's. Moral life in bad circumstances can be messy; Kant is often accused of denying this point. But I actually think it is a strength of his view that it allows us to see how one form of messiness arises – and that it does so without resorting to the pat explanation that we happen to be subject to an unsystematic plurality of duties that can of course conflict.[31] In the case of the conscientious revolutionary, the problem is not a conflict between different duties but rather the fact that a single duty – the duty to care for the rights of humanity – implodes when we try to act on it in an unjust world. But could Kant have recognized this? It is hard to know for sure, for the fact is that Kant never discusses the question whether the *ethical* duty not to revolt is always in place. His discussions of revolution are all concerned with the duty of justice, and it is, interestingly, the punishability of revolution that he always emphasizes. My view that he did recognize the possibility I've described here comes for the most part not from his published writings, but from what we know about his attitude toward the revolutions of his day. But there is one thing in the published writings that does support my claim. Listen again to part of the passage from "An Old Question Raised Again" where Kant praises the enthusiasm of the spectators of the French Revolution. Listen, in particular, to the way Kant imagines the deliberations of the would-be revolutionary himself:

The revolution of a gifted people which we have seen unfolding in our day may succeed or miscarry; it may be filled with misery and atrocities to the point that a sensible man, were he boldly to hope to execute it successfully the second time, would never resolve to make the experiment at such cost. (*OQ* 85)

Kant's revolutionary considers the prospects of success and views the costs of failure as his own. In this, he follows the pattern I have described.

VIII CONCLUSION

The Kingdom of Ends is an ideal, not a goal. For the most part, our duty is to live as if it were real, not to bring it about that it is so. A Kantian doesn't paternalize every time a loved one makes a poor choice; a Kantian doesn't revolt every time the government makes a wrong decision. In the one case, respect for autonomy, in the other, respect for the rule of law, matter to her more than the content of the particular decisions which are made.

But in some cases, respect for autonomy, or respect for the rule of law, can be turned against themselves. When autonomy is used self-destructively, and law turns against the rights it is there to protect, morality ceases to give us clear guidance how to proceed. The claims of right remain clear, but the demands of virtue become ambiguous. In such cases, good people may do things that are, in one fairly clear sense, wrong.[32] A dogmatist may deny that a good person would ever do this; a skeptic may think such actions are unproblematic, showing only that morality is not unconditional after all. I believe that both views over-simplify our moral situation: the world is a less comfortable home for morality than they suppose. Skepticism and dogmatism are attempts to evade one of the most important facts about moral responsibility. The moral life can contain moments when responsibility is so deep that even a justification is denied us. The agent who can save morality only by violating its principles faces such a moment. At such moments the virtuous person may find that he must take morality itself under his own protection, and so take even the moral law into his own hands.

IX AFTERWORD: WHY WE FIND REVOLUTION THRILLING

Earlier I claimed that the moment of revolution, though hard and full of pain for the revolutionary himself, is thrilling to the spectator. I also claimed that neither skepticism nor dogmatism could give an adequate account of the thrill. How should a Kantian account for it?

Kant, as we have seen, had his own explanation, detailed in the essay "An Old Question Raised Again." There Kant argues that revolutionaries of his day sought republican forms of government, the only form under which Kant thought real justice and peace could possibly be secured. With peace and justice would come enlightenment. The nations would be able to guarantee civil liberties and spend money on education rather than on arms (*IUH* 26–28; *CBHH* 121). Enlightenment, the condition in which people think for themselves (*WE* 35), leads to morality, the condition in which people live by the laws of their own autonomy. Thus enthusiasm for the revolution can be understood as enthusiasm for the future of morality itself.

My explanation is different, though not incompatible with Kant's. If Kant is right, human freedom is autonomy and autonomy is morality. This makes human freedom a paradoxical thing. In everyday life, it consists to a surprising extent in having to do things. When we are dealing with evil, it consists to a tragic extent in having to put up with things. When faced with oppression, bullying, and heartbreaking unfairness, freedom can appear as helplessness; autonomy as a terrifying defenselessness. There's a real antinomy here, a natural dialectic that throws us into doubt about the nature and the value of our own moral capacity. Plato gave voice to this worry in the very earliest works of Western moral philosophy: Thrasymachus laughs at the just person as someone easily tricked into serving the interests of the stronger; Callicles argues that even self-government is merely a form of slavery.[33] Freud and Nietzsche recast the worry in more psychological terms. Morality is an expression of strength, the will to power, the aggressive instincts, turned inward. It is the magical transformation of masterfulness into self-mastery that makes us human. But morality is a form of weakness, for the will to power, the aggressive instincts, are eating us alive from the inside out, sapping our strength, making us herd animals, victims, sickly prey.[34] Autonomy gives life meaning, showing us that the world is ours to create; but autonomy is morality and morality leads to nihilism, for the good have no option but surrender.

The moment of revolution is a vindication of morality, and so of our humanity. We are the masters of our own self-mastery in control of our self-control. Being human is not sapping our strength, for we still know when to fight. The revolutionary does not *become* strong and free when he picks up his gun. Instead, he proves to us that he's been free all along. It is because the law of morality are his own laws that he is finally prepared to fight for them. The doubt created by the antinomy is dispelled. Revolution teaches us nothing but what we have known all along: that the good person and the free person are one and the same.

NOTES

Versions of this paper were delivered at the Central Division meeting of the American Philosophical Association in the spring of 1991, where I had the benefit of a helpful and sympathetic commentary by Andrews Reath; at the Kantian Ethics Workshop in Chapel Hill in the fall of 1993, where I received challenging comments from Simon Blackburn; and at the Political Philosophy Colloquium in Princeton in the fall of 1995. I am grateful to the audiences at all three occasions for many illuminating comments and useful objections; I would like especially to thank Stephen Engstrom, Avishai Margalit, and Arthur Ripstein. I have benefited from discussing the issues of the paper with Charlotte Brown, Daniel Brudney, Peter Hylton, Arthur Kuflik, Tamar Schapiro, and Jay Schleusenser, and from written comments sent to me by Kenneth Westphal. The paper was completed while I was a Laurence S. Rockefeller Visiting Fellow at the University Center for Human Values in Princeton in 1995–1996; I am deeply grateful both for the time the Center provided me to finish the paper, and for the useful discussions of it I had with the Fellows there. But my primary debt, here as in everything that I write, is to the example and inspiration of my teacher, John Rawls.

1 Friedrich Nietzsche, *On the Genealogy of Morals*, trans. Walter Kaufmann and R.J. Hollingdale. In *On the Genealogy of Morals and Ecce Homo*, ed. Walter Kaufmann (New York: Random House, 1967), p. 59.

2 This use of the terms dogmatism and skepticism is of course borrowed from Kant. Kant characterizes the dogmatist as one who assumes "that it is possible to make progress with pure knowledge, according to principles, from concepts alone" (*KrV* Bxxxv; see note 5 for an explanation of the system used for referring to Kant's works). Dogmatism itself produces skepticism when dogmatic claims are found to be defeasible, or, as in the case of antinomy, when dogmatic arguments can be made on both sides of a question. The alternative is criticism, which calls into question reason's jurisdiction over the matter at hand; and *sometimes* ends by establishing only a more limited jurisdiction than reason had originally claimed. I leave the reader to judge for herself the extent to which these characterizations are apt for the work of this paper. Kant also characterizes dogmatism as despotic and suggests that skepticism, by contrast, is anarchic (*KrV* Aix). In these terms, it is apt to characterize the two views about the nature of morality's rule over us that I am discussing here as dogmatic and skeptical.

3 See, for instance, Williams's essays "Persons, Character, and Morality" and "Moral Luck" in *Moral Luck* (Cambridge University Press, 1981).

4 In the well-known story *Mutiny on the Bounty*, and in the movie, *The Man Who Shot Liberty Valance*, directed by John Ford. There are certain other popular characters whose appeal is certainly related to that of the good person who takes the law into his own hands. For example there is the hotdog cop, who uses irregular methods to catch bad guys. He doesn't take the law into his own hands on some particular occasion, but rather lives that way. Indeed, we are fascinated by the police in general, who, as Nietzsche points out, use all the same methods as criminals (*The Genealogy of Morals*, p. 82). Then there's the revenge film hero, who is, so to speak, *released* from the usual restraints of morality by a terrible crime committed against someone in his family. As we go down this list, a more deflationary account of the source of our pleasure becomes more plausible: the hero's plight serves merely to give us a kind of permission to enjoy the spectacle of violence wholeheartedly. But that's not what's going on in the cases mentioned in the text; and I think that an explanation of the phenomenon I discuss in the text should throw some light on the various pleasures we take in some of these stock figures.

5 References to and citations of Kant's works are given parenthetically in the text, using the abbreviations below, and for most works citing the page numbers of the relevant volume of *Kants gesammelte Schriften* (published by the Preussische Akademie der Wissenschaften, Berlin), which appear in the margins of most translations. The *Critique of Pure Reason*, however, is cited in its own standard way, by the page numbers of both the first (A) and second (B) editions. The *Lectures on Ethics* and the essay "On the Common Saying: 'This May Be True in Theory but It Does Not Apply in Practice'" are cited only by the page number of the translation. The translations of works from which I have quoted are also listed below.

KrV   *Critique of Pure Reason* (1st ed. 1781, 2d ed. 1787), trans. Norman Kemp Smith (New York: Macmillan, St. Martin's Press, 1965)

KpV   *Critique of Practical Reason* (1788)

CBHH   "Conjectural Beginning of Human History" (1786). Available in English translation in *Kant On History*, ed. Lewis White Beck (New York: Macmillan Library of Liberal Arts, 1963) or in *Kant's Political Writings*, 2d ed., trans. H.B. Nisbet, ed. Hans Reiss (Cambridge University Press, 1991).

G   *Groundwork of the Metaphysics of Morals* (1785)

IUH   "Idea for a Universal History from a Cosmopolitan Point of View" (1784). Available in English translation in *Kant On History*, ed. Lewis White Beck, cited above; or in *Kant's Political Writings*, 2d ed., trans. H.B. Nisbet, ed. Hans Reiss, cited above.

LE   *Lectures on Ethics* (1775–1780). Drawn from the lecture notes of Theodor Friedrich Brauer, Gottlieb Kutzner, and Chr. Mrongovious by Paul Menzer in 1924; trans. Louis Infeld (Indianapolis: Hackett Publishing, 1980).

MM   The General Introduction to *The Metaphysics of Morals* (1797), trans. James Ellington, in *Immanuel Kant: Ethical Philosophy* (Indianapolis: Hackett Publishing, 1983). The two main parts of the work are listed below.

MPJ   *The Metaphysical Principles of Justice* (1797), trans. John Ladd as *The Metaphysical Elements of Justice* (New York: Macmillan Library of Liberal Arts, 1965).

MPV   *The Metaphysical Principles of Virtue* (1797), trans. James Ellington, in *Immanuel Kant: Ethical Philosophy*, cited above.

OQ   "An Old Question Raised Again: Is the Human Race Constantly Progressing?" trans. Robert Anchor in *Kant On History*, ed. Lewis White Beck, cited above.

PP   *Perpetual Peace* (1795), trans. Lewis White Beck in *Kant On History*, ed. Lewis White Beck, cited above.

R   *Religion within the Limits of Reason Alone* (1793), trans. Theodore M. Greene and Hoyt H. Hudson (La Salle, IL: Open Court, 1934; rpt. New York: Harper Torchbooks, 1960).

TP   "On the Common Saying: 'This May Be True in Theory but It Does not Apply in Practice'" (1793), in *Kant's Political Writings*, 2d ed., trans. H.B. Nisbet, ed. Hans Reiss, cited above.

WE   "What is Enlightenment?" (1784). Available in English translation in *Kant On History*, ed. Lewis White Beck, cited above; or in *Kant's Political Writings*, 2d ed., trans H.B. Nisbet, ed Hans Reiss, cited above.

6 G.P. Gooch, *Germany and the French Revolution* (New York: Russell and Russell, 1966), p. 269.

7 Locke, *The Second Treatise of Government: An Essay Concerning the Original, Extent, and End of Civil Government*. For the discussion of rights in the state of nature, see Chapter II; for our reasons for leaving the state of nature, see Chapter IX.

8 Why must things be property in order for us to use them? In the case of immediate consumables, it is of course true that by using them we make them our own; we make them part of ourselves in the most literal way, so

that interfering with our use of them becomes in the most literal way interfering with ourselves. If we could not make them our own in this way, we could not use them. In the case of "the means of production" a simpler and more practical argument can be made: we cannot make *effective* use of them without some guarantee that they will be reserved for us exclusively during the time of use, since, for example, I cannot effectively grow corn in the same field where you are trying, at the same time, to grow barley. It is worth pointing out that this argument, if it works, does not establish the necessity of "private property" in any controversial sense; it establishes only that the means of production and action must be reserved to the exclusive use of certain individuals in certain times and places. This applies even to things owned communally – for instance, library books are reserved to particular patrons for speci- fied amounts of time. Your right to the exclusive use of a book, for reading only, and for a certain length of time, still counts as a form of "property" in Kant's sense. In the same way, the means of production might be communally owned and "lent out" to particular users.

9 Rousseau, Jean-Jacques, *On the Social Contract*, Book I, Chapter IX.

10 Of course it may be argued that Lockean rights also depend on human relationships, because of the proviso that the laborer should leave "enough and as good" for others, which seems to substitute for making agreements with others. But Locke seems to take it for granted that this proviso not only can be but is met, whereas the relationships on which rights are built in the accounts of Kant and Rousseau are ones that people must actually enter into. See Locke's *Second Treatise*, Chapter V.

11 Following Rousseau, Kant argues that a republican constitution must provide for the separation of the three powers, since when they are united in one person the state is effectively despotic (*MPJ* 316–19; *PP* 352). Rousseau argues that legislation must be couched in general terms, while it is the business of the executive to apply the law to particular cases (see *On the Social Contract*, Book II, Chapter IV). This makes it easy to see why unification of the powers leads to despotism. Suppose we legislate by majority vote, and suppose that the majority would like to institute a majority religion as the official church of the state. In their capacity as legislators, they cannot name a particular religion, but they could make a law that, say, everyone is to practice the one true faith. It will be left to the executive to determine which faith that is. Under these circumstances, it is plausible to suppose that individual citizens would have reason *not* to vote for such a law – the same sorts of reasons that the parties in Rawls's original position have for upholding freedom of

conscience (see John Rawls, *Political Liberalism* [New York: Columbia University Press, 1993], pp. 310–15). But now suppose that the majority is also the executive, who will choose the one true faith. Then they can make the law in question with impunity. In this way the unification of the legislative and executive powers makes democracy degenerate into a form of despotism – the tyranny of the majority.

12 In reconstructing Kant's complex account of these matters, I have drawn on the discussion in Howard Williams, *Kant's Political Philosophy* (New York: St. Martin's Press, 1983), pp. 173–8.

13 Kant argues that morality requires us to make the "Highest Good" – a state of affairs in which we all attain a virtuous disposition and happiness proportionate to that disposition – the end of our moral practice, and that we cannot conceive how such a state could be brought about unless God exists and we are immortal. We are therefore licensed to postulate that these things are so.

14 Kant does not say this directly, but he appeals to considerations of exactly this kind in explaining why in civil society we take long possession to establish a property claim (*MPJ* 292–3) and how we deal with cases in which someone has come into possession of stolen property (*MPJ* 302–3).

15 According to Kant himself, the review appeared in the *Göttingen Journal*, Number 28, February 18, 1797.

16 This criterion seems called for by Kant's account of citizenship as fitness for voting. Kant himself attempted to argue that some adults – apprentices, servants, and "all women" – could still count as "passive citizens" even though we are (rightly, according to Kant) not allowed to vote because of our "dependence" on others. But, in a textually rather unsteady moment, he also conceded that this is only legitimate if the laws chosen by the active citizens allow "everyone" to "work up" from a passive to an active status (*MPJ* 314–15).

17 Kant himself associates his use of the terms "Idea" and "Ideal" with Platonic forms at *KrV* A313/B370 ff., and A568–9/B596–7; and in the earlier discussion, he explicitly compares his own idea of a republic to Plato's (*KrV* A316/B373).

18 See Plato, *Phaedo*, lines 74a–76a, and *Republic*, especially books II–VII.

19 Kant himself says, "Even if the sovereign were to decide to transform himself into a democracy, he would still be doing the people an injustice, because the people themselves might abhor this kind of constitution and might find that one of the other two was more advantageous for them"

(*MPJ* 340). Of course Kant is talking here not about whether the state should be a republic, but about which of the three "empirical" forms it should take. The remark raises odd problems about whether Kant thinks there is *any* legitimate way for a state to change its basic form of government, but I leave those aside here.

20 When thinking about the terms on which we interact with other nations, as when thinking about the terms on which we interact with other people, it is important to distinguish two different issues: one is whether you disapprove of the way they go on, and the other is whether the way they go on prevents you from interacting with them on terms that are honorable in your own eyes.

21 As a citizen, rather than merely as a subject, he is sometimes entitled to act on his own substantive views. For instance, they determine who and what he votes for. But the cases in which he is permitted in this way to act on his private views must be constitutionally defined.

22 Hobbes makes essentially the same argument in *Leviathan*, Chapter XVIII.

23 Rousseau, *On the Social Contract*, Book II, Chapter III.

24 For Kant's own reflections on this point, see note 28 below.

25 One standard response to this point is that it shows only that there cannot be a legal right to revolution, but not that there cannot be a moral right. Kant's system makes no use of any distinctive category of moral right; for him, a right is by definition the kind of moral claim that can legitimately be coercively enforced and so can be legalized. There are claims in Kant's system that it is tempting to identify with moral rights. Kant distinguishes duties of justice from duties of virtue on the grounds that the former are, and the latter are not, both legitimate and possible to enforce coercively. We *may not* force people to be virtuous because virtue is a matter of inner motives and attitudes, and your having a bad attitude toward me does not hinder my freedom. But we also *cannot* force people to do the duties of virtue, because we cannot control the motives from which they act. Yet one of the duties of virtue – the duty to respect others – seems to be a perfect duty and seems to establish a kind of claim, so that we might say that we have a moral right to the respect of others. This will not help us here, however. It is, though, related to what I take to be the most plausible grounds for claiming a "moral right" to revolution – namely, exclusion from full citizenship on arbitrary grounds. The most extreme case is that of slaves, but victims of apartheid, and Kant's so-called passive citizens (see note 16 above) may also plausibly claim that the general will is not their will, that they have been left outside of the

commonwealth. So let me just say that the case of the conscientious revolutionary that I will shortly examine, the one I think morally interesting, is not that of someone who himself can plausibly claim to be excluded from the commonwealth, but rather someone who is part of the commonwealth but objects to its actions. One obvious reason why he might object is that some others are arbitrarily excluded.

26 For a further explanation of the basis and meaning of this view, see my "The Right to Lie: Kant on Dealing with Evil" in Korsgaard, *Creating the Kingdom of Ends* (Cambridge University Press, 1996), pp. 141–3.

27 For discussion, see my "Morality as Freedom" in *Creating the Kingdom of Ends*, pp. 176–83.

28 Kant explicitly acknowledges the existence of conscientious revolutionaries in the course of a rather odd discussion of the morality of the death penalty at *MPJ* 333–4. People join rebellions both for honorable and for venal motives, Kant notices, and we might think that the former should be punished less severely than the latter. But applying the death penalty to all concerned achieves this, Kant argues, since "a man of honor would choose death and ... the knave would choose servitude." The knave therefore *is* punished more severely.

29 I owe this formulation to Andrews Reath.

30 See Bernard Williams, "Moral Luck."

31 An account that, to my mind, makes sense of the complexity of morality at the expense of depriving morality itself of sense. I am indebted to Tamar Schapiro for illuminating discussions of this topic.

32 What fairly clear sense? Not universalizable, certainly; but the more important point is what that shows: that such an action relates us wrongly to others. Almost any moral philosopher would grant that wrong actions relate us wrongly to others, of course, but I mean something different. I don't regard that as an incidental feature of wrong actions, a mere effect of the fact that the actions are wrong and therefore others don't want us to do them. I regard the way it relates you to yourself and others as *of the essence* of the morality of an action. See my "The Reasons We Can Share" in *Creating the Kingdom of Ends*, pp. 275–6 and 300–2; and *The Sources of Normativity* (Cambridge University Press, 1996), p. 114 n. 26.

33 Plato, *Republic*, lines 338ff.; *Gorgias*, lines 491–2.

34 See Friedrich Nietzsche, *On the Genealogy of Morals* (cited in note 2 above). Essay 2, and Sigmund Freud, in, for example, *Civilization and Its Discontents*, trans. James Strachey (New York: W.W. Norton & Co., 1961), Chapter 7.

READING QUESTIONS ON KORSGAARD

1 John Locke, in chapter 19 of his *Second Treatise of Government*, says that "whenever the legislators endeavor to take away, and destroy the property of the people ... by this breach of trust they forfeit their right to rule." He appears to be defending both a moral and a legal right to revolution. How would Korsgaard or Kant respond?

2 Is Korsgaard right to claim that an unjust regime is still a legal regime, no matter how atrocious its policies? If the policies are bad enough, does there come a point at which it falls into a "state of nature" in which one group of people is simply making war on another? If so, what would Korsgaard or Kant recommend? How would one decide whether this was in fact the case?

3 Korsgaard argues that our conception of justice includes both formal and substantive concerns, and argues that these are in tension when one is dealing with an unjust regime. Are they in tension more generally? Is this tension relevant to *Sim's Case*? To *Billy Budd*? To *Riggs v Palmer*?

Reference re Secession of Quebec [1998] 2 SCR 217

The *Quebec Secession Reference* concerned the legality of any secession from Canada by Quebec. The matter came to Court through a special process known as the reference procedure. The essence of a reference is that it asks the Court to give an advisory opinion on important legal questions that may or may not have arisen in the context of concrete disputes between interested parties, without the benefit of findings of fact made at trial. Quebec refused to appear in the proceedings before the Court, alleging that the Court lacked the jurisdiction to consider a matter that was fundamentally political in nature, and that was for the population of Quebec to decide itself. The Court did wish to hear all sides of the legal argument and so took the unusual step of appointing a lawyer to make arguments on Quebec's behalf. It also rejected in its judgment the argument that the issue was too political in nature to be adjudicated by a Court.

The Court (Lamer, CJC and L'Heureux-Dubé, Gonthier, Cory, Mc-Lachlin, Iacobucci, Major, Bastarache and Binnie, JJ): –

I INTRODUCTION

[1] This Reference requires us to consider momentous questions that go to the heart of our system of constitutional government. The observation we made more than a decade ago in *Reference re Manitoba Language Rights*, [1985] 1 SCR 721 (*Manitoba Language Rights Reference*), at p. 728, applies with equal force here: as in that case, the present one "combines legal and constitutional questions of the utmost subtlety and complexity with political questions of great sensitivity." In our view, it is not possible to answer the questions that have been put to us without a consideration of a number of underlying principles. An exploration of the meaning and nature of these underlying principles is not merely of academic interest. On the contrary, such an exploration is of immense practical utility. Only once those underlying principles have been examined and delineated may a considered response to the questions we are required to answer emerge.

[2] The questions posed by the Governor in Council by way of Order in Council P.C. 1996-1497, dated September 30, 1996, read as follows:

1 Under the Constitution of Canada, can the National Assembly, legislature or government of Quebec effect the secession of Quebec from Canada unilaterally?
2 Does international law give the National Assembly, legislature or government of Quebec the right to effect the secession of Quebec from Canada unilaterally? In this regard, is there a right to self-determination under international law that would give the National Assembly, legislature or government of Quebec the right to effect the secession of Quebec from Canada unilaterally?
3 In the event of a conflict between domestic and international law on the right of the National Assembly, legislature or government of Quebec to effect the secession of Quebec from Canada unilaterally, which would take precedence in Canada?

. . .

III REFERENCE QUESTIONS

A Question 1

Under the Constitution of Canada, can the National Assembly, legislature or government of Quebec effect the secession of Quebec from Canada unilaterally?

(1) Introduction

[32] As we confirmed in *Reference re Objection by Quebec to a Resolution to amend the Constitution*, [1982] 2 SCR 793, at p. 806, "The *Constitution Act, 1982* is now in force. Its legality is neither challenged nor assailable." The "Constitution of Canada" certainly includes the constitutional texts enumerated in s. 52(2) of the *Constitution Act, 1982.* Although these texts have a primary place in determining constitutional rules, they are not exhaustive. The Constitution also "embraces unwritten, as well as written rules," as we recently observed in the *Provincial Judges Reference*, [1997] 3 SCR 3, at para. 92. Finally, as was said in the *Patriation Reference*, [1981] 1 SCR 753, at p. 874, the Constitution of Canada includes

the global system of rules and principles which govern the exercise of constitutional authority in the whole and in every part of the Canadian state.

These supporting principles and rules, which include constitutional conventions and the workings of Parliament, are a necessary part of our Constitution because problems or situations may arise which are not expressly dealt with by the text of the Constitution. In order to endure over time, a constitution must contain a comprehensive set of rules and principles which are capable of providing an exhaustive legal framework for our system of government. Such principles and rules emerge from an understanding of the constitutional text itself, the historical context, and previous judicial interpretations of constitutional meaning. In our view, there are four fundamental and organizing principles of the Constitution which are relevant to addressing the question before us (although this enumeration is by no means exhaustive): federalism; democracy; constitutionalism and the rule of law; and respect for minorities. The foundation and substance of these principles are addressed in the following paragraphs. We will then turn to their specific application to the first reference question before us.

(2) Historical Context: The Significance of Confederation

[33] In our constitutional tradition, legality and legitimacy are linked. The precise nature of this link will be discussed below. However, at this stage, we wish to emphasize only that our constitutional history demonstrates that our governing institutions have adapted and changed

to reflect changing social and political values. This has generally been accomplished by methods that have ensured continuity, stability and legal order.

[34] Because this Reference deals with questions fundamental to the nature of Canada, it should not be surprising that it is necessary to review the context in which the Canadian union has evolved. To this end, we will briefly describe the legal evolution of the Constitution and the foundational principles governing constitutional amendments. Our purpose is not to be exhaustive, but to highlight the features most relevant in the context of this Reference.

[35] Confederation was an initiative of elected representatives of the people then living in the colonies scattered across part of what is now Canada. It was not initiated by Imperial fiat. In March 1864, a select committee of the Legislative Assembly of the Province of Canada, chaired by George Brown, began to explore prospects for constitutional reform. The committee's report, released in June 1864, recommended that a federal union encompassing Canada East and Canada West, and perhaps the other British North American colonies, be pursued. A group of Reformers from Canada West, led by Brown, joined with Étienne P. Taché and John A. Macdonald in a coalition government for the purpose of engaging in constitutional reform along the lines of the federal model proposed by the committee's report.

[36] An opening to pursue federal union soon arose. The leaders of the maritime colonies had planned to meet at Charlottetown in the fall to discuss the perennial topic of maritime union. The Province of Canada secured invitations to send a Canadian delegation. On September 1, 1864, 23 delegates (five from New Brunswick, five from Nova Scotia, five from Prince Edward Island, and eight from the Province of Canada) met in Charlottetown. After five days of discussion, the delegates reached agreement on a plan for federal union.

[37] The salient aspects of the agreement may be briefly outlined. There was to be a federal union featuring a bicameral central legislature. Representation in the Lower House was to be based on population, whereas in the Upper House it was to be based on regional equality, the regions comprising Canada East, Canada West and the Maritimes. The significance of the adoption of a federal form of government cannot be exaggerated. Without it, neither the agreement of the delegates from Canada East nor that of the delegates from the maritime colonies could have been obtained.

[38] Several matters remained to be resolved, and so the Charlotte-town delegates agreed to meet again at Quebec in October, and to invite Newfoundland to send a delegation to join them. The Quebec Conference began on October 10, 1864. Thirty-three delegates (two from New-foundland, seven from New Brunswick, five from Nova Scotia, seven from Prince Edward Island, and twelve from the Province of Canada) met over a two and a half week period. Precise consideration of each aspect of the federal structure preoccupied the political agenda. The delegates approved 72 resolutions, addressing almost all of what subsequently made its way into the final text of the *Constitution Act, 1867*. These included guarantees to protect French language and culture, both directly (by making French an official language in Quebec and Canada as a whole) and indirectly (by allocating jurisdiction over education and "Property and Civil Rights in the Province" to the provinces). The protection of minorities was thus reaffirmed.

[39] Legally, there remained only the requirement to have the Quebec Resolutions put into proper form and passed by the Imperial Parliament in London. However, politically, it was thought that more was required. Indeed, Resolution 70 provided that "The Sanction of the Imperial and *Local Parliaments* shall be sought for the Union of the Provinces, on the principles adopted by the Conference." (Cited in J. Pope, ed., *Confederation: Being a Series of Hitherto Unpublished Documents Bearing on the British North America Act* (1895), at p. 52 (emphasis added).)

[40] Confirmation of the Quebec Resolutions was achieved more smoothly in central Canada than in the Maritimes. In February and March 1865, the Quebec Resolutions were the subject of almost six weeks of sustained debate in both houses of the Canadian legislature. The Canadian Legislative Assembly approved the Quebec Resolutions in March 1865 with the support of a majority of members from both Canada East and Canada West. The governments of both Prince Edward Island and Newfoundland chose, in accordance with popular sentiment in both colonies, not to accede to the Quebec Resolutions. In New Brunswick, a general election was required before Premier Tilley's pro-Confederation party prevailed. In Nova Scotia, Premier Tupper ultimately obtained a resolution from the House of Assembly favouring Confederation.

[41] Sixteen delegates (five from New Brunswick, five from Nova Scotia, and six from the Province of Canada) met in London in December 1866 to finalize the plan for Confederation. To this end, they

agreed to some slight modifications and additions to the Quebec Resolutions. Minor changes were made to the distribution of powers, provision was made for the appointment of extra senators in the event of a deadlock between the House of Commons and the Senate, and certain religious minorities were given the right to appeal to the federal government where their denominational school rights were adversely affected by provincial legislation. The British North America Bill was drafted after the London Conference with the assistance of the Colonial Office, and was introduced into the House of Lords in February 1867. The Act passed third reading in the House of Commons on March 8, received royal assent on March 29, and was proclaimed on July 1, 1867. The Dominion of Canada thus became a reality.

[42] There was an early attempt at secession. In the first Dominion election in September 1867, Premier Tupper's forces were decimated: members opposed to Confederation won 18 of Nova Scotia's 19 federal seats, and in the simultaneous provincial election, 36 of the 38 seats in the provincial legislature. Newly-elected Premier Joseph Howe led a delegation to the Imperial Parliament in London in an effort to undo the new constitutional arrangements, but it was too late. The Colonial Office rejected Premier Howe's plea to permit Nova Scotia to withdraw from Confederation. As the Colonial Secretary wrote in 1868:

The neighbouring province of New Brunswick has entered into the union in reliance on having with it the sister province of Nova Scotia; and vast obligations, political and commercial, have already been contracted on the faith of a measure so long discussed and so solemnly adopted. . . . I trust that the Assembly and the people of Nova Scotia will not be surprised that the Queen's government feel that they would not be warranted in advising the reversal of a great measure of state, attended by so many extensive consequences already in operation ... (Quoted in H. Wade MacLauchlan, "Accounting for Democracy and the Rule of Law in the Quebec Secession Reference," [1997], 76 *Can Bar Rev* 155, at p. 168.)

The interdependence characterized by "vast obligations, political and commercial," referred to by the Colonial Secretary in 1868, has, of course, multiplied immeasurably in the last 130 years.

[43] Federalism was a legal response to the underlying political and cultural realities that existed at Confederation and continue to exist today. At Confederation, political leaders told their respective communities that the Canadian union would be able to reconcile diversity with

unity. It is pertinent, in the context of the present Reference, to mention the words of George-Étienne Cartier (cited in the *Parliamentary Debates on the subject of the Confederation* (1865), at p. 60):

Now, when we [are] united together, if union [is] attained, we [shall] form a political nationality with which neither the national origin, nor the religion of any individual, [will] interfere. It was lamented by some that we had this diversity of races, and hopes were expressed that this distinctive feature would cease. The idea of unity of races [is] utopian – it [is] impossible. Distinctions of this kind [will] always exist. Dissimilarity, in fact, appear[s] to be the order of the physical world and of the moral world, as well as in the political world. But with regard to the objection based on this fact, to the effect that a great nation [can]not be formed because Lower Canada [is] in great part French and Catholic, and Upper Canada [is] British and Protestant, and the Lower Provinces [are] mixed, it [is] futile and worthless in the extreme ... In our own Federation we [will] have Catholic and Protestant, English, French, Irish and Scotch, and each by his efforts and his success [will] increase the prosperity and glory of the new Confederacy. ... [W]e [are] of different races, not for the purpose of warring against each other, but in order to compete and emulate for the general welfare.

The federal-provincial division of powers was a legal recognition of the diversity that existed among the initial members of Confederation, and manifested a concern to accommodate that diversity within a single nation by granting significant powers to provincial governments. The *Constitution Act, 1867* was an act of nation-building. It was the first step in the transition from colonies separately dependent on the Imperial Parliament for their governance to a unified and independent political state in which different peoples could resolve their disagreements and work together toward common goals and a common interest. Federalism was the political mechanism by which diversity could be reconciled with unity.

[44] A federal-provincial division of powers necessitated a written constitution which circumscribed the powers of the new Dominion and Provinces of Canada. Despite its federal structure, the new Dominion was to have "a Constitution similar in Principle to that of the United Kingdom" (*Constitution Act, 1867*, preamble). Allowing for the obvious differences between the governance of Canada and the United Kingdom, it was nevertheless thought important to thus emphasize the continuity of constitutional principles, including democratic institutions

and the rule of law; and the continuity of the exercise of sovereign power transferred from Westminster to the federal and provincial capitals of Canada.

[45] After 1867, the Canadian federation continued to evolve both territorially and politically. New territories were admitted to the union and new provinces were formed. In 1870, Rupert's Land and the Northwest Territories were admitted and Manitoba was formed as a province. British Columbia was admitted in 1871, Prince Edward Island in 1873, and the Arctic Islands were added in 1880. In 1898, the Yukon Territory and in 1905, the provinces of Alberta and Saskatchewan were formed from the Northwest Territories. Newfoundland was admitted in 1949 by an amendment to the *Constitution Act, 1867*. The new territory of Nunavut was carved out of the Northwest Territories in 1993 with the partition to become effective in April 1999.

[46] Canada's evolution from colony to fully independent state was gradual. The Imperial Parliament's passage of the *Statute of Westminster, 1931* (U.K.), 22 & 23 Geo. 5, c. 4, confirmed in law what had earlier been confirmed in fact by the Balfour Declaration of 1926, namely, that Canada was an independent country. Thereafter, Canadian law alone governed in Canada, except where Canada expressly consented to the continued application of Imperial legislation. Canada's independence from Britain was achieved through legal and political evolution with an adherence to the rule of law and stability. The proclamation of the *Constitution Act, 1982* removed the last vestige of British authority over the Canadian Constitution and re-affirmed Canada's commitment to the protection of its minority, aboriginal, equality, legal and language rights, and fundamental freedoms as set out in the *Canadian Charter of Rights and Freedoms*.

[47] Legal continuity, which requires an orderly transfer of authority, necessitated that the 1982 amendments be made by the Westminster Parliament, but the legitimacy as distinguished from the formal legality of the amendments derived from political decisions taken in Canada within a legal framework which this Court, in the *Patriation Reference*, had ruled was in accordance with our Constitution. It should be noted, parenthetically, that the 1982 amendments did not alter the basic division of powers in ss. 91 and 92 of the *Constitution Act, 1867*, which is the primary textual expression of the principle of federalism in our Constitution, agreed upon at Confederation. It did, however, have the important effect that, despite the refusal of the government of Quebec

to join in its adoption, Quebec has become bound to the terms of a Constitution that is different from that which prevailed previously, particularly as regards provisions governing its amendment, and the *Canadian Charter of Rights and Freedoms*. As to the latter, to the extent that the scope of legislative powers was thereafter to be constrained by the *Charter*, the constraint operated as much against federal legislative powers as against provincial legislative powers. Moreover, it is to be remembered that s. 33, the "notwithstanding clause," gives Parliament and the provincial legislatures authority to legislate on matters within their jurisdiction in derogation of the fundamental freedoms (s. 2), legal rights (ss. 7 to 14) and equality rights (s. 15) provisions of the *Charter*.

[48] We think it apparent from even this brief historical review that the evolution of our constitutional arrangements has been characterized by adherence to the rule of law, respect for democratic institutions, the accommodation of minorities, insistence that governments adhere to constitutional conduct and a desire for continuity and stability. We now turn to a discussion of the general constitutional principles that bear on the present Reference.

(3) Analysis of the Constitutional Principles

(a) Nature of the Principles. [49] What are those underlying principles? Our Constitution is primarily a written one, the product of 131 years of evolution. Behind the written word is an historical lineage stretching back through the ages, which aids in the consideration of the underlying constitutional principles. These principles inform and sustain the constitutional text: they are the vital unstated assumptions upon which the text is based. The following discussion addresses the four foundational constitutional principles that are most germane for resolution of this Reference: federalism, democracy, constitutionalism and the rule of law, and respect for minority rights. These defining principles function in symbiosis. No single principle can be defined in isolation from the others, nor does any one principle trump or exclude the operation of any other.

[50] Our Constitution has an internal architecture, or what the majority of this Court in *OPSEU v Ontario (Attorney General)*, [1987] 2 SCR 2, at p. 57, called a "basic constitutional structure." The individual elements of the Constitution are linked to the others, and must be interpreted by reference to the structure of the Constitution as a whole.

As we recently emphasized in the *Provincial Judges Reference*, certain underlying principles infuse our Constitution and breathe life into it. Speaking of the rule of law principle in the *Manitoba Language Rights Reference, supra*, at p. 750, we held that "the principle is clearly implicit in the very nature of a Constitution." The same may be said of the other three constitutional principles we underscore today.

[51] Although these underlying principles are not explicitly made part of the Constitution by any written provision, other than in some respects by the oblique reference in the preamble to the *Constitution Act, 1867*, it would be impossible to conceive of our constitutional structure without them. The principles dictate major elements of the architecture of the Constitution itself and are as such its lifeblood.

[52] The principles assist in the interpretation of the text and the delineation of spheres of jurisdiction, the scope of rights and obligations, and the role of our political institutions. Equally important, observance of and respect for these principles is essential to the ongoing process of constitutional development and evolution of our Constitution as a "living tree," to invoke the famous description in *Edwards v Attorney-General for Canada*, [1930] AC 124 (PC), at p. 136. As this Court indicated in *New Brunswick Broadcasting Co. v Nova Scotia (Speaker of the House of Assembly)*, [1993] 1 SCR 319, Canadians have long recognized the existence and importance of unwritten constitutional principles in our system of government.

[53] Given the existence of these underlying constitutional principles, what use may the Court make of them? In the *Provincial Judges Reference, supra*, at paras. 93 and 104, we cautioned that the recognition of these constitutional principles (the majority opinion referred to them as "organizing principles" and described one of them, judicial independence, as an "unwritten norm") could not be taken as an invitation to dispense with the written text of the Constitution. On the contrary, we confirmed that there are compelling reasons to insist upon the primacy of our written constitution. A written constitution promotes legal certainty and predictability, and it provides a foundation and a touchstone for the exercise of constitutional judicial review. However, we also observed in the *Provincial Judges Reference* that the effect of the preamble to the *Constitution Act, 1867* was to incorporate certain constitutional principles by reference, a point made earlier in *Fraser v Public Service Staff Relations Board*, [1985] 2 SCR 455, at pp. 462–3. In the *Provincial Judges Reference*, at para. 104, we determined that the pre-

amble "invites the courts to turn those principles into the premises of a constitutional argument that culminates in the filling of gaps in the express terms of the constitutional text."

[54] Underlying constitutional principles may in certain circumstances give rise to substantive legal obligations (have "full legal force," as we described it in the *Patriation Reference, supra*, at p. 845), which constitute substantive limitations upon government action. These principles may give rise to very abstract and general obligations, or they may be more specific and precise in nature. The principles are not merely descriptive, but are also invested with a powerful normative force, and are binding upon both courts and governments. "In other words," as this Court confirmed in the *Manitoba Language Rights Reference, supra*, at p. 752, "in the process of Constitutional adjudication, the Court may have regard to unwritten postulates which form the very foundation of the Constitution of Canada." It is to a discussion of those underlying constitutional principles that we now turn.

(b) Federalism. [55] It is undisputed that Canada is a federal state. Yet many commentators have observed that, according to the precise terms of the *Constitution Act, 1867*, the federal system was only partial. See, e.g., K.C. Wheare, *Federal Government* (4th ed. 1963), at pp. 18–20. This was so because, on paper, the federal government retained sweeping powers which threatened to undermine the autonomy of the provinces. Here again, however, a review of the written provisions of the Constitution does not provide the entire picture. Our political and constitutional practice has adhered to an underlying principle of federalism, and has interpreted the written provisions of the Constitution in this light. For example, although the federal power of disallowance was included in the *Constitution Act, 1867*, the underlying principle of federalism triumphed early. Many constitutional scholars contend that the federal power of disallowance has been abandoned (e.g., P.W. Hogg, *Constitutional Law of Canada* (4th ed. 1997), at p. 120).

[56] In a federal system of government such as ours, political power is shared by two orders of government: the federal government on the one hand, and the provinces on the other. Each is assigned respective spheres of jurisdiction by the *Constitution Act, 1867*. See, e.g., *Liquidators of the Maritime Bank of Canada v Receiver-General of New Brunswick*, [1892] AC 437 (PC), at pp. 441–2. It is up to the courts "to control the limits of the respective sovereignties": *Northern Telecom Canada Ltd. v Communica-*

tion Workers of Canada, [1983] 1 SCR 733, at p. 741. In interpreting our Constitution, the courts have always been concerned with the federalism principle, inherent in the structure of our constitutional arrangements, which has from the beginning been the lodestar by which the courts have been guided.

[57] This underlying principle of federalism, then, has exercised a role of considerable importance in the interpretation of the written provisions of our Constitution. In the *Patriation Reference, supra,* at pp. 905–9, we confirmed that the principle of federalism runs through the political and legal systems of Canada. Indeed, Martland and Ritchie JJ, dissenting in the *Patriation Reference,* at p. 821, considered federalism to be "the dominant principle of Canadian constitutional law." With the enactment of the *Charter,* that proposition may have less force than it once did, but there can be little doubt that the principle of federalism remains a central organizational theme of our Constitution. Less obviously, perhaps, but certainly of equal importance, federalism is a political and legal response to underlying social and political realities.

[58] The principle of federalism recognizes the diversity of the component parts of Confederation, and the autonomy of provincial governments to develop their societies within their respective spheres of jurisdiction. The federal structure of our country also facilitates democratic participation by distributing power to the government thought to be most suited to achieving the particular societal objective having regard to this diversity. The scheme of the *Constitution Act, 1867,* it was said in *Re the Initiative and Referendum Act,* [1919] AC 935 (PC), at p. 942, was

not to weld the Provinces into one, nor to subordinate Provincial Governments to a central authority, but to establish a central government in which these Provinces should be represented, entrusted with exclusive authority only in affairs in which they had a common interest. Subject to this each Province was to retain its independence and autonomy and to be directly under the Crown as its head.

More recently, in *Haig v Canada,* [1993] 2 SCR 995, at p. 1047, the majority of this Court held that differences between provinces "are a rational part of the political reality in the federal process." It was referring to the differential application of federal law in individual provinces, but the point applies more generally. A unanimous Court expressed similar views in *R. v S. (S.),* [1990] 2 SCR 254, at pp. 287–8.

[59] The principle of federalism facilitates the pursuit of collective goals by cultural and linguistic minorities which form the majority within a particular province. This is the case in Quebec, where the majority of the population is French-speaking, and which possesses a distinct culture. This is not merely the result of chance. The social and demographic reality of Quebec explains the existence of the province of Quebec as a political unit and indeed, was one of the essential reasons for establishing a federal structure for the Canadian union in 1867. The experience of both Canada East and Canada West under the *Union Act, 1840* (U.K.), 3–4 Vict., c. 35, had not been satisfactory. The federal structure adopted at Confederation enabled French-speaking Canadians to form a numerical majority in the province of Quebec, and so exercise the considerable provincial powers conferred by the *Constitution Act, 1867* in such a way as to promote their language and culture. It also made provision for certain guaranteed representation within the federal Parliament itself.

[60] Federalism was also welcomed by Nova Scotia and New Brunswick, both of which also affirmed their will to protect their individual cultures and their autonomy over local matters. All new provinces joining the federation sought to achieve similar objectives, which are no less vigorously pursued by the provinces and territories as we approach the new millennium.

(c) Democracy. [61] Democracy is a fundamental value in our constitutional law and political culture. While it has both an institutional and an individual aspect, the democratic principle was also argued before us in the sense of the supremacy of the sovereign will of a people, in this case potentially to be expressed by Quebecers in support of unilateral secession. It is useful to explore in a summary way these different aspects of the democratic principle.

[62] The principle of democracy has always informed the design of our constitutional structure, and continues to act as an essential interpretive consideration to this day. A majority of this Court in *OPSEU v Ontario, supra,* at p. 57, confirmed that "the basic structure of our Constitution, as established by the *Constitution Act, 1867,* contemplates the existence of certain political institutions, including freely elected legislative bodies at the federal and provincial levels." As is apparent from an earlier line of decisions emanating from this Court, including *Switzman v. Elbling,* [1957] SCR 285, *Saumur v City of Quebec,* [1953] 2 SCR 299, *Boucher v The King,* [1951] SCR 265, and *Reference re*

Alberta Statutes, [1938] SCR 100, the democracy principle can best be understood as a sort of baseline against which the framers of our Constitution, and subsequently, our elected representatives under it, have always operated. It is perhaps for this reason that the principle was not explicitly identified in the text of the *Constitution Act, 1867* itself. To have done so might have appeared redundant, even silly, to the framers. As explained in the *Provincial Judges Reference, supra*, at para. 100, it is evident that our Constitution contemplates that Canada shall be a constitutional democracy. Yet this merely demonstrates the importance of underlying constitutional principles that are nowhere explicitly described in our constitutional texts. The representative and democratic nature of our political institutions was simply assumed.

[63] Democracy is commonly understood as being a political system of majority rule. It is essential to be clear what this means. The evolution of our democratic tradition can be traced back to the *Magna Carta* (1215) and before, through the long struggle for Parliamentary supremacy which culminated in the English *Bill of Rights* of 1689, the emergence of representative political institutions in the colonial era, the development of responsible government in the 19th century, and eventually, the achievement of Confederation itself in 1867. "[T]he Canadian tradition," the majority of this Court held in *Reference re Provincial Electoral Boundaries (Sask.)*, [1991] 2 SCR 158, at p. 186, is "one of evolutionary democracy moving in uneven steps toward the goal of universal suffrage and more effective representation." Since Confederation, efforts to extend the franchise to those unjustly excluded from participation in our political system – such as women, minorities, and aboriginal peoples – have continued, with some success, to the present day.

[64] Democracy is not simply concerned with the process of government. On the contrary, as suggested in *Switzman v Elbling, supra*, at p. 306, democracy is fundamentally connected to substantive goals, most importantly, the promotion of self-government. Democracy accommodates cultural and group identities: *Reference re Provincial Electoral Boundaries*, at p. 188. Put another way, a sovereign people exercises its right to self-government through the democratic process. In considering the scope and purpose of the *Charter*, the Court in *R. v Oakes*, [1986] 1 SCR 103, articulated some of the values inherent in the notion of democracy (at p. 136):

The Court must be guided by the values and principles essential to a free and democratic society which I believe to embody, to name but a few, respect for the inherent dignity of the human person, commitment to social justice and equality, accommodation of a wide variety of beliefs, respect for cultural and group identity, and faith in social and political institutions which enhance the participation of individuals and groups in society.

[65]   In institutional terms, democracy means that each of the provincial legislatures and the federal Parliament is elected by popular franchise. These legislatures, we have said, are "at the core of the system of representative government": *New Brunswick Broadcasting, supra*, at p. 387. In individual terms, the right to vote in elections to the House of Commons and the provincial legislatures, and to be candidates in those elections, is guaranteed to "Every citizen of Canada" by virtue of s. 3 of the *Charter*. Historically, this Court has interpreted democracy to mean the process of representative and responsible government and the right of citizens to participate in the political process as voters (*Reference re Provincial Electoral Boundaries, supra*) and as candidates (*Harvey v New Brunswick (Attorney General)*, [1996] 2 SCR 876). In addition, the effect of s. 4 of the *Charter* is to oblige the House of Commons and the provincial legislatures to hold regular elections and to permit citizens to elect representatives to their political institutions. The democratic principle is affirmed with particular clarity in that s. 4 is not subject to the notwithstanding power contained in s. 33.

[66] It is, of course, true that democracy expresses the sovereign will of the people. Yet this expression, too, must be taken in the context of the other institutional values we have identified as pertinent to this Reference. The relationship between democracy and federalism means, for example, that in Canada there may be different and equally legitimate majorities in different provinces and territories and at the federal level. No one majority is more or less "legitimate" than the others as an expression of democratic opinion, although, of course, the consequences will vary with the subject matter. A federal system of government enables different provinces to pursue policies responsive to the particular concerns and interests of people in that province. At the same time, Canada as a whole is also a democratic community in which citizens construct and achieve goals on a national scale through a federal government acting within the limits of its jurisdiction. The function of federalism is to enable citizens to participate concurrently in different collectivities and to pursue goals at both a provincial and a federal level.

[67] The consent of the governed is a value that is basic to our understanding of a free and democratic society. Yet democracy in any real sense of the word cannot exist without the rule of law. It is the law

that creates the framework within which the "sovereign will" is to be ascertained and implemented. To be accorded legitimacy, democratic institutions must rest, ultimately, on a legal foundation. That is, they must allow for the participation of, and accountability to, the people, through public institutions created under the Constitution. Equally, however, a system of government cannot survive through adherence to the law alone. A political system must also possess legitimacy, and in our political culture, that requires an interaction between the rule of law and the democratic principle. The system must be capable of reflecting the aspirations of the people. But there is more. Our law's claim to legitimacy also rests on an appeal to moral values, many of which are imbedded in our constitutional structure. It would be a grave mistake to equate legitimacy with the "sovereign will" or majority rule alone, to the exclusion of other constitutional values.

[68] Finally, we highlight that a functioning democracy requires a continuous process of discussion. The Constitution mandates government by democratic legislatures, and an executive accountable to them, "resting ultimately on public opinion reached by discussion and the interplay of ideas" (*Saumur v City of Quebec, supra*, at p. 330). At both the federal and provincial level, by its very nature, the need to build majorities necessitates compromise, negotiation, and deliberation. No one has a monopoly on truth, and our system is predicated on the faith that in the marketplace of ideas, the best solutions to public problems will rise to the top. Inevitably, there will be dissenting voices. A democratic system of government is committed to considering those dissenting voices, and seeking to acknowledge and address those voices in the laws by which all in the community must live.

[69] The *Constitution Act, 1982* gives expression to this principle, by conferring a right to initiate constitutional change on each participant in Confederation. In our view, the existence of this right imposes a corresponding duty on the participants in Confederation to engage in constitutional discussions in order to acknowledge and address democratic expressions of a desire for change in other provinces. This duty is inherent in the democratic principle which is a fundamental predicate of our system of governance.

(d) Constitutionalism and the Rule of Law. [70] The principles of constitutionalism and the rule of law lie at the root of our system of government. The rule of law, as observed in *Roncarelli v Duplessis*, [1959] SCR 121, at p. 142, is "a fundamental postulate of our constitutional struc-

ture." As we noted in the *Patriation Reference, supra,* at pp. 805–6, "[t]he 'rule of law' is a highly textured expression, importing many things which are beyond the need of these reasons to explore but conveying, for example, a sense of orderliness, of subjection to known legal rules and of executive accountability to legal authority." At its most basic level, the rule of law vouchsafes to the citizens and residents of the country a stable, predictable and ordered society in which to conduct their affairs. It provides a shield for individuals from arbitrary state action.

[71] In the *Manitoba Language Rights Reference, supra,* at pp. 747–52, this Court outlined the elements of the rule of law. We emphasized, first, that the rule of law provides that the law is supreme over the acts of both government and private persons. There is, in short, one law for all. Second, we explained, at p. 749, that "the rule of law requires the creation and maintenance of an actual order of positive laws which preserves and embodies the more general principle of normative order." It was this second aspect of the rule of law that was primarily at issue in the *Manitoba Language Rights Reference* itself. A third aspect of the rule of law is, as recently confirmed in the *Provincial Judges Reference, supra,* at para. 10, that "the exercise of all public power must find its ultimate source in a legal rule." Put another way, the relationship between the state and the individual must be regulated by law. Taken together, these three considerations make up a principle of profound constitutional and political significance.

[72] The constitutionalism principle bears considerable similarity to the rule of law, although they are not identical. The essence of constitutionalism in Canada is embodied in s. 52(1) of the *Constitution Act, 1982,* which provides that "[t]he Constitution of Canada is the supreme law of Canada, and any law that is inconsistent with the provisions of the Constitution is, to the extent of the inconsistency, of no force or effect." Simply put, the constitutionalism principle requires that all government action comply with the Constitution. The rule of law principle requires that all government action must comply with the law, including the Constitution. This Court has noted on several occasions that with the adoption of the *Charter,* the Canadian system of government was transformed to a significant extent from a system of Parliamentary supremacy to one of constitutional supremacy. The Constitution binds all governments, both federal and provincial, including the executive branch (*Operation Dismantle Inc. v The Queen,* [1985] 1 SCR 441, at p. 455). They may not transgress its provisions: indeed, their sole

claim to exercise lawful authority rests in the powers allocated to them under the Constitution, and can come from no other source.

[73] An understanding of the scope and importance of the principles of the rule of law and constitutionalism is aided by acknowledging explicitly why a constitution is entrenched beyond the reach of simple majority rule. There are three overlapping reasons.

[74] First, a constitution may provide an added safeguard for fundamental human rights and individual freedoms which might otherwise be susceptible to government interference. Although democratic government is generally solicitous of those rights, there are occasions when the majority will be tempted to ignore fundamental rights in order to accomplish collective goals more easily or effectively. Constitutional entrenchment ensures that those rights will be given due regard and protection. Second, a constitution may seek to ensure that vulnerable minority groups are endowed with the institutions and rights necessary to maintain and promote their identities against the assimilative pressures of the majority. And third, a constitution may provide for a division of political power that allocates political power amongst different levels of government. That purpose would be defeated if one of those democratically elected levels of government could usurp the powers of the other simply by exercising its legislative power to allocate additional political power to itself unilaterally.

[75] The argument that the Constitution may be legitimately circumvented by resort to a majority vote in a province-wide referendum is superficially persuasive, in large measure because it seems to appeal to some of the same principles that underlie the legitimacy of the Constitution itself, namely, democracy and self-government. In short, it is suggested that as the notion of popular sovereignty underlies the legitimacy of our existing constitutional arrangements, so the same popular sovereignty that originally led to the present Constitution must (it is argued) also permit "the people" in their exercise of popular sovereignty to secede by majority vote alone. However, closer analysis reveals that this argument is unsound, because it misunderstands the meaning of popular sovereignty and the essence of a constitutional democracy.

[76] Canadians have never accepted that ours is a system of simple majority rule. Our principle of democracy, taken in conjunction with the other constitutional principles discussed here, is richer. Constitutional government is necessarily predicated on the idea that the political representatives of the people of a province have the capacity and the

power to commit the province to be bound into the future by the constitutional rules being adopted. These rules are "binding" not in the sense of frustrating the will of a majority of a province, but as defining the majority which must be consulted in order to alter the fundamental balances of political power (including the spheres of autonomy guaranteed by the principle of federalism), individual rights, and minority rights in our society. Of course, those constitutional rules are themselves amenable to amendment, but only through a process of negotiation which ensures that there is an opportunity for the constitutionally defined rights of all the parties to be respected and reconciled.

[77] In this way, our belief in democracy may be harmonized with our belief in constitutionalism. Constitutional amendment often requires some form of substantial consensus precisely because the content of the underlying principles of our Constitution demand it. By requiring broad support in the form of an "enhanced majority" to achieve constitutional change, the Constitution ensures that minority interests must be addressed before proposed changes which would affect them may be enacted.

[78] It might be objected, then, that constitutionalism is therefore incompatible with democratic government. This would be an erroneous view. Constitutionalism facilitates – indeed, makes possible – a democratic political system by creating an orderly framework within which people may make political decisions. Viewed correctly, constitutionalism and the rule of law are not in conflict with democracy; rather, they are essential to it. Without that relationship, the political will upon which democratic decisions are taken would itself be undermined.

(e) Protection of Minorities. [79] The fourth underlying constitutional principle we address here concerns the protection of minorities. There are a number of specific constitutional provisions protecting minority language, religion and education rights. Some of those provisions are, as we have recognized on a number of occasions, the product of historical compromises. As this Court observed in *Reference re Bill 30, An Act to amend the Education Act (Ont.)*, [1987] 1 SCR 1148, at p. 1173, and in *Reference re Education Act (Que.)*, [1993] 2 SCR 511, at pp. 529–30, the protection of minority religious education rights was a central consideration in the negotiations leading to Confederation. In the absence of such protection, it was felt that the minorities in what was then Canada East and Canada West would be submerged and assimilated. See also

Greater Montreal Protestant School Board v Quebec (Attorney General), [1989] 1 SCR 377, at pp. 401–2, and *Adler v Ontario,* [1996] 3 SCR 609. Similar concerns animated the provisions protecting minority language rights, as noted in *Société des Acadiens du Nouveau-Brunswick Inc. v Association of Parents for Fairness in Education,* [1986] 1 SCR 549, at p. 564.

[80] However, we highlight that even though those provisions were the product of negotiation and political compromise, that does not render them unprincipled. Rather, such a concern reflects a broader principle related to the protection of minority rights. Undoubtedly, the three other constitutional principles inform the scope and operation of the specific provisions that protect the rights of minorities. We emphasize that the protection of minority rights is itself an independent principle underlying our constitutional order. The principle is clearly reflected in the *Charter's* provisions for the protection of minority rights. See, e.g., *Reference re Public Schools Act (Man.), s. 79(3), (4) and (7),* [1993] 1 SCR 839, and *Mahe v Alberta,* [1990] 1 SCR 342.

[81] The concern of our courts and governments to protect minorities has been prominent in recent years, particularly following the enactment of the *Charter.* Undoubtedly, one of the key considerations motivating the enactment of the *Charter,* and the process of constitutional judicial review that it entails, is the protection of minorities. However, it should not be forgotten that the protection of minority rights had a long history before the enactment of the *Charter.* Indeed, the protection of minority rights was clearly an essential consideration in the design of our constitutional structure even at the time of Confederation: *Senate Reference,* [1980] 1 SCR 54, at p. 71. Although Canada's record of upholding the rights of minorities is not a spotless one, that goal is one towards which Canadians have been striving since Confederation, and the process has not been without successes. The principle of protecting minority rights continues to exercise influence in the operation and interpretation of our Constitution.

[82] Consistent with this long tradition of respect for minorities, which is at least as old as Canada itself, the framers of the *Constitution Act, 1982* included in s. 35 explicit protection for existing aboriginal and treaty rights, and in s. 25, a non-derogation clause in favour of the rights of aboriginal peoples. The "promise" of s. 35, as it was termed in *R. v Sparrow,* [1990] 1 SCR 1075, at p. 1083, recognized not only the ancient occupation of land by aboriginal peoples, but their contribution to the building of Canada, and the special commitments made to them by successive governments. The protection of these rights, so recently and

arduously achieved, whether looked at in their own right or as part of the larger concern with minorities, reflects an important underlying constitutional value.

(4) The Operation of the Constitutional Principles in the Secession Context

[83] Secession is the effort of a group or section of a state to withdraw itself from the political and constitutional authority of that state, with a view to achieving statehood for a new territorial unit on the international plane. In a federal state, secession typically takes the form of a territorial unit seeking to withdraw from the federation. Secession is a legal act as much as a political one. By the terms of Question 1 of this Reference, we are asked to rule on the legality of unilateral secession "[u]nder the Constitution of Canada." This is an appropriate question, as the legality of unilateral secession must be evaluated, at least in the first instance, from the perspective of the domestic legal order of the state from which the unit seeks to withdraw. As we shall see below, it is also argued that international law is a relevant standard by which the legality of a purported act of secession may be measured.

[84] The secession of a province from Canada must be considered, in legal terms, to require an amendment to the Constitution, which perforce requires negotiation. The amendments necessary to achieve a secession could be radical and extensive. Some commentators have suggested that secession could be a change of such a magnitude that it could not be considered to be merely an amendment to the Constitution. We are not persuaded by this contention. It is of course true that the Constitution is silent as to the ability of a province to secede from Confederation but, although the Constitution neither expressly authorizes nor prohibits secession, an act of secession would purport to alter the governance of Canadian territory in a manner which undoubtedly is inconsistent with our current constitutional arrangements. The fact that those changes would be profound, or that they would purport to have a significance with respect to international law, does not negate their nature as amendments to the Constitution of Canada.

[85] The Constitution is the expression of the sovereignty of the people of Canada. It lies within the power of the people of Canada, acting through their various governments duly elected and recognized under the Constitution, to effect whatever constitutional arrangements are desired within Canadian territory, including, should it be so

desired, the secession of Quebec from Canada. As this Court held in the *Manitoba Language Rights Reference, supra*, at p. 745, "[t]he Constitution of a country is a statement of the will of the people to be governed in accordance with certain principles held as fundamental and certain prescriptions restrictive of the powers of the legislature and government." The manner in which such a political will could be formed and mobilized is a somewhat speculative exercise, though we are asked to assume the existence of such a political will for the purpose of answering the question before us. By the terms of this Reference, we have been asked to consider whether it would be constitutional in such a circumstance for the National Assembly, legislature or government of Quebec to effect the secession of Quebec from Canada unilaterally.

[86] The "unilateral" nature of the act is of cardinal importance and we must be clear as to what is understood by this term. In one sense, any step towards a constitutional amendment initiated by a single actor on the constitutional stage is "unilateral." We do not believe that this is the meaning contemplated by Question 1, nor is this the sense in which the term has been used in argument before us. Rather, what is claimed by a right to secede "unilaterally" is the right to effectuate secession without prior negotiations with the other provinces and the federal government. At issue is not the legality of the first step but the legality of the final act of purported unilateral secession. The supposed juridical basis for such an act is said to be a clear expression of democratic will in a referendum in the province of Quebec. This claim requires us to examine the possible juridical impact, if any, of such a referendum on the functioning of our Constitution, and on the claimed legality of a unilateral act of secession.

[87] Although the Constitution does not itself address the use of a referendum procedure, and the results of a referendum have no direct role or legal effect in our constitutional scheme, a referendum undoubtedly may provide a democratic method of ascertaining the views of the electorate on important political questions on a particular occasion. The democratic principle identified above would demand that considerable weight be given to a clear expression by the people of Quebec of their will to secede from Canada, even though a referendum, in itself and without more, has no direct legal effect, and could not in itself bring about unilateral secession. Our political institutions are premised on the democratic principle, and so an expression of the democratic will of the people of a province carries weight, in that it would confer legitimacy on the efforts of the government of Quebec to initiate the Constitution's

amendment process in order to secede by constitutional means. In this context, we refer to a "clear" majority as a qualitative evaluation. The referendum result, if it is to be taken as an expression of the democratic will, must be free of ambiguity both in terms of the question asked and in terms of the support it achieves.

[88] The federalism principle, in conjunction with the democratic principle, dictates that the clear repudiation of the existing constitutional order and the clear expression of the desire to pursue secession by the population of a province would give rise to a reciprocal obligation on all parties to Confederation to negotiate constitutional changes to respond to that desire. The amendment of the Constitution begins with a political process undertaken pursuant to the Constitution itself. In Canada, the initiative for constitutional amendment is the responsibility of democratically elected representatives of the participants in Confederation. Those representatives may, of course, take their cue from a referendum, but in legal terms, constitution-making in Canada, as in many countries, is undertaken by the democratically elected representatives of the people. The corollary of a legitimate attempt by one participant in Confederation to seek an amendment to the Constitution is an obligation on all parties to come to the negotiating table. The clear repudiation by the people of Quebec of the existing constitutional order would confer legitimacy on demands for secession, and place an obligation on the other provinces and the federal government to acknowledge and respect that expression of democratic will by entering into negotiations and conducting them in accordance with the underlying constitutional principles already discussed.

[89] What is the content of this obligation to negotiate? At this juncture, we confront the difficult inter-relationship between substantive obligations flowing from the Constitution and questions of judicial competence and restraint in supervising or enforcing those obligations. This is mirrored by the distinction between the legality and the legitimacy of actions taken under the Constitution. We propose to focus first on the substantive obligations flowing from this obligation to negotiate; once the nature of those obligations has been described, it is easier to assess the appropriate means of enforcement of those obligations, and to comment on the distinction between legality and legitimacy.

[90] The conduct of the parties in such negotiations would be governed by the same constitutional principles which give rise to the duty to negotiate: federalism, democracy, constitutionalism and the rule

of law, and the protection of minorities. Those principles lead us to reject two absolutist propositions. One of those propositions is that there would be a legal obligation on the other provinces and federal government to accede to the secession of a province, subject only to negotiation of the logistical details of secession. This proposition is attributed either to the supposed implications of the democratic principle of the Constitution, or to the international law principle of self-determination of peoples.

[91] For both theoretical and practical reasons, we cannot accept this view. We hold that Quebec could not purport to invoke a right of self-determination such as to dictate the terms of a proposed secession to the other parties: that would not be a negotiation at all. As well, it would be naive to expect that the substantive goal of secession could readily be distinguished from the practical details of secession. The devil would be in the details. The democracy principle, as we have emphasized, cannot be invoked to trump the principles of federalism and rule of law, the rights of individuals and minorities, or the operation of democracy in the other provinces or in Canada as a whole. No negotiations could be effective if their ultimate outcome, secession, is cast as an absolute legal entitlement based upon an obligation to give effect to that act of secession in the Constitution. Such a foregone conclusion would actually undermine the obligation to negotiate and render it hollow.

[92] However, we are equally unable to accept the reverse proposition, that a clear expression of self-determination by the people of Quebec would impose no obligations upon the other provinces or the federal government. The continued existence and operation of the Canadian constitutional order cannot remain indifferent to the clear expression of a clear majority of Quebecers that they no longer wish to remain in Canada. This would amount to the assertion that other constitutionally recognized principles necessarily trump the clearly expressed democratic will of the people of Quebec. Such a proposition fails to give sufficient weight to the underlying constitutional principles that must inform the amendment process, including the principles of democracy and federalism. The rights of other provinces and the federal government cannot deny the right of the government of Quebec to pursue secession, should a clear majority of the people of Quebec choose that goal, so long as in doing so, Quebec respects the rights of others. Negotiations would be necessary to address the interests of the federal government, of Quebec and the other provinces, and other participants, as well as the rights of all Canadians both within and outside Quebec.

[93] Is the rejection of both of these propositions reconcilable? Yes, once it is realized that none of the rights or principles under discussion is absolute to the exclusion of the others. This observation suggests that other parties cannot exercise their rights in such a way as to amount to an absolute denial of Quebec's rights, and similarly, that so long as Quebec exercises its rights while respecting the rights of others, it may propose secession and seek to achieve it through negotiation. The negotiation process precipitated by a decision of a clear majority of the population of Quebec on a clear question to pursue secession would require the reconciliation of various rights and obligations by the representatives of two legitimate majorities, namely, the clear majority of the population of Quebec, and the clear majority of Canada as a whole, whatever that may be. There can be no suggestion that either of these majorities "trumps" the other. A political majority that does not act in accordance with the underlying constitutional principles we have identified puts at risk the legitimacy of the exercise of its rights.

[94] In such circumstances, the conduct of the parties assumes primary constitutional significance. The negotiation process must be conducted with an eye to the constitutional principles we have outlined, which must inform the actions of all the participants in the negotiation process.

[95] Refusal of a party to conduct negotiations in a manner consistent with constitutional principles and values would seriously put at risk the legitimacy of that party's assertion of its rights, and perhaps the negotiation process as a whole. Those who quite legitimately insist upon the importance of upholding the rule of law cannot at the same time be oblivious to the need to act in conformity with constitutional principles and values, and so do their part to contribute to the maintenance and promotion of an environment in which the rule of law may flourish.

[96] No one can predict the course that such negotiations might take. The possibility that they might not lead to an agreement amongst the parties must be recognized. Negotiations following a referendum vote in favour of seeking secession would inevitably address a wide range of issues, many of great import. After 131 years of Confederation, there exists, inevitably, a high level of integration in economic, political and social institutions across Canada. The vision of those who brought about Confederation was to create a unified country, not a loose alliance of autonomous provinces. Accordingly, while there are regional economic interests, which sometimes coincide with provincial boundaries, there are also national interests and enterprises (both public and

private) that would face potential dismemberment. There is a national economy and a national debt. Arguments were raised before us regarding boundary issues. There are linguistic and cultural minorities, including aboriginal peoples, unevenly distributed across the country who look to the Constitution of Canada for the protection of their rights. Of course, secession would give rise to many issues of great complexity and difficulty. These would have to be resolved within the overall framework of the rule of law, thereby assuring Canadians resident in Quebec and elsewhere a measure of stability in what would likely be a period of considerable upheaval and uncertainty. Nobody seriously suggests that our national existence, seamless in so many aspects, could be effortlessly separated along what are now the provincial boundaries of Quebec. As the Attorney General of Saskatchewan put it in his oral submission:

A nation is built when the communities that comprise it make commitments to it, when they forego choices and opportunities on behalf of a nation, ... when the communities that comprise it make compromises, when they offer each other guarantees, when they make transfers and perhaps most pointedly, when they receive from others the benefits of national solidarity. The threads of a thousand acts of accommodation are the fabric of a nation ...

[97] In the circumstances, negotiations following such a referendum would undoubtedly be difficult. While the negotiators would have to contemplate the possibility of secession, there would be no absolute legal entitlement to it and no assumption that an agreement reconciling all relevant rights and obligations would actually be reached. It is foreseeable that even negotiations carried out in conformity with the underlying constitutional principles could reach an impasse. We need not speculate here as to what would then transpire. Under the Constitution, secession requires that an amendment be negotiated.

[98] The respective roles of the courts and political actors in discharging the constitutional obligations we have identified follows ineluctably from the foregoing observations. In the *Patriation Reference*, a distinction was drawn between the law of the Constitution, which, generally speaking, will be enforced by the courts, and other constitutional rules, such as the conventions of the Constitution, which carry only political sanctions. It is also the case, however, that judicial intervention, even in relation to the law of the Constitution, is subject to the Court's appreciation of its proper role in the constitutional scheme.

[99] The notion of justiciability is, as we earlier pointed out in dealing with the preliminary objection, linked to the notion of appropriate judicial restraint. We earlier made reference to the discussion of justiciability in *Reference re Canada Assistance Plan*, [1991] 2 SCR 525, at p. 545:

In exercising its discretion whether to determine a matter that is alleged to be non-justiciable, the Court's primary concern is to retain its proper role within the constitutional framework of our democratic form of government.

In *Operation Dismantle, supra*, at p. 459, it was pointed out that justiciability is a "doctrine ... founded upon a concern with the appropriate role of the courts as the forum for the resolution of different types of disputes." An analogous doctrine of judicial restraint operates here. Also, as observed in *Canada (Auditor General) v Canada (Minister of Energy, Mines and Resources)*, [1989] 2 SCR 49 (the *Auditor General's* case), at p. 91:

There is an array of issues which calls for the exercise of judicial judgment on whether the questions are properly cognizable by the courts. Ultimately, such judgment depends on the appreciation by the judiciary of its own position in the constitutional scheme.

[100] The role of the Court in this Reference is limited to the identification of the relevant aspects of the Constitution in their broadest sense. We have interpreted the questions as relating to the constitutional framework within which political decisions may ultimately be made. Within that framework, the workings of the political process are complex and can only be resolved by means of political judgments and evaluations. The Court has no supervisory role over the political aspects of constitutional negotiations. Equally, the initial impetus for negotiation, namely a clear majority on a clear question in favour of secession, is subject only to political evaluation, and properly so. A right and a corresponding duty to negotiate secession cannot be built on an alleged expression of democratic will if the expression of democratic will is itself fraught with ambiguities. Only the political actors would have the information and expertise to make the appropriate judgment as to the point at which, and the circumstances in which, those ambiguities are resolved one way or the other.

[101] If the circumstances giving rise to the duty to negotiate were to arise, the distinction between the strong defence of legitimate

interests and the taking of positions which, in fact, ignore the legitimate interests of others is one that also defies legal analysis. The Court would not have access to all of the information available to the political actors, and the methods appropriate for the search for truth in a court of law are ill-suited to getting to the bottom of constitutional negotiations. To the extent that the questions are political in nature, it is not the role of the judiciary to interpose its own views on the different negotiating positions of the parties, even were it invited to do so. Rather, it is the obligation of the elected representatives to give concrete form to the discharge of their constitutional obligations which only they and their electors can ultimately assess. The reconciliation of the various legitimate constitutional interests outlined above is necessarily committed to the political rather than the judicial realm, precisely because that reconciliation can only be achieved through the give and take of the negotiation process. Having established the legal framework, it would be for the democratically elected leadership of the various participants to resolve their differences.

[102] The non-justiciability of political issues that lack a legal component does not deprive the surrounding constitutional framework of its binding status, nor does this mean that constitutional obligations could be breached without incurring serious legal repercussions. Where there are legal rights there are remedies, but as we explained in the *Auditor General's* case, *supra*, at p. 90, and *New Brunswick Broadcasting*, *supra*, the appropriate recourse in some circumstances lies through the workings of the political process rather than the courts ...

[104] Accordingly, the secession of Quebec from Canada cannot be accomplished by the National Assembly, the legislature or government of Quebec unilaterally, that is to say, without principled negotiations, and be considered a lawful act. Any attempt to effect the secession of a province from Canada must be undertaken pursuant to the Constitution of Canada, or else violate the Canadian legal order. However, the continued existence and operation of the Canadian constitutional order cannot remain unaffected by the unambiguous expression of a clear majority of Quebecers that they no longer wish to remain in Canada. The primary means by which that expression is given effect is the constitutional duty to negotiate in accordance with the constitutional principles that we have described herein. In the event secession negotiations are initiated, our Constitution, no less than our history, would call on the participants to work to reconcile the rights, obligations and legitimate aspirations of all Canadians within a framework

that emphasizes constitutional responsibilities as much as it does constitutional rights.

[105] It will be noted that Question 1 does not ask how secession could be achieved in a constitutional manner, but addresses one form of secession only, namely unilateral secession. Although the applicability of various procedures to achieve lawful secession was raised in argument, each option would require us to assume the existence of facts that at this stage are unknown. In accordance with the usual rule of prudence in constitutional cases, we refrain from pronouncing on the applicability of any particular constitutional procedure to effect secession unless and until sufficiently clear facts exist to squarely raise an issue for judicial determination.

(5) Suggested Principle of Effectivity

[106] In the foregoing discussion we have not overlooked the principle of effectivity, which was placed at the forefront in argument before us. For the reasons that follow, we do not think that the principle of effectivity has any application to the issues raised by Question 1. A distinction must be drawn between the right of a people to act, and their power to do so. They are not identical. A right is recognized in law: mere physical ability is not necessarily given status as a right. The fact that an individual or group can act in a certain way says nothing at all about the legal status or consequences of the act. A power may be exercised even in the absence of a right to do so, but if it is, then it is exercised without legal foundation. Our Constitution does not address powers in this sense. On the contrary, the Constitution is concerned only with the rights and obligations of individuals, groups and governments, and the structure of our institutions. It was suggested before us that the National Assembly, legislature or government of Quebec could unilaterally effect the secession of that province from Canada, but it was not suggested that they might do so as a matter of law: rather, it was contended that they simply could do so as a matter of fact. Although under the Constitution there is no right to pursue secession unilaterally, that is secession without principled negotiation, this does not rule out the possibility of an unconstitutional declaration of secession leading to a de facto secession ...

[107] In our view, the alleged principle of effectivity has no constitutional or legal status in the sense that it does not provide an *ex ante* explanation or justification for an act. In essence, acceptance of a

principle of effectivity would be tantamount to accepting that the National Assembly, legislature or government of Quebec may act without regard to the law, simply because it asserts the power to do so. So viewed, the suggestion is that the National Assembly, legislature or government of Quebec could purport to secede the province unilaterally from Canada in disregard of Canadian ... law. It is further suggested that if the secession bid was successful, a new legal order would be created in that province, which would then be considered an independent state.

[108] Such a proposition is an assertion of fact, not a statement of law. It may or may not be true; in any event it is irrelevant to the questions of law before us. If, on the other hand, it is put forward as an assertion of law, then it simply amounts to the contention that the law may be broken as long as it can be broken successfully. Such a notion is contrary to the rule of law, and must be rejected ...

READING QUESTIONS ON QUEBEC SECESSION REFERENCE

1 What do you make of the fact that no judge's name is affixed to the judgment, that is, that it purports to be the judgment of an impersonal Court?
2 Do you think the judgment is firmly based on principles of Canadian law or do you think the judges merely cloaked their political stance, one supportive of the Federal Government's political aims, in legal language?
3 If you are dealing with the Supreme Court's judgment in *Vriend*, ask yourself whether in both this decision and *Vriend* the judges went beyond their legitimate role.

Sujit Choudhry and Robert Howse
Constitutional Theory and the *Quebec Secession Reference* (2000)

1 INTRODUCTION: THE *QUEBEC SECESSION REFERENCE* AND THE POVERTY OF THEORY IN CANADIAN CONSTITUTIONAL DISCOURSE

From the moment that it was handed down, the judgment of the Supreme Court in Canada in the *Quebec Secession Reference* produced a torrent of public commentary.[1] Journalists, politicians, and legal academics have debated the consequences, and the merits and demerits of the result. The judgment has been read as a statute that lays down the roadmap to referendum and secession. If one of the Court's goals was to secure a central place for the judgment in the ongoing debate over the future of the country, that goal has surely been met.

Remarkable as the decision is, however, and given the fundamental issues about the relationship between law and politics that it raises, the discussion in question has remained almost entirely in what we describe as the *pragmatic perspective*, which asks how positive politics entered into the motivations and justifications of the Court, and looks at the results in terms of their political consequences, without deep or sustained reflection on the ultimate grounds for the role the Court took upon itself, or on the normative sources of its reasoning. The preoccupations of this perspective are along the following lines:

- What were the political *origins* of the judgment? More specifically, what circumstances led the Court to be thrust into the political morass of constitutional reform, and how did the Court respond? It is fairly clear that the reference to the Supreme Court was a centre-piece of the federal government's strategy to get tough with Quebec – widely known as "Plan B." Moreover, rather than shying away from the task thrust upon it, the Court interposed itself into the political thicket, and fundamentally altered the rules of the game.
- What were the political *effects* of the judgment? On this point, there seems to be a consensus that the judgment was a success. It has been widely accepted by political actors across the political spectrum. Moreover, it has shaped the terms of debate in a stability-promoting way. It has eliminated extreme opinions – that a yes vote would effect a unilateral secession, or could be ignored by the federal government with impunity. Additionally, it has focused debate over certain issues, such as what constitutes a clear majority and a clear question.
- Who were the political *winners and losers*? Here, the picture is mixed. As expected, the Court summarily rejected arguments made on Quebec's behalf that it would be legal for Quebec to unilaterally secede from Canada, decisively refuting the claim that Quebec possessed a right to self-determination cognizable in Canadian constitutional law. Contrary to expectations, though, the Court decided that in the event of a yes vote, the federal

government would be under a constitutional duty to negotiate in good faith. The uncertainty of the federal response to a positive referendum result – a source of strategic power for the federal government in the past – has been eliminated. Moreover, Quebec nationalists now have an incentive to hold referenda repeatedly until they achieve a positive result.

- What political issues remain *unresolved*? The Court left many questions unanswered, creating ongoing uncertainty – the borders of an independent Quebec, the division of the national debt, citizenship, and the rights of aboriginal peoples in northern Quebec, to name a few. More accurately, the Court relegated these issues to constitutional negotiations, and steadfastly refused to speculate on the implications of a breakdown in those discussions.

The domination of the pragmatic perspective in public discourse about the judgment is perhaps understandable, given the political context in which the Court was asked to decide and the obviously high stakes in Canadian constitutional politics. But this dominance also reflects an abdication of intellectual responsibility on the part of the Canadian academy, and the traditional poverty of theory in Canadian constitutional law. Apart from some rather crude attacks on the "politicization of the law" through activist judicial review,[2] with some important exceptions,[3] analysis of Canadian constitutional law and jurisprudence based on systematic reflection concerning the relationship between constitutional adjudication and democratic politics has been, for the most part, sorely lacking. While some of the crucial elements of the judgment beg for adequate theorization – especially the reliance on unwritten constitutional principles and the Court's self-limitation of its judicial review function with respect to the application of the law by the political actors – it has of course been possible either to embrace or reject these features of the decision, understanding them cynically as the Court seeking an "old-fashioned" Canadian compromise, or getting itself out of a political bind into which the government awkwardly and unjustifiably put it.

Yet the respect of citizens for the Court depends importantly on their view of it as a forum of principle and of reason. Indeed, absent such a belief, it is doubtful that the judgment of the Court could play any role whatever in restraining or informing political behaviour in the circumstances of the secession, where hateful passion and prejudice are likely to be running at their highest, and the potential "end game" nature of the situation removes many of the usual pragmatic constraints on the degeneration of political action into force and fraud.

Thus, even from a pragmatic perspective dominated by a concern with political effects, the question of the legitimacy of the Court's decision, the "compliance pull" of its reasons even and especially in the presence of potentially overmastering passion, deserves serious attention. And this question, especially given the apparent novelty and anomaly of some of the Court's holdings in this case, can only be answered through an excursion into constitutional theory of the kind dreaded by many Canadian legal academics.

The premise of this paper is that for constitutional adjudication to be a legitimate practice, it must be supported by reasons that justify the judicial role. Although courts may not be forthright in providing these reasons, the task of the constitutional theorist is to identify whatever justifications the courts may provide, and to weave those justifications into coherent accounts. Constitutional theories emerge from and seek to justify our interpretive practice. Only then can we examine the ability of that theory to provide satisfactory explanations of the salient features of particular constitutional decisions, such as the *Quebec Secession Reference*. Practically, a theoretical account is valuable for two reasons: it helps us to better identify in what respects the Court owes us more detail on the legal framework governing secession, and more generally, it helps us to grasp the Court's understanding of its own role in the Canadian constitutional scheme.

2 THE THEORETICAL CONTEXT

Our excursus into constitutional theory takes place against the background of a voluminous critical literature. Not surprisingly given what we have already said about the relative poverty of theory in Canadian constitutional scholarship, much of that literature is American, and is framed around that nation's constitutional practice. Nevertheless, that literature is general in aspiration, and accordingly may be of relevance to other jurisdictions, including Canada. What we do here is to briefly mention some of the relevant debates in American constitutional theory. In section 3, we develop an analytical framework to organize these debates; in sections 4 and 5, we examine the *Quebec Secession Reference* in the light of that framework.

The Political Questions Doctrine

A long-standing dispute among American constitutional scholars is the question of whether some constitutional provisions, or some constitutional disputes, are by their very nature non-justiciable and hence beyond the ambit of constitutional adjudication, because they are perceived as being fundamentally political in nature. Well-known examples of such political questions are impeachment trials by the Senate and House of Representatives, and the interpretation of the Guarantee Clause (Article IV, section 4) and the Privileges and Immunities Clause (Amendment XIV, section 1).[4]

Although there is general agreement that such a doctrine – known as the political questions doctrine – exists, scholars and courts are divided over its rationale and scope. Some scholars ground the political questions doctrine in constitutional text, claiming that some provisions of the U.S. Constitution commit an issue to the legislative and executive branches for their final determination.[5] Given that constitutional texts are rarely so explicit or unambiguous, though, other scholars have turned instead to the apparent lack of judicially manageable standards for interpreting open-ended constitutional language as a rationale for the doctrine.[6] However, in the face of the development of large and complex bodies of jurisprudence to implement open-ended guarantees such as "equal protection" and "due process" in the U.S. Constitution, defenders of the political questions doctrine have been pushed back to prudential concerns regarding the legitimate scope of judicial review. At this level, critics of the political questions doctrine raise the stakes by arguing that a commitment to judicial review is logically incompatible with the political questions doctrine, because the legitimacy concerns that drive the latter in fact undermine the justification of the former.[7] Proponents of the political questions doctrine respond in two different ways – that a political questions doctrine protects the legitimacy of judicial review by avoiding disputes that would undermine it; and that the political questions doctrine acknowledges that constitutional supremacy does not necessarily lead to an exclusive power for courts to interpret and apply the constitution.[8]

The Judicial Supremacy & Exclusivity Debate

Related to the political questions doctrine is the issue of the proper scope of the power of judicial review first asserted by the U.S. Supreme

Court in *Marbury v Madison*.[9] *Marbury* stands for the proposition that the power of courts to interpret constitutional provisions, and to give them priority over conflicting legislation, follows from the combination of (i) the notion of constitutional supremacy (i.e., that the constitution is supreme law), and (ii) the power of the courts to resolve legal disputes before them on the basis of the relevant legal materials, including the Constitution. *Marbury* is the source of on-going controversy, because it infers that courts are *competent* to interpret and enforce written constitutions (point (ii)) from the very idea of a written constitution that creates institutions and confers limited powers upon them (point (i)). The notion of constitutional supremacy, though, is agnostic on the practical question of which institution is best suited to enforce constitutional provisions.[10] Driven by the suspicion that *Marbury* may have amounted to a judicial usurpation of constitutional power, critics of the decision read it narrowly, by highlighting that it is ambiguous on two critical questions. The first is whether judicial competence implies judicial *supremacy*, i.e., whether judicial interpretations of the Constitution bind other institutions whose own interpretations of the Constitution may differ. The second is whether judicial competence implies judicial *exclusivity*, i.e., whether only the courts have the power to interpret the Constitution.

Debate on the first issue has revolved around the relationship between the doctrine of precedent and the separation of powers. Proponents of a narrow reading of *Marbury* have suggested that court decisions only bind the parties to a lawsuit (Jefferson), or both the parties and the executive with respect to the enforcement of that decision (Lincoln). However, they stress that precedent does not operate to preclude independent executive or legislative consideration of a constitutional issue.[11] Proponents of a broad reading of *Marbury* argue that judicial supremacy is important because it settles legal disputes with finality, and hence argue that judgments in constitutional cases establish precedents binding on the other branches of government.[12] Debate on the second issue is focused on whether courts are uniquely qualified to interpret the Constitution. Proponents of exclusivity have argued that certain institutional features of courts (judicial independence and impartiality, the requirement of reasoned decisions) give them a comparative advantage in matters of constitutional adjudication.[13] Critics of exclusivity argue both empirically, positing that non-judicial actors are capable of constitutional interpretation, and normatively, asserting that constitutional discourse should not be confined to legal fora.[14]

The Theory v Anti-Theory Debate[15]

The last debate of relevance revolves around the role of normative political, social, and economic theory in adjudication. Over the course of the last half-century, the most imaginative and influential legal scholarship has applied normative theories to the analysis of legal doctrine, statutes and institutions. Normative law and economics is a prominent example;[16] another is scholarship that relies on the liberal tradition defined by Kant and Rawls[17] or Locke and Nozick.[18] The rise of normative theory in law can in part be understood as a response to an intellectual movement known as Legal Realism. Put simply, the Realists proposed that formal sources of law – legal texts and precedents – did not contain within them the resources to provide "the sort of determinate and defensible answers to concrete and controverted normative questions required by the very idea of law and its rule."[19] Realists attributed this deficiency to the vagueness, abstractness or indeterminacy of legal terms and categories. These features of legal language served as a cloak for judges to implement their own preferences through adjudication, often at the price of important rule of law values such as consistency. In response, scholars invoked normative theories as a means to constrain judicial discretion, to pursue important social goals, and to protect important values.[20]

In recent years, though, scholars have begun to question the appropriate role of normative theory in legal interpretation generally, and constitutional interpretation in particular. There are two versions of this criticism. Strong critics argue that moral theories do not and should not play a role in adjudication.[21] Instead, adjudication should be conceived of pragmatically, relying not on moral theory but on common sense, professionalism, and a sense of people's needs, wants, and expectations. Weak critics argue that given the fact of reasonable pluralism in modern societies, adjudicating on the basis of particular moral theories lacks legitimacy.[22] Courts should resist the tendency to ascend to abstract normativity, and instead ground their judgments on "incompletely theorized agreements" that can secure the consent of persons holding divergent and mutually irreconcilable conceptions of the good.

The relevance of these debates among American constitutional theorists to an analysis of the *Quebec Secession Reference* is clear. The judgment, for example, vests primary responsibility for contextualizing the constitutional rules governing secession with the political organs of the Constitution, and eschews any supervisory role for the courts. This part of the judgment is reminiscent of the political questions doctrine, and therefore implicates issues regarding that doctrine's scope and rationale. Similarly, by dividing interpretive responsibility for the norms of the Canadian Constitution between the judicial and political branches, the judgment invites an examination of the issues of interpretive supremacy and exclusivity. This is an issue with far broader implications than the constitutional framework governing the secession of Quebec.

Finally, the Court's reliance on abstract, unwritten constitutional principles implicates the place of normative political theory in its crafting of the decision. It may be that the intuitively plausible appeal of these principles in the context of secession comes not so much from their implicit source in the constitutional text taken as a whole – the constitution that is being *rejected* by one of the parties in this dispute – but from their place in a certain kind of regime, a liberal democratic one, which the majority of both federalists and secessionists are compelled to accept as legitimate. Here, it may be that one of the most important lessons of the *Reference* for debates in constitutional theory about the role of abstract argument in the presence of normative controversy, is that there are some situations where the problem of agreement under conditions of normative dissensus actually points to a solution at a higher rather than lower level of abstraction. Because of historical disagreements and grievances about Quebec's acceptance of the written constitutional text, including and especially an amending formula that did not give it a veto over most constitutional changes, reliance on the text would have accentuated normative dissensus, while reliance on basic liberal democratic principles did not.

3 A FRAMEWORK FOR ANALYSIS

We propose to examine these questions by using the following analytical framework. Our claim is that despite fundamental differences in methodology and outlook, every theory of constitutional interpretation has the following three components. First, a theory of constitutional interpretation must contain an account of *sources*, that is, it must specify criteria for the identification of the constitutional norms which are the objects of constitutional interpretation. Although an emphasis on sources is a prominent feature of positivist jurisprudence,[23] any theory of legal interpretation must address the issue of which materials may properly figure into interpretation, even if the criteria so specified do not sharply distinguish between the law and normativity more generally.[24] An account of sources, in turn, will usually contain a theory of *amendment*, which specifies criteria for the adoption of new constitutional norms, or the removal of existing ones. Again, it may be that a particular theory denies the possibility of amendment[25] but nevertheless in so stating touches on the issue.

Second, a theory of constitutional interpretation must also contain an account of *interpretive responsibility*, which specifies which institutions are charged with the task of constitutional interpretation. Interpretive responsibility can be understood in two different but equally important senses. It can be understood as *jurisdiction*, that is, whether interpretive responsibility for constitutional norms is exclusive to, divided among, or shared by certain institutions. But interpretive responsibility can also be understood as *supremacy*, which addresses the question of whether the constitutional interpretations of an institution or of institutions vested with interpretive jurisdiction bind other institutions. Although jurisdiction and supremacy are different dimensions of interpretive responsibility, jurisdiction is of primary importance, because exclusive jurisdiction over constitutional interpretation obviates an assessment of which competing interpretation is supreme.

Third, a theory of constitutional interpretation must contain an account of *interpretive style*. Given the identification of constitutional norms, and the allocation of interpretive responsibility, the question which remains is how those norms are to be interpreted and applied. For most of the half century, American constitutionalists have hotly debated whether the text, original intent, or various versions of substantive political morality should be given pride of place in constitutional interpretation. It is important to recognize that interpretive methodology or style is to a large extent indissociable from the first two features of theories of constitutional interpretation. Debates over style, in essence, have revolved around the identification of the sources of constitutional norms, and the relative importance of these various sources. Similarly, style may be driven by the institutional allocation of interpretive responsibility, so that, for example, a court may decline to articulate a complete theory of a constitutional provision in order to prompt a political actor to do so.[26]

4 THE POSITIVIST UNDERSTANDING OF CONSTITUTIONAL INTERPRETATION

Utilizing this framework, we now detail what we call the *positivist account* of constitutional interpretation. This account cannot be found in any canonical texts or judicial decisions. Rather, it is a composite that we have constructed on the basis of our understanding of Canadian constitutional culture. The positivist account, in other words, articulates many of the intuitions held by the various actors in the Canadian constitutional scheme, but in a systematic way. Although this account is descriptively inaccurate of actual Canadian constitutional practice, the enterprise is nevertheless valuable because it serves to highlight the distinctive features of the judgment in the *Quebec Secession Reference*. In important ways, although not more than crudely theorized, this account is *presupposed* in the attack on "activist" judicial review by right-wing scholars such as Morton and Knopf, who adopt a conservative variation of the positivist account, in which ambiguous constitutional language is construed by reference to original intent, or failing that, the "traditional understanding" of the concepts invoked by constitutional provisions, as revealed by political practice.[27]

Sources

According to the positivist account, the sources of constitutional norms in Canada are limited to the express provisions of the *Constitution Acts* (this account has, of course, to deal in some way with important rules of Canadian constitutional law, for example concerning the prerogative powers of the Crown and the doctrine of parliamentary privilege, that are not specified in the constitutional text; this element in the Canadian constitutional system drives something of a wedge, however narrow, between positivism and textualism *tout court*). One textual basis for the textualism of the positivists is s. 52(2) of the *Constitution Act, 1982*,[28] which lists the legal documents that together make up the Constitution of Canada.[29] This is not to say that the *Constitution Acts* are exhaustive of constitutional law; the positivist account also gives an important place to past interpretations of those provisions, which have precedential force. However, those precedents derive their legitimacy from the fact that they represent authoritative interpretations of the constitutional text, and applications of the constitutional text to the facts of particular cases.

The centrality of text to the positivist account of constitutional interpretation has three important implications for the relationship between the norms of constitutional law, and normativity at large. First, it suggests a sharp distinction between the former and the latter. The latter lies outside the law; in constitutional terms, it lies in the world of politics. The former, by contrast, lies within and defines the boundaries of the world of the Constitution. Secondly, positivism has to cope with the possibility that no written text can explicitly contain rules for all those situations in which it would be desirable for the text to be governing of the controversy. One answer to this dilemma is to revert to original intent, asking how the framers would have wished a controversy to be resolved given what *is* explicitly specified in the text. An alternative answer, more characteristic of Canadian than American constitutionalism, is to simply say that, after a point, the law runs out. The constitutional order contains gaps, in which the law is silent, and politics reigns supreme, absent an explicit choice to amend the Constitution to deal explicitly with that situation. Thus, amendment to the Constitution requires express additions to the constitutional text, themselves the product of textually specified processes of amendment. As it turns out, Part V of the *Constitution Act, 1982* contains a variety of procedures to amend the Constitution. The relevant point for our discussion is that amendment is exclusively the domain of the political institutions (Parliament and the provincial legislatures).

Interpretive Responsibility

The positivist account is clear on the allocation of interpretive responsibility, in both of its senses. The task of constitutional interpretation is vested with the judiciary, and, ultimately, the Supreme Court of Canada. Moreover, the responsibility of the Supreme Court is both exclusive and supreme. It has exclusive jurisdiction over constitutional interpretation because no other actors in the constitutional scheme – neither executives nor legislatures at the provincial or federal level – have any kind of interpretive responsibility with respect to constitutional norms. To adapt a distinction most famously made by Ronald Dworkin, the political organs are uniquely qualified and hence confined to examine considerations of policy, whereas courts are expert in and limited to examining questions of constitutional principle.[30] Because the Supreme Court has exclusive jurisdiction over constitutional interpretation, its interpretations also enjoy supremacy; more accurately, the issue of supremacy among competing interpretations does not really arise, because the Court's jurisdiction is exclusive.[31]

Interpretive Style

Finally, the positivist account contains a view of interpretive style. Legal interpretation is delimited by the text of the Constitution, so that the beginning and ending points of constitutional interpretation are the express terms of individual constitutional provisions. This is not to say that principles of substantive political morality should not play a role in constitutional interpretation. As Fred Schauer persuasively argues, some constitutional provisions appear to incorporate principles of political morality "by reference," and therefore invite (but do not compel) courts to engage in the type of normative reasoning characteristic of moral and political philosophy.[32] Schauer's point, though, is that not all provisions are worded in this way. Setting to one side the inherent limitations of legal language to address factual situations that were unanticipated when that language was framed (the problem of open-texturedness), some provisions are relatively specific and precise, and admit of a narrower range of interpretive choices. The interpretive frames surrounding such terms is narrow enough to create a strong presumption against the recourse to normative reasoning.[33] Given the primacy of text in signaling the appropriate style of interpretation, the positivist account defends the possibility of distinguishing the construction of constitutional provisions from moral reasoning writ-large.

The positivist account has a number of important features worth emphasizing because of their relevance to our analysis of the *Quebec Secession Reference*. First, a central tenet of legal positivism is a sharp distinction between legality and legitimacy. A legal regime may conform with legality if it complies with the formal rules and procedures laid down in the constitution. But such a legal regime may nonetheless lack legitimacy if it fails to accord with principles of political justice that can justify the coercive use of state power. Legitimacy and legality may coincide; indeed, it is the ambition of liberal democracy to make the latter a condition of the former.[34] However, in cases where they diverge (as occurred in the *Quebec Secession Reference*), the positivist account denies courts the power to draw them together.

Second, the special role of the Supreme Court in constitutional interpretation yields a view on justiciability. Since the interpretive responsibility of the Court is both exclusive and supreme, every rule of constitutional law in principle can be the subject of adjudication. As a consequence, every rule of constitutional law is justiciable, and a dispute that is non-justiciable lies outside the grounds of constitutional law.

Finally, the positivist account, by implication, suggests what inappropriate judicial behaviour consists of. Courts that look beyond the text of the Constitution as a source of constitutional norms, that engage in amendment under the guise of interpretation, that surrender interpretive authority to other organs of government, or that engage in grand theorizing in a manner not invited by the constitutional text, have contravened the constitutional norms defining the judicial role.

5 PARTNERSHIP AND INSTITUTIONAL DIALOGUE

Sources

What is particularly striking about the *Quebec Secession Reference* is that it rejects each of the features of the positivist account. Consider the judgment's conception of sources. The Court considered and rejected the notion that the text of the *Constitution Acts* were exhaustive of Canadian constitutional law. Rather, at the outset of its answer to the reference questions, the Court stated:

The "Constitution of Canada" certainly includes the constitutional texts enumerated in s. 52(2) of the *Constitution Act, 1982*. Although these texts have a primary place in determining constitutional rules, they are not exhaustive. The Constitution also "embraces unwritten, as well as written rules."[35]

The Court's assertion that the Canadian Constitution contains unwritten rules of "principles" (terms which the Court used interchangeably, without reference to the technical distinction between the two drawn by legal theorists)[36] required some sort of justification. Indeed, given the Court's statements in a recent judgment that written constitutions ground the legitimacy of judicial review in liberal democracies, and promote legal certainty and predictability[37] – elements of the positivist account – the Court needed to explain *why* the conventional account was inadequate. Unless, of course, what it meant by "unwritten rules" was confined to those rules that have long existed as part of Canadian constitutional law, concerning, for example, the prerogative powers of the Crown and the doctrine of parliamentary privilege, and which were not extinguished by the creation of the *Constitution Act, 1982*.[38]

In its defense of the presence of unwritten rules or principles in the Canadian constitutional scheme, though, it is clear that the Court had in mind much more than these well-established rules. Upon close reading, it appears that the Court offered two different defenses. The first justification attempted to tie the written text and the unwritten *principles* of the Constitution together. According to the Court, the unwritten principles "inform and sustain the constitutional text: they are the vital unstated assumptions upon which the text is based."[39] This formulation suggests that the principles are general or abstract in nature, and the specific provisions of the constitutional text implement or actualize them. Indeed, the unwritten norms identified by the Court – federalism, democracy, constitutionalism and the rule of law, and respect for minority rights – *were* general or abstract. These principles, in the Court's words, formed the Constitution's "internal architecture" or "basic constitutional structure," around which the specified provisions of the Constitution were framed.[40] This justification of unwritten constitutional principles also suggests that they play a rather limited practical role – as aids to the construction of ambiguous constitutional provisions or the harmonious interpretation of different and perhaps apparently divergent or conflicting constitutional provisions. Again, the Courts said as much, when it stated that these principles "assist in the interpretation of the text and the delineation of spheres of jurisdiction, the scope of rights and obligations, and the role of our political institutions."[41]

The difficulty with the first justification is that it cannot explain the Court's judgment, for the Court went far beyond using unwritten principles to construe ambiguous constitutional provisions or reconcile provisions that were in conflict. In fact, the constitutional text contains no references, explicit or implicit, to the legal principles governing secession. Moreover, in contrast to the generality or abstractness of the unwritten norms of federalism, the rule of law, etc., the rules governing secession laid down by the Court are rather specific. What must be acknowledged is that the Court engaged in a style of constitutional interpretation which on any positivist account would be characterized as making constitutional rules, as opposed to merely applying them. In effect, the Court wove a secession clause[s] into the Constitution through the use of unwritten constitutional norms. It seems that the Court acknowledged this, when it quoted, with approval, a statement in an earlier judgment that the unwritten principles could be used to fill the "gaps in the express terms of the constitutional text."[42]

Faced with the inadequacy of its first justification to make sense of its judgment, the Court offered another. It defended the use of unwritten rules to not only clarify the written Constitution, but also to augment it. This argument was functional. In the Court's words, the unwritten rules of Canadian constitutional law exist:

because problems or situations may arise which are not expressly dealt with by the text of the Constitution. In order to endure over time, a constitution must contain a comprehensive set of rules and principles which are capable of providing an exhaustive legal framework for our system of government.[43]

The Court's argument appeared to be that the written text of the Constitution cannot possibly specify in advance adequate rules to govern all the situations that may arise in the future in which the constitutional order has a stake or interest. The difficulty with this argument, though, is that it appears to beg the question as to why the appropriate solution to this in a given case would be to evolve the Constitution through judicial interpretation of the underlying principles at its foundation, rather than to turn responsibility over to the political actors to effect an amendment of the Constitution, pursuant to the procedures provided in Part V of the *Constitution Act, 1982*. Here one kind of institutional answer that might have at least limited theoretical force is that the practice reference of questions from the political branch to the Court gives it a place, where invited by the political branch to do so, in charting the future influence of the Constitution on political events that the court might not possess when deciding cases and controversies. It should be noted that, in the *Secession Reference*, the very constitutional basis for references was challenged, and the Court had to provide an explicit affirmation of the legitimacy of the institutional role thrust upon it through the practice of the reference. Yet, in that part of the judgment as well, the Court remained largely unforthcoming with any general theory about the significance of the reference for the balance of judicial and political action in charting the future evolution of constitutional law and politics.

Thus, what the Court required, but what its judgment did not provide, is an account of sources that justifies the recourse to unwritten constitutional norms. In our view, the theory that best justifies the judgment is one we call dualist interpretation.[44] The dualist scheme comprehends two different interpretive roles for courts. First, there is the task of *ordinary interpretation*, whereby courts interpret and apply the constitutional text in the fashion suggested by the conventional account. The existence of unwritten norms is acknowledged here; however, their role is limited to resolving textual ambiguities and reconciling conflicting provisions. Ordinary interpretation covers day-to-day matters in the life-cycle of modern constitutions – specifically, the resolution of concrete legal disputes before courts of law where the parties do not challenge the very legitimacy of the constitutional order itself.

However, at exceptional moments, a court may engage in *extra-ordinary interpretation*, in which the text assumes secondary importance. Here, the Constitution is comprehended as a scheme of principle organized around unwritten norms that explain, and are implemented by, the constitutional text. These norms are regarded as providing "an exhaustive legal framework for our system of government," and as a consequence, invite the courts to interpret them in a manner that, in positivist eyes, would resemble amendment, and lead to the fashioning of new constitutional rules. We would classify the Court's judgment in the *Quebec Secession Reference* as a paradigmatic case of extra-ordinary interpretation.

The dualist scheme raises a number of questions that revolve around the relationship between the power of the courts to engage in extra-ordinary interpretation, and the power of political institutions to alter the Constitution through formal amendment. The first concerns the respective roles of extra-ordinary interpretation and formal amendment: has extra-ordinary interpretation displaced the need for ordinary amendment, and if not, how do we determine which one applies? The second question raised by the dualist scheme concerns the distinction between extra-ordinary interpretation and formal amendment: are extra-ordinary interpretations of the Constitution equivalent to amendments, or are they something different? Again, the Court was woefully unclear, in large part because while at some points it recognizes the extra-ordinary nature of the context, in many other places it seeks to present its judgment as quite ordinary, rather than acknowledging that it had shifted gears into an extra-ordinary mode. Thus, for example, at one point it stated that the duty to negotiate flowed not from a positive referendum result that amounted to a repudiation of the existing constitutional order, but rather from any proposals for constitutional amendment.[45]

Nonetheless, some points are clear. Extra-ordinary interpretations, in strictly legal terms, are not formal amendments to the constitutional text. But extra-ordinary interpretation does force the positivist distinction between amendment and interpretation, and replaces it with a broader notion of constitutional evolution. Instead of imagining the Constitution as bounded or as containing gaps, that must be added to by constitutional amendment, dualist interpretation views the Constitution as a dynamic entity that aspires to exhaustiveness. In one narrow sense, the written Constitution does "run out," because the textual provisions may not address a particular scenario. But in a more fundamental sense, it does not, because the internal logic of the constitutional document is capable of governing those situations. The extension of the internal logic of the Constitution occurs either through formal amendment or extra-ordinary interpretation.[46]

Interpretive Responsibility

Another distinctive feature of the judgment is that it vests substantial, if not exclusive, responsibility for interpreting the constitutional rules on secession in particular situations or contexts with political organs, not the courts. This is a break with the Canadian constitutional tradition, which, as the Court itself noted, has hitherto drawn a distinction between the law of the Constitution, which was judicially enforceable, and the political conventions of the Constitution, which were only subject to political sanctions. Indeed, given that the operation of the unwritten rules on secession was held to impose binding legal obligations on the federal and provincial governments, one might have expected the Court to hold that the application of those rules to particular situations related to secession would be a matter of judicial interpretive responsibility. However, the Court noted "that judicial intervention, even in relation to the *law* of the Constitution, is subject to the Court's appreciation of its proper role in the constitutional scheme."[47]

The Court then went to hold that its role was "limited to the identification of the relevant aspects of the Constitution in their broadest sense."[48] The relevant constitutional rules – defined in earlier passages – fell into two categories. First, there were the pre-requisites to the duty to engage in constitutional negotiations: a referendum voted by "a clear majority [of the population of Quebec] on a clear question" that evinced their intention to secede from Canada. Second, there were the rules governing both the process and outcome of the negotiations themselves. The Court's governing premise appeared to be that those negotiations must be conducted "in accordance with the underlying constitutional principles already discussed," such as democracy.[49] This premise led the Court to reject the view that a positive referendum would impose a "legal obligation on the other provinces and federal government to accede to the secession of a province."[50] But it also rejected "the reverse proposition, that a clear expression of self-determination by the people of Quebec would impose *no* obligations upon the other provinces or the federal government."[51] Instead, the Court held that a positive referendum vote for secession triggers "a reciprocal obligation on all parties to Confederation to negotiate constitutional changes to respond to that desire," which seems to amount to an obligation not only to negotiate, but to negotiate in good faith.[52] Moreover, the judgment seemed to suggest that the substantive outcome of any agreement must show adequate respect for the unwritten constitutional principles. Thus, the Court stated that "[t]he negotiation process must be conducted with an eye for the constitutional principles we have outlined, which must inform the actions of *all* the participants in the negotiation process."[53] Beyond specifying these constitutional rules, the Court stated that it had "no supervisory role."[54]

Given this radical departure from normal constitutional practice, the Court owed us an account of how it understood its role in the Canadian constitutional scheme. The Court offered two such explanations. The first, oddly enough, reverted to the traditional distinction between the law of the Constitution and "the workings of the political process."[55] The former defines the constitutional framework within which the latter sorts of non-constitutional decisions are made. Moreover, because those latter decisions are non-constitutional, they are beyond the scope of judicial review and non-justiciable. As the Court stated:

The Court has no supervisory role over the *political aspects* of constitutional negotiations. Equally, the initial impetus for negotiation, namely a clear majority on a clear question in favour of secession, is subject only to *political evaluation*, and properly so.[56]

A few sentences later, the Court reiterated the distinction between the legal framework governing secession and the non-justiciability of the political judgments that must be made within that framework, when it added, "[t]o the extent that the questions are political in nature, it is not the role of the judiciary to interpose its own views on the different negotiating positions of the parties."[57] Finally, the Court clarified that non-legal was synonymous with non-justiciable, when it referred to "[t]he non-justiciability of political issues that lack a legal component."[58]

The difficulty with this justification is that it does not yield the Court's innovative holding that the rules governing secession are at once legally binding and non-justiciable. Rather, the Court appears to have regressed to the standard view that the law of the Constitution is the business of the Courts, and defines the decisional space within which the political process can proceed unimpeded aside from those constraints. Judicial interpretation of the Constitution, in other words, is both exclusive and supreme. This sort of analysis suggests the following *ratio* – that the legal rules governing secession are fully justiciable, but that beyond those legal requirements, political actors may act unconstrained. The Court, though, held exactly the opposite – that the legal rules governing secession are non-justiciable (or at least not fully justiciable), but that those rules are legally binding on all parties to the negotiating process and must guide their deliberations. In other words, the Court's judgment modified the traditional approach to interpretive responsibility in two different respects. First, it replaced exclusive with shared interpretive jurisdiction, giving the political actors a role in constitutional interpretation. Moreover, by eschewing a "supervisory role," the Court may have even divided interpretive supremacy over the Constitution, at least with respect to the rules governing secession.

The Court's second justification spoke directly to these novel aspects of its judgment. Instead of sharply distinguishing between law and politics, the Court relied on the comparative institutional advantage of the political actors in this area of constitutional interpretation, stating that the Court itself lacked the requisite "information and expertise."[59] Elaborating upon the informational limitations of the litigation process, the Court explained that "the methods appropriate for the search for truth in a court of law are ill-suited to getting to the bottom of constitutional negotiations."[60] Clarifying the limitations of its expertise, the Court reasoned that "the strong defence of legitimate interests and the taking of positions which, in fact, ignore the legitimate interests of others is one that also defies legal analysis."[61] In other words, judicially enforceable standards are absent. Presumably, shared jurisdiction and divided supremacy are suitable responses to these institutional considerations.

Unfortunately, the Court's second justification is problematic as well. It is not at all clear, for example, that the Court is incapable of adjudicating upon both the preconditions to, and the process and outcome of, constitutional negotiations. The interpretation of the terms "clear majority" and "clear question," the enforcement of the obligation to negotiate in good faith, and even the compliance of a negotiated agreement with certain basic constitutional principles, are not totally beyond the realm of judicial competence.[62] As the debate over the political questions doctrine illustrates, judicially enforceable standards can always be developed. Moreover, assuming these institutional considerations to be valid, they fail to define the Court's role. Although the Court has eschewed the prospect of supervision, it nevertheless articulated the justifications behind the rules governing secession. Although this feature of the judgment may be necessary in cases of extra-ordinary interpretation, one gets the sense that the Court would have offered these justifications regardless.

The account which best explains the Court's judgment is one we call the model of *joint constitutional responsibility*. It is inspired by Lawrence Sager's theory of the underenforced constitutional norm. Sager's basic claim is that there are situations where the U.S. Supreme Court, "because of institutional concerns, has failed to enforce a provision of the Constitution to its full conceptual boundaries."[63] That norm is legally valid to its full conceptual limits. Judicial decisions only demarcate the limits of its judicial enforcement, and reflect the practical limitations on the ability of courts to translate abstract constitutional ideals into judicially enforceable standards. Beyond the boundaries of judicial competence, then, it is for the political organs of the Constitution to frame their own interpretations of those norms and assess their own compliance with them. Thus, interpretive responsibility for particular constitutional norms is both shared and divided. It is shared to the extent that courts are responsible for articulating constitutional norms in their conceptually abstract form. But interpretive responsibility is divided because beyond the limits of doctrine, constitutional interpretation is left to the political organs. The image which emerges is one of "judicial and legislative cooperation in the molding of concrete standards through which elusive and complex constitutional norms come to be applied."[64]

The model of joint constitutional responsibility also draws a distinction between the full conceptual limits of a constitutional norm and the boundaries of judicial enforceability. The limits of justiciability, though, turn not on competence but on legitimacy. Vesting the courts with exclusive and supreme interpretive responsibility creates the danger of marginalizing the Constitution in public discourse. By denying democratic institutions any role in constitutional interpretation, those institutions may fail to examine constitutional considerations at all in the legislative process. As a consequence, the Constitution may recede from importance in public life. This is a particular problem for liberal democracies like Canada, for which constitutions are a central component of national self-understanding. We adopt here the (admittedly simplifying) distinction between civic nations, which are founded on the basis of a shared commitment to principles of political justice, and ethnic nations, that are viewed as instruments to ensure the survival and flourishing of a particular people or *Volk*. In civic nations like Canada, the principles of political justice often take the form of written constitutions. Written constitutions, then, serve as the cement of social solidarity, and can give rise to a constitutional patriotism. However, for that constitutional patriotism to be sustained, it is imperative that constitutional discourse take place not just in the courts, but in democratic institutions, giving concrete political existence to the common values and principles that underpin such constitutional patriotism.[65]

The model of joint constitutional responsibility raises a number of difficult questions. The first is the question of *which* constitutional norms should be subject to this shared and divided jurisdiction, as opposed to exclusive judicial interpretation. The judgment itself offers little assistance in this regard. By focusing on institutional considerations to the exclusion of the larger issues of political legitimacy raised by involving the courts in the future of the federation, the Court deprived itself of the opportunity to address this issue. It may be that what drove the Court was a sense that the judicial interpretation of the rules governing secession would have failed to generate widespread acceptance in the political community. This is yet another part of the judgment where the Court owed us a better explanation than it provided.

The second question raised by the model of joint constitutional responsibility concerns the interpretive responsibility of political institutions.[66] That responsibility entails an obligation for the political organs to lay down relatively concrete principles that interpret and apply the constitutional rules governing secession. This obligation follows from the general principle that rules of constitutional law often must be interpreted and specified to be fully implemented. Courts do this through the development of doctrine. Political institutions, by contrast, may do this through statutes, resolutions, or declarations. In the wake of the *Quebec Secession Reference*, for example, political institutions must now define what a clear majority and a clear question mean. These terms are not self-defining, and require elaboration. This, of course, is the best way to understand the proposed *Clarity Act* (Bill C-20), the long title of which is "An Act *to give effect to* the requirement for clarity as set out in the opinion of the Supreme Court of Canada in the *Quebec Secession Reference*."[67] Indeed, one effect of the judgment has been to force these issues onto the forefront of the political agenda. Bill C-20 takes up this challenge, by spelling out procedures and criteria according to which the House of Commons will determine whether a clear majority has voted in favour of a clear question in favour of secession. The more general point is that the vesting of interpretive responsibility with political institutions enhances political accountability. The Court's simultaneous statement that it lacked the power to interpret the rules governing secession, but that the political institutions *were* charged with this task, had the effect of clarifying the lines of responsibility.[68] Thus, coupled with a much clearer legal framework governing secession, the judgment means that political institutions can no longer avoid difficult questions on the pretext that they are clouded in constitutional uncertainty. Indeed, there is no doubt that *Quebec Secession Reference* gave rise to a political dynamic that made the enactment of Bill C-20 both politically inevitable and constitutionally required.

A further perspective on the Court's view of interpretative responsibility is provided by Sunstein's observation that certain judicial outcomes can be understood as democracy-promoting, or even democracy-forcing.[69] The Court may further a conception of deliberative democracy by deciding in such a way as to require democratic deliberation, or to improve its quality. In some instances, where positions are entrenched and common ground elusive, there may not be an evident starting point or even rules of the game for democratic deliberation, the idea of a "clear background" against which democratic institutions can work. By specifying some general rules or norms that can constitute legitimate common ground on which deliberation might occur, but by refusing to decide in such a way as to foreclose the possible outcomes of deliberation, the Court promotes democracy. In fact, the duty to negotiate – the most striking unwritten rule elaborated by the Court in this decision – could well be described as "democracy-forcing." The democratic angle is useful, particularly, in pointing out the oversimplification in the positivist account that suggests the appropriate posture for the Court, where the existing law "runs out," is to leave matters to the political process or constitutional amendment. But by failing to act at all, the Court may, in certain situations, actually worsen, or increase the transaction costs, of the political actors resolving the controversy, or agreeing to new explicit constitutional rules for future resolution of this kind of controversy by the judiciary.

The final question is whether the model of joint constitutional responsibility excludes the possibility of judicial review entirely. Recall that constitutional rules are valid to their conceptual limits, but are underenforced for reasons of legitimacy. It is not inconceivable, then, that a situation might arise where an interpretation put on an underenforced constitutional rule by a political institution might be conceptually invalid. This is a hard case, because the courts defer matters to the political institutions precisely because a judicial decision would lack the requisite legitimacy. But if a political institution's interpretation is conceptually flawed, then its decision may lack legitimacy as well. It may be in these exceptional cases that the courts would retain the power to strike down political decisions. Indeed, one of the justifications for allowing courts to articulate a theory underlying a provision may be to put political institutions on notice that such judicial review is still available. What this suggests is that the model of joint responsibility is ultimately founded on judicial self-restraint, rather than the abdication of the power of judicial review in deference to the prerogatives of the other branches of government. Thus, we are somewhat skeptical that the Court has washed its hands entirely of the rules governing secession.[70] In this regard, the enactment of Bill C-20 may rather unexpectedly give the courts an opening to re-enter the legal fray over the constitutional framework regarding secession, because it provides a statutory basis for judicial intervention.[71] Indeed, interpreting the Court to have closed off further *dialogue ex ante* with the political branches by permanently renouncing interpretive responsibility over certain subject-matter – pre-judging its competence, as it were, without being willing to consider, based on the issues that emerge, which have sufficient legal elements to warrant further intervention – would suggest not joint responsibility, but abdication of responsibility, at odds with the Court's own substantive criteria for sharing.[72]

Interpretive Style

The final issue we address in this section is the Court's interpretive methodology. Instead of sticking closely to the constitutional text, as the conventional account urges courts to do, the Court articulated a normative vison of the Canadian constitutional order. This is evident from the outset of the judgment, where the Court stated that this case presented "momentous questions that go to the heart of our system of constitutional government."[73] After dealing with some preliminary objections to its reference jurisdiction, the Court then turned not to the text of the *Constitution Acts*, but to the unwritten principles of constitutional law that lay at the foundation of the Canadian constitutional order. The Court then went on to discuss each principle in considerable detail, both at the level of theory and practice. Thus, the Court took pains to distinguish constitutional democracy subject to the rule of law from simple majority rule. Out of these principles, the Court then fashioned the constitutional rules governing secession.

The Court offered little in the way of justification for its ascent to abstract normativity. This is rather unfortunate, given its departure from its normal practice – to begin with the relevant provisions of the Constitution. The Court came closest to providing a justification, though, in its scattered references to the relationship between legality and legitimacy. To the Court, legality stood for the compliance of public decision-making with the institutional formalities and procedures laid down by the constitutional text. Legitimacy, by contrast, referred to the justness or rightness of a constitutional regime. A constitution is legitimate if it reflects "the aspirations of the people," suggesting that a democratic pedigree is one condition of legitimacy.[74] Another condition of legitimacy, though, is compliance with "moral values, many of which are imbedded in our constitutional structure," including values which presumably do not merely reflect majority preferences.[75]

The Court's statements on the relationship between legality and legitimacy are hard to interpret, because they point to two rather different conceptions of that relationship. At times, the Court argued that legality and legitimacy are both necessary, but not sufficient, criteria for the survival of a constitutional system. On this account, legitimacy and legality are analytically distinct. Thus, the Court was careful to point out that the partition of the Constitution in 1982 complied both with requirements of legality (adoption by the Imperial Parliament) and legitimacy (the conventions governing constitutional amendments); by implication, had either been absent, the 1982 amendments might not have taken hold. At other times, though, the Court seemed to suggest that legality is a necessary means to securing legitimacy. As we noted earlier, this is the aspiration of liberal democracy. We take this to be the meaning of the Court's obscure statement that in the Canadian constitutional tradition "legality and legitimacy are linked."[76]

The Court's apparently contradictory statements on the relationship between legitimacy and legality can be reconciled in the following way. On most occasions in the day-to-day operations of the state, legality is sufficient to secure the legitimacy of liberal democratic regimes. However, in exceptional circumstances, legality and legitimacy may come apart, so that the issue of legitimacy must be addressed directly. It is readily apparent from the judgment that a positive referendum vote in favour of secession would force apart legitimacy and legality in this manner. Thus, while the Court noted that "the results of a referendum have no direct role or legal effect," it also noted that the "continued existence and operation of the Canadian constitutional order cannot remain indifferent to the clear expression of a clear majority of Quebecois that they no longer wish to remain in Canada," because the latter amounted to a "clear repudiation of the existing constitutional order."[77]

The coming apart of legality and legitimacy in exceptional circumstances raises the question of how the legitimacy of a constitutional order could be restored. The positivist account, for example, suggests that the express exclusion of the courts from the amending procedures reflects an institutional division of labour between the courts and the political organs of the Constitution in the protection of legality and legitimacy. Courts ensure fidelity to legality through judicial review; Parliament and the provincial legislatures use the amending power to ensure that the constitutional scheme as a whole is legitimate. The special role of institutions that are politically accountable in constitutional change might in fact render judicial amendment illegitimate. What the Court had to explain, then, is why it did not allow the normal processes of constitutional politics and amendment to operate, and instead took on the task of restoring the legitimacy of the Canadian Constitution itself. Indeed, how could the principles of the Canadian constitutional order legitimately govern or structure a process whose starting premise was, in the Court's own admission, a clear repudiation of that order? It would seem that only constitutional amendment by the political actors could reconcile the repudiation of the constitutional order by one province with the overall legality and integrity of that order, through formalizing the response to repudiation in a constitutional amendment.

However, once we examine the political context surrounding the *Quebec Secession Reference*, it becomes evident that the Court acted in the face of the failure of federal political institutions to face the challenge posed by the referendum process in Quebec to the legitimacy of the Canadian constitutional order, and the comparable failure of the Quebec separatists to even engage the issue of the legitimacy of secession in terms of Canadian constitutional principles, rights, and interests, claiming that the choice to make a state is a matter of the will of a *Volk*, impervious to any effects on "others" who are not members of the *Volk*. Before the reference questions had been issued, it was entirely open to the federal government to lay down principles governing referenda and secession. To do so, however, would have been to confront the Schmittean extra-legalism of the Quebec separatists with a unilateral claim of the "enemy" (the federal authorities) about legitimacy. This would have reinforced the notion, propounded by separatists, that what was at stake was merely a clash of wills, unresolvable by any agreed or shared legal principles or conception of legitimacy.

In thus referring the matter to the Supreme Court, the federal government made a brilliant institutional wager – that the Court would not simply be identified by those whom it sought to persuade of the illegitimacy of unilateral secession, with the federal authorities *and* with one side in a boundless political struggle. The Court could effectively play a political role that the federal government would fail at precisely because of the Court's observance, historically and in this very case, of institutional constraints on its interpretive authority that would allow it to be fairly perceived as not "politicized" in the sense that separatists initially *claimed* that it would inevitably be if it chose to adjudicate the matter. In sum, the Court had to play a political role, which it could only legitimately and effectively do through setting institutional bounds around its engagement with the political choices of political actors.

The political context, and the Court's response to it, explains the shift to extra-ordinary interpretation. Moreover, the challenge to the legitimacy of the Canadian Constitution raised by the case also makes sense of the Court's ascent to abstract normativity. In the submissions of the parties, the Court was presented with two dramatically different and mutually incompatible accounts of the legitimacy of the Canadian constitutional order. On the one hand, the federal government took the position that democratic expressions of the will of the people of a province in themselves were of no significance to the legitimacy of the constitutional scheme. Rather, what was dispositive was adherence to legality, which, in the case of secession, was adherence to the amending procedures laid down in Part V of the *Constitution Act, 1982*. On the other hand, the amicus curiae took exactly the opposite position – that the legitimacy of the Canadian constitutional order was entirely dependent on expressions of democratic will, and that constitutional procedures could not fetter the right of Quebec to self-determination.

This clash of constitutional visions placed the Court in an extraordinarily difficult position. Choosing one position by necessity entailed the rejection of the other. Had the Court sided with one of the parties, its judgment would have, in effect, rendered the Constitution illegitimate in the eyes of a large segment of Canadians. But nor was it open to the Court to avoid the abstract normative dispute at the heart of the litigation, in a manner akin to that suggested by Cass Sunstein. Sunstein proposes that, in normal cases, courts should be averse to grounding their decisions in controversial moral or political theories, because those theories are unlikely to secure wide agreement in liberal societies characterized by the fact of reasonable pluralism. He argues, though, that it may be possible that persons who disagree on a fundamental level may nevertheless agree on particular results, and on reasons that operate at a relatively low level of abstraction to justify them. Sunstein also acknowledges, however, that there are other cases, rather atypical of the daily fare of public law litigation, where it is inappropriate, or unrealistic, to seek low-level, untheorized or undertheorized agreement. He remarks that there are occasions where deciding cases on the basis of abstract, "relatively large-scale principles" is "legitimate and even glorious," referring to "rare occasions when more ambitious thinking becomes necessary to resolve a case or when the case for ambitious theory is so insistent that a range of judges can converge on it."[78]

The limitation of Sunstein's account (as he himself acknowledges) is that low-level agreement may not always be possible, especially when disagreements on fundamental questions of principle produce disagreements on specific outcomes. In the *Quebec Secession Reference*, for example, the normative dispute was of this nature, because the competing constitutional visions of the parties dictated dramatically different positions on the question of unilateral secession. Indeed, had the Court tried to follow Sunstein's advice on how *normal* cases should be adjudicated, it would have courted disaster. Justifying its decision on the basis of a theoretical account that was obscure and underdeveloped might have created the misunderstanding that it was applying one's party's view by stealth, throwing into question the very legitimacy of its judgment. In fact, in a more recent articulation of his theory of adjudication, Sunstein actually raises the possibility that higher level agreement about general norms may exactly be what is required, where sharp divergences of perspective exist at a more concrete level. However, Sunstein identifies this situation strongly with constitution-making, not interpretation.[79] Yet, while this observation may be sound, there is no intrinsic reason why the only situation where agreement is easier with respect to abstract principles and harder with respect to particulars is that of constitution-making.

If one understands the Court's task as to provide a judgment that is legitimate in the eyes of Canadians on both sides of the secession debate, then we can see clearly why it resorted to general principles to craft its ruling. In the perspective of the divide between federalists and secessionists, these principles could enjoy the reasonable assent of everyone, whereas at the core of the debate over secession is in fact the moral bindingness of the constitutional *text* on Quebec, given the secessionist historical narrative of Quebec's "exclusion" in the creation of a self-standing written constitution in 1982, and the failure to remedy this exclusion in subsequent rounds of constitutional negotiations (Meech Lake, Charlottetown). Indeed, one could even say that in appealing to the four principles, the Supreme Court was appealing to the pride of the separatists that, contrary to the suspicions of many of their opponents, their movement is entirely liberal democratic. How then could they really repudiate the principles in question? And if they could not repudiate the principles, then how could they not accept the proposition that secession itself must take place in accordance with those principles? Thus, while in this case the Court's formal legitimacy was weak, given the secessionist repudiation of the formal text of the Constitution as a basis for deciding Quebec's future in relation to Canada, its substantive legitimacy was strong. Yet the Court apparently saw how easily this substantive legitimacy would slip away, were it required to apply in detail the abstract principles upon which it relied, and therefore enunciated its refusal to do so.

The judgment in the *Quebec Secession Reference* accordingly suggests the possibility of a dynamic interaction between sources, interpretive responsibility, and interpretive style. The idea is that only particular combinations of conceptions of sources, interpretive responsibility, and interpretive style will together secure the legitimacy of judicial review. These different components balance each other, together constituting a theory of constitutional interpretation. Moreover, altering a conception of one element in this package necessitates the modification of the others. The positivist account, for example, balances a robust notion of interpretive responsibility – judicial interpretation of the Constitution is both exclusive and supreme – against a view of interpretive style that sharply distinguishes adjudication from normative reasoning writ large, and a narrow view of legal sources. The ascent to abstract normativity in the *Quebec Secession Reference*, along with an expansive view of sources, accordingly required an adjustment in the Court's conception of interpretive responsibility, to one where interpretive jurisdiction is both shared and divided.

The resort to abstract normativity in the *Quebec Secession Reference* raises the interesting question of *when* such a shift is justified. In this judgment, for example, the ascent to abstract normativity went hand-in-hand with extra-ordinary adjudication. In this judgment, the two were part and parcel of the same phenomenon. But one could imagine situations where the sort of institutional failure that gave rise to extra-ordinary interpretation here did not exist, but the Court nevertheless ascended to abstract normativity. Novel cases, cases where there are conflicting lines of authority, or cases where the established case-law seems to run counter to widely held moral and political values – different varieties of hard cases – all might invite the court to engage in what Ronald Dworkin calls a process of "justificatory assent."[80]

Another question which emerges is whether the phenomenon of institutional failure explains some of the more dramatic judicial decisions in Canadian constitutional history. The failure of the Trudeau government and the provinces to agree on a set of principles regarding provincial participation in the partition of the Canadian Constitution may account for the holding on constitutional conventions in the *Partition Reference*. The goal of relying on conventions was to combine an ambitious normative account of the Canadian federation with institutional self-restraints in the enforcement of those norms, albeit in a different manner from the *Quebec Secession Reference*. However, the use of conventions created serious problems of its own, because it conferred constitutional significance and normative force on mere political practice and tradition without any further considerations. Likewise, the inability of the federal and provincial governments to strengthen the economic union may have motivated the Court to step into the breach, with a series of ambitious judgments on the federal trade and commerce power, federal jurisdiction over peace, order and good government, mobility rights, and the constitutional aspects of conflicts of law.[81] This suggestion is speculative, but we raise it for discussion.

ACKNOWLEDGMENTS

We thank Ira Parghi and Amir Sperling for extremely helpful comments on an earlier draft. Amir Sperling also provided excellent research assistance. Robert Howse, in particular, would like to thank Annalise Acorn, Andrew Coyne, and Senators Gerard Beaudoin, Serge Joyal, and Lowell Murray for stimulating exchanges on the issues surrounding the Court's role in the secession debate. The usual disclaimer applies. We acknowledge the financial support of the Harvard University Center for Ethics and the Professions (SC).

NOTES

1 *Reference re Secession of Quebec*, [1998] 2 SCR 217 [hereinafter *Quebec Secession Reference*]; A.C. Cairns, "The Quebec Secession Reference: The Constitutional Obligation to Negotiate" (1998) 10:1 *Constitutional Forum* 26; Editorial, "Court Answers Succeed" *The Kitchener-Waterloo Record* (25 August 1998) A6; D. Greschner, "The Quebec Secession Reference: Goodbye to Part V?" (1998) 10:1 *Constitutional Forum* 19; P. Joffe, "Quebec's Sovereignty Project and Aboriginal Rights" (1999) 7 *Canada Watch* 6; J. Legault, "How to deny Quebec's right to self-determination: With the Supreme Court's opinion, we have entered the realm of colonial federalism" *The Globe and Mail* (21 August 1998) A19; P.J. Monahan, "Doing the Rules: An Assessment of the Federal *Clarity Act* in Light of the *Quebec Secession Reference*" (2000) 135 *C.D. Howe Institute Commentary* 3; P.J. Monahan, "The Public Policy Role of the Supreme Court of Canada in the *Secession Reference*" (1999) 11 NJCL 65; J. Morin, "L'avis de la Cour supreme: Une sécession légitime et réalisable en théorie" *Le Devoir* (31 August 1998) A7; T. Morton, "A ticket to separate: Has the Supreme Court curbed separatism? No, says Ted Morton" *Ottawa Citizen* (22 August 1998) B7; P. Oliver, "Canada's Two Solitudes: Constitutional and International Law in *Reference re Secession of Quebec*" (1999) 6:1 *Int'l J. on Minority and Group Rights* 65; C. Ryan, "What if Quebeckers voted clearly for secession? While the Supreme Court did a good job of defining broad principles, it left a great contradiction hanging in the air" *The Globe and Mail* (27 August 1998) A12; D. Turp, "Globalizing Sovereignty" (1999) 7 *Canada Watch* 4; W. Walker, "Difficult Questions Remain for the Politi-

cians to Resolve" *The Toronto Star* (21 August 1998) A9; J.D. Whyte, "The Secession Reference and Constitutional Paradox" in D. Schneiderman, ed., *The Quebec Decision: Perspectives on the Supreme Court Ruling on Secession* (Toronto: Lorimer, 1999) 130; J. Woehrling, "Unexpected Consequences of Constitutional First Principles" (1999) 7:1–2 *Canada Watch* 18; R.A. Young, "A Most Politic Judgment" (1998) 10:1 *Constitutional Forum* 14.

2 The foremost work here is F.L. Morton & R. Knopff, *The Charter Revolution and the Court Party* (Peterborough, ON: Broadview Press, 2000).

3 Some notable exceptions are: J. Bakan, *Just Words: Constitutional Rights and Social Wrongs* (Toronto: University of Toronto Press, 1997); D. Beatty, *Constitutional Law in Theory and Practice* (Toronto: University of Toronto Press, 1995); R.F. Devlin, ed., *Canadian Perspectives on Legal Theory* (Toronto: E. Montgomery Publications, 1991); R.F. Devlin, "Some Recent Developments in Canadian Constitutional Theory with Particular Reference to Beatty and Hutchinson" (1996) 22:1 Queen's LJ 81; D. Dyzenhaus, "The New Positivists" (1989) 39 UTLJ 361; J. Fudge, "The Public/Private Distinction: The Possibilities of and the Limits of the Use of *Charter* Litigation to Further Feminist Struggles" (1987) 25:3 Osgoode Hall LJ 485; P. Horwitz, "The Sources and Limits of Freedom of Religion in a Liberal Democracy: Section 2(a) and Beyond" (1996) 54:1 UT Fac L Rev 1; A. Hutchinson & A. Petter, "Private Rights/Public Wrongs: The Liberal Lie of the *Charter*" (1988) 38:3 UTLJ 288; A.C. Hutchinson, *Waiting for Coraf: A Critique of Law and Rights* (Toronto: University of Toronto Press, 1995); P. Macklem, "Constitutional Ideologies" (1988) 20:1 Ottawa L Rev 117; P. Macklem, "Normative Dimensions of an Aboriginal Right of Self-Government" (1995) 21:1 Queen's LJ 173; P.J. Monahan & A. Petter, "Developments in Constitutional Law: the 1985–86 Term" (1987) 9 Supreme Court LR 69; P. Monahan, *Politics and the Constitution: The Charter, Federalism and the Supreme Court of Canada* (Scarborough, ON: Carswell, 1987); D. Réaume & L. Green, "Education and Linguistic Security in the Charter" (1989) 34:4 McGill LJ 777; B. Ryder, "The Demise and Rise of the Classical Paradigm in Canadian Federalism: Promoting Autonomy for the Provinces and First Nations" (1991) 36:2 McGill LJ 309; D. Schneiderman, "Economic Citizenship and Deliberative Democracy: An Inquiry Into Constitutional Limitations on Economic Regulation" (1995) 21:1 Queen's LJ 125; B. Slattery, "A Theory of the *Charter*" (1987) 25:4 Osgoode Hall LJ 701; L. Weinrib, "Limitations on Rights in a Constitutional Democracy" (1996) 6 Caribbean L Rev 428.

4 *Baker v Carr*, 369 U.S. 186 (1962).

5 H. Wechsler, "Toward Neutral Principles of Constitutional Law" (1959) 73:1 Harv L Rev 1.

6 A.M. Bickel, *The Least Dangerous branch: the Supreme Court at the Bar of Politics* (Indianapolis, IN: Bobbs-Merrill, 1962).

7 M.H. Redish, "Judicial Review and the 'Political Question'" (1984) 79 Nw UL Rev 1031.

8 M. Tushnet, "Principles, Politics, and Constitutional Law" (1989) 88:1 Mich L Rev 49.

9 5 U.S. (1 Cranch) 137 (1803), 31 U.S. (6 Pet.) 515 (1832) [hereinafter *Marbury*].

10 R.M. Dworkin, *Freedom's Law: The Moral Reading of the American Constitution* (Cambridge, MA: Harvard University Press, 1996) at 33–4.

11 See generally, G. Gunther & K. Sullivan, *Constitutional Law*, 13th ed. (Westbury, NY: Foundation Press, 1997) at 20–7.

12 L. Alexander & F. Schauer, "On Extrajudicial Constitutional Interpretation" (1997) 110:7 Harv L Rev 1359.

13 O.M. Fiss, "Foreword: The Forms of Justice" (1979) 93:1 Harv L Rev 1.

14 M.V. Tushnet, "The Hardest Question in Constitutional Law" (1996) 81:1 Minn L Rev 1; N. Devins & L. Fisher, "Judicial Exclusivity and Political Instability" (1998) 84:1 Va L Rev 83. To some extent, the American debate over the scope and extent of *Marbury* is inapplicable to Canada, because there is clear support in both the constitutional text and in the Canadian constitutional tradition, for the practice of judicial review. Section 52(1) declares the *Constitution Act, 1982* to be the supreme law of Canada, and provides that laws inconsistent with it are of no force or effect; moreover, the status of the *Constitution Acts* as enactments of the Imperial Parliament justifies judicial review as a means to pursuing the traditional goals of parliamentary supremacy and legislative intent. By contrast, since Alexander Bickel's examination of the question in the *Least Dangerous Branch*, there is a broad consensus that neither the text of the U.S. Constitution nor the intent of the framers expressly or impliedly authorizes judicial review. Judicial review must therefore be justified as a matter of first principle. Nevertheless, the institutional questions raised by *Marbury* with respect to the interpretive responsibility of courts are relevant to the Canadian context, because the scope and extent of judicial review are open to differing interpretations.
 In this connection, we mention the important work of Brian Slattery. In "A Theory of the *Charter*," *supra* note 3, Slattery argues for a theory of

judicial review in Canada in which courts, executives and legislatures all share the responsibility of interpreting the *Canadian Charter of Rights and Freedoms*. Moreover, he suggests, barring exceptional circumstances, that judicial interpretations of the *Charter* may not even be supreme. Slattery in effect resists a conception of judicial review in Canada that would be identical to a broad reading of *Marbury* in the United States. Slattery's argument is novel, because it is premised not only on the institutional considerations at play in the American discourse, but on the nature of law itself. For Slattery, the very idea of law is that it possesses a normative force that makes it a guide for conduct, a standard for evaluation, and a reason for compliance, in the minds of the persons to whom it is addressed. The role of coercive sanctions to ensure compliance with the law is secondary, or parasitic. In the constitutional context, this means that the rules of constitutional law are addressed primarily not to the courts that enforce them, but to political institutions that are bound by them. Inasmuch as coming to terms with constitutional norms is an inherently interpretive act, Slattery accordingly argues that executives and legislatures have an important role to playing constitutional interpretation, and that the power of courts to interpret the Constitution is not exclusive. Moreover, since political institutions are presumed to give due consideration to constitutional questions in arriving at their decisions, Slattery suggests that their constitutional interpretations be given deference in certain circumstances defined by relative institutional competence.

15 We draw this account from F. Michelman, "Normative Theory in Legal Scholarship: Moral and Related Political Philosophy" [unpublished].

16 E.g., R.A. Posner, *The Economics of Justice* (Cambridge, MA: Harvard University Press, 1981).

17 E.g., R.M. Dworkin, *Taking Rights Seriously* (Cambridge, MA: Harvard University Press, 1978); F. Michelman: "Constitutional Welfare Rights and *A Theory of Justice*: in N. Daniels, ed., *Reading Rawls: Critical Studies on Rawls'* A Theory of Justice (Oxford: Basil Blackwell, 1975).

18 R.A. Epstein, *Takings: Private Property and the Power of Eminent Domain* (Cambridge, MA: Harvard University Press, 1985).

19 Michelman, *supra* note 17, section 2 at 2.

20 Set against this background, the debate between non-interpretivists and interpretivists – between scholars who endorsed the reliance in adjudication on substantive principles of political morality not expressed in the written text of the Constitution (T.C. Grey, "Do We Have an Unwritten Constitution?" (1975) 27:3 Stan L Rev 703) and those who did not (Justice

H.L. Black, "The Bill of Rights" (1990) 35 NYUL Rev 865) can easily be seen as part of the larger debate over Legal Realism.

21 R.A. Posner, "The Problematics of Moral and Legal Theory" (1998) 111:7 Harv L Rev 1637. Also see the following commentaries on Posner's lecture in the same issue of the Harvard Law Review: R.M. Dworkin, "Darwin's New Bulldog" (1998) 111:7 Harv L Rev 1718 [hereinafter *Darwin's New Bulldog*]; C. Fried, "Philosophy Matters" (1998) 111:7 Harv L Rev 1739; M.C. Nussbaum, "Still Worthy of Praise" (998) 111:7 Harv L Rev 1776.

22 C.R. Sunstein, "Incompletely Theorized Agreements" (1995) 108:7 Harv L Rev 1733; C.R. Sunstein, *Legal Reasoning & Political Conflict* (New York: Oxford University Press, 1996) [hereinafter *Legal Reasoning*]; R.H. Fallon, Jr., "Foreword: Implementing the Constitution" (1997) 111:1 Harv L Rev 54.

23 E.g., H.L.A. Hart, *The Concept of Law* (Oxford: Clarendon Press, 1961) (the rule of recognition); H. Kelsen, *General Theory of Law and State*, trans. A. Wedberg (Cambridge, MA: Harvard University Press, 1945) (the grundnorm).

24 E.g., *Taking Rights Seriously, supra* note 17 at 344; R.M. Dworkin, *Law's Empire* (Cambridge, MA: Belknap Press, 1986).

25 E.g., the view of the German Constitutional Court that certain articles of the German Basic Law are unamendable (see D.P. Kommers, *The Constitutional Jurisprudence of the Federal Republic of Germany* (Durham, NC: Duke University Press, 1989) at 76.

26 N.K. Katyal, "Judges as Advicegivers" (1998) 50:6 Stan L Rev 1709.

27 R. Knopff & F.L. Morton, *Charter Politics* (Scarborough, ON: Nelson Canada, 1992) at 130.

28 *Constitution Act, 1982*, being Schedule B to the *Canada Act 1982* (U.K.), 1982, c. 11 [hereinafter *Constitution Act, 1982*].

29 Section 52(2) of the *Constitution Act, 1982*, provides that:

The Constitution of Canada includes:
(a) the *Canada Act 1982*, including this Act;
(b) the Acts and orders referred to in the schedule; and
(c) any amendment to any Act or order referred to in paragraph (a) or (b).

Note, though, that the Supreme Court of Canada held in *New Brunswick Broadcasting Co. v Nova Scotia*, [1993] 1 SCR 319 that s. 52(2) should not be read exhaustively (i.e., that "includes" is not synonymous with "means"), and as a consequence, that the doctrine of parliamentary privilege constituted part of the Constitution of Canada. The source of this unwritten rule was the preamble to the *Constitution Act, 1867* (U.K.), 20 & 31 Vict., c. 3, which states that the Constitution of Canada is "a Constitution similar in Principle to that of the United Kingdom."

30 *Taking Rights Seriously, supra* note 17 at ch. 4.

31 For a similar account, see "A Theory of the *Charter*," *supra* note 3.

32 F. Schauer, "Constitutional Invocations" (1997) 65:4 Fordham L Rev 1295.

33 F. Schauer, "Easy Cases" (1985) 58:1 S Cal L Rev 399.

34 J. Habermas, *Between Facts and Norms: Contributions to a Discourse Theory of Law and Democracy* (Cambridge, MA: MIT Press, 1996); D. Dyzenhaus, "The Legitimacy of Legality" (1996) 46:1 UTLJ 129.

35 *Quebec Secession Reference, supra* note 1 at para. 32, quoting s. 52(2) of the *Constitution Act, 1982, supra* note 28 and *Reference re Remuneration of Judges of the Provincial Court of Prince Edward Island,* [1977] 3 SCR 3 [hereinafter *Provincial Judges Reference*] at para. 92.

36 E.g., *Taking Rights Seriously, supra* note 17 at ch. 2.

37 *Provincial Judges Reference, supra* note 35 at para. 93.

38 P.W. Hogg, *Constitutional Law of Canada*, Student ed. (Scarborough, ON: Carswell 2000) at c. 1.7 and 1.9.

39 *Quebec Secession Reference, supra* note 1 at para. 49.

40 Ibid. at para. 50; the second quotation is from *OPSEU v Ontario (A.G.),* [1987] 2 SCR 2 at 57.

41 *Quebec Secession Reference, supra* note 1 at para. 52.

42 Ibid. at para. 53, citing *Provincial Judges Reference, supra* note 35 at para. 104.

43 Ibid. at para. 32.

44 As will become apparent, our account of dualist interpretation differs sharply from Bruce Ackerman's account of dualist democracy in *We the People*, Vol. 1: *Foundations* (Cambridge, MA: Belknap Press of Harvard University Press, 1991).

45 *Quebec Secession Reference, supra* note 1 at para. 69.

46 Compare this account with Ackerman's in *We the People, supra* note 44 – ours is almost a mirror image of his dualist account.

47 *Quebec Secession Reference, supra* note 1 at para. 98 [emphasis in original].

48 Ibid. at para. 100.

49 Ibid. at para. 88. Also see ibid. at para. 90: "The conduct of the parties in such negotiations would be governed by the same constitutional principles which give rise to the duty to negotiate: federalism, democracy, constitutionalism and the rule of law, and the protection of minorities."

50 Ibid. at para. 90.

51 Ibid. at para. 92 [emphasis in original]. The Court went on to say (in ibid. at para. 92) that "[t]he continued existence and operation of the Canadian constitutional order cannot remain indifferent to the clear expression of a clear majority of Quebecers that they no longer wish to remain in Canada."

52 Ibid. at para. 88. It is noteworthy that "[w]hile the negotiators would have to contemplate the possibility of secession," the Court clearly envisions that the negotiations may not reach agreement (ibid. at para. 97). Also see ibid. at para. 96: "No one can predict the course that such negotiations might take. The possibility that they might not lead to an agreement amongst the parties must be recognized." Thus, the Court never endorses the proposition that, at the end of the day, good faith in negotiation extends to actually offering or acceding to secession. The possibility of impasse, even in the case that the constitutional principles are respected by all parties to the negotiations, clearly implies that these principles do not contain a decision-rule able to break such an impasse. An example of such a decision-rule would be that Quebec must be offered secession if it agrees to terms consistent with the four principles. But the Court clearly preferred to accept the possibility of an impasse, with a judgment on the responsibility for the impasse to be left to the world community, than to tilt even that far in implying a right to secede. On these points, see *Special Senate Committee on Bill C-20 Debates* (8 June 2000) (R. Howse), online: Proceedings of the Special Committee on Bill C-20 <http://www.parl.gc.ca/36/2/parlbus/commbus/senate/com-e/clar-e/04ev-e.htm>.

53 Ibid. at para. 94 [emphasis in original].

54 Ibid. at para. 100.

55 Ibid.

56 Ibid. [emphasis added].

57 Ibid. at para. 101.

58 Ibid. at para. 102.

59 Ibid. at para. 100.

60 Ibid. at para. 101.

61 Ibid.

62 For example, see the judgement of the Constitutional Court of South Africa in *Certification of the Constitution of South Africa, 1996 (Re)*, [1966] SAJ No. 19, where that court measured the compliance of the Final South African Constitution with a list of "constitutional principles" spelled out in the Interim Constitution.

63 L.G. Sager, "Fair Measure: The Legal Status of Underenforced Constitutional Norms" (1978) 91:6 Harv L Rev 1212 at 1213.

64 Ibid. at 1240.

65 This understanding of the importance of constitutional politics – by necessity, a politics of principle – amounts to a rejection of the view that politics is merely about registering and aggregating the preferences of citizens. See generally, J. Cohen, "Deliberation and Democratic Legitimacy" in A. Hamlin & P. Pettit, eds., *The Good Polity: Normative Analysis of the State* (New York: Basil Blackwell, 1989); J. Cohen, "Procedure and Substance in Deliberative Democracy" in S. Benhabib, ed., *Democracy and Difference: Contesting the Boundaries of the Political* (Princeton, NJ: Princeton University Press, 1996); J. Elster, "The Market and the Forum" in J. Elster & A. Hylland, eds., *Foundations of Social Choice Theory* (New York: Cambridge University Press, 1986); C.R. Sunstein, "Preferences and Politics" (1991) 20 Phil & Publ Affairs 3 at 20.

66 For interesting discussions of this issue in the American context, see D.A. Strauss, "Presidential Interpretation of the Constitution" (1993) 15 Cardoza L Rev 113; P. Brest, "The Conscientious Legislator's Guide to Constitutional Interpretation" (1975) 27:3 Stan L Rev 585.

67 Bill C-20, *An Act to give effect to the requirement for clarity as set out in the opinion of the Supreme Court of Canada in the Quebec Secession Reference*, 2d Sess., 36th Parl., 1999 (as passed by the House of Commons 15 March 2000 [emphasis added].

68 Katyal, *supra* note 26.

69 C.R. Sunstein, *One Case at a Time: Judicial Minimalism on the Supreme Court* (Cambridge, MA: Harvard University Press, 1999).

70 Compare *Nixon v United States*, 506 U.S. 224 (1993) (various justices expressing the view that Congressional interpretations of the term "trial" in the Impeachment Clause are subject to judicial review in extreme circumstances, such as the adoption of Senate rules providing for automatic convictions without any formal proceedings).

The question of whether the Court will second-guess interpretations of the rules governing secession adopted by the political actors is distinct from another issue – whether the Court will enforce the provisions of Part V of the *Constitution Act, 1982* to ensure that the correct amending formulas are applied to effectuate constitutional change. Unfortunately, the judgment is extremely ambiguous on this point. On the one hand, the failure of the Court to mention the amending procedures in Part V, coupled with its disavowal of any supervisory role in constitutional negotiations, suggests that unwritten norms subject to political interpretation alone will guide the process of secession. The centrality of referenda to constitutional change, despite the lack of any textual support for that view, also lends support to this interpretation. On the other hand, the Court does consider constitutional changes as drastic as secession to still fall within the definition of a constitutional amendment (*Quebec Secession Reference, supra* note 1 at para. 84), and emphasizes that secession will require an amendment (ibid. at para. 97). Coupled with the Court's reference to "the applicability of various procedures to achieve lawful secession" (ibid. at para. 105), the Court might be suggesting that Part V will be engaged. However, even here, the Court does not identify the relevant amending formula, or even refer to Part V explicitly, suggesting that the existing formulas may be inadequate.

71 We owe this point to Amir Sperling.

72 This point was suggested to us by Annalise Acorn.

73 *Quebec Secession Reference, supra* note 1 at para. 1.

74 Ibid. at para. 67.

75 Ibid.

76 *Quebec Secession Reference, supra* note 1 at para. 33.

77 Ibid. at paras. 87, 92, 88. For a discussion of the challenge for constitutional interpretation posed by the coming apart of legitimacy and legality, and the need to have recourse to an adjudicative approach of the kind we describe in this article, see R.J. Howse & A. Malkin, "Canadians are a sovereign people: how the Supreme Court should approach the reference on Quebec secession" (1997) 76 Can Bar Rev 186.

78 *Legal Reasoning, supra* note 22 at 46.

79 *One Case at a Time, supra* note 69 at 11–12.

80 *Darwin's New Bulldog, supra* note 21.

81 *General Motors of Canada Ltd. v City National Leasing Ltd.*, [1989] 1 SCR 641; *R. v Crown Zellerbach Canada Ltd.*, [1988] 1 SCR 401; *Black v Law Society of Alberta*, [1989] 1 SCR 591; *De Savoye v Morguard Investments Ltd.*, [1990] 3 SCR 1077; *Hunt v T & N Plc*, [1993] 4 SCR 289.

READING QUESTION ON CHOUDHRY AND HOWSE

1 Choudhry and Howse argue that the Supreme Court rejected a positivist stance in the *Quebec Secession Reference* in order to restore the legitimacy of the constitutional order. They also claim that this restoration was achieved on the basis of legal principles – no step outside of the law was required. Is there a tension, even a contradiction, lurking here?

John Borrows
"Frozen Rights in Canada: Constitutional Interpretation and the Trickster" (1998)

Borrows and Macklem address the difficult issue of whether and how (if at all) the Canadian legal order can cope with the fundamental challenge posed by the aspirations of Aboriginal people.

The trickster is alive and well. The Supreme Court of Canada illustrated this in the recent cases of *R. v Vanderpeet*,[1] *R. v Gladstone*,[2] *R v N.T.C. Smokehouse*[3] and *R. v Pamajewon*[4] when it considered how it would define Aboriginal rights "recognized and affirmed" under section 35(1) of the Canadian Constitution.[5] Until these judgments were released, the country's highest court had supplied very little guidance concerning the test it would use to identify those rights protected by section 35(1). In 1982 Aboriginal rights were placed within Canada's newly patriated Constitutional Act, and outside of its Charter of Rights and Freedoms,[6] at the insistence of many Aboriginal governments.[7] Section 35(1) protected these rights by stating "[t]he existing [A]boriginal and treaty rights of the [A]boriginal people of Canada are hereby recognized and affirmed."[8] The problem with this language was that no one was quite sure what Aboriginal rights were, and therefore what, if anything, was being protected.[9]

After the failure to define these rights through four high profile First Ministers conferences, and a nationally negotiated Charlottetown Accord,[10] the task of defining Aboriginal rights passed to the country's highest Court. The Supreme Court of Canada's definitions of Aboriginal rights in these cases fell far short of the large, liberal and generous interpretations of Aboriginal rights considered throughout the political process,[11] and urged by previous court judgments.[12]

The Supreme Court was asked to consider the meaning of Aboriginal rights in the context of criminal charges brought against Aboriginal people under sections of the Fisheries Act and Criminal Code. In the *Pamajewon* case, charges were laid under the Canadian Criminal Code for keeping a common gaming house and conducting a scheme for the purposes of determining the winners of property.[13] The Canadian Supreme Court held that Aboriginal rights did not include "high stakes gambling" and were not a defense to the convictions entered under the Criminal Code. In the *Vanderpeet, Smokehouse* and *Gladstone* cases charges were laid under the Fisheries Act for exchanging fish for money without possessing a commercial fishing license. These cases were more varied in their results.

In *Vanderpeet* and *Smokehouse*, the Court held that these particular groups did not have an Aboriginal right to sell and exchange fish, while in *Gladstone* the Court ruled that the group in question did possess such a right. This latter ruling was significant in Canadian jurisprudence because for the first time the Court held that it is possible for Aboriginal peoples to possess commercial-like rights to harvest and sell resources within their territories. However, these rulings are also important because in arriving at these conclusions the Court seriously undermined the future commercial competitiveness and survival of Aboriginal nations in contemporary Canadian society. This comment will focus on the Court's partiality concerning the contemporary nature of Aboriginal rights.

First Nations have an intellectual tradition that teaches about ideas and principles that are partial and incomplete. The elders teach these traditions through a character known as the trickster.[14] He has various persona in different cultures. The Anishinabe (Ojibway) of the Great Lakes call the trickster Nanabush; the First Nations people of the coastal North-west know him as Raven; he is known as Glooscap by the Mi'kmaq of the Maritimes; and as Coyote, Crow, Wisakedjak, Badger, or Old Man among other First Nations people in North America. The trickster offers insights through encounters which are simultaneously altruistic and self-interested.[15] In his adventures the trickster roams from place to place and fulfills his goals by using ostensibly contradictory behaviors such as charm and cunning, honesty and deception, kindness and mean tricks.[16] The trickster also displays transformative power as he takes on new persona in the manipulation of these behaviors and in the achievement of his objectives.[17] Lessons are learned as the trickster engages in actions which in some particulars are representative of the listener's behavior, and on other points are uncharacteristic of their comportment.[18] The trickster encourages an awakening of understanding because listeners are compelled to interpret and reconcile the notion that their ideas may be partial. As such, the trickster assists people in conceiving of the limited viewpoint they possess. The trickster is able to kindle these understandings because his actions take place in a perplexing realm that partially escapes the structures of society and the order of cultural things.[19] The trickster's interaction with the Supreme Court of Canada demonstrates these insights.[20]

This comment draws upon this intellectual tradition and sites Nanabush as the center and edge of recent Aboriginal rights cases from the Supreme Court of Canada. It examines these judgements by alternatively interchanging Anishinabe and Canadian jurisprudential narratives and providing commentary on what this exchange reveals. The distinctions highlighted within these encounters accentuate where confusion, misinformation and self-contradiction appear in the Supreme Court's story about Aboriginal rights.[21] The trickster's unique placement generates a language between "western" and "Aboriginal" accounts of law[22] which incorporates intersecting and oppositional cultural perspectives.[23] Following this approach develops a perspicuous contrast, or vocabulary of comparison, between the Court's narration and First Nation understandings, and renders a clearer reflection on the appropriateness of the cases' analysis and effects.[24] Thus, this methodology simultaneously frames and centers the judgments as the trickster stands inside and outside the court, both as a member and as one of its critics. His appearance provides alternative constitutional interpretations,[25] and reveals the cultural construction and contingency of law.[26] The trickster's incongruous entry into legal discourse presents law from a perspective which is outside of the conventional structure of legal argument and exposes its hidden cultural (dis)order.[27]

SEEGWUN

Seegwun – spring. Nanabus is walking up a stream. Around his ankles the water breaks free and flees to the Nottawasaga River. Imprisoned as ice for too long it hurries its escape towards Georgian Bay and Lake Huron. He notices the water's rush is met by travelers going in the opposite direction. Fish run into and through the water's swollen charge. In the midst of his collision there are periods of rest. In a shallow pool Nanabush spots a solitary rainbow trout. He breaks the walls of a downstream beaver dam. He waits. Within a few minutes the water in the pool goes down. Trapped, the fish has nowhere to go. Another prisoner caught on life's precarious road. He walks towards it, slowly puts his fingers under its belly, and feels the weight of life within. Nanabush lifts the fish into the next pool and watches it swim away.

NEEBIN

Neebin – summer. Nine people are dressed in red, with white ermine framing their costumes. They are wearing their traditional regalia.[28] It is the members of the Supreme Court of Canada, asked to consider the meaning of Aboriginal rights in the context of criminal charges laid against Aboriginal people exchanging fish for money. Their Chief Justice, Antonio Lamer, is delegated to speak for the group. The Chief Justice steps into court. He notices that Aboriginal rights are "held by [A]boriginal people because they are [A]boriginal."[29] With this as his starting point, to define Aboriginal rights he is going to have to tell us what Aboriginal means. How is he going to do this? Maybe he knows what it means to be Aboriginal. He writes: "The Court must define the scope of section 35(1) in a way which captures both the [A]boriginal and the rights in [A]boriginal rights."[30] He will define Aboriginal by "capturing" the Aboriginal and the right? How is he going to do this? What will he do once he captures it? He searches for a purpose, that might help him. In the jurisprudential stream behind him, he sees a purposive rationale and a foundation to explain "the special status that [A]boriginal peoples have within Canadian society."[31] He pulls the sticks from this structure; a deluge ensues. Aboriginal rights in section 35(1) exist "because of one simple fact: when Europeans arrived in North America, [A]boriginal peoples were already here, living in communities on the land, and participating in distinctive cultures, as they had done for centuries."[32]

The Chief Justice is nearly washed away by this flood. When he pulled the sticks he was standing on the wrong side of their weir and could have been knocked over. If Aboriginal peoples have prior rights to land and participatory governance, how did the Crown and Court gain their right to adjudicate here? He has to stem the flow. He has to regain his footing. He plants a flag. "[A]boriginal rights recognized and affirmed by section 35(1) must be directed towards their reconciliation of the pre-existence of [A]boriginal societies with the sovereignty of the Crown."[33] He now has a purpose with which to capture both the Aboriginal and the right – "the reconciliation of pre-existing claims to the territory that now constitutes Canada, with the assertion of British sovereignty over that territory."[34] The assertion of non-aboriginal sovereignty provides familiar ground from which to define Aboriginal.[35]

Now comes the clairvoyant moment when he will tell us what Aboriginal means. He reaches his fingers into the cold stream of past decisions; but there is only one judgment he relies on to define Aboriginal. At his feet, in a shallow pool of reasoning, the Chief Justice finds the *Sparrow* Court's acknowledgment that the Aboriginal right to fish for food was considered to "ha[ve] always constituted an integral part of this distinctive culture."[36] From this solitary line, where the Court never doubted the Aboriginal's right to fish for food, the Chief Justice tells us what Aboriginal means, and by extension what rights Aboriginals possess. Aboriginal rights are those activities that are "integral to the distinctive culture of the [A]boriginal group claiming the right."[37] But what is integral to being Aboriginal, and claiming rights? He takes another step, and sets out to explain what is integral to Aboriginal people.

[T]he test for identifying the [A]boriginal rights recognized and affirmed by s[ection] 35(1) must be directed at identifying the crucial elements of those pre-existing distinctive societies. It must, in other words, aim at identifying the practices, traditions and customs central to the Aboriginal societies that existed in North America prior to contact with Europeans.[38]

Integral thus means central, significant, distinctive, defining. The Chief Justice notes: "a practical way of thinking about this problem is to ask whether, without this practice, tradition or custom, the culture in question would be fundamentally altered or other than what it WAS."[39]

With this test, as promised, Chief Justice Antonio Lamer has now told us what Aboriginal means. Aboriginal is retrospective. It is about what was, "once upon a time," central to the survival of community, not necessarily about what is central, significant and distinctive to the survival of these communities today. His test invites stories about the past.[40]

These stories speak about whether a protected Aboriginal right has its "origins pre-contact",[41] prior to the arrival of Europeans",[42] because "it is the fact that distinctive [A]boriginal societies lived on the land prior to the arrival of Europeans that underlies the [A]boriginal rights protected by section 35(1), it is to that pre-contact period that the courts must look in identifying [A]boriginal rights."[43] Aboriginal means a long time ago; pre-contact. Aboriginal rights protect only those customs which have continuity with practices existing before the arrival of Europeans. Aboriginal rights do not sustain central and significant Aboriginal practices which developed solely as a result of their contact with European cultures.[44] The jurisprudential dam is now back in place.

A stagnant pool is once again beginning to fill. With this judgment, the Chief Justice lifts the Aboriginal right and gently places it back in this pool, behind some of its centuries long, common law encumbrances. As he set out to do, he has captured both the Aboriginal and the right. Nanabush waits.

A NEW TEST FOR DEFINING ABORIGINAL RIGHTS

As the above account reveals, the Canadian Supreme Court developed its definition of Aboriginal rights by using a questionable definition of Aboriginality. However, the Court's initial inquiry was appropriate, as it sought to discover "the purposes behind section 35(1) as they relate to the scope of the rights the provision is intended to protect."[45] The Court properly found that the "special legal and constitutional status of [A]boriginal peoples" existed to reconcile "pre-existing [A]boriginal rights with the assertion of Crown sovereignty."[46]

Two reasons were advanced in support of this proposition. First, Aboriginal people enjoy Constitutional protection "because of one simple fact: when Europeans arrived in North America, [A]boriginal peoples were already here, living in communities on the land, and participating in distinctive cultures, as they had done for centuries."[47] Second, Aboriginal rights were also placed within the Constitution to reconcile the assertion of British sovereignty with the pre-existing rights of Aboriginal peoples.[48] The decision might not have been as troubling had the Court stopped there, since its reasons seem to recognize legal equality for Aboriginal people. However, in further searching for the intention behind the entrenchment of Aboriginal rights, the Court applied disturbing stereotypes of Aboriginal culture to frame the reconciliation it suggested. It defined Aboriginal practices "prior contact with Europeans" as the legally relevant date for reconciliation.[49] As a result, to establish an Aboriginal right, Aboriginal peoples have to demonstrate that the practices for which they seek protection are a "central and significant part of the society's distinctive culture,"[50] "prior to the arrival of Europeans."[51] In so ruling, the Court placed the protection those activities that developed solely as a result of European culture outside of the protection of the Canadian Constitution.[52] This was reflected in Nanabush's walk through the water, and the Chief Justice's walk through the jurisprudence. This decision relegated Aboriginal peoples to the backwaters of social development, deprived them of protection for practices that grew through intercultural exchange, and minimized the impact of Aboriginal rights on non-Aboriginal people.

In its reasons for judgment, the Court elaborated upon ten factors it would consider in the application of the integral to a distinctive culture test. These factors were articulated to provide guidance for future courts in defining Aboriginal rights. They form an important insight on how the Court developed the integral test. They also demonstrate the Court's limited cultural understanding of Indigenous communities.[53]

First, in applying this new test the Court noted that it must consider the perspective of Aboriginal peoples themselves on the meaning of the rights at stake. This factor for defining Aboriginal rights was first spoken of in the path-breaking case of *R. v Sparrow*[54] and was elaborated upon in *Vanderpeet*. While the *Sparrow* Court observed that the Aboriginal perspective on their rights was crucial, in *Vanderpeet* they modified this approach and stated that the Aboriginal perspective must be "framed in terms cognizable to the Canadian legal and constitutional structure,"[55] to incorporate both Aboriginal and non-Aboriginal legal perspectives. This reformulation substantially weakened the potential for Aboriginal claimants to express the law on their own terms, according to their own customs. To facilitate an understanding among Canadian judges, Aboriginal laws will need reframing and reinterpretation. This creates the very real danger of mischaracterizing Aboriginal law in order to make it "fit" another system, and thus not accurately protect the underlying context and reason for the rule's existence within the Aboriginal community.[56] Curiously, the Court reasoned that this approach best reconciles the prior occupation of Canada with Crown sovereignty because it bridges two legal perspectives.[57] It seems unusual that the Aboriginal perspective on the meaning of their rights must incorporate non-Aboriginal legal perspectives. One would think that the Aboriginal perspective is needed precisely because the non-Aboriginal perspective does not effectively reconcile the prior occupation of Canada with assertions of Crown sovereignty. In the end, however, even the limited protection of a mediated Aboriginal perspective may provide few benefits for Aboriginal litigants, as the Court failed to invoke the Aboriginal perspective of the rights in question in its subsequent decisions of *Pamajewon, R. v Cote*[58] and *R. v Adams*.[59]

The second factor the Court identified in determining integral Aboriginal practices concerns the nature of the claim being made. The Court narrowed the nature of claim being put forward, as it often does when considering collective rights.[60] The Chief Justice wrote that to define integral Aboriginal rights one must identify the precise nature of the claim to determine whether the evidence provided supports its recognition. The correct characterization of a claim involved three considerations: "the nature of the action which the applicant [was] claiming was done pursuant to an [A]boriginal right, the nature of the governmental regulation, statute or action being impugned, and the tradition, custom or practice being relied upon to establish the right."[61] The application of these steps in determining the precise nature of the claim asserted was a very significant activity in all four cases. The Court's characterization of the claim in some instances changed the very question the people were attempting to litigate.[62]

For example, in *Pamajewon* it would not be an unfair reading of the case to observe that the appellants were asserting a right to self-government. However, since rights to Indian self-government have not yet been explicitly recognized in Canadian jurisprudence,[63] the Supreme Court considered that assertions of Aboriginal rights to self-government were cast at a level of "excessive generality."[64] The Court observed that if section 35(1) rights encompass claims to self-government, which it did not decide, one must consider these claims in the light of specific practices integral to the pre-contact Aboriginal culture. The Court's re-characterization of the right illustrated its unwillingness to consider self-government rights on any general basis.

This approach defeats many Aboriginal peoples' aspirations for a fuller articulation of powers relative to the federal and provincial governments.[65] It is clear that the current Court was unwilling to consider Aboriginal rights to self-government on any global basis. Thus, in the *Pamajewon* case, the precise nature of the right was characterized as a right to "participate in, and to regulate, high stakes gambling activities on the reservation."[66] The Court rejected this claim as an Aboriginal right and refused to consider it on a broader basis.

Similarly, in the *Vanderpeet* and *Smokehouse* cases, the Court also narrowed the consideration of the claimed practice to a more precise articulation of the potential right. These two cases held that the most accurate characterization of the Aboriginal position consisted of a right "to exchange fish for money or other goods."[67] Since the evidence in these cases did not support this more limited right, it was not necessary to consider the nature of this right at a more general level. However, in the *Gladstone* case, compelling evidence existed that the sale and exchange of fish was integral to the Nation's culture, and thus the Court looked even further to determine whether there was an associated Aboriginal right to trade on a commercial basis. It found that such a right existed, which was a significant finding because it confirmed that Aboriginal peoples can possess constitutionally-protected commercial rights. By holding that an Aboriginal right could exist at this level of generality, the Court held out a thin thread of hope for Aboriginal peoples seeking more encompassing rights. The *Gladstone* case demonstrated that precise rights to a practice may also evidence more general rights. This step by step approach to defining Aboriginal rights underlines the Court's hesitancy to articulate them more broadly.

The third factor the Court considered in the application of the integral to a distinctive culture test concerned the centrality of the practice to the group claiming the right. The majority wrote that "the claimant must demonstrate that the practice, tradition or custom was a central and significant part of the society's distinctive culture."[68] As noted previously, to have a practice protected as a right the group must show that the activity was distinctive – a defining feature of the culture." A practical way of thinking about this problem is to ask whether, without this practice, tradition or custom, the culture in question would be fundamentally altered or other than what it [was]."[69] This element of the Court's test was based on a passage in *Sparrow* where the Musqueam right to fish for food was stated to "ha[ve] always constituted an integral part of their distinctive culture".[70]

One might question whether it was appropriate for the Court in *Vanderpeet* to develop its test for the definition of Aboriginal rights from these observations, since the Aboriginal right to fish for food in *Sparrow* was never open to serious question. Furthermore, in the same paragraph, the *Sparrow* Court also wrote, with equal authority, that the Musqueam "always fished for reasons connected to their cultural and physical survival", and noted that "the right to do so may be exercised in a contemporary manner."[71] This raises an additional question about why, in *Vanderpeet*, notions of survival and the contemporary exercise of rights did not form part of the integral to a distinctive culture test, since the idea of "integral" in *Sparrow* included the contemporary exercise of rights necessary for physical and cultural survival. Aboriginal rights should exist to ensure Indigenous peoples' physical and cultural survival, not necessarily to preserve distinctive elements of pre-contact culture. The acceptance of these considerations would have strengthened Aboriginal peoples interactions with other Canadians, and been more consistent with the Court's previous rulings.

The fourth factor the Court articulated in determining whether an Aboriginal practice is integral to distinctive culture was whether they had continuity with the activities which existed "prior to the arrival of the Europeans in North America."[72] The focus on pre-contact practices restricts contemporary Aboriginal development. The rights of other Canadians are not limited to those practices which have continuity with their activities prior to their first arrival in North America. They would find such a limitation as the gravest form of injustice. However, for the Court this factor was relevant to defining Aboriginal rights "[b]ecause it [was] the fact that distinctive [A]boriginal societies lived on the land prior to the arrival of Europeans that underlies the [A]boriginal rights protected by section 35(1), it [was] to that pre-contact period that the courts must look in identifying [A]boriginal rights."[73] The two dissenting judgments criticized this part of the majority's test as "freezing" Aboriginal rights, contrary to the admonition found within *Sparrow*.[74] Justice L'Heureux-Dubé noted that the definition of Aboriginal rights by reference to pre-contact practices inappropriately crystallized Aboriginal rights at an arbitrary date.[75] She argued this was contrary to the perspective of Aboriginal peoples, and overstated the impact of European influence on Aboriginal peoples.[76] Similarly, Justice McLachlin stated that the majority's failure to recognize the distinction between rights and contemporary form "freeze[s] [A]boriginal societies in their ancient modes and den[ies] to them the right to adapt, as all peoples must, to the changes in the society in which they live."[77] These dissenting judgments implicitly recognize the inequity in creating non-Aboriginal rights following contact and not extending the same entitlement to Aboriginal peoples.

After exploring the above four factors relevant to the application of the integral to a distinctive culture test in some detail, the Court breezed through a list of six other considerations appropriate to defining Aboriginal rights. They wrote that in defining Aboriginal rights "[t]he courts must not undervalue the evidence presented by the [A]boriginal claimants," simply because it did not conform precisely with evidentiary standards in private litigation.[78] This was an important subsidiary qualification in defining integral rights noted in the ancient practices because difficulties will arise in obtaining certain evidence of pre-contact European practices.[79] The Court eased the evidentiary burden by this admonishment.

The Court then stated that claims to Aboriginal rights were not general and universal, but related to the specific history of the group claiming the right.[80] The Court's failure to articulate general features of Aboriginal claims prevented their expansion. If claimants cannot rely on the victories of other communities, because cases may always be distinguishable through particular histories, then this provides very little basis for Aboriginal peoples to build a principled, protective jurisprudence. Yet, despite this disadvantage the Chief Justice wrote that "[t]he fact that one group of [A]boriginal people has an [A]boriginal right to do a particular thing will not be, without something more, sufficient to demonstrate that another Aboriginal community has the same [A]boriginal right."[81] While there was a certain amount of truth in this statement that Aboriginal rights are fact and site specific, these reasons ignore a more global basis for Aboriginal rights. "Aboriginal rights are rooted in an overarching jurisprudential infrastructure ... First Nation's laws are integral to the exercise of all Aboriginal rights."[82] The Court failed to recognize that one right that all Aboriginal peoples possess as an integral right was their organization in societies according to their traditions, customs and laws.[83] The organization and laws of Aboriginal peoples were universally protected as something each group could successfully claim, though it was true their content varied from group to group.

A seventh factor to consider in applying the integral test was that the claimed practice contain independent significance to the community, and not be a mere incidence to another tradition. Without providing justification or reasons the Court wrote that "[i]ncidental practices, customs and traditions cannot qualify as [A]boriginal rights through a process of piggybacking on integral practices, customs and traditions."[84] This assertion seems contrary to the Court's earlier ruling in *R. v Simon*, where incidental practices were protected as Aboriginal rights.[85] It also suggests that, while the Court was willing to protect independent rights in the abstract, it was unwilling to preserve the place and means necessary to make the exercise or rights meaningful. Only the culture will reveal if and how the Court will resolve this seeming contradiction.

The other three factors the Court identified as important in determining Aboriginal rights involved the "distinctive" nature of the Aboriginal practice.[86] A distinctive practice is one that does not arise solely as a response to European influences,[87] and which can arise separately from the Aboriginal group's relationship to the land.[88] Distinctiveness and the European influence on Aboriginal rights have been touched upon elsewhere in this comment and will receive no further attention at this point. However, the idea that Aboriginal rights may arise not only from prior occupation of land, but from the prior social organization and distinctive cultures of Aboriginal people is novel. Prior to these cases it was not clear whether Aboriginal rights arose only through claims to Aboriginal title.[89] Now it is clear that Aboriginal title does not necessarily need the requisite proof to sustain other Aboriginal rights. Section 35(1) of the Constitution is emerging as the most relevant criteria in defining Aboriginal rights in Canada. The subsequent Supreme Court cases of *Adams* and *Cote* followed this approach, wherein it was held that Aboriginal peoples in Quebec could claim food fishing rights, even if they had not established Aboriginal title in the area in question.[90]

The net effect of these ten considerations is to circumscribe Aboriginal rights and bring them more fully under the cultural assumptions of the common law. They establish non-Aboriginal characterizations of Aboriginality,[91] evidence,[92] and law[93] as the standards against which Aboriginal rights are measured. Taken together, these factors compel the conformity of Aboriginal rights to "western" formulations of law in order to find recognition and affirmation in Canada's constitution. This creates problems for Aboriginal groups since these norms are generally not sensitive to the Aboriginal perspective on the meaning of the rights at stake[94] and consequently constrain the reception of Aboriginal viewpoints. Yet, the Court should not interpret these rights in such an inflexible and narrow manner.[95] The trickster conveys this principle.

TAHWAHGI

Tahwahgi – Fall. The Couchiching Narrows, Orillia, Ontario. Nanabush has recently presided over the opening of the casino on the Chippewas of the Rama reservation. Confined for over a century, Anishinabe self-government has escaped federalism's cells and now spills into the surrounding communities. Over one-hundred thousand people travel to Rama and drop quarters in the Casino's well. The Woodland art of its outer walls encloses the interaction of mean tricks and kindness, help and neglect, charm and cunning. The rush to get into self-government's outward flow has its periods of rest too. Nanabush takes the three minutes walk to the Lake. On the water the boat's sails hang loosely. For 4000 years an Aboriginal weir raked these Narrows to trap fish behind its wooden bars. Now behind the Lake's shores the fingers of a new presence reach out. Nanabus looks back towards it; thinks about how he placed it perfectly. Buses disgorge their contents, cars and trains arrive every few minutes, the people of the reserve are also swept into its flow; its grasp is extensive.

North of Rama, Chief Justice Antonio Lamer presides over the fate of two casinos on the Shawanaga and Eagle Lake reservations. It is the *Pamajewon* case. The communities have risked asking the Court to rule that Aboriginal rights to self-government include high-stakes gambling. The outward rush into these communities is just beginning to build. The land is cleared for a new gaming hall and hotel, and signs on the highway announce the arrival of monster bingo. The Chief Justice takes a thirty-two paragraph stroll around the place. With *Vanderpeet* as a companion – a "legal standard against which the appellants' claim must be measured"[96] – he tells us the character of Aboriginal rights. Once again he gets to decide the character traits. He not only defines the character of an Aboriginal, he defines the character of an entire Aboriginal community. How is he going to do this? Can he identify the character of another culture? He consults his companion. *Vanderpeet* has some words of advice: change the characterization of what the Aboriginal people are claiming. The Chief Justice agrees; that makes it easier. He confides:

To characterize an applicant's claim correctly, a court should consider such factors as the nature of the action which the applicant is claiming was done pursuant to an [A]boriginal right, the nature of the governmental regulation, statute or action being impugned, and the tradition, custom or practice being relied upon to establish the right.[97]

The Chief Justice provides three factors to consider in developing the correct characterization of a claim, there is no mention of standards by which one should judge these factors. What principles will guide judgments about the characterization of these factors? Should Aboriginal claims be characterized in a large, liberal and generous manner,[98] with sensitivity to the "[A]boriginal perspective on the meaning of the rights at state"?[99] Nope. No mention of that here. With that out of the way, the Chief Justice provides his own characterization of what is being claimed.

He walks on. The people want him to see how the band participates in deciding who lives where on the reserve, and under what conditions. He is invited to tour the band council office, read their governing bylaws, see how the people depend on them. He declines. He stays out near the road. The Chief Justice turns his attention to the empty casino land, sees the monster being advertised. In the next breath, he states, "When these factors are considered in this case it can be seen that the correct characterization of the applicants' claim [is] that they [are] claiming the right to participate in, and to regulate, high stakes gambling activities on the reservation".[100] His short promenade sidesteps claims about Aboriginal rights to self-government. "The appellants themselves would have this Court characterize their claim as to 'a broad right to manage the use of their reserve lands.' To so characterize the appellants' claim would be to cast the Court's inquiry at a level of excessive generality."[101] This is a comfortable pace. One needs to get a little exercise, but no use over-extending yourself. "The factors laid out in *Vanderpeet*, and applied, *supra*, allow the Court to consider the appellants' claim at the appropriate level of specificity; the characterization put forward by the appellants would not allow the Court to do so."[102] It is too high a level of generality to think that Aboriginal people would actually have a broad right to manage the use of their own lands.

The Chief Justice is almost through with his visit. It is getting dark. He just has something to dispose of before he leaves – whether Shawanaga and Eagle Lake's "participation in, and regulation of, gambling on reserve lands was an integral part of their distinctive culture."[103] The evidence "d[oes] not demonstrate that gambling , or that the regulation of gambling, was of central significance to the Ojibway people." Prior to contact, informal gambling activities took place on a "small scale." The Chief Justice refers to a prior visitor: "I also agree with the observation made by Flaherty Prov. Ct. J ... commercial lotteries such as bingo [were] a twentieth century phenomena and nothing of the kind existed amongst [A]boriginal peoples and was never part of the means by which these societies were traditionally sustained or socialized."[104] Done. End of the trail. The claim is defeated since Anishinabe gambling, prior to contact, was not done on a twentieth century scale. Hardly surprising that this standard of evidence could not be met. Not many activities in any society, prior to this century, took place on a twentieth-century scale. It is a good thing the rights of other Canadians do not depend on whether such rights were important to them two to three hundred years ago. What would it be like for Canadians to have their fundamental rights defined by what *was* integral to European people's distinctive culture prior to their arrival in North America?[105]

The door slams. The Chief Justice drives away. Self-government will serve more time in isolation, locked within federalism's cells. Very few people will visit Shawanaga and Eagle Lake, even fewer will leave their money behind. The people of Shawanaga and Eagle Lake will not spend the rest of their lives, and that of their children's children, caught inside a casino.[106] The fresh October wind is brisk. Clear. Orange and yellow leaves dance in this breeze, and mimic the setting autumn sun. A walk to shore reveals Indian fishers pulling in their nets. Whitefish and trout will be served tonight. Lake Huron has witnessed this activity for centuries. No buses, trains or cars crowding the life out of the community. No new presence – no grasping; quiet settles back into the familiar rhythms of activity.

AN ALTERNATIVE BASIS FOR THE CONSTITUTIONAL ENTRENCHMENT OF ABORIGINAL RIGHTS

As the preceding account reveals, the idea that Aboriginal peoples will have to base the source and temporal roots of their rights in their historic presence – their ancestry – in North America and reconcile these with Crown sovereignty is disputed.[107] As Justice McLachlin noted in dissent,

Aboriginal rights find their source not in a magic moment of European contact, but in the traditional laws and customs of the [A]boriginal people in question ... One finds no mention in the text of s[ection] 35(1) or in the jurisprudence of the moment of European contact as the definitive all-or-nothing time for establishing an [A]boriginal right.[108]

Even the majority judgment in these cases mentioned the fact that traditional laws and customs were the basis for Aboriginal rights.[109] The current Supreme Court test defines Aboriginal rights as those rooted in practices which were central to their societies prior to the arrival of European culture, and not solely a result of European influence. Therefore, if the purposes underlying the existence of section 35(1) in the Constitution were even slightly differently conceived, then the test defining an Aboriginal right would vary accordingly. This was illustrated in Nanabush and the Chief Justice's visit to the casino.

Furthermore, the Aboriginal right's nexus to "crucial elements" of pre-existing societies is, in the words of Justice McLachlin, too broad a characterization of the rights, too indeterminate and too categorical.[110] The first criticism of this new test involved the over-broad denotation because "integral is a wide concept, capable of embracing virtually everything that an Aboriginal people customarily did."[111] Moreover, the integral test is too indeterminate because "one encounters the problem that different people may entertain different ideas of what is distinctive, specific or central. To use such concepts as the markers of legal rights is to permit the determination of rights to be coloured by the subjective views of the decision maker."[112] Finally, the integral to a distinctive culture test is inappropriately categorical because "[w]hether something is integral is an all or nothing test. Once it is concluded that a practice is integral to the people's culture, the right to pursue it obtains unlimited protection, subject only to the Crown's right to impose limits on the grounds of justification."[113]

An alternative basis for defining Aboriginal rights is the common law's recognition of the ancestral laws and customs "of the [A]boriginal peoples who occupied land prior to European settlement."[114] This basis for Aboriginal rights is preferred to that of the majority because it is more in line with the existing case law and the "time honoured methodology of the common law."[115] Under this new methodology, the Court would evaluate new situations by reference to what the law recognized in the past. The Chief Justice did not follow this methodology, but engaged in a more theoretical approach to Aboriginal rights which reasoned from broad principles which found little or no support in past judgments. On the other hand, Madam Justice McLachlin's methodology and reasons followed a "golden thread" of case law which defined the nature and incidents of Aboriginal rights by reference to the laws and customs of Indigenous people.[116] Her reasons led her to hold that the purpose of section 35(1) was, first, to protect the existing customary laws and rights of Aboriginal peoples and, second, to ensure that such customs and rights remain in the Aboriginal people until extinguished or surrendered by treaty. These two principles, according to McLachlin, were supported by the common law and history, and "may safely be said to be enshrined in s[ection] 35(1) of the Constitution Act, 1982."[117] Thus for McLachlin, since Aboriginal rights rested on Aboriginal laws, section 35(1) must define these rights by reference to these pre-existing laws.

Yet, the Chief Justice's test defines Aboriginal rights according to stereotypical perceptions of Aboriginal characteristics, rather than by their nature and source. This approach freezes the development of certain Aboriginal practices in the distant past. For example, under the Chief Justice's reasoning, an Aboriginal right does not include Aboriginal hunting rights to sell and exchange furs because some argue this practice developed solely as a result of European influence.[118] This understanding of Aboriginal rights cannot be correct. The idea that Aboriginal people do not have rights which developed solely in response to European influences is contrary to the history and the very possibility of the exploration and early development of many parts of North America.[119] This restriction of Aboriginal rights goes against the Chief Justice's own observation that the rights developed from the "peculiar meeting of two vastly different legal cultures."[120] If Aboriginal rights developed through the meeting of two cultures, then surely those practices which resulted solely in response to European culture must encompass this legal regime. Otherwise, it is difficult to see how the law is "intersocietal."[121] Early European presence in North America would have been frustrated if Aboriginal people did not have rights to hunt and trade because some of these practices developed through contact with Europeans. Europeans relied on the profit from the fur trade and would have been seriously handicapped in asserting sovereignty in North America if Aboriginal people had no rights to sell furs to them.[122] Furthermore, Aboriginal people themselves would have also rebelled or refused to trade if anyone would have seriously suggested that they had no rights to exchange or sell animals.[123] Such a policy would have undermined one of the principal reasons underlying colonial policy in the settlement of Canada found in the Royal Proclamation's assertion that the "[t]rade with the said Indians shall be free and open to all."[124] As such, the Lamer's holding does not comport with history or Aboriginal law if the development of Crown/Aboriginal relations, which he himself described as "intersocietal law," was predicated on this denial of the continued development of Aboriginal practices solely as a result of European influence.[125]

To take away the possibility that Aboriginal laws, traditions and practices could develop and receive protection as rights in relation to the appearance of European cultures is to take away the means to allow Aboriginal people to compete on the same basis, with equal power, with the settling peoples. Why is it that European laws, practices and traditions, some of which developed solely through contact with Aboriginal peoples, are allowed to grow and develop from the moment of contact, while Aboriginal laws and practices, which also developed from the same moment of contact, are stifled in their progression? Such a holding is contrary to the Chief Justice's assertion that "the essence of [A]boriginal rights is their bridging of [A]boriginal and non-[A]boriginal cultures."[126] To accomplish this bridging of cultures and truly render the Aboriginal perspective of Aboriginal rights in terms "cognizable to Canadian law," as required by Lamer in the *Vanderpeet* case, true reconciliation requires those in power to give "equal weight" to Aboriginal law.[127]

The downgrading of Aboriginal rights is even more apparent in the greater power given to Canadian governments to infringe Aboriginal rights in these cases. In *Gladstone*, the majority provided strong obiter dicta stating that Aboriginal rights must be capable of being limited and, as such, could be infringed by justifiable government legislation.[128] This potentially widens the government's power to interfere with Aboriginal rights. Justifiable legislative objectives could include "the pursuit of economic and regional fairness, and the recognition of the historic reliance upon, and participation in, the fishery by non-[A]boriginal groups."[129] This further potential for the infringement of Aboriginal rights must be considered in the light of the fact that government already has a generous two-step chance for justifying interference with Aboriginal rights outlined in *Sparrow*.[130] The concern that motivated the widening of permissible legislative infringement in *Gladstone* was the lack of any inherent limitation for Aboriginal people on the exercise of their rights. This concern is curious, from an Aboriginal perspective, because there are imitations placed on these rights – the laws and traditions of Aboriginal peoples.[131] Aboriginal peoples have laws which dictate the appropriate exercise of a right.[132] Furthermore, non-Aboriginal peoples exercise exclusive rights all the time. In fact, exclusive rights are one of the distinguishing features of western legal ,systems. Why should an extra concern arise when Aboriginal peoples exercise exclusive rights? What can explain the concern in assigning Aboriginal peoples exclusive rights, when the Court generally shows no anxiety when allotting them to non-Aboriginal peoples?

The Chief Justice's failure to place equal weight on Aboriginal practices, customs and traditions contradicts his stated purpose for the inclusion of section 35(1) in the Constitution. The downgrading of Aboriginal practices severely constrains true reconciliation between the assertion of Crown sovereignty and the pre-existing rights of Aboriginal peoples. Reconciliation usually requires that each party to a relationship concede something to the other, and the majority's test does not require any relinquishment on the part of the Crown in accomplishing this objective. Lamer's test compels only Aboriginal peoples to give something up in reconciling the assertion of Crown sovereignty with pre-existing Aboriginal occupation. For example, the integral to a distinctive culture test requires Aboriginal peoples to concede any protection for practices which may have developed solely as response to European cultures. Yet since the adoption of new practices, traditions and laws in response to new influences is integral to the survival of Aboriginal communities, reconciliation should not require a concession of those practices which allow them to survive as a contemporary community.[133] By limiting Aboriginal rights to integral practices not developed solely as a result of European influences, the Court is denying these cultures the right to survive by adapting to new situations never before encountered. This test appears to work against Aboriginal peoples competing on an equal footing within Canadian society, and extinguishes their contemporary vigor as dynamic, competitive communities. Surely the Chief Justice could not have meant to uphold such a result for the avowed noble purpose underlying section 35(1) of the Constitution.[134] Once again, the trickster's engagement with the Court can help identify whether the Court has upheld such a purpose.

PEEBON

Peebon – Winter. Frozen nights. Peebon's return always brings hardship, decay and dissolution. His perpetual defeat of Neebin withers the plants, hardens the ground and sends white beings through the skies. With his approach the animals sleep, and fish return to deep lakes escaping the rivers' congealing arteries. To the north, the ancient grandfathers retreat to their lodges. Their fires reflect on the sky – blue, white and cold red, and illuminate the path of souls for those traveling to the land of the dead. Some time will pass before the grandfathers' voices again accompany the clouds and let their fire fall across the earth. For now, they remain in their lodges, protect their fires, and await the return of Neebin. Peebon and Neebin's perpetual quest for supremacy continually enforces this cycle on the Anishinabe. While Peebon is in the ascendancy, Nanabush looks for ways to steal fire from the grandfathers, to bring it back to the Anishinabe and keep them warm.

Peebon's frigid sovereignty has wide dominion. Aboriginal practices that developed solely as a response to European culture are now frozen, courtesy of the "integral test." How can one reconcile this with Chief Justice Antonio Lamer's own observation that Aboriginal rights developed form the "peculiar meeting of two vastly different legal cultures."[135] Nanabush stalks the land and looks for ways to steal fire.

He approaches the common law warily. He might get burned. With suspicion that comes from experience, he knows the danger of trying to take something of value from that which can harm him so greatly. Yet he is both brave and foolish, so he tries.

Nanabush reasons that if Aboriginal rights emerged through the meeting of two legal cultures, then Aboriginal rights must be litigated by reference to both societies' laws. The Chief Justice would appear to agree: "[T]he law of [A]boriginal rights is neither English or [A]boriginal in origin: it is a form of intersocietal law that evolved from long-standing practices linking the various communities."[136] Yet, despite this endorsement of Aboriginal law, in developing the "integral to a distinctive culture" test Nanabush observes that the Chief Justice did not consult or apply Sto:lo, Nuu-Chah-Nulth, Heiltsuk or Ojibway law in defining Aboriginal rights under section 35(1) of the Constitution.[137]

While the Court asserted that Aboriginal rights are based on traditional laws and customs "passed down, and arising from, the pre-existing culture and customs of [A]boriginal peoples,"[138] nowhere in these cases does the Chief Justice use the laws of the people charged, or the laws of any other Aboriginal people, to arrive at the standards through which he will define these rights.[139] As such, the Court does not use "intersocietal" law in developing its test for Aboriginal rights.[140] In so observing Nanabush has peered into the fire and found a branch sufficiently dense in its grain to keep a flame burning while he brings it back home to his people.

Nanabush reaches in through the smoke and observes that the Chief Justice engaged in an abstract, theoretical approach to define Aboriginal rights. He did not fully reference the "long-standing practices linking the various communities" in defining Aboriginal rights.[141] Vacuous reasons about section 35(1) reconciling Crown assertions of sovereignty with the fact that Aboriginal peoples were here first, may at the most elementary level qualify as an application of intersocietal law. However, the idea that this reconciliation should take place upon contact finds no support in either Aboriginal or non-Aboriginal law. It is the Chief Justice's invention. Nanabush has firmly grasped the branch and taken it from the fire. The smoke is clearing. Nanabush then finds a confederate, quoting from Madam Justice McLachlin's dissent in *Vanderpeet*, he states:

Aboriginal rights find their source not in a magic moment of European contact, but in the traditional laws and customs of the [A]boriginal people in question ... One finds no mention in the text of s[ection] 35(1), or in the jurisprudence, of the moment of European contact as the definitive all-or-nothing time for establishing an [A]boriginal right.[142]

Nanabush finds in this statement a more substantial basis upon which to define Aboriginal rights. A "morally and politically defensible conception of [A]boriginal rights will incorporate both legal perspectives."[143] The development of the "integral to a distinctive culture test" does not incorporate either legal perspective because neither the common law nor Aboriginal law held that the "moment of European contact" was the "definitive" time for establishing an Aboriginal right.

It is now time for Nanabush to run for home. The fires of his people are almost extinguished. What he has found may re-kindle them. The common law's recognition of Aboriginal ancestral laws and customs, and their continual evolution and interaction with the Crown, is preferred as a basis for defining Aboriginal rights because it is more in line with the existing case law and the "time honoured methodology of the common law."[144] This methodology follows a "golden thread" of case law which defines the nature and incidents of Aboriginal rights by reference to the laws and customs of Indigenous people.[145] This methodology also fans the embers of Aboriginal law and encourages its development as a greater source of authority for Aboriginal and non-Aboriginal Canadians.[146] With this basis for defining Aboriginal rights, the purpose of section 35(1) becomes truly "intersocietal." It also strengthens the continued interaction of these laws because Constitutional protection of the existing customary laws and rights of Aboriginal peoples ensures that such customs and rights remain in the Aboriginal people until extinguished or surrendered by treaty. Since Aboriginal rights rest on Aboriginal laws, section 35(1) must define these rights by reference to these pre-existing laws.

While Nanabush steals fire, Peebon's chilling pervasiveness is felt all around. Nanabush's solitary actions may not be enough to help the thaw. The Supreme Court of Canada's interpretations of Aboriginal rights remain restrictive and burdensome. The integral to a distinctive culture test freezes the protection of practices which may have developed solely as response to European cultures. Yet the adoption of new practices, traditions and laws in response to new influences is always integral to the survival of any community in its relations with another. Reconciliation should not require Aboriginal peoples to concede those practices which allow them to survive as a contemporary community.

However, the Court's new test threatens Aboriginal cultures precisely on this point, since in adapting to new situations they do not have protection for the practices devised in meeting challenges solely as a result of European influence.[147] Such a restriction is contrary to the Chief Justice's assertion that "equal weight" be placed on Aboriginal law[148] by rendering it in terms "cognizable to Canadian law." The "integral to a distinctive culture" test does not place equal weight on traditional Aboriginal law,[149] and denies legal equality to Aboriginal peoples in their relationship with Canada.[150]

Peebon remains ascendant. His icy embrace chills. The dissolution and decay continue. Throughout the land Aboriginal practices are coldly suspended. Have to wait for the thaw again. It may be a long winter.

CONCLUSION

This comment has attempted to show how Aboriginal rights in Canada's Constitution remain partial and incomplete. The Court's integral to a distinctive culture test does not extend protection to Aboriginal practices that developed solely as a result of European influence – even if those practices are crucial to their contemporary physical and cultural survival. Surely this result is less than a full recognition and affirmation of Aboriginal rights. Aboriginal peoples are entitled to expect legal protection for their existence as communities and nations within North America. Otherwise, what is the value of entrenching Aboriginal rights in the Constitution if the societies these rights were meant to protect cannot survive? Canadian courts have not yet come to terms with the fact that, like others, Aboriginal people are traditional, modern and post-modern. Physical and cultural survival depends as much on attracting legal protection for contemporary activities, as it does on gaining recognition for traditional practices. The courts need to recognize that Aboriginal rights attach to Aboriginal activities, whether making moccasins or marketing computers. It is not specific practices that are necessarily important to the definition of Aboriginal rights; what counts in determining Aboriginal rights is whether these practices contribute to the survival of the group. The rights exist first and foremost to protect the group, and are only incidentally concerned with the protection of specific practices. However, the courts are operating under the assumption that protecting specific "[A]boriginal" activities satisfies the Constitutional purpose for the entrenchment of Aboriginal rights (and they get to decide what is Aboriginal). They do not interpret Aboriginal in a "large, liberal and generous manner," with "sensitivity to the [A]boriginal perspective on the meaning of the rights at stake."[151] Thus, they interpret Aboriginal in an incomplete way, and do not take account of their physical and cultural survival in North America.

The courts need to embrace broader notions of Indian rights. As I have tried to demonstrate, Native peoples of the Americas can use their intellectual traditions to assist in this venture. Our ideologies and approaches to law may yield important insights on the partiality of current legal discourse. The trickster's deployment represents one such methodology and illustrates the relevance of First Nations inquiry in understanding the law. Indigenous traditions are not static and their strength lies in their ability to survive through the power of tribal memory and renew themselves by incorporating new elements.[152] By intermingling these approaches with the law, the trickster and other traditions can speak as strongly to the continent's dominant legal institutions, as they can to long-standing tribal relationships. Their vitality and authenticity points us beyond ourselves.[153] Their power lies not in how closely they adhere to their original form, but in how well they are able to develop and remain relevant under changing circumstances.[154]

Aboriginal ideologies are jurisprudentially relevant in reflecting upon the law in its general and specific contexts. Aboriginal ideologies, like Aboriginal practices, are not frozen. Their practice is integral to the distinctive culture of Aboriginal people today, even if these narratives may have developed as a result of colonial influence. Their use is vital to physical and cultural survival. The trickster is alive and well. His travels, insights and experiences still have much to teach us about this survival.

NOTES

* B.A., M.A., LL.B., LL.M., D.Jur., Associate Professor and Director of First Nations Legal Studies, Faculty of Law at the University of British Columbia, of the Chippewas of the Nawash, Ojibway/Anishinabe Nation. Thanks to Joel Bakan, Susan Boyd, Christine Boyle, Ron Delisle, Doug Harris, Sakej Henderson, Nitya Iyer, Alan Manson, Kent McNeil, David Schneiderman, and Don Stuart for their encouragement and comments on earlier drafts of this article.

1 137 DLR 4th 289, 9 WWR 1 (Can. 1996). In *Vanderpeet* the accused was charged under section 61(1) of the Fisheries Act, RSC ch. F-14 (1970), with selling salmon caught under the authority of an Indian food fishing license, contrary to section 27(5) of the British Columbia Fishery (General) Regulations at SOR/84–248, which prohibited the sale or barter of fish caught under such a license.

2 137 DLR 4th 648, 9 WWR 1 (Can. 1996). In *Gladstone* the accused was charged under section 61(1) of the Fisheries Act with attempting to sell herring spawn on kelp caught under the authority of an Indian food fish license, contrary to the same regulations used to charge *Vanderpeet*, and of attempting to sell herring spawn on kelp caught without a license, contrary to section 20(3) of the Pacific Herring Fishery Regulations at SOR/83–324.

3 137 DLR 4th 528, 9 WWR 114 (Can. 1996). In *Smokehouse* the accused was an incorporated company which owned and operated a food processing plant. They were charged under section 61(1) of the Fisheries Act with selling and purchasing fish not caught under the authority of a commercial fishing license, contrary to section 4(5) of the British Columbia (General) Regulations, and of selling and purchasing fish contrary to section 27(5) of these same regulations.

4 138 DLR 4th 204 (Can. 1996). In *Pamajewon* the accused were charged under sections 201(1) and 206(1) of the Criminal Code with the offense of keeping a common gaming house and conducting a scheme for the purposes of determining the winners of property.

5 Section 35(1) states: "The existing [A]boriginal and treaty rights of the [A]boriginal peoples of Canada are hereby recognized and affirmed." Canadian Charter of Rights and Freedoms, Part I of the Constitution Act, 1982, being Schedule B to the Canadian Act of 1982, (U.K.), 1982, ch. 11. For information on the enactment of section 35(1), see Brian Slattery, "The Constitutional Guarantee of Aboriginal and Treaty Rights," 8 Queen's LJ 232 (1983); Kent McNeil, "The Constitutional Rights of the Aboriginal Peoples of Canada," 4 Sup Ct L Rev 255 (1982); Douglas Sanders, "The Rights of the Aboriginal Peoples of Canada," 61 Can Bar Rev 314 (1983).

6 Aboriginal rights were placed outside of the Canadian Charter to shield collective Aboriginal rights from erosion due to its individualist orientation. See William Pentney, "The Rights of the Aboriginal Peoples of Canada and the Constitution Act 1982," Part I: "The Interpretive Prism of s. 25," 22 UBC L Rev 21 (1988). Section 25 of the Constitutional Act reflects this concern:

> The guarantee in this Charter of certain rights and freedoms shall not be construed so as to abrogate or derogate from any [A]boriginal peoples of Canada including
> (a) any rights or freedoms that have been recognized by the Royal Proclamation of October 7, 1763; and
> (b) any rights or freedoms that now exist by way of land claims agreements or may be so acquired

For judicial interpretation confirming this protection, see *R. v Stienhuaer*, [1985] 3 CNLR 187, 191 (Alta QB); *Barlow v R.*, [1987] 1 CNLR 20, 44 (NBCA). For an excellent article discussing the problems of imposing individual rights on Canadian Aboriginal peoples, see Mary Ellen Turpel, "Aboriginal Peoples and the Canadian Charter: Interpretive Monopolies, Cultural Differences," 6 Can Hum Rts YB 3 (1989–1990).

7 Douglas Sanders, "The Indian Lobby," in *And No One Cheered: Federalism, Democracy and the Constitutional Act* 301–32 (Keith Banting & Richard Simeon eds., 1983).

8 *Canadian Charter of Rights and Freedoms*, Part I of the Constitutional Act, 1982, being Schedule B to the *Canadian Act, 1982* (U.K.), 1982, ch. 11.

9 Bryan Schwartz, "Unstarted Business: Two Approaches to Defining s. 35 – What's in the Box, and What Kind of Box?," in *First Principles, Second Thoughts* 353–64 (1986).

10 For an analysis of the First Ministers Conferences mandated by section 37 of the Constitution, see Kathy Brock, "The Politics of Aboriginal Self-Government: A Canadian Paradox," 34 Can Pub Admin 272 (1991). For suggestions building upon the Charlottetown Accord, see Peter Hogg & Mary Ellen Turpel, "Implementing Aboriginal Self-Government: Constitutional and Jurisdictional Issues," 74 Can Bar Rev 187 (1995).

11 The most recent example of the wider view of Aboriginal rights which can emerge from the political process is found in the final report of The Royal Commission on Aboriginal Peoples. 1–5 *Report of the Royal Commission on Aboriginal Peoples* (1996). This report summarizes and extends many ideas for protecting and improving Aboriginal rights within Canada.

12 Previous cases which held that Aboriginal rights should be given a large, liberal and generous interpretation include *Jones v Meechan*, 175 US 1, 10–11 (1899); *Nowegijck v The Queen*, 144 DLR 3rd 193, 198 (Can. 1983); *R. v Simon*, 24 DLR 4th 390, 435 (Can. 1985); *R. v Sioui*, 70 DLR 4th 427, 453 (Can. 1990).

13 RSC ch. C-46 (1985).

14 The trickster's role is revealed in a brief exchange from an interview between Lenore Keeshig-Tobias (an Anishinabe story-teller from my reservation) and Harmut Lutz:

> HL: Was that your idea, founding the society for the Reawakening of the Trickster?
> LKT: The Committee to Re-Establish the Trickster. You know, this is to learn from mistakes. The Trickster, The Teacher is a paradox: Christ-like in a way. Except that from our Teacher, we learn through the Teacher's mistakes as well as the Teacher's virtues.
> Harmut Lutz, *Contemporary Challenges: Conversations with Canadian Authors* 85 (1991).

15 Penny Petrone, *Native Literature in Canada: From Oral Tradition to the Present* 16 (1990).

16 Gerald Vizenor, *The People Named the Chippewa: Narrative Histories* 3–4 (1984). Vizenor states:

> Naanabozho, the compassionate woodland trickster, wanders in mythic time and transformational space between tribal experiences and dreams. The trickster is related to plants and animals and trees; he is a teacher and healer in various personalities who, as numerous stories reveal, explains the values of healing ... More than a magnanimous teacher and transformer, the trickster is capable of violence, deceptions, and cruelties: the realities of human imperfections. The woodland trickster is an existential shaman in the comic mode, not an isolated and sentimental tragic hero in conflict with nature.

17 For a composite Trickster Story, see Thomas King, "The One About Coyote Going West," in *All My Relations: An Anthology of Canadian Native Fiction* 89 (William Hebert New ed., 1990).

18 Daniel David Moses, "The Trickster Theatre of Tomson Highway," 60 Can Fiction Mag 83 (1987).

19 See Barbara Babcock Adams, "A Tolerated Margin of Mess: The Trickster and His Tales Reconsidered," 11 J of Folklore Inst 147 (1975); Henry Rowe Schoolcraft, "Historical and Methodological Perspectives," in Andrew Wiget, *Critical Essays on Native American Literature* 21 (1985); John Borrows, "Constitutional Law From a First Nations Perspective: Self-Government and the Royal Proclamation," 28 UBC L Rev 1, 6–10 (1994); Gerald Vizenor, *The Trickster of Liberty: Tribal Heirs to a Wild Baronage* (1988).

20 The trickster's interaction with the court is an effective vehicle for examining law because: "Stories are a great device for probing the

dominant narrative. We use them to examine presupposition, the body of received wisdoms that pass as truth but actually are contingent, power-serving, and drastically disadvantage our people." Richard Delgado, "Rodrigo's Final Chronicle: Cultural Power, The Law Reviews, and the Attack on Narrative Jurisprudence," 68 S Cal L Rev 545, 549 (1995); *see also* Jane B. Baron & Julia Epstein, "Is Law Narrative?" 45 Buff L Rev 141 (1997) (describing foundationalist and anti-foundationalist uses of narrative in law).

21 For a series of articles that examines the similarities and differences between jurisprudence and stories, see Peter Gewirtz, *Law's Stories* (1966).

22 See James Boyd White, *Justice as Translation: An Essay in Cultural and Legal Criticism* (1990). "To attempt to translate puts you in a place between texts, between languages." *Id*. at 255.

23 See Jurgen Habermas, *Justification and Application: Remarks on Discourse Ethics* (1993).

24 For further discussion on the use of this methodology, see 2 Charles Taylor, "Understanding and Ethnocentricity," in *Philosophy and the Human Science: Philosophical Papers* 116–33 (1985); Charles Taylor, "The Politics of Recognition," in *Multiculturalism and the Politics of Recognition* (Amy Gutman & Charles Taylor eds., 1992); Borrows, *supra* note 19, at 1–10.

25 For a discussion of how racialized perspectives can create alternative legal interpretations, see Richard Devlin, "We Can't Go On Together with Suspicious Minds: Judicial Bias and Racialized Perspective in R v RDS," 18 Dalhousie LJ 408 (1995).

26 See John Borrows, *Living Between Water and Rocks: First Nations, Environmental Planning and Democracy*, 47 UTLJ 417 (1997).

27 In this sense the Trickster's methodology has similarities with objectives often associated with critical race theory, see *Introduction* in Mari Matsuda et al., *Words That Wound: Critical Race Theory, Assaultive Speech, and the First Amendment* 4–7 (Charles Lawrence et al., eds., 1993); Richard Delgado & Jean Stephanic, *Failed Revolutions: Social Reform and the Limits of Legal Imagination* (1994).

28 The Supreme Court of Canada wear these robes as a symbol of respect for the judicial office.

29 See Vanderpeet, 137 DLR 4th 289, at para. 19 (Lamer, CJC).

30 *Id*. at para. 20.

31 *Id*. at para. 27.

32 *Id*. at para. 30.

33 *Id*. at para. 31.

34 *Id*. at para. 36.

35 See *Johnson v McIntosh*, 21 U.S. (8 Wheat) 543, 572–4 (1823); *Worchester v Georgia*, 31 U.S. (6 Pet.) 515, 542–3 & 559 (1832); *R. v Sparrow*, 70 DLR 4th 385 (Can. 1990). "[T]here was from the outset, never any doubt, that sovereignty and legislative power, and indeed the underlying title to such lands vested in the Crown." *Id*. at 404.

36 *Sparrow*, 70 DLR 4th at 398.

37 See Vanderpeet, 137 DLR 4th 289, at para. 46 (Lamer, CJC).

38 *Id*. at para 44.

39 *Id*. at para. 59 (emphasis added); see also *Id*. at paras. 55–8.

40 This test has the potential to reinforce stereotypes about Indians. In order to claim an Aboriginal right, these determinations of Aboriginal will become more important than what it means to be Aboriginal today. The notion of what was integral to Aboriginal societies is steeped in questionable North American cultural images. See Daniel Francis, *The Imaginary Indian: The Image of the Indian in Canadian Culture* (1992).

41 See Vanderpeet, 137 DLR 4th 289, at para. 62 (Lamer, CJC).

42 *Id*. at para. 61.

43 *Id*. at para. 60

44 *Id*. at para. 73.

45 *Id*. at para. 22.

46 The articulation of this second purpose, reconciliation, as a reason for the entrenchment of section 35(1) in the Constitution was unexpected because it was not formerly a part of Aboriginal rights jurisprudence.

47 See *Vanderpeet*, 137 DLR 4th 289, at para. 30 (Lamer, CJC). The justification for this reason drew strongly from early U.S. jurisprudence in the Marshall cases. For commentary on the Marshall cases, see Rennard Strickland, "A Tale of Two Marshalls: Reflections on Indian Law and Policy, The Cherokee Cases and the Cruel Irony of Supreme Court Victories," 47 Okla L Rev 111 (1994); Philip Frickey, "Marshalling the Past and Present: Colonialism, Constitutionalism and Interpretation in Federal Indian Law," 107 Harv L Rev 381 (1993).

48 It is ironic that this assertion of British sovereignty should form one of the principal bases and underlying purposes for the existence of Aboriginal rights. At its most simple level, one might have thought that the assertion of British sovereignty was the last thing that would inform the constitutionalized protection of Aboriginal rights, since it is almost always British sovereignty that most severely threatens these rights. For criticism of the law's artificial and self-serving acceptance of the Crown

claims of sovereignty, see Brian Slattery, *Understanding Aboriginal Rights*, 66 Can Bar Rev 727, 730 (1987).

49 See *Vanderpeet*, 137 DLR 4th 289, at para. 44 (Lamer, CJC).

50 *Id*. at para. 46.

51 *Id*. at paras. 55, 60.

52 Or to put the question affirmatively, in recognizing Aboriginal rights, one must ask "whether or not a practice, tradition or custom was a defining feature of the culture in question" prior to European influences. See *Vanderpeet*, 137 DLR 4th 289, at para. 59 (Lamer, CJC).

53 For a discussion of the Court's limited understanding of Aboriginal culture, see Turpel.

54 70 DLR 4th 385, 411 (Can. 1990). For an excellent commentary on this case, see Michael Asch & Patrick Macklem, *Aboriginal Rights and Canadian Sovereignty: An Essay on R.. v Sparrow*, 29 Alta L Rev 498 (1991). For a comparison with U.S. law, see Matthew D. Wells, *Sparrow and Lone Wolf: Honoring Tribal Rights in Canada and the United States*, 66 Wash L Rev 1119 (1991).

55 See *Vanderpeet*, 137 DLR 4th 289, at para. 49 (Lamer CJC).

56 For an elaboration of the difficulties encountered in articulating Aboriginal world-views before common law courts, see Robin Riddington, "Cultures in Conflict: The Problem of Discourse," in *Native Writers and Canadian Writing* 273 (William Herbert New ed., 1990); Leslie H. Pinder, *The Carriers of No: After the Land Claims Trial* (1991); Joan Ryan & Bernard Ominayak, "The Cultural Effects of Judicial Bias," in *Equality and Judicial Neutrality* 346 (Kathleen Mahoney & Sheilah Martin eds., 1987); Louise Mandell, "Native Culture on Trial," in *Equality and Judicial Neutrality* 358 (Kathleen Mahoney & Sheilah Martin eds., 1989); Michael Jackson, "The Case in Context," in *Colonialism on Trial: Indigenous Land Rights and the Gitksan and Wet'Suwet'en Sovereignty Case* x–xi (Don Monet & Sakau'u eds., 1992).

57 In dissent, Madam Justice L'Heureux-Dubé stated "I do not think it appropriate to qualify this proposition by saying that the perspective of the common law matters as much as the perspective of the native when defining [A]boriginal rights." *Vanderpeet*, 137 DLR 4th 289, at para. 145 (L'Heureux-Dubé, J).

58 138 DLR 4th 385 (Can. 1996)l. In the *Cote* case, the issues were: whether an Aboriginal right to fish must be necessarily incidental to a claim of Aboriginal title, and whether section 35(1) protections outlined in *Vanderpeet* extended to areas included with the former colonial regime of New France. The Court held that "[A]boriginal rights may exist

independently of [A]boriginal title" and that section 35(1) "would fail to achieve its noble purpose [if it] only protected those defining features [of Aboriginal societies] which were fortunate enough to receive the protection of European colonizers." *Id.* at paras. 38, 52, (Lamer, CJC). Thus, Aboriginal rights could extend to areas within the former colonial regime of New France.

59　138 DLR 4th 657 (Can. 1996). The *Adams* case also addressed the issue of whether Aboriginal rights are inherently based in claims to land, or whether claims to land are simply one manifestation of a broader concept of Aboriginal rights. The Court held "[A]boriginal rights do not exist solely where a claim to Aboriginal title has been made out." *Id.* at para. 26 (Lamer, CJC). It stated that the *Vanderpeet* test does not require that an Aboriginal group satisfy a further hurdle of demonstrating that their connection to land where the activity was taking place was of central significance to their distinctive culture.

60　For a discussion on the willingness of courts to alter the nature of claims to collective rights, see Leon Trakman, "Native Cultures in a Rights Empire: Ending the Dominion," 45 Buff L Rev 189, 196–212 (1997).

61　See *Vanderpeet*, 137 DLR 4th 289, at para. 53 (Lamer CJC).

62　For a perceptive article that discusses the law's re-characterization of Aboriginal claims because of its inability to directly address colonialism, see Mary Ellen Turpel, *Home/Land*, 10 Can J Fam L 17, 34 (1991).

63　But see *R. v Sioui*, 70 DLR 4th 427 (Can. 1990). Sioui provides for a recognition of the existence of Aboriginal self-government in the historic period.

64　See *Pamajewon*, 138 DLR 4th 204, para. 27 (Lamer, CJC).

65　The legal basis for broader claims to self-government is set out in *Royal Comm'n of Aboriginal Peoples, Partners in Confederation: Aboriginal, Peoples, Self-Government and the Constitution* (1993).

66　See *Pamajewon*, 138 DLR 4th 204, at para. 26 (Lamer, CJC).

67　See *Vanderpeet*, 137 DLR 4th 289, at para. 76 (Lamer, CJC); *Smokehouse*, 137 DLR 4th 528, at para. 21 (Lamer CJC).

68　See *Vanderpeet*, 137 DLR 4th 289, at para. 58 (Lamer, CJC).

69　*Id.* at para. 59 (Lamer, CJC).

70　*R. v Sparrow*, 70 DLR 4th 385, 401 (Can. 1990).

71　*Id.*

72　See *Vanderpeet*, 137 DLR 4th 289, at para. 60 (Lamer CJC).

73　*Id.*

74　"[T]he phrase 'existing [A]boriginal rights' must be interpreted flexibly so as to permit their evolution over time." *Sparrow*, 70 DLR 4th at 397.

75 See *Vanderpeet*, 137 DLR 4th 289, at para. 167 (L'Heureux-Dubé, J).

76 *Id*. at paras. 165–7.

77 *Id*. at para. 240 (McLachlin, J).

78 *Id*. at para. 68 (Lamer, CJC).

79 For evidentiary problems in Aboriginal rights litigation, see Michael Asch & Catherine Bell, "Definition and Interpretation of Fact in Canadian Aboriginal Title Litigation: An Analysis of Delgamuukw," 19 Queen's LJ 503 (1993–1994); Clay McLeod, "The Oral Histories of Canada's Northern Peoples, Anglo-Canadian Evidence Law, and Canada's Fiduciary Duty to First Nations: Breaking Down the Barriers of the Past," 30 Alta L Rev 1276 (1992).

80 See *Vanderpeet*, 137 DLR 4th 289, at para. 69 (Lamer CJC).

81 *Id*.

82 John Borrows, "With or Without You: First Nations Law (in Canada)," 41 McGill LJ 631, 645–6 (1996) [hereinafter Borrows II].

83 The Court does not recognize that Aboriginal laws are universally protected Aboriginal rights even though they note that traditional laws form the basis of Aboriginal rights in an earlier part of the judgment. See *Vanderpeet*, 137 DLR 4th 289, at para. 42 (Lamer CJC).

84 *Id*. at para. 70.

85 *R. v Simon*, 24 DLR 4th 390 (Can. 1985) (the Aboriginal accused had a right to carry a gun in closed season on his hunting grounds because its possession was reasonably incidental to his protected treaty right to hunt in all seasons).

86 See *Vanderpeet*, 137 DLR 4th 289, at paras. 71–2 (Lamer, CJC).

87 *Id*. at para. 73.

88 *Id*. at para. 74.

89 For the inappropriateness of applying the "integral" test to aboriginal life, see Kent McNeil, "The Meaning of Aboriginal Title," in *Aboriginal and Treaty Rights in Canada: Essays on Law, Equality, and Respect for Difference* 135–54 (Michael Asch ed. 1997).

90 See *R. v Cote*, 138 DLR 4th 385 (Can. 1996); *R. v Adams*, 138 DRL 4th 657 (Can. 1996).

91 For accounts that problematize non-Aboriginal accounts of Aboriginality, see Ghislain Otis, "Opposing Aboriginality to Modernity: The Doctrine of Aboriginal Rights in Canada," 12 British J Canadian Stud 1 (1997), and Gillian Cowlishaw, "Did the Earth Move for You? The Anti-Mabo Debate," 6 Australian J Anthropology 32 (1995).

92 For commentary on non-Aboriginal interpretations of Aboriginal evidence, see Geoff Sherrott, "The Court's Treatment of the Evidence in

Delgamuukw v BC" 56 Sask L Rev 41 (1992); Louis Assier-Andrieu, "Anthropology as the Eye of the Law: Comment on Canadian Jurisprudence," 33 J Legal Pluralism 179 (1993); Marlee Kline, "The Colour of Law: Ideological Representations of First Nations in Legal Discourse," 3 Social & Legal Stud 451 (1994).

93 For a critique of the application of non-Aboriginal characterizations of Aboriginal law, see *Colonialism on Trial: Indigenous Land Rights and the Gitksan and Wet'suwet'en Sovereignty Case* (Don Monet & Sakau'u eds., 1992).

94 *R. v Sparrow*, 70 DLR 4th 385, 411 (Can. 1990).

95 See John Borrows, "Contemporary Traditional Equality: The Effect of the Charter on First Nation Politics," 43 UNBLJ 19 (1994).

96 See *Pamajewon*, 138 DLR 4th 204, at para. 23 (Lamer, CJC).

97 *Id.* at para. 26.

98 *R. v Sioui*, 70 DLR 4th 427, 453 (Can. 1990).

99 *R. v Sparrow*, 70 DLR 4th 385, 404 (Can. 1990).

100 See *Pamajewon*, 138 DLR 4th 204, at para. 26 (Lamer, CJC).

101 *Id.* at para. 27.

102 *Id.*

103 *Id.* at para. 28.

104 *Id.* at para. 29.

105 Unfortunately, some Canadians may know exactly what it is like to have fundamental rights defined by what was integral to European culture prior to its arrival in North America. People disadvantaged on the basis of sex, class, race, etc., may well feel their rights depend on what was defining European culture 200–300 years ago.

106 For an excellent novel where an Anishinabe writer has described this experience, see Louise Erdrich, *The Bingo Palace* (1994). For United States statute and case law dealing with Indian gaming, see Naomi Mezey, "The Distribution of Wealth, Sovereignty and Culture Through Indian Gaming," 48 Stan L Rev 711 (1996); Kathryn Rand & Steven Light, "Virtue of Vice? How IGRA Shapes the Politics of Native American Gaming, Sovereignty, and Identity," 4 Va J Soc Pol'y & L 380 (1997).

107 See *Vanderpeet*, 137 DLR 4th 289, at para. 32 (Lamer, CJC).

108 *Id.* at para. 247 (McLachlin, J).

109 *Id.* at para. 40 (Lamer, CJC).

110 *Id.* at paras. 256–60 (McLachin, J).

111 *Id.* at para. 256.

112 *Id.* at para. 257.

113 *Id.* at para. 258.

114 *Id.* at para. 263.
115 *Id.* at para. 261.
116 *Id.* at para. 265.
117 *Id.* at para. 275.
118 Arthur J. Ray, *Indians in the Fur Trade: Their Role as Trappers, Hunters, and Middlemen in the Lands Southwest of Hudson Bay 1660–1870,* at 51–7 (1974).
119 Richard White, *The Middle Ground: Indians, Empires and Republics in the Great Lake Region, 1650–1815,* at 50–142 (1991); James Rodger Miller, *Skyscrapers Hide the Heavens* 23–82 (1989); Olive P. Dickason, *Canada's First Nations: A History of Founding Peoples from Earliest Times* 86–215 (1992); 1 *Report of the Royal Commission on Aboriginal Peoples* 99–137 (1996).
120 See *Vanderpeet,* 137 DLR 4th 289, at para. 42 (Lamer, CJC) (quoting Mark Walter, "British Imperial Constitutional Law and Aboriginal Rights: A Comment on *Delagamuukw v British Columbia,*" 17 Queen's LJ 412–13 (1992)).
121 *Id.* (citing Brian Slatterly, "The Legal Basis of Aboriginal Title," in *Aboriginal Title in British Columbia;* Delgamuukw v The Queen 121–2 (1992)).
122 See generally, Harold Adams Innis, *Fur Trade in Canada: An Introduction to Canadian Economic History* (1956).
123 In fact, Indians did rebel on those occasions where they were told they had no rights to occupy and use their lands, see Francis Jennings, *The Ambiguous Iroquois Empire* (1975); Cornelius Jaenen, *Friend or Foe: Aspects of French-Amerindian Cultural Contact in the Sixteenth and Seventeenth Centuries* (1976); Leslie Stokes Upton, *Micmacs and Colonists, Indian-White Relations in the Maritimes* (1979).
124 The Royal Proclamation of October 7, 1763, RSC 1985, App. II, No. 1; See Borrows, *supra* note 19.
125 A holding that denies the protection of Aboriginal practices which developed solely as a result of European contact would also violate Canada's fiduciary obligation towards Aboriginal peoples, to maintain the honor of the Crown in dealings with Aboriginal peoples. For discussion of this doctrine, see Leo Rotman, *Parallel Paths: Fiduciary Doctrine and the Crown–Native Relationship in Canada* (1996); David Elliot, "Aboriginal Peoples in Canada and the United States and the Scope of the Fiduciary Relationship," 24 Man LJ 137 (1996); Peter W. Hutchins et al., "When Do Special Fiduciary Obligations to Aboriginal Peoples Arise?," 59 Sask L Rev 97 (1995).
126 See *Vanderpeet,* 137 DLR 4th 289, at para. 42 (Lamer CJC).

127 *Id.* at paras. 59–60.

128 See *Gladstone*, 137 DLR 4th 648, at para. 73 (Lamer, CJC)

129 *Id.* at para. 75.

130 Under the *Sparrow* test for infringement, first, the Aboriginal group must demonstrate a prima facie interference with their rights because legislation is either unreasonable, causes undue hardship, or denies the preferred means of exercising rights. If the group passes this test the court still may hold that interference is justified if the Crown can show a valid legislative objective for infringing the law, and demonstrate that the honor of the Crown was preserved in the enactment.

131 Although the Supreme Court of Canada has recently narrowed the bounds in which First Nations laws can apply, see *R. v Nikal*, 133 DLR 4th 658 (Can. 1996); *R. v Lewis*, 133 DLR 700 (Can. 1996).

132 Borrows II, *supra* note 82, at 646–57.

133 For a discussion about the importance of the continued interaction of state law and customary Indigenous law, see Maria Teresa Sierra, "Indian Rights and Customary Law in Mexico: A Study of the Nahuas in the Sierra De Pueblo," 29 Law & Soc'y Rev 227 (1995).

134 See *Cote*, 138 DLR 4th 385, at para. 52 (Lamer, CJC).

135 See *Vanderpeet*, 137 DLR 4th 289, at para. 42 (Lamer, CJC).

136 *Id.*

137 These communities have laws relating to selling fish and gambling that the Court could receive and consider in develop its sui generis Aboriginal rights jurisprudence. These laws "may be helpful by way of analogy" in defining and interpreting Aboriginal rights, see *R. v Simon*, 24 DLR 4th 390, 404 (Can. 1985).

138 *Id.* at 40.

139 For an excellent discussion of the persistence of customary tribal law, see Gloria Valencia-Weber, "Tribal Courts: Custom and Innovative Law," 24 NM L Rev 225 (1994).

140 For a discussion of the diverse sources of law in Canada, including Aboriginal law, see Patrick Glenn, "The Common Law in Canada," 74 Can Bar Rev 261 (1995).

141 See *Vanderpeet*, 137 DLR 4th 289, at para. 42 (Lamer CJC) (citing Brian Slatterly, "The Legal Basis of Aboriginal Title," in *British Columbia: Delgamuukw v The Queen* 121–22 (1992)).

142 *Id.* at para. 247 (McLachlin, J).

143 *Id.* at para. 42 (Lamer, CJC).

144 *Id.* at para. 261 (McLachlin, J).

145 *Id.* at para. 265.

146 For supporting argument, see Sakej Henderson, "First Nations Legal

Inheritances: The Mikmaq Model," 23 Man LJ 1 (1996); Sakej Henderson, "Micmaw Tenure in Atlantic Canada," 18 Dalhousie LJ 196 (1995);
Borrows II, *supra* note 82.

147 If reconciliation is to be used to define Aboriginal rights at all, a better
approach to reconciliation would have made 1982 the effective date for
the definition of rights. The Constitution Act recognized and affirmed
those rights which were existing in 1982, NOT at the date when Europeans asserted sovereignty in what is now Canada.

148 See *Vanderpeet*, 137 DLR 4th 289, at paras. 59–60 (Lamer, CJC).

149 The downgrading of Aboriginal rights is even more apparent in the
greater power given to Canadian governments to infringe Aboriginal
rights in these cases. For further comment, see Kent McNeil, "How Can
Infringements of the Constitutional Rights of the Aboriginal Peoples Be
Justified," 8 Const F 33 (1997).

150 For an argument which develops the equality of peoples as central to
reconciling Crown/Aboriginal relationships, see Patrick Macklem,
"Narrative Dimensions of an Aboriginal Right of Self-Government,"
Queen's LJ 173 (1995); Patrick Macklem, "Disturbing Sovereignty:
Indian Nations and the Equality of Peoples," 45 Stan L Rev 1311 (1993).

151 See *R. v Sioui*, 70 DLR 4th 427, 453 (Can. 1990); *R. v Sparrow*, 70 DLR 4th
385, 404 (Can. 1990).

152 Penny Petrone, *Native Literature in Canada: From Oral Tradition to the
Present* 17 (1990).

153 Jarislav Pelikan, *The Vindication of Tradition* 54 (1984).

154 Katharine T. Barlett, "Tradition, Change, and the Idea of Progress in
Feminist Legal Thought," 1995 Wis L Rev 303, 306–19.

Patrick Macklem
Indigenous Difference and the Constitution of Canada (2000)

CHAPTER 1: METHOD

*The wild requires that we learn the terrain, nod to all the plants and animals and
birds, ford the streams and cross the ridges, and tell a good story when we get
back home.*

Gary Snyder, *The Practice of the Wild*[1]

The existence of a unique constitutional relationship between Aboriginal people and the Canadian state turns on what the constitution has to say about the matter. Yet determining the meaning of the constitution immediately raises matters of method. By "method," I refer to investigatory approaches to a number of interpretive and theoretical questions that are analytically prior to an inquiry into the constitutional status of Aboriginal people. For example, is the written text of the constitution clear, vague, or silent on the relationship between Aboriginal people and the Canadian state? Does the text exhaust the constitution's meaning? What role do judicial decisions play in determining the constitutional status of Aboriginal people? What does it mean to say that certain social facts – in our case, the four facts that comprise indigenous difference – possess constitutional significance? More generally, how do claims of justice relate to constitutional interpretation? And what is the relevance to this inquiry of the debate between those who argue that a universal set of standards exists for assessing the justice of constitutional arrangements and those who claim that normative standards are relative to specific cultural contexts?

In this chapter, I first examine what the text and structure of the constitution have to say about the constitutional position of Aboriginal people and the role that precedent plays in my inquiry. I then explore a common way of understanding constitutional law, known as positivism, that treats constitutional law as a set of textual and structural imperatives and rules promulgated by the judiciary. From a positivist perspective, whether Aboriginal people enjoy a unique constitutional relationship with the Canadian state depends solely on whether the text and structure of the constitution as interpreted by the judiciary support such a claim. I outline a number of positivism's deficiencies, not the least of which is its insistence on a radical separation between law and justice. I also navigate the debate between universalism and relativism and lay the theoretical groundwork for the claim that constitutional recognition of indigenous difference furthers equality. In addition, I explore the utility of the distinction between individual and collective rights and examine the relationship between equality and distributive justice. Each of these topics raises fundamental questions concerning the nature of law and justice and merits a more exhaustive discussion than it receives in this study. But I hope to provide an explanation of the method that informs my analysis in the chapters that follow.

Text, Structure, Precedent

Three provisions of the Constitution of Canada frame my inquiry. First, subsection 35(1) of the Constitution Act, 1982 provides that the "existing aboriginal and treaty rights of the Aboriginal peoples of Canada are hereby recognized and affirmed." By recognizing and affirming existing Aboriginal and treaty rights, subsection 35(1) provides explicit textual support for the proposition that Aboriginal people possess a unique constitutional status in Canadian law. Moreover, the fact that Aboriginal and treaty rights are "recognized and affirmed," as opposed to created or conferred, implies that such rights owe their existence not to subsection 35(1) but to some other source of law. Second, subsection 91(24) of the Constitution Act, 1867 authorizes Parliament to enact laws in relation to "Indians, and Lands reserved for the Indians." By referring to two classes of subject matters that fall within federal legislative authority – Indians and Indian lands – subsection 91(24) authorizes special legislative measures aimed at both a class of persons who can claim Indian legal status and territory set aside for such persons. And, third, section 25 of the Canadian Charter of Rights and Freedoms provides that "[t]he guarantee in this Charter of certain rights and freedoms shall not be construed so as to abrogate or derogate from any aboriginal, treaty or other rights or freedoms that pertain to the aboriginal peoples of Canada." By insulating Aboriginal and treaty rights from the constraints of the Charter of Rights, section 25 signals that Aboriginal people merit unique constitutional consideration.

The structure of the constitution also suggests that Aboriginal people enjoy a unique constitutional relationship with the Canadian state. Reasoning from structure is a mode of interpretation that derives the existence of particular constitutional entitlements from structural presuppositions of the constitution itself.[2] A structural account of a unique constitutional relationship between Aboriginal people and Canada starts with the presupposition that Canada is a federal state. Parliament and provincial legislatures possess exclusive authority to enact laws in relation to certain classes of subject matters. As noted, the Constitution Act, 1867 assigns two such classes of subject matters, Indians and lands reserved for the Indians, to Parliament. If Aboriginal people did not possess a unique constitutional status in Canada, each province would be entitled to enact laws in relation to Indians and Indian lands located in that province. This result would be at odds not only with the text of subsection 91(24) but, more importantly from a structural perspective, with the federal system of government in Canada. Thus one of the basic structures of the constitution – the federal distribution of legislative authority – suggests that Aboriginal people enjoy a unique constitutional relationship with the Canadian state.

Given the text and structure of the constitution, why is there a need to demonstrate the constitutional significance of indigenous difference? This need arises in part because reliance on text and structure that intimate that Aboriginal people enjoy a unique constitutional status in Canada raises more questions than it answers.[3] Neither text nor structure provides insight into a wide range of issues critical to understanding the constitutional status of Aboriginal people. For example, what types of activities do Aboriginal and treaty rights authorize? Are Aboriginal and treaty rights individual or collective rights? Do Aboriginal and treaty rights constrain the exercise of legislative power? What is the precise relation between Aboriginal and treaty rights and rights guaranteed by the Charter of Rights? What is the nature and scope of federal legislative authority with respect to Aboriginal people? The written text provides guidance on but ultimately underdetermines both the nature and scope of Aboriginal and treaty rights and the nature and scope of federal legislative authority. The structure of the constitution may provide interpretive assistance, but in no way does it resolve these questions.

The judiciary, through detailed interpretations of the provisions identified above, has begun to explore and resolve some of these issues. For example, the Supreme Court of Canada has held that the legal relationship between Canada and Aboriginal people is "trust-like, rather than adversarial, and contemporary recognition of Aboriginal rights must be defined in light of this historic relationship."[4] It has also held that the constitution provides a framework to reconcile the fact that Aboriginal peoples lived on the continent in distinctive societies before European contact with the fact of Canadian sovereignty, and that Aboriginal rights recognized by subsection 35(1) relate to practices, customs, or traditions integral to the distinctive culture of Aboriginal peoples.[5] Treaty rights have been held to constrain the exercise of federal and provincial legislative authority.[6] And provincial legislatures have been held to exceed their legislative authority when they enact laws that single out Indian people,[7] or when provincial laws of general application touch on matters that go to the core of federal jurisdiction over Indians and lands reserved for the Indians.[8]

Precedent thus supports the view that Aboriginal people enjoy a unique constitutional relationship with the Canadian state. Judicial decisions also suggest the role that precedent can play in fixing the meaning of otherwise generally worded and open-ended constitutional provisions.[9] But many questions remain. For example, what does it mean to speak of practices integral to an Aboriginal culture? Do Aboriginal and treaty rights inhere in individuals or collectivities? What is the relation between Aboriginal rights and treaty rights? The judiciary will probably be afforded opportunities to rule on these and related questions, but until this occurs, the constitutional position of Aboriginal people requires elaboration. And even if the judiciary were to establish precedent on these issues, any certainty would be more illusory than real. New cases present different sets of facts, and the judiciary often departs from precedent when it views prior holdings as unsound. More important, precedent does not eliminate normative concerns surrounding the legitimacy of judicial interpretations.[10] Whether the judiciary has provided a legitimate account of the constitutional relationship between Canada and Aboriginal people or convincingly explained the justice of constitutionally recognizing this relationship are questions that cannot be answered by precedent alone. Unless and until these normative questions are addressed, they will continue to threaten the legitimacy of judicial inquiries into the constitutional status of Aboriginal people in Canada.

Positivism and Distributive Justice

By engaging these normative questions directly, this book strays from the well-travelled path of what legal philosophers call legal positivism – the view that legal rights and relationships exist solely because of positive legislative or judicial action.[11] Positivism insists on a sharp distinction between description and evaluation, or between what the law is and what the law ought to be. In the words of John Austin, a classical positivist scholar, "[t]he existence of the law is one thing; its merit or demerit is another."[12] A positivist account of constitutional law strives to describe an objectively ascertainable set of rules, generated by legislative or judicial action and understood as constitutional in nature, that govern the exercise of state authority.[13] From a positivist perspective, whether a unique constitutional relationship between Aboriginal people and the Canadian state exists depends on whether the text and structure of the constitution as understood by the judiciary mandates such a relationship. Whether, as a matter of justice or morality, Canadian law ought to recognize such a relationship is an entirely different matter.

The drawbacks of positivism in this context are fivefold. First, by assuming that the constitution is comprised solely of formal rules generated by positive legislative or judicial action, positivism at best dimly comprehends a perspective alluded to earlier, namely, that at least some Aboriginal rights are inherent rights and not contingent on Canadian law. This perspective suggests that although the constitution recognizes and affirms Aboriginal rights, at least some Aboriginal rights owe their origins to the presence of Aboriginal law, not Canadian law,[14] and that, as a result, the Canadian constitutional order houses a plurality of legal systems.[15] Positivism does not dismiss the possibilities of describing Aboriginal rights in this manner, in so far as Aboriginal rights can be defined by reference to legal rights and relationships recognized by Aboriginal legal regimes,[16] but its emphasis on legislative and judicial rule-making is not immediately receptive to legal pluralism in general and an inherent understanding of Aboriginal rights in particular.

Second, positivist accounts of law typically obscure but do not eliminate normative concerns about the legitimacy of particular judicial decisions and reasons offered in support of such decisions. Specifically, in positivist descriptions of Aboriginal rights (for example, "precedent holds that Aboriginal rights are practices integral to Aboriginal identity that existed pre-contact")[17] normative concerns invariably re-emerge (for example, "is it just or appropriate to restrict Aboriginal rights to practices that existed pre-contact?"). Such concerns are often addressed by reasons judges offer in support of their rulings, but reasons for decision tend to play a secondary role in positivist accounts. Because they are rendered by the judiciary, reasons for decision no doubt form part of a positivist account of the nature of law, but they tend not to enjoy the same ascribed status as judicial rules or holdings. Yet reasons for decision provide an opportunity for the judiciary to justify its own rulings. As such, they are central to law's legitimacy, belying positivist attempts to maintain a bright line between legality and normativity. Positivist accounts of the legitimacy of constitutional law – wherein decisions are legitimate if they are authorized by the constitution – do not help matters much.[18] Such accounts too often appear to be question-begging; constitutional law is justified simply because it is law.

Third, positivist accounts of law tend to assume a degree of determinacy in law that on many occasions does not exist.[19] Legal indeterminacy in this context exists in relation to both the choice of constitutional norm and the constitutional norm chosen. With respect to the former, the constitution invariably offers an array of norms from which to begin an inquiry and does not dictate how to choose among them. Is the constitutional status of religious schooling, for example, to be determined by reference to freedom of religion, freedom of association, equal protection of the law, or all three? With respect to the latter, the constitutional norm chosen to guide the inquiry often turns out to be a highly abstract principle which could logically be used both to support and to criticize the specific proposition under scrutiny. The establishment of religious schools both furthers and frustrates values underlying freedom of religion, freedom of association and equal protection of the law. In other words, because abstract constitutional norms often turn out to be contested sites of interpretation, normative stances are necessary to render them useful in particular circumstances. This is not to say that positivist scholarship is unaware of legal indeterminacy. H.L.A. Hart, for example, acknowledges that judges exercise "discretion" when text or precedent do not provide clear direction.[20] And scholars have argued that the law requires that discretion be exercised in particular ways and for specific ends,[21] and that the law itself authorizes the judiciary to rely on normative considerations when exercising discretion.[22] But legal indeterminacy nonetheless destabilizes the distinction that lies at the heart of positivism, namely, the distinction between description and evaluation, or between what the law is and what the law ought to be.

Fourth, positivist modes of reasoning can lead to the trap of thinking that constitutional rights do not exist if precedent is silent on the matter. But judicial silence should not be automatically equated with constitutional silence.[23] As stated, the judiciary has yet to confront many issues involving the constitutional status of Aboriginal people, and the possibility that a unique constitutional relationship exists between Aboriginal people and the Canadian state in itself does not necessarily entail that the judiciary should immediately recognize this relationship in its entirety. There may be independent reasons for taking a minimalist approach to its recognition. In Chapters 8 and 9, for example, I argue that Aboriginal and treaty rights do more than restrict governmental action; properly understood, they impose certain positive social, fiscal, and institutional obligations on federal, provincial, and territorial governments. Yet the positive dimensions of Aboriginal and treaty rights pose complex questions of legislative and social policy that are not amenable to judicial assessment. In such circumstances, a minimalist interpretive strategy may well be warranted.[24] However, where few formal legal sources can be found in support of recognizing positive dimensions of a constitutional right, an undue emphasis on positivist modes of reasoning may prematurely terminate the inquiry. In such cases, positivism tends to generate unduly conservative, and often inaccurate, descriptions of the law. This risk of inaccuracy arises as a result of erroneously treating constitutional law as a static body of manifest legal rules instead of an active, evolving, and interpretive inquiry into not only what constitutional law is but what it ought to become.

Finally, even where the judiciary has not remained silent on the matter, the constitution is more than what judges say it is.[25] Precedent has a unique way of infiltrating and shaping inquiries into the justice of certain constitutional arrangements not only by virtue of the normative force of its content but also because of its ability to provide a ready-made set of legal categories with which to begin an inquiry. As stated by Abram Chayes, "the ability of a judicial pronouncement to sustain itself ... and the power of judicial action to generate assent over the long haul become the ultimate touchstones of legitimacy."[26] As such, judicial decision making is deeply implicated in the conceptualization of the constitutional status of Aboriginal people in Canada. But in as much as Canadians seek a just constitutional order, the possibility that the judiciary has spoken on the subject will not end the inquiry. In Chayes's words, "judicial action only achieves such legitimacy by responding to and indeed stirring the deep and durable demands for a just society."[27] Judicial rulings at best are contributions to an ongoing debate concerning constitutional justice. Blind acceptance of the validity of judicially generated legal categories and constructions is especially fatal in the context of the constitutional relationship between Aboriginal people and the Canadian state – a relationship that raises profound normative questions concerning the legitimacy of assertions of Canadian sovereignty over Aboriginal societies that predate the emergence of the Canadian state.

This book treats constitutional law as more than a limited number of textual and structural imperatives and a finite set of legal rules that passively constrain the exercise of political power. Constitutional law is an enterprise that actively distributes power, primarily in the form of rights and jurisdiction, among a variety of legal actors, including individuals, groups, institutions, and governments. By "power," I mean the constitutional authority not only to engage or not to engage in certain activities but also to mobilize what Joel Handler describes as "the rules of the game – values, beliefs, rituals, as well as institutional procedures – which systematically benefit certain groups at the expense of others."[28] The fact that a legal actor possesses a measure of constitutional authority does not mean it possesses the material ability to accomplish what the constitution authorizes. A myriad of factors – economic, social, political, and legal – affects the ability of a legal actor to translate formal constitutional authority into material reality. But constitutional law distributes fundamental baseline entitlements among legal actors and, in so doing, it can have profound effects on the material circumstances of individuals and groups in society. This is especially true in the context of Aboriginal and treaty rights, which confer explicit territorial and law-making authority on Aboriginal people. Aboriginal title, for example, in so far as it vests an exclusive right to land in an Aboriginal nation, enables that nation to engage in or authorize and share in the proceeds arising from the development of renewable and non-renewable resources, including mineral resources, timber, and wildlife.

Judges may not experience their actions as possessing distributive dimensions; judges typically describe their constitutional role in supervisory terms. As guardians of the constitution, they see themselves as responsible for ensuring that exercises of political power comply with constitutional requirements. That judges experience their actions in this manner and in fact perform this task is no doubt true, but such descriptions obscure the distributive consequences of the supervisory role. When the judiciary rules on the division of legislative authority between Parliament and provincial legislatures, for example, it is not simply constraining the exercise of legislative power. It is distributing power between two levels of government. Nor are the distributive dimensions of constitutional law restricted to jurisdictional disputes. The judiciary also distributes power, in the form of rights and freedoms, among individuals and groups, through its interpretations of rights and freedoms guaranteed by the Charter of Rights and Aboriginal and treaty rights guaranteed by section 35 of the constitution.

A focus on the distributive dimensions of constitutional law reveals its relation to distributive justice. As a distributive enterprise, constitutional law implicates an aspiration that power be distributed in a just manner. This aspiration is often expressed positively in the form of constitutional rules, either by explicit textual reference or by judicial interpretation. For example, section 15 of the Charter guarantees equality before and under the law and the equal protection and benefit of the law, thereby instructing the judiciary to ensure that legislatures distribute statutory power in a manner consistent with principles of equality. But the constitutional aspiration that power be distributed in a just manner is not exhausted by section 15. Nor does it depend merely on text or precedent. Instead, it operates as a "background norm" in that it illuminates the legitimacy or illegitimacy of a wide array of particular distributions of power.[29] The legitimacy of the constitutional distribution of voting rights, for example, turns not simply on whether it is mandated by text, structure, or precedent, but also on whether the principle of "one citizen, one vote"[30] is a distributively just means of allocating votes. Similarly, whether provincial legislatures deserve equal treatment in the distribution of legislative authority or whether Quebec ought to possess special status within the Canadian federation is a question that implicates the justice of the existing distribution of legislative authority. Debates over the distributive justice of "one citizen, one vote" or of special status for Quebec illustrate the fact that Canadians aspire to belong to a just constitutional order. "In such discussions," in the words of Jürgen Habermas, "participants clarify the way they want to understand themselves as citizens of a specific republic, as inhabitants of a specific region, as heirs to a specific culture, which traditions they want to perpetuate and which they want to discontinue."[31] Constitutional law, on this account, refers to an ongoing project of aspiring to distributive justice, disciplined but not determined by text, structure, or precedent.

This is not to say that comprehending constitutional law in terms of a commitment to distributive justice either resolves constitutional indeterminacy or insulates constitutional law from political controversy.[32] Those in favour of special status for Quebec typically identify certain aspects of Québécois identity, such as its culture and civil law tradition, as worthy of constitutional recognition. Those who advocate equality of the provinces typically deny that Québécois culture and tradition merit differential treatment in the distribution of legislative authority. Whether the former or the latter position constitutes a just distribution of legislative authority is deeply contestable and shot through with political considerations. Equally controversial is the claim that constitutional recognition of indigenous difference promotes a just distribution of constitutional power. As stated in the Introduction, many Canadians regard constitutional recognition of indigenous difference to be incompatible with individual equality. But the contestability of the justice of particular distributive outcomes should not impede an inquiry into the constitutional significance of indigenous difference.

In fact, it underscores the need to determine what distributive outcomes might follow from constitutional recognition of indigenous difference and whether such outcomes are consistent or inconsistent with a commitment to distributive justice.

THE ROLE OF EXTERNAL THEORY

In recent years, there has been an explosion of interest among philosophers and legal theorists in the conditions of a just constitutional order. Two scholars dominate the field. John Rawls has argued that a just constitutional order is one in which each person possess an equal right to the most extensive set of equal basic liberties compatible with a similar system of liberty for all, and that social and economic inequalities are to be arranged so that they are to the greatest benefit of the least advantaged.[33] Rawls derives these two principles of justice by arguing that equally situated free and rational individuals, stripped of any specific knowledge of their society and of their individual circumstances, would agree that they constitute just principles of determining how basic institutions should be arranged to distribute benefits and burdens through social cooperation.[34] Ronald Dworkin has argued that a just constitutional order is one that accords individuals "equal concern and respect."[35] He argues that much of democratic life rightly involves the enactment of laws that strive to satisfy the preferences of citizens. But he distinguishes between personal preferences, which call for the assignment of a set of goods or opportunities to the preference holder, and external preferences, which call for an assignment of a set of goods or opportunities not to the preference holder but to other members of the community. Dworkin calls for constitutional rights to be entrenched and interpreted in a manner that prevents the state from constraining the liberty of some in order to satisfy the external preferences of others.[36]

Scholarship on the subject often appears to bracket social reality when working out the normative content of constitutional law.[37] Bracketing social reality tends to spawn a methodology that generates abstract, acontextual, and ahistorical principles that are then used to assess whether existing institutions meet the requirements of a just constitutional order. Rawls places hypothetical individuals behind a "veil of ignorance" concerning their "place in society" to determine the components of a just constitutional order;[38] Dworkin speaks of the need to ground the justice of constitutional law in a "vast over-arching theoretical system of complex principles."[39] Such a methodology often supports the conclusion that just institutions already exist in Western constitutional orders,[40] thereby providing little assistance in determining how they can be promoted or established in the event that existing institutions are found wanting.[41] And it does not lend itself easily to assessing whether existing institutional arrangements were established in a manner consistent with principles of justice.

This book claims that the conditions of a just constitutional order cannot be determined without paying close attention to aspects of social reality – in particular, the four complex facts that comprise indigenous difference. Close attention to social reality entails a method that is consciously empirical, historical, contextual, and critical. It is empirical in its assumption that part of the task of constitutional theory is to determine whether and which social facts possess constitutional significance. It is historical through its inquiry into the birth and development of Canada as a sovereign state. It is contextual in its presumption that the conditions of a just constitutional order may vary from country to country, and in its claim that the specific distributive principle brought to bear on the justice of particular distributions depends on the nature of the good in question.[42] And it is critical in its assessment of the justice of existing distributions of constitutional power and in its determination of how just distributions can be established or promoted in light of contemporary social reality.[43]

This book thus shares much with what several scholars have referred to as external theories of law.[44] In contrast to an internal perspective, which seeks to understand law on its own terms, an external perspective treats law as a component of social reality and attempts to explicate its sociological functions. Some argue that law works to institutionalize and legitimate a market economy at the expense of alternative economic arrangements;[45] others argue that law works to institutionalize and legitimate patriarchal values at the expense of feminist aspirations;[46] still others argue that law works to institutionalize and legitimate dominant cultural values at the expense of marginalized systems of belief.[47] However diverse such stances may appear at first glance, they share a methodology that describes law in terms of its sociological functions, thereby treating law as part of a broader set of economic, social, and political practices that comprise social reality.

I adopt an external perspective on constitutional law in three respects. First, by arguing that the Canadian constitutional order can and ought to be understood in light of certain social facts, I place constitutional law alongside social life and argue that the meaning of the constitution is in part a function of certain aspects of social reality. Second, by focusing on the distributive dimensions of constitutional law, I hope to illuminate the relationship between constitutional law and the material circumstances facing Aboriginal people in Canadian society. Third, I argue that the justice of particular distributions of power, whether in the form of rights or jurisdiction, turns in part on the extent to which legal authority materially empowers those entitled to its exercise. In each respect, I view constitutional law in light of its functions and as comprehensible in terms of a broader set of practices that constitute social life.

In other respects, however, this book stands at a distance from external theory. Despite my focus on the distributive dimensions of constitutional law, I do not attempt to reduce constitutional law's functions to a singular performance, nor do I view them as immutable. My account does not treat constitutional law solely as a function of social reality, nor does it reduce the normative implications of constitutional law to its distributive consequences. Instead, I seek to split the difference between internal and external perspectives on law.[48] Pure externalism ultimately disables one from judging the justice of existing distributions by reference to ideals internal to the constitutional enterprise and from proposing ways in which constitutional law can better achieve just distributions of power. Pure internalism, by turning constitutional law inside out, fails to explain what aspects of social reality receive constitutional attention and ignores the distributive consequences of constitutional law. I acknowledge constitutional law's external dimensions in so far as I argue that the meaning of the constitution turns on the existence of certain social facts and that constitutional law operates to distribute power among legal actors in society, and I identify external factors that might explain why Aboriginal interests receive insufficient constitutional attention. But I also acknowledge that constitutional law possesses an internal dimension in so far as it is an enterprise that implicates an aspiration to distributive justice.[49] Given that "power is maintained partly on the acceptance of its justifications,"[50] I critically examine justifications supporting existing distributions of power that affect Aboriginal interests. I also argue that alternative distributions that conform to principles of distributive justice can be established or promoted which will have a material effect on contemporary Aboriginal reality.

Equality as an Organizing Principle

If constitutional law implicates an aspiration that power be distributed in a just manner, what constitutes a just distribution of power? A short answer to this question is that an equal distribution is a just distribution.[51] But a longer answer acknowledges that the concept of equality itself does not appear to supply the criteria by which to determine the justice of particular distributions. Equality is said to exist simply when equals are treated equally and unequals are treated unequally.[52] In general, when used descriptively, equality refers to the relationship that exists between two things measured by a common standard and found to be indistinguishable by reference to that standard.[53] Used prescriptively, equality refers to a relation that ought to exist between two classes of people who are similar or different in relevant respects.[54] Equality therefore requires that distributive outcomes reflect relevant similarities and differences that exist among people, but it does not specify which similarities or differences might be relevant to the justice of any given distribution.

It is often said that all Canadian citizens are equal before and under the law and that constitutional recognition of indigenous difference runs counter to fundamental principles of individual equality. According to this perspective, indigenous difference is not a relevant difference among citizens for the purpose of distributing constitutional rights. In contrast, I argue that indigenous difference is constitutionally relevant to the distribution of rights that protect interests associated with Aboriginal cultural difference, territory, sovereignty, and the treaty process. Arguments to the contrary tend wrongly to reduce indigenous difference to racial or cultural difference,[55] overlook the fact that similar treatment of people who possess relevant differences can constitute inequality, and ignore scholarship that defends Aboriginal rights on the basis that they further principles of equality.[56]

Two concerns appear to underpin the claim that indigenous difference is not a relevant difference for the purpose of distributing constitutional rights among Canadian citizens. First, constitutional recognition of indigenous difference might be thought illegitimate because it privileges the collective over the individual by attaching rights to individuals by virtue of their membership in a group. Second, collective differences between Aboriginal and non-Aboriginal people arguably are not relevant for the purpose of distributing constitutional rights. The first concern should be dispensed with at the outset. In so far as they attach to collectivities and protect interests that individuals share with others,[57] Aboriginal and treaty rights are often described as collective, as opposed to individual, rights.[58] But to suggest that collective rights are incompatible with notions of individual equality ignores the fact that equality itself possesses collective dimensions. If equality requires determining relevant similarities and differences among individuals, it requires determining whether two classes of people are sufficiently similar in relevant respects to warrant similar treatment or sufficiently different in relevant respects to warrant differential treatment. Equality, in other words, requires regarding people in light of the fact that they belong to particular collectivities or classes of persons and determining which similarities and differences warrant legal protection.[59]

The second concern is more challenging. Why is indigenous difference a relevant difference for the purpose of distributing constitutional entitlements? The relevance of certain similarities or differences among individuals seems to turn on what standard or criterion is employed to structure distributions. "To each according to his or her need," for example, identifies need as a standard or criterion to be employed in distributions, which in turn deems certain similarities and differences to be relevant to distributive outcomes. Similarly, merit as a distributive criterion renders relevant certain similarities and differences among people, namely, their ability or skill at performing or accomplishing certain activities or tasks. Criteria such as need and merit call for distributions on the basis of particular attributes of classes of people; they stipulate that people are equal and deserving of equal treatment when they share such attributes and that people are unequal and deserving of differential treatment when they do not share such attributes. Assessing the justice of a distributive outcome thus involves determining whether it has taken into account similarities and differences deemed relevant by the criterion structuring the distribution in question. Whether indigenous difference possesses constitutional relevance, according to this line of reasoning, depends on the criteria chosen to structure the distribution of constitutional rights.

But, as stated by Douglas Rae, "the question is not 'Whether equality,' but 'Which equality?'"[60] Beyond a certain level of generality, equality admits of many specific conceptions that attempt to supply criteria capable of assessing the justice of particular distributive outcomes.[61] Accordingly, distributive justice does not turn solely on fidelity to the criteria employed in particular distributions. It also turns on the appropriateness of the criteria themselves. In other words, what counts as a relevant similarity or difference among people also depends on the object of the distribution under assessment. In the words of Charles Taylor, "[c]riteria of distributive justice are meant to give us the basis for knowing what our share is, and therefore when we are being grasping."[62] But the fairness of a share, and who ought to receive one, cannot be determined without reference to what is being shared. A focus on certain similarities or differences among people may do justice in relation to some goods, but can be at best irrelevant or at worst unjust in relation to the distribution of other goods.[63]

For example, need may well be an appropriate distributive principle in relation to the distribution of health care, but less relevant in relation to the distribution of other types of goods, such as the right to vote. Similarly, certain differences among people may well be irrelevant when distributing political rights within a particular collectivity, but relevant when distributing political power among collectivities.[64] Assessing the justice of the latter type of distribution requires asking which collectivities ought to be entitled to exercise political power. Asserting that certain differences are irrelevant to this inquiry because they are irrelevant to the distribution of political rights within particular collectivities often tends to assume the legitimacy of including a group that seeks political autonomy in the very collectivity from which it seeks distance. Whether indigenous difference is a relevant difference for the purpose of distributing constitutional entitlements thus depends on the nature of the entitlement in question. If indigenous difference is relevant to the distribution of constitutional entitlements, then taking indigenous difference into account will further, not frustrate, equality. And to the extent that equal distributions are consistent with distributive justice, acknowledging the constitutional significance of indigenous difference is consistent with the aspiration that power be distributed in a just manner.

What of the fact that Aboriginal people in Canada and elsewhere constitute peoples, in the sense that "they comprise distinct communities with a continuity of existence and identity that links them to the communities, tribes, or nations of their ancestral past?"[65] That Aboriginal people constitute peoples is relevant to many areas of the law, especially international law, which regards a people as possessing a right of self-determination.[66] In the following section, I explore the significance of self-determination discourse to the task of determining the extent to which indigenous difference merits constitutional protection.

But whether Aboriginal people constitute peoples in international law is of secondary importance to this task. The concept of indigenous difference includes many of the factors that lead scholars to conclude that Aboriginal people comprise peoples, including aspects of Aboriginal ancestry and continuity of identity, but the term "people," like the terms "minority" and "nation," serves little purpose in my inquiry, other than providing a shorthand for the proposition that Aboriginal people constitute a class or classes of people who occupy a unique position in the Canadian constitutional order.

The Significance of Self-Determination

Although equality is the primary focus of this book, the constitutional relevance of indigenous difference can be articulated by reference to other fundamental values,[67] such as respect for life,[68] liberty,[69] freedom of association,[70] or self-determination.[71] Of these other values, self-determination is perhaps the most significant, given its place as a core legal principle of international law. International law is often invoked in support of the normative proposition that all peoples, or nations, should be entitled to determine their own political future or destiny free of external interference.[72] The principle of self-determination, in the words of James Anaya, has arisen "within international law's expanding lexicon of human rights concerns and accordingly is posited as a fundamental right that attaches collectively to groups of living human beings."[73]

International legal sources supporting a right of self-determination include article 1(2) of the United Nations Charter, which lists the principle of self-determination as one of the purposes of the United Nations.[74] Article 55 of the Charter calls for the promotion of a number of social and economic goals "[w]ith a view to the creation of conditions of stability and well-being which are necessary for peaceful and friendly relations among nations based on respect for the principle of equal rights and self-determination of peoples."[75] Similarly, the International Covenant on Civil and Political Rights provides that "[a]ll peoples have the right of self-determination ... [and to] freely determine their political status and freely pursue their economic, social and cultural development."[76] Self-determination has also been described as a right by the International Court of Justice.[77]

At its inception in the early twentieth century, the principle of self-determination was primarily invoked in the international sphere as a political justification for the liberation of Eastern European nations under the yoke of foreign domination.[78] It later served increasingly as a clarion call for colonies seeking to shed imperial shackles and assume independent statehood. In the 1950s, Belgium attempted to extend the principle of self-determination not only to colonies that wished to rid themselves of their imperial masters, but also to populations within independent states, so that indigenous populations and cultural minorities could assert a right of self-determination under international law.[79] The Belgian initiative was unsuccessful; in passing the Declaration on the Granting of Independence to Colonial Territories,[80] the General Assembly of the United Nations implemented what is known as the "salt water thesis," which restricts the right of self-determination to overseas colonies. The Declaration stated that "[a]ny attempt aimed at the partial or total disruption of the national unity and the territorial integrity of a country is incompatible with the Purposes and Principles of the Charter of the United Nations."[81] In the words of Patrick Thornberry, "The effect is that colonial boundaries function as the boundaries of the emerging States. Minorities, therefore, may not secede from States, at least, international law gives them no right to do so. The logic of the resolution is relatively simple: peoples hold the right of self-determination; a people is the whole people of a territory; a people exercises its right through the achievement of independence."[82]

As with constitutional law, international law is not a static body of manifest legal rules but an active, evolving, and interpretive inquiry into both what the law is and what it ought to become. And international law increasingly is acknowledging the arbitrariness of restricting the right of self-determination to overseas colonies. Positivistic limitations on the principle of self-determination under international law, such as the salt water thesis, should not obscure its normative dimensions[83] or the emergence of a more flexible formulation of the principle of self-determination based in part on the relevance of indigenous difference. Indigenous organizations themselves certainly describe their objectives in terms of self-determination. The World Council of Indigenous Peoples, at its second general assembly, described self-determination as one of the "irrevocable and inborn rights which are due to us in our capacity as Aboriginals."[84] The International Indian Treaty Council described indigenous populations as "composed of nations and peoples, which are collective entities entitled to and requiring self-determination," which in turn is described as including external and internal features.[85] External self-determination encompasses all the features of independent statehood, whereas internal self-determination includes rights to maintain and promote interests associated with indigenous difference through parallel political institutions.[86]

The emergence of a more flexible formulation of the principle of self-determination is also reflected in the Draft Declaration on the Rights of Indigenous Peoples, prepared by a subcommission of the United Nations Commission on Human Rights. The Draft Declaration proposes to recognize that "Indigenous peoples have the right to self-determination" and "[b]y virtue of that right they freely determine their political status and freely determine their economic, social and cultural development."[87] Accordingly, the Draft Declaration proposes to recognize indigenous rights of autonomy and self-government, the right to manifest, practice and teach spiritual and religious traditions, rights to territory, education, language, and cultural property, and the right to maintain and develop indigenous economic and social systems.[88]

An explanatory note accompanying an earlier version of the Draft Declaration draws the aforementioned distinction between "external" and "internal" self-determination. It defines internal self-determination as "entitling a people to choose its political allegiance, to influence the political order in which it lives and to preserve its cultural, ethnic, historical or territorial identity."[89] An indigenous right of external self-determination is contingent upon the failure of the state in which indigenous peoples live to accommodate indigenous aspirations for internal self-determination: "Once an independent State has been established and recognized, its constituent peoples must try to express their aspirations through the national political system, and not through the creation of new States. This requirement continues unless the national political system becomes so exclusive and non-democratic that it no longer can be said to be representing the whole people. At that point, and if all international and diplomatic measures fail to protect the peoples concerned from the State, they may perhaps be justified in creating a new State."[90] Acceptance by the world community of the Draft Declaration would usher in a new international legal order, one in which indigenous peoples would no longer be denied the right of self-determination simply because they live within existing state structures.

What is the relevance of these developments to the claim that Aboriginal nations ought to be treated as independent of the Canadian constitutional order? They suggest the emergence of a more flexible formulation of the principle of self-determination in international law, one that extends to Aboriginal people in Canada and that calibrates its content to the capacity and willingness of the Canadian state to protect interests associated with indigenous difference. Under this formulation, a failure by Canada to constitutionally protect interests associated with indigenous difference increases the likelihood that Aboriginal nations possess a right of external self-determination under international law. However, if Canada protects interests associated with indigenous difference in accordance with the right of internal self-determination, it is unlikely that international law, under this formulation, would treat Aboriginal nations as independent of the Canadian constitutional order. Canada's international legal obligations, in other words, require domestic constitutional arrangements that implement the right of internal self-determination that Aboriginal peoples possess under international law. In Chapter 4, I argue that these domestic arrangements must be predicated on a non-absolute, pragmatic conception of sovereignty that contemplates a plurality of entities wielding sovereign authority within the Canadian constitutional order.[91]

Notwithstanding the emerging distinction between external and internal self-determination in international law, the discourse of self-determination is difficult to adapt to the objective of allowing Aboriginal peoples to participate in Canadian, as well as their own, forms of government. The principle of self-determination supports constitutional recognition of Aboriginal governmental authority but it is not clear why, having exercised rights of self-determination, Aboriginal peoples ought also to possess the right to continue to enjoy benefits associated with Canadian citizenship.[92] In other words, the principle of self-determination yields a group right to decide to be self-governing,[93] but it does not appear to confer a right on the group in question to unilaterally decide the extent to which it is entitled to participate in the polity from which it seeks a measure of distance. If a group exercises its right to exclude others from its political institutions, on what basis can it demand representation in the political institutions of those whom it has excluded? Although there may be normative reasons in support of continued representation, the principle of self-determination, standing alone, does not appear to provide them.

The distinction between internal and external self-determination avoids this concern by defining internal self-determination as including rights of political participation within the state structure in which indigenous peoples find themselves in addition to rights of self-government and political autonomy. But simply redefining the principle as including that which it appears to exclude does not eliminate the necessity of normatively justifying such a definition. The question remains: why should indigenous peoples be entitled both to rights of self-government and autonomy and the right to continue to participate in political structures from which they seek a measure of distance? In light of concerns that constitutional protection of interests associated with indigenous difference clashes with the fundamental ideal of equal citizenship, an answer to this question cannot rest solely on an assertion of a flexible international right of self-determination. As will be seen, it also rests on the constitutional significance of the four social facts that comprise indigenous difference.

Universalism and Relativism

This book stakes out what I believe is a distinct position among current debates concerning the justice of constitutional arrangements by sidestepping an important debate concerning the nature of human rights. Some scholars believe in the existence of certain values so fundamental to humanity that they provide universal standards for determining the justice of particular constitutional arrangements.[94] Others believe that normative standards are relative to specific cultural contexts,[95] and that there exists no universal means of judging the merits of culturally specific ways of life. Universalists charge that relativists sanction violations of human rights in the name of cultural difference, whereas relativists argue that universalism is a cloak for the projection of culturally specific beliefs onto cultures that possess different inner logics.[96]

Rights to be free of racial or cultural discrimination are often posited as universal human rights, inhering in all persons as a prerequisite to human dignity and freedom. The Universal Declaration of Human Rights, to take one international legal instrument, recognizes that all individuals "are equal before the law and are entitled without any discrimination to equal protection of the law," and that every individual possesses the right to vote and to take part in government.[97] The Universal Declaration suggests the existence of a "limited international normative order"[98] that treats equality and antidiscrimination rights as universally shared by all individuals and to be respected by all governments. Constitutional recognition of Aboriginal-specific cultural, territorial, and self-government rights appears to threaten not only domestic constitutional commitments to the ideal of equality of citizenship but also universal commitments to equality and human rights.

Universality, however, is often purchased at the expense of determinacy, resulting in principles pitched at such an abstract level that they are of limited use in assessing the justice of particular constitutional arrangements. For example, it is not difficult to construct arguments that "the will to live and to be free," one basis for the assertion of universal rights,[99] both undercuts and underpins the legitimacy of a unique constitutional relationship between Aboriginal people and the Canadian state. One variant would stress the relationship between Aboriginal forms of government and individual and collective identities; the other would stress values of antidiscrimination and individual autonomy. Deriving one conclusion instead of the other requires the injection of normative concerns that cannot claim the same degree of universality that might attach to the more abstract premise of the will to live and be free.

Moreover, there is no universally accepted way to choose which universal norm ought to govern the assessment of the legitimacy of particular constitutional arrangements. For example, how does the right to equal protection of the law and the right to vote and take part in government, to the extent that they are interpreted as hostile to constitutional recognition of Aboriginal forms of government, square with article 27 of the International Covenant on Civil and Political Rights, which provides that "persons belonging to [ethnic] minorities shall not be denied the right, in community with the other members of their group, to enjoy their own culture"?[100] Those in favour of constitutional recognition of Aboriginal forms of government would enlist article 27 in its defence; those opposed would refer to equal protection. It is true that contestability in relation to the choice of the governing universal norm does not itself refute universalism. However, as we have seen, a flexible formulation of the right of self-determination is emerging in international law, making it difficult to determine on which side of the dispute universalism lies.

One strength of cultural relativism lies in its ability to circumvent problems of indeterminacy that bedevil any attempt to establish universality. The relativist can concede that some principles may be shared by all but argue that they exist at a level of abstraction so high that their articulation is of no use in assessing the legitimacy of particular constitutional arrangements. Any principle that deserves the mantle of universality does so by virtue of its indeterminacy. Because its meaning will be rendered concrete in radically diverse ways by different communities, any attempt to insist on one particular interpretation constitutes interpretive imperialism. Specifically, cultural relativism often underpins challenges to the legitimacy of constitutional principles and practices that do not take into account Aboriginal world-views and ways of life.[101] It is often said that because Aboriginal people have different ways of relating to others and to the world, as well as different ways of resolving disputes, it is unjust to govern Aboriginal people by normative standards that emanate from, and are only meaningful to, non-Aboriginal society. Rupert Ross, for example, writes eloquently of the injustices invariably produced when the Canadian legal system fails to acknowledge cultural differences between Aboriginal and non-Aboriginal people. He argues for reforms that respect such cultural differences and facilitate cross-cultural communication.[102]

I do not challenge the fact that Aboriginal people have culturally different ways of relating to others and to the world; in fact, in the next chapter, I argue that interests associated with Aboriginal cultural difference merit constitutional protection. But cultural relativism, as opposed to cultural difference, is an unstable perspective on which to rest constitutional recognition of indigenous difference. First, there is nothing logically necessary about equating cultural relativism with the protection of cultural difference. One could derive a denial of the relevance of cultural difference from some versions of cultural relativism,[103] namely, those that claim that different moral beliefs are the products of differing cultural contexts but do not ascribe normative significance to this fact.[104] Second, at least some versions of relativism are self-refuting. For example, should relative or universal status be ascribed to the relativist's claim that "evaluations are relative to the cultural background out of which they arise"?[105] It cannot be a universal truth, for relativism dismisses such a concept; on the other hand, if it is relative to a particular culture, then relativism itself is relative.[106]

Many critics have argued that adhering to cultural relativism forces the toleration of intolerance. With its premise that moral values are contingent on cultural practices, relativism disarms social criticism; as one critic writes, "[i]ts tolerance might be less charitably interpreted as the cowardice of moral abstention."[107] The critic is disarmed because once the wall of cultural autonomy is raised as a defence, little more can be said on a matter.[108] One version of this charge notes that relativism does not have egalitarian consequences; since all it does is assert that values are culturally specific, it provides no means of challenging culturally specific inegalitarianism.[109] Another scholar has even argued that, pushed to its extreme, relativism permits intolerance on the part of the external observer: if all moral beliefs are relative, "[w]e might just as well hate them all."[110] Still others have claimed that, by elevating principles of tolerance to the international context, cultural relativists commit the very sin they accuse universalists of committing, namely, the imposition of ethnocentric views about how groups ought to relate to one another.[111]

Relativist claims tend to totalize the concept of culture – as if one single uniform, dominant culture exists within a particular society instead of intersecting and competing structures of belief.[112] When people have conflicting or overlapping collective affiliations, an assertion of cultural relativism adds little insight and may justify protecting only those aspects of a culture that differ from those of the observer, resulting in only traditional forms of culture being respected by external observers. Cultural relativism may ignore how powerful cultures exercise power over weak ones. Interactions with external forces, including legal norms, often tend to reverberate through cultures in unpredictable ways and leave lasting imprints on cultural identities. Aboriginal practices that arose in response and in reaction to European contact, such as participating in the fur trade or incorporating elements of European religious beliefs into Aboriginal consciousness,[113] and that ensured the continuation and survival of Aboriginal communities, may not be shielded by blanket assertions of cultural relativism. As discussed in the following chapter, the boundaries of culture are more porous than cultural relativism presupposes. A particular culture that is both similar to and different from a more dominant culture may only be able to assert its identity in terms of its difference and not in its more subtle variations of difference and similarity.

The debate between universalism and relativism shows no sign of abating in the near future. Pending its outcome, grounding the constitutional significance of indigenous difference in either relativist or universalist premises is inherently unstable.[114] The risk of constitutional instability is sufficient justification, if not to "move beyond" it,[115] then at least to put the debate aside and engage in the more immediate task of assessing the constitutional relevance of indigenous difference in light of principles that potentially possess normative significance to Aboriginal and non-Aboriginal people alike.[116] Such principles can serve as standards for determining the justice of existing constitutional arrangements and suggest ways in which just distributions of power can be established or promoted in light of contemporary social reality without having to wait for a conclusive determination of whether universalism or cultural relativism is actually "true." In the next chapter, I argue that interests associated with Aboriginal cultural difference warrant constitutional protection not because of any incommensurability between Aboriginal and non-Aboriginal values, but because such protection promotes a just distribution of constitutional power. By proceeding in this way, I hope to capture a measure of intercultural agreement among Aboriginal people and non-Aboriginal people on the constitutional significance of indigenous difference.

NOTES

1 Gary Snyder, *The Practice of the Wild* (New York: North Point Press, 1990), at 24.
2 See Charles L. Black Jr, *Structure and Relationship in Constitutional Law* (Woodbridge: Ox Bow Press, 1968), at 7 (describing constitutional interpretation as including "a method of inference from the structures and relationships created by the constitution in all its parts or in some principal part"). Some define structural theory more broadly to include what are often referred to as procedural theories. See, for example, Louis Michael Seidman and Mark V. Tushnet, *Remnants of Belief: Contemporary Constitutional Issues* (Oxford: Oxford University Press, 1996), at 166–89. For a classic procedural theory, known as "legal process," see Henry Melvin Hart and Albert M. Sacks, *The Legal Process* (Westbury: Foundation Press, 1994) (judicial decision-making ought to attempt to find consensus on a set of jurisdictional and procedural rules concerning which institution should decide particular issues and how such decisions ought to be made, as opposed to substantive principles that purport to dictate what those decisions ought to be); for a modern procedural account, known as "representation-reinforcing theory," see John Hart Ely, *Democracy and Distrust* (Cambridge: Harvard University Press, 1980) (the primary role of constitutional review is to ensure the fairness of the political process by making certain that everyone has fair access).
3 For analysis of the limits of textual reasoning, see Eric J. Segall, "The Skeptic's Constitution," 44 U.C.L.A. L. Rev. 1467, at 1502 (1997) ("[t]he constitutional text is irrelevant to virtually every case the Supreme Court decides"); David A. Strauss, "Common Law Constitutional Interpretation," 63 U. Chi. L. Rev. 877, 883 (1996) ("[i]n practice constitutional law generally has little to do with the text"). For analysis of the limitations of structural reasoning, see Seidman and Tushnet, *Remnants of Belief*, at 180 ("it is hard to choose between structural theories or to

give the theories determinate content without reference to disputed value judgments"). See, generally, Paul Brest, "The Fundamental Rights Controversy: The Essential Contradictions of Normative Constitutional Scholarship," 90 Yale L.J. 1063 (1981).

4 R. v. Sparrow, [1990] 1 S.C.R. 1075 at 1108.

5 R. v. Van der Peet, [1996] 2 S.C.R. 507.

6 R. v. Badger, [1996] 1 S.C.R. 771.

7 See, for example, R. v. Sutherland, [1980] 2 S.C.R. 451.

8 See, for example, Kruger and Manuel v. The Queen, [1978] 1 S.C.R. 104; Four B Manufacturing v. United Garment Workers of America, [1980] 1 S.C.R. 1031.

9 See specifically Catherine Bell and Michael Asch, "Challenging Assumptions: The Impact of Precedent in Aboriginal Rights Litigation," in Michael Asch, ed., Aboriginal and Treaty Rights in Canada: Essays on Law, Equality, and Respect for Difference (Vancouver: UBC Press, 1997), 38–74. See generally F. Schauer, "Precedent," 39 Stan. L. Rev. 571 (1987); Henry P. Monaghan, "Our Perfect Constitution," 56 N.Y.U. L. Rev. 353 (1981).

10 See Schauer, "Precedent," at 576 ("a pure argument from precedent depends only on the results of [previous] decisions, and not only [on] the validity of reasons supporting those results").

11 See generally, John Austin, The Province of Jurisprudence Determined, ed. W.E. Rumble (Cambridge: Cambridge University Press, 1995); Hans Kelsen, General Theory of Law and State, trans. A. Nedberg (Cambridge: Harvard University Press, 1945); H.L.A. Hart, The Concept of Law (Oxford: Clarendon Press, 1961). See also Owen Fiss, "The Varieties of Positivism," 90 Yale L.J. 1007 (1981).

12 Austin, The Province of Jurisprudence Determined, at 157.

13 Compare Luc B. Tremblay, The Rule of Law, Justice, and Interpretation (Montreal and Kingston: McGill-Queen's University Press, 1997), at 25 (positivist constitutional theory regards "a given legal doctrine as true if its main propositions correspond to a subset of valid material rules of constitutional law laid down in recognized legal sources such as the constitution, a statute, or a case").

14 See, for example, Coté v. The Queen, [1996] 3 S.C.R. 139 at 174 (s. 35 protection is not restricted to "those defining features [of Aboriginal societies] which were fortunate enough to have received the legal recognition and approval of European colonizers").

15 For scholarship on legal pluralism generally, see John Griffiths, "What Is Legal Pluralism?" 24 Journal of Legal Pluralism 1(1986); Martha-Marie

Kleinhans and Roderick A. Macdonald, "What Is a *Critical* Legal Plural-ism?" 12 Can. J. Law & Soc. 25 (1997); see, specifically, John Borrows, "With or without You: First Nations (in Canada)," 41 McGill L.J. 630 (1996); Natalie Oman, "The Role of Recognition in the Delgamuukw Case," in Jill Oakes et al., eds., *Sacred Lands: Aboriginal World Views, Claims, and Conflicts* (Edmonton: Canadian Circumpolar Institute, 1998), 243–56.

16 See, for example, *Mabo v. Queensland* [No. 2] (1992), 175 C.L.R. 1 at 58, per Brennan J. ("Native title has its origin in and is given content by the traditional laws acknowledged by and the traditional customs observed by the indigenous inhabitants of a territory" and "[t]he nature and incidents of native title must be ascertained as a matter of fact by refer-ence to those laws and customs"). For discussion, see Kent McNeil, "The Meaning of Aboriginal Title," in Asch, ed., *Aboriginal and Treaty Rights in Canada*, 135 at 137–41. See also Ian Hamnett, *Chieftainship and Legitimacy* (Boston: Routledge and Kegan Paul, 1975), at 14 ("customary law can be regarded as a set of norms which the actors in a social situation abstract from practice and which they invest with binding authority"); Marc Galanter, "Justice in Many Rooms: Courts, Private Ordering, and Indige-nous Law," 19 Journal of Legal Pluralism 1 (1981) ("indigenous law" refers to "concrete patterns of social ordering").

17 See, for example, *R. v. Van der Peet, supra.*

18 See, for example, Austin, *The Province of Jurisprudence Determined* (a law is valid because it is the command of a sovereign); Kelsen, *General Theory of Law and State* (a legal norm is valid if authorized by another legal norm of a higher rank); Hart, *The Concept of Law* (a law is valid if it complies with "secondary rules" or laws that authorize the enactment of law).

19 For scholarship addressing legal indeterminacy, see Duncan Kennedy, *A Critique of Adjudication* (Cambridge: Harvard University Press, 1997); Robert W. Gordon, "Critical Legal Histories," 36 Stan. L. Rev. 57 (1984); Joseph Singer, "The Player and the Cards: Nihilism and Legal Theory," 94 Yale L.J. 1 (1984); Karl Klare, "Law-Making as Praxis," 40 Telos 123 (1979); and Duncan Kennedy, "Legal Formality," 2 J. Legal Studies 351 (1973).

20 See Hart, *The Concept of Law.*

21 See, for example, Neil MacCormick, *Legal Reasoning and Legal Theory* (Oxford: Clarendon Press, 1978) (arguing judges decide hard cases under a detailed judicial duty to do justice according to law).

22 For an extensive discussion of positivist theory in this regard, see An-thony J. Sebok, *Legal Positivism in American Jurisprudence* (Cambridge:

Cambridge University Press, 1998) (arguing that positivism can explain how law can both incorporate and cabin normative considerations).

23 For a discussion of judicial minimalism, see Cass R. Sunstein, *One Case at a Time: Judicial Minimalism on the Supreme Court* (Cambridge: Harvard University Press, 1999).

24 See Lawrence G. Sager, "Justice in Plain Clothes: Reflections on the Thinness of Constitutional Law," 88 Northwestern U.L. Rev. 410 (arguing that social and economic rights call for a minimalist approach to constitutional enforcement). See also Lawrence G. Sager, "Fair Measure: The Legal Status of Underenforced Constitutional Norms," 91 Harv. L. Rev. 1212 (1978) (arguing that the legal scope of constitutional norms often is not coterminous with the scope of judicial enforcement).

25 Compare Paul Brest, "Constitutional Citizenship," 34 Cleveland State L. Rev. 175 at 181 (1986) ("[I]f the judges exercise a monopoly over constitutional decisionmaking, then other citizens and their representatives are excluded from participating in what are among the polity's most fundamental decisions"); Sager, "Fair Measure," at 1264 ("the Court should welcome the efforts of Congress and the state courts to shape elusive constitutional norms at their margins").

26 Abram Chayes, "The Role of the Judge in Public Law Litigation," 89 Harv. L. Rev. 1281 at 1316 (1976).

27 Ibid. For a detailed examination of the merits and demerits of the judicial arena in relation to Aboriginal claims, see Lisa Marie Strelein, "Indigenous Self-Determination Claims and the Common Law in Australia" (PhD thesis, Australian National University, 1998) (on file with author).

28 Joel Handler, "Poverty, Dependency, and Social Welfare: Procedural Justice for the Poor," in Bryant G. Garth and Austin Sarat, eds., *Justice and Power in Sociolegal Studies* (Evanston: Northwestern University Press, 1998), 136–65 at 140.

29 Cass R. Sunstein, *After the Rights Revolution: Reconceiving the Regulatory State* (Cambridge: Harvard University Press, 1990), at 157 (discussing the role of contestable background norms in legal interpretation).

30 See Constitution Act, 1982, s. 3 ("[e]very citizen of Canada has the right to vote in an election of members of the House of Commons or of a legislative assembly").

31 Jürgen Habermas, "Struggles for Recognition in the Democratic Constitutional State," in Amy Gutman, ed., *Multiculturalism: Examining the Politics of Recognition* (Princeton: Princeton University Press, 1994), at 125.

32 See Tom Campbell, *Justice* (Atlantic Highlands: Humanities Press International, 1988), at 3 (principles of distributive justice "are ideological

battlegrounds which exhibit some of the most basic differences in moral and political outlook").

33 See John Rawls, *A Theory of Justice* (Cambridge: Harvard University Press, 1971).

34 Ibid., at 153–6. In his recent writings Rawls has introduced the idea of an "overlapping consensus," consisting of "all the reasonable opposing religious, philosophical, and moral doctrines likely to persist over generations and to gain a sizable body of adherents," which can support a political conception of justice: see John Rawls, *Political Liberalism* (New York: Columbia University Press, 1993), at 15.

35 See Ronald Dworkin, *Taking Rights Seriously* (Cambridge: Harvard University Press, 1977), at 277.

36 Ibid., at 275–8. In more recent writings, Dworkin has introduced the idea of "law as integrity," which posits that "rights and responsibilities flow from past decisions and so count as legal, not just when they are explicit in these decisions but also when they follow from the principles of personal and political morality the explicit decisions presupposed by way of justification": see *Law's Empire* (Cambridge: Harvard University Press, 1986), at 96. He has also sought to advance the view that his work does not endorse any particular set of moral values: see ibid., at 358–9; but see Ronald Dworkin, *Freedom's Law: The Moral Reading of the American Constitution* (Cambridge: Harvard University Press, 1996), at 75 ("the Constitution guarantees the rights required by the best conceptions of the political ideals of equal concern and basic liberty").

37 For the view that much of contemporary constitutional theory brackets social reality, see Jürgen Habermas, *Between Facts and Norms: Contributions to a Discourse Theory of Law and Democracy* (Cambridge: MIT Press, 1996), at 43 (criticizing philosophical theories of justice for "los[ing] touch with contemporary societies").

38 Rawls, *A Theory of Justice*, at 12.

39 Ronald Dworkin, "In Praise of Theory," 29 Ariz. L.J. 353 at 354 (1997).

40 Compare Stanley Fish, *Doing What Comes Naturally: Change, Rhetoric, and the Practice of Theory in Literary and Legal Studies* (Durham: Duke University Press, 1989), at 370 (*Law's Empire* "urges us to adopt 'law as integrity,' but since that is the form our judicial practice already and necessarily takes, the urging is superfluous"); Pierre Schlag, "Normativity and the Politics of Form," in Paul F. Campos, Pierre Schlag, and Steven D. Smith, *Against the Law* (Durham: Duke University Press, 1996), 29–99 at 56, n. 74 ("as jurisprudence goes, [*Law's Empire*] is in the genre of cheerleading").

41 Habermas, *Between Facts and Norms*, at 58 ("all this holds only on the assumption that just institutions already exist .... [I]t is another question how these can be *established* or at least promoted in present circumstances") (emphasis in original).

42 For analyses of contextual methodologies, see Martha Minow and Elizabeth Spelman, "In Context," 63 S. Cal. L. Rev. 1597 (1990); C. Wells, "Situated Decisionmaking," 63 S. Cal. L. Rev. 1727 (1990); Thomas Grey, "Holmes and Legal Pragmatism," 41 Stan. L. Rev. 787 (1989).

43 Compare Roberto Mangabeira Unger, *What Should Legal Analysis Become?* (London: Verso, 1996), at 132 ("[c]riticism explores the disharmonies between the professed social ideals and programmatic commitments of society, as well as the recognized group interests, and the detailed institutional arrangements that not only constrain the realization of those ideals, programs, and interests but also give them their developed meaning").

44 See Dworkin, *Law's Empire*, at 13–14 (drawing a distinction between internal and external points of view on law); Hart, *The Concept of Law*, at 86–8 (drawing a distinction between the external observer who does not accept the rules and the internal participant who uses the rules as guides to conduct).

45 Some advance this claim with praise: see, for example, Richard Epstein, *Takings: Private Property and the Power of Eminent Domain* (Cambridge: Harvard University Press, 1985), at 332 ("[a] system of private rights provides an exhaustive and internally consistent normative baseline of entitlements against which all the complex schemes of justice can be tested"). Others decry it: see Joel Bakan, *Just Words: Constitutional Rights and Social Wrongs* (Toronto: University of Toronto Press, 1997), at 61 ("[l]iberal rights discourse is sustained by, and helps sustain, the various elements of liberal and capitalist hegemony").

46 Catherine MacKinnon, *Toward a Feminist Theory of the State* (Cambridge: Harvard University Press, 1989), at 224 (law conceals "the substantive way in which man has become the measure of all things").

47 See, for example, Kenneth B. Nunn, "Law as a Eurocentric Enterprise," 15 Law & Inequality 323 at 328 (1997) ("law is part of a broader cultural endeavor that attempts to promote European values and interests at the expense of all others"); see also Mary Ellen Turpel, "Aboriginal Peoples and the Canadian Charter: Interpretive Monopolies, Cultural Differences," 6 Can. Human Rights Yearbook 3 (1989–90) ("[t]he rights paradigm and interpretive context of Canadian constitutional law is so

unreceptive to cultural differences that, as a result, it is oppressively hegemonic in its perception of its own cultural authority").

48 Compare Schlag, "Normativity and the Politics of Form," at 89 ("law has an *inside* and an *outside*; it is bounded") (emphasis in original); Unger, *What Should Legal Analysis Become?* at 179 (calling for legal scholarship to "split the difference between rationalism and historicism"); Habermas, *Between Facts and Norms*, at 79 ("[l]aw is two things at the same time: a system of knowledge and a system of action" and "[i]t is equally possible to understand law as a text, composed of legal propositions and their interpretations, and to view it as an institution, that is, as a complex of normatively regulated action"); and Sally Falk Moore, *Law as Process* (Cambridge: Harvard University Press, 1978), at 57 (law "can generate rules and customs and symbols internally, but ... it is also vulnerable to rules and decisions and other forces emanating from the larger world by which it is surrounded").

49 Compare Klare, "Law-Making as Praxis," at 134 ("Must we not recognize that legal culture can and has provided a context and a moral basis for resistance to injustice?").

50 Robert Gordon, "Unfreezing Critical Reality: Critical Approaches to Law," 15 Florida State U. L. Rev. 196 at 217 (1987). See also Habermas, *Between Facts and Norms*, at 36 ("the acceptance of validity claims, which generates and perpetuates social facts, rests on the context-dependent acceptability of reasons that are constantly exposed to the risk of being invalidated by better reasons").

51 See, e.g., Aristotle, *Politics*, ed. G.P. Gould, trans. H. Rackham (Cambridge: Harvard University Press, 1990), at 370–3; Aristotle, *Nichomachean Ethics*, ed. and trans. Martin Ostwald (Indianapolis: Bobbs-Merrill, 1962), at 119–20 (distributive justice produces equality). Following Plato, Aristotle divided equality into numerical and proportional equality, the former referring to distributions that treat all individuals within the set as indistinguishable, and the latter referring to distributions that treat all individuals within the set in proportion to a relevant characteristic, such as merit. See Plato, *Laws*, ed. G.P. Goold, trans. R.G. Bury (London: Heinemann, 1984), at 412–15. Aristotle confined proportional equality to distributive justice and numerical equality to corrective justice. See Aristotle, *Nichomachean Ethics*, at 118–19; see also Michael Walzer, *Spheres of Justice: A Defense of Pluralism and Equality* (New York: Basic Books, 1983), at xv ("distributive justice is ... an art of differentiation ... [a]nd equality is simply the outcome of that art"). For a detailed discussion of Aristotelian theories of equality, see Wolfgang von Leyden, *Aristotle on*

Equality and Justice: His Political Argument (Houndsmills: Macmillan, 1985).

52 Aristotle, *Nichomachean Ethics*, at 118–20. Compare Hart, *The Concept of Law*, at 155 ("justice is traditionally thought of as maintaining or restoring a *balance* or *proportion*, and its leading precept is often formulated as 'Treat like cases alike'; although we need to add to the latter 'and treat different cases differently'") (emphasis in original).

53 Peter Westen, *Speaking of Equality: An Analysis of the Rhetorical Force of "Equality" in Moral and Legal Discourse* (Princeton: Princeton University Press, 1990), at 40–1.

54 Ibid., at 61.

55 Compare Adeno Addis, "Individualism, Communitarianism, and the Rights of Ethnic Minorities," 66 Notre Dame L. Rev. 1219 (1991) (cultural difference should not be reduced to racial difference); Turpel, "Aboriginal Peoples and the Canadian Charter" (indigenous difference should not be reduced to racial difference); David Schneiderman, "Theorists of Difference and the Interpretation of Aboriginal and Treaty Rights," 14 Int'l J. Can Stud. 35 (1996) (indigenous difference should not be reduced to cultural difference); and Isabelle Schulte-Tenckhoff, "Reassessing the Paradigm of Domestication: The Problematic of Indigenous Treaties," 4 Rev. Const. Stud. 239 (1998) (indigenous difference should not be reduced to cultural difference). See also Chapter 2, below.

56 See, for example, Will Kymlicka, *Multicultural Citizenship: A Liberal Theory of Minority Rights* (Oxford: Clarendon Press, 1995). See also Duncan Ivison, "Decolonizing the Rule of Law: Mabo's Case and Postcolonial Constitutionalism," 17 Oxford J. Leg. Stud. 252 at 254 (1997) (arguing that "accommodation of differences is essential to treating [Aboriginal] people equally in diverse political communities").

57 For the view that some individual interests possess collective aspects, see Leslie Green, "Two Views of Collective Rights," 4 Can. J. Law & Jur. 315 (1991); see also Leighton McDonald, "Can Collective and Individual Rights Coexist?" 22 Melbourne U. L. Rev. 310 (1998). For a collective interest analysis of "cultural autonomy" see Denise Réaume, "Justice between Cultures: Autonomy and the Protection of Cultural Affiliation," 29 U.B.C. L. Rev. 117 (1995).

58 See, for example, *Delgamuukw v. British Columbia*, [1997] 3 S.C.R. 1010; see also *Amodu Tijani v. Secretary, Southern Nigeria*, [1921] 2 A.C. 399 (P.C.).

59 Joseph Tussman and Jacobus TenBroek, "The Equal Protection of Laws," 37 Cal. L. Rev. 341, at 343 (1949) ("the demand for equal protection cannot be a demand that laws apply universally to all persons. The legisla-

ture, if it is to act at all, must impose special burdens upon or grant special benefits to special groups or classes of individuals").

60 Douglas Rae, et al., *Equalities* (Cambridge: Harvard University Press, 1981), at 19 (emphasis deleted). See also Westen, *Speaking of Equality*, at 126 ("[e]very normative dispute can be framed as a contest between ... one proposed equality and another"); David E. Cooper, *The Illusions of Equality* (London: Routledge and Kegan Paul, 1980), at 14 ("many of the interesting debates are not about the bare question, 'should we have equality?,' but about which of the various competing equalities we should have").

61 Westen, *Speaking of Equality*, at 61. Compare Rawls, *A Theory of Justice*, at 4–5 (distinction between concept of justice and conceptions of justice); Dworkin, *Law's Empire*, at 70–2, 134–6 (distinction between concept of equality and conceptions of equality).

62 Charles Taylor, *Philosophy and the Human Sciences: Philosophical Papers* (Cambridge: Cambridge University Press, 1985), at 2:300. Compare James Boyd White, *Justice as Translation: An Essay in Cultural and Legal Criticism* (Chicago: University of Chicago Press, 1990), at 233 ("the radical question of justice ... [is] not, 'How much do I get?' but 'Who are we to each other?'").

63 See Walzer, *Spheres of Justice*, at 6 ("principles of justice are themselves pluralistic in form; ... different social goods ought to be distributed for different reasons, in accordance with different procedures, by different agents; and ... all these differences derive from different understandings of the social goods themselves").

64 For an apparent endorsement of this claim, see Walzer, *Spheres of Justice*, at 62. While Walzer argues that American political culture is premised on equal treatment of citizens without regard to racial or cultural difference, he appears to accept that this particular conception of equality is of little use in determining whether a group or collectivity has the right to govern itself.

65 S. James Anaya, *Indigenous Peoples in International Law* (Oxford: Oxford University Press, 1996), at 3. See also U.N. Subcommission on Prevention of Discrimination and Protection of Minorities, *Study of the Problem of Discrimination Against Indigenous Populations*, U.N. Doc. E/CN.4/ Sub.2/1986/7/Add. 4, para. 379 (1986) ("Indigenous ... peoples ... are those which, having a historical continuity with pre-invasion and pre-colonial societies that developed on their territories, consider themselves distinct from the other sectors of the societies now prevailing in those territories").

66 Articles 1(2) and 55 of the United Nations Charter refer to "the principle of equal rights and self-determination of peoples." However, articles 2(1) and 2(4) of the Charter also affirm the "sovereign equality" and "territorial integrity" of member states: Charter of the United Nations, adopted 26 June 1945, entered into force 24 Oct. 1945, as amended.

67 Compare Schlag, "Normativity and the Politics of Form," at 39 (criticizing normative legal thought as monistic, for seeking "to prescribe a single authoritative norm to rule within the described jurisdiction of the enterprise"); Cass R. Sunstein, "General Propositions and Concrete Cases (With Special Reference to Affirmative Action and Free Speech)," 31 Wake Forest L. Rev. 369 at 381 (1996) ("Human morality recognizes irreducibly diverse goods, which cannot be subsumed under a single 'master' value. The same is true for the moral values reflected in law. ... It would be absurd to try to organize legal judgments through a single conception of value").

68 See Brian Slattery, "Aboriginal Sovereignty and Imperial Claims," 29 Osgoode Hall L.J. 681 (1991) (rights to life and basic necessities ground Aboriginal rights of self-government).

69 See Leon Trakman, "Native Cultures in a Rights Empire Ending the Dominion," 45 Buff. L. Rev. 189 (1997) (liberty should be understood as encompassing a responsibility to respect Aboriginal interests).

70 See Aviam Soifer, *Law and the Company We Keep* (Cambridge: Harvard University Press, 1995), at 542 ("if ever freedom of association should have constitutional clout, it ought to be in cases brought by remaining Native Americans that assert tribal rights").

71 See Anaya, *Indigenous Peoples in International Law*; see also Royal Commission on Aboriginal Peoples, *Final Report*, vol. 2, *Restructuring the Relationship* (Ottawa: Minister of Supply and Services Canada, 1996).

72 See, generally, Antonio Cassese, *Self-Determination of Peoples: A Legal Reappraisal* (Cambridge: Cambridge University Press, 1995); Martti Koskenniemi, "National Self-Determination Today: Problems of Legal Theory and Practice," 43 Int'l & Comp. L.Q. 241 (1994); Guyora Binder, "The Case for Self-Determination," 29 Stan. J. Int'l Law 223 (1993); Edward M. Morgan, "The Imagery and Meaning of Self-Determination," 20 N.Y.U. J. Int'l Law 355 (1988); Nathaniel Berman, "Sovereignty in Abeyance: Self-Determination and International Law," 7 Wisc. Int'l L.J. 51 (1988). See, specifically, Russel Lawrence Barsh, "Indigenous Peoples in the 1990s: From Object to Subject of International Law?," 7 Harv. Human Rights J. 33 (1994); Mary Ellen Turpel, "Indigenous Peoples' Rights of Political Participation and Self-Determination: Recent Interna-

tional Legal Developments and the Continuing Struggle for Recognition," 25 Cornell Int'l L.J. 579 (1992); Maivân Clech Lâm, "Making Room for Peoples at the United Nations: Thoughts Provoked by Indigenous Claims to Self-Determination," 25 Cornell Int'l L.J. 603 (1992); Catherine J. Iorns, "Indigenous Peoples and Self-Determination: Challenging State Sovereignty," 24 Case Western. Res. J. Int'l L. 199 (1992).

73 S. James Anaya, "The Capacity of International Law to Advance Ethnic or Nationality Rights Claims," 75 Iowa L. Rev. 837 at 841 (1990).

74 U.N. Charter, ("[t]he purposes of the United Nations are ... [t]o develop friendly relations among nations based on respect for the principle of equal rights and self-determination of peoples").

75 Ibid., art. 55.

76 International Covenant on Civil and Political Rights, art. 1, opened for signature 19 Dec. 1966, 999 U.N.T.S. 171 (entered into force 23 Mar. 1976). Article 1 of the International Covenant on Economic, Social and Cultural Rights contains identical language. Opened for signature 19 Dec. 1966, 993 U.N.T.S. 3 (entered into force 3 Jan. 1976).

77 *Namibia*, [1971] I.C.J. 16 at 31; *Western Sahara*, [1975] I.C.J. 12 at 31.

78 See, generally, Umozurike Oji Umozurike, *Self-Determination in International Law* (Hamden: Archon, 1972), at 11–26.

79 See, generally, Fernand van Langenhove, *The Question of Aborigines before the United Nations: The Belgian Thesis* (Brussels: Royal Colonial Institute, 1954).

80 G.A. Res. 1514, 15 U.N. GAOR Supp. (No. 16), at 66, U.N. Doc. A/7218 (1969).

81 GAOR 15th Session, Supplement 16, 66.

82 Patrick Thornberry, *International Law and the Rights of Minorities* (Oxford: Clarendon Press, 1991), at 18 (emphasis deleted). For critiques of the "salt water" thesis, see, generally, Lung-Chu Chen, "Self-Determination and World Public Order," 66 Notre Dame L. Rev. 1287 (1991); see, specifically, Russel Lawrence Barsh, "Indigenous Peoples and the Right to Self-Determination in International Law," in Barbara Hocking, ed., *International Law and Aboriginal Human Rights* (Sidney: Law Book, 1988), at 68.

83 See, generally, Dov Ronen, *The Quest for Self-Determination* (New Haven: Yale University Press, 1979), at 7 (self-determination "is an expression, in succinct form, of the aspiration to rule one's self and not to be ruled by others"); see, specifically, Iorns, *Indigenous Peoples*, at 225 (indigenous self-determination refers to "the idea of freedom from oppressors and

the right to determine their future, their own form of government, as well as the extent of self-government").

84 Quoted in Thornberry, *International Law and the Rights of Minorities*, at 18.

85 U.N. Doc. E/CN.4/Sub.2/476/Add.5, Annex III, 2. See also Grand Council of the Crees (of Quebec), *Submission: Status and Rights of the James Bay Crees in the Context of Quebec's Secession from Canada* (Commission on Human Rights, 48th Sess., 1992).

86 For an illuminating analysis of external self-determination, see Karen C. Knop, "The Making of Difference in International Law: Interpretation, Identity and Participation in the Discourse of Self-Determination" (S.J.D. thesis, Faculty of Law, University of Toronto, 1998) (on file with author). For discussions of internal self-determination, see Patrick Thornberry, "The Democratic or Internal Aspect of Self-Determination with Some Remarks on Federalism," in C. Tomuschat, ed., *Modern Law of Self-Determination* (Dordrecht: Martinus Nijhoff, 1993); Thomas Franck, "The Emerging Right to Democratic Governance," 86 Amer.J. Int'l L. 46 (1992). See also *Reference re Secession of Quebec*, [1998] 2 S.C.R. 217.

87 Draft Declaration on the Rights of Indigenous Peoples (as agreed to by the members of the working group at its 11th session) E/CN.4/Sub.2/1994/2/Add.1 (20 Apr. 1994), art. 3.

88 Ibid.

89 Erica-Irene Daes, Chairperson of the Working Group on Indigenous Populations, *Explanatory Note concerning the Draft Declaration on the Rights of Indigenous Peoples*, E/CN.4/Sub.2/1993/26/Add.1 (released 19 July 1993).

90 Ibid.

91 Compare James Tully, "The Struggles of Indigenous Peoples for and of Freedom," in D. Ivison et al., eds., *Political Theory and the Rights of Indigenous Peoples* (Oakleigh: Cambridge University Press, forthcoming), at 33 (internal self-determination coupled with an absolute conception of state sovereignty constitutes "indirect colonial rule").

92 Compare Jeremy Waldron, "Minority Cultures and the Cosmopolitan Alternative," 25 U. Mich. L. Rev. 751, at 779 (1992) ("Indigenous communities ... are not entitled to accept the benefits of ... protection and subsidization and at the same time disparage and neglect the structures, institutions, and activities that make it possible for indigenous communities to secure the aid, toleration, and forebearance of the large numbers of other citizens and other small communities by which they are surrounded").

93 See Avishai Margalit and Joseph Raz, "National Self-Determination," 87 J. Philo. 439 (1990).

94 See, for example, Jack Donnelly, *Universal Human Rights in Theory and Practice* (Ithaca: Cornell University Press, 1989).

95 See, generally, Alison Dundes Renteln, *International Human Rights: Universalism versus Relativism* (Newbury Park: Sage Publications, 1990).

96 See Iris Marion Young, *Justice and the Politics of Difference* (Princeton: Princeton University Press, 1990), at 59 (defining cultural imperialism as the establishment of a dominant group's experience and culture as a universal norm).

97 G.A. Res. 217A, U.N. GAOR, 3d Sess., pt. 1, at 71, U.N. Doc. A/810 (1948), arts. 7 and 21, respectively.

98 Douglas Lee Donoho, "Relativism versus Universalism in Human Rights: The Search for Meaningful Standards," 27 Stan. J. Int'l L. 345, at 357 (1991).

99 Abdullahi Ahmed An-Na'im, *Toward an Islamic Reformation: Civil Liberties, Human Rights, and International Law* (Syracuse: Syracuse University Press, 1990), at 164 ("universal human rights are based on the two primary forces that motivate all human behavior, the will to live and the will to be free").

100 19 Dec. 1966, art. 27, 999 U.N.T.S. 171.

101 See, for example, Turpel, "Aboriginal Peoples and the Canadian Charter" (challenging the cultural authority of Canadian constitutional law as it relates to Aboriginal people). See more generally, Nunn, "Law as a Eurocentric Enterprise," at 324 ("law is the creation of a particular *type* of culture") (emphasis in original).

102 Rupert Ross, *Dancing with a Ghost: Exploring Indian Reality* (Markham: Octopus, 1992), at 186.

103 Cultural relativism is often broken down into a number of different versions. A common list includes descriptive relativism, normative relativism, and meta-ethical relativism. Descriptive relativism is factual in nature: it points out that as a matter of fact different moral beliefs exist by virtue of differing cultural contexts. For refinements of this version, see M. Spiro, "Cultural Relativism and the Future of Anthropology," 1 Cultural Anthropology 259 at 260–1 (1986). Normative relativism is based on the more contentious claim that differing moral values have no validity outside of their particular cultural contexts and, as such, are incommensurable. The work of Ruth Benedict is often associated with this view. See Ruth Benedict, *Patterns of Culture* (Boston: Houghton Mifflin, 1934), at 278 (there are "coexisting and equally valid patterns of

life"). Meta-ethical relativism holds that one cannot objectively justify the moral beliefs of one culture over the moral beliefs of another, although there may exist certain shared or universal values. See, generally, Donoho, "Relativism versus Universalism in Human Rights," at 351–2; William K. Frankena, *Ethics* (Englewood Cliffs, N.J.: Prentice-Hall, 1973), at 109–10; Paul F. Schmidt, "Some Criticisms of Cultural Relativism," 70 J. Philo. 780 (1955).

104 Similarly, one could derive recognition of the relevance of indigenous difference from some versions of universalism: see, e.g., Anaya, *Indigenous Peoples in International Law*, at 75–96.

105 Melville J. Herskovits, *Man and His Works: The Science of Cultural Anthropology* (New York: Knopf, 1948), at 63.

106 Many have made this point. See for example, Schmidt, "Some Criticisms of Cultural Relativism," 70 J. Phil. 780 at 781 (1955) ("the cultural relativist cannot have it both ways: he cannot claim that the truth of factual judgments is relative to their cultural background and at the same time believe in the objectivity of sociological and anthropological investigations"). See also Grace A. de Laguna, "Cultural Relativism and Science," 51 Phil. Rev. 141 (1942).

107 R.J. Vincent, *Human Rights and International Relations* (Cambridge: Cambridge University Press, 1986), at 55; I.C. Jarvis, "Rationalism and Relativism," 34 Brit. J. Sociology 44 at 46 (1983) ("behind relativism nihilism looms"); Clyde Kluckhohn, "Ethical Relativity: Sic et Non," 52 J. Phil. 663 (1995) ("one is compelled to accept any cultural pattern as vindicated precisely by its cultural status"). But see Herskovits, *Man and His Works*, at 245 ("To recognize that right, and justice, and beauty may have as many manifestations as there are cultures is to express tolerance, not nihilism").

108 Compare Donnelly, *Universal Human Rights*, at 116 ("no matter how firmly someone else, or even a whole culture, believes differently, at some point we simply must say that those contrary beliefs are wrong"); and Vincent, *Human Rights and International Relations*, at 55 ("[h]owever true it is that we all tend to devolve upon our own worlds the responsibility of being in the right against others, this is not a reason to withdraw from moral argument in world politics all together").

109 See Clifford Geertz, *The Interpretation of Cultures* (New York: Basic Books, 1973), at 192–200; see also Fish, *Doing What Comes Naturally*, at 351–4 (non-foundationalism does not entail any particular political consequences).

110 Robert Redfield, *The Primitive World and Its Transformations* (Ithaca: Cornell University Press, 1962), at 147.

111 See, e.g., Frank E. Hartung, "Cultural Relativity and Moral Judgments," 21 Phil. Sci. 118 at 121 (1954) (relativism "is an ethnocentric circumlocution, a round-about way of saying that our liberal tradition is the best tradition, and that all ought to follow").

112 See Rhoda Howard, *Human Rights in Commonwealth Africa* (Totowa N.J.: Rowman & Littlefield, 1986), at 23–5; see also Annie Bunting, "Theorizing Women's Cultural Diversity in Feminist International Human Rights Strategies," 20 J. Law & Society 6 at 9 (1993) ("multiply-constituted nature and competing understandings of any given culture are rarely discussed" in relativistic accounts).

113 See, e.g., John Borrows, "A Genealogy of Law: Inherent Sovereignty and First Nations Self-Government," 30 Osgoode Hall L.J. 291 (1992).

114 But see Donnelly, *Universal Human Rights in Theory and Practice*, at 118 ("where there is a thriving indigenous cultural tradition and community, arguments of cultural relativism offer a strong defense against outside interference – including disruptions that might be caused by introducing 'universal' human rights").

115 See Richard J. Bernstein, *Beyond Objectivism and Relativism: Science, Hermeneutics, and Praxis* (Philadelphia: University of Pennsylvania Press, 1983) at 1–44 (arguing that a new understanding of rationality permits one to move beyond philosophical debates concerning objectivism and relativism).

116 Compare Abdullahi Ahmed An-Na'im, "Toward a Cross-Cultural Approach to Defining International Standards of Human Rights: The Meaning of Cruel, Inhuman or Degrading Treatment or Punishment," in An-Na'im, ed., *Human Rights in Cross-Cultural Perspective: A Quest for Consensus* (Philadelphia: University of Pennsylvania Press, 1992), at 19, 27 ("[C]ultural consensus on the goals and methods of cooperation in the protection and promotion of human rights ... can be achieved through internal cultural discourse and cross-cultural dialogue ... Cross-cultural dialogue should be aimed at broadening and deepening international ... consensus"); Amelie Oskenberg Rorty, "Relativism, Persons, and Practices," in Michael Kraus, ed., *Relativism: Interpretation and Confrontation* (Notre Dame: University of Notre Dame Press, 1989), 418–40, at 418 ("nothing follows from [relativism] about the impossibility of cross-cultural interpretation, communication, or evaluation, particularly among cultures engaged in practical interactions with one another").

READING QUESTIONS ON BORROWS AND MACKLEM

1 Do Borrows and Macklem share the same hopes for the ability of law to accommodate the challenge posed by the aspirations of Aboriginal people?
2 Which conceptions of the rule of law are more helpful to their particular arguments?
3 Does the reasoning in *The Quebec Secession Reference* help in considering the problems posed by the aspirations of Aboriginal people?

8

Speech, Hate Propaganda, and Pornography

Freedom of expression is a central value in a free and democratic society. Indeed, it is so important that some people have suggested that it is entirely without exceptions. Despite its high-minded tone, such a view is probably unrealistic. As the American judge Oliver Wendell Holmes famously put it, even the most stringent protection of free speech will not extend to the person falsely shouting "fire" in a crowded theatre. There are plainly exceptions to free expression; the problem for philosophers is to come up with a principled way of thinking about them. Unfortunately, much of the public debate about free expression consists in exaggerated claims about the harmful effects of either speech or censorship. The readings in this section offer some more sophisticated accounts of the basis and limits of the protection of expression.

Joel Feinberg
"Pornography and the Criminal Law" (1979)

Feinberg argues that offensive material should be treated as a private matter. As a result, regulations are only legitimate if they aim to protect those who are offended from materials that bother them.

When the possession, use, or display of sexually explicit materials is prohibited by law, and violations are punished by fine or imprisonment, many thousands of persons are prevented from doing what they would otherwise freely choose to do. Such forceful interference in private affairs seems morally outrageous, unless, of course, it is supported by special justifying reasons. In the absence of appropriate reasons, the coercive use of governmental power, based ultimately on guns and clubs, is merely arbitrary and as such is always morally illegitimate. Criminal prohibitions, of course, are sometimes backed by appropriate reasons, and when that is the case, they are not morally illicit uses of force but rather reasonable regulations of our social activities.

What then are "appropriate reasons" for criminal prohibitions? Surely the need to prevent harm or injury to persons other than the one interfered with is one kind of legitimate reason. Some actions, however, while harmless in themselves, are great nuisances to those who are affected by them, and the law from time immemorial has provided remedies, some civil and some criminal, for actions in this category. So a second kind of legitimate reason for prohibiting conduct is the need to protect others from certain sorts of offensive, irritating, or inconveniencing experiences. Extreme nuisances can actually reach the threshold of harm, as when noises from the house next door prevent a student from studying at all on the evening before an examination, or when an obstructed road causes a person to be late for an important appointment. But we are not very happy with nuisances even when they do not harm our interests, but only cause irritations to our senses, or inconvenient detours from our normal course. The offending conduct produces unpleasant or uncomfortable experiences – affronts to sense or sensibility, disgust, shock, shame, embarrassment, annoyance, boredom, anger, or humiliation – from which one cannot escape without unreasonable inconvenience or even harm.

We demand protection from nuisances when we think of ourselves as *trapped* by them, and we think it unfair that we should pay the cost in inconvenience that is required to escape them. In extreme cases, the offending conduct commandeers our attention from the outside, forcing us to relinquish control of our inner states, and drop what we were doing in order to cope, when it is greatly inconvenient to do so. That is why laws prohibiting nuisances are sometimes said to protect our interest in "privacy."

What distinguishes the "liberal position" on this question is the insistence that the need to prevent harm to others and the need to prevent offensive nuisances to others between them exhaust all the types of reasons which may appropriately support criminal prohibitions. Insofar as a criminal statute is unsupported by reasons of either of these two kinds, it tends to be arbitrary and hence morally illicit. In this respect certain commonly proffered reasons are no better than no reasons at all. The need to protect either the interests or the character of the actor himself from his own folly, does not, according to the liberal, confer moral legitimacy on a criminal statute, nor does the need to prevent inherently sinful or immoral conduct as such. Liberalism so construed does not purport to be a guide to useful public policy for the utilitarian legislator, nor does it claim to provide a key to the interpretation of the American, or any other, constitution. (It is entirely possible that the moral restrictions liberalism would place on legislative discretion are not always socially useful, and also that the Constitution itself allows some morally illegitimate statutes to remain as valid laws.) Instead liberalism purports to indicate to the legislator where the moral limits to government coercion are located.

Let me state from the outset that I am a committed liberal, in this sense, on the question of the legal regulation of pornography. Like the late Herbert Packer, I believe that pornography, at its worst, is not so much a menace as a nuisance, and that the moral right of legislatures to restrict it derives from, and is limited by, the same principles that morally entitle the state to command owners of howling dogs to stop their racket, to punish owners of fertilizing plants for letting odors escape over a whole town, to prohibit indecent exposure and public defecation, and so on. It is absurd to punish nuisances as severely as harmful or injurious conduct, however, and unless certain well-understood conditions are satisfied, it may be illegitimate to punish a given nuisance at all. For that reason it may be useful, before looking at the pornography problem, to examine the restrictions recognized by legislatures and courts on the proper regulation of harmless but offensive nuisances.

I

The most interesting aspect of the law of nuisance is its version of the unavoidable legal balancing act. Both legislatures, when they formulate statutes that define public nuisances, and courts, when they adjudicate conflicts between neighboring landowners in "private nuisance" cases, must weigh opposing considerations. Establishing that one person's conduct is or would be a nuisance to someone else is by no means sufficient to warrant legal interference. First one must compare carefully the magnitude of the nuisance to the one against the reasonableness of the conduct of the other, and the necessity "that all may get on together."[1]

William Prosser, describing the various factors that weigh on one side of the scale, tells us that the magnitude of the nuisance (or "seriousness of the inconvenience") to the plaintiff in a private nuisance action depends upon (1) the extent, duration, and character of the interference, (2) the social value of the use the plaintiff makes of his land, and (3) the extent to which the plaintiff can, without undue burden or hardship, avoid the offense by taking precautions against it.[2] These three factors yield the weight to be assigned to the "seriousness" of the inconvenience. They must be weighed against the reasonableness of the defendant's conduct, which is determined by (1) "the social value of its ultimate purpose, (2) the motive of the defendant [in particular its character as innocent or spiteful], and (3) whether the defendant by taking reasonable steps can avoid or reduce the inconvenience to the plaintiff without undue burden or inconvenience to himself."[3] Finally Prosser would have us throw on to the scale the interests of the "public at large," in particular its interest in "the nature of the locality" where the nuisance occurred – to "what paramount use it is already devoted" and given that background, "the suitability of the use made of the land by both plaintiff and defendant."[4] In sum, the more extended, durable, and severe the inconvenience to the plaintiff, and the greater the social value of the land uses interfered with, then the greater is the magnitude of the nuisance, while the greater the ease with which the plaintiff can avoid the nuisance, the smaller its magnitude. Similarly, the greater the social value of the defendant's conduct[5] and the freer his motives of spite toward the plaintiff, the more reasonable is his conduct, despite its inconvenience to the plaintiff, while the easier it is for him to achieve his goals by means that do not inconvenience the plaintiff, the less reasonable is his offending conduct. Finally, the prevalent character of the neighborhood weighs heavily, so that a householder who takes up residence in a manufacturing district cannot complain, as a plaintiff in a private nuisance suit, of the noise, dust, or vibration, whereas the same amount of disturbance caused by a factory in a primarily residential district, will be declared a nuisance to the landowners in its vicinity.

If, as I recommend, we think of pornographic exhibitions and publications as nuisances which may properly be controlled by the law under certain very strict conditions, we shall have to posit a similar set of conflicting considerations to be weighed carefully, not only by juries in private tort suits, but also by legislatures in their deliberations over the wording of criminal statutes designed to prohibit and punish pornography. Let me suggest that legislators who are impressed by the model of "public nuisance" should weigh, in the case of each main category and context of pornography, the seriousness of the offense caused to unwilling witnesses against the reasonableness of the offender's conduct. The magnitude of the offensiveness would be determined by (1) the intensity and durability of the repugnance the material produces, and the extent to which repugnance could be anticipated to be the general reaction of strangers to the conduct displayed or represented (conduct offensive only to persons with an abnormal susceptibility to offense would not count as *very* offensive), (2) the ease with which unwilling witnesses can avoid the offensive displays, and (3) whether or not the witnesses have willingly assumed the risk of being offended either through curiosity or the anticipation of pleasure. (The maxim *volenti non fit injuria* applies to offense as well as to harm.) We can refer to these norms, in order, as "the extent of offense standard" (with its "exclusion of abnormal susceptibility corollary"), "the reasonable avoidability standard," and "the *volenti* standard."

These factors would be weighed as a group against the reasonableness of the pornographers' conduct as determined by (1) its personal importance to the exhibitors themselves and its social value generally, remembering always the enormous social utility of unhampered expression (in those cases where expression is involved), (2) the availability of alternative times and places where the conduct in question would cause less offense, and (3) the extent if any to which the offense is caused by spiteful motives. In addition, the legislature would examine the prior established character of various neighborhoods, and consider establishing licensed zones in areas where the conduct in question is known to be already prevalent, so that people inclined to be offended are not likely to stumble on it to their surprise.

A legislature, of course, does not concern itself with judging specific actions and specific offended states after they have occurred. Rather its eyes are to the future, and it must weigh against one another, or authorize courts to weigh against one another, generalized *types* of conduct and offense. In hard cases this balancing procedure can be very complex and uncertain, but there are some cases that fall clearly within one or another standard in such a way as to leave no doubt how they must be decided. Thus, the *volenti* standard, for example, preempts all the others when it clearly applies. Film exhibitors cannot reasonably be charged with criminally offensive conduct when they have seen to it that the only people who witness their films are those adults who voluntarily purchased tickets to do so, knowing full well what sort of film they were about to see. One cannot be *wrongfully* offended by that to which one fully consents. Similarly, bans on *books* must fail to be morally legitimate in view of the ease with which offense at printed passages can be avoided. Since potential readers are not "captive audiences," here the reasonable avoidability standard is preemptive. So also do inoffensively expressed political or theological opinions fail to qualify as "criminal nuisances," by virtue of their personal and social importance as "free expression." On the other side, purely spiteful motives in the offender can be a preemptive consideration weighting the balance scale decisively on the side of unreasonableness.

In some cases, no one standard is preemptive, but nevertheless all applicable standards pull together towards one inevitable decision. The public eating of excrement (coprophagia) fully and unambiguously satisfies the extent of offense standard. One doesn't have to be abnormally squeamish to be offended by the very sight of it. If it is done (say) on a public bus, it definitely fails to win the support of the reasonable avoidability and *volenti* standards, which is to say that it causes intense disgust to captive observers. Hence, by *all* the relevant criteria, it is seriously offensive. By all the criteria for weighing reasonableness, public coprophagia does poorly too. It cannot be very important to the neurotic person who does it (not as important, for example, as earning a living, or eating fresh food); it has a definitely limited social utility; it is not the expression in language of an opinion, nor does it fall into a recognized genre of aesthetic expression; and it could as well be done in private. Hence it is both seriously offensive and unredeemed by independent "reasonableness." It would not of course be called "pornography," but its criminal proscription under another name would be morally legitimate in principle, even though in practice it might be unwise, uneconomical, or unnecessary.

NOTES

1 Practically all human activities, unless carried on in a wilderness, interfere to some extent with others or involve some risk of interference, and these interferences range from mere trifling annoyances to serious harms. It is an obvious truth that each individual in a community must put up with a certain amount of annoyance, inconvenience and interference, and must take a certain amount of risk in order that all may get on together. The very existence of organized society depends upon the principle of "give and take, live and let live," and therefore the law of torts does not

attempt to impose liability or shift the loss in every case where one person's conduct has some detrimental effect on another. Liability is imposed only in those cases where the harm or risk [or inconvenience or offense] to one is greater than he ought to be required to bear under the circumstances ... Restatement of Torts s. 822, comment j (1939).
2 W. Prosser, *Handbook of the Law of Torts* 597 (4th ed. 1971).
3 Ibid., at 597–9.
4 Ibid., at 599–600.
5 "The world must have factories, smelters, oil refineries, noisy machinery, and blasting, as well as airports, even at the expense of some inconvenience to those in the vicinity, and the plaintiff may be required to accept and tolerate some not unreasonable discomfort for the general good ... On the other hand, a foul pond, or a vicious or noisy dog, will have little if any social value, and relatively slight annoyance from it may justify relief." Ibid. at 597–8 (footnotes omitted).

READING QUESTIONS ON FEINBERG

1 Feinberg seems to suppose that the liberal commitment to individual autonomy survives confining one's expression of important aspects of one's personality to the private. Is this adequate, or do you suppose that public expression is sometimes important to autonomy?
2 As you go through the readings below, think about the implications of Feinberg's distinction between offence and harm. How should such a distinction be drawn in particular cases?

T.M. Scanlon
"A Theory of Freedom of Expression" (1972)

Scanlon argues that the need to protect freedom of expression follows from the importance of individual autonomy. The state must treat citizens as capable of making up their own minds. As a result, it cannot hold one person responsible for something that others do because of reasons they have offered them.

... Typically, the acts of expression with which a theory of "free speech" is concerned are addressed to a large (if not the widest possible) audience, and express propositions or attitudes thought to have a certain generality of interest. This accounts, I think, for our reluctance to regard as an act of expression in the relevant sense the communication between the average bank robber and the teller he confronts. This reluctance is diminished somewhat if the note the robber hands the teller contains, in addition to the usual threat, some political justification for his act and an exhortation to others to follow his example. What this addition does is to broaden the projected audience and increase the generality of the message's interest. The relevance of these features is certainly something which an adequate theory of freedom of expression should explain, but it will be simpler at present not to make them part of the definition of the class of acts of expression.

Almost everyone would agree, I think, that the acts which are protected by a doctrine of freedom of expression will all be acts of expression in the sense I have defined. However, since acts of expression can be both violent and arbitrarily destructive, it seems unlikely that anyone would maintain that as a class they were immune from legal restrictions. Thus the class of protected acts must be some proper subset of this class. It is sometimes held that the relevant subclass consists of those acts of expression which are instances of "speech" as opposed to "action." But those who put forward such a view have generally wanted to include within the class of protected acts some which are not speech in any normal sense of the word (for instance, mime and certain forms of printed communication) and to exclude from it some which clearly are speech in the normal sense (talking in libraries, falsely shouting "fire" in crowded theatres etc.). Thus if acts of speech are the relevant subclass of acts of expression, then "speech" is here functioning as a term of art which needs to be defined. To construct a theory following these traditional lines we might proceed to work out a technical correlate to the distinction between speech and action which seemed to fit our clearest intuitions about which acts do and which do not qualify for protection.[1]

To proceed in this way seems to me, however, to be a serious mistake. It seems clear that the intuitions we appeal to in deciding whether a given restriction infringes freedom of expression are not intuitions about which things are properly called speech as opposed to action, even in some refined sense of "speech." The feeling that we must look for a definition of this kind has its roots, I think, in the view that since any adequate doctrine of freedom of expression must extend to some acts a privilege not enjoyed by all, such a doctrine must have its theoretical basis in some difference between the protected acts and others, i.e., in some definition of the protected class. But this is clearly wrong. It could be, and I think is, the case that the theoretical bases of the doctrine of freedom of expression are multiple and diverse, and while the net effect of these elements taken together is to extend to some acts a certain privileged status, there is no theoretically interesting (and certainly no simple and intuitive) definition of the class of acts which enjoys this privilege. Rather than trying at the outset to carve out the privileged subset of acts of expression, then, I propose to consider the class as a whole and to look for ways in which the charge of irrationality brought against the doctrine of freedom of expression might be answered without reference to a single class of privileged acts.

As I mentioned at the start, this charge arises from the fact that under any nontrivial form of the doctrine there will be cases in which acts of expression are held to be immune from legal restriction despite the fact that they give rise to undoubted harms which would in other cases be sufficient to justify such restriction. (The "legal restriction" involved here may take the form either of the imposition of criminal sanctions or of the general recognition by the courts of the right of persons affected by the acts to recover through civil suits for damages.) Now it is not in general sufficient justification for a legal restriction on a certain class of acts to show that certain harms will be prevented if this restriction is enforced. It might happen that the costs of enforcing the restriction outweigh the benefits to be gained, or that the enforcement of the restriction infringes some right either directly (e.g., a right to the unimpeded performance of exactly those acts to which the restriction applies) or indirectly (e.g., a right which under prevailing circumstances can be secured by many only through acts to which the restriction applies). Alternatively, it may be that while certain harms could be prevented by placing legal restrictions on a class of acts, those to whom the restriction would apply are not responsible for those harms and hence cannot be restricted in order to prevent them.

Most defences of freedom of expression have rested upon arguments of the first two of these three forms. In arguments of both these forms factors which taken in isolation might have been sufficient to justify restrictions on a given class of acts are held in certain cases to be overridden by other considerations. As will become clear later, I think that appeals both to rights and to the balancing of competing goals are essential components of a complete theory of freedom of expression. But I want to begin by considering arguments which, like disclaimers of responsibility, have the effect of showing that what might at first seem to be reasons for restricting a class of acts cannot be taken as such reasons at all.

My main reason for beginning in this way is this: it is easier to say what the classic violations of freedom of expression have in common than it is to define the class of acts which is protected by that doctrine. What distinguishes these violations from innocent regulation of expression is not the character of the acts they interfere with but rather what they hope to achieve – for instance, the halting of the spread of heretical notions. This suggests that an important component of our intuitions about freedom of expression has to do not with the illegitimacy of certain restrictions but with the illegitimacy of certain justifications for restrictions. Very crudely, the intuition seems to be something like this: those justifications are illegitimate which appeal to the fact that it would be a bad thing if the view communicated by certain acts of expression were to become generally believed; justifications which are legitimate, though they may sometimes be overridden, are those that appeal to features of acts of expression (time, place, loudness) other than the views they communicate.

As a principle of freedom of expression this is obviously unsatisfactory as it stands. For one thing, it rests on a rather unclear notion of "the view communicated" by an act of expression; for another, it seems too restrictive, since, for example, it appears to rule out any justification for laws against defamation. In order to improve upon this crude formulation, I want to consider a number of different ways in which acts of expression can bring about harms, concentrating on cases where these harms clearly can be counted as reasons for restricting the acts that give rise to them. I will then try to formulate the principle in a way which accommodates these cases. I emphasize at the outset that I am not maintaining in any of these cases that the harms in question are always sufficient justification for restrictions on expression, but only that they can always be taken into account.

1 Like other acts, acts of expression can bring about injury or damage as a direct physical consequence. This is obviously true of the more bizarre forms of expression mentioned above, but no less true of more pedestrian forms: the sound of my voice can break

glass, wake the sleeping, trigger an avalanche, or keep you from paying attention to something else you would rather hear. It seems clear that when harms brought about in this way are intended by the person performing an act of expression, or when he is reckless or negligent with respect to their occurrence, then no infringement of freedom of expression is involved in considering them as possible grounds for criminal penalty or civil action.

2 It is typical of the harms just considered that their production is in general quite independent of the view which the given act of expression is intended to communicate. This is not generally true of a second class of harms, an example of which is provided by the common-law notion of assault. In at least one of the recognized senses of the term, an assault (as distinct from a battery) is committed when one person intentionally places another in apprehension of imminent bodily harm. Since assault in this sense involves an element of successful communication, instances of assault may necessarily involve expression. But assaults and related acts can also be part of larger acts of expression, as for example when a guerrilla theatre production takes the form of a mock bank robbery which starts off looking like the real thing, or when a bomb scare is used to gain attention for a political cause. Assault is sometimes treated as inchoate battery, but it can also be viewed as a separate offence which consists in actually bringing about a specific kind of harm. Under this analysis, assault is only one of a large class of possible crimes which consist in the production in others of harmful or unpleasant states of mind, such as fear, shock, and perhaps certain kinds of offence. One may have doubts as to whether most of these harms are serious enough to be recognized by the law or whether standards of proof could be established for dealing with them in court. In principle, however, there seems to be no alternative to including them among the possible justifications for restrictions on expression.

3 Another way in which an act of expression can harm a person is by causing others to form an adverse opinion of him or by making him an object of public ridicule. Obvious examples of this are defamation and interference with the right to a fair trial.

4 As Justice Holmes said, "The most stringent protection of free speech would not protect a man in falsely shouting fire in a theatre and causing a panic."[2]

5 One person may through an act of expression contribute to the production of a harmful act by someone else, and at least in some cases the harmful consequences of the latter act may justify making the former a crime as well. This seems to many people to be the case when the act of expression is the issuance of an order or the making of a threat or when it is a signal or other communication between confederates.

6 Suppose some misanthropic inventor were to discover a simple method whereby anyone could make nerve gas in his kitchen out of gasoline, table salt, and urine. It seems just as clear to me that he could be prohibited by law from passing out his recipe on handbills or broadcasting it on television as that he could be prohibited from passing out free samples of his product in aerosol cans or putting it on sale at Abercrombie and Fitch. In either case his action would bring about a drastic decrease in the general level of personal safety by radically increasing the capacity of most citizens to inflict harm on each other. The fact that he does this in one case through an act of expression and in the other through some other form of action seems to me not to matter.

It might happen, however, that a comparable decrease in the general level of personal safety could be just as reliably predicted to result from the distribution of a particularly effective piece of political propaganda which would undermine the authority of the government, or from the publication of a theological tract which would lead to a schism and a bloody civil war. In these cases the matter seems to me to be entirely different, and the harmful consequence seems clearly not to be a justification for restricting the acts of expression.

What I conclude from this is that the distinction between expression and other forms of action is less important than the distinction between expression which moves others to act by pointing out what they take to be good reasons for action and expression which gives rise to action by others in other ways, e.g., by providing them with the means to do what they wanted to do anyway. This conclusion is supported, I think, by our normal views about legal responsibility.

If I were to say to you, an adult in full possession of your faculties, "What you ought to do is rob a bank," and you were subsequently to act on this advice, I could not be held legally responsible for your act, nor could my act legitimately be made a separate crime. This remains true if I supplement my advice with a battery of arguments about why banks should be robbed or even about why a certain bank in particular should be robbed and why you in particular are entitled to rob it. It might become false – what I did might legitimately be made a crime – if certain further conditions held: for example, if you were a child, or so weak-minded as to be legally incompetent, and I knew this or ought to have known it; or if you were my subordinate in some organization and what I said to you was not advice but an order, backed by the discipline of the group; or if I went on to make further contributions to your act, such as aiding you in preparations or providing you with tools or giving you crucial information about the bank.

The explanation for these differences seems to me to be this. A person who acts on reasons he has acquired from another's act of expression acts on what *he* has come to believe and has judged to be a sufficient basis for action. The contribution to the genesis of his action made by the act of expression is, so to speak, superseded by the agent's own judgment. This is not true of the contribution made by an accomplice, or by a person who knowingly provides the agent with tools (the key to the bank) or with technical information (the combination of the safe) which he uses to achieve his ends. Nor would it be true of my contribution to your act if, instead of providing you with reasons for thinking bank robbery a good thing, I issued orders or commands backed by threats, thus changing your circumstances so as to *make* it a (comparatively) good thing for you to do.

It is a difficult matter to say exactly when legal liability arises in these cases, and I am not here offering any positive thesis about what constitutes being an accessory, inciting, conspiring, etc. I am interested only in maintaining the negative thesis that whatever these crimes involve, it has to be something more than merely the communication of persuasive reasons for action (or perhaps some special circumstances, such as diminished capacity of the person persuaded).

I will now state the principle of freedom of expression which was promised at the beginning of this section. The principle, which seems to me to be a natural extension of the thesis Mill defends in Chapter II of *On Liberty*, and which I will therefore call the Millian Principle, is the following:

There are certain harms which, although they would not occur but for certain acts of expression, nonetheless cannot be taken as part of a justification for legal restrictions on these acts. There harms are: (a) harms to certain individuals which consist in their coming to have false beliefs as a result of those acts of expression; (b) harmful consequences of acts performed as a result of those acts of expression, where the connection between the acts of expression and the subsequent harmful acts consists merely in the fact that the act of expression led the agents to believe (or increased their tendency to believe) these acts to be worth performing.

I hope it is obvious that this principle is compatible with the examples of acceptable reasons for restricting expression presented in 1 through 6 above. (One case in which this may not be obvious, that of the man who falsely shouts "fire," will be discussed more fully below.) The preceding discussion, which appealed in part to intuitions about legal responsibility, was intended to make plausible the distinction on which the second part of the Millian Principle rests and, in general, to suggest how the principle could be reconciled with cases of the sort included in 5 and 6. But the principle itself goes beyond questions of responsibility. In order for a class of harms to provide a justification for restricting a person's act it is not necessary that he fulfil conditions for being legally responsible for any of the individual acts which actually produce those harms. In the nerve-gas case, for example, to claim that distribution of the recipe may be prevented one need not claim that a person who distributed it could be held legally responsible (even as an accessory) for any of the particular murders the gas is used to commit. Consequently, to explain why this case differs from sedition it would not be sufficient to claim that providing means involves responsibility while providing reasons does not.

I would like to believe that the general observance of the Millian Principle by governments would, in the long run, have more good consequences than bad. But my defence of the principle does not rest on this optimistic outlook. I will argue in the next section that the Millian Principle, as a general principle about how governmental restrictions on the liberty of citizens may be justified, is a consequence of the view, coming down to us from Kant and others, that a legitimate government is one whose authority citizens can recognize while still regarding themselves as equal, autonomous, rational agents. Thus, while it is not a principle about legal responsibility, the Millian Principle has its origins in a certain view of human agency from which many of our ideas about responsibility also derive.

Taken by itself, the Millian Principle obviously does not constitute an adequate theory of freedom of expression. Much more needs to be said about when the kinds of harmful consequences which the principle allows us to consider can be taken to be sufficient justification for restrictions on expression. Nonetheless, it seems to me fair to call the Millian Principle the basic principle of freedom of expression. This is so, first, because a successful defence of the principle would provide us with an answer to the charge of irrationality by explaining why certain of the most obvious consequences of acts of expression cannot be appealed to as a justification for legal restrictions against them. Second, the Millian Principle is the only plausible principle of freedom of expression I can think of which applies to expression in general and makes no appeal to special rights (e.g., political rights) or to the value to be attached to expression in some particular domain (e.g., artistic expression or the discussion of scientific ideas). It thus specifies what is special about acts of expression as opposed to other acts and constitutes in this sense the usable residue of the distinction between speech and action.

I will have more to say in Section IV about how the Millian Principle is to be supplemented to obtain a full account of freedom of expression. Before that, however, I want to consider in more detail how the principle can be justified.

III

As I have already mentioned, I will defend the Millian Principle by showing it to be a consequence of the view that the powers of a state are limited to those that citizens could recognize while still regarding themselves as equal, autonomous, rational agents. Since the sense of autonomy to which I will appeal is extremely weak, this seems to me to constitute a strong defence of the Millian Principle as an exceptionless restriction on governmental authority. I will consider briefly in section V, however, whether there are situations in which the principle should be suspended.

To regard himself as autonomous in the sense I have in mind a person must see himself as sovereign in deciding what to believe and in weighing competing reasons for action. He must apply to these tasks his own canons of rationality, and must recognize the need to defend his beliefs and decisions in accordance with these canons. This does not mean, of course, that he must be perfectly rational, even by his own standard of rationality, or that his standard of rationality must be exactly ours. Obviously the content of this notion of autonomy will vary according to the range of variation we are willing to allow in canons of rational decision. If just anything counts as such a canon then the requirements I have mentioned will become mere tautologies: an autonomous man believes what he believes and decides to do what he decides to do. I am sure I could not describe a set of limits on what can count as canons of rationality which would secure general agreement, and I will not try, since I am sure that the area of agreement on this question extends far beyond anything which will be relevant to the applications of the notion of autonomy that I intend to make. For present purposes what will be important is this. An autonomous person cannot accept without independent consideration the judgment of others as to what he should believe or what he should do. He may rely on the judgment of others, but when he does so he must be prepared to advance independent reasons for thinking their judgment likely to be correct, and to weigh the evidential value of their opinion against contrary evidence.

The requirements of autonomy as I have so far described them are extremely weak. They are much weaker than the requirements Kant draws from essentially the same notion,[3] in that being autonomous in my sense (like being free in Hobbes's) is quite consistent with being subject to coercion with respect to one's actions. A coercer merely changes the considerations which militate for or against a certain course of action; weighing these conflicting considerations is still up to you.

An autonomous man may, if he believes the appropriate arguments, believe that the state has a distinctive right to command him. That is, he may believe that (within certain limits, perhaps) the fact that the law requires a certain action provides him with a very strong reason for performing that action, a reason which is quite independent of the consequences, for him or others, of his performing it or refraining. How strong this reason is – what, if anything, could override it – will depend on his view of the arguments for obedience to law. What is essential to the person's remaining autonomous is that in any given case his mere recognition that a certain action is required by law does not settle the question of whether he will do it. That question is settled only by his own decision, which may take into account his current assessment of the general case for obedience and the exceptions it admits, consideration of his other duties and obligations, and his estimate of the consequences of obedience and disobedience in this particular case.[4]

Thus, while it is not obviously inconsistent with being autonomous to recognize a special obligation to obey the commands of the state, there are limits on the *kind* of obligation which autonomous citizens could recognize. In particular, they could not regard themselves as being under an "obligation" to believe the decrees of the state to be correct, nor could they concede to the state the right to have its decrees obeyed without deliberation. The Millian Principle can be seen as a refinement of these limitations.

The apparent irrationality of the doctrine of freedom of expression derives from its apparent conflict with the principle that it is the prerogative of a state – indeed, part if its duty to its citizens – to decide when the threat of certain harms is great enough to warrant legal action, and when it is, to make laws adequate to meet this threat. (Thus Holmes's famous reference to "substantive evils that Congress has a right to prevent."[5]) Obviously this principle is not acceptable in the crude form in which I have just stated it; no one thinks that Congress can do *anything* it judges to be required to save us from "substantive evils." The Millian Principle specifies two ways in which this prerogative must be limited if the state is to be acceptable to autonomous subjects. The argument for the first part of the principle is as follows.

The harm of coming to have false beliefs is not one that an autonomous man could allow the state to protect him against through restrictions on expression. For a law to provide such protection it would have to be in effect and deterring potential misleaders while the potentially misled remained susceptible to persuasion by them. In order to be protected by such a law a person would thus have to concede to the state the right to decide that certain views were false and, once it had so decided, to prevent him from hearing them advocated even if he might wish to. The conflict between doing this and remaining autonomous would be direct if a person who authorized the state to protect him in this way necessarily also bound himself to accept the state's judgment about which views were false. The matter is not quite this simple, however, since it is conceivable that a person might authorize the state to act for him in this way while still reserving to himself the prerogative of deciding, on the basis of the arguments and evidence left available to him, where the truth was to be found. But such a person would be "deciding for himself" only in an empty sense, since in any case where the state exercised its prerogative he would be "deciding" on the basis of evidence preselected to include only that which supported one conclusion. While he would not be under an obligation to accept the state's judgment as correct, he would have conceded to the state the right to deprive him of grounds for making an independent judgement.

The argument for the second half of the Millian Principle is parallel to this one. What must be argued against is the view that the state, once it has declared certain conduct to be illegal, may when necessary move to prevent that conduct by outlawing its advocacy. The conflict between this thesis and the autonomy of citizens is, just as in the previous one, slightly oblique. Conceding to the state the right to use this means to secure compliance with its laws does not immediately involve conceding to it the right to require citizens to believe that what the law says ought not to be done ought not to be done. None the less, it is a concession that autonomous citizens could not make, since it gives the state the right to deprive citizens of the grounds for arriving at an independent judgement as to whether the law should be obeyed.

These arguments both depend on the thesis that to defend a certain belief as reasonable a person must be prepared to defend the grounds of his belief as not obviously skewed or otherwise suspect. There is a clear parallel between this thesis and Mill's famous argument that if we are interested in having truth prevail we should allow all available arguments to be heard.[6] But the present argument does not depend, as Mill's may appear to, on an empirical claim that the truth is in fact more likely to win out if free discussion is allowed. Nor does it depend on the perhaps more plausible claim that, given the nature of people and governments, to concede to governments the power in question would be an outstandingly poor strategy for bringing about a situation in which true opinions prevail.

It is quite conceivable that a person who recognized in himself a fatal weakness for certain kinds of bad arguments might conclude that everyone would be better off if he were to rely entirely on the judgment of his friends in certain crucial matters. Acting on this conclusion, he might enter into an agreement, subject to periodic review by him, empowering them to shield him from any sources of information likely to divert him from their counsel on the matters in question. Such an agreement is not obviously irrational, nor, if it is entered into voluntarily, for a limited time, and on the basis of the person's own knowledge of himself and those he proposes to trust, does it appear to be inconsistent with his autonomy. The same would be true if the proposed trustees were in fact the authorities of the state. But the question we have been considering is quite different: Could an autonomous individual regard the state as having, not as part of a special voluntary agreement with him but as part of its normal powers *qua* state, the power to put such an arrangement into effect without his consent whenever *it* (i.e., the legislative authority) judged that to be advisable? The answer to this question seems to me to be quite clearly no.

Someone might object to this answer on the following grounds. I have allowed for the possibility that an autonomous man might accept a general argument to the effect that the fact that the state commands a certain thing is in and of itself a reason why that thing should be done. Why couldn't he also accept a similar argument to the effect that the state *qua* state is in the best position to decide when certain counsel is best ignored?

I have already argued that the parallel suggested here between the state's right to command action and a right to restrict expression does not hold. But there is a further problem with this objection. What saves temporary, voluntary arrangements of the kind considered above from being obvious violations of autonomy is the fact that they can be based on a firsthand estimation of the relative reliability of the trustee's judgment and that of the "patient." Thus the person whose information is restricted by such an arrangement has what he judges to be good grounds for thinking the evidence he does receive to be a sound basis for judgment. A principle which provided a corresponding basis for relying on the state *qua* state would have to be extremely general, applying to all states of a certain kind, regardless of who occupied positions of authority in them, and to all citizens of such states. Such a principle would have to be one which admitted variation in individual cases and rested its claim on what worked out best "in the long run." Even if some generalization of this kind were true, it seems to me altogether implausible to suppose that it could be rational to rely on such a general principle when detailed knowledge of the individuals involved in a particular case suggested a contrary conclusion.

A more limited case for allowing states the power in question might rest not on particular virtues of governments but on the recognized fact that under certain circumstances individuals are quite incapable of acting rationally. Something like this may seem to apply in the case of the man who falsely shouts "fire" in a crowded theatre. Here a restriction on expression is justified by the fact that such acts would lead others (give them reason) to perform harmful actions. Part of what makes the restriction acceptable is the idea that the persons in the theatre who react to the shout are under conditions that diminish their capacity for rational deliberation. This case strikes us as a trivial one. What makes it trivial is, first, the fact that only in a very far-fetched sense is a person who is prevented from hearing the false shout under such circumstances prevented from making up his own mind about some question. Second, the diminished capacity attributed to those in the theatre is extremely brief, and applies equally to anyone under the relevant conditions. Third, the harm to be prevented by the restriction is not subject to any doubt or controversy, even by those who are temporarily "deluded." In view of all these facts, the restriction is undoubtedly one which would receive unanimous consent if that were asked.[7]

This is not true, however, of most of the other exceptions to the Millian Principle that might be justified by appeal to "diminished rationality." It is doubtful, for example, whether any of the three conditions I have mentioned would apply to a case in which political debate was to be suspended during a period of turmoil and impending revolution. I cannot see how nontrivial cases of this kind could be made compatible with autonomy.

The arguments I have given may sound like familiar arguments against paternalism, but the issue involved is not simply that. First, a restriction on expression justified on grounds contrary to the Millian Principle is not necessarily paternalistic, since those who are to be protected by such a restriction may be other than those (the speaker and his audience) whose liberty is restricted. When such a restriction is paternalistic, however, it represents a particularly strong form of paternalism, and the arguments I have given are arguments against paternalism only in this strong form. It is quite consistent with a person's autonomy, in the limited sense I have employed, for the law to restrict his freedom of action "for his own good," for instance by requiring him to wear a helmet while riding his motorcycle. The conflict arises only if compliance with this law is then promoted by forbidding, for example, expression of the view that wearing a helmet isn't worth it, or is only for sissies.

It is important to see that the argument for the Millian Principle rests on a limitation of the authority of states to command their subjects rather than on a right of individuals. For one thing, this explains why this particular principle of freedom of expression applies to governments rather than to individuals, who do not have such authority to begin with. There are surely cases in which individuals have the right not to have their acts of expression interfered with by other individuals, but these rights presumably flow from a general right to be free from arbitrary interference, together with considerations which make certain kinds of expression particularly important forms of activity.

If the argument for the Millian Principle were thought to rest on a right, "the right of citizens to make up their own minds," then that argument might be thought to proceed as follows. Persons who see themselves as autonomous see themselves as having a right to make up their own minds, hence also a right to whatever is necessary for them to do this; what is wrong with violations of the Millian Principle is that they infringe this right.

A right of this kind would certainly support a healthy doctrine of freedom of expression, but it is not required for one. The argument given above was much more limited. Its aim was to establish that the authority of governments to restrict the liberty of citizens in order to prevent certain harms does not include authority to prevent these harms by controlling people's sources of information to ensure that they will maintain certain beliefs. It is a long step from this conclusion to a right which is violated whenever someone is deprived of information necessary for him to make an informed decision on some matter that concerns him.

There are clearly cases in which individuals have a right to the information necessary to make informed choices and can claim this right against the government. This is true in the case of political decisions, for example, when the right flows from a certain conception of the relation between a democratic government and its citizens. Even where there is no such right, the provision of information and other conditions for the exercise of autonomy is an important task for states to pursue. But these matters take us beyond the Millian Principle.

IV

The Millian Principle is obviously incapable of accounting for all of the cases that strike us as infringements of freedom of expression. On the basis of this principle alone we would raise no objection against a government that banned all parades or demonstrations (they interfere with traffic), outlawed posters and handbills (too messy), banned public meetings of more than 10 people (likely to be unruly), and restricted newspaper publication to one page per week (to save trees). Yet such policies surely strike us as intolerable. That they so strike us is a reflection of our belief that free expression is a good which ranks above the maintenance of absolute peace and quiet, clean streets, smoothly flowing traffic, and rock-bottom taxes.

Thus there is a part of our intuitive view of freedom of expression which rests upon a balancing of competing goods. By contrast with the Millian Principle, which provides a single defence for all kinds of expression, here it does not seem to be a matter of the value to be placed on expression (in general) as opposed to other goods. The case seems to be different for, say, artistic expression than for the discussion of scientific matters, and different still for expression of political views.

Within certain limits, it seems clear that the value to be placed on having various kinds of expression flourish is something which should be subject to popular will in the society in question. The limits I have in mind here are, first, those imposed by considerations of distributive justice. Access to means of expression for whatever purposes one may have in mind is a good which can be fairly or unfairly distributed among the members of a society, and many cases which strike us as violations of freedom of expression are in fact instances of distributive injustice. This would be true of a case where, in an economically inegalitarian society, access to the principal means of expression was controlled by the government and auctioned off by it to the highest bidders, as is essentially the case with broadcasting licences in the United States today. The same might be said of a parade ordinance which allowed the town council to forbid parades by unpopular groups because they were too expensive to police.

But to call either of these cases instances of unjust distribution tells only part of the story. Access to means of expression is in many cases a necessary condition for participation in the political process of the country, and therefore something to which citizens have an independent right. At the very least the recognition of such rights will require governments to ensure that means of expression are readily available through which individuals and small groups can make their views on political issues known, and to ensure that the principal means of expression in the society do not fall under the control of any particular segment of the community. But exactly what rights of access to means of expression follow in this way from political rights will depend to some extent on the political institutions in question. Political participation may take different forms under different institutions, even under equally just institutions.

The theory of freedom of expression which I am offering, then, consists of at least four distinguishable elements. It is based upon the Millian Principle, which is absolute but serves only to rule out certain justifications for legal restrictions on acts of expression. Within the limits set by this principle the whole range of governmental policies affecting opportunities for expression, whether by restriction, positive intervention, or failure to intervene, are subject to justification and criticism on a number of diverse grounds. First, on grounds of whether they reflect an appropriate balancing of the value of certain kinds of expression relative to other social goods; second, whether they ensure equitable distribution of access to means of expression throughout the society; and third, whether they are compatible with the recognition of certain special rights, particularly political rights.

This mixed theory is somewhat cumbersome, but the various parts seem to me both mutually irreducible and essential if we are to account for the full range of cases which seem intuitively to constitute violations of "free speech."

V

The failure of the Millian Principle to allow certain kinds of exceptions may seem to many the most implausible feature of the theory I have offered. In addition to the possibility mentioned earlier, that exceptions should be allowed in cases of diminished rationality, there may seem to be an obvious case for allowing deviations from the principle in time of war or other grave emergency.

It should be noticed that because the Millian Principle is much narrower than, say, a blanket protection of "speech," the theory I have offered can already accommodate some of the restrictions on expression which wartime conditions may be thought to justify. The Millian Principle allows one, even in normal times, to consider whether the publication of certain information might present serious hazards to public safety by giving people the capacity to inflict certain harms. It seems likely that risks of this kind which are worth taking in time of peace in order to allow full discussion of, say, certain scientific questions, might be intolerable in wartime.

But the kind of emergency powers that governments feel entitled to invoke often go beyond this and include, for example, the power to cut off political debate when such debate threatens to divide the country or otherwise to undermine its capacity to meet a present threat. The obvious justification for such powers is clearly disallowed by the Millian Principle, and the theory I have offered provides for no exceptions of this kind.

It is hard for me at the present moment to conceive of a case in which I would think the invocation of such powers by a government right. I am willing to admit that there might be such cases, but even if there are I do not think that they should be seen as "exceptions" to be incorporated within the Millian Principle.

That principle, it will be recalled, does not rest on a right of citizens but rather expresses a limitation on the authority governments can be supposed to have. The authority in question here is that provided by a particular kind of political theory, one which has its starting point in the question: How could citizens recognize a right of governments to command them while still regarding themselves as equal, autonomous, rational agents? The theory is normally thought to yield the answer that this is possible if, but only if, that right is limited in certain ways, and if certain other conditions, supposed to ensure citizen control over government, are fulfilled. I have argued that one of the necessary limitations is expressed by the Millian Principle. If I am right, then the claim of a government to rule by virtue of this particular kind of authority is undermined, I think completely, if it undertakes to control its citizens in the ways that the Millian Principle is intended to exclude.

This does not mean, however, that it could not in an extreme case be right for certain people, who normally exercised the kind of authority held to be legitimate by democratic political theory, to take measures which this authority does not justify. These actions would have to be justified on some other ground (e.g., utilitarian), and the claim of their agents to be obeyed would not be that of a legitimate government in the usual (democratic) sense. None the less most citizens might, under the circumstances, have good reason to obey.

There are a number of different justifications for the exercise of coercive authority. In a situation of extreme peril to a group, those in the group who are in a position to avert disaster by exercising a certain kind of control over the others may be justified in using force to do so, and there may be good reason for their commands to be obeyed. But this kind of authority differs both in justification and extent from that which, if democratic political theory is correct, a legitimate democratic government enjoys. What I am suggesting is that if there are situations in which a general suspension of civil liberties is justified – and, I repeat, it is not clear to me that there are such – these situations constitute a shift from one kind of authority to another. The people involved will probably continue to wear the same hats, but this does not mean that they still rule with the same title.

It should not be thought that I am here giving governments licence to kick over the traces of constitutional rule whenever this is required by the "national interest." It would take a situation of near catastrophe to justify a move of the kind I have described, and if governments know what they are doing it would take such a situation to make a move of this sort inviting. For a great deal is given up in such a move, including any notion that the commands of government have a claim to be obeyed which goes beyond the relative advantages of obedience and disobedience.

When the situation is grave and the price of disorder enormous, such utilitarian considerations may give the government's commands very real binding force. But continuing rule on this basis would be acceptable only for a society in permanent crisis or for a group of people who, because they could see each other only as obedient servants or as threatening foes, could not be ruled on any other.

NOTES

1 This task is carried out by Thomas Emerson in *Toward a General Theory of the First Amendment* (New York, 1966). See esp. pp. 60–2.
2 In *Schenck v United States*, 249 US 47 (1919).
3 Kant's notion of autonomy goes beyond the one I employ in that for him there are special requirements regarding the reasons which an autonomous being can act on. (See the second and third sections of *Foundations of the Metaphysics of Morals.*) While his notion of autonomy is stronger than mine, Kant does not draw from it the same limitations on the authority of states (see *Metaphysical Elements of Justice*, sections 46–9).
4 I am not certain whether I am here agreeing or disagreeing with Robert Paul Wolff (*In Defense of Anarchism*, New York, 1970). At any rate I would not call what I am maintaining anarchism. The limitation on state power I have in mind is that described by John Rawls in the closing paragraphs of 'The Justification of Civil Disobedience," in *Civil Disobedience: Theory and Practice*, ed. Hugo Bedau (New York, 1969).
5 In *Schenck v United States*.
6 In Ch. II of *On Liberty*.
7 This test is developed as a criterion for justifiable paternalism by Gerald Dworkin in his essay "Paternalism," in *Morality and the Law*, ed. Richard Wasserstrom (Belmont, Calif., 1971).

READING QUESTIONS ON SCANLON

1 Does Scanlon's argument apply to all types of speech that claims to offer reasons?
2 Do all forms of speech purport to offer reasons to be evaluated? Think about pornography and hate speech.
3 Reread Mill's discussion of speech, above. How is Scanlon's view related to Mill's?

Mayo Moran
"Talking about Hate Speech: A Rhetorical Analysis of American and Canadian Approaches to the Regulation of Hate Speech" (1994)

Moran contrasts the visions of the state which distinguish American and Canadian jurisprudence on free speech.

THE CONTEXT

As is apparent in American cases, much depends upon the context in which the court chooses to situate the problem of hate speech. The *Keegstra* majority selected a very different context in which to analyze the problem of hate speech than that chosen in the American cases. It is telling that Chief Justice Dickson, speaking for the majority, begins his analysis of the constitutionality of the legislation by focusing on why the legislature thought regulation of this speech was important. Since the legislation was developed following the Second World War and the discovery of the horrors of Nazi Germany, the historical analysis naturally leads into a discussion of discrimination, racial and religious relations, and the violent activities of hate groups, including the Ku Klux Klan. This in turns leads to a discussion of the harms of hate speech.

Several things are accomplished by situating hate speech in this context. Linking hate speech to a history of genocide and discrimination makes the speech appear violent and dangerous, rather than innocuous. However, it does more than this. The conflict made visible by situating hate speech in the context of racial and religious discrimination is not the conflict between the individual and the state, but rather between private individuals within society. The relevant source of danger is not the coercive state but violent individuals. Describing civil society in this way also allows for the possibility of casting the state in the benevolent role of attempting to ensure a society in which the vulnerable as well as the powerful can be free.

CHARACTERS

As with the American cases, the choice of context has an important bearing not merely on how the characters are depicted but even more fundamentally on what characters are depicted. Given the significantly different context chosen by the Canadian majority, it is unsurprising that these characterizations are very different from those found in the American cases.

The most significant and far-reaching difference is the treatment of the state. The American discourse characterizes the state as the ominous police power, acting arbitrarily and clumsily overreaching its constitutional confines. In sharp contrast to this is the Canadian majority's vision of the state. This state appears calm and deliberative rather than unwieldy and threatening. It is conscientiously pursuing public good, not placating narrow factional interests. And far from overreaching its constitutional limits, the state here appears to be acting upon prudent legal considerations.

The majority in *Keegstra* and the other decisions conveys the image of a restrained and prudent state in part by carefully chronicling the legal sources that both inspire and constrain official action. By emphasizing that the Holocaust was the impetus for the legislation, the Court casts the state in the role of protector rather than destroyer of individual freedom. However, the Court does not rely simply on a sympathetic rendering of history to support this characterization of the state. It also finds justifications for state action in what might be termed persuasive legal authority.

The Court finds one such legal source in international law. For example, the Court outlines the development of the internationally based obligation to prohibit the dissemination of hate propaganda. The codification of the obligation to prevent the dissemination of hate propaganda is found in the International Convention on the Elimination of All Forms of Racial Discrimination, International Covenant on Civil and Political Rights, and in documents such as the European Convention for the Protection of Human Rights and Fundamental Freedoms. These documents are used to emphasize that, in legislating against the dissemination of hate propaganda, the Canadian government was not acting rashly or out of narrow self-interest. Rather, it was proceeding on the basis of a broad consensus borne of both historical experience and of the efforts of human rights scholars over the last several decades.

The Court finds another legal argument in support of the regulation of hate speech. In the section 1 inquiry, the Court insists that a particular right or freedom should not be viewed in isolation, but rather should be seen in the context of the broader obligations which the *Charter* as a whole imposes on the state. The Court finds the equality guarantee in section 15 and the obligation to respect and enhance the multicultural heritage of Canada in section 27 particularly relevant to hate speech:

The message of [hate speech] is that members of identifiable groups are not to be given equal standing in society, and are not human beings equally deserving of concern, respect and consideration. The harms caused by this message run directly counter to the values central to a free and democratic society, and in restricting the promotion of hatred Parliament is therefore seeking to bolster the notion of mutual respect necessary in a nation which venerates the equality of all persons.[1]

By emphasizing these legal obligations, the Court advances a justification for official action that goes beyond an empathic response to the plight of the targets. The use of historical and legal precedents does more than draw attention to the moral and other-directed impetus behind the regulation of hate speech. It also makes the crucial point that in regulating hate speech the state is not unconstrained, nor is it acting arbitrarily and merely protecting its own self-interest or playing favorites. Instead, the state is seeking, within the confines of an extensive system of legal obligations, to further public good by securing the most fundamental of constitutional values.

In addition to identifying various legal motivations behind the regulation of hate speech, the Court depicts the state in a positive light in other related ways. The Court broadens the inquiry by focusing on the dialogical situation, thus recasting the question that confronted the legislature. So the issue is not simply the narrow question of how to ensure that the speaker is as free as possible, but rather the broader question of how to ensure that public debate is as free as possible. And of necessity, this broader inquiry must take into consideration the effect of hate speech on the ability of the targets to speak, act, and participate in the world.

This dialogical focus is crucial to the Court's analysis of the extent to which the traditional rationales for protecting freedom of expression justify protecting hate speech. Once the inquiry is broadened to include the target's interests as well as the speaker's, justifying tolerance of hate speech on traditional freedom of expression rationales becomes problematic.[2] So, for instance, the Court finds that hate speech cannot be upheld on the self-actualization rationale because its "extreme opposition" to the "process of individual self-development and human flourishing among all members of society" inhibits the targets of the speech from being self-actualized.[3]

This broader focus also makes the hate speech's effect on the target relevant to the analysis of the justifiability of regulation. By describing hate speech from the target's point of view, the Court is able to identify the distinctive harms that justify the regulation of such speech, even according to the liberal harm principle. Thus, the Court's language associates the harms of hate speech with the most elemental aspects of personhood. Hate speech does not simply offend sensibilities, it also attacks "human dignity" and "an individual's sense of self-worth,"[4] values which resonate with liberalism's emphasis on human equality and autonomy. Including the vantage point of the target supports the harm principle justification in another way, for it undermines the pure speech argument by illuminating the link between racist speech and exclusion, racial violence and even genocide.

While the Court does discuss how the liberal harm principle can justify the regulation of hate speech, the plight of the target is not the exclusive, or even the primary, focus of the analysis. Rather, the Court carefully explains that in legislating against hate speech, the legislature is not merely protecting a private party, no matter how deserving of protection that person might be. By identifying the link between individual and collective identity, the Court illustrates how protecting particular individuals can also further constitutional interests. The Court notes that the hate speech attack is not simply an individual affront – it also undermines social and even constitutional values, such as the "relations between the various cultural and religious groups in Canadian society."[5] In this way, the Court uncovers how the legislation not only protects the dignity of individual targets, but also supports vital public interests.

The Court finds another public interest behind the regulation by describing the regulation itself as a form of "expression" inspired by constitutional ambitions: "[T]he reaction to various types of expression by a democratic government may be perceived as meaningful expression on behalf of the vast majority of citizens."[6] Such regulation provides society with an opportunity to "illustrate" and to publicize "the values beneficial to a free and democratic society."[7] Similarly, the Court insists that the regulation encourages "the values central to freedom of expression, while simultaneously demonstrating dislike for the vision forwarded by the hate-mongers."[8] In this way, the Court identifies expressive rights of constitutional dimension on both sides of the hate speech equation.

Throughout this discussion, the Court invokes the image of an even more important public good ensured by the regulation of hate speech.

The point of hate speech regulation is not simply to fulfill various legal obligations, nor just to protect the target. Behind these aims the Court discerns and gives voice to a deeper ambition, an ambition that is at the heart of who we are as a community. It is, at bottom, an image of a certain kind of public world, a conception of democracy. This public world is not a rough and tumble place where only the loudest survive. If it is a "marketplace of ideas," it is the regulated marketplace of the late twentieth century, not the Darwinian marketplace of nineteenth-century capitalism.

However, the public world that the Supreme Court of Canada both describes and helps to create seems more aptly described in conversational or deliberative terms. For while the marketplace metaphor imagines ideal (efficient) results emerging from the wholly separate actions of self-interested individuals, the rhetoric of the Canadian Supreme Court rests on a fundamentally different notion. In this more Aristotelian public world it is the "open participation" of all persons in the processes of collective deliberation that forms the heart of the democratic ideal. This can only be achieved, the Court suggests, through observance of the fundamental tenet, the animating idea, of democracy: the notion that "all persons are equally deserving of respect and dignity."[9] Because the regulation of hate speech bolsters these democratic values, the Court is able to identify such regulation with a fundamental public interest – the protection of democracy. Thus, our treatment of the target is the barometer of the strength of our democratic convictions.[10] According to this view, democracy requires more than simply the absence of official obstacles to participation; it must also enshrine the fundamental commitment to equal respect and dignity that is the substantive heart of the democratic ideal.

The sharp contrast between how the Canadian and American states are depicted derives at least in part from the language used to describe the state. For the courts do not merely analyze, but actually recreate, the deliberations of the state. It is not coincidental that American courts convey the state's unwieldy ambitions partly through dramatic and even feverish rhetoric in which the judges imagine an apparently endless array of potentially silenced speakers and threats to democracy. Part of the sense that the state is dangerous comes precisely from this anxious language. Conversely, the deliberative and careful terms in which the *Keegstra* majority recreates legislative motivation and traces out the sources and justifications for the regulation of hate speech help to create a very different image of the state. The language is not sensational or dramatic, but calm and reasoned. It is less overtly metaphorical and less figurative than the language in the American cases. The state is depicted as careful and responsible, and the measured rhetoric of the Court subtly reinforces this image.

But for all of this restraint, there is also rhetorical power in the Canadian Supreme Court's discussion of the state. The organic connection between the government and the people is conveyed partly through language that emphasizes the unity of the government and the governed. Both the Court's vision and its language refute the notion of a state-society dichotomy, of an opposition between the people and their government. Over and over again, the term "community" and references to "collective" values and ambitions are used to describe the unified collectivity of state and society. Additionally, the language of shared moral ambition is used to describe the aspirations of the legislation: the purpose of the legislation is to foster "harmonious social relations in a community dedicated to equality and multiculturalism,"[11] our "aspirations" include "fostering a vibrant democracy where the participation of all individuals is accepted and encouraged,"[12] the ambition of Parliament is to "bolster the notion of mutual respect necessary in a nation which venerates the equality of all persons."[13] References to the fundamental democratic values of equality and human dignity that we all share also reinforce the sense of a unified and morally engaged communal life.

The Court's extensive and laudatory discussion of the state stands in sharp contrast to its characterization of the speaker. The speaker appears as the violent enemy of the target, partly because the Court brings the target much more into view in discussing the speaker. When the effect on the target is treated as a structural part of assessing the claim that the speech deserves protection, the speaker appears less like a free-thinking zealot and more like a threatening hate-monger. However, the Court depicts the speaker not only as inflicting injury on the target, but also as striving to undermine our worthy communal aspirations. Thus, the language used to describe the proponents of hate speech draws attention to the impact of their speech both on the targets and on the fundamental values which define our legal and political community.

Unlike the calm and deliberative language used to describe the state, the language used to describe the speaker is strong, negative and extreme. Those who promote hate speech are routinely described as "hate-mongers" who advocate their views with "inordinate vitriol."[14] The whole aim of their speech is to "subvert" and "repudiate" and "undermine" democracy, which they do with "unparalleled vigor."[15] Since their ideas are "anathemic" and "inimical" to our fundamental values, we view them with "severe reprobation."[16] In this way, the Court characterizes the speaker as the enemy of democracy, not its litmus test, a hypocrite using democracy's most cherished ideal of free speech to undermine the freedom and democracy of others.

JUDICIAL VOICE

The judicial voice that dominates the Canadian hate speech cases provides an interesting contrast with the American jurisprudence. The majority in the Canadian hate speech decisions conceives of constitutional adjudication and of the role of judges in a very different way. According to this view, good judging is a matter of defensible value choices, rather than of steering a neutral course among (or perhaps above) particular value choices. And since there is no elevated position above all value choices, the judge cannot avoid making choices. Thus, the Court must come to terms with the value conflict in all of its particularity.[17] Only in this way, the Court insists, can the normative issues inherent in the conflict properly come into view. It is partly this close scrutiny that accounts for the concerned and engaged tone of the Canadian Supreme Court.

Thus, the Canadian cases discuss the speech in great detail, focusing on its specific content. Indeed, the majority's focus on the specific message of hate speech is crucial to its conclusion that such speech is appropriately regulated. By characterizing hate speech as "deeply offensive, hurtful and damaging to target group members, misleading to ... listeners, and antithetical to the furtherance of tolerance and understanding in society," the Court helps to settle the question of the normative value of the speech. Indeed, in the companion case of *Canada (HRC) v Taylor*,[18] Chief Justice Dickson expresses a certain frustration with the dissent's abstract characterization of the speech. After noting that he "cannot ignore the setting" in which freedom of expression is raised, he continues:

It is not enough to simply balance or reconcile those interests promoted by a government objective with abstract panegyrics to the value of open expression. Rather, a contextual approach to s. 1 demands an appreciation of the extent to which a restriction of the activity at issue on the facts of the particular case debilitates or compromises the principles underlying the broad guarantee of freedom of expression.[19]

This careful inquiry into the particulars of the speech at issue is crucial to the Court's resolution of the problem. It also helps to account for the less detached tone of the *Keegstra* majority's legal analysis.

The Court's admission that it too must engage in a process of mediating different values also helps to create a more egalitarian relationship with the reader. Although the Court must try to fairly assess the conflict and understand both perspectives, it does not and indeed cannot view the conflict from a privileged, neutral position above the particular sides in the debate. So, while the American hate speech cases suggest that it is incumbent upon judges to set aside their personal assessments of the speech in favor of a more objective point of view, the rhetoric of the Canadian Supreme Court clearly illustrates that the Court's considered response to the speech is a relevant factor in determining whether the speech should be protected. Since the Court does not claim that it has a privileged perspective from which it can see what hate speech really is (although it does have an institutional tradition of fairness and even-handedness to respect), it must justify its decision on normative grounds. And this justification inevitably implicates the Court's own determinations of value, determinations which must themselves be assessed and either justified or rejected.

The Court strengthens this egalitarian relationship with the reader by exposing her to some of the difficulties inherent in the position it ultimately defends. Throughout the opinion one has a sense of intellectual struggle ... So, in considering the appropriate course of action, the Chief Justice admits that the state "cannot act to hinder or condemn a political view without to some extent harming the openness of Canadian democracy."[20] Similarly, after illustrating that no course of action can completely protect the values underlying freedom of expression, he wonders how to deal with the possibility that his ruling weakens our communal commitment to freedom of expression, albeit in a different way than does the toleration of hate speech.[21] By thus exposing the weaknesses of the position ultimately adopted,[22] the Court encourages the reader to participate in the process of thinking through the best approach to this difficult problem. And the Court refuses to allow easy equivalences to obscure the difficulty of the choices we all, judges and citizens, face:

While we must guard carefully against judging expression according to its popularity, it is equally destructive of free expression values, as well as the other values which underlie a free and democratic society, to treat all expression as equally crucial [to the values of freedom of expression].[23]

Even the language of the Canadian Supreme Court's hate speech opinions creates the sense that the Court hopes to forge a different relationship with its audience, for the Court chooses language that reaches beyond the legal community to the citizen. These opinions, although dauntingly long, are generally written in language which makes sense to the ordinary person. There is little technical language, and when legal doctrines are discussed, they are discussed in accessible rather than esoteric language. Reading these cases, one feels that the Court was aware that it was crafting an important cultural document, creating our most basic cultural values, even as it expressed them. In its eloquent statements about Canadians' traditional beliefs in equality and tolerance, the Court not only expresses but also encourages us to strengthen those beliefs, to become more fully who we like to think we are.

COMPARATIVE JURISPRUDENCE AND THE PROBLEM OF TRANSLATION

... Naturally, we all speak languages that are largely inherited. Particularly – but by no means solely – in the field of law, the established language is powerful, ordering our existence and our relations with others, but also obscuring certain aspects of our world. Power has a way of concealing point of view and making a particular understanding of reality look simply neutral and true. And the realities our languages obscure remain invisible; the possibility of change, however necessary, seems elusive. But power cannot be exercised responsibly, nor perhaps even impartially, until this is recognized. The American discourse of hate speech that has developed in the past few decades is so powerful, so formulaic, that it indeed becomes difficult to conceive of alternative understandings. Much of it seems to insiders, even critical ones, to be so natural and inevitable as to be unquestionable. For this reason, comparing the American discourse of hate speech with the recent hate speech decisions of the Canadian Supreme Court may be a useful way of revivifying the American hate speech debate and enabling it to move forward.

Part of the potency of encountering another's way of speaking about the world is that it makes apparent the conditions on which our own language operates; it renders visible what our own languages make invisible. Clifford Geertz suggest that to grasp concepts that, for another people are "experience-near" (in the sense that they are so foundational, so un-self-conscious that they do not appear as concepts at all), may enable us to move towards a more nuanced understanding of both ourselves and others. In this comparative activity we may begin to discover not only the value of other languages, but also the strictures of our own. Our own rhetorical choices, which inevitably privilege certain points of view and make others implausible, become matters to be discussed and justified rather than simply assumed. In this process of normative justification, we engage in the ongoing human task of fashioning a language adequate to our changing world.

There is a pragmatic reason why it can be valuable to compare the way different legal systems approach a similar problem. As discussed above, the dominant American discourse on the issue of hate speech makes a persuasive rendering of the alternative perspective within the system all but impossible. For this reason, it can be helpful to those seeking to articulate a subjugated perspective to look to comparative jurisprudence. The decisions of the Canadian Supreme Court provide a useful illustration of how one might go about making a persuasive case for the constitutionality of the regulation of hate speech.

In particular, the Canadian hate speech decisions are helpful because they illustrate the kinds of sources that might be called upon to make a case for the regulation of hate speech. For example, as noted above, the Canadian Supreme Court finds several legal sources, including international human rights instruments and the equality guarantee of the *Charter*, which foster respect for the legislature's decision to prohibit hate speech. On the critical issue of how the facts of a hate speech case are constructed, it may also be helpful that the majority of the Canadian Supreme Court implicitly and explicitly challenges the use of the vagueness and overbreadth arguments to shift the focus from actual litigants to more attractive constitutional stand-ins. The decisions of the Canadian Supreme Court also provide some guidance for how the regulation of hate speech might be understood to further a public interest. The American approach to hate speech classifies the target's interest in protection as purely private. The predominant technique of critics, which relies on storytelling and the creation of empathy, implicitly accepts that classification and hopes to generate enough sympathy to make the private plight a matter of public concern. But the failure to challenge the implicit classification of that interest as purely private allows the official discourse to characterize regulation as illegitimate favoritism and to ignore the alternative perspectives. In contrast, the Canadian hate speech cases find that the regulation of hate speech protects not just the targets, but also important public interests, including equal participation in public life, democracy and respect for human dignity and equality. These arguments may further a richer discussion of the potential public – as opposed to merely private – issues in the regulation of hate speech.

However, comparative jurisprudence offers more than practical benefits. In the context of hate speech, for instance, comparing the Canadian and American approaches can reveal the crucial yet unstated assumptions which underlie each discussion.

Judicial construction of the facts is one of the most decisive elements of a legal opinion. In a sense, the war over hate speech is largely fought on the battleground of what will be considered the relevant facts. Paradoxically, justification for any particular construction of the facts is one of the most neglected issues in both judicial opinions and theoretical writings. But this poverty of discussion means that the war is largely a guerilla war – the opinions state only the bare result of any particular battle. Judges do not tell us why they situate facts in a particular way, nor why certain facts are relevant but others are not. Yet, comparing the American and the Canadian descriptions of the very similar facts of a hate speech case uncovers the vital choices judges nonetheless make in finding the facts.[24]

Perhaps most importantly, the Canadian and American cases come to very different conclusions on the crucial determination of how to situate the hate speech problem. While the American courts treat hate speech as an unproblematic extension of the subversive advocacy cases, the Canadian Supreme Court instead situates it in the context of racial and religious discrimination. This demonstrates that although the choice of context is indeed crucial to the resolution of the issue, hate speech can plausibly be understood in the context of either subversive advocacy or of racial discrimination. Comparison of the Canadian and the American discussions also uncovers a whole range of choices about how to characterize hate speech. The American cases characterize the speech in very general terms and dwell very little on its specific content. In contrast, the Canadian cases focus closely on the specific content of the speech. There is an important link between how the speech is described and the resolution of the case. Focusing on its specific content makes hate speech seem like violent harassment, so that protecting it in freedom's name seems dubious. Conversely, describing the speech in general terms as political or even philosophical speech makes any regulation of it appear unjustifiable. But there does not seem to be any objective or neutral way to choose between the various levels of specificity at which speech can be described. Nor can it plausibly be said that general descriptions are more objective, particularly when it is necessary to select among general descriptions like "racial harassment" or "political speech."

Similar choices become apparent when one compares the points of view adopted by the courts. The American hate speech cases talk about the vantage point of the judge as if it were above the messy events of history, where the judge can see what hate speech really is. When one compares this vantage point with the Canadian cases, however, the particularity of this apparently neutral perspective becomes apparent. It is point of view that seems to distinguish the context and the description of the facts adopted by the American courts from those adopted by the Canadian courts. Seeing the problem as one of subversive advocacy and political speech casts the speaker as an idealistic dissident and thus tracks his or her self-understanding. In contrast, describing the issue as racial harassment and focusing on the impact of the hate message on the target implicitly identifies the target's perspective as the normatively relevant point of view. The different treatments of democracy in the Canadian and American cases also privilege different perspectives. If, as the American cases suggest, democracy requires the unfettered airing of all ideas, then the speaker's interest in participation in the "marketplace of ideas" is privileged. In contrast, a view of democracy that protects each member's equality and dignity gives greater priority to the interests of the targets. But in what meaningful sense can one of these perspectives be said to be more neutral than the other?

The way a court describes the facts of a case always has an intimate relationship to the legal conclusion. It is partly by adopting apt descriptions of the facts that courts so often are able to plausibly invoke precedent without any discussion. So, for example, in the American cases on hate speech, the fact that the speech is described as symbolic and political speech involving philosophical ideas helps to determine whether the law of subversive advocacy or the law concerning racial harassment and civil rights will be relevant. If the speaker is described as an idealistic radical, cases about war protesters and civil rights activists naturally seem applicable. In contrast, as the Canadian cases illustrate, if the speech and the speaker are characterized in terms of discrimination and harassment, then it is precisely the precedents on discrimination and human rights that seem applicable.

This comparison also reveals an absence that is at least as relevant as the fact of these choices. Courts make crucial choices in their descriptions of the facts and invocation of precedent, but they do not justify those choices. Instead, they rely on rhetoric that makes their understanding appear natural and even inevitable – rhetoric that obscures the fact of choice and thus avoids responsibility. Comparison illustrates that these questions cannot be adjudicated simply by resort to truth claims. The issue is not whether a particular description or classification is true, but whether it is illuminating. This requires a substantive discussion of the merits of viewing hate speech in one context or another. How does it further understanding, for instance, to treat hate speech as morally and legally equivalent to the speech of idealistic anarchists like Jacob Abrams? There are at least as many discontinuities as continuities in the analogy, so the argument cannot simply be that it is the same. So why exactly do courts think that the continuities are more deserving of judicial attention? There may be good reasons why, but the hate speech cases do not divulge them. And if justification is crucial to judicial decision making, then this cannot be adequate. It is also necessary to justify why any one particular perspective is a better way of viewing the problem than another, or perhaps more optimistically, whether it isn't possible to take multiple perspectives into consideration. Since one body of law cannot simply be assumed to apply, courts must explain what makes one body of law more applicable than another. Such a discussion would most certainly not only enrich decisions but might also inspire more meaningful conversations by enabling the participants to concur on what truly divides them.

Comparing the Canadian and the American discussions of hate speech is also illuminating because the rhetoric provides a window to the deepest commitments of the two discourses. The two sides in the American hate speech debate often fail to engage at all on the deepest issues that divide them. However, uncovering the fundamental assumptions that underlie the official American discourse on hate speech by contrasting that discourse with the Canadian approach may at least make discussion possible. Comparison reveals that the two discourses rest on very different understandings of the nature of the state, the concept of freedom, and even the concept of democracy itself. These understandings are "experience-near" – so fundamental that they are not mentioned, so constitutive of our ways of speaking about and living in the world that they do not seem to be assumptions at all.

The notion of the state is the most fundamental concept underlying the competing discussions of hate speech. While neither the American nor the Canadian cases explicitly discuss their views of the state, these unarticulated views profoundly inform the way the problem of hate speech is discussed. Indeed, the very unselfconsciousness of the concept is testimony to its power. Unifying much of the discussion of hate speech in the American cases is the premise that the state is profoundly dangerous. A belief that no private actor, however threatening, could ever be as dangerous as the state underlies much of both the rhetoric and the results in the American hate speech cases. The very language used to describe the state invokes this image – it is the menacing police power, exercising thought control, playing favorites, and likely to use even the most apparently innocuous regulation for its own selfish purposes. This state is characterized by pluralist politics and dominated by factions. It is this vision of the state, and of official psychology, that underlies the all too prevalent slippery slope argument, for the assumption that the state is a dangerous megalomaniac is what gives force to the concern with the precision and clarity of the legal line. This is also what makes plausible the depiction of the speaker as beleaguered. In a political culture dominated by this conception of the state, the threat one private individual poses to another inevitably appears insignificant. For this reason, courts characterize the state as the dangerous discriminator. In this sense too, the language of "mere offensiveness" and other attempts to minimize the harm of the speech can be seen as an attempt of the part of the judiciary to convince the audience that abuses of private power pale in comparison with abuses of state power. As Justice Scalia's warning against adding the First Amendment to the fire so aptly illustrates, in this discourse the state is a kind of super-individual, like other individuals in its pursuit of its own selfish ambitions, but profoundly more dangerous because of its relative power.

In contrast, the Canadian hate speech cases rest on a much more positive understanding of the state. The descriptions of the state and of official motivation in the Canadian cases convey an image of the orderly and rational pursuit of public interest. According to this view, given constitutional expression in section 1 of the *Charter*, the state is not a super-individual necessarily concerned with selfish motives. Instead, the state can be public-spirited, and, as the Court describes it, the state does indeed seem to be pursuing a conception of the public good. This conception emphasizes both the centrality of equal citizenship as well as the responsibility of the state to ensure that this kind of equality can be realized. It is to make this point that the opinions emphasize the equality-seeking and the freedom-enhancing nature of official action. And it is in part this possibility of benevolent state action that makes the dissent's slippery slope arguments ring hollow. Culturally, even if

Canadians do not particularly like the government, we do not tend to see it as dangerous – foolish and bumbling, yes, but rarely dangerous.

This difference in the understanding of the state also has important implications for the concept of freedom at work in the two narratives. If the state is the fundamental threat to freedom, then freedom is secured by restraining the state and giving full play to forces in the private sphere. This classic "negative liberty"[25] view of freedom and of the state forms the conceptual underpinning of the way that hate speech is discussed in the American cases. Its implicit distinction between the freedom of civil society and the coerciveness of public authority makes plausible the notion that the courts are preserving freedom, even as they uphold the rights of groups like the Nazis and the Ku Klux Klan, for what the courts are preserving is a sphere in which individuals may act free of government interference. This view of the freedom of the private sphere is also apparent in the judicial rhetoric that identifies the speaker with the cause of freedom and the state with oppressive constraint. If government intervention is seen as an inevitable threat to liberty, then keeping government out will be seen as freedom. Preserving freedom of speech thus requires the courts to keep the meddlesome and dangerous state at a safe distance from the free interplay of ideas.

Underlying the Canadian discourse is a profoundly different vision of freedom. Indeed, it is perhaps unsurprising given the long tradition of public involvement in medical care, higher education, public broadcasting and many other areas of life, that Canadians generally embrace not only negative but also positive liberty. Since the state is not seen as necessarily threatening, freedom is not automatically equated with the state staying out. This conception of freedom has more in common with the "exercise-concept" of positive liberty, according to which freedom is not merely the absence of external constraint, but is instead the effective exercise of control over one's life.[26] Even the structure of the *Charter* is illustrative of this. If many of the guarantees of the *Charter* protect the classic negative liberties, section 1 gives expression to Canada's belief in positive liberty. This is because section 1 embodies the recognition that the state may well be *acting*, and even limiting, some *Charter* rights and freedoms, in an attempt to secure a more positive form of freedom not sufficiently safeguarded in private ordering. When seen in light of this more positive conception of liberty, section 1's reference to those limits on rights which are justified by a free and democratic society is not incoherent. Instead, it expresses the "uniquely Canadian"[27] vision of a free society – a society in which members have not merely the opportunity to be free, but also the means of exercising that freedom. This accounts for the necessity of looking at the effects of speech and of legislation in order to determine how much effective self-determination people can actually exercise in the private realm, under conditions not only of state intervention, but also of non-intervention. The Canadian Supreme Court does exactly this in the hate speech cases by describing the speaker as destructive of freedom and the regulation as supportive of it.

Perhaps most interesting of the underlying assumptions at work in the two discussions of hate speech is the vision of democracy. In both the American and Canadian cases, identification of the overwhelming public interest is crucial. Interestingly, both approaches accomplish this identification primarily through their notions of democracy. However, the visions of democracy invoked by the two courts are strikingly different.

An important part of the rationale at work in the American cases is the view that if the state is allowed to silence anyone, it will inevitably distort the processes of democracy. This embodies a certain ideal of democracy as a process by which all ideas are presented so that the populace can select among them. Like the market metaphor on which this view is based, democracy itself is a mechanism neutral as among the contending ideas. In this sense, the prevalence of the "marketplace of ideas" metaphor is anything but accidental. According to this Schumpeterean model, democracy consists purely of the unfettered process by which the people choose among contending views: "The main stipulations of this model are, first, that democracy is simply a mechanism for choosing and authorizing governments, not a kind of society nor a set of moral ends; and second, that the mechanism consists of a competition between two or more self-chosen sets of politicians ..."[28] Under this model, the purpose of democracy is not to assess but simply to register preferences, and therefore any restriction of the market options inevitably undermines democracy. Thus, judges indicate that only the protection of hate speech can safeguard democracy, for such protection ensures that the market will proffer the widest possible array of options. This model also underlies the claim that the refusal to regulate hate speech distinguishes the American way of life from totalitarian societies – that is, from societies where the state dictates what options can and cannot enter the democratic marketplace. It is this view of democracy that gives force to the normative identification of anarchists with members of the Klan and Nazis. They are equally legitimate representatives of democracy, for they bring ideas to the marketplace. Indeed, they are even plausibly the litmus test for the extent of a society's commitment to democracy, since they test its devotion to the unfettered airing of ideas and thus to democracy itself. Politics is conceived as a competition among interest groups and whoever wins rules legitimately, for the touchstone of legitimacy is the unfettered process which guarantees the citizens' ability to replace one government with another of their choice.

The Canadian view of democracy sharply contrasts with this vision. The democratic ideal that animates the Canadian hate speech decisions is at its core concerned with the substantive value commitments democracy entails, including most prominently an overriding belief in the dignity and equal worth of each human being. This model of democracy, which has John Stuart Mill and the ethical-liberal democrats of the late nineteenth and early twentieth centuries as it philosophical ancestors, aims toward a society where all people are equally free to realize their capabilities. Therefore, the democratic process must be measured against the substantive commitments to human dignity and equality which infuse the democratic ideal. For example, the Canadian Chief Justice argues that the open participation so crucial to democracy is not simply procedural, but instead relies on the substantive belief that "all persons are equally deserving of respect and dignity." It is this understanding of democracy which enables the Supreme Court of Canada to find that hate speech subverts and repudiates the democratic ideal. This focus on substantive results also underlies the distinction that the Canadian Supreme Court draws between Canada and totalitarian or undemocratic regimes. The Court points out that hate speech aims to undermine not only the democratic process but also the substantive belief in equal humanity and dignity that underlies that ideal, thus suggesting that restricting hate speech supports rather than undermines the democratic ideal.

So, there are very fundamental differences underlying the rhetoric of the American and the Canadian hate speech cases. But this may call into question whether the two discourses are in fact so divergent that the Canadian approach cannot serve as a useful means of revivifying the American debate on hate speech and suggesting some new directions. Are the differences simply too great to make comparison useful?

Canadian legal and political institutions have developed in a political culture that has imbued them with certain ideals well suited to their allotted role. And the same is true of the American institutions. More-over, the histories of the two countries are very different despite many obvious similarities. In particular, Canada has no true equivalent of the McCarthy era and the subversive advocacy cases which seem to be the impetus for the judicial concern with the regulation of speech. It may be the case that when it comes to political freedoms, the American state is more dangerous than the Canadian state. There may be other significant differences between the two countries that are important for the issue of hate speech regulation. For instance, it is possible that Canadians are more tolerant of certain kinds of differences. It is noteworthy, for example, that the Canadian political culture is typically described in terms of a cultural mosaic while the American political culture is de-scribed as a melting pot. While these characterizations are obviously simplistic, and probably overplay the real differences, it may nonethe-less be true that there is in Canada greater tolerance for a wide range of political opinions, as well as for various cultural differences. Thus, pro-moting tolerance through non-regulation of hate speech may not seem as crucial to Canadians. To the extent that Canadian and American political culture differ on this point, then, the approach of the Canadian hate speech cases may not be persuasive in the American situation.

It is also important to note the very different institutional histories that inform the two judicial approaches. The rhetoric of the Canadian Supreme Court betrays some of the zeal of the newcomer to the exhila-rating language which the *Charter* puts at the disposal of the courts. Until 1982, discussions of individual rights by the Canadian judiciary were lodged in the oblique language of federalism and the division of powers. Perhaps for this reason, Canadian courts, and the Supreme Court in particular, have enthusiastically embraced the more appropri-ate language of the *Charter*. Conversely, it is certainly of some relevance that American judicial history is much more extensive and naturally contains episodes that make contemporary courts aware of the dangers of wholeheartedly embracing an interpretive position that acknowl-edges that constitutional interpretation ultimately requires judges to make substantive value choices. Though Canadian courts will no doubt at some point have their own equivalent of the *Lochner* era or the subversive advocacy era, they have no such troubling judicial history under the *Charter* at this point, and this is reflected in their understand-ing of the judicial role.

No doubt these are but a few of the reasons why, even if one were so inclined, it would not be possible to simply transpose the Canadian approach to the regulation of hate speech to the United States. Nonetheless, comparative jurisprudence can be illuminating, perhaps most of all because it makes us aware of the most fundamental commitments we make when we invoke – as we inevitably do – an inherited way of speaking about the world. Ironically, in studying the approach that another country takes to a problem we all face, the most valuable knowledge we gain may be self-knowledge. What always seemed simple and natural becomes, through force of comparison, complex and problematic ...

Certainly we cannot simply import wholesale the approach of one country's jurisprudence into that of our own. Indeed, this would undermine the whole point of trying to shape a language adequate to one's own world. There is, in fact, no easy way around this enduring human struggle. It is no more adequate to simply transpose the approach of another country than it is to hold blindly onto inherited understandings. Like the growth and development of the old city that Wittgenstein described, revivifying our languages proceeds by means more piecemeal, more uncertain. Difficult as it is, even as we work within our own languages, we must struggle against them and question what they enable us to see of our world. In this arduous task, comparative jurisprudence can be useful. It makes visible possibilities obscured by our way of speaking about the world, makes problematic what had always seemed simple, and thus helps us to become aware of the straightjackets of our once liberating ideas. But this rediscovery of complexity and ambiguity is only the beginning. Ultimately we must ask what makes sense now, in our time. No matter what the outcome, this is a crucial part of each citizen's moral education.

Comparing the American and Canadian approaches to the regulation of hate speech can therefore be instructive. Uncovering some of the differences also illustrates that the construction of the state, of the private realm, and of democracy are choices about how to understand and speak about the world, not unassailable truths. This, process helps to uncover – and thus enables discussion about – the complexities that the reductionist pressures of legal language work to suppress. This comparison may also be helpful in another way. The energetic American debate on freedom of speech is frustrating for several reasons, among them the fact that the contending perspectives do not seem to address each other at all. Examining another way of approaching the problem may help to uncover the invisible assumptions and therefore make it possible to identify some of the fundamental points of contention. In this way, the two sides may, at least, begin to really speak about what divides them. Such a discussion cannot help but enrich the debate, even if the result remains the same.

This process of questioning is also crucial to the democratic ideal, for, as John Dewey said, "democracy begins in conversation." Our constitutional provisions themselves can never be considered completely defined by history, for we are responsible for interpreting that history and its import for our time. Our forbearers inhabited a certain world and fashioned their ideals accordingly. Our world is in some respects the same and in some different. It is our responsibility to reexamine that world and struggle with how we can best live together. And in that process, in reexamining the way we understand and speak about the world, we begin the conversation that begins democracy.

NOTES

1 *R. v Keegstra*, [1990] 3 SCR 697, at 756 (Can.).
2 Lee Bollinger makes a similar point.
3 *Keegstra*, [1990] 3 SCR at 763.
4 Ibid. at 746.
5 Ibid. at 767.
6 Ibid. at 764–5.
7 Ibid. at 769.
8 Ibid. at 764.
9 Ibid.
10 Interestingly, the Court implies here that part of what makes Canada different from South Africa or Nazi Germany is the fact that the state not only does not itself engage in violent discrimination, but it also does not tolerate others doing so. The distinction that the Canadian Supreme Court implicitly makes between states such as Nazi Germany and Apartheid South Africa on one hand, and Canada on the other, is that in Canada, individuals should never have to live under the shadow of racial hatred. In contrast, as noted above, several of the American cases suggest that what separates the U.S. from Nazi Germany is the fact that in the U.S. one can say what one thinks, while in Nazi Germany, one could not.
11 *Keegstra*, at 767.
12 Ibid. at 766.
13 Ibid. at 756.
14 Ibid. at 763
15 Ibid. at 764–5.

16 Ibid. at 769.

17 So, for example, the Supreme Court has insisted that section 1 requires a contextual approach in order to "[b]ring into sharp relief the aspect of the right or freedom which is truly at stake in the case as well as the aspects of any values in competition with it." *Keegstra*, at 737 (quoting *Edmonton Journal v Alberta*, [1989] 2 SCR 1326 at 1335–6).

18 [1990] 3 SCR 892 (Can.).

19 Ibid. at 922.

20 *Keegstra*, at 764.

21 Ibid. at 766.

22 This is not to suggest, however, that the judgments are in all respects ideal. They particularly seem to fall short in their treatment of the hate speech proponent. While the Court allows the target a certain kind of personhood not granted in the American case law, it does not seem willing to go the final step and also grant the proponent of hate speech the status of personhood. Instead, he is routinely described as a violent hate-monger. There may be a fair middle ground available between the American approach, which minimizes the harm and venerates open expression, and the Canadian approach, which reduces the speaker to a violent hate-monger. Of course, these speakers may be violent hate-mongers, but they are also individuals even if they are profoundly misguided and dangerous. Watching a film like *Blood in the Face* or the trial of someone like Jim Keegstra should make anyone but the ideologue feel some sense of sorrow for people who are so racked by hatred, and some sense of concern about how we have failed them (for instance, the class dynamics of this kind of racial hatred are often troubling). Thus, I think the Canadian hate speech opinions would be strengthened by recognizing that judgments upholding the regulation of hate speech do inflict a certain amount of real suffering on the proponent of hate speech. Surely we do not have to deny this in order to say that the regulation is nonetheless justified. There is something elitist, and even authoritarian, about the fact that courts do not seem to trust their audiences to feel some sympathy for the proponents of hate speech, and yet to feel that legislation is justified. This all too common technique of simplifying the moral equation by allowing personhood to only one party does not do us justice. A related difficulty is found in the Canadian Supreme Court's decision to uphold pornography legislation. *R. v Butler*, [1992] 1 SCR 452 (Can.). In *Butler*, a unanimous Court simply dismissed far more serious problems of vagueness, and did not even address indications that the legislation had been disproportionately applied to gay bookstores. Since

Butler, there have been continuing complaints about the unfair enforcement of pornography laws against gay and lesbian bookstores, as well as discontent about the failure to enforce the legislation against "mainstream" pornography. A lesbian bookstore in Vancouver B.C. called "The Little Sister Cooperative" has just commenced litigation in which it alleges that the practices of customs officials in enforcing the pornography provisions discriminate against lesbians. Arguments in the case concluded in the late fall of 1994.

23 *Keegstra*, at 760.

24 This is not to suggest that this is a conscious choice. Indeed, part of the invisible power of an established language is its ability to make choices not seem like choices, even to those who make them. Further, as noted above, there also seems to be at work a desire to minimize the sense that the decision inflicts harm, and this is achieved partly by creating sympathy for the speaker and avoiding serious discussion of the plight of the target.

25 Sir Isaiah Berlin describes negative liberty in the following terms: "By being free in this sense I mean not being interfered with by others. The wider the area of non-interference the wider my freedom." Isaiah Berlin, "Two Concepts of Liberty," in *Four Essays on Liberty* 123 (1979). Berlin notes that since, as Hobbes argued, 'Law is always a 'fetter,' even if it protects you from being bound in chains that are heavier than those of law," there must be a frontier "drawn between the area of private life and that of public authority." Otherwise, there will be no personal freedom. Ibid. at 124. Charles Taylor describes – and critically discusses – this "opportunity concept" of negative liberty in "What's Wrong with Negative Liberty," in *Philosophy and the Human Sciences: Philosophical Papers* 2, 213 (1985).

26 Taylor, *supra* note 25, at 213.

27 *Keegstra*, at 743. The Court seems to be referring to the uniqueness of section 1 as compared with the American view of rights and liberty.

28 C.B. MacPherson, *The Life and Times of Liberal Democracy* 78 (1977).

READING QUESTIONS ON MORAN

1 Moran suggests that American hate speech jurisprudence views the state with suspicion. To what extent is this an appropriate starting point for a view about regulation?

2 How are the views of democracy which Moran contrasts related to the debates about positive and negative liberty considered above?

R v Keegstra [1990] 3 SCR 697

The Supreme Court of Canada upheld the section of the *Criminal Code* outlawing the incitement of hatred. Writing for the majority, Dickson, CJC argued that the reasons for limiting expression in this case were the same as the reasons for protecting it more generally.

Dickson, CJC: – This appeal ... raises a delicate and highly controversial issue as to the constitutional validity of s. 319(2) of the *Criminal Code*, RSC, 1985, c. C-46, a legislative provision which prohibits the wilful promotion of hatred, other than in private conversation, towards any section of the public distinguished by colour, race, religion or ethnic origin. In particular, the court must decide whether this section infringes the guarantee of freedom of expression found in s. 2(b) of the *Canadian Charter of Rights and Freedoms* in a manner that cannot be justified under s. 1 of the *Charter*. A secondary issue arises as to whether the presumption of innocence protected in the *Charter's* s. 11(d) is unjustifiably breached by reason of s. 319(3)(a) of the *Code*, which affords a defence of "truth" to the wilful promotion of hatred, but only where the accused proves the truth of the communicated statements on the balance of probabilities.

FACTS

Mr James Keegstra was a high school teacher in Eckville, Alberta, from the early 1970s until his dismissal in 1982. In 1984, Mr Keegstra was charged under s. 319(2) (then 281.2(2)) of the *Criminal Code* with unlawfully promoting hatred against an identifiable group by communicating anti-Semitic statements to his students. He was convicted by a jury in a trial before McKenzie, J of the Alberta Court of Queen's Bench.

Mr Keegstra's teachings attributed various evil qualities to Jews. He thus described Jews to his pupils as "treacherous," "subversive," "sadistic," "money-loving," "power hungry," and "child killers." He taught his classes that Jewish people seek to destroy Christianity and are responsible for depressions, anarchy, chaos, wars, and revolution. According to Mr Keegstra, Jews "created the Holocaust to gain sympathy" and, in contrast to the open and honest Christians, were said to be deceptive, secretive, and inherently evil. Mr Keegstra expected his students to reproduce his teachings in class and on exams. If they failed to do so, their marks suffered.

Prior to his trial, Mr Keegstra applied to the Court of Queen's Bench in Alberta for an order quashing the charge on a number of grounds, the primary one being that s. 319(2) of the *Criminal Code* unjustifiably infringed his freedom of expression as guaranteed by s. 2(b) of the *Charter*. Among the other grounds of appeal was the allegation that the defence of truth found in s. 319(3)(a) of the *Code* violates the *Charter's* presumption of innocence. The application was dismissed by Quigley, J, and Mr Keegstra was thereafter tried and convicted. He then appealed his conviction to the Alberta Court of Appeal, raising the same *Charter* issues. The Court of Appeal unanimously accepted his argument, and it is from this judgment that the Crown appeals.

RELEVANT STATUTORY AND CONSTITUTIONAL PROVISIONS

The relevant legislative and Charter provisions are set out below:

Criminal Code
319(2) Every one who, by communicating statements, other than in private conversation, wilfully promotes hatred against any identifiable group is guilty of
(a) an indictable offence and is liable to imprisonment for a term not exceeding two years; or
(b) an offence punishable on summary conviction.

(3) No person shall be convicted of an offence under subsection (2)
(a) if he establishes that the statements communicated were true;
(b) if, in good faith, he expressed or attempted to establish by argument an opinion upon a religious subject;
(c) if the statements were relevant to any subject of public interest, the discussion of which was for the public benefit, and if on reasonable grounds he believed them to be true; or
(d) if, in good faith, he intended to point out, for the purpose of removal, matters producing or tending to produce feelings of hatred towards an identifiable group in Canada.

(6) No proceeding for an offence under subsection (2) shall be instituted without the consent of the Attorney General.

(7) In this section,
"communicating" includes communicating by telephone, broadcasting or other audible or visible means;
"identifiable group" has the same meaning as in section 318;
"public place" includes any place to which the public have access as of right or by invitation, express or implied;
"statements" includes words spoken or written or recorded electronically or electromagnetically or otherwise, and gestures, signs or other visible representations.

318(4) In this section, "identifiable group" means any section of the public distinguished by colour, race, religion or ethnic origin.

Canadian Bill of Rights, RSC 1985, App. III

1. It is hereby recognized and declared that in Canada there have existed and shall continue to exist without discrimination by reason of race, national origin, colour, religion or sex, the following human rights and fundamental freedoms, namely, ...
(d) freedom of speech;

Canadian Charter of Rights and Freedoms

1. *The Canadian Charter of Rights and Freedoms* guarantees the rights and freedoms set out in it subject only to such reasonable limits prescribed by law as can be demonstrably justified in a free and democratic society.

2. Everyone has the following fundamental freedoms:
(b) freedom of thought, belief, opinion and expression, including freedom of the press and other media of communication;

11. Any person charged with an offence has the right
(d) to be presumed innocent until proven guilty according to law in a fair and public hearing by an independent and impartial tribunal;

15(1) Every individual is equal before and under the law and has the right to the equal protection and equal benefit of the law without discrimination and, in particular, without discrimination based on race, national and ethnic origin, colour, religion, sex, age or mental or physical disability.

27. This *Charter* shall be interpreted in a manner consistent with the preservation and enhancement of the multicultural heritage of Canadians.

THE HISTORY OF HATE PROPAGANDA CRIMES IN CANADA

While the history of attempts to prosecute criminally the libel of groups is lengthy, the *Criminal Code* provisions discussed so far do not focus specifically upon expression propagated with the intent of causing hatred against racial, ethnic, or religious groups. Even before the Second World War, however, fears began to surface concerning the inadequacy of Canadian criminal law in this regard. In the 1930s, for example, Manitoba passed a statute combatting a perceived rise in the dissemination of Nazi propaganda. Following the Second World War and revelation of the Holocaust, in Canada and throughout the world a desire grew to protect human rights, and especially to guard against discrimination. Internationally, this desire led to the landmark *Universal Declaration of Human Rights* in 1948, and, with reference to hate propaganda, was eventually manifested in two international human rights instruments ...

The Special Committee on Hate Propaganda in Canada, usually referred to as the Cohen Committee ...

The tenor of the report is reflected in the opening paragraph of its preface, which reads:

This Report is a study in the power of words to maim, and what it is that a civilized society can do about it. Not every abuse of human communication can or should be controlled by law or custom. But every society from time to time draws lines at the point where the intolerable and the impermissible coincide. In a free society such as our own, where the privilege of speech can induce ideas that may change the very order itself, there is bias weighted heavily in favour of the maximum of rhetoric whatever the cost and consequences. But that bias stops this side of injury to the community itself and to individual members or identifiable groups innocently caught in verbal crossfire that goes beyond legitimate debate.

In keeping with these remarks, the recurrent theme running throughout the report is the need to prevent the dissemination of hate propaganda without unduly infringing the freedom of expression ...

SECTION 2(B) OF THE *CHARTER* – FREEDOM OF EXPRESSION

Obviously, one's conception of the freedom of expression provides a crucial backdrop to any s. 2(b) inquiry; the values promoted by the freedom help not only to define the ambit of s. 2(b), but also come to the forefront when discussing how competing interests might co-exist with the freedom under s. 1 of the *Charter*.

In the recent past, this court has had the opportunity to hear and decide a number of freedom of expression cases ... Together, the judgments in these cases provide guidance as to the values informing the freedom of expression, and additionally indicate the relationship between ss. 2(b) and 1 of the *Charter*.

It was argued before this court that the wilful promotion of hatred is an activity the form and consequences of which are analogous to those associated with violence or threats of violence. This argument contends that Supreme Court of Canada precedent excludes violence and threats of violence from the ambit of s. 2(b), and that the reason for such exclusion must lie in the fact that these forms of expression are inimical to the values supporting freedom of speech. Indeed, in support of this view it was pointed out to us that the court in *Irwin Toy* stated that "freedom of expression ensures that we can convey our thoughts and feelings in non-violent ways without fear of censure" (p. 607). Accordingly, we were urged to find that hate propaganda of the type caught by s. 319(2), insofar as it imperils the ability of target group members themselves to convey thoughts and feelings in non-violent ways without fear of censure, is analogous to violence and threats of violence and hence does not fall within s. 2(b).

Turning specifically to the proposition that hate propaganda should be excluded from the coverage of s. 2(b), I begin by stating that the communications restricted by s. 319(2) cannot be considered as violence, which on a reading of *Irwin Toy* I find to refer to expression communicated directly through physical harm. Nor do I find hate propaganda to be analogous to violence, and through this route exclude it from the protection of the guarantee of freedom of expression. As I have explained, the starting proposition in *Irwin Toy* is that all activities conveying or attempting to convey meaning are considered expression for the purposes of s. 2(b); the content of expression is irrelevant in determining the scope of this *Charter* provision. Stated at its highest, an exception has been suggested where meaning is communicated directly via physical violence, the extreme repugnance of this form to free expression values justifying such an extraordinary step. Section 319(2) of the *Criminal Code* prohibits the communication of meaning that is repugnant, but the repugnance stems from the content of the message as opposed to its form. For this reason, I am of the view that hate propaganda is to be categorized as expression so as to bring it within the coverage of s. 2(b).

As for threats of violence, *Irwin Toy* spoke only of restricting s. 2(b) to certain forms of expression, stating at p. 607 that,

While the guarantee of free expression protects all content of expression, certainly violence as a form of expression receives no such protection. It is not necessary here to delineate precisely when and on what basis a form of expression chosen to convey a meaning falls outside the sphere of the guarantee. But it is clear, for example, that a murderer or rapist cannot invoke the freedom of expression in justification of the form of expression he has chosen.

While the line between form and content is not always easily drawn, in my opinion threats of violence can only be so classified by reference to the content of their meaning. As such, they do not fall within the exception spoken of in *Irwin Toy*, and their suppression must be justified under s. 1. As I do not find threats of violence to be excluded from the definition of expression envisioned by s. 2(b), it is unnecessary to determine whether the threatening aspects of hate propaganda can be seen as threats of violence, or analogous to such threats, so as to deny it protection under s. 2(b).

The second matter which I wish to address before leaving the s. 2(b) inquiry concerns the relevance of other *Charter* provisions and international agreements to which Canada is a party in interpreting the coverage of the freedom of expression guarantee. It has been argued in support of excluding hate propaganda from the coverage of s. 2(b) that the use of ss. 15 and 27 of the *Charter* – dealing respectively with equality and multiculturalism – and Canada's acceptance of international agreements requiring the prohibition of racist statements make s. 319(2) incompatible with even a large and liberal definition of the freedom: The general tenor of this argument is that these interpretive aids inextricably infuse each constitutional guarantee with values supporting equal societal participation and the security and dignity of all persons. Consequently, it is said that s. 2(b) must be curtailed so as not to extend to communications which seriously undermine the equality, security, and dignity of others ...

I thus conclude on the issue of s. 2(b) by finding that s. 319(2) of the *Criminal Code* constitutes an infringement of the *Charter* guarantee of freedom of expression, and turn to examine whether such an infringement is justifiable under s. 1 as a reasonable limit in a free and democratic society.

SECTION 1 ANALYSIS OF SECTION 319(2)

General Approach to Section 1

Though the language of s. 1 appears earlier in these reasons, it is appropriate to repeat its words:

1. *The Canadian Charter of Rights and Freedoms* guarantees the rights and freedoms set out in it subject only to such reasonable limits prescribed by law as can be demonstrably justified in a free and democratic society.

In *R v Oakes* (1986), 24 CCC (3d) 321, this court offered a course of analysis to be employed in determining whether a limit on a right or freedom can be demonstrably justified in a free and democratic society. Under the approach in *Oakes*, it must first be established that impugned state action has an objective of pressing and substantial concern in a free and democratic society. Only such an objective is of sufficient stature to warrant overriding a constitutionally protected right or freedom. The second feature of the *Oakes* test involves assessing the proportionality between the objective and the impugned measure. The inquiry as to proportionality attempts to guide the balancing of individual and group interests protected in s. 1, and in *Oakes* was broken down into the following three segments:

First, the measures adopted must be carefully designed to achieve the objective in question. They must not be arbitrary, unfair or based on irrational considerations. In short, they must be rationally connected to the objective. Secondly, the means, even if rationally connected to the objective in this first sense, should impair "as little as possible" the right or freedom in question ... Thirdly, there must be a proportionality between the effects of the measures which are responsible for limiting the *Charter* right or freedom, and the objective which has been identified as of "sufficient importance."

The analytical framework of *Oakes* has been continually reaffirmed by this court, yet it is dangerously misleading to conceive of s. 1 as a rigid and technical provision, offering nothing more than a last chance for the state to justify incursions into the realm of fundamental rights. From a crudely practical standpoint, *Charter* litigants sometimes may perceive s. 1 in this manner, but in the body of our nation's constitutional law it plays an immeasurably richer role, one of great magnitude and sophistication ... As this court has said before, the premier article of the *Charter* has a dual function, operating both to activate *Charter* rights and freedoms and to permit such reasonable limits as a free and democratic society may have occasion to place upon them *(Oakes,* at pp. 343–4). What seems to me to be of significance in this dual function is the commonality that links the guarantee of rights and freedoms to their limitation. This commonality lies in the phrase "free and democratic society."

Obviously, a practical application of s. 1 requires more than an incantation of the words "free and democratic society." These words require some definition, an elucidation as to the values that they invoke. To a large extent, a free and democratic society embraces the very values and principles which Canadians have sought to protect and further by entrenching specific rights and freedoms in the Constitution, although the balancing exercise in s. 1 is not restricted to values expressly set out in the *Charter*. With this guideline in mind, in *Oakes* I commented upon some of the ideals that inform our understanding of a free and democratic society, saying (at p. 346):

> The court must be guided by the values and principles essential to a free and democratic society which I believe embody, to name but a few, respect for the inherent dignity of the human person, commitment to social justice and equality, accommodation of a wide variety of beliefs, respect for cultural and group identity, and faith in social and political institutions which enhance the participation of individuals and groups in society. The underlying values and principles of a free and democratic society are the genesis of the rights and freedoms guaranteed by the *Charter* and the ultimate standard against which a limit on a right or freedom must be shown, despite its effect, to be reasonable and demonstrably justified.

Undoubtedly these values and principles are numerous, covering the guarantees enumerated in the *Charter* and more. Equally, they may well deserve different emphases, and certainly will assume varying degrees of importance depending upon the circumstances of a particular case.

It is important not to lose sight of factual circumstances in undertaking a s. 1 analysis, for these shape a court's view of both the right or freedom at stake and the limit proposed by the state; neither can be surveyed in the abstract. As Wilson, J said in *Edmonton Journal, supra,* referring to what she termed the "contextual approach" to *Charter* interpretation (at p. 584):

... a particular right or freedom may have a different value depending on the context. It may be, for example, that freedom of expression has greater value in a political context than it does in the context of disclosure of the details of a matrimonial dispute.

Though Wilson, J was speaking with reference to the task of balancing enumerated rights and freedoms, I see no reason why her view should not apply to all values associated with a free and democratic society. Clearly, the proper judicial perspective under s. 1 must be derived from an awareness of the synergetic relation between two elements: the values underlying the *Charter* and the circumstances of the particular case.

The Use of American Constitutional Jurisprudence

Having discussed the unique and unifying role of s. 1, I think it appropriate to address a tangential matter, yet one nonetheless crucial to the disposition of this appeal: the relationship between Canadian and American approaches to the constitutional protection of free expression, most notably in the realm of hate propaganda. Those who attack the constitutionality of s. 319(2) draw heavily on the tenor of First Amendment jurisprudence in weighing the competing freedoms and interests in this appeal, a reliance which is understandable given the prevalent opinion that the criminalization of hate propaganda violates the Bill of Rights ... In response to the emphasis placed upon this jurisprudence, I find it helpful to summarize the American position and to determine the extent to which it should influence the s. 1 analysis in the circumstances of this appeal.

A myriad of sources – both judicial and academic – offer reviews of First Amendment jurisprudence as it pertains to hate propaganda. Central to most discussions is the 1952 case of *Beauharnais v Illinois*, 343 US 250, where the Supreme Court of the United States upheld as constitutional a criminal statute forbidding certain types of group defamation. Though never overruled, *Beauharnais* appears to have been weakened by later pronouncements of the Supreme Court: The trend reflected in many of these pronouncements is to protect offensive, public invective as long as the speaker has not knowingly lied and there exists no clear and present danger of violence or insurrection.

In the wake of subsequent developments in the Supreme Court, on several occasions *Beauharnais* has been distinguished and doubted by lower courts.

The question that concerns us in this appeal is not, of course, what the law is or should be in the United States. But it is important to be explicit as to the reasons why or why not American experience may be useful in the s. 1 analysis of s. 319(2) of the *Criminal Code*. In the United States, a collection of fundamental rights has been constitutionally protected for over 200 years. The resulting practical and theoretical experience is immense, and should not be overlooked by Canadian courts. On the other hand, we must examine American constitutional law with a critical eye, and in this respect La Forest, J has noted:

While it is natural and even desirable for Canadian courts to refer to American constitutional jurisprudence in seeking to elucidate the meaning of *Charter* guarantees that have counterparts in the United States Constitution, they should be wary of drawing too ready a parallel between constitutions born to different countries in different ages and in very different circumstances ...

Having examined the American cases relevant to First Amendment jurisprudence and legislation criminalizing hate propaganda, I would be adverse to following too closely the line of argument that would overrule *Beauharnais* on the ground that incursions placed upon free expression are only justified where there is a clear and present danger of imminent breach of peace. Equally, I am unwilling to embrace various categorizations and guiding rules generated by American law without careful consideration of their appropriateness to Canadian constitutional theory. Though I have found the American experience tremendously helpful in coming to my own conclusions regarding this appeal, and by no means reject the whole of the First Amendment doctrine, in a number of respects I am thus dubious as to the applicability of this doctrine in the context of a challenge to hate propaganda legislation.

... [A]pplying the *Charter* to the legislation challenged in this appeal reveals important differences between Canadian and American constitutional perspectives. I have already discussed in some detail the special role of s. 1 in determining the protective scope of *Charter* rights and freedoms. Section 1 has no equivalent in the United States, a fact previously alluded to by this court in selectively utilizing American constitutional jurisprudence. Of course, American experience should never be rejected simply because the *Charter* contains a balancing provision, for it is well known that American courts have fashioned compromises between conflicting interests despite what appears to be the absolute guarantee of constitutional rights. Where s. 1 operates to accentuate a uniquely Canadian vision of a free and democratic society, however, we must not hesitate to depart from the path taken in the United States. Far from requiring a less solicitous protection of *Charter* rights and freedoms, such independence of vision protects these rights and freedoms in a different way. As will be seen below, in my view the international commitment to eradicate hate propaganda and, most importantly, the special role given equality and multiculturalism in the Canadian Constitution necessitate a departure from the view, reasonably prevalent in America at present, that the suppression of hate propaganda is incompatible with the guarantee of free expression.

Most importantly, the nature of the s. 1 test as applied in the context of a challenge to s. 319(2) may well demand a perspective particular to Canadian constitutional jurisprudence when weighing competing interests. If values fundamental to the Canadian conception of a free and democratic society suggest an approach that denies hate propaganda the highest degree of constitutional protection, it is this approach which must be employed.

Objective of Section 319(2)

I now turn to the specific requirements of the *Oakes* approach in deciding whether the infringement of s. 2(b) occasioned by s. 319(2) is justifiable in a free and democratic society. According to *Oakes*, the first aspect of the s. 1 analysis is to examine the objective of the impugned legislation. Only if the objective relates to concerns which are pressing and substantial in a free and democratic society can the legislative limit on a right or freedom hope to be permissible under the *Charter*. In examining the objective of s. 319(2), I will begin by discussing the harm caused by hate propaganda as identified by the Cohen Committee and subsequent study groups, and then review in turn the impact upon this objective of international human rights instruments and ss. 15 and 27 of the *Charter*.

Harm Caused by Expression Promoting the Hatred of Identifiable Groups

Looking to the legislation challenged in this appeal, one must ask whether the amount of hate propaganda in Canada causes sufficient harm to justify legislative intervention of some type. The Cohen Committee, speaking in 1965, found that the incidence of hate propaganda in Canada was not insignificant (at p. 24):

... there exists in Canada a small number of persons and a somewhat larger number of organizations, extremist in outlook and dedicated to the preaching and spreading of hatred and contempt against certain identifiable minority groups in Canada. It is easy to conclude that because the number of persons and organizations is not very large, they should not be taken too seriously. The Committee is of the opinion that this line of analysis is no longer tenable after what is known to have been the result of hate propaganda in other countries, particularly in the 1930s when such material and ideas played a significant role in the creation of a climate of malice, destructive to the central values of Judaic-Christian society, the values of our civilization. The Committee believes, therefore, that the actual and potential danger caused by present hate activities in Canada cannot be measured by statistics alone.

Even the statistics, however, are not unimpressive, because while activities have centered heavily in Ontario, they nevertheless have extended from Nova Scotia to British Columbia and minority groups in at least eight Provinces have been subjected to these vicious attacks.

In 1984, the House of Commons Special Committee on Participation of Visible Minorities in Canadian Society in its report, entitled *Equality Now!*, observed that increased immigration and periods of economic difficulty "have produced an atmosphere that may be ripe for racially motivated incidents" (p. 69). With regard to the dissemination of hate propaganda, the Special Committee found that the prevalence and scope of such material had risen since the Cohen Committee made its report, stating (at p. 69):

There has been a recent upsurge in hate propaganda. It has been found in virtually every part of Canada. Not only is it anti-semitic and anti-black, as in the 1960s, but it is also now anti-Roman Catholic, anti-East Indian, anti-aboriginal people and anti-French. Some of this material is imported from the United States but much of it is produced in Canada. Most worrisome of all is that in recent years Canada has become a major source of supply of hate propaganda that finds its way to Europe, and especially to West Germany.

As the quotations above indicate, the presence of hate propaganda in Canada is sufficiently substantial to warrant concern. Disquiet caused by the existence of such material is not simply the product of its offensiveness, however, but stems from the very real harm which it causes. Essentially, there are two sorts of injury caused by hate propaganda. First, there is harm done to members of the target group. It is indisputable that the emotional damage caused by words may be of grave psychological and social consequence. In the context of sexual harassment, for example, this court has found that words can in themselves constitute harassment: *Janzen v Platy Enterprises Ltd* (1989), 59 DLR (4th) 352. In a similar manner, words and writings that wilfully promote hatred can constitute a serious attack on persons belonging to a racial or religious group, and in this regard the Cohen Committee noted that these persons are humiliated and degraded (p. 214).

In my opinion, a response of humiliation and degradation from an individual targeted by hate propaganda is to be expected. A person's sense of human dignity and belonging to the community at large is closely linked to the concern and respect accorded the groups to which he or she belongs. The derision, hostility and abuse encouraged by hate propaganda therefore have a severely negative impact on the individual's sense of self-worth and acceptance. This impact may cause target group members to take drastic measures in reaction, perhaps avoiding activities which bring them into contact with non-group members or adopting attitudes and postures directed towards blending in with the majority. Such consequences bear heavily in a nation that prides itself on tolerance and the fostering of human dignity through, among other things, respect for the many racial, religious, and cultural groups in our society.

A second harmful effect of hate propaganda which is of pressing and substantial concern is its influence upon society at large. The Cohen Committee noted that individuals can be persuaded to believe "almost anything" (p. 30) if information or ideas are communicated using the right technique and in the proper circumstances (at p. 8):

... we are less confident in the 20th century that the critical faculties of individuals will be brought to bear on the speech and writing which is directed at them. In the 18th and 19th centuries, there was a widespread belief that man was a rational creature, and that if his mind was trained and liberated from superstition by education, he would always distinguish truth from falsehood, good from evil. So Milton, who said "let truth and falsehood grapple: who ever knew truth put to the worse in a free and open encounter."

We cannot share this faith today in such a simple form. While holding that over the long run, the human mind is repelled by blatant falsehood and seeks the good, it is too often true, in the short run, that emotion displaces reason and individuals perversely reject the demonstrations of truth put before them and forsake the good they know. The successes of modern advertising, the triumphs of impudent propaganda such as Hitler's, have qualified sharply our belief in the rationality of man. We know that under the strain and pressure in times of irritation and frustration, the individual is swayed and even swept away by hysterical, emotional appeals. We act irresponsibly if we ignore the way in which emotion can drive reason from the field.

It is thus not inconceivable that the active dissemination of hate propaganda can attract individuals to its cause, and in the process create serious discord between various cultural groups in society. Moreover, the alteration of views held by the recipients of hate propaganda may occur subtly, and is not always attendant upon conscious acceptance of the communicated ideas. Even if the message of hate propaganda is outwardly rejected, there is evidence that its premise of racial or religious inferiority may persist in a recipient's mind as an idea that holds some truth, an incipient effect not to be entirely discounted.

The threat to the self-dignity of target group members is thus matched by the possibility that prejudiced messages will gain some credence, with the attendant result of discrimination, and perhaps even violence, against minority groups in Canadian society. With these dangers in mind, the Cohen Committee made clear in its conclusions that the presence of hate propaganda existed as a baleful and pernicious element, and hence a serious problem, in Canada (at p. 59):

We believe that, given a certain set of socioeconomic circumstances, such as a deepening of the emotional tensions or the setting in of a severe business recession, public susceptibility might well increase significantly. Moreover, the potential psychological and social damage of hate propaganda, both to a desensitized majority and to sensitive minority target groups, is incalculable.

As noted previously, in articulating concern about hate propaganda and its contribution to racial and religious tension in Canada, the Cohen

Committee recommended that Parliament use the *Criminal Code* in order to prohibit wilful, hate-promoting expression and underline Canada's commitment to end prejudice and intolerance ...

International Human Rights Instruments

There is a great deal of support, both in the submissions made by those seeking to uphold s. 319(2) in this appeal and in the numerous studies of racial and religious hatred in Canada, for the conclusion that the harm caused by hate propaganda represents a pressing and substantial concern in a free and democratic society. I would also refer to international human rights principles, however, for guidance with respect to assessing the legislative objective.

Generally speaking, the international human rights obligations taken on by Canada reflect the values and principles of a free and democratic society, and thus those values and principles that underlie the *Charter* itself ...

No aspect of international human rights has been given attention greater than that focused upon discrimination ... In 1966, the United Nations adopted the international *Convention on the Elimination of All Forms of Racial Discrimination*, 1970, Can. TS, No. 28 (hereinafter CERD). The convention, in force since 1969 and including Canada among its signatory members, contains a resolution that states parties agree to:

... adopt all necessary measures for speedily eliminating racial discrimination in all its forms and manifestations, and to prevent and combat racist doctrines and practices in order to promote understanding between races and to build an international community free from all forms of racial segregation and racial discrimination ...

Article 4 of the *CERD* is of special interest, providing that:

States Parties condemn all propaganda and all organizations which are based on ideas or theories of superiority of one race or group of persons of one colour or ethnic origin, or which attempt to justify or promote racial hatred and discrimination in any form, and undertake to adopt immediate and positive measures designed to eradicate all incitement to, or acts of, such discrimination and, to this end, with due regard to the principles embodied in the *Universal Declaration of Human Rights* and the rights expressly set forth in article 5 of this *Convention*, inter alia:

(a) Shall declare an offence punishable by law all dissemination of ideas based on racial superiority or hatred, incitement to racial discrimination, as well as all acts of violence or incitement to such acts against any race or group of persons of another colour or ethnic origin, and also the provision of any assistance to racist activities, including the financing thereof;

Further, the *International Covenant on Civil and Political Rights,* 1966, 999 UNTS 171 (hereinafter *ICCPR*) , adopted by the United Nations in 1966 and in force in Canada since 1976, in the following two articles guarantees the freedom of expression while simultaneously prohibiting the advocacy of hatred.

It appears that the protection provided freedom of expression by *CERD* and ICCPR does not extend to cover communications advocating racial or religious hatred ...

Other Provisions of the *Charter*

Significant indicia of the strength of the objective behind s. 319(2) are gleaned not only from the international arena, but are also expressly evident in various provisions of the *Charter* itself. As Wilson, J noted in *Singh v Canada (Minister of Employment and Immigration)* (1985), 17 DLR (4th) 422 at p. 468, [1985] 1 SCR 177, 14 CRR 13:

... it is important to bear in mind that the rights and freedoms set out in the *Charter* are fundamental to the political structure of Canada and are guaranteed by the *Charter* as part of the supreme law of our nation. I think that in determining whether a particular limitation is a reasonable limit prescribed by law which can be "demonstrably justified in a free and democratic society" it is important to remember that the courts are conducting this inquiry in light of a commitment to uphold the rights and freedoms set out in other sections of the *Charter.*

Most importantly for the purposes of this appeal, ss. 15 and 27 represent a strong commitment to the values of equality and multiculturalism, and hence underline the great importance of Parliament's objective in prohibiting hate propaganda.

[T]he effects of entrenching a guarantee of equality in the *Charter* are not confined to those instances where it can be invoked by an individual against the state. Insofar as it indicates our society's dedication to promoting equality, s. 15 is also relevant in assessing the aims of s. 319(2) of the *Criminal Code* under s. 1. In *Andrews v Law Society of British Columbia* (1989), 56 DLR (4th) 1 at p. 15, this court examined the equality guarantee of s. 15, McIntyre, J noting:

It is clear that the purpose of s. 15 is to ensure equality in the formulation and application of the law. The promotion of equality entails the promotion of a society in which all are secure in the knowledge that they are recognized at law as human beings equally deserving of concern, respect and consideration. It has a large remedial component.

... The principles underlying s. 15 of the *Charter* are thus integral to the s. 1 analysis.

In its written submission to the court, the intervenor LEAF [Women's Legal Education and Action Fund *(eds.)*] made the following comment in support of the view that the public and wilful promotion of group hatred is properly understood as a practice of inequality:

Government sponsored hatred on group grounds would violate section 15 of the Charter. Parliament promotes equality and moves against inequality when it prohibits the wilful public promotion of group hatred on these grounds. It follows that government action against group hate, because it promotes social equality as guaranteed by the *Charter*, deserves special constitutional consideration under section 15.

I agree with this statement. In light of the *Charter* commitment to equality, and the reflection of this commitment in the framework of s. 1, the objective of the impugned legislation is enhanced insofar as it seeks to ensure the equality of all individuals in Canadian society. The message of the expressive activity covered by s. 319(2) is that members of identifiable groups are not to be given equal standing in society, and are not human beings equally deserving of concern, respect, and consideration. The harms caused by this message run directly counter to the values central to a free and democratic society, and in restricting the promotion of hatred Parliament is therefore seeking to bolster the notion of mutual respect necessary in a nation which venerates the equality of all persons.

Section 15 is not the only *Charter* provision which emphasizes values both important to a free and democratic society and pertinent to the disposition of this appeal under s. 1. Section 27 states that:

27. This *Charter* shall be interpreted in a manner consistent with the preservation and enhancement of the multicultural heritage of Canadians.

This court has where possible taken account of s. 27 and its recognition that Canada possesses a multicultural society in which the diversity and richness of various cultural groups is a value to be protected and enhanced ... The value expressed in s. 27 cannot be casually dismissed in assessing the validity of s. 319(2) under s. 1, and I am of the belief that s. 27 and the commitment to a multicultural vision of our nation bears notice in emphasizing the acute importance of the objective of eradicating hate propaganda from society.

Hate propaganda seriously threatens both the enthusiasm with which the value of equality is accepted and acted upon by society and the connection of target group members to their community. I thus agree with the sentiments of Cory, JA who, in writing to uphold s. 319(2) in *R v Andrews* (1988), 43 CCC (3d) 193 at p. 213, said: "Multiculturalism cannot be preserved let alone enhanced if free rein is given to the promotion of hatred against identifiable cultural groups." When the prohibition of expressive activity that promotes hatred of groups identifiable on the basis of colour, race, religion, or ethnic origin is considered in light of s. 27, the legitimacy and substantial nature of the government objective is therefore considerably strengthened.

Conclusion Respecting Objective of Section 319(2)

In my opinion, it would be impossible to deny that Parliament's objective in enacting s. 319(2) is of the utmost importance ...

Proportionality

The second branch of the *Oakes* test – proportionality – poses the most challenging questions with respect to the validity of s. 319(2) as a reasonable limit on freedom of expression in a free and democratic society. It is therefore not surprising to find most commentators, as well as the litigants in the case at bar, agreeing that the objective of the provision is of great importance, but to observe considerable disagreement when it comes to deciding whether the means chosen to further the objective are proportional to the ends.

Relation of the Expression at Stake to Free Expression Values

In discussing the nature of the government objective, I have commented at length upon the way in which the suppression of hate propaganda furthers values basic to a free and democratic society. I have said little, however, regarding the extent to which these same values, including the freedom of expression, are furthered by permitting the exposition of such expressive activity. This lacuna is explicable when one realizes that the interpretation of s. 2(b) under *Irwin Toy, supra*, gives protection to a very wide range of expression. Content is irrelevant to this interpretation, the result of a high value being placed upon freedom of expression in the abstract. This approach to s. 2(b) often operates to leave unexamined the extent to which the expression at stake in a particular case promotes freedom of expression principles. In my opinion, however, the s. 1 analysis of a limit upon s. 2(b) cannot ignore the nature of the expressive activity which the state seeks to restrict. While we must guard carefully against judging expression according to its popularity, it is equally destructive of free expression values, as well as the other values which underlie a free and democratic society, to treat all expression as equally crucial to those principles at the core of s. 2(b).

In *Rocket v Royal College of Dental Surgeons of Ontario, supra*, McLachlin, J recognized the importance of context in evaluating expressive activity under s. 1, stating with regard to commercial speech (at p. 78):

While the Canadian approach does not apply special tests to restrictions on commercial expression, our method of analysis does permit a sensitive, case-oriented approach to the determination of their constitutionality. Placing the conflicting values in their factual and social context when performing the s. 1 analysis permits the courts to have regard to special features of the expression in question.

Royal College dealt with provincial limitations upon the freedom of dentists to impart information to patients and potential patients via advertisements. In these circumstances, the court found that the expression regulated was of a nature that made its curtailment something less than a most serious infringement of the freedom of expression, the limitation affecting neither participation in the political process nor the ability of the individual to achieve spiritual or artistic self-fulfilment.

Applying the *Royal College* approach to the context of this appeal is a key aspect of the s. 1 analysis. One must ask whether the expression prohibited by s. 319(2) is tenuously connected to the values underlying s. 2(b) so as to make the restriction "easier to justify than other infringements." In this regard, let me begin by saying that, in my opinion, there can be no real disagreement about the subject-matter of the messages and teachings communicated by the respondent, Mr Keegstra: it is deeply offensive, hurtful and damaging to target group members, misleading to his listeners, and antithetical to the furtherance of tolerance and understanding in society. Furthermore, as will be clear when I come to discuss in detail the interpretation of s. 319(2), there is no doubt that all expression fitting within the terms of the offence can be similarly described. To say merely that expression is offensive and disturbing, however, fails to address satisfactorily the question of whether, and to what extent, the expressive activity prohibited by s. 319(2) promotes the values underlying the freedom of expression. It is to this difficult and complex question that I now turn.

From the outset, I wish to make clear that in my opinion the expression prohibited by s. 319(2) is not closely linked to the rationale underlying s. 2(b). Examining the values identified in *Ford* and *Irwin Toy* as fundamental to the protection of free expression, arguments can be made for the proposition that each of these values is diminished by the suppression of hate propaganda. While none of these arguments is spurious, I am of the opinion that expression intended to promote the hatred of identifiable groups is of limited importance when measured against free expression values.

At the core of freedom of expression lies the need to ensure that truth and the common good are attained, whether in scientific and artistic endeavors or in the process of determining the best course to take in our political affairs. Since truth and the ideal form of political and social organization can rarely, if at all, be identified with absolute certainty, it is difficult to prohibit expression without impeding the free exchange of potentially valuable information. Nevertheless, the argument from truth does not provide convincing support for the protection of hate propaganda. Taken to its extreme, this argument would require us to permit the communication of all expression, it being impossible to know with absolute certainty which factual statements are true, or which ideas obtain the greatest good. The problem with this extreme position, however, is that the greater the degree of certainty that a statement is erroneous or mendacious, the less its value in the quest for truth. Indeed, expression can be used to the detriment of our search for truth; the state should not be the sole arbiter of truth, but neither should we overplay the view that rationality will overcome all falsehoods in the unregulated market-place of ideas. There is very little chance that statements intended to promote hatred against an identifiable group are true, or that their vision of society will lead to a better world. To portray such statements as crucial to truth and the betterment of the political and social milieu is therefore misguided.

Another component central to the rationale underlying s. 2(b) concerns the vital role of free expression as a means of ensuring individuals the ability to gain self-fulfilment by developing and articulating thoughts and ideas as they see fit. It is true that s. 319(2) inhibits this process among those individuals whose expression it limits, and hence arguably works against freedom of expression values. On the other hand, such self-autonomy stems in large part from one's ability to articulate and nurture an identity derived from membership in a cultural or religious group. The message put forth by individuals who fall within the ambit of s. 319(2) represents a most extreme opposition to the idea that members of identifiable groups should enjoy this aspect of the s. 2(b) benefit. The extent to which the unhindered promotion of this message furthers free expression values must therefore be tempered insofar as it advocates with inordinate vitriol an intolerance and prejudice which views as execrable the process of individual self-development and human flourishing among all members of society.

Moving on to a third strain of thought said to justify the protection of free expression, one's attention is brought specifically to the political realm. The connection between freedom of expression and the political process is perhaps the linchpin of the s. 2(b) guarantee, and the nature of this connection is largely derived from the Canadian commitment to democracy. Freedom of expression is a crucial aspect of the democratic commitment, not merely because it permits the best policies to be chosen from among a wide array of proffered options, but additionally because it helps to ensure that participation in the political process is open to all persons. Such open participation must involve to a substantial degree the notion that all persons are equally deserving of respect and dignity. The state therefore cannot act to hinder or condemn a political view without to some extent harming the openness of Canadian democracy and its associated tenet of equality for all.

The suppression of hate propaganda undeniably muzzles the participation of a few individuals in the democratic process, and hence detracts somewhat from free expression values, but the degree of this limitation is not substantial. I am aware that the use of strong language in political and social debate – indeed, perhaps even language intended to promote hatred – is an unavoidable part of the democratic process. Moreover, I recognize that hate propaganda is expression of a type which would generally be categorized as "political," thus putatively placing it at the very heart of the principle extolling freedom of expression as vital to the democratic process. Nonetheless, expression can work to undermine our commitment to democracy where employed to propagate ideas anathemic to democratic values. Hate propaganda works in just such a way, arguing as it does for a society in which the democratic process is subverted and individuals are denied respect and dignity simply because of racial or religious characteristics. This brand of expressive activity is thus wholly inimical to the democratic aspirations of the free expression guarantee.

Indeed, one may quite plausibly contend that it is through rejecting hate propaganda that the state can best encourage the protection of values central to freedom of expression, while simultaneously demonstrating dislike for the vision forwarded by hate-mongers. In this regard, the reaction to various types of expression by a democratic government may be perceived as meaningful expression on behalf of the vast majority of citizens. I do not wish to be construed as saying that an infringement of s. 2(b) can be justified under s. 1 merely because it is the product of a democratic process; the *Charter* will not permit even the democratically elected legislature to restrict the rights and freedoms crucial to a free and democratic society. What I do wish to emphasize, however, is that one must be careful not to accept blindly that the suppression of expression must always and unremittingly detract from values central to freedom of expression.

I am very reluctant to attach anything but the highest importance to expression relevant to political matters. But given the unparalleled vigour with which hate propaganda repudiates and undermines democratic values, and in particular its condemnation of the view that all citizens need be treated with equal respect and dignity so as to make participation in the political process meaningful, I am unable to see the protection of such expression as integral to the democratic ideal so central to the s. 2(b) rationale ... In my view, hate propaganda should not be accorded the greatest of weight in the s. 1 analysis.

As a caveat, it must be emphasized that the protection of extreme statements, even where they attack those principles underlying the freedom of expression, is not completely divorced from the aims of s. 2(b) of the *Charter*. As noted already, suppressing the expression covered by s. 319(2) does to some extent weaken these principles. It can also be argued that it is partly through a clash with extreme and erroneous views that truth and the democratic vision remain vigorous and alive. In this regard, judicial pronouncements strongly advocating the importance of free expression values might be seen as helping to expose prejudiced statements as valueless even while striking down legislative restrictions that proscribe such expression. Additionally, condoning a democracy's collective decision to protect itself from certain types of expression may lead to a slippery slope on which encroachments on expression central to s. 2(b) values are permitted. To guard against such a result, the protection of communications virulently unsupportive of free expression values may be necessary in order to ensure that expression more compatible with these values is never unjustifiably limited.

None of these arguments is devoid of merit, and each must be taken into account in determining whether an infringement of s. 2(b) can be justified under s. 1. It need not be, however, that they apply equally or with the greatest of strength in every instance ... While I cannot conclude that hate propaganda deserves only marginal protection under the s. 1 analysis, I can take cognizance of the fact that limitations upon hate propaganda are directed at a special category of expression which strays some distance from the spirit of s. 2(b), and hence conclude that "restrictions on expression of this kind might be easier to justify than other infringements of s. 2(b)": *Royal College, supra,* at p. 79.

As a final point, it should be stressed that in discussing the relationship between hate propaganda and freedom of expression values I do not wish to be taken as advocating an inflexible "levels of scrutiny" categorization of expressive activity. The contextual approach necessitates an open discussion of the manner in which s. 2(b) values are engaged in the circumstances of an appeal. To become transfixed with categorization schemes risks losing the advantage associated with this sensitive examination of free expression principles, and I would be loath to sanction such a result.

Having made some preliminary comments as to the nature of the expression at stake in this appeal, it is now possible to ask whether s. 319(2) is an acceptably proportional response to Parliament's valid objective. As stated above, the proportionality aspect of the *Oakes* test requires the court to decide whether the impugned state action: (i) is rationally connected to the objective; (ii) minimally impairs the *Charter* right or freedom at issue, and (iii) does not produce effects of such severity so as to make the impairment unjustifiable.

Rational Connection

... Doubts have been raised, however, as to whether the actual effect of s. 319(2) is to undermine any rational connection between it and Parliament's objective. As stated in the reasons of McLachlin, J, there are three primary ways in which the effect of the impugned legislation might be seen as an irrational means of carrying out the Parliamentary purpose. First, it is argued that the provision may actually promote the cause of hate-mongers by earning them extensive media attention. In this vein, it is also suggested that persons accused of intentionally promoting hatred often see themselves as martyrs, and may actually generate sympathy from the community in the role of underdogs engaged in battle against the immense powers of the state. Secondly, the public may view the suppression of expression by the government with suspicion, making it possible that such expression – even if it be hate propaganda – is perceived as containing an element of truth. Finally, it is often noted that Germany of the 1920s and 1930s possessed and used hate propaganda laws similar to those existing in Canada, and yet these laws did nothing to stop the triumph of a racist philosophy under the Nazis.

If s. 319(2) can be said to have no impact in the quest to achieve Parliament's admirable objectives, or in fact works in opposition to these objectives, then I agree that the provision could be described as "arbitrary, unfair or based on irrational considerations": (*Oakes, supra,* at p. 348). I recognize that the effect of s. 319(2) is impossible to define with exact precision – the same can be said for many laws, criminal or otherwise. In my view, however, the position that there is no strong and evident connection between the criminalization of hate propaganda and its suppression is unconvincing. I come to this conclusion for a number of reasons, and will elucidate these by answering in turn the three arguments just mentioned ...

It is undeniable that media attention has been extensive on those occasions when s. 319(2) has been used. Yet from my perspective, s. 319(2) serves to illustrate to the public the severe reprobation with which society holds messages of hate directed towards racial and religious groups. The existence of a particular criminal law, and the process of holding a trial when that law is used, is thus itself a form of expression, and the message sent out is that hate propaganda is harmful to target group members and threatening to a harmonious society: The many, many Canadians who belong to identifiable groups surely gain a great deal of comfort from the knowledge that the hate-monger is criminally prosecuted and his or her ideas rejected. Equally, the community as a whole is reminded of the importance of diversity and multiculturalism in Canada, the value of equality and the worth and dignity of each human person being particularly emphasized.

In this context, it can also be said that government suppression of hate propaganda will not make the expression attractive and hence increase acceptance of its content. Similarly, it is very doubtful that Canadians will have sympathy for either propagators of hatred or their ideas. Governmental disapproval of hate propaganda does not invariably result in dignifying the suppressed ideology. Pornography is not dignified by its suppression, nor are defamatory statements against individuals seen as meritorious because the common law lends its support to their prohibition. Again, I stress my belief that hate propaganda legislation and trials are a means by which the values beneficial to a free and democratic society can be publicized. In this context, no dignity will be unwittingly foisted upon the convicted hate-monger or his or her philosophy, and that a hate-monger might see him or herself as a martyr is of no matter to the content of the state's message.

As for the use of hate propaganda laws in pre–World War Two Germany, I am skeptical as to the relevance of the observation that legislation similar to s. 319(2) proved ineffective in curbing the racism of the Nazis. No one is contending that hate propaganda laws can in themselves prevent the tragedy of a Holocaust; conditions particular to Germany made the rise of Nazi ideology possible despite the existence and use of these laws. Rather, hate propaganda laws are one part of a free and democratic society's bid to prevent the spread of racism, and their rational connection to this objective must be seen in such a context. Certainly West Germany has not reacted to the failure of pre-war laws by seeking their removal, a new set of criminal offences having been implemented as recently as 1985: In sum, having found that the purpose of the challenged legislation is valid, I also find that the means chosen to further this purpose are rational in both theory and operation, and therefore conclude that the first branch of the proportionality test has been met.

Minimal Impairment of the Section 2(b) Freedom

The criminal nature of the impugned provision, involving the associated risks of prejudice through prosecution, conviction, and the imposition of up to two years' imprisonment, indicates that the means embodied in hate propaganda legislation should be carefully tailored so as to minimize impairment of the freedom of expression. It therefore must be shown that s. 319(2) is a measured and appropriate response to the phenomenon of hate propaganda, and that it does not overly circumscribe the s. 2(b) guarantee.

The main argument of those who would strike down s. 319(2) is that it creates a real possibility of punishing expression that is not hate propaganda. It is thus submitted that the legislation is overbroad, its terms so wide as to include expression which does not relate to Parliament's objective, and also unduly vague, in that a lack of clarity and precision in its words prevents individuals from discerning its meaning with any accuracy. In either instance, it is said that the effect of s. 319(2) is to limit the expression of merely unpopular or unconventional communications. Such communications may present no risk of causing the harm which Parliament seeks to prevent, and will perhaps be closely associated with the core values of s. 2(b). This overbreadth and vagueness could consequently allow the state to employ s. 319(2) to infringe excessively the freedom of expression or, what is more likely, could have a chilling effect whereby persons potentially within s. 319(2) would exercise self-censorship. Accordingly, those attacking the validity of s. 319(2) contend that vigorous debate on important political and social issues, so highly valued in a society that prizes a diversity of ideas, is unacceptably suppressed by the provision.

The question to be answered, then, is whether s. 319(2) indeed fails to distinguish between low value expression that is squarely within the focus of Parliament's valid objective and that which does not invoke the need for the severe response of criminal sanction.

Terms of Section 319(2). In assessing the constitutionality of s. 319(2), especially as concerns arguments of overbreadth and vagueness, an immediate observation is that statements made "in private conversation" are not included in the criminalized expression. The provision thus does not prohibit views expressed with an intention to promote hatred if made privately, indicating Parliament's concern not to intrude upon the privacy of the individual. Indeed, that the legislation excludes private conversation, rather than including communications made in a public forum, suggests that the expression of hatred in a place accessible to the public is not sufficient to activate the legislation. This observation is supported by comparing the words of s. 319(2) with those of the prohibition against the incitement of hatred likely to lead to a breach of peace in s. 319(1). Section 319(1) covers statements communicated "in a public place," suggesting that a wider scope of prohibition was intended where the danger occasioned by the statements was of an immediate nature, while the wording of s. 319(2) indicates that private conversations taking place in public areas are not prohibited. Moreover, it is reasonable to infer a subjective *mens rea* requirement regarding the type of conversation covered by s. 319(2), an inference supported by the definition of "private communications" contained in s. 183 of the *Criminal Code*. Consequently, a conversation or communication intended to be private does not satisfy the requirements of the provision if through accident or negligence an individual's expression of hatred for an identifiable group is made public.

Is s. 319(2) nevertheless overbroad because it captures all public expression intended to promote hatred? It would appear not, for the harm which the government seeks to prevent is not restricted to certain mediums and/or locations. To attempt to distinguish between various forms and fora would therefore be incongruent with Parliament's legitimate objective.

The way in which I have defined the s. 319(2) offence, in the context of the objective sought by society and the value of the prohibited expression, gives me some doubt as to whether the *Charter* mandates that truthful statements communicated with an intention to promote hatred need be excepted from criminal condemnation. Truth may be used for widely disparate ends, and I find it difficult to accept that circumstances exist where factually accurate statements can be used for no other purpose than to stir up hatred against a racial or religious group. It would seem to follow that there is no reason why the individual who intentionally employs such statements to achieve harmful ends must under the *Charter* be protected from criminal censure.

Nevertheless, it is open to Parliament to make a concession to free expression values, whether or not such is required by the *Charter*. Deference to truth as a value central to free expression has thus led Parliament to include the defence in s. 319(3)(a), even though the accused has used truthful statements to cause harm of the type falling squarely within the objective of the legislation. When the statement contains no truth, however, this flicker of justification for the intentional promotion of hatred is extinguished, and the harmful malice of the disseminator stands alone. The relationship between the value of hate propaganda as expression and the parliamentary objective of eradicating harm, slightly altered so as to increase the magnitude of the former where the statement of the accused is truthful, thus returns to its more usual condition, a condition in which it is permissible to suppress the expression.

Because the presence of truth, though legally a defence to a charge under s. 319(2), does not change the fact that the accused has intended to promote the hatred of an identifiable group, I cannot find excessive impairment of the freedom of expression merely because s. 319(3)(a) does not cover negligent or innocent error. Whether or not a statement is susceptible to classification as true or false, my inclination is therefore to accept that such error should not excuse an accused who has wilfully used a statement in order to promote hatred against an identifiable group.

That s. 319(2) may in the past have led authorities to restrict expression offering valuable contributions to the arts, education, or politics in Canada is surely worrying. I hope, however, that my comments as to the scope of the provision make it obvious that only the most intentionally extreme forms of expression will find a place within s. 319(2). In this light, one can safely say that the incidents mentioned above illustrate not over-expansive breadth and vagueness in the law, but rather actions by the state which cannot be lawfully taken pursuant to s. 319(2). The possibility of illegal police harassment clearly has minimal bearing on the proportionality of hate propaganda legislation to legitimate parliamentary objectives, and hence the argument based on such harassment can be rejected.

Alternative Modes of Furthering Parliament's Objective. Given the stigma and punishment associated with a criminal conviction and the presence of other modes of government response in the fight against intolerance, it is proper to ask whether s. 319(2) can be said to impair minimally the freedom of expression. With respect to the efficacy of criminal legislation in advancing the goals of equality and multicultural tolerance in Canada, I agree that the role of s. 319(2) will be limited. It is important, in my opinion, not to hold any illusions about the ability of this one provision to rid our society of hate propaganda and its associated harms. Indeed, to become overly complacent, forgetting that there are a great many ways in which to address the problem of racial and religious intolerance, could be dangerous. Obviously, a variety of measures need be employed in the quest to achieve such lofty and important goals.

In assessing the proportionality of a legislative enactment to a valid governmental objective, however, s. 1 should not operate in every instance so as to force the government to rely upon only the mode of intervention least intrusive of a *Charter* right or freedom. It may be that a number of courses of action are available in the furtherance of a pressing and substantial objective, each imposing a varying degree of restriction upon a right or freedom. In such circumstances, the government may legitimately employ a more restrictive measure, either alone or as part of a larger program of action, if that measure is not redundant, furthering the objective in ways that alternative responses could not, and is in all other respects proportionate to a valid s. 1 aim.

Analysis of Section 319(2) under Section 1 of the Charter: *Conclusion*

I find that the infringement of the respondent's freedom of expression as guaranteed by s. 2(b) should be upheld as a reasonable limit prescribed by law in a free and democratic society. Furthering an immensely important objective and directed at expression distant from the core of free expression values, s. 319(2) satisfies each of the components of the proportionality inquiry. I thus disagree with the Alberta Court of Appeal's conclusion that this criminal prohibition of hate propaganda violates the *Charter*, and would allow the appeal in this respect.

McLachlin, J (dissenting): – ...

Hate Propaganda and Freedom of Speech – An Overview

Before entering upon the analysis of whether s. 319(2) of the *Criminal Code* is inconsistent with the *Charter* and must be struck down, it may be useful to consider the conflicting values underlying the question of the prohibition of hate literature and how the issue has been treated in other jurisdictions.

Hate literature presents a great challenge to our conceptions about the value of free expression. Its offensive content often constitutes a direct attack on many of the other principles which are cherished by our society. Tolerance, the dignity and equality of all individuals; these and other values are all adversely affected by the propagation of hateful sentiment. The problem is not peculiarly Canadian; it is universal. Wherever racially or culturally distinct groups of people live together, one finds people, usually a small minority of the population, who take it upon themselves to denigrate members of a group other than theirs. Canada is no stranger to this conduct. Our history is replete with examples of discriminatory communications. In their time, Canadians of Asian and East Indian descent, black, and native people have been the objects of communications tending to foster hate. In the case at bar it is the Jewish people who have been singled out as objects of calumny.

The evil of hate propaganda is beyond doubt. It inflicts pain and indignity upon 'individuals who are members of the group in question. Insofar as it may persuade others to the same point of view, it may threaten social stability. And it is intrinsically offensive to people – the majority in most democratic countries – who believe in the equality of all people regardless of race or creed.

For these reasons, governments have legislated against the dissemination of propaganda directed against racial groups, and in some cases this legislation has been tested in the courts. Perhaps the experience most relevant to Canada is that of the United States, since its Constitution, like ours, places a high value on free expression, raising starkly the conflict between freedom of speech and the countervailing values of individual dignity and social harmony. Like s. 2(b), the First Amendment guarantee is conveyed in broad, unrestricted language, stating that "Congress shall make no law ... abridging the freedom of speech, or of the press." The relevance of aspects of the American experience to this case is underlined by the factums and submissions, which borrowed heavily from ideas which may be traced to the United States.

The protections of the First Amendment to the U.S. Constitution, and in particular free speech, have always assumed a particular importance within the U.S. constitutional scheme, being regarded as the cornerstone of all other democratic freedoms. As expressed by Jackson, J, in *West Virginia State Board of Education v Barnette*, 319 US 624 (1943), "[i]f there is any fixed star in our constitutional constellation, it is that no official, high or petty, can prescribe what shall be orthodox in politics, nationalism, religion, or other matters of opinion or force citizens to confess by word or act their faith therein" (p. 642). The U.S. Supreme Court, particularly in recent years, has pronounced itself strongly on the need to protect speech even at the expense of other worthy competing values.

In the United States, a provision similar to s. 319(2) of the *Criminal Code* was struck down in *Collin v Smith, supra,* on the ground that is was fatally overbroad. In addition, the Seventh Circuit Court of Appeals hinted that the provision might also be void for vagueness. The ordinance in *Collin* prohibited "[t]he dissemination of any materials within the Village of Skokie which promotes and incites hatred against persons by reason of their race, national origin, or religion, and is intended to do so." The court found that the activity in question in the case – a proposed neo-Nazi demonstration in Skokie, Illinois – was a form of expression entitled to protection under the First Amendment. The ordinance, it found, was overbroad in that it "could conceivably be applied to criminalize dissemination of *The Merchant of Venice* or a vigorous discussion of the merits of reverse racial discrimination in Skokie" (p. 1207).

The *Charter* follows the American approach in method, affirming freedom of expression as a broadly defined and fundamental right, and contemplating balancing the values protected by and inherent in freedom of expression against the benefit conferred by the legislation limiting that freedom under s. 1 of the *Charter*. This is in keeping with the strong liberal tradition favouring free speech in this country – a tradition which had led to conferring quasi-constitutional status on free expression in this country prior to any bill of rights or *Charter*. At the same time, the tests are not necessarily the same as in the United States ...

The Construction Arguments

These submissions urge that s. 2(b) of the *Charter* should not be construed as extending to statements which offend s. 319(2) of the *Criminal Code*. The arguments are founded on three distinct considerations: s. 15 of the *Charter*, s. 27 of the *Charter*; and Canada's international obligations.

The Argument Based on Section 15 of the *Charter*

The first argument is that the scope of s. 2(b) is diminished by s. 15 of the *Charter*. This argument is based on the principle of construction that where possible, the provisions of a statute should be read together so as to avoid conflict. The guarantee of equality in s. 15, it is submitted, is offended by speech which denigrates a particular ethnic or religious group. The competing values reflected by the two sections might therefore be reconciled by informing the content of s. 2(b) with the values of s. 15. Accordingly, the freedom of expression guarantee should be read down to exclude from protected expression statements whose content promotes such inequality.

It is important initially to define the nature of the potential conflict between s. 2(b) and s. 15 of the *Charter*. This is not a case of the collision of two rights which are put into conflict by the facts of the case. There is no violation of s. 15 in the case at bar, since there is no law or state action which puts the guarantee of equality into issue. The right granted by s. 15 is the right to be free from inequality and discrimination effected by the state. That right is not violated in the case at bar. The conflict, then, is not between rights, but rather between philosophies ...

There are two significant considerations which militate against an acceptance of the argument based on s. 15. First, it is important to consider the nature of the two guarantees in question. On the one hand, s. 2(b) confers on each individual freedom of expression, unconstrained by state regulation or action, and subject only to a possible limitation under s. 1. On the other hand s. 15 grants the right to be free from inequality and discrimination effected by the state. Given that the protection under s. 2(b) is aimed at protecting individuals from having their expression infringed by the government, it seems a misapplication of *Charter* values to thereby limit the scope of that individual guarantee with an argument based on s. 15, which is also aimed at circumscribing the power of the state.

This conclusion is supported by a second factor which weighs against limiting the scope of freedom of expression on the basis of the guarantee of s. 15. The cases where this court has considered the meaning of s. 2(b) have expressly rejected the suggestion that certain statements should be denied the protection of the guarantee on the basis of their content. This court has repeatedly affirmed that no matter how offensive or disagreeable the content of the expression, it cannot on that account be denied protection under s. 2(b) of the *Charter*: see *Irwin Toy* and *Reference re ss. 193 and 195.1(1)(c) of the Criminal Code* (Man.), *supra*. The argument based on s. 15 is clearly opposed to this principle, as it suggests that protection be denied expression whose content conflicts with the values underlying the s. 15 guarantee.

Even if these difficulties could be surmounted, one would be faced with the prospect of cutting back a freedom guaranteed by the *Charter* on the basis that the exercise of the freedom may run counter to the philosophy behind another section of the *Charter*. The alleged breach of s. 2(b) can be placed in a factual context. But since there is no breach of s. 15, the value to be weighed on that side of the balance cannot be placed in a factual context. This would render the exercise of balancing the conflicting values extremely difficult.

I conclude that this court should not reduce the scope of expression protected by s. 2(b) of the *Charter* because of s. 15 of the *Charter*.

The Argument Based on Section 27 of the *Charter*

Section 27 states that the *Charter* shall be interpreted in a manner consistent with the preservation and enhancement of the multicultural heritage of Canadians. Similar considerations apply here as applied to the argument based on s. 15 of the *Charter*. As in the case of the s. 15 argument, there is no conflict of rights, s. 27 embodying not a right or freedom but a principle of construction. As in the case of the s. 15 argument, the submission under s. 27 amounts to advocating that certain statements be denied protection under s. 2(b) because of their content, an approach which this court has rejected. Using s. 27 to limit the protection guaranteed by s. 2(b) is likewise subject to the objection that it would leave unprotected a large area of arguably legitimate social and political debate. All this is not to mention the difficulty of weighing abstract values such as multiculturalism in the balance against freedom of speech.

Further difficulties are not hard to conjure up. Different people may have different ideas about what undermines multiculturalism. The issue is inherently vague and to some extent a matter of personal opinion. For example, it might be suggested that a statement that Canada should not permit immigration from a certain part of the world is inconsistent with the preservation and enhancement of multiculturalism. Is s. 2(b) to be cut back to eliminate protection for such a statement, given the differing opinions one might expect on such a matter? It may be argued, moreover, that a certain latitude for expression of derogatory opinion about other groups is a necessary correlative of a multicultural society, where different groups compete for limited resources.

Before leaving this point I would add that there is no evidence that the impugned legislation in fact contributes to the enhancement and preservation of multiculturalism in Canada. Reliance, therefore, on s. 27 to tailor or otherwise cut back the protection afforded by s. 2(b) risks undercutting the fundamental freedom with no guarantee of a tangible benefit in return. In my opinion, the weighing of interests and values implicit in questions such as these is better accomplished under s. 1 of the *Charter*.

The Argument Based on International Law

... Canada's international obligations, and the accords negotiated between international governments may well be helpful in placing *Charter* interpretation in a larger context. Principles agreed upon by free and democratic societies may inform the reading given to certain of its guarantees. It would be wrong, however, to consider these obligations as determinative of or limiting the scope of those guarantees. The provisions of the *Charter*, though drawing on a political and social philosophy shared with other democratic societies, are uniquely Canadian. As a result, considerations may point, as they do in this case, to a conclusion regarding a rights violation which is not necessarily in accord with those international covenants.

I should add that I am not of the view that any measures taken to implement Canada's international obligations to combat racial discrimination and hate propaganda must necessarily be unconstitutional. The obligations expressed in the *International Covenant on Civil and Political Rights* (to prohibit by law "[a]ny advocacy of national, racial or religious hatred that constitutes incitement to discrimination, hostility or violence") and the *International Convention on the Elimination of All Forms of Racial Discrimination* (to "declare an offence punishable by law all dissemination of ideas based on racial superiority or hatred") are general in nature. Details of methods to be used are not specified. Nothing in those instruments compels enactment of s. 319(2), as opposed to other provisions combating racism.

I conclude that none of the arguments which are advanced for construing s. 2(b) of the *Charter* narrowly to exclude from its protection, statements offending s. 319(2) of the *Criminal Code* can prevail.

THE ANALYSIS UNDER SECTION 1

Section 1 and the Infringement of Freedom of Expression

The court's function under s. 1 of the *Charter* is that of weighing and balancing. Before reaching s. 1, the court must already have determined that the law in question infringes a right or freedom guaranteed by the *Charter*. The infringement alone, however, does not mandate that the law must fall. If the limit the law imposes on the right infringed is "reasonable" and "can be demonstrably justified in a free and democratic society," the law is valid. The demonstration of this justification, the burden of which lies on the state, involves proving that there are other rights or interests which outweigh the right infringed in the context of that case ...

The Objective of Section 319(2) of the *Criminal Code*

The objective of s. 319(2) of the *Criminal Code* is to prevent the promotion of hatred towards identifiable groups within our society. As the Attorney-General of Canada puts it, the objective of the legislation is, "among other things, to protect racial, religious and other groups from the wilful promotion of hatred against them, to prevent the spread of hatred and the breakdown of racial and social harmony," and "to prevent the destruction of our multicultural society." These aims are subsumed in the twin values of social harmony and individual dignity.

Given the problem of racial and religious prejudice in this country, I am satisfied that the objective of the legislation is of sufficient gravity to be capable of justifying limitations on constitutionally protected rights and freedoms.

Proportionality

General Considerations. The real question in this case, as I see it, is whether the means – the criminal prohibition of wilfully promoting hatred – are proportional and appropriate to the ends of suppressing hate propaganda in order to maintain social harmony and individual dignity. The objective of the legislation is one of great significance, such significance that it is capable of outweighing the fundamental values protected by the *Charter.* The ultimate question is whether this objective is of sufficient importance to justify the limitation on free expression effected by s. 319(2) of the *Criminal Code.* In answering this question, the court must consider not only the importance of the right or freedom in question and the significance of its limitation, but whether the way in which the limitation is imposed is justifiable. How serious is the infringement of the constitutionally guaranteed freedom, in this case freedom of expression? Is the limiting measure likely to further the objective in practice? Is the limiting measure overbroad or unnecessarily invasive? In the final analysis, bearing all these things in mind, does the benefit to be derived from the legislation outweigh the seriousness of the infringement? These are the considerations relevant to the question of the proportionality of the limiting law.

I have said that the contest in this case lies between the fundamental right of free expression on the one hand, and the values of social harmony and individual liberty on the other. In approaching the difficult task of determining where the balance lies in the context of this case, it is important not to be diverted by the offensive content of much of the speech in question. As this court has repeatedly stated, even the most reprehensible or disagreeable comments are prima facie entitled to the protection of s. 2(b). It is not the statements of Mr Keegstra which are at issue in this case, but rather the constitutionality of s. 319(2) of the *Criminal Code*. That must be our focus ...

Another general consideration relevant to the balancing of values involved in the proportionality test in this case relates peculiarly to the nature of freedom of expression. Freedom of expression is unique among the rights and freedoms guaranteed by the *Charter* in two ways.

The first way in which freedom of expression may be unique was alluded to earlier in the context of the philosophical underpinnings of freedom of expression. The right to fully and openly express one's views on social and political issues is fundamental to our democracy and hence to all the other rights and freedoms guaranteed by the *Charter*. Without free expression, the vigorous debate on policies and values that underlies participatory government is lacking. Without free expression, rights may be trammelled with no recourse in the court of public opinion. Some restrictions on free expression may be necessary and justified and entirely compatible with a free and democratic society. But restrictions which touch the critical core of social and political debate require particularly close consideration because of the dangers inherent in state censorship of such debate. This is of particular importance under s. 1 of the *Charter* which expressly requires the court to have regard to whether the limits are reasonable and justified in a free and democratic society.

A second characteristic peculiar to freedom of expression is that limitations on expression tend to have an effect on expression other than that which is their target. In the United States this is referred to as the chilling effect. Unless the limitation is drafted with great precision, there will always be doubt about whether a particular form of expression offends the prohibition. There will always be limitations inherent in the use of language, but that must not discourage the pursuit of the greatest drafting precision possible. The result of a failure to do so may be to deter not only the expression which the prohibition was aimed at, but legitimate expression. The law-abiding citizen who does not wish to run afoul of the law will decide not to take the chance in a doubtful case. Creativity and the beneficial exchange of ideas will be adversely affected. This chilling effect must be taken into account in performing the balancing required by the analysis under s. 1. It mandates that in weighing the intrusiveness of a limitation on freedom of expression our consideration cannot be confined to those who may ultimately be convicted under the limit, but must extend to those who may be deterred from legitimate expression by uncertainty as to whether they might be convicted.

I make one final point before entering on the specific tests for proportionality proposed in *Oakes*. In determining whether the particular limitation of a right or freedom is justified under s. 1, it is important to consider not only the proportionality and effectiveness of the particular law in question, but alternative ways of furthering the objective. This is particularly important at stages two (minimum impairment) and three (balancing the infringement against the objective) of the proportionality analysis proposed in *Oakes*.

Against this background, I turn to the three considerations critical to determining whether the limitation on freedom of expression effected by s. 319(2) of the *Criminal Code* is reasonably and demonstrably justifiable in a free and democratic society.

Rational Connection. The first question is whether s. 319(2) of the *Criminal Code* may be seen as carefully designed or rationally connected to the objectives which it is aimed at promoting. This may be viewed in two ways.

The first is whether Parliament carefully designed s. 319(2) to meet the objectives it is enacted to promote.

Although some evidence of care in linking s. 319(2) to its objectives is clear, it has been argued that it is overbroad, an allegation which I will consider in greater detail in discussing whether s. 319(2) represents a "minimum impairment" of the right of free speech guaranteed by s. 2(b) of the *Charter*. Nevertheless it is clear that the legislation does, at least at one level, further Parliament's objectives. Prosecutions of individuals for offensive material directed at a particular group may bolster its members' beliefs that they are valued and respected in their community, and that the views of a malicious few do not reflect those of the population as a whole. Such a use of the criminal law may well affirm certain values and priorities which are of a pressing and substantial nature.

It is necessary, however, to go further, and consider not only Parliament's intention, but whether, given the actual effect of the legislation, a rational connection exists between it and its objectives. Legislation designed to promote an objective may in fact impede that objective.

Section 319(2) may well have a chilling effect on defensible expression by law-abiding citizens. At the same time, it is far from clear that it provides an effective way of curbing hate-mongers. Indeed, many have suggested it may promote their cause. Prosecutions under the *Criminal Code* for racist expression have attracted extensive media coverage. Zundel, prosecuted not under s. 319(2), but for the crime of spreading false news (s. 181), claimed that his court battle had given him "a million dollars worth of publicity" (*Globe and Mail*, March 1, 1985, p. 1).

Not only does the criminal process confer on the accused publicity for his dubious causes – it may even bring him sympathy. The criminal process is cast as a conflict between the accused and the state, a conflict in which the accused may appear at his most sympathetic. Franz Kafka was not being entirely whimsical when he wrote, "If you have the right eye for these things, you can see that accused men are often attractive" (*The Trial*, 1976, p. 203).

The argument that criminal prosecutions for this kind of expression will reduce racism and foster multiculturalism depends on the assumption that some listeners are gullible enough to believe the expression if exposed to it. But if this assumption is valid, these listeners might be just as likely to believe that there must be some truth in the racist expression because the government is trying to suppress it. Theories of a grand conspiracy between government and elements of society wrongly perceived as malevolent can become all too appealing if government dignifies them by completely suppressing their utterance. It is therefore not surprising that the criminalization of hate propaganda and prosecutions under such legislation have been subject to so much controversy in this country.

Minimum Impairment. The second matter which must be considered in determining whether the infringement represented by the legislation is proportionate to its ends is whether the legislation impairs the right to the minimum extent possible.

Those supporting s. 319(2) of the *Criminal Code* point to the fact that it applies only to wilful promotion of hatred, and not to promotion of any lesser emotion. Hatred, they argue, is the most extreme and reprehensible of human emotions. They also point out that s. 319(2) provides a number of defences, including the truth of the statements made, discussion for public benefit of a subject of public importance (provided the statements were believed to be true on reasonable grounds), and good faith opinion on a religious subject. They add that s. 319(2) does no more than fulfil Canada's international obligations and that similar provisions apply in other Western democracies.

Despite the limitations found in s. 319(2), a strong case can be made that it is overbroad in that its definition of offending speech may catch many expressions which should be protected. The first difficulty lies in the different interpretations which may be placed on the word "hatred." The *Shorter Oxford English Dictionary* defines "hatred" as: "The condition or state of relations in which one person hates another; the emotion of hate; active dislike, detestation; enmity, ill-will, malevolence." The wide range of diverse emotions which the word "hatred" is capable of denoting is evident from this definition. Those who defend its use in s. 319(2) of the *Criminal Code* emphasize one end of this range   hatred, they say, indicates the most powerful of virulent emotions lying beyond the bounds of human decency and limiting s. 319(2) to extreme materials. Those who object to its use point to the other end of the range, insisting that "active dislike" is not an emotion for the promotion of which a person should be convicted as a criminal. To state the arguments is to make the case; "hatred" is a broad term capable of catching a wide variety of emotion.

It is not only the breadth of the term "hatred" which presents dangers; it is its subjectivity. "Hatred" is proved by inference   the inference of the jury or the judge who sits as trier of fact   and inferences are more likely to be drawn when the speech is unpopular. The subjective and emotional nature of the concept of promoting hatred compounds the difficulty of ensuring that only cases meriting prosecution are pursued and that only those whose conduct is calculated to dissolve the social bonds of society are convicted.

The absence of any requirement that actual harm or incitement to hatred be shown further broadens the scope of s. 319(2) of the *Criminal Code*. This, in the view of the Court of Appeal, was the section's main defect. In effect, the provision makes a crime not only of actually inciting others to hatred, but also of attempting to do so. The Court of Appeal accepted the argument that this made the crime, at least potentially, a victimless one. In the view of Kerans, JA, while a prohibition on expression that actually spread hatred would be justified, a prohibition on attempts to spread hatred was not.

Not only is the category of speech caught by s. 319(2) defined broadly. The application of the definition of offending speech, i.e., the circumstances in which the offending statements are prohibited, is virtually unlimited. Only private conversations are exempt from state scrutiny. Section 319(2) is calculated to prevent absolutely expression of the offending ideas in any and all public forums through any and all mediums. Speeches are caught. The corner soap-box is no longer open. Books, films, and works of art   all these fall under the censor's scrutiny because of s. 319(2) of the *Criminal Code*.

The real answer to the debate about whether s. 319(2) is overbroad is provided by the section's track record. Although the section is of relatively recent origin, it has provoked many questionable actions on the part of the authorities. There have been no reported convictions, other than the instant appeals. But the record amply demonstrates that intemperate statements about identifiable groups, particularly if they represent an unpopular viewpoint, may attract state involvement or calls for police action.

The combination of overbreadth and criminalization may well lead people desirous of avoiding even the slightest brush with the criminal law to protect themselves in the best way they can – by confining their expression to non-controversial matters. Novelists may steer clear of controversial characterizations of ethnic characteristics, such as Shakespeare's portrayal of Shylock in *The Merchant of Venice.* Scientists may well think twice before researching and publishing results of research suggesting difference between ethnic or racial groups. Given the serious consequences of criminal prosecution, it is not entirely speculative to suppose that even political debate on crucial issues such as immigration, educational language rights, foreign ownership, and trade may be tempered. These matters go to the heart of the traditional justifications for protecting freedom of expression.

This brings me to the second aspect of minimum impairment. The examples I have just given suggest that the very fact of criminalization itself may be argued to represent an excessive response to the problem of hate propagation. The procedures and sanctions associated with the criminal law are comparatively severe. Given the stigma that attaches and the freedom which is at stake, the contest between the individual and the state imposed by a criminal trial must be regarded as difficult and harrowing in the extreme. The seriousness of the imprisonment which may follow conviction requires no comment. Moreover, the chilling effect of prohibitions on expression is at its most severe where they are effected by means of the criminal law. It is this branch of the law more than any other which the ordinary, law-abiding citizen seeks to avoid. The additional sanction of the criminal law may pose little deterrent to a convinced hate-monger who may welcome the publicity it brings; it may, however, deter the ordinary individual.

Moreover, it is arguable whether criminalization of expression calculated to promote racial hatred is necessary. Other remedies are perhaps more appropriate and more effective. Discrimination on grounds of race and religion is worthy of suppression. Human rights legislation, focusing on reparation rather than punishment, has had considerable success in discouraging such conduct ...

Finally, it can be argued that greater precision is required in the criminal law than, for example, in human rights legislation because of the different character of the two types of proceedings. The consequences of alleging a violation of s. 319(2) of the *Criminal Code* are direct and serious in the extreme. Under the human rights process a tribunal has considerable discretion in determining what messages or conduct should be banned and by its order may indicate more precisely their exact nature, all of which occurs before any consequences inure to the alleged violator.

In summary, s. 319(2) of the *Criminal Code* catches a broad range of speech and prohibits it in a broad manner, allowing only private conversations to escape scrutiny. Moreover, the process by which the prohibition is effected – the criminal law – is the severest our society can impose and is arguably unnecessary given the availability of alternate remedies. I conclude that the criminalization of hate statements does not impair free speech to the minimum extent permitted by its objectives.

READING QUESTIONS ON *KEEGSTRA*

1 What does Dickson, CJC mean in saying that the reasons for limiting expression in this case are the same as those for protecting it more generally?
2 How are Dickson's reasons related to Minow's arguments?
3 Both the majority and the dissent appeal to the consequences of the law. How are considerations of equality and consequences related in the competing arguments?
4 How are McLachlin, J's arguments about statutory construction related to libertarian views about the rule of law?

RAV v City of St Paul 112 S Ct 2538 (1992)

The U.S. Supreme Court overturned a Minnesota ordinance prohibiting displays of racial hatred on the grounds that it advocated a particular viewpoint. In the instant case, the law would have punished white youths for burning a cross on the lawn of an African American family.

Justice Scalia delivered the opinion of the Court.

In the predawn hours of June 21, 1990, petitioner and several other teenagers allegedly assembled a crudely made cross by taping together broken chair legs. They then allegedly burned the cross inside the fenced yard of a black family that lived across the street from the house where petitioner was staying. Although this conduct could have been punished under any of a number of laws, one of the two provisions under which respondent city of St. Paul chose to charge petitioner (then a juvenile) was the St. Paul Bias-Motivated Crime Ordinance, St. Paul, Minn., Legis.Code § 292.02 (1990), which provides:

Whoever places on public or private property a symbol, object, appellation, characterization or graffiti, including, but not limited to, a burning cross or Nazi swastika, which one knows or has reasonable grounds to know arouses anger, alarm or resentment in others on the basis of race, color, creed, religion or gender commits disorderly conduct and shall be guilty of a misdemeanor.

Petitioner moved to dismiss this count on the ground that the St. Paul ordinance was substantially overbroad and impermissibly content based and therefore facially invalid under the First Amendment ...

In construing the St. Paul ordinance, we accept the Minnesota Supreme Court's authoritative statement that the ordinance reaches only those expressions that constitute "fighting words" within the meaning of *Chaplinsky*. 464 N.W.2d, at 510–11. Petitioner and his amici urge us to modify the scope of the *Chaplinsky* formulation, thereby invalidating the ordinance as "substantially overbroad," *Broadrick v Oklahoma*, 413 U.S. 601, 610, 93 S.Ct. 2908, 2914–15, 37 L.Ed.2d 830 (1973). We find it unnecessary to consider this issue. Assuming, arguendo, that all of the expression reached by the ordinance is proscribable under the "fighting words" doctrine, we nonetheless conclude that the ordinance is facially unconstitutional in that it prohibits otherwise permitted speech solely on the basis of the subjects the speech addresses.

The First Amendment generally prevents government from pro-scribing speech ... Content-based regulations are presumptively invalid. From 1791 to the present, however, our society, like other free but civilized societies, has permitted restrictions upon the content of speech in a few limited areas, which are "of such slight social value as a step to truth that any benefit that may be derived from them is clearly outweighed by the social interest in order and morality." ... We have recognized that "the freedom of speech" referred to by the First Amendment does not include a freedom to disregard these traditional limitations. Our decisions since the 1960's have narrowed the scope of the traditional categorical exceptions for defamation ... but a limited categorical approach has remained an important part of our First Amendment jurisprudence.

We have sometimes said that these categories of expression are "not within the area of constitutionally protected speech," ... or that the "protection of the First Amendment does not extend" to them ... Such statements must be taken in context, however, and are no more literally true than is the occasionally repeated shorthand characterizing obscenity "as not being speech at all," ... What they mean is that these areas of speech can, consistently with the First Amendment, be regulated because of their constitutionally proscribable content (obscenity, defamation, etc.) – not that they are categories of speech entirely invisible to the Constitution, so that they may be made the vehicles for content discrimination unrelated to their distinctively proscribable content. Thus, the government may proscribe libel; but it may not make the further content discrimination of proscribing only libel critical of the government. We recently acknowledged this distinction ... where, in upholding New York's child pornography law, we expressly recognized that there was no "question here of censoring a particular literary theme ..."

Our cases surely do not establish the proposition that the First Amendment imposes no obstacle whatsoever to regulation of particular instances of such proscribable expression, so that the government "may regulate [them] freely," ... That would mean that a city council could enact an ordinance prohibiting only those legally obscene works that contain criticism of the city government or, indeed, that do not include endorsement of the city government. Such a simplistic, all-or- nothing-at-all approach to First Amendment protection is at odds with common sense and with our jurisprudence as well. It is not true that "fighting words" have at most a *"de minimis"* expressive content, ibid., or that their content is in all respects "worthless and undeserving of constitutional protection," ... sometimes they are quite expressive indeed. We have not said that they constitute "no part of the expression of ideas," but only that they constitute "no essential part of any exposition of ideas." ...

The proposition that a particular instance of speech can be proscrib-able on the basis of one feature (e.g., obscenity) but not on the basis of another (e.g., opposition to the city government) is commonplace and has found application in many contexts. We have long held, for example, that nonverbal expressive activity can be banned because of the action it entails, but not because of the ideas it expresses – so that burning a flag in violation of an ordinance against outdoor fires could be punishable, whereas burning a flag in violation of an ordinance against dishonoring the flag is not. Similarly, we have upheld reason-able "time, place, or manner" restrictions, but only if they are "justified without reference to the content of the regulated speech." ... And just as the power to proscribe particular speech on the basis of a noncontent element (e.g., noise) does not entail the power to proscribe the same speech on the basis of a content element; so also, the power to proscribe it on the basis of one content element (e.g., obscenity) does not entail the power to proscribe it on the basis of other content elements.

In other words, the exclusion of "fighting words" from the scope of the First Amendment simply means that, for purposes of that Amend-ment, the unprotected features of the words are, despite their verbal character, essentially a "nonspeech" element of communication. Fighting words are thus analogous to a noisy sound truck: Each is, as Justice Frankfurter recognized, a "mode of speech," ... both can be used to convey an idea; but neither has, in and of itself, a claim upon the First Amendment. As with the sound truck, however, so also with fighting words: The government may not regulate use based on hostility – or favoritism – towards the underlying message expressed ...

Even the prohibition against content discrimination that we assert the First Amendment requires is not absolute. It applies differently in the context of proscribable speech than in the area of fully protected speech. The rationale of the general prohibition, after all, is that content discrimination "raises the specter that the Government may effectively drive certain ideas or viewpoints from the marketplace," ... But content discrimination among various instances of a class of proscribable speech often does not pose this threat.

When the basis for the content discrimination consists entirely of the very reason the entire class of speech at issue is proscribable, no significant danger of idea or viewpoint discrimination exists. Such a reason, having been adjudged neutral enough to support exclusion of the entire class of speech from First Amendment protection, is also neutral enough to form the basis of distinction within the class. To illustrate: A State might choose to prohibit only that obscenity which is the most patently offensive in its prurience – i.e., that which involves the most lascivious displays of sexual activity. But it may not prohibit, for example, only that obscenity which includes offensive political messages. And the Federal Government can criminalize only those threats of violence that are directed against the President, see 18 U.S.C. § 871 – since the reasons why threats of violence are outside the First Amendment (protecting individuals from the fear of violence, from the disruption that fear engenders, and from the possibility that the threatened violence will occur) have special force when applied to the person of the President. But the Federal Government may not criminalize only those threats against the President that mention his policy on aid to inner cities. And to take a final example ... a State may choose to regulate price advertising in one industry but not in others, because the risk of fraud (one of the characteristics of commercial speech that justifies depriving it of full First Amendment protection) but it may not prohibit only that commercial advertising that depicts men in a demeaning fashion.

Another valid basis for according differential treatment to even a content-defined subclass of proscribable speech is that the subclass happens to be associated with particular "secondary effects" of the speech, so that the regulation is "justified without reference to the content of the ... speech," ... A State could, for example, permit all obscene live performances except those involving minors. Moreover, since words can in some circumstances violate laws directed not against speech but against conduct (a law against treason, for example, is violated by telling the enemy the Nation's defense secrets), a particular content-based subcategory of a proscribable class of speech can be swept up incidentally within the reach of a statute directed at conduct rather than speech ... Thus, for example, sexually derogatory "fighting words," among other words, may produce a violation of Title VII's general prohibition against sexual discrimination in employment practices ... Where the government does not target conduct on the basis of its expressive content, acts are not shielded from regulation merely because they express a discriminatory idea or philosophy.

These bases for distinction refute the proposition that the selectivity of the restriction is "even arguably 'conditioned upon the sovereign's agreement with what a speaker may intend to say.'" ... There may be other such bases as well. Indeed, to validate such selectivity (where totally proscribable speech is at issue) it may not even be necessary to identify any particular "neutral" basis, so long as the nature of the content discrimination is such that there is no realistic possibility that official suppression of ideas is afoot. (We cannot think of any First Amendment interest that would stand in the way of a State's prohibiting only those obscene motion pictures with blue-eyed actresses.) Save for that limitation, the regulation of "fighting words," like the regulation of noisy speech, may address some offensive instances and leave other, equally offensive, instances alone.

Applying these principles to the St. Paul ordinance, we conclude that, even as narrowly construed by the Minnesota Supreme Court, the ordinance is facially unconstitutional. Although the phrase in the ordinance, "arouses anger, alarm or resentment in others," has been limited by the Minnesota Supreme Court's construction to reach only those symbols or displays that amount to "fighting words," the remaining, unmodified terms make clear that the ordinance applies only to "fighting words" that insult, or provoke violence, "on the basis of race, color, creed, religion or gender." Displays containing abusive invective, no matter how vicious or severe, are permissible unless they are addressed to one of the specified disfavored topics. Those who wish to use "fighting words" in connection with other ideas – to express hostility, for example, on the basis of political affiliation, union membership, or homosexuality – are not covered. The First Amendment does not permit St. Paul to impose special prohibitions on those speakers who express views on disfavored subjects.

In its practical operation, moreover, the ordinance goes even beyond mere content discrimination, to actual viewpoint discrimination. Displays containing some words – odious racial epithets, for example – would be prohibited to proponents of all views. But "fighting words" that do not themselves invoke race, color, creed, religion, or gender – aspersions upon a person's mother, for example – would seemingly be usable *ad libitum* in the placards of those arguing in favor of racial, color, etc., tolerance and equality, but could not be used by those speakers' opponents. One could hold up a sign saying, for example, that all "anti-Catholic bigots" are misbegotten; but not that all "papists" are, for that would insult and provoke violence "on the basis of religion." St. Paul has no such authority to license one side of a debate to fight free-style, while requiring the other to follow Marquis of Queensberry rules.

What we have here, it must be emphasized, is not a prohibition of fighting words that are directed at certain persons or groups (which would be facially valid if it met the requirements of the Equal Protection Clause); but rather, a prohibition of fighting words that contain (as the Minnesota Supreme Court repeatedly emphasized) messages of "bias-motivated" hatred and in particular, as applied to this case, messages "based on virulent notions of racial supremacy." One must wholeheartedly agree with the Minnesota Supreme Court that "[i]t is the responsibility, even the obligation, of diverse communities to confront such notions in whatever form they appear," ... but the manner of that confrontation cannot consist of selective limitations upon speech. St. Paul's brief asserts that a general "fighting words" law would not meet the city's needs because only a content-specific measure can communicate to minority groups that the "group hatred" aspect of such speech "is not condoned by the majority." The point of the First Amendment is that majority preferences must be expressed in some fashion other than silencing speech on the basis of its content.

The content-based discrimination reflected in the St. Paul ordinance comes within neither any of the specific exceptions to the First Amendment prohibition we discussed earlier nor a more general exception for content discrimination that does not threaten censorship of ideas. It assuredly does not fall within the exception for content discrimination based on the very reasons why the particular class of speech at issue (here, fighting words) is proscribable. As explained earlier ... the reason why fighting words are categorically excluded from the protection of the First Amendment is not that their content communicates any particular idea, but that their content embodies a particularly intolerable (and socially unnecessary) mode of expressing whatever idea the speaker wishes to convey. St. Paul has not singled out an especially offensive mode of expression – it has not, for example, selected for prohibition only those fighting words that communicate ideas in a threatening (as opposed to a merely obnoxious) manner. Rather, it has proscribed fighting words of whatever manner that communicate messages of racial, gender, or religious intolerance. Selectivity of this sort creates the possibility that the city is seeking to handicap the expression of particular ideas. That possibility would alone be enough to render the ordinance presumptively invalid, but St. Paul's comments and concessions in this case elevate the possibility to a certainty ...

Finally, St. Paul and its amici defend the conclusion of the Minnesota Supreme Court that, even if the ordinance regulates expression based on hostility towards its protected ideological content, this discrimination is nonetheless justified because it is narrowly tailored to serve compelling state interests. Specifically, they assert that the ordinance helps to ensure the basic human rights of members of groups that have historically been subjected to discrimination, including the right of such group members to live in peace where they wish. We do not doubt that these interests are compelling, and that the ordinance can be said to promote them. But the "danger of censorship" presented by a facially content-based statute ... requires that that weapon be employed only where it is "necessary to serve the asserted [compelling] interest." The existence of adequate content-neutral alternatives thus "undercut[s] significantly" any defense of such a statute ... The dispositive question in this case, therefore, is whether content discrimination is reasonably necessary to achieve St. Paul's compelling interests; it plainly is not. An ordinance not limited to the favored topics, for example, would have precisely the same beneficial effect. In fact the only interest distinctively served by the content limitation is that of displaying the city council's special hostility towards the particular biases thus singled out. That is precisely what the First Amendment forbids. The politicians of St. Paul are entitled to express that hostility – but not through the means of imposing unique limitations upon speakers who (however benightedly) disagree.

* * *

Let there be no mistake about our belief that burning a cross in someone's front yard is reprehensible. But St. Paul has sufficient means at its disposal to prevent such behavior without adding the First Amendment to the fire.

The judgment of the Minnesota Supreme Court is reversed, and the case is remanded for proceedings not inconsistent with this opinion.

It is so ordered.

Justice White, (concurring)
Although I disagree with the Court's analysis, I do agree with its conclusion: The St. Paul ordinance is unconstitutional. However, I would decide the case on overbreadth grounds.

We have emphasized time and again that overbreadth doctrine is an exception to the established principle that "a person to whom a statute may constitutionally be applied will not be heard to challenge that statute on the ground that it may conceivably be applied unconstitutionally to others, in other situations not before the Court." ... A defendant being prosecuted for speech or expressive conduct may challenge the law on its face if it reaches protected expression, even when that person's activities are not protected by the First Amendment. This is because "the possible harm to society in permitting some unprotected speech to go unpunished is outweighed by the possibility that protected speech of others may be muted." ...

The St. Paul antibias ordinance is such a law. Although the ordinance reaches conduct that is unprotected, it also makes criminal expressive conduct that causes only hurt feelings, offense, or resentment, and is protected by the First Amendment ... The ordinance is therefore fatally overbroad and invalid on its face.

Justice Stevens, with whom Justice White and Justice Blackmun join as to Part I, concurring in the judgment.

Conduct that creates special risks or causes special harms may be prohibited by special rules. Lighting a fire near an ammunition dump or a gasoline storage tank is especially dangerous; such behavior may be punished more severely than burning trash in a vacant lot. Threatening someone because of her race or religious beliefs may cause particularly severe trauma or touch off a riot, and threatening a high public official may cause substantial social disruption; such threats may be punished more severely than threats against someone based on, say, his support of a particular athletic team. There are legitimate, reasonable, and neutral justifications for such special rules.

This case involves the constitutionality of one such ordinance. Because the regulated conduct has some communicative content – a message of racial, religious, or gender hostility – the ordinance raises two quite different First Amendment questions. Is the ordinance "overbroad" because it prohibits too much speech? If not, is it "underbroad" because it does not prohibit enough speech?

In answering these questions, my colleagues today wrestle with two broad principles: first, that certain "categories of expression [including 'fighting words'] are 'not within the area of constitutionally protected speech,'" ... and second, that "[c]ontent-based regulations [of expression] are presumptively invalid." Although in past opinions the Court has repeated both of these maxims, it has – quite rightly – adhered to neither with the absolutism suggested by my colleagues. Thus, while I agree that the St. Paul ordinance is unconstitutionally overbroad for the reasons stated in Part II of Justice White's opinion, I write separately to suggest how the allure of absolute principles has skewed the analysis of both the majority and Justice White's opinions.

Fifty years ago, the Court articulated a categorical approach to First Amendment jurisprudence ... The Court today revises this categorical approach. It is not, the Court rules, that certain "categories" of expression are "unprotected," but rather that certain "elements" of expression are wholly "proscribable." To the Court, an expressive act, like a chemical compound, consists of more than one element. Although the act may be regulated because it contains a proscribable element, it may not be regulated on the basis of another (nonproscribable) element it also contains. Thus, obscene antigovernment speech may be regulated because it is obscene, but not because it is antigovernment. ... It is this revision of the categorical approach that allows the Court to assume that the St. Paul ordinance proscribes only fighting words, while at the same time concluding that the ordinance is invalid because it imposes a content-based regulation on expressive activity.

As an initial matter, the Court's revision of the categorical approach seems to me something of an adventure in a doctrinal wonderland, for the concept of "obscene anti-government" speech is fantastical. The category of the obscene is very narrow; to be obscene, expression must be found by the trier of fact to "appea[l] to the prurient interest, ... depic[t] or describ[e], in a patently offensive way, sexual conduct, [and], taken as a whole, lac[k] serious literary, artistic, political, or scientific value." *Miller v California*, 413 U.S. 15, 24. "Obscene antigovernment" speech, then, is a contradiction in terms: If expression is antigovernment, it does not "lac[k] serious ... political ... value" and cannot be obscene.

The Court attempts to bolster its argument by likening its novel analysis to that applied to restrictions on the time, place, or manner of expression or on expressive conduct. It is true that loud speech in favor of the Republican Party can be regulated because it is loud, but not because it is pro-Republican; and it is true that the public burning of the American flag can be regulated because it involves public burning and not because it involves the flag. But these analogies are inapposite. In each of these examples, the two elements (e.g., loudness and pro-Republican orientation) can coexist; in the case of "obscene antigovernment" speech, however, the presence of one element ("obscenity") by definition means the absence of the other. To my mind, it is unwise and unsound to craft a new doctrine based on such highly speculative hypotheticals.

I am, however, even more troubled by the second step of the Court's analysis – namely, its conclusion that the St. Paul ordinance is an unconstitutional content-based regulation of speech. Drawing on broadly worded dicta, the Court establishes a near-absolute ban on content-based regulations of expression and holds that the First Amendment prohibits the regulation of fighting words by subject matter. Thus, while the Court rejects the "all-or-nothing-at-all" nature of the categorical approach, ante, at 2543, it promptly embraces an absolutism of its own: Within a particular "proscribable" category of expression, the Court holds, a government must either proscribe all speech or no speech at all. This aspect of the Court's ruling fundamentally misunderstands the role and constitutional status of content-based regulations on speech, conflicts with the very nature of First Amendment jurisprudence, and disrupts well-settled principles of First Amendment law.

Although the Court has, on occasion, declared that content-based regulations of speech are "never permitted," ... such claims are overstated ... [O]ur decisions demonstrate that content-based distinctions, far from being presumptively invalid, are an inevitable and indispensable aspect of a coherent understanding of the First Amendment.

This is true at every level of First Amendment law. In broadest terms, our entire First Amendment jurisprudence creates a regime based on the content of speech. The scope of the First Amendment is determined by the content of expressive activity: Although the First Amendment broadly protects "speech," it does not protect the right to "fix prices, breach contracts, make false warranties, place bets with bookies, threaten, [or] extort" ...

Likewise, whether speech falls within one of the categories of "unprotected" or "proscribable" expression is determined, in part, by its content. Whether a magazine is obscene, a gesture a fighting word, or a photograph child pornography is determined, in part, by its content. Even within categories of protected expression, the First Amendment status of speech is fixed by its content ... Speech about public officials or matters of public concern receives greater protection than speech about other topics. It can, therefore, scarcely be said that the regulation of expressive activity cannot be predicated on its content: Much of our First Amendment jurisprudence is premised on the assumption that content makes a difference.

Consistent with this general premise, we have frequently upheld content-based regulations of speech. For example, in *Young v American Mini Theatres*, the Court upheld zoning ordinances that regulated movie theaters based on the content of the films shown ... We have long recognized the power of the Federal Trade Commission to regulate misleading advertising and labeling ... It is also beyond question that the Government may choose to limit advertisements for cigarettes, but not for cigars; choose to regulate airline advertising ... but not bus advertising; or choose to monitor solicitation by lawyers ... but not by doctors.

All of these cases involved the selective regulation of speech based on content – precisely the sort of regulation the Court invalidates today. Such selective regulations are unavoidably content based, but they are not, in my opinion, "presumptively invalid" ...

Our First Amendment decisions have created a rough hierarchy in the constitutional protection of speech. Core political speech occupies the highest, most protected position; commercial speech and nonobscene, sexually explicit speech are regarded as a sort of second-class expression; obscenity and fighting words receive the least protection of all. Assuming that the Court is correct that this last class of speech is not wholly "unprotected," it certainly does not follow that fighting words and obscenity receive the same sort of protection afforded core political speech. Yet in ruling that proscribable speech cannot be regulated based on subject matter, the Court does just that. Perversely, this gives fighting words greater protection than is afforded commercial speech. If Congress can prohibit false advertising directed at airline passengers without also prohibiting false advertising directed at bus passengers and if a city can prohibit political advertisements in its buses while allowing other advertisements, it is ironic to hold that a city cannot regulate fighting words based on "race, color, creed, religion or gender" while leaving unregulated fighting words based on "union membership ... or homosexuality." The Court today turns First Amendment law on its head: Communication that was once entirely unprotected (and that still can be wholly proscribed) is now entitled to greater protection than commercial speech – and possibly greater protection than core political speech.

In a pivotal passage, the Court writes: "[T]he Federal Government can criminalize only those threats of violence that are directed against the President, see 18 U.S.C. § 871 – since the reasons why threats of violence are outside the First Amendment (protecting individuals from the fear of violence, from the disruption that fear engenders, and from the possibility that the threatened violence will occur) have special force when applied to the ... President" ...

As I understand this opaque passage, Congress may choose from the set of unprotected speech (all threats) to proscribe only a subset (threats against the President) because those threats are particularly likely to cause "fear of violence," "disruption," and actual "violence."

Precisely this same reasoning, however, compels the conclusion that St. Paul's ordinance is constitutional. Just as Congress may determine that threats against the President entail more severe consequences than other threats, so St. Paul's City Council may determine that threats based on the target's race, religion, or gender cause more severe harm to both the target and to society than other threats. This latter judgment – that harms caused by racial, religious, and gender-based invective are qualitatively different from that caused by other fighting words – seems to me eminently reasonable and realistic.

Similarly, it is impossible to reconcile the Court's analysis of the St. Paul ordinance with its recognition that "a prohibition of fighting words that are directed at certain persons or groups ... would be facially valid." Ante, at 2548 (emphasis deleted). A selective proscription of unprotected expression designed to protect "certain persons or groups" (for example, a law proscribing threats directed at the elderly) would be constitutional if it were based on a legitimate determination that the harm created by the regulated expression differs from that created by the unregulated expression (that is, if the elderly are more severely injured by threats than are the nonelderly). Such selective protection is no different from a law prohibiting minors (and only minors) from obtaining obscene publications ... St. Paul has determined – reasonably in my judgment – that fighting-word injuries "based on race, color, creed, religion or gender" are qualitatively different and more severe than fighting-word injuries based on other characteristics. Whether the selective proscription of proscribable speech is defined by the protected target ("certain persons or groups") or the basis of the harm (injuries "based on race, color, creed, religion or gender") makes no constitutional difference: What matters is whether the legislature's selection is based on a legitimate, neutral, and reasonable distinction.

In sum, the central premise of the Court's ruling – that "[c]ontent-based regulations are presumptively invalid" – has simplistic appeal, but lacks support in our First Amendment jurisprudence. To make matters worse, the Court today extends this overstated claim to reach categories of hitherto unprotected speech and, in doing so, wreaks havoc in an area of settled law. Finally, although the Court recognizes exceptions to its new principle, those exceptions undermine its very conclusion that the St. Paul ordinance is unconstitutional. Stated directly, the majority's position cannot withstand scrutiny ...

In sum, the St. Paul ordinance (as construed by the Court) regulates expressive activity that is wholly proscribable and does so not on the basis of viewpoint, but rather in recognition of the different harms caused by such activity. Taken together, these several considerations persuade me that the St. Paul ordinance is not an unconstitutional content-based regulation of speech. Thus, were the ordinance not overbroad, I would vote to uphold it.

READING QUESTIONS ON *RAV*

1 How does the court distinguish between expression and action? Is their distinction tenable?

American Booksellers v Hudnut 771 F.2d 323 (7th Cir. 1985), excerpts

This American case struck down as unconstitutional an ordinance which dealt with pornography as a violation of civil rights.

... Easterbrook, Circuit Judge: – Indianapolis enacted an ordinance defining "pornography" as a practice that discriminates against women. "Pornography" is to be redressed through the administrative and judicial methods used for other discrimination. The City's definition of "pornography" is considerably different from "obscenity," which the Supreme Court held is not protected by the First Amendment ...

"Pornography" under the ordinance is "the graphic sexually explicit subordination of women, whether in pictures or in words, that also includes one or more of the following:

(1) Women are presented as sexual objects who enjoy pain or humiliation or
(2) Women are presented as sexual objects who experience sexual pleasure in being raped; or

(3) Women are presented as sexual objects tied up or cut up or mutilated or bruised or physically hurt, or as dismembered or truncated or fragmented or severed into body parts; or
(4) Women are presented as being penetrated by objects or animals; or
(5) Women are presented in scenarios of degradation, injury, abasement, torture, shown as filthy or inferior, bleeding, bruised, or hurt in a context that makes these conditions sexual; or
(6) Woman are presented as sexual objects for domination, conquest, violation, exploitation, possession, or use, or through postures or positions of servility or submission or display."

Indianapolis Code s. 16-3(q). The statute provides that the "use of men, children, or transsexuals in the place of women in paragraphs (1) through (6) shall also constitute pornography under this section."

The ordinance as passed in April 1984 defined "sexually explicit" to mean actual or simulated intercourse or the uncovered exhibition of the genitals, buttocks or anus. An amendment in June 1984 deleted this provision, leaving the term undefined.

The Indianapolis ordinance does not refer to the prurient interest, to offensiveness, or to the standards of the community. It demands attention to particular depictions, not to the work judged as a whole. It is irrelevant under the ordinance whether the work has literary, artistic, political, or scientific value. The City and many amici point to these omissions as virtues. They maintain that pornography influences attitudes, and the statute is a way to alter the socialization of men and women rather than to vindicate community standards of offensiveness. And as one of the principal drafters of the ordinance has asserted, "if a woman is subjected, why should it matter that the work has other value?" Catharine A. MacKinnon, *Pornography, Civil Rights, and Speech*, 20 Harv.Civ.Rts. – Civ.Lib.L.Rev. 1, 21 (1985).

Civil rights groups and feminists have entered this case as amici on both sides. Those supporting the ordinance say that it will play an important role in reducing the tendency of men to view women as sexual objects, a tendency that leads to both unacceptable attitudes and discrimination in the workplace and violence away from it. Those opposing the ordinance point out that much radical feminist literature is explicit and depicts women in ways forbidden by the ordinance and that the ordinance would reopen old battles. It is unclear how Indianapolis would treat works from James Joyce's *Ulysses* to Homer's *Iliad;* both depict women as submissive objects for conquest and domination.

We do not try to balance the arguments for and against an ordinance such as this. The ordinance discriminates on the ground of the content of the speech. Speech treating women in the approved way – in sexual encounters "premised on equality" (MacKinnon, *supra*, at 22) – is lawful no matter how sexually explicit. Speech treating women in the disapproved way – as submissive in matters sexual or as enjoying humiliation – is unlawful no matter how significant the literary, artistic, or political qualities of the work taken as a whole. The state may not ordain preferred viewpoints in this way. The Constitution forbids the state to declare one perspective right and silence opponents ...

"If there is any fixed star in our constitutional constellation, it is that no official, high or petty, can prescribe what shall be orthodox in politics, nationalism, religion, or other matters of opinion or force citizens to confess by word or act their faith therein." *West Virginia State Board of Education v Barnette*, 319 US 624, 642, 63 SCt 1178, 1187, 87 L.Ed. 1628 (1943). Under the First Amendment the government must leave to the people the evaluation of ideas. Bald or subtle, an idea is as powerful as the audience allows it to be. A belief may be pernicious – the beliefs of Nazis led to the death of millions, those of the Klan to the repression of millions. A pernicious belief may prevail. Totalitarian governments today rule much of the planet, practicing suppression of billions and spreading dogma that may enslave others. One of the things that separates our society from theirs is our absolute right to propagate opinions that the government finds wrong or even hateful ...

Under the ordinance graphic sexually explicit speech is "pornography" or not depending on the perspective the author adopts. Speech that "subordinates" women and also, for example, presents women as enjoying pain, humiliation, or rape, or even simply presents women in "positions of servility or submission or display" is forbidden, no matter how great the literary or political value of the work taken as a whole. Speech that portrays women in positions of equality is lawful, no matter how graphic the sexual content. This is thought control. It establishes an "approved" view of women, of how they may react to sexual encounters, of how the sexes may relate to each other. Those who espouse the approved view may use sexual images; those who do not, may not.

Indianapolis justifies the ordinance on the ground that pornography affects thoughts. Men who see women depicted as subordinate are more likely to treat them so. Pornography is an aspect of dominance. It does not persuade people so much as change them. It works by socializing, by establishing the expected and the permissible. In this view pornography is not an idea; pornography is the injury.

There is much to this perspective. Beliefs are also facts. People often act in accordance with the images and patterns they find around them. People raised in a religion tend to accept the tenets of that religion, often without independent examination. People taught from birth that black people are fit only for slavery rarely rebelled against that creed; beliefs coupled with the self-interest of the masters established a social structure that inflicted great harm while enduring for centuries. Words and images act at the level of the subconscious before they persuade at the level of the conscious. Even the truth has little chance unless a statement fits within the framework of beliefs that may never have been subjected to rational study.

Therefore we accept the premises of this legislation. Depictions of subordination tend to perpetuate subordination. The subordinate status of women in turn leads to affront and lower pay at work, insult and injury at home, battery and rape on the streets. In the language of the legislature, "[p]ornography is central in creating and maintaining sex as a basis of discrimination. Pornography is a systematic practice of exploitation and subordination based on sex which differentially harms women. The bigotry and contempt it produces, with the acts of aggression it fosters, harm women's opportunities for equality and rights [of all kinds]." Indianapolis Code s. 16-1(a)(2).

Yet this simply demonstrates the power of pornography as speech. All of these unhappy effects depend on mental intermediation. Pornography affects how people see the world, their fellows, and social relations. If pornography is what pornography does, so is other speech. Hitler's orations affected how some Germans saw Jews. Communism is a world view, not simply a *Manifesto* by Marx and Engels or a set of speeches. Efforts to suppress communist speech in the United States were based on the belief that the public acceptability of such ideas would increase the likelihood of totalitarian government. Religions affect socialization in the most pervasive way...

Many people believe that the existence of television, apart from the content of specific programs, leads to intellectual laziness, to a penchant for violence, to many other ills. The Alien and Sedition Acts passed during the administration of John Adams rested on a sincerely held belief that disrespect for the government leads to social collapse and revolution – a belief with support in the history of many nations. Most governments of the world act on this empirical regularity, suppressing critical speech. In the United States, however, the strength of the support for this belief is irrelevant. Seditious libel is protected speech unless the danger is not only grave but also imminent ...

Sexual responses often are unthinking responses, and the association of sexual arousal with the subordination of women therefore may have a substantial effect. But almost all cultural stimuli provoke unconscious responses ...

Much of Indianapolis's argument rests on the belief that when speech is "unanswerable," and the metaphor that there is a "marketplace of ideas" does not apply, the First Amendment does not apply either. The metaphor is honored; Milton's *Aeropagitica* and John Stuart Mill's *On Liberty* defend freedom of speech on the ground that the truth will prevail, and many of the most important cases under the First Amendment recite this position. The Framers undoubtedly believed it. As a general matter it is true. But the Constitution does not make the dominance of truth a necessary condition of freedom of speech. To say that it does would be to confuse an outcome of free speech with a necessary condition for the application of the amendment.

A power to limit speech on the ground that truth has not yet prevailed and is not likely to prevail implies the power to declare truth. At some point the government must be able to say (as Indianapolis has said): "We know what the truth is, yet a free exchange of speech has not driven out falsity, so that we must now prohibit falsity" ...

At all events, "pornography" is not low value speech within the meaning of these cases. Indianapolis seeks to prohibit certain speech because it believes this speech influences social relations and politics on a grand scale, that it controls attitudes at home and in the legislature. This precludes a characterization of the speech as low value. True, pornography and obscenity have sex in common. But Indianapolis left out of its definition any reference to literary, artistic, political, or scientific value. The ordinance applies to graphic sexually explicit subordination in words great and small.[1] The Court sometimes balances the value of speech against the costs of its restriction, but it does this by category of speech and not by the content of particular works ...

Any rationale we could imagine in support of this ordinance could not be limited to sex discrimination. Free speech has been on balance an ally of those seeking change. Governments that want stasis start by restricting speech. Culture is a powerful force of continuity; Indianapolis paints pornography as part of the culture of power. Change in any complex system ultimately depends on the ability of outsiders to challenge accepted views and the reigning institutions. Without a strong guarantee of freedom of speech, there is no effective right to challenge what is.

The definition of "pornography" is unconstitutional. No construction or excision of particular terms could save it ...

But the ... Indianapolis ordinance is not neutral with respect to viewpoint. The ban on distribution of works containing coerced performances is limited to pornography; coercion is irrelevant if the work is not "pornography," and we have held the definition of "pornography" to be defective root and branch. A legislature might replace "pornography" in s. 16-3(g)(4) with "any film containing explicit sex" or some similar expression, but even the broadest severability clause does not permit a federal court to rewrite as opposed to excise. Rewriting is work for the legislature of Indianapolis ...

Much speech is dangerous. Chemists whose work might help someone build a bomb, political theorists whose papers might start political movements that lead to riots, speakers whose ideas attract violent protesters, all these and more leave loss in their wake. Unless the remedy is very closely confined, it could be more dangerous to speech than all the libel judgments in history. The constitutional requirements for a valid recovery for assault caused by speech might turn out to be too rigorous for any plaintiff to meet.[2] But the Indianapolis ordinance requires the complainant to show that the attack was "directly caused by specific pornography" (s. 16-3(g)(7)), and it is not beyond the realm of possibility that a state court could construe this limitation in a way that would make the statute constitutional. We are not authorized to prevent the state from trying.

Again, however, the assault statute is tied to "pornography," and we cannot find a sensible way to repair the defect without seizing power that belongs elsewhere. Indianapolis might choose to have no ordinance if it cannot be limited to viewpoint-specific harms, or it might choose to extend the scope to all speech, just as the law of libel applies to all speech. An attempt to repair this ordinance would be nothing but a blind guess.

No amount of struggle with particular words and phrases in this ordinance can leave anything in effect. The district court came to the same conclusion. Its judgment is therefore

Affirmed.

NOTES

1 Indianapolis briefly argues that *Beauharnais v Illinois*, 343 US 250, 72 SCt 725, 96 L.Ed. 919 (1952), which allowed a state to penalize "group libel," supports the ordinance. In *Colin v Smith, supra,* 578 F.2d at 1205, we concluded that cases such as *New York Times v Sullivan* had so washed away the foundations of *Beauharnais* that it could not be considered authoritative. If we are wrong in this, however, the case still does not support the ordinance. It is not clear that depicting women as subordinate in sexually explicit ways, even combined with a depiction of pleasure in rape, would fit within the definition of a group libel. The well received film *Swept Away* used explicit sex, plus taking pleasure in rape, to make a political statement, not to defame. Work must be an insult or slur for its own sake to come within the ambit of *Beauharnais,* and a work need not be scurrilous at all to be "pornography" under the ordinance.

2 See, e.g., *Zamora v CBS*, 480 F.Supp. 199 (S.D.Fla.1979), among the many cases concluding that particular plaintiffs could not show a connection sufficiently direct to permit liability consistent with the First Amendment.

READING QUESTIONS ON *HUDNUT*

1 Why does Judge Easterbrook put so much weight on the idea that the ordinance is "viewpoint based"? Is it viewpoint based in the sense he suggests?
2 Should speech be protected even when it is harmful? How serious must the harm be to justify censorship?

R v Butler [1992] 1 SCR 452

A decision of the Canadian Supreme Court upholding Canada's obscenity law.

Sopinka, J for the majority: – This appeal calls into question the constitutionality of the obscenity provisions of the *Criminal Code*, RSC 1985, c. C-46, s. 163. They are attacked on the ground that they contravene

s. 2(b) of the *Canadian Charter of Rights and Freedoms*. The case requires the Court to address one of the most difficult and controversial of contemporary issues, that of determining whether, and to what extent, Parliament may legitimately criminalize obscenity. I propose to begin with a review of the facts which gave rise to this appeal, as well of the proceedings in the lower courts.

FACTS AND PROCEEDINGS

In August, 1987, the appellant, Donald Victor Butler, opened the Avenue Video Boutique located in Winnipeg, Manitoba. The shop sells and rents "hard core" videotapes and magazines as well as sexual paraphernalia. Outside the store is a sign which reads:

Avenue Video Boutique; a private members only adult video/visual club.

Notice: if sex oriented material offends you, please do not enter.

No admittance to persons under 18 years.

On August 21, 1987, the City of Winnipeg Police entered the appellant's store with a search warrant and seized all the inventory. The appellant was charged with 173 counts in the first indictment: three counts of selling obscene material contrary to s. 159(2)(a) of the *Criminal Code*, RSC 1970, c. C-34 (now s. 163(2)(a)), 41 counts of possessing obscene material for the purpose of distribution contrary to s. 159(l)(a) (now s. 163(l)(a)) of the *Criminal Code*, 128 counts of possessing obscene material for the purpose of sale contrary to s. 159(2)(a) of the *Criminal Code*, and one count of exposing obscene material to public view contrary to s. 159(2)(a) of the *Criminal Code*.

On October 19, 1987, the appellant re-opened the store at the same location. As a result of a police operation a search warrant was executed on October 29, 1987, resulting in the arrest of an employee, Norma McCord. The appellant was arrested at a later date.

A joint indictment was laid against the appellant doing business as Avenue Video Boutique and Norma McCord. The joint indictment contains 77 counts under s. 159 (now s. 163) of the *Criminal Code*: two counts of selling obscene material contrary to s. 159(2)(a), 73 counts of possessing obscene material for the purpose of distribution contrary to s. 159(l)(a), one count of possessing obscene material for the purpose of sale contrary to s. 159(2)(a), and one count of exposing obscene material to public view contrary to s. 159(2)(a).

The trial judge convicted the appellant on eight counts relating to eight films. Convictions were entered against the co-accused McCord with respect to two counts relating to two of the films. Fines of $1,000 per offence were imposed on the appellant. Acquittals were entered on the remaining charges.

The Crown appealed the 242 acquittals with respect to the appellant, and the appellant cross-appealed the convictions. The majority of the Manitoba Court of Appeal allowed the appeal of the Crown and entered convictions for the appellant with respect to all of the counts ...

RELEVANT LEGISLATION

Criminal Code, RSC 1985, c. C-46.

163. (1) Everyone commits an offence who,
(a) makes, prints, publishes, distributes, circulates or has in his possession for the purpose of publication, distribution or circulation any obscene written matter, picture, model, phonograph record or other thing whatever; or
(b) makes, prints, publishes, distributes, sells or has in his possession for the purpose of publication, distribution or circulation a crime comic.
(2) Every one commits an offence who knowingly, without lawful justification or excuse,
(a) sells, exposes to public view or has in his possession for such a purpose any obscene written matter, picture, model, phonograph record or other thing whatever;
(b) publicly exhibits a disgusting object or an indecent show;
(c) offers to sell, advertises or publishes an advertisement of, or has for sale or disposal, any means, instructions, medicine, drug or article intended or represented as a method of causing abortion or miscarriage; or
(d) advertises or publishes an advertisement of any means, instructions, medicine, drug or article intended or represented as a method for restoring sexual virility or curing venereal diseases or diseases of the generative organs.
(3) No person shall be convicted of an offence under this section if he establishes that the public good was served by the acts that are alleged to constitute the offence and that the acts alleged did not extend beyond what served the public good.

(4) For the purposes of this section, it is a question of law whether an act served the public good and whether there is evidence that the act alleged went beyond what served the public good, but it is a question of fact whether the acts did or did not extend beyond what served the public good.

(5) For the purposes of this section, the motives of an accused are irrelevant.

(6) Where an accused is charged with an offence under subsection (1), the fact that the accused was ignorant of the nature or presence of the matter, picture, model, phonograph record, crime comic or other thing by means of or in relation to which the offence was committed is not a defence to the charge.

(7) In this section, "crime comic" means a magazine, periodical or book that exclusively or substantially comprises matter depicting pictorially
(a) the commission of crimes, real or fictitious; or
(b) events connected with the commission of crimes, real or fictitious, whether occurring before of after the commission of the crime.

(8) For the purposes of this Act, any publication a dominant characteristic of which is the undue exploitation of sex, or of sex and any one or more of the following subjects, namely, crime, horror, cruelty and violence, shall be deemed to be obscene.

ISSUES

The following constitutional questions are raised by this appeal:

1 Does s. 163 of the *Criminal Code* of Canada, RSC 1985, c. C-46, violate s. 2(b) of the *Canadian Charter of Rights and Freedoms*?
2 If s. 163 of the *Criminal Code* of Canada, RSC 1985, c. C-46, violates s. 2(b) of the *Canadian Charter of Rights and Freedoms*, can s. 163 of the *Criminal Code* of Canada be demonstrably justified under s. 1 of the *Canadian Charter of Rights and Freedoms* as a reasonable limit prescribed by law?

ANALYSIS

... In my view, in the circumstances, this appeal should be confined to the examination of the constitutional validity of s. 163(8) only.

Before proceeding to consider the constitutional questions, it will be helpful to review the legislative history of the provision as well as the extensive judicial interpretation and analysis which have infused meaning into the bare words of the statute.

Legislative History

The *Criminal Code* did not [in the past] provide a definition of any of the operative terms, "obscene," "indecent," or "disgusting." The notion of obscenity embodied in these provisions was based on the test formulated by Cockburn, CJ in *R v Hicklin* (1868), LR 3 QB 360:

I think the test of obscenity is this, whether the tendency of the matter charged as obscenity is to deprave and corrupt those whose minds are open to such immoral influences, and into whose hands a publication of this sort may fall. (At p. 371)

The focus on the "corruption of morals" in the earlier legislation grew out of the English obscenity law which made the Court the "guardian of public morals" ...

The current provision, which is the subject of this appeal, entered into force in 1959 in response to the much criticized former version ... Unlike the previous statutes, s-s. (8) provided a statutory definition of "obscene":

(8) For the purposes of this Act, any publication a dominant characteristic of which is the undue exploitation of sex, or of sex and any one or more of the following subjects, namely, crime, horror, cruelty and violence, shall be deemed to be obscene.

As will be discussed further, the introduction of the statutory definition had the effect of replacing the *Hicklin* test with a series of rules developed by the courts. The provision must be considered in light of these tests.

Judicial Interpretation of Section 163(8)

The first case to consider the current provision was *Brodie v The Queen*, [1962] SCR 681. The majority of this Court found in that case that D.H. Lawrence's novel, *Lady Chatterley's Lover*, was not obscene within the meaning of the *Code*. The *Brodie* case lay the groundwork for the interpretation of s. 163(8) by setting out the principal tests which should govern the determination of what is obscene for the purposes of criminal prosecution. The first step was to discard the *Hicklin* test.

Section 163(8) to be Exclusive Test

In examining the definition provided by s-s. (8), the majority of this Court was of the view that the new provision provided a clean slate and had the effect of bringing in an "objective standard of obscenity" which rendered all the jurisprudence under the *Hicklin* definition obsolete. In the words of Judson, J:

> I think that the new statutory definition does give the Court an opportunity to apply tests which have some certainty of meaning and are capable of objective application and which do not so much depend as before upon the idiosyncrasies and sensitivities of the tribunal of fact, whether judge or jury. We are now concerned with a Canadian statute which is exclusive of all others. [At p. 702]

...

Tests of "Undue Exploitation of Sex"

In order for the work or material to qualify as "obscene," the exploitation of sex must not only be its dominant characteristic, but such exploitation must be "undue." In determining when the exploitation of sex will be considered "undue," the courts have attempted to formulate workable tests. The most important of these is the "community standard of tolerance" test.

"Community Standard of Tolerance" Test. In *Brodie,* Judson, J accepted the view espoused notably by the Australian and New Zealand courts that obscenity is to be measured against "community standards." He cited the following passage in the judgment of Fullager, J in *R v Close,* [1948] VLR 445:

> There does exist in any community at all times – however the standard may vary from time to time – a general instinctive sense of what is decent and what is indecent, of what is clean and what is dirty, and when the distinction has to be drawn, I do not know that today there is any better tribunal than a jury to draw it ... I am very far from attempting to lay down a model direction, but a judge might perhaps, in the case of a novel, say something like this: "It would not be true to say that any publication dealing with

sexual relations is obscene. The relations of the sexes are, of course, legitimate matters for discussion everywhere ... There are certain standards of decency which prevail in the community, and you are really called upon to try this case because you are regarded as representing, and capable of justly applying, those standards. What is obscene is something which offends against those standards." [At pp. 705–6]

The community standards test has been the subject of extensive judicial analysis. It is the standards of the community as a whole which must be considered and not the standards of a small segment of that community such as the university community where a film was shown ... The standard to be applied is a national one ... With respect to expert evidence, it is not necessary and is not a fact which the Crown is obliged to prove as part of its case ... In *R v Dominion News & Gifts (1962) Ltd*, [1963] 2 CCC 103 (Man. CA), Freedman, JA (dissenting) emphasized that the community standards test must necessarily respond to changing mores:

Community standards must be contemporary. Times change, and ideas change with them. Compared to the Victorian era this is a liberal age in which we live. One manifestation of it is the relative freedom with which the whole question of sex is discussed. In books, magazines, movies, television, and sometimes even in parlour conversation, various aspects of sex are made the subject of comment, with a candour that in an earlier day would have been regarded as indecent and intolerable. We cannot and should not ignore these present-day attitudes when we face the question whether [the subject materials] are obscene according to our criminal law. [At pp. 116–17]

Our Court was called upon to elaborate the community standards test in *Towne Cinema Theatres Ltd v The Queen*, [1985] 1 SCR 494. Dickson, CJ reviewed the case law and found:

The cases all emphasize that it is a standard of *tolerance*, not taste, that is relevant. What matters is not what Canadians think is right for themselves to see. What matters is what Canadians would not abide other Canadians seeing because it would be beyond the contemporary Canadian standard of tolerance to allow them to see it. Since the standard is tolerance, I think the audience to which the allegedly obscene material is targeted must be relevant. The operative standards are those of the Canadian community as a whole, but since what matters is what other people may see, it is quite conceivable that the Canadian community would tolerate varying degrees of explicitness depending upon the audience and the circumstances. [Emphasis in original; at pp. 508–9]

Therefore, the community standards test is concerned not with what Canadians would not tolerate being exposed to themselves, but what they would not tolerate other Canadians being exposed to. The minority view was that the tolerance level will vary depending on the manner, time, and place in which the material is presented as well as the audience to whom it is directed. The majority opinion on this point was expressed by Wilson, J in the following passage:

It is not, in my opinion, open to the courts under s. 159(8) of the *Criminal Code* to characterize a movie as obscene if shown to one constituency but not if shown to another ... In my view, a movie is either obscene under the *Code* based on a national community standard of tolerance or it is not. If it is not, it may still be the subject of provincial regulatory control. [At p. 521]

"Degradation or Dehumanization" Test. There has been a growing recognition in recent cases that material which may be said to exploit sex in a "degrading or dehumanizing" manner will necessarily fail the community standards test ...

Among other things, degrading or dehumanizing materials place women (and sometimes men) in positions of subordination, servile submission, or humiliation. They run against the principles of equality and dignity of all human beings. In the appreciation of whether material is degrading or dehumanizing, the appearance of consent is not necessarily determinative. Consent cannot save materials that otherwise contain degrading or dehumanizing scenes. Sometimes the very appearance of consent makes the depicted acts even more degrading or dehumanizing.

This type of material would, apparently, fail the community standards test not because it offends against morals but because it is perceived by public opinion to be harmful to society, particularly to women. While the accuracy of this perception is not susceptible of exact proof, there is a substantial body of opinion that holds that the portrayal of persons being subjected to degrading or dehumanizing sexual treatment results in harm, particularly to women and therefore to society as a whole ... It would be reasonable to conclude that there is an appreciable risk of harm to society in the portrayal of such material.

The effect of the evidence on public opinion was summed up by Wilson, J in *Towne Cinema, supra,* as follows:

The most that can be said, I think, is that the public has concluded that exposure to material which degrades the human dimensions of life to a subhuman or merely physical dimension and thereby contributes to a process of moral desensitization must be harmful in some way. [At p. 524]

In *Towne Cinema,* Dickson, CJ considered the "degradation" or "dehumanization" test to be the principal indicator of "undueness" without specifying what role the community tolerance test plays in respect of this issue. He did observe, however, that the community might tolerate some forms of exploitation that caused harm that was nevertheless undue. The relevant passages appear at p. 505:

There are other ways in which exploitation of sex might be "undue." Ours is not a perfect society and it is unfortunate but true that the community may tolerate publications that cause harm to members of society and therefore to society as a whole. Even if, at certain times, there is a coincidence between what is not tolerated and what is harmful to society, there is no necessary connection between these two concepts. Thus, a legal definition of "undue" must also encompass publications harmful to members of society and, therefore, to society as a whole.

Sex related publications which portray persons in a degrading manner as objects of violence, cruelty or other forms of dehumanizing treatment, may be "undue" for the purpose of s. 159(8). No one should be subject to the degradation and humiliation inherent in publications which link sex with violence, cruelty, and other forms of dehumanizing treatment. It is not likely that at a given moment in a society's history, such publications will be tolerated ...

However, as I have noted above, there is no *necessary* coincidence between the undueness of publications which degrade people by linking violence, cruelty or other forms of dehumanizing treatment with sex, and the community standard of tolerance. Even if certain sex related materials were found to be within the standard of tolerance of the community, it would still be necessary to ensure that they were not "undue" in some other sense, for example, in the sense that they portray persons in a degrading manner as objects of violence, cruelty, or other forms of dehumanizing treatment. [Emphasis in original]

In the reasons of Wilson, J concurring in the result, the line between the mere portrayal of sex and the dehumanization of people is drawn by the "undueness" concept. The community is the arbiter as to what is harmful to it. She states:

As I see it, the essential difficulty with the definition of obscenity is that "undueness" must presumably be assessed in relation to consequences. It is implicit in the definition that at some point the exploitation of sex becomes harmful to the public or at least the public believes that to be so. It is therefore necessary for the protection of the public to put limits on the degree of exploitation and, through the application of the community standard test, the public is made the arbiter of what is harmful to it and what is not. The problem is that we know so little of the consequences we are seeking to avoid. Do obscene movies spawn immoral conduct? Do they degrade women? Do they promote violence? The most that can be said, I think, is that the public has concluded that exposure to material which degrades the human dimensions of life to a subhuman or merely physical dimension and thereby contributes to a process of moral desensitization must be harmful in some way. It must therefore be controlled when it gets out of hand, when it becomes "undue." [At p. 524]

"Internal Necessities Test" or "Artistic Defence." In determining whether the exploitation of sex is "undue," Judson, J set out the test of "internal necessities" in *Brodie, supra:*

What I think is aimed at is excessive emphasis on the theme for a base purpose. But I do not think that there is undue exploitation if there is no more emphasis on the theme than is required in the serious treatment of the theme of a novel with honesty and uprightness. That the work under attack is a serious work of fiction is to me beyond question. It has none of the characteristics that are often described in judgments dealing with obscenity – dirt for dirt's sake, the leer of the sensualist, depravity in the mind of an author with an obsession for dirt, pornography, an appeal to a prurient interest, etc. The section recognizes that the serious-minded author must have freedom in the production of a work of genuine artistic and literary merit and the quality of the work, as the witnesses point out and common sense indicates, must have real relevance in determining not only a dominant characteristic but also whether there is undue exploitation. [At pp. 704–5]

As counsel for the Crown pointed out in his oral submissions, the artistic defence is the last step in the analysis of whether the exploitation of sex is undue. Even material which by itself offends community standards will not be considered "undue," if it is required for the serious treatment of a theme ...

Accordingly, the "internal necessities" test, or what has been referred to as the "artistic defence," has been interpreted to assess whether the exploitation of sex has a justifiable role in advancing the plot or the theme, and in considering the work as a whole, does not merely represent "dirt for dirt's sake" but has a legitimate role when measured by the internal necessities of the work itself.

The Relationship of the Tests to Each Other. This review of jurisprudence shows that it fails to specify the relationship of the tests one to another. Failure to do so with respect to the community standards test and the degrading or dehumanizing test, for example, raises a serious question as to the basis on which the community acts in determining whether the impugned material will be tolerated. With both these tests being applied to the same material and apparently independently, we do not know whether the community found the material to be intolerable because it was degrading or dehumanizing, because it offended against morals or on some other basis. In some circumstances a finding that the material is tolerable can be overruled by the conclusion by the court that it causes harm and is therefore undue. Moreover, is the internal necessities test dominant so that it will redeem material that would otherwise be undue or is it just one factor? Is this test applied by the community or is it determined by the court without regard for the community? This hiatus in the jurisprudence has left the legislation open to attack on the ground of vagueness and uncertainty. That attack is made in this case. This lacuna in the interpretation of the legislation must, if possible, be filled before subjecting the legislation to *Charter* scrutiny. The necessity to do so was foreseen by Wilson, J in *Towne Cinema* when she stated:

The test of the community standard is helpful to the extent that it provides a norm against which impugned material may be assessed but it does little to elucidate the underlying question as to why some exploitation of sex falls on the permitted side of the line under s. 159(8) and some on the prohibited side. No doubt this question will have to be addressed when the validity of the obscenity provisions of the *Code* is subjected to attack as an infringement on freedom of speech and the infringement is sought to be justified as reasonable. [At p. 525]

Pornography can be usefully divided into three categories: (1) explicit sex with violence, (2) explicit sex without violence but which subjects people to treatment that is degrading or dehumanizing, and (3) explicit sex without violence that is neither degrading nor dehumanizing. Violence in this context includes both actual physical violence and threats of physical violence. Relating these three categories to the terms of s. 163(8) of the *Code*, the first, explicit sex coupled with violence, is expressly mentioned. Sex coupled with crime, horror, or cruelty will sometimes involve violence. Cruelty, for instance, will usually do so. But, even in the absence of violence, sex coupled with crime, horror, or cruelty may fall within the second category. As for category (3), subject to the exception referred to below, it is not covered.

Some segments of society would consider that all three categories of pornography cause harm to society because they tend to undermine its moral fibre. Others would contend that none of the categories cause harm. Furthermore, there is a range of opinion as to what is degrading or dehumanizing ... Because this is not a matter that is susceptible of proof in the traditional way and because we do not wish to leave it to the individual tastes of judges, we must have a norm that will serve as an arbiter in determining what amounts to an undue exploitation of sex. That arbiter is the community as a whole.

The courts must determine as best they can what the community would tolerate others being exposed to on the basis of the degree of harm that may flow from such exposure. Harm in this context means that it predisposes persons to act in an anti-social manner as, for example, the physical or mental mistreatment of women by men, or, what is perhaps debatable, the reverse. Anti-social conduct for this purpose is conduct which society formally recognizes as incompatible with its proper functioning. The stronger the inference of a risk of harm the lesser the likelihood of tolerance. The inference may be drawn from the material itself or from the material and other evidence. Similarly evidence as to the community standards is desirable but not essential.

In making this determination with respect to the three categories of pornography referred to above, the portrayal of sex coupled with violence will almost always constitute the undue exploitation of sex. Explicit sex which is degrading or dehumanizing may be undue if the risk of harm is substantial. Finally, explicit sex that is not violent and neither degrading nor dehumanizing is generally tolerated in our society and will not qualify as the undue exploitation of sex unless it employs children in its production.

If material is not obscene under this framework, it does not become so by reason of the person to whom it is or may be shown or exposed nor by reason of the place or manner in which it is shown. The availability of sexually explicit materials in theatres and other public places is subject to regulation by competent provincial legislation. Typically such legislation imposes restrictions on the material available to children ...

The foregoing deals with the inter-relationship of the "community standards test" and "the degrading or dehumanizing" test. How does the "internal necessities" test fit into this scheme? The need to apply this test only arises if a work contains sexually explicit material that by itself would constitute the undue exploitation of sex. The portrayal of sex must then be viewed in context to determine whether that is the dominant theme of the work as a whole. Put another way, is undue exploitation of sex the main object of the work or is this portrayal of sex essential to a wider artistic, literary, or other similar purpose? Since the threshold determination must be made on the basis of community standards, that is, whether the sexually explicit aspect is undue, its impact when considered in context must be determined on the same basis. The court must determine whether the sexually explicit material when viewed in the context of the whole work would be tolerated by the community as a whole. Artistic expression rests at the heart of freedom of expression values and any doubt in this regard must be resolved in favour of freedom of expression.

Does Section 163 Violate Section 2(b) of the Charter?

The majority of the Court of Appeal in this case allowed the appeal of the Crown on the ground that s. 163 does not violate freedom of expression as guaranteed under s. 2(b) of the *Charter* ... [However] [t]he form of activity in this case is the medium through which the meaning sought to be conveyed is expressed, namely, the film, magazine, written matter, or sexual gadget. There is nothing inherently violent in the vehicle of expression, and it accordingly does not fall outside the protected sphere of activity.

In light of our recent decision in *R v Keegstra*, [1990] 3 SCR 697, the respondent, and most of the parties intervening in support of the respondent, do not take issue with the proposition that s. 163 of the *Criminal Code* violates s. 2(b) of the *Charter*. In *Keegstra*, we were unanimous in advocating a generous approach to the protection afforded by

s. 2(b) of the *Charter*. Our Court confirmed the view ... that activities cannot be excluded from the scope of the guaranteed freedom on the basis of the content or meaning being conveyed ...

With respect, the majority of the Court of Appeal did not sufficiently distance itself from the content of the materials ...

Meaning sought to be expressed need not be "redeeming" in the eyes of the Court to merit the protection of s. 2(b) whose purpose is to ensure that thoughts and feelings may be conveyed freely in non-violent ways without fear of censure.

In this case, both the purpose and effect of s. 163 is specifically to restrict the communication of certain types of materials based on their content. In my view, there is no doubt that s. 163 seeks to prohibit certain types of expressive activity and thereby infringes s. 2(b) of the *Charter* ...

I would conclude that the first constitutional question should be answered in the affirmative.

Is Section 163 Justified under Section 1 of the Charter?

Is Section 163 a Limit Prescribed by Law?

The appellant argues that the provision is so vague that it is impossible to apply it. Vagueness must be considered in relation to two issues in this appeal: (1) is the law so vague that it does not qualify as "a limit prescribed by law"; and (2) is it so imprecise that it is not a reasonable limit ...

In assessing whether s. 163(8) prescribes an intelligible standard, consideration must be given to the manner in which the provision has been judicially interpreted ...

The fact that a particular legislative term is open to varying interpretations by the courts is not fatal ... Therefore the question at hand is whether the impugned sections of the *Criminal Code* can be or have been given sensible meanings by the courts ...

Standards which escape precise technical definition, such as "undue," are an inevitable part of the law. The *Criminal Code* contains other such standards. Without commenting on their constitutional validity, I note that the terms "indecent," "immoral," or "scurrilous," found in ss. 167, 168, 173, and 175, are nowhere defined in the *Code*. It is within the role of the judiciary to attempt to interpret these terms. If such interpretation yields an intelligible standard, the threshold test for the application of s. 1 is met. In my opinion, the interpretation of s. 163(8) in prior judgments which I have reviewed, as supplemented by these reasons, provides an intelligible standard.

Objective

The respondent argues that there are several pressing and substantial objectives which justify overriding the freedom to distribute obscene materials. Essentially, these objectives are the avoidance of harm resulting from antisocial attitudinal changes that exposure to obscene material causes and the public interest in maintaining a "decent society." On the other hand, the appellant argues that the objective of s. 163 is to have the state act as "moral custodian" in sexual matters and to impose subjective standards of morality.

The obscenity legislation and jurisprudence prior to the enactment of s. 163 were evidently concerned with prohibiting the "immoral influences" of obscene publications and safeguarding the morals of individuals into whose hands such works could fall. The *Hicklin* philosophy posits that explicit sexual depictions, particularly outside the sanctioned contexts of marriage and procreation, threatened the morals or the fabric of society ... In this sense, its dominant, if not exclusive, purpose was to advance a particular conception of morality. Any deviation from such morality was considered to be inherently undesirable, independently of any harm to society ... [T]his particular objective is no longer defensible in view of the *Charter*. To impose a certain standard of public and sexual morality, solely because it reflects the conventions of a given community, is inimical to the exercise and enjoyment of individual freedoms, which form the basis of our social contract. D. Dyzenhaus, "Obscenity and the Charter: Autonomy and Equality" (1991), 1 CR (4th) 367, at p. 370, refers to this as "legal moralism," of a majority deciding what values should inform individual lives and then coercively imposing those values on minorities. The prevention of "dirt for dirt's sake" is not a legitimate objective which would justify the violation of one of the most fundamental freedoms enshrined in the *Charter*.

On the other hand, I cannot agree with the suggestion of the appellant that Parliament does not have the right to legislate on the basis of some fundamental conception of morality for the purposes of safeguarding the values which are integral to a free and democratic society. As Dyzenhaus, *supra*, writes:

Moral disapprobation is recognized as an appropriate response when it has its basis in *Charter* values. (At p. 376)

As the respondent and many of the interveners have pointed out, much of the criminal law is based on moral conceptions of right and wrong and the mere fact that a law is grounded in morality does not automatically render it illegitimate. In this regard, criminalizing the proliferation of materials which undermine another basic *Charter* right may indeed be a legitimate objective.

In my view, however, the overriding objective of s. 163 is not moral disapprobation but the avoidance of harm to society. In *Towne Cinema,* Dickson, CJ stated:

It is harm to society from undue exploitation that is aimed at by the section, not simply lapses in propriety or good taste. (At p. 507)

The harm was described in the following way in the *Report on Pornography by the Standing Committee on Justice and Legal Affairs* (MacGuigan Report) (1978):

The clear and unquestionable danger of this type of material is that it reinforces some unhealthy tendencies in Canadian society. The effect of this type of material is to reinforce male-female stereotypes to the detriment of both sexes. It attempts to make degradation, humiliation, victimization, and violence in human relationships appear normal and acceptable. A society which holds that egalitarianism, non-violence, consensualism, and mutuality are basic to any human interaction, whether sexual or other, is clearly justified in controlling and prohibiting any medium of depiction, description or advocacy which violates these principles.

The appellant argues that to accept the objective of the provision as being related to the harm associated with obscenity would be to adopt the "shifting purpose" doctrine explicitly rejected in *R v Big M Drug Mart Ltd,* [1985] 1 SCR 295. This Court concluded in that case that a finding that the *Lord's Day Act* has a secular purpose was not possible given that its religious purpose, in compelling sabbatical observance, has been long-established and consistently maintained by the courts. The appellant relies on the words of Dickson, J (as he then was):

... the theory of a shifting purpose stands in stark contrast to fundamental notions developed in our law concerning the nature of "Parliamentary intention." Purpose is a function of the intent of those who drafted and enacted the legislation at the time, and not of any shifting variable.

While the effect of such legislation as the *Lord's Day Act* may be more secular today than it was in 1677 or in 1906, such a finding cannot justify a conclusion that its purpose has similarly changed. In result, therefore, the *Lord's Day Act* must be characterized as it has always been, a law the primary purpose of which is the compulsion of sabbatical observance. [At pp. 335–6]

I do not agree that to identify the objective of the impugned legislation as the prevention of harm to society, one must resort to the "shifting purpose" doctrine. First, the notions of moral corruption and harm to society are not distinct, as the appellant suggests, but are inextricably linked. It is moral corruption of a certain kind which leads to the detrimental effect on society. Second, and more importantly, I am of the view that with the enactment of s. 163, Parliament explicitly sought to address the harms which are linked to certain types of obscene materials. The prohibition of such materials was based on a belief that they had a detrimental impact on individuals exposed to them and consequently on society as a whole. Our understanding of the harms caused by these materials has developed considerably since that time; however, this does not detract from the fact that the purpose of this legislation remains, as it was in 1959, the protection of society from harms caused by the exposure to obscene materials ...

It is the harm to society resulting from the undue exploitation of such matters which is aimed at by the section. The "harm" conceived by Parliament in 1959 may not have been expressed in the same words as one would today. The Court is not limited to a 1959 perspective in the determination of this matter ...

A permissible shift in emphasis was built into the legislation when, as interpreted by the courts, it adopted the community standards test. Community standards as to what is harmful have changed since 1959.

This being the objective, is it pressing and substantial? Does the prevention of the harm associated with the dissemination of certain obscene materials constitute a sufficiently pressing and substantial concern to warrant a restriction on the freedom of expression? In this regard, it should be recalled that in *Keegstra, supra,* this Court unanimously accepted that the prevention of the influence of hate propaganda on society at large was a legitimate objective ...

This Court has thus recognized that the harm caused by the proliferation of materials which seriously offend the values fundamental to our society is a substantial concern which justifies restricting the otherwise full exercise of the freedom of expression. In my view, the harm sought to be avoided in the case of the dissemination of obscene materials is similar ... [I]f true equality between male and female persons is to be achieved, we cannot ignore the threat to equality resulting from exposure to audiences of certain types of violent and degrading material. Materials portraying women as a class as objects for sexual exploitation and abuse have a negative impact on "the individual's sense of self-worth and acceptance."

In reaching the conclusion that legislation proscribing obscenity is a valid objective which justifies some encroachment of the right to freedom of expression, I am persuaded in part that such legislation may be found in most free and democratic societies.

The advent of the *Charter* did not have the effect of dramatically depriving Parliament of a power which it has historically enjoyed ...

Finally, it should be noted that the burgeoning pornography industry renders the concern even more pressing and substantial than when the impugned provisions were first enacted. I would therefore conclude that the objective of avoiding the harm associated with the dissemination of pornography in this case is sufficiently pressing and substantial to warrant some restriction on full exercise of the right to freedom of expression. The analysis of whether the measure is proportional to the objective must, in my view, be undertaken in light of the conclusion that the objective of the impugned section is valid only insofar as it relates to the harm to society associated with obscene materials. Indeed, the section as interpreted in previous decisions and in these reasons is fully consistent with that objective. The objective of maintaining conventional standards of propriety, independently of any harm to society, is no longer justified in light of the values of individual liberty which underlie the *Charter*. This, then, being the objective of s. 163, which I have found to be pressing and substantial, I must now determine whether the section is rationally connected and proportional to this objective. As outlined above, s. 163(8) criminalizes the exploitation of sex and sex and violence, when, on the basis of the community test, it is undue. The determination of when such exploitation is undue is directly related to the immediacy of a risk of harm to society which is reasonably perceived as arising from its dissemination.

Proportionality

General. The proportionality requirement has three aspects:

1 the existence of a rational connection between the impugned measures and the objective;
2 minimal impairment of the right or freedom; and
3 a proper balance between the effects of the limiting measures and the legislative objective.

In assessing whether the proportionality test is met, it is important to keep in mind the nature of expression which has been infringed ...

The values which underlie the protection of freedom of expression relate to the search for truth, participation in the political process, and individual self-fulfilment. The Attorney General for Ontario argues that of these, only "individual self-fulfilment," and only in its most base aspect, that of physical arousal, is engaged by pornography. On the other hand, the civil liberties groups argue that pornography forces us to question conventional notions of sexuality and thereby launches us into an inherently political discourse. In their factum, the *BC Civil Liberties Association* adopts a passage from R. West, "The Feminist-Conservative Anti-Pornography Alliance and the 1986 Attorney General's Commission on Pornography Report" (1987), 4 *American Bar Foundation Research Journal* 681, at p. 696:

Good pornography has value because it validates women's will to pleasure. It celebrates female nature. It validates a range of female sexuality that is wider and truer than that legitimated by the non-pornographic culture. Pornography when it is good celebrates both female pleasure and male rationality.

A proper application of the test should not suppress what West refers to as "good pornography." The objective of the impugned provision is not to inhibit the celebration of human sexuality. However, it cannot be ignored that the realities of the pornography industry are far from the picture which the *BC Civil Liberties Association* would have us paint ...

In my view, the kind of expression which is sought to be advanced does not stand on equal footing with other kinds of expression which directly engage the "core" of the freedom of expression values.

This conclusion is further buttressed by the fact that the targeted material is expression which is motivated, in the overwhelming majority of cases, by economic profit ...

I will now turn to an examination of the three basic aspects of the proportionality test.

Rational Connection. The message of obscenity which degrades and dehumanizes is analogous to that of hate propaganda. As the Attorney General of Ontario has argued in its factum, obscenity wields the power to wreak social damage in that a significant portion of the population is humiliated by its gross misrepresentations ...

Accordingly, the rational link between s. 163 and the objective of Parliament relates to the actual causal relationship between obscenity and the risk of harm to society at large. On this point, it is clear that the literature of the social sciences remains subject to controversy ...

While a direct link between obscenity and harm to society may be difficult, if not impossible, to establish, it is reasonable to presume that exposure to images bears a causal relationship to changes in attitudes and beliefs ...

I am in agreement with ... the view that Parliament was entitled to have a "reasoned apprehension of harm" resulting from the desensitization of individuals exposed to materials which depict violence, cruelty, and dehumanization in sexual relations.

Accordingly, I am of the view that there is a sufficiently rational link between the criminal sanction, which demonstrates our community's disapproval of the dissemination of materials which potentially victimize women and which restricts the negative influence which such materials have on changes in attitudes and behaviour, and the objective.

Finally, I wish to distinguish this case from *Keegstra*, in which the minority adopted the view that there was no rational connection between the criminalization of hate propaganda and its suppression. As McLachlin, J noted, prosecutions under the *Criminal Code* for racist expression have attracted extensive media coverage. The criminal process confers on the accused publicity for his or her causes and succeeds even in generating sympathy. The same cannot be said of the kinds of expression sought to be suppressed in the present case. The general availability of the subject materials and the rampant pornography industry are such that, in the words of Dickson, CJ in *Keegstra*, "pornography is not dignified by its suppression." In contrast to the hate-monger who may succeed, by the sudden media attention, in gaining an audience, the prohibition of obscene materials does nothing to promote the pornographer's cause.

Minimal Impairment. In determining whether less intrusive legislation may be imagined ... it is not necessary that the legislative scheme be the "perfect" scheme, but that it be appropriately tailored in the context of the infringed right ...

There are several factors which contribute to the finding that the provision minimally impairs the freedom which is infringed.

First, the impugned provision does not proscribe sexually explicit erotica without violence that is not degrading or dehumanizing. It is designed to catch material that creates a risk of harm to society. It might be suggested that proof of actual harm should be required. It is apparent from what I have said above that it is sufficient in this regard for Parliament to have a reasonable basis for concluding that harm will result and this requirement does not demand actual proof of harm.

Second, materials which have scientific, artistic, or literary merit are not captured by the provision. As discussed above, the court must be generous in its application of the "artistic defence." For example, in certain cases, materials such as photographs, prints, books, and films which may undoubtedly be produced with some motive for economic profit, may nonetheless claim the protection of the *Charter* insofar as their defining characteristic is that of aesthetic expression, and thus represent the artist's attempt at individual fulfilment. The existence of an accompanying economic motive does not, of itself, deprive a work of significance as an example of individual artistic or self-fulfilment.

Third, in considering whether the provision minimally impairs the freedom in question, it is legitimate for the court to take into account Parliament's past abortive attempts to replace the definition with one that is more explicit ... The attempt to provide exhaustive instances of obscenity has been shown to be destined to fail ... It seems that the only practicable alternative is to strive towards a more abstract definition of obscenity which is contextually sensitive and responsive to progress in the knowledge and understanding of the phenomenon to which the legislation is directed. In my view, the standard of "undue exploitation" is therefore appropriate. The intractable nature of the problem and the impossibility of precisely defining a notion which is inherently elusive makes the possibility of a more explicit provision remote. In this light, it is appropriate to question whether, and at what cost, greater legislative precision can be demanded.

Fourth, while the discussion in this appeal has been limited to the definition portion of s. 163, 1 would note that the impugned section, with the possible exception of s-s. 1 which is not in issue here, has been held by this Court not to extend its reach to the private use or viewing of obscene materials ...

Accordingly, it is only the public distribution and exhibition of obscene materials which is in issue here.

Finally, I wish to address the arguments of the interveners, *Canadian Civil Liberties Association* and *Manitoba Association for Rights and Liberties*, that the objectives of this kind of legislation may be met by alternative, less intrusive measures. First, it is submitted that reasonable time, manner, and place restrictions would be preferable to outright prohibition. I am of the view that this argument should be rejected. Once it has been established that the objective is the avoidance of harm caused by the degradation which many women feel as "victims" of the message of obscenity, and of the negative impact exposure to such material has on perceptions and attitudes towards women, it is untenable to argue that these harms could be avoided by placing restrictions on access to such material. Making the materials more difficult to obtain by increasing their cost and reducing their availability does not achieve the same objective. Once Parliament has reasonably concluded that certain acts are harmful to certain groups in society and to society in general, it would be inconsistent, if not hypocritical, to argue that such acts could be committed in more restrictive conditions. The harm sought to be avoided would remain the same in either case.

It is also submitted that there are more effective techniques to promote the objectives of Parliament. For example, if pornography is seen as encouraging violence against women, there are certain activities which discourage it – counselling rape victims to charge their assailants, provision of shelter and assistance for battered women, campaigns for laws against discrimination on the grounds of sex, education to increase the sensitivity of law enforcement agencies and other governmental authorities. In addition, it is submitted that education is an under-used response.

It is noteworthy that many of the above-suggested alternatives are in the form of responses to the harm engendered by negative attitudes against women. The role of the impugned provision is to control the dissemination of the very images that contribute to such attitudes. Moreover, it is true that there are additional measures which could alleviate the problem of violence against women. However, given the gravity of the harm, and the threat to the values at stake, I do not believe that the measure chosen by Parliament is equalled by the alternatives which have been suggested. Education, too, may offer a means of combating negative attitudes to women, just as it is currently used as a means of addressing other problems dealt with in the *Code*. However, there is no reason to rely on education alone. It should be emphasized that this is in no way intended to deny the value of other educational and counselling measures to deal with the roots and effects of negative attitudes. Rather, it is only to stress the arbitrariness and unacceptability of the claim that such measures represent the sole legitimate means of addressing the phenomenon. Serious social problems such as violence against women require multi-pronged approaches by government. Education and legislation are not alternatives but complements in addressing such problems. There is nothing in the *Charter* which requires Parliament to choose between such complementary measures.

Balance between Effects of Limiting Measures and Legislative Objective. The final question to be answered in the proportionality test is whether the effects of the law so severely trench on a protected right that the legislative objective is outweighed by the infringement. The infringement on freedom of expression is confined to a measure designed to prohibit the distribution of sexually explicit materials accompanied by violence, and those without violence that are degrading or dehumanizing. As I have already concluded, this kind of expression lies far from the core of the guarantee of freedom on expression. It appeals only to the most base aspect of individual fulfilment, and it is primarily economically motivated.

The objective of the legislation, on the other hand, is of fundamental importance in a free and democratic society. It is aimed at avoiding harm, which Parliament has reasonably concluded will be caused directly or indirectly, to individuals, groups such as women and children, and consequently to society as a whole, by the distribution of these materials. It thus seeks to enhance respect for all members of society, and non-violence and equality in their relations with each other. I therefore conclude that the restriction on freedom of expression does not outweigh the importance of the legislative objective.

CONCLUSION

I conclude that while s. 163(8) infringes s. 2(b) of the *Charter*, freedom of expression, it constitutes a reasonable limit and is saved by virtue of the provisions of s. 1. The trial judge convicted the appellant only with respect to materials which contained scenes involving violence or cruelty intermingled with sexual activity or depicted lack of consent to sexual contact or otherwise could be said to dehumanize men or women in a sexual context. The majority of the Court of Appeal, on the other hand, convicted the appellant on all charges.

While the trial judge concluded that the material for which the accused were acquitted was not degrading or dehumanizing, he did so in the context of s. 1 of the *Charter*. In effect, he asked himself whether, if the material was proscribed by s. 163(8), that section would still be supportable under s. 1. In this context, he considered the government objectives of s. 163(8) and measured the material which was the subject of the charges against this objective. The findings at trial were therefore made in a legal framework that is different from that outlined in these reasons. Specifically, in considering whether the materials were degrading or dehumanizing, he did not address the issue of harm. Accordingly, it would be speculation to conclude that the same result would have been obtained if the definition of obscenity contained in these reasons had been applied. The test applied by the majority of the Court of Appeal also differed significantly from these reasons. I therefore cannot accept their conclusion that all of the materials are obscene. Accordingly, I would allow the appeal and direct a new trial on all charges. I note, however, that I am in agreement with Wright, J's conclusion that, in the case of material found to be obscene, there should only be one conviction imposed with respect to a single tape.

I would answer the constitutional questions as follows:

Question 1: Does s. 163 of the *Criminal Code* of Canada, RSC 1985, c. C-46, violate s. 2(b) of the *Canadian Charter of Rights and Freedoms*?
Answer: Yes.
Question 2: If s. 163 of the *Criminal Code* of Canada, RSC 1985, c. C-46, violates s. 2(b) of the *Canadian Charter of Rights and Freedoms*, can s. 163 of the

Criminal Code of Canada be demonstrably justified under s. 1 of the *Canadian Charter of Rights and Freedoms* as a reasonable limit prescribed by law? Answer: Yes.

READING QUESTION ON *BUTLER*

1 MacKinnon, as you will see below, approves of this decision. Is there a covert legal moralism of the kind Devlin advocates in Sopinka, J's reasoning?

Catharine MacKinnon
Only Words (1993)

MacKinnon defends the court's approach in *Butler* against the approach taken in *Hudnut*.

The pornography issue, far more than the political speech cases, has provided the setting for the definitive development of the absolutist approach to speech. First Amendment absolutism did not begin in obscenity cases, but it is in explaining why obscenity should be protected speech, and how it cannot be distinguished from art and literature, that much of the work of absolutism has been done, taking as its point of departure and arrival the position that whatever is expressive should be constitutionally protected. In pornography, absolutism found, gained, and consolidated its ground and hit its emotional nerve. It began as a dissenting position of intellectual extremists and ended by reducing the regulation of obscenity to window dressing on violence against women.

Concretely, observe that it was the prospect of losing access to pornography that impelled the social and legal development of absolutism as a bottom line for the First Amendment, as well as occasioned bursts of passionate eloquence on behalf of speech per se; if we can't have this, they seem to say, what can we have? During the same twenty-year period of struggle over obscenity standards, the Court was watching more and more pornography as its mass-marketed forms became more and more intrusive and aggressive. Observing this process from its end point of state protection of pornography, I have come to think that the main principle at work here is that, once pornography becomes pervasive, speech will be defined so that men can have their pornography. American obscenity law merely illustrates one adaptation of this principle: some men ineffectually prohibit it while others vaunt it openly as the standard for speech as such.

Consider the picture. The law against pornography was not designed to see harm to women in the first place. It is further weakened as pornography spreads, expanding into new markets (such as video and computers) and more legitimate forums and making abuse of women more and more invisible as abuse, as that abuse becomes more and more visible as sex. So the Court becomes increasingly *unable to tell* what is pornography and what is not, a failing it laments not as a consequence of the saturation of society by pornography, but as a specifically judicial failure, then finally as an impossibility of line-drawing. The stage is thus set for the transformation of pornography into political speech: the excluded and stigmatized "ideas" we love to hate. Obscured is the way this protects what pornography says and ignores what it does, or, alternatively, protects what pornography says as a means of protecting what it does. Thus can a law develop which prohibits restricting a film because it advocates adultery, but does not even notice a film that is made from a rape.

Nothing in the American law of obscenity is designed to perceive the rape, sexual abuse of children, battering, sexual harassment, prostitution, or sexual murder in pornography. This becomes insulting upon encountering obscenity law's search for harm and failure to find any. The law of child pornography, by contrast – based as it is on the assumption that children are harmed by having sex pictures made of them – applies a test developed in areas of speech other than the sexual: if the harm of speech outweighs its value, it can be restricted by properly targeted means. Given the history of the law of pornography of adult women, it is tempting to regard this as a miracle. Child pornography is not considered the speech of a sexually dissident minority, which it is, advocating "ideas" about children and sex, which it does. Perhaps the fact that boys were used in the film in the test case has something to do with it. The ability to see that child pornography is harmful has everything to do with a visceral sense of the inequality in power between children and adults, yet inequality is never mentioned.

Now, in this context of speech and equality concerns, consider again the judicial opinion of the law Andrea Dworkin and I wrote and Indianapolis passed. This law defines the documented harms pornography does as violations of equality rights and makes them actionable as practices of discrimination, of second-class citizenship. This ordinance allows anyone hurt through pornography to prove its role in their abuse, to recover for the deprivation of their civil rights, and to stop it from continuing. Judicially, this was rendered as censorship of ideas.

In *American Booksellers v Hudnut,* the Court of Appeals for the Seventh Circuit found that this law violated the First Amendment. It began by recognizing that the harm pornography does is real, conceding that the legislative finding of a causal link was judicially adequate: "... we accept the premises of this legislation. Depictions of subordination tend to perpetuate subordination. The subordinate status of women in turn leads to affront and lower pay at work, insult and injury at home, battery and rape on the streets. In the language of the legislature, "pornography is central in creating and maintaining sex as a basis of discrimination."[1] Writing for the panel, Judge Easterbrook got, off and on, that "subordination" is something pornography does, not something it just says, and that its active role had to be proven in each case brought under the ordinance. But he kept losing his mental bearings and referring to pornography as an "idea,"[2] finally concluding that the harm it does "demonstrates the power, of pornography as speech."[3] This is like saying that the more a libel destroys a reputation, the greater is its power as speech. To say that the more harm speech does, the more protected it is, is legally wrong, even in this country.

Implicitly applying the political speech model, Judge Easterbrook said that the law restricted the marketplace of ideas, the speech of outcast dissenters – referring presumably to those poor heads of organized crime families making ten billion dollars a year trafficking women. He said the law discriminated on the basis of point of view, establishing an approved view of what could be said and thought about women and sex. He failed to note at this point that the invalidated causes of action included coercion, force, and assault, rather a far cry from saying and thinking. He reminded us of *Sullivan,* whose most famous dictum is that to flourish, debate must be "uninhibited, robust, and wide-open."[4] Behind his First Amendment façade, women were being transformed into ideas, sexual traffic in whom was protected as if it were a discussion, the men uninhibited and robust, the women wide-open.

Judge Easterbrook did not say this law was not a sex discrimination law, but he gave the state interest it therefore served – opposition to sex inequality – no constitutional weight. He did this by treating it as if it were a group defamation law, holding that no amount of harm of discrimination can outweigh the speech interests of bigots, so long as they say something while doing it. Besides, if we restrict this, who knows where it will end. He is sure it will end with "Leda and the Swan." He did not suggest that bestiality statutes also had to go, along with obscenity's restrictions on depictions of sex between humans and animals. Both restrict a disapproved sexuality that, no doubt, contains an element of "mental intermediation."[5] Nothing in *Hudnut* explains why, if pornography is protected speech based on its mental elements, rape and sexual murder, which have mental elements, are not as well.

A dissent in a recent case invalidating sentence enhancements for crimes of bias could have been a dissent here: "The majority rationalizes their conclusion [that the statute violates the First Amendment] by insisting that this statute punishes bigoted thought. Not so. The statute does not impede or punish the right of persons to have bigoted thoughts or to express themselves in a bigoted fashion or otherwise, regarding the race, religion, or other status of a person. It does attempt to limit the effects of bigotry. What the statute does punish is acting upon those thoughts. It punishes the act of [discrimination] not the thought or expression of bigotry."[6]

Perhaps it is the nature of legal inequality that was missed by the Seventh Circuit. Discrimination has always been illegal because it is based on a prohibited motive: "an evil eye and an unequal hand,"[7] what the perpetrator is thinking while doing, what the acts mean. Racial classifications are thought illegal because they "supply a reason to infer antipathy."[8] A showing of discriminatory intent is required under the Fourteenth Amendment. Now we are told that this same motive, this same participation in a context of meaning, this same hatred and bigotry, these same purposes and thoughts, presumably this same intent, *protect* this same activity under the First Amendment. The courts cannot have it both ways, protecting discriminatory activity under the First Amendment on the same ground they make a requirement for its illegality under the Fourteenth. To put it another way, it is the "idea" of discrimination in the perpetrator's mind that courts have required be proven before the acts that effectuate it will be considered discriminatory. Surely, if acts that are otherwise legal, like hiring employees or renting rooms or admitting students, are made illegal under the Constitution by being based on race or sex because of what those who engage in this think about race or sex, acts that are otherwise *il*legal, like coercion, force, and assault, do not become constitutionally protected because they are done with the same thoughts in mind ...

That these tortured consequences result from the lack of an equality context in which to interpret expressive freedoms is clear from the fact that the same issues produced exactly the opposite results in Canada. Canada's new constitution, the *Charter of Rights and Freedoms*, includes an expansive equality guarantee and a serious entrenchment of freedom of expression. The Supreme Court of Canada's first move was to define equality in a meaningful way – one more substantive than formal, directed toward changing unequal social relations rather than monitoring their equal positioning before the law. The United States, by contrast, remains in the grip of what I affectionately call the stupid theory of equality. Inequality here is defined as distinction, as differentiation, indifferent to whether dominant or subordinated groups are hurt or helped. Canada, by contrast, following the argument of the Women's Legal Education and Action Fund (LEAF), repudiated this view in so many words, taking as its touchstone the treatment of historically disadvantaged groups and aiming to alter their status. The positive spin of the Canadian interpretation holds the law to promoting equality, projecting the law into a more equal future, rather than remaining rigidly neutral in ways that either reinforce existing social inequality or prohibit changing it, as the American constitutional perspective has increasingly done in recent years.

The first case to confront expressive guarantees with equality requirements under the new constitution came in the case of James Keegstra, an anti-Semite who taught Holocaust revisionism to schoolchildren in Alberta. Prosecuted and convicted under Canada's hate propaganda provision, Keegstra challenged the statute as a violation of the new freedom of expression guarantee. LEAF intervened to argue that the hate propaganda law promoted equality. We argued that group libel, most of it concededly expression, promotes the disadvantage of unequal groups; that group-based enmity, ill will, intolerance, and prejudice are the attitudinal engines of the exclusion, denigration, and subordination that make up and propel social inequality; that without bigotry, social systems of enforced separation, ghettoization, and apartheid would be unnecessary, impossible, and unthinkable; that stereotyping and stigmatization of historically disadvantaged groups through group hate propaganda shape their social image and reputation, which controls their access to opportunities more powerfully than their individual abilities ever do; and that it is impossible for an individual to receive equality of opportunity when surrounded by an atmosphere of group hate.

We argued that group defamation is a verbal form inequality takes, that just as white supremacy promotes inequality on the basis of race, color, and sometimes ethnic or national origin, anti-Semitism promotes the inequality of Jews on the basis of religion and ethnicity. We argued that group defamation in this sense is not a mere expression of opinion but a practice of discrimination in verbal form, a link in systemic discrimination that keeps target groups in subordinated positions through the promotion of terror, intolerance, degradation, segregation, exclusion, vilification, violence, and genocide. We said that the nature of the practice can be understood and its impact measured from the damage it causes, from immediate psychic wounding to consequent physical aggression. Where advocacy of genocide is included in group defamation, we said an equality approach to such speech would observe that to be liquidated because of the group you belong to is the ultimate inequality.

The Supreme Court of Canada agreed with this approach, a majority upholding the hate propaganda provision, substantially on equality grounds. The Court recognized the provision as a content restriction – content that had to be stopped because of its anti-egalitarian meaning and devastating consequences.[9]

Subsequently, the Winnipeg authorities arrested a whole pornography book store and prosecuted the owner, Donald Victor Butler, for obscenity. Butler was convicted but said the obscenity law was an unconstitutional restriction on his Charter-based right of freedom of expression. LEAF argued that if Canada's obscenity statute, substantially different from U.S. obscenity law in prohibiting "undue exploitation of sex, or sex and violence, cruelty, horror, or crime," was interpreted to institutionalize some people's views about women and sex over others, it would be unconstitutional. But if the community standards applied were interpreted to prohibit harm to women as harm to the community, it was constitutional because it promoted sex equality.

The Supreme Court of Canada essentially agreed, upholding the obscenity provision on sex equality grounds.[10] It said that harm to women – which the Court was careful to make "contextually sensitive" and found could include humiliation, degradation, and subordination – *was* harm to society as a whole. The evidence on the harm of pornography was sufficient for a law against it. Violent materials always present this risk of harm, the Court said; explicit sexual materials that are degrading or dehumanizing (but not violent) could also unduly exploit sex under the obscenity provision if the risk of harm was substantial. Harm in this context was defined as "predispos[ing] persons to act in an anti-social manner, as, for example, the physical or mental mistreatment of women by men, or, what is perhaps debatable, the reverse." The unanimous Court noted that "if true equality between male and female persons is to be achieved, we cannot ignore the threat to equality resulting from exposure to audiences of certain types of violent and degrading material." The result rested in part on *Keegstra* but also observed that the harms attendant to the production of pornography situated the problem of pornography differently, such that the appearance of consent by women in such materials could exacerbate its injury. Recognizing that education could be helpful in combating this harm, the Court held that that fact did not make the provision unconstitutional.[11]

Although the Canadians considered the U.S. experience on these issues closely in both cases, the striking absence of a U.S.-style political speech litany suggests that taking equality seriously precludes it, or makes it look like the excuse for enforcing inequality that it has become. The decision did not mention the marketplace of ideas. Maybe in Canada, people talk to each other, rather than buy and sell each other as ideas. In an equality context, it becomes obvious that those with the most power buy the most speech, and that the marketplace rewards the powerful, whose views then become established as truth. We were subjected to "Let [Truth] and falsehood grapple; who ever knew Truth put to the worse, in a free and open encounter." Milton had not been around for the success of the Big Lie technique, but this Court had.

Nor did the Canadian Court even consider the "slippery slope," a largely phony scruple impossible to sustain under a contextually sensitive equality rule. With inequality, the problem is not where intervention will end, but when it will ever begin. Equality is the law; if the slippery slope worked, the ineluctable logic of principle would have slid us into equality by now. Also, perhaps, because the Canadian law of equality is moored in the world, and knows the difference between disadvantaged groups and advantaged ones, it is less worried about the misfiring of restrictions against the powerless and more concerned about having nothing to fire against abuses of power by the powerful.

Fundamentally, the Supreme Court of Canada recognized the reality of inequality in the issues before it: this was not big bad state power jumping on poor powerless individual citizen, but a law passed to stand behind a comparatively powerless group in its social fight for equality against socially powerful and exploitative groups. This positioning of forces – which makes the hate propaganda prohibition and the obscenity law of Canada (properly interpreted) into equality laws, although neither was called such by Parliament – made the invocation of a tradition designed to keep government off the backs of people totally inappropriate. The Court also did not say that Parliament had to limit its efforts to stop the harm of inequality by talking to it. *What* it did was make more space for the unequal to find voice.

Nor did the Canadians intone, with Brandeis and nearly every American court that has ruled on a seriously contested speech issue since, that "[f]ear of serious injury cannot alone justify suppression of free speech ... Men feared witches and burnt women."[12] I have never understood this argument, other than as a way of saying that zealots misidentify the causes of their woes and hurt the wrong people. What has to be added to fear of serious injury to justify doing something about the speech that causes it? *Proof* of serious injury? If we can't restrict it then, when can we? Isn't fear of serious injury the concern behind restricting publication of the dates on which troop ships sail? Is it mere "fear" of injury to children that supports the law against the use of children to make pornography? If that isn't enough, why isn't proof of injury required? "Men feared witches and burnt women." Where is the speech here? Promoting the fear? Nobody tried to suppress tracts against witches. If somebody had, would some women not have been burnt? Or was it the witches' writings? Did they write? So burning their writings is part of the witch-hunt aspect of the fear? The women who are being burned as witches these days are the women in the pornography, and their burning is sex and entertainment and protected as speech. Those who are hunted down, stigmatized, excluded, and unpublished are the women who oppose their burning.

Neither Canadian decision reduces the harm of hate propaganda or pornography to its "offensiveness." When you hear the women next door screaming as she is bounced off the walls by a man she lives with, are you "offended"? Hate speech and pornography do the same thing: enact the abuse. Women's reactions to the presentation of other women being sexually abused in pornography, and the reactions of Jews living in Skokie to having Nazis march through their town, are routinely trivialized in the United States as "being offended." The position of those with less power is equated with the position of those with more power, as if sexual epithets against straight white men were equivalent to sexual epithets against women, as if breaking the window of a Jewish-owned business in the world after Kristallnacht were just so much breaking glass.

In the cases both of pornography and of the Nazi march in Skokie, it is striking how the so-called speech reenacts the original experience of the abuse, and how its defense as speech does as well. It is not only that both groups, through the so-called speech, are forcibly subjected to the spectacle of their abuse, legally legitimized. Both have their response to it trivialized as "being offended," that response then used to support its speech value, hence its legal protection. Both are also told that what they can do about it is avert their eyes, lock their doors, stay home, stay silent, and hope the assault, and the animus it makes tangible, end when the film or the march ends. This is exactly what perpetrators of rape and child sexual abuse tell their victims and what the Jews in Germany were told by the Nazis (and the rest of the world) in the 1930s. Accept the freedom of your abusers. This best protects you in the end. Let it happen. You are not really being hurt. When sexually abused women are told to let the system work and tolerate the pornography, this is what they are being told. The Jews in Germany, and the Jews in Skokie, were told to let the system work. At least this time around, the Jews of Canada were not, nor were sexually abused women.

The final absence in the Canadian decisions, perhaps the most startling, is the failure to mention any equivalent to the notion that, under the First Amendment, there is no such thing as a false idea. Perhaps under equality law, in some sense there is. When equality is recognized as a constitutional value and mandate, the idea that some people are inferior to others on the basis of group membership is authoritatively rejected as the basis for public policy. This does not mean that ideas to the contrary cannot be debated or expressed. It should mean, however, that social inferiority cannot be imposed through any means, including expressive ones.

Because society is made of language, distinguishing talk about inferiority from verbal imposition of inferiority may be complicated at the edges, but it is clear enough at the center with sexual and racial harassment, pornography, and hate propaganda. At the very least, when equality is taken seriously in expressive settings, such practices are not constitutionally insulated from regulation on the ground that the ideas they express cannot be regarded as false. Attempts to address them would not be prohibited – as they were in rejecting the Indianapolis pornography ordinance, for example – on the ground that, in taking a position in favor of equality, such attempts assume that the idea of human equality is true. The legal equality guarantee has already decided that. There is no requirement that the state remain neutral as between equality and inequality – quite the contrary. Equality is a "compelling state interest" that can already outweigh First Amendment rights in certain settings. In other words, expressive means of practicing inequality can be prohibited.

This is not the place to spell out in detail all the policy implications of such a view. Suffice it to say that those who wish to keep materials that promote inequality from being imposed on students – such as academic books purporting to document women's biological inferiority to men, or arguing that slavery of Africans should return, or that Fourteenth Amendment equality should be repealed, or that reports of rape are routinely fabricated – especially without critical commentary, should not be legally precluded from trying on the grounds that the ideas contained in them cannot be assumed false. No teacher should be forced to teach falsehoods as if they must be considered provisionally true, just because bigots who have managed to get published have made their lies part of a debate. Teachers who wish to teach such materials should be prepared to explain what they are doing to avoid creating a hostile learning environment and to provide all students the equal benefit of an education. Wherever equality is mandated, racial and sexual epithets, vilification, and abuse should be able to be prohibited, unprotected by the First Amendment. The current legal distinction between screaming "go kill that nigger" and advocating the view that African-Americans should be eliminated from parts of the United States needs to be seriously reconsidered, if real equality is ever to be achieved. So, too, the current line separating pornography from hate speech and what is done to make pornography from the materials themselves.

Pornography, under current conditions, *is* largely its own context. Many believe that in settings that encourage critical distance, its showing does not damage women as much as it sensitizes viewers to the damage it does to women. My experience, as well as all the information available, makes me think that it is naive to believe that anything other words can do is as powerful as what pornography itself does. At the very least, pornography should never be imposed on a viewer who does not choose – then and there, without pressure of any kind – to be exposed to it. Tom Emerson said a long time ago that imposing what he called "erotic material" on individuals against their will is a form of action that "has all the characteristics of a physical assault."[13] Equality on campuses, in workplaces, everywhere, would be promoted if such assaults were actionable. Why any women should have to attend school in a setting stacked against her equality by the showing of pornography – especially when authoritatively permitted by those who are legally obligated to take her equality seriously – is a question that those who support its showing should have to answer. The answer is not that she should have to wait for the resulting abuse or leave.

Where is all this leading? To a new model for freedom of expression in which the free speech position no longer supports social dominance, as it does now; in which free speech does not most readily protect the activities of Nazis, Klansmen, and pornographers, while doing nothing for their victims, as it does now; in which defending free speech is not speaking on behalf of a large pile of money in the hands of a small group of people, as it is now. In this new model, principle will be defined in terms of specific experiences, the particularity of history, substantively rather than abstractly. It will notice who is being hurt and never forget who they are. The state will have as great a role in providing relief from injury to equality through speech and in giving equal access to speech as it now has in disciplining its power to intervene in that speech that manages to get expressed.

In a society in which equality is a fact, not merely a word, words of racial or sexual assault and humiliation will be nonsense syllables. Sex between people and things, human beings and pieces of paper, real men and unreal women, will be a turn-off. Artifacts of these abuses will reside in a glass case next to the dinosaur skeletons in the Smithsonian. When this day comes, silence will be neither an act of power, as it is now for those who hide behind it, nor an experience of imposed powerlessness, as it is now for those who are submerged in it, but a context of repose into which thought can expand, an invitation that gives speech its shape, an opening to a new conversation.

NOTES

1 Hudnut, 771 F.2d at 328–9.
2 "... above all else, the First Amendment means that government has no power to restrict expression because of its message [or] ideas ..." Ibid. at 328.
3 Hudnut, 771 F.2d at 329.
4 Sullivan, 376 US at 270.

5 Hudnut, 771 F.2d at 329.

6 *State v Mitchell*, 485 NW2d at 820 (Bablitch, J, dissenting).

7 *Yick Wo v Hopkins*, 118 US 356 (1886).

8 *Personnel Administrator v Feeney*, 442 US 256 at 272 (1979); *Vance v Bradley*, 440 US 93 at 97 (1979).

9 *R. v Keegstra*, [1991] 2 WWR 1 (1990) (Can.).

10 *Butler v Regina* [1992] 2 WWR 577 (Can.).

11 Ibid. at 594-7, 601, 609.

12 *Whitney v California*, 274 US 357 at 376 (1927) (Brandeis, J, concurring).

13 Thomas I. Emerson, *The System of Freedom of Expression* 496 (1970): "A communication of this [erotic] nature, imposed upon a person contrary to his wishes, has all the characteristics of a physical assault" and "can therefore realistically be classified as action." A comparison with his preliminary formulation in *Toward a General Theory of the First Amendment* 91 (1963) suggests that his view on this subject became stronger by his 1970 revisiting of the issue.

READING QUESTION ON MACKINNON

1   What does MacKinnon mean by "silencing"? What view of freedom of expression does her argument rest on? What view of equality does her argument rest on, and what is the relation between equality and freedom of expression on her theory?

Ronald Dworkin, "Two Concepts of Liberty" (1991)

Dworkin charges that MacKinnon's approach is undemocratic.

When Isaiah Berlin delivered his famous Inaugural Lecture as Chichele Professor of Social and Political Theory at Oxford, in 1958, he felt it necessary to acknowledge that politics did not attract the professional attention of most serious philosophers in Britain and America. They thought philosophy had no place in politics and *vice versa*; that political philosophy could be nothing more than a parade of the theorist's own preferences and allegiances with no supporting argument of any rigour or respectability. That gloomy picture is unrecognisable now. Political philosophy thrives as a mature industry; it dominates many distinguished philosophy departments and attracts a large share of the best graduate students almost everywhere.

Berlin's lecture, "Two Concepts of Liberty," played an important and distinctive role in this renaissance. It provoked immediate, continuing, heated and mainly illuminating controversy. It became, almost at once, a staple of graduate and undergraduate reading lists, as it still is. Its scope and erudition, its historical sweep and evident contemporary force, its sheer interest, made political ideas suddenly seem exciting and fun. Its main polemical message – that it is fatally dangerous for philosophers to ignore either the complexity or the power of those ideas – was both compelling and overdue. But chiefly, or so I think, its importance lay in the force of its central argument. For though Berlin began by conceding to the disdaining philosophers that political philosophy could not match logic or the philosophy of language as a theatre for "radical discoveries" in which "talent for minute analyses is likely to be rewarded," he continued by analysing subtle distinctions that, as it happens, are even more important now, in the Western democracies at least, than when he first called our attention to them.

I must try to describe two central features of his argument, though in this short note I shall have to leave out much that is important to them. The first is the celebrated distinction described in the lecture's title: between two (closely allied) senses of liberty. Negative liberty (as Berlin came later to restate it) means not being obstructed by others in doing whatever one might wish to do. We count some negative liberties – like the freedom to speak our mind without censorship – as very important, and others – like driving at very fast speeds – as trivial. But they are both instances of negative freedom, and though a state may be justified in imposing speed limits, for example, on grounds of safety and convenience, that is nevertheless an instance of restricting negative liberty. Positive liberty, on the other hand, is the power to control or participate in public decisions, including the decision how far to curtail negative liberty. In an ideal democracy, whatever that is, the people govern themselves. Each is master to the same degree, and positive liberty is secured for all.

In the Inaugural Lecture Berlin described the historical corruption of the idea of positive liberty, a corruption that began in the idea that someone's true liberty lies in control by his rational self rather than his empirical self, that is, in control that aims at securing goals other than those the person himself recognises. Freedom, on that conception, is possible only when people are governed, ruthlessly if necessary, by rulers who know their true, metaphysical, will. Only then are people truly free, albeit against their will. That deeply confused and dangerous, but nevertheless potent, chain of argument had in many parts of the world tuned positive liberty into the most terrible tyranny. Of course, Berlin did not mean, by calling attention to this corruption of positive liberty, that negative liberty was an unalloyed blessing, and should be protected in all its forms in all circumstances at all costs. He said, later, that on the contrary the vices of excessive and indiscriminate negative liberty were so evident, particularly in the form of savage economic inequality, that he had not thought it necessary much to describe them.

The second feature of Berlin's argument I have in mind is a theme repeated throughout his writing on political topics. He insists on the complexity of political value, and the fallacy of supposing that all the political virtues that are attractive in themselves can be realised in a single political structure. The ancient Platonic ideal, of some master accommodation of all attractive virtues and goals, combined in institutions satisfying each in the right proportion and sacrificing none, is in Berlin's view, for all its imaginative power and historical influence, only a seductive myth.

One freedom may abort another; [he said, summing up later] one freedom may obstruct or fail to create conditions which make other freedoms, or a larger degree of freedom, or freedom for more persons, possible; positive and negative freedom may collide; the freedom of the individual or the group may not be fully compatible with a full degree of participation in a common life, with its demands for cooperation, solidarity, fraternity. But beyond all these there is an acuter issue: the paramount need to satisfy the claims of other, no less ultimate, values: justice, happiness, love, the realisation of capacities to create new things and experiences and ideas, the discovery of the truth. Nothing is gained by identifying freedom proper, in either of its senses, with these values, or with the conditions of freedom, or by confounding types of freedom with one another.[1]

Berlin's warnings about conflating positive and negative liberty, and liberty itself with other values, seemed to students of political philosophy in the great Western democracies in the 1950s to provide important lessons about authoritarian regimes in other times and places. Though cherished liberties were very much under attack in both American and Britain in that decade, the attack was not grounded in or defended through either form of confusion. The enemies of negative liberty were powerful, but they were also crude and undisguised. Joseph McCarthy and his allies did not rely on a Kantian or Hegelian or Marxist concept of metaphysical selves to justify censorship or blacklists. They distinguished liberty not from itself, but from security; they claimed that too much free speech made us vulnerable to spies and intellectual saboteurs and ultimately to conquest. In both Britain and America, in spite of limited reforms, the state still sought to enforce conventional sexual morality about pornography, contraception, prostitution and homosexuality. Conservatives who defended these invasions of negative liberty appealed not to some higher or different sense of freedom, however, but to values that were plainly distinct from and in conflict with freedom: religion, true morality, and traditional and proper family values. The wars over liberty were fought, or so it seemed, by clearly divided armies. Liberals were for liberty, except for the negative liberty of economic entrepreneurs. Conservatives were for that liberty, but against other forms when these collided with security or their view of decency and morality.

But now the political maps have radically changed and some forms of negative liberty have acquired new opponents. Both in America and Britain, though in different ways, racial and gender conflicts have transformed old alliances and divisions. Speech that expresses racial hatred, or a degrading attitude toward women, or that threatens environmental destruction has come to seem intolerable to many people whose convictions are otherwise traditionally liberal. It is hardly surprising that they should try to reduce the conflict between their old liberal ideals and their new acceptance of censorship by some redefinition of what liberty, properly understood, really is. It is hardly surprising, but the result is dangerous confusion, and Berlin's warnings, framed with different problems in minds, are directly in point.

I shall try to illustrate that point with a single example: a lawsuit arising out of the attempt by certain feminist groups in America to outlaw what they consider a particularly objectionable from of pornography. I select this example not because pornography is more important or dangerous or objectionable than racist invective or other highly distasteful kinds of speech, but because the debate over pornography has been the subject of the fullest and most comprehensive scholarly discussion.

Through the efforts of Catharine MacKinnon and other prominent feminists, Indianapolis in Indiana enacted an anti-pornography ordinance. The ordinance defined pornography as "the graphic sexually explicit subordination of women, whether in pictures or words ...," and it specified, as among pornographic materials falling within that definition, those that present women as enjoying pain or humiliation or rape, or as degraded or tortured or filthy, bruised or bleeding, or in postures of servility or submission or display. It included no exception for literary or artistic value, and opponents claimed that applied literally it would outlaw James Joyce's *Ulysses*, John Cleland's *Memoirs*, various works of D.H. Lawrence, and even Yeat's *Leda and the Swan*. But the groups who sponsored the ordinance were anxious to establish that their objection was not to obscenity or indecency, as such, but to the consequences of a particular kind of pornography, and they presumably thought that an exception for artistic value would undermine that claim.

Publishers and members of the public who claimed a desire to read the banned material arranged a prompt constitutional challenge. The federal district court held that the ordinance was unconstitutional because it violated the First Amendment to the United States Constitution, which guarantees the negative liberty of free speech.[2] The Circuit Court for the Seventh Circuit upheld the district court's decision,[3] and the Supreme Court of the United States declined to review that holding. The Circuit Court's decision, in an opinion by Judge Easterbrook, noticed that the ordinance did not outlaw obscene or indecent material generally but only material reflecting the opinion that women are submissive, or enjoy being dominated, or should be treated as if they did. Easterbrook said that the central point of the First Amendment was exactly to protect speech from content-based regulation of that sort. Censorship may on some occasions be permitted if it aims to prohibit directly dangerous speech – crying fire in a crowded theatre or inciting a crowd to violence, for example – or speech particularly and unnecessarily inconvenient – broadcasting from sound trucks patrolling residential streets at night, for instance. But nothing must be censored because the message it seeks to deliver is a bad one, because it expresses ideas that should not be heard at all.

It is by no means universally agreed that censorship should never be based on content. The British Race Relations Act, for example, forbids speech of racial hatred, not only when it is likely to lead to violence, but generally, on the grounds that members of minority races should be protected from racial insults. In America, however, it is a fixed principle of constitutional law that regulation is unconstitutional unless some compelling necessity, not just official or majority disapproval of the message, requires it. Pornography is often grotesquely offensive; it is insulting, not only to women but to men as well. But we cannot consider that a sufficient reason for banning it without destroying the principle that the speech we hate is as much entitled to protection as any other. The essence of negative liberty is freedom to offend, and that applies to the tawdry as well as the heroic.

Lawyers who defend the Indianapolis ordinance argue that society does have a further justification for outlawing pornography: that it causes great harm as well as offence to women. But their arguments mix together claims about different types of kinds of harm, and it is necessary to distinguish these. They argue, first, that some forms of pornography significantly increase the danger that women will be raped or physically assaulted. If that were true, and the danger were clear and present, then it would indeed justify censorship of those forms, unless less stringent methods of control, such as restricting pornographer's audience, would be feasible, appropriate and effective. In fact, however, though there is some evidence that exposure to pornography weakens people's critical attitudes toward sexual violence, there is no persuasive evidence that it causes more actual incidents of assault. The Seventh Circuit cited a variety of studies (including that of the Williams Commission in Britain in 1979) all of which concluded, the Court said, "that it is not possible to demonstrate a direct link between obscenity and rape ..."[4] A recent and guarded report on a year's research in Britain said: "The evidence does not point to pornography as a cause of deviant sexual orientation in offenders. Rather, it seems to be used as part of that deviant sexual orientation."[5]

Some feminist groups argue, however, that pornography causes not just physical violence but a more general and endemic subordination of women. In that way, they say, pornography makes for inequality. But even if it could be shown, as a matter of causal connection, that pornography is in part responsible for the economic structure in which few women attain top jobs or equal pay for the same work, that would not justify censorship under the Constitution. It would plainly be unconstitutional to ban speech directly *advocating* that women occupy inferior roles, or none at all, in commerce and the professions, even if that speech fell on willing male ears and achieved its goals. So it cannot be a reason for banning pornography that it contributes to an unequal economic or social structure, even if we think that it does.

But the most imaginative feminist literature for censorship makes a further and different argument: that negative liberty for pornographers conflicts not just with equality but with positive liberty as well, because pornography leads to women's *political* as well as economic or social subordination. Of course pornography does not take the vote from women, or somehow make their votes count less. But it produces a climate, according to this argument, in which women cannot have genuine political power or authority because they are perceived and understood unauthentically, made over by male fantasy into people very different, and of much less consequence, than the people they really are. Consider, for example, these remarks from the work of the principal sponsor of the Indianapolis ordinance. "[Pornography] institutionalizes the sexuality of male supremacy, fusing the eroticization of dominance and submission with the social construction of male and female ... Men treat women as who they see women as being. Pornography constructs who that is. Men's power over women means that the way men see women defines who women can be."

Pornography, on this view, denies the positive liberty of women; it denies them the right to be their own masters by recreating them, for politics and society, in the shapes of male fantasy. That is a powerful argument, even in constitutional terms, because it asserts a conflict not just between liberty and equality but within liberty itself, that is, a conflict that cannot be resolved simply on the ground that liberty must be sovereign. What shall we make of the argument understood that way? We must notice, first, that it remains a causal argument. It claims not that pornography is a consequence or symptom or symbol of how the identify of women has been reconstructed by men, but an important cause or vehicle of that reconstruction.

That seems strikingly implausible. Sadistic pornography is revolting, but it is not in any general circulation, except for its milder, soft-pom manifestations. It seems unlikely that it has remotely the influence over how women's sexuality or character or talents are conceived by men, and indeed by women, that commercial advertising and soap operas have. Television and other parts of popular culture use sex to sell everything, and they show women as experts in domestic detail and unreasoned intuition and nothing else. The images they create are subtle and ubiquitous, and it would not be surprising to learn, through whatever research might establish this, that they do indeed do great damage to the way women are understood and allowed to be influential in politics. Sadistic pornography, though much more offensive and disturbing, is greatly overshadowed by these dismal cultural influences as a causal force.

Judge Easterbrook's opinion for the Seventh Circuit assumed *arguendo*, however, that pornography did have the consequences the defenders of the ordinance claimed. He said that nevertheless the argument failed because the point of free speech is precisely to allow ideas to have whatever consequences follows from their dissemination, including undesirable consequences for positive liberty. "Under the First Amendment," he said, "the government must leave to the people the evaluation of ideas. Bald or subtle, an idea is as powerful as the audience allows it to be ... [The assumed result] simply demonstrates the power of pornography as speech. All of these unhappy effects depend on mental intermediation."

That is right as a matter of American constitutional law. The Ku Klux Klan and the American Nazi Party are allowed to propagate their ideas in America, and the British Race Relations Act, so far as it forbids abstract speech of racial hatred, would be unconstitutional there. But does the American attitude represent the kind of Platonic absolutism Berlin warned against? No, because there is an important difference between the idea he thinks absurd, that all ideals attractive in themselves can be perfectly reconciled within a single utopian political order, and the different idea he thought essential, that we must, as individuals and nations, choose among possible combinations of ideals a coherent, even though inevitably and regrettably limited, set of these to define our own individual or national way of life. Freedom of speech, conceived and protected as a fundamental negative liberty, is the core of the choice modern democracies have made, a choice we must now honour in finding our own ways to combat the shaming inequalities women still suffer.

This reply depends, however, on seeing the alleged conflict within liberty as a conflict between the negative and positive senses of that virtue. We must consider yet another argument which, if successful, could not be met in the same way, because it claims that pornography presents a conflict within the negative liberty of speech itself. Berlin said that the character, at least, of negative liberty was reasonably clear, that although excessive claims of negative liberty were dangerous, they could at least always be seen for what they were. But the argument I have in mind, which has been offered, among others, by Frank Michelman of the Harvard Law School, expands the idea of the negative liberty in an unanticipated way. He argues that some speech, including pornography, may be itself "silencing," so that its effect is to prevent other people from exercising their negative freedom to speak.

Of course it is fully recognised in First Amendment jurisprudence that some speech is silencing in that way. Government must indeed balance negative liberties when it prevents heckling or other demonstrative speech designed to stop others from speaking or being heard. But Michelman has something different in mind. He says that a woman's speech may be silenced not just by noise intended to drown her out but also by argument and image that change her audience's perceptions of her character, needs, desires and standing, and also, perhaps, change her own sense of who she is and what she wants. Speech with that consequence silences her, Michelman supposes, by making it impossible for her effectively to contribute to the process Judge Easterbrook said the First Amendment protected, the process through which ideas battle for the public's favour. "[I]t is a highly plausible claim," Michelman writes, "[that] pornography [is] a cause of women's subordination and silencing ... It is a fair and obvious question why our society's openness to challenge does not need protection against repressive private as well as public action."[6]

He argues that if our commitment to negative freedom of speech is consequentialist – if we want free speech in order to have a society in which no idea is barred from entry – then we must censor some ideas in order to make entry possible for other ones. He protests that the distinction American constitutional law makes, between the suppression of ideas by the effect of public criminal law and by the consequences of private speech, is arbitrary, and that a sound concern for openness would be equally concerned about both forms of control. But the distinction the law makes is not between public and private power, as such, but between negative liberty and other virtues, including positive liberty. It would indeed be contradictory for a constitution to prohibit official censorship but also to protect the right of private citizens physically to prevent other citizens from publishing or broadcasting specified ideas. That would allow private citizens to violate the negative liberty of other citizens by preventing them from saying what they wish. But there is no contradiction in insisting that every idea must be allowed to be heard, even those whose consequence is that other ideas will be misunderstood, or given little consideration, or even not be spoken at all because those who might speak them are not in control of their own public identifies and therefore cannot be understood as they wish to be. These are very bad consequences, and they must be resisted by whatever means our constitution permits. But they are not the same thing as depriving others of their negative liberty to speak, and the distinction, as Berlin insisted, is very far from arbitrary or inconsequential.

It is of course understandable why Michelman and others should want to expand the idea of negative liberty in the way they try to do. Only by characterising certain ideas as themselves "silencing" ideas, only by supposing that censoring pornography is the same thing as stopping people from drowning out other speakers, can they hope to justify censorship within the constitutional scheme that assigns a pre-eminent place to free speech. But the assimilation is nevertheless a confusion, exactly the kind of confusion Berlin warned against in his original lecture, because it obscures the true political choice that must be made. I return to Berlin's lecture, which put the point with that striking combination of clarity and sweep I have been celebrating. "I should be guilt-stricken, and rightly so, if I were not, in some circumstances, ready to make [some] sacrifice [of freedom]. But a sacrifice is not an increase in what is being sacrificed, namely freedom, however great the moral need or the compensation for it. Everything is what it is: liberty is liberty, not equality or fairness or justice or culture, or human happiness or a quiet conscience."

NOTES

1 Berlin, *Four Essays on Liberty*, Oxford Paperbacks, 1969, p. lvi.
2 *American Booksellers Association, Inc et al. v William Hudnut, III, Mayor, City of Indianapolis et al.*, 598 F. Supp. 1316 (S.D. Ind. 1984).
3 771 F2d 323 (US Court Appeals, Seventh Circuit).
4 That court, in a confused passage, said that it nevertheless accepted "the premises of this legislation, which included the claims about a causal connection with sexual violence. But it seemed to mean that it was accepting the rather different causal claim considered in the next paragraph, about subordination. In any case, it said that it accepted those premises only arguendo, since it thought it had no authority to reject decisions of Indianapolis based on its interpretation of empirical evidence.
5 See *Daily Telegraph*, December 23, 1990.
6 Frank Michelman, "Conceptions of Democracy in American Constitutional Argument: The Case of Pornography Regulation," 57 *Tennessee Law Review* 291, 1989, pp. 303–4.

READING QUESTIONS ON DWORKIN

1 Should the law in a society marked by pervasive inequalities be the same as it would in a society of equals? Can you think of any exceptions to this claim?
2 Can MacKinnon's argument be restated so that it passes the test for an acceptable moral argument that Dworkin outlines in his response to Devlin?
3 Does the view of politics and law which Dworkin articulates here strengthen the arguments Hutchinson and Monahan make against liberalism and the rule of law?
4 Does Dworkin tacitly rely on a positivistic conception of law in this essay?

Brenda Cossman
Bad Attitude/s on Trial: Pornography, Feminism, and the **Butler** *Decision* **(1997)**

Cossman argues that *Butler* serves a conservative agenda, something revealed by a careful analysis of its text. Her argument, though, is that it could not help but serve such an agenda because of the distinction between good and bad sex which it presupposes.

CHAPTER 3: FEMINIST FASHION OR MORALITY IN DRAG? THE SEXUAL SUBTEXT OF THE *BUTLER* DECISION

In *R. v Butler* (1992), the Supreme Court of Canada upheld the constitutionality of the criminal prohibition of obscenity under section 163 of the *Criminal Code* of Canada (RSC 1985, c. c–46). The Court held that although this provision violated free speech as guaranteed by section 2 of the *Canadian Charter of Rights and Freedoms*, it was a reasonable limit under section 1. In so doing, the Supreme Court tries to tell us that the obscenity laws are no longer concerned with corrupting morals, or with courts as the guardians of public morality. Rather, in the Court's view, the obscenity law is justifiable in its objective of preventing harm, particularly harm towards women, and in promoting the equality and dignity of women.

This has become the official story of *Butler* – it is the story that the Court tries to tell within the text of the decision, and it is the story that feminists who support the obscenity provisions have told before, during, and after the decision (McAllister 1992–3; Busby 1994; Landsberg 1992). But there is another story to be told about the *Butler* decision. *Butler* is also a decision about sex: it is a decision about the role and status of sex, sexuality, and the representation of sexual practices in our society. When we scratch beneath the surface, we find a conservative sexual morality that sees sex as bad, physical, shameful, dangerous, base, guilty until proved innocent, and redeemable only if it transcends its base nature. It is a sexual subtext informed by the basic assumptions that have traditionally informed the dominant ideological discourses of sexuality in Western society: sexual negativity <sex is bad>, sexual essentialism <sex is biological>, sexual monism <there is one way to have sex>, and sexual hierarchy <some sex is better than others>.

In this chapter, I will deconstruct the *Butler* decision in an effort to reveal this sexual subtext. A textual analysis of the decision will reveal the extent to which the discourse of the decision is informed by the same conservative sexual morality that has traditionally framed obscenity law in Canada, with its problematic assumptions about the nature of sex and sexuality. The chapter will argue that, contrary to the claims of anti-pornography feminists, the most significant change in the law represented by the *Butler* decision is one of language alone. Now the law is dressed up in feminist discourse, that of preventing harm towards women, of equality and dignity. The test for obscenity as reviewed and synthesized by the Supreme Court of Canada in *Butler* simply provides a new discourse for what is in fact a very old objective – the legal regulation of sexual morality, and the legal repression of sexual representation. The *Butler* decision and its discourse of harm against women is really just sexual morality in drag.

Further, I will argue that this sexual subtext is essential in understanding how *Butler* has set the discursive stage for the subsequent judicial applications of the *Butler* test, in which gay and lesbian sexual representations have been held to be obscene. The first two obscenity cases to have reached the courts since *Butler* were both against Glad Day Bookshop – a gay and lesbian bookstore in Toronto. While prosecutions have since been brought against heterosexual pornography as well, the particular way in which this law has been used against gay and lesbian sexual representations should alert us to this discursive drag. Yet, feminists who support the *Butler* decision continue to argue that this targeting of gay and lesbian sexual representations constitutes a misapplication of the *Butler* test (Busby 1994, 185). Contrary to these arguments, I will argue that the underlying conservative sexual morality of *Butler* has set the discursive framework for this targeting. The sexual subtext and its good sex / bad sex distinction is particularly dangerous in the context of gay and lesbian sexual representations. The heterosexist assumptions informing this sexual morality operate to locate these representations on the bad side of the dichotomy, and thus pave the road for a particular judicial determination of obscenity.

The Butler *Decision: Sex and the Supreme Court*

The majority decision of the Supreme Court of Canada in the *Butler* case was written by Mr. Justice Sopinka.[1] The decision is divided into two parts. In the first part, the court reviews and clarifies the law of obscenity. In the second part, the court then examines whether this law of obscenity is constitutional, that is, whether it violates the right to freedom of expression guarantees of the *Charter*, and if so, whether it is a reasonable limit on that right. In reviewing the text of both parts of the decision, this section will challenge the dominant representation of the *Butler* decision, by illustrating the sexual subtext of the decision – a sexual subtext informed by the same assumptions of sexual morality that prevailed before the *Butler* decision.

The Law of Obscenity

In the first part of the decision, the Court reviews and clarifies the law of obscenity as set out in s. 163 of the Criminal Code. Obscenity is defined in subsection 163(8) as "any publication a dominant characteristic of which is the undue exploitation of sex, or of sex and any one or more of the following subjects, namely, crime, horror, cruelty and violence." The question of what constitutes the "undue exploitation of sex" has been the subject of considerable judicial analysis. Sopinka J thus begins by reviewing the various tests that have emerged to determine whether the exploitation of sex is undue.

Community Standards. The first and most important test developed by the courts to determine when the exploitation of sex is undue is the community standards of tolerance. The Court begins by quoting a passage from *R. v Close* (1948), which was first adopted by the Supreme Court in *R. v Brodie* (1962) and has been cited by the Supreme Court of Canada in its obscenity case law ever since: "There does exist in any community at all times – however the standard may vary from time to time – a general instinctive sense of what is decent and what is indecent, of what is clean and what is dirty" (as cited in *Butler* 1992, 464). Within this passage, which has set the discursive framework within which the Supreme Court of Canada has repeatedly interpreted the undue exploitation of sex, obscenity is cast in the language of indecency and dirt. Not all sexual representations are obscene; only indecent or dirty sexual representations are obscene.[2] Within this framework, there is a distinction made between good and bad sex – a binary opposition between clean and dirty, decent and indecent. Bad sex is dirty sex. There is no positive theory of sexual expression that tells us what makes good sex. The best the courts have been able to do is establish a test of some generality to defer to community standards – that is, to allow "the community" to draw the lines between clean and dirty sex.

Sopinka J further observed that this community standard has been found to be a national standard; that expert evidence is not required to establish the community standard, and that the community standard may change over time (*Butler* 1992, 465). Finally, the community-standards test is not based on taste, but tolerance, and the measure of tolerance is not what Canadians would themselves tolerate, but "what they would tolerate other Canadians being exposed to" (ibid., 465–6). It attempts to escape the subjective nature of individual taste by directing attention away from "what Canadians think is right for themselves" to the ostensibly broader standard of "what Canadians would not abide other Canadians seeing because it would be beyond the contemporary Canadian standard of tolerance to allow them to see it[3] (*Towne Cinema* 1985, as cited in *Butler* 1992, 465–6).

According to this test, individual Canadians may have different tastes, but we all subscribe to the same standard of tolerance. Although this standard of tolerance may change over time, at any one moment it is monolithic. In other words, at any moment in time, there is in the eyes of all Canadians a clear and singular distinction between what we will tolerate others seeing and what we will not – between what is clean (good sex) and what is dirty (bad sex) – even though this may not correspond to each of our own personal tastes of good sex and bad sex. And the obviousness of this distinction is underscored by the fact that no expert evidence is required to establish it. The line between good sex and bad sex is an "instinctive" matter – a matter of common sense for a judge who will, presumably, simply recognize it when he sees it.

Degradation and Dehumanization. The Court examines a second and more recent test for determining whether the exploitation of sex is undue. This test emerged in the 1980s, as anti-pornography feminism began to shape the discourse within which pornography was debated, and was first endorsed by the Supreme Court of Canada in *R. v Towne Cinema* (*Towne Cinema* 1985, 202–3). According to this test, materials that "may be said to exploit sex in a degrading or dehumanizing manner will ... fail the community standards test" (*Butler* 1992, 466). In elaborating on the meaning of this test, the Court tells us that it means materials that harm women: "Among other things, degrading or dehumanizing materials place women (and sometimes men) in positions of subordination, servile submission or humiliation. They run against the principles of equality and dignity" (ibid., 466). According to this approach, material that is degrading and dehumanizing fails the community-standards test, "not because it offends morals," but because these materials are "perceived by public opinion to be harmful to society, particularly to women" (ibid., 467). The Court notes that although "this perception is not susceptible to exact proof," there is nevertheless a body of literature that supports the view that these materials are harmful to women.[4]

In this passage, the Court has begun its attempt to shift the objective of obscenity law from the legal regulation of morality to the legal regulation of material that is harmful to women. It emphasizes that material is obscene not because it offends morals, but because it is harmful to women. The shift in the discourse used to articulate and justify the obscenity provisions obscures the extent to which, as Lise Gotell has argued in chapter 2, the feminist discourse of harm does represent a moral claim. Moreover, this effort to shift the discourse from morality to harm has not displaced the underlying conservative sexual morality that has informed the law before *Butler*. Rather, this sexual morality – its opposition between good and bad sex and its strictly negative theory of sexual expression – continues to inform the Court's approach. According to this degrading and dehumanizing test, any sexual representation involving aspects of dominance is bad sex. But this test does not tell us what is good about sex, or what good sex is. By implication, good sex must be the opposite of bad sex. If bad sex is sex that places any of its subjects "in positions of subordination, servile submission or humiliation," then good sex must be sex that does not place its subjects in such positions. Good sex must be what bad sex is not.

In this good sex/bad sex distinction, the Court tells us that consent is not necessarily determinative. "Consent cannot save materials that otherwise contain degrading or dehumanizing scenes. Sometimes the very appearance of consent makes the depicted acts even more degrading or dehumanizing" (*Butler* 1992, 466–7). Again, the Court does not tell us what good sex is, but, simply, what it is not. Good sex is not necessarily sex with consent. Sex with consent can be really bad sex; in fact, it can make bad sex even worse. There is no positive theory of what makes sex good; only the further articulation of sex that might be bad. The good sex/bad sex distinction continues to appear in even more troubling forms. It is seen in the passage cited from Madam Justice Wilson, in *Towne Cinema*: "the public has concluded that exposure to material which degrades the human dimensions of life to a subhuman or merely physical dimension and thereby contributes to a process of moral desensitization must be harmful in some way" (*Towne Cinema* 1985, 217–18, as quoted in *Butler* 1992, 468). We see in this passage from Wilson J as affirmed by Sopinka J, a particular vision of sex and sexual representation. The merely physical dimension of sex is subhuman. The opposition of good and bad sex reappears in a somewhat different guise. Bad sex is subhuman sex. Bad sex is sex that emphasizes the merely physical dimension of sex.

We begin to see here the underlying binary opposition. It is the distinction between mind and body, between the intellectual and physical, between the emotional and sensual, that has long informed Western thought.[5] In this opposition, the body, the physical, the sensual, are seen as base, as bad, in need of control and, ultimately, transcendence. Sex is physical, it is about the body and the sensual pleasures of the body. Being of the body, it is natural, essential, and unchanging[6] (Rubin 1989, 275). And, being of the body, it is, by reference to the mind/body opposition, bad. This conflation of sex with the physical operates to sustain what Gayle Rubin describes as sex negativity, that is, the idea deeply rooted in Western culture that sex is "a dangerous, destructive, negative force" (ibid., 278; Weeks 1986). But sex is saved from complete damnation by another opposition. Good sex, then, is sex that is not only physical; it is not only sensual. Good sex must transcend the very nature of sex as physical pleasure. Good sex, then, must be sex with more, it must appeal to the other side of the opposition, and thus be part of the mind, the intellect, the soul.

The interaction between these two oppositions, while saving sex from itself, operates to destabilize the underlying assumptions about sex, and to constitute sex and sexuality as a highly contradictory category. The good sex/bad sex opposition, for example, brings into question the assumption of sex negativity <that sex is always bad>, as well as that of sexual essentialism <that sex is physical, natural, and unchanging>. If sex is, by definition, bad, how can it be made good? If sex is of the body, how can it be made not of the body? And if sex is unchanging, how can it change? The good sex/bad sex opposition introduces all of these possibilities – possibilities that sit awkwardly with the underlying assumptions about the nature of sex. Yet, these assumptions are never completely undermined. Sex continues to be presumed to be bad, unless it can be made good.[7] Sex continues to be of the body, unless it can be made to be of the mind. And sex continues to be natural and unchanging, unless it is changed <that is, made good and of the mind>. According to the good sex/bad sex distinction, sex can now become that which, by definition, it is not. Sex can now become more than sex.

Internal Necessities/Artistic Defence. The theme of "sex with more" is continued in the third and final test reviewed by the Court. Sopinka J begins by quoting the internal-necessities test as set out in *Brodie*: "What I think is aimed at is excessive emphasis on the theme for a base purpose. But I do not think that there is undue exploitation if there is no more emphasis on the theme than is required in the serious treatment of the theme of a novel with honesty and uprightness" (*Brodie* 1962, 181, as quoted in *Butler* 1992, 468). The Court in *Brodie*, in evaluating the work in question – D.H. Lawrence's *Lady Chatterley's Lover* – held: "It has none of the characteristics that are often described in judgments dealing with obscenity – dirt for dirt's sake, the leer of the sensualist, depravity of the mind of an author with an obsession for dirt, pornography, an appeal to a prurient interest etc. The section recognizes that the serious-minded author must have freedom in the protection of work of genuine artistic and literary merit and the quality of the work must have real relevance in determining not only a dominant characteristic but also whether there is undue exploitation" (*Brodie* 1962, 181 quoted in *Butler* 1992, 468). According to the Court, this artistic defence has been considered to be the last step in determining whether the exploitation of sex is undue. If sexual material is "required for the serious treatment of a theme," then it will not be held to be "undue." "[T]he internal necessities test ... has been interpreted to assess whether the exploitation of sex has a justifiable role in advancing the plot or the theme, and in considering the work as a whole, does not merely represent 'dirt for dirt's sake' but has a legitimate role when measured by the internal necessities of the work itself" (*Butler* 1992, 469). According to this test, the representation of sex in and of itself constitutes "dirt for dirt's sake."[8] We again see the view that sex is dirt – it is dirty, it is bad. Within this vision, art cannot be sex for sex's sake. By definition, sex is not art. Sex is not a legitimate focus for art. It can at most be part of the larger artistic purpose, but sexuality in and of itself is not art. Within the courts' view, this is one area of human activity (or subhuman activity) that is inappropriate for artistic portrayal.

Art, like good sex, is defined in relation to the mind/body opposition. Art is that which appeals to more than our physical nature. It is, by definition, that which appeals to our higher dimensions – to our intellectual, emotional or spiritual aspirations (Nead 1993a, 145; 1993b, 281–2). Accordingly, only sex with more, sex that appeals to the other side of the mind/body distinction – that is, sex that transcends its physical nature by appealing to the intellect, the emotions, the soul – can become good sex and, thus, be the subject of art. In other words, only sex that is not sex can be a legitimate focus for art.[9]

Relationship between the Tests. Sopinka J then attempts to clarify the relationship between these tests, which he acknowledges has been unclear in the case law. He begins by dividing pornography into three categories: "(1) explicit sex with violence (2) explicit sex without violence but which subjects people to treatment that is degrading or dehumanizing and (3) explicit sex without violence that is neither degrading nor dehumanizing" (*Butler* 1992, 470). The Court notes that there is some disagreement in society as to which materials would constitute the undue exploitation of sex. Some would argue that all three categories should be prohibited; others would argue that none of these categories should be prohibited. Sopinka J further observes that this is not an issue "that is susceptible to proof in the traditional way" (ibid.). In order to avoid these determinations being made according to the subjective opinions of individual judges, there must be a "norm that will serve as an arbiter in determining what amounts to an undue exploitation of sex. That arbiter is the community as a whole" (ibid.). According to the community-standards test, the courts must decide what "the community would tolerate others being exposed to on the basis of the degree of harm that may flow from such exposure" (ibid.). "Harm in this context means that it predisposes persons to act in an antisocial manner as, for example, the physical or mental mistreatment of women by men, or what is perhaps debatable, the reverse. Antisocial conduct for this purpose is conduct which society formally recognizes as incompatible with its proper functioning" (ibid. 470–1). The community standards test continues to play a central role in the *Butler* test for obscenity, although it is now more carefully articulated in the discourse of harm, avoiding any obvious references to morality. Under the revised test, the guideline of community standards is intended to allow courts to categorize pornography into one of the three discrete categories, according to an objective legal norm. This categorization approach is based on the assumption that the meaning of pornography can be objectively established. We can begin to see in this test the Court's literalist approach to representation. Like the approach of anti-pornography feminism discussed in the previous chapter, in the Court's view, the meaning of sexual images can be determined in isolation from the context of these images; meaning is thus separated from context.

The Court then returns to the three categories of pornography. In Sopinka J's view, the first category <sex with violence> is explicitly mentioned within s. 163(8) and will almost always constitute the undue exploitation of sex. The second category <sex without violence, but that is degrading or dehumanizing> may be undue exploitation of sex if the risk of harm is substantial. The third category <sex without violence, and that is not degrading or dehumanizing> is generally tolerated, and will not, with the exception of the involvement of children, constitute undue exploitation of sex. The Court then turns to the question of the internal-necessities test, and how it fits into this new scheme. Sopinka J states that the artistic defence – that is, whether the undue exploitation of sex is the main object of the work, or whether the portrayal of sex is essential to a wider artistic, literary, or other similar purpose – remains the last step in determining if the material is obscene. "The portrayal of sex must then be viewed in context to determine whether that is the dominant theme of the work as a whole. Put another way, is undue exploitation of sex the main object of the work or is this portrayal of sex essential to a wider artistic, literary, or other similar purpose" (*Butler* 1992, 471). The court must determine whether the community would tolerate the sexually explicit materials when seen within the broader context of the work as a whole.

According to this test, not only can pornography be objectively and unequivocally classified into one of three discrete categories, but this categorization becomes determinative as to whether the material will be considered to be obscene. This categorization further underscores the absence of a positive theory of sex and sexual expression in *Butler*. The very definition of good sex – the third category – is framed in purely negative terms. Good sex does *not* involve violence, it does *not* involve children, it is *not* degrading or dehumanizing, and it does *not* create a risk of harm. The Court does not tell us what makes sex good; it only tells us what makes sex bad. Good sex, then, is defined only in opposition to what it is not: bad sex. Within this categorization of pornography, the major contested site of sexual representation is degrading and dehumanizing sex.[10] The courts must determine whether particular sexual representations are degrading and dehumanizing, and if so, whether these degrading and dehumanizing representations are likely to cause harm. This is the dividing line between good and bad sex. Drawing the line between good and bad sex continues to be the job of the community-standards test. Notwithstanding the repeated claims to the contrary, this determination can only be made by reference to an underlying sexual morality. The very exercise of drawing a line between good sex and bad sex presumes an underlying conservative sexual morality in which sex is divided between good and bad, and in which there is a hierarchy of sexual practices.

The use of a community standard in this exercise further presumes an underlying sexual morality in which sex and sexual practices are, or should be, essential and monolithic. It continues to assume that there is a national standard that can judge which sexual practices are acceptable and which are not; a national standard that presumes that there is, or should be, a monolithic view of good and bad sex. Not only is sex simply of the body, but this biological imperative is such that sex always and only ever takes one form. As Gayle Rubin has argued, "sexuality is supposed to conform to a single standard. One of the most tenacious ideas about sex is that there is one best way to do it, and that everyone should do it that way" (Rubin 1989, 283). These assumptions of sexual essentialism and sexual monism – of a single and essential nature of sex, any deviation from which is condemned as "unnatural," and thus bad – continue to operate, barely beneath the surface of the *Butler* test.

Finally, by simply incorporating the artistic defence as the last step in determining whether material is obscene, the Supreme Court has reinscribed the underlying oppositions of sex and art, of good and bad sex, of mind and body, that have long informed the internal-necessities test. Indeed, in articulating the new relationship between these various tests, the Supreme Court can be seen to have rearticulated the sexual subtext, and its underlying oppositions, that has long informed each of these tests. Sex remains a highly contradictory category. Sex is of the body, it is physical, not mental, it is sensual not intellectual, it is pleasure, not pursuit. Sex, being of the body, is bad unless it can be made good, by transcending the body and its physical pleasures. Sex can only be made good by transcending its very nature. Good sex is discursively constituted as a contradictory category – it is sex (which is of the body) that has been made of the mind: it is sex that is not sex. According to the test set out in *Butler*, drawing the line between good sex and bad sex continues to be a determination made by reference to this underlying sexual morality.

The Constitutionality of Obscenity

In the second part of the decision, the Court examines whether s. 163 violates the right to freedom of expression guaranteed by the Charter. The Court's discussion of the constitutionality of obscenity is divided into two parts, which will be examined in turn: (1) whether the law violates the right to freedom of expression as guaranteed by s. 2(b) of the Charter, and (2) if so, whether the violation is a reasonable limit on the right, as contemplated by section 1 of the *Charter*. In upholding the law from the constitutional challenge, the Court tells us, over and over again, that the objective of the obscenity law is preventing harm, particularly harm towards women. At the same time, in taking a deeper look at why the criminalization of sexual expression is justifiable, the Court continues to expose its views on the value of sex, sexuality, and sexual expression. As I will attempt to illustrate, beneath the official story of preventing harm and promoting equality is the same sexual subtext as found in the first part of the decision, and the same sexual morality that informed the law of obscenity before *Butler*.

Sexual Representation as Expression. The Court first considers whether s. 163 violates freedom of expression as guaranteed by section 2(b) of the Charter. Sopinka J rejected the argument made by the government that physical activity, such as sexual activity, could not be considered expression. In the Court's view, the fact that the subject matter of the materials was "clearly physical" did not mean that the materials did not "convey or attempt to convey meaning" (*Butler* 1992, 472). In previous decisions, the Supreme Court of Canada has consistently adopted an expansive approach to the protection provided by s. 2(b), holding that the content or meaning cannot exclude the activities or statements from the scope of protection accorded by s. 2(b), no matter how offensive those activities or statements may be to the Court.[11] "Meaning sought to be expressed need not be 'redeeming' in the eyes of the court to merit the protection of s. 2(b) whose purpose is to ensure that thoughts and feelings may be conveyed freely in non-violent ways without fear of censure" (ibid., 473). Sopinka J held that both the purpose and effect of s. 163 was to restrict "the communication of certain types of materials based on their content" (ibid.). As a result, the law prohibited expressive activity, and violated s. 2(b) of the Charter.

While the Court rejected the view that "purely physical activity does not convey meaning," implicit in the Court's language is the view that sex constitutes purely physical activity.[12] It is of, and only of, the body. At the same time, however, the Court recognizes that the portrayal of this physical activity "conveys ideas, opinions, or feeling" (*Butler* 1992, 472). For example, the Court notes that the portrayal of this physical activity involves the production of meaning by film-makers: "in creating a film, regardless of its content, the maker of the film is consciously choosing the particular images which together constitute the film. In choosing his or her images, the creator of the film is attempting to convey some meaning" (ibid., 474). In the Court's view, although sex is purely physical, sexual representations are not. Rather, the process of representation necessarily involves the other side of the mind/body distinction, and thus constitutes expression, regardless of the content of that expression.

Obscenity as a Reasonable Limit. The Court then considered whether this violation of s. 2(b) by s. 163 of the *Criminal Code* is a reasonable limit within the meaning of section 1 of the *Charter*. The discussion proceeds along the lines of the well-established *Oakes* test, which requires that there be an objective that is sufficiently pressing and substantial to justify the violation of the *Charter* right, and that the violation of the right be proportional to the objective.[13] In addressing the question of objective, Sopinka J observed that, historically, the objective of obscenity legislation was the prohibition of "immoral influences" and the imposition of a "standard of public and sexual morality" (*Butler* 1992, 476). In the Court's view, this objective is no longer sustainable. "The prevention of 'dirt for dirt's sake' is not a legitimate objective which would justify the violation of one of the most fundamental freedoms enshrined in the *Charter*" (ibid.). The Court does not say that Parliament cannot legislate on the basis of morality. However, it does say that the objective of s. 163 "is not moral disapprobation but the avoidance of harm to society" (ibid., 477). The Court cited with approval the description of the harm of pornography in the Report of the Standing Committee on Justice and Legal Affairs (1978, 18:4). "The clear and unquestionable danger of this type of material is that it reinforces some unhealthy tendencies in Canadian society. The effect of this type of material is to reinforce male-female stereotypes to the detriment of both sexes. It attempts to make degradation, humiliation, victimization and violence in human relationships appear normal and acceptable. A society which holds that egalitarian, non-violence, consensualism and mutuality are basic to any human interaction, whether sexual or other, is clearly justified in controlling and prohibiting any medium of depiction, description or advocacy which violates these principles" (*Butler* 1991, 477). The objective of s. 163 is thus not the imposition of a sexual morality but, rather, the prevention of the harm that pornography causes to women.

Much has been made of these statements of the objective of s. 163, particularly by feminists, who support the *Butler* decision. LEAF, for example, has argued that this represents a fundamental shift in obscenity law, away from the regulation of sexual morality and towards a feminist reformulation of the harm of pornography (Busby 1994, 176). However, the Court's effort to reconceptualize the objective must be read within the framework of the decision as a whole. It must be considered alongside the actual test for obscenity set out by the Court in the first part of the decision, as well as considered in light of the rest of section 1 analysis. When evaluated within the discursive framework of the decision as a whole, and its sexual subtext, the assertion that the statement of objective signifies a radical transformation in the law of obscenity is, at the very least, contestable.

Indeed, even the discussion of the objective of the law itself is contradictory, in so far as the Court is not able to sustain the distinction it is attempting to make between morality <the old law> and harm <the new law>. The sexual morality of the old law is apparent even in the language of the decision. Although the Court specifically states that regulating a standard of public and sexual morality would be inappropriate – that is, it is not an acceptable objective to prohibit "dirt for dirt's sake" – the Court continues to sue the term "dirt for dirt's sake" as a synonym for pornography in several places in the decision. Again we see the extent to which, in the eyes of the Court, sexually explicit materials constitute dirt. Of course, according to the official story, the point is that the Court has to find another reason to regulate and prohibit this "dirt."

In attempting to locate the harm as something other than moral disapprobation, the distinction between morality and harm is further disrupted. In previous decisions, the Supreme Court has held that the purpose of a law cannot be seen to change or shift over time.[14] The purpose of a law is, in effect, written in stone at the time that the legislation was drafted and enacted. As a result, the Court in *Butler* was confronted with a problem: did this effort to recast the objective of the law as preventing harm, particularly harm against women, violate this shifting-purpose doctrine – that is, did it constitute an effort to change the purpose of the law from the regulation of morality to the prevention of harm? The Supreme Court of Canada said no. Yet, in so doing, the Court is forced to retreat from its earlier position that morality and harm were distinct. "[T]he notions of moral corruption and harm to society are not distinct ... but are inextricably linked. It is a moral corruption of a certain kind which leads to the detrimental effect on society" (*Butler* 1992, 427). Since the objective of the law cannot change, Sopinka J holds that the prevention of harm is intricately related to morality. Now, morality and harm are not different. According to Sopinka J the only thing that has changed is our understanding of the harm caused by pornography. "The prohibition of such materials was based on the belief that they had a detrimental impact on individuals exposed to them and consequently on society as a whole. Our understanding of the harms caused by these materials has developed considerably since that time; however, this does not detract from the fact that the purpose of this legislation remains, as it was in 1959, the protection of society from harms caused by the exposure to obscene materials" (ibid., 478). The Court spins around a tautological circle: the harms that are intended to be addressed by obscenity legislation are the harms that are caused by obscenity. If this circular reasoning is valid, we now have a generic objective so broad that it can be applied to virtually any piece of legislation. Just fill in the blank: the objective of the <pornography, traffic congestion, security fraud> law is to prevent the harm that <pornography, traffic congestion, security fraud> causes to society. According to this generic, or "no-name" objective of preventing harm, there will be little difficulty avoiding the net of the shifting-purpose doctrine whenever it is convenient to do so.[15]

Further, in these passages, the Court's views on the relationship between harm and morality is inconsistent. First, Sopinka J tells us that the law is not about morality, but about harm (morality is bad, and distinct from harm). But, then he tells us that harm is not actually distinct from morality, so there is no shifting purpose (morality is OK, and related to harm). And, finally, he tells us that the harm intended to be addressed is the harm caused by pornography, which used to be immorality but now is harm to women (morality is bad, and distinct from harm). So morality is bad, except when it is related to harm, in which case it is no longer morality. The Court's effort to cast the objective of s. 163 as something other than moral approbation is, at best, on rather shaky ground.

The sexual morality underlying the decision is made further manifest in the subsequent analysis of the proportionality requirement.[16] This sexual morality is most clearly revealed in the Court's brief discussion of the nature of the expression at stake in the legal regulation of pornography, which in its view is important in deciding whether the proportionality requirement has been met. Sopinka J examines whether the nature of the expression at issue in the regulation of pornography is in any way related to the three values that underlie the right to freedom of expression, namely, "the search for truth, participation in the political process, and individual self-fulfilment" (*Butler* 1992, 481). In evaluating the nature of the expression, the Court reviews the contrasting positions of the Ontario Attorney General and the British Columbia Civil Liberties Association. The former argued that "only individual self fulfilment and only as its most base aspect, that of physical arousal, is engaged by pornography" (ibid.). The latter argued that "pornography forces us to question conventional notions of sexuality and thereby launches us into an inherently political discourse" (ibid.). Interestingly, the Court then quotes a passage from Robin West (cited in the BCCLA factum), who argues, "Good pornography has value because it validates women's will to pleasure. It celebrates female nature. It validates a range of female sexuality that is wider and truer than that legitimated by the non-pornographic culture. Pornography when it is good celebrates both female pleasure and male rationality" (Robin West as quoted in *Butler* 1992, 481). The Court seems to adopt West's view of the position value of sexual expression, in noting that "[a] proper application of the test should not suppress what West refers to as "good pornography." The objective of the impugned provision is not to inhibit the celebration of human sexuality" (*Butler* 1992, 481).

This is as close as the Court comes to articulating a positive theory of sexual expression. Pornography is divided into good pornography and bad pornography (good sex/bad sex). Good pornography is sexual expression that affirm women's agency (*will* to pleasure, not just pleasure). It is the will, the appeal to agency that comes from the intellect, the mind that transforms sex from bad to good. It is good because it has transcended its purely physical nature. It is also good because it "celebrates female nature" – a nature that although unarticulated is more than the body; it is of the whole female person – which must include the mind, the spirit. Female pleasure rooted in female nature seems to be posited as something more than physical self-fulfilment. Finally, sexual expression is good when it affirms "male rationality" – that is, when male sexuality transcends its base and cor-poreal nature; when it is no longer just of the body, but of the mind. We catch a glimpse of the deeply gendered nature of these oppositions: men are associated with rationality <which is of the mind> and women with pleasure <which is of the body> (Hekman 1990). This articulation of a positive theory of sexual expression is thus firmly rooted in the underlying conservative sexual morality and its good sex/bad sex, mind/body oppositions.

This positive theory of sexual expression is further limited when the Court shifts back, in the next sentence to its focus on the negative value of sexual expression. "[I]t cannot be ignored that the realities of the pornography industry are far from the picture which the B.C. Civil Liberties Association would have us paint" (*Butler* 1992, 481). This assertion of "the realities of the pornography industry" is supported only by reference to another court decision that describes pornographic materials; it is a reality apparently so obvious that the Court does not even have to take judicial notice, nor refer to expert evidence or secondary literature. These "realities of the pornography industry" are such that the Court is compelled to adopt the position of the Ontario Attorney General on the nature of the expression, namely, that it appeals only to the most base aspect of individual self-fulfilment. Sopinka J concludes: "the kind of expression which is sought to be advanced does not stand on equal footing with other kinds of expres-sion which directly engage with 'core' of the freedom of expression values" (ibid., 482). While the Court had found that sexual expression was expression within the meaning of s. 2(b) of the Charter, it subse-quently holds that sexual expression is an inferior form of expression, and thus not entitled to the same degree of protection. While, for the purpose of s. 2(b), all expression is equal, for the purpose of s. 1, the Court appears to be of the view that some expression is more equal than others.[17]

Why is sexual expression a lesser form of expression? All the Court tells us is that it is not related to any of the three core values underlying expression – the pursuit of truth, participation in the political process, or individual self-fulfilment. The Court's answer begs the deeper question – that is, why is sexual expression not related to the pursuit of truth, or to political participation, or to individual self-fulfilment?

Sopinka J only addresses the third value, that of individual self-fulfilment. In his view, "this kind of expression is far from the core of the guarantee of freedom of expression. It appeals only to the most base aspect of individual fulfilment" (*Butler* 1992, 488). In this passage, Sopinka J seems to endorse the position advocated by the Ontario Attorney General, which, as noted, described this most base aspect of self-fulfilment as physical arousal. Sexual expression is a lesser form of expression because it appeals only to our most base – that is, our physical – dimension.

A now familiar subtext emerges: sexual arousal, rather than being an important part of our human dimension, is seen as base. And sexual arousal is seen as purely physical arousal – as a purely physiological reaction devoid of any mental elements. Again, sex is only of the body, not of the mind. Since individual self-fulfilment is valued only when it is promoting arousal of something more than the body – arousal of the mind or the spirit – it does not apply to sexual arousal or fulfilment. And again, we see the mind/body opposition, in which sex is located firmly within the body; it is bad unless it can be made good by transcending its corporeal nature. It is, then, this appeal to the body that makes sexual expression a lesser form of expression. As Linda Williams has argued, we can begin to see the extent to which pornography is "a volatile issue not simply because it represents sexual acts and fantasies, but because in that representation it frankly seeks to arouse viewers. Perhaps more than any other genre its pleasures are aimed at the body" (Williams 1989, 46). It is the very fact that this expression is directed at the pleasures of the body that makes it a lesser form of expression. It is based on an understanding of sex and sexual pleasure as being only of the body. There is no recognition of the role of our minds or our imaginations in sexual arousal and sexual pleasure. Nor is there any recognition of the social construction of sexuality. We again see the assumption of sexual essentialism operating: sex is biological, it is of and only of the body and, as such, unaffected by social relationships or culture.

Ironically, this assumption of sexual essentialism sits in stark contrast to the understanding of sexuality that informs the feminist anti-pornography position. The work of anti-pornography feminists has been based on the idea that sexuality is socially constructed – that sex and sexual desire are a product of the patriarchal society in which we live, and that sexual arousal (particularly, male sexual arousal) is negatively affected by images that represent women as sexual objects. Indeed, the sexual essentialism of the decision sits awkwardly with the

Court's own assertion of the relationship between pornography and harm to women. Yet, it is only through this biological essentialism of sex, as of and only of the body, that the Court can sustain the assertion that sex appeals only to the most base aspect of physical fulfilment, and, in turn, the conclusion that sexual expression is a lesser form of expression.

The question of why sexual expression is not related to the other two values of expression – the search for truth and political participation – is not directly addressed by the Court. This silence, however, speaks volumes as to the underlying sexual morality. It is based on an unstated understanding of the truth about pornography – what it is, and what it is not; a "truth" that upon further deconstruction reveals a multiplicity of assumptions about sex and sexuality. In the Court's view, there is a "truth" to pornography, which is asserted to dismiss the idea that it could in any way be related to the values underlying freedom of expression. It was the truth about pornography – that it appeals only to the most base dimension of physical fulfilment – that allowed the Court to reject any connection between sexual expression and individual self-fulfilment. It is similarly this truth about pornography that allows the Court to implicitly reject any connection between sexual expression and the pursuit of truth.

For example, the efforts of the BC Civil Liberties Association to frame sexual expression as a challenge to conventional sexuality and, in turn, as a political discourse (see Gotell), were simply rejected on the basis of the "realities" of the pornography industry. According to the Court, the realities or truth of the pornography industry are that it is characterized by a particular form of sexual representations of women, that is, of women as sexual objects for men. In this view, there is no possibility of a diversity of sexual representations within the pornography industry. Nor is there any room to admit that these sexual representations may be subject to different interpretations (Williams 1989). Again, we see the Court's literalist approach to representation, according to which pornography is seen to have a single and universal meaning, readily available to any viewer. This reality of the pornography industry, along with the monolithic nature of its representations, the meaning of which is uncontestable, precludes the possibility that pornography could be implicated in what we otherwise value – the search for truth. The "truth" of the pornography industry is in effect asserted to preclude the possibility that pornography could be implicated in the search for truth.

It is similarly the truth about pornography that precludes the possibility that pornography could in any way be involved in promoting the second value of freedom of expression – that is, participation in the political process. Pornography, or more specifically the pornography industry, which by definition undermines women's equality and dignity, becomes the antithesis of participation. The arguments that sexual representation is for some communities part of an inherently political process of forging community identities were not, in the Court's view, even deemed worthy of mention. The question "participation for whom?" thus remains unaddressed, as does the question of participation in relation to what issues.

. This rejection of the potential value of sexual expression in promoting participation in the political process also implies that sex is not worthy of the political process – that sex is not a matter for the political process. Yet the very history of the legal regulation of sex demonstrates how extensive this regulation has been. The failure to consider any possible connection between sexual expression and political participation obscures the extent to which sex has long been a subject of legal regulation and repression. Indeed, the sexualities of the very individuals who are now seeking to forge their identities in and through these sexual presentations – lesbians and gay men, sex-trade workers, feminist artists – have long been the subject of legal regulation and repression, without their consent.

Contrary to the historical realities of legal regulation, the sexual subtext of the decision is based on the idea that sex is not a matter for politics, or for political debate. Not only is the subject not worthy of politics, but we see again the underlying assumptions of the monolithic nature of sexuality. The truth about sex is that sex is just sex – basically it's bad, unless it's good, and we all know which one it is when we see it. There is no room for disagreement or dissent, or for the possibility that there may be diverse sexualities. Nor is there any room to acknowledge that the exploration of diverse sexualities may have value in and of itself.

Sex, being of the body, cannot be the subject of debate. As a function of biology, of pure physical arousal, there is nothing to debate. This sexual essentialism is further reinforced by the assumption of sexual monism. Because there is only one way to have sex, or at least, one good way to have sex, there is nothing to be gained from sexual expression. It is not a subject that can contribute to or be advanced by political debate. These various assumptions of sexual morality – sexual essentialism, sexual monism, and sexual negativity – combine and interact to produce a truth about the nature of sexual expression, a truth according to which sexual expression is not in any way related to political participation, or to any of the other core values that underlie freedom of expression.

Again, we can begin to see the tensions in this sexual subtext. The assumption of sexual monism sits awkwardly with the good sex/bad sex distinction and the sexual hierarchy implicit in this distinction. The idea that there is only one way to have sex is at odds with the idea that there is good sex and bad sex. The latter suggests that there is in fact more than one way to have sex, although one way is good and the other bad. Notwithstanding this tension, these two assumptions – of sexual monism and sexual negativity – operate together to the effect that there is only one way that we should have sex.

In the context of sexual expression, this sexual subtext operates to reinforce the idea that nothing is to be gained from such expression, and, in fact, much is to be lost. Since there is only one way to have sex, sexual expression may only lead others astray; it may encourage people to have bad sex (which in the Court's view is what pornography does). This view is reinforced by the truth about the pornography industry – that is, that it only represents bad sex. The very problem with sexual expression, then, is that it will cause people to have sex or sexual desire in ways that they should not. The repression of such expression, by contrast, will ensure that sex will be as it should be, in the natural order of things, which is still bad, unless it can become good, which if left to the natural order of things <marriage, heterosexuality, and reproduc­tion> it can.

In the subsequent discussion of the three dimensions of the proportionality test, the Court continues to articulate its now popular refrain – obscenity laws do not prohibit all sexual materials, only those sexual materials that cause harm, particularly harm towards women. The sexual subtext of this refrain is also articulated again and again. On the question of minimum impairment, for example, the Court finds that s. 163(8) does not proscribe all sexually explicit material, but only that which is violent, degrading, and/or dehumanizing. The provision does not prohibit good sex, that is, "sexually explicit erotica without violence, that is not degrading or dehumanizing" (*Butler* 1992, 485). Nor does the section include sexually explicit materials that have scientific, artistic, or literary merit. The Court here rearticulates the distinction between sex and art, noting that materials that involve "aesthetic expression," and thus "represent the artist's attempt at individual fulfilment" would not be captured by the provision. The same good sex/bad sex, mind/body, art/sex distinctions continue to appear.

Concluding Remarks on the *Butler* Decision

The result of the *Butler* decision was twofold. The Supreme Court reformulated the test for obscenity under s. 163 and subsequently found that although s. 163 violated the right to freedom of expression, it was a reasonable limit on this right, and thus constitutional. The meaning of the decision remains highly contested. Those who take the position that *Butler* represents a feminist victory have argued that the objectives of s. 163 now require that degrading and dehumanizing be read in a new light, and that the meaning of community standards has been so fundamentally transformed as to resemble the previous test in name alone (Busby 1994, 176). I have tried to map out a very different reading of the *Butler* decision, within which the underlying sexual morality, and its assumptions of sexual negativity, sexual essentialism, and sexual monism, can be seen to leave s. 163 transformed in language alone. The classification of sexual representations into one of the three categories of pornography according to the community-standards test of harm can only be done by an implicit reliance on an underlying sexual morality. The very concept of sex that is or could be degrading and dehumanizing only makes sense through the underlying discourses on sexuality – of good sex/bad sex, of min/body distinctions, and of the assumptions of sexual negativity, essentialism, monism, and hierarchy on which these distinctions are based. Similarly, community standards only make sense in relation to a prevailing, and generally accepted, understanding of sexual morality, in which some sex is good and some sex is not.

In this reading of the *Butler* decision, the sexual subtext can be seen to inform the Court's discussion of the objective of the legislation, and indeed the discussion of the constitutionality of the law as a whole. Notwithstanding the Court's best efforts to cast the objective of the law as the prevention of harm, particularly of harm towards women, the underlying sexual morality continues to infuse and shape the discourse of the decision. We do not have to look very far to find the continued references to morality, to sexual morality, to good sex and bad sex, to sex being of the body and thus bad, unless it can be made something more, and thereby good. Yet, there is no explicit articulation of what makes sex good. Rather, good sex is simply implied as that which bad sex is not: not base, not physical, not violent, not degrading or dehumanizing, not involving children. The sexual subtext of the *Butler* decision is informed by the discourses on sexuality that have dominated Western thought since the nineteenth century: sexual negativity <sex is bad>, sexual essentialism <sex is biological>, sexual monism <sex is singular>, and sexual hierarchy <some sex is better than other>.

These different assumptions informing prevailing understandings of sexuality sit in awkward relationship to one another, and operate to constitute sex as a highly unstable category. For example, the idea that sex is bad sits in awkward juxtaposition to the idea that it can be made good, which in turn does not seem consistent with the idea that sex being of the body can be made good only by becoming that which is not of the mind. The very idea of sexual hierarchy – that some sex <marital, heterosexual, reproductive> is better than other <non-marital, non-reproductive, homosexual> sits inconsistently with the idea of sexual monism – that there is only one sexuality. Sexual hierarchy seems to be based on an implicit notion of sexual diversity, and yet operates at the same time to condemn that diversity. The diversity is reduced to a simple binary opposition of good and bad sex. In *Butler*, these assumptions interact in multiple and seemingly contradictory ways to constitute sex as a highly unstable category – yet not so unstable as to be easily displaced. This unstated sexual morality remains powerfully entrenched as the ideologically dominant discourse of sexuality.

Beyond Butler: *Obscenity and the Representation of Gay and Lesbian Sexuality*

Since the *Butler* decision, gay and lesbian sexually explicit materials continue to be targeted by customs officials and police. The continued criminalization of gay and lesbian sexual representations raises some difficult questions around the ostensible rejection of sexual morality in obscenity law. According to *Butler*, the purpose of s. 163 is to prevent harm, particularly harm towards women. The understanding of harm is based on the tenuous, but judicially accepted, link between pornography and violence against women. Men watching pictures in which women are objectified as sex objects is seen to cause men to mistreat women. It is an understanding of harm set in a heterosexual framework. The pornography is male heterosexual pornography, and its harm is that heterosexual men are likely to mistreat women. The feminist literature on which this understanding of harm is based has similarly operated within this heterosexual discursive framework. In the work of its leading exponents, (hetero)sexuality is identified as the site of women's oppression. It is in and through (hetero)sexuality that men are constituted as aggressive and dominant, and women are constituted as passive and subordinate (MacKinnon 1987, Dworkin 1981).

This heterosexual framework raises a serious question about applying the *Butler* test, and its conception of harm, to gay and lesbian materials. Many gay men and lesbians have argued that gay or lesbian sexual representations have absolute nothing to do with the harm towards women associated with heterosexual pornography. Carl Stychin has contended, for example, that the sexually explicit images of gay male pornography do not reinforce patriarchal male sexuality, but, rather, directly challenge dominant constructs of masculinity by displacing the heterosexual norm (Stychin 1992, 857). Lesbian writers, such as Barbara Smith and Lisa Henderson, have similarly resisted the equation of lesbian pornography and heterosexual pornography, insisting instead on the cultural specificity and the cultural transgression of sexually explicit imagery created for, by, and about lesbians (Smith 1988; Henderson 1992). Within this view, since gay and lesbian sexual representations do not operate within a heterosexual framework, these images cannot and should not be measured against a heterosexual norm.

It would therefore not be unreasonable to suggest that the heterosexual framework of the *Butler* test should limit the applicability of this obscenity doctrine to heterosexual pornography. At a minimum, this heterosexual framework would seem to require that courts at least address the question of how the understanding of harm could be applied to gay and lesbian sex. How does men watching pictures of men having sex with men, or women watching pictures of women having sex with women, contribute to the type of harm to women identified in *Butler*? In the case law that followed on the heels of the *Butler* decision, however, the courts have neither limited the *Butler* test to heterosexual materials nor explored how this heterosexually defined concept of harm can be applied to gay and lesbian imagery. The first two obscenity cases after *Butler* involved Glad Day Bookshop (a gay and lesbian bookstore), and the courts used the obscenity test as set out by the Supreme Court of Canada to find sexually explicit gay and lesbian materials to be obscene. Not only was the question of the relationship between gay and lesbian sexual imagery and harm to women not answered in these cases – the question was not even posed.

Indeed, it is in this application of the *Butler* test, and of its model of harm to gay and lesbian sexual representations, that the discursive drag of the *Butler* decision can be most directly challenged. It is within the context of gay and lesbian materials that the distinction between morality and harm is most difficult to sustain, and that we can most clearly see the extent to which obscenity laws are still predicated on the legal regulation of sexual morality. Gay and lesbian sexual representations are not produced within the heterosexual framework of the more mainstream pornography to which the *Butler* decision addressed itself – the images are of gay/lesbian sexuality, produced by gay men/lesbians, to be consumed by gay men/lesbians. Yet, these sexual representations have been charged and found guilty pursuant to the *Butler* test for obscenity. In this section, I will argue that the criminalization of these gay and lesbian sexual materials does, however, make sense within the discursive context of the sexual subtext of the *Butler* decision. I will illustrate the extent to which the sexual morality underlying the *Butler* decision has framed and informed these two obscenity decisions against Glad Day Bookshop. The sexual subtext, and its good sex/bad sex oppositions is particularly dangerous in the context of gay and lesbian sexual representations. The heterosexist and often homophobic discourses of this conservative sexual morality operate to locate these representations on the bad-sex side of the dichotomy.

Glad Day Bookshop v Canada

In the case of *Glad Day Bookshop* (1992), the dangerous implications of the *Butler* decision, and of its understanding of sex and sexuality, for gay and lesbian sexual representation has begun to come clear. This case arose in the context of a customs seizure of gay male pornography en route to Glad Day Bookshop. Glad Day appealed from a determination of the deputy minister of National Revenue for Customs and Excise, declaring the materials to be obscene and, thus, prohibited from import into Canada.[18]

After reviewing the case in considerable detail (and dismissing the expert evidence called by the defence) and the law of obscenity as established in *Butler*, Hayes J turned to the material in question. The Ontario Court (General Division) reviewed each of the seized materials. Hayes J briefly described each publication, and concluded that each magazine, story, and comic strip was "degrading and dehumanizing." Throughout the decision, each publication is dealt with in two or three paragraphs: one paragraph describes the sexual representation; the second paragraph is conclusory in nature – that is, the Court concludes that the material is degrading, that the material does violate community standards. For example, in relation to *Oriental Guys* no. 4 (Spring 1989), which contains explicit representations of gay oral and anal sex with no violence, the Court held: "The description in the magazine of this sexual activity is degrading, I am of the opinion that this particular material does indicate a strong inference of a risk of harm that might flow from the community being exposed to this material. I am of the opinion that the community would not tolerate others being exposed to this item. The dominant characteristic is an undue exploitation of sex. It is obscene" (*Glad Day Bookshop* 1992, 15). There is almost no analysis as to why particular materials are degrading. Rather, in each case, the Court simply asserts that the material is degrading, that there is a risk of harm, that the community would not tolerate others being exposed to it.

To the extent that the Court gives any reason as to why the material is degrading, the theme that emerges, in single sentences and passages, is the ostensible absence of "real human relationships." For example, with regard to *Movie Star Confidential*, a sexually explicit comic strip, the Court writes "It does not contain any real human relationship. In its grotesque figures and their sexual activity, it is completely degrading and dehumanizing" (*Glad Day Bookshop* 1992, 16). On *Spartan's Quest*, Hayes J writes: "It is a sexual encounter without any real meaningful human relationship" (ibid.). On *Humongous – True Gay Encounters*, a collection of short stories, which includes explicit gay sex with strangers: "The manner in which they express explicit sexual activity is described is degrading [sic] to human beings. *There is no real human relationship*" (ibid., 17; emphasis added). On *Sex Stop*: "The introduction to this book ... clearly indicates the base purpose of the material which has no human dimension and is degrading and dehumanizing" (ibid., 18). On *Advocate Men*, a magazine with explicit representations of oral and anal sex: "The description and activities are degrading and without any human dimension. The dominant characteristic is the undue exploitation of sex" (ibid., 19).

According to Hayes J any explicit sexual representation without a "human dimension" or "human relationship" is degrading and dehumanizing, and constitutes the undue exploitation of sex. The implication throughout the decision is that sex is not human – a sexual relationship is not a human relationship. Our sexual dimension is not part of our human dimension – our sexual dimension makes us base, makes us subhuman. This understanding of sex is informed by and reinforces the binary opposition between good and bad sex, in which sex – which in and of itself is bad – gets to become good if it can transcend its subhuman nature and become human. Sex becomes good if it can transcend the purely physical, purely pleasurable, dimension and become something more. Sex becomes good if it can become that which by definition it is not.

In Hayes J's view, sexual representations are bad, unless they can be redeemed by emotional relationships. The *Glad Day Bookshop* decision makes clear that what is needed to make sex (which is inherently bad) good is an intimate, loving, monogamous relationship. However, since even *Advocate Men*, the gay male equivalent to *Playboy*, was found to be obscene, it is difficult to imagine what, if any, representations of gay male sex and sexuality would meet this test. It seems as if it is the representation of gay male sex in and of itself that is without a "human dimension" and thus degrading and dehumanizing.

According to the *Glad Day Bookshop* decision, sex with strangers, group sex, sex with bondage are all degrading and dehumanizing. Not only are the actual sexual practices considered to be inappropriate, but the mere representation of sexual fantasies are also prohibited (such as comic books, which represent the fantastical, not the real). Even the fantastical "without a human dimension" is degrading and dehumanizing. There is, in Hayes J's sexual morality, no distinction between the real and the fantastical, between reality and fantasy. The *Glad Day Bookshop* decision has been argued by some to be a misapplication of the *Butler* test, and it is currently under appeal. There is no question that the Court failed to engage with the *Butler* test. There was no consideration of why particular materials were degrading and dehumanizing, nor why these materials would cause harm. They were simply deemed to be degrading and dehumanizing and, in turn, deemed to cause harm. However, the failure of the Court to engage with the *Butler* test should not be taken as vindication of the *Butler* test. First, the *Glad Day Bookshop* decision exemplifies what lower courts can do with an inherently vague test like "degrading and dehumanizing," and with a community-standards test that does not require evidence. The vagueness of the test opens the door to, and invites the application of, a subjective determination on the nature of the sexually explicit materials. Second, it is not at all clear that the finding in Hayes is at odds with the sexual subtext of the *Butler* decision. Rather, in its assumptions of sexual negativity and sexual essentialism – sex is of the body and bad, unless it can be made good – Hayes decision is quite consistent with the sexual morality of *Butler*.

The main point of potential conflict between the *Glad Day Bookshop* decision and the *Butler* decision is in the application of a heterosexist model of harm to gay sexual representations. The Court does not engage with the fundamental question of what the *Butler* model of harm has to do with gay sexual representations. Indeed, the Court makes no reference to harm in terms of harm towards women. The only reference to harm by Hayes J is in terms of causing "anti-social conduct." The ostensibly feminist objective of the law evaporates. Rather, the application of the law is simply the application of a conservative sexual morality. The harm, according to the Court, is the harm of sexually explicit materials. The sexual subtext of the *Butler* decision – the good sex/bad sex distinction – is given a particularly homophobic spin in *Glad Day Bookshop*, whereby the representation of explicit gay sexuality becomes, by definition, bad sex.

R. v Scythes, Glad Day Bookshop

On 30 April 1992, two months after the *Butler* decision, the Toronto police seized the magazine *Bad Attitude* – a magazine of "lesbian erotic fiction" – from Toronto's Glad Day Bookshop, and charged the store and the store's owner, John Scythes, with the possession and sale of obscene material, in contravention of s. 163 of the *Criminal Code*. After a five-day trial in December 1992, Justice Paris of the Ontario Court (Provincial Division) delivered a six page judgement in February 1993, in which he found *Bad Attitude* to be obscene, and the accuseds were convicted of violating s. 163.

At trial, the Crown focused on a number of parts of the magazine: the fictional articles containing accounts of lesbian sadomasochist sex, and the accompanying photographs of explicit lesbian sex. In the decision, however, the Court focused on one article entitled "Wunna My Fantasies," in which writer Trish Thomas tells a story about the sexual practices of two fictional lesbian characters. One lesbian character stalks another in a shower room, and the two women engage in s/m sex.

The brief decision is a journey through heterosexual assumptions and neo-Victoria sexual morality. Interestingly, after briefly reviewing the *Butler* decision, the Court specifically turns to the question of heterosexuality. Paris J denies that the "sexual orientation" of the sexual representations have anything to do with his decision.

I have detected during this trial a concern that the Court will find relevant the sexual orientation of Bad Attitude. In recent years, many courts and tribunals have struck down laws and practices held to discriminate against gays. This is an indication that our society has moved beyond tolerance to the actual recognition that homosexuals form an essential part of our community. It follows then that as members of a sexual minority they have the right to communicate publicly on the subject that bind together. That right however will on occasion be curtailed in the public interest. The community tolerance test is blind to sexual orientation or practices. Its only focus is the potential harm to the public. Any consideration given to the sexual orientation of the material would constitute an unwarranted application of the test. (*Scythes* 1993, 4)

In the Court's view, sexual orientation is irrelevant, and the community-standards test must be applied in a formally equal manner. In the name of formal equality   which does not exist for gays and lesbians in Canadian law   the Court has ensured that the particular context of lesbian sexuality and representations will not be considered relevant. The test for community standards is supposed to be formally neutral to sexual orientation. But what this standard of formal neutrality obscures is the extent to which the standard is one deeply informed by heterosexual assumptions. The community standard is a heterosexual standard, and it is this heterosexual standard that becomes the norm by which all representations of sexuality are to be judged.

In the next paragraph, Paris J finds that the article contains representations of both sex and violence, and thus falls within the definition of s. 163(8). He then briefly turns his attention to the question of consent: "The consent in this case, far from redeeming the material makes it degrading and dehumanizing" (*Scythes* 1993, 4). In a slick discursive move, provided courtesy of the Supreme Court of Canada in *Butler*, the consensual nature of the sexual practices is not simply rendered irrelevant, but, in the Court's view, actually contributes to making the material degrading and dehumanizing. This discursive shift, in which consent becomes degradation, ensures the erasure of the specificity of lesbian sexual practices.

Consent is a cornerstone in lesbian s/m sexual practices, and in lesbian sexual/cultural production. As Lisa Henderson has argued, consent appears as a subtext throughout lesbian s/m sexual/cultural production.[19] As Becki Ross discusses in greater detail in the next chapter, the defence counsel in the case tried to explain this consensual nature of sex in "Wunna My Fantasies" to the Court. This attempt to explain the importance of consent within lesbian s/m culture, however, proved futile.[20] Even if established, in the reasoning of the *Butler* decision, consent only makes the sexual representation more degrading. After citing the *Butler* decision's passage on consent, Paris J writes: "This material flashes every light and blows every whistle of obscenity. Enjoyable sex after subordination by bondage and physical abuse at the hands of a total stranger" (*Scythes* 1993, 5). In Paris J's sexual world, there is no legitimate space for s/m sex, no room for bondage, no room for fantasizing about sex with a stranger. None of these sexual practices and fantasies could or should lead to enjoyable sex. Moreover, Paris J seems unable to comprehend the extent to which the story represents a sexual fantasy. In the Court's view, the sexual representations combined too many elements of bad sex: sex with strangers, sex with bondage, sex with submission, or even sexual fantasy.

Paris J then commits the ultimate act of judicial heterosexism: "If I replaced the aggressor in this article with a man there would be very few people in the community who would not recognize the potential for harm. The fact that the aggressor is a female is irrelevant because the potential for harm remains" (*Scythes* 1993, 5). To determine whether the text in question is obscene, the Court replaces the woman aggressor with a male aggressor. This substitution is allowed by the framework that the Court sets out at the beginning of the decision, which insists that sexual orientation is not relevant in determining community standards. Since sexual orientation is not relevant, then, in the Court's eyes, it does not matter whether the sex is occurring between two women, or between a woman and a man. The court is able to use its understanding of heterosexual sex to evaluate whether the representation of lesbian sex is obscene.[21] Through this judicial technique of heteroswitching, the specificity of lesbian sexuality, and of lesbian s/m cultural practices, are negated. All the arguments of the defence counsel, on the need to consider the specific cultural and ideological context under which lesbian sexual images are produced and given meaning, are, in a single heterosexual sweep, rendered irrelevant. And the heterosexual norm of the ostensibly neutral community standards is thereby reinforced.

In the final paragraph of the decision, the Court rejects the comparison the defence attempted to make between *Bad Attitude* and Madonna's book *Sex*. Defence counsel argued that the sexually explicit representations in *Sex*, which includes both heterosexual and homosexual s/m practices, demonstrated a shift in community standards. The commercial success of *Sex* in the Canadian market was presented as evidence that these kinds of sexually explicit representations do not violate community standards. The Court, however, was unpersuaded. "Madonna's book called Sex was offered to show the public tolerance to this type of material. One photograph of particular relevance shows a so called playful rape in a school gymnasium. I received very little information on the distribution of this book. I am told however that few were available and were sold immediately. I find the sample too small to be a reliable indication of the public's reaction to is distribution" (*Scythes* 1993, 6). The strongest argument on the nature of community standards, and the challenge to the assumed heterosexism of the standards, was simply rejected on the grounds that there was not enough evidence. The *Butler* test reaffirmed that there is no need to enter evidence of the community standard. Yet, here, the arbitrary and discretionary nature of the community-standards test is used to say that there was not enough evidence to show that the community standard has been changed. In other words, while no evidence is required to prove community standards, evidence is required to prove that these standards have changed.

In *Bad Attitude*, the representation of s/m lesbian sex, which in the Court's view involves explicit sex with violence, is, by the standards laid down by the Supreme Court of Canada, bad sex. There was no need to entertain the question of whether the representation constituted good sex, because the representation "blows every whistle of obscenity." Again, we see the Court expound on the negative values of sexual expression, on what is bad about sex. Sex with bondage, with domination, with strangers, is bad sex. And in order to insulate itself from charges that it was reverting back to the regulation of sexual morality, and not the prevention of harm towards women, the Court simply turned lesbian sex into heterosexual sex. It was only by virtue of this heteroswitching that the Court was able to conclude that the sexual representations harmed women, within the heterosexual framework of the *Butler* decision. Indeed, within this framework, no gay or lesbian sexual representations will be safe from review on the ground that there is no harm towards women. Rather, through this new-found judicial technique of heteroswitching, gay sexual representations can always be transformed by replacing a man with a woman; and lesbian sexual representations transformed by replacing one of the women with a man.[22]

R. v 931536 Ontario

Gay and lesbian sexual representations have not been the only focus of criminal prosecutions. Heterosexual pornography has also been subject to prosecution under s. 163 in the aftermath of *Butler*. Interestingly, some of the so-called straight porn that has been prosecuted has included scenes of lesbian or gay sexuality.[23] In *R. v 931536 Ontario*, this lesbian imagery played a central role in the Court's finding of the material to be degrading and dehumanizing. In this case, eight videos were alleged to be obscene. At trial, the court held that seven of the videos did exploit sex, and thus had to determine whether this exploitation was "undue." According to the Court, six of the remaining videos did not fall within the categories proscribed by *Butler*: they did not involve sex with violence, they were not degrading or dehumanizing, and did not create a substantial risk of harm. But one video, entitled *Cherry Tricks*, was held to be obscene on the basis that "its dominant theme is the degrading and demeaning treatment of women, combined with unobjectionable heterosexual and lesbian acts of sex." While this reference to lesbian acts of sex as unobjectionable might suggest that lesbian sexuality was not a relevant factor in the case, a deeper look at the reasoning brings this claim into at least some doubt.

In reviewing the video, the Court tells us that women are degraded throughout the video in their portrayal as "stupid, with no skills or ability, except sex." The women are "required to and are prepared to have sex with men who are either their employers, acting teachers, or men in positions to give them a job." The Court describes that each sex act begins *after* a scene in which a woman is humiliated. "The only actual overlapping of sex and humiliation occurs when two women are requested to suck and lick each other so that the men can choose the appropriate person for a job (a pun made in the movie), while the men look on. The women in the scene are shown as consenting and enjoying the sex" (*R. v 931536*). The Court concludes, on the basis of *Butler*, that the "film is degrading and dehumanizing because it places women in positions of subordination or humiliation, and runs against the principles of equality and dignity of all human beings." The Court repeats that "the sexual acts, themselves, taken in isolation, are not degrading.'

It is the lesbian sex act that nevertheless stands out. It is in this sequence that women are humiliated at the same time as they perform an otherwise "unobjectionable sex act." In the Court's view, there is a connection between the degrading mental treatment and the sex act. "There is the false consent, and the sex is always related to the woman's servile and subordinate position in relation to the men. The non-degrading sex taken in isolation is so interwoven with the reasons the women are having sex that it becomes degrading itself (*R. v 931536*). It is interesting that this ostensibly "false consent" and the depiction of women in subordinate positions is present in other scenes, which the Court describes but does not focus on in finding the video to be an "undue" exploitation of sex. Women are shown as only able to advance in their modelling or acting careers by having sex with their male employers or teachers. There is also the depiction of what the Court describes as "non-violent sexual assault," in which a woman consents to sex with a man on the basis of mistaking his identity. Yet, these are not the images that attract the Court's attention – apparently because the humiliation immediately precedes the sex. The Court does not tell us why humiliating women just before sex (and, presumably, into having sex) is any less degrading and dehumanizing to women than if the act of humiliation continues during the sex.

Nor does the Court tell us why this particular sex act is any more humiliating than the others, in which women are compelled to have sex with their male employers or teachers. The Court insists that it is not because the act is a lesbian act. Lesbian sex is, according to the Court, unobjectionable in isolation. This position is consistent with the Court's conclusion on two of the other videos, which also contain scenes of explicit sex between women, but which were not held to be degrading and dehumanizing. While lesbian sex may be unobjectionable, forcing women to have lesbian sex is, apparently, a different story. Indeed, it appears to be a different story than forcing women to have sex with men. The subtext is difficult to escape: what is particular objectionable is coercing women to have lesbian sex.

Lesbian sexuality is not irrelevant. While it may not be sufficient in itself to make sexual representations bad sex (which is certainly a step forward from the *Glad Day Bookshop* decision), it does operate as a factor that pushes sex across the line into bad sex. Compelling women to have sex with male employers to get a job may not exactly be good sex – in the Court's view, it is clearly sexist – but it is not sufficient to push the sex into the bad-sex category. Compelling women to have sex with other women to get a job, however, is bad sex. This is not to suggest that if the court had focused on the other scenes in *Cherry Tricks*, then the finding that the video was degrading and dehumanizing would have been justified. It is simply an attempt to illustrate the underlying assumptions of sexual morality that continue to operate – assumptions in which sexual orientation is not a neutral factor. Neither the *Butler* test nor the sexual morality within which it interpreted or applied is neutral on sexual orientation. While the decision in *Cherry Tricks* is evidence that this sexual morality has shifted, in so far as the Court is willing to say that lesbian sexuality is not in and of itself obscene, this is not the end of the story. Underlying the decision is still a sexual morality informed by the assumption of sexual hierarchy, in which some sex is better than others. Lesbian and gay sex may not be bad sex in and of itself, but it is certainly not as good as straight sex.

Good Girls (and Boys) Don't: Gay and Lesbian Sexual Representations as Bad Sex

The question that remains unanswered in these cases is what gay and lesbian sexual representations have to do with harm against women? While in *Cherry Tricks* the sexual representations of women having sex with women were, arguably, not inappropriately interpreted within the heterosexual context of the video, the same does not apply to the first two cases involving specifically gay and lesbian material. In the *Glad Day Bookshop* decision, the Court did not even attempt to answer the question. In *Scythes*, the Court engages with the question, although it hardly provides an acceptable answer. The Court simply falls back on the heterosexual discursive framework of *Butler*, and assumes that the same harms would flow. At this level, it would seem that both of these obscenity charges against Glad Day Bookshop could reasonably be seen as a misapplication of the *Butler* test. And this is the view taken by feminists who support the *Butler* decision: that *Butler* has been misapplied, and that gay and lesbian representations are being unfairly targeted (Busby 1994, 184–7).

At a deeper level, however, it is considerably less clear that these cases can simply be dismissed as a misapplication. The sexual subtexts of the cases is quite consistent with the sexual subtext of the *Butler* decision. Each of these cases is characterized by assumptions of sexual negativity, sexual essentialism, sexual monism, and sexual hierarchy. While these assumptions are troubling enough in a heterosexual context, they are disastrous in a gay or lesbian context. If heterosexual sex is at risk of being bad sex, then gay or lesbian sex is most certain to be bad sex (sexual negativity). If (hetero) sex is a natural force, then gay or lesbian sex is most likely to be unnatural (sexual essentialism). If there is only one way to have (hetero) sex, then it is almost certain that it is not the way of gay or lesbian sex. And in the hierarchy of sexual activity, gay or lesbian sex most certainly ranks well below heterosexual sex.

Gayle Rubin, in her description of the sex hierarchy, observes that some areas of previously contested sex are now "inching across the line of acceptability": "Unmarried couples living together, masturbation, and some forms of homosexuality are moving in the direction of respectability. Most homosexuality is still on the bad side of the line. But if it is coupled and monogamous, the society is beginning to recognize that it includes the full range of human interaction" (Rubin 1989, 283). In the context of representations of gay and lesbian sexuality, sexually explicit representations risk pushing this sex back across the line of bad sex. Sexually explicit materials focus attention on sexual interaction, which, in turn, seems to detract from viewing gay and lesbian sexuality within this fuller "range of human interaction." Good sex for gay men and lesbians must not only be monogamous and loving – it must also be private and, preferably, in the absence of cameras. The mere representation of gay and lesbian sex risks pushing the new-found acceptability back across the line of bad sex. Gay sexuality can be represented within a higher artistic context – witness films such as *M. Butterfly, The Wedding Banquet, Torch Song Trilogy*, and *Strawberry and Chocolate*, which illustrate the so-called fuller human dimension of gay men's lives, in which sex is only a small part. But, the representation of gay and lesbian sex for the explicit purpose of sexual arousal is in a different category – a category more likely than not to fall on the side of bad sex. Gay and lesbian sexuality may not be degrading and dehumanizing in and of itself – it is just the *representation* of gay and lesbian sexuality that is degrading and dehumanizing. Gay and lesbian sex is not bad sex, but representations of gay and lesbian sex might be. And the more the representation hints of other forms of traditionally "deviant" sexuality, the more likely it is to be bad sex. Bondage and leather is virtually guaranteed to be bad sex. However, even non-monogamous or non-intimate sex, which abounds in heterosexual pornography, risks becoming bad sex if it is situated in the context of gay and lesbian explicit sexual representations.

As I have tried to argue, the *Butler* decision is not neutral on sexual orientation. The analysis of harm within *Butler* is based on a particular analysis of heterosexual sexuality. Yet, it is being deployed in ways that assume that the analysis of harm can be applied to all sexually explicit representations. And as such, the decisions are beginning to expose this underlying heterosexism of the *Butler* test. In *Glad Day Bookshop*, this heterosexual norm was most notoriously exposed: it was simply the representation of gay sex that made the sex bad. In *Bad Attitude*, the heterosexism was somewhat less visible, but no less significant. Lesbian sex was not in and of itself degrading and dehumanizing. Rather, lesbian sex was turned into heterosexual sex, and then judged by heterosexual norms. Even in *Cherry Tricks*, a "straight porn" video, the heterosexual norm of the degrading and dehumanizing test was again apparent, in so far as "otherwise unobjectionable" lesbian sex was judged by harsher standards than heterosexual sex.

Neither the discursive framework of the *Butler* test, nor the dominant sexual morality within which this test is applied, is neutral on the question or sexual orientation. The relevance of sexual orientation within this sexual morality has shifted over time, to the extent that sexual orientation has now become a contested site. It is a sexual morality in which some courts are willing to state that gay and lesbian sexuality is not in and of itself obscene. This is an important change, but it does not signal the end of sexual orientation's relevance. There is still a conservative sexual morality informed by the assumption of sexual hierarchy, in which some sex is better than others. Lesbian and gay sex may not (always) be bad sex in and of itself, but it is certainly not as good as straight sex. Lesbian and gay sex continues to run a much higher risk of being pushed back across the dividing line between good and bad sex, back from its tenuous legitimacy, into its all-too-familiar condemnation as bad sex.

To return to the argument that some feminists have made that the gay and lesbian community is being unfairly targeted and that these decisions by lower courts are a misapplication of the *Butler* decision, I believe that a different reading is possible. While I agree that these are not particularly exceptional examples of judicial decision-making, I disagree that these decisions represent some fundamental deviation from the principles established in *Butler*. The very argument that gay and lesbian sexual representations have been misclassified by the courts – that these representations should not be bad sex – is based on the tacit acceptance of the good sex/bad sex distinction of the *Butler* test, a distinction that only makes sense when put within the framework of the dominant discourses of sexuality. Further, the *Butler* decision still involves an appeal to a community standard – a standard that is national in scope and can be established without evidence. It is a standard that only makes sense in the context of dominant discourses of sexuality that remain informed by a profoundly conservative sexuality morality, in which heterosexuality, and only certain forms of heterosexuality, remain privileged.

While the discourse of *Butler* justifies the law of obscenity in relation to harm towards women, and the promotion of equality and dignity, the sexual subtext of the decision has provided the lower courts with the arsenal they need to repress sexual representation – particularly, sexual representation by sexual minorities. The anti-sex agenda of the *Butler* decision paved the road for the particular judicial approach to gay and lesbian sexual representation.

At the same time, it is important to recognize that the legal regulation of sexual representations in the post-*Butler* era continues to be a site of contest, conflict, and change. Neither the Supreme Court of Canada nor any of the lower courts has yet had their last word in the development and application of obscenity doctrine. In *R. v Hawkins*, the Ontario Court of Appeal entered the fray and attempted to correct what it considered to be evidentiary problems in the early application of the *Butler* test.[24] The site of contest in *Hawkins* was, again, the second category of the *Butler* typography of pornography – degrading and dehumanizing. The Court of Appeal revisited the specific requirements set out in *Butler* for this category of materials. The Court emphasized that not all sexually explicit materials that are degrading and dehumanizing are obscene, but rather must also, according to the *Butler* test, create a substantial risk of harm to society. And, like any element in a criminal trial, "such risk must be proved beyond a reasonable doubt and that proof must be found in the evidence adduced at trial." In considering the facts of each case, and whether sufficient evidence has been adduced at trial to conclude that the materials did create a substantial risk of harm, the Court of Appeal dismissed all but one appeal, in which the Court held that the trial court had incorrectly found the materials to be obscene.[25]

Hawkins is an important development in the post-*Butler* obscenity jurisprudence, particularly in its re-emphasis that the Crown must prove that degrading and dehumanizing materials create a substantial risk of harm. In so doing, it may operate to protect against some of the more flagrant abuses of *Butler*, by ensuring that the Crown meets the regular standard of proof in a criminal case. The ruling casts further doubt on the *Glad Day Bookshop* decision, in which there is a strong argument to be made that the trial judge erred in finding the materials to be obscene, without adequate evidence that the materials caused harm.

However, *Hawkins* does not represent a departure from the *Butler* test, nor from its sexual subtext. It simply re-emphasizes the objective elements of the crime that the Crown must establish. And in so doing, the Court of Appeal can be seen to be reinscribing the good sex/bad sex distinctions that underlie *Butler*. For example, in attempting to clarify the degree of proof that is required to establish the material causes harm, the Court held:

In some cases, as, for example, in films portraying necrophilia, bondage or bestiality, or sex associated with crime, horror, cruelty, coercion or children, it may be concluded from the contents of the films themselves, without expert or other evidence, that they may predispose persons to act in the antisocial manner contemplated by *Butler*. In other cases, as, for example, in films in which the participants appear as fully willing participants occupying substantially equal roles in a setting devoid of violence or the other kinds of conducts just noted, the risk of societal harm may not be evident. Further evidence may be required to prove that exposure to the impugned materials will create a substantial risk of an identifiable harm that may cause persons to act in a manner inimical to the proper functioning of society. (*Hawkins*)

According to the Court of Appeal, some sexual representations are so bad that no further evidence is required to prove that they are bad. Other sexual representations that are not so bad will require further evidence in order to prove that they are bad sex. A new dualism thus arrives on the obscenity scene: bad sex that is really bad, and bad sex that is not really bad. This somewhat recast good sex/bad sex distinction (really bad sex/not really bad sex) is thus deployed to establish the degree of proof required to draw the lines between good and bad sex. In other words, the line between good and bad sex is used to help draw the line between good and bad sex. Ironically, the more the Court attempts to establish objective standards of proof, the more it falls back on it subjective distinctions between good and bad sex.[26]

Hawkins, then, is at best a cause for cautious optimism, in the continuing conflict over the legitimacy of sexual representations. As a legal text, it too is the site of contradictory assumptions about the place and status of sexual representations, assumptions that include instinctive notions about what is good and what is bad. And leave to appeal to the Supreme Court of Canada has been granted in one of the cases included within the *Hawkins* appeal.[27] This appeal means that within the foreseeable future, the Supreme Court of Canada will have another opportunity to address the law of obscenity. And more generally, the appeal is yet another indication that the struggle over the legal representation of sexual representation is far from over. The law of obscenity, along with the place and status of sexual representations in our society, continues to be a site of contest and change.

Conclusion

My efforts in this chapter to reveal and deconstruct the conservative sexual morality of the *Butler* decision should not be seen as a condemnation of any concept of sexual morality. To critique the conservative sexual morality is not necessarily to adopt a position of sexual libertarianism according to which "anything goes." My argument is not that we can transcend sexual morality, and that the Supreme Court of Canada has failed in not doing so. Rather, my concern is with the content of that sexual morality. We delude ourselves with the attempt to cast the legal regulation of sex as something other than what it is. We must, as Carol Smart has argued, recognize that feminism has not transcended moral questions, and begin to address feminism's failure to confront moral questions "sufficiently reflexively" (Smart 1993, 187; see also Gotell in this volume). The legal regulation of sex will necessarily involve a sexual morality – of what is good and what is bad about sex. My point is that the sexual morality of the *Butler* decision is one about which we should be very concerned.

I believe that we need to turn our minds to the question of sexual morality, not away from it. Recognizing and critiquing the deeply problematic nature of the dominant sexual morality that informs the *Butler* decision need not mean that we relinquish the terrain of discursive struggle about sexuality. As feminists and queer theorists have revealed, our sexualities are deeply political. We can and must continue to engage in political argument about the sexual world that we want to inhabit. We need to re-image our sexualities in ways that embrace their deeply political nature and the diversity of human sexual experiences. We need to develop more positive theories of sex and sexual expression; of what makes sex a good and positive dimension to our humanity. We need to move beyond the assumptions of sexual essentialism and sexual monism – to recognize the ways in which our sexualities are products of the communities in which we live, and the ways in which our sexual desires and practices are different. We must transcend the mere denunciation of diversity if we are to construct a sexual morality that is based on respect.

A revisioned sexual morality, based on a radical sexual pluralism, could still allow us to be attentive to the subtle workings of power in sexual discourses. We can still be attentive to the ways in which these subtle workings of power deprive many women from engaging in consensual sex. Yet, we must do so in a way that does not make sweeping generalizations about the way other people engage in consensual sex, including s/m practices of consensual nonconsensuality. Such a sexual morality would further allow us to rethink the legal regulation of sex. Sex laws that seek to impose a conservative sexual morality, in which sex is bad – such as obscenity and the criminalization of prostitution – should be abolished. Sex laws, by contrast that seek to eliminate coercive sex – sexual assault and child sexual abuse – should be retained, and even strengthened. We need not relinquish normative judgment, nor even the drawing of lines between good and bad sex, and, in turn, between good sex laws and bad sex laws. But, we must radically rethink the way in which we do so.

NOTES

1   Lamer, CJC, LaForest, Cory, McLachlin, Stevenson, and Iacobucci, JJ concurred with Sopinka, J. Gonthier, J wrote a minority decision, in which he agreed in the result of the majority, although he offered different reasons. L'Heureux-Dubé, J concurred in this minority decision. It is the majority decision that is the focus of this discussion.

2   In this respect, the community-standard test did represent a significant change from the *Hicklin* test. Under *Hicklin*, virtually any sexual representation could be (and was) found to be obscene, since it was sexual images themselves that were bad. With the community-standards test, it was no longer necessarily the case that sexual representations were in and of themselves bad, but only those representations that were dirty, indecent, or illicit. The community-standards test introduced into obscenity law the possibility of distinguishing between good sex and bad sex. See Kendrick 1987.

3   Another assumption underlying this test seems to be that tolerance is not only more objective than taste, but that it is also broader. This distinction flies in the face of the history of the legal regulation of

obscenity, where the explicit justification of prohibiting its distribution was that certain particularly vulnerable groups in society – notably, poor, uneducated men, and all women, particularly young women – must not be exposed to its influences. Although pornographic images were acceptable for the educated male elites, they must not be massly distributed. The history of pornography reveals that tolerance was in fact considerably more narrow than taste.

4   The Court cites some of the literature that has been seen to establish a connection between pornography and violence against women, includ- ing the U.S. Attorney General's Commission on Pornography (the Meese Commission) of 1986. For a critique of the Meese Commission in particular, see Vance 1993b. For a critique of the literature attempting to find a casual connection between pornography and violence, see Segal 1993 and Thelma McCormack, "Making Sense of the Research on Por- nography," in *Women Against Censorship*, ed. V. Vurstyn (Vancouver: Douglas and McIntyre 1985).

5   This mind/body opposition, which has formed a cornerstone of West- ern thought since Descartes, rests on and reinforces a series of founda- tional dualisms: rational/irrational, culture/nature, subject/object. As feminist theorists have argued, these oppositions are also deeply gen- dered. "In each of the dualisms on which Enlightenment thought rests, rational/irrational, subject/object, and culture/nature, the male is asso- ciated with the first element, the female with the second. And in each case, the male element is privileged over the female" (Hekman 1990, 5). The gendered nature of the mind/body distinction, in which men are associated with the mind, and women with the body, makes several brief, but significant, appearances in the text of the decision.

6   Gayle Rubin describes this assumption of sexual essentialism as "the idea that sex is a natural fore that exists prior to social life and shapes institutions ... [it] consider[s] sex to be eternally unchanging, asocial and transhistorical" (Rubin 1989, 275).

7   As Gayle Rubin argues, "[s]ex is presumed guilty until proven innocent. Virtually all erotic behavior is considered bad unless a specific reason to exempt it has been established" (Rubin 1989, 278). And that reason must have something to do with the other side of the mind/body distinction.

8   Some readers might be inclined to dismiss the relevance of this lan- guage – since it comes, after all, from an old case, which the Court is only reviewing, not unequivocally adopting. Indeed, some commenta- tors point to the fact that the Court expressly rejects this objective of obscenity law later in the decision. However, I believe that this language

is not insignificant. Similar language is deployed through the decision. Sopinka, J resorts to the language of sex as dirty, of "dirt for dirt's sake," on several occasions in the decision. His use of quotation marks, signalling both the adoption of this language from earlier decisions and, presumably, his distance from this language, is somehow intended to sanitize his deployment of the language. These are not his words, after all. Yet, he chooses to use them – again and again. Even in quotation marks, the effect of the repetition of this phrase is to reinforce the underlying binary opposition between good and bad sex (between dirty and clean sex). This repeated deployment of the discourse of sex as dirty is significant in the production of meaning, and in revealing the sexual subtext of the decision.

9   As Lynda Nead's work has illustrated, pornography and art have been set up as binary oppositions, in which each is defined as that which the other is not. "If art is a reflection of the highest social values, then pornography is a symptom of a rotten society; if art stands for lasting, universal values, then pornography represents disposability, trash. Art is a sign of cleanliness and licit morality, whereas pornography symbolizes filth and the illicit" (Nead 1993b, 282).

10   This second category is not the only contested site. Rather, the question of what constitutes "sex with violence" within the first category is also a highly contested site, particularly within the context of s/m sex. S/m-sex advocates argue that s/m sex is not violence, and thus ought not to be classified as "sex with violence." Gayle Rubin, for example, writes "S/M materials are aimed at an audience that understand a set of conventions for interpreting them. Sadomasochism is not a form of violence, but is rather a type of ritual and contractual sex play whose aficionados go to great lengths in order to do it and to ensure the safety and enjoyment of one another. S/m fantasy does involve images of coercion and sexual activities that may appear violent to outsiders" (Rubin 1993a, 22). Yet the mere appearance of these images is within the context of the *Butler* test, likely to lead to their classification as "sex with violence." As a result, consensual s/m sex, as well as depictions of sex with bondage, is (mis)classified as "sex with violence."

11   *See R. v Keegstra* (1990), 61 CCC (3d) 1; *Reference re:ss.193 and 195.1(1)(c) of the Criminal Code* (1990), 56 CCC (3d) 65.

12   There is some inconsistency in the Court's description of sex as physical activity. At 472, the Court distinguishes between purely physical activity, like parking a car, and physical activity, such as sex. However, at 474, the Court again uses the phrase "purely physical activity" as

synonymous with "purely sexual activity." The point seems to be that although sex may not be so purely physical as to be devoid of any expression, it is, nevertheless, still physical. In relation to the mind/body distinction, it remains of the body, which foreshadows the Court's subsequent discussion of the "nature of expression."

13 Section 1 of the *Charter* provides that all rights and freedoms are "subject only to such reasonable limits, prescribed by law, as can be demonstrably justified in a free and democratic society." The Supreme Court of Canada has established a test for this section 1 analysis (*R. v Oakes*). According to this test, the Government must first establish that there is a pressing and substantial objective that justifies overriding the violation of the *Charter* right. Second, the government must establish that the violation of the *Charter* right is proportional with the objective of the legislation.

14 Although the Court tends to use the words "objective" and "purpose" interchangeably, the word "purpose" is often used specifically in relation to the "shifting purpose doctrine." Shifting-purpose doctrine refers to the idea that the purpose of a law can change over time. This doctrine was rejected by the Supreme Court in *R. v Big M Drug Mart Ltd* [1985] 1 SCR 295. Dickson J (as he then was) held that "Purpose is a function of the intent of those who drafted and enacted the legislation at the time and not of any shifting variable." In considering the objective of the legislation, courts are thus not permitted to consider a new purpose, but rather must focus only on the purpose of the drafters of the legislation.

15 It is interesting to note, however, the way in which the shifting-purpose doctrine has been used in other cases by the Supreme Court of Canada. In a subsequent s. 2(b) case, *R. v Zundel* (1992), in which neo-Nazi Ernst Zundel was charged with the crime of spreading false news for this publication of Holocaust denials, the Supreme Court of Canada struck down s. 181 of the *Criminal Code*, on the basis that it violated freedom of expression and was not justifiable under section 1. The shifting-purpose doctrine was an important factor in the decision. The Court rejected the arguments of the Government that the objective of the legislation could be seen. On the basis of *Butler*, it was open to the Court to cast the objective of the legislation more broadly. Indeed, it is difficult to reconcile the decisions of the Court in *Butler* with its decision in *Zundel* on the shifting-purpose doctrine.

In comparing the use of the shifting-purpose doctrine in these two cases, I do not mean to conflate the regulation of sexual expression with the regulation of hate expression. These two areas, which are often conflated in procensorship arguments <pornography is framed as hate speech>, have very different histories, with very distinct legislative objectives. A position for or against the censorship of sexual representations should be seen and evaluated quite separately from a position for or against the censorship of hate speech. Although there may be similar arguments in terms of the relative legitimacy and efficacy of state censorship, the arguments are otherwise quite distinct. As discussed in the introduction, it is not our intention in this book to evaluate the relative merits of the regulation of hate speech.

16 This proportionality requirement involves a three-step test: (1) there must be a rational connection between the legislative provision violating the right of the objective; (2) there must be a minimum impairment of the right; and (3) there must be proper balance between the effect of the legislative provision and the legislative objective.

17 For a further discussion of this marginalization of the s. 2(b) guarantees through the section 1 analysis, see Jamie Cameron, "Abstract Principle v Contextual Conceptions of Harm: A Comment on R. v Butler," (1992) 37 *McGill LJ* 1135.

18 Tariff Code 9956 prohibits the importation of obscene materials, as defined by s. 163 of the *Criminal Code* into Canada. When materials are seized by Canada Customs, the importer has a right of appeal. The first step involves a request for redetermination, after which ensues an appeal to the deputy minister of National Revenue for Customs and Excise, and, subsequently, to court.

19 Henderson examines the lesbian s/m imagery in *On Our Backs*, a lesbian sex magazine, and Pat Califia's *Macho Sluts*, a collection of short stories about lesbian s/m. She argues that both are filled with references to the consensual nature of the sexual practices of the women. "*Macho Sluts* also addresses a range of readers through its demystifications of s/m practice, particularly around images of consent. Indeed, in her introduction, Califia challenges critics who would argue that amid the sexual coercions of patriarchal society, women cannot truly consent to sadomasochism: "If you don't believe we choose to do s/m, you aren't using the term 'consent' in any meaningful way, but rather, as a synonym for 'mature,' 'socially acceptable' and 'politically correct' ... Virtually all the stories ... make pointed distinctions between sadomasochism and sexual coersion" (Henderson 1992, 184).

20 This issue of consent in lesbian sexual representations is explored more fully by Becki Ross in chapter 4.

21 We are at least partially indebted to LEAF for this heteroswitching

technique. In the *Butler* case, LEAF attempted to support their arguments of the degrading and dehumanizing nature of pornography to
women with reference to gay male pornography. Kathleen Mahoney,
quoted in *MS Magazine*, explained: "We showed them the porn – and
among the seized videos were some horrifically violent and degrading
gay movies. We made the point that the abused men in these films were
being treated like women – and the judges got it. Otherwise, men can't
put themselves in our shoes. Porn makes women's subordination look
sexy and appealing; it doesn't threaten men's jobs, safety, rights, or
credibility" (Landsberg 1992, 14).

Karen Busby, however, denies that LEAF played into homophobic
discourses in its arguments, and she specifically takes issue with the
allegations that LEAF showed videos of gay sex to the Court, which she
insists is categorically untrue, and simply the product of media misrep-
resentation. It is difficult to know what to make of Mahoney's quote in
the Landsberg article, since neither Mahoney, Landsberg, or *MS Maga-*
zine appear to have retracted the comments. While LEAF did not in fact
show videos in Court, Mahoney's words suggest that LEAF may have
simply tried to make this connection in oral argument. Busby admits
that LEAF did refer to gay male pornography, but that the arguments in
no way collapsed these materials with the harms-based analysis of
heterosexual pornography (Busby 1994, 179–80). It is difficult, however,
to reconcile Busby's argument with the submission in LEAF's factum,
which Busby herself cites – that is, that "LEAF submits that some of the
subject of pornography of men for men, in addition to abusing some
men in ways that is more common to abuse women through sex, arguably contributes to abuse and homophobia as it normalizes sexual
aggression generally." The submission seems more in line with Mahoney's quote than with Busby's explanation.

22 The technique of heteroswitching can be related to what Eve Sedgwick
has described as the trope of "gender inversion," according to which
lesbians have long been constructed as virile and masculine (and conversely, gay men as effeminate) in order to maintain "the essential
heterosexuality within desire itself" (*Epistemology of the Closet* [Berkeley:
University of California Press, 1990] at 87). The construction of sexuality
as heterosexuality is thereby not threatened or displaced by the recognition of same-sex sexuality. The heteroswitching is perhaps a particular
manifestation of this gender inversion, which within the context of
obscenity leaves the heterosexual norm of both sexuality and its model
of harm unchallenged.

23 This is hardly a surprising factor, in so far as much straight pornography includes depictions of women having sex with women. The discursive distinction between these sexual representations and the representations of specifically lesbian sexuality is discussed in greater length by Becki Ross in chapter 4.

24 *R. v Hawkins* involved appeals from five separate criminal charges, in relation to four different accused persons: Hawkins, Ronish, Smeek, and Jorgensen: Jorgenson had two different charges against him – one against his adult video store in Hamilton, and one against his store in Scarborough. The Crown appealed the acquittals of Hawkins and Ronish at trial. The defendants Jorgensen and Smeek appealed their convictions.

25 In *Hawkins*, the Crown had adduced no evidence to establish harmful effects, and the material had been approved by the Ontario Film Review Board for "restricted audiences," which absent any evidence rebutting this finding could be taken as a significant indication of the community standard of tolerance. The Crown's appeal of the acquittal was dismissed.

In *Ronish*, the evidence adduced by the Crown did not prove to the satisfaction of the judge that social harm would result from exposure to the films. The Crown's appeal of the acquittal was dismissed.

In *Jorgensen* (Scarborough), the trial judge correctly concluded that the content of the three videos included the depiction of sex coupled with violence and coercion and created the requisite risk of harm. The approval of the materials by the OFRB was found not to be determinative. Rather, the trial judge had properly treated this evidence as indicative of community standards of tolerance, but concluded that it did not outweigh the evidence before her that the material coupled sex with violence and created a substantial risk of harm. The defendant's appeal was dismissed. In *Jorgensen* (Hamilton), the record in the case did not contain evidence to support the conclusion that community standards require that "sexual activity take place within the context of love, affection, commitment, or emotional involvement." The evidence, including the testimony of the Chair of the OFRB, indicated the opposite – that is, that "explicit depiction of human sexuality in a context devoid of any meaningful relationship does not exceed contemporary national community standards of tolerance." The defendant's appeal was allowed.

In *Smeek*, the violence, vampirism, and necrophilia depicted in the films was, according to the Court of Appeal, "patently such as to bring the films within the second of the *Butler* categories." The depictions were degrading and dehumanizing, and created a risk of harm. The defendant's appeal was dismissed.

26 Further, in this passage, the Court articulates its own view of which particular sexual practices constitute really bad sex. These bad representations include those specifically mentioned in s. 163 – sex with "crime, horror, cruelty," as well as those specifically mentioned in *Butler* – sex with children. But, these representations also include sexual practices that are not explicitly mentioned in s. 163, or by the Supreme court of Canada in the *Butler* test – necrophilia, bondage, bestiality, coercion. There may in fact be a strong argument to be made on the face of the *Butler* reasoning, and its underlying sexual morality, that these practices are within these categories of bad sex. But, these practices were not specifically so designated within the *Butler* decision. Nor does the Court of Appeal articulate its reasoning for including these practices within these proscribed categories. Rather, it simply asserts these practices as obvious examples of really bad sex – so obvious, that no reasoning is required to bring them within the *Butler* categories.

27 The Crown's application for leave to appeal in the acquittals of *Hawkins* and *Ronish* was dismissed, but the defendant's applications for leave to appeal their convictions in *Jorgensen* was allowed.

READING QUESTION ON COSSMAN

1 Do Dworkin and Cossman arrive at the same conclusion by very different routes or do they share more in common that at first sight appears to be the case?

Little Sisters Book and Art Emporium v Canada (Minister of Justice) 2000 SCC 69

Little Sisters, a bookstore in Vancouver, challenged the right of Canadian customs officers to seize gay and lesbian materials at the border. The officers believed it was their mandate to do so under the *Butler* decision, above.

Binnie, J: – Little Sisters is a lesbian and gay bookshop ... The store carried a specialized inventory catering to the gay and lesbian community which consisted largely of books that included, but was not limited to, gay and lesbian literature, travel information, general interest periodicals, academic studies related to homosexuality, AIDS/HIV safe sex advisory material and gay and lesbian erotica. It was not in the nature of a "XXX Adult" store. It was and is a boutique carrying a fairly broad range of inventory of interest to a special clientele. It was considered something of a "community centre" for Vancouver's gay and lesbian population.

The appellants concede that much of the material imported by Little Sisters consisted of erotica but have denied throughout that anything it has imported is obscene ... We are told that Canada produces very little gay and lesbian erotica, obscene or otherwise, and Little Sisters therefore depends on foreign suppliers, mainly in the United States. The appeal therefore requires us to consider what limitations may constitutionally be placed on freedom of expression when "expression" crosses international boundaries, and to what extent the rights of importers must be balanced against the state's interest in preventing the importation of materials that the state considers to be harmful to society ...

Section 99 of the *Customs Act* authorizes customs officers to examine imported goods and mail and to open packages that they reasonably suspect may contain goods referred to in the Customs Tariff, RSC 1985, c. 41 (3rd Supp.) ... At the entry level, Customs Inspectors determine the appropriate tariff classification (s. 58). At the relevant time, an item considered "obscene" and thus prohibited was subject to a re-determination upon request, by a specialized Customs unit and upon a further appeal subject to a further re-determination by the Deputy Minister or designate ...

Government interference with freedom of expression in any form calls for vigilance. Where, as here, a trial judge finds that such interference is accompanied "by the systemic targeting" of a particular group in society (in this case individuals who were seen as standardbearers for the gay and lesbian community), the issue takes on a further and even more serious dimension. Sexuality is a source of profound vulnerability, and the appellants reasonably concluded that they were in many ways being treated by Customs officials as sexual outcasts ... In this Court the Crown acknowledges that errors were made in the classification of the appellants' imported materials, but says that such errors were only to be expected given the huge volume of cross-border mail handled at the Vancouver Customs Mail Centre each day ...

I propose first to deal with the relationship between the Customs legislation and the obscenity provisions of the *Criminal Code* as interpreted in *Butler*. My conclusion is that the Customs legislation violates the appellants' freedom of expression, as the Crown is prepared to concede, but with the exception of the reverse onus provision in s. 152(3) of the *Customs Act*, it constitutes a reasonable limit prescribed by law which the Crown has justified under s. 1 of the *Charter* ...

The administration of the Act, however, was characterized by conduct of Customs officials that was oppressive and dismissive of the appellants' freedom of expression. Its effect – whether intended or not – was to isolate and disparage the appellants on the basis of their sexual orientation ...

My conclusion on the first branch of the appellants' attack is that the *Butler* analysis does not discriminate against the gay and lesbian community. *Butler* is directed to the prevention of harm, and is indifferent to whether such harm arises in the context of heterosexuality or homosexuality. Nor in my view is the gay and lesbian community discriminated against in the Customs legislation, which is quite capable of being administered in a manner that respects *Charter* rights. The government is entitled to impose border inspections of expressive material. The obstacles experienced by the appellants and detailed at length by the trial judge were not inherent in the statutory scheme. The obstacles were, however, very real and in the end quite unjustified ...

The appellants contend that importing a majoritarian analysis into the definition of obscenity (e.g., what the broader Canadian community will tolerate), inevitably creates prejudice against non-mainstream, minority representations of sex and sexuality. They argue that the "national" community is by definition majoritarian and is more likely than the homosexual community itself to view gay and lesbian imagery as degrading and dehumanizing. The whole idea of a community standards test, they say, is incompatible with *Charter* values that were enacted to protect minority rights. The fact that no particular evidence to define the community standard is required to support a successful prosecution heightens the vulnerability of minorities ... What makes this standard even more problematic in the context of gay and lesbian erotica is that where expression is suppressed on the basis of sexual orientation, so goes the argument, it silences voices that are already suppressed and subject to discrimination ...

This line of argument simply rejects the idea that *Butler* means what it says, i.e., that the community standard of tolerance is based on the reasonable apprehension of harm, not on morality. The arguments assume that any appeal to a national community standard cannot be targeted on harm and will inevitably be overwhelmed by majoritarian taste. This approach presupposes that the arbiter (the broader community) is incapable of being focussed on the task that it is required to address (harm). We have no evidence that the courts are not able to apply the *Butler* test, and the reported decisions seem to confirm that the identification of harm is a well understood requirement ...

The constitutional question challenges the validity of s. 71 of the Customs Act, on which the redetermination and court proceedings are based. In part, the challenge relies on the "reverse onus" provision applied in such proceedings by virtue of s. 152(3) of the *Customs Act*, as explained in oral argument by counsel for the appellants:

We challenge the entire scheme, not just the power of the Customs officer at the front line to do that detention and prohibition, but the scheme insofar as it puts the onus on the importer, whether the importer is a bookstore or a regular individual to seek a redetermination, or review, or appeal, would have you through a byzantine bureaucratic process and ultimately to the Courts in order to prove that the material is not obscene.

Section 152(3) is not specific to obscenity or even to prohibited goods generally, but applies to "any proceeding under this Act," including the appeals process authorized by s. 71. Section 152(3) directs the decision-maker to assume that Customs officials are right unless and until the importer proves them to be wrong. It provides:

(3) Subject to subsection (4), in any proceeding under this Act, the burden of proof in any question relating to ...

(d) the compliance with any of the provisions of this Act or the regulations in respect of any goods lies on the person, other than Her Majesty, who is a party to the proceeding or the person who is accused of an offence, and not on Her Majesty.

The appellants did not directly impugn the constitutionality of the reverse onus provision in their application to state the constitutional questions, presumably because they intended to rely on its continued validity as a lever to overturn the rest of the Customs legislation in relation to expressive materials. In my view, however, the appellants' attack on s. 71 and the procedures it authorizes is inextricably bound up with the reverse onus provision, and the Court is not bound to accept the application of the latter as valid when considering the constitutionality of the former. The constitutional question in relation to s. 71 encompasses both aspects of the appellants' argument.

The first step is to identify which of the various remedies afforded by s. 71 attract the s. 152(3) onus. Where applicable, it would put on the importer the burden of establishing a negative, i.e., that the expressive material is more likely than not to be non-obscene.

The word "proceeding" is of course apt to apply to any court action that may follow an in-house Customs determination. In my view, however, the provision cannot constitutionally apply to put on the importer the onus of disproving obscenity. Otherwise entry of expressive materials could be denied by reason of the onus even where the standard of obscenity is not met, as for example, where an importer lacks the resources or the stamina to contest an initial determination. An importer has a *Charter* right to receive expressive material unless the state can justify its denial. It is not open to the state to put the onus on an individual to show why he or she should be allowed to exercise a *Charter* right. It is for the state to establish that a limitation on the *Charter* right is justified: *R. v Oakes*, per Dickson, CJ at pp. 136–7: "The onus of proving that a limit on a right or freedom guaranteed by the *Charter* is reasonable and demonstrably justified in a free and democratic society rests upon the party seeking to uphold the limitation."

As to the obscenity determination at the departmental level, I do not think s. 152(3) applies at all. The Crown does not contend that all expressive material entering Canada is presumptively obscene until shown to be otherwise. The earliest the reverse onus could apply with any logic is in the re-determination, but at that stage the importer is given neither sufficient notice nor a sufficient opportunity to be heard to discharge the onus. The reality is that once the front-line officer has made the initial determination that he or she considers the publication to be obscene, the question for the Deputy Minister or designate on the re-determination is whether the Department is ready, willing and able, if required, to establish in court that the detained material is obscene.

As mentioned, s. 152(3) is not restricted to obscenity but has a broad application across the whole Customs process. It may be appropriate when dealing with imports of materials that ordinarily would not have much constitutional sensitivity (such as Minister Nowlan's "cabbages and cucumbers") to put the onus on the importer at the court level to show that the Customs official has made an erroneous tariff classification. What may work as a general rule in circumstances where Customs procedures are not limited by constitutional rights does not, however, work in relation to constitutionally protected expressive materials. In these circumstances, however, the proper order should be limited to the matters pertinent to the disposition of this appeal. I would therefore declare that s. 152(3) is not to be construed and applied so as to place on an importer the onus to establish that goods are not obscene within the meaning of s. 163(8) of the *Criminal Code*. The burden of proving obscenity rests on the Crown or other person who alleges it ...

Iacobucci, J: – The Customs Tariff, s. 114, states that "[t]he importation into Canada of any goods enumerated or referred to in Schedule VII is prohibited." Schedule VII, Code 9956(a), prohibits importation of:

Books, printed paper, drawings, paintings, prints, photographs or representations of any kind that
(a) are deemed to be obscene under subsection 163(8) of the *Criminal Code*.

Several aspects of this regulatory scheme warrant comment. The first is that the initial classification decision, according to s. 58 of the *Customs Act*, is to be made by "[a]n officer." Section 2 of the Act states that a customs officer includes any "person employed in the administration or enforcement" of the *Customs Act*, and any member of the Royal Canadian Mounted Police. In practice, these decisions are made by Customs Inspectors and Commodity Specialists, the front-line customs officers. The statute does not designate any specialized officers to make obscenity determinations. Instead, any one of the approximately 4,000 customs officers working at the border can prohibit a book from entering the country. The officers receive minimal training with regard to obscenity determinations and are not required to have any specialized knowledge of art or literature.

At high-volume border crossings, such as the Toronto region, certain Commodity Specialists are given special responsibilities over obscenity determinations. Goods suspected of being obscene are detained and forwarded to a Commodity Specialist for classification. However, John Shearer, the Director General of the Tariff Programs Division, testified that working on obscenity classifications is perceived to be more stressful and limiting career-wise. As a result, as Smith, J recognized, "Customs employees generally consider this work to be undesirable, not all officers participate in it and those assigned to it are regularly moved from these duties into other areas, generally after three to six months" ((1996), 18 BCLR (3d) 241, at para. 44).

Section 58 is also notable for its failure to offer any guidance as to how the tariff classification is to be made. It does not provide for even the simplest of hearings. It does not allow the importer to present evidence, call witnesses, or submit written arguments. It does not require the officer to provide reasons for the decision to prohibit. It does not even require the officer to read or view the material in question ... Customs officers' review of imported materials is frequently superficial and context-insensitive. A typical example is provided by the testimony of Scenery Slater, a Customs Inspector at the Vancouver Mail Centre, describing how she would review a videotape:

[W]e would view it on fast forward. And if there was – there was a scene or scenes we deemed might be potentially prohibited, we rewind and slow it down to verify, and do this through the entirety of the tape.

When asked whether she would typically read a book in its entirety, she responded as follows:

That was rarely necessary. It's – what you – what you would initially do is you would try to determine the gist of the book ... If you started reading it and the general nature was sort of sensationalistic in a sexual manner, and you might flip through to make sure the entirety is like that, go to various sections throughout ... You would find – try to find at least two to three instances of having something prohibited and then once you hit three in the – it was deemed that the rest of the book was of the same nature you would prohibit it there without reading the rest of it.

Several Customs officers testified that they did not even attempt to judge the political, artistic, or literary merit of a particular work. Mr Shearer freely admitted that customs officers do not hold themselves out to be experts on artistic or literary merit. Moreover, Customs officers often do not understand the context in which a book was written. For example, Linda Murphy, the Director of the PID, admitted her lack of understanding of "the S and M practices engaged in by some people in our society." Another Customs officer admitted that she had not recognized Marguerite Duras as a major French novelist of the twentieth century, and that she generally did not have enough time to investigate the literary credentials of the authors whose books appear before her for review ... Incorrect determinations are the inevitable result of these factors ... Behind the statistics are countless anecdotes of incorrect seizures ... An importer or exporter with a history of dealing in pornography is also susceptible to increased scrutiny. During the time period relevant to this appeal, Customs officers in British Columbia inspected virtually every shipment of books and magazines headed to Little Sisters ... While Little Sisters and its suppliers are routinely targeted, mainstream bookstores receive more favourable treatment ... Similarly, books that were prohibited when destined for Little Sisters were widely available at other general interest bookstores in Vancouver, and even at the Vancouver Public Library ... A discussion of the facts as brief as this cannot capture adequately the complexities of the record compiled in this appeal. Nevertheless, I hope to have conveyed a basic portrayal of the Customs legislation and its enforcement.

III ANALYSIS ...

I agree with my colleague Binnie, J's defence of the harm-based approach to obscenity set out by this Court in *Butler, supra*. In particular, I agree with his conclusions that the *Butler* test does not distinguish between materials based on the sexual orientation of the individuals involved or characters depicted. It seems to me that the *Butler* test applies equally to heterosexual, homosexual and bisexual materials ... We differ, however, over the crucial issue of whether the Customs legislation itself is responsible for the constitutional violations documented in this case, or whether it is only the legislation's application that was at fault ... Consequently, I disagree with my colleague Binnie, J's interpretation of this Court's decisions in *Hunter v Southam Inc.*, [1984] 2 SCR 145, *R. v Morgentaler*, [1988] 1 SCR 30, and *R. v Bain*, [1992] 1 SCR 91. In my opinion, these cases illustrate the vigilance of this Court in protecting *Charter* rights when the legislative scheme in question is being applied in an unconstitutional fashion. Regardless of whether the legislation is under- or over-inclusive, if it lends itself to the repeated violations of *Charter* rights, as does the legislative scheme here, the legislation itself is partially responsible and must be remedied ... *Morgentaler* also rejected the argument that any problems were a product of maladministration, not the legislation itself.

In this case, Binnie, J argues that a failure at the implementation level can be addressed at that level. As will be discussed below, however, the government has provided little reason to believe that reforms at the implementation level will adequately protect the expressive rights involved or that any such reforms will not be dependent on exemplary conduct by Customs officials to avoid future violations of constitutional rights ... When the problems at the review stages are also taken into consideration, it is clear that the legislative scheme must take significant responsibility for the violations of expressive rights that have been documented in this case. This is not surprising when one considers that the Customs legislation was designed to deal with mechanical, objective determinations under a taxing regime and not nuanced judgments on literary and expressive values that are inherently subjective. I therefore conclude that it is the Customs legislation itself which is largely responsible for the infringement of s. 2(b) *Charter* rights in this case.

E Is the Violation of Section 2(b) Justified Under Section 1?

The government's burden under s. 1 is to justify the actual infringement on rights occasioned by the impugned legislation, not simply that occasioned by some hypothetical ideal of the legislation. In my view, my colleague Binnie, J incorrectly analyzes the s. 1 justification with regard only to the Customs legislation when properly administered. Examining such a hypothetical ideal runs the risk of allowing even egregious violations of *Charter* rights to go unaddressed. Obviously any substantive standard for obscenity will have difficulties in application, regardless of the institutional setting in which it is applied. As we recognized in *Butler* and *Keegstra*, this will not necessarily be cause for concern. Where, however, the challenge is to the procedures by which the law is enforced, the fact that far more materials are prohibited than intended is extremely relevant ...

What is challenged primarily in this appeal is not the exclusion of obscenity from this country; instead, it is the legislation which establishes the procedural mechanism for doing so, by which a great deal of non-obscene works are detained or prohibited. The narrow ambit of the government's legitimate purpose will be important to remember when determining whether the Customs legislation is a proportional response to the danger posed by the entry of obscene materials to Canada ...

In light of the Customs legislation's failure to acknowledge effectively the unique *Charter* concerns raised by expressive materials, I conclude that it is not minimally intrusive. As noted above, the only accommodation made for expressive materials is that their review under s. 67 is done by a superior court rather than by the Canadian International Trade Tribunal. In my view, this is insufficient to safeguard the fundamental *Charter* rights at stake. The sheer number of contested prohibitions, and the cost of challenging them through the various levels of administrative review, make it completely impracticable for the appellants to contest each one of them up to the s. 67 level. Thus the accommodation provided is not even triggered for the vast majority of prohibitions ...

The common law has a long tradition disfavouring prior restraint ... As Thomas Emerson argued in "The Doctrine of Prior Restraint" ... the "worst evils of the system are likely to accumulate" where the system "entrusts the prevention of communication to an executive official." This is not to criticize the character of those charged with enforcing the Customs legislation. I have no doubt that they are generally honest, well-intentioned, hard-working civil servants. Emerson's point, to the contrary, is that the institutional dynamics of prior restraint commonly produce the kinds of "grave systemic problems" found in this case ... The flaws in the Customs regime are not the product of simple bad faith or maladministration, but rather flow from the very nature of prior restraint itself.

READING QUESTIONS ON *LITTLE SISTERS*

1 Do you agree with Iacobucci, J that the fault lies with the legislation, not just with its administration? Are his arguments specific to prior restraint of free expression, or more general? How are they related to the views of Hobbes and Fuller, above?
2 Do you agree with Binnie, J that a reverse onus is appropriate for "cabbages and cucumbers"? Or would that too violate values related to the rule of law?
3 In evaluating legislation, should judges assume it will be administered perfectly? Imperfectly? Sloppily? How might one justify the appropriate standard?
4 Both Iacobucci, J and Binnie, J say that *Butler* applies to homosexual as well as heterosexual materials. Is this claim convincing? How might one apply it, given the role that the court, following MacKinnon, gives to pornography in the subordination of women?
5 How do you suppose Cossman, above, would respond to the decision?

9

Abortion

Political debate about abortion has raged for decades. As such, it probably needs no introduction. The selections included here attempt to articulate views of abortion that treat its regulation as a special case of more general legal principles.

Judith Jarvis Thomson[1]
"A Defence of Abortion" (1971)

Thomson argues that, even if we suppose the foetus to be a person, the limits of moral and legal duties to aid others ensure that abortion cannot be prohibited.

Most opposition to abortion relies on the premise that the foetus is a human being, a person, from the moment of conception. The premise is argued for, but, as I think, not well. Take, for example, the most common argument. We are asked to notice that the development of a human being from conception through birth into childhood is continuous; then it is said that to draw a line, to choose a point in this development and say "before this point the thing is not a person, after this point it is a person" is to make an arbitrary choice, a choice for which in the nature of things no good reason can be given. It is concluded that the foetus is, or anyway that we had better say it is, a person from the moment of conception. But this conclusion does not follow. Similar things might be said about the development of an acorn into an oak tree, and it does not follow that acorns are oak trees, or that we had better say they are. Arguments of this form are sometimes called "slippery slope arguments" – the phrase is perhaps self-explanatory – and it is dismaying that opponents of abortion rely on them so heavily and uncritically.

I am inclined to agree, however, that the prospects for "drawing a line" in the development of the foetus look dim. I am inclined to think also that we shall probably have to agree that the foetus has already become a human person well before birth. Indeed, it comes as a surprise when one first learns how early in its life it begins to acquire human characteristics. By the tenth week, for example, it already has a face, arms and legs, fingers and toes; it has internal organs, and brain activity is detectable.[2] On the other hand, I think that the premise is false, that the foetus is not a person from the moment of conception. A newly fertilized ovum, a newly implanted clump of cells, is no more a person than an acorn is an oak tree. But I shall not discuss any of this. For it seems to me to be of great interest to ask what happens if, for the sake of argument, we allow the premise. How, precisely, are we supposed to get from there to the conclusion that abortion is morally impermissible? Opponents of abortion commonly spend most of their time establishing that the foetus is a person, and hardly any time explaining the step from there to the impermissibility of abortion. Perhaps they think the step too simple and obvious to require much comment. Or perhaps instead they are simply being economical in argument. Many of those who defend abortion rely on the premise that the foetus is not a person, but only a bit of tissue that will become a person at birth; and why pay out more arguments than you have to? Whatever the explanation, I suggest that the step they take is neither easy nor obvious, that it calls for closer examination than it is commonly given, and that when we do give it this closer examination we shall feel inclined to reject it.

I propose, then, that we grant that the foetus is a person from the moment of conception. How does the argument go from here? Something like this, I take it. Every person has a right to life. So the foetus has a right to life. No doubt the mother has a right to decide what happens in and to her body; everyone would grant that. But surely a person's right to life is stronger and more stringent than the mother's right to decide what happens in and to her body, and so outweighs it. So the foetus may not be killed; an abortion may not be performed.

It sounds plausible. But now let me ask you to imagine this. You wake up in the morning and find yourself back to back in bed with an unconscious violinist. A famous unconscious violinist. He has been found to have a fatal kidney ailment, and the Society of Music Lovers has canvassed all the available medical records and found that you alone have the right blood type to help. They have therefore kidnapped you, and last night the violinist's circulatory system was plugged into yours, so that your kidneys can be used to extract poisons from his blood as well as your own. The director of the hospital now tells you, "Look, we're sorry the Society of Music Lovers did this to you – we would never have permitted it if we had known. But still, they did it, and the violinist now is plugged into you. To unplug you would be to kill him. But never mind, it's only for nine months. By then he will have recovered from his ailment, and can safely be unplugged from you." Is it morally incumbent on you to accede to this situation? No doubt it would be very nice of you if you did, a great kindness. But do you *have* to accede to it? What if it were not nine months, but nine years? Or longer still? What if the director of the hospital says, "Tough luck, I agree, but you've now got to stay in bed, with the violinist plugged into you, for the rest of your life. Because remember this. All persons have a right to life, and violinists are persons. Granted you have a right to decide what happens in and to your body, but a person's right to life outweighs your right to decide what happens in and to your body. So you cannot ever be unplugged from him." I imagine you would regard this as outrageous, which suggests that something really is wrong with that plausible-sounding argument I mentioned a moment ago.

In this case, of course, you were kidnapped; you didn't volunteer for the operation that plugged the violinist into your kidneys. Can those who oppose abortion on the ground I mentioned make an exception for a pregnancy due to rape? Certainly. They can say that persons have a right to life only if they didn't come into existence because of rape; or they can say that all persons have a right to life, but that some have less of a right to life than others, in particular, that those who came into existence because of rape have less. But these statements have a rather unpleasant sound. Surely the question of whether you have a right to life at all, or how much of it you have, shouldn't turn on the question of whether or not you are the product of a rape. And in fact the people who oppose abortion on the ground I mentioned do not make this distinction, and hence do not make an exception in case of rape.

Nor do they make an exception for a case in which the mother has to spend the nine months of her pregnancy in bed. They would agree that would be a great pity, and hard on the mother; but all the same, all persons have a right to life, the foetus is a person, and so on. I suspect, in fact, that they would not make an exception for a case in which, miraculously enough, the pregnancy went on for nine years, or even the rest of the mother's life.

Some won't even make an exception for a case in which continuation of the pregnancy is likely to shorten the mother's life; they regard abortion as impermissible even to save the mother's life. Such cases are nowadays very rare, and many opponents of abortion do not accept this extreme view. All the same, it is a good place to begin: a number of points of interest come out in respect to it.

1. Let us call the view that abortion is impermissible even to save the mother's life "the extreme view." I want to suggest that it does not issue from the argument I mentioned earlier without the addition of some fairly powerful premises. Suppose a woman has become pregnant, and now learns that she has a cardiac condition such that she will die if she carries the baby to term. What may be done for her? The foetus, being a person, has a right to life, but as the mother is a person too, so has she a right to life. Presumably they have an equal right to life. How is it supposed to come out that an abortion may not be performed? If mother and child have an equal right to life, shouldn't we perhaps flip a coin? Or should we add to the mother's right to life her right to decide what happens in and to her body, which everybody seems to be ready to grant – the sum of her rights now outweighing the foetus's right to life?

The most familiar argument here is the following. We are told that performing the abortion would be directly killing[3] the child, whereas doing nothing would not be killing the mother, but only letting her die. Moreover, in killing the child, one would be killing an innocent person, for the child has committed no crime, and is not aiming at his mother's death. And then there are a variety of ways in which this might be continued. (1) But as directly killing an innocent person is always and absolutely impermissible, an abortion may not be performed. Or, (2) as directly killing an innocent person is murder, and murder is always and absolutely impermissible, an abortion may not be performed.[4] or, (3) as one's duty to refrain from directly killing an innocent person is more stringent than one's duty to keep a person from dying, an abortion may not be performed. Or, (4) if one's only options are directly killing an innocent person or letting a person die, one must prefer letting the person die, and thus an abortion may not be performed.[5]

Some people seem to have thought that these are not further premises which must be added if the conclusion is to be reached, but that they follow from the very fact that an innocent person has a right to life.[6] But this seems to me to be a mistake, and perhaps the simplest way to show this is to bring out that while we must certainly grant that innocent persons have a right to life, the theses in (1) through (4) are all false. Take (2), for example. If directly killing an innocent person is murder, and thus is impermissible, then the mother's directly killing the innocent person inside her is murder, and thus is impermissible. But it cannot seriously be thought to be murder if the mother performs an abortion on herself to save her life. It cannot seriously be said that she must refrain, that she *must* sit passively by and wait for her death. Let us look again at the case of you and the violinist. There you are, in bed with the violinist, and the director of the hospital says to you, "It's all most distressing, and I deeply sympathize, but you see this is putting an additional strain on your kidneys, and you'll be dead within the month. But you *have* to stay where you are all the same. Because unplugging you would be directly killing an innocent violinist, and that's murder, and that's impermissible." If anything in the world is true, it is that you do not commit murder, you do not do what is impermissible, if you reach around to your back and unplug yourself from that violinist to save your life.

The main focus of attention in writing on abortion has been on what a third party may or may not do in answer to a request from a woman for an abortion. This is in a way understandable. Things being as they are, there isn't much a woman can safely do to abort herself. So the question asked is what a third party may do, and what the mother may do, if it is mentioned at all, is deduced, almost as an afterthought, from what it is concluded that third parties may do. But it seems to me that to treat the matter in this way is to refuse to grant to the mother that very status of person which is so firmly insisted on for the foetus. For we cannot simply read off what a person may do from what a third party may do. Suppose you find yourself trapped in a tiny house with a growing child. I mean a very tiny house, and a rapidly growing child – you are already up against the wall of the house and in a few minutes you'll be crushed to death. The child on the other hand won't be crushed to death; if nothing is done to stop him from growing he'll be hurt, but in the end he'll simply burst open the house and walk out a free man. Now I could well understand it if a bystander were to say, "There's nothing we can do for you. We cannot choose between your life and his, we cannot be the ones to decide who is to live, we cannot intervene." But it cannot be concluded that you too can do nothing, that you cannot attack it to save your life. However innocent the child may be, you do not have to wait passively while it crushes you to death. Perhaps a pregnant woman is vaguely felt to have the status of house, to which we don't allow the right of self-defence. But if the woman houses the child, it should be remembered that she is a person who houses it.

I should perhaps stop to say explicitly that I am not claiming that people have a right to do anything whatever to save their lives. I think, rather, that there are drastic limits to the right of self-defence. If someone threatens you with death unless you torture someone else to death, I think you have not the right, even to save your life, to do so. But the case under consideration here is very different. In our case there are only two people involved, one whose life is threatened, and one who threatens it. Both are innocent: the one who is threatened is not threatened because of any fault, the one who threatens does not threaten because of any fault. For this reason we may feel that we bystanders cannot intervene. But the person threatened can.

In sum, a woman surely can defend her life against the threat to it posed by the unborn child, even if doing so involves its death. And this shows not merely that the theses in (1) through (4) are false; it shows also that the extreme view of abortion is false, and so we need not canvass any other possible ways of arriving at it from the argument I mentioned at the outset.

2. The extreme view could of course be weakened to say that while abortion is permissible to save the mother's life, it may not be performed by a third party, but only by the mother itself. But this cannot be right either. For what we have to keep in mind is that the mother and the unborn child are not like two tenants in a small house which has, by an unfortunate mistake, been rented to both: the mother *owns* the house. The fact that she does adds to the offensiveness of deducing that the mother can do nothing from the supposition that third parties can do nothing. But it does more than this: it casts a bright light on the supposition that third parties can do nothing. Certainly it lets us see that a third party who says "I cannot choose between you" is fooling himself if he thinks this is impartiality. If Jones has found and fastened on a certain coat, which he needs to keep him from freezing, but which Smith also needs to keep him from freezing, then it is not impartiality that says "I cannot choose between you" when Smith owns the coat. Women have said again and again "This body is my body!" and they have reason to feel angry, reason to feel that it has been like shouting into the wind. Smith, after all, is hardly likely to bless us if we say to

him, "Of course it's your coat, anybody would grant that it is. But no one may choose between you and Jones who is to have it."

We should really ask what it is that says "no one may choose" in the face of the fact that the body that houses the child is the mother's body. It may be simply a failure to appreciate this fact. But it may be something more interesting, namely the sense that one has a right to refuse to lay hands on people, even where it would be just and fair to do so, even where justice seems to require that somebody do so. Thus justice might call for somebody to get Smith's coat back from Jones, and yet you have a right to refuse to be the one to lay hands on Jones, a right to refuse to do physical violence to him. This, I think, must be granted. But then what should be said is not "no one may choose," but only, "I cannot choose," and indeed not even this, but "I will not *act*," leaving it open that somebody else can or should, and in particular that anyone in a position of authority, with the job of securing people's rights, both can and should. So this is no difficulty. I have not been arguing that any given third party must accede to the mother's request that he perform an abortion to save her life, but only that he may.

I suppose that in some views of human life the mother's body is only on loan to her, the loan not being one which gives her any prior claim to it. One who held this view might well think it impartiality to say "I cannot choose." But I shall simply ignore this possibility. My own view is that if a human being has any just, prior claim to anything at all, he has a just, prior claim to his own body. And perhaps this needn't be argued for here anyway, since, as I mentioned, the arguments against abortion we are looking at do grant that the woman has a right to decide what happens in and to her body.

But although they do grant it, I have tried to show that they do not take seriously what is done in granting it. I suggest the same thing will reappear even more clearly when we turn away from cases in which the mother's life is at stake, and attend, as I propose we now do, to the vastly more common cases in which a woman wants an abortion for some less weighty reason than preserving her own life.

3. Where the mother's life is not at stake, the argument I mentioned at the outset seems to have a much stronger pull. "Everyone has a right to life, so the unborn person has a right to life." And isn't the child's right to life weightier than anything other than the mother's own right to life, which she might put forward as ground for an abortion?

This argument treats the right to life as it if were unproblematic. It is not, and this seems to me to be precisely the source of the mistake.

For we should now, at long last, ask what it comes to, to have a right to life. In some views having a right to life includes having a right to be given at least the bare minimum one needs for continued life. But suppose that what in fact *is* the bare minimum a man needs for continued life is something he has no right at all to be given? If I am sick unto death, and the only thing that will save my life is the touch of Henry Fonda's cool hand on my fevered brow, then all the same, I have no right to be given the touch of Henry Fonda's cool hand on my fevered brow. It would be frightfully nice of him to fly in from the West Coast to provide it. It would be less nice, though no doubt well meant, if my friends flew out to the West Coast and carried Henry Fonda back with them. But I have no right at all against anybody that he should do this for me. Or again, to return to the story I told earlier, the fact that for continued life that violinist needs the continued use of your kidneys does not establish that he has a right to be given the continued use of your kidneys. He certainly has no right against you that you should give him continued use of your kidneys. For nobody has any right to use your kidneys unless you give him such a right; and nobody has the right against you that you shall give him this right – if you do allow him to go on using your kidneys, this is a kindness on your part, and not something he can claim from you as his due. Nor has he any right against anybody else that they should give him continued use of your kidneys. Certainly he had no right against the Society of Music Lovers that they should plug him into you in the first place. And if you now start to unplug yourself, having learned that you will otherwise have to spend nine years in bed with him, there is nobody in the world who must try to prevent you, in order to see to it that he is given something he has a right to be given.

Some people are rather stricter about the right to life. In their view, it does not include the right to be given anything, but amounts to, and only to, the right not to be killed by anybody. But here a related difficulty arises. If everybody is to refrain from killing that violinist, then everybody must refrain from doing a great many different sorts of things. Everybody must refrain from slitting his throat, everybody must refrain from shooting him – and everybody must refrain from unplugging you from him. But does he have a right against everybody that they shall refrain from unplugging you from him? To refrain from doing this is to allow him to continue to use your kidneys. It could be argued that he has a right against us that *we* should allow him to continue to use your kidneys. That is, while he had no right against us that we should give him the use of your kidneys, it might be argued that he anyway has a right against us that we shall not now intervene and deprive him of the use of your kidneys. I shall come back to third-party interventions later. But certainly the violinist has no right against you that you shall allow him to continue to use your kidneys. As I said, if you do allow him to use them, it is a kindness on your part, and not something you owe him.

The difficulty I point to here is not peculiar to the right to life. It reappears in connection with all the other natural rights; and it is something which an adequate account of rights must deal with. For present purposes it is enough just to draw attention to it. But I would stress that I am not arguing that people do not have a right to life – quite to the contrary, it seems to me that the primary control we must place on the acceptability of an account of rights is that it should turn out in that account to be a truth that all persons have a right to life. I am arguing only that having a right to life does not guarantee having either a right to be given the use of or a right to be allowed continued use of another person's body – even if one needs it for life itself. So the right to life will not serve the opponents of abortion in the very simple and clear way in which they seem to have thought it would.

4. There is another way to bring out the difficulty. In the most ordinary sort of case, to deprive someone of what he has a right to is to treat him unjustly. Suppose a boy and his small brother are jointly given a box of chocolates for Christmas. If the older boy takes the box and refuses to give his brother any of the chocolates, he is unjust to him, for the brother has been given a right to half of them. But suppose that, having learned that otherwise it means nine years in bed with that violinist, you unplug yourself from him. You surely are not being unjust to him, for you gave him no right to use your kidneys, and no one else can have given him any such right. But we have to notice that in unplugging yourself, you are killing him; and violinists, like everybody else, have a right to life, and thus in the view we were considering just now, the right not to be killed. So here you do what he supposedly has a right you shall not do, but you do not act unjustly to him in doing it.

The emendation which may be made at this point is this: the right to life consists not in the right not to be killed, but rather in the right not to be killed unjustly. This runs a risk of circularity, but never mind: it would enable us to square the fact that the violinist has a right to life with the fact that you do not act unjustly toward him in unplugging yourself, thereby killing him. For if you do not kill him unjustly, you do not violate his right of life, and so it is no wonder you do him no injustice.

But if this emendation is accepted, the gap in the argument against abortion stares us plainly in the face: it is by no means enough to show that the foetus is a person, and to remind us that all persons have a right to life – we need to be shown also that killing the foetus violates its right to life, i.e., that abortion is unjust killing. And is it?

I suppose we may take it as a datum that in a case of pregnancy due to rape the mother has not given the unborn person a right to the use of her body for food and shelter. Indeed, in what pregnancy could it be supposed that the mother has given the unborn person such a right? It is not as if there were unborn persons drifting about the world, to whom a woman who wants a child says "I invite you in."

But it might be argued that there are other ways one can have acquired a right to the use of another person's body than by having been invited to use it by that person. Suppose a woman voluntarily indulges in intercourse, knowing of the chance it will issue in pregnancy, and then she does become pregnant; is she not in part responsible for the presence, in fact the very existence, of the unborn person inside here? No doubt she did not invite it in. But doesn't her partial responsibility for its being there itself give it a right to the use of her body?[7] If so, then her aborting it would be more like the boy's taking away the chocolates, and less like your unplugging yourself from the violinist – doing so would be depriving it of what it does have a right to, and thus would be doing it an injustice.

And then, too, it might be asked whether or not she can kill it even to save her own life: If she voluntarily called it into existence, how can she now kill it, even in self-defence?

The first thing to be said about this is that it is something new. Opponents of abortion have been so concerned to make out the independence of the foetus, in order to establish that it has a right to life, just as its mother does, that they have tended to overlook the possible support they might gain from making out that the foetus is *dependent* on the mother, in order to establish that she has a special kind of responsibility for it, a responsibility that gives it rights against her which are not possessed by any independent person – such as an ailing violinist who is a stranger to her.

On the other hand, this argument would give the unborn person a right to its mother's body only if her pregnancy resulted from a voluntary act, undertaken in full knowledge of the chance a pregnancy might result from it. It would leave out entirely the unborn person whose existence is due to rape. Pending the availability of some further argument, then, we would be left with the conclusion that unborn persons whose existence is due to rape have no right to the use of their mothers' bodies, and thus that aborting them is not depriving them of anything they have a right to and hence is not unjust killing.

And we should also notice that it is not at all plain that this argument really does go even as far as it purports to. For there are cases and cases, and the details make a difference. If the room is stuffy, and I therefore open a window to air it, and a burglar climbs in, it would be absurd to say, "Ah, now he can stay, she's given him a right to the use of her house – for she is partially responsible for his presence there, having voluntarily done what enabled him to get in, in full knowledge that there are such things as burglars, and that burglars burgle." It would be still more absurd to say this if I had had bars installed outside my windows, precisely to prevent burglars from getting in, and a burglar got in only because of a defect in the bars. It remains equally absurd if we imagine it is not a burglar who climbs in, but an innocent person who blunders or falls in. Again, suppose it were like this: people-seeds drift about in the air like pollen, and if you open your windows, one may drift in and take root in your carpets or upholstery. You don't want children, so you fix up your windows with fine mesh screens, the very best you can buy. As can happen, however, and on very, very rare occasions does happen, one of the screens is defective; and a seed drifts in and takes root. Does the person-plant who now develops have a right to the use of your house? Surely not – despite the fact that you voluntarily opened your windows, you knowingly kept carpets and upholstered furniture, and you knew that screens were sometimes defective. Someone may argue that you are responsible for its rooting, that it does have a right to your house, because after all you *could* have lived your life with bare floors and furniture, or with sealed windows and doors. But this won't do – for by the same token anyone can avoid a pregnancy due to rape by having a hysterectomy, or anyway by never leaving home without a (reliable!) army.

It seems to me that the argument we are looking at can establish at most that there are *some* cases in which the unborn person has a right to the use of its mother's body, and therefore *some* cases in which abortion is unjust killing. There is room for much discussion and argument as to precisely which, if any. But I think we should side-step this issue and leave it open, for at any rate the argument certainly does not establish that all abortion is unjust killing.

5. There is room for yet another argument here, however. We surely must all grant that there may be cases in which it would be morally indecent to detach a person from your body at the cost of his life. Suppose you learn that what the violinist needs is not nine years of your life, but only one hour: all you need do to save his life is to spend one hour in that bed with him. Suppose also that letting him use your kidneys for that one hour would not affect your health in the slightest. Admittedly you were kidnapped. Admittedly you did not give anyone permission to plug him into you. Nevertheless it seems to me plain you *ought* to allow him to use your kidneys for that hour – it would be indecent to refuse.

Again, suppose pregnancy lasted only an hour, and constituted no threat to life or health. And suppose that a woman becomes pregnant as a result of rape. Admittedly she did not voluntarily do anything to bring about the existence of a child. Admittedly she did nothing at all which would give the unborn person a right to the use of her body. All the same it might well be said, as in the newly emended violinist story, that she *ought* to allow it to remain for that hour – that it would be indecent in her to refuse.

Now some people are inclined to use the term "right" in such a way that it follows from the fact that you ought to allow a person to use your body for the hour he needs, that he has a right to use your body for the hour he needs, even though he has not been given that right by any person or act. They may say that it follows also that if you refuse, you act unjustly toward him. This use of the term is perhaps so common that it cannot be called wrong; nevertheless it seems to me to be an unfortunate loosening of what we would do better to keep a tight rein on. Suppose that box of chocolates I mentioned earlier had not been given to both boys jointly, but was given only to the older boy. There he sits, stolidly eating his way through the box, his small brother watching enviously. Here we are likely to say "You ought not to be so mean. You ought to give your brother some of those chocolates." My own view is that it just does not follow from the truth of this that the brother has any right to any of the chocolates. If the boy refuses to give his brother any, he is greedy, stingy, callous – but not unjust. I suppose that the people I have in mind will say it does follow that the brother has a right to some of the chocolates, and thus that the boy does act unjustly if he refuses to give his brother any. But the effect of saying this is to obscure what we should keep distinct, namely the difference between the boy's refusal in this case and the boy's refusal in the earlier case, in which the box was given to both boys jointly, and in which the small brother thus had what was from any point of view clear title to half.

A further objection to so using the term "right" that from the fact that A ought to do a thing for B, it follows that B has a right against A that A do it for him, is that it is going to make the question of whether or not a man has a right to a thing turn on how easy it is to provide him with it; and this seems not merely unfortunate, but morally unacceptable. Take the case of Henry Fonda again. I said earlier that I had no right to the touch of his cool hand on my fevered brow, even though I needed it to save my life. I said it would be frightfully nice of him to fly in from the West Coast to provide me with it, but that I had no right against him that he should do so. But suppose he isn't on the West Coast. Suppose he has only to walk across the room, place a hand briefly on my brow and lo, my life is saved. Then surely he ought to do it, it would be indecent to refuse. Is it to be said "Ah, well, it follows that in this case she has a right to the touch of his hand on her brow, and so it would be an injustice in him to refuse"? So that I have a right to it when it is easy for him to provide it, though no right when it's hard? It's rather a shocking idea that anyone's rights should fade away and disappear as it gets harder and harder to accord them to him.

So my own view is that even though you ought to let the violinist use your kidneys for the one hour he needs, we should not conclude that he has a right to do so – we should say that if you refuse, you are, like the boy who owns all the chocolates and will give none away, self-centred and callous, indecent in fact, but not unjust. And similarly, that even supposing a case in which a women pregnant due to rape ought to allow the unborn person use her body for the hour he needs, we should not conclude that he has a right to do so; we should conclude that she is self-centred, callous, indecent, but not unjust, if she refuses. The complaints are no less grave; they are just different. However, there is no need to insist on this point. If anyone does wish to deduce "he has a right" from "you ought," then all the same he must surely grant that there are cases in which it is not morally required of you that you allow that violinist to use your kidneys, and in which he does not have a right to use them, and in which you do not do him an injustice if you refuse. And so also for mother and unborn child. Except in such cases as the unborn person has a right to demand it – and we were leaving open the possibility that there may be such cases – nobody is morally *required to* make large sacrifices, of health, of all other interests and concerns, of all other duties and commitments, for nine years, or even for nine months, in order to keep another person alive.

6. We have in fact to distinguish between two kinds of Samaritan: the Good Samaritan and what we might call the Minimally Decent Samaritan. The story of the Good Samaritan, you will remember, goes like this:

A certain man went down from Jerusalem to Jericho, and fell among thieves, which stripped him of his raiment, and wounded him, and departed, leaving him half dead.

And by chance there came down a certain priest that way; and when he saw him, he passed by on the other side.

And likewise a Levite, when he was at the place, came and looked on him, and passed by on the other side.

But a certain Samaritan, as he journeyed, came where he was; and when he saw him he had compassion on him.

And went to him, and bound up his wounds, pouring in oil and wine, and set him on his own beast, and brought him to an inn, and took care of him.

And on the morrow, when he departed, he took out two pence, and gave them to the host, and said unto him, "Take care of him; and whatsoever thou spendest more, when I come again, I will repay thee."

(Luke 10:30–5)

The Good Samaritan went out of his way, at some cost to himself, to help one in need of it. We are not told what the options were, that is, whether or not the priest and the Levite could have helped by doing less than the Good Samaritan did, but assuming they could have, then the fact they did nothing at all shows they were not even Minimally Decent Samaritans, not because they were not Samaritans, but because they were not even minimally decent.

These things are a matter of degree, of course, but there is a difference, and it comes out perhaps most clearly in the story of Kitty Genovese, who, as you will remember, was murdered while thirty-eight people watched or listened, and did nothing at all to help her. A Good Samaritan would have rushed out to give direct assistance against the murderer. Or perhaps we had better allow that it would have been a Splendid Samaritan who did this, on the ground that it would have involved a risk of death for himself. But the thirty-eight not only did not do this, they did not even trouble to pick up a phone to call the police. Minimally Decent Samaritanism would call for doing at least that, and their not having done it was monstrous.

After telling the story of the Good Samaritan, Jesus said "Go, and do thou likewise." Perhaps he meant that we are morally required to act as the Good Samaritan did. Perhaps he was urging people to do more than is morally required of them. At all events it seems plain that it was not morally required of any of the thirty-eight that he rush out to give direct assistance at the risk of his own life, and that it is not morally required of anyone that he give long stretches of his life – nine years or nine months – to sustaining the life of a person who has no special right (we were leaving open the possibility of this) to demand it.

Indeed, with one rather striking class of exceptions, no one in any country in the world is legally required to do anywhere near as much as this for anyone else. The class of exceptions is obvious. My main concern here is not the state of the law in respect to abortion, but it is worth drawing attention to the fact that in none of the United States is any man compelled by law to be even a Minimally Decent Samaritan to any person; there is no law under which charges could be brought against the thirty-eight who stood by while Kitty Genovese died. By contrast, in most states in this country women are compelled by law to be not merely Minimally Decent Samaritans, but Good Samaritans to unborn persons inside them. This doesn't by itself settle anything one way or the other, because it may well be argued that there should be laws in this country – as there are in many European countries – compelling at least Minimally Decent Samaritanism.[8] But it does show that there is a gross injustice in the existing state of the law. And it shows also that the groups currently working against liberalization of abortion laws, in fact working toward having it declared unconstitutional for a state to permit abortion, had better start working for the adoption of Good Samaritan laws generally, or earn the charge that they are acting in bad faith.

I should think, myself, that Minimally Decent Samaritan laws would be one thing, Good Samaritan laws quite another, and in fact highly improper. But we are not here concerned with the law. What we should ask is not whether anybody should be compelled by law to be a Good Samaritan, but whether we must accede to a situation in which somebody is being compelled – by nature, perhaps – to be a Good Samaritan. We have, in other words, to look now at third-party interventions. I have been arguing that no person is morally required to make large sacrifices to sustain the life of another who has no right to demand them, and this even where the sacrifices do not include life itself; we are not morally required to be Good Samaritans or anyway Very Good Samaritans to one another. But what if a man cannot extricate himself from such a situation? What if he appeals to us to extricate him? It seems to me plain that there are cases in which we can, cases in which a Good Samaritan would extricate him. There you are, you were kidnapped, and nine years in bed with that violinist lie ahead of you. You have your own life to lead. You are sorry, but you simply cannot see giving up so much of your life to the sustaining of his. You cannot extricate yourself, and ask us to do so. I should have thought that in light of his having no right to the use of your body – it was obvious that we do not have to accede to your being forced to give up so much. We can do what you ask. There is no injustice to the violinist in our doing so.

7. Following the lead of the opponents of abortion, I have throughout been speaking of the foetus merely as a person, and what I have been asking is whether or not the argument we began with, which proceeds only from the foetus's being a person, really does establish its conclusion. I have argued that it does not.

But of course there are arguments and arguments, and it may be said that I have simply fastened on the wrong one. It may be said that what is important is not merely the fact that the foetus is a person, but that it is a person for whom the woman has a special kind of responsibility issuing from the fact that she is its mother. And it might be argued that all my analogies are therefore irrelevant – for you do not have that special kind of responsibility for that violinist, Henry Fonda does not have that special kind of responsibility for me. And our attention might be drawn to the fact that men and women both *are* compelled by law to provide support for their children.

I have in effect dealt (briefly) with this argument in section 4 above; but a (still briefer) recapitulation now may be in order. Surely we do not have any such "such responsibility" for a person unless we have assumed it, explicitly or implicitly. If a set of parents do not try to prevent pregnancy, do not obtain an abortion, and then at the time of birth of the child do not put it out for adoption, but rather take it home with them, then they have assumed responsibility for it, they have given it rights, and they cannot now withdraw support from it at the cost of its life because they now find it difficult to go on providing for it. But if they have taken all reasonable precautions against having a child, they do not simply by virtue of their biological relationship to the child who comes into existence have a special responsibility for it. They may wish to assume responsibility for it, or they may not wish to. And I am suggesting that if assuming responsibility for it would require large sacrifices, then they may refuse. A Good Samaritan would not refuse or anyway, a Splendid Samaritan, if the sacrifices that had to be made were enormous. But then so would a Good Samaritan assume responsibility for that violinist; so would Henry Fonda, if he is a Good Samaritan, fly in from the West Coast and assume responsibility for me.

8. My argument will be found unsatisfactory on two counts by many of those who want to regard abortion as morally permissible. First, while I do argue that abortion is not impermissible, I do not argue that it is always permissible. There may well be cases in which carrying the child to term requires only Minimally Decent Samaritanism of the mother, and this is a standard we must not fall below. I am inclined to think it a merit of my account precisely that it does not give a general yes or a general no. It allows for and supports our sense that, for example, a sick and desperately frightened fourteen-year-old schoolgirl, pregnant due to rape, may *of course* choose abortion, and that any law which rules this out is an insane law. And it also allows for and supports our sense that in other cases resort to abortion is even positively indecent. It would be indecent in the woman to request an abortion, and indecent in a doctor to perform it, if she is in her seventh month, and wants the abortion just to avoid the nuisance of postponing a trip abroad. The very fact that the arguments I have been drawing attention to treat all cases of abortion, or even all cases of abortion in which the mother's life is not at stake, as morally on a par ought to have made them suspect at the outset.

Secondly, while I am arguing for the permissibility of abortion in some cases, I am not arguing for the right to secure the death of the unborn child. It is easy to confuse these two things in that up to a certain point in the life of the foetus it is not able to survive outside the mother's body; hence removing it from her body guarantees its death. But they are importantly different. I have argued that you are not morally required to spend nine months in bed, sustaining the life of that violinist; but to say this is by no means to say that if, when you unplug yourself, there is a miracle and he survives, you then have a right to turn round and slit his throat. You may detach yourself even if this costs him his life; you have no right to be guaranteed his death, by some other means, if unplugging yourself does not kill him. There are some people who will feel dissatisfied by this feature of my argument. A woman may be utterly devastated by the thought of a child, a bit of herself, put out for adoption and never seen or heard of again. She may therefore want not merely that the child be detached from her, but more, that it die. Some opponents of abortion are inclined to regard this as beneath contempt – thereby showing insensitivity to what is surely a powerful source of despair. All the same, I agree that the desire for the child's death is not one which anybody may gratify, should it turn out to be possible to detach the child alive.

At this place, however, it should be remembered that we have only been pretending throughout that the foetus is a human being from the moment of conception. A very early abortion is surely not the killing of a person, and so is not dealt with by anything I have said here.

NOTES

1   I am much indebted to James Thomson for discussion, criticism, and many helpful suggestions.
2   Daniel Callahan, *Abortion: Law, Choice and Morality* (New York, 1970), p. 373. This book gives a fascinating survey of the available information on abortion. The Jewish tradition is surveyed in David M. Feldman, *Birth Control in Jewish Law* (New York, 1968). Part 5, the Catholic tradition in John T. Noonan, Jr, "An Almost Absolute Value in History," in *The Morality of Abortion*, ed. John T. Noonan, Jr. (Cambridge, Mass., 1970).
3   The term "direct" in the arguments I refer to is a technical one. Roughly, what is meant by "direct killing" is either killing as an end in itself, or killing as a means to some end, for example, the end of saving someone's life. See n.6, below, for an example of its use.
4   Cf. *Encyclical Letter of Pope Pius XI on Christian Marriage*, St Paul Editions (Boston, n.d.), p. 32: "however much we may pity the mother whose health and even life is gravely imperiled in the performance of the duty allotted to her by nature, nevertheless what could ever be a sufficient reason for excusing in any way the direct murder of the innocent? This is precisely what we are dealing with here." Noonan *(The Morality of Abortion*, p. 43) reads this as follows: "What cause can ever avail to excuse in any way the direct killing of the innocent? For it is a question of that."
5   The thesis in (4) is in an interesting way weaker than those in (1), (2), and (3): they rule out abortion even in cases in which both mother and child will die if the abortion is not performed. By contrast, one who held the view expressed in (4) could consistently say that one needn't prefer letting two persons die to killing one.
6   Cf. the following passage from Pius XII, *Address to the Italian Catholic Society of Midwives:* "The baby in the maternal breast has the right to life immediately from God. – Hence there is no man, no human authority, no science, no medical, eugenic, social, economic or moral 'indication' which can establish or grant a valid juridical ground for a direct deliber-

ate disposition of an innocent human life, that is a disposition which looks to its destruction either as an end or as a means to another end perhaps in itself not illicit. – The baby, still not born, is a man in the same degree and for the same reason as the mother" (quoted in Noonan, *The Morality of Abortion*, p. 45).

7   The need for a discussion of this argument was brought home to me by members of the Society for Ethical and Legal Philosophy, to whom this was originally presented as a paper.

8   For a discussion of the difficulties involved, and a survey of the European experience with such laws, see *The Good Samaritan and the Law*, ed. James M. Ratcliffe (New York, 1966).

READING QUESTIONS ON THOMSON

1   Is it appropriate to think of the relation between a pregnant woman and a foetus in the terms Thomson suggests?
2   Why does Thomson talk so much about avoidability? How does it change the rights of the parties involved?
3   Thomson maintains that the law should not place larger burdens on women than on men. How is this claim related to the rest of her argument?

John Finnis
"The Rights and Wrongs of Abortion: A Reply to Judith Jarvis Thomson" (1973)

Finnis appeals to traditional moral understandings to argue that abortion is indistinguishable from murder because it requires the intentional taking of life.

Fortunately, none of the arguments for and against abortion *need* be expressed in terms of "rights." As we shall see, Judith Thomson virtually admits as much in her "A Defence of Abortion."[1] But since she has chosen to conduct her case by playing off a "right to decide what happens in and to one's body," I shall begin by showing how this way of arguing about the rights and wrongs of abortion needlessly complicates and confuses the issue. It is convenient and appropriate to speak of "rights" for purposes and in contexts which I shall try to identify; it is most inconvenient and inappropriate when one is debating the moral permissibility of types of action – types such as "abortions performed without the desire to kill," which is the type of action Thomson wishes to defend as morally permissible under most circumstances. So in section I of this essay I shall show how her specification and moral characterization of this type of action are logically independent of her discussion of "rights." Then in section II I shall outline at some principles of moral characterization and of moral permissibility, principles capable of explaining some of the moral condemnations which Thomson expresses but which remain all too vulnerable and obscure in her paper. In section III I shall show how the elaboration of those principles warrants those condemnations of abortion which Thomson thinks mistaken as well as many of those attributions of human rights which she so much takes for granted. In section IV I briefly state the reason (misstated by Thomson and also by Wertheimer[2]) why the foetus from conception has human rights, i.e., should be given the same consideration as other human beings.

I

Thomson's reflections on rights develop in three states. (A) She indicates a knot of problems about what rights are rights to; she dwells particularly on the problem "what it comes to, to have a right to life" (p. 959). (B) She indicates, rather less clearly, a knot of problems about the source of rights; in particular she suggests that, over a wide range (left unspecified by her) of types of right, a person has a right only to what he has "title" to by reason of some gift, concession, grant or undertaking to him by another person. (C) She cuts both these knots by admitting (but all too quietly) that her whole argument about abortion concerns simply what is "morally required" or "morally permissible"; that what is in question is really the scope and source of the mother's responsibility (and only derivatively, by entailment, the scope and source of the unborn child's rights). I shall now examine these three stages a little more closely, and (D) indicate why I think it useful to have done so.

(A) How do we specify the content of a right? What is a right a right to? Thomson mentions at least nine different rights which a person might rightly or wrongly be said to have.[3] Of these nine, seven have the same logical structure,[4] viz., in each instance, the alleged right is a right with respect to P's action (performance, omission) as an action which may affect Q. In some of these seven instances,[5] the right with respect to P's action is P's right (which Hohfeld[6] called a privilege and Hohfeldians call a liberty). In the other instances[7] "the right with respect to P's action is Q's right (which Hohfeldians call a "claim-right"). But in all these seven instances there is what I shall call a "Hohfeldian right": to assert a Hohfeldian right is to assert a three-term relation between two persons and the action of one of those persons in so far as that action concerns the other person.

The other two rights mentioned by Thomson have a different logical structure.[8] In both these instances, the alleged right is a right with respect to a thing (one's "own body," or the state of affairs referred to as one's "life"). Here the relation is two-term: between one person and some thing or state of affairs. Rights in this sense cannot be completely analysed in terms of some unique combination of Hohfeldian rights.[9] P's right to a thing (land, body, life) can and normally should be secured by granting or attributing Hohfeldian rights to him or to others; but just which combination of such Hohfeldian rights will properly or best secure his single right to the thing in question will vary according to time, place, person, and circumstance. And since moral judgments centrally concern *actions*, it is this specification of Hohfeldian rights that we need for moral purposes, rather than invocations of rights to things.

Since Thomson concentrates on the problematic character of the "right to life," I shall illustrate what I have just said by reference to the "right to one's own body," which she should (but seems, in practice, not to) regard as equally problematic. Now her two explicit versions of this right are: one's "just, prior claim to his own body," and one's "right to decide what happens in and to one's body." But both versions need much specification[10] before they can warrant moral judgments about particular sorts of action. For example, the "right to decide" may be *either* (i) a right (Hohfeldian liberty) to do things to or with one's own body (e.g., to remove those kidney plugs, or that baby, from it – but what else? anything? do I have the moral liberty to decide not to raise my hand to the telephone to save Kitty Genovese from her murderers?); *or* (ii) a right (Hohfeldian claim-right) that other people shall not (at least without one's permission) do things to or with one's own body (e.g., draw sustenance from, or inhabit, it – but what else? anything?); *or* (iii) some combination of these forms of right with each other or with other forms of right such as (a) the right (Hohfeldian power) to change another person's right (liberty) to use one's body by making a grant of or permitting such use (*any* such use?), or (b) the right (Hohfeldian immunity) not to have one's right (claim-right) to be free from others' use of one's body diminished or affected by purported grants or permissions by third parties. And as soon as we thus identify these possible sorts of right, available to give concrete moral content to the "right to one's body," it becomes obvious that the actions which the right entitles, disentitles, or requires one to perform (or entitles, disentitles, or requires others to perform) vary according to the identity and circumstances of the two parties to each available and relevant Hohfeldian right. And this, though she didn't recognize it, is the reason why Thomson found the "right to life" problematic, too.

(B) I suspect it was her concentration on non-Hohfeldian rights ("title" to things like chocolates or bodies) that led Thomson to make the curious suggestion which appears and reappears, though with a very uncertain role, in her article. I mean, her suggestion that we should speak of "rights" only in respect of what a man has "title" to (usually, if not necessarily, by reason of gift, concession, or grant to him).

This suggestion[11] quite apart from the dubious centrality it accords to ownership and property in the spectrum of rights, causes needless confusion in the presentation of Thomson's defence of abortion. For if the term "right" were to be kept on the "tight rein" which she suggests (p. 963), then (a) the Popes and others whose appeal to the "right to life" she is questioning would deprive her paper of its starting-point and indeed its pivot by simply rephrasing their appeal so as to eliminate all reference to rights (for, as I show in the next section, they are not alleging that the impropriety of abortion follows from any grant, gift, or concession of "rights" to the unborn child); and (b) Thomson would likewise have to rephrase claims she herself makes, such as that innocent persons certainly have a right to life, that mothers have the right to abort themselves to save their lives, that P has a right not to be tortured to death by Q even if R is threatening to kill Q unless Q does so, and so on. But if such rephrasing is possible (as indeed it is), then it is obvious that suggestions about the proper or best way to use the term "a right" are irrelevant to the substantive moral defence or critique of abortion.

But this terminological suggestion is linked closely with Thomson's substantive thesis that we do not have any "special [sc. Good Samaritan or Splendid Samaritan] responsibility" for the life or well-being of others "unless we have assumed it, explicitly or implicitly" (p. 967). It is this (or some such) thesis about *responsibility* on which Thomson's whole argument, in the end, rests.

(C) Thomson's explicit recognition that her defence of abortion *need* not have turned on the assertion or denial of rights comes rather late in her paper, when she says that there is "no need to insist on" her suggested reined-in use of the term "right":

If anyone does wish to deduce "he has a right" from "you ought", then all the same he must surely grant that there are cases in which it is not morally required of you that you allow that violinist to use your kidneys ...[12] And so also for mother and unborn child. Except in such cases as the unborn person has a right to demand it ... nobody is morally *required* to make large sacrifices ... in order to keep another person alive. (p. 964)

In short, the dispute is about what is "morally required" (i.e., about what one "must" and, for that matter, "may" or "can" [not] do: see p. 958; that is to say, about the rights and wrongs of abortion. True, on page 968 there is still that "right to demand large sacrifices" cluttering up the margins of the picture. But when we come to the last pages of her paper (p. 969) even that has been set aside, and the real question is identified as not whether the child has a "right to demand large sacrifices" of its mother, but whether the other has a "special responsibility" to or for the child (since, if she has, then she may be morally required to make large sacrifices for it and *therefore* we will be able to assert, by a convenient locution, the child's "right to [demand] those sacrifices").

(D) So in the end most of the argument about rights was a red herring. I have bothered to track down this false trail, not merely to identify some very common sorts and sources of equivocation (more will come to light in the next two sections), but also to show how Thomson's decision to conduct her defence in terms of "rights" makes it peculiarly easy to miss a most important weak point in her defence. This weak point is the connection or relation between one's "special responsibilities" and one's ordinary (not special) responsibilities; and one is enabled to miss it easily if one thinks (a) that the whole problem is essentially one of rights, (b) that rights typically or even essentially depend on grant, concession, assumption, etc., (c) that special responsibilities likewise depend on grants, concessions, assumptions, etc., and

(d) that therefore the whole moral problem here concerns one's *special* responsibilities. Such a train of thought is indeed an enthymeme, if not a downright fallacy; but that is not surprising, since I am commenting here not on an argument offered by Thomson but on a likely effect of her "rhetoric."

What Thomson, then, fails to attend to adequately is the claim (one of the claims implicit, I think, in the papal and conservative rhetoric of rights) that the mother's duty not to abort herself is *not* an incident of any special responsibility which she assumed or undertook for the child, but is a straight-forward incident of an ordinary duty everyone owes to his neighbour. Thomson indeed acknowledges that such ordinary nonassumed duties exist and are as morally weighty as duties of justice in her reined-in sense of "justice"; but I cannot discern the principles on which she bases, and (confidently) delimits the range of, these duties.[13]

She speaks, for instance, about "the drastic limits to the right of self-defence": "If someone threatens you with death unless you torture someone else to death, I think you have not the right, even to save your life, to do so" (p. 957). Yet she also says: "If anything in the world is true, it is that you do not ... do what is impermissible, if you reach around to your back and unplug yourself from that violinist to save your life" (p. 957). So why, in the first case, has one the strict responsibility not to bring about the death demanded? Surely she is not suggesting that the pain ("torture") makes the difference, or that it *is* morally permissible to kill *painlessly* another person on the orders of a third party who threatens you with death for noncompliance? And, since she thinks that "nobody is morally *required* to make large sacrifices, of health, of all other interests and concerns, of all other duties and commitments, for nine years, or even for nine months, in order to keep another person alive" (p. 964), will she go on to say that it is permissible, when a third party threatens you with such "large sacrifices" (though well short of your life), to *kill* (painlessly) another person, or two or ten other persons?

If Thomson balks at such suggestions, I think it must be because she does in the end rely on some version of the distinction, forced underground in her paper, between "direct killing" and "not keeping another person alive."

The more one reflects on Thomson's argument, the more it seems to turn and trade on some version of this distinction. Of course she starts by rejecting the view that it is always wrong to directly kill, because that view would (she thinks) condemn one to a lifetime plugged into the violinist. But she proceeds, as we have noted, to reject at least one form of killing to save one's life, on grounds that seem to have nothing to do with consequences and everything to do with the formal context and thus structure of one's action (the sort of formal considerations that usually are wrapped up, as we shall see, in the word "direct"). And indeed the whole movement of her argument in defence of abortion is to assimilate abortion to the range of Samaritan problems, on the basis that having an abortion is, or can be, justified as *merely* a way of *not rendering special assistance.* Again, the argument turns, not on a calculus of consequences, but on the formal characteristics of one's choice itself.

Well, why should this apparently *formal* aspect of one's choice determine one's precise responsibilities in a certain situation whatever the other circumstances and expected consequences or upshots? When we know why, on both sides of the debate about abortion, we draw and rely on these distinctions, then we will be better placed to consider (i) whether or not unplugging from the violinist is, after all, direct killing in the sense alleged to be relevant by Popes and others, and (ii) whether or not abortion is, after all, just like unplugging the captive philosopher from the moribund musician.

II

Like Thomson's moral language (setting off the "permissible" against the "impermissible"), the traditional rule about killing doubtless gets its peremptory sharpness primarily (historically speaking) from the injunction, respected as divine and revealed: "Do not kill the innocent and just."[14] But the handful of peremptory negative moral principles correspond to the handful of really basic aspects of human flourishing, which in turn correspond to the handful of really basic and controlling human needs and human inclinations. To be fully reasonable, one must remain *open* to every basic aspect of human flourishing, to every basic form of human good. For is not each irreducibly basic, and none merely means to end? Are not the basic goods incommensurable? Of course it is reasonable to concentrate on realizing those forms of good, in or for those particular communities and persons (first of all oneself, which one's situation, talents, and opportunities most fit one for. But concentration, specialization, particularization is one thing; it is quite another thing, rationally and thus morally speaking, to make a choice which cannot but be characterized as a choice *against* life (to kill), *against* communicable knowledge of truth (to lie, where truth is at stake in communication), *against* procreation, *against* friendship and the justice that is bound up with friendship. Hence the strict negative percepts.[15]

The general sense of "responsibility," "duty," "obligation," "permissibility" is not my concern here, but rather the *content* of our responsibilities, duties, obligations, of the demands which human good makes on each of us. The general demand is that we remain adequately open to, attentive to, respectful of, and willing to pursue human good in so far as it can be realized and respected in our choices and dispositions. Now most moral failings are not by way of violation of strict negative precepts – i.e., are not straightforward choices against basic values. Rather, they are forms of negligence, of *insufficient* regard for these basic goods, or for the derivative structures reasonably created to support the basic goods. And when someone is accused of violating directly a basic good, he will usually plead that he was acting out of a proper care and concern for the realization of that or another basic value in the *consequences* of his chosen act though not in the act itself. For example, an experimenter accused of killing children in order to conduct medical tests will point out that these deaths are necessary to these tests, and these tests to medical discoveries, and the discoveries to the saving of many more lives – so that, in view of the foreseeable consequences of his deed, he displays (he will argue) a fully adequate (indeed, the only adequate) and reasonable regard for the value of human life.

But to appeal to consequences in this fashion is to set aside one criterion of practical reasonableness and hence of morality – namely, that one remain open to each basic value, and attentive to some basic value, in each of one's chosen acts – in favour of quite another criterion – namely, that one choose so to act as to bring about consequences involving a greater balance of good over bad than could be expected to be brought about by doing any alternative action open to one. Hare has observed that *"for practical purposes* there is no important difference" between most of the currently advocated theories in ethics; they all are "utilitarian," a term he uses to embrace Brandt's ideal observer theory, Richards's (Rawls's?) rational contractor theory, specific rule-utilitarianism, universalistic act-utilitarianism and his own universal prescriptivism.[16] All justify and require, he argues, the adoption of "the principles whose general inculcation will have, all in all, the best consequences."[17] I offer no critique of this utilitarianism here; Thomson's article is not, on its face, consequentialist. Suffice it to inquire how Hare and his fellow consequentialists know the future that to most of us is hidden. How do they know what unit of computation to select from among the incommensurable and irreducible basic aspects of human flourishing; what principle of distribution of goods to commend to an individual considering his own interests, those of his friends, his family, his enemies, his *patria* and those of all men present and future? How do they know how to define the "situation" whose universal specification will appear in the principle whose adoption (singly? in conjunction with other principles?) "will" have best consequences;[18] whether and how to weigh future and uncertain consequences against present and certain consequences? And how do they know that net good consequences would in fact be maximized (even if *per impossible* they were calculable) by general adoption of consequentialist principles of action along with consequentialist "principles" to justify nonobservance of consequentialist "principles" in hard cases?[19] One cannot understand the Western moral tradition, with its peremptory negative (forbearance-requiring) principles (the positive principles being relevant in all, but peremptory in few, particular situations), unless one sees why that tradition rejected consequentialism as mere self-delusion – for Hare and his fellow consequentialists can provide no satisfactory answer to any of the foregoing lines of inquiry, and have no coherent rational account to give of any level of moral thought above that of the man who thinks how good it would be to act "for the best."[20] Expected total consequences of one's action do not provide a sufficient ground for making a choice that cannot but be regarded as *itself* a choice directly against a basic value (even that basic value which it is hoped will be realized in the *consequences)* – for expected total consequences cannot be given an evaluation sufficiently reasonable and definitive to be the decisive measure of our response to the call of human values, while a choice directly against a basic good provides, one might say, its own definitive evaluation of itself.

I do not expect these isolated and fragmentary remarks to be in themselves persuasive. I do not deny that the traditional Western willingness (in theory) to discount expected consequences wherever the action itself could not but be characterized as against a basic value, is or was supported by the belief that Providence would inevitably provide that "all manner of things shall be well" (i.e., that the whole course of history would turn out to have been a fine thing, indisputably evil deeds and their consequences turning out to have been "all to the good" like indisputably saintly deeds and their consequences). Indeed, the consequentialist moralist, who nourishes his moral imagination on scenarios in which by killing an innocent or two he saves scores, thousands, millions, or even the race itself, rather obviously is a post-Christian phenomenon – such an assumption of the role of Providence would have seemed absurd to the pre-Christian philosophers[21] known to Cicero and Augustine. I am content to suggest the theoretical and moral context in which the casuistry of "direct" and "indirect" develops, within the wider context of *types* of action to be considered "impermissible" (I leave the term incompletely accounted for) because *inescapably* (i.e., whatever the hoped-for consequences) choices *against* a basic value of human living and doing. In short, one's responsibility for the realization of human good, one's fostering of or respect for human flourishing in future states of affairs at some greater or lesser remove from one's present action, does not override one's responsibility to respect each basic form of human good which comes directly in question in one's present action itself.

But how does one choose "directly against" a basic form of good? When is it the case, for example, that one's choice, one's intentional act, "cannot but be" characterized as "inescapably" anti-life? Is abortion always (or ever) such a case? A way to tackle these questions can be illustrated by reference to three hard cases whose traditional "solutions" contributed decisively to the traditional judgment about abortion. The relevance of these "hard cases" and "solutions" to the discussion with Thomson should be apparent in each case, but will become even more apparent in the next section.

(I) Suicide

Considered as a fully deliberate choice (which it doubtless only rather rarely is), suicide is a paradigm case of an action that is always wrong because it cannot but be characterized as a choice directly against a fundamental value, life. The characterization is significant, for what makes the killing of oneself attractive is usually, no doubt, the prospect of peace, relief, even a kind of freedom or personal integration, and sometimes is an admirable concern for others; but no amount of concentration on the allure of these positive values can disguise from a clear-headed practical reasoner that it is *by* and *in* killing himself that he intends or hopes to realize those goods. And the characterization is given sharpness and definition by the contrast with heroic self-sacrifices in battle or with willing martyrdom.[22] Where Durkheim treated martyrdom as a case of suicide,[23] anybody concerned with the intentional structure of actions (rather than with a simplistic analysis of movements with foreseen upshots) will grant that the martyr is not directly choosing death, either as end or as means. For, however certainly death may be expected to ensue from the martyr's choice not to accede to the tyrant's threats, still it will ensue through, and as the point of, *someone else's* deliberate act (the tyrant's or the executioner's), and thus the martyr's chosen act of defiance need not be interpreted as itself a choice against the good of life.

The case of suicide has a further significance. The judgments, the characterizations, and the distinctions made in respect of someone's choices involving his *own* death will be used in respect of choices involving the death of *others*. In other words, *rights* (such as the "right to life") are not the fundamental rationale for the judgment that the killing of other (innocent) persons is impermissible. What is impermissible is an intention set against the value of human life where that value is directly at stake in any action by virtue of the intentional and causal structure of that action; and such an impermissible intention may concern my life or yours – and no one speaks of his "right to life" as against himself, as something that would explain why *his* act of self-killing would be wrongful.

Indeed, I think the real justification for speaking of "rights" is to make the point that, when it comes to characterizing intentional actions in terms of their openness to basic human values, those human values are, and are to be, realized in the lives and well-being of others as well as in the life and well-being of the actor. That is, the point of speaking of "rights" is to stake out the relevant claims to equality and nondiscrimination (claims that are not to absolute equality, since my life and my well-being have some reasonable priority in the direction of my practical effort, if only because I am better placed to secure them). But the claims are to equality of *treatment*; so, rather than speak emptily of (say) a "right to life," it would be better to speak of (say, *inter alia*) a "right not to be killed intentionally" – where the meaning and significance of "intentional killing" can be illuminated by consideration of the right and wrong of killing oneself (i.e., of a situation where no "rights" are in question and one is alone with the bare problem of the right relation between one's acts and the basic values that can be realized or spurned in human actions).

Finally, the case of suicide and its traditional solution remind us forcefully that traditional Western ethics simply does not accept that a person has "a right to decide what shall happen in and to his body," a right which Thomson thinks, astonishingly (since she is talking of Pius XI and Pius XII), that "everybody seems to be ready to grant." Indeed, one might go so far as to say that traditional Western ethics holds that, because and to the extent that one does not have the "right" to decide what shall happen in and to one's body, one *therefore* and to that extent does not have the right to decide what shall, by way of one's own acts, happen in and to anyone else's body. As I have already hinted, and shall elaborate later, this would be something of an oversimplification, since one's responsibility for one's own life, health, etc. is reasonably regarded as prior to one's concern for the life, health, etc. of others. But the oversimplification is worth risking in order to make the point that the traditional condemnation of abortion (as something one makes happen in and to a baby's body) *starts* by rejecting what Thomson thinks everyone will admit.

(ii) D's Killing an Innocent V in Order to Escape Death at the Hands of P, Who Has Ordered D to Kill V

This case has been traditionally treated on the same footing as cases such as D's killing V in order to save Q (or Ql, Q, ... Qn) from death (perhaps at the hands of P) or from disease (where D is a medical researcher); for all such cases cannot but be characterized as choices to act directly against human life. Of course, in each case, the reason for making the choice is to save life; but such saving of life will be effected, if at all, through the choices of other actors (e.g., P's choice not to kill D where D has killed V; or P's choice not to kill Q) or through quite distinct sequences of events (e.g., Q's being given life-saving drugs discovered by D).

Hence the traditional ethics affirms that "there are drastic limits to the right of self-defence" in much the same terms as Thomson. "If someone threatens you with death unless you torture someone else to death ... you have not the right, even to save your own life, to do so" (p. 957). And it was this very problem that occasioned the first ecclesiastical pronouncement on abortion in the modern era, denying that "it is licit to procure abortion before animation of the foetus in order to prevent a girl, caught pregnant, being killed or dishonoured.[24] The choice to abort here cannot but be characterized as a choice against life, since its intended good life- or reputation-saving effects are merely expected consequences, occurring if at all through the further acts of other persons, and thus are not what is being *done* in and by the act of abortion itself. But I do not know how one could arrive at any view of this second sort of hard case by juggling, as Thomson seems to be willing to, with a "right to life," a "right to determine what happens in and to your own body," a "right to self-defence" and a "right to refuse to lay hands on other people" – all rights shared equally by D, V, P, and Q, Q_1, Q_2, ... !

(iii) Killing the Mother to Save the Child

This was the only aspect of abortion that Thomas Aquinas touched on, but he discussed it thrice.[25] For if it is accepted that eternal death is worse than mere bodily death, shouldn't one choose the lesser evil? So if the unborn child is likely to die unbaptized, shouldn't one open up the mother, rip out the child and save-it-from-eternal-death-by-baptizing-it? (If you find Aquinas's problems unreal, amend it – consider instead the cases where the child's life seems so much more valuable, whether to itself or to others, than the life of its sick or old or low-born mother.) No, says Aquinas. He evidently considers (for reasons I consider in section III) that the project involves a direct choice against life and is straightforwardly wrong, notwithstanding the good consequences.

So the traditional condemnation of therapeutic abortion flows not from a prejudice against women or in favour of children but from a straightforward application of the solution in the one case to the other case, on the basis that mother and child are *equally* persons in whom the value of human life is to be realized (or the "right to life" respected) and not directly attacked.[26]

III

But now at last let us look at this "traditional condemnation of abortion" a little more closely that Thomson does. It is not a condemnation of the administration of medications to a pregnant mother whose life is threatened by, say, a high fever (whether brought on by pregnancy or not), in an effort to reduce the fever, even if it is known that such medications have the side effect of inducing miscarriage. It is not a condemnation of the removal of the malignantly cancerous womb of a pregnant woman, even if it is known that the foetus within is not of viable age and so will die. It is quite doubtful whether it is a condemnation of an operation to put back in its place the displaced womb of a pregnant woman whose life is threatened by the displacement, even though the operation necessitates the draining off of the amniotic fluids necessary to the survival of the foetus.[27]

But why are these operations not condemned? As Foot has remarked, the distinction drawn between these and other death-dealing operations "has evoked particularly bitter reactions on the part of non-Catholics. If you are permitted to bring about the death of the child, what does it matter how it is done?"[28] Still, she goes some way to answering her own question; she is not content to let the matter rest where Hart had left it, when he said:

Perhaps the most perplexing feature of these cases is that the overriding aim in all of them is the same good result, namely ... to save the mother's life. The differences between the cases are differences of causal structure leading up to the applicability of different verbal distinctions. There seems to be no relevant moral difference between them on any theory of morality ... [to attribute moral relevance to distinctions drawn in this way] in cases where the ultimate purpose is the same can only be explained as the result of a legalistic conception of morality as if it were conceived in the form of a law in rigid form prohibiting all intentional killing as distinct from knowingly causing death.[29]

Foot recognizes that attention to "overriding aim" and "ultimate purpose" is not enough if we are to keep clear of moral horrors such as saving life by killing innocent hostages, etc. As a general though not exclusive and not (it seems) at-all-costs principle, she proposes that one has a duty to refrain from doing injury to innocent people and that this duty is stricter than one's duty to aid others; this enables her to see that "we might find" the traditional conclusion correct, that we must not crush the unborn child's skull in order to save the mother (in a case where the child could be saved if one let the mother die): "for in general we do not think that we can kill one innocent person to rescue other."[30] But what is it to "do injury to" innocent people? She does not think it an injury to blow a man to pieces, or kill and eat him, in order to save others trapped with him in a cave, *if he is certain to die soon anyway*.[31] So I suppose that, after all, she *would* be willing (however reluctantly) to justify the killing by D of hostages V, V_1, V_2, whenever the blackmailer P threatened to kill *them too*, along with Q, Q_1, Q_2, unless D killed them himself. One wonders whether this is not an unwarranted though plausible concession to consequentialism.

In any event, Foot was aware, not only that the "doctrine of the double effect" "should be taken seriously in spite of the fact that it sounds rather odd,"[32] but also of what Thomson has not recorded in her brief footnote (p. 697, n. 3) on the technical meaning given to the term "direct" by moralists using the "doctrine" to analyse the relation between choices and basic values, namely that the "doctrine" requires more than that a certain bad effect or aspect (say, someone's being killed) of one's deed be not intended either as end or as means. If one is to establish that one's death-dealing deed need not be characterized as directly or intentionally against the good of human life, the "doctrine" requires further that the good effect or aspect, which is intended, should be proportionate (say, saving someone's life), i.e., sufficiently good and important relative to the bad effect or aspect: otherwise (we may add, in our own words) one's choice, although not directly and intentionally to kill, will reasonably be counted as a choice inadequately open to the value of life.[33] And this consideration alone might well suffice to rule out abortions performed in order simply to remove the unwanted foetus from the body of women who conceived as a result of forcible rape, even if one were to explicate the phrase "intended directly as end or as means" in such a way that the abortion did not amount to a directly intended killing (e.g., because the mother desired only the removal, not the death of the foetus, and would have been willing to have the foetus reared in an artificial womb had one been available).[34]

Well, how *should* one explicate these central requirements of the "doctrine" of double effect? When *should* one say that the expected bad effect or aspect of an action is not intended either as end or as means and hence does not determine the moral character of the act as a choice not to respect one of the basic human values? Since it is in any case impossible to undertake a full discussion of this question here, let me narrow the issue down to the more difficult and controverted problem of "means." Clearly enough, D intends the death of V *as a means* when he kills him in order to conform to the orders of the blackmailer P (with the object of thereby saving the lives of Q et al.), since the good effect of D's act will follow only by virtue of *another* human act (here P's). But Grisez (no consequentialist!) argues that the bad effects or aspects of some *natural* process or chain of causation need not be regarded as intended as means to the good effects or aspects of that process even if the good effects or aspects *depend* on them in the causal sense (and provided that those good effects could not have been attained in some other way by that agent in those circumstances).[35] So he would, I think, say that Thomson could rightly unplug herself from the violinist (at least where the hook-up endangered her life) even if "unplugging" could only be effected by chopping the violinist in pieces. He treats the life-saving abortion operation in the same way, holding that there is no direct choice against life involved in chopping up the foetus if what is intended as end is to save the life of the mother and what is intended as means is no more than the removal of the foetus and the consequential relief to the mother's body.[36] As a suasive, he points again to the fact that *if* an artificial womb or restorative operation were available for the aborted foetus, a right-thinking mother and doctor in such a case would wish to make these available to the foetus; this shows, he says, that a right-thinking mother and doctor, even where such facilities are *not* in fact available, need not be regarded as intending the death of the foetus they kill.[37] For my part, I think Grisez's reliance on such counter-factual hypotheses to specify the morally relevant meaning or intention of human acts is excessive, for it removes morally relevant "intention" too far from common-sense intention, tends to unravel the traditional and common-sense moral judgments on suicide (someone would say: "It's not death I'm choosing, only a long space of peace and quiet, after which I'd willingly be revived, if that were possible"!), and likewise disturbs our judgments on murder and in particular on the difference between administering (death-hastening) drugs to relieve pain and administering drugs to relieve-pain-by-killing.

In any event, the version of traditional nonconsequentialist ethics which has gained explicit ecclesiastical approval in the Roman church these last ninety years treats the matter differently; it treats a bad or unwanted aspect or effect of act A_1 as an *intended* aspect of A_1, not only when the good effect (unlike the bad) follows only by virtue of another human act A_2, but also *sometimes* when both the good effect and the bad effect are parts of one natural causal process requiring no further human act to achieve its effect. *Sometimes*, but not always; so when?

A variety of factors are appealed to explicitly or relied on implicitly in making a judgment that the bad effect is to count as intended-as-a-means; Bennett would call the set of factors a "jumble,"[38] but they are even more various than he has noted. It will be convenient to set them out while at the same time observing their bearing on the two cases centrally in dispute, the craniotomy to save a mother's life and that notable scenario in which "you reach around to your back and unplug yourself from that violinist to save your life."

(1) Would the chosen action have been chosen if the victim had not been present? If it would, this is ground for saying that the bad aspects of the action, viz. its death-dealing effects on the victim (child or violinist), are not being intended or chosen either as end or means, but are genuinely incidental side effects that do not necessarily determine the character of one's action as (not) respectful of human life. This was the principal reason the ecclesiastical moralists had for regarding as permissible the operation to remove the cancerous womb of the pregnant woman.[39] And the "bitter" reaction which Foot cites and endorses – "If you are permitted to bring about the death of the child, what does it matter how it is done?" – seems, here, to miss the point. For what is in question, here, is not a mere matter of technique, or different ways of doing something. Rather it is a matter of the very reason one has for acting in the way one does, and such reasons can be constitutive of the act as an intentional performance. One has no reason even to want to be rid of the foetus within the womb, let alone to want to kill it; and so one's act, though certain, causally, to kill, is not, intentionally, a choice against life.

But of course, *this* factor does not serve to distinguish a craniotomy from unplugging that violinist; in both situations, the oppressive presence of the victim is what makes one minded to do the act in question.

(2) Is the person making the choice the one whose life is threatened by the presence of the victim? Thomson rightly sees that this is a relevant question, and Thomas Aquinas makes it the pivot of his discussion of self-defensive killing (the discussion from which the "doctrine" of double effect, as a theoretically elaborated way of analysing intention, can be said to have arisen). He says:

Although it is not permissible to intend to kill someone else in order to defend oneself (since it is not right to do the act "killing a human being", except [in some cases of unjust aggression] by public authority and for the general welfare), still it is not morally necessary to omit to do what is strictly appropriate to securing one's own life simply in order to avoid killing another, for to make provision for one's own life is more strictly one's moral concern than to make provision for the life of another person.[40]

As Thomson has suggested, a bystander, confronted with a situation in which one innocent person's presence is endangering the life of another innocent person, is in a different position; to choose to intervene, in order to kill one person to save the other, involves a choice to make himself a master of life and death, a judge of who lives and who dies; and (we may say) this context of his choice prevents him from saying, reasonably, what the man defending himself can say: "I am not choosing to kill; I am just doing what – as a single act and not simply by virtue of remote consequences or of someone else's subsequent act – is strictly needful to protect my own life, by forcefully removing what is threatening it." Now the traditional condemnation of abortion[41] concerns the bystander's situation: a bystander cannot but be choosing to kill if (a) he rips open the mother, in a way foreseeably fatal to her, in order to save the child from the threatening enveloping presence of the mother (say, because the placenta has come adrift and the viable child is trapped and doomed unless it can be rescued, or because the mother's blood is poisoning the child, in a situation in which the bystander would prefer to save the child, either because he wants to save it from eternal damnation, or because the child is of royal blood and the mother low born, or because the mother is in any case sick, or old, or useless, or "has had her turn", while the child has a whole rich life before it); or if (b) he cuts up or drowns the child in order to save the mother from the child's threatening presence. "Things being as they are, there isn't much a woman can safely do to abort herself," as Thomson says (p. 684) – at least, not without the help of bystanders, who by helping (directly) would be making the same choice as if they did it themselves. But the unplugging of the violinist is done by the very person defending herself. Thomson admits that this gives quite a different flavour to the situation, but she thinks that the difference is not decisive, since bystanders have a decisive reason to intervene in favour of the *mother* threatened by her child's presence. And she finds this reason in the fact that the mother *owns* her body, just as the person plugged in to the violinist owns his own kidneys and is entitled to their unencumbered use. Well, this too has always been accounted a factor in these problems, as we can see by turning to the following question.

(3) Does the chosen action involve not merely a denial of aid and succour to someone but an actual intervention that amounts to an assault on the body of that person? Bennett wanted to deny all relevance to any such question,[42] but Foot[43] and Thomson have rightly seen that in the ticklish matter of respecting human life in the persons of others, and of characterising choices with a view to assessing their respect for life, it can matter that one is directly injuring and not merely failing to maintain a life-preserving level of assistance to another. Some-

times, as here, it is the causal structure of one's activity that involves one willy-nilly in a choice for or against a basic value. The connection between one's activity and the destruction of life may be so close and direct that intentions and considerations which would give a different dominant character to mere nonpreservation of life are incapable of affecting the dominant character of a straightforward taking of life. This surely is the reason why Thomson goes about and about to represent a choice to have an abortion as a choice *not* to provide assistance or facilities, not to be a Good or at any rate a Splendid Samaritan; and why too, she carefully describes the violinist affair so as to minimize the degree of intervention against the violinist's body, and to maximize the analogy with simply refusing an invitation to volunteer one's kidneys for this welfare (like Henry Fonda's declining to cross America to save Judith Thomson's life). "If anything in the world is true, it is that you do not commit murder, you do not do what is impermissible, if you reach around to your back and unplug yourself from that violinist to say your life." Quite so. It might nevertheless be useful to test one's moral reactions a little further: suppose, not simply that "unplugging" required a *bystander's* intervention, but also that (for medical reasons, poison in the bloodstream, shock, etc.) unplugging could not safely be performed unless and until the violinist had first been dead for six hours and had moreover been killed outright, say by drowning or decapitation (though not necessarily while conscious). Could one then be *so* confident, as a bystander, that it was right to kill the violinist in order to save the philosopher? But I put forward this revised version principally to illustrate *another* reason for thinking that, within the traditional casuistry, the violinist-unplugging in Thomson's version is *not* the "direct killing" which she claims it is, and which she must claim it is if she is to make out her case for rejecting the traditional principle about direct killing.

Let us now look back to the traditional rule about abortion. If the mother needs medical treatment to save her life, she gets it, subject to one proviso, even if the treatment is certain to kill the unborn child – for after all, her body is *her* body, as "women have said again and again" (and they have been heard by the traditional casuists!). And the proviso? That the medical treatment not be *via* a straightforward assault on or intervention against the child's body. For after all *the child's body is the child's body, not the woman's.* The traditional casuists have admitted the claims made on behalf of one "body" up to the very limit where those claims became *mere (understandable) bias, mere (understandable) self-*

interested refusal to listen to the *very same* claim ("This body is my body") when it is made by or on behalf of another person.[44] Of course, a traditional casuist would display an utter want of feeling if he didn't most profoundly sympathise with women in the desperate circumstances under discussion. But it is vexing to find a philosophical Judith Thomson, in a cool hour, unable to see when an argument cuts both ways, and unaware that the casuists have seen the point before her and have, unlike her, allowed the argument to cut both ways impartially. The child, like his mother, has a "just prior claim to his own body," and abortion involves laying hands on, manipulating, that body. And here we have perhaps the decisive reason why abortion cannot be assimilated to the range of Samaritan problems and why Thomson's location of it within that range is a mere (ingenious) novelty.

(4) But is the action against someone who had a duty not to be doing what he is doing, or not to be present where he is present? There seems no doubt that the "innocence" of the victim whose life is taken makes a difference to the characterizing of an action as open to and respectful of the good of human life, and as an intentional killing. Just how and why it makes a difference is difficult to unravel; I shall not attempt an unravelling here. We all, for whatever reasons, recognize the difference and Thomson has expressly allowed its relevance.

But her way of speaking of "rights" has a final unfortunate effect at this point. We can grant, and have granted, that the unborn child has no Hohfeldian *claim-right* to be allowed to stay within the mother's body under all circumstances; the mother is not under a strict duty to allow it to stay under all circumstances. In *that* sense, the child "has no right to be there." But Thomson discusses also the case of the burglar in the house; and he, too, has "no right to be there", even when she opens the window! But beware of the equivocation! The burglar not merely has no claim-right to be allowed to enter or stay; he also has a strict duty *not* to enter or stay; i.e., he has no Hohfeldian *liberty* – and it is *this* that is uppermost in our minds when we think that he "has no right to be there": it is actually unjust for him to be there. Similarly with Jones who takes Smith's coat, leaving Smith freezing. And similarly with the violinist. He and his agents had a strict duty not to make the hook-up to Judith Thomson or her gentle reader. Of course, the violinist himself may have been unconscious and so not himself at fault; but the whole affair is a gross injustice to the person whose kidneys are made free with, and the injustice to that person is not measured simply by the degree of moral fault of one of the parties to the injustice. Our whole view of the violinist's situation is coloured by this burglarious and persisting wrongfulness of his presence plugged into his victim.

But can any of this reasonably be said or thought of the unborn child? True, the child had no *claim-right* to be allowed to come into being within the mother. But it was not in breach of any *duty* in coming into being nor in remaining present within the mother; Thomson gives no arguments at all in favour of the view that the child is in breach of duty in being present (though her counter examples show that she is often tacitly assuming this). (Indeed, if we are going to use the wretched analogy of owning houses, I fail to see why the unborn child should not with justice say of the body around it: "That is my house. No one *granted* me property rights in it, but equally no one *granted* my mother any property rights in it." The fact is that both persons *share* in the use of this body, both by the same sort of title, viz, that this is the way they happened to come into being. But it would be better to drop this ill-fitting talk of "ownership" and "property rights" altogether). So though the unborn child "had no right to be there" (in the sense that it never had a claim-right to be allowed to *begin* to be there), in another straight-forward and more important sense it *did* "have a right to be there" (in the sense that it was not in breach of duty in being or continuing to be there). All this is, I think, clear and clearly different from the violinist's case. Perhaps forcible rape is a special case; but even then it seems fanciful to say that the child is or could be in any way at fault, as the violinist is at fault or would be but for the adventitious circumstance that he was unconscious at the time.

Still, I don't want to be dogmatic about the justice or injustice, innocence or fault, involved in a rape conception. (I have already remarked that the impermissibility of abortion in any such case where the mother's life is not in danger, does not depend necessarily on showing that the act is a choice directly to kill.) It is enough that I have shown how in three admittedly important respects the violinist case differs from the therapeutic abortion performed to save the life of the mother. As presented by Thomson, the violinist's case involves (i) no bystander, (ii) no intervention against or assault upon the body of the violinist, and (iii) an indisputable injustice to the agent in question. Each of these three factors is absent from the abortion cases in dispute. Each has been treated as relevant by the traditional casuists whose condemnations Thomson was seeking to contest when she plugged us into the violinist.

When all is said and done, however, I haven't rigorously answered my own question. When should one say that the expected bad effect or aspect of an act is not intended even as a means and hence does not determine the moral character of the act as a choice not to respect one of the basic human values? I have done no more than list some factors. I have not discussed how one decides which combinations of these factors suffice to answer the question one way rather than the other. I have not discussed the man on the plank, or the man off the plank; or the woman who leaves her baby behind as she flees from the lion, or the other women who feeds her baby to the lion in order to make good her own escape; or the "innocent" child who threatens to shoot a man dead, or the man who shoots that child to save himself;[45] or the starving explorer who kills himself to provide food for his fellows, or the other explorer who wanders away from the party so as not to hold them up or diminish their rations. The cases are many, various, instructive. Too generalized or rule-governed an application of the notion of "double effect" would offend against the Aristotelian, common-law, Wittgensteinian wisdom that here "we do not know how to draw the boundaries of the concept" – of intention, or respect for the good of life, and of action as distinct from consequences – "except for a special purpose."[46] But I think that those whom Aristotle bluntly calls wise can come to clear judgments on most of the abortion problems, judgments that will not coincide with Thomson's.

IV

I have been assuming that the unborn child is, from conception, a person and hence is not to be discriminated against on account of age, appearance, or other such factors in so far as such factors are reasonably considered irrelevant where respect for basic human values is in question. Thomson argues against this assumption, but not, as I think, well. She thinks (like Wertheimer[47] mutatis mutandis) that the argument in favour of treating a newly conceived child as a person is merely a "slippery slope" argument (p. 953), rather like (I suppose) saying that one should call all men bearded because there is no line one can confidently draw between beard and clean shavenness. More precisely, she thinks that a newly conceived child is like an acorn, which after all is not an oak! It is discouraging to see her relying so heavily and uncritically on this hoary muddle. An acorn can remain for years in a stable state, simply but completely an acorn. Plant it and from it will sprout an oak sapling, a new, dynamic biological system that has nothing much in common with an acorn save that it came from an acorn and is capable of generating new acorns. Suppose an acorn is formed in September 1971, picked up on 1 February 1972, and stored under good conditions for three years, then planted in January 1975; it sprouts on 1 March 1975 and fifty years later is a fully mature oak tree. Now suppose I ask: When did that oak begin to grow? Will anyone say September 1971 or February 1972? Will anyone look for the date on which it was first noticed in the garden? Surely not. If we know it sprouted from the acorn on 1 March 1975, that is enough (though a biologist could be a trifle more exact about "sprouting"); that is when *the oak* began. *A fortiori* with the conception of a child, which is no *mere* germination of a seed. Two cells, each with only twenty-three chromosomes, unite and more or less immediately fuse to become a new cell with forty-six chromosomes providing a unique genetic constitution (not the father's, not the mother's, and not a mere juxtaposition of the parents') which thenceforth throughout its life, however long, will substantially determine the new individual's makeup.[48] This new cell is the first stage in a dynamic integrated system that has nothing much in common with the individual male and female sex cells, save that it sprang from a pair of them and will in time produce new sets of them. To say that *this* is when a person's life began is not to work backwards from maturity, sophistically asking at each point "How can one draw the line *here?*" Rather it is to point to a perfectly clear-cut beginning to which each one of us can look back and in looking back see how, in a vividly intelligible sense, "in my beginning is my end." Judith Thomson thinks she began to "acquire human characteristics" "by the tenth week" (when fingers, toes, etc. became visible). I cannot think why she overlooks the most radically and distinctively human characteristic of all – the fact that she was conceived of human parents. And then there is Henry Fonda. From the time of his conception, though not before, one could say, looking at his unique personal genetic constitution, not only that "by the tenth week" Henry Fonda would have fingers, but also that in his fortieth year he would have a cool hand. That is why there seems no rhyme or reason in waiting "ten weeks" until his fingers and so on actually become visible before declaring that he *now* has the human rights which Judith Thomson rightly but incompletely recognizes.

NOTES

1 *Philosophy and Public Affairs,* vol. 1, no. l (Fall 1971), 47–66. Otherwise unidentified page references in the text are to this article.

2 Roger Wertheimer, "Understanding the Abortion Argument," *Philosophy and Public Affairs,* vol. 1, no. 1 (Fall 1971), pp. 67–95.

3 Rights which Thomson is willing to allow that a person has:

R1. a right to life (p. 954);

R2. a right to decide what happens in and to one's body (p. 954) (to be equated, apparently, with a just prior claim to one's own body, p. 958);

R3. a right to defend oneself (i.e., to self-defence, p. 957);

R4. a right to refuse to lay hands on other people (even when it would be just and fair to do so, p. 958) – more precisely, a right not to lay hands on other people.

Rights which she thinks it would be coherent but mistaken to claim that a person has or in any event always has:

R5. a right to demand that someone else give one assistance (p. 964) – more precisely, a right to be given assistance by ... ;

R6. a right to be given whatever one needs for continued life (p. 959);

R7. a right to the use of (or to be given, or to be allowed to continue, the use of) someone else's body (or house) (p. 958);

R8. a right not to be killed by anybody (p. 959);

R9. a right to slit another's throat (an instance, apparently, of a "right to be guaranteed his death") (p. 958);

4 Namely, R3 through R9 in the list of note 3 above.

5 Namely, R3, R4, and, in one of their senses, R7 and R9.

6 W.H. Hohfeld, *Fundamental Legal Conceptions* (New Haven, 1923).

7 Namely, R5, R6, R8, and, in another of their senses, R7 and R9.

8 Namely, R1 and R2.

9 This proposition is elaborated in a juridicial context by A.M. Honore, "Rights of Exclusion and Immunities against Divesting," *University of Tulane Law Review,* vol. 34 (1960), p. 453.

10 Insufficient specification causes needless problems, besides those mentioned in the text. For example, against "so using the term 'right' that from the fact that A ought to do a thing for B, it follows that B has a right against A that A do it for him," Thomson objects that any such use of the term "right" is "going to make the question of whether or not a man has a right to a thing turn on how easy it is to provide him with it" (p. 964); and she adds that it's "rather a shocking idea that anybody's rights

should fade away and disappear as it gets harder and harder to accord them to him" (p. 964). So she says she has no "right" to the touch of Henry Fonda's cool hand, *because,* although he ought to cross the room to touch her brow (and thus save her life), he is not morally obliged to cross America to do so. But this objection rests merely on inadequate specification of the right as against Henry Fonda. For if we say that she has a right that Henry Fonda should cross-the-room-to-touch-her-fevered-brow, and that she has no right that he should cross-America-to-touch-her-fevered-brow, then we can (if we like!) continue to deduce rights from duties.

11 It is perhaps worth pointing out that, even if we restrict our attention to the rights involved in gifts, concessions, grants, trusts, and the like, Thomson's proposed reining-in of the term "right" will be rather inconvenient. Does only the donee have the "rights"? Suppose that uncle U gives a box of chocolates to nephew Nl, with instructions to share it with nephew N2, and asks father F to see that this sharing is done. Then we want to be able to say that U has a right that Nl and N2 shall each get their share, that Nl shall give N2 that share, that F shall see to it that this is done, and so on; and that Nl has the right to his share, the right not to be interfered with by F or N2 or anyone else in eating his share, and so on; and that N2 has a similar set of rights; and that F has the right to take steps to enforce a fair distribution, the right not to be interfered with in taking those steps, and so on. Since disputes may arise about any one of these relations between the various persons and their actions and the chocolates thereby affected, it is convenient to have the term "right" on a loose rein, to let it ride round the circle of relations, picking up the action in dispute and fitting the competing Claims about the "right thing to do" into intelligible and typical three-term relationships. Yet some of the rights involved in the gift of the chocolates, for example U's rights, are not acquired by any grant to the right-holder.

12 The sentence continues: "and in which he does not have a right to use them, and in which you do not do him an injustice if you refuse." But these are merely remnants of the "rhetoric" in which she has cast her argument. Notice, incidentally, that her suggestion that "justice" and "injustice" should be restricted to respect for and violation of rights in her reined-in sense is of no importance since she grants that actions not in her sense unjust may be self-centred, callous, and indecent, and that these vices are "no less grave."

13 Perhaps this is the point at which to note how dubious is Thomson's assertion that "in no state in this country is any man compelled by law to be even a Minimally Decent Samaritan to any person," and her insinua-

tion that this is a manifestation of a discrimination against women. This sounds so odd coming from a country in which a young man, not a young woman, is compelled by law to "give up long stretches of his life" to defending his country at considerable "risk of death for himself." True, he is not doing this for "a person who has no special right to demand it"; indeed, what makes active military service tough is that one is not risking one's life to save *anybody* in particular from any *particular* risk. And are we to say that young men have *assumed* a "special responsibility" for defending other people? Wouldn't that be a gross fiction which only a lame moral theory could tempt us to indulge in? But it is just this sort of social contractarianism that Thomson is tempting us with.

14 Exodus 23:7; cf. Exodus 20:13, Deuteronomy 5:17, Genesis 9:6, Jeremiah 7:6 and 22:3.

15 These remarks are filled out somewhat in my "Natural Law and Unnatural Acts," *Heythrop Journal* 11 (1970): 365. See also Germain Grisez, *Abortion: the Myths, the Realities and the Arguments* (New York 1970), Ch. 6. My argument owes much to this and other works by Grisez.

16 R.M. Hare, "Rules of War and Moral Reasoning," *Philosophy and Public Affairs*, vol. 1, no. 2 (winter 1972), pp. 167, 168.

17 Ibid., p. 174.

18 Cf. H.-N. Castaneda, "On the Problem of Formulating a Coherent Act-Utilitarianism," *Analysis* 32 (1972), p. 118; Harold M. Zellner, "Utilitarianism and Derived Obligation,"*Analysis* 32 (1972), p. 124.

19 See D.H. Hodgson, *Consequences of Utilitarianism* (Oxford, 1967).

20 Cf. Hare, op. cit, p. 174: "The defect in most deontological theories ... is that they have no coherent rational account to give of, any level of moral thought above that of the man who knows some good simple moral principles and sticks to them ... [The] simple principles of the deontologist ... are what we should be trying to inculcate into ourselves and our children if we want to stand the best chance ... of doing what is for the best."

21 Not to mention the Jewish moralists: see D. Daube, *Collaboration with Tyranny in Rabbinic Law* (Oxford, 1965).

22 Note that I am not asserting (or denying) that self-sacrificial heroism and martyrdom are moral duties; I am explaining why they need not be regarded as moral faults.

23 *Le Suicide* (Paris, 1897), p. 5. Cf. also Daube's remarks on Donne in "The Linguistics of Suicide," *Philosophy and Public Affairs*, vol. 1, no. 4 (summer 1972), pp. 418ff.

24 Decree of the Holy Office. 2 March 1679, error no 34; see Denzinger and Schönmetzer, *Enchiridion symbolorum definitionum et declaratjonum de rebus*

fidei er morum (Barcelona, 1967), par. 2134; Grisez, *Abortion: the Myths, the Realities and the Arguments*, p. 174; John T. Noonan, Jr., "An Almost Absolute Value in History," in *The Morality of Abortion*, ed. John T. Noonan, Jr. (Cambridge, Mass., 1970), p. 34.

25 See *Summa Theologiae III*, q. 468, art. II; in *4 Sententiarum* d. 6, q. 1, a. 1, q. 1, ad. 4; d. 23, q. 2. a. 2, 1. q. 1, ad 1 & 2; Grisez, op. cit., p. 154; Noonan, op. cit., p. 24.

26 Pius XII's remark, quoted by Thomson, that "the baby in the maternal breast has the right to life immediately from God" has its principal point, not (*pace* Thomson, p. 683) in the assertion of a premise from which one could deduce the wrongfulness of direct killing, but in the assertion that if anybody – e.g., the mother – has the right not to be directly killed, *then* the baby has the same right, since as Pius XII goes on immediately "the baby, still not born, is a man in the same degree and for the same reason as the mother."

27 The three cases mentioned in this paragraph are discussed in a standard and conservative Roman Catholic textbook: Marcellino Zalba, *Theologiae Moralis Compendium* (Madrid, 1958), i. 885.

28 Philippa Foot, "The Problem of Abortion and the Doctrine of Double Effect," *The Oxford Review*, vol. 5 (1967), p. 6.

29 H.L.A. Hart, "Intention and Punishment," *The Oxford Review*, vol. 4 (1967), p. 13; reprinted in Hart, *Punishment and Responsibility* (Oxford, 1968), pp. 124–5.

30 Foot, op. cit., p. 15.

31 Ibid., p. 14.

32 Ibid., p. 8.

33 Ibid., p. 7. This is the fourth of the four usual conditions for the application of the "Doctrine of Double Effect"; see, e.g., Grisez, op. cit., p. 329. G.E.M. Anscombe, "War and Murder," in *Nuclear Weapons and Christian Conscience*, ed. W. Stein (London, 1961), p. 57, formulates the "principle of double effect," in relation to the situation where "someone innocent will die unless I do a wicked thing," thus: "you are no murderer if a man's death was neither your aim nor your chosen means, *and if you had to act in the way that led to it or else do something absolutely forbidden*" (emphasis added).

34 Grisez argues thus, op. cit., p. 343; also in "Toward a Consistent Natural-Law Ethics of Killing," *American Journal of Jurisprudence*, vol. 15 (1970), p. 95.

35 Ibid., p. 333 and pp. 89–90 respectively.

36 Ibid., p. 341 and p. 94 respectively.
37 Ibid., p. 341 and p. 95 respectively. I agree with Grisez that the fact that, if an artificial womb were available, many women would *not* transfer their aborted offspring to it shows that those women are directly and wrongfully intending the *death* of their offspring. I suspect Judith Thomson would agree.
38 Jonathan Bennett, "'Whatever the Consequences," *Analysis*, vol. 26 (1966), p. 92 n. 1.
39 See the debate between A. Gemelli and P. Vermeersch, summarized in *Ephemerides Theologicae Lovaniensis*, ii (1934), 525–61; see also Noonan, op. cit., p. 49; Zalba, *Theologiae Moralis Compendium*, i. 885.
40 *Summa Theologiae* II–II, q. 64, art. 7: "Nec est nesessarium ad salutem ut homo actum moderatae tuterae practermittat ad evitandum occisionem alterius; quia plus tenetur homo vitae suae providers quam vitae alienae. Sed quia occidere hominem non licet nisi publica auctoritate propter bonum commune, ut ex supra dictis patet [art. 3], illicitum est quod homo intendat occidere hominem ut seipsum defendat."
41 Ibid., arts. 2 and 3.
42 Bennett, op. cit.
43 Foot, op. cit, pp. 11–13.
44 Not, of course, that they have used Thomson's curious talk of "owning" one's own body with its distracting and legalistic connotations and its dualistic reduction of subjects of justice to objects.
45 This case is (too casually) used in Brody, "Thomson on Abortion," 11 *Philosophy and Public Affairs*, vol. 1, no. 3 (spring 1972), p. 335.
46 Cf. Wittgenstein, *Philosophical Investigations* (Oxford, 1953), sec. 69.
47 "Understanding the Abortion Argument."
48 See Grisez, op. cit., Ch. 1 and pp. 273–87, with literature there cited.

READING QUESTIONS ON FINNIS

1 Finnis distinguishes between takings of life that are intended and those that are merely foreseen. Explain the distinction.
2 How does Finnis know that it is right to classify abortion as an intentional taking of life rather than a foreseeable loss of life? How might Thomson reply?
3 Suppose that Finnis is right about the moral significance of the distinction he draws. Does he need to show anything further to conclude that it ought to be the basis for legal enforcement?

Morgentaler, Smolling and Scott v The Queen [1988] 1 SCR 30

The Supreme Court of Canada case overturning the *Criminal Code* provision outlawing abortion. The Court held that the law violated women's equality rights.

Dickson, CJC: – The principal issue raised by this appeal is whether the abortion provisions of the *Criminal Code* infringe the "right to life, liberty and security of the person and the right not to be deprived thereof except in accordance with the principles of fundamental justice" as formulated in s. 7 of the *Canadian Charter of Rights and Freedoms*. The appellants, Dr Henry Morgentaler, Dr Leslie Frank Smoling, and Dr Robert Scott, have raised 13 distinct grounds of appeal. During oral submissions, however, it became apparent that the primary focus of the case was upon the s. 7 argument. It is submitted by the appellants that s. 251 of the *Criminal Code*, RSC 1970, c. C-34, contravenes s. 7 of the *Canadian Charter of Rights and Freedoms* and that s. 251 should be struck down. Counsel for the Crown admitted during the course of her submissions that s. 7 of the *Charter* was indeed "the key" to the entire appeal. As for the remaining grounds of appeal, only a few brief comments are necessary. First of all, I agree with the disposition made by the Court of Appeal of the non-*Charter* issues, many of which have already been adequately dealt with in earlier cases by this court. I am also of the view that the arguments concerning the alleged invalidity of s. 605 under ss. 7 and 11 of the *Charter* are unfounded. In view of my resolution of the s. 7 issue, it will not be necessary for me to address the appellants' other *Charter* arguments and I expressly refrain from commenting upon their merits ...

SECTION 7 OF THE *CHARTER*

In his submissions, counsel for the appellants argued that the court should recognize a very wide ambit for the rights protected under s. 7 of the *Charter*. Basing his argument largely on American constitutional theories and authorities, Mr Manning submitted that the right to "life, liberty and security of the person" is a wide-ranging right to control one's own life and to promote one's individual autonomy. The right would therefore include a right to privacy and a right to make unfettered decisions about one's own life.

In my opinion, it is neither necessary nor wise in this appeal to explore the broadest implications of s. 7 as counsel would wish us to do. I prefer to rest my conclusions on a narrower analysis than that put forward on behalf of the appellants. I do not think it would be appropriate to attempt an all-encompassing explication of so important a provision as s. 7 so early in the history of *Charter* interpretation. The court should be presented with a wide variety of claims and factual situations before articulating the full range of s. 7 rights. I will therefore limit my comments to some interpretive principles already set down by the court and to an analysis of only two aspects of s. 7, the right to "security of the person" and "the principles of fundamental justice."

Interpreting Section 7

The goal of *Charter* interpretation is to secure for all people "the full benefit of the Charter's protection": To attain that goal, this court has held consistently that the proper technique for the interpretation of *Charter* provisions is to pursue a "purposive" analysis of the right guaranteed.

In *Re Singh and Minister of Employment and Immigration* (1985), 17 DLR (4th) 422 at p. 458, Justice Wilson emphasized that there are three distinct elements to the s. 7 right, that "life, liberty, and security of the person" are independent interests, each of which must be given independent significance by the court (pp. 458–9 DLR, p. 205 SCR). It is therefore possible to treat only one aspect of the first part of s. 7 before determining whether any infringement of that interest accords with the principles of fundamental justice ...

I have no doubt that s. 7 does impose upon courts the duty to review the substance of legislation once it has been determined that the legislation infringes an individual's right to "life, liberty and security of the person." The section states clearly that those interests may only be impaired if the principles of fundamental justice are respected. Lamer J emphasized, however, that the courts should avoid "adjudication of the merits of public policy" (p. 299 CCC, p. 546 DLR, p. 499 SCR). In the present case, I do not believe that it is necessary for the court to tread the fine line between substantive review and the adjudication of public policy. As in the *Singh* case, it will be sufficient to investigate whether or not the impugned legislative provisions meet the procedural standards of fundamental justice. First it is necessary to determine whether s. 251 of the *Criminal Code* impairs the security of the person.

Security of the Person

The law has long recognized that the human body ought to be protected from interference by others. At common law, for example, any medical procedure carried out on a person without that person's consent is an assault. Only in emergency circumstances does the law allow others to make decisions of this nature. Similarly, art. 19 of the *Civil Code of Lower Canada* provides that "[t]he human person is inviolable" and that "[n]o person may cause harm to the person of another without his consent or without being authorized by law to do so." "Security of the person," in other words, is not a value alien to our legal landscape. With the advent of the *Charter*, security of the person has been elevated to the status of a constitutional norm. This is not to say that the various forms of protection accorded to the human body by the common and civil law occupy a similar status. "Security of the person" must be given content in a manner sensitive to its constitutional position. The above examples are simply illustrative of our respect for individual physical integrity.

The appellants submitted that the "security of the person" protected by the *Charter* is an explicit right to control one's body and to make fundamental decisions about one's life. The Crown contended that "security of the person" is a more circumscribed interest and that, like all of the elements of s. 7, it at most relates to the concept of physical control, simply protecting the individual's interest in his or her bodily integrity.

The case law leads me to the conclusion that state interference with bodily integrity and serious state-imposed psychological stress, at least in the criminal law context, constitute a breach of security of the person. It is not necessary in this case to determine whether the right extends further, to protect either interests central to personal autonomy, such as a right to privacy, or interests unrelated to criminal justice.

I wish to reiterate that finding a violation of security of the person does not end the s. 7 inquiry. Parliament could choose to infringe security of the person if it did so in a manner consistent with the principles of fundamental justice. The present discussion should therefore be seen as a threshold inquiry and the conclusions do not dispose definitively of all the issues relevant to s. 7. With that caution, I have no difficulty in concluding that the encyclopedic factual submissions addressed to us by counsel in the present appeal establish beyond any doubt that s. 251 of the *Criminal Code* is prima facie a violation of the security of the person of thousands of Canadian women who have made the difficult decision that they do not wish to continue with a pregnancy ...

At the most basic, physical and emotional level, every pregnant woman is told by the section that she cannot submit to a generally safe medical procedure that might be of clear benefit to her unless she meets criteria entirely unrelated to her own priorities and aspirations. Not only does the removal of decision-making power threaten women in a physical sense; the indecision of knowing whether an abortion will be granted inflicts emotional stress. Section 251 clearly interferes with a woman's bodily integrity in both a physical and emotional sense. Forcing a woman, by threat of criminal sanction, to carry a foetus to term unless she meets certain criteria unrelated to her own priorities and aspirations, is a profound interference with a woman's body and thus a violation of security of the person. Section 251, therefore, is required by the *Charter* to comport with the principles of fundamental justice.

Although this interference with physical and emotional integrity is sufficient in itself to trigger a review of s. 251 against the principles of fundamental justice, the operation of the decision-making mechanism set out in s. 251 creates additional glaring breaches of security of the person. The evidence indicates that s. 251 causes a certain amount of delay for women who are successful in meeting its criteria. In the context of abortion any unnecessary delay can have profound consequences on the woman's physical and emotional well-being.

If forced to apply to several different therapeutic abortion committees, there can be no doubt that a woman will experience serious delay in obtaining a therapeutic abortion ... [T]he implications of any delay, according to the evidence, are potentially devastating. The first factor to consider is that different medical techniques are employed to perform abortions at different stages of pregnancy. The testimony of expert doctors at trial indicated that in the first 12 weeks of pregnancy, the relatively safe and simple suction dilation and curettage method of abortion is typically used in North America. From the 13th to the 16th week, the more dangerous dilation and evacuation procedure is performed, although much less often in Canada than in the United States. From the 16th week of pregnancy, the instillation method is commonly employed in Canada. This method requires the intra-amniotic introduction of prostaglandin, urea, or a saline solution, which causes a woman to go into labour, giving birth to a foetus which is usually dead, but not invariably so. The uncontroverted evidence showed that each method of abortion progressively increases risks to the woman.

The second consideration is that even within the periods appropriate to each method of abortion the evidence indicated that the earlier the abortion was performed, the fewer the complications and the lower the risk of mortality.

It is no doubt true that the over-all complication and mortality rates for women who undergo abortions are very low, but the increasing risks caused by delay are so clearly established that I have no difficulty in concluding that the delay in obtaining therapeutic abortions caused by the mandatory procedures of s. 251 is an infringement of the purely physical aspect of the individual's right to security of the person.

Secondly, were it nevertheless possible in this case to dissociate purpose and administration, this court has already held as a matter of law that purpose is not the only appropriate criterion in evaluating the constitutionality of legislation under the *Charter*. Even if the purpose of legislation is unobjectionable, the administrative procedures created by law to bring that purpose into operation may produce unconstitutional effects, and the legislation should then be struck down.

In summary, s. 251 is a law which forces women to carry a foetus to term contrary to their own priorities and aspirations and which imposes serious delay causing increased physical and psychological trauma to those women who meet its criteria. It must, therefore, be determined whether that infringement is accomplished in accordance with the principles of fundamental justice, thereby saving s. 251 under the second part of s. 7.

The Principles of Fundamental Justice

Although the "principles of fundamental justice" referred to in s. 7 have both a substantive and a procedural component, I have already indicated that it is not necessary in this appeal to evaluate the substantive content of s. 251 of the *Criminal Code*. My discussion will therefore be limited to various aspects of the administrative structure and procedure set down in s. 251 for access to therapeutic abortions.

In outline, s. 251 operates in the following manner. Subsection (1) creates an indictable offence for any person to use any means with the intent "to procure the miscarriage of a female person." Subsection (2) establishes a parallel indictable offence for any pregnant woman to use or to permit any means to be used with the intent "to procure her own miscarriage." The "means" referred to in s-ss. (1) and (2) are defined in s-s. (3) as the administration of a drug or "other noxious thing," the use of an instrument, and "manipulation of any kind." The crucial provision for the purposes of the present appeal is s-s. (4) which states that the offences created in s-ss. (1) and (2) "do not apply" in certain circumstances.

The procedure surrounding the defence is rather complex. A pregnant woman who desires to have an abortion must apply to the "therapeutic abortion committee" of an "accredited or approved hospital." Such a committee is empowered to issue a certificate in writing stating that in the opinion of a majority of the committee, the continuation of the pregnancy would be likely to endanger the pregnant woman's life or health. Once a copy of the certificate is given to a qualified medical practitioner who is not a member of the therapeutic abortion committee, he or she is permitted to perform an abortion on the pregnant woman and both the doctor and the woman are freed from any criminal liability ...

As is so often the case in matters of interpretation, however, the straightforward reading of this statutory scheme is not fully revealing. In order to understand the true nature and scope of s. 251, it is necessary to investigate the practical operation of the provisions. The court has been provided with a myriad of factual submissions in this area ... In other words, the seemingly neutral requirement of s. 251(4) that at least four physicians be available to authorize and to perform an abortion meant in practice that abortions would be absolutely unavailable in almost one-quarter of all hospitals in Canada.

Other administrative and procedural requirements of s. 251(4) reduce the availability of therapeutic abortions even further. For the purposes of s. 251, therapeutic abortions can only be performed in "accredited" or "approved" hospitals. As noted above, an "approved" hospital is one which a provincial minister of health has designated as such for the purpose of performing therapeutic abortions. The minister is under no obligation to grant any such approval. Furthermore, an "accredited" hospital must not only be accredited by the Canadian Council on Hospital Accreditation, it must also provide specified services. Many Canadian hospitals do not provide all of the required services, thereby being automatically disqualified from undertaking therapeutic abortions. Moreover, even if a hospital is eligible to create a therapeutic abortion committee, there is no requirement in s. 251 that the hospital need do so.

A further flaw with the administrative system established in s. 251(4) is the failure to provide an adequate standard for therapeutic abortion committees which must determine when a therapeutic abortion should, as a matter of law, be granted. Subsection (4) states simply that a therapeutic abortion committee may grant a certificate when it determines that a continuation of a pregnancy would be likely to endanger the "life or health" of the pregnant woman. It was noted above that "health" is not defined for the purposes of the section. The Crown admitted in its supplementary factum that the medical witnesses at trial testified uniformly that the "health" standard was ambiguous, but the Crown derives comfort from the fact that "the medical witnesses were unanimous in their approval of the broad World Health Organization definition of health." The World Health Organization defines "health" not merely as the absence of disease or infirmity, but as a state of physical, mental, and social well-being.

I do not understand how the mere existence of a workable definition of "health" can make the use of the word in s. 251(4) any less ambiguous when that definition is nowhere referred to in the section. There is no evidence that therapeutic abortion committees are commonly applying the World Health Organization definition.

Various expert doctors testified at trial that therapeutic abortion committees apply widely differing definitions of health. For some committees, psychological health is a justification for therapeutic abortion; for others it is not. Some committees routinely refuse abortions to married women unless they are in physical danger, while for other committees it is possible for a married woman to show that she would suffer psychological harm if she continued with a pregnancy, thereby justifying an abortion. It is not typically possible for women to know in advance what standard of health will be applied by any given committee.

When the decision of the therapeutic abortion committee is so directly laden with legal consequences, the absence of any clear legal standard to be applied by the committee in reaching its decision is a serious procedural flaw ... The combined effect of all of these problems with the procedure stipulated in s. 251 for access to therapeutic abortions is a failure to comply with the principles of fundamental justice. One of the basic tenets of our system of criminal justice is that when Parliament creates a defence to a criminal charge, the defence should not be illusory or so difficult to attain as to be practically illusory. The criminal law is a very special form of governmental regulation, for it seeks to express our society's collective disapprobation of certain acts and omissions. When a defence is provided, especially a specifically tailored defence to a particular charge, it is because the legislator has determined that the disapprobation of society is not warranted when the conditions of the defence are met.

The Crown argues in its supplementary factum that women who face difficulties in obtaining abortions at home can simply travel elsewhere in Canada to procure a therapeutic abortion. That submission would not be especially troubling if the difficulties facing women were not in large measure created by the procedural requirements of s. 251 itself. If women were seeking anonymity outside their home town or were simply confronting the reality that it is often difficult to obtain medical services in rural areas, it might be appropriate to say "let them travel." But the evidence establishes convincingly that it is the law itself which in many ways prevents access to local therapeutic abortion facilities. The enormous emotional and financial burden placed upon women who must travel long distances from home to obtain an abortion is a burden created in many instances by Parliament.

SECTION 1 ANALYSIS

Section 1 of the *Charter* can potentially be used to "salvage" a legislative provision which breaches s. 7.

The appellants contended that the sole purpose of s. 251 of the *Criminal Code* is to protect the life and health of pregnant women. The respondent Crown submitted that s. 251 seeks to protect not only the life and health of pregnant women, but also the interests of the foetus. On the other hand, the Crown conceded that the court is not called upon in this appeal to evaluate any claim to "foetal rights" or to assess the meaning of "the right to life." I expressly refrain from so doing. In my view, it is unnecessary for the purpose of deciding this appeal to evaluate or assess "foetal rights" as an independent constitutional value. Nor are we required to measure the full extent of the state's interest in establishing criteria unrelated to the pregnant woman's own priorities and aspirations. What we must do is evaluate the particular balance struck by Parliament in s. 251, as it relates to the priorities and aspirations of pregnant women and the government's interests in the protection of the foetus.

Section 251 provides that foetal interests are not to be protected where the "life or health" of the woman is threatened. Thus, Parliament itself has expressly stated in s. 251 that the "life or health" of pregnant women is paramount. The procedures of s. 251(4) are clearly related to the pregnant woman's "life or health" for that is the very phrase used by the subsection. As McIntyre, J states in his reasons, the aim of s. 251(4) is "to restrict abortion to cases where the continuation of the pregnancy would, or would likely, be injurious to the life or health of the woman concerned, not to provide unrestricted access to abortion." I have no difficulty in concluding that the objective of s. 251 as a whole, namely, to balance the competing interests identified by Parliament, is sufficiently important to meet the requirements of the first step in the Oakes inquiry under s. 1. I think the protection of the interests of pregnant women is a valid governmental objective, where life and health can be jeopardized by criminal sanctions. Like Beetz and Wilson, JJ, I agree that protection of foetal interests by Parliament is also a valid governmental objective. It follows that balancing these interests, with the lives and health of women a major factor, is clearly an important governmental objective.

I am equally convinced, however, that the means chosen to advance the legislative objectives of s. 251 do not satisfy any of the three elements of the proportionality component of *R v Oakes*. The evidence has led me to conclude that the infringement of the security of the person of pregnant women caused by s. 251 is not accomplished in accordance with the principles of fundamental justice. It has been demonstrated that the procedures and administrative structures created by s. 251 are often arbitrary and unfair. The procedures established to implement the policy of s. 251 impair s. 7 rights far more than is necessary because they hold out an illusory defence to many women who would prima facie qualify under the exculpatory provisions of s. 251(4). In other words, many women whom Parliament professes not to wish to subject to criminal liability will nevertheless be forced by the practical unavailability of the supposed defence to risk liability or to suffer other harm such as a traumatic late abortion caused by the delay inherent in the s. 251 system. Finally, the effects of the limitation upon the s. 7 rights of many pregnant women are out of proportion to the objective sought to be achieved. Indeed, to the extent that s. 251(4) is designed to protect the life and health of women, the procedures it establishes may actually defeat that objective. The administrative structures of s. 251(4) are so cumbersome that women whose health is endangered by pregnancy may not be able to gain a therapeutic abortion, at least without great trauma, expense and inconvenience. Section 251 of the *Criminal Code* cannot be saved, therefore, under s. 1 of the *Charter*.

Beetz, J:– I have had the advantage of reading the reasons for judgment written by the Chief Justice, as well as the reasons written by Mr Justice McIntyre and Madam Justice Wilson.

Like the Chief Justice and Wilson, J, I would allow the appeal and answer the first constitutional question in the affirmative and the second constitutional question in the negative. This, however, is a result which I reach for reasons which differ from those of the Chief Justice and those of Wilson, J.

I find it convenient to outline at the outset the steps which lead me to this result:

Before the advent of the *Charter*, Parliament recognized, in adopting s. 251(4) of the *Criminal Code*, that the interest in the life or health of the pregnant woman takes precedence over the interest in prohibiting abortions, including the interest of the state in the protection of the foetus, when "the continuation of the pregnancy of such female person would or would be likely to endanger her life or health." In my view, this standard in s. 251(4) became entrenched at least as a minimum when the "right to life, liberty and security of the person" was enshrined in the *Canadian Charter of Rights and Freedoms* at s. 7.

"Security of the person" within the meaning of s. 7 of the *Charter* must include a right of access to medical treatment for a condition representing a danger to life or health without fear of criminal sanction. If an Act of Parliament forces a pregnant woman whose life or health is in danger to choose between, on the one hand, the commission of a crime to obtain effective and timely medical treatment and, on the other hand, inadequate treatment or no treatment at all, her right to security of the person has been violated.

According to the evidence, the procedural requirements of s. 251 of the *Criminal Code* significantly delay pregnant women's access to medical treatment resulting in an additional danger to their health, thereby depriving them of their right to security of the person.

The deprivation referred to in the preceding proposition does not accord with the principles of fundamental justice. While Parliament is justified in requiring a reliable, independent, and medically sound opinion as to the "life or health" of the pregnant woman in order to protect the state interest in the foetus, and while any such statutory mechanism will inevitably result in some delay, certain of the procedural requirements of s. 251 of the *Criminal Code* are nevertheless manifestly unfair. These requirements are manifestly unfair in that they are unnecessary in respect of Parliament's objectives in establishing the administrative structure and that they result in additional risks to the health of pregnant women.

The primary objective of s. 251 of the *Criminal Code* is the protection of the foetus. The protection of the life and health of the pregnant woman is an ancillary objective. The primary objective does relate to concerns which are pressing and substantial in a free and democratic society and which, pursuant to s. 1 of the *Charter*, justify reasonable limits to be put on a woman's right. However, rules unnecessary in respect of the primary and ancillary objectives which they are designed to serve, such as some of the rules contained in s. 251, cannot be said to be rationally connected to these objectives under s. 1 of the *Charter*. Consequently, s. 251 does not constitute a reasonable limit to the security of the person.

It is not necessary to decide whether there is a proportionality between the effects of s. 251 and the objective of protecting the foetus, nor is it necessary to answer the question concerning the circumstances in which there is a proportionality between the effects of s. 251 which limit the right of pregnant women to security of the person and the objective of the protection of the foetus. But I feel bound to observe that the objective of protecting the foetus would not justify the severity of the breach of pregnant women's right to security of the person which would result if the exculpatory provision of s. 251 was completely removed from the *Criminal Code*. However, a rule that would require a higher degree of danger to health in the latter months of pregnancy, as opposed to the early months, for an abortion to be lawful, could possibly achieve a proportionality which would be acceptable under s. 1 of the *Charter* ...

If a rule of criminal law precludes a person from obtaining appropriate medical treatment when his or her life or health is in danger, then the state has intervened and this intervention constitutes a violation of that man's or that woman's security of the person. "Security of the person" must include a right of access to medical treatment for a condition representing a danger to life or health without fear of criminal sanction. If an Act of Parliament forces a person whose life or health is in danger to choose between, on the one hand, the commission of a crime to obtain effective and timely medical treatment and, on the other hand, inadequate treatment or no treatment at all, the right to security of the person has been violated.

This interpretation of s. 7 of the *Charter* is sufficient to measure the content of s. 251 of the *Criminal Code* against that of the *Charter* in order to dispose of this appeal. While I agree with McIntyre, J that a breach of a right to security must be "based upon an infringement of some interest which would be of such nature and such importance as to warrant constitutional protection," I am of the view that the protection of life or health is an interest of sufficient importance in this regard.

McIntyre, J (dissenting): – I have read the reasons for judgment prepared by my colleagues, the Chief Justice and Beetz and Wilson, JJ. I agree that the principal issue which arises is whether s. 251 of the *Criminal Code*, RSC 1970, c. C-34, contravenes s. 7 of the *Canadian Charter of Rights and Freedoms*. I will make some comments later on other issues put forward by the appellants. The Chief Justice has set out the constitutional questions and the relevant statutory provisions, as well as the facts and procedural history. He has considered the scope of s. 7 of the *Charter* and, having found that it has been offended, he would allow the appeal. I am unable to agree with his reasons or his disposition of the appeal. I find myself in broad general agreement with the reasons of the Court of Appeal, and I would dismiss the appeal on that basis and for reasons that I will endeavour to set forth.

PROCEDURAL FAIRNESS

I now turn to the appellant's argument regarding the procedural fairness of s. 251 of the *Criminal Code*. The basis of the argument is that the exemption provisions of s-s. (4) are such as to render illusory or practically illusory any defence arising from the subsection for many women who seek abortions. It is pointed out that therapeutic abortions are available only in accredited or approved hospitals, that hospitals so accredited or approved may or may not appoint abortion committees, and that "health" is defined in vague terms which afford no clear guide to its meaning. Statistically, it was said that abortions could be lawfully performed in only 20 per cent of all hospitals in Canada. Because abortions are not generally available to all women who seek them, the argument goes, the defence is illusory, or practically so, and the section therefore fails to comport with the principles of fundamental justice ...

It would seem to me that a defence created by Parliament could only be said to be illusory or practically so when the defence is not available in the circumstances in which it is held out as being available. The very nature of the test assumes, of course, that it is for Parliament to define the defence and, in so doing, to designate the terms and conditions upon which it may be available.

[I]t is apparent that the court's role is not to second-guess Parliament's policy choice as to how broad or how narrow the defence should be. The determination of when "the disapprobation of society is not warranted" is in Parliament's hands. The Court's role when the enactment is attacked on the basis that the defence is illusory is to determine whether the defence is available in the circumstances in which it was intended to apply. Parliament has set out the conditions, in s. 251(4), under which a therapeutic abortion may be obtained, free from criminal sanction. It is patent on the face of the legislation that the defence is circumscribed and narrow. It is clear that this was the Parliamentary intent and it was expressed with precision. I am not able to accept the contention that the defence has been held out to be generally available. It is, on the contrary, carefully tailored and limited to special circumstances. Therapeutic abortions may be performed only in certain hospitals and in accordance with certain specified provisions. It could only be classed as illusory or practically so if it could be found that it does not provide lawful access to abortions in circumstances described in the section. No such finding should be made upon the material before this court. The evidence will not support the proposition that significant numbers of those who meet the conditions imposed in s. 251 of the *Criminal Code* are denied abortions.

It is evident that what the appellants advocate is not the therapeutic abortion referred to in s. 251 of the *Code*. Their clinic was called into being because of the perceived inadequacies of s. 251. They propose and seek to justify "abortion on demand." The defence in s. 251(4) was not intended to meet the views of the appellants and provide a defence at large which would effectively repeal the operative subsections of s. 251. Some feel strongly that s. 251 is not adequate in today's society. Be that as it may, it does not follow that the defence provisions of s. 251(4) are illusory. They represent the legislative choice on this question and, as noted, it has not been shown that therapeutic abortions have not been available in cases contemplated by the provision.

Wilson, J: – At the heart of this appeal is the question whether a pregnant woman can, as a constitutional matter, be compelled by law to carry the foetus to term. The legislature has proceeded on the basis that she can be so compelled and, indeed, has made it a criminal offence punishable by imprisonment under s. 251 of the *Criminal Code*, RSC

1970, c. C-34, for her or her physician to terminate the pregnancy unless the procedural requirements of the section are complied with.

My colleagues, the Chief Justice and Beetz, J, have attacked those requirements in reasons which I have had the privilege of reading. They have found that the requirements do not comport with the principles of fundamental justice in the procedural sense and have concluded that, since they cannot be severed from the provisions creating the substantive offence, the whole of s. 251 must fall.

With all due respect, I think that the court must tackle the primary issue first. A consideration as to whether or not the procedural requirements for obtaining or performing an abortion comport with fundamental justice is purely academic if such requirements cannot as a constitutional matter be imposed at all. If a pregnant woman cannot, as a constitutional matter, be compelled by law to carry the foetus to term against her will, a review of the procedural requirements by which she may be compelled to do so seems pointless. Moreover, it would, in my opinion, be an exercise in futility for the legislature to expend its time and energy in attempting to remedy the defects in the procedural requirements unless it has some assurance that this process will, at the end of the day, result in the creation of a valid criminal offence. I turn, therefore, to what I believe is the central issue that must be addressed.

THE RIGHT OF ACCESS TO ABORTION

Section 7 of the *Canadian Charter of Rights and Freedoms* provides:

7. Everyone has the right to life, liberty and security of the person and the right not to be deprived thereof except in accordance with the principles of fundamental justice.

I agree with the Chief Justice that we are not called upon in this case to delineate the full content of the right to life, liberty, and security of the person. This would be an impossible task because we cannot envisage all the contexts in which such a right might be asserted. What we are asked to do, I believe, is define the content of the right in the context of the legislation under attack. Does s. 251 of the *Criminal Code* which limits the pregnant woman's access to abortion violate her right to life, liberty, and security of the person within the meaning of s. 7?

Leaving aside for the moment the implications of the section for the foetus and addressing only the s. 7 right of the pregnant woman, it seems to me that we can say with a fair degree of confidence that a legislative scheme for the obtaining of an abortion which exposes the pregnant woman to a threat to her security of the person would violate her right under s. 7 ... But this, of course, does not answer the question whether even the ideal legislative scheme, assuming that it is one which poses no threat to the physical and psychological security of the person of the pregnant woman, would be valid under s. 7. I say this for two reasons: (1) because s. 7 encompasses more than the right to security of the person; it speaks also of the right to liberty, and (2) because security of the person may encompass more than physical and psychological security; this we have yet to decide.

It seems to me, therefore, that to commence the analysis with the premise that the s. 7 right encompasses only a right to physical and psychological security and to fail to deal with the right to liberty in the context of "life, liberty and security of the person" begs the central issue in the case. If either the right to liberty or the right to security of the person or a combination of both confers on the pregnant woman the right to decide for herself (with the guidance of her physician) whether or not to have an abortion then we have to examine the legislative scheme not only from the point of view of fundamental justice in the procedural sense but in the substantive sense as well. I think, therefore, that we must answer the question: what is meant by the right to liberty in the context of the abortion issue? Does it give the pregnant woman control over decisions affecting her own body? If not, does her right to security of the person give her such control? I turn first to the right to liberty.

The Right to Liberty

In order to ascertain the content of the right to liberty, we must commence with an analysis of the purpose of the right. We are invited, therefore, to consider the purpose of the *Charter* in general and of the right to liberty in particular.

The *Charter* is predicated on a particular conception of the place of the individual in society. An individual is not a totally independent entity disconnected from the society in which he or she lives. Neither, however, is the individual a mere cog in an impersonal machine in which his or her values, goals, and aspirations are subordinated to those of the collectivity. The individual is a bit of both. The *Charter* reflects this reality by leaving a wide range of activities and decisions open to legitimate government control while at the same time placing limits on the proper scope of that control. Thus, the rights guaranteed in the *Charter* erect around each individual, metaphorically speaking, an invisible fence over which the state will not be allowed to trespass. The role of the courts is to map out, piece by piece, the parameters of the fence ...

The idea of human dignity finds expression in almost every right and freedom guaranteed in the Charter. Individuals are afforded the right to choose their own religion and their own philosophy of life, the right to choose with whom they will associate and how they will express themselves, the right to choose where they will live and what occupation they will pursue. These are all examples of the basic theory underlying the *Charter*, namely, that the state will respect choices made by individuals and, to the greatest extent possible, will avoid subordinating these choices to any one conception of the good life.

Thus, an aspect of the respect for human dignity on which the *Charter* is founded is the right to make fundamental personal decisions without interference from the state ... In my view, this right, properly construed, grants the individual a degree of autonomy in making decisions of fundamental personal importance ... Liberty in a free and democratic society does not require the state to approve the personal decisions made by its citizens; it does, however, require the state to respect them.

In my opinion, the respect for individual decision making in matters of fundamental personal importance reflected in the American jurisprudence also informs the Canadian *Charter*. Indeed, as Chief Justice pointed out in *R v Big M Drug Mart Ltd,* beliefs about human worth and dignity "are the *sine qua non* of the political tradition underlying the *Charter.*" I would conclude, therefore, that the right to liberty contained in s. 7 guarantees to every individual a degree of personal autonomy over important decisions intimately affecting their private lives.

The question then becomes whether the decision of a woman to terminate her pregnancy falls within this class of protected decisions. I have no doubt that it does. This decision is one that will have profound psychological, economic, and social consequences for the pregnant woman. The circumstances giving rise to it can be complex and varied and there may be, and usually are, powerful considerations militating in opposite directions. It is a decision that deeply reflects the way the woman thinks about herself and her relationship to others and to society at large. It is not just a medical decision; it is a profound social and ethical one as well. Her response to it will be the response of the whole person.

It is probably impossible for a man to respond, even imaginatively, to such a dilemma not just because it is outside the realm of his personal experience (although this is, of course, the case) but because he can relate to it only by objectifying it, thereby eliminating the subjective elements of the female psyche which are at the heart of the dilemma ...

[T]he history of the struggle for human rights from the eighteenth century on has been the history of men struggling to assert their dignity and common humanity against an overbearing state apparatus. The more recent struggle for women's rights has been a struggle to eliminate discrimination, to achieve a place for women in a man's world, to develop a set of legislative reforms in order to place women in the same position as men. It has not been a struggle to define the rights of women in relation to their special place in the societal structure and in relation to the biological distinction between the two sexes. Thus, women's needs and aspirations are only now being translated into protected rights. The right to reproduce or not to reproduce which is in issue in this case is one such right and is properly perceived as an integral part of modern woman's struggle to assert her dignity and worth as a human being ...

Given then that the right to liberty guaranteed by s. 7 of the *Charter* gives a woman the right to decide for herself whether or not to terminate her pregnancy, does s. 251 of the *Criminal Code* violate this right? Clearly it does. The purpose of the section is to take the decision away from the woman and give it to a committee. Furthermore, as the Chief Justice correctly points out, the committee bases its decision on "criteria entirely unrelated to [the pregnant woman's] priorities and aspirations." The fact that the decision whether a woman will be allowed to terminate her pregnancy is in the hands of a committee is just as great a violation of the woman's right to personal autonomy in decisions of an intimate and private nature as it would be if a committee were established to decide whether a woman should be allowed to continue her pregnancy. Both these arrangements violate the woman's right to liberty by deciding for her something that she has the right to decide for herself.

The Right to Security of the Person

Section 7 of the *Charter* also guarantees everyone the right to security of the person. Does this, as Mr Manning suggests, extend to the right of control over their own bodies?

I agree with the Chief Justice and with Beetz, J that the right to "security of the person" under s. 7 of the *Charter* protects both the physical and psychological integrity of the individual. State-enforced medical or surgical treatment comes readily to mind as an obvious invasion of physical integrity. [T]he present legislative scheme for the obtaining of an abortion clearly subjects pregnant women to considerable emotional stress as well as to unnecessary physical risk. I believe, however, that the flaw in the present legislative scheme goes much deeper than that. In essence, what it does is assert that the woman's capacity to reproduce is not to be subject to her own control. It is to be subject to the control of the state. She may not choose whether to exercise her existing capacity or not to exercise it. This is not, in my view, just a matter of interfering with her right to liberty in the sense (already discussed) of her right to personal autonomy in decision-making, it is a direct interference with her physical "person" as well. She is truly being treated as a means – a means to an end which she does not desire but, over which she has no control. She is the passive recipient of a decision made by others as to whether her body is to be used to nurture a new life. Can there be anything that comports less with human dignity and self-respect? How can a woman in this position have any sense of security with respect to her person? I believe that s. 251 of the *Criminal Code* deprives the pregnant woman of her right to security of the person as well as her right to liberty.

THE SCOPE OF THE RIGHT UNDER SECTION 7

I turn now to a consideration of the degree of personal autonomy the pregnant woman has under s. 7 of the *Charter* when faced with a decision whether or not to have an abortion or, to put it into the legislative context, the degree to which the legislature can deny the pregnant woman access to abortion without violating her s. 7 right. This involves a consideration of the extent to which the legislature can "deprive" her of it under the second part of s. 7 and the extent to which it can put "limits" on it under s. 1.

The Principles of Fundamental Justice

Does s. 251 deprive women of their right to liberty and to security of the person "in accordance with the principles of fundamental justice"? I agree with Lamer, J who stated in *Reference re s. 94(2) of Motor Vehicle*

Act (1985), 23 CCC (3d) 289 at p. 311, that the principles of fundamental justice "cannot be given any exhaustive content or simple enumerative definition, but will take on concrete meaning as the courts address alleged violations of s. 7." In the same judgment Lamer, J also stated at p. 302 CCC, p. 550:

In other words, the principles of fundamental justice are to be found in the basic tenets of our legal system. They do not lie in the realm of general public policy but in the inherent domain of the judiciary as guardian of the justice system ...

While Lamer, J draws mainly upon ss. 8 to 14 of the *Charter* to give substantive content to the principles of fundamental justice, he does not preclude, but seems rather to encourage, the idea that recourse may be had to other rights guaranteed by the *Charter* for the same purpose. The question, therefore, is whether the deprivation of the s. 7 right is in accordance not only with procedural fairness (and I agree with the Chief Justice and Beetz, J for the reasons they give that it is not) but also with the fundamental rights and freedoms laid down elsewhere in the *Charter*.

In my view, the deprivation of the s. 7 right with which we are concerned in this case offends s. 2(a) of the *Charter*. I say this because I believe that the decision whether or not to terminate a pregnancy is essentially a moral decision, a matter of conscience. I do not think there is or can be any dispute about that. The question is: whose conscience? Is the conscience of the woman to be paramount or the conscience of the state? I believe, for the reasons I gave in discussing the right to liberty, that in a free and democratic society it must be the conscience of the individual. Indeed, s. 2(a) makes it clear that this freedom belongs to "everyone," i.e., to each of us individually. I quote the section for conveniences

2. Everyone has the following fundamental freedoms:
(a) freedom of conscience and religion;

It seems to me, therefore, that in a free and democratic society "freedom of conscience and religion" should be broadly construed to extend to conscientiously held beliefs, whether grounded in religion or in a secular morality. Indeed, as a matter of statutory interpretation, "conscience" and "religion" should not be treated as tautologous if capable of independent, although related, meaning. Accordingly, for the state to take sides on the issue of abortion as it does in the impugned legislation by making it a criminal offence for the pregnant woman to exercise one of her options, is not only to endorse but also to enforce, on pain of a further loss of liberty through actual imprisonment, one conscientiously held view at the expense of another. Legislation which violates freedom of conscience in this manner cannot, in my view, be in accordance with the principles of fundamental justice within the meaning of s. 7.

READING QUESTIONS ON MORGENTALER

1 Can you think of a statute regulating abortion that would pass the tests the court outlines?
2 Wilson, J uses the metaphor of a "fence" protecting individual rights. How is this type of argument related to the debate about negative liberty, above?

Lorraine Weinrib
"The Morgentaler Judgment: Constitutional Rights, Legislative Intention, and Institutional Design" (1992)

Weinrib examines the consequences of the court's decision in Morgentaler. She criticizes the judgment, although she argues that it is the beginning of the realization that women are rights-holders first, breeders second.

IV THE FUTURE OF CANADIAN ABORTION LAW

The *Morgentaler* judgment does not incapacitate our legislatures from regulating abortion or even prohibiting abortion in some circumstances. Nor is there in the absence of legislation, a legal vacuum, as repeatedly declared by the press in the aftermath of the decision. On the contrary, we have abundant law on the subject of abortion – constitutional law that circumscribes the permissible exercise of state power. Any state action must honour the *Charter* guarantee of expeditious access to therapeutic health care for women throughout pregnancy, without prejudice attaching to gender and without moral overtones.

The diversity of analysis in the three majority judgments is often cited as proof that *Charter* analysis lies in the subjective leanings of the individual judge rather than in the realm of legal discourse. But diversity is not disparity. Each opinion is a study in legal, rather than political or moral, analysis; each presents a distinctively judicial approach to elaboration of guaranteed rights; each expresses disdain for the subordination of the substantive rights of women to therapeutic health care to the lesser ranked interests of doctors, hospitals, and politicians. The taint of subjectivism lies, if anywhere, in the dissent.

Proof of a majority consensus as to the substantive dictates of the supreme law of Canada lies in the remedy afforded. If Justice Beetz's concern applied only to the procedural delivery of the therapeutic standard, he would have left that standard in place, leaving those charged with the offence of procuring miscarriages with the defence of therapeutic need. Similarly, if Chief Justice Dickson's interest was limited to securing a fair procedure unrelated to the "priorities and aspirations" of the pregnant woman, he too would have left women and doctors with the defence of therapeutic cause. The working of the criminal law system would have been an orderly reprieve from the lottery established by section 251. In sum, if the Court's concerns had really been restricted to procedure, four members of the Court's panel of seven should have been satisfied with a more minimal remedy than invalidation of section 251 in toto.

The remedy accords best with the reasoning of Justice Wilson, the view that a pregnant woman's liberty includes the right to access in early abortion, period. This result may appear startling, until one comes to appreciate that the positions of the other judges in the majority are closer to her view than generally understood. The logic of the Chief Justice's approach as well as the remedy he affirms take him to autonomy over procreation, because "priorities and aspirations" are subjective values and thus inappropriate to substitute decision-making, especially by doctors. Justice Beetz is not far from this camp. His acceptance of a non-stringent therapeutic standard for early pregnancy, which appears to include reactive stress, as an exercise of medical judgment unsupervised by the institutions of public hospital administration or the politics of the medical profession, his rejection of any conditions unrelated to therapeutic concerns, his refusal to rule out liberty as a ground for access to abortion, and his insistence upon a therapeutic exemption as a *Charter* right, all suggest how he agreed to invalidate section 251 in its entirety. The majority opinions also share another important element. They accord a woman's claim to therapeutic health care the highest constitutional stature, above the claims of the foetus and above the conscientious, political and economic claims of the public, the medical profession, and politicians.[1]

The majority position therefore precludes, on *Charter* grounds, the blanket criminalization of abortion. It also precludes restriction without a therapeutic exemption in early pregnancy, at least on the common law standard. In later pregnancy, the state may impose a more stringent therapeutic standard. There need be no legislated abortion policy, least of all in exercise of the federal jurisdiction over criminal law.

It was in this mesh of constitutional strictures that the federal government proposed Bill C-43 as an exercise of its criminal law jurisdiction. Its conformity to the principles established by the majority in *Morgentaler* is not clear. In my view, features of Bill C-43, the proposed amendment to the *Criminal Code* that failed to pass the Senate in January of 1991, ran contrary to the Supreme Court of Canada's reasons for judgment.

The Infirmities of Bill C-43

General Conditions

Bill C-43 contained no conditions unrelated to the delivery of therapeutic health care.[2] The absence of such requirements reflected the denunciation by Beetz, J and Dickson, CJC of general conditions that restricted access to abortion in the name of health and professional standards, financial constraints, and ease of enforcement.

Personal Standards

The proposed bill would have extended the personal therapeutic standard in section 251.[3] In addition to retaining the terms included in section 251, Bill C-43 specified that physical, mental, and psychological health were included. Interpretive material provided by the minister of justice incorporated a wider range of circumstances than accepted by the Court as coming within the therapeutic standard.[4] Some may use this extended usage of the word "health" to argue that the statutory standard moves beyond therapeutic health care (by including stress reaction to the pregnancy due to socioeconomic circumstances, for example) into the realm connoted by the terms "priorities and aspirations" or even "abortion on demand." If so, one may question, on

Charter grounds, whether the state can require women to seek permission from doctors for abortions that are based on subjective considerations rather than grounds recognizable by medical expertise.

One can also question whether this kind of prohibition-exception undermines the jurisdiction of Parliament to enact the law in exercise of its criminal law power. At issue is the elastic quality of the category of "therapy" in the current societal context, reflected in the federal government's interpretation of the proposed legislation and medical practice. While the Parliament of Canada can say that a cow is a pig, it cannot alter its legislative jurisdiction by so doing.

When doctors and the health-care system deal not only with disease and its prevention, but also with well-being on a broader socio-economic basis, including consideration of an individual's relationships and life circumstances, then the concept of therapy loses its hard edges. Consequently, one cannot continue to differentiate between expert medical assessments of the presence of illness or likely deleterious impact on health, on the one hand, and findings that a pregnant woman is suffering stress because she sincerely believes that she should not continue a pregnancy, on the other.

The wide understanding of therapy impinges on the criminal quality of the prohibition-exemption in the following way. *Morgentaler* establishes that any prohibition against abortion must include a therapeutic exemption. But if therapy is as expansive a category as indicated, then the criminal prohibition admits an exemption based on expert determination that the individual is experiencing reactive stress. This condition combines a reaction to the situation of unwanted pregnancy as well as to the prohibition itself. One satisfies the exemption by reacting negatively to the prohibition, and its attendant interruption of one's control over intimate decision-making. In result, the most basic understanding of the nature of criminal law, that it condemns certain conduct as unacceptable to the fabric of society, is abandoned. The norm established by the prohibition is self-contradictory to the extent it admits of an exception that is merely an objection to the norm.[5]

This feature of the proposed legislation also undercuts the argument for foetal protection under section 1 of the *Charter*. The majority opinions in *Morgentaler* accept the claims on behalf of the foetus as grounds for justifying restrictions in later pregnancy on the pregnant woman's access to therapeutic health care. To the extent that the grounds for permitted abortion are relaxed to include what is in effect elective abortion, the credibility of the state's argument that it acts to protect the foetus in any meaningful way is weakened.

This same difficulty follows from another feature of the proposed legislation, the inapplicability of the prohibition before implantation.[6] While this window of opportunity may lessen the impact of criminalization by increasing the frequency of very early pregnancy termination, it may also weaken the state's claim to act to protect the foetus.

The majority judges each justified encroachment upon women's rights in terms of foetal interests. While formulated differently by each judge, the common ground appears to be that the state can provide increasing protection to the foetus as the pregnancy progresses against the pregnant women's constitutional rights to security of the person and/or to liberty.[7] None of the judgments, however, adequately addresses the principled basis for this position.

The task of articulating the principled grounds of justification for increasing recognition of foetal claims, however, is made all the more difficult by the proposed open-ended "therapeutic" standard and the early dispensation period, generally accepted as part of pregnancy, in which no protection is afforded whatsoever. The pre-implantation dispensation suggests that the state's interest is not in the fertilized ovum that develops into the foetus, but in the pregnancy. The argument for increasing foetal rights was beyond the majority's grasp in *Morgentaler*. Bridging the gap between no protection and protection is a greater challenge.[8]

Decision-Making

If *Morgentaler* makes anything clear, it is the requirement of an accessible, expeditious, and medically expert decision-making instrumentality where a therapeutic standard is imposed as a precondition for access to legal abortion. Justice Beetz gives the clearest direction in suggesting that the attending doctor solicit a second opinion from another doctor and that permission be transferable. The proposed legislation, however, would have required even less: the opinion of the doctor performing or overseeing the abortion, on generally accepted professional standards.

This arrangement might appear to provide the ready access that *Morgentaler* demands. However, appearances are often deceptive. It is true that the proposed legislation would not have imposed the infamous general conditions that formerly impeded and restricted decision-making. But it contained another feature of the invalidated legislative arrangements, one that might impede decision-making in an equally impermissible way although not to the same extent. The reasons for judgment in *Morgentaler* did not dwell on this deficiency because the gross deficiencies of section 251 rendered more subtle analysis unnecessary. The offensive feature in the new legislation is once again the unconstrained discretion given to doctors.

One of the primary desiderata in the formulation of the provision invalidated in *Morgentaler* was the delegation of complete authority over abortions to the medical profession in large public hospitals. That discretion included freedom to establish therapeutic committees, or not, as well as the authority to set the acceptable attitudes for members of those committees, the basis for permitting abortions, the conditions attached to permission, the eligible population of applicants, the mode of application, the number of abortions, and the abortion methods. The 1969 amendment, it must be emphasized, created *no entitlement* to abortion for women who could satisfy the therapeutic standard. There was only "permission," as the minister of justice had made clear in 1969, for doctors to operate within the statutory arrangements prescribed.

In formulating the therapeutic exemption, legislators took care that doctors retained discretion on grounds of conscience. No doctor was to be forced against conscience to participate in the decision-making process or in the provision of abortion services. Amendments to make this protection explicit were abandoned only on the assurance of the minister of justice that they were unnecessary.[9]

The infirmity of the proposed legislation was not that it failed to honour the conscience of doctors in regard to abortion, but that it maintained the doctors' option on access to the exemption beyond the exercise of conscience. Even though the Supreme Court of Canada made it clear that the exemption must be easily and widely available, because otherwise the securing of therapeutic health care is constitutionally fettered by criminal sanction, Parliament in Bill C-43 made no arrangements to provide a functioning and accessible decision-making process. Nor did it ensure that, once permission was given, abortion would be available.

Much of the discussion about Bill C-43 focused on the possible criminal and civil liability of doctors who perform abortions. In addition to exposure to criminal liability[10] for failing to apply the therapeutic standard properly, or at all, the spectre of civil proceedings[11] put doctors on guard. The only response of the federal government was to stress that the provincial attorneys general would exercise discretion as to criminal proceedings.

This response was unsatisfactory for two reasons. First, in practical terms, it did not diminish the anxiety of doctors who did not want exposure to criminal liability to cast a pall over their practices. Second, on a more legal plane, it manifested an odd reluctance by the federal government to make clear that it would exercise its prosecutorial responsibility to stop frivolous or vexatious prosecutions.[12] This reluctance to give some direct and meaningful assurance to doctors in order to guarantee that the new system would accommodate all applicants demonstrated, at least, a failure to appreciate the constitutional obligation that follows from the creation of an exemption from criminalization.

To no one's surprise, many doctors and groups of doctors indicated that they would no longer provide abortions and thereby reduce and delay the availability of abortion beyond the well-known problem areas, for example, in the Atlantic provinces and non-urban centres generally. In the light of this development it was highly unrealistic for the federal government to assume that the day-to-day functioning of the medical system would accommodate the constituency with constitutional claim to its services.

Without legislated assurance that such accommodation was in place, Bill C-43 would put pregnant women in the same situation in which they found themselves under section 251, namely, hostage to the monopoly of a medical profession under no statutory or constitutional obligation to provide abortion.

The Parliament of Canada, however, enjoys no such option. Once it embarks on criminalization, it must provide a therapeutic exemption, the administration of which dictates exercise of medical expertise. It is not enough to refrain from imposing impediments. No considerations in conflict with the right of access to therapeutic health care – expense constraint, the exclusive legislative jurisdiction of the provinces over the health-care system, garden-variety paternalism, or reluctance to conscript the medical profession – dissolve that obligation. *Morgentaler* makes that abundantly clear.

It is unreasonable, unfair, and unconstitutional to leave the administration of an exemption from criminal liability to the unconstrained discretion of the medical profession. It is unreasonable because members of the profession, licensed and professionally bound to offer healthcare services, also stand liable to prosecution for every asserted or manipulated misstep. Moreover, doctors' behaviour under section 251 signals that they are not better able than anyone else to put personal prejudices, stereotypes, and self-interest before constitutional rights. It is unfair because giving doctors the authority, but not the duty, to consider applications for exemption renders the proposed system potentially as arbitrary, unpredictable, and mysterious as that rejected by the Supreme Court. And, one must remember, women seeking abortion approach the medical profession in the physical and emotional throes of early and unwanted pregnancy. Finally, it is unconstitutional because the federal government assumes constitutional responsibility to provide access to therapeutic health care if it chooses to criminalize abortions that do not pass this standard.[13]

Beyond Bill C-43

If the federal government chose not to act under the *Criminal Code*, each province would regulate abortion, either specifically or within the larger organization of the health-care system. Could a province establish criteria for abortion, such as a therapeutic standard? That would depend on the grounds for the standard. The province cannot legislate criminal law, although it can enforce its own regulatory schemes.[14] Accordingly, it could not impose criteria for abortion reflecting the disapproval of society, for example, in respect to the "proper" role for procreation in the lives of women or the morality of abortion. The *Morgentaler* judgment also precludes giving priority to foetal interests at the expense of therapeutic health care for pregnant women.

The provinces are also subject to the *Charter's* equality guarantees. The stipulation of equality before and under the law, without discrimination on the ground of sex, in section 15, precludes any fetter upon access to abortion as a matter of therapeutic health care that is not generally applicable to other therapeutic and elective services.

Similarly, payment for the procedure under provincial health-care plans would also have to be consistent with payment for any comparable therapeutic or elective treatment. To the extent that treatment for birth control, sterilization, infertility, and birth are funded, therapeutic abortion should be as well. Also, since early abortion is less expensive than late abortion and much less expensive than medical supervision of a pregnancy, birth, and infant care, expeditious access is required, without restrictions or rationing for the sake of reducing health-care expenditures.

V CONCLUSION: WOMEN AND THE CONSTITUTION

No one should regret the demise of section 251, an ill-conceived and manifestly unfair legislation provision. The ability of the Court to decide *Morgentaler* as it did, given the political volatility of the issue, stands to its credit. In the future it may be obvious that women are *Charter* rights-holders first, breeders second. As we look back on *Morgentaler*, we will see the preliminary attempts to give shape to that idea as constitutional law.

NOTES

1 For the view that the anti-abortion argument, that the foetus's right to life trumps all other claims, is "on very weak ground" because the right of a mature moral agent must prevail over the right of an unborn, potential person, see R. Whitaker "Rights in a 'Free and Democratic Society': Abortion" in *Federalism and Political Community* 331. Once one looks at the abortion issue from the point of view of women as gestators, birth-givers, and primary caretakers of children, especially in a society that devalues and disadvantages women because of the procreative role, this conclusion seems to follow. The weakness of the position in terms of legal argument is also demonstrated by written argument submitted to the Supreme Court of Canada in *R v Borowski* [1989] 1 SCR 342, 57 DLR (4th) 231 by Borowski and by REAL Women.

2 An Act Respecting Abortion

1. S. 287 & 288 of the *Criminal Code* are repealed and the following substituted therefore:

s. 287(1) Every person who induced an abortion on a female person is guilty of an indictable offence and liable to imprisonment for a term not exceeding 2 years, unless the abortion is induced by or under the direction of a medical practitioner who is of the opinion that, if the abortion were not induced, the health or life of the female person would be likely to be threatened.

(2) For the purposes of this section, "health" includes, for general certainty, physical, mental and psychological health; "medical practitioner," in respect of an abortion induced in a province, means a person who is entitled to practice medicine under the laws of that province; "opinion" means an opinion formed using generally accepted standards of the medical profession;

(3) For the purposes of this section and s. 288, inducing an abortion does not include using a drug, device or other means on a female person that is likely to prevent implantation of a fertilized ovum.

s. 288 Everyone who unlawfully supplies or procures a drug or other noxious thing or an instrument or thing, knowing that it is intended to be used or employed to induce an abortion on a female person, is guilty of an indictable offence and liable to imprisonment for a term not exceeding two years.

2. This Act shall come into force on a day to be fixed by order of the Governor in Council.

3 Four judges approved this standard: Justices Beetz, Estey, McIntyre, and La Forest. The Chief Justice and Justice Lamer would form part of this group if one reads their judgment as dispensing with wider grounds for the exemption, that is, accepting therapeutic grounds rather than the applicant's "priorities and aspirations," positing fair access to the exemption. While this is a possible reading of the Dickson judgment, his unswerving commitment to the status of women as free and equal members of the polity militates against it. I would argue that the Dickson opinion should be read as mandating the therapeutic exemption.

4 In correspondence to the medical profession Justice Minister Kim Campbell expressed the view that Bill C-43 would permit doctors to consider "such factors as rape, incest, genetic defects and socioeconomic factors" with their opinion on "health." This view was also contained in explanatory material released with Bill C-43 on 3 November 1989. Both documents are on file with the author.

5 An analogy might clarify this argument. The insanity defence to a criminal charge denotes some sort of mental or emotional disability relating to the essential features of the offence. Such a condition is understood to be beyond the individual's control and to vitiate responsibility for the commission of the offence. If the range of the defence were expanded to include stress reaction to the urge to commit the offence or to the prohibition against commission of the act, then the defence itself would swallow up the prohibition.

6 Bill C-43, *supra* note 2, new section 287(3). The dispensation from criminalization is significant. Most abortions are now performed in early pregnancy at the time when the procedure is simple, inexpensive, and minimally traumatic. Most women prefer very early abortion. Later abortions under the regime of section 251, as the Beetz and Dickson judgments make clear, were a function of statute-induced and other delay. Relatively recent developments, such as the morning-after pill (routinely administered to rape victims in many centres) and the abortion pill, facilitate early, non-surgical intervention. Later abortions are usually precipitated by acquisition of information as to the health of the pregnant woman or of the foetus, which was unavailable earlier. Foetal abnormality, although per se not a therapeutic indication for the gestator, was

widely understood in medical practice to satisfy the therapeutic standard under section 251, because of its traumatic effect upon the pregnant woman. Breakthroughs in medical science that advance the detection of foetal abnormality at earlier stages of pregnancy will lead to earlier abortions. (One unresolved issue is the use of abortion for gender selection, a practice that might slip into the therapeutic stress reaction category. This possibility could be eliminated by provincial regulations prohibiting reporting of the gender of the foetus unless the information is related to the likelihood of transmission of genetic defects or disease. Such a prohibition might also be promulgated by medical associations and regulatory bodies as a matter of professional ethics. Any resistance to such a regulation could be met by section 15(2) of the *Charter*, which provides a basis for state action that works against discrimination based, inter alia, on sex.)

7 For Justice Beetz this justification applies, on a rising scale of therapeutic cause; for the Chief Justice this justification is a balance between the interests of pregnant women and the unborn. For Justice Wilson the justification arises in the latter half of pregnancy, on therapeutic grounds.

8 Principled argumentation in favour of an autonomy approach is not diminished but that is of no assistance because Bill C-43, *supra* note 2, as a criminal formulation, does not and cannot accommodate an autonomy-based right.

9 Justice Beetz confirmed this right to conscience under the *Charter*; see text, *supra*.

10 One can imagine, in the intense atmosphere infusing this issue, that anti-abortion activists might attempt to "trap" doctors into decisions that could be the basis for laying private informations.

11 Civil proceedings might arise at the initiative of third parties to stop abortions or by successful but regretful applicants, after the fact, for negligent exercise of the decision-making function. While it is exceedingly unlikely that any would succeed, the nuisance value of instituting proceedings might prove very effective in inducing doctors to withdraw their services.

12 See *A.G. Can. v C.N. Transportation* [1983] 2 SCR 206, 3 DLR (4th) 16 and *R v Wetmore* [1983] 2 SCR 284, 2 DLR (4th) 577.

13 Analogies may clarify the argument. If the government criminalized the possession, sale, and use of proscribed drugs, with an exemption based on a determination of eligibility by qualified medical practitioners, it would be constitutionally obligated to ensure that persons who wanted to qualify for the exemption could have their eligibility determined. If the

determination process was time consuming, tedious, and involved the doctor in long-term supervision, and also provided inadequate remuneration, doctors might decide not to provide the service. Persons for whom an exemption to criminal liability had been provided by Parliament would thus find themselves exposed to criminal liability. Here, where there is a much weaker case for constitutional claim to the exemption than in the context of abortion, one can see the contours of a credible section 7 argument. Another analogy, perhaps closer to the abortion issue, would involve claims of insanity at the time of commission of an offence. Imagine a requirement that an individual, who committed an offence involving serious bodily harm and wanted to make an insanity defence, consult a psychiatrist within two months of the commission of the offence. (This time frame is close to the time frame for securing a first-trimester abortion.) And let us say that psychiatrists did not want to be burdened with the public outcry that medical practitioners would be harbouring the incriminating secrets of persons who had committed criminal acts, but had not yet been charged. If many psychiatrists refused to do this work and persons were for that reason denied access to defences to criminal charges, a credible section 7 argument could be made.

14 This power is provided in section 92(15) of the *Constitution Act, 1867*.

READING QUESTION ON WEINRIB

1 Why does Weinrib insist that any abortion law must contain a therapeutic exemption? Do you agree?

Winnipeg Child and Family Services (Northwest Area) v D.F.G. [1997] 3 SCR

D.F.G. was pregnant for the fourth time. She was addicted to the inhalation of solvent fumes over a long period. Two of her previous children were born permanently disabled as a result of her addiction and became permanent wards of the state. In August 1996, a judge of the Manitoba Court of Queen's Bench ordered that D.F.G. be detained at the Health Sciences Centre until the birth of her child.

McLachlin, J: – I would dismiss the appeal on the ground that an order detaining a pregnant woman for the purpose of protecting her foetus would require changes to the law which cannot properly be made by the courts and should be left to the legislature.

I

This appeal raises two legal issues:

(1) Does tort law, as it exists or may properly be extended by the Court, permit an order detaining a pregnant woman against her will in order to protect her unborn child from conduct that may harm the child?

(2) Alternatively, does the power of a court to make orders for the protection of children (its *parens patriae* jurisdiction), as it exists or may properly be extended by the Court, permit an order detaining a pregnant woman against her will in order to protect her unborn child from conduct that may harm the child?

Before dealing with the cases treating the issue in tort law, I turn to the general proposition that the law of Canada does not recognize the unborn child as a legal or juridical person. Once a child is born, alive and viable, the law may recognize that its existence began before birth for certain limited purposes. But the only right recognized is that of the born person. This is a general proposition, applicable to all aspects of the law, including the law of torts ...

By way of preamble, two points may be made. First, we are concerned with the common law, not statute. If Parliament or the legislatures wish to legislate legal rights for unborn children or other protective measures, that is open to them, subject to any limitations imposed by the Constitution of Canada. Further, the fact that particular statutes may touch on the interests of the unborn need not concern us. Second, the issue is not one of biological status, nor indeed spiritual status, but of legal status. ... What then is the status of the foetus at common law? ... [U]nder the law as it presently stands, the foetus on whose behalf the agency purported to act in seeking the order for the respondent's detention was not a legal person and possessed no legal rights. If it was not a legal person and possessed no legal rights at the time of the application, then there was no legal person in whose interests the agency could act or in whose interests a court order could be made.

Putting the matter in terms of tort, there was no right to sue, whether for an injunction or damages, until the child was born alive and viable. The law of tort as it presently stands might permit an action for injury to the foetus to be brought in the child's name *after its birth*. But there is no power in the courts to entertain such an action before the child's birth ...

The changes which the agency asks this Court to make to the law of tort may be summarized as follows:

1 Overturn the rule that rights accrue to a person only at birth (the "live-birth" rule);
2 Recognize a fetal right to sue the mother carrying the foetus;
3 Recognize a cause of action for lifestyle choices which may adversely affect others;
4 Recognize an injunctive remedy which deprives a defendant of important liberties, including her involuntary confinement.

The proposed changes to the law of tort are major, affecting the rights and remedies available in many other areas of tort law. They involve moral choices and would create conflicts between fundamental interests and rights. They would have an immediate and drastic impact on the lives of women as well as men who might find themselves incarcerated and treated against their will for conduct alleged to harm others. And, they possess complex ramifications impossible for this Court to fully assess, giving rise to the danger that the proposed order might impede the goal of healthy infants more than it would promote it. In short, these are not the sort of changes which common law courts can or should make. These are the sort of changes which should be left to the legislature.

...

This change to the law of tort is fraught with complexities and ramifications, the consequences of which cannot be precisely foretold. At what stage would a foetus acquire rights? Could women who choose to terminate a pregnancy face injunctive relief prohibiting termination, relief which this Court rejected in *Tremblay v Daigle*? Alternatively, could they face an action for damages brought on behalf of the foetus for its lost life? If a pregnant woman is killed as a consequence of negligence on the highway, may a family sue not only for her death, but for that of the unborn child? If it is established that a foetus can feel discomfort, can it sue its mother (or perhaps her doctor) and claim damages for the discomfort? If the unborn child is a legal person with legal rights, arguments can be made in favour of all these propositions. Some might endorse such changes, others deplore them. The point is that they are major changes attracting an array of consequences that would place the courts at the heart of a web of thorny moral and social issues which are better dealt with by elected legislators than by the courts. Having broken the time-honoured rule that legal rights accrue only upon live birth, the courts would find it difficult to limit application of the new principle to particular cases. By contrast, the legislature, should it choose to introduce a law permitting action to protect unborn children against substance abuse, could limit the law to that precise case ...

(c) Recognizing a Cause of Action for Lifestyle Choices Which May Adversely Affect Others

If the problem of permitting an unborn child to sue its future mother could be surmounted, a further difficulty presents itself: could the unborn child sue her for lifestyle choices? The difficulty of this question may be discerned from the cases considering the right of born children to sue their mothers for prenatal injuries. To date, courts and legislatures have confined the right to the child suing its mother for prenatal injuries to injuries due to motor vehicle accidents.

...

Behind the refusal of the courts and at least one legislature to permit a child to sue its mother for prenatal injuries related to her lifestyle, lies the fear that such suits would take the courts into the difficult policy issue of the extent to which a mother's lifestyle is actionable. Leaving the special relationship between mother and unborn child aside for the moment, there is little precedent for suing any defendant in tort for damages one has suffered as a consequence of his or her lifestyle. While it is not inconceivable that the courts, proceeding properly in their incremental law-making capacity, may one day recognize such claims, the appellant agency faces the difficulty that on this point too it is asking this Court to break new ground in a controversial area. Once again, the consequences for the law of tort generally might be great. Are children to be permitted to sue their parents for second-hand smoke inhaled around the family dinner table? Could any cohabitant bring such an action? Are children to be permitted to sue their parents for spanking causing psychological trauma or poor grades due to alcoholism or a parent's undue fondness for the office or the golf course? If we permit lifestyle actions, where do we draw the line?

The difficulties multiply when the lifestyle in question is that of a pregnant woman whose liberty is intimately and inescapably bound to her unborn child. One faces, to borrow the words of Hoyt, CJNB in *Dobson, supra*, the "spectre of mothers being sued by their children for various activities or lifestyle choices, such as smoking, drinking and the taking or refusal of medication, during pregnancy that injure the child, with the result that mothers will be unable to control their own bodies and make autonomous choices" ... (p. 336) ... Before imposing a duty of care in a new situation, the court must be satisfied: (1) that there is a sufficiently close relationship between the parties to give rise to the duty of care; and (2) that there are no considerations which ought to negative or limit the scope of the duty, the class of persons to whom it is owed or the damages to which a breach of it may give rise: *City of Kamloops v Nielsen*, [1984] 2 SCR 2.

The first criterion is met in the present case. The relationship between a woman and her foetus (assuming for the purposes of argument that they can be treated as separate legal entities) is sufficiently close that in the reasonable contemplation of the woman, carelessness on her part might cause damage to the foetus. The more difficult questions arise within the second branch of the test. A host of policy considerations may be raised against the imposition of tort liability on a pregnant woman for lifestyle choices that may affect her unborn child.

Most obviously, recognizing a duty of care owed by a mother to her child for negligent prenatal behaviour may create a conflict between the pregnant woman as an autonomous decision-maker and her foetus. ... The potential for intrusions on a woman's right to make choices concerning herself is considerable. The foetus' complete physical existence is dependent on the body of the woman. As a result, any intervention to further the foetus' interests will necessarily implicate, and possibly conflict with the mother's interests. Similarly, each choice made by the woman in relation to her body will affect the foetus and potentially attract tort liability.

The appellant agency argues that the potential intrusions would be minimal because the duty of care could be defined very narrowly. It submits that the duty of care should be to refrain from activities that have no substantial value to a pregnant woman's well-being or right of self-determination and that have the potential to cause grave and irreparable harm to the child's life, health and ability to function after birth.

II

The problem with this test lies in the terms "substantial value" and "well-being or right of self-determination." They are vague and broad and may not be adequate by themselves to narrowly confine the duty of care. What does substantial value to a woman's well-being mean? What does a woman's well-being include? What is involved in a woman's right of self-determination – all her choices, or merely some of them? And if some only, what is the criterion of distinction? Although it may be easy to determine that abusing solvents does not add substantial value to a pregnant woman's well-being and may not be the type of self-determination that deserves protection, other behaviours are not as easily classified. At what point does consumption of alcohol fail to add substantial value to a pregnant woman's well-being? Or cigarette smoking? Or strenuous exercise? No bright lines emerge to distinguish tortious behaviour from non-tortious once the door is opened to suing a pregnant mother for lifestyle choices adversely affecting the foetus ... Indeed, changing tort law to make a pregnant mother liable for lifestyle-related foetal damage may be counterproductive in at least two ways. First, it may tend to drive the problems underground. Pregnant women suffering from alcohol or substance abuse addictions may not seek prenatal care for fear that their problems would be detected and they would be confined involuntarily and/or ordered to undergo mandatory treatment. As a result, there is a real possibility that those women most in need of proper prenatal care may be the ones who will go without and a judicial intervention designed to improve the health of the foetus and the mother may actually put both at serious health risk. Second, changing the law of tort as advocated by the agency might persuade women who would otherwise choose to continue their pregnancies to undergo an abortion. Women under the control of a substance addiction may be unable to face the prospect of being without their addicting substance and may find terminating the pregnancy a preferable alternative. In the end, orders made to protect a foetus' health could ultimately result in its destruction ...

(d) The Extension of Injunctive Relief in Civil Cases to Detention of the Person

In Canada, tort law permits injunctions to detain goods (the *Mareva* injunction), to restrain activities such as unlawful picketing, and sometimes to mandate certain positive action to prevent the occurrence of serious damage. But the principles of tort law have never been used to justify the forcible detention and mandatory treatment of a person.

(e) Conclusion as to Whether the Law of Tort Should Be Extended as Proposed

Taken together, the changes to the law of tort that would be required to support the order for detention at issue are of such magnitude, consequence, and policy difficulty that they exceed the proper incremental law-making powers of the courts. Whether such changes should be made, and if so, how far the law should go in making them, is a task more appropriate to the legislatures than the courts. I conclude that the order for detention cannot be upheld as an application of tort law.

B Does the Power of the Court in Parens Patriae Support an Order for the Detention and Treatment of a Pregnant Woman for the Purpose of Preventing Harm to the Unborn Child?

Alternatively, the appellant agency seeks to sustain the order for the detention of the respondent by an extension of the court's *parens patriae* jurisdiction to permit protection of unborn children. Courts have the power to step into the shoes of the parent and make orders in the best interests of the child: *E. (Mrs.) v Eve*, [1986] 2 SCR 388. The agency argues that this power should be extended to orders on behalf of unborn children.

I would reject this submission for reasons similar to those enunciated in connection with the submission that the law of tort should be extended to the unborn. The submission requires a major change to the law of *parens patriae*. The ramifications of the change would be significant and complex. The change involves conflicts of fundamental rights and interests and difficult policy issues. Not surprisingly these difficulties have led all appellate courts that have considered the extension to reject it. I share their view.

The law as it stands is clear: the courts do not have *parens patriae* or wardship jurisdiction over unborn children ...

[There are] four reasons for limiting the court's jurisdiction to born children. First, a foetus does not attain legal personhood until birth and therefore, the order would be contrary to that principle ... Second, applying the principle that the interests of the child are to be predominant would create conflict between the existing legal interests of the mother and those of the unborn child. Third, there could be difficulties in enforcing against the mother any order in respect of an unborn child. And finally, he held that under the *Supreme Court Act 1981* only "minors" could be made wards of the court and that in light of the *Family Law Reform Act 1969*, a "minor" could only be a person, in the sense that he or she had been born.

It is argued that the *parens patriae* jurisdiction over children necessarily involves overriding the liberty of parents, and that there is nothing new in this. This argument overlooks the fact that the invasion of liberty involved in making court orders affecting the unborn child, is of a different order than the invasion of liberty involved in court orders relating to born children. The *parens patriae* power over born children permits the courts to override the liberty of the parents to make decisions on behalf of their children where a parental choice may result in harm to a child: *B. (R.) v Children's Aid Society of Metropolitan Toronto,* [1995] 1 SCR 315. The only liberty interest affected is the parent's interest in making decisions for *his or her child*. By contrast, extension of the *parens patriae* jurisdiction of the court to unborn children has the potential to affect a much broader range of liberty interests. The court cannot make decisions for the unborn child without inevitably making decisions for the mother herself. The intrusion is therefore far greater than simply limiting the mother's choices concerning her child. Any choice concerning her child inevitably affects her. For example, to sustain the order requested in the case at bar would interfere with the pregnant woman's ability to choose where to live and what medical treatment to undergo. The *parens patriae* jurisdiction has never been used to permit a court to make such decisions for competent women, whether pregnant or not. Such a change would not be an incremental change within *Watkins v Olafson, supra,* but a generic change of major impact and consequence. It would seriously intrude on the rights of women. If anything is to be done, the legislature is in a much better position to weigh the competing interests and arrive at a solution that is principled and minimally intrusive to pregnant women.

Major, J (dissenting): – I respectfully disagree with the conclusion of McLachlin, J that an order detaining a pregnant woman addicted to glue sniffing for which she has rejected abortion and/or medical treatment and decided to carry her child to term, would require a change to the law which cannot be properly made other than by legislation.

The law of this country is consistent with the grant of a remedy in this case. The *parens patriae* jurisdiction of the superior courts is of undefined and undefinable breadth. This Court's decision in *E. (Mrs.) v Eve*, [1986] 2 SCR 388, indicates that inherent power resides in the provincial superior courts to act on behalf of those who cannot act to protect themselves. A foetus suffering from its mother's abusive behaviour is particularly within this class and deserves protection.

It has been submitted, however, that a foetus acquires no actionable rights in our law until it is born alive. In my view, the "born alive" rule, as it is known, is a common law evidentiary presumption rooted in rudimentary medical knowledge that has long since been overtaken by modern science and should be set aside for purpose of this appeal.

This means that a superior court, on proper motion, should be able to exercise its *parens patriae* jurisdiction to restrain a mother's conduct when there is a reasonable probability of that conduct causing serious and irreparable harm to the foetus within her. While the granting of this type of remedy may interfere with the mother's liberty interests, in my view, those interests must bend when faced with a situation where devastating harm and a life of suffering can so easily be prevented. In any event, this interference is always subject to the mother's right to end it by deciding to have an abortion.

...

If a foetus is a "person" for purposes of the *parens patriae* jurisdiction, he or she is in a particularly vulnerable position. A foetus, absent outside assistance, has no means of escape from toxins ingested by its mother. The *parens patriae* jurisdiction exists for the stated purpose of doing what is necessary to protect the interests of those who are unable to protect themselves. Society does not simply sit by and allow a mother to abuse her child after birth. How then should serious abuse be allowed to occur before the child is born?

...

However, clearly, the only person by law able to choose between an abortion or carrying to term is the mother. She too has the right to decide her lifestyle whether pregnant or not. The court's ability to intervene must therefore be limited. *It will only be in extreme cases, where the conduct of the mother has a reasonable probability of causing serious irreparable harm to the unborn child, that a court should assume jurisdiction to intervene.*

In the Court of Appeal, Twaddle, JA grounded his decision denying jurisdiction in part upon a type of "slippery slope" argument (at p. 260 DLR):

The mother's right to sniff solvents may not seem of much importance, but I do not see how a court can select which conduct harmful to an unborn child should be restrained and which not.

This concern was expressed in a variety of ways at the appeal. Serious substance abuse that has a reasonable probability of causing serious and irreparable harm to the foetus should be restrained. Simply because there may be hard cases on other facts not before the Court does not mean we should ignore what is obvious from the evidence in this case. The damage caused to children by serious substance abuse is well documented. It seems derelict to suggest that we should not restrain this abuse because we can imagine some other cases that may not be as clear.

Taking Twaddle, JA's argument to its logical extreme, we would be faced with some strange results. It is interesting speculation to wonder what the result of this appeal might have been, had the state been trying to restrain a pregnant mother from taking thalidomide to deal with her morning sickness.

...

In cases such as this any remedy of confinement must be for purposes of treatment, and not punishment. It follows that the situs of the confinement should be a residential treatment facility or hospital which can offer a treatment program. The mother remains free to reject all suggested medical treatment. The confinement serves only to prevent her using toxins strong enough to cause serious and permanent damage to the foetus.

...

The threshold for state intervention is high. In this case the difficult test is met but each case will have to be decided on its facts. The failure of a pregnant woman to quit smoking or act in some way that is optimum for fetal health would not meet the test for state intervention. The familiar "slippery slope" argument has some points of value, however, it cannot be raised as a principled bar to granting an injunction in this case. The "slippery slope" argument if not carefully assessed can easily become a *in terrorem* argument and lose whatever value it may legitimately possess.

In the present case it is clear that D.F.G. has had ample knowledge of the effects of substance abuse on her foetus. She was sadly aware of giving birth to two permanently handicapped children. D.F.G. had been offered counselling and education of various kinds to no apparent avail.

...

It is a fundamental precept of our society and justice system that society *can* restrict an individual's right to autonomy where the exercise of that right causes harm to others. Conversely, it would be unjust *not* to restrict one person's right of autonomy when the exercise of that right causes harm to others.

QUESTIONS ON WINNIPEG CHILD AND FAMILY SERVICES

1 What would Thomson say about this case? Would the availability of abortion shape her view?
2 What would Finnis say about this case? Would the fact that the pregnant woman intended no harm to the foetus be relevant to his answer?

The Canada Act and the Canadian Charter of Rights and Freedoms

CANADA ACT 1982
U.K., 1982, c.11
An Act to give effect to a request by the Senate and
House of Commons of Canada

Whereas Canada has requested and consented to the enactment of an Act of the Parliament of the United Kingdom to give effect to the provisions hereinafter set forth and the Senate and the House of Commons of Canada in Parliament assembled have submitted an address to Her Majesty requesting that Her Majesty may graciously be pleased to cause a Bill to be laid before the Parliament of the United Kingdom for that puzpose.

Be it therefore enacted by the Queen's Most Excellent Majesty, by and with the advice and consent of the Lords Spiritual and Temporal, and Commons, in this present Parliament assembled, and by the authority of the same as follows:

1. *The Constitution Act, 1982* set out in Schedule B to this Act is hereby enacted for and enacted shall have the force of law in Canada and shall come into force as provided in that Act.

2. No Act of the Parliament of the United Kingdom passed after the *Constitution Act, 1982* comes into force shall extend to Canada as part of its law.

3. So far as it is not contained in Schedule B, the French version of this Act is set out in Schedule A to this Act and has the same authority in Canada as the English version thereof.

4. This Act may be cited as the *Canada Act 1982*.

CONSTITUTION ACT, 1982
Schedule B to Canada Act 1982 (U.K.)

PART I
CANADIAN CHARTER OF RIGHTS AND FREEDOMS

Whereas Canada is founded upon principles that recognize the supremacy of God and the rule of law:

Guarantee of Rights and Freedoms

1. *The Canadian Charter of Rights and Freedoms* guarantees the rights and freedoms set out in it subject only to such reasonable limits prescribed by law as can be demonstrably justified in a free and democratic society.

Fundamental Freedoms

2. Everyone has the following freedoms:
- (a) freedom of conscience and religion;
- (b) freedom of thought, belief, opinion and expression, including freedom of the press and other media of communication;
- (c) freedom of peaceful assembly; and
- (d) freedom of association.

Democratic Rights

3. Every citizen of Canada has the right to vote in an election of members of the House of Commons or of a legislative assembly and to be qualified for membership therein.

4. (1) No House of Commons and no legislative assembly shall continue for longer than five years from the date fixed for the return of the writs at a general election of its members.

(2) In time of real or apprehended war, invasion or insurrection, a House of Commons may be continued by Parliament and a legislative assembly may be continued by the legislature beyond five years if such continuation is not opposed by the votes of more than one-third of the members of the House of Commons or the legislative assembly, as the case may be.

5. There shall be a sitting of Parliament and of each legislature at least once every twelve months.

Mobility Rights

6. (1) Every citizen of Canada has the right to enter, remain in and leave Canada.

(2) Every citizen of Canada and every person who has the status of a permanent resident of Canada has the right
(a) to move and to take up residence in any province; and
(b) to pursue the gaining of a livelihood in any province.

(3) The rights specified in subsection (2) are subject to
(a) any laws or practices of general application in force in a province other than those that discriminate among persons primarily on the basis of province of present or previous residence; and
(b) any laws providing for reasonable residency requirements as a qualification for the receipt of publicly provided social services.

(4) Subsections (2) and (3) do not preclude any law, program or activity that has as its object the amelioration in a province of conditions of individuals in that province who are socially or economically disadvantaged if the rate of employment in that province is below the rate of employment in Canada.

Legal Rights

7. Everyone has the right to life, liberty and security of the person and the right not to be deprived thereof except in accordance with the principles of fundamental justice.

8. Everyone has the right to be secure against unreasonable search or seizure.

9. Everyone has the right not to be arbitrarily detained or imprisoned.

10. Everyone has the right on arrest or detention
(a) to be informed promptly of the reasons therefor;
(b) to retain and instruct counsel without delay and to be informed of that right; and
(c) to have the validity of the detention determined by way of *habeas corpus* and to be released if the detention is not lawful.

11. Any person charged with an offence has the right
(a) to be informed without unreasonable delay of the specific offence;
(b) to be tried within a reasonable time;

(c) not to be compelled to be a witness in proceedings against that person in respect of the offence;

(d) to be presumed innocent until proven guilty according to law in a fair and public hearing by an independent and impartial tribunal;

(e) not to be denied reasonable bail without just cause;

(f) except in the case of an offence under military law tried before a military tribunal, to the benefit of trial by jury where the maximum punishment for the offence is imprisonment for five years or a more severe punishment;

(g) not to be found guilty on account of any act or omission unless, at the time of the act or omission, it constituted an offence under Canadian or international law or was criminal according to the general principles of law recognized by the community of nations;

(h) if finally acquitted of the offence, not to be tried for it again and, if finally found guilty and punished for the offence, not to be tried or punished for it again; and

(i) if found guilty of the offence and if the punishment for the offence has been varied between the time of commission and the time of sentencing, to the benefit of the lesser punishment.

12. Everyone has the right not to be subjected to any cruel and unusual treatment or punishment.

13. A witness who testifies in any proceedings has the right not to have any incriminating evidence so given used to incriminate that witness in any other proceedings, except in a prosecution for perjury or for the giving of contradictory evidence.

14. A party or witness in any proceedings who does not understand or speak the language in which the proceedings are conducted or who is deaf has the right to the assistance of an interpreter.

Equality Rights

15. (1) Every individual is equal before and under the law and has the right to the equal protection and equal benefit of the law without discrimination and, in particular, without discrimination based on race, national or ethnic origin, colour, religion, sex, age or mental or physical disability.

(2) Subsection (1) does not preclude any law, program or activity that has as its object the amelioration of conditions of disadvantaged individuals or groups including those that are disadvantaged because of race, national or ethnic origin, colour, religion, sex, age or mental or physical disability.

Official Languages of Canada

16. (1) English and French are the official languages of Canada and have equality of status and equal rights and privileges as to their use in all institutions of the Parliament and government of Canada.

(2) English and French are the official languages of New Brunswick and have equality of status and equal rights and privileges as to their use in all institutions of the legislature and government of New Brunswick.

(3) Nothing in this Charter limits the authority of Parliament or a legislature to advance the equality of status or use of English and French.

17. (1) Everyone has the right to use English or French in any debates and other proceedings of Parliament.

(2) Everyone has the right to use English or French in any debates and other proceedings of the legislature of New Brunswick.

18. (1) The statutes, records and journals of Parliament shall be printed and published in English and French and both language versions are equally authoritative.

(2) The statutes, records and journals of the legislature of New Brunswick shall be printed and published in English and French and both language versions are equally authoritative.

19. (1) Either English or French may be used by any person in, or in any pleading in or process issuing from, any court established by Parliament.

(2) Either English or French may be used by any person in, or in any pleading in or process issuing from, any court of New Brunswick.

20. (1) Any member of the public in Canada has the right to communicate with, and to receive available services from, any head or central office of an institution of the Parliament or government of Canada in English or French, and has the same right with respect to any other office of any such institution where

> (a) there is a significant demand for communications with and services from that office in such language; or
> (b) due to the nature of the office, it is reasonable that communications with and services from that office be available in both English and French.

(2) Any member of the public in New Brunswick has the right to communicate with, and to receive available services from, any office of an institution of the legislature or government of New Brunswick in English or French.

21. Nothing in sections 16 to 20 abrogates or derogates from any right, privilege or obligation with respect to the English and French languages, or either of them, that exists or is continued by virtue of any other provision of the Constitution of Canada.

22. Nothing in sections 16 to 20 abrogates or derogates from any legal or customary right or privilege acquired or enjoyed either before or after the coming into force of this Charter with respect to any language that is not English or French.

Minority Language Educational Rights

23. (1) Citizens of Canada

(a) whose first language learned and still understood is that of the English or French linguistic minority population of the province in which they reside, or

(b) who have received their primary school instruction in Canada in English or French and reside in a province where the language in which they received that instruction is the language of the English or French linguistic minority population of the province,

have the right to have their children receive primary and secondary school instruction in that language in that province.

(2) Citizens of Canada of whom any child has received or is receiving primary or secondary school instruction in English or French in Canada, have the right to have all their children receive primary and secondary school instruction in the same language.

(3) The right of citizens of Canada under subsections (1) and (2) to have their children receive primary and secondary school instruction in the language of the English or French linguistic minority population of a province

(a) applies wherever in the province the number of children of citizens who have such a right is sufficient to warrant the provision to them out of public funds of minority language instruction; and

(b) includes, where the number of those children so warrants, the right to have them receive that instruction in minority language educational facilities provided out of public funds.

24. (1) Anyone whose rights or freedoms, as guaranteed by this Charter, have been infringed or denied may apply to a court of competent jurisdiction to obtain such remedy as the court considers appropriate and just in the circumstances.

(2) Where, in proceedings under subsection (1), a court concludes that evidence was obtained in a manner that infringed or denied any rights or freedoms guaranteed by this Charter, the evidence shall be excluded if it is established that, having regard to all the circumstances, the admission of it in the proceedings would bring the administration of justice into disrepute.

General

25. The guarantee in this Charter of certain rights and freedoms shall not be construed so as to abrogate or derogate from any aboriginal, treaty or other rights or freedoms that pertain to the aboriginal peoples of Canada including

(a) any rights or freedoms that have been recognized by the Royal Proclamation of October 7,1763; and

(b) any rights or freedoms that now exist by way of land claims agreements or may be so acquired.[1]

26. The guarantee in this Charter of certain rights and freedoms shall not be construed as denying the existence of any other rights or freedoms that exist in Canada.

27. This Charter shall be interpreted in a manner consistent with the preservation and enhancement of the multicultural heritage of Canadians.

28. Notwithstanding anything in this Charter, the rights and freedoms referred to in it are guaranteed equally to male and female persons.

29. Nothing in this Charter abrogates or derogates from any rights or privileges guaranteed by or under the Constitution of Canada in respect of denominational, separate or dissentient schools.

30. A reference in this Charter to a province or to the legislative assembly or legislature of a province shall be deemed to include a reference to the Yukon Territory and the Northwest Territories, or to the appropriate legislative authority thereof, as the case may be.

31. Nothing in this Charter extends the legislative powers of any body or authority.

Application of Charter

32. (1) This Charter applies

(a) to the Parliament and government of Canada in respect of all matters within the authority of parliament including all matters relating to the Yukon Territory and Northwest Territories; and

(b) to the legislature and government of each province in respect of all matters within the authority of the legislature of each province.

(2) Notwithstanding subsection (1), section 15 shall not have effect until three years after this section comes into force.

33. (1) Parliament or the legislature of a province may expressly declare in an Act of Parliament or of the legislature, as the case may be, that the Act or a provision thereof shall operate notwithstanding a provision included in section 2 or sections 7 to 15 of this Charter.

(2) An Act or a provision of an Act in respect of which a declaration made under this section is in effect shall have such operation as it would have but for the provision of this Charter referred to in the declaration.

(3) A declaration made under subsection (1) shall cease to have effect five years after it comes into force or on such earlier date as may be specified in the declaration.

(4) Parliament or the legislature of a province may re-enact a declaration made under subsection (1).

(5) Subsection (3) applies in respect of a re-enactment made under subsection (4).

Citation

34. This Part may be cited as the *Canadian Charter of Rights and Freedoms.*

NOTE

1   Paragraph 25 (b) was amended by the *Constitution Amendment Proclamation, 1983.* It originally read "(b) any rights or freedoms that may be acquired by the aboriginal peoples of Canada by way of land claims settlement."

APPENDIX 2

An Overview of the Canadian Legal System: Division of Powers and Essentials of Procedure

While the focus of most of the readings in this book is the role of moral reasoning in the law, understanding of those issues is enhanced by an understanding of the ways in which particular issues arise and are resolved within a legal order. Not every dispute involves legal rights, and not every dispute involving legal rights makes it to trial. Canada's legal order shares important features with many of the world's legal systems, though it differs from other systems in various ways. This appendix is meant as a quick tour through the structure of legal order in general and in particular the structure of the Canadian legal order.

The Canadian legal system exhibits the classic liberal division of powers between three branches of government – the legislature, the executive, and the judiciary. According to the doctrine of the division of powers, the legislature – the democratically elected representatives of the people – make law, while the executive – a body of professional government employees – implement and enforce the law. The judiciary, who in Canada are unelected officials appointed by the government, interpret the law when a question arises about what it requires in a particular case.

The rationale for dividing power in this way is doing so secures the rule of law. Law is legitimate when it is made by the legislature for it then reflects the will of the people. Executive action to implement and enforce the law is legitimate as long as the officials stay within the limits set by the law. Thus, civil servants are charged with carrying out broadly defined government policies. Judicial interpretation of the law is legitimate as long as it is confined to seeing to it that the executive officials stay within the limits set by the law rather than whatever they would themselves consider appropriate.

In this scheme, judges are given the role of ultimately determining what the law is, but are subject to the duty to confine their determinations to what the law requires. If they confine their interpretative role in this way, society is governed by laws rather than by the personal whims of people holding power. Citizens can be secure in the knowledge that government officials may not act except when the law gives them the warrant to do so.

In Canada, the role of determining the law is the task of the superior courts of general jurisdiction of each province. These have different names according to the province, for example, Ontario Court (General Division), or in Alberta and other provinces, the Court of Queen's Bench. These courts have general jurisdiction in that they have the power to hear and decide any question of law. Appeals against their decisions are to the provincial courts of appeal. In addition, federal courts hear some cases in specialized areas of the law. Appeals against the decisions of both provincial and federal courts can be made to the Supreme Court of Canada. The Supreme Court agrees to hear only a small proportion of the cases appealed to it, and normally decides which cases to hear based on the legal significance of the issues they raise. Judges are appointed to all of these courts by the federal government, and enjoy lifetime tenure so as to protect their independence.

In order to bring a case before a court, the person bringing it must have *standing*. In private disputes, private citizens who claim to have been wronged by others have standing to sue. In general private citizens only have standing to challenge government action if they can claim that some right of theirs is jeopardized by it. However, in certain circumstances, parties before a court can argue on the basis of the constitutional rights of third parties. Also, courts have discretion to grant intervenor status to interested parties in appellate cases in which they have an indirect interest. Intervenors can raise broader constitutional issues that the parties to the dispute may not have raised themselves.

Public law governs the relationship between government and citizen as well as between the different branches of government. But judges also decide cases arising in private law, the law which regulates the interactions between individuals. The courts may have to decide whether an agreement between two people is a valid contract, or who is liable in the case of an unintended injury. They may have to determine who owns a piece of land, or whether someone can recover from someone else who was unjustly enriched at their expense. In Canada (unlike the United States) questions of private law are always tried by judges rather than juries. In answering questions in a private law case, judges often need to sort out difficult questions of fact – who did what, and when – as well as questions of law concerning the legal rights and duties of the parties. In considering facts in matters of private law, judges decide in favor of the party whose claim is supported by the balance of the evidence. Since one of the two parties will lose in a private dispute, fairness requires that the one with the stronger case should prevail. In order to limit frivolous litigation, the losing party in a private suit must pay the legal expenses of the winner. In private law cases, both parties enjoy the right of appeal. However, only issues of law can be raised on appeal. Facts must be taken to be as the trial court found them.

Canada has two distinctive systems of private law. In Quebec, private law is codified in the *Code Civile*. In the rest of Canada, private law is largely a matter of common law. The difference is important, because at the core of common-law reasoning is the appeal to precedent – the way cases have been decided before. Precedents can be drawn from other common-law jurisdictions, including foreign ones. By contrast, decisions in civil law systems are presented as the consequences of the explicit provisions of the civil code. As a result, decisions sometimes look as though they are the result of a straightforward deductive process. However, the generality with which such provisions must be framed still leaves space for judicial creativity, and judges are aware of prior judicial understandings of how the law should be interpreted.

In private law, judges are upholding the rule of law because individuals know that any private dispute which the law regulates will be settled by an impartial application of the law. Just as it is essential that citizens know that judges will keep government officials within the law, so it is essential that individuals know that their fellows will have to deal with them in the manner prescribed by law.

Criminal law falls into public rather than private law, because the state investigates and prosecutes criminal offences. Because of the grave consequences which attend criminal conviction, the standard of proof is higher in criminal law – facts must be proven beyond a reasonable doubt. For the same reasons, people accused of crimes are presumed innocent until proven guilty. Those accused of crimes with sentences of less than two years are subject to summary trial without a jury. Those accused of more serious crimes are entitled to trial by jury, though they may elect to be tried by a judge. In a jury trial, the jury's role is limited to determining facts. In Canada (unlike the United States) both the Crown and the accused are allowed to appeal a criminal decision, but only on the basis of questions of law. Often the grounds for appeal turn on the judge's instruction to the jury, or on the trial judge's decisions about the admissibility of evidence. The criminal law in Canada is codified in a single federal *Criminal Code*.

In common-law systems, it is sometimes difficult to determine what principle or principles a judicial decision stands for, since principles must be inferred from the judge's reasoning or argument justifying the decision. If several judges hear the matter, some might dissent from the majority on some issues but not others, while others concur with the result, but offer different reasons for it. Finally, even when all the judges support the judgment given by one judge, the opinion might include arguments which are in tension with each other. The common law is found in the judgments of the superior courts and changes over time at the hands of judges. When a judge decides an issue in a common-law legal order, that judgment becomes a precedent – it has authority for judges deciding similar issues. The weight of the authority it has will vary on a number of dimensions, the extent to which it has been followed, the place of the judge in the judicial hierarchy, and, indeed, the merits of the judgment. In some parts of the law, especially private law, the law in a common-law legal order might be made almost entirely by judges. In other parts, such as the criminal law, the common law will be a complex overlay of judicial interpretation of statutory codification. But it will also serve as an underlay, or a background for interpretation, since the principles that were codified were in the first instance principles developed by judges. The role of precedent in common-law systems means that the subsequent development of the law will often depend on the particular cases that make it to trial, which in turn depends in part on the resources available to the parties.

Public law includes the rules of public international law, the law which governs relations between states. Public international law also governs the interpretation of treaties. For example, if Canada and the United States have an extradition treaty, and some American states have the death penalty while Canada does not, does Canada need to send an American fugitive convicted of a capital crime in one of those states to certain death? (In private matters, the rules governing the choice of laws are no less complex, and govern such questions as which law applies to the property of a couple married in France, but residing in Canada at the time of their divorce.) Public law also includes constitutional law and administrative law. Some issues in constitutional law seem to have little to do with particular individuals, as in the questions relating to the division of political power in the Canadian federal system between the central federal government and the provincial governments. But the division of powers is important to the ability of various bodies to make law. If a lawmaking body overreaches its mandate, individuals may be illegally deprived of advantages to which they are entitled. Since the enactment of the *Charter* in 1982, Canada has had a written constitution. Even in jurisdictions without a written constitution (such as Britain), courts sometimes engage in constitutional review.

Issues of public law reveal the complexities of the division of powers. Governments often enact statutes which delegate broad powers to officials to elaborate and implement policies, rather than attempting to anticipate details in advance. In order to protect their agencies from the intrusion of the superior courts into this kind of policy making, governments have often at the same time set up tribunals to decide the legal questions which arise in the course of elaborating and implementing the statute. For example, questions of labor law are decided by provincially appointed labor relations boards, and human rights codes by specially appointed tribunals. To what extent can the decisions of such bodies be immunized from the supervision by the superior courts? Courts have generally recognized the authority of tribunals to decide such issues, subject to their own "review power." Courts will intervene if the tribunal either overreaches what the court deems to be its statutory authority, or offends against any of the procedural values – the values of fair process which the courts deem it their constitutional duty to protect. Courts always retain a residual power of review because of their role as final arbiters of the boundaries between the branches of government.

Since the enactment of the *Charter of Rights and Freedoms* in 1982, a new range of constitutional issues has preoccupied the courts. These of course pertain to whether statutes or official action under statutes offend against *Charter*-protected rights and values. The Canadian *Charter* has an unusual structure in two respects. First, Section 1 requires a court to ask a further question after a finding that a Charter-protected right or value has been violated. This is the question whether that violation can itself be justified by the values of a "free and democratic society," and whether the violation is proportional to the problem it is supposed to address. Second, Section 33 permits a legislature or parliament to "override" a judicial determination of constitutionality subject to the conditions set out in the section. Thus, while judges have the final say over what the law is, legislatures retain the power to temporarily override those decisions.

The *Charter* may seem to undermine the division of powers. It clearly gives judges the power to decide on whether the laws made by democratically elected parliaments are valid in accordance with their interpretation of very broadly defined values, for example, the right to free speech. That is, judges may not merely be keeping officials within the limits of the law as it is, but deciding what the law ought to be. In this the *Charter* only makes more visible and dramatic a pervasive feature of legal orders. Virtually all legal systems include such concepts as "good faith," "reasonableness," and 'fair play,' all of which are open to moral interpretation. That judicial interpretation is partly creative and not merely deductive is explicitly recognized in the Canadian legal system.

APPENDIX 3

Glossary of Legal and Philosophical Terms

Terms and Definitions

This section contains some technical terms that will be found in the readings. The definitions and discussions are intended to give a bare handle on the terms, and thus are an aid to the readings rather than a replacement for them.

Atomism. The view that the social world is made up of isolated individuals each making perfectly independent choices about how to live. The label "atomism" is more often offered as a criticism of others' view than as a view put forward by anyone.

Autonomy. The individual's right to decide for herself how to live her life.

Comity. The recognition by one legal system of another legal system's laws. Extradition treaties are one example of comity; the acceptance of marriages or divorces made abroad is another.

Common law. Systems of law descended from the British common-law system. (The common law was originally the law common to the King's courts, and thus contrasted with manorial and cannon law.) The distinctive feature of common-law systems is the way in which judges appeal to previously decided cases in deciding novel ones. The law is to be found in cases, rather than statutes. Most modern common-law systems include statutes as well, but these are standardly interpreted in light of settled cases.

Commensurability. Two things are said to be commensurable if there is some basis for comparing them. Things are said to be incommensurable if no such basis exists. For example, love and money are usually thought to be incommensurable, because no amount of money can replace a lost love.

Communitarianism. The view that an individual is the product of a particular social and cultural environment. The meaningful choices as to how to live for an individual are the choices informed by this environment. Thus, communitarians suppose that choices to reject the ways of one's culture are often not worthy of protection.

Consequentialism. The moral position which evaluates actions based on the balance of good over bad consequences which they bring or might bring about. An argument in favor of something that claims its implementation would reduce violent crime is consequentialist. Consequentialist arguments always require factual support because they depend on claims about what would happen if various policies were adopted.

Constitutionalism. The view that the basic essentials of a political regime should lie outside the reach of ordinary processes of majority rule. Not all advocates of constitutional democracy suppose a written constitution is necessary. In Britain, for example, there is no written constitution, but the powers of government are limited.

Deontological. The moral position that supposes that acts should be evaluated on the basis of some intrinsic quality. For example, claims about rights, and appeals to fairness and desert are deontological. Both deontological and consequentialist arguments can be found on both sides of almost every political debate. Many complex positions will appeal to both kinds of arguments.

Egalitarianism. The view that the allocation of resources and opportunities has to be substantially equal.

Habeas corpus. The right against unlawful imprisonment. For example, prisoners who have not been promptly charged with any crime can be freed under *habeas corpus.*

Legal moralism. The position that the state can legitimately coerce people into ways that do not accord with their own views of the best way to live. *Pure* legal moralists suppose that there is a correct answer about how best to live; *impure* legal moralists suppose it is up to each society to answer questions about the appropriate moral content of law for itself. Opponents of legal moralism often appeal to the "harm principle," which holds that the only legitimate basis for restrictions on liberty is the prevention of harm to others.

Legal positivism. The view that the law that exists on any matter exists as a matter of publicly ascertainable fact. That is, finding out what the law is does not require any sort of controversial moral argument.

Liberalism. The view that the fundamental role of the state is to enable people to freely decide how best to live their own lives. Different liberals have very different views about how best to protect individual liberty, as well as different views about which individual choices are most important. Some suppose that liberty requires an unregulated capitalist market; others that the state must make sure that individuals have a fair share of resources and opportunities in order to be able to freely decide what life is best for them. All liberals share an abstract commitment to rejecting paternalism, though they disagree about the implications of this commitment.

Libertarianism. The view that the only legitimate role of the state is in protecting negative liberty. Libertarians standardly reject economic redistribution as an illicit interference with property rights.

Majoritarianism. The view that the law should implement the preferences of the majority whatever these happen to be. Majoritarianism can be understood as a democratic position, but is at odds with the view that democracy requires certain constitutional safeguards.

Natural law. Defenders of natural law insist that whether or not anything counts as law will depend on its specific content. For the natural lawyer, wicked legal systems are not legal systems at all; they need to be understood as exercises of naked power. Natural lawyers disagree among themselves about just what moral content a legal system must have, but they agree that the proper role of positive law is to articulate and implement natural law.

Negative liberty. Defenders of negative liberty understand liberty as the absence of external impediments to individual preferences. One has this kind of liberty when the state limits its coercive interference in the lives of individual to the minimum necessary to prevent individuals from harming each other.

Neutrality. The refusal by the state to take a stand on contested views about the good life. A neutral state will not treat opera any differently than it does football. A difficult question for theories of liberal neutrality is whether traditional practices that discriminate against women are best thought of as contested conceptions of the good which the state has no business correcting, or as injustices which are within the scope of its proper concern.

Normative claim. A claim about how things should be. Normative claims aim to guide action. Thus, they contrast with descriptions of how things are. There are a wide variety of types of normative claims. Moral claims are normative, as are aesthetic claims and claims of etiquette, though few suppose that any of these is simply a special case of the others. Legal claims are also action-guiding. One of the central questions of jurisprudence concerns the nature of legal normativity. The dispute between positivists and anti-positivists turns on whether the normative element in legal claims is a special case of the normativity of moral claims.

Paternalism. Actions by the state that are done to protect people from themselves. For example, a law outlawing bungee-jumping is paternalistic because it seeks to protect people from the consequences of their own choices. By contrast, drunk-driving laws are not paternalistic because one of their aims is to protect people from the choices of others.

Perfectionism. The position which requires the state to aid or even coerce people into living out their lives in accordance with some ideal of what makes life valuable. For example, state support of the arts is sometimes defended on perfectionist grounds.

Positive liberty. The view that individuals have to have certain things before the idea of negative liberty and autonomy makes any sense. Defenders of positive liberty differ in their views about what it requires. Some emphasize the role of various social conditions that are said to enable individual choice. Others stress the importance of such things as political participation or community to any life that is truly free.

Reasonable person. Anglo-American legal systems use the construct of a reasonable person to articulate standards of care and judgment. The reasonable person is neither the rational person who acts effectively to realize his or her ends, nor the typical or average person. Instead, the reasonable person is the person who shows appropriate regard for the interests of others, and takes appropriate care in avoiding injury to them. Reasonableness standards reflect views both about what is important to the security of those who might be harmed, and about the importance of people being able to go about their own affairs. The reasonable person also appears in the law of self-defence, as the measure of the care one must take in assessing whether one's life is in peril. The reasonable person standard is sometimes called an *objective* standard because it abstracts away from the personal features of the person being judged.

Utilitarianism. The most prominent kind of consequentialist position. Utilitarians say that policies and institutions should be assessed on the basis of their ability to bring about the best overall balance of good over bad consequences. The most popular candidate for good consequences is the satisfaction of people's preferences – that is, the aggregate sum of what various people in fact want and desire.

Sources and Credits

H.L.A. Hart, "Positivism and the Separation of Law and Morals," *Essays in Jurisprudence and Philosophy* (1983) 49–87 (some notes omitted, remaining notes renumbered), and *The Concept of Law* (1961) 89–95, 107–14, reprinted by permission of Oxford University Press.

Lon L. Fuller, *The Morality of Law* (1969) 33–44, 200–17 (some notes omitted; remaining notes renumbered), reprinted by permission of Yale University Press; copyright by Yale University Press; this extract may not be reproduced in whole or in part, in any form without written permission from the publishers.

Ronald Dworkin, "Law's Ambitions for Itself" (1985) 71 *Virginia Law Review* 173–87, reprinted by permission of the editors of the *Virginia Law Review* and by Fred B. Rothman and Company, and *Law's Empire* (1986) 228–33 (some notes omitted; remaining notes renumbered), reprinted by permission of Harvard University Press; copyright by Harvard University Press; this extract may not be reproduced in whole or in part, in any form without written permission from the publishers.

Mark Tushnet, "Following the Rules Laid Down: A Critique of Interpretivism and Neutral Principles" (1983) 96 *Harvard Law Review* 781–826. Reprinted by permission of the author and the Harvard Law Review Association.

Robert Cover, "Of Creon and Captain Vere," from *Justice Accused* (1976) 1–7 (notes omitted), reprinted by permission of Yale Univer-

Patrick Devlin, "Morals and the Criminal Law," in *The Enforcement of Morals* (1965) 1–25 (some notes omitted; remaining notes renumbered), reprinted by permission of Oxford University Press.

Allan C. Hutchinson and Patrick Monahan, "Democracy and the Rule of Law," in Hutchinson and Monahan, eds., *The Rule of Law: Ideal or Ideology* (1987) 97–123, reprinted by permission of the authors and of Carswell.

Jean Hampton, "Democracy and the Rule of Law," in Ian Shapiro, ed., *The Rule of Law: Nomos* vol. 36 (1994) 13–44, reprinted by permission of New York University Press.

Jody Freeman, "Defining Family in *Mossop v DSS*: The Challenge of Anti-Essentialism and Interactive Discrimination for Human Rights Litigation" (1994) 44 *University of Toronto Law Journal* 42–92 (some notes omitted; remaining notes renumbered), reprinted by permission of the author and of University of Toronto Press.

John Finnis, "Law, Morality and 'Sexual Orientation,'" (1994) 69 *Notre Dame Law Review* 1049–76, reprinted by permission of the author and the editors of the *Notre Dame Review*.

John Rawls, "Civil Disobedience," in *A Theory of Justice* (1971) 36–91 (notes omitted), reprinted by permission of Harvard University Press; copyright by Harvard University Press; this extract may not be reproduced in whole or in part, in any form without written permission from the publishers.

Ronald Dworkin, "Civil Disobedience," in *Taking Rights Seriously* (1977) 206–22 , reprinted by permission of Duckworth and Company.

Christine M. Korsgaard, "Taking the Law into Our Own Hands: Kant on the Right of Revolution," in Korsgaard et al., eds., *Reclaiming the History of Ethics: Essays for John Rawls* (1997) reprinted by permission of the author.

Sujit Choudhry and Robert Howse, "Constitutional Theory and the *Quebec Secession Reference*" (2000) 13 *Canadian Journal of Law and Jurisprudence* 143–69, reprinted by permission of the authors.

John Borrows, "Frozen Rights in Canada: Constitutional Interpretation and the Trickster" (1998) 22 *American Indian Law Review* 37–64, reprinted by permission of the author.

Patrick Macklem, *Indigenous Difference and the Constitution of Canada* (2000), 11–46, reprinted by permission of University of Toronto Press.

Joel Feinberg, "Pornography and the Criminal Law" (1979) 40 *University of Pittsburgh Law Review* 567–73, reprinted by permission of the author and of the editors of the *University of Pittsburgh Law Review*.

T.M. Scanlon, "A Theory of Freedom of Expression," *Philosophy and Public Affairs* vol. 1, no. 2 (winter 1972) 204–26 (some notes omitted; remaining notes renumbered), reprinted by permission of Princeton University Press.

Mayo Moran, "Talking about Hate Speech: A Rhetorical Analysis of American and Canadian Approaches to the Regulation of Hate Speech" (1994) 6 *Wisconsin Law Review* 1497–1514 (some notes omitted; remaining notes renumbered), reprinted by permission of the author and of the editors of the *Wisconsin Law Review*.

Catharine A. MacKinnon, *Only Words* (1993) 89–110 (some notes omitted; remaining notes renumbered), reprinted by permission of Harvard University Press and the author; copyright by Harvard University Press; this extract may not be reproduced in whole or in part, in any form without written permission from the publishers.

Ronald Dworkin, "Two Concepts of Liberty," in Edna Ulman-Margalit and Avishai Margalit, eds., *Isaiah Berlin: A Celebration* (Hogarth Press, Chatto and Windus, 1991), 100–9, reprinted by permission of the author.

Brenda Cossman, et al., *Bad Attitude/s on Trial: Pornography, Feminism and the Butler Decision* (1997) 107–51, reprinted by permission of University of Toronto Press.

Judith Jarvis Thomson, "A Defence of Abortion," *Philosophy and Public Affairs* vol. 1, no. 1 (Fall 1971) 47–66, reprinted by permission of Princeton University Press.

John Finnis, "The Rights and Wrongs of Abortion: A Reply to Judith Jarvis Thomson," *Philosophy and Public Affairs* vol. 2. no. 2 (Winter 1973) 117–45, reprinted by permission of Princeton University Press.